My Virtual Child

My Virtual Child is an interactive web-based simulation that allows students to raise a child from birth to age 18 and monitor the effects of their parenting decisions over time. This engaging resource is fully integrated into MyDevelopmentLab and is also available to package with any Pearson text or as a stand-alone item.

For additional information, visit us at **www.myvirtualchild.com.**

www.myvirtualchild.com

Child Development

Child Development

FIFTH EDITION

Robert S. Feldman

University of Massachusetts at Amherst

Prentice Hall

Upper Saddle River   London   Singapore
Toronto   Tokyo   Sydney   Hong Kong   Mexico City

VP, Editorial Director: Leah Jewell
Editor in Chief: Jessica Mosher
Executive Editor: Jeff Marshall
Editorial Project Manager: Judy Casillo
Editorial Assistant: Aaron Talwar
Director of Marketing: Brandy Dawson
Marketing Manager: Nicole Kunzmann
Assistant Marketing Manager: Laura Kennedy
Managing Editor: Maureen Richardson
Project Manager: Shelly Kupperman
Senior Operations Supervisor: Sherry Lewis
Operations Specialist: Christina Amato
Senior Art Director: Nancy Wells
Art Director: Anne Bonanno Nieglos

Text and Cover Designer: Ilze Lemesis
AV Project Manager: Maria Piper
Manager, Visual Research: Beth Brenzel
Manager, Rights and Permissions: Zina Arabia
Image Permission Coordinator: Michelina Viscusi
Manager, Cover Visual Research and Permissions:
   Karen Sanatar
Cover Art: Caracler Design/iStockphoto
Senior Media Project Manager: Paul De Luca
Managing Supplements Editor: Ginny Livsey
Full-Service Project Management/
   Composition: Francesca Monaco, Prepare Inc.
Printer/Binder: Courier Companies Inc.
Cover Printer: Lehigh—Phoenix Color

This book was set in 10/11 Minion.

Credits and acknowledgments borrowed from other sources and reproduced, with permission, in this textbook appear on appropriate page within text (or on page 481).

Library of Congress Cataloging-in-Publication Data

Feldman, Robert S. (Robert Stephen)
   Child development / Robert S. Feldman.—5th ed.
      p. cm.
   ISBN 0-205-65502-5
1. Child development. 2. Child psychology. 3. Adolescence. 4. Adolescent psychology.
   I. Title.

HQ767.9.F43 2009
305.231—dc 22

                                                      2008031520

Prentice Hall
is an imprint of

www.pearsonhighered.com

10 9 8 7 6 5 4 3 2 1
Student Edition ISBN-13: 978-0-205-65502-1
                ISBN-10:   0-205-65502-5
Exam   ISBN-13: 978-0-205-65603-5
                ISBN-10:   0-205-65603-X

Contents

PART 2 Infancy

13 Social and Personality Development in Middle Childhood 308

PART 5 Adolescence

14 Physical Development in Adolescence 332

15 Cognitive Development in Adolescence   356

16 Social and Personality Development in Adolescence   382

Child development is a unique field of study. Unlike other academic disciplines, each of us has experience with its subject matter in very personal ways. It is a discipline that deals not only with ideas and concepts and theories, but has at its heart the forces that have made each of us who we are.

This text, *Child Development*, Fifth Edition, seeks to capture the discipline in a way that sparks and nurtures and shapes readers' interest. It is meant to excite students about the field, to draw them into its way of looking at the world, and to mold their understanding of developmental issues. By exposing readers to both the current content and the promise inherent in child and adolescent development, the text is designed to keep interest in the discipline alive long after students' formal study of the field has ended.

Overview

Child Development, Fifth Edition, provides a broad overview of the field of development. It covers the full range of childhood and adolescence, from the moment of conception through the end of adolescence. The text furnishes a broad, comprehensive introduction to the field, discussing basic theories and research findings, and highlighting current applications outside the laboratory. It covers childhood and adolescence chronologically, encompassing the prenatal period, infancy and toddlerhood, the preschool years, middle childhood, and adolescence. Within these periods, the text focuses on physical, cognitive, and social and personality development.

The book seeks to accomplish the following four major goals:

- First and foremost, the book is designed to provide a broad, balanced overview of the field of child development. It introduces readers to the theories, research, and applications that constitute the discipline, examining both the traditional areas of the field as well as more recent innovations.

  The book pays particular attention to the applications developed by child and adolescent development specialists. While not slighting theoretical material, the text emphasizes what we know about development across childhood and adolescence, rather than focusing on unanswered questions. It demonstrates how this knowledge may be applied to real-world problems.

  In sum, the book highlights the interrelationships between theory, research, and application, accentuating the scope and diversity of the field. It also illustrates how child developmentalists use theory, research, and applications to help solve significant social problems.

- The second major goal of the text is to explicitly tie development to students' lives. Findings from the study of child and adolescent development have a significant degree of relevance to students, and this text illustrates how these findings can be applied in a meaningful, practical sense. Applications are presented in a contemporaneous framework, including current news items, timely world events, and contemporary uses of child development that draw readers into the field. Numerous descriptive scenarios and vignettes reflect everyday situations in people's lives, and discussion explores how they relate to the field.

  For example, each chapter begins with an opening prologue that provides a real-life situation relating to the chapter subject area. All chapters have a "Becoming an Informed Consumer of Development" feature, which explicitly suggests ways to apply developmental findings to students' experience in a practical, hands-on way. Each chapter also includes a selection called "From Research to Practice" that discusses ways that developmental research is being used to answer problems that society faces.

  In addition, the text contains several interviews, "Careers in Child Development," highlighting a person working in a profession related to that chapter's topic. These interviews illustrate how a background in child development can be beneficial in a variety of vocations. Also included are numerous questions in figure and photo captions asking readers to take the perspective of people in a variety of professions that make use of child development, including health-care professionals, educators, and social workers.

- The third goal of this book is to highlight both the commonalties and diversity of today's multicultural society. Consequently, every chapter has at least one "Developmental Diversity" section. These features explicitly consider how cultural factors relevant to development both unite and diversify our contemporary, global society. In addition, the book incorporates material relevant to diversity throughout every chapter.

- Finally, the fourth goal of the text is one that underlies the other three: making the field of child development engaging, accessible, and interesting to students. Child development is a joy both to study and teach, because so much of it has direct, immediate meaning to our lives. Because each of us is involved in our own developmental path, we are tied in very personal ways to the content areas covered by the book. *Child Development*, Fifth Edition, then, is meant to engage and nurture this interest, planting a seed that will develop and flourish throughout a reader's lifetime.

  To accomplish this fourth goal, the book is "user friendly." Written in a direct, conversational voice, it replicates as much as possible a dialogue between author and student.

The text is meant to be understood and mastered on its own, without the intervention of an instructor. To that end, it includes a variety of pedagogical features. Each chapter contains a "Looking Ahead" overview that sets the stage for the chapter; "application perspective" questions, in the margins, that promote and test critical thinking and application of the material; a running glossary; a "Looking Back" summary; a list of key terms and concepts; and an epilogue containing critical thinking questions. In addition, each chapter has several "Review" sections that provide an enumeration of the key concepts. NEW to this edition, every chapter ends with a Case Study followed by related critical thinking questions.

The Philosophy Behind *Child Development*, Fifth Edition   *Child Development*, Fifth Edition, blends and integrates theory, research, and applications. It is *not* an applied development book, focused solely on techniques for translating the knowledge base of development into answers to societal problems. Nor is it a theory-oriented volume, concentrating primarily on the field's abstract theories. Instead, the text focuses on the scope and breadth of human development during childhood and adolescence. The strategy of concentrating on the scope of the field permits the text to examine both the traditional core areas of the field, as well as evolving, nontraditional areas of development.

Furthermore, the book concentrates on the here and now, rather than attempting to provide a detailed historical record of the field. Although it draws on the past where appropriate, it does so with a view toward delineating the field as it now stands and the directions toward which it is evolving. Similarly, while providing descriptions of classic studies, the emphasis is more on current research findings and trends.

Overall, then, the book provides a broad overview of child and adolescent development, integrating the theory, research, and applications of the discipline. It is meant to be a book that readers will want to keep in their own personal libraries, one that they will take off the shelf when considering problems related to that most intriguing of questions: How do people get to be the way they are?

What's New in This Edition?

A number of new topics and areas have been added in this edition. A sampling of topics that have been either newly included or expanded also illustrates the scope of the revision:

Chapter 1

Cohort effects

Terrorism

Rousseau

Locke

Noble savage

Tabula rasa

Physical abuse as risk factors for violence

Psychological abuse and childhood violence

Chapter 2

Replication

Meta-analysis

Chapter 3

Intergenerational effects of smoking

Psychological consequences of abortion

Prenatal vitamins and folic acid

Prenatal testing

Chapter 4

U.S. *Family and Medical Leave Act*

American Academy of Pediatrics guidelines on hospital discharge following birth

Bradley method

Hypnobirthing

Side effects of birthing drugs

Postpartum depression

Circumcision

Chapter 5

Gender/ethnic differences in height and weight

Shaken baby syndrome

Obesity in infants

New data on underweight children

New data on child poverty rates

Chapter 6

Baby Einstein

Value of educational media

Neurodevelopment aspects of memory

Chapter 7

Mirror neurons

Reactive attachment disorder

Findings on low-quality group child care

Chapter 8

Children's participation in medical decision making

Brain growth and nutrition

Brain growth and cognitive and motor skills

Malnutrition and brain development

Agility

Spanking and parental reactions to stress

Chapter 9

Montessori school effectiveness

Cost-benefit analysis of pre-kindergarten

Educational television outcomes

Television viewing and obesity

Chapter 10

Play and cognitive and brain development

Racial and ethnic identity development

In addition, a wealth of contemporary research is cited in this edition—hundreds of new citations have been added, most from the last few years.

The new edition of *Child Development* includes an increased emphasis on integrating the huge array of electronic media in *My Virtual Child* and *MyDevelopmentLab,* Pearson's all-inclusive online resource. These sites provide online electronic exercises, videos, sample tests, and literally hundreds of activities that extend the text and make concepts come alive. The online material is referenced throughout the book in an engaging way, enticing students to go online to make use of the electronic tools that will help them understand the material in the book more deeply. To further promote the use of online resources, questions in the "Review" sections are drawn from *MyDevelopmentLab.*

Teaching and Learning Resources

Child Development, Fifth Edition, is accompanied by a superb set of ancillary materials. They include the following.

Print and Media Supplements for the Instructor

Download Instructor Resources at the Instructor's Resource Center Register or log in to the Instructor Resource Center to download textbook supplements from our online catalog or request premium content for your school's course management system. Go to: http://www.pearsonhighered.com/educator

This time-saving resource provides you with electronic versions of a variety of teaching resources all in one place allowing you to customize your lecture notes, PowerPoint slides, and media presentations. The PowerPoint slides are customized for *Child Development,* Fifth Edition, providing electronic versions of the artwork from the text, the *Instructor's Resource Manual,* and the Test Item File.

For technical support for any of your Pearson products, you and your students can contact http://247.pearsoned.com.

Save time, improve results with MyDevelopmentLab PEARSON mydevelopmentlab **www.mydevelopmentlab.com** MyDevelopmentLab is a learning and assessment tool that enables instructors to assess student performance and adapt course content—without investing additional time or resources. Students benefit from an easy-to-use site where they can test themselves on key content, track their progress, and utilize individually tailored study plans. NEW to MyDevelopmentLab:

- NEW more easily navigated eBook with great highlight features and powerful embedded media
- NEW timeline feature
- NEW survey tool
- NEW flashcards
- NEW podcasting tool
- NEW video clips, animations, and podcasts
- Improvements to design, course content, and grading system based on direct customer feedback

Assessment and Ability to Adapt MyDevelopmentLab is designed with instructor flexibility in mind—you decide the extent of integration into your course—from independent self-assessment for students, to total course management. By transferring faculty members' most time-consuming tasks—content delivery, student assessment, and grading—to automated tools, MyDevelopmentLab enables faculty to spend more quality time with students.

Some time-saving features for instructors integrating MyDevelopmentLab: Instructors are provided with the results of the diagnostic tests—by student or by class. In addition to the activities students can access in their customized study plans, instructors are provided with extra lecture notes, video clips, and activities that reflect the content areas their class is still struggling with. Instructors can bring these resources to class, or easily post them online for students to access.

If this text did not come with a MyDevelopmentLab access code, visit www.mydevelopmentlab.com to purchase a subscription.

www.MyVirtualChild.com
Let your students raise a child and monitor the effects of their parenting decisions over time.

MyVirtualChild is an interactive simulation that allows students to raise a child from birth to age 18 and to monitor the effects of their parenting decisions. This engaging resource is fully integrated into MyDevelopmentLab—Pearson's innovative online learning system—and is also available to package with any Pearson child development text or as a stand-alone item.

Lecture Launcher Video Adopters can receive this new video that includes short clips covering all major topics in developmental psychology. The videos have been carefully selected from the *Films for Humanities and Sciences* library and edited to provide brief and compelling video content to enhance your lectures. Contact your local representative for a full list of the video clips on this tape.

Observation Video for Child Development (CD-ROM) ISBN 0-205-65602-1 These videos bring to life many key concepts discussed in the text. Students get to view each video twice: once with an introduction to the concept being illustrated and again with commentary describing what is taking place at crucial points in the video. Whether your course has an observation component or not, this CD-ROM provides your students the opportunity to see children in action.

Instructor's Resource Manual—ISBN 0-205-65504-1
Each chapter in the manual includes the following resources: Chapter Learning Objectives; Lecture Suggestions and Discussion Topics; Classroom Activities, Demonstrations, and Exercises; Out-of-Class Assignments and Projects; Lecture Notes; Multimedia Resources; Video Resources; and Handouts. Designed to make your lectures more effective and to save you preparation time, this extensive resource gathers together the most effective activities and strategies for teaching your developmental psychology course. Also included in the *Instructor's Resource Manual* are answers to the "Case Study" questions presented at the end of each chapter of the text. Available in print and online at http://www.pearsonhighered.com/education

Test Item File—ISBN 0-205-65505-X This test bank contains over 2,500 multiple choice, true/false, and short-answer essay questions, and *many enhancements*. The Total Assessment Guide *test planner chapter overview* makes creating tests easier by listing all of the test items in an easy-to-reference grid. The Total Assessment Guide organizes all test items by text section, question type, and level of difficulty. Available in print and online at http://www.pearsonhighered.com/education

MyTest

The new edition test bank comes with NEW Pearson MyTest (ISBN 0205656250), a powerful assessment generation program that helps instructors easily create and print quizzes and exams. Questions and tests can be authored online, allowing instructors ultimate flexibility and the ability to efficiently manage assessments anytime, anywhere! Instructors can easily access existing questions, edit, create, and store using simple drag-and-drop and Word-like controls. Data on each question includes information on difficulty level and page number cross reference to the textbook. In addition, each question maps to the text's major section and learning objective. For more information go to www.PearsonMyTest.com

PowerPoint Slides for *Child Development,* Fifth Edition—ISBN 0-205-65506-8 Each chapter's PowerPoint presentation highlights the key points covered in the text. Provided in two versions—one with the chapter graphics and one without—to give you flexibility in preparing your lectures. Available online at http://www.pearsonhighered.com/educator

Print and Media Supplements for the Student

CourseSmart eBook

CourseSmart Textbooks Online is an exciting new *choice* for students wanting to save money. As an alternative to purchasing the print textbook, students can *subscribe* to the same content online and save up to 50% off the suggested list price of the print text. With a CourseSmart etextbook, students can search the text, make notes online, print out reading assignments that incorporate lecture notes, and bookmark important passages for later review. For more information, or to subscribe to the CourseSmart eTextbook, visit www.coursesmart.com

Study Guide ISBN 0-205-65503-3 The study guide helps students master the core concepts presented in each chapter. The guide includes learning objectives, a brief chapter summary, and practice tests to help them master the content and concepts in each chapter of *Child Development.*

MyDevelopmentLab

Want to save time and improve results?

MyDevelopmentLab is a dynamic, interactive, online resource that gives you everything you need to ace this psychology course—all in one easy-to-use Web site. Log on to www.mydevelopmentlab.com and find a wealth of activities, practice exams and tests, interactive maps, and much more!

Find answers to your concerns . . .

I want to practice the kinds of questions we'll get on the test.

I need extra review of certain chapter sections.

Video clips and simulations help me learn the material better!

I don't understand some of the terms my instructor uses.

If this text did not come with a MyDevelopmentLab access code, visit www.mydevelopmentlab.com to purchase a subscription.

www.MyVirtualChild.com
Raise a child of your own and monitor the effects of your parenting decisions over time. MyVirtualChild is an interactive simulation that allows students to raise a child from birth to age 18 and monitor the effects of parenting decisions. This engaging resource is fully integrated into MyDevelopmentLab—Pearson's innovative online learning system.

For a list of all student resources available with Feldman's *Child Development*, Fifth Edition, go to www.mypearsonstore.com, enter the text ISBN (0-205-65502-5) and check out the "Everything That Goes With It" section under the book cover.

Supplementary Texts

Contact your Pearson Education representative to package this supplementary text with *Child Development*, Fifth Edition.

***Current Directions in Developmental Psychology: Readings from the Association for Psychological Science*, Edited by Lynn S. Liben—ISBN 0-205-59750-5** This updated and exciting reader includes 30 articles that have been carefully selected for the undergraduate audience, and taken from the very accessible *Current Directions in Psychological Science* journal. These timely, cutting-edge articles allow instructors to bring their students real-world perspective—from a reliable source—about today's most current and pressing issues in developmental psychology. For details or to find out how to get these readers at no additional cost when purchased with Pearson psychology texts, please contact your local Pearson sales representative.

Acknowledgments

I am grateful to the following reviewers who provided a wealth of comments, criticism, and encouragement in the development of this edition and previous editions of this text:

Kristi Almeida-Bowin, Moorpark College; Heidi Burross, University of Arizona; Myra Cox, Harold Washington College; Roseanne L. Flores, Hunter College, CUNY; Nadine Garner, Millersville University; Michael Green, University of North Carolina, Charlotte; Sandra Hellyer, Ball State University; Mary Hughes Stone, San Francisco State University; Mary Clare Munger, Amarillo College; Patricia Weaver, Fayetteville Technical Community College; Alesia Williams Richardson, Chicago State University; Earleen Huff, Amarillo College; Sara Lawrence, California State University; Mary Kay Reed, York College of Pennsylvania; Charlene A. Drake, UMASS Lowell; Susan Bowers, Northern Illinois University; Marguerite Clark, California State Polytechnic University, Pomona; Pamela Chibucos, Owens Community College; Vivian Harper, San Joaquin Delta College; Karen Frye, University of Nevada, Reno; Bruce Anthony, Tabor College; and Eugene Grist, Ohio University.

Many others deserve a great deal of thanks. I am indebted to all those who provided me with a superb education, first at Wesleyan University and later at the University of Wisconsin. Specifically, Karl Scheibe played a pivotal role in my undergraduate education, and the late Vernon Allen acted as mentor and guide through my graduate years. It was in graduate school that I learned about development, being exposed to such experts as Ross Parke, Joel Levin, Herb Klausmeier, and many others.

My education continued when I became a professor. I am especially grateful to my colleagues and students at the University of Massachusetts, who make the university such a wonderful place in which to teach and do research.

Several people played central roles in the development of this book. My gratitude goes to John Bickford, who provided significant editorial support. In addition, Christopher Poirier provided important advice, and I am thankful for his work on this and on other projects for which he provided help. Tolley Jones and John Graiff were essential in juggling and coordinating the multiple aspects of writing this book, and I am so grateful for the role they played.

I am also indebted to the superb Pearson Education team that was instrumental in the development of this book. Jeff Marshall, my terrific editor, always provided support and direction. I am grateful for his enthusiasm, intelligence, and creativity. Managing Editor Judy Casillo's unceasing attention to detail and concern for the book never faltered, and the book is stronger because of her efforts. Finally, I'd like to thank marketing manager Nicole Kunzmann, on whose skills I'm counting. It's a privilege to be part of this world-class team.

I also wish to acknowledge the members of my family, who play such a central role in my life. My brother, Michael, my sisters-in-law and brothers-in-law, my nieces and nephews, all make up an important part of my life. In addition, I am always indebted to the older generation of my family, who led the way in a manner I can only hope to emulate. I will always be obligated to Harry Brochstein for his wisdom and support, as well as to the late Mary Vorwerk and Ethel Radler. Most of all, this list is headed by my father, the late Saul Feldman, and my mother, Leah Brochstein.

In the end, it is my immediate family who deserve the greatest thanks. My son Jon, his wife, Leigh, and my grandson Alex; my son Josh and his wife Julie; and my daughter Sarah—not only are they nice, smart, and good-looking, but my pride and joy. And ultimately my wife, Katherine Vorwerk, provides the love and grounding that makes everything worthwhile. I thank them, with all my love.

Robert S. Feldman
University of Massachusetts at Amherst

About the Author

ROBERT S. FELDMAN is Professor of Psychology and Associate Dean of the College of Social and Behavioral Sciences at the University of Massachusetts, Amherst. A recipient of the College Distinguished Teacher Award, he teaches psychology classes ranging in size from 15 to nearly 500 students. During the course of more than 2 decades as a college instructor, he has taught both undergraduate and graduate courses at Mount Holyoke College, Wesleyan University, Virginia Commonwealth University, in addition to the University of Massachusetts.

Feldman, who initiated the Minority Mentoring Program at the University of Massachusetts, also has served as a Hewlett Teaching Fellow and Senior Online Teaching Fellow. He also is actively involved in promoting the field of psychology. He is on the Board of Directors of the Federation of Behavioral, Psychological, and Cognitive Sciences, and the Board of the Foundation for the Advancement of Behavioral and Brain Sciences.

A Fellow of both the American Psychological Association and the Association for Psychological Science, Feldman received a B.A. with High Honors from Wesleyan University and an M.S. and Ph.D. from the University of Wisconsin–Madison.

Feldman is a winner of a Fulbright Senior Research Scholar and Lecturer Award, and he has written more than 100 books, book chapters, and scientific articles. He has edited *Development of Nonverbal Behavior in Children, Applications of Nonverbal Behavioral Theory and Research*, and coedited *Fundamentals of Nonverbal Behavior*. He is also author of *Development Across the Life Span, Understanding Psychology,* and *P.O.W.E.R. Learning: Strategies for Success in College and Life*. His books have been translated into many languages, including Spanish, French, Portuguese, Dutch, Chinese, and Japanese.

His research interests include honesty and deception in everyday life. His research has been supported by grants from the National Institute of Mental Health and the National Institute on Disabilities and Rehabilitation Research.

Feldman loves music, is an enthusiastic, if not exactly expert, pianist, and he enjoys cooking and traveling. He has three children, and he and his wife, a psychologist, live in western Massachusetts in a home overlooking the Holyoke mountain range.

Child Development

chapter one

An Introduction to Child Development

PROLOGUE: NEW CONCEPTIONS

What if for your entire life, the image that others held of you was colored by the way in which you were conceived?

In some ways, that's what it has been like for Louise Brown, who was the world's first "test tube baby," born by *in vitro fertilization* (*IVF*), a procedure in which fertilization of a mother's egg by a father's sperm takes place outside of the mother's body.

Louise was a preschooler when her parents told her about how she was conceived, and throughout her childhood she was bombarded with questions. It became routine to explain to her classmates that she in fact was not born in a laboratory.

As a child, Louise sometimes felt completely alone. "I thought it was something peculiar to me," she recalled. But as she grew older, her isolation declined as more and more children were born in the same manner.

Louise Brown (foreground) and friends

In fact, today Louise is hardly isolated. More than 1.5 million babies have been born using the procedure, which has become almost routine. And at the age of 28, Louise became a mother herself, giving birth to a baby boy name Cameron—conceived, by the way, in the old-fashioned way (Moreton, 2007; Sanderson, 2007; Lawrance, 2008).

► Looking Ahead

Louise Brown's conception may have been novel, but her development, from infancy onward, has followed predictable patterns. While the specifics of our development vary—some people encounter economic deprivation or live in war-torn territories; others contend with family issues like divorce and stepparents—the broad strokes of the development set in motion in that test tube 28 years ago are remarkably similar for all of us.

Louise Brown's conception in the lab is just one of the brave new worlds of the 21st century. Issues ranging from cloning to the consequences of poverty on development to the effects of culture and race raise significant developmental concerns. Underlying these are even more fundamental issues: How do children develop physically? How does their understanding of the world grow and change over time? And how do our personalities and our social world develop as we move from birth through adolescence?

Each of these questions, and many others that we'll encounter throughout this book, are central to the field of child development. Consider, for example, the range of approaches that different specialists in child development might take when considering the story of Louise Brown:

- Child-development researchers who investigate behavior at the level of biological processes might determine if Louise's functioning prior to birth was affected by her conception outside the womb.

Child development The field that involves the scientific study of the patterns of growth, change, and stability that occur from conception through adolescence

- Specialists in child development who study genetics might examine how the biological endowment from Louise's parents affected her later behavior.

- For child development specialists who investigate the ways thinking changes over the course of childhood, Louise's life might be examined in terms of how her understanding of the nature of her conception changed as she grew older.

- Other researchers in child development who focus on physical growth might consider whether her growth rate differed from children conceived more traditionally.

- Child development experts who specialize in the social world of children might look at the ways that Louise interacted with other children and the kinds of friendships she developed.

Although their interests take many forms, all these specialists in child development share one concern: to understand the growth and change that occur during the course of childhood and adolescence. Taking many differing approaches, developmentalists study how both our biological inheritance from our parents and the environment in which we live jointly affect our behavior.

Some researchers in child development focus on explaining how our genetic background can determine not only how we look but also how we behave and how we relate to others—that is, they study personality. These professionals explore ways to identify how much of our potential as human beings is provided—or limited—by heredity. Other child development specialists look to the environment in which we are raised, exploring ways in which our lives are shaped by the world that we encounter. They investigate the extent to which we are shaped by our early environments and how our current circumstances influence our behavior in both subtle and obvious ways.

Whether they focus on heredity or environment, all child-development specialists hope that their work will ultimately inform and support the efforts of professionals whose careers are devoted to improving the lives of children. Practioners, in fields ranging from education to health care to social work, draw on the studies of child developmentalists and use those research findings to advance children's welfare.

In this chapter, we orient ourselves to the field of child development. We begin with a discussion of the scope of the discipline, illustrating the wide array of topics it covers and the range of ages it examines, from the moment of conception through the end of adolescence. We also survey the foundations of the field and examine the key issues and questions that underlie child development. Finally, we consider future trends in the child-development field. After reading this chapter, you will be able to answer these questions:

- *What is child development?*
- *What is the scope of the field?*
- *What are the key issues and questions in the field of child development?*
- *What is the future of child development likely to hold?*

An Orientation to Child Development

Have you ever wondered how it is possible that an infant tightly grips your finger with tiny, perfectly formed hands? Or marveled at how a preschooler methodically draws a picture? Or considered the way an adolescent can make involved decisions about whom to invite to a party or can discuss the ethics of downloading music files?

If you've ever pondered such things, you are asking the kinds of questions that scientists pose in the field of child development. **Child development** is the scientific study of the patterns of growth, change, and stability that occur from conception through adolescence. And although the definition of the field seems straightforward, its simplicity is somewhat misleading. To thoroughly understand what child development is actually about, we need to look deeper into the various parts of the definition.

Child development takes a scientific approach to the study of growth, change, and stability. Like members of other scientific disciplines, researchers in child development test their assumptions about the nature and course of human development by applying scientific methods. As we'll see in the next chapter, reasearchers in the field formulate theories about development, and then use methodical, scientific techniques to systematically validate the accuracy of their assumptions.

Child development focuses on human development. Although there are some developmentalists who study the course of development in nonhuman species, the vast majority examine growth and change in people. Some seek to understand universal principles of development, while others focus on how cultural, racial, and ethnic differences affect the course of development. Still others aim to understand the unique aspects of individuals, looking at the traits and characteristics that differentiate one person from

4 **PART ONE** Beginnings

Physical development Development involving the body's physical makeup, including the brain, nervous system, muscles, and senses and the need for food, drink, and sleep

Cognitive development Development involving the ways that growth and change in intellectual capabilities influence a person's behavior

Personality development Development involving the ways that the enduring characteristics that differentiate one person from another change over the life span

Social development The way in which individuals' interactions with others and their social relationships grow, change, and remain stable over the course of life

another. Regardless of approach, however, all child developmentalists view development as a continuing process throughout childhood and adolescence.

As developmental specialists focus on the ways people change and grow during their lives, they also consider stability in children's and adolescents' lives. They ask in which areas and in what periods of life people show change and growth, as well as when and how their behavior reveals consistency and continuity.

Finally, although child development focuses on childhood and adolescence, the process of development persists throughout every part of people's lives, beginning with the moment of conception and continuing until death. Developmental specialists assume that in some ways people continue to grow and change up to the end of their lives, while in other respects their behavior remains stable. At the same time, developmentalists believe that no particular, single period of life governs all development. Instead, they hold that every period of life contains the potential for both growth and decline in abilities and that individuals maintain the capacity for substantial growth and change throughout their lives.

Characterizing Child Development: The Scope of the Field

Clearly, the definition of child development is broad and the scope of the field is extensive. Consequently, professionals in child development cover several quite diverse areas, and a typical developmentalist will specialize in both a topical area and age range.

Topical Areas in Child Development The field of child development includes three major topics or approaches:

- Physical development
- Cognitive development
- Social and personality development.

A child developmentalist might specialize in a particular one of these topical areas. For example, some developmentalists focus on **physical development**, examining the ways in which the body's makeup—the brain, nervous system, muscles, and senses and the need for food, drink, and sleep—helps determine behavior. For example, one specialist in physical development might examine the effects of malnutrition on the pace of growth in children, while another might look at how an athlete's physical performance changes during adolescence.

Other developmental specialists examine **cognitive development**, seeking to understand how growth and change in intellectual capabilities influence a person's behavior. Cognitive developmentalists examine learning, memory, problem solving, and intelligence. For example, specialists in cognitive development might want to see how

problem solving changes over the course of childhood or if cultural differences exist in the way people explain the reasons for their academic successes and failures. Researchers in this area would also be interested in how a person who experiences significant or traumatic events at an early age would remember those experiences later in life.

Finally, some developmental specialists focus on personality and social development. **Personality development** is the study of stability and change in the enduring characteristics that differentiate one person from another. **Social development** is the way in which individuals' interactions with others and their social relationships grow, change, and remain stable over the course of life. A researcher interested in personality development might ask whether there are stable, enduring personality traits throughout the life span, while a specialist in social development might examine the effects of racism, poverty, or divorce on development. The major approaches to child development are summarized in Table 1-1.

Age Ranges and Individual Differences As they specialize in chosen topical areas, child developmentalists typically look at particular age ranges. These researchers usually divide childhood and adolescence into broad age ranges: the prenatal period (the period from conception to birth), infancy and toddlerhood (birth to age 3), the preschool period (ages 3 to 6), middle childhood (ages 6 to 12), and adolescence (ages 12 to 20).

Although most child developmentalists accept these broad periods, the age ranges themselves are in many ways arbitrary. Although some periods have one clear-cut boundary (infancy begins with birth, the preschool period ends with entry into public school, and adolescence starts with sexual maturity), others do not.

For instance, consider the separation between middle childhood and adolescence, which usually occurs around the age of 12. Because the boundary between these two periods is based on a biological change—the onset of sexual maturation—the time one enters adolescence can vary greatly from person to person.

In short, there are substantial individual differences in the timing of events in people's lives. In part, this is a biological fact of life: People mature at different rates and reach developmental milestones at different points. However, environmental factors also play a significant role in determining the age at which a particular event is likely to occur. For example, the typical age at which people develop romantic attachments varies substantially from one culture to another, depending in part on the way that relationships are viewed in a given culture.

It is important to keep in mind, then, that when developmental specialists discuss age ranges, they are talking about averages—the times when people, on average, reach particular milestones. Some children will reach the milestone earlier,

TABLE 1-1 Approaches to Child Development

Orientation	Defining Characteristics	Examples of Questions Asked[a]
Physical development	Examines how brain, nervous system, muscles, sensory capabilities, and needs for food, drink, and sleep affect behavior	What determines the sex of a child? (3) What are the long-term consequences of premature birth? (4) What are the benefits of breast-feeding? (5) What are the consequences of early or late sexual maturation? (14)
Cognitive development	Emphasizes intellectual abilities, including learning, memory, language development, problem solving, and intelligence	What are the earliest memories that can be recalled from infancy? (6) What are the consequences of watching television? (9) Are there benefits to bilingualism? (12) Are there ethnic and racial differences in intelligence? (12) How does an adolescent's egocentrism affect his or her view of the world? (15)
Personality and social development	Examines enduring characteristics that differentiate one person from another and how interactions with others and social relationships grow and change over the life span	Do newborns respond differently to their mothers than to others? (4) What is the best procedure for disciplining children? (10) When does a sense of gender develop? (10) How can we promote cross-race friendships? (13) What are the causes of adolescent suicide? (16)

[a]Numbers in parenthesis indicate in which chapter the question is addressed.

This wedding of two children in India is an example of how cultural factors play a significant role in determining the age when a particular even is likely to occur.

some later, and many—in fact, most—will reach it around the time of the average. Such variation becomes noteworthy only when children show substantial deviation from the average. For example, parents whose child begins to speak at a much later age than average might decide to have their son or daughter evaluated by a speech therapist.

Furthermore, as children grow older, they become more likely to deviate from the average and exhibit individual differences. In very young children, a good part of developmental change is genetically determined and unfolds automatically, making development fairly similar in different children. But as children age, environmental factors become more potent, leading to greater variability and individual differences as time passes.

The Links Between Topics and Ages Each of the broad topical areas of child development—physical, cognitive, and social and personality development—plays a role throughout childhood and adolescence. Consequently, some developmental experts focus on physical development during the prenatal period and others on what occurs during adolescence. Some might specialize in social development during the preschool years, while others look at social relationships in middle childhood. And still others might take a broader approach, looking at cognitive development through every period of childhood and adolescence (and beyond).

The variety of topical areas and age ranges studied within the field of child development means that specialists from many diverse backgrounds and areas of expertise consider themselves child developmentalists. Psychologists who study behavior and mental processes, educational researchers, geneticists, and physicians are only some of the people who specialize and conduct research in child development. Furthermore, developmentalists work in a variety of settings, including university departments of psychology, education, human development, and medicine, as well as nonacademic settings as varied as human-service agencies and child-care centers.

The diversity of specialists working under the broad umbrella of child development brings a variety of perspectives and intellectual richness to the field of child development.

In addition, it permits the research findings of the field to be used by practitioners in a wide array of applied professions. Teachers, nurses, social workers, child-care providers, and social-policy experts all rely on the findings of child development to make decisions about how to improve children's welfare.

DEVELOPMENTAL DIVERSITY

How Culture, Ethnicity, and Race Influence Development

Mayan mothers in Central America are certain that almost constant contact between themselves and their infant children is necessary for good parenting, and they are physically upset if contact is not possible. They are shocked when they see a North American mother lay her infant down, and they attribute the baby's crying to the poor parenting of the North American (Morelli et al., 1992).

What are we to make of the two views of parenting expressed in this passage? Is one right and the other wrong? Probably not, if we take into consideration the cultural context in which the mothers are operating. In fact, different cultures and subcultures have their own views of appropriate and inappropriate child rearing, just as they have different developmental goals for children (Haight, 2002; Tolchinsky, 2003; Feldman & Masalha, 2007).

Specialists in child development must consider broad cultural factors, such as an orientation toward individualism or collectivism. In addition, they must also take into account ethnic, racial, socioeconomic, and gender differences if they are to achieve an understanding of how people change and grow throughout the life span. If these specialists succeed in doing so, not only can they achieve a better understanding of human development, but they may also be able to derive more precise applications for improving the human social condition.

Efforts to understand how diversity affects development have been hindered by difficulties in finding an appropriate vocabulary. For example, members of the research community—as well as society at large—have sometimes used terms such as *race* and *ethnic group* in inappropriate ways. Race is a biological concept, which should be employed to refer to classifications based on physical and structural characteristics of species. In contrast, *ethnic group* and *ethnicity* are broader terms, referring to cultural background, nationality, religion, and language.

The concept of race has proven particularly problematic. Although it formally refers to biological factors, race has taken on substantially more meanings—many of them inappropriate—that range from skin color to religion to culture. Moreover, the concept of race is exceedingly imprecise; depending on how it is defined, there are between 3 and 300 races, and no race is genetically distinct. The fact that 99.9% of humans' genetic makeup is identical across the species, makes the question of race seem comparatively insignificant (Bamshad & Olson, 2003; Helms, Jernigan, & Mascher, 2005; Smedley & Smedley, 2005).

In addition, there is little agreement about which names best reflect different races and ethnic groups. Should the term

The face of the United States is changing as the proportion of children from different backgrounds is increasing.

African American—which has geographical and cultural implications—be preferred over *black*, which focuses primarily on skin color? Is *Native American* preferable to *Indian*? Is *Hispanic* more appropriate than *Latino*? And how can researchers accurately categorize people with multiethnic backgrounds? The choice of category has important implications for the validity and usefulness of research. The choice even has political implications. For example, the decision to permit people to identify themselves as "multiracial" on U.S. government forms and in the 2000 U.S. Census was highly controversial (Perlmann & Waters, 2002).

As the proportion of minorities in U.S. society continues to increase, it becomes crucial to consider the complex issues associated with human diversity in order to fully understand development. In fact, it is only by looking for similarities and differences among various ethnic, cultural, and racial groups that developmental researchers can distinguish principles of development that are universal from ones that are culturally determined. In the years ahead, it is likely that child development will move from a discipline that primarily focuses on children with North American and European backgrounds to one that encompasses the development of children around the globe (Fowers & Davidov, 2006; Matsumoto & Yoo, 2006; Wardle, 2007).

Cohort Influences on Development: Developing With Others in a Social World

Bob, born in 1947, is a baby boomer. He was born soon after the end of World War II, when an enormous bulge in the birthrate occurred as soldiers returned to the United States from overseas. He was an adolescent at the height of the civil rights movement and the beginning of protests against the Vietnam War. His mother, Leah, was born in 1922; she is part of the generation that passed its childhood and teenage years in the shadow of the Great Depression. Bob's son, Jon, was born in 1975. Now building a career after graduating from college and starting his own family, he is a member of what has been called Generation X. Jon's younger sister, Sarah, who was born in 1982, is part of the next generation, which sociologists have called the Millennial Generation. These people are, in part, products of the social times in which they live. Each belongs to a particular **cohort**, a group of people born at around the same time in the same place. Such major social events as wars, economic upturns and depressions, famines, and epidemics (like the one due to the AIDS virus) work similar influences on members of a particular cohort (Mitchell, 2002; Dittmann, 2005).

Cohort effects provide an example of *history-graded influences*, which are biological and environmental influences associated with a particular historical moment. For instance, children who lived in New York City during the 9/11 terrorist attack on the World Trade Center experienced shared biological and environmental challenges due to the event. Their development is going to be affected by this normative history-graded event (Bonanno, Galea, & Bucciarelli, 2006; Laugharne, Janca, & Widiger, 2007).

From an educator's perspective:
How would a student's cohort membership affect his or her readiness for school?

Society's view of childhood and what is appropriate to ask of children has changed through the ages. These children worked full time in mines in the early 1900s.

In contrast, *age-graded influences* are biological and environmental influences that are similar for individuals in a particular age group, regardless of when or where they are raised. For example, biological events such as puberty and menopause are universal events that occur at relatively the same time throughout all societies. Similarly, a sociocultural event such as entry into formal education can be considered a normative age-graded influence because it occurs in most cultures around age 6.

Development is also affected by *sociocultural-graded influences*, which include ethnicity, social class, subcultural membership, and other factors. For example, sociocultural-graded influences will be considerably different for immigrant children who speak English as a second language than it will be for children born in the United States who speak English as their first language (Rose et al., 2003).

Finally, *non-normative life events* also influence development. Non-normative life events are specific, atypical events that occur in a particular person's life at a time when such events do not happen to most people. For instance, the experience of Louise Brown, who grew up with the knowledge that she was the first person to be conceived using in vitro fertilization, constitutes a non-normative life event. In addition, children can create their own non-normative life events. For instance, a high school girl who enters and wins a national science competition produces a non-normative life event for herself. In a very real sense, she is actively constructing her own environment, thereby participating in her own development.

REVIEW ↵ mydevelopmentlab

1. Child development takes a scientific approach to development, and it considers _____ as well as change, in the lives of children and adolescents.

   Answer: stability

2. The field of child development includes three major topics or approaches: physical development, _____ development, and social and personality development.

   Answer: cognitive

3. Specialists in child development must take into consideration broad _____ factors and account for ethnic, racial, socioeconomic, and gender differences if they are to understand how people change and grow throughout the life span.

   Answer: cultural

4. Major social events have similar influences on members of a particular _____, a group of people born at around the same time in the same place.

   Answer: cohort

To see more review questions, log on to MyDevelopmentLab.

Children: Past, Present, and Future

Children have been the target of study from the time that humans have walked the planet. Parents are endlessly fascinated by their children, and the growth displayed throughout childhood and adolescence is a source of both curiosity and wonderment. But it is relatively recent in the course of history that children have been studied from a scientific vantage point. Even a brief look at how the field of child development has progressed shows that there has been considerable advancement in the way that children are viewed.

Early Views of Children

Although it is hard to imagine, some scholars believe that there was a time when childhood didn't even exist, at least in the minds of adults. According to Philippe Ariès, who studied paintings and other forms of art, children in medieval Europe were not given any special status before 1600. Instead, they were viewed as miniature, somewhat imperfect adults. They were dressed in adult clothing and not treated specially in any significant way. Childhood was seen as a stage, not qualitatively different from adulthood (Ariès, 1962; Acocella, 2003; Hutton, 2004).

The view that children during the Middle Ages were seen simply as miniature adults may be somewhat exaggerated—Ariès's arguments were based primarily on art depicting the European aristocracy, a very limited sample of Western culture. However, it is clear that childhood had a considerably different meaning than it does now. Moreover, the idea that childhood could be studied systematically did not take hold until later.

Philosophers' Views of Children   During the 16th and 17th centuries, philosophers took the lead in thinking about the nature of childhood. For example, English philosopher John Locke (1632–1704) considered a child to be a *tabula rasa*—which is Latin for "blank slate." In this view, children entered the world with no specific characteristics or personalities. Instead, they were entirely shaped by their experiences as they grew up. As we'll see in the next chapter, this view was the precursor of the modern perspective known as behaviorism.

French philosopher Jean-Jacques Rousseau (1712–1778) had an entirely different view of the nature of children. He argued that children were *noble savages*, meaning that they were born with an innate sense of right and wrong and morality. Seeing humans as basically good, he argued that infants developed into admirable and worthy children and adults unless corrupted by negative circumstances in their lives. Rousseau was one of the first observers of childhood to suggest that growth occurred in distinct, discontinuous stages that unfolded automatically—a concept that is reflected in some contemporary theories of child development that we'll discuss in the next chapter.

Baby Biographies   Among the first instances in which children were methodically studied came in the form of *baby*

During medieval times in Europe, children were thought of as miniature, although imperfect, adults. This view of childhood was reflected in how children were dressed—identically as adults.

biographies, which were popular in the late 1700s in Germany. Observers—typically parents—tried to trace the growth of a single child, recording the physical and linguistic milestones achieved by their child.

But it was not until Charles Darwin, who developed the theory of evolution, that observation of children took a more systematic turn. Darwin was convinced that understanding the development of individuals within a species could help identify how the species itself had developed. He made baby biographies more scientifically respectable by producing one of his own, a record of his own son's development during his first year.

A wave of baby biographies were produced following publication of Darwin's book. Furthermore, other historical trends were helping propel the development of a new scientific discipline focusing on children. Scientists were discovering the mechanisms behind conception, and geneticists were beginning to unlock the mysteries of heredity. Philosophers were arguing about the relative influences of nature (heredity) and nurture (influences in the environment).

Focus on Childhood   As the adult labor pool increased, children were no longer needed as a source of inexpensive labor, paving the way for laws that protected children from exploitation. The advent of more universal education meant that children were separated from adults for more of the day, and educators sought to identify better ways of teaching children.

Advances in psychology led people to focus on the ways that events that had occurred during childhood influenced them during their adult lives. As a consequence of these significant social changes, child development became recognized as a field of its own.

The 20th Century: Child Development as a Discipline

Several figures became central to the emerging field of child development. For example, Alfred Binet, a French psychologist, not only pioneered work on children's intelligence but

Continuous change
Gradual development in which achievements at one level build on those of previous levels

Discontinuous change
Development that occurs in distinct steps or stages, with each stage bringing about behavior that is assumed to be qualitatively different from behavior at earlier stages

Critical period   A specific time during development when a particular event has its greatest consequences

also investigated memory and mental calculation. G. Stanley Hall pioneered the use of questionnaires to illuminate children's thinking and behavior. He also wrote the first book that targeted adolescence as a distinct period of development, aptly titled *Adolescence* (Hall, 1904/1916).

Contributions of Women   Even though prejudice hindered women in their pursuit of academic careers, they made significant contributions to the discipline of child development during the early part of the 1900s. For example, Leta Stetter Hollingworth was one of the first psychologists to focus on child development (Hollingworth, 1943/1990; Denmark & Fernandez, 1993).

During the first decades of the 1900s, one emerging trend that had enormous impact on our understanding of children's development was the rise of large-scale, systematic, and ongoing investigations of children and their development throughout the life span. For example, the Stanford Studies of Gifted Children began in the early 1920s and continue today. Similarly, the Fels Research Institute Study and the Berkeley Growth and Guidance Studies helped identify the nature of change in children's lives as they became older. Using a normative approach, they studied large numbers of children in order to determine the nature of normal growth (Dixon & Lerner, 1999).

The women and men who built the foundations of child development shared a common goal: to scientifically study the nature of growth, change, and stability throughout childhood and adolescence. They brought the field to where it is today.

Today's Key Issues and Questions: Child Development's Underlying Themes

Several key issues and questions dominate the field of child development today. Among the major issues (summarized in Table 1-2) are the nature of developmental change, the importance of critical and sensitive periods, life span approaches versus more focused approaches, and the nature–nurture issue.

Continuous Change Versus Discontinuous Change

One of the primary issues challenging child developmentalists is whether development proceeds in a continuous or discontinuous fashion (illustrated in Figure 1-1). In **continuous change**, development is gradual, with achievements at one level building on those of previous levels. Continuous change is quantitative; the basic underlying developmental processes that drive change remain the same over the course of the life span. Continuous change, then, produces changes that are a matter of degree, not of kind. Changes in height prior to adulthood, for example, are continuous. Similarly, as we'll see later in the chapter, some theorists suggest that changes in people's thinking capabilities are also continuous, showing gradual quantitative improvements rather than developing entirely new cognitive processing capabilities.

In contrast, **discontinuous change** occurs in distinct steps or stages. Each stage brings about behavior that is assumed to be qualitatively different from behavior at earlier stages. Consider the example of cognitive development. We'll see in Chapter 2 that some cognitive developmentalists suggest that our thinking changes in fundamental ways as children develop and that such development is not just a matter of quantitative change but also one of qualitative change.

Most developmentalists agree that taking an either–or position on the continuous–discontinuous issue is inappropriate. While many types of developmental change are continuous, others are clearly discontinuous (Flavell, 1994; Heimann, 2003).

Critical and Sensitive Periods: Gauging the Impact of Environmental Events   If a woman comes down with a case of rubella (German measles) in the 11th week of pregnancy, the consequences for the child she is carrying are likely to be devastating and include the possibility of blindness, deafness, and heart defects. However, if she comes down with the same strain of rubella in the 30th week of pregnancy, damage to the child is unlikely.

The differing outcomes of the disease in the two periods demonstrate the concept of critical periods. A **critical period** is a specific time during development when a particular event

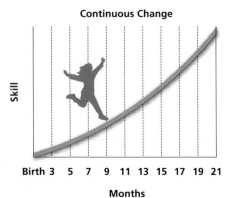

Continuous Change

Skill

Birth 3   5   7   9   11 13 15 17 19 21

Months

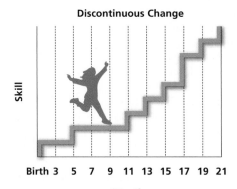

Discontinuous Change

Skill

Birth 3   5   7   9   11 13 15 17 19 21

Months

FIGURE 1-1 Two Approaches to Developmental Change

The two approaches to development are *continuous change*, which is gradual, with achievements at one level building on those of previous levels, and *discontinuous change*, which occurs in distinct steps or stages.

Plasticity The degree to which a developing behavior or physical structure is modifiable

Sensitive period A specific time when organisms are particularly susceptible to certain kinds of stimuli in their environment

TABLE 1-2	Major Issues in Child Development	

Continuous Change	Discontinuous Change
• Change is gradual. • Achievements at one level build on previous level. • Underlying developmental processes remain the same over the life span.	• Change occurs in distinct steps or stages. • Behavior and processes are qualitatively different at different stages.
Critical Periods	**Sensitive Periods**
• Certain environmental stimuli are necessary for normal development. • Emphasized by early developmentalists.	• People are susceptible to certain environmental stimuli, but consequences of absent stimuli are reversible. • Current emphasis in life span development.
Life Span Approach	**Focus on Particular Periods**
• Current theories emphasize growth and change throughout life, relatedness of different periods.	• Infancy and adolescence emphasized by early developmentalists as most important periods.
Nature (Genetic Factors)	**Nurture (Environmental Factors)**
• Emphasis is on discovering inherited genetic traits and abilities.	• Emphasis is on environmental influences that affect a person's development.

has its greatest consequences. Critical periods occur when the presence of certain kinds of environmental stimuli are necessary for development to proceed normally (Uylings, 2006).

Although early specialists in child development placed great emphasis on the importance of critical periods, more recent thinking suggests that in many realms, individuals may be more flexible than was first thought, particularly in the domains of cognitive, personality, and social development. In these areas, there is a significant degree of **plasticity**, the degree to which a developing behavior or physical structure is modifiable. For instance, rather than suffering permanent damage from a lack of certain kinds of early social experiences, there is increasing evidence that children can use later experiences to help overcome earlier deficits.

Consequently, developmentalists are now more likely to speak of sensitive periods rather than critical periods. In a **sensitive period**, organisms are particularly susceptible to certain kinds of stimuli in their environment. A sensitive period represents the optimal period for particular capacities to emerge, and children are particularly sensitive to environmental influences.

It is important to understand the difference between the concepts of critical periods and sensitive periods: In critical periods, it is assumed that the absence of certain kinds of environmental influences is likely to produce permanent, irreversible consequences for the developing individual. In contrast, although the absence of particular environmental influences during a sensitive period may hinder develop-

ment, it is possible for later experiences to overcome the earlier deficits. In other words, the concept of sensitive periods recognizes the plasticity of developing humans (Beauchaine, 2003; Armstrong, et al., 2006).

Life Span Approaches Versus a Focus on Particular Periods

On what part of the life span should child developmentalists focus their attention? For early developmentalists, the answers tended to be infancy and adolescence. Most attention was clearly concentrated on those two periods, largely to the exclusion of other parts of childhood.

Today, however, the story is different. The entire period encompassing conception through adolescence is now regarded as important, for several reasons. First, with the discovery that growth and change continue over the entire life span, modern research has broadened to focus on development through all the stages of life. Furthermore, to understand the social influences on children of a given age, we need to understand the people who make up their social environment. These are the people, who in large measure, have the greatest opportunity to influence children's development. For instance, to understand development in infants, we need to unravel the effects of their parents' age on each baby's social environment. It is likely that a 15-year-old mother will provide parental influences of a very different sort from those provided by an experienced 37-year-old

> **From a child-care worker's perspective:** What might you do to take advantage of a sensitive period?

Maturation   The process of
the predetermined unfolding of
genetic information

mother. Consequently, infant development is in part a consequence of adult development.

The Relative Influence of Nature and Nurture on Development

One of the enduring questions of child development involves how much of people's behavior is due to their genetically determined nature and how much is due to nurture, the influences of the physical and social environment in which a child is raised. This issue, which has deep philosophical and historical roots, has dominated much work in child development (Wexler, 2006).

In this context, *nature* refers to traits, abilities, and capacities that are inherited from one's parents. It encompasses any factor that is produced by the predetermined unfolding of genetic information—a process known as **maturation**. These genetic, inherited influences are at work as we move from the one-cell organism that is created at the moment of conception to the billions of cells that make up a fully formed human. Nature influences whether our eyes are blue or brown, whether we have thick hair throughout life or eventually go bald, and how good we are at athletics. Nature allows our brains to develop in such a way that we can read the words on this page.

In contrast, *nurture* refers to the environmental influences that shape behavior. Some of these influences may be biological, such as the impact of a pregnant mother's cocaine use on her unborn child, or the amounts and kinds of food that are available to children. Other environmental influences are more social, such as the ways parents discipline their children or the effects of peer pressure on an adolescent. Finally, some influences are a result of larger, societal-level factors, such as the socioeconomic circumstances in which people find themselves.

If our traits and behavior were determined solely by either nature or nurture, there would probably be little debate regarding the issue. However, for most critical behaviors, this is hardly the case. Take, for instance, one of the most controversial arenas: intelligence. As we'll consider in detail in Chapter 12, the question of whether intelligence is determined primarily by inherited, genetic factors—nature—or is shaped by environmental factors—nurture—has caused lively and often bitter arguments. Largely because of its social implications, the issue has spilled out of the scientific arena and into the realm of politics and social policy.

Implications for Child Rearing and Social Policy

Consider the implications of the nature-versus-nurture issue: If the extent of one's intelligence is primarily determined by heredity and consequently is largely fixed at birth, then efforts to improve intellectual performance later in life may be doomed to failure. In contrast, if intelligence is primarily a result of environmental factors, such as the amount and quality of schooling and stimulation to which one is exposed, then we would expect that an improvement in social conditions could bring about an increase in intelligence.

The extent of social policy affected by ideas about the origins of intelligence illustrates the significance of issues that involve the nature–nurture question. As we address it in relation to several topical areas throughout this book, we should keep in mind that specialists in child development reject the notion that behavior is the result solely of either nature or nurture. Instead, the question is one of degree—and the specifics of that, too, are hotly debated.

Furthermore, the interaction of genetic and environmental factors is complex, in part because certain genetically determined traits have not only a direct influence on children's behavior but an indirect influence in shaping children's environments as well. For example, a child who is consistently cranky and who cries a great deal—a trait that may be produced by genetic factors—may influence her environment by making her parents so highly responsive to her insistent crying that they rush to comfort her whenever she cries. Their responsivity to the child's genetically determined behavior consequently becomes an environmental influence on her subsequent development.

Similarly, although our genetic background orients us toward particular behaviors, those behaviors will not necessarily occur without an appropriate environment. People with similar genetic backgrounds (such as identical twins) may behave in very different ways; and people with highly dissimilar genetic backgrounds can behave quite similarly to one another in certain areas (Coll, Bearer, & Lerner, 2004; Kato & Pedersen, 2005).

In sum, the question of how much of a given behavior is due to nature and how much to nurture is a challenging one. Ultimately, we should consider the two sides of the nature–nurture issue as opposite ends of a continuum, with particular behaviors falling somewhere between the two ends. We can say something similar about the other controversies that we have considered. For instance, continuous versus discontinuous development is not an either–or proposition; some forms of development fall toward the continuous end of the continuum, while others lie closer to the discontinuous end. In short, few statements about development involve either–or absolutes (Rutter, 2006; Deater-Deckard & Cahill, 2007).

The Future of Child Development

We've examined the foundations of the field of child development, along with the key issues and questions that underlie the discipline. But what lies ahead? Several trends appear likely to emerge:

- As research in development continues to be amassed, the field will become increasingly specialized. New areas of study and perspectives will emerge.

- The explosion in information about genes and the genetic foundations of behavior will influence all spheres of child development. Increasingly, developmentalists will link work

Preventing Violence in Children

When other children were hearing fairy tales, Garland Hampton heard bedtime stories about the day Uncle Robert killed two Milwaukee police officers, or the time Grandma, with both barrels, blew away the father of two of her children back in '62. By the time he was 9, he had seen his mother kill her boyfriend.

Now, at 15, locked up in the County Jail and awaiting trial on murder charges, Garland is still enough of a child that he is afraid he might cry when darkness falls.

But he is old enough to have had a nasty past of his own, too: at 10, there was trouble about stolen bicycles; at 12, he was picked up for shooting and wounding a gang rival; at 14, for carrying a .357 Magnum and a bag of cocaine, and now, gunning down a fellow gang member. Prosecutors say he is an adolescent menace to society, who must pay for his sins like a man.

Garland just says he is scared. (Terry, 1994, p. A1)

Garland's descent into violence is representative of the lives of too many children and adolescents in the United States today. Many observers have called the level of violence nothing less than an epidemic. In fact, surveys find that violence and crime rank as the issues of greatest concern to most U.S. citizens (Mehran, 1997; National Coalition Against Domestic Violence, 2003).

How can we explain the level of violence? How do people learn to be violent? How can we control and remedy aggression? And how can we discourage violence from occurring in the first place? Child development has sought to answer such questions from several different perspectives. Consider these examples:

- **Explaining the roots of violence.** Some child developmentalists have looked at how early behavioral and physical problems may be associated with later difficulties in controlling aggression. For instance, researchers have found links between early maltreatment, physical and psychological abuse, and neglect of children to their subsequent aggressive behavior. Others have looked at hormonal influences on violent behavior (Gagné et al., 2007; Maas, Herrenkohl, & Sousa, 2008).

- **Examining how exposure to aggression may lead to violence.** Other psychologists have examined how exposure to violence in the media and in video games may lead to aggression. For example, Brad Bushman and Craig Anderson have found that people who play violent video games have an altered view of the world, seeing it as more violent than those who do not play such games. In addition, those who play such violent video games are more easily triggered into aggressive behavior (Bushman & Anderson, 2002; Anderson, Funk, & Griffiths, 2004; Barlett, Harris, & Baldassaro, 2007).

- **Developing programs to reduce aggression.** According to psychologists Ervin Staub and Darren Spielman, schoolteachers and school administrators must be on the lookout for even milder forms of aggression, such as bullying. Unless such forms of aggression are checked, they are likely to endure and to escalate into more blatant forms. To combat aggression, Staub and Spielman devised a program to help children develop constructive ways of fulfilling their basic needs. After involvement in an intervention that included role paying, videotaping, and structured discussions, participants' aggressive behavior declined (Spielman & Staub, 2003).

As these examples illustrate, developmental researchers are making progress in understanding and dealing with the violence that is increasingly part of modern society. Furthermore, violence is just one example of the areas in which experts in child development are contributing their skills for the betterment of human society. As we'll see throughout this book, the field has much to offer.

- Why does violence remain such a problem in the United States, and why are the levels of violence (as measured by crime statistics) worse in the United States than in other industrialized countries?

- Because research shows that exposure to violent video games raises the level of aggression in players, do you think there should be legal limitations on the sale and distribution of such games? Why or why not?

---

across biological, cognitive, and social domains, and the boundaries between different subdisciplines will be blurred.
- The increasing diversity of the population of the United States in terms of race, ethnicity, language, and culture will lead the field to focus greater attention on issues of diversity.
- A growing number of professionals in a variety of fields will make use of child development's research and findings. Educators, social workers, nurses and other health-care providers, genetic counselors, toy designers, child-care providers, cereal manufacturers, social ethicists, and members of dozens of other professions will all draw on the field of child development.

- Work on child development will increasingly influence public-interest issues. Discussion of many of the major social concerns of our time, including violence, prejudice and discrimination, poverty, changes in family life, child care, schooling, and even terrorism, can be informed by research in child development. Consequently, child developmentalists are likely to make important contributions to 21st-century society (Pyszczynski, Solomon, & Greenberg, 2004; Block, Weinstein, & Seitz, 2005). (For one example of the current contributions of work in child development, see the *From Research to Practice* box.)

Becoming an Informed Consumer of Development

Assessing Information on Child Development

If you immediately comfort crying babies, you'll spoil them.

If you let babies cry without comforting them, they'll be untrusting and clingy as adults.

Spanking is one of the best ways to discipline your child.

Never hit your child.

If a marriage is unhappy, children are better off if their parents divorce than if they stay together.

No matter how difficult a marriage is, parents should avoid divorce for the sake of their children.

There is no lack of advice on the best way to raise a child or, more generally, to lead one's life. From best sellers with titles such as *The No-Cry Sleep Solution* to magazine and newspaper columns that provide advice on every imaginable topic, each of us is exposed to tremendous amounts of information.

Yet not all advice is equally valid. The mere fact that something is in print, on television, or on the Internet does not automatically make it legitimate or accurate. Fortunately, some guidelines can help distinguish when recommendations and suggestions are reasonable and when they are not. Here are a few:

- **Consider the source of the advice.** Information from established, respected organizations such as the American Medical Association, the American Psychological Association, and the American Academy of Pediatrics is likely to be the result of years of study, and its accuracy is probably high.

- **Evaluate the credentials of the person providing advice.** Information coming from established, acknowledged researchers and experts in a field is likely to be more accurate than that coming from a person whose credentials are obscure.

- **Understand the difference between anecdotal evidence and scientific evidence.** Anecdotal evidence is based on one or two instances of a phenomenon, haphazardly discovered or encountered; scientific evidence is based on careful, systematic procedures.

- **Keep cultural context in mind.** Although an assertion may be valid in some contexts, it may not be true in all. For example, it is typically assumed that providing infants the freedom to move about and exercise their limbs facilitates their muscular development and mobility. Yet in some cultures, infants spend most of their time closely bound to their mothers with no apparent long-term damage (Kaplan & Dove, 1987; Tronick, Thomas, & Daltabuit, 1994).

- **Don't assume that because many people believe something, it is necessarily true.** Scientific evaluation has often proved that some of the most basic presumptions about the effectiveness of various techniques are invalid. For instance, consider DARE, the Drug Abuse Resistance Education antidrug program that is used in about half the school systems in the United States. DARE is designed to prevent the spread of drugs through lectures and question-and-answer sessions run by police officers. Careful evaluation, however, finds no evidence that the program is effective in reducing drug use (Rhule, 2005).

In short, the key to evaluating information relating to child development is to maintain a healthy dose of skepticism. No source of information is invariably, unfailingly accurate. By keeping a critical eye on the statements you encounter, you'll be in a better position to determine the very real contributions made by child developmentalists in understanding how we change and grow over the course of childhood and adolescence.

REVIEW mydevelopmentlab

1. The predetermined unfolding of genetic information is
   _____ .

   Answer: maturation

2. One key issue in child development today includes the comparison and contrast between continuous versus _____ change.

   Answer: discontinuous

3. Another important issue involves the understanding of critical and _____ periods.

   Answer: sensitive

4. The relative influence of nature versus _____ on development illustrates a key question in child development.

   Answer: nurture

To see more review questions, log on to MyDevelopmentLab.

CASE STUDY

The Case of... Too Many Choices

Jenny Claymore, midway through her 3rd year of college, is desperate to pick a career, but hasn't a clue. The problem isn't that nothing interests her; it's that too many things do. From her reading, radio listening, and TV watching, her head is full of ideas for great-sounding careers.

Jenny loves children, having always enjoyed babysitting and her summer work as a camp counselor—so maybe she should be a teacher. She is fascinated by all she hears about DNA and genetic research—so maybe she should be a biologist or a doctor. She is concerned when she hears about school violence—from bullying to shootings—so maybe she should go into school administration or law enforcement. She is curious about how children learn language—so maybe she should go into speech pathology or, again, teaching. She is fascinated by court cases that rely on the testimony of young children, and how experts on both sides contradict each other—so maybe she should become a lawyer.

Her college counselor once said "Begin your search for a career by thinking about the classes you've taken in high school and college." Jenny recalls a high school course in early child-hood that she loved, and she knows that her favorite class in college is her child development course. Would considering a career in child development make sense?

1. How well might a career in the field of child development address her love of children and her interest in genetic research?

2. What sort of career might focus on the prevention of school violence?

3. How might child development relate to her interest in eyewitness testimony and memory?

4. Overall, how many careers could you think of that would fit Jenny's interests?

◄ Looking Back

What is child development?

- Child development is a scientific approach to questions about growth, change, and stability that occur from conception to adolescence.

What is the scope of the field?

- The scope of the field encompasses physical, cognitive, and social and personality development at all ages from conception through adolescence.

- Culture—both broad and narrow—is an important issue in child development. Many aspects of development are influenced not only by broad cultural differences but also by ethnic, racial, and socioeconomic differences within a particular culture.

- Every person is subject to history-graded influences, age-graded influences, sociocultural-graded influences, and non-normative life events.

What are the key issues and questions in the field of child development?

- Four key issues in child development are (1) whether developmental change is continuous or discontinuous, (2) whether development is largely governed by critical or sensitive periods during which certain influences or experiences must occur for development to be normal, (3) whether to focus on certain particularly important periods in human development or on the entire life span, and (4) the nature–nurture question, which focuses on the relative importance of genetic versus environmental influences.

What is the future of child development likely to hold?

- Future trends in the field are likely to include increasing specialization, the blurring of boundaries between different areas, increasing attention to issues involving diversity, and an increasing influence on public-interest issues. ∎

Epilogue

We have covered a lot of ground in our introduction to the growing field of child development. We have reviewed the broad scope of the field, touching on the wide range of topics that child developmentalists may address, and have discussed the key issues and questions that have shaped the field since its inception.

Before proceeding to the next chapter, take a few minutes to reconsider the prologue of this chapter—about the case of Louise Brown, the first child to be born through in vitro fertilization. Based on what you now know about child development, answer the following questions:

1. What are some of the potential benefits, and the costs, of in vitro fertilization, that was carried out for Louise's parents?

2. What are some questions that researchers who study either physical, cognitive, or personality and social development might ask about the effects on Louise of being conceived via in vitro fertilization?

3. The creation of complete human clones, exact genetic replicas of an individual, is still in the realm of science fiction, but the theoretical possibility does raise some important questions. For example, what would be the psychological consequences of being a clone?

4. If clones could actually be produced, how might it help scientists understand the relative impact of heredity and environment on development?

Key Terms and Concepts

child development (p. 4)
physical development (p. 5)
cognitive development (p. 5)
personality development (p. 5)

social development (p. 5)
cohort (p. 8)
continuous change (p. 10)
discontinuous change (p. 10)

critical period (p. 10)
plasticity (p. 11)
sensitive period (p. 11)
maturation (p. 12)

chapter two

Theoretical Perspectives and Research

PROLOGUE: AGAINST THE ODDS

Recently, a student was shot dead by a classmate during lunch period outside Frank W. Ballou Senior High. It didn't come as much of a surprise to anyone at the school, in this city's most crime-infested ward. Just during the current school year, one boy was hacked by a student with an ax, a girl was badly wounded in a knife fight with another female student, five fires were set by arsonists, and an unidentified body was dumped next to the parking lot.

But all is quiet in the echoing hallways at 7:15 A.M., long before classes start on a spring morning. The only sound comes from the computer lab, where 16-year-old Cedric Jennings is already at work on an extra-credit project, a program to bill patients at a hospital. Later, he will work on his science-fair project, a chemical analysis of acid rain.

He arrives every day this early and often doesn't leave until dark. The high-school junior with the perfect grades has big dreams: He wants to go to Massachusetts Institute of Technology. (Suskind, 1994, p. 1; Suskind, 1999)

► Looking Ahead

Cedric Jennings was one of a tiny group of students who had an average of B or better at their huge inner-city high school in Washington, D.C. These achievers were a lonely group, the frequent target of threats and actual violence. Yet Cedric persevered, intent on getting a college education and succeeding academically and, ultimately, in life—something that he would eventually accomplish.

How do individuals such as Cedric overcome the extremes of poverty and violence that they face? Why are others less successful? More broadly, how do all children and adolescents navigate the challenges they each face?

The ability to answer these questions depends on the accumulated findings from literally thousands of developmental research studies. These studies have looked at questions ranging from brain development to the nature of social relationships to the way in which cognitive abilities grow throughout childhood and adolescence. The common challenge of these studies is to pose and answer questions of interest in child development.

Like all of us, these developmentalists ask questions about people's bodies, minds, and social interactions—and about how these aspects of human life change as people age. But to the natural curiosity that we all share, developmental scientists add one important ingredient that makes a difference in how they ask—and try to answer—questions. This ingredient is the scientific method. This structured but straightforward way of looking at phenomena elevates questioning from mere curiosity to purposeful learning. With this powerful tool, developmentalists are able not only to ask good questions but also to begin to answer them systematically.

In this chapter, we consider the way in which developmentalists ask and answer questions about the world. We begin with a discussion of the broad perspectives used in understanding children and their behavior. These outlooks provide broad approaches from which to view the development along multiple dimensions. We then turn to the basic building blocks of the science of child development: research. We describe the major types of research that developmentalists perform to pursue their research and get answers to their questions. Finally, we focus on

Theories Explanations and predictions concerning phenomena of interest, providing a framework for understanding the relationships among an organized set of facts or principles

Psychodynamic perspective The approach to the study of development that states behavior is motivated by inner forces, memories, and conflicts of which a person has little awareness or control

Psychoanalytic theory The theory proposed by Freud that suggests that unconscious forces act to determine personality and behavior

two important issues in developmental research: how to choose research participants so that results can be applied beyond the study setting, and the central issue of research ethics.

In sum, after reading this chapter, you will be able to answer these questions:

- *What are the major perspectives on child development?*
- *What is the scientific method, and how does it help answer questions about child development?*
- *What are the major research strategies and challenges?*

Perspectives on Children

When Roddy McDougall said his first word, his parents were elated—and relieved. They had anticipated the moment for what seemed a long time; most of the children of his age had already uttered their first word. In addition, his grandparents had weighed in with their concerns, his grandmother going so far as to suggest that he might be suffering from some sort of developmental delay, although that was based solely on a "feeling" she had. But the moment Roddy spoke, his parents' and grandparents' anxieties fell away, and they all simply experienced great pride in Roddy's accomplishment.

The concerns Roddy's relatives felt were based on their vague conceptions of how a normal child's development proceeds. Each of us has established ideas about the course of development, and we use them to make judgments and develop hunches about the meaning of children's behavior. Our experience orients us to certain types of behavior that we see as particularly important. For some people, it may be when a child says his or her first word; for others, it may be the way a child interacts with others.

Like laypeople, child developmentalists approach the field from a number of different perspectives. Each broad perspective encompasses one or more **theories**, broad, organized explanations and predictions concerning phenomena of interest. A theory provides a framework for understanding the relationships among a seemingly unorganized set of facts or principles.

We all create theories about development, based on

Sigmund Freud

our experience, folklore, and articles in magazines and newspapers. However, theories in the discipline of child development are different. Whereas our own personal theories are built on unverified observations that are developed haphazardly, child developmentalists' theories are more formal, based on a systematic integration of prior findings and theorizing. These theories allow developmentalists to summarize and organize prior observations, and allow them to move beyond existing observations to draw deductions that may not be immediately apparent. In addition, these theories are then subject to rigorous testing in the form of research. By contrast, the developmental theories of individuals are not subject to such testing and may never be questioned at all (R. Thomas, 2001).

We'll consider five major perspectives used in child development: the psychodynamic, behavioral, cognitive, contextual, and evolutionary perspectives. These diverse outlooks emphasize somewhat different aspects of development that steer inquiry in particular directions. Just as we can use multiple maps to find our way around a region—for example, one map might show the roadways and another might focus on key landmarks—the various developmental perspectives provide us with different views of child and adolescent behavior. And just as maps must continually be revised, each perspective continues to evolve and change, as befits a growing and dynamic discipline.

The Psychodynamic Perspective: Focusing on Internal Forces

When Marisol was 6 months old, she was involved in a bloody automobile accident—or so her parents tell her, since she has no conscious recollection of it. Now, however, at age 24, she is having difficulty maintaining relationships, and her therapist is seeking to determine whether her current problems are a result of the early accident.

Looking for such a link might seem a bit far-fetched, but to proponents of the **psychodynamic perspective**, it is not so improbable. Advocates of the psychodynamic perspective believe that behavior is motivated by inner forces, memories, and conflicts of which a person has little awareness or control. The inner forces, which may stem from one's childhood, continually influence behavior throughout the life span.

Freud's Psychoanalytic Theory The psychodynamic perspective is most closely associated with Sigmund Freud and his psychoanalytic theory. Freud, who lived from 1856 to 1939, was a Viennese physician whose revolutionary ideas ultimately had a profound effect not just on the fields of psychology and psychiatry but on Western thought in general (Masling & Bornstein, 1996).

Freud's **psychoanalytic theory** suggests that unconscious forces act to determine personality and behavior. To Freud, the *unconscious* is a part of the personality about which a person is unaware. It contains infantile wishes, desires, demands, and needs that are hidden, because of their disturbing nature, from conscious awareness. Freud suggested that the unconscious is responsible for a good part of our everyday behavior.

According to Freud, everyone's personality has three aspects: id, ego, and superego. The *id* is the raw, unorganized, inborn part of personality that is present at birth. It represents primitive drives related to hunger, sex, aggression, and irrational impulses. The id operates according to the *pleasure principle*, in which the goal is to maximize satisfaction and reduce tension.

The *ego* is the part of personality that is rational and reasonable. The ego acts as a buffer between the real world outside of us and the primitive id. The ego operates on the *reality principle*, in which instinctual energy is restrained to maintain the safety of the individual and help integrate the person into society.

Finally, Freud proposed that the *superego* represents a person's conscience, incorporating distinctions between right and wrong. It develops around age 5 or 6 and is learned from an individual's parents, teachers, and other significant figures.

In addition to providing an account of the various parts of the personality, Freud also suggested the ways in which personality developed during childhood. He argued that **psychosexual development** occurred as children passed through a series of stages, in which pleasure, or gratification, was focused on a particular biological function and body part. As illustrated in Table 2-1, he suggested that pleasure shifted from the mouth (the *oral stage*) to the anus (the *anal stage*) and eventually to the genitals (the *phallic stage* and the *genital stage*).

According to Freud, if children are unable to gratify themselves sufficiently during a particular stage, or conversely, if they receive too much gratification, fixation may occur. *Fixation* is behavior reflecting an earlier stage of development due to an unresolved conflict. For instance, fixation at the oral stage might produce an adult unusually absorbed in oral activities—eating, talking, or chewing gum. Freud also argued that fixation is represented through symbolic sorts of oral activities, such as the use of "biting" sarcasm.

Erikson's Psychosocial Theory Psychoanalyst Erik Erikson, who lived from 1902 to 1994, provided an alternative psychodynamic view in his theory of psychosocial development, which emphasizes our social interaction with other people. In Erikson's view, society and culture both challenge and shape us. **Psychosocial development** encompasses changes in our interactions with and understandings of one another, as well as in our knowledge and understanding of ourselves as members of society (Erikson, 1963; Côté, 2005).

Erikson's theory suggests that developmental change occurs throughout our lives in eight distinct

stages (see Table 2-1). The stages emerge in a fixed pattern and are similar for all people.

Erikson argued that each stage presents a crisis or conflict that the individual must resolve. Although no crisis is ever fully resolved, making life increasingly complicated, the individual must at least address the crisis of each stage sufficiently to deal with demands made during the next stage of development.

Erik Erikson

Unlike Freud, who regarded development as relatively complete by adolescence, Erikson suggested that growth and change continue throughout the life span. For instance, he suggested that during middle adulthood, people pass through the *generativity-versus-stagnation stage*, in which their contributions to family, community, and society can produce either positive feelings about the continuity of life or a sense of stagnation and disappointment about what they are passing on to future generations (De St. Aubin, McAdams, & Kim, 2004).

Assessing the Psychodynamic Perspective It is hard for us to grasp the full significance of psychodynamic theories, represented by Freud's psychoanalytic theory and Erikson's theory of psychosocial development. Freud's introduction of the notion that unconscious influences affect behavior was a monumental accomplishment, and that it seems at all reasonable to us shows how extensively the idea of the unconscious has pervaded thinking in Western cultures. In fact, work by contemporary researchers studying memory and learning suggests that we carry with us memories—of which we are not consciously aware—that have a significant impact on our behavior. The example of Marisol, who was in a car accident when she was a baby, shows one application of psychodynamically based thinking and research.

However, some of the most basic principles of Freud's psychoanalytic theory have been called into question because they have not been validated by subsequent research. In particular, the notion that people pass through stages in childhood that determine their adult personalities has little definitive research support. In addition, because much of Freud's theory was based on a limited population of upper-middle-class Austrians living during a strict, puritanical era, its application to broad, multicultural populations is questionable. Finally, because Freud's theory focuses primarily on male development, it has been criticized as sexist and may be interpreted as devaluing women. For such reasons, many

TABLE 2-1   Freud's and Erikson's Theories

Approximate Age	Freud's Stages of Psychosexual Development	Major Characteristics of Freud's Stages	Erikson's Stages of Psychosocial Development	Positive and Negative Outcomes of Erikson's Stages
Birth to 12–18 months	Oral	Interest in oral gratification from sucking, eating, mouthing, biting	Trust vs. mistrust	*Positive:* Feelings of trust from environmental support *Negative:* Fear and concern regarding others
12–18 months to 3 years	Anal	Gratification from expelling and withholding feces; coming to terms with society's controls relating to toilet training	Autonomy vs. shame and doubt	*Positive:* Self-sufficiency if exploration is encouraged *Negative:* Doubts about self, lack of independence
3 to 5–6 years	Phallic	Interest in the genitals; coming to terms with Oedipal conflict, leading to identification with same sex parent	Initiative vs. guilt	*Positive:* Discovery of ways to initiate actions *Negative:* Guilt from actions and thoughts
5–6 years to adolescence	Latency	Sexual concerns largely unimportant	Industry vs. inferiority	*Positive:* Development of sense of competence *Negative:* Feelings of inferiority, no sense of mastery
Adolescence to adulthood (Freud) Adolescence (Erikson)	Genital	Reemergence of sexual interests and establishment of mature sexual relationships	Identity vs. role diffusion	*Positive:* Awareness of uniqueness of self, knowledge of role to be followed *Negative:* Inability to identify appropriate roles in life
Early adulthood (Erikson)			Intimacy vs. isolation	*Positive:* Development of loving, sexual relationships and close friendships *Negative:* Fear of relationships with others
Middle adulthood (Erikson)			Generativity vs. stagnation	*Positive:* Sense of contribution to continuity of life *Negative:* Trivialization of one's activities
Late adulthood (Erikson)			Ego-integrity vs. despair	*Positive:* Sense of unity in life's accomplishments *Negative:* Regret over lost opportunities of life

developmentalists question Freud's theory (Guterl, 2002; Messer & McWilliams, 2003; Schachter, 2005).

Erikson's view that development continues throughout the life span is an important one, and it influenced a good deal of thinking about how developmental change unfolds during life. On the other hand, the theory is vague and hard to test in a rigorous manner. Furthermore, like Freud's theory, it focuses more on male than female development. In sum, although the psychodynamic perspective provides reasonably good descriptions of past behavior, its predictions of future behavior are imprecise (Zauszniewski & Martin, 1999; De St. Aubin et al., 2004).

Behavioral perspective
The approach to the study of development that suggests that the keys to understanding development are observable behavior and outside stimuli in the environment

Classical conditioning
A type of learning in which an organism responds in a particular way to a neutral stimulus that normally does not bring about that type of response

Operant conditioning A form of learning in which a voluntary response is strengthened or weakened, depending on its association with positive or negative consequences

The Behavioral Perspective: Focusing on Observable Behavior

When Elissa Sheehan was 3, a large brown dog bit her, and she needed dozens of stitches and several operations. Since the time she was bitten, she broke into a sweat whenever she saw a dog and, in fact never enjoyed being around any pet.

To a child development specialist using the behavioral perspective, the explanation for Elissa's behavior is straightforward: She has a learned fear of dogs. Rather than looking inside the organism at unconscious processes, the **behavioral perspective** suggests that the keys to understanding development are observable behavior and outside stimuli in the environment. If we know the stimuli, we can predict the behavior. In this respect, the behavioral perspective reflects the view that nurture is more important to development than nature.

Behavioral theories reject the notion that people universally pass through a series of stages. Instead, people are assumed to be affected by the environmental stimuli to which they happen to be exposed. Developmental patterns, then, are personal, reflecting a particular set of environmental stimuli, and behavior is the result of continuing exposure to specific factors in the environment. Furthermore, developmental change is viewed in quantitative, rather than qualitative, terms. For instance, behavioral theories hold that advances in problem-solving capabilities as children age are largely a result of greater mental *capacities* rather than changes in the *kind* of thinking that children are able to bring to bear on a problem.

Classical Conditioning: Stimulus Substitution

> Give me a dozen healthy infants, well-formed, and my own specified world to bring them up in and I'll guarantee to take any one at random and train him to become any type of specialist I might select—doctor, lawyer, artist, merchant-chief, and yes, even beggar-man and thief, regardless of his talents, penchants, tendencies, abilities ... (J. B. Watson, 1925, p. 14).

With these words, John B. Watson, one of the first American psychologists to advocate a behavioral approach, summed up the behavioral perspective. Watson, who lived from 1878 to 1958, believed strongly that we could gain a full understanding of development by carefully studying the stimuli that make up the environment. In fact, he argued that by effectively controlling a person's environment, it was possible to produce virtually any behavior.

As we will consider further in Chapter 4, **classical conditioning** occurs when an organism learns to respond in a particular way to a neutral stimulus that normally does not evoke that type of response. For instance, if a dog is repeatedly exposed to the pairing of the sound of a bell and the presentation of meat, it may learn to react to the bell alone in the same way it reacts to the meat—by salivating and

wagging its tail with excitement. Dogs don't typically respond to bells in this way; the behavior is a result of conditioning, a form of learning in which the response associated with one stimulus (food) comes to be connected to another—in this case, the bell.

The same process of classical conditioning explains how we learn emotional responses. In the case of dog-bite victim Elissa Sheehan, for instance, Watson would say that one stimulus has been substituted for another: Elissa's unpleasant experience with a particular dog (the initial stimulus) has been transferred to other dogs and to pets in general.

John B. Watson

Operant Conditioning In addition to classical conditioning, other types of learning are found within the behavioral perspective. For example, **operant conditioning** is a form of learning in which a voluntary response is strengthened or weakened by its association with positive or negative consequences. It differs from classical conditioning in that the response being conditioned is voluntary and purposeful rather than automatic (such as salivating).

In operant conditioning, formulated and championed by psychologist B. F. Skinner (1904–1990), individuals learn to act deliberately on their environments in order to bring about desired consequences (Skinner, 1975). In a sense, then, children *operate* on their environments to bring about a desired state of affairs.

Whether children will seek to repeat a behavior depends on whether it is followed by reinforcement. *Reinforcement* is

B. F. Skinner

the process by which a stimulus is provided that increases the probability that a preceding behavior will be repeated. Hence a student is apt to work harder in school if he or she receives good grades, workers are likely to labor harder at their jobs if their efforts are tied to pay increases, and people are more apt to buy lottery tickets if they are reinforced by winning at least occasionally. In addition, *punishment*, the introduction of an unpleasant or painful stimulus or the removal of a desirable stimulus, will decrease the probability that a preceding behavior will occur in the future.

Behavior that is reinforced, then, is more likely to be repeated in the future, while behavior that receives no reinforcement or is punished is likely to be discontinued, or in the language of operant conditioning, *extinguished*. Principles of operant conditioning are used in **behavior modification**, a formal technique for promoting the frequency of desirable behaviors and decreasing the incidence of unwanted ones. Behavior modification has been used in a variety of situations, ranging from teaching severely retarded people the rudiments of language to helping people stick to diets (Christophersen & Mortweet, 2003; Matson & LoVullo, 2008).

Social-Cognitive Learning Theory: Learning Through Imitation

A five-year-old boy seriously injures his 22-month-old cousin while imitating a violent wrestling move he had seen on television. Although the infant sustained spinal cord injuries, he improved and was discharged 5 weeks after his hospital admission (Health eLine, 2003).

Cause and effect? We can't know for sure, but it certainly seems possible, especially looking at the situation from the perspective of social-cognitive learning theory. According to developmental psychologist Albert Bandura and colleagues, a significant amount of learning is explained by **social-cognitive learning theory**, an approach that emphasizes learning by observing the behavior of another person, called a *model* (Bandura, 1994, 2002).

Rather than viewing learning to be a matter of trial and error, as it is with operant conditioning, according to social-cognitive learning theory, behavior is learned through observation. We don't need to experience the consequences of a behavior ourselves to learn it. Social-cognitive learning theory holds that when we see the behavior of a model being rewarded, we are likely to imitate that behavior. For instance, in one classic experiment, children who were afraid of dogs were exposed to a

According to social-cognitive learning theory, observation of television programs such as *Jackass* can produce significant amounts of learning—not all of it positive.

model, nicknamed the "Fearless Peer," who was seen playing happily with a dog (Bandura, Grusec, & Menlove, 1967). After exposure, the children who previously had been afraid were more likely to approach a strange dog than were children who had not seen the model.

Bandura suggests that social-cognitive learning proceeds in four steps (Bandura, 1986). First, an observer must pay attention and perceive the most critical features of a model's behavior. Second, the observer must successfully recall the behavior. Third, the observer must reproduce the behavior accurately. And finally, the observer must be motivated to learn and carry out the behavior.

Assessing the Behavioral Perspective Research based on the behavioral perspective has made significant contributions, ranging from techniques for educating children with severe mental retardation to identifying procedures for curbing aggression. At the same time, there are controversies regarding the behavioral perspective. For example, although they are part of the same general behavioral perspective, classical and operant conditioning, on the one hand, and social learning theory, on the other, disagree in some basic ways. Both classical and operant conditioning consider learning in terms of external stimuli and responses, in which the only important factors are the observable features of the environment. In such an analysis, people and other organisms are like inanimate "black boxes"; nothing that occurs inside the box is understood, nor much cared about, for that matter.

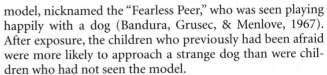

From an educator's perspective:
How might the kind of social learning that comes from viewing television influence children's behavior?

To social learning theorists, such an analysis is an oversimplification. They argue that what makes people different from rats and pigeons is mental activity, in the form of thoughts and expectations. A full understanding of people's development, they maintain, cannot occur without moving beyond external stimuli and responses.

In many ways, social learning theory has come to predominate in recent decades over classical and operant conditioning theories. In fact, another perspective that focuses explicitly on internal mental activity has become enormously influential. This is the cognitive approach, which we consider next.

The Cognitive Perspective: Examining the Roots of Understanding

When 3-year-old Jake is asked why it sometimes rains, he answers, "So the flowers can grow." When his 11-year-old sister Lila is asked the same question, she responds, "Because of evaporation from the surface of the earth." And when their cousin Ajima, who is studying meteorology in her high school science class, considers the same question, her extended answer includes a discussion of cumulonimbus clouds, the Coriolis effect, and synoptic charts.

To a developmental theorist using the cognitive perspective, the difference in the sophistication of these answers is evidence of a different degree of knowledge and understanding, or cognition. The **cognitive perspective** focuses on the processes that allow people to know, understand, and think about the world.

The cognitive perspective emphasizes how people internally represent and think about their environment. By using this perspective, developmental researchers hope to understand how children and adults process information and how their ways of thinking and understanding affect their behavior. They also seek to learn how cognitive abilities change as people develop, the degree to which cognitive development represents quantitative and qualitative growth in intellectual abilities, and how different cognitive abilities are related to one another.

Piaget's Theory of Cognitive Development No single person has had a greater impact on the study of cognitive development than Jean Piaget. A Swiss psychologist who lived from 1896 to 1980, Piaget proposed that all people passed in a fixed sequence through a series of universal stages of cognitive development (summarized in Table 2-2). He suggested that not only did the quantity of information increase in each stage, but the quality of knowledge and understanding changed as well. His focus was on the change in cognition that occurred as children moved from one stage to the next (Piaget, 1952, 1962, 1983).

We'll consider Piaget's theory in detail beginning in Chapter 6, but we can get a broad sense of it now by looking at some of its main features. Piaget suggested that human thinking is arranged into *schemes*, organized mental patterns that represent behaviors and actions. In infants, such schemes represent concrete behavior—a scheme for sucking, for reaching, and for each separate behavior. In older children, the schemes become more sophisticated and abstract. Schemes are like intellectual computer software that directs and determines how data from the world are looked at and dealt with (Parker, 2005).

Piaget suggests that children's *adaptation*—his term for the way in which children respond and adjust to new information—can be explained by two basic principles. *Assimilation* is the process in which people understand an experience in terms of their current stage of cognitive development and way of thinking. In contrast, *accommodation* refers to changes in existing ways of thinking in response to encounters with new stimuli or events.

Assimilation occurs when people use their current ways of thinking about and understanding the world to perceive and understand a new experience. For example, a young child who has not yet learned to count will look at two rows of buttons, each containing the same number of buttons, and say that a row in which the buttons are closely spaced together has fewer buttons in it than a row in which the buttons are more spread out. The experience of counting buttons, then, is assimilated to already existing schemes that contain the principle "bigger is more."

Later, however, when the child is older and has had sufficient exposure to new experiences, the content of the scheme will undergo change. In understanding that the quantity of buttons is identical whether they are spread out or closely spaced, the child has *accommodated* to the experience. Assimilation and accommodation work in tandem to bring about cognitive development.

Assessing Piaget's Theory Piaget has profoundly influenced our understanding of cognitive development and is one of the towering figures in child development. He provided masterful descriptions of how intellectual growth

TABLE 2-2 Piaget's Stages of Cognitive Development

Cognitive Stage	Approximate Age Range	Major Characteristics
Sensorimotor	Birth–2 years	Development of object permanence (idea that people/objects exist even when they can't be seen); development of motor skills; little or no capacity for symbolic representation
Preoperational	2–7 years	Development of language and symbolic thinking; egocentric thinking
Concrete operational	7–12 years	Development of conservation (idea that quantity is unrelated to physical appearance); mastery of concept of reversibility
Formal operational	12 years–adulthood	Development of logical and abstract thinking

proceeds during childhood—descriptions that have stood the test of literally thousands of investigations. By and large, Piaget's broad view of the sequence of cognitive development is accurate. However, the specifics of the theory, particularly in terms of change in cognitive capabilities over time, have been called into question. For instance, some cognitive skills clearly emerge earlier than Piaget suggested. Furthermore, the universality of Piaget's stages has been disputed. A growing amount of evidence suggests that the emergence of particular cognitive skills occurs according to a different timetable in non-Western cultures. And in every culture, some people never seem to reach Piaget's highest level of cognitive sophistication: formal, logical thought (McDonald & Stuart-Hamilton, 2003; Genovese, 2006).

Ultimately, the greatest criticism leveled at the Piagetian perspective is that cognitive development is not necessarily as discontinuous as Piaget's stage theory suggests. Remember that Piaget argued that growth proceeds in four distinct stages in which the quality of cognition differs from one stage to the next. However, many developmental researchers argue that growth is considerably more continuous. These critics have suggested an alternative perspective, known as the information-processing approach, which focuses on the processes that underlie learning, memory, and thinking throughout the life span.

Information-Processing Approaches Information-processing approaches have become an important alternative to Piagetian approaches. **Information-processing approaches** to cognitive development seek to identify the ways individuals take in, use, and store information.

Information-processing approaches grew out of developments in the electronic processing of information, particularly as carried out by computers. These perspectives assume that even complex behavior such as learning, remembering, categorizing, and thinking can be broken down into a series of individual, specific steps. And like computers, children are assumed by information-processing approaches to have limited capacity for processing information. Although as they develop, children employ increasingly sophisticated strategies that allow them to process information more efficiently.

In stark contrast to Piaget's view that thinking undergoes qualitative advances as children age, information-processing approaches assume that development is marked more by quantitative advances. Our capacity to handle information changes with age, as do our processing speed and efficiency. Furthermore, information-processing approaches suggest that as people age, they are better able to control the nature of processing, and that they can change in the strategies they choose to process information.

An information-processing approach that builds on Piaget's research is known as neo-Piagetian theory. In contrast to Piaget's original work, which viewed cognition as a single system of increasingly sophisticated general cognitive abilities, neo-Piagetian theory considers cognition as made up of different types of individual skills. Using the terminology of information-processing approaches, neo-Piagetian theory suggests that cognitive development proceeds quickly in certain areas and more slowly in others. For example, reading ability and the skills needed to recall stories may progress sooner than the sorts of abstract computational abilities used in algebra or trigonometry. Furthermore, neo-Piagetian theorists believe that experience plays a greater role than traditional Piagetian approaches in advancing cognitive development (Case, Demetriou, & Platsidou, 2001; Yan & Fischer, 2002; Loewen, 2006).

Assessing Information-Processing Approaches As we'll see in future chapters, information-processing approaches have become a central part of our understanding of development. At the same time, they do not offer a complete explanation for behavior. For example, information-processing approaches have paid little attention to behavior such as creativity, in which the most profound ideas often are developed in a seemingly nonlogical, nonlinear manner. In addition, they do not take into account the social context in which development takes place. That's one of the reasons that theories that emphasize the social and cultural aspects of development have become increasingly popular—as we discuss next.

Cognitive Neuroscience Approaches One of the most recent additions to the array of approaches taken by child developmentalists are **cognitive neuroscience approaches**, which look at cognitive development through the lens of brain processes. Like other cognitive perspectives, cognitive neuroscience approaches consider internal, mental processes, but they focus specifically on the neurological activity that underlies thinking, problem solving, and other cognitive behavior.

Cognitive neuroscientists seek to identify actual locations and functions within the brain that are related to different types of cognitive activity, rather than simply assuming that there are hypothetical or theoretical cognitive structures related to thinking. For example, using sophisticated brain-scanning techniques, cognitive neuroscientists have demonstrated that thinking about the meaning of a word activates different areas of the brain than are activated when thinking about how the word sounds when it is spoken.

Work of cognitive neuroscientists is also providing clues to the cause of *autism*, a major developmental disability that can produce profound language deficits and self-injurious behavior in young children. For example, neuroscientists have found that the brains of children with the disorder show explosive, dramatic growth in the 1st year of life, making their heads significantly larger than those of children without the disorder. By identifying children with the disorder very early in their lives, health-care providers can provide

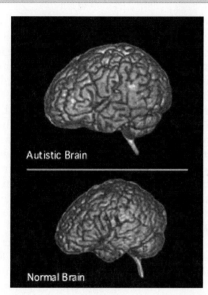

The brains of children with autism show a different pattern of networks of neurons and appear structurally different from those without the disorder.

crucial early intervention (Nadel & Poss, 2007; Lewis J. & Elman, 2008).

Cognitive neuroscience approaches are also on the forefront of cutting edge research that has identified specific genes associated with disorders ranging from physical problems such as breast cancer to psychological disorders like schizophrenia (DeLisi & Fleischhaker, 2007; Strobel et al., 2007). Identifying the genes that make one vulnerable to such disorders is the first step in genetic engineering in which gene therapy can reduce or even prevent the disorder from occurring, as we'll discuss in Chapter 3.

Assessing Cognitive Neuroscience Approaches

Cognitive neuroscience approaches represent a new frontier in the study of child and adolescent development. Using sophisticated measurement techniques, many of them developed only in the last few years, cognitive neuroscientists are able to peer into the inner functioning of the brain. Advances in our understanding of genetics also has opened a new window into both normal and abnormal development and has suggested a variety of treatments for abnormalities.

Critics of the cognitive neuroscience approach have suggested that it sometimes provides a better description than an explanation of developmental phenomena. For instance, finding that children with autism have larger brains than those without the disorder does not provide an explanation of why their brains became larger—that's a question that remains to be answered. Still, such work not only offers important clues to appropriate treatments but ultimately it can lead to a full understanding of a range of developmental phenomena.

The Contextual Perspective: Taking a Broad Approach to Development

Although child developmentalists often consider the course of development in terms of physical, cognitive, and personality and social factors separately, such categorization has one serious drawback: In the real world, none of these broad influences occurs in isolation from any other. Instead, there is a constant, ongoing interaction between the different types of influence.

The **contextual perspective** considers the relationship between individuals and their physical, cognitive, personality, and social worlds. It suggests that a child's unique development cannot be properly viewed without seeing the child enmeshed within a complex social and cultural context. We'll consider two major theories that fall into this category: Bronfenbrenner's bioecological approach and Vygotsky's sociocultural theory.

The Bioecological Approach to Development In acknowledging the problem with traditional approaches to life span development, psychologist Urie Bronfenbrenner (1989, 2000, 2002) has proposed an alternative perspective, called the bioecological approach. The **bioecological approach** suggests there are five levels of the environment that simultaneously influence individuals. Bronfenbrenner suggests that we cannot fully understand development without considering how a person is influenced by each of these levels (illustrated in Figure 2-1).

- The *microsystem* is the everyday, immediate environment in which children lead their daily lives. Homes, caregivers, friends, and teachers all are influences that are part of the microsystem. But the child is not just a passive recipient of these influences. Instead, children actively help construct the microsystem, shaping the immediate world in which they live. The microsystem is the level at which most traditional work in child development has been directed.

- The *mesosystem* provides connections among the various aspects of the microsystem. Like links in a chain, the mesosystem binds children to parents, students to teachers, employees to bosses, friends to friends. It acknowledges the direct and indirect influences that bind us to one another, such as those that affect a mother who has a bad day at the office and then is short-tempered with her son or daughter at home.

- The *exosystem* represents broader influences, encompassing societal institutions such as local government, the community, schools, places of worship, and the local media. Each of these larger institutions of society can have an immediate, and major, impact on personal development, and each affects how the microsystem and mesosystem operate. For example, the quality of a school will affect a child's cognitive development and potentially can have long-term consequences.

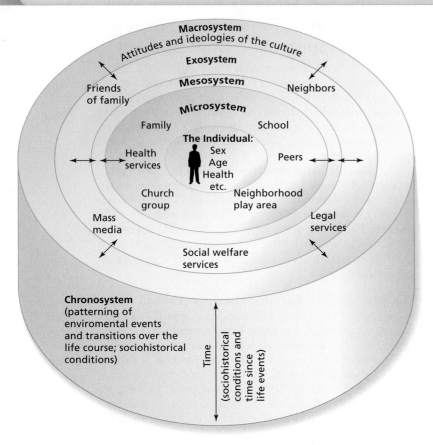

FIGURE 2-1 Bronfenbrenner's Approach to Development

Urie Bronfenbrenner's bioecological approach to development offers five levels of the environment that simultaneously influence individuals: the macrosystem, exosystem, mesosystem, microsystem, and chronosystem.
(*Source:* Adapted from Bronfenbrenner & Morris, 1998)

- The *macrosystem* represents the larger cultural influences on an individual. Society in general, types of governments, religious and political value systems, and other broad, encompassing factors are parts of the macrosystem. For example, the value a culture or society places on education or the family will affect the values of the people who live in that society. Children are part of a broader culture (such as Western culture) and are influenced by their membership in a particular subculture (for instance, being part of Mexican American subculture).

- Finally, the *chronosystem* underlies each of the previous systems. It involves the way the passage of time, including historical events (such as the terrorist attacks in September 2001) and more gradual historical changes (such as changes in the number of women who work outside of the home), affects children's development.

The bioecological approach emphasizes the *interconnectedness of the influences on development*. Because the various levels are related to one another, a change in one part of the system affects other parts of the system. For instance, a parent's loss of a job (involving the mesosystem) has an impact on a child's microsystem.

Conversely, changes on one environmental level may make little difference if other levels are not also changed. For instance, improving the school environment may have a negligible effect on academic performance if children receive little support for academic success at home. Similarly, the bioecological approach illustrates that the influences among different family members are multidirectional. Parents don't just influence their child's behavior—the child also influences the parents' behavior.

Finally, the bioecological approach stresses the importance of broad cultural factors that affect development. Researchers in child development increasingly look at how membership in cultural and subcultural groups influences behavior.

The Influence of Culture Consider whether you agree that children should be taught that their classmates' assistance is indispensable to getting good grades in school, or that they should definitely plan to continue their fathers' business, or that children should follow their parents' advice when determining their own career plans. If you have been raised in the widespread North American culture, you would likely disagree with all three statements, because they violate the premises of *individualism*, the dominant Western philosophy that emphasizes personal identity, uniqueness, freedom, and the worth of the individual.

By contrast, if you were raised in a traditional Asian culture, it is considerably more likely that you will agree with the three statements. Why? The statements reflect the value orientation known as collectivism. *Collectivism* is the notion that the well-being of the group is more important than that of the individual. People raised in collectivistic cultures tend to emphasize the welfare of the groups to which they belong, sometimes even at the expense of their own personal well-being.

The individualism–collectivism spectrum is one of several dimensions along which cultures differ, and it illustrates differences in the cultural contexts in which people operate. Such broad cultural values play an important role in shaping the ways people view the world and how they behave (Leung, 2005; Garcia & Saewyc, 2007; Yu & Stiffman, 2007).

Assessing the Bioecological Approach Although Bronfenbrenner considers biological influences an important component of the bioecological approach, ecological influences are central to the theory. In fact, some critics argue that the perspective pays insufficient attention to biological factors. Still, the bioecological approach is of considerable importance to child development, suggesting as it does the

CAREERS *in* CHILD DEVELOPMENT

Judy Coleman Brinich

Position: Director, Bloomsburg University Campus Child Center, Bloomsburg, Pennsylvania

Education: Bloomsburg University: BS, Early Childhood Education, M.E.D., Elementary Education, M.S., Exceptionalities

Home: Bloomsburg, PA

Current child-care providers are far more than the babysitters they often were in the past. Greater societal demands from parents needing to work full time has required the establishment of appropriate care for children and infants.

At the Bloomsburg University Campus Child Center, Judy Coleman Brinich oversees a program that serves 46 children, nine of them infants. The Center provides a safe, comfortable, stimulating yet calm and loving environment, according to Brinich.

"Our infants enjoy a relaxing environment, each with individualized schedules," said Brinich. "They are held frequently and pleasant conversation, music, and literature is common. For their play we provide interactive, tactile, colorful, and interesting toys."

Parent involvement is very important, according to Brinich, and it forms the basic foundation of the care provided for the infants.

"The parent's place is extremely important because we are a community helping one another take care of our children," she noted. "We begin the process with a parent/child care-staff interview and we learn from each other our expectations and determine whether or not the parent, child, facility, and child-care team are the right fit."

Parents are then invited to visit the child's classroom and then given access to the center, Brinich said. "Their input, advice, and wisdom are valued components to the child's day."

As infants move into toddlerhood the approach and care shifts according to need.

"At this stage they are learning to walk and talk and approach life in new and exciting ways," Brinich explained. "Everything they do is a unique experience that they will build upon to create meaning in their world."

"Music and literature is provided in abundance, and opportunities are provided for the growth and development of their bodies through large muscle activities and outdoor play," she added. In addition, "we provide the children with consistent opportunities for health social and emotional growth along with a daily routine that encourages the use of good manners, taking care of themselves, their belongings, and each other," she said.

Through each age group the children's interests and actions influence the direction of the teachers as their guide.

---

multiple levels at which the environment affects children's development. (Also see the *Careers in Child Development* box, which describes a director of a child-care center whose work involves children and their parents, taking the contextual perspective into account.)

Vygotsky's Sociocultural Theory To Russian developmentalist Lev Semenovich Vygotsky, a full understanding of development was impossible without taking into account the culture in which children develop. Vygotsky's **sociocultural theory** emphasizes how cognitive development proceeds as a result of social interactions between members of a culture (Vygotsky, 1979, 1926/1997; Winsler, 2003; S. Edwards, 2005).

Vygotsky, who lived a brief life from 1896 to 1934, argued that children's understanding of the world is acquired through their problem-solving interactions with adults and other children. As children play and cooperate with others, they learn what is important in their society and, at the same time, advance cognitively in their understanding of the world. Consequently, to understand the course of development, we must consider what is meaningful to members of a given culture.

More than most other theories, sociocultural theory emphasizes that development is a *reciprocal transaction* between the people in a child's environment and the child. Vygotsky believed that people and settings influence the child, who in turn influences the people and settings. This pattern continues in an endless loop, with children being both recipients of socialization influences and sources of influence. For example, a child raised with his or her extended family nearby will grow up with a different sense of family life than a child whose relatives live a considerable distance away. Those relatives, too, are affected by that situation and that child, depending upon how close and frequent their contact is with the child.

According to Vygotsky, through play and cooperation with others, children can develop cognitively in their understanding of the world and learn what is important in society.

Assessing Vygotsky's Theory Sociocultural theory has become increasingly influential, despite Vygotsky's death almost 8 decades ago. The reason is the growing acknowledgment of the central importance of cultural factors in development. Children do not develop in a cultural vacuum. Instead, their attention is directed by society to certain areas, and as a consequence, they develop particular kinds of skills that are an outcome of their cultural environment. Vygotsky was one of the first developmentalists to recognize and acknowledge the importance of culture, and—as today's society becomes increasingly multicultural—sociocultural theory is helping us to understand the rich and varied influences that shape development (Koshmanova, 2007; Rogan, 2007).

Evolutionary Perspectives: Our Ancestors' Contributions to Behavior

One increasingly influential approach is the evolutionary perspective, the final developmental perspective that we will consider. The **evolutionary perspective** seeks to identify behavior that is the result of our genetic inheritance from our ancestors. It focuses on how genetics and environmental factors combine to influence behavior (Bjorklund, 2006; Goetz & Shackelford, 2006).

Evolutionary approaches grow out of the groundbreaking work of Charles Darwin. In 1859, Darwin argued in his book *On the Origin of Species* that a process of natural selection creates traits in a species that are adaptive to its environment. Using Darwin's arguments, evolutionary approaches contend that our genetic inheritance not only determines such physical traits as skin and eye color, but certain personality traits and social behaviors as well. For instance, some evolutionary developmentalists suggest that behaviors such as shyness and jealousy are produced in part by genetic causes, presumably because they helped increase survival rates of humans' ancient relatives (D.M. Buss, 2003; Easton, Schipper, & Shackelford, 2007).

The evolutionary perspective draws heavily on the field of *ethology*, which examines the ways in which our biological makeup influences our behavior. A primary proponent of ethology was Konrad Lorenz (1903–1989), who discovered that newborn geese are genetically preprogrammed to become attached to the first moving object they see after birth. His work, which demonstrated the importance of biological determinants in influencing behavior patterns, ultimately led developmentalists to consider the ways in which human behavior might reflect inborn genetic patterns.

As we'll consider later in the chapter, the evolutionary perspective encompasses behavioral genetics, which is one of the fastest growing areas within the field of life span development. *Behavioral genetics* studies the effects of heredity on behavior. Behavioral geneticists seek to understand how we might inherit certain behavioral traits and how the environment influences whether we actually display such traits. This perspective also considers how genetic factors may produce psychological disorders such as schizophrenia (Eley, Lichtenstein, & Moffitt, 2003; Gottlieb, 2003; Li, 2003; Bjorklund, 2006).

Assessing the Evolutionary Perspective There is little argument among child developmentalists that Darwin's evolutionary theory provides an accurate description of basic genetic processes, and the evolutionary perspective is increasingly visible in the field of life span development. However, applications of the evolutionary perspective have been subjected to considerable criticism.

Some developmentalists are concerned that because of its focus on genetic and biological aspects of behavior, the evolutionary perspective pays insufficient attention to the environmental and social factors involved in producing human behavior. Other critics argue that there is no good way to experimentally test theories derived from the evolutionary approach because the biological development and inheritance of traits happened so long ago. For example, it is one thing to say that jealousy helped individuals to survive more effectively but it is another thing to prove it. Still, the evolutionary approach has stimulated a significant amount of research on how our biological inheritance influences at least partially our traits and behaviors (D.M. Buss & Reeve, 2003; Bjorklund, 2006; Baptista et al., 2008).

Konrad Lorenz, seen here with geese imprinted to him, considered the ways in which behavior reflects inborn genetic patterns.

Why "Which Perspective Is Right?" Is the Wrong Question

We have considered five major perspectives on development: psychodynamic, behavioral, cognitive, contextual, and evolutionary (summarized in Table 2-3). It would be natural to wonder which approach provides the most accurate account of child development.

For several reasons, this is not an entirely appropriate question. For one thing, each perspective emphasizes somewhat different aspects of development. For instance, the psychodynamic approach emphasizes emotions, motivational conflicts, and unconscious determinants of behavior. In contrast, behavioral perspectives emphasize overt behavior, paying far more attention to what people *do* than to what goes on inside their heads, which is deemed largely irrelevant. The cognitive perspective takes quite the opposite tack, looking more at what people *think* than at what they do. Finally, while the contextual perspective focuses on the interaction of environmental influences, the evolutionary perspective focuses on how inherited biological factors underlie development.

For example, a developmentalist using the psychodynamic approach might consider how the 9/11 terrorist attacks on the World Trade Center and Pentagon might affect children, unconsciously, for their entire life span. A cognitive approach might focus on how children perceived and came to interpret and understand the terrorism, while a contextual approach might consider what personality and social factors led the perpetrators to adopt terrorist tactics.

Clearly, each perspective is based on its own premises and focuses on different aspects of development. Furthermore, the same developmental phenomenon can be looked at from a number of perspectives simultaneously. In fact, some life span developmentalists use an *eclectic* approach, drawing on several perspectives simultaneously.

We can think of the different perspectives as analogous to a set of maps of the same general geographical area. One map may contain detailed depictions of roads; another map may show geographical features; another may show political subdivisions, such as cities, towns, and counties; and still another may highlight particular points of interest, such as scenic areas and historic landmarks. Each of the maps is accurate, but each provides a different point of view and way of thinking. No one map is "complete," but by considering

TABLE 2-3	Major Perspectives on Child Development		
Perspective	Key Ideas About Human Behavior and Development	Major Proponents	Example
Psychodynamic	Behavior throughout life is motivated by inner, unconscious forces, stemming from childhood, over which we have little control.	Sigmund Freud, Erik Erikson	This view might suggest that an adolescent who is overweight has a fixation in the oral stage of development.
Behavioral	Development can be understood through studying observable behavior and environmental stimuli.	John B. Watson, B. F. Skinner, Albert Bandura	In this perspective, an adolescent who is overweight might be seen as not being rewarded for good nutritional and exercise habits.
Cognitive	Emphasis is on how changes or growth in the ways people know, understand, and think about the world affect behavior.	Jean Piaget	This view might suggest that an adolescent who is overweight hasn't learned effective ways to stay at a healthy weight and doesn't value good nutrition.
Contextual	Behavior is determined by the relationship between individuals and their physical, cognitive, personality, social, and physical worlds.	Lev Vygotsky, Uric Bronfenbrenner	In this perspective an adolescent may become overweight because of a family environment in which food and meals are unusually important and intertwined with family rituals.
Evolutionary	Behavior is the result of genetic inheritance from our ancestors; traits and behavior that are adaptive for promoting the survival of our species have been inherited through natural selection.	Konrad Lorenz; influenced by early work of Charles Darwin	This view might suggest that an adolescent might have a genetic tendency toward obesity because extra fat helped his or her ancestors to survive in times of famine.

Scientific method
The process of posing and
answering questions using
careful, controlled techniques
that include systematic, orderly
observation and the collection of
data

them together, we can come to a fuller understanding of
the area.

In the same way, the various theoretical perspectives
provide different ways of looking at development. Considering them together paints a fuller portrait of the myriad ways
human beings change and grow over the course of their lives.
However, not all theories and claims derived from the various perspectives are accurate. How do we choose among
competing explanations? The answer is *research*, which we
consider in the final part of this chapter.

REVIEW ↵ mydevelopmentlab

1. The five major theoretical perspectives that guide the
   study of child development are: the psychodynamic,
   the _____, the cognitive, the contextual, and the
   evolutionary perspectives.

   Answer: behavioral

2. The _____ perspective identifies behaviors that
   are the result of genetic inheritance.

   Answer: evolutionary

3. Erikson's _____ _____ theory was created as an alternative psychodynamic view and emphasizes social interaction with other people.

   Answer: psychosocial development

4. Vygotsky's sociocultural theory emphasizes how cognitive development proceeds as a result of _____
   _____ between members of a culture.

   Answer: social interactions

To see more review questions, log on to MyDevelopmentLab.

The Scientific Method and Research

The Egyptians had long believed that they were the most
ancient race on earth, and Psamtik [king of Egypt in the
7th century B.C.], driven by intellectual curiosity, wanted
to prove that flattering belief. Like a good researcher, he
began with a hypothesis: If children had no opportunity
to learn a language from older people around them, they
would spontaneously speak the primal, inborn language
of humankind—the natural language of its most ancient
people—which, he expected to show, was Egyptian.

To test his hypothesis, Psamtik commandeered two
infants of a lower-class mother and turned them over to a
herdsman to bring up in a remote area. They were to be
kept in a sequestered cottage [and] properly fed and
cared for but were never to hear anyone speak so much as
a word. The Greek historian Herodotus, who tracked the

story down and learned what he calls "the real facts" from
priests of Hephaestus in Memphis, says that Psamtik's
goal "was to know, after the indistinct babblings of infancy were over, what word they would first articulate."

The experiment, he tells us, worked. One day, when the
children were two years old, they ran up to the herdsman as
he opened the door of their cottage and cried out "Becos!"
Since this meant nothing to him, he paid no attention, but
when it happened repeatedly, he sent word to Psamtik, who
at once ordered the children brought to him. When he too
heard them say it, Psamtik made inquiries and learned that
becos was the Phrygian word for bread. He concluded
that, disappointingly, the Phrygians were an older race
than the Egyptians. (M. Hunt, 1993, pp. 1–2)

With the perspective of several thousand years, we can easily
see the shortcomings—both scientific and ethical—in
Psamtik's approach. Yet his procedure represents an improvement over mere speculation and as such is sometimes
regarded as the first developmental experiment in recorded
history (M. Hunt, 1993).

Theories and Hypotheses: Posing Developmental Questions

Questions such as those raised by Psamtik lie at the heart of
the study of child development. Is language innate? What are
the effects of malnutrition on later intellectual performance?
How do infants form relationships with their parents, and
does participation in day care disrupt such relationships?
Why are adolescents susceptible to peer pressure?

To answer such questions, specialists in child development rely on the scientific method. The **scientific method** is
the process of posing and answering questions using careful,
controlled techniques that include systematic, orderly observation and the collection of data. As shown in Figure 2-2, the
scientific method involves three major steps: (1) identifying
questions of interest, (2) formulating an explanation, and
(3) carrying out research that either lends support to the explanation or refutes it.

Why use the scientific method, when our own experiences and common sense might seem to provide reasonable
answers to questions? One important reason is that our own
experience is limited; most of us encounter only a relatively
small number of people and situations, and drawing suppo-
sitions from that restricted sample may lead us to the wrong
conclusion.

Similarly, although common sense may seem helpful, it
turns out that common sense often makes contradictory
predictions. For example, common sense tells us that "birds
of a feather flock together." But it also says that "opposites
attract." You see the problem: Because common sense is
often contradictory, we can't rely on it to provide objective
answers to questions. That's why developmental psychologists insist on using the controlled methods of the scientific
method.

Theories: Framing Broad Explanations

The first step in the scientific method, the identification of questions of interest, begins when an observer puzzles over some aspect of behavior. Perhaps it is an infant who cries when she is picked up by a stranger, or a child who is doing poorly in school, or an adolescent who engages in risky behavior. Developmentalists, like all of us, ponder such everyday aspects of behavior, and—also like all of us—they seek to determine answers to these questions.

However, it is the way that developmental researchers try to find answers that differentiates them from more casual observers. Developmental researchers formulate *theories*, broad explanations and predictions about phenomena of interest. Using one of the major perspectives that we discussed earlier, researchers develop more specific theories.

In fact, all of us develop theories about development, based on our experience, folklore, and articles in magazines and newspapers. For instance, many people theorize that there is a crucial bonding period between parent and child immediately after birth, which is a necessary ingredient in forming a lasting parent–child relationship. Without such a bonding period, they assume, the parent–child relationship will be forever compromised.

Whenever we employ such explanations, we are developing our own theories. However, the theories in child development are different. Whereas our own personal theories are built on unverified observations that are developed haphazardly, developmentalists' theories are more formal, based on a systematic integration of prior findings and theorizing. These theories allow developmental researchers to summarize and organize prior observations and to move beyond existing observations to draw deductions that may not be immediately apparent.

Hypotheses: Specifying Testable Predictions

Although the development of theories provides a general approach to a problem, it is only the first step. To determine the validity of a theory, developmental researchers must test it scientifically. To do that, they develop hypotheses based on their theories. A **hypothesis** is a prediction stated in a way that permits it to be tested. For instance, someone who subscribes to the general theory that bonding is a crucial ingredient in the parent–child relationship might derive the more specific hypothesis that adopted children whose adoptive parents never had the chance to bond with them immediately after birth may ultimately have less secure relationships with their adoptive parents.

Other researchers might derive different hypotheses, such as that effective bonding occurs only if it lasts for a certain length of time or that bonding affects the mother–child

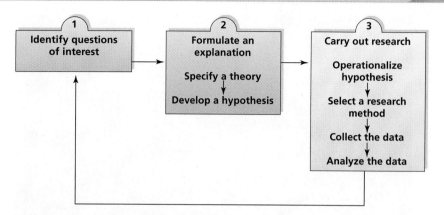

FIGURE 2-2 The Scientific Method

A cornerstone of research, the scientific method is used by psychologists as well as researchers from all other scientific disciplines.

relationship but not the father–child relationship. (In case you're wondering, as we'll discuss in Chapter 4, these particular hypotheses have *not* been upheld; there are no long-term reactions to the separation of parent and child immediately after birth, even if the separation lasts several days, and there is no difference in the strength of bonds with mothers and bonds with fathers.)

Choosing a Research Strategy: Answering Questions

Once researchers have formed a hypothesis, they must develop a strategy for testing its validity. As we mentioned earlier, the first step is to state the hypothesis in a way that will allow it to be tested. *Operationalization* is the process of translating a hypothesis into specific, testable procedures that can be measured and observed. For example, a researcher interested in testing the hypothesis that "being evaluated leads to anxiety" might operationalize "being evaluated" as a teacher's giving a grade to a student or in terms of a child's commenting on a friend's athletic skills. Similarly, "anxiety" could be operationalized in terms of responses on a questionnaire or as measurements of biological reactions by an electronic instrument.

The choice of how to operationalize a variable often reflects the kind of research that is to be conducted. There are two major categories of research: correlational research and experimental research. **Correlational research** seeks to identify whether an association or relationship between two factors exists. As we'll see, correlational research cannot be used to determine whether one factor causes changes in the other. For instance, correlational research could tell us if there is an association between the number of minutes a mother and her newborn child are together immediately after birth and the quality of the mother–child relationship when the child

Experimental research
Research designed to discover
causal relationships between
various factors

Researchers use a wide
range of procedures to study
human development.

reaches 2 years of age. Such correlational research indicates whether the two factors are *associated* or *related* to one another but not whether the initial contact caused the relationship to develop in a particular way (Schutt, 2001).

In contrast, **experimental research** is designed to discover *causal* relationships between various factors. In experimental research, scientists deliberately introduce a change in a carefully structured situation in order to see the consequences of that change. For instance, a researcher conducting an experiment might vary the number of minutes that mothers and children interact immediately following birth in an attempt to see whether the amount of bonding time affects the mother–child relationship.

Because experimental research is able to answer questions of causality, it represents the heart of developmental research. However, some research questions cannot be answered through experiments, for either technical or ethical reasons (for example, it would be unethical to design an experiment in which a group of infants was offered no chance to bond with a caregiver). In fact, a great deal of pioneering developmental research—such as that conducted by Piaget and Vygotsky—employed correlational techniques.

Consequently, correlational research remains an important tool in the developmental researcher's toolbox.

Correlational Studies

As we've noted, correlational research examines the relationship between two variables to determine whether they are associated, or *correlated*. For instance, researchers interested in the relationship between televised aggression and subsequent behavior have found that children who watch a substantial amount of aggression on television—murders, crime, shootings, and the like—tend to be more aggressive than those who watch only a little. In other words, as we'll discuss in greater detail in Chapter 10, viewing of aggression and actual aggression are strongly associated, or correlated, with each other (C.A. Anderson, Funk, & Griffiths, 2004; Donnerstein, 2005; Brady, 2007).

But does this mean we can conclude that the viewing of televised aggression *causes* the more aggressive behavior of the viewers? Not at all. Consider some of the other possibilities: Perhaps being aggressive in the first place makes children more likely to choose to watch violent programs. In such a case, then, it is the aggressive tendency that causes the viewing behavior, not the other way around.

Or consider another possibility. Suppose that children who are raised in poverty are more likely to behave aggressively *and* to watch higher levels of aggressive television than are youngsters raised in more affluent settings. In this case, it is socioeconomic status that causes *both* the aggressive behavior and the television viewing. (The various possibilities are illustrated in Figure 2-3).

In short, finding that two variables are correlated proves nothing about causality. Although it is possible that the variables are linked causally, this is not necessarily the case. Nevertheless, correlational studies can provide important information. For instance, as we'll see in later chapters, we know from correlational studies that the closer the genetic link between two people, the more highly associated their intelligence. We have learned that the more parents speak to their young children, the more extensive the children's vocabularies. And we know from correlational studies that the better the nutrition that infants receive, the fewer cognitive and social problems they experience later (Plomin, 1994c; B. Hart, 2004; Colom, Lluis-Font, & Andrés-Pueyo, 2005).

The Correlation Coefficient The strength and direction of a relationship between two factors is represented by a mathematical score, called a *correlation coefficient*, that ranges from +1.0 to −1.0. A positive correlation indicates that as the value of one factor increases, it can be predicted that the value of the other will also increase. For instance, if we find that the more calories children eat, the better their school performance, and the fewer calories children eat, the worse their school performance, we have found a positive correlation. (Higher values of the factor "calories" are associated

Naturalistic observation
Studies in which researchers observe some naturally occurring behavior without intervening or making changes in the situation

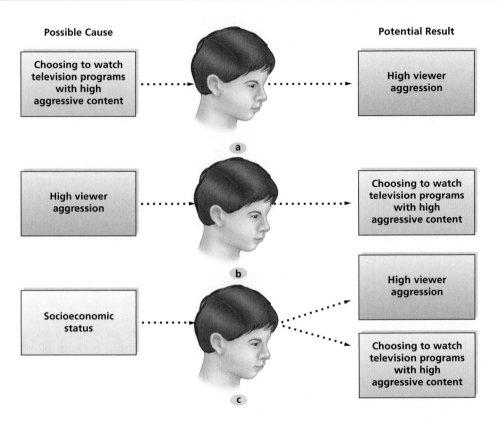

Possible Cause | Potential Result

FIGURE 2-3

Finding a Correlation

Finding a correlation between two factors does not imply that one factor causes the other factor to vary. For instance, suppose that a study found that viewing television programs with high levels of aggression is correlated with actual aggression in children. The correlation might reflect at least three possibilities: (a) watching television programs containing high levels of aggression causes aggression in viewers; (b) children who behave aggressively choose to watch television programs with high levels of aggression; or (c) some third factor, such as a child's socioeconomic status, leads to both high viewer aggression and choosing to watch television programs with high aggression.

with higher values of the factor "school performance," and lower values of the factor "calories" are associated with lower values of the factor "school performance.") The correlation coefficient, then, would be indicated by a positive number, and the stronger the association between calories and school performance, the closer the number would be to +1.0.

In contrast, a correlation coefficient with a negative value informs us that as the value of one factor increases, the value of the other factor declines. For example, suppose we found that the greater the number of hours adolescents spend using instant messaging on their computers, the worse their academic performance. Such a finding would result in a negative correlation, ranging between 0 and −1.0. More instant messaging is associated with lower performance, and less instant messaging is associated with better performance. The stronger the association between instant messaging and school performance, the closer the correlation coefficient will be to −1.0.

Finally, it is possible that two factors are unrelated to each other. For example, it is unlikely that we would find a correlation between school performance and shoe size. In this case, the lack of a relationship would be indicated by a correlation coefficient close to 0.

It is important to reiterate what we noted earlier: Even if the correlation coefficient involving two variables is very strong, there is no way we can know whether one factor causes another factor to vary. It simply means that the two factors are associated with one another in a predictable way.

Types of Correlational Studies   There are several types of correlational studies.

Naturalistic obvservation.   **Naturalistic observation** is the observation of a naturally occurring behavior without intervention in the situation. For instance, an investigator who wishes to learn how often preschool children share toys with one another might observe a classroom over a 3-week period, recording how often the preschoolers spontaneously share with one another. The key point about naturalistic observation is that the investigator simply observes the children without interfering with the situation in any way (e.g., Prezbindowski & Lederberg, 2003; Rustin, 2006).

Naturalistic observation has the advantage of identifying what children do in their "natural habitat," and it offers an excellent way for researchers to develop questions of interest. However, natural observation has a considerable drawback: Researchers are unable to exert control over factors of interest. For instance, in some cases, researchers might find so few naturally occurring instances of the behavior of interest that they are unable to draw any conclusions at all. In addition, children who know they are being watched may modify their behavior as a result of the observation. Consequently, their

Case studies Extensive, in-depth interviews with a particular individual or small group of individuals

Survey research Research in which a group of people chosen to represent some larger population are asked questions about their attitudes, behavior, or thinking on a given topic

Psychophysiological methods A research approach that focuses on the relationship between physiological processes and behavior

Naturalistic observation is used to examine a situation in its natural habitat without interference of any sort. What are some disadvantages of naturalistic observation?

behavior may not be representative of how they would behave if they were not being watched.

Ethnography. Increasingly, naturalistic observation employs *ethnography*, a method borrowed from the field of anthropology and used to investigate cultural questions. In ethnography, a researcher's goal is to understand a culture's values and attitudes through careful, extended examination. Typically, researchers using ethnography act as *participant observers*, living for a period of weeks, months, or even years in another culture. By carefully observing everyday life and conducting in-depth interviews, researchers are able to obtain a deep understanding of life in another culture (Dyson, 2003).

Ethnographic studies can provide important information, because they offer a fine-grained view of everyday behavior in another culture. However, they also have some limitations. As in naturalistic observation, the presence of a participant observer may influence the behavior of the individuals being studied. Furthermore, because only a small number of individuals are studied, it may be hard to generalize the findings to people in other cultures. Finally, ethnographers may misinterpret and misconceive what they are observing, particularly in cultures that are very different from their own (Polkinghome, 2005).

Case studies. Case studies involve extensive, in-depth interviews with a particular individual or small group of individuals. They are often used not just to learn about the individual who is being interviewed but also to derive broader principles or draw tentative conclusions that might apply to others. For example, case studies have been conducted on children who display unusual genius and on children who have spent their early years in the wild without human contact. These case studies have provided important information to researchers and have suggested hypotheses for future investigation (L. T. Goldsmith, 2000; L. Cohen, & Cashon, 2003; S. L. Wilson, 2003).

Using *diaries*, participants are asked to keep a record of their behavior on a regular basis. For example, a group of adolescents may be asked to record each time they interact with friends for more than 5 minutes, thereby providing a way to track their social behavior.

Survey research. You're probably familiar with an additional research strategy called survey research. In **survey research**, a group of individuals chosen to represent some larger population are asked questions about their attitudes, behavior, or thinking on a given topic. For instance, surveys have been conducted about parents' use of punishment on their children and on attitudes toward breast-feeding. From the responses, inferences are drawn regarding the larger population represented by the individuals being surveyed.

Although the most straightforward way to determine what people think and do is to ask them directly about their behavior, it is not always an effective technique. For instance, adolescents asked about their sex lives may be unwilling to admit to various sexual practices for fear that confidentiality will not be complete. In addition, if the sample of people surveyed is not representative of the broader population of interest, the results of the survey have little meaning.

Psychophysiological methods. Some developmental researchers, particularly those using a cognitive neuroscience approach, make use of psychophysiological methods. **Psychophysiological methods** focus on the relationship between physiological processes and behavior. For instance, a researcher might examine the relationship between blood flow within the brain and problem-solving capabilities. Similarly, some studies use infants' heart rate as a measure of their interest in stimuli to which they are exposed.

Among the most frequently used psychophysiological measures:

- **Electroencephalogram (EEG).** The EEG records electrical activity within the brain recorded by electrodes placed on the outside of the skull. That brain acitivity is transformed into a pictorial representation of the brain, permitting the representation of brain wave patterns and diagnosis of disorders such as epilepsy and learning disabilities.

- **Computerized Axial Tomography (CAT) Scan.** In a CAT scan, a computer constructs an image of the brain by

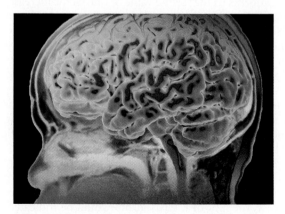

A functional magnetic resonance image (fMRI) of the brain shows brain activity at a given moment.

Experiment A process in which an investigator, called an experimenter, devises two different experiences for subjects or participants

Treatment A procedure applied by an experimental investigator based on two different experiences devised for subjects or participants

Treatment group The group in an experiment that receives the treatment

Control group The group in an experiment that receives either no treatment or an alternative treatment

Independent variable The variable in an experiment that is manipulated by researchers

Dependent variable The variable in an experiment that is measured and is expected to change as a result of the experimental manipulation

combining thousands of individual X-rays taken at slightly different angles. Although it does not show brain activity, it does illuminate the structure of the brain.

- **Functional Magnetic Resonance Imaging (fMRI) Scan.** An fMRI provides a detailed, three-dimensional computer-generated image of brain activity by aiming a powerful magnetic field at the brain. It offers one of the best ways of learning about the operation of the brain, and provides imaging to the level of individual nerves.

Experiments: Determining Cause and Effect

In an **experiment**, an investigator, called an *experimenter*, typically devises two different experiences for *participants*, or *subjects*. These two different experiences are called treatments. A **treatment** is a procedure applied by an investigator. One group of participants receives one of the treatments, whereas another group of participants receives either no treatment or an alternative treatment. The group receiving the treatment is known as the **treatment group** (sometimes called the *experimental group*), whereas the no-treatment or alternative-treatment group is called the **control group**.

Although the terminology may seem daunting at first, there is an underlying logic to help sort it out. Think in terms of a medical experiment in which the aim is to test the effectiveness of a new drug. In testing the drug, we wish to see if the drug successfully *treats* the disease. Consequently, the group that receives the drug would be called the *treatment group*. In comparison, another group of participants would not receive the drug treatment. Instead, they would be part of the no-treatment *control* group.

Similarly, suppose we wish to explore the consequences of exposure to movie violence on viewers' subsequent aggression. We might take a group of adolescents and show them a series of movies that contain a great deal of violent imagery. We would then measure their subsequent aggression. This group would constitute the treatment group. But we would also need another group—a control group. To fulfill this need, we might take a second group of adolescents, show them movies that contain no aggressive imagery, and then measure their subsequent aggression. This would be the control group.

By comparing the amount of aggression displayed by members of the treatment and control groups, we would be able to determine if exposure to violent imagery produces aggression in viewers. And this is just what a group of researchers found: Running an experiment of this very sort, psychologist Jacques-Philippe Leyens and colleagues at the University of Louvain in Belgium found that the level of aggression rose significantly for the adolescents who had seen the movies containing violence (Leyens et al., 1975).

Designing an Experiment The central feature of this experiment—and all other experiments—is the comparison of the consequences of different treatments. The use of both treatment and control groups allows researchers to rule out the possibility that something other than the experimental manipulation produced the results found in the experiment. For instance, if a control group was not used, experiments could not be certain that some other factor, such as the time of day the movies were shown, the need to sit still during the movie, or even the mere passage of time, produced the changes that were observed. By employing a control group experimenters can draw accurate conclusions about causes and effects.

The formation of treatment and control groups represents the independent variable in an experiment. The **independent variable** is the variable that researchers manipulate in the experiment. In contrast, the **dependent variable** is the variable that researchers measure in an experiment and expect to change as a result of the experimental manipulation. (One way to remember the difference: A hypothesis predicts how a dependent variable *depends* on the manipulation of the independent variable.) For instance, in an experiment studying the effects of taking a drug, manipulating whether participants receive or do not receive a drug is the independent variable. Measurement of the effectiveness of the drug or no-drug treatment is the dependent variable.

To consider another example, let's take the Belgian study of the consequences of observing filmed aggression on future aggression. In this experiment the independent variable is the *level of aggressive imagery* viewed by participants—determined by whether they viewed films containing aggressive imagery (the treatment group) or devoid of aggressive imagery (the control group). The dependent variable in the study? It was what the experimenters expected to vary as a consequence of viewing a film: the measurable *aggressive behavior* shown by participants after they had viewed the films. Every experiment has an independent and dependent variable.

Random Assignment One critical step in the design of experiments is to assign participants to different treatment groups. The procedure that is used is known as random assignment. In *random assignment*, participants are assigned to different experimental groups or conditions strictly on the basis of chance. By using this technique, the laws of statistics ensure that personal characteristics that might affect the outcome of the experiment are divided proportionally among the participants in the different groups. In other words, the groups are equivalent to one another in terms of the personal characteristics of the participants. Equivalent groups achieved by random assignment allow an experimenter to draw conclusions with confidence.

Given the advantage of experimental research—that it provides a means of determining causality—why aren't experiments always used? The answer is that there are some

Sample A group of participants chosen for an experiment

Field study A research investigation carried out in a naturally occurring setting

TABLE 2-4 Types of Research

Research Method	Description	Example
Naturalistic observation	An investigator systematically observes naturally occurring behavior and does not make a change in the situation.	A researcher investigating bullying carefully observes and records instances of bullying on elementary school playgrounds.
Archival research	Existing data such as census documents, college records, and newspaper clippings are examined to test a hypothesis.	College records are used to determine whether gender differences exist in math grades.
Ethnography	Careful study of a culture's values and attitudes through careful, extended examination.	A researcher lives for 6 months among families in a remote African village in order to study child-rearing practices.
Survey research	Individuals chosen to represent a larger population are asked a series of questions about their behavior, thoughts, or attitudes.	A researcher conducts a comprehensive poll asking a large group of adolescents about their attitudes toward exercise.
Case study	An in-depth, intensive investigation of an individual or small group of people.	An intensive study of a child involved in a school shooting is carried out by an investigator.
Psychophysiological research	A study of the relationship between physiological processes and behavior.	A researcher examines brain scans of children who are unusually violent to see whether there are abnormalities in brain structures and functioning.

situations that a researcher, no matter how ingenious, simply cannot control; and there are some situations that would be unethical to control, even if it were possible. For instance, no researcher would be able to assign different groups of infants to parents of high- and low-socioeconomic status in order to learn the effects of such status on subsequent development. Similarly, we cannot control what a group of children watch on television throughout their childhood years to learn if childhood exposure to televised aggression leads to aggressive behavior later in life. Consequently, in situations in which experiments are logistically or ethically impossible, developmentalists employ correlational research. (See Table 2-4 for a summary of the major research strategies.)

Furthermore, keep in mind that a single experiment is insufficient to answer a research question definitively. Before complete confidence can be placed in a conclusion, research must be *replicated*, or repeated, sometimes using other procedures and techniques with other participants. Sometimes developmentalists use a procedure called *meta-analysis*, which permits the combination of results of many studies into one overall conclusion (Shelby & Vaske, 2008).

Choosing a Research Setting Deciding where to conduct a study may be as important as determining what to do. In the Belgian experiment on the influence of exposure to media aggression, the researchers used a real-world setting—a group home for boys who had been convicted of juvenile delinquency. They chose this **sample**, the group of participants chosen for the experiment, because it was useful to have adolescents whose normal level of aggression was relatively high, and because experimenters could incorporate showing the films into the everyday life of the home with minimal disruption.

Using a real-world setting like the one in the aggression experiment is the hallmark of a field study. A **field study** is a research investigation carried out in a naturally occurring setting. Field studies may be carried out in preschool classrooms, at community playgrounds, on school buses, or on street corners. Field studies capture

Developmentalists work in such diverse settings as in a laboratory preschool on a college campus and in human service agencies.

Laboratory study A research investigation conducted in a controlled setting explicitly designed to hold events constant

behavior in real-life settings, and research participants may behave more naturally than they would if they were brought into a laboratory.

Field studies may be used in both correlational studies and experiments. Field studies typically employ naturalistic observation, the technique we discussed previously in which researchers observe some naturally occurring behavior without intervening or making changes in the situation. For instance, a researcher might examine behavior in a child-care center, view the groupings of adolescents in high school corridors, or observe elderly adults in a senior center.

However, it is often difficult to run an experiment in real-world settings, where it is hard to exert control over the situation and environment. Consequently, field studies are more typical of correlational designs than of experimental designs, and most developmental research experiments are conducted in laboratory settings. A **laboratory study** is a research investigation conducted in a controlled setting explicitly designed to hold events constant. The laboratory may be a room or building designed for research, as in a university's psychology department. The controlled settings of laboratory studies allow researchers to learn more clearly how their treatments affect participants.

From an educator's perspective:

Why might you criticize theories that are supported only by data collected from laboratory studies, rather than from field studies? Would such criticism be valid?

In order to understand development in all children, researchers must include participants in their studies that represent the diversity of humanity.

transportation capabilities to bring their infants into a research center. In contrast, African Americans (as well as members of other groups) who are relatively poor will face more hurdles when it comes to participating in research.

Something is amiss when a science that seeks to explain children's behavior—as is the case with child development—disregards significant groups of individuals. Child developmentalists are aware of this issue, and they have become increasingly sensitive to the importance of using participants who are fully representative of the general population (H. Fitzgerald, 2006).

DEVELOPMENTAL DIVERSITY

Choosing Research Participants Who Represent the Diversity of Children

For child development to represent the full range of humanity, its research must incorporate children of different races, ethnicities, cultures, genders, and other categories. However, although the field of child development is increasingly concerned with issues of human diversity, its actual progress in this domain has been slow, and in some ways, it has actually regressed.

For instance, between 1970 and 1989, only 4.6% of the articles published in *Developmental Psychology*, one of the premier journals of the discipline, focused on African American participants. Moreover, the number of published studies involving African American participants of all ages actually declined over that 20-year period (S. Graham, 1992; MacPhee, Kreutzer, & Fritz, 1994).

Even when minority groups are included in research, the particular participants may not represent the full range of variation that actually exists within the group. For example, African American infants used in a research study might well be disproportionally upper- and middle-class, because parents in higher socioeconomic groups may be more likely to have the time and

REVIEW mydevelopmentlab

1. The _____ _____ is the process of posing and answering questions using controlled techniques that include systematic, orderly observation and the collection of data.

   Answer: scientific method

2. A _____ is a prediction stated in a way that permits it to be tested.

   Answer: hypothesis

3. _____ are systematically derived explanations of facts or phenomena.

   Answer: Theories

4. The major research strategies associated with social science research are _____ and correlational studies.

   Answer: experimental

To see more review questions, log on to MyDevelopmentLab.

Theoretical research
Research designed specifically to test some developmental explanation and expand scientific knowledge

Applied research   Research meant to provide practical solutions to immediate problems

Longitudinal research
Research in which the behavior of one or more individuals is measured as the subjects age

Research Strategies and Challenges

Developmental researchers typically focus on either theoretical research or applied research, although the two approaches are complementary.

Theoretical and Applied Research: Complementary Approaches

Theoretical research is designed specifically to test some developmental explanation and expand scientific knowledge, whereas **applied research** is meant to provide practical solutions to immediate problems. For instance, if we were interested in the processes of cognitive change during childhood, we might carry out a study of how many digits children of various ages can remember after one exposure to multidigit numbers—a theoretical approach. Alternatively, we might focus on how children learn by examining ways in which elementary school instructors can teach children to remember information more easily. Such a study would represent applied research, because the findings are applied to a particular setting and problem.

Often the distinctions between theoretical and applied research are blurred. For instance, should a study that examines the consequences of ear infections in infancy on future hearing loss be considered theoretical or applied research? Because such a study may help illuminate the basic processes involved in hearing, it can be considered theoretical. But to the extent that the study helps us understand how to prevent hearing loss in children and how various medicines may ease the consequences of the infection, it may be considered applied research (Lerner, Fisher, & Weinberg, 2000).

In short, even the most applied research can help advance our theoretical understanding of a particular topical area, and theoretical research can provide concrete solutions to a range of practical problems. In fact, as discussed in the accompanying *From Research to Practice* box, research of both a theoretical and an applied nature has played a significant role in shaping and resolving a variety of public policy questions.

Measuring Developmental Change

For developmental researchers, the question of how people grow and change throughout the life span is central to their discipline. Consequently, one of the thorniest research issues they face concerns the measurement of change and differences over age and time. To solve this problem, researchers have developed three major strategies: longitudinal research, cross-sectional research, and sequential research.

Longitudinal Studies: Measuring Individual Change

If you were interested in learning how a child's moral development changes between the ages of 3 and 5, the most direct approach would be to take a group of 3-year-olds and follow them until they were age 5, testing them periodically.

Such a strategy illustrates longitudinal research. In **longitudinal research**, the behavior of one or more study participants is measured as they age. Thus longitudinal research measures change over time. By following many individuals over an extended time, researchers can understand the general course of change across some period of life.

The granddaddy of longitudinal studies, which has become a classic, is a study of gifted children begun by Lewis Terman around 80 years ago. In the study—which has yet to be concluded—a group of 1,500 children with high IQs were tested about every 5 years. Now in their 80s, the participants—who call themselves "Termites"—have provided information on everything from intellectual accomplishment to personality and longevity (Feldhusen, 2003; McCullough, Tsang, & Brion, 2003; Subotnik, 2006).

Longitudinal research has also provided great insight into language development. For instance, by tracing how children's vocabularies increase on a day-by-day basis, researchers have been able to understand the processes that underlie the human ability to become competent in using language (Gershkoff-Stowe & Hahn, 2007; Oliver & Plomin, 2007).

Longitudinal studies can provide a wealth of information about change over time. However, they have several drawbacks. For one thing, they require a tremendous investment of time, because researchers must wait for participants to become older. Furthermore, over the course of the research participants may drop out of a study, move away, become ill, or die as the research proceeds.

Finally, subjects who are observed or tested repeatedly may become "test-wise" and perform better each time they are assessed as they become familiarized with the procedure. Even if the process of observation in a study is not particularly intrusive for participants (such as simply recording, over a lengthy period of time, vocabulary increases in infants and preschoolers), the participants may be affected by the repeated presence of an experimenter or observer.

Consequently, despite the benefits of longitudinal research, particularly its ability to look at change within individuals, developmental researchers often turn to other methods in conducting research. The alternative they choose most often is the cross-sectional study.

Cross-Sectional Studies   Suppose again that you want to consider how children's moral development—their sense of right and wrong—changes from ages 3 to 5. Instead of using a longitudinal approach and following the same children over several years, we might conduct the study by simultaneously looking at three groups of children: 3-year-olds, 4-year-olds, and 5-year-olds, perhaps presenting each group with the same problem, and then seeing how they respond to it and explain their choices.

FROM RESEARCH to PRACTICE
Using Developmental Research to Improve Public Policy

- Is national legislation designed to "leave no child behind" effective in improving the lives of children?
- Does research support the legalization of marijuana?
- What are the effects of gay marriage on children in such unions?
- Should preschoolers diagnosed with attention deficit hyperactivity disorder receive drugs to treat their condition?

Each of these questions represents a national policy issue that can be answered only by considering the results of relevant research studies. By conducting controlled studies, developmental researchers have made a number of important contributions affecting education, family life, and health on a national scale. Consider the variety of ways that public policy issues have been informed by various types of research findings (Brooks-Gunn, 2003; Maton et al., 2004; Mervis, 2004; Jones, Brown, & Aber, 2008):

- **Research findings can provide policymakers a means of determining what questions to ask in the first place.** For example, studies of children's caregivers (some of which we'll consider in Chapter 7) have led policymakers to question whether the benefits of infant day care are outweighed by possible deterioration in parent–child bonds.

- **Research findings and the testimony of researchers are often part of the process by which laws are drafted.** A good deal of legislation has been passed based on findings from developmental researchers. For example, research revealed that children with developmental disabilities benefit from exposure to children without special needs, ultimately leading to passage of national legislation mandating that children with disabilities be placed in regular school classes as much as possible.

- **Policymakers and other professionals use research findings to determine how best to implement programs.** Research has shaped programs designed to reduce the incidence of unsafe sex among teenagers, to increase the level of prenatal care for pregnant mothers, to raise class attendance rates in school-age children, and to promote flu shots for older adults. The common thread among such programs is that many of their details are built upon basic research findings.

- **Research techniques are used to evaluate the effectiveness of existing programs and policies.** Once a public policy has been implemented, it is necessary to determine whether it has been effective and successful in accomplishing its goals. To do this, researchers employ formal evaluation techniques, developed from basic research procedures. For instance, researchers have continually scrutinized the Head Start preschool program, which has received massive federal funding, to ensure that it really does what it is supposed to do—improve children's academic performance.

Developmentalists have worked hand in hand with policymakers, and the resulting research findings have had a substantial impact on public policies, creating potential benefits for all of us. (To learn about some of the public policies that have been most effective, go to the the U.S. Education Department Web site, "What Works Clearinghouse" at *www.whatworks.ed.gov*.)

- What are some policy issues affecting children that are currently being debated nationally?

- Despite the existence of research data that might inform policy about development, politicians rarely discuss such data in their speeches. Why do you think this is?

Such an approach typifies cross-sectional research. In **cross-sectional research**, people of different ages are compared at the same point in time. Cross-sectional studies provide information about differences in development among different age groups.

Cross-sectional research is considerably more economical than longitudinal research in terms of time: Participants are tested at just one point in time. For instance, Terman's study conceivably might have been completed 75 years ago if Terman had simply looked at a group of gifted 15-year-olds, 20-year-olds, 25-year-olds, and so forth, all the way through a group of 80-year-olds. Because the participants would not be periodically tested, there would be no chance that they would become test-wise, and problems of participant attrition would not occur. Why, then, would anyone choose to use a procedure other than cross-sectional research?

The answer is that cross-sectional research brings its own set of difficulties. Recall that every person belongs to a particular *cohort*, the group of people born at around the same time in the same place. If we find that people of different ages vary along some dimension, it may be due to differences in cohort membership, not age per se.

Consider a concrete example: If we find in a correlational study that people who are 25 years old perform better on a test of intelligence than those who are 75 years old, there are several explanations. Although the finding may be due to decreased intelligence in older people, it may also be attributable to cohort differences. The group of 75-year-olds may

Cross-sectional research allows researchers to compare representatives of different age groups at the same time.

Sequential studies Studies in which researchers examine members of a number of different age groups at several points in time

have had less formal education than the 15-year-olds, because members of the older cohort were less likely to have finished high school or attended college than were members of the younger group. Or perhaps the older participants performed less well because as infants they received less adequate nutrition than did members of the younger group. In short, we cannot fully rule out the possibility that differences we find among people of different age groups in cross-sectional studies are due to cohort differences.

Cross-sectional studies also may suffer from *selective dropout*, in which participants in some age groups are more likely than others to quit participating in a study. For example, suppose a study of cognitive development in preschoolers includes a lengthy assessment of cognitive abilities. It is possible that young preschoolers would find the task more difficult and demanding than older preschoolers. As a result, the younger children would be more likely than the older preschoolers to discontinue participation in the study. If the least competent young preschoolers are the ones who drop out, then the remaining sample of participants in the study will consist of the more competent young preschoolers—together with a broader and more representative sample of older preschoolers. The results of such a study would be questionable (Mazumdar et al., 2007).

Finally, cross-sectional studies have an additional, more basic, disadvantage: They are unable to inform us about changes in individuals or groups. If longitudinal studies are like videos taken of a person at various ages, cross-sectional studies are like snapshots of entirely different groups. Although we can establish differences related to age, we cannot fully determine if such differences are related to change over time.

Sequential Studies Because both longitudinal and cross-sectional studies have drawbacks, researchers have turned to some compromise techniques. Among the most frequently employed are sequential studies, which are essentially a combination of longitudinal and cross-sectional studies.

In **sequential studies**, researchers examine a number of different age groups at several points in time. For instance, an investigator interested in children's moral behavior might begin a sequential study by examining the behavior of three groups of children, who are 3 years old, 4 years old, or 5 years old at the time the study begins. (This is no different from the way a cross-sectional study would be done.)

However, the study wouldn't stop there, but would continue for the next several years. During this period, each of the research participants would be tested annually. Thus, the 3-year-olds would be tested at ages 3, 4, and 5; the 4-year-olds at ages 4, 5, and 6; and the 5-year-olds at ages 5, 6, and 7. Such an approach combines the advantages of longitudinal and cross-sectional research, and it permits developmental researchers to tease out the consequences of age *change*

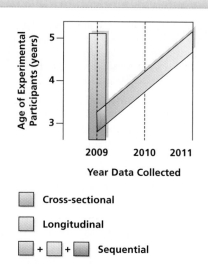

FIGURE 2-4 Research Techniques for Studying Development

In a cross-sectional study, 3-, 4- and 5-year-olds are compared at a similar point in time (in the year 2009). In longitudinal research, a set of participants who are 3 years old in the year 2009 are studied when they are 4 years old (in 2010) and when they are 5 years old (in 2011). A sequential study combines cross-sectional and longitudinal techniques; here, a group of 3-year-olds would be compared initially in 2009 with 4- and 5-year-olds but would also be studied 1 and 2 years later, when they themselves were 4 and 5 years old. Although the graph does not illustrate this, researchers carrying out this sequential study might also choose to retest the children who were 4 and 5 in 2009 for the next 2 years. What advantages do the three kinds of studies offer?

versus age *difference*. (The major research techniques for studying development are summarized in Figure 2-4.)

Becoming an Informed Consumer of Development

Critically Evaluating Developmental Research

"Study Shows Adolescent Suicide Reaches New Peaks"

"Genetic Basis Found for Children's Obesity"

"New Research Points to Cure for Sudden Infant Death Syndrome"

We've all seen headlines like these, which at first glance seem to herald important, meaningful discoveries. But before we accept the findings, it is important to think critically about the research on which the headlines are based. Among the most important questions that we should consider are the following:

• Is the study grounded in theory, and what are the underlying hypotheses about the research? Research should flow from theoretical foundations, and hypotheses should be logical and based on some underlying theory. Only by considering the results in terms of theory and hypotheses can we determine how successful the research has been.

- Is this an isolated research study, or does it fit into a series of investigations addressing the same general problem? A one-time study is far less meaningful than a series of studies that build upon one another. By placing research in the context of other studies, we can be much more confident regarding the validity of the findings of a new study.

- Who took part in the study, and how far can we generalize the results beyond the participants? As we discussed earlier in the chapter, conclusions about the meaning of research can only be generalized to people who are similar to the participants in a study.

- Was the study carried out appropriately? Although it is often difficult to know the details of a study from media summaries, it is important to learn as much as possible about who did the study and how it was done. For instance, did it include appropriate control groups, and are the researchers who conducted it reputable? One clue that a study meets these criteria and is well done is whether the findings reported in the media are based on a study published in a major journal such as *Developmental Psychology, Adolescence, Child Development*, or *Science*. Each of these journals is carefully edited, and only the best, most rigorous research is reported in them.

- Were the participants studied long enough to draw reasonable developmental implications? A study that purports to study long-term development should encompass a reasonably long time frame. Furthermore, developmental implications beyond the age span studied should not be drawn. ●

Ethics and Research

In the "study" conducted by Egyptian King Psamtik presented earlier in the chapter, two children were removed from their mothers and held in isolation in an effort to learn about the roots of language. If you found yourself thinking this was extraordinarily cruel, you are in good company. Clearly, such an experiment raises blatant ethical concerns, and nothing like it would ever be done today.

But sometimes ethical issues are more subtle. For instance, in seeking to understand the roots of aggressive behavior, U.S. government researchers proposed holding a conference to examine possible genetic roots of aggression. Based on work conducted by neuroscientists and geneticists, some researchers had begun to raise the possibility that genetic markers might be found that would allow the identification of children as being particularly violence-prone. In such cases, it might be possible to track these violence-prone children and provide interventions that might reduce the likelihood of later violence.

Critics objected strenuously, however. They argued that such identification might lead to a self-fulfilling prophecy. Children labeled as violence-prone might be treated in a way that would actually cause them to be more aggressive than if they hadn't been so labeled. Ultimately, under intense political pressure, the conference was canceled (R. Wright, 1995).

To help researchers deal with such ethical problems, the major organizations of developmentalists, including the Society for Research in Child Development and the American Psychological Association, have developed comprehensive ethical guidelines for researchers. Among the basic principles that must be followed are those involving freedom from harm, informed consent, the use of deception, and maintenance of participants' privacy (Sales & Folkman, 2000; American Psychological Association [APA], 2008; Fisher, 2003, 2004):

- **Researchers must protect participants from physical and psychological harm.** Their welfare, interests, and rights come before those of researchers. In research, participants' rights always come first (Sieber, 2000; C. B. Fisher, 2004).

- **Researchers must obtain informed consent from participants before their involvement in a study.** If they are over the age of 7, participants must voluntarily agree to be in a study. For those under 18, their parents or guardians must also provide consent.

  The requirement for informed consent raises some difficult issues. Suppose, for instance, researchers want to study the psychological effects of abortion on adolescents. Although they may be able to obtain the consent of an adolescent who has had an abortion, the researchers may need to get her parents' permission as well, because she is a minor. But if the adolescent hasn't told her parents about the abortion, the mere request for permission from the parents would violate her privacy—leading to a breach of ethics.

- **The use of deception in research must be justified and cause no harm.** Although deception to disguise the true purpose of an experiment is permissible, any experiment that uses deception must undergo careful scrutiny by an independent panel before it is conducted. Suppose, for example, we want to know the reaction of participants to success and failure. It is ethical to tell participants that they will be playing a game when the true purpose is actually to observe how they respond to doing well or poorly on the task. However, such a procedure is ethical only if it causes no harm to participants, has been approved by a review panel, and ultimately includes a full debriefing, or explanation, for participants when the study is over.

- **Participants' privacy must be maintained.** For example, if participants are videotaped during the course of a study, they must give their permission for the videotapes to be viewed. Furthermore, access to the tapes must be carefully restricted.

From a health-care provider's perspective: Are there some special circumstances involving adolescents (who are not legally adults) that would justify allowing them to participate in a study without obtaining their parents' permission?

1. Developmental researchers focus on _____ and applied research.

   Answer: theoretical

2. _____ research measures change over time.

   Answer: Longitudinal

To see more review questions, log on to MyDevelopmentLab.

3. The research method in which researchers examine a number of different age groups at a single point in time is called _____-_____ research

   Answer: cross-sectional

4. Among the basic ethical principles that protect research participants are those involving freedom from harm, _____ _____, and maintenance of participants' privacy.

   Answer: informed consent

CASE STUDY

The Case of... A Study in Violence

Don Callan loves his new job teaching fourth grade at a large public school. Lately, though, he has been concerned about the aggression he sees on the playground. He hears his students talking about movies, TV shows, and games that sound very violent. As a result, Don decides to conduct a research study. He theorizes that "indirect" media violence causes actual violence and aggression. His hypothesis is that children who encounter indirect violence at home will prefer violent images and behaviors at school.

He prepares a note for parents describing his experiment, asking them to indicate how often their children play with violent games and watch TV shows and movies that contain violence. He then plans to observe all his students for 2 weeks on the playground, keeping a record of any time they act aggressively. In addition, he plans to place violent and nonviolent games, comic books, and DVDs on a table and ask each child to pick one to borrow. He plans to tally their choices to see whether they choose a violent or nonviolent game.

He shows his experimental plan to his instructional supervisor and awaits her reaction.

1. Do you think Don's theory is a good example of a theory? Is his hypothesis sound?

2. Is his study an experiment or a correlational study? Why or why not?

3. Do you think Don's fourth graders would be able to understand and participate in the study and provide informed consent for their participation?

4. Do you think Don's method will yield reliable results? Why or why not?

5. What do you suppose the students' parents will think of the study? What will his instructional supervisor think? What do you think?

◀ Looking Back

What are the major perspectives on child development?

- Five major theoretical perspectives guide the study of child development: the psychodynamic, behavioral, cognitive, contextual, and evolutionary perspectives.

- The psychodynamic perspective is exemplified by the psychoanalytic theory of Freud and the psychosocial theory of Erikson. Freud focused attention on the unconscious and on stages through which children must pass successfully to avoid harmful fixations. Erikson identified eight distinct stages of development, each characterized by a conflict, or crisis, to work through.

- The behavioral perspective typically concerns stimulus–response learning, exemplified by classical conditioning, the operant conditioning of Skinner, and Bandura's social-cognitive learning theory.

- The cognitive perspective focuses on the processes that allow people to know, understand, and think about the world. For example, Piaget identified developmental stages through which all children are assumed to pass. Each stage involves qualitative differences in thinking. In contrast, information processing approaches attribute cognitive growth to quantitative changes in mental processes and capacities. Cognitive neuroscientists seek to identify locations and functions within the brain that are related to different types of cognitive activity.

- The contextual perspective stresses the interrelatedness of developmental areas and the importance of broad cultural factors in human development. Bronfenbrenner's ecological approach focuses on the microsystem, mesosystem, exosystem, macrosystem, and chronosystem. Vygotsky's sociocultural theory emphasizes the central influence on cognitive development exerted by social interactions between members of a culture.

- The evolutionary perspective attributes behavior to genetic inheritance from our ancestors, contending that genes determine not only traits such as skin color and eye color but also certain personality traits and social behaviors.

What is the scientific method, and how does it help answer questions about child development?

- The scientific method is the process of posing and answering questions using careful, controlled techniques that include systematic, orderly observation and the collection of data.
- Theories are broad explanations of facts or phenomena of interest, based on a systematic integration of prior findings and theories. Hypotheses are theory-based predictions that can be tested. Operationalization is the process of translating a hypothesis into specific, testable procedures that can be measured and observed.
- Researchers test hypotheses by correlational research (to determine if two factors are associated) and experimental research (to discover cause-and-effect relationships).
- Correlational studies use naturalistic observation, case studies, diaries, survey research, and psychophysiological methods to investigate whether certain characteristics of interest are associated with other characteristics.

Correlational studies lead to no direct conclusions about cause and effect.

- Typically, experimental research studies are conducted on participants in a treatment group, who receive the experimental treatment, and participants in a control group, who do not. Following the treatment, differences between the two groups can help the experimenter determine the effects of the treatment. Experiments may be conducted in a laboratory or in a real-world setting.

What are the major research strategies and challenges?

- Theoretical research is designed specifically to test some developmental explanation and expand scientific knowledge, whereas applied research is meant to provide practical solutions to immediate problems.
- To measure change at different ages, researchers use longitudinal studies of the same participants over time, cross-sectional studies of different-age participants conducted at one time, and sequential studies of different-age participants at several points in time.
- Ethical guidelines for research include the protection of participants from harm, informed consent of participants, limits on the use of deception, and the maintenance of privacy. ∎

Epilogue

This chapter examined the way developmentalists use theory and research to understand child development. We reviewed the broad approaches to study children, examining the theories that each has produced. In addition, we looked at the ways in which research is conducted.

Before proceeding to the next chapter, think about the Prologue of this chapter, which told about Cedric Jennings. In light of what you now know about theories and research, consider the following questions about Cedric:

1. How might child developmentalists from the psychodynamic, behavioral, cognitive, contextual, and evolutionary perspectives explain Cedric's motivation to succeed?
2. What differences might there be in the questions that would interest them and the studies they might wish to conduct?
3. Formulate one hypothesis using either the behavioral or cognitive perspective to explain Cedric's motivation.
4. Try to design a research study to test the hypothesis you generated in response to question 3.

Key Terms and Concepts

theories (p. 18)
psychodynamic perspective (p. 18)
psychoanalytic theory (p. 18)
psychosexual development (p. 19)
psychosocial development (p. 19)
behavioral perspective (p. 21)
classical conditioning (p. 21)
operant conditioning (p. 21)
behavior modification (p. 22)
social-cognitive learning theory (p. 22)
cognitive perspective (p. 23)
information-processing approaches (p. 24)

cognitive neuroscience approaches (p. 24)
contextual perspective (p. 25)
bioecological approach (p. 25)
sociocultural theory (p. 27)
evolutionary perspective (p. 28)
scientific method (p. 30)
hypothesis (p. 31)
correlational research (p. 31)
experimental research (p. 32)
naturalistic observation (p. 33)
case studies (p. 34)
survey research (p. 34)
psychophysiological methods (p. 34)

experiment (p. 35)
treatment (p. 35)
treatment group (p. 35)
control group (p. 35)
independent variable (p. 35)
dependent variable (p. 35)
sample (p. 36)
field study (p. 36)
laboratory study (p. 37)
theoretical research (p. 38)
applied research (p. 38)
longitudinal research (p. 38)
cross-sectional research (p. 39)
sequential studies (p. 40)

3

The Start of Life: Genetics and Prenatal Development

PROLOGUE: THE FUTURE IS NOW

It came out of the blue: Jana and Tom Monaco's seemingly healthy 3-year-old son Stephen developed a life-threatening stomach virus that led to severe brain damage. His diagnosis: a rare but treatable disease called isovaleric acidemia (IVA), marked by the body's inability to metabolize an amino acid found in dietary protein. Jana and Tom were unknowing carriers of the disease. . . . The Monacos had no warning whatsoever.

Not so when Jana got pregnant again. Her daughter, Caroline, was tested by amniocentesis while still in the womb. Knowing Caroline had the mutation, doctors were able to administer medication the day she was born—and the Monacos were prepared to monitor her diet immediately to keep her healthy. Today Stephen, 9, is unable to walk, talk or feed himself. Caroline, meanwhile, is an active, healthy 4-year-old. Genetic testing, says Jana, "gives Caroline the future that Stephen didn't get to have." (Kalb, 2006, p. 52)

► Looking Ahead

A hidden genetic disorder robbed Jana and Tom Monaco's first child of a normal, healthy life. Their second child was

spared the same fate by advances in genetic testing, which gave the Monacos a chance to intervene before the damage was done. They were able to stop Caroline's inherited disorder from doing the same damage by controlling aspects of her environment.

In this chapter, we'll examine what developmental researchers and other scientists have learned about ways that heredity and the environment work in tandem to create and shape human beings. We begin with the basics of heredity, the genetic transmission of characteristics from biological parents to their children, by examining how we receive our genetic endowment. We consider behavioral genetics, an area of study that specializes in the consequences of heredity on behavior. We also discuss what happens when genetic factors cause development to go awry, and how such problems are dealt with through genetic counseling and gene therapy.

But genes are only one part of the story of prenatal development. We also consider the ways in which a child's genetic heritage interacts with her environment: In other words, how one's family, socioeconomic status, and life events can affect a variety of characteristics, including physical traits, intelligence, and even personality.

Finally, we focus on the very first stage of development, tracing prenatal growth and change. We review some of the alternatives available to couples who find it difficult to conceive. We also talk about the stages of the prenatal period and how the prenatal environment offers both threats to—and the promise of—future growth.

After reading this chapter, you will be able to answer these questions:

- *What is our basic genetic endowment, and how can human development go off track?*
- *How do the environment and genetics work together to determine human characteristics?*

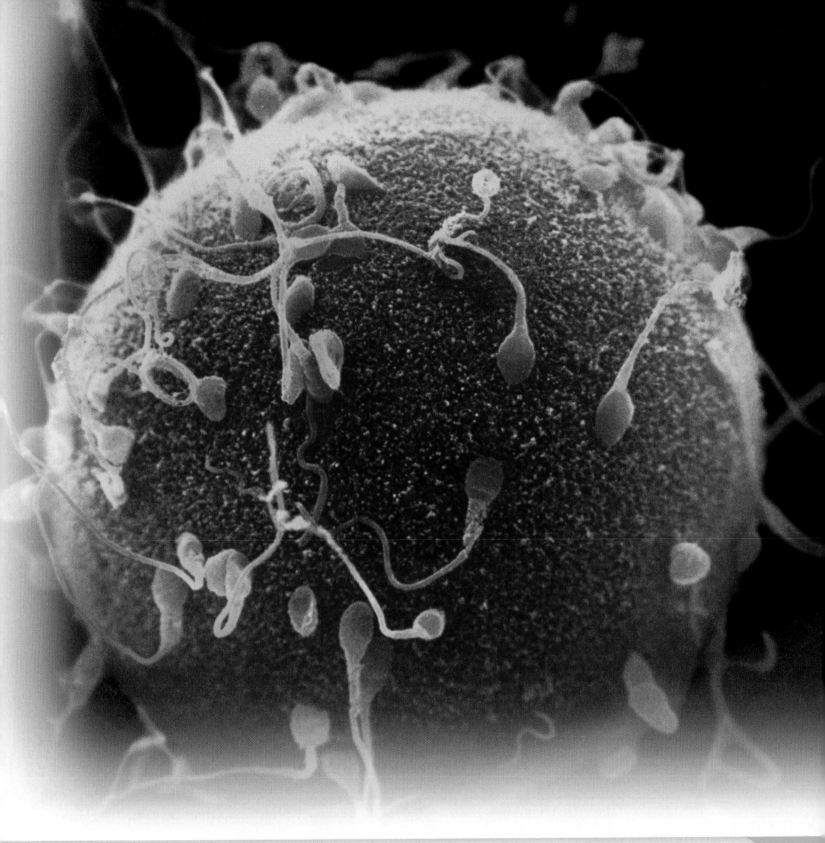

Gametes The sex cells from the mother and father that form a new cell at conception

Zygote The new cell formed by the process of fertilization

Genes The basic unit of genetic information

DNA (deoxyribonucleic acid) molecules The substance that genes are composed of that determines the nature of every cell in the body and how it will function

Chromosomes Rod-shaped portions of DNA that are organized in 23 pairs

Monozygotic twins Twins who are genetically identical

Dizygotic twins Twins who are produced when two separate ova are fertilized by two separate sperm at roughly the same time

- *Which human characteristics are significantly influenced by heredity?*
- *What happens during the prenatal stages of development?*
- *What are the threats to the fetal environment, and what can be done about them?*

Earliest Development

We humans begin the course of our lives simply.

Like individuals from tens of thousands of other species, we start as a single cell, a tiny speck probably weighing no more than 1/20-millionth of an ounce. But from this humble beginning, in relatively few months, a living, breathing, unique infant is born. This first cell is created when a male reproductive cell, a *sperm*, pushes through the membrane of the *ovum*, the female reproductive cell. These **gametes**, as the male and female reproductive cells are also known, each contain huge amounts of genetic information. About an hour or so after the sperm enters the ovum, the two gametes suddenly fuse, becoming one cell, a **zygote**. The resulting combination of their genetic instructions—over 2 billion chemically coded messages—is sufficient to begin creating a whole person.

Genes and Chromosomes: The Code of Life

The blueprints for creating a person are stored and communicated in our **genes**, the basic units of genetic information. The roughly 25,000 human genes are the biological equivalent of "software" that programs the future development of all parts of the body's "hardware."

All genes are composed of specific sequences of **DNA (deoxyribonucleic acid) molecules**. The genes are arranged in specific locations and in a specific order along 46 **chromosomes**, rod-shaped portions of DNA that are organized in 23 pairs. Only sex cells— the ova and the sperm—contain half this number, so that a child's mother and father each provide one of the two chromosomes in each of the 23 pairs. The 46 chromosomes (in 23 pairs) in the new zygote contain the genetic blueprint that will guide cell activity for the rest of the individual's life (Pennisi, 2000; International Human Genome Sequencing Consortium, 2001; see Figure 3-1). Through a process called *mitosis*, which accounts for the replication of most types of cells, nearly all the cells of the body will contain the same 46 chromosomes as the zygote.

70,000–100,000 Genes	=
46 Chromosomes	=
23 Chromosome Pairs	=
One Human Cell	

FIGURE 3-1

The Contents of a Single Human Cell

At the moment of conception, humans receive 70,000 to 100,000 genes, contained on 46 chromosomes in 23 pairs.

Specific genes in precise locations on the chain of chromosomes determine the nature and function of every cell in the body. For instance, genes determine which cells will ultimately become part of the heart and which will become part of the muscles of the leg. Genes also establish how different parts of the body will function: how rapidly the heart will beat, or how much strength a muscle will have.

If each parent provides just 23 chromosomes, where does the potential for the vast diversity of human beings come from? The answer resides primarily in the nature of the processes that underlie the cell division of the gametes. When the sperm and ova are formed in the adult human body in a process called *meiosis*, each gamete receives one of the two chromosomes that make up each of the 23 pairs. Because for each of the 23 pairs it is largely a matter of chance which member of the pair is contributed, there are 2^{23}, or about 8 million combinations possible. Furthermore, other processes, such as random transformations of particular genes, add to the variability of the genetic brew. The ultimate outcome: tens of *trillions* of possible genetic combinations.

With so many possible genetic mixtures provided by heredity, there is no likelihood that someday you'll bump into a genetic duplicate of yourself—with one exception: an identical twin.

Multiple Births: Two—or More— For the Genetic Price of One

Although it doesn't seem surprising when dogs and cats give birth to several offspring at one time, in humans, multiple births are cause for comment. And they should be: Less than 3% of all pregnancies produce twins, and the odds are even slimmer for three or more children.

Why do multiple births occur? Some occur when a cluster of cells in the ovum splits off within the first 2 weeks after fertilization. The result is two genetically identical zygotes, which are called *monozygotic* because they come from the same original zygote. **Monozygotic twins** are twins who are genetically identical. Any differences in their future development can be attributed only to environmental factors, because genetically they are exactly the same.

There is a second, and actually more common, mechanism that produces multiple births. In these cases, two separate ova are fertilized by two separate sperm at roughly the same time. Twins produced in this fashion are known as **dizygotic twins**. Because they are the result of two separate ovum–sperm combinations, they are no more genetically similar than two siblings born at different times.

Of course, not all multiple births produce only two babies. Triplets, quadruplets, and even more births are produced by either (or both) of the mechanisms that yield twins. Thus, triplets may be some combination of monozygotic, dizygotic, or trizygotic.

Although the chances of having a multiple birth are typically slim, the odds rise considerably when couples use fertility drugs to improve the probability of conceiving a child. For example, 1 in 10 couples using fertility drugs have dizygotic twins, compared to an overall figure of 1 in 86 for Caucasian couples in the United States. Older women, too, are more likely to have multiple births, and multiple births are also more common in some families than they are in others. The increased use of fertility drugs and rising average age of mothers giving birth has meant that multiple births have increased in the last 25 years (see Figure 3-2; Martin et al., 2005).

There are also racial, ethnic, and national differences in the rate of multiple births; this is probably due to inherited differences in the likelihood that more than one ovum will be released at a time. One out of 70 African American couples have dizygotic births, compared with the 1 out of 86 figure for White American couples (Vaughan, McKay, & Behrman, 1979; Wood, 1997).

Mothers carrying multiple children run a higher than average risk of premature delivery and birth complications. Consequently, these mothers must be particularly concerned about their prenatal care.

Monozygotic and dizygotic twins present opportunities to learn about the relative contributions of heredity and situational factors. What kinds of things can psychologists learn from studying twins?

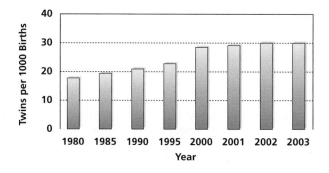

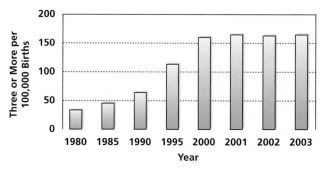

FIGURE 3-2 Rising Multiples

Multiple births have increased significantly over the last 25 years. What are some of the reasons for this phenomenon?
(*Source*: Martin et al., 2005)

Boy or Girl? Establishing the Sex of the Child   Recall that there are 23 matched pairs of chromosomes. In 22 of these pairs, each chromosome is similar to the other member of its pair. The one exception is the 23rd pair, which is the one that determines the sex of the child. In females, the 23rd pair consists of two matching, relatively large X-shaped chromosomes, appropriately identified as XX. In males, on the other hand, the members of the pair are dissimilar. One consists of an X-shaped chromosome, but the other is a shorter, smaller Y-shaped chromosome. This pair is identified as XY.

As we discussed earlier, each gamete carries one chromosome from each of the parent's 23 pairs of chromosomes. Because a female's 23rd pair of chromosomes are both Xs, an ovum will always carry an X chromosome, no matter which chromosome of the 23rd pair it gets. A male's 23rd pair is XY, so each sperm could carry either an X or a Y chromosome.

If the sperm contributes an X chromosome when it meets an ovum (which, remember, will always contribute an X chromosome), the child will have an XX pairing on the 23rd chromosome and will be a female. If the sperm contributes a Y chromosome, the result will be an XY pairing and will be a male (see Figure 3-3).

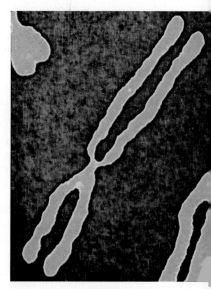

Not only is the X chromosome important in determining gender, but it is also the site of genes controlling other aspects of development.

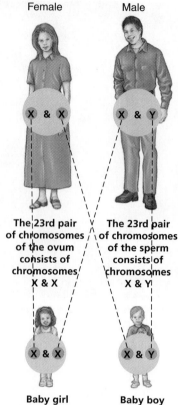

Female   Male

X & X   X & Y

The 23rd pair of chromosomes of the ovum consists of chromosomes X & X

The 23rd pair of chromosomes of the sperm consists of chromosomes X & Y

X & X   X & Y

Baby girl   Baby boy

FIGURE 3-3
Determining Sex

When an ovum and sperm meet at the moment of fertilization, the ovum is certain to provide an X chromosome, whereas the sperm will provide either an X or a Y chromosome. If the sperm contributes its X chromosome, the child will have an XX pairing on the 23rd chromosome and will be a girl. If the sperm contributes a Y chromosome, the result will be an XY pairing and will be a boy. Does this mean that girls are more likely to be conceived than are boys?

It is clear from this process that the father's sperm determines the gender of the child. This fact is leading to the development of techniques that will allow parents to increase the chances of specifying the gender of their child. In one new technique, lasers measure the DNA in sperm. By discarding sperm that harbor the unwanted sex chromosome, the chances of having a child of the desired sex increase dramatically (Belkin, 1999; Van Balen, 2005).

Of course, procedures for choosing a child's sex raise ethical and practical issues. For example, in cultures that value one gender over the other, might there be a kind of gender discrimination prior to birth? Furthermore, a shortage of children of the less preferred sex might ultimately emerge. Many questions remain, then, before sex selection becomes routine (Sharma, 2008).

The Basics of Genetics: The Mixing and Matching of Traits

What determined the color of your hair? Why are you tall or short? What made you susceptible to hay fever? And why do you have so many freckles? To answer these questions, we need to consider the basic mechanisms involved in the way that the genes we inherit from our parents transmit information.

We can start by examining the discoveries of an Austrian monk, Gregor Mendel, in the mid-1800s. In a series of simple yet convincing experiments, Mendel cross-pollinated pea plants that always produced yellow seeds with pea plants that always produced green seeds. The result was not, as one might guess, a plant with a combination of yellow and green seeds. Instead, all of the resulting plants had yellow seeds. At first it appeared that the green-seeded plants had had no influence.

However, additional research on Mendel's part proved this was not true. He bred together plants from the new, yellow-seeded generation that had resulted from his original cross-breeding of the green-seeded and yellow-seeded plants. The consistent result was a ratio of three-fourths yellow seeds to one-fourth green seeds.

Why did this 3-to-1 ratio of yellow to green seeds appear so consistently? It was Mendel's genius to provide an answer. Based on his experiments with pea plants, he argued that

Gregor Mendel's pioneering experiments on pea plants provided the foundation for the study of genetics.

when two competing traits, such as a green or yellow coloring of seeds, were both present, only one could be expressed (displayed). The one that was expressed was called a **dominant trait**. Meanwhile, the other trait remained present in the organism, although not expressed. This was called a **recessive trait**. In the case of Mendel's original pea plants, the offspring plants received genetic information from both the green-seeded and the yellow-seeded parents. However, the yellow trait was dominant, and consequently the recessive green trait did not assert itself.

Keep in mind, however, that genetic material relating to both parent plants is present in the offspring, even though it cannot be seen. The genetic information is known as the organism's genotype. A **genotype** is the underlying combination of genetic material present (but outwardly invisible) in an organism. In contrast, a **phenotype** is the observable trait, the trait that actually is seen. Although the offspring of the yellow-seeded and green-seeded pea plants all have yellow seeds (i.e., they have a yellow-seeded phenotype), the genotype consists of genetic information relating to both parents.

And what is the nature of the information in the genotype? To answer that question, let's turn from peas to people. In fact, the principles are the same not only for plants and humans but also for the majority of species.

Recall that parents transmit genetic information to their offspring via the chromosomes they contribute through the gamete they provide during fertilization. Some of the genes form pairs called *alleles*, genes governing traits that may take alternate forms, such as hair or eye color. For example, brown eye color is a dominant trait (B); blue eyes are recessive (b). A child's allele may contain similar or dissimilar genes from each parent. If the child receives similar genes, he is said to be **homozygous** for the trait. On the other hand, if the child receives different forms of the gene from his parents, he is said to be **heterozygous**. In the case of heterozygous alleles (Bb), the dominant characteristic, brown eyes, is expressed. However, if the child happens to receive a recessive allele from each of his parents, and therefore lacks a dominant characteristic (bb), he will display the recessive characteristic, such as blue eyes.

Transmission of Genetic Information

We can see this process at work in humans by considering the transmission of *phenylketonuria (PKU)*, an inherited disorder in which a child is unable to make use of phenylalanine, an essential amino acid present in proteins found in milk and other foods. If left untreated, PKU allows phenylalanine to build up to toxic levels, causing brain damage and mental retardation.

PKU is produced by a single allele, or pair of genes. As shown in Figure 3-4, we can label each gene of the pair with a *P* if it carries a dominant gene, which causes the normal production of phenylalanine, or a *p* if it carries the recessive gene that produces PKU. In cases in which neither parent is a PKU carrier, both the mother's and the father's pairs of genes are the dominant form, symbolized as *PP*. Consequently, no matter which member of the pair is contributed by the mother and father, the resulting pair of genes in the child will be *PP*, and the child will not have PKU.

However, consider what happens if one of the parents has a recessive *p* gene. In this case, which we can we symbolize as *Pp*, the parent will not have PKU, because the normal *P* gene is dominant. But the recessive gene can be passed down to the child. This is not so bad: If the child has only one recessive gene, it will not suffer from PKU. But what if both parents carry a recessive *p* gene? In this case, although neither parent has the disorder, it is possible for the child to receive a recessive gene from both parents. The child's genotype for PKU then will be *pp*, and he or she will have the disorder.

Remember, though, that even children whose parents both have the recessive gene for PKU have only a 25% chance of inheriting the disorder. Due to the laws of probability, 25% of children with *Pp* parents will receive the dominant gene from each parent (these children's genotype would be *PP*), and 50% will receive the dominant gene from one parent and the recessive gene from the other (their genotypes would be either *Pp* or *pP*). Only the unlucky 25% who receive the recessive gene from each parent and have the genotype *pp* will suffer from PKU.

Polygenic Traits The transmission of PKU is a good way to illustrate the basic principles of how genetic information passes from parent to child, although the case of PKU is simpler than most cases of genetic transmission. Relatively few traits are governed by a single pair of genes. Instead, most

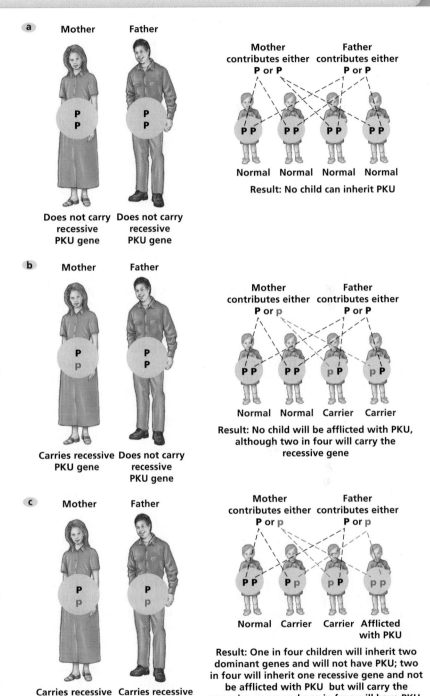

FIGURE 3-4 PKU Probabilities

PKU, a disease that causes brain damage and mental retardation, is produced by a single pair of genes inherited from one's mother and father. If neither parent carries a gene for the disease (a), a child cannot develop PKU. Even if one parent carries the recessive gene, but the other doesn't (b), the child cannot inherit the disease. However, if both parents carry the recessive gene (c), there is a one in four chance that the child will have PKU.

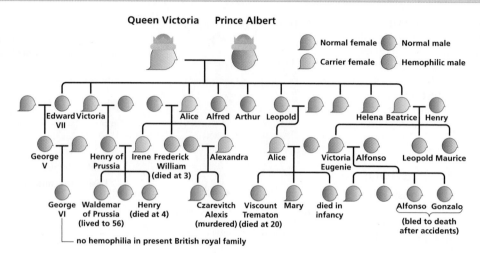

Queen Victoria   Prince Albert

Normal female   Normal male
Carrier female   Hemophilic male

no hemophilia in present British royal family

FIGURE 3-5
Inheriting Hemophilia

Hemophilia, a blood-clotting disorder, has been an inherited problem throughout the royal families of Europe, as illustrated by the descendants of Queen Victoria of Britain.

(*Source:* Adapted from Kimball, 1983)

traits are the result of polygenic inheritance. In **polygenic inheritance**, a combination of multiple gene pairs is responsible for the production of a particular trait.

Furthermore, some genes come in several alternate forms, and still others act to modify the way that particular genetic traits (produced by other alleles) are displayed. Genes also vary in terms of their *reaction range*, the potential degree of variability in the actual expression of a trait due to environmental conditions. And some traits, such as blood type, are produced by genes in which neither member of a pair of genes can be classified as purely dominant or recessive. Instead, the trait is expressed in terms of a combination of the two genes—such as type AB blood.

A number of recessive genes, called **X-linked genes**, are located only on the X chromosome. Recall that in females, the 23rd pair of chromosomes is an XX pair, whereas in males it is an XY pair. One result is that males have a higher risk for a variety of X-linked disorders, because males lack a second X chromosome that can counteract the genetic information that produces the disorder. For example, males are significantly more apt to have red–green color blindness, a disorder produced by a set of genes on the X chromosome.

Similarly, the blood disorder *hemophilia* is produced by X-linked genes. Hemophilia has been a recurrent problem in the royal families of Europe, as illustrated in Figure 3-5, which shows the inheritance of hemophilia in the descendants of Queen Victoria of Great Britain.

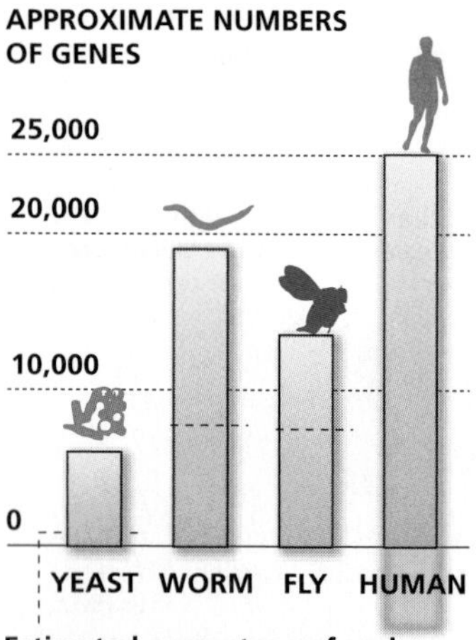

APPROXIMATE NUMBERS OF GENES

25,000
20,000
10,000
0

YEAST   WORM   FLY   HUMAN

Estimated percentage of each creature's total genes found in humans are indicated by the dotted line.

FIGURE 3-6
Uniquely Human?

Humans have about 25,000 genes, making them not much more genetically complex than some primitive species.

(*Source:* Celera Genomics: International Human Genome Sequencing Consortium, 2001)

The Human Genome and Behavioral Genetics: Cracking the Genetic Code

Mendel's achievements in recognizing the basics of genetic transmission of traits were trailblazing. However, they mark only the beginning of our understanding of the ways those particular sorts of characteristics are passed on from one generation to the next. The most recent milestone in understanding genetics was reached in early 2001, when molecular geneticists succeeded in mapping the specific sequence of genes on each chromosome. This accomplishment stands as one of the most important moments in the history of genetics, and, for that matter, all of biology (International Human Genome Sequencing Consortium, 2001).

Already, the mapping of the gene sequence has provided important advances in our understanding of genetics. For instance, the number of human genes, long thought to be 100,000, has been revised downward to 25,000—not many more than is found in organisms that are far less complex (see Figure 3-6). Furthermore, scientists have discovered that 99.9% of the gene sequence is shared by all humans. In short, this means that we humans are far more similar to one another than we are different. It also indicates that many of the differences that seemingly separate people—such as race—are, literally, only skin deep. Human genome mapping will also help identify particular disorders to which a given individual is susceptible (Gee, 2004; DeLisi & Fleischhaker, 2007; Gupta & State, 2007).

The mapping of the human gene sequence is supporting the field of behavioral genetics. As the name implies, **behavioral genetics** studies the effects of heredity on psychological characteristics. Rather than simply examine stable, unchanging characteristics such as hair or eye color, behavioral geneticists take a broader approach and consider how our personality and behavioral habits are affected by genetic factors. Personality traits such as shyness or sociability, moodiness and assertiveness are among the areas being studied. Other behavioral geneticists study psychological

TABLE 3-1 The Genetic Basis of Selected Behavioral Disorders and Traits

Behavioral Trait	Current Ideas of Genetic Basis
Huntington's disease	Huntington gene has been identified.
Early-onset (familial) Alzheimer's disease	Three distinct genes have been identified.
Fragile X mental retardation	Two genes have been identified.
Late-onset Alzheimer's disease	One set of genes has been associated with increased risk.
Attention-deficit/hyperactivity disorder	Three locations related to the genetics involved with the neurotransmitter dopamine may contribute.
Dyslexia	Relationships to two locations, on chromosomes 6 and 15, have been suggested.
Schizophrenia	There is no consensus, but links to numerous chromosomes, including 1, 5, 6, 10, 13, 15, and 22 have been reported.

(*Source*: Adapted from McGulfin, Riley, & Plomin, 2001)

disorders such as depression, attention-deficit/hyperactivity disorder, and schizophrenia, looking for possible genetic links (Baker, Mazzeo, & Kendler, 2007; DeYoung, Quilty, & Peterson, 2007; Haeffel et al., 2008; see Table 3-1).

The promise of behavioral genetics is substantial. For one thing, researchers working within the field are gaining a better understanding of the specifics of the genetic code that underlie human behavior and development. Even more important, researchers are seeking to identify how genetic defects may be remedied (Plomin & Rutter, 1998; Peltonen & McKusick, 2001). To understand how that goal might be reached, we need to consider the ways in which genetic factors, which normally cause development to proceed so smoothly, may falter.

Inherited and Genetic Disorders: When Development Goes Awry

PKU is just one of several disorders that may be inherited. Like a bomb that is harmless until its fuse is lit, a recessive gene responsible for a disorder may be passed on unknowingly from one generation to the next, revealing itself only when, by chance, it is paired with another recessive gene. It is only when two recessive genes come together like a match and a fuse that the gene will express itself and a child will inherit the genetic disorder.

But there is another reason that genes can be a source of concern: In some cases, genes become physically damaged. For instance, genes may break down due to wear-and-tear or to chance events occurring during the cell-division processes of meiosis and mitosis. And sometimes, for no known reason, genes spontaneously change their form, a process called *spontaneous mutation*.

Alternatively, certain environmental factors, such as exposure to X-rays or even to highly polluted air, may produce a malformation of genetic material (see Figure 3-7). When such damaged genes are passed on to a child, the

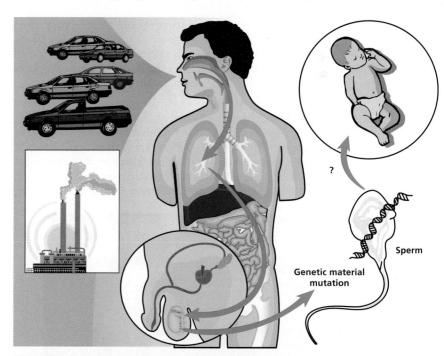

FIGURE 3-7 Inhaled Air and Genetic Mutations

Inhalation of unhealthy, polluted air may lead to mutations in genetic material in sperm. These mutations may be passed on, damaging the fetus and affecting future generations. (*Source:* Based on Samet, DeMarini, & Malling, 2004, p. 971)

results can be disastrous in terms of future physical and cognitive development (Samet, DeMarini, & Malling, 2004).

In addition to PKU, which occurs once in 10,000 to 20,000 births, other inherited and genetic disorders include:

- *Down syndrome.* As we noted earlier, most people have 46 chromosomes, arranged in 23 pairs. One exception is individuals with **Down syndrome**, a disorder produced by the presence of an extra chromosome on the 21st pair. Once referred to as mongolism, Down syndrome is the most frequent cause of mental retardation. It occurs in about 1 out of 500 births, although the risk is much greater in mothers who are unusually young or old (Crane & Morris, 2006).

- *Fragile X syndrome.* **Fragile X syndrome** occurs when a particular gene is injured on the X chromosome. The result is mild to moderate mental retardation.

- *Sickle-cell anemia.* Around one-tenth of the African American population carries genes that produce sickle-cell anemia, and 1 African American in 400 actually has the disease. **Sickle-cell anemia** is a blood disorder that gets its name from the shape of the red blood cells in those who have it. Symptoms include poor appetite, stunted growth, swollen stomach, and yellowish eyes. People afflicted with the most severe form of the disease rarely live beyond childhood. However, for those with less severe cases, medical advances have produced significant increases in life expectancy.

- *Tay-Sachs disease.* Occurring mainly in Jews of eastern European ancestry and in French Canadians, **Tay-Sachs disease** usually causes death before its victims reach school age. There is no treatment for the disorder, which produces blindness and muscle degeneration prior to death.

- *Klinefelter's syndrome.* One male out of every 400 is born with **Klinefelter's syndrome**, an abnormality resulting from the presence of an extra X chromosome. The resulting XXY complement produces underdeveloped genitals, extreme height, and enlarged breasts. Klinefelter's syndrome is one of a number of genetic abnormalities that result from receiving the improper number of sex chromosomes. For instance,

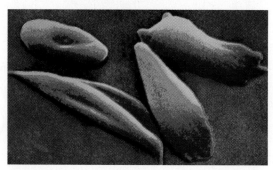

Sickle-cell anemia, named for the presence of misshapen red blood cells, is carried in the genes of 1 in 10 African Americans.

there are disorders produced by an extra Y chromosome (XYY), a missing second chromosome (called *Turner syndrome*; X0), and three X chromosomes (XXX). Such disorders are typically characterized by problems relating to sexual characteristics and by intellectual deficits (Kesler, 2007; J. Ross, Stefanatos, & Roeltgen, 2007).

It is important to keep in mind that the mere fact a disorder has genetic roots does not mean that environmental factors do not also play a role (Moldin & Gottesman, 1997). Consider, for instance, sickle-cell anemia, which primarily afflicts people of African descent. Because the disease can be fatal in childhood, we'd expect that those who suffer from it would be unlikely to live long enough to pass it on. And this does seem to be true, at least in the United States: Compared with parts of West Africa, the incidence in the United States is much lower.

But why shouldn't the incidence of sickle-cell anemia also be gradually reduced for people in West Africa? This question proved puzzling for many years, until scientists determined that carrying the sickle-cell gene raises immunity to malaria, which is a common disease in West Africa (Allison, 1954). This heightened immunity means that people with the sickle-cell gene have a genetic advantage (in terms of resistance to malaria) that offsets, to some degree, the disadvantage of being a carrier of the sickle-cell gene.

The lesson of sickle-cell anemia is that genetic factors are intertwined with environmental considerations and can't be looked at in isolation. Furthermore, we need to remember that although we've been focusing on inherited factors that can go awry, in the vast majority of cases the genetic mechanisms with which we are endowed work quite well. Overall, 95% of children born in the United States are healthy and normal. For the some 250,000 who are born with some sort of physical or mental disorder, appropriate intervention often can help treat and, in some cases, cure the problem.

Moreover, due to advances in behavioral genetics, genetic difficulties increasingly can be forecast, anticipated, and planned for before a child's birth, enabling parents to take steps before the child is born to reduce the severity of certain genetic conditions. In fact, as scientists' knowledge regarding the specific location of particular genes expands, predictions of what the genetic future may hold are becoming increasingly exact, as we discuss next (Plomin & Rutter, 1998).

Genetic Counseling: Predicting the Future From the Genes of the Present

If you knew that your mother and grandmother had died of Huntington's disease—a devastating, always fatal inherited disorder marked by tremors and intellectual deterioration—to

Genetic counseling
The discipline that focuses on helping people deal with issues relating to inherited disorders

Ultrasound sonography
A process in which high-frequency sound waves scan the mother's womb to produce an image of the unborn baby, whose size and shape can then be assessed

Chorionic villus sampling (CVS) A test used to find genetic defects that involves taking samples of hairlike material that surrounds the embryo

whom could you turn to learn your own chances of coming down with the disease? The best person to seek would be a genetic counselor, a member of a field that, until a few decades ago, was nonexistent. **Genetic counseling** focuses on helping people deal with issues relating to inherited disorders.

Genetic counselors use a variety of data in their work. For instance, couples contemplating having a child may seek to determine the risks involved in a future pregnancy. In such a case, a counselor will take a thorough family history, seeking any familial incidence of birth defects that might indicate a pattern of recessive or X-linked genes. In addition, the counselor will assess factors such as the age of the mother and father and any previous abnormalities in other children they may have already had (Resta et al., 2006).

Typically, genetic counselors suggest a thorough physical examination. Such an exam may identify physical abnormalities that potential parents may have and not be aware of. In addition, samples of blood, skin, and urine may be used to isolate and examine specific chromosomes. Possible genetic defects, such as the presence of an extra sex chromosome,

can be identified by assembling a *karyotype*, a chart containing enlarged photos of each of the chromosomes.

Prenatal Testing A variety of techniques can be used to assess the health of an unborn child if a woman is already pregnant (see Table 3-2 for a list of currently available tests). The earliest test is a *first-trimester screen*, which combines a blood test and ultrasound sonography in the 11th to 13th week of pregnancy. In **ultrasound sonography**, high-frequency sound waves bombard the mother's womb. These waves produce a rather indistinct, but useful, image of the unborn baby, whose size and shape can then be assessed. Repeated use of ultrasound sonography can reveal developmental patterns. Although the accuracy of blood tests and ultrasound in identifying abnormalities is not high early in pregnancy, it becomes more accurate later on.

A more invasive test, **chorionic villus sampling (CVS)**, can be employed in the 11th to 13th week if blood tests and ultrasound have identified a potential problem.

TABLE 3-2	Fetal Development Monitoring Techniques
Technique	Description
Amniocentesis	Done between the 15th and 20th week of pregnancy, this procedure examines a sample of the amniotic fluid, which contains fetal cells. Recommended if either parent carries Tay-Sachs, spina bifida, sickle-cell, Down syndrome, muscular dystrophy, or Rh disease.
Chorionic villus sampling (CVS)	Done at 8 to 11 weeks, either transabdominally or transcervically, depending on where the placenta is located. Involves inserting a needle (abdominally) or a catheter (cervically) into the substance of the placenta but staying outside the amniotic sac and removing 10 to 15 milligrams of tissue. This tissue is manually cleaned of maternal uterine tissue and then grown in culture, and a karyotype is made, as with amniocentesis.
Embryoscopy	Examines the embryo or fetus during the first 12 weeks of pregnancy by means of a fiber-optic endoscope inserted through the cervix. Can be performed as early as week 5. Access to the fetal circulation may be obtained through the instrument, and direct visualization of the embryo permits the diagnosis of malformations.
Fetal blood sampling (FBS)	Performed after 18 weeks of pregnancy by collecting a small amount of blood from the umbilical cord for testing. Used to detect Down syndrome and most other chromosome abnormalities in the fetuses of couples who are at increased risk of having an affected child. Many other diseases can be diagnosed using this technique.
Sonoembryology	Used to detect abnormalities in the first trimester of pregnancy. Involves high-frequency transvaginal probes and digital image processing. In combination with ultrasound, can detect more than 80% of all malformations during the second trimester.
Sonogram	Uses ultrasound to produce a visual image of the uterus, fetus, and placenta.
Ultrasound sonography	Uses very high-frequency sound waves to detect structural abnormalities or multiple pregnancies, measure fetal growth, judge gestational age, and evaluate uterine abnormalities. Also used as an adjunct to other procedures such as amniocentesis.

Amniocentesis The process of identifying genetic defects by examining a small sample of fetal cells drawn by a needle inserted into the amniotic fluid surrounding the unborn fetus

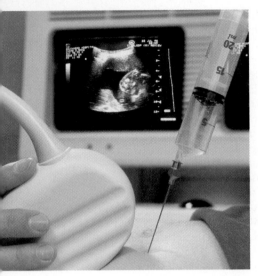

In amniocentesis, a sample of fetal cells is withdrawn from the amniotic sac and used to identify a number of genetic defects.

This procedure involves inserting a thin needle into the fetus and extracting small samples of hairlike material that surrounds the embryo. The test can be done between the 8th and 11th week of pregnancy. However, it produces a risk of miscarriage of 1 in 100 to 1 in 200; because of the risk, its use is relatively infrequent.

In **amniocentesis**, a small sample of fetal cells is drawn by a tiny needle inserted into the amniotic fluid surrounding the unborn fetus. Carried out 15 to 20 weeks into the pregnancy, amniocentesis allows the analysis of the fetal cells that can identify a variety of genetic defects with nearly 100% accuracy. In addition, this test can determine the sex of the child. Although there is always a danger to the fetus in an invasive procedure such as amniocentesis, it is generally safe.

After the various tests are complete and all possible information is available, the couple will meet with the genetic counselor again. Typically, counselors avoid giving specific recommendations. Instead, they lay out the facts and present various options, ranging from doing nothing to taking more drastic steps, such as terminating the pregnancy through abortion. Ultimately, it is the parents who must decide what course of action to follow.

Screening for Future Problems   The newest role for genetic counselors involves testing people to identify whether they themselves, rather than their children, are susceptible to future disorders because of genetic abnormalities. For instance, Huntington's disease typically does not appear until people reach their 40s. However, genetic testing can identify much earlier whether a person carries the flawed gene that produces Huntington's disease. Presumably, people's knowledge that they carry the gene can help them prepare themselves for the future (Ensenauer, Michels, & Reinke, 2005; Cina & Fellmann, 2006).

In addition to Huntington's disease, more than 1,000 disorders can be predicted on the basis of genetic testing (see Table 3-3). Although such testing may bring welcome relief from future worries—if the results are negative—positive results may produce just the opposite effect. In fact, genetic testing raises difficult practical and ethical questions (Johannes, 2003; Twomey, 2006).

Suppose, for instance, a woman who thought she was susceptible to Huntington's disease was tested in her 20s and found that she did not carry the defective gene. Obviously, she would experience tremendous relief. But suppose she found that she did carry the flawed gene and was therefore going to get the disease. In this case, she might well experience depression and remorse. In fact, some studies show that 10% of people who find they have the flawed gene that leads to Huntington's disease never recover fully on an emotional level (Groopman, 1998; Wahlin, 2007).

Clearly, genetic testing is a complicated issue. It rarely provides a simple yes or no answer as to whether an individual will be susceptible to a disorder. Instead, typically it presents a range of probabilities. In some cases, the likelihood of actually becoming ill depends on the type of environmental stressors to which a person is exposed. Personal differences also affect a given person's susceptibility to a disorder (Patenaude, Guttmacher, & Collins, 2002; Bonke et al., 2005).

As our understanding of genetics continues to grow, researchers and medical practitioners have moved beyond testing and counseling to actively working to change flawed genes. The possibilities for genetic intervention and manipulation increasingly border on what once was science fiction—as we consider in the *From Research to Practice* box on page 56 about preimplantation genetic diagnosis.

From a health-care provider's perspective: What are some ethical and philosophical questions that surround the issue of genetic counseling? Might it sometimes be unwise to know ahead of time about possible genetically linked disorders that might afflict your child or yourself?

REVIEW ↵ mydevelopmentlab

1. The human genetic code, transmitted at the moment of conception, is stored in our genes and is composed of specific sequences of _____.

   Answer: DNA

2. _____ twins are genetically identical and come from the same zygote.

   Answer: Monozygotic

3. A _____ is the underlying combination of genetic material present (but outwardly invisible) in an organism, while a phenotype is the observable trait.

   Answer: genotype

To see more review questions, log on to MyDevelopmentLab.

TABLE 3-3 Some Currently Available DNA-Based Genetic Tests

Disease	Description
Adult polycystic kidney disease	Kidney failure and liver disease
Alpha-1-antitrypsin deficiency	Emphysema and liver disease
Alzheimer's disease	Late-onset variety of senile dementia
Amyotrophic lateral sclerosis (Lou Gehrig's disease)	Progressive motor function loss leading to paralysis and death
Ataxia telangiectasia	Progressive brain disorder resulting in loss of muscle control and cancers
Breast and ovarian cancer (inherited)	Early-onset tumors of breasts and ovaries
Charcot-Marie-Tooth	Loss of feeling in ends of limbs
Congenital adrenal hyperplasia	Hormone deficiency; ambiguous genitalia and male pseudohermaphroditism
Cystic fibrosis	Thick mucus accumulations in lungs and chronic infections in lungs and pancreas
Duchenne muscular dystrophy (Becker muscular dystrophy)	Severe to mild muscle wasting, deterioration, weakness
Dystonia	Muscle rigidity, repetitive twisting movements
Factor V-Leiden	Blood-clotting disorder
Fanconi anemia, group	Anemia, leukemia, skeletal deformities
Fragile X syndrome	Mental retardation
Gaucher disease	Enlarged liver and spleen, bone degeneration
Hemophilia A and B	Bleeding disorders
Hereditary nonpolyposis colon cancer [a]	Early-onset tumors of colon and sometimes other organs
Huntington's disease	Progressive neurological degeneration, usually beginning in midlife
Myotonic dystrophy	Progressive muscle weakness
Neurofibromatosis, type 1	Multiple benign nervous system tumors that can be disfiguring; cancers
Phenylketonuria	Progressive mental retardation due to missing enzyme; correctable by diet
Prader Willi/Angelman syndromes	Decreased motor skills, cognitive impairment, early death
Sickle-cell disease	Blood cell disorder; chronic pain and infections
Spinal muscular atrophy	Severe, usually lethal progressive muscle-wasting disorder in children
Spinocerebellar ataxia, type 1	Involuntary muscle movements, reflex disorders, explosive speech
Tay-Sachs disease	Seizures, paralysis; fatal neurological disease of early childhood
Thalassemias	Anemias

[a] These are susceptibility tests that provide only an estimated risk for developing the disorder.
(*Source*: Human Genome Project, 2006, http://www.oml.gov/scl/techresources/Human_Genome/medicine/genetest.shtml.)

The Interaction of Heredity and Environment

Like many other parents, Jared's mother, Leesha, and his father, Jamal, tried to figure out which one of them their new baby resembled the most. He seemed to have Leesha's big, wide eyes, and Jamal's generous smile. As he grew, Jared grew to resemble his mother and father even more. His hair grew in with a hairline just like Leesha's, and his teeth, when they came, made his smile resemble Jamal's even more. He also seemed to act like his parents. For example, he was a charming little baby, always ready to smile at people who visited the house—just like his friendly, jovial dad. He seemed to sleep like his mom which was lucky because Jamal was an extremely light sleeper who could do with as little as 4 hours a night, whereas Leesha liked a regular 7 or 8 hours.

Were Jared's ready smile and regular sleeping habits something he just luckily inherited from his parents? Or did Jamal and Leesha provide a happy and stable home that encouraged

Temperament Patterns of arousal and emotionality that represent consistent and enduring characteristics in an individual

FROM RESEARCH to PRACTICE
Are "Designer Babies" in Our Future?

Adam Nash was born to save his older sister Molly's life—literally. Molly was suffering from a rare disorder called Fanconi anemia, which meant that her bone marrow was failing to produce blood cells. This disease can have devastating effects on young children, including birth defects and certain cancers. Many don't survive to adulthood. Molly's best hope for overcoming this disease was to grow healthy bone marrow by receiving a transplant of immature blood cells from the placenta of a newborn sibling. But not just any sibling would do—it had to be one with compatible cells that would not be rejected by Molly's immune system. So Molly's parents turned to a new and risky technique that had the potential to save Molly by using cells from her unborn brother.

Molly's parents were the first to use a genetic screening technique called *preimplantation genetic diagnosis* (PGD) to ensure that their next child would be free of Fanconi anemia. With PGD, a newly fertilized embryo can be screened for a variety of genetic diseases before it is implanted in the mother's uterus to develop. Doctors fertilized several of Molly's mother's eggs with her husband's sperm in a test tube. They then examined the embryos to ensure that they would only implant the embryo that PGD revealed to be both genetically healthy and a match for Molly. When Adam was born 9 months later, Molly got a new lease on life, too: The transplant was a success, and Molly was cured of her disease.

Molly's parents were understandably focused on saving their seriously ill daughter's life, but they and their doctors also opened a controversial new chapter in genetic engineering involving the use of advances in reproductive medicine that give parents a degree of prenatal control over the traits of their children. Another procedure that makes this level of genetic control possible is *germ line therapy*, in which cells are taken from an embryo and then replaced after the defective genes they contain have been repaired.

While PGD and germ line therapy have important uses in the prevention and treatment of serious genetic disorders, concerns have been raised over whether such scientific advances can lead to the development of "designer babies"—infants that have been genetically manipulated to have traits their parents wish for. The question is whether these procedures can and should be used not only to correct undesirable genetic defects, but also to breed infants for specific purposes or to "improve" future generations on a genetic level.

The ethical concerns are numerous: Is it right to tailor babies to serve a specific purpose, however noble? Does this kind of genetic control pose any dangers to the human gene pool? Would unfair advantages be conferred on the offspring of those who are wealthy or privileged enough to have access to these procedures? (Sheldon & Wilkinson, 2004).

Designer babies aren't with us yet; currently, scientists do not understand enough about the human genome to identify the genes that control most traits, nor are they able to make genetic modifications to control how those traits will be expressed. Moreover, the term itself is a bit misleading. For one thing, babies aren't being genetically engineered; PGD merely entails selecting an embryo that already has the desired genetic makeup. For another thing, it's a difficult and expensive procedure that does not lend itself to casual use. Still, as Adam Nash's case reveals, we are inching closer to a day when it is possible for parents to decide what genes their children will and will not have.

- How might the circumstances of Adam's birth affect the relationship between him and Molly as they grow up?

- How might Adam feel when he learns that he was selected to be born in order to save his sister?

- What if our understanding of the human genome develops to the point that it becomes possible to use PGD to control the future intelligence, attractiveness, or sexuality of one's children? Where should we draw the line on parents' ability to dictate what traits their children will have?

these welcome traits? What causes our behavior? Nature or nurture? Is behavior produced by inherited, genetic influences, or is it triggered by factors in the environment?

The simple answer is: There is no simple answer.

The Role of the Environment in Determining the Expression of Genes: From Genotypes to Phenotypes

As developmental research accumulates, it is becoming increasingly clear that to view behavior as due to *either* genetic *or* environmental factors is inappropriate. A given behavior is not caused just by genetic factors; nor is it caused solely by environmental forces. Instead, as we first discussed in Chapter 1, the behavior is the product of some combination of the two.

For instance, consider **temperament**, patterns of arousal and emotionality that represent consistent and enduring characteristics in an individual. Suppose we found—as increasing evidence suggests is the case—that a small percentage of children are born with temperaments that produce an unusual degree of physiological reactivity. Having a tendency to shrink from anything unusual, such infants react to novel stimuli with a rapid increase in heartbeat and unusual excitability of the limbic system of the brain. Such heightened reactivity to stimuli at the start of life, which seems to be linked to inherited factors, is also likely to cause children, by the time they are 4 or 5 years old, to be considered shy by their parents and teachers. But not always: Some of them

Multifactorial transmission The determination of traits by a combination of genetic and environmental factors in which a genotype provides a range within which a phenotype may be expressed

behave indistinguishably from their peers at the same age (Kagan & Snidman, 1991; McCrae et al., 2000).

What makes the difference? The answer seems to be the environment in which the children are raised. Children, whose parents encourage them to be outgoing by arranging new opportunities for them, may overcome their shyness. In contrast, children raised in a stressful environment marked by marital discord or a prolonged illness may be more likely to retain their shyness later in life (Kagan, Arcus, & Snidman, 1993; R. Joseph, 1999; Propper & Moore, 2006). Jared, described earlier, may have been born with an easy temperament, which was readily reinforced by his caring parents.

Interaction of Factors Such findings illustrate that many traits reflect **multifactorial transmission**, meaning that they are determined by a combination of both genetic and environmental factors. In multifactorial transmission, a genotype provides a particular range within which a phenotype may achieve expression. For instance, people with a genotype that permits them to gain weight easily may never be slim, no matter how much they diet. They may be *relatively* slim, given their genetic heritage, but they may never be able to get beyond a certain degree of thinness (Faith, Johnson, & Allison, 1997). In many cases, then, it is the environment that determines the way in which a particular genotype will be expressed as a phenotype (Wachs, 1992, 1993, 1996; Plomin, 1994b).

On the other hand, certain genotypes are relatively unaffected by environmental factors. In such cases, development follows a preordained pattern, relatively independent of the specific environment in which a person is raised. For instance, research on pregnant women who were severely malnourished during famines caused by World War II found that their children were, on average, unaffected physically or intellectually as adults (Z. Stein et al., 1975). Similarly, no matter how much health food people eat, they are not going to grow beyond certain genetically imposed limitations in height. Little Jared's hairline will probably be affected very little by any actions on the part of his parents. Ultimately, of course, it is the unique interaction of inherited and environmental factors that determines people's patterns of development.

The more appropriate question, then, is *how much* of the behavior is caused by genetic factors, and *how much* by environmental factors? (See, for example the range of possibilities for the determinants of intelligence, illustrated in Figure 3-8.) At one extreme is the idea that opportunities in the environment are solely responsible for intelligence; on the other, that intelligence is purely genetic—you either have it or you don't. The usefulness of such extremes seems to point us toward the middle ground—that intelligence is the result of some combination of natural mental ability and environmental opportunity.

Studying Development: How Much Is Nature? How Much Is Nurture?

Developmental researchers use several strategies to try to resolve the question of the degree to which traits, characteristics, and behavior are produced by genetic or environmental factors. Their studies involve both nonhuman species and humans.

Nonhuman Animal Studies: Controlling Both Genetics and Environment It is relatively simple to develop breeds of animals that are genetically similar to one another in terms of specific traits. The people who raise Butterball turkeys for

Nature				Nurture
Intelligence is provided entirely by genetic factors; environment plays no role. Even a highly enriched environment and excellent education make no difference.	Although largely inherited, intelligence is affected by an extremely enriched or deprived environment.	Intelligence is affected both by a person's genetic endowment and environment. A person genetically predisposed to low intelligence may perform better if raised in an enriched environment or worse in a deprived environment. Similarly, a person genetically predisposed to higher intelligence may perform worse in a deprived environment or better in an enriched environment.	Although intelligence is largely a result of environment, genetic abnormalities may produce mental retardation.	Intelligence depends entirely on the environment. Genetics plays no role in determining intellectual success.

Possible Causes

FIGURE 3-8 Possible Causes of Intelligence

Intelligence may be explained by a range of differing possible sources, spanning the nature–nurture continuum. Which of these explanations do you find most convincing, given the evidence discussed in the chapter?

"The title of my science project is 'My Little Brother: Nature or Nurture.'"

Thanksgiving do it all the time, producing turkeys that grow especially rapidly so that they can be brought to market inexpensively. Similarly, strains of laboratory animals can be bred to share similar genetic backgrounds.

By observing animals with similar genetic backgrounds in different environments, scientists can determine, with reasonable precision, the effects of specific kinds of environmental stimulation. For example, animals can be raised in unusually stimulating environments, with lots of items to climb over or through, or they can be raised in relatively barren environments, to determine the results of living in such different settings. Conversely, researchers can examine groups of animals that have been bred to have significantly *different* genetic backgrounds on particular traits. Then, by exposing such animals to identical environments, they can determine the role that genetic background plays.

Of course, the drawback to using nonhumans as research subjects is that we can't be sure how well the findings we obtain can be generalized to people. Still, the opportunities that animal research offers are substantial.

Contrasting Relatedness and Behavior: Adoption, Twin, and Family Studies

Obviously, researchers can't control either the genetic backgrounds or the environments of humans in the way they can with nonhumans. However, nature conveniently has provided the potential to carry out various kinds of "natural experiments"—in the form of twins.

Recall that identical, monozygotic twins are also identical genetically. Because their inherited backgrounds are precisely the same, any variations in their behavior must be due entirely to environmental factors.

It would be rather simple for researchers to make use of identical twins to draw unequivocal conclusions about the roles of nature and nurture. For instance, by separating identical twins at birth and placing them in totally different environments, researchers could assess the impact of environment unambiguously. Of course, ethical considerations make this impossible. However, what researchers can—and do—study, are cases in which identical twins have been put up for adoption at birth and are raised in substantially different environments. Such instances allow us to draw fairly confident conclusions about the relative contributions of genetics and environment (Bailey et al., 2000; Richardson & Norgate, 2007).

The data from such studies of identical twins raised in different environments are not always without bias. Adoption agencies typically take the characteristics (and wishes) of birth mothers into account when they place babies in adoptive homes. For instance, children tend to be placed with families of the same race and religion. Consequently, even when monozygotic twins are placed in different adoptive homes, there are often similarities between the two home environments. As a result, researchers can't always be certain that differences in behavior are due to differences in the environment.

Studies of nonidentical, dizygotic twins also present opportunities to learn about the relative contributions of nature and nurture. Recall that dizygotic twins are genetically no more similar than siblings in a family born at different times. By comparing behavior within pairs of dizygotic twins with that of pairs of monozygotic twins (who are genetically identical) researchers can determine whether monozygotic twins are more similar on a particular trait, on average, than dizygotic twins. If so, they can assume that genetics plays an important role in determining the expression of that trait.

Still another approach is to study people who are totally unrelated to one another and who therefore have dissimilar genetic backgrounds, but who share an environmental background. For instance, a family that adopts, at the same time, two very young unrelated children probably will provide them with quite similar environments throughout their childhood. In this case, similarities in the children's characteristics and behavior can be attributed with some confidence to environmental influences (N. L. Segal, 1993, 2000).

Finally, developmental researchers have examined groups of people in light of their degree of genetic similarity. For instance, if we find a high association on a particular trait between biological parents and their children, but a weaker association between adoptive parents and their children, we have evidence for the importance of genetics in determining the expression of that trait. On the other hand, if there is a stronger association on a trait between adoptive parents and their children than between biological parents and their children, we have evidence for the importance of the environment in determining that trait. If a particular trait tends to occur at similar levels among genetically similar individuals, but occurs at different levels among genetically more distant individuals, signs point to the fact that genetics plays an important role in the development of that trait (Rowe, 1994).

Developmental researchers have used these approaches and others to study the relative impact of genetic and environmental factors. What have they found?

Before turning to specific findings, here's the general conclusion resulting from decades of research: Virtually all traits, characteristics, and behaviors are the joint result of the combination and interaction of nature and nurture. Genetic and environmental factors work in tandem, each affecting and being affected by the other, creating the unique individual that each of us is and will become (G. E. Robinson, 2004; Waterland & Jirtle, 2004).

Physical Traits: Family Resemblances

When patients entered the examining room of Dr. Cyril Marcus, they didn't realize that sometimes they were actually being treated by his identical twin brother, Dr. Stewart Marcus. So similar in appearance and manner were the twins that even long-time patients were fooled by this admittedly unethical behavior, which occurred in a bizarre case made famous in the film *Dead Ringers*.

Monozygotic twins are merely the most extreme example of the fact that the more genetically similar two people are, the more likely they are to share physical characteristics. Tall parents tend to have tall children, and short ones tend to have short children. Obesity, which is defined as being more than 20% above the average weight for a given height, also has a strong genetic component. For example, in one study, pairs of identical twins were put on diets that contained an extra 1,000 calories a day—and ordered not to exercise.

Over a 3-month period, the twins gained almost identical amounts of weight. Moreover, different pairs of twins varied substantially in how much weight they gained, with some pairs gaining almost three times as much weight as other pairs (Bouchard et al., 1990).

Other, less obvious physical characteristics also show strong genetic influences. For instance, blood pressure, respiration rates, and even the age at which life ends are more similar in closely related individuals than in those who are less genetically alike (Sorensen et al., 1988; Price & Gottesman, 1991).

Intelligence: More Research, More Controversy

No other issue involving the relative influence of heredity and environment has generated more research than the topic of intelligence. Why? The main reason is that intelligence, generally measured in terms of an IQ score, is a central human characteristic that differentiates humans from other species. In addition, intelligence is strongly related to success in scholastic endeavors and, somewhat less strongly, to other types of achievement.

Genetics plays a significant role in intelligence. In studies of both general intelligence and of specific subcomponents of intelligence (such as spatial skills, verbal skills, and memory), the closer the genetic link between two individuals, the greater the correspondence of their overall IQ scores. (See Figure 3-9)

Some traits—like curly hair—have a clear genetic component.

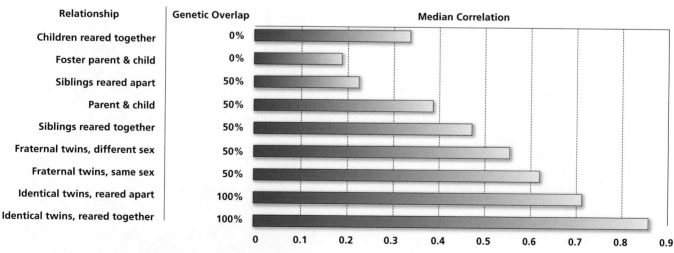

Relationship	Genetic Overlap	Median Correlation
Children reared together	0%	
Foster parent & child	0%	
Siblings reared apart	50%	
Parent & child	50%	
Siblings reared together	50%	
Fraternal twins, different sex	50%	
Fraternal twins, same sex	50%	
Identical twins, reared apart	100%	
Identical twins, reared together	100%	

FIGURE 3-9 Genetics and IQ

The closer the genetic link between two individuals, the greater the correspondence between their IQ scores. Why do you think there is a sex difference in the fraternal twins' figures? Might there be other sex differences in other sets of twins or siblings, not shown on this chart? (*Source:* Bouchard & McGue, 1981)

Some people have used the proven genetic basis of intelligence to argue against strenuous educational efforts on behalf of individuals with below-average IQs. Does this viewpoint make sense based on what you have learned about heredity and environment? Why or why not?

From an educator's perspective:

Not only is genetics an important influence on intelligence but also the impact increases with age. For instance, as fraternal (i.e., dizygotic) twins move from infancy to adolescence, their IQ scores become less similar. In contrast, the IQ scores of identical (monozygotic) twins become increasingly similar over the course of time. These opposite patterns suggest the intensifying influence of inherited factors with increasing age (Brody, 1993; McGue et al., 1993).

Although it is clear that heredity plays an important role in intelligence, investigators are much more divided on the question of the degree to which it is inherited. Perhaps the most extreme view is held by psychologist Arthur Jensen (2003), who argued that as much as 80% of intelligence is a result of heredity. Others have suggested more modest figures, ranging from 50% to 70%. It is critical to keep in mind that such figures are averages across large groups of people, and any particular individual's degree of inheritance cannot be predicted from these averages (e.g., Herrnstein & Murray, 1994; Devlin, Daniels, & Roeder, 1997).

It is important to keep in mind that although heredity clearly plays an important role in intelligence, environmental factors such as exposure to books, good educational experiences, and intelligent peers are profoundly influential. Even those like Jensen who make the most extreme estimates of the role of genetics still allow for environmental factors to play a significant role. In fact, in terms of public policy, environmental influences are the focus of efforts geared toward maximizing people's intellectual success. As developmental psychologist Sandra Scarr suggests, we should be asking what can be done to maximize the intellectual development of each individual (Scarr & Carter-Saltzman, 1982; Storfer, 1990; Bouchard, 1997).

Genetic and Environmental Influences on Personality: Born to Be Outgoing?

Do we inherit our personality?

At least in part. There's increasing research evidence suggesting that some of our most basic personality traits have genetic roots. For example, two of the key "Big Five" personality traits, neuroticism and extroversion, have been linked to genetic factors. *Neuroticism*, as used by personality researchers, is the degree of emotional stability an individual characteristically displays. *Extroversion* is the degree to which a person seeks to be with others, to behave in an outgoing manner, and generally to be sociable. For instance, Jared, the baby described earlier in this chapter, may have inherited a tendency to be outgoing from his

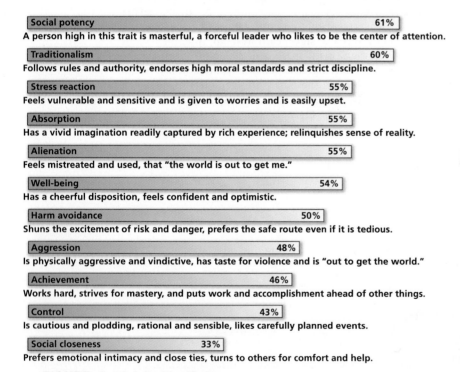

Trait	%
Social potency	61%

A person high in this trait is masterful, a forceful leader who likes to be the center of attention.

Traditionalism	60%

Follows rules and authority, endorses high moral standards and strict discipline.

Stress reaction	55%

Feels vulnerable and sensitive and is given to worries and is easily upset.

Absorption	55%

Has a vivid imagination readily captured by rich experience; relinquishes sense of reality.

Alienation	55%

Feels mistreated and used, that "the world is out to get me."

Well-being	54%

Has a cheerful disposition, feels confident and optimistic.

Harm avoidance	50%

Shuns the excitement of risk and danger, prefers the safe route even if it is tedious.

Aggression	48%

Is physically aggressive and vindictive, has taste for violence and is "out to get the world."

Achievement	46%

Works hard, strives for mastery, and puts work and accomplishment ahead of other things.

Control	43%

Is cautious and plodding, rational and sensible, likes carefully planned events.

Social closeness	33%

Prefers emotional intimacy and close ties, turns to others for comfort and help.

FIGURE 3-10 Inheriting Traits

These traits are among the personality factors that are related most closely to genetic factors. The higher the percentage, the greater the degree to which the trait reflects the influence of heredity. Do these figures mean that "leaders are born, not made"? Why or why not?
(*Source:* Adapted from Tellegen et al., 1988)

"*The good news is that you will have a healthy baby girl. The bad news is that she is a congenital liar.*"

extroverted father, Jamal (Plomin & Caspi, 1998; Benjamin, Ebstein, & Belmaker, 2002; Zuckerman, 2003).

How do we know which personality traits reflect genetics? Some evidence comes from direct examination of genes themselves. For instance, it appears that a specific gene is very influential in determining risk-taking behavior. This novelty-seeking gene affects the production of the brain chemical dopamine, making some people more prone than others to seek out novel situations and to take risks (Ebstein et al., 1996; Gillespie et al, 2003; Serretti et al., 2007).

Other evidence for the role of genetics in the determination of personality traits comes from studies of twins. For instance, in one major study, researchers looked at the personality traits of hundreds of pairs of twins. Because a good number of the twins were genetically identical but had been raised apart, it was possible to determine with some confidence the influence of genetic factors (Tellegen et al., 1988). The researchers found that certain traits reflected the contribution of genetics considerably more than others. As you can see in Figure 3-10, social potency (the tendency to be a masterful, forceful leader who enjoys being the center of attention) and traditionalism (strict endorsement of rules and authority) are strongly associated with genetic factors (Harris, Vernon, & Jang, 2007).

Even less basic personality traits are linked to genetics. For example, political attitudes, religious interests and values, and even attitudes toward human sexuality have genetic components (Eley, 2003; Bouchard, 2004; Koenig et al., 2005).

Clearly, genetic factors play a role in determining personality. At the same time, the environment in which a child is raised also affects personality development. For example, some parents encourage high activity levels, seeing activity as a manifestation of independence and intelligence. Other parents may encourage lower levels of activity on the part of their children, feeling that more passive children will get along better in society. Part of these parental attitudes are culturally determined; parents in the United States may encourage higher activity levels, whereas parents in Asian cultures

may encourage greater passivity. In both cases, children's personalities will be shaped in part by their parents' attitudes.

Because both genetic and environmental factors have consequences for a child's personality, personality development is a perfect example of a central fact of child development: the interplay between nature and nurture. Furthermore, the way in which nature and nurture interact can be reflected not only in the behavior of individuals, but also in the very foundations of a culture, as we see next.

DEVELOPMENTAL DIVERSITY

Cultural Differences in Physical Arousal: Might a Culture's Philosophical Outlook Be Determined by Genetics?

The Buddhist philosophy, an inherent part of many Asian cultures, emphasizes harmony and peacefulness. In contrast, some traditional Western philosophies, such as those of Martin Luther and John Calvin, accentuate the importance of controlling the anxiety, fear, and guilt that they assume to be basic parts of the human condition.

Could such philosophical approaches reflect, in part, genetic factors? That is the controversial suggestion made by developmental psychologist Jerome Kagan and his colleagues. They speculate that the underlying temperament of a given society, determined genetically, may predispose people in that society toward a particular philosophy (Kagan, Arcus, & Snidman, 1993; Kagan, 2003).

Kagan bases his admittedly speculative suggestion on well-confirmed findings that show clear differences in temperament between Caucasian and Asian children. For instance, one study that compared 4-month-old infants in China, Ireland, and the United States found several relevant differences. In comparison to the Caucasian American babies and the Irish babies, the Chinese babies had significantly lower motor activity, irritability, and vocalization (see Table 3-4).

Kagan suggests that the Chinese, who enter the world temperamentally calmer, may find Buddhist philosophical notions of

TABLE 3-4	Mean Behavioral Scores for Caucasian American, Irish, and Chinese 4-Month-Old Infants		
Behavior	**American**	**Irish**	**Chinese**
Motor activity score	48.6	36.7	11.2
Crying (in seconds)	7.0	2.9	1.1
Fretting (% trials)	10.0	6.0	1.9
Vocalizing (% trials)	31.4	31.1	8.1
Smiling (% trials)	4.1	2.6	3.6

(*Source*: Kagan, Arcus, & Snidman, 1993)

serenity more in tune with their natural inclinations. In contrast, Westerners, who are emotionally more volatile and tense, and who report higher levels of guilt, are more likely to be attracted to philosophies that articulate the necessity of controlling the unpleasant feelings that they are more apt to encounter in their everyday experience (Kagan et al., 1994; Kagan, 2003).

It is important to note that this does not mean that one philosophical approach is necessarily better or worse than the other. Nor does it mean that either of the temperaments from which the philosophies are thought to spring is superior or inferior to the other. Similarly, we must keep in mind that any single individual within a culture can be more or less temperamentally volatile and that the range of temperaments found even within a particular culture is vast. Finally, as we noted in our initial discussion of temperament, environmental conditions can have a significant effect on the portion of a person's temperament that is not genetically determined. But what Kagan and his colleagues' speculation does attempt to address is the back and forth between culture and temperament. As religion may help mold temperament, so may temperament make certain religious ideals more attractive.

The notion that the very basis of culture—its philosophical traditions—may be affected by genetic factors is intriguing. More research is necessary to determine just how the unique interaction of heredity and environment within a given culture may produce a framework for viewing and understanding the world. ———●

Psychological Disorders: The Role of Genetics and Environment

> Lori Schiller began to hear voices when she was a teenager in summer camp. Without warning, the voices screamed "You must die! Die! Die!" She ran from her bunk into the darkness, where she thought she could get away. Camp counselors found her screaming as she jumped wildly on a trampoline, "I thought I was possessed," she said later. (Bennett, 1992)

In a sense, she was possessed: possessed with schizophrenia, one of the severest types of psychological disorder. Normal and happy through childhood, Schiller's world took a tumble during adolescence as she increasingly lost her hold on reality. For the next 2 decades, she would be in and out of institutions, struggling to ward off the ravages of the disorder.

What was the cause of Schiller's mental disorder? Increasing evidence suggests that schizophrenia is brought about by genetic factors. The disorder runs in families, with some families showing an unusually high incidence. Moreover, the closer the genetic links between someone with schizophrenia and another family member, the more likely it is that the other person will also develop schizophrenia. For instance, a monozygotic twin has close to a 50% risk of developing schizophrenia when the other twin develops the disorder (see Figure 3-11). On the other hand, a niece or nephew of a person with schizophrenia has less than a 5% chance of developing the disorder (Prescott & Gottesman, 1993; Hanson & Gottesman, 2005).

However, these data also illustrate that genetics alone does not influence the development of the disorder. If genetics were the sole cause, the risk for an identical twin would

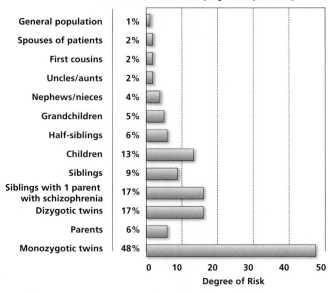

Lifetime Risk of Developing Schizophrenia (percent)

General population	1%
Spouses of patients	2%
First cousins	2%
Uncles/aunts	2%
Nephews/nieces	4%
Grandchildren	5%
Half-siblings	6%
Children	13%
Siblings	9%
Siblings with 1 parent with schizophrenia	17%
Dizygotic twins	17%
Parents	6%
Monozygotic twins	48%

Degree of Risk

FIGURE 3-11 **The Genetics of Schizophrenia**

The psychological disorder of schizophrenia has clear genetic components. The closer the genetic links between someone with schizophrenia and another family member, the more likely it is that the other person will also develop schizophrenia.
(*Source:* Gottesman, 1991)

be 100%. Consequently, other factors account for the disorder, ranging from structural abnormalities in the brain to a biochemical imbalance (e.g., Lyons, Bar, & Kremen, 2002; Hietala, Cannon, & van Erp, 2003).

It also seems that even if individuals harbor a genetic predisposition toward schizophrenia, they are not destined to develop the disorder. Instead, they may inherit an unusual sensitivity to stress in the environment. If stress is low, schizophrenia will not occur. But if stress is sufficiently strong, it will lead to schizophrenia. On the other hand, for someone with a strong genetic predisposition toward the disorder, even relatively weak environmental stressors may lead to schizophrenia (Paris, 1999; Norman & Malla, 2001).

Several other psychological disorders have been shown to be related, at least in part, to genetic factors. For instance, major depression, alcoholism, autism, and attention-deficit/hyperactivity disorder have significant inherited components (Prescott et al., 2005; Dick, Rose, & Kaprio, 2006; Monastra, 2008).

The example of schizophrenia and other genetically related psychological disorders also illustrates a fundamental principle regarding the relationship between heredity and environment, one that underlies much of our previous discussion. Specifically, the role of genetics is often to produce tendency toward a future course of development. When and whether a certain behavioral characteristic will actually be displayed depends on the nature of the environment. Thus, although a predisposition

Developmental psychologist Sandra Scarr argues that children's genetic characteristics actively influence and shape their environment.

for schizophrenia may be present at birth, typically people do not show the disorder until adolescence—if at all.

Similarly, certain other kinds of traits are more likely to be displayed as the influence of parents and other socializing factors declines. For example, adopted children may, early in their lives, display traits that are relatively similar to their adoptive parents' traits, given the overwhelming influence of the environment on young children. As they get older and their parents' day-to-day influence declines, genetically influenced traits may begin to manifest themselves as unseen genetic factors begin to play a greater role (Caspi & Moffitt, 1993; Arsenault et al., 2003; Poulton & Caspi, 2005).

Can Genes Influence the Environment?

According to developmental psychologist Sandra Scarr (1993, 1998), the genetic endowment provided to children by their parents not only determines their genetic characteristics, but also actively influences their environment. Scarr suggests three ways a child's genetic predisposition might influence his or her environment.

Children tend to actively focus on those aspects of their environment that are most connected with their genetically determined abilities. For example, an active, more aggressive child will gravitate toward sports, while a more reserved child will be more engaged by academics or solitary pursuits like computer games or drawing. Children also pay less attention to those aspects of the environment that are less compatible with their genetic endowment. For instance, two girls may be reading the same school bulletin board. One may notice the sign advertising tryouts for Little League baseball, whereas her less coordinated but more musically endowed friend might be more apt to spot the notice recruiting students for an after-school chorus. In each case, the child is attending to those aspects of the environment in which her genetically determined abilities can flourish.

In some cases, the gene–environment influence is more passive and less direct. For example, a particularly sports-oriented parent, who has genes that promote good physical coordination, may provide many opportunities for a child to play sports.

Finally, the genetically driven temperament of a child may *evoke* certain environmental influences. For instance, an infant's demanding behavior may cause parents to be more attentive to the infant's needs than they would be if the infant were less demanding. Or, for instance, a child who is genetically inclined to be well coordinated may play ball with anything in the house so often that her parents notice. They may then decide that she should have some sports equipment.

In sum, determining whether behavior is primarily attributable to nature or nurture is a bit like shooting at a moving target. Not only are behaviors and traits a joint outcome of genetic and environmental factors, but also the relative influence of genes and environment for specific characteristics shifts over the course of people's lives. Although the pool of genes we inherit at birth sets the stage for our future development, the constantly shifting scenery and the other characters in our lives determine just how our development eventually plays out. The environment both influences our experiences and is molded by the choices we are temperamentally inclined to make.

REVIEW ↵ mydevelopmentlab

1. Mapping the gene sequence has provided support for the field of _____ genetics, which studies the effects of heredity on psychological characteristics.

   Answer: behavioral

2. _____ counseling focuses on helping people deal with issues related to inherited disorders.

   Answer: Genetic

3. Examples of inherited disorders are _____ syndrome, once referred to as mongolism; fragile X syndrome; sickle-cell anemia; and Tay-Sachs disease.

   Answer: Down

4. For women who are already pregnant, the health of the unborn child can be assessed using _____, chorionic villus sampling, or ultrasound sonography.

   Answer: amniocentesis

To see more review questions, log on to MyDevelopmentLab.

Prenatal Growth and Change

Robert accompanied Lisa to her first appointment with the midwife. The midwife checked the results of tests done to confirm the couple's own positive home pregnancy test. "Yep, you're going to have a baby," she confirmed, speaking to Lisa. "You'll need to set up monthly visits for the next 6 months, then more frequently as your due date approaches. You can get this prescription for prenatal vitamins filled at any pharmacy, and here are some guidelines about diet and exercise. You don't smoke, do you?

That's good." Then she turned to Robert. "How about you? Do you smoke?" After giving lots of instructions and advice, she left the couple feeling slightly dazed, but ready to do whatever they could to have a healthy baby.

From the moment of conception, development proceeds relentlessly. As we've seen, many aspects are guided by the complex set of genetic guidelines inherited from the parents. Of course, prenatal growth, like all development, is also influenced from the start by environmental factors. As we will see later, both parents, like Lisa and Robert, can take part in providing a good prenatal environment.

Fertilization: The Moment of Conception

When most of us think about the facts of life, we tend to focus on the events that cause a male's sperm cells to begin their journey toward a female's ovum. Yet the act of sex that brings about the potential for conception is both the consequence and the start of a long string of events that precede and follow **fertilization**, or conception: the joining of sperm and ovum to create the single-celled zygote from which each of us began our lives.

Both the male's sperm and the female's ovum come with a history of their own. Females are born with around 400,000 ova located in the two ovaries (see Figure 3-12 for the basic anatomy of the female reproductive organs). However, the ova do not mature until the female reaches puberty. From that point until she reaches menopause, the female will ovulate about every 28 days. During ovulation, an egg is released from one of the ovaries and pushed by minute hair cells through the fallopian tube toward the uterus. If the ovum meets a sperm in the fallopian tube, fertilization takes place (Aitken, 1995).

Sperm, which look a little like microscopic tadpoles, have a shorter life span. They are created by the testicles at a rapid rate: An adult male typically produces several hundred million sperm a day. Consequently, the sperm ejaculated during sexual intercourse are of considerably more recent origin than the ovum to which they are heading.

When sperm enter the vagina, they begin a winding journey that takes them through the cervix, the opening into the uterus, and into the fallopian tube, where fertilization may take place. However, only a tiny fraction of the 300 million cells that are typically ejaculated during sexual intercourse ultimately survive the arduous journey. That's usually okay, though: It takes only one sperm to fertilize an ovum, and each sperm and ovum contains all the genetic data necessary to produce a new human.

The Stages of the Prenatal Period: The Onset of Development

The prenatal period consists of three phases: the germinal, embryonic, and fetal stages. They are summarized in Table 3-5.

The Germinal Stage: Fertilization to 2 Weeks In the **germinal stage**, the first—and shortest—stage of the prenatal period, the zygote begins to divide and grow in complexity during the first 2 weeks following conception. During the germinal stage, the fertilized egg (now called a *blastocyst*) travels toward the *uterus*, where it becomes implanted in the uterus's wall, which is rich in nutrients. The germinal stage is characterized by methodical cell division, which gets off to a quick start: Three days after fertilization, the organism consists of some 32 cells, and by the next day the number doubles. Within a week, it is made up of 100 to 150 cells, and the number rises with increasing rapidity.

In addition to increasing in number, the cells of the organism become increasingly specialized. For instance, some cells form a protective layer around the mass of cells, whereas others begin to establish the rudiments of a placenta and umbilical cord. When fully developed, the **placenta** serves as a conduit between the mother and fetus, providing nourishment and oxygen via the *umbilical cord*. In addition, waste materials from the developing child are removed through the umbilical cord.

The Embryonic Stage: 2 Weeks to 8 Weeks By the end of the germinal period, just 2 weeks after conception, the organism is firmly secured to the wall of the mother's uterus. At this point, the child is called an *embryo*. The **embryonic stage** is the period from 2 to 8 weeks following fertilization. One of the highlights of this stage is the development of the major organs and basic anatomy.

At the beginning of the embryonic stage, the developing child has three distinct layers, each of which will ultimately form a different set of structures as development proceeds.

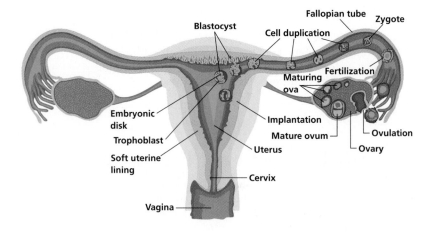

FIGURE 3-12 Anatomy of the Female Reproductive Organs

The basic anatomy of the female reproductive organs is illustrated in this cutaway view. (*Source:* Moore & Persaud, 2003)

TABLE 3-5 Stages of the Prenatal Period

Germinal (Fertilization–2 Weeks)	Embryonic (2 Weeks–8 Weeks)	Fetal (8 Weeks–Birth)
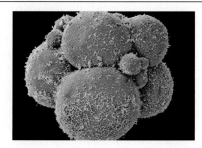	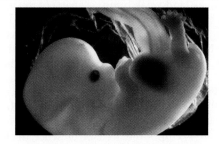	
The germinal stage is the first and shortest, characterized by methodical cell division and the attachment of the organism to the wall of the uterus. Three days after fertilization, the zygote consists of 32 cells, a number that doubles by the next day. Within a week, the zygote multiplies to 100 to 150 cells. The cells become specialized, with some forming a protective layer around the zygote.	The zygote is now designated an embryo. The embryo develops three layers, which ultimately form a different set of structures as development proceeds. The layers are as follows: Ectoderm: Skin, sense organs, brain, spinal cord; Endoderm: Digestive system, liver, respiratory system; Mesoderm: Muscles, blood, circulatory system. At 8 weeks, the embryo is 1 inch long.	The fetal stage formally starts when the differentiation of the major organs has occurred. Now called a fetus, the individual grows rapidly as length increases 20 times. At 4 months, the fetus weighs an average of 4 ounces; at 7 months, 3 pounds; and at the time of birth, the average child weighs just over 7 pounds.

The outer layer of the embryo, the *ectoderm*, will form skin, hair, teeth, sense organs, and the brain and spinal cord. The *endoderm*, the inner layer, produces the digestive system, liver, pancreas, and respiratory system. Sandwiched between the ectoderm and endoderm is the *mesoderm*, from which the muscles, bones, blood and circulatory system are forged. Every part of the body is formed from these three layers.

If you were looking at an embryo at the end of the embryonic stage, you might be hard-pressed to identify it as human. Only an inch long, an 8-week-old embryo has what appear to be gills and a tail-like structure. On the other hand, a closer look reveals several familiar features. Rudimentary eyes, nose, lips, and even teeth can be recognized, and the embryo has stubby bulges that will form arms and legs.

The head and brain undergo rapid growth during the embryonic period. The head begins to represent a significant proportion of the embryo's size, encompassing about 50% of its total length. The growth of nerve cells, called *neurons*, is

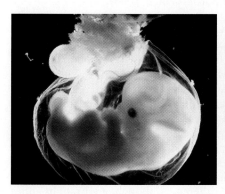

Fetus at 5–6 weeks

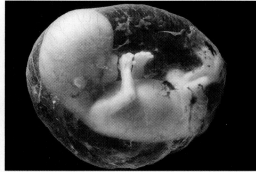

Fetus at 8 weeks

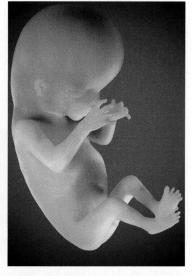

Fetus at 12 weeks

Fetal stage The stage that begins at about 8 weeks after conception and continues until birth

Fetus A developing child, from 8 weeks after conception until birth

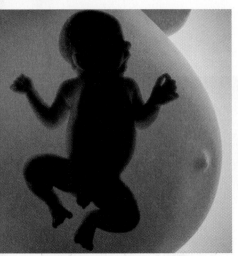

As with adults, there are broad differences in the nature of fetuses. Some are very active while others are more reserved, and these characteristics can continue after birth.

astonishing: As many as 100,000 neurons are produced every minute during the second month of life! The nervous system begins to function around the 5th week, and weak brain waves begin to be produced as the nervous system starts to function (Lauter, 1998; Nelson & Bosquet, 2000).

The Fetal Stage: 8 Weeks to Birth It is not until the final period of prenatal development, the fetal stage, that the developing child becomes easily recognizable. The **fetal stage** starts at about 8 weeks after conception and continues until birth. The fetal stage formally starts when the differentiation of the major organs has occurred.

Now called a **fetus**, the developing child undergoes astoundingly rapid change. For instance, it increases in length approximately 20 times, and its proportions change dramatically. At 2 months, approximately one-half of the fetus is what will ultimately be its head; 5 months, the head accounts for just over one-fourth of its total size (see Figure 3-13). The fetus also substantially increases in weight. At 4 months, the fetus weighs an average of about 4 ounces; at 7 months, it weighs about 3 pounds; and at the time of birth the average child weighs just over 7 pounds.

At the same time, the developing child is rapidly becoming more complex. Organs become more differentiated and start to work. By 3 months, for example, the fetus swallows and urinates. In addition, the interconnections between the different parts of the body become more complex and integrated. Arms develop hands; hands develop fingers; fingers develop nails.

As this is happening, the fetus makes itself known to the outside world. In the earliest stages of pregnancy, mothers may be unaware that they are, in fact, pregnant. As the fetus becomes increasingly active, however, most mothers certainly take notice. By 4 months, a mother can feel the movement of her child, and several months later, others can feel the baby's kicks through the mother's skin. In addition to the kicks that alert its mother to its presence, the fetus can turn, do somersaults, cry, hiccup, clench its fist, open and close its eyes, and suck its thumb.

The brain becomes increasingly sophisticated during the fetal stage. The two symmetrical left and right halves of the brain, known as *hemispheres*, grow rapidly, and the interconnections between neurons become more complex. The neurons become coated with an insulating material called *myelin* which helps speed the transmission of messages from the brain to the rest of the body.

By the end of the fetal period, brain waves are produced that indicate the fetus passes through different stages of sleep and wakefulness. The fetus is also able to hear (and feel the vibrations of) sounds to which it is exposed. For instance, researchers Anthony DeCasper and Melanie Spence (1986) asked a group of pregnant mothers to read aloud the Dr. Seuss story *The Cat in the Hat* two times a day during the latter months of pregnancy. Three days after the babies were born, they appeared to recognize the story they had heard, responding more to it than to another story that had a different rhythm.

In weeks 8 to 24 following conception, hormones are released that lead to the increasing differentiation of male and female fetuses. For example, high levels of androgen are produced in males that affect the size of brain cells and the growth of neural connections, which, some scientists speculate, ultimately may lead to differences in male and female brain structure and even later variations in gender-related behavior (Berenbaum & Bailey, 2003; Reiner & Gearhart, 2004; Knickmeyer & Baron-Cohen, 2006).

Just as no two adults are alike, no two fetuses are the same. Although development during the prenatal period follows the broad patterns outlined here, there are significant differences in the specific nature of individual fetuses' behavior. Some fetuses are exceedingly active, whereas others are more sedentary. (The more active fetuses will probably be more active after birth.) Some have relatively quick heart rates, whereas others' heart rates are slower, with the typical range varying between 120 and 160 beats per minute (DiPietro et al., 2002; Niederhofer, 2004; Tongsong et al., 2005).

Such differences in fetal behavior are due in part to genetic characteristics inherited at the moment of fertilization. Other kinds of differences, though, are brought about by the nature of the environment in which the child spends

1/2	3/8	1/4

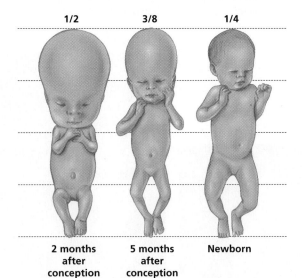

2 months after conception	5 months after conception	Newborn

FIGURE 3-13 Body Proportions

During the fetal period, the proportions of the body change dramatically. At 2 months, the head represents approximately half the fetus, but by the time of birth, it is one fourth of its total size.

Infertility The inability to conceive after 12 to 18 months of trying to become pregnant

Artificial insemination A process of fertilization in which a man's sperm is placed directly into a woman's vagina by a physician

In vitro fertilization (IVF) A procedure in which a woman's ova are removed from her ovaries, and a man's sperm are used to fertilize the ova in a laboratory

its first 9 months of life. As we will see, there are numerous ways in which the prenatal environment of infants affects their development—in good ways and bad.

Pregnancy Problems

For some couples, conception presents a major challenge. Let's consider some of the challenges—both physical and ethical—that relate to pregnancy.

Infertility Some 15% of couples suffer from **infertility**, the inability to conceive after 12 to 18 months of trying to become pregnant. Infertility is negatively correlated with age. The older the parents, the more likely infertility will occur; see Figure 3-14.

In men, infertility is typically a result of producing too few sperm. Use of illicit drugs or cigarettes and previous bouts of sexually transmitted diseases also increase infertility. For women, the most common cause of infertility is failure to release an egg through ovulation. This may occur because of a hormone imbalance, a damaged fallopian tube or uterus, stress, or abuse of alcohol or drugs (Pasqualotto et al., 2005; Lewis, Legato, & Fisch, 2006; Kelly-Weeder & Cox, 2007).

Several treatments for infertility exist. Some difficulties can be corrected through the use of drugs or surgery. Another option may be **artificial insemination**, a procedure in which a man's sperm is placed directly into a woman's vagina by a physician. In some situations, the woman's husband provides the sperm, whereas in others it is an anonymous donor from a sperm bank.

In other cases, fertilization takes place outside of the mother's body. **In vitro fertilization (IVF)** is a procedure in

"I'm their real child, and you're just a frozen embryo thingy they bought from some laboratory."

which a woman's ova are removed from her ovaries, and a man's sperm are used to fertilize the ova in a laboratory. The fertilized egg is then implanted in a woman's uterus. Similarly, *gamete intrafallopian transfer (GIFT)* and *zygote intrafallopian transfer (ZIFT)* are procedures in which an egg and sperm or fertilized egg are implanted in a woman's fallopian tubes. In IVF, GIFT, and ZIFT, implantation is done either in the woman who provided the donor eggs or, in rarer instances, in

FIGURE 3-14

Older Women and Risks of Pregnancy

Not only does the rate of infertility increase as women get older, but also the risk of chromosomal abnormality.

(*Source:* Reproductive Medicine Associates of New Jersey, 2002)

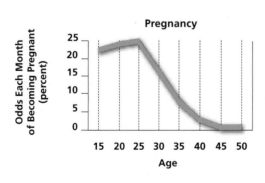

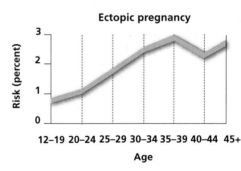

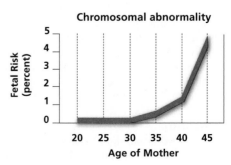

a *surrogate mother*, a woman who agrees to carry the child to term. Surrogate mothers may also be used in cases in which the mother is unable to conceive; the surrogate mother is artificially inseminated by the biological father, and she agrees to give up rights to the infant (Frazier et al., 2004; Kolata, 2004).

In vitro fertilization is increasingly successful, with success rates of as high 33% for younger women (but with lower rates for older women). Furthermore, reproductive technologies are becoming increasingly sophisticated, permitting parents to choose the sex of their baby. One technique is to separate sperm carrying the X and Y chromosome and later implanting the desired type into a woman's uterus. In another technique, eggs are removed from a woman and fertilized with sperm using in vitro fertilization. Three days after fertilization, the embryos are tested to determine their sex. If they are the desired gender, they are then implanted into the mother (Duenwald, 2003, 2004; Kalb, 2004).

Ethical Issues The use of surrogate mothers, in vitro fertilization, and sex selection techniques present a web of ethical and legal issues, as well as many emotional concerns. In some cases, surrogate mothers have refused to give up the child after its birth, whereas in others the surrogate mother has sought to have a role in the child's life. In such cases, the rights of the mother, the father, the surrogate mother, and ultimately the baby are in conflict.

Even more troubling are concerns raised by sex selection techniques. Is it ethical to terminate the life of an embryo based on its sex? Do cultural pressures that may favor boys over girls make it permissible to seek medical intervention to produce male offspring? And—even more disturbing—if it is permissible to intervene in the reproductive process to obtain a favored sex, what about other characteristics determined by genetics that it may be possible to preselect for in the future? For instance, assuming the technology advances, would it be ethical to select for a favored eye or hair color, a certain level of intelligence, or a particular kind of personality? That's not feasible now, but it is not out of the realm of possibility in the future (Bonnicksen, 2007; Mameli, 2007; E. Roberts, 2007).

For the moment, many of these ethical issues remain unresolved. But we can answer one question: How do children conceived using emerging reproductive technologies such as in vitro fertilization fare?

Research shows that they do quite well. In fact, some studies find that the quality of family life for those who have used such techniques may be superior to that in families with naturally conceived children. Furthermore, the later psychological adjustment of children conceived using in vitro fertilization and artificial insemination is no different from that of children conceived using natural techniques (Hahn & DiPietro, 2001; Golumbok et al., 2004; DiPietro, Costigan, & Gurewitsch, 2005; Hjelmstedt, Widstrom, & Collins, 2006).

On the other hand, the increasing use of IVF techniques by older individuals (who might be quite elderly when their children reach adolescence) may change these positive findings. Because widespread use of IVF is only recent, we just don't know yet what will happen with aging parents (Colpin & Soenen, 2002).

Miscarriage and Abortion A *miscarriage*—known as a spontaneous abortion—occurs when pregnancy ends before the developing child is able to survive outside the mother's womb. The embryo detaches from the wall of the uterus and is expelled.

Some 15% to 20% of all pregnancies end in miscarriage, usually in the first several months of pregnancy. Many occur so early that the mother is not even aware she was pregnant and may not even know she has suffered a miscarriage. Typically, miscarriages are attributable to some sort of genetic abnormality.

In *abortion*, a mother voluntarily chooses to terminate pregnancy. Involving a complex set of physical, psychological, legal, and ethical issues, abortion is a difficult choice for every woman. A task force of the American Psychological Association (APA), which looked at the aftereffects of abortion, found that, following an abortion, most women experienced a combination of relief over terminating an unwanted pregnancy, and regret and guilt. However, in most cases, the negative psychological aftereffects did not last, except for a small proportion of women who already had serious emotional problems (APA Reproductive Choice Working Group, 2000).

Other research finds that abortion may be associated with an increased risk of future psychological problems. However, the findings are mixed, and there are significant individual differences in how women respond to the experience of abortion. What is clear is that in all cases, abortion is a difficult decision (Fergusson, Horwood, & Ridder, 2006).

The Prenatal Environment: Threats to Development

According to the Siriono people of South America, if a pregnant woman eats the meat of certain kinds of animals, she runs the risk of having a child who may act and look like those animals. According to opinions offered on daytime television talk, a pregnant mother should avoid getting angry in order to spare her child from entering the world with anger (Cole, 1992).

Such views are largely the stuff of folklore, although there is some evidence that a mother's anxiety during pregnancy may affect the sleeping patterns of the fetus prior to birth. There are certain aspects of a mothers' and fathers' behavior, both before and after conception, that can produce lifelong consequences for the child. Some consequences show up immediately, but half the possible problems aren't apparent before birth. Other problems, more insidious, may not appear until years after birth (Groome et al., 1995; Couzin, 2002). Some of the most profound consequences are brought about by teratogenic agents. A **teratogen** is an environmental agent such as a drug, chemical, virus, or other factor that produces a birth defect. Although it is the job of the placenta to keep teratogens from reaching the fetus, the placenta is not entirely successful at this, and probably every fetus is exposed to some teratogens.

The timing and quantity of exposure to a teratogen are crucial. At some phases of prenatal development, a certain teratogen may have only a minimal impact. At other periods, however, the same teratogen may have profound consequences. Generally, teratogens have their largest effects during periods of especially rapid prenatal development. Sensitivity to specific teratogens is also related to racial and cultural background. For example, Native American fetuses are more susceptible to the effects of alcohol than those of European American descent (Kinney et al., 2003; Winger & Woods, 2004).

Furthermore, different organ systems are vulnerable to teratogens at different times during development. For exam-ple, the brain is most susceptible 15 to 25 days after conception, whereas the heart is most vulnerable 20 to 40 days following conception (see Figure 3-15; Bookstein et al., 1996; Pakjrt, 2004).

We will consider the findings relating to specific teratogens next. As we do, we keep in mind the broader social and cultural context in which teratogen exposure occurs. For example, living in poverty increases the chances of exposure to teratogens. Mothers who are poor may not be able to afford adequate diets, nor may they be able to afford adequate medical care, making them more susceptible to illness that can damage a developing fetus. They are more likely to be exposed to pollution. Consequently, it is important to consider the social factors that permit exposure to teratogens.

Mother's Diet Most of our knowledge of the environmental factors that affect the developing fetus comes from the study of the mother. For instance, as the midwife pointed

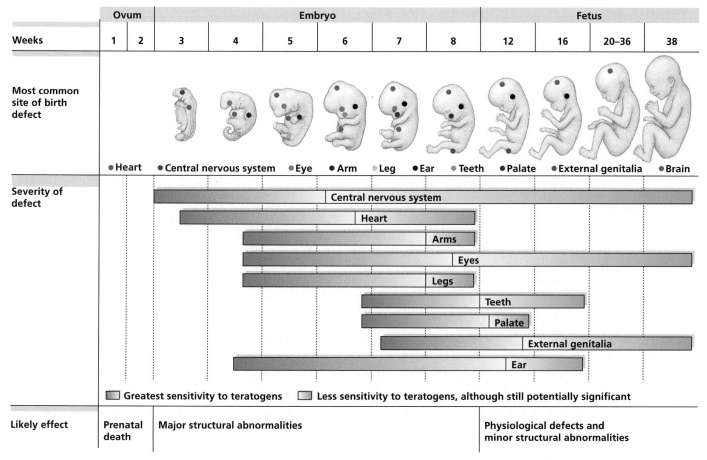

FIGURE 3-15 Teratogen Sensitivity

Depending on their state of development, some parts of the body vary in their sensitivity to teratogens. (*Source:* Moore, 1974)

out in our earlier example of Lisa and Robert, a mother's diet clearly plays an important role in bolstering the development of the fetus. A mother who eats a varied diet high in nutrients is apt to have fewer complications during pregnancy, an easier labor, and a generally healthier baby than a mother whose diet is restricted in nutrients (Kaiser & Allen, 2002; Guerrini, Thomson, & Gurling, 2007).

The problem of diet is of immense global concern, with 800 million hungry people in the world. Even worse, the number of people vulnerable to hunger is close to 1 *billion*. Clearly, restrictions in diet that bring about hunger on such a massive scale affect millions of children born to women living under such conditions (United Nations, 2004).

Fortunately, there are ways to counteract the types of maternal malnourishment that affect prenatal development. Dietary supplements given to mothers can reverse some of the problems produced by a poor diet. Furthermore, research shows that babies who were malnourished as fetuses, but who are subsequently raised in enriched environments, can overcome some of the effects of their early malnourishment. However, the reality is that few of the world's children whose mothers were malnourished *before* their birth are apt to find themselves in enriched environments after birth (Grantham-McGregor et al., 1994; Kramer, 2003; Olness, 2003).

Mother's Age More women are giving birth later in life than was true just 2 or 3 decades ago. The cause for this change is largely due to transformations in society, as more women choose to continue their education with advanced degrees and to start careers prior to giving birth to their first child (Gibbs, 2002; Wildberger, 2003; Bornstein et al., 2006).

Consequently, the number of women who give birth in their 30s and 40s has grown considerably since the 1970s. However, this delay in childbirth has potential consequences for both mothers' and children's health. Women who give birth when over the age of 30 are at greater risk for a variety of pregnancy and birth complications than are younger mothers. For instance, they are more apt to give birth prematurely, and their children are more likely to have low birth weights. This occurs in part because of a decline in the condition of a woman's eggs. For example, by the time they are 42 years old, 90% of a woman's eggs are no longer normal (Cnattingius, Berendes, & Forman, 1993; Gibbs, 2002). Older mothers are also considerably more likely to give birth to children with Down syndrome, a form of mental retardation. About 1 out of 100 babies born to mothers over 40 years of age has Down syndrome; for mothers over 50, the incidence increases to 25%, or 1 in 4 (Gaulden, 1992). On the other hand, some research shows that older mothers are not automatically at risk for more pregnancy problems. For instance, one study found that when women in their 40s who had not experienced health difficulties were considered, they were no more likely than women in their 20s to have prenatal problems (Ales, Druzin, & Santini, 1990; Dildy et al., 1996).

The risks involved in pregnancy are greater not only for older mothers but also for atypically young women. Women who become pregnant during adolescence—and such pregnancies actually encompass 20% of all pregnancies—are more likely to have premature deliveries. Furthermore, the mortality rate of infants born to adolescent mothers is double that for mothers in their 20s (Kirchengast & Hartmann, 2003).

Mother's Prenatal Support Keep in mind, though, that the higher mortality rate for babies of adolescent mothers reflects more than just physiological problems related to the mothers' young age. Young mothers often face adverse social and economic factors which can affect infant health. Many teenage mothers do not have enough money or social support, a situation that prevents them from getting good prenatal care and parenting support after the baby is born. Poverty or social circumstances, such as a lack of parental involvement or supervision may even have set the stage for the adolescent to become pregnant in the first place (DiPietro, 2004; Huizink, Mulder, & Buitelaar, 2004).

Mother's Health Mothers who eat the right foods, maintain an acceptable weight, and who exercise appropriately maximize the chances of having a healthy baby. Furthermore, they can reduce the lifetime risk of obesity, high blood pressure, and heart disease in their children by maintaining a healthy lifestyle (Walker & Humphries, 2005, 2007).

In contrast, illness in a pregnant woman can have devastating consequences. For instance, the onset of *rubella* (German measles) in the mother prior to the 11th week of pregnancy is likely to cause serious consequences in the baby, including blindness, deafness, heart defects, or brain damage. In later stages of a pregnancy, however, adverse consequences of rubella become increasingly less likely.

Several other diseases may affect a developing fetus, again depending on when the illness is contracted. For instance, *chicken pox* may produce birth defects, whereas *mumps* may increase the risk of miscarriage.

Some sexually transmitted diseases such as *syphilis* can be passed directly to the fetus, who will be born suffering from the disease. In some cases, sexually transmitted diseases such as *gonorrhea* are communicated to the child as it passes through the birth canal to be born. *Acquired immune deficiency syndrome (AIDS)* is the newest of the diseases to affect a newborn. Mothers who have the disease or who merely are carriers of the virus may pass it on to their fetuses through the blood that reaches the placenta. However, if mothers with AIDS are treated with antiviral drugs such as AZT during pregnancy, less than 5% of those infants are born with the disease. Infants who are born with AIDS must remain on antiviral drugs their entire lives (Nesheim et al., 2004).

Mothers' Drug Use Mothers' use of many kinds of drugs—both legal and illegal—poses serious risks to the unborn child. Even over-the-counter remedies for common

Fetal alcohol syndrome (FAS)
A disorder caused by the pregnant mother consuming substantial quantities of alcohol during pregnancy, potentially resulting in mental retardation and delayed growth in the child

Fetal alcohol effects (FAE)
A condition in which children display some, although not all, of the problems of fetal alcohol syndrome due to the mother's consumption of alcohol during pregnancy

ailments can have surprisingly injurious consequences. For instance, aspirin taken for a headache can lead to fetal bleeding and growth impairments (Griffith, Azuma, & Chasnoff, 1994).

Even drugs prescribed by medical professionals have sometimes had disastrous consequences. In the 1950s, many women who were told to take *thalidomide* for morning sickness during their pregnancies gave birth to children with stumps instead of arms and legs. Although the physicians who prescribed the drug did not know it, thalidomide inhibited the growth of limbs that normally would have occurred during the first 3 months of pregnancy.

Some drugs taken by mothers cause difficulties in their children literally decades after they were taken. As recently as the 1970s, the artificial hormone *diethylstilbestrol (DES)* was frequently prescribed to prevent miscarriage. Only later was it found that the daughters of mothers who took DES stood a much higher than normal chance of developing a rare form of vaginal or cervical cancer and had more difficulties during their pregnancies. Sons of the mothers who had taken DES had their own problems, including a higher rate than average of reproductive difficulties (Schechter, Finkelstein, & Koren, 2005).

Birth control or fertility pills taken by pregnant women before they are aware of their pregnancy can also cause fetal damage. Such medicines contain sex hormones that affect developing brain structures in the fetus. These hormones, which when produced naturally are related to sexual differentiation in the fetus and gender differences after birth, can cause significant damage (Miller, 1998; Brown, Hines, & Fane, 2002).

Illicit drugs may pose equally great, and sometimes even greater, risks for the environments of prenatal children. For one thing, the purity of drugs purchased illegally varies significantly, so drug users can never be quite sure what specifically they are ingesting. Furthermore, the effects of some commonly used illicit drugs can be particularly devastating (Mayes et al., 2007).

Consider, for instance, the use of *marijuana*; it is certainly one of the most commonly used illegal drugs—millions of people in the United States have admitted trying it. Marijuana used during pregnancy can restrict the oxygen that reaches the fetus. Its use can lead to infants who are irritable, nervous, and easily disturbed. Children exposed to marijuana prenatally show learning and memory deficits at the age of 10 (Huizink & Mulder, 2006; Smith et al., 2006; Williams & Ross, 2007).

During the early 1990s, *cocaine* use by pregnant women led to an epidemic of thousands of so-called "crack babies." Cocaine produces an intense restriction of the arteries leading to the fetus, causing a significant reduction in the flow of blood and oxygen, increasing the risks of fetal death and a number of birth defects and disabilities (Schuetze, Eiden, & Coles, 2007).

Children whose mothers were addicted to cocaine may themselves be born addicted to the drug and may have to suffer through the pain of withdrawal. Even if not addicted, they may be born with significant problems. They are often shorter and their weight is less than average, and they may have serious respiratory problems, visible birth defects, or seizures. They behave quite differently from other infants: Their reactions to stimulation are muted, but once they start to cry, it may be hard to soothe them (Singer et al., 2000; Eiden, Foote, & Schuetze, 2007).

It is difficult to determine the long-term effects of maternal cocaine use in isolation, because such drug use is often accompanied by poor prenatal care and impaired nurturing following birth. In fact, in many cases it is the poor caregiving by mothers who use cocaine that results in children's problems, and not exposure to the drug. Treatment of children exposed to cocaine consequently requires not only that the child's mother stop using the drug but also a positive improvement in the level of infant care that the mother or other caregivers provide. (Brown et al., 2004; Schempf, 2007).

Mothers' Use of Alcohol and Tobacco A pregnant woman who reasons that having a drink every once in a while or smoking an occasional cigarette has no appreciable effect on her unborn child is, in all likelihood, kidding herself: Increasing evidence suggests that even small amounts of alcohol and nicotine can disrupt the development of the fetus.

Maternal use of alcohol can have profound consequences for the unborn child. Alcoholics who consume substantial quantities of alcohol during pregnancy, place their children at the greatest risk. Approximately 1 out of every 750 infants in the United States is born with **fetal alcohol syndrome (FAS)**, a disorder that may include below-average intelligence and sometimes mental retardation, delayed growth, and facial deformities. FAS is now the primary preventable cause of mental retardation (Steinhausen & Spohr, 1998; Burd et al., 2003; Calhoun & Warren, 2007).

Even mothers who use smaller amounts of alcohol during pregnancy place their child at risk. **Fetal alcohol effects (FAE)** is a condition in which children display some, although not all, of the problems of FAS due to their mother's consumption of alcohol during pregnancy (Baer et al., 2003; Molina et al., 2007).

Children who do not have FAE may still be affected by their mothers' use of alcohol. Studies have found that maternal consumption of an average of just two alcoholic drinks a day during pregnancy is associated with lower intelligence in their offspring at age 7. Other research concurs, suggesting that relatively small quantities of alcohol taken during pregnancy can have future adverse effects on children's behavior and psychological functioning. Furthermore, the consequences of alcohol ingestion during pregnancy are long lasting. For example, one study found that 14-year-olds' success on a test involving spatial and visual reasoning was related to their mothers' alcohol consumption during pregnancy. The more the mothers reported drinking, the less accurately their children responded (Johnson et al., 2001; Lynch et al., 2003; Mattson, Calarco, & Lang, 2006).

Because of the risks associated with alcohol, physicians today counsel pregnant women (and even those who are trying to become pregnant) to avoid drinking any alcoholic beverages. In addition, they caution against smoking—another practice proven to have an adverse effect on an unborn child. Smoking produces several consequences, none good. For starters, smoking reduces the oxygen content and increases the carbon monoxide in the mother's blood, which quickly reduces the oxygen available to the fetus. In addition, the nicotine and other toxins in cigarettes slow the respiration rate of the fetus and speed up its heart.

The ultimate result is an increased possibility of miscarriage and a higher likelihood of death during infancy. In fact, estimates suggest that smoking by pregnant women leads to more than 100,000 miscarriages and the deaths of 5,600 babies in the United States alone each year (Haslam & Lawrence, 2004; Triche & Hossain, 2007).

Smokers are two times as likely as nonsmokers to have babies with an abnormally low birthweight, and smokers' babies are shorter, on average, than those of nonsmokers. Furthermore, women who smoke during pregnancy are 50% more likely to have mentally retarded children. Finally, mothers who smoke are more likely to have children who exhibit disruptive behavior during childhood (Drews et al., 1996; Dejin-Karlsson et al., 1998; Wakschalg et al., 2006).

The consequences of smoking are so profound that it may affect not only a mother's children, but her grandchildren. For example, children whose *grandmothers* smoked during pregnancy are more than twice as likely to develop childhood asthma than are children of grandmothers who did not smoke (Li et al., 2005).

Do Fathers Affect the Prenatal Environment? It would be easy to reason that once the father has done his part in the sequence of events leading to conception, he would have no role in the *prenatal* environment of the fetus. In the past, developmental researchers have generally shared this view, and there is relatively little research investigating it.

However, it is becoming increasingly clear that fathers' behavior may indeed influence the prenatal environment. Consequently, health practitioners are utilizing available research to suggest ways fathers can support healthy prenatal development, as our story of Lisa and Robert's visit to the midwife illustrated.

From a health-care provider's perspective: In addition to avoiding smoking, what other sorts of things might fathers-to-be do to help their unborn children develop normally in the womb?

For instance, fathers-to-be should avoid smoking. Secondhand smoke from a father's cigarettes may affect the mother's health, which in turn influences her unborn child. The greater the level of a father's smoking, the lower the birthweight of his children (Hyssaelae, Rautava, & Helenius, 1995; Tomblin, Hammer, & Zhang, 1998).

Similarly, a father's use of alcohol and illegal drugs can have significant effects on the fetus. Alcohol and drug use impairs sperm and may lead to chromosomal damage that may affect the fetus at conception. In addition, alcohol and drug use during pregnancy may also affect the prenatal environment by creating stress in the mother and generally producing an unhealthy environment. A father's exposure to environmental toxins in the workplace, such as lead or mercury, may bind themselves to sperm and cause birth defects (Wakefield et al., 1998; Dare et al., 2002; Choy et al., 2002).

Finally, fathers who are physically or emotionally abusive to their pregnant wives can damage their unborn children. By increasing the level of maternal stress, or actually causing physical damage, abusive fathers increase the risk of harm to their unborn children. In fact, 4% to 8% of women face physical abuse during pregnancy (Gazmarian et al., 2000; Bacchus, Mezey, & Bewley, 2006; Martin et al., 2006).

Becoming an Informed Consumer of Development

Optimizing the Prenatal Environment

If you are contemplating ever having a child, you may be overwhelmed, at this point in the chapter, by the number of things that can go wrong. Don't be. Although both genetics and the environment pose their share of risks, in the vast majority of cases, pregnancy and birth proceed without mishap. Moreover, there are several things that women can do—both before and during pregnancy—to optimize the probability that pregnancy will progress smoothly (Massaro, Rothbaum, & Aly, 2006). Among them:

- For women who are planning to become pregnant, several precautions are in order. First, women should have non-emergency X-rays only during the first 2 weeks after their menstrual periods. Second, women should be vaccinated against rubella (German measles) at least 3 and preferably 6 months before getting pregnant. Finally, women who are planning to become pregnant should avoid the use of birth control pills at least 3 months before trying to conceive, because of disruptions to hormonal production caused by the pills.

- Eat well, both before and during (and after, for that matter!) pregnancy. Pregnant mothers are, as the saying goes, eating for two. This means that it is more essential than ever to eat regular, well-balanced meals. In addition, physicians typically recommend taking prenatal vitamins which include folic acids, which can decrease the likelihood of birth defects (Amitai et al., 2004).

- Don't use alcohol and other drugs. The evidence is clear that many drugs pass directly to the fetus and may cause birth defects. It is also clear that the more one drinks, the greater the risk to the fetus. The best advice, whether you are already pregnant or planning to have a child: Don't use *any* drug unless directed by a physician. If you are planning to get pregnant, encourage your partner to avoid using alcohol or other drugs too (O'Connor & Whaley, 2006).

- Monitor caffeine intake. Although it is still unclear whether caffeine produces birth defects, it is known that the caffeine found in coffee, tea, and chocolate can pass to the fetus, acting as a stimulant. Because of this, you probably shouldn't drink more than a few cups of coffee a day (Wisborg et al., 2003).

- Whether pregnant or not, don't smoke. This holds true for mothers, fathers, and anyone else in the vicinity of the pregnant mother, because research suggests that smoke in the fetal environment can affect birthweight.

- Exercise regularly. In most cases, women can continue to exercise, particularly exercises involving low-impact routines. On the other hand, extreme exercise should be avoided, especially on very hot or very cold days. "No pain, no gain" isn't applicable during pregnancy (Paisley, Joy, & Price, 2003; Schmidt et al., 2006).

REVIEW ⏎ mydevelopmentlab

1. When sperm enter the vagina, they travel through the cervix and into the fallopian tube where _____ may take place.

Answer: fertilization

2. A _____ occurs when pregnancy ends before the developing child is able to survive outside the mother's womb.

Answer: miscarriage

3. An environmental agent such as a drug, chemical, virus, or other factor that produces a birth defect is called a _____.

Answer: teratogen

To see more review questions, log on to MyDevelopmentLab.

CASE STUDY

The Case of... The Genetic Finger of Fate

Melindah and Jermain Tessel were incredibly happy last week when they learned that Melindah was pregnant with their first child, but now they're so worried they can't sleep.

When they got home from the physican's visit, they began to jokingly consider such characteristics as height (tall like Melindah or on the short side, like Jermain), tendency to obesity (like Jermain), athletic ability (like Melindah), intelligence (high, of course, like both of them), and so on. But then they turned to other traits.

Even as adults, both Melindah and Jermain are overly shy and quiet, and they wish they were more assertive. Neither is a natural leader or confident public speaker, but they want their children to be. Both were loners when they were younger, and they agree that their kids would have an easier time if they turned out to be more sociable and outgoing. They worry whether these personality traits are predetermined, or if their kids' fates can be different.

Later, the conversation got even more unsettling. Melindah remembered that there was some mental illness in her family and there were even rumors of violent behavior by one of her uncles. This prompted Jermain to recall an alcoholic cousin and a more distant relative who, he thought, had died early from sickle-cell anemia.

There seems to be so many things that could go wrong—all because of the baggage they carry in their genes!

1. How would you begin to reassure Melindah and Jermain about their worries?

2. Which characteristics that they discussed are largely genetic, and which are more environmentally influenced? Are the genetic traits equivalent to fate, or can their expression be modified? Why or why not?

3. How much should Melindah worry about the mental illness and violence in her family? What would you tell her?

4. How much should Jermain worry about his children inheriting sickle-cell anemia?

5. Would you advise Melindah and Jermain to seek genetic counseling? Why or why not? What factors would you consider in advising them to visit or not to visit a counselor?

What is our basic genetic endowment, and how can human development go off track?

- A child receives 23 chromosomes from each parent. These 46 chromosomes provide the genetic blueprint that will guide cell activity for the rest of the individual's life.

- Gregor Mendel discovered an important genetic mechanism that governs the interactions of dominant and recessive genes and their expression in alleles. Traits such as hair and eye color and the presence of phenylketonuria (PKU) are alleles and follow this pattern.

- Genes may become physically damaged or may spontaneously mutate. If damaged genes are passed on to the child, the result can be a genetic disorder.

- Behavioral genetics, which studies the genetic basis of human behavior, focuses on personality characteristics and behaviors, and on psychological disorders such as schizophrenia. Researchers are now discovering how to remedy certain genetic defects through gene therapy.

- Genetic counselors use data from tests and other sources to identify potential genetic abnormalities in women and men who plan to have children. Recently, they have begun testing individuals for genetically based disorders that may eventually appear in the individuals themselves.

How do the environment and genetics work together to determine human characteristics?

- Behavioral characteristics are often determined by a combination of genetics and environment. Genetically based traits represent a potential, called the genotype, which may be affected by the environment and is ultimately expressed in the phenotype.

- To work out the different influences of heredity and environment, researchers use nonhuman studies and human studies, particularly the studies of twins.

Which human characteristics are significantly influenced by heredity?

- Virtually all human traits, characteristics, and behaviors are the result of the combination and interaction of nature and nurture. Many physical characteristics show strong genetic influences. Intelligence contains a strong genetic component, but can be significantly influenced by environmental factors.

- Some personality traits, including neuroticism and extroversion, have been linked to genetic factors, and even attitudes, values, and interests have a genetic component. Some personal behaviors may be genetically influenced through the mediation of inherited personality traits.

What happens during the prenatal stages of development?

- The union of a sperm and ovum at the moment of fertilization, which begins the process of prenatal development, can be difficult for some couples. Infertility, which occurs in some 15% of couples, can be treated by drugs, surgery, artificial insemination, and in vitro fertilization.

- The germinal stage (fertilization–2 weeks) is marked by rapid cell division and specialization, and the attachment of the zygote to the wall of the uterus. During the embryonic stage (2–8 weeks), the ectoderm, the mesoderm, and the endoderm begin to grow and specialize. The fetal stage (8 weeks–birth) is characterized by a rapid increase in complexity and differentiation of the organs. The fetus becomes active and most of its systems operational.

What are the threats to the fetal environment, and what can be done about them?

- Factors in the mother that may affect the unborn child include diet, age, illnesses, and drug, alcohol, and tobacco use. The behaviors of fathers and others in the mother's environment may also affect the health and development of the unborn child. ■

Epilogue

In this chapter, we have discussed the basics of heredity and genetics, including the way in which the code of life is transmitted across generations through DNA. We have also seen how genetic transmission can go wrong, and we have discussed ways in which genetic disorders can be treated—and perhaps prevented—through new interventions such as genetic counseling and gene therapy.

One important theme considered in this chapter has been the interaction between hereditary and environmental factors in the determination of a number of human traits. While we have encountered a number of surprising instances in which heredity plays a part—including in the development of personality traits and even personal preferences and tastes—we have also seen that heredity is virtually never the sole factor in any complex trait. Environment nearly always plays an important role.

Finally, we reviewed the main stages of prenatal growth—germinal, embryonic, and fetal—and examined threats to the prenatal environment and ways to optimize that environment for the fetus.

Before moving on, return to the Prologue of this chapter—about the Monaco siblings with IVA—and answer the following questions based on your understanding of genetics and prenatal development.

1. How could Jana and Tom Monaco have passed on a rare genetic disease to their children without knowing that they were carriers?

2. From the Monacos's story, would you guess that IVA is an X-linked trait or not?

3. What evidence is there in the story of the Monacos's children that the debilitating effects of IVA are determined by a combination of both genetic and environmental factors?

4. Could the Monacos have learned that they were carriers of IVA before their son Stephen was born? How?

Key Terms and Concepts

gametes (p. 46)
zygote (p. 46)
genes (p. 46)
DNA (deoxyribonucleic acid)
    molecules (p. 46)
chromosomes (p. 46)
monozygotic twins (p. 46)
dizygotic twins (p. 46)
dominant trait (p. 48)
recessive trait (p. 48)
genotype (p. 48)
phenotype (p. 48)
homozygous (p. 49)
heterozygous (p. 49)

polygenic inheritance (p. 50)
X-linked genes (p. 50)
behavioral genetics (p. 50)
Down syndrome (p. 52)
fragile X syndrome (p. 52)
sickle-cell anemia (p. 52)
Tay-Sachs disease (p. 52)
Klinefelter's syndrome (p. 52)
genetic counseling (p. 53)
ultrasound sonography (p. 53)
chorionic villus sampling
    (CVS) (p. 53)
amniocentesis (p. 54)
temperament (p. 56)

multifactorial transmission (p. 57)
fertilization (p. 64)
germinal stage (p. 64)
placenta (p. 64)
embryonic stage (p. 64)
fetal stage (p. 66)
fetus (p. 66)
infertility (p. 67)
artificial insemination (p. 67)
in vitro fertilization (IVF) (p. 67)
teratogen (p. 68)
fetal alcohol syndrome
    (FAS) (p. 71)
fetal alcohol effects (FAE) (p. 71)

4 Birth and the Newborn Infant

PROLOGUE: A 22-OUNCE MIRACLE

"She looked like a little old man," says Elizabeth Thatcher of her daughter, Hattie, who was born at 25 weeks, weighing 1 pound, 6 ounces. "She wasn't plump like a baby should be. She was skin and bones."

Hattie, Elizabeth and husband Brad's firstborn, faced tough odds, but the Montclair, N.J., couple held out hope. A friend's baby born at 23 weeks was doing fine—so, too, the Thatchers prayed, would their little girl. . . .

The Thatchers visited Hattie every day, singing and talking to her. Preemies can't handle much stimulation, so instead of holding her, they lovingly cupped her head and body with their hands.

A fighter from the start, today Hattie, 6, is an outgoing little girl who loves pretending to be a lion. She's eagerly looking forward to Valentine's Day, busy making paper hearts for everyone in her family and "all my neighbors." "On Feb. 14, my mom will get a Valentine under her pillow," she says. Hattie plays soccer every Monday. "I like kicking the ball," she says.

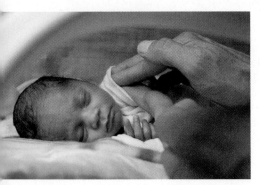

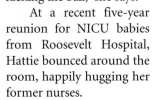

At a recent five-year reunion for NICU babies from Roosevelt Hospital, Hattie bounced around the room, happily hugging her former nurses.

Some children came in wheelchairs. "It made us realize how lucky we really are," says Brad gratefully (Kelly, 2006, p. 26).

▶ Looking Ahead

Infants were not meant to be born as early as Hattie. Yet, for a variety of reasons, more than 10% of all babies today are born prematurely, and the outlook for them to lead a normal life is improving dramatically.

All births, even those that reach full term, are tinged with a combination of excitement and some degree of anxiety. In the vast majority of cases delivery goes smoothly, and it is an amazing and joyous moment when a new being enters the world. The excitement of birth is soon replaced by wonder at the extraordinary nature of newborns themselves. Babies enter the world with a surprising array of capabilities, ready from the first moments of life outside the womb to respond to the world and the people in it.

In this chapter we examine the events that lead to the delivery and birth of a child, and take an initial look at the newborn. We first consider labor and delivery, exploring how the process usually proceeds, as well as several alternative approaches.

We next examine some of the possible complications of birth. Problems that can occur range from premature births to infant mortality. Finally, we consider the extraordinary range of capabilities of newborns. We look not only at their physical and perceptual abilities but also at the way they enter the world with the capacity to learn and with skills that help form the foundations of their future relationships with others.

After reading this chapter, you will be able to answer these questions:

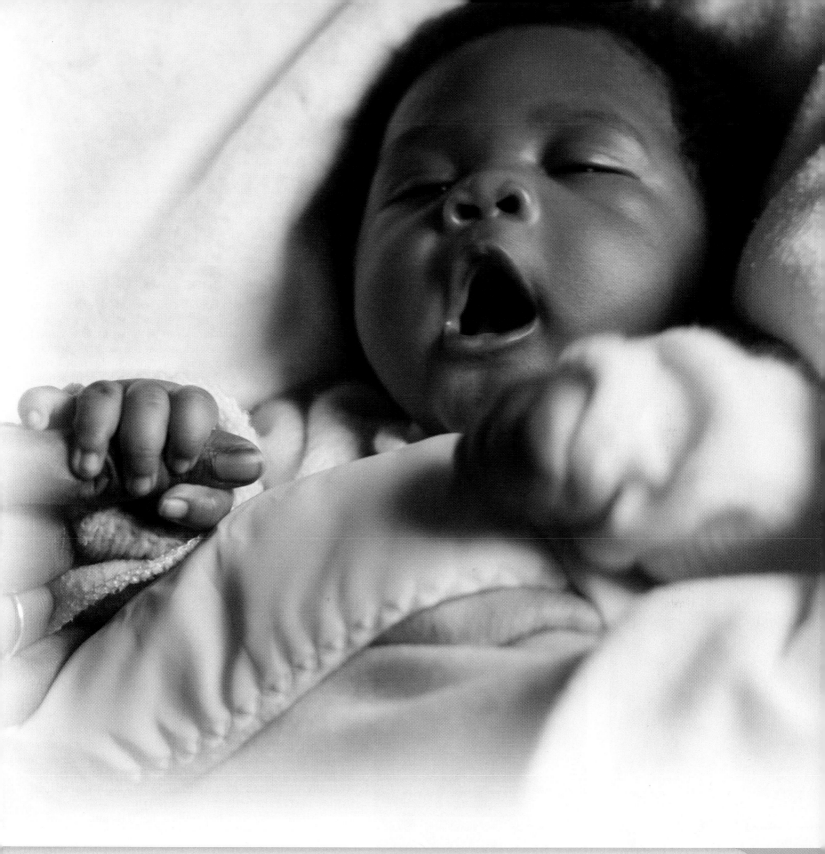

- *What is the normal process of labor?*
- *What complications can occur at birth, and what are their causes, effects, and treatments?*
- *What capabilities does the newborn have?*

Birth

Her head was cone-shaped at the top. Although I knew this was due to the normal movement of the head bones as she came through the birth canal and that this would change in a few days, I was still startled. She also had some blood on the top of her head and was damp, a result of the amniotic fluid in which she had spent the last 9 months. There was some white, cheesy substance over her body, which the nurse wiped off just before she placed her in my arms. I could see a bit of downy hair on her ears, but I knew that this too would disappear before long. Her nose looked a little as if she had been on the losing end of a fistfight: It was squashed into her face, flattened by its trip through the birth canal. But as she seemed to fix her eyes on me and grasped my finger, it was clear that she was nothing short of perfect (Adapted from Brazelton, 1983).

For those of us accustomed to thinking of newborns based on images used in baby-food commercials, this scenario describing a typical newborn may be surprising. Yet most **neonates**—the term used for newborns—are born resembling this one. Make no mistake, however: Despite their

temporary blemishes, babies are a welcome sight to their parents from the moment of their birth.

The neonate's outward appearance is caused by a variety of factors in its journey from the mother's uterus, down the birth canal, and out into the world. We can trace its passage, beginning with the release of the chemicals that initiate the process of labor.

Labor: The Process of Birth Begins

About 266 days after conception, a protein called *corticotropin-releasing hormone* (CRH) triggers the release of various hormones, and the process that leads to birth begins. One critical hormone is *oxytocin*, which is released by the mother's pituitary gland. When the concentration of oxytocin becomes high enough, the mother's uterus begins periodic contractions (Heterelendy & Zakar, 2004; Terzidou, 2007).

During the prenatal period, the uterus, which is composed of muscle tissue, slowly expands as the fetus grows. Although for most of the pregnancy it is inactive, after the 4th month it occasionally contracts in order to ready itself for the eventual delivery. These contractions, called *Braxton-Hicks contractions*, are sometimes called "false labor," because while they can fool eager and anxious expectant parents, they do not signify that the baby will be born soon.

When birth is actually imminent, the uterus begins to contract intermittently. Its increasingly intense contractions act as if it were a vise, opening and closing to force the head of the fetus against the *cervix*, the neck of the uterus that separates it from the vagina. Eventually, the force of the contractions becomes strong enough to propel the fetus slowly down the birth canal until it enters the world as a newborn. It is this exertion and the narrow birth passageway that often gives newborns the battered conehead appearance described earlier.

Labor proceeds in three stages (see Figure 4-1). In the *first stage of labor*, the uterine contractions initially occur around every 8 to 10 minutes and last about 30 seconds. As labor proceeds, the contractions occur more frequently and last longer. Toward the end of labor, the contractions may occur every 2 minutes and last almost 2 minutes. During the final part of the first stage of labor, the contractions increase to their greatest intensity, a period known as *transition*. The mother's cervix fully opens, eventually expanding enough (usually to around 10 cm) to allow the baby's head (the widest part of the body) to pass through.

This first stage of labor is the longest. Its duration varies significantly, depending on the mother's age, race, ethnicity, number of prior pregnancies, and a variety of other factors involving both the fetus and the mother. Typically, labor takes 16 to 24 hours for firstborn children, but there are wide variations. Births of subsequent children usually involve shorter periods of labor.

During the *second stage of labor*, which typically lasts around 90 minutes, the baby's head emerges further with each contraction, increasing the size of the vaginal opening.

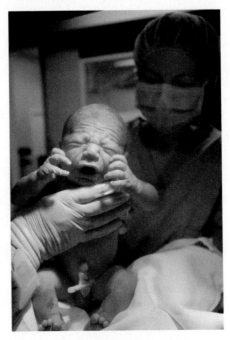

The image of newborns portrayed in commercials differs dramatically from reality.

Episiotomy An incision sometimes made to increase the size of the opening of the vagina to allow the baby to pass

Apgar scale A standard measurement system that looks for a variety of indications of good health in newborns

Stage 1

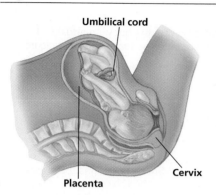

Umbilical cord

Cervix

Placenta

Uterine contractions initially occur every 8 to 10 minutes and last 30 seconds. Toward the end of labor, contractions may occur every 2 minutes and last as long as 2 minutes. As the contractions increase, the cervix, which separates the uterus from the vagina, becomes wider, eventually expanding to allow the baby's head to pass through.

Stage 2

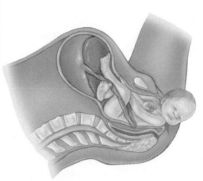

The baby's head starts to move through the cervix and birth canal. Typically lasting around 90 minutes, the second stage ends when the baby has completely left the mother's body.

Stage 3

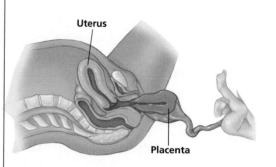

Uterus

Placenta

The child's umbilical cord (still attached to the neonate) and the placenta are expelled from the mother. This stage is the quickest and easiest, taking just a few minutes.

FIGURE 4-1 The Three Stages of Labor

Because the area between the vagina and rectum must stretch a good deal, an incision called an **episiotomy** is sometimes made to increase the size of the opening of the vagina. However, this practice has been increasingly criticized in recent years as potentially causing more harm than good, and the number of episiotomies has fallen drastically in the last decades (Goldberg et al., 2002; Dudding, Vaizey, & Kamm, 2008).

The second stage of labor ends when the baby has completely left the mother's body. Finally, the *third stage of labor* occurs when the child's umbilical cord (still attached to the neonate) and the placenta are expelled from the mother. This stage is the quickest and easiest, taking just a few minutes.

How a woman reacts to labor reflects, in part, cultural factors. Although there is no evidence that the physiological aspects of labor differ among women of different cultures, expectations about labor and interpretations of its pain do vary significantly from one culture to another (Callister et al., 2003; Fisher, Hauck, & Fenwick, 2006).

For instance, there is a kernel of truth to popular stories of pregnant women in certain societies putting down the tools with which they are tilling their fields, stepping aside and giving birth, and immediately returning to work with their neonates wrapped and bundled on their backs. Accounts of the !Kung people in Africa describe the woman in labor sitting calmly beside a tree and without much ado—or assistance—successfully giving birth to a child and quickly recovering. On the other hand, many societies regard childbirth

as dangerous, and some even view it in terms befitting an illness. Such cultural perspectives color the way that people in a given society view the experience of childbirth.

Birth: From Fetus to Neonate

The exact moment of birth occurs when the fetus, having left the uterus through the cervix, passes through the vagina to emerge fully from its mother's body. In most cases, babies automatically make the transition from taking in oxygen via the placenta to using their lungs to breathe air. Consequently, as soon as they are outside the mother's body, most newborns spontaneously cry. This helps them clear their lungs and breathe on their own.

What happens next varies from situation to situation and from culture to culture. In Western cultures, health-care workers are almost always on hand to assist with the birth. In the United States, 99% of births are attended by professional health-care workers, but worldwide only about 50% of births have professional health-care workers in attendance (United Nations, 1990).

The Apgar Scale In most cases, the newborn infant first undergoes a quick visual inspection. Parents may be counting fingers and toes, but trained health-care workers look for something more. Typically, they employ the **Apgar scale**, a standard measurement system that looks for a variety of indications of good health (see Table 4-1). Developed by physician Virginia Apgar, the scale directs attention to five

Anoxia A restriction of oxygen to the baby, lasting a few minutes during the birth process, which can produce brain damage

Bonding Close physical and emotional contact between parent and child during the period immediately following birth, argued by some to affect later relationship strength

---

TABLE 4-1	Apgar Scale

A score is given for each sign at 1 minute and 5 minutes after the birth. If there are problems with the baby, an additional score is given at 10 minutes. A score of 7–10 is considered normal, whereas 4–7 might require some resuscitative measures, and a baby with an Apgar score under 4 requires immediate resuscitation.

	Sign	0 Points	1 Point	2 Points
A	Appearance (skin color)	Blue-gray, pale all over	Normal, except for extremities	Normal over entire body
P	Pulse	Absent	Below 100 bpm	Above 100 bpm
G	Grimace (reflex irritability)	No response	Grimace	Sneezes, coughs, pulls away
A	Activity (muscle tone)	Absent	Arms and legs flexed	Active movement
R	Respiration	Absent	Slow, irregular	Good, crying

(*Source*: Apgar, 1953)

---

basic qualities, recalled most easily by using Apgar's name as a guide: *a*ppearance (color), *p*ulse (heart rate), *g*rimace (reflex irritability), *a*ctivity (muscle tone), and *r*espiration (respiratory effort).

Using the scale, health-care workers assign the newborn a score ranging from 0 to 2 on each of the five qualities, producing an overall score that can range from 0 to 10. The vast majority of children score 7 or above. The 10% of neonates who score under 7 require help to start breathing. Newborns who score under 4 need immediate, life-saving intervention.

Low Apgar scores (or low scores on other neonatal assessments, such as the *Brazelton Neonatal Behavioral Assessment Scale*, which we discuss in the next chapter) may indicate problems or birth defects that were already present in the fetus. However, the process of birth itself may sometimes cause difficulties. Among the most profound are those relating to a temporary deprivation of oxygen.

At various junctures during labor, the fetus may not get sufficient oxygen. This can happen for any of a number of reasons. For instance, the umbilical cord may get wrapped around the neck of the fetus. The cord can also be pinched during a prolonged contraction, thereby cutting off the supply of oxygen that flows through it.

Lack of oxygen for a few seconds is not harmful to the fetus, but deprivation for any longer time may cause serious harm. A restriction of oxygen, or **anoxia**, lasting a few minutes can produce cognitive deficits such as language delays and even mental retardation due to brain-cell death (Hopkins-Golightly, Raz, & Sander, 2003).

Physical Appearance and Initial Encounters After assessing the newborn's health, health-care workers next deal with the remnants of the child's passage through the birth canal. You'll recall the description of the thick, greasy substance (like cottage cheese) that covers the newborn. This material, called *vernix*, smoothes the passage through the birth canal; it is no longer needed once the child is born and is easily cleaned away. Newborns' bodies are also covered with a fine, dark fuzz known as *lanugo*; this soon disappears. The newborn's eyelids may be puffy due to an accumulation of fluids during labor, and the newborn may have blood or other fluids on parts of its body.

After being cleansed, the newborn is usually returned to the mother and the father, if he is present. The everyday and universal occurrence of childbirth makes it no less miraculous to parents, and most cherish this time to make their first acquaintance with their child.

The importance of this initial encounter between parent and child has become a matter of considerable controversy. Some psychologists and physicians argued that **bonding**, the close physical and emotional contact between parent and child during the period immediately following birth, was a crucial ingredient for forming a lasting relationship between parent and child (Lorenz, 1957). Their arguments were based in part on research conducted on nonhuman species such as ducklings. This work showed that there was a critical period just after birth when organisms showed a particular readiness to learn, or imprint, from other members of their species who happened to be present.

According to the concept of bonding applied to humans, a critical period begins just after birth and lasts only a few hours. During this period actual skin-to-skin contact between mother and child supposedly leads to deep, emotional bonding. The corollary to this assumption is that if circumstances prevent such contact, the bond between mother and child will forever be lacking in some way. Because so many babies were taken from their mothers and placed in incubators or in the hospital nursery, the fear was that medical practices prevalent at the time often left little opportunity for sustained mother and child physical contact immediately after birth.

However, when developmental researchers carefully reviewed the research literature, they found little support for the existence of a critical period for bonding at birth. Although it does appear that mothers who have early physical contact with their babies are more responsive to them than those who don't have such contact, the difference lasts only a few days. Such news is reassuring to parents whose children must receive immediate, intensive medical attention just after birth, such as in the case of Hattie Thatcher, described in the chapter Prologue. It is also comforting to parents who adopt children and are not present at their births (Else-Quest, Hyde, & Clark, 2003; Weinberg, 2004; Miles et al., 2006).

Although mother–child bonding does not seem critical, it is important for newborns to be gently touched and massaged soon after birth. The physical stimulation they receive stimulates the production of chemicals in the brain that instigate growth (Field, 2001).

Approaches to Childbirth: Where Medicine and Attitudes Meet

Ester Iverem knew herself well enough to know that she didn't like the interaction she had with medical doctors. So she opted for a nurse-midwife at Manhattan's Maternity Center where she was free to use a birthing stool and to have her husband, Nick Chiles, by her side. When contractions began, Iverem and Chiles went for a walk, stopping periodically to rock—a motion, she says, "similar to the way children dance when they first learn how, shifting from foot to foot." That helped her work through the really powerful contractions.

"I sat on the birthing chair [a Western version of the traditional African stool, which lies low to the ground and has an opening in the middle for the baby to come through] and Nick was sitting right behind me. When the midwife said 'Push!' the baby's head just went 'pop!' and out he came." Their son, Mazi (which means "Sir" in Ibo) Iverem Chiles, was placed on Ester's breast while the midwives went to prepare for his routine examination. (Knight, 1994, p. 122)

Parents in the Western world have developed a variety of strategies—and some very strong opinions—to help them deal with something as natural as giving birth, which occurs apparently without much thought throughout the nonhuman animal world. Today parents need to decide: Should the birth take place in a hospital or in the home? Should a physician, a nurse, or a midwife assist? Is the father's presence desirable? Should siblings and other family members be on hand to participate in the birth?

Most of these questions cannot be answered definitively, primarily because the choice of childbirth techniques often comes down to a matter of values and opinions. No single procedure will be effective for all mothers and fathers, and no conclusive research evidence has proven that one procedure is significantly more effective than another. As we'll see, there is a wide variety of different issues and options involved, and certainly one's culture plays a role in choices of birthing procedures.

The abundance of choices is largely due to a reaction to traditional medical practices that had been common in the United States until the early 1970s. Before that time, the typical birth went something like this: A woman in labor was placed in a room with many other women, all of whom were in various stages of childbirth, and some of whom were screaming in pain. Fathers and other family members were not allowed to be present. Just before delivery, the woman was rolled into a delivery room, where the birth took place. Often she was so drugged that she was not aware of the birth at all.

At the time, physicians argued that such procedures were necessary to ensure the health of the newborn and the mother. However, critics charged that alternatives were available that not only would maximize the medical well-being of the participants in the birth but also would represent an emotional and psychological improvement (Curl et al., 2004; Hotelling & Humenick, 2005).

Alternative Birthing Procedures   Not all mothers give birth in hospitals, and not all births follow a traditional course. Among the major alternatives to traditional birthing practices are the following:

In Lamaze classes, parents are taught relaxation techniques to prepare for childbirth and to reduce the need for anesthetics.

- **Lamaze birthing techniques.** The Lamaze method has achieved widespread popularity in the United States. Based on the writings of Dr. Fernand Lamaze, the method makes use of breathing techniques and relaxation training. Typically, mothers-to-be participate in a series of weekly training sessions in which they learn exercises that help them relax various parts of the body on command. A "coach," most typically the father, is trained along with the future mother. The training allows women to cope with painful contractions by concentrating on their breathing and producing relaxation response, rather than by tensing up, which can make the pain more acute. Women learn to to focus on a relaxing stimulus, such as a tranquil scene in a picture. The goal is to learn how to deal positively with pain and to relax at the onset of a contraction (Lothian, 2005).

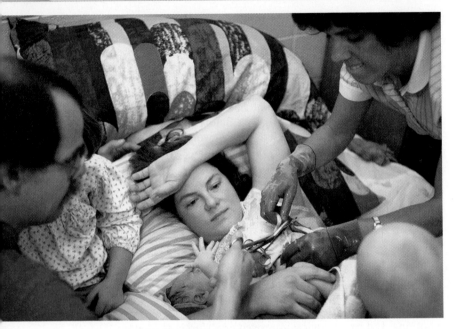

A midwife helps in this home delivery.

- **Bradley Method.** The Bradley Method, which is sometimes known as "husband-coached childbirth," is based on the principle that childbirth should be as natural as possible and involve no medication or medical interventions. Women are taught to "tune in to" their bodies in order to deal with the pain of childbirth.

  To prepare for childbirth, mothers-to-be are taught muscle relaxation techniques, similar to Lamaze procedures, and good nutrition and exercise during pregnancy are seen as important to prepare for delivery. Parents are urged to take responsibility for childbirth, and the use of physicians is viewed as unnecessary and sometimes even dangerous. As you might expect, the discouragement of traditional medical interventions is quite controversial (McCutcheon-Rosegg, Ingraham, & Bradley, 1996; Reed, 2005).

- **Hypnobirthing.** Hypnobirthing is a new, but increasingly popular, technique. It involves a form of self-hypnosis during delivery which produces a sense of peace and calm, thereby reducing pain. The basic concept is to produce a state of focused concentration in which a mother relaxes her body while focusing inward. Increasing research evidence shows the technique can be effective in reducing pain (Mongan, 2005; Cyna, Andrew, & McAuliffe, 2006; Olson, 2006).

Childbirth Attendants: Who Delivers? Traditionally, *obstetricians*, physicians who specialize in delivering babies, have been the childbirth attendants of choice. In the last few decades, more mothers have chosen to use a *midwife*, a childbirth attendant who stays with the mother throughout labor and delivery. Midwives—most often nurses specializing in childbirth—are used primarily for pregnancies in which no complications are expected. The use of midwives has increased steadily in the United States—there are now 7,000 of them—and they are employed in 10% of births. Midwives help deliver some 80% of babies in other parts of the world, often at home. Home birth is common in countries at all levels of economic development. For instance, a third of all births in the Netherlands occur at home (Ayoub, 2005).

The newest trend in childbirth assistance is also one of the oldest: the doula (pronounced doo-lah). A *doula* is trained to provide emotional, psychological, and educational support during birth. A doula does not replace an obstetrician or midwife, and does not perform medical exams. Instead, doulas, who are often well-versed in birthing alternatives, provide the mother with support and ensures that parents are aware of alternatives and possibilities regarding the birth process.

Although the use of doulas is new in the United States, they represent a return to an older tradition that has existed for centuries in other cultures. Although they may not be called "doulas," supportive, experienced older women have helped mothers as they give birth in non-Western cultures for centuries.

A growing body of research indicates the presence of a doula is beneficial to the birth process, speeding deliveries and reducing reliance on drugs. Yet concerns remain about

Does the procedure work? Most mothers, as well as fathers, report that a Lamaze birth is a very positive experience. They enjoy the sense of mastery that they gain over the process of labor, a feeling of being able to exert some control over what can be a formidable experience. On the other hand, we can't be sure that parents who choose the Lamaze method aren't already more highly motivated about the experience of childbirth than are parents who do not choose the technique. It is therefore possible that the accolades they express after Lamaze births are due to their initial enthusiasm, and not to the Lamaze procedures themselves (Larsen, 2001; Zwelling, 2006).

Participation in Lamaze procedures—as well as other natural childbirth techniques in which the emphasis is on educating the parents about the process of birth and minimizing the use of drugs—is relatively rare among members of lower income groups, including many members of ethnic minorities. Parents in these groups may not have the transportation, time, or financial resources to attend childbirth preparation classes. The result is that women in lower income groups tend to be less prepared for the events of labor and consequently may suffer more pain during childbirth (Brueggemann, 1999; Lu et al., 2003).

From a health-care worker's perspective: Although 99% of U.S. births are attended by professional medical workers or birthing attendants, this is the case in only about half of births worldwide. What do you think are some reasons for this, and what are the implications of this statistic?

their use. Unlike certified midwives, who are nurses and receive an additional year or two of training, doulas do not need to be certified or have any particular level of education. (Breedlove, 2005; Ballen & Fulcher, 2006; Campbell et al., 2007).

Pain and Childbirth Any woman who has delivered a baby will agree that childbirth is painful. But exactly how painful is it?

Such a question is largely unanswerable. One reason is that pain is a subjective, psychological phenomenon that cannot be easily measured. No one is able to answer the question of whether their pain is "greater" or "worse" than someone else's pain, although some studies have tried to quantify it. For instance, in one survey women were asked to rate the pain they experienced during labor on a 1-to-5 scale, with 5 being the most painful (Yarrow, 1992). Nearly half (44%) said "5," and an additional one-quarter said "4."

Because pain is usually a sign that something is wrong in one's body, we have learned to react to pain with fear and concern. Yet during childbirth, pain is actually a signal that the body is working appropriately and that the contractions that are meant to propel the baby through the birth canal are doing their job. Consequently, the experience of pain during labor is difficult for women in labor to interpret, thereby potentially increasing their anxiety and making the contractions seem even more painful. Ultimately, every woman's delivery depends on such variables as how much preparation and support she has before and during delivery, her culture's view of pregnancy and delivery, and the specific nature of the delivery itself (DiMatteo & Kahn, 1997; Walker & O'Brien, 1999; Abushaikha, 2007).

Use of Anesthesia and Pain-Reducing Drugs
Among the greatest advances of modern medicine is the ongoing discovery of drugs that reduce pain. However, the use of medication during childbirth is a practice that holds both benefits and pitfalls.

About a third of women who receive anesthesia do so in the form of *epidural anesthesia*, which produces numbness from the waist down. Traditional epidurals produce an inability to walk and in some cases prevent women from helping to push the baby out during delivery. However, a newer form of epidural, known as a *walking epidural* or *dual spinal-epidural*, uses smaller needles and a system for administering continuous doses of anesthetic. It permits women to move about more freely during labor and has fewer side effects than traditional epidural anesthesia (Simmons et al., 2007).

It is clear that drugs hold the promise of greatly reducing, and even eliminating, pain associated with labor, which can be extreme and exhausting. However, pain reduction comes at a cost: Drugs administered during labor reach not just the mother but the fetus as well. The stronger the drug, the greater its effects on the fetus and neonate. Because of the small size of the fetus relative to the mother, drug doses that might have only a minimal effect on the mother can have a magnified effect on the fetus.

Anesthetics may temporarily depress the flow of oxygen to the fetus and slow labor. In addition, newborns whose mothers have been anesthetized are less physiologically responsive, show poorer motor control during the first days of life after birth, cry more, and may have more difficulty in initiating breast-feeding (Walker & O'Brien, 1999; Torvaldsen et al., 2006).

However, most research suggests that drugs, as they are currently employed during labor, produce only minimal risks to the fetus and neonate. Guidelines issued by the American College of Obstetricians and Gynecologists (ACOG) suggest that a woman's request for pain relief at any stage of labor should be honored, and that the proper use of minimal amounts of drugs for pain relief is reasonable and has no significant effect on a child's later well-being (ACOG, 2002; Alberst et al., 2007).

Postdelivery Hospital Stay: Deliver, Then Depart?
When New Jersey mother Diane Mensch was sent home from the hospital just a day after the birth of her third child, she still felt exhausted. But her insurance company insisted that 24 hours was sufficient time to recover, and it refused to pay for more. Three days later, her newborn was back in the hospital, suffering from jaundice. Mensch is convinced the problem would have been discovered and treated sooner had she and her newborn been allowed to remain in the hospital longer (Begley, 1995).

Mensch's experience was not unusual. In the 1970s the average hospital stay for a normal birth was 3.9 days. By the 1990s, it was 2 days. These changes were prompted in large part by medical insurance companies, who advocated hospital stays of only 24 hours following birth in order to reduce costs.

Medical care providers have fought against this trend, believing that there are definite risks involved, both for mothers and for their newborns. For instance, mothers may begin to bleed if they tear tissue injured during childbirth. It is also riskier for newborns to be discharged prematurely from the intensive medical care that hospitals can provide. Furthermore, mothers are better rested and more satisfied with their medical care when they stay longer (Finkelstein, Harper, & Rosenthal, 1998; see Figure 4-2).

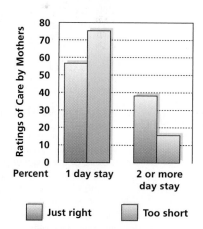

FIGURE 4-2 Longer Is Better

Clearly, mothers are most satisfied with their medical care if they stay longer following a birth than if they are discharged after only 1 day. However, some medical insurance companies prefer a reduction to a stay of only 24 hours following a birth. Do you think such a reduction is justified?
(*Source:* Finkelstein, Harper, & Rosenthal, 1998)

In accordance with these views, the American Academy of Pediatrics states that except in unusual cases, women should stay in the hospital no less than 48 hours after giving birth. Furthermore, the U.S. Congress passed legislation mandating a minimum insurance coverage of 48 hours for childbirth (American Academy of Pediatrics Committee on Fetus and Newborn, 2004).

Newborn Medical Screening Just after birth, newborns typically are tested for a variety of diseases and genetic conditions. The American College of Medical Genetics recommends that all newborns be screened for 29 disorders, ranging from hearing difficulties and sickle-cell anemia to extremely rare conditions such as isovaleric academia, a disorder involving metabolism. These disorders can be detected from a tiny quantity of blood drawn from an infant's heel (American College of Medical Genetics, 2006).

The advantage of newborn screening is that it permits early treatment of problems that might go undetected for years. In some cases, devastating conditions can be prevented through early treatment of the disorder, such as the implementation of a particular kind of diet (Goldfarb, 2005; Kayton, 2007).

The exact number of tests that a newborn experiences varies drastically from state to state. In some states, only three tests are mandated, while in others over 30 are required. In jurisdictions with only a few tests, many disorders go undiagnosed. In fact, each year around 1,000 infants in the United States suffer from disorders that could have been detected at birth if appropriate screening had been conducted at that time (American Academy of Pediatrics, 2005).

Becoming an Informed Consumer of Development

Dealing With Labor

Every woman who is soon to give birth has some fear of labor. Most have heard gripping tales of extended, 48-hour labors or vivid descriptions of the pain that accompanies labor. Still, few mothers would dispute the notion that the rewards of giving birth are worth the effort.

There is no single right or wrong way to deal with labor. However, several strategies can help make the process as positive as possible:

- **Be flexible.** Although you may have carefully worked out what to do during labor, don't feel an obligation to follow through exactly. If a strategy is ineffective, turn to another one.

- **Communicate with your health-care providers.** Let them know what you are experiencing. They may be able to suggest ways to deal with what you are encountering. As your labor progresses, they may also be able to give you a fairly clear idea of how much longer you will be in labor. Knowing the worst of the pain is going to last only another 20 minutes or so, you may feel you can handle it.

- **Remember that labor is . . . laborious.** Expect that you may become fatigued, but realize that as the final stages of labor occur, you may well get a second wind.

- **Accept your partner's support.** If a spouse or other partner is present, allow that person to make you comfortable and provide support. Research has shown that women who are supported by a spouse or partner have a more comfortable birth experience (Bader, 1995; Kennell, 2002).

- **Be realistic and honest about your reactions to pain.** Even if you had planned an unmedicated delivery, realize that you may find the pain difficult to tolerate. At that point, consider the use of drugs. Above all, don't feel that asking for pain medication is a sign of failure. It isn't.

- **Focus on the big picture.** Keep in mind that labor is part of a process that ultimately leads to an event unmatched in the joy it can bring.

REVIEW ↵ mydevelopmentlab

1. About 266 days after conception, _____ - _____ _____ triggers the process that leads to birth.

   Answer: corticotrophin-releasing hormone (CRH)

2. The _____ scale is a standard measurement system designed to assess five basic qualities in a newborn: appearance (color), pulse (heart rate), grimace (reflex irritability), activity (muscle tone), and respiration (respiratory effort).

   Answer: Apgar

3. During delivery, a restriction of oxygen, known as _____, can last only a few minutes but can produce long-term cognitive deficits.

   Answer: anoxia

To see more review questions, log on to MyDevelopmentLab.

Birth Complications

In addition to the usual complimentary baby supplies that most hospitals bestow on new mothers, the maternity nurses at Greater Southeast Hospital have become practiced in handing out "grief baskets."

Inside are items memorializing one of [Washington, D.C.'s] grimmest statistics—an infant mortality rate that's more than twice the national average. The baskets contain a photograph of the dead newborn, a snip of its hair, the tiny cap it wore, and a yellow rose (P. Thomas, 1994, p. A14).

The infant mortality rate in Washington, D.C., capital of the richest country in the world, is 12.2 deaths per 1,000 births, exceeding the rate of countries such as Hungary, Cuba, Kuwait, and Costa Rica. Overall, the United States ranks 22nd among industrialized countries, with 6.37 deaths for every 1,000 live births (*Washington Post*, 2007; World Factbook, 2007; see Figure 4-3).

Why is infant survival less likely in the United States than in other, less developed countries? To answer this question, we need to consider the nature of the problems that can occur during labor and delivery.

Preterm Infants: Too Soon, Too Small

Like Hattie Thatcher, whose birth was described in the chapter Prologue, 11% of infants are born earlier than normal. **Preterm infants**, or premature infants, are born prior to 38 weeks after conception. Because they have not had time to develop fully as fetuses, preterm infants are at high risk for illness and death.

The extent of danger faced by preterm babies largely depends on the child's weight at birth, which has great significance as an indicator of the extent of the baby's development. Although the average newborn weighs around 3,400 grams (about 7 1/2 pounds), **low-birthweight infants** weigh less than 2,500 grams (around 5 1/2 pounds). Although only 7% of all newborns in the United States fall into the low-birthweight category, they account for the majority of newborn deaths (Gross, Spiker, & Haynes, 1997; DeVader et al., 2007).

Although most low-birthweight infants are preterm, some are small-for-gestational-age babies. **Small-for-gestational-age infants** are infants who, because of delayed fetal growth, weigh 90% (or less) of the average weight of infants of the same gestational age. Small-for-gestational-age infants are sometimes also preterm, but may not be. The syndrome may be caused by inadequate nutrition during pregnancy (Bergmann, Bergmann, & Dudenhausen, 2008).

If the degree of prematurity is not too great and weight at birth is not extremely low, the threat to the child's well-being is relatively minor. In such cases, the main treatment may be to keep the baby in the hospital to gain weight. Additional weight is critical because fat layers help prevent chilling in neonates, who are not particularly efficient at regulating body temperature.

Newborns who are born more prematurely and who have birthweights significantly below average face a tougher road. For them, simply staying alive is a major task. For instance, low-birthweight infants are highly vulnerable to infection, and because their lungs have not had sufficient time to develop completely, they have problems taking in sufficient oxygen. As a consequence, they may experience *respiratory distress syndrome (RDS)*, with potentially fatal consequences.

To deal with respiratory distress syndrome, low-birthweight infants are often placed in incubators, enclosures in which temperature and oxygen content are controlled. The exact amount of oxygen is carefully monitored. Too low a concentration of oxygen will not provide relief, and too high a concentration can damage the delicate retinas of the eyes, leading to permanent blindness.

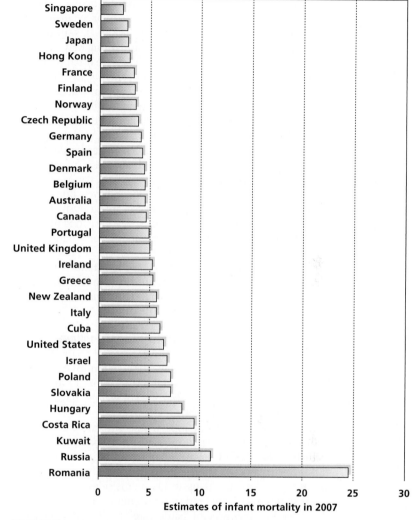

FIGURE 4-3 International Infant Mortality

While the United States has greatly reduced its infant mortality rate in the past 25 years, it ranks only 22nd among industrialized countries as of 2007. What are some of the reasons for this?
(*Source:* World Factbook, 2007)

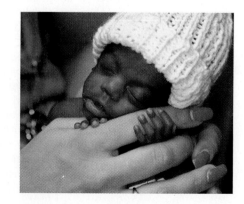

Preterm infants stand a much greater chance of survival today than they did even a decade ago.

Very-low-birthweight infants
Infants who weigh less than
1,250 grams (around 2 1/4
pounds) or, regardless of weight,
have been in the womb fewer
than 30 weeks

The immature development of preterm neonates makes them unusually sensitive to stimuli in their environment. They can easily be overwhelmed by the sights, sounds, and sensations they experience, and their breathing may be interrupted or their heart rates may slow. They are often unable to move smoothly; their arm and leg movements are uncoordinated, causing them to jerk about and appear startled. Such behavior is quite disconcerting to parents (Miles et al., 2006).

Despite the difficulties they experience at birth, the majority of preterm infants eventually develop normally in the long run. However, the tempo of development often proceeds more slowly for preterm children compared to children born at full term, and more subtle problems sometimes emerge later. For example, by the end of their 1st year, only 10% of prematurely born infants display significant problems, and only 5% are seriously disabled. By the age of 6, however, approximately 38% have mild problems that call for special educational interventions. For instance, some preterm children show learning disabilities, behavior disorders, or lower-than-average IQ scores. Others have difficulties with physical coordination. Still, around 60% of preterm infants are free of even minor problems (Nadeau et al., 2001; Arseneault et al., 2002; Dombrowski, Noonan, & Martin, 2006).

Very-Low-Birthweight Infants: The Smallest of the Small

The story is less positive for the most extreme cases of prematurity—very-low-birthweight infants. **Very-low-birthweight infants** weigh less than 1250 grams (around 2 1/4 pounds) or, regardless of weight, have been in the womb less than 30 weeks.

Very-low-birthweight infants not only are tiny—some, like little Hattie Thatcher, fitting easily in the palm of the hand at birth—they hardly seem to belong to the same species as full-term newborns. Their eyes may be fused shut and their earlobes may look like flaps of skin on the sides of their heads. Their skin is a darkened red color, whatever their race.

Very-low-birthweight babies are in grave danger from the moment they are born, due to the immaturity of their organ systems. Before the mid-1980s, these babies would not have survived outside their mothers' wombs. However, medical advances have led to a higher chance of survival, pushing the *age of viability*, the point at which an infant can survive prematurely, to about 22 weeks—some 4 months earlier than the term of a normal delivery. Of course, the longer the period of development beyond conception, the higher are a newborn's chances of survival. A baby born earlier than 25 weeks has less than a 50–50 chance of survival (see Figure 4-4).

The physical and cognitive problems experienced by low-birthweight and preterm babies are even more pronounced in very-low-birthweight infants, with astonishing financial consequences. A 4-month stay in an incubator in an intensive care unit can run hundreds of thousands of dollars, and about half of these newborns ultimately die, despite massive medical intervention (Taylor et al., 2000).

Even if a very-low-birthweight preterm infant survives, the medical costs can continue to mount. For instance, one

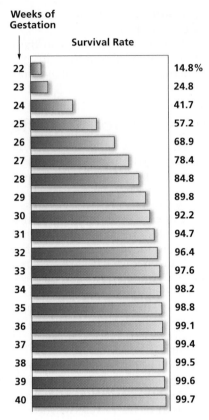

FIGURE 4-4 Survival and Gestational Age

Chances of a fetus surviving greatly improve after 28 to 32 weeks. Rates shown are the percentages of babies born in the United States after specified lengths of gestation who survive the first year of life. (*Source:* Stolberg, 1997)

estimate suggests that the average monthly cost of medical care for such infants during the first 3 years of life may be between 3 and 50 times higher than the medical costs for a full-term child. Such astronomical costs have raised ethical debates about the expenditure of substantial financial and human resources in cases in which a positive outcome may be unlikely (Prince, 2000; Doyle, 2004; Petrou, 2006).

As medical capabilities progress and developmental researchers come up with new strategies for dealing with preterm infants and improving their lives, the age of viability is likely to be pushed even earlier. Emerging evidence suggests that high-quality care can provide protection from some of the risks associated with prematurity, and that by the time they reach adulthood, premature babies may be little different from other adults (Hack et al., 2002).

Research also shows that preterm infants who receive more responsive, stimulating, and organized care are apt to show more positive outcomes than those children whose care is not as good. Some of these interventions are quite simple. For example, "Kangaroo Care" in which infants are held skin-to-skin against their parents' chests, appears to be effective in helping preterm infants develop. Massaging preterm infants several times a day triggers the release of hormones that promote weight gain, muscle development, and abilities to cope with stress (Feldman et al., 2003; Tallandini & Scalembra, 2006; Erlandsson et al., 2007).

What Causes Preterm and Low-Birthweight Deliveries? About half of preterm and low-birthweight births are unexplained, but several known causes account for the remainder. In some cases, premature labor results from difficulties relating to the mother's reproductive system. For instance, mothers carrying twins have unusual stress placed on them, which can lead to early labor. In fact, most multiple births are preterm to some degree (Tan et al., 2004; Luke & Brown, 2008).

In other cases, preterm and low-birthweight babies are a result of the immaturity of the mother's reproductive system. Young mothers—under the age of 15—are more prone

to deliver prematurely than are older ones. In addition, a woman who becomes pregnant within 6 months of her previous delivery is more likely to bear a preterm or low-birthweight infant than a woman whose reproductive system has had a chance to recover from a prior delivery. Father's age matters, too: wives of older fathers are more likely to have preterm deliveries (Zhu, 2005; Branum, 2006).

Finally, factors that affect the general health of the mother, such as nutrition, level of medical care, amount of stress in the environment, and economic support, all are related to prematurity and low birthweight. Rates of preterm births differ between racial groups, not because of race per se, but because members of racial minorities have disproportionately lower incomes and higher stress as a result. For instance, the percentage of low-birthweight infants born to African American mothers is double that for Caucasian American mothers. (A summary of the factors associated with increased risk of low birthweight is shown in Table 4-2;

TABLE 4-2   Factors Associated With Increased Risk of Low Birthweight

I. **Demographic Risks**

  a. Age (less than 17; over 34)

  b. Race (minority)

  c. Low socioeconomic status

  d. Unmarried

  e. Low level of education

II. **Medical Risks Predating Pregnancy**

  a. Number of previous pregnancies (0 or more than 4)

  b. Low weight for height

  c. Genitourinary anomalies/surgery

  d. Selected diseases such as diabetes, chronic hypertension

  e. Nonimmune status for selected infections such as rubella

  f. Poor obstetric history, including previous low-birthweight infant or multiple spontaneous abortions

  g. Maternal genetic factors (such as low weight at own birth)

III. **Medical Risks in Current Pregnancy**

  a. Multiple pregnancy

  b. Poor weight gain

  c. Short interpregnancy interval

  d. Low blood pressure

  e. Hypertension/preeclampsia/toxemia

  f. Selected infections such as asymptomatic bacteriuria, rubella, and cytomegalovirus

  g. First or second trimester bleeding

  h. Placental problems such as placenta previa, abruptio placentae

  i. Severe morning sickness

  j. Anemia/abnormal hemoglobin

  k. Severe anemia in a developing baby

  l. Fetal anomalies

  m. Incompetent cervix

  n. Spontaneous premature rupture of membrane

IV. **Behavioral and Environmental Risks**

  a. Smoking

  b. Poor nutritional status

  c. Alcohol and other substance abuse

  d. DES exposure and other toxic exposure, including occupational hazards

  e. High altitude

V. **Health-Care Risks**

  a. Absent or inadequate prenatal care

  b. Iatrogenic prematurity

VI. **Evolving Concepts of Risks**

  a. Stress, physical and psychosocial

  b. Uterine irritability

  c. Events triggering uterine contractions

  d. Cervical changes detected before onset of labor

  e. Selected infections such as mycoplasma and chlamydia trachomatis

  f. Inadequate plasma volume expansion

  g. Progesterone deficiency

(*Source:* Adapted from Committee to Study the Prevention of Low Birthweight, 1985)

CAREERS *in* CHILD DEVELOPMENT

Diana Hegger, R.N., B.S.N.

Education: B.S.N., San Diego State University, San Diego, California

Position: Neonatal Nurse and Educator at Children's Healthcare of Atlanta hospital

Home: Ryoston, Georgia

The care and treatment of preterm infants as young as 23 weeks not only calls for the most sophisticated use of modern medicine, but for dedicated and skilled professionals such as Diana Hegger.

Hegger, a neonatal nurse and educator at Children's Healthcare of Atlanta hospital, says that the treatment of preterm newborns begins immediately upon birth, right in the delivery room.

"Because their breathing capacity is not well developed, we immediately put them on a ventilator and give them a medication so that their lungs do not stick together," she noted.

"We also put them in an isolette (incubator), which provides an environment close to body temperature. This is because they are constantly trying to keep warm, and in the process they are using precious calories and require more oxygen," Hegger noted.

These are just two of the many vital signs that are monitored in the preterm infant, according to Hegger.

"We also have to think about maintaining blood pressure, and because the skin is not developed there is water loss. Since they cannot eat, everything has to be provided intravenously" she said. "The blood–brain barrier is very fragile, and if you have a fluctuation in blood pressure, it can result in bleeding in the head, which can lead to mental retardation and cerebral palsy."

Only a quarter of those born at 23 weeks survive, and a substantial number are subject to a variety of ailments that range from blindness to cerebral palsy. Because of the magnitude of the problems, Hegger and her colleagues pay almost as much attention to parents as to their children.

"We pride ourselves in reaching and meeting with parents," Hegger said. Before a child is born, and if we have prior knowledge of a known disease, counseling is provided," she said. "After the child is born, we have what we call Heart-to-Heart groups where parents can meet with social workers, lactation consultants, as well as clergy."

"We also do baby showers—or follow-ups if a baby has died. We also provide memory boxes that contain a lock of the child's hair and other mementos. Some parents do not want them, but we keep them and have found that sometimes a year later they will ask for them. The strength of the human parent still amazes me," Hegger said.

Field, Diego, & Hernandex-Reif, 2006; Bergmann, Bergmann, & Dudenhausen, 2008.) (Also see the Careers in Child Development interview with a nurse who cares for preterm and low-birthweight babies.)

Postmature Babies: Too Late, Too Large

One might imagine that a baby who spends extra time in the womb might have some advantages, given the opportunity to continue growth undisturbed by the outside world. Yet **postmature infants**—those still unborn 2 weeks after the mother's due date—face several risks.

For example, the blood supply from the placenta may become insufficient to adequately nourish the still-growing fetus. Consequently, the blood supply to the brain may be decreased, leading to the potential of brain damage. Similarly, labor becomes riskier (for both the child and the mother) as a fetus who may be equivalent in size to a 1-month-old infant has to make its way through the birth canal (Shea, Wilcox, & Little, 1998; Fok, 2006).

Difficulties involving postmature infants are more easily prevented than those involving preterm babies, since medical practitioners can induce labor artificially if the pregnancy continues too long. Not only can certain drugs bring on labor, but physicians also have the option of performing cesarean deliveries, a form of delivery we consider next.

Cesarean Delivery: Intervening in the Process of Birth

As Elena entered her 18th hour of labor, the obstetrician who was monitoring her progress began to look concerned. She told Elena and her husband, Pablo, that the fetal monitor revealed that the fetus's heart rate had begun to repeatedly fall after each contraction. After trying some simple remedies, such as repositioning Elena on her side, the obstetrician came to the conclusion that the fetus was in distress. She told them that the baby should be delivered immediately, and to accomplish that, she would have to carry out a Cesarean delivery.

Elena became one of the more than 1 million mothers in the United States who have a cesarean delivery each year. In a **cesarean delivery** (sometimes known as a *c-section*), the baby is surgically removed from the uterus, rather than traveling through the birth canal.

Cesarean deliveries occur most frequently when the fetus shows distress of some sort. For instance, if the fetus appears to be in danger, as indicated by a sudden rise in its

TABLE 4-3   Childbirth-Related Leave Policies in the United States and 10 Peer Nations

Country	Type of Leave Provided	Total Duration (in months)	Payment Rate
United States	12 weeks of family leave	2.8	Unpaid
Canada	17 weeks maternity leave 10 weeks parental leave	6.2	15 weeks at 55% of prior earnings 55% of prior earnings
Denmark	28 weeks maternity leave 1 year parental leave	18.5	60% of prior earnings 90% of unemployment benefit rate
Finland	18 weeks maternity leave 26 weeks parental leave Child rearing leave until child is 3	36.0	70% of prior earnings 70% of prior earnings Flat rate
Norway	52 weeks parental leave 2 years child rearing leave	36.0	80% of prior earnings Flat rate
Sweden	18 months parental leave	18.0	12 months at 80% of prior earnings, 3 months flat rate, 3 months unpaid
Austria	16 weeks maternity leave 2 years parental leave	27.7	100% of prior earnings 18 months of unemployment benefit rate, 6 months unpaid
France	16 weeks maternity leave Parental leave until child is 3	36.0	100% of prior earnings Unpaid for one child; paid at flat rate (income is tested) for two or more
Germany	14 weeks maternity leave 3 years parental leave	39.2	100% of prior earnings Flat rate (income-tested) for 2 years, unpaid for 3rd year
Italy	5 months maternity leave 6 months parental leave	11.0	80% of prior earnings 30% of prior earnings
United Kingdom	18 weeks maternity leave 13 weeks parental leave	7.2	90% for 6 weeks and flat rate for 12 weeks, if sufficient work history; otherwise, flat rate

(*Source:* "From Maternity to Parental Leave Policies: Women's Health, Employment and Child and Family Well-Being," by S. B. Kamerman, 2000 (Spring), *The Journal of the American Women's Medical Association*, p. 55, table 1; "Parental Leave Policies: An Essential Ingredient in Early Childhood Education and Care Policies," by S. B. Kamerman, 2000. *Social Policy Report*, p. 14. Table 1.0)

high-quality medical care from the very beginning of pregnancy. Furthermore, barriers that prevent poor women from receiving such care should be reduced. For instance, programs can be developed that help pay for transportation to a health facility or for the care of older children while the mother is making a health-care visit. The cost of these programs is likely to be offset by the savings they make possible—healthy babies cost less than infants with chronic problems as a result of poor nutrition and prenatal care (Fangman et al., 1994; Kronenfeld, 2002).

Postpartum Depression: Moving from the Heights of Joy to the Depths of Despair

Renata had been overjoyed when she found out that she was pregnant and had spent the months of her pregnancy happily preparing for her baby's arrival. The birth was routine, the baby a healthy, pink-cheeked boy. But a few days after her son's birth, she sank into the depths of depression. Constantly crying, confused, feeling incapable of caring for her child, she was experiencing unshakable despair.

The diagnosis: a classic case of postpartum depression. *Postpartum depression*, a period of deep depression following the birth of a child, affects some 10% of all new mothers. Although it takes several forms, its main symptom is an enduring, deep feeling of sadness and unhappiness, lasting in some cases for months or even years. In about 1 in 500 cases, the symptoms are even worse, evolving into a total break with reality. In extremely rare instances, postpartum depression may turn deadly. For example, Andrea Yates, a mother in Texas who was charged with drowning all five of her children in a bathtub, was diagnosed with postpartum depression (Yardley, 2001; Misri, 2007).

For mothers who suffer from postpartum depression, the symptoms are often bewildering. The onset of depression usually comes as a complete surprise. Certain mothers do seem more likely to become depressed, such as those who have been clinically depressed at some point in the past or who have depressed family members. Furthermore, women who are unprepared for the range of emotions that follow the birth of a child—some positive, some negative—may be more prone to depression.

Finally, postpartum depression may be triggered by the pronounced swings in hormone production that occur after birth. During pregnancy, the production of the female hormones of estrogen and progesterone increase significantly. However, within the first 24 hours following birth, they plunge to normal levels. This rapid change may result in depression (Honey, Bennett, & Morgan, 2003; Klier et al., 2007).

Whatever the cause, maternal depression leaves its marks on the infant. As we'll see later in the chapter, babies are born with impressive social capacities, and they are highly attuned to the moods of their mothers. When depressed mothers interact with their infants, they are likely to display little emotion and to act detached and withdrawn. This lack of responsiveness leads infants to display fewer positive emotions and to withdraw from contact not only with their mothers but with other adults as well. In addition, children of depressed mothers are more prone to antisocial activities such as violence (Weinberg & Tronick, 1996; Hay et al., 2003; Nylen et al., 2006).

From an educator's perspective:

Why do you think the United States lacks effective educational and health-care policies that could reduce infant mortality rates overall and among poorer people? What arguments would you make to change this situation?

REVIEW ↵ mydevelopmentlab

1. Preterm infants, or premature infants, are born prior to _____ weeks after conception.

   Answer: 38

2. _____-_____-_____ infants weigh less than 1250 grams (around 2 1/4 pounds) or have been in the womb less than 30 weeks.

   Answer: Very-low-birthweight

3. In a _____ delivery, the baby is surgically removed from the uterus, rather than traveling through the birth canal.

   Answer: cesarean (or c-section)

4. Symptoms of _____ _____ include an enduring, deep feeling of sadness and unhappiness following the birth of a child.

   Answer: postpartum depression

To see more review questions, log on to MyDevelopmentLab.

The Competent Newborn

Relatives gathered around the infant car seat and its occupant, Kaita Castro. Born just 2 days ago, this is Kaita's 1st day home from the hospital with her mother. Kaita's nearest cousin, 4-year-old Tabor, seems uninterested in the new arrival. "Babies can't do anything fun. They can't even do anything at all," he says.

Kaita's cousin Tabor is partly right. There are many things babies cannot do. Neonates arrive in the world quite incapable of successfully caring for themselves, for example. Why are human infants born so dependent, whereas members of other species seem to arrive much better equipped for their lives?

One reason is that, in one sense, humans are born too soon. The brain of the average newborn is just one-fourth of what it will be at adulthood. In comparison, the brain of the macaque monkey, which is born after just 24 weeks of gestation, is 65% of its adult size. Because of the relative puniness of the infant human brain, some observers have suggested that we are propelled out of the womb some 6 to 12 months sooner than we ought to be.

In reality, if we stayed inside our mothers' bodies an additional half-year to a year, our heads would be so large that we'd never manage to get through the birth canal (Gould, 1977; Kotre & Hall, 1990). The relatively underdeveloped brain of the human newborn helps explain the infant's apparent helplessness. Because of this, the earliest views of newborns

focused on the things that they could not do, comparing them rather unfavorably to older members of the human species.

Today, however, such beliefs have taken a backseat to more favorable views of the neonate. As developmental researchers have begun to understand more about the nature of newborns, they have come to realize that infants enter this world with an astounding array of capabilities in all domains of development: physical, cognitive, and social.

Physical Competence: Meeting the Demands of a New Environment

The world faced by a neonate is remarkably different from the one it experienced in the womb. Consider, for instance, the significant changes in functioning that Kaita Castro encountered as she began the first moments of life in her new environment (summarized in Table 4-4).

Kaita's most immediate task was to bring sufficient air into her body. Inside her mother, oxygen was delivered through the umbilical cord, which also provided a means for taking away carbon dioxide. The realities of the outside world are different: Once the umbilical cord was cut, Kaita's respiratory system needed to begin its lifetime's work.

For Kaita, the task was automatic. As we noted earlier, most newborn babies begin to breathe on their own as soon as they are exposed to air. The ability to breathe immediately is a good indication that the respiratory system of the normal neonate is reasonably well developed, despite its lack of rehearsal in the womb.

Neonates emerge from the uterus more practiced in other types of physical activities. For example, newborns such as Kaita show several **reflexes**—unlearned, organized involuntary responses that occur automatically in the presence of certain stimuli. Some of these reflexes are well re-

hearsed, having been present for several months before birth. The *sucking reflex* and the *swallowing reflex* permit Kaita to begin right away to ingest food. The *rooting reflex*, which involves turning in the direction of a source of stimulation (such as a light touch) near the mouth, is also related to eating. It guides the infant toward potential sources of food that are near its mouth, such as a mother's nipple.

Not all of the reflexes that are present at birth lead the newborn to seek out desired stimuli such as food. For instance, Kaita can cough, sneeze, and blink—reflexes that help her to avoid stimuli that are potentially bothersome or hazardous. (We discuss more reflexes in Chapter 5.)

Kaita's sucking and swallowing reflexes, which help her to consume her mother's milk, are coupled with the newfound ability to digest nutriments. The newborn's digestive system initially produces feces in the form of *meconium*, a greenish-black material that is a remnant of the neonate's days as a fetus.

Because the liver, a critical component of the digestive system, does not always work effectively at first, almost half of all newborns develop a distinctly yellowish tinge to their bodies and eyes. This change in color is a symptom of *neonatal jaundice*. It is most likely to occur in preterm and low-weight neonates, and it is typically not dangerous. Treatment most often consists of placing the baby under fluorescent lights or administering medicine.

Newborns enter the world preprogrammed to find, take in, and digest food in the form of the rooting, sucking, and swallowing reflexes.

TABLE 4-4	Kaita Castro's First Encounters Upon Birth

1. As soon as she is through the birth canal, Kaita automatically begins to breathe on her own after no longer being attached to the umbilical cord that provided precious oxygen in the womb.

2. Reflexes—unlearned, organized involuntary responses that occur in the presence of stimuli—begin to take over. Sucking and swallowing reflexes permit Kaita immediately to ingest food.

3. The rooting reflex, which involves turning in the direction of a source of stimulation, guides Kaita toward potential sources of food that are near her mouth, such as her mother's nipple.

4. Kaita begins to cough, sneeze, and blink—reflexes that help her avoid stimuli that are potentially bothersome or hazardous.

5. Her senses of smell and taste are highly developed. Physical activities and sucking increase when she smells peppermint. Her lips pucker when a sour taste is placed on her lips.

6. Objects with colors of blue and green seem to catch Kaita's attention more than other colors, and she reacts sharply to loud, sudden noises. She will also continue to cry if she hears other newborns cry, but will stop if she hears a recording of her own voice crying.

Sensory Capabilities: Experiencing the World

Just after Kaita was born, her father was certain that she looked directly at him. Did she, in fact, see him?

This is a hard question to answer for several reasons. For one thing, when sensory experts talk of "seeing," they mean both a sensory reaction due to the stimulation of the visual sensory organs and an interpretation of that stimulation (the distinction, as you might recall from an introductory psychology class, between sensation and perception). In addition, as we'll discuss further when we consider sensory capabilities during infancy in Chapter 5, it is tricky, to say the least, to pinpoint the specific sensory skills of newborns who lack the ability to explain what they are experiencing.

Still, we do have some answers to the question of what newborns are capable of seeing and, for that matter, questions about their other sensory capabilities. For example, it is clear that neonates such as Kaita can see to some extent. Although their visual acuity is not fully developed, newborns actively pay attention to certain types of information in their environment.

For instance, neonates pay closest attention to portions of scenes in their field of vision that are highest in information, such as objects that sharply contrast with the rest of their environment. Furthermore, infants can discriminate different levels of brightness. There is even evidence suggesting that newborns have a sense of size constancy. They seem aware that objects stay the same size even though the size of the image on the retina varies with distance (A. Slater, Mattock, & Brown, 1990; A. Slater & Johnson, 1998; Chien et al., 2006).

In addition, not only can newborn babies distinguish different colors but also they seem to prefer particular ones. For example, they are able to distinguish among red, green, yellow, and blue, and they take more time staring at blue and green objects—suggesting a partiality for those colors (Adams, Mauer, & Davis, 1986; Dobson, 2000; Alexander & Hines, 2002).

Newborns are clearly capable of hearing. They react to certain kinds of sounds, showing startle reactions to loud, sudden noises, for instance. They also exhibit familiarity with certain sounds. For example, a crying newborn will continue to cry when he or she hears other newborns crying. If the baby hears a recording of its own crying, on the other hand, he or she is more likely to stop crying, as if recognizing the familiar sound (Dondi, Simion, & Caltran, 1999; Fernald, 2001).

As with vision, however, the degree of auditory acuity is not as great as it will be later. The auditory system is not completely developed. Moreover, amniotic fluid, which is initially trapped in the middle ear, must drain out before the newborn can fully hear. In addition to sight and hearing, the other senses also function quite adequately in the newborn. It is obvious that newborns are sensitive to

Starting at birth, infants are able to distinguish colors and even show preferences for particular ones.

touch. For instance, they respond to stimuli such as the hairs of a brush, and they are aware of puffs of air so weak that adults cannot notice them. (In fact, the newborn's sensitivity to touch—and to pain—is part of the controversy surrounding circumcision of male infants, as we consider in the *From Research to Practice* box).

At birth, the senses of smell and taste are also well developed. Newborns suck and increase other physical activity when the odor of peppermint is placed near the nose. They also pucker their lips when a sour taste is placed on them, and respond with appropriate facial expressions to other tastes as well. Such findings clearly indicate that the senses of touch, smell, and taste not only are present at birth but also are reasonably sophisticated (Marlier, Schaal, & Soussignan, 1998; Cohen & Cashon, 2003).

In one sense, the sophistication of the sensory systems of newborns such as Kaita is not surprising. After all, the typical neonate has had 9 months to prepare for his or her encounter with the outside world. As we discussed in Chapter 2, human sensory systems begin their development well before birth. Furthermore, the passage through the birth canal may place babies in a state of heightened sensory awareness, preparing them for the world that they are about to encounter for the first time.

Early Learning Capabilities

One-month-old Michael Samedi was on a car ride with his family when a thunderstorm suddenly began. The storm rapidly became violent, and flashes of lightning were quickly followed by loud thunderclaps. Michael was clearly disturbed and began to sob. With each new thunderclap, the pitch and fervor of his crying increased. Unfortunately, before very long it wasn't just the sound of the thunder that would raise Michael's anxiety; the sight of the lightning alone was enough to make him cry out in fear. In fact, even as an adult, Michael feels his chest tighten and his stomach churn at the mere sight of lightning.

Classical Conditioning The source of Michael's fear is classical conditioning, a basic type of learning first identified by Ivan Pavlov (and first discussed in Chapter 2). In **classical conditioning**, an organism learns to respond in a particular way to a neutral stimulus that normally does not bring about that type of response. Pavlov discovered that by repeatedly pairing two stimuli, such as the sound of a bell and the arrival of meat, he could make hungry dogs learn to respond (in this case by salivating) not only when the meat was presented but also even when the bell was sounded without the presence of meat (Pavlov, 1927).

The key feature of classical conditioning is stimulus substitution, in which a stimulus that doesn't naturally bring about a particular response is paired with a stimulus that does evoke that response. Repeatedly presenting the two stimuli together results in the second stimulus taking on the properties of the first. In effect, the second stimulus is substituted for the first.

Operant conditioning A form of learning in which a voluntary response is strengthened or weakened, depending on its association with positive or negative consequences

FROM RESEARCH to PRACTICE
Circumcision of Newborn Male Infants: The Unkindest Cut?

Throughout much of her pregnancy, Sandi Levine and her husband Jim were worried about the health of their unborn son. Genetic testing and other diagnostic procedures revealed no genetic disorders, and the birth of Adam Levine was uneventful. Yet they were barely out of the delivery room before Jim and Sandi were confronted with a difficult decision they had been avoiding.

"I don't see the problem," Jim argued. "It's just tradition. Millions of boys are circumcised and they grow up just fine."

"Tradition or not, Adam's our son," countered Sandi. "I feel like we're forcing our will on him. I just don't know if one of his first experiences in life should be a painful, irreversible surgical procedure. I mean, tradition aside, what's the point?"

The Levines' dilemma is not an unusual one. More than a million male newborn infants—over 57%—are circumcised every year in the United States. *Circumcision* is the surgical removal of part or all of the foreskin from the penis. Although the procedure may be performed on males of any age, it is most commonly performed shortly after birth (National Center for Health Statistics, 2006).

Until recently, the arguments in favor of circumcision have sounded a lot like Jim Levine's. Parents usually choose to have their newborn sons circumcised for a combination of health, religious, cultural, or traditional reasons. But although it is one of the most commonly performed surgical procedures in the United States, national medical associations such as the American Medical Association, the American Academy of Pediatrics, and the American Academy of Family Physicians have long maintained that circumcision is not medically necessary and do not recommend that it be performed routinely (American Academy of Pediatrics, 1999a; American Academy of Family Physicians, 2002).

But emerging research findings have added a new twist to the controversy: Circumcision provides protection against future sexually transmitted diseases. A number of studies conducted in Africa (where HIV infection rates are high) have found that circumcised men are less likely to become infected with HIV, even when other factors such as hygiene are controlled. In fact, large experimental studies being conducted in Kenya and Uganda were stopped early when the researchers found compelling evidence that circumcision

of healthy adult males approximately cut their risk of subsequent HIV infection in half (the studies were stopped early to allow the uncircumcised men in the control groups to get circumcised for the same protective benefits) (National Institutes of Health, 2006; Rennie, Muula, & Westreich, 2007; Shaffer et al., 2007).

Circumcision may produce other medical benefits as well. The risk of urinary tract infections is reduced in circumcised males, especially during the 1st year of life. The benefit is small, however, given that this risk is already low in uncircumcised males. The risk of penile cancer is about 3 times higher in uncircumcised men than in men who were circumcised at birth, but again, the overall risk is already very low even for uncircumcised men (Frisch et al., 1995; American Academy of Pediatrics, 1999a).

Circumcision opponents nevertheless raise some important concerns. Estimates range widely on the rate at which complications arise from circumcision, but the most common ones are bleeding and infection, both of which are usually minor and easily treated. More serious complications, such as failure to remove enough of the foreskin or inflammation of the urinary opening, occur more rarely. Furthermore, as we'll discuss in the next chapter, the procedure is also painful and stressful to the infant, as it is typically done without general anesthesia. Some experts believe that circumcision reduces sensation and sexual pleasure later in life, while others argue that the overriding concern is the ethicality of removing a healthy, intact part of a person's body without his own consent when there is no medical need to do so (American Academy of Pediatrics, 1999a; American Academy of Family Physicians, 2002; Payne et al., 2007).

One thing is clear: Circumcision is a controversial practice that evokes strong emotions on both sides of the debate. The decision to circumcise a newborn son or not is a complex one that may ultimately come down to personal preferences and values (Goldman, 2004).

- Do you agree that tradition alone is enough of a reason to circumcise a male infant? Why or why not?

- Considering that men can be circumcised at any age, is protection against HIV infection enough of a medical reason to circumcise a male infant? Why or why not?

One of the earliest examples of the power of classical conditioning in shaping human emotions was demonstrated in the case of an 11-month-old infant known by researchers as "Little Albert" (Watson & Rayner, 1920). Although he initially adored furry animals and showed no fear of rats, Little Albert learned to fear them when, during a laboratory demonstration, a loud noise was sounded every time he played with a cute and harmless white rat. In fact, the fear generalized to other furry objects, including rabbits and even a Santa Claus mask. (By the way, such a demonstration would be considered unethical today, and it would never be conducted.)

Infants are capable of learning very early through classical conditioning. For instance, 1- and 2-day-old newborns who are

stroked on the head just before being given a drop of a sweet-tasting liquid soon learn to turn their heads and suck at the head-stroking alone. Clearly, classical conditioning is in operation from the time of birth (Blass, Ganchrow, & Steiner, 1984; Dominguez, Lopez, & Molina, 1999).

Operant Conditioning But classical conditioning is not the only mechanism through which infants learn; they also respond to **operant conditioning**. As noted in Chapter 2, operant conditioning is a form of learning in which a voluntary response is strengthened or weakened, depending on its association with positive or negative consequences. In operant conditioning, infants learn to act deliberately on their environments in order to

Developmental psychologist Tiffany Field carried out pioneering work on infants' facial expressions.

bring about some desired consequence. An infant who learns that crying in a certain way is apt to bring her parents' immediate attention is displaying operant conditioning.

Like classical conditioning, operant conditioning functions from the earliest days of life. For instance, researchers have found that even newborns readily learn through operant conditioning to keep sucking on a nipple when it permits them to continue hearing their mothers read a story or to listen to music (DeCasper & Fifer, 1980; Lipsitt, 1986).

Habituation Probably the most primitive form of learning is demonstrated by the phenomenon of habituation. **Habituation** is the decrease in the response to a stimulus that occurs after repeated presentations of the same stimulus.

Habituation in infants relies on the fact that when newborns are presented with a new stimulus, they produce an *orienting response*, in which they become quiet, attentive, and experience a slowed heart rate as they take in the novel stimulus. When the novelty wears off due to repeated exposure to the stimulus, the infant no longer reacts with this orienting response. If a new and different stimulus is presented, the infant once again reacts with an orienting response. When this happens, we can say that the infant has learned to recognize the original stimulus and to distinguish it from others.

Habituation occurs in every sensory system, and researchers have studied it in several ways. One is to examine changes in sucking, which stops temporarily when a new stimulus is presented. This reaction is not unlike that of an adult who temporarily puts down her knife and fork when a dinner companion makes an interesting statement to which she wishes to pay particular attention. Other measures of habituation include changes in heart rate, respiration rate, and the length of time an infant looks at a particular stimulus (Schöner & Thelen, 2006; Brune & Woodward, 2007; Farroni et al., 2007).

The development of habituation is linked to physical and cognitive maturation. It is present at birth and becomes more pronounced over the first 12 weeks of infancy. Difficulties involving habituation represent a signal of developmental problems such as mental retardation (Moon, 2002). (The three basic processes of learning that we've considered—classical conditioning, operant conditioning, and habituation are summarized in Table 4-5)

Social Competence: Responding to Others

Soon after Kaita was born, her older brother looked down at her in her crib and opened his mouth wide, pretending to be surprised. Kaita's mother, looking on, was amazed when it appeared that Kaita imitated his expression, opening her mouth as if *she* were surprised.

Researchers registered surprise of their own when they first found that newborns did indeed have the capability to imitate others' behavior. Although infants were known to have all the muscles in place to produce facial expressions related to basic emotions, the actual appearance of such expressions was assumed to be largely random.

However, research beginning in the late 1970s began to suggest a different conclusion. For instance, developmental researchers found that, when exposed to an adult modeling a behavior that the infant already performed spontaneously, such as opening the mouth or sticking out the tongue, the newborn appeared to imitate the behavior (Meltzoff & Moore, 1977; Meltzoff & Moore, 2002; Nagy, 2006).

Even more exciting were findings from a series of studies conducted by developmental psychologist Tiffany Field and her colleagues (Field, 1982; Field & Walden, 1982; Field et al., 1984). They initially showed that infants could discriminate among such basic facial expressions as happiness, sadness, and surprise. They then exposed newborns to an adult model with a happy, sad, or surprised facial expression.

TABLE 4-5	Learning in Infancy: Some Basic Processes	
Type	**Description**	**Example**
Classical Conditioning	A situation in which an organism learns to respond in a particular way to a neutral stimulus that normally does not bring about that type of response.	A hungry baby stops crying when her mother picks her up because she has learned to associate being picked up with subsequent feeding.
Operant Conditioning	A form of learning in which a voluntary response is strengthened or weakened, depending on its positive or negative consequences.	An infant who learns that smiling at his or her parents brings positive attention and may smile more often.
Habituation	The decrease in the response to a stimulus that occurs after repeated presentations of the same stimulus.	A baby who showed interest and surprise at first seeing a novel toy may show no interest after seeing the same toy several times.

States of arousal Different degrees of sleep and wakefulness through which newborns cycle, ranging from deep sleep to great agitation

TABLE 4-6	Factors That Encourage Social Interaction Between Full-Term Newborns and Their Parents	

Full-Term Newborn	Parent
Has organized states	Helps regulate infant's states
Attends selectively to certain stimuli	Provides these stimuli
Behaves in ways interpretable as specific communicative intent	Searches for communicative intent
Responds systematically to parent's acts	Wants to influence newborn, feel effective
Acts in temporally predictable ways	Adjusts actions to newborn's temporal rhythms
Learns from, adapts to parent's behavior	Acts repetitively and predictably

(*Source:* Eckerman & Oehler, 1992)

The results suggested that newborns produced a reasonably accurate imitation of the adult's expression.

However, subsequent research seemed to point to a different conclusion, as other investigators found consistent evidence only for a single imitative movement: sticking out the tongue. And even that response seemed to disappear around the age of 2 months. Because it seems unlikely that imitation would be limited to a single gesture and only appear for a few months, some researchers began to question the earlier findings. In fact, some researchers suggested that even sticking out the tongue was not imitation, but merely an exploratory behavior (Anisfeld, 1996; Bjorklund, 1997a; Jones, 2006, 2007; Tissaw, 2007).

The jury is still out on exactly when true imitation begins, although it seems clear that some forms of imitation begin very early in life. Such imitative skills are important, because effective social interaction with others relies in part on the ability to react to other people in an appropriate manner and to understand the meaning of others' emotional states. Consequently, newborns' ability to imitate provides them with an important foundation for social interaction later in life (Rogers & Williams, 2006; Zeedyk & Heimann, 2006; Legerstee & Markova, 2008).

Several other aspects of newborns' behavior also act as forerunners for more formal types of social interaction that they will develop as they grow. As shown in Table 4-6, certain characteristics of neonates mesh with parental behavior to help produce a social relationship between child and parent, as well as social relationships with others (C. O. Eckerman & Oehler, 1992).

For example, newborns cycle through various **states of arousal**, different degrees of sleep and wakefulness, ranging from deep sleep to great agitation. Although these cycles are disrupted immediately after birth, they quickly become more regularized. Caregivers become involved when they seek to aid the infant in transitions from one state to another. For instance, a father who rhythmically rocks his crying daughter in an effort to calm her is engaged in a joint activity that is a prelude to future social interactions of different sorts. Similarly, newborns tend to pay particular attention to their mothers' voices In turn, parents and others modify their speech when talking to infants, using a different pitch and tempo than they use with older children and adults (De Casper & Fifer, 1980; Trainor, Austin, & Desjardins, 2000; Kisilevsky, 2003; Newman & Hussain, 2006).

The ultimate outcome of the social interactive capabilities of the newborn infant, and the responses such behavior brings about from parents, is to pave the way for future social interactions. Just as the neonate shows remarkable skills on a physical and perceptual level, its social capabilities are no less sophisticated.

From a child-care worker's perspective: Developmental researchers no longer view the neonate as a helpless, incompetent creature, but rather as a remarkably competent, developing human being. What do you think are some implications of this change in viewpoint for methods of child rearing and child care?

REVIEW ↵ mydevelopmentlab

1. Infants learn through both classical and _____ conditioning.

   Answer: operant

2. The decrease in the response to a stimulus that occurs after repeated presentations of the same stimulus is called _____.

   Answer: habituation

3. The ability to _____ others' behavior and facial expressions provides the newborn with an important foundation for social interaction later in life.

   Answer: imitate

4. Newborns cycle through various _____, different degrees of sleep and wakefulness, ranging from deep sleep to great agitation.

   Answer: states of arousal

*To see more review questions, log on to MyDevelopmentLab

CASE STUDY

The Case of. . . No Place Like Home?

James and Roberta Calder can't quite agree on the best way for Roberta to give birth to her first child. James is enthralled by the idea of a natural, midwife-directed, at-home childbirth. His child by his first wife was born in a hospital, and he remembers the entire experience as impersonal, overmanaged, and excessively mechanical. He can still see his first wife's frightened, bewildered face as she watched dozens of people bustling about, treating her as a passive participant on what was, after all, her big day. If possible, he would like to spare Roberta that experience. After all, babies are born every day in all parts of the world, at home or out in a field—and usually without a doctor's intervention. Why should this birth be so different?

Roberta, in contrast, wants to give birth in a hospital. She approves of the idea of midwife deliveries and wants her birthing experience to be as natural as possible, but she knows too many women who tried the at-home route and ended up wishing they had the support personnel and equipment of a hospital. She knows many cases of delayed or denied anesthesia, breakneck trips to the emergency room for an unplanned cesarean, the sudden loss of a newborn's heartbeat, and the need for heavy intervention by a team of obstetricians. These stories have made her less than entirely comfortable with a home delivery.

Both Calders want to be understanding and cooperative, but both have clear ideas about how childbirth should proceed.

1. What ideas might Roberta suggest to help James overcome his distaste for hospital deliveries? Can the hospital experience be made more personal and natural?

2. Conversely, what ideas might James propose to address Roberta's fears about at-home delivery? Are there ways to make a home birth as safe as a hospital birth?

3. If you were asked to make a recommendation for Roberta and James, what questions would you ask them?

4. Roberta and James seem stuck on the question of at-home versus in-hospital birth. Are there other options that might address both parents' concerns? What are they, and how would they address those concerns?

5. Would your recommendation change if you found out that Roberta's mother and sisters all experienced long and painful labor and ultimately had to have cesareans? Why or why not?

◄ Looking Back

What is the normal process of labor?

- In the first stage of labor contractions occur about every 8 to 10 minutes, increasing in frequency, duration, and intensity until the mother's cervix expands. In the second stage of labor, which lasts about 90 minutes, the baby begins to move through the cervix and birth canal and ultimately leaves the mother's body. In the third stage of labor, which lasts only a few minutes, the umbilical cord and placenta are expelled from the mother.

- After it emerges, the newborn, or neonate, is usually inspected for irregularities, cleaned, and returned to its mother and father.

- Parents-to-be have a variety of choices regarding the setting for the birth, medical attendants, and whether to use pain-reducing medication. Sometimes, medical intervention, such as cesarean birth, becomes necessary.

What complications can occur at birth, and what are their causes, effects, and treatments?

- Preterm, or premature, infants, born fewer than 38 weeks following conception, generally have low birthweight, which can cause vulnerability to infection, respiratory distress syndrome, and hypersensitivity to environmental stimuli. They may even show adverse effects later in life, including slowed development, learning disabilities, behavior disorders, below-average IQ scores, and problems with physical coordination.

- Very-low-birthweight infants are in special danger because of the immaturity of their organ systems. However, medical advances have pushed the age of viability of the infant back to about 22 weeks following conception.

- Postmature babies, who spend extra time in their mothers' wombs, are also at risk. However, physicians can artificially induce labor or perform a cesarean delivery to address this situation. Cesarean deliveries are performed when the fetus is in distress, in the wrong position, or unable to progress through the birth canal.

- The infant mortality rate in the United States is higher than the rate in many other countries, and higher for low-income families than for higher income families.

- Postpartum depression, an enduring, deep feeling of sadness, affects about 10% of new mothers. In severe cases, its effects can be harmful to the mother and the child, and aggressive treatment may be employed.

What capabilities does the newborn have?

- Human newborns quickly master breathing through the lungs, and they are equipped with reflexes to help them eat, swallow, find food, and avoid unpleasant stimuli. Their sensory capabilities are also sophisticated.

- From birth, infants learn through habituation, classical conditioning, and operant conditioning. Newborns are able to imitate the behavior of others, a capability that helps them form social relationships and facilitates the development of social competence. ■

Epilogue

This chapter has covered the amazing and intense processes of labor and birth. There are a number of birthing options that are available to parents, and these options need to be weighed in light of possible complications that can arise during the birthing process. In addition to considering the remarkable progress that has been made regarding the various treatments and interventions available for babies that are too early or too late, we examined the grim topics of still-birth and infant mortality. We concluded with a discussion of the surprising capabilities of newborns and their early development of social competence.

Before we move on to a more detailed discussion of infants' physical development, return for a moment to the case of the premature birth of Hattie Thatcher, discussed in the Prologue. Using your understanding of the issues discussed in this chapter, answer the following questions.

1. Hattie was born more than 3 months early. Why was the fact that she was born alive so surprising? Can you discuss her birth in terms of "the age of viability"?

2. What procedures and activities were most likely set into motion immediately after her birth?

3. What dangers was Hattie subject to immediately after birth because of her high degree of prematurity? What dangers would be likely to continue into her childhood?

4. What ethical considerations affect the decision of whether the high costs of medical interventions for highly premature babies are justifiable? Who should pay those costs? ○

Key Terms and Concepts

neonate (p. 78)
episiotomy (p. 79)
Apgar scale (p. 79)
anoxia (p. 80)
bonding (p. 80)
preterm infants (p. 85)
low-birthweight infants (p. 85)
small-for-gestational-age infants (p. 85)
very-low-birthweight infants (p. 86)
postmature infants (p. 88)

cesarean delivery (p. 88)
fetal monitor (p. 89)
stillbirth (p. 89)
infant mortality (p. 89)
reflexes (p. 93)
classical conditioning (p. 94)
operant conditioning (p. 95)
habituation (p. 96)
states of arousal (p. 97)

○

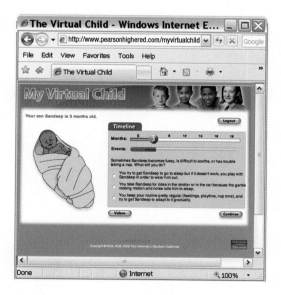

What decisions would you make while raising a child? What would the consequences of those decisions be?

Find out by logging onto **My Virtual Child** and raising your child from birth to 18 years.

1

Beginnings

Parents-to-be typically look forward to the birth of their child. They may speculate—just as developmentalists do—about the role of genetics and environment in their children's development, considering issues like intelligence, resemblance, personality, schooling, and neighborhood. For the birth itself, they have many options available. Some may choose to use a midwife rather than an obstetrician, an/or to give birth at a traditional hospital, but in a nontraditional way. And when the baby is born, the baby reacts to the sound of the mother's voice, which he or she first heard from inside the womb. This, in turn, fosters the bond between parents and infant.

What decisions would you make while raising a child? What would the consequences of those decisions be?

Find out by logging onto **My Virtual Child** and raising your child from birth to 18 years.

From a **Parent's** perspective

What strategies would you use to prepare yourself for the upcoming birth of your child? How would you evaluate the different options for prenatal care and delivery? How would you prepare your older child for the birth of a new baby?

HINT **Review pages 81–84**

Your response?

From a **Healthcare Provider's** perspective

How would you prepare new parents for the upcoming birth of their baby? How would you respond to their concerns and anxieties? What would you tell them about the different options they have for giving birth?

HINT **Review pages 81–84**

Your response?

Beginnings

Introduction to Development

- New parents may consider the role of genetics (nature) versus environment (nurture) in thinking about what their child would be like (p. 56)

- They also may consider how their new child will develop physically, intellectually (or cognitively), and socially (p. 56)

Prenatal Development

- All parents contribute 23 chromosomes each at conception. Their baby's sex is determined from the particular mix of one pair of chromosomes (p. 47)

- Many of an infant's characteristics will have a strong genetic component, but virtually all of them will represent some combination of genetics and environment (p. 55)

- An infant's prenatal development started as a fetus and progressed through a number of stages (p. 64)

Birth and the Newborn

- Some women's labor is intense and painful, although others experience labor in different ways due to individual and cultural differences (p. 78)

- Some choose to use a midwife, or one of several new birthing methods (p. 81)

- The vast majority of births are completely normal and successful (p. 72)

- Although a newborn seems helpless and dependent, from birth she actually possesses an array of useful capabilities and skills (p. 92)

From an **Educator's** perspective

What strategies might you use to teach parents-to-be about the stages of pregnancy and the process of birth? What might you tell them about infancy to prepare them for caring for their child?

HINT **Review pages 83–97**

Your response?

From **Your** perspective

What would you say to new parents about the impending birth of their child? What advice would you give them about prenatal care and their decision about the use of a midwife?

HINT **Review pages 63–84**

Your response?

5 Physical Development in Infancy

PROLOGUE: FIRST STEPS

We had warnings that his first steps would not be too far in the future. Josh had previously dragged himself up, and, clutching the side of chairs and tables, managed to progress slowly around our living room. For the last few weeks, he'd even been able to stand, unmoving, for several moments without holding on.

But walking? It seemed too early: Josh was only 10 months old, and the books we read told us that most children would not take their first steps on their own until they were a year old. And our older son, Jon, hadn't walked until he was 14 months of age.

So, when Josh suddenly lurched forward, taking one awkward step after another away from the safety of the furniture and moved toward the center of the room, we were astounded. Despite the appearance that he was about to keel over at any second, he moved one, then two, then three steps forward, until our awe at his accomplishment overtook our ability to count each step.

Josh tottered all the way across the room, until he reached the other side. Not quite knowing how to stop, he toppled over, landing in a happy heap. It was moment of pure glory.

▶ Looking Ahead

Josh's first steps at the age of 10 months was just one of the succession of milestones that characterize the dramatic physical attainments during infancy. In this chapter we consider the nature of physical development during infancy, a period that starts at birth and continues until the second birthday. We begin by discussing the pace of growth during infancy, noting obvious changes in height and weight as well as less apparent changes in the nervous system. We also consider how infants quickly develop increasingly stable patterns in such basic activities as sleeping, eating, and attending to the world.

Our discussion then turns to infants' thrilling gains in motor development as skills emerge that eventually will allow an infant to roll over, take the first step, and pick up a cookie crumb from the floor—skills that ultimately form the basis of later, even more complex behaviors. We start with basic, genetically determined reflexes and consider how even these may be modified through experience. We also discuss the nature and timing of the development of particular physical skills, look at whether their emergence can be speeded up, and consider the importance of early nutrition to their development.

Finally, we explore how infants' senses develop. We investigate how sensory systems such as hearing and vision operate, and how infants sort through the raw data from their sense organs and transform it into meaningful information.

After reading this chapter, you will be able to answer these questions:

- *How do the human body and nervous system develop?*
- *Does the environment affect the pattern of development?*
- *What developmental tasks must infants accomplish in this period?*
- *How does nutrition affect physical development?*
- *What sensory capabilities do infants possess?*

Growth and Stability

The average newborn weighs just over 7 pounds, which is less than the weight of the average Thanksgiving turkey. Its length is about 20 inches, shorter than a loaf of French bread. A newborn is helpless; if left to fend for itself, an infant could not survive.

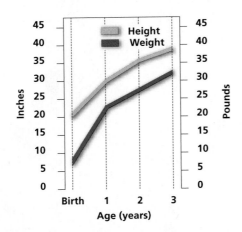

FIGURE 5-1 Height and Weight Growth

Although the greatest increase in height and weight occurs during the 1st year of life, children continue to grow throughout infancy and toddlerhood.
(*Source:* Cratty, 1979)

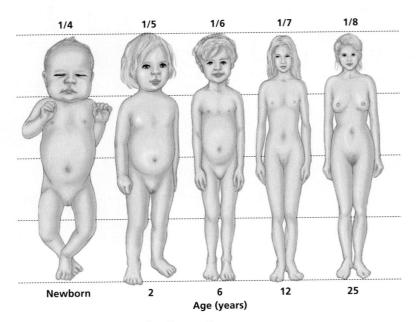

FIGURE 5-2 Decreasing Proportions

At birth, the head represents one-quarter of the neonate's body. By adulthood, the head is only one-eighth the size of the body. Why is the neonate's head so large?

Yet after just a few years, the story is very different. Babies become much larger, they are mobile, and they become increasingly independent. How does this growth happen? We can answer this question first by describing the changes in weight and height that occur over the first 2 years of life, and then by examining some of the principles that underlie and direct that growth.

Physical Growth: The Rapid Advances of Infancy

Infants grow at a rapid pace over the first 2 years of their lives (see Figure 5-1). By the age of 5 months, the average infant's birthweight has doubled to around 15 pounds. By the first birthday, the baby's weight has tripled to about 22 pounds. Although the pace of weight gain slows during the 2nd year, it still continues to increase. By the end of his or her 2nd year, the average child weighs around four times as much as he or she did at birth. Of course, there is a good deal of variation among infants. Height and weight measurements, which are taken regularly during physician's visits during a baby's 1st year, provide a way to spot problems in development.

The weight gains of infancy are matched by increased length. By the end of the 1st year, the typical baby grows almost a foot and is about 30 inches tall. By their second birthdays, children average a height of 3 feet.

Not all parts of an infant's body grow at the same rate. As we saw in Chapter 2, at birth, the head accounts for one-quarter of the newborn's entire body size. During the first 2 years of life, the rest of the body begins to catch up. By the age of 2 the baby's head is only one fifth of body length, and by adulthood it is only one-eighth (see Figure 5-2).

There also are gender and ethnic differences in weight and length. Girls generally are slightly shorter and weigh slightly less than boys, and these differences remain throughout childhood (and, as we will see later in the book, the disparities become considerably greater during adolescence). Furthermore, Asian infants tend to be slightly smaller than North American Caucasian infants, and African American infants tend to be slightly bigger than North American Caucasian infants.

Four Principles of Growth The disproportionately large size of infants' heads at birth is an example of one of four major principles that govern growth. The **cephalocaudal principle** states that growth follows a direction and pattern that begins with the head and upper body parts and then proceeds to the rest of the body. The word *cephalocaudal* is derived from Greek and Latin roots meaning "head-to-tail." The cephalocaudal growth principle means that we develop visual abilities (located in the head) well before we master the ability to walk (closer to the end of the body). The cephalocaudal principle operates both prenatally and after birth.

Proximodistal principle The principle that development proceeds from the center of the body outward	Principle of hierarchical integration The principle that simple skills typically develop separately and independently but are later integrated into more complex skills	Principle of the independence of systems The principle that different body systems grow at different rates	Neuron The basic nerve cell of the nervous system

TABLE 5-1 The Major Principles Governing Growth

Cephalocaudal Principle	Proximodistal Principle	Principle of Hierarchical Integration	Principle of the Independence of Systems
Growth follows a pattern that begins with the head and upper body parts and then proceeds to the rest of the body. Based on Greek and Latin roots meaning "head-to-tail."	Development proceeds from the center of the body outward. Based on the Latin words for "near" and "far."	Simple skills typically develop separately and independently. Later they are integrated into more complex skills.	Different body systems grow at different rates.

Three other principles (summarized in Table 5-1) help explain the patterns by which growth occurs. The **proximodistal principle** states that development proceeds from the center of the body outward. Based on the Latin words for "near" and "far," the proximodistal principle means that the trunk of the body grows before the extremities of the arms and legs. Similarly, it is only after growth has occurred in the arms and legs that the fingers and toes can grow. Furthermore, the development of the ability to use various parts of the body also follows the proximodistal principle. For instance, the effective use of the arms precedes the ability to use the hands.

Related to this is the way complex skills build upon simpler ones. The **principle of hierarchical integration** states that simple skills typically develop separately and independently. Later, however, these simple skills are integrated into more complex ones. Thus, the relatively complex skill of grasping something in the hand cannot be mastered until the developing infant learns how to control—and integrate—the movements of the individual fingers.

Finally, the fourth and last major principle of growth is the **principle of the independence of systems**, which suggests that different body systems grow at different rates. This principle means that growth in one system does not necessarily imply that growth is occurring in others. For instance, Figure 5-3 illustrates the patterns of growth for three very different systems: body size, which we've already discussed; the nervous system; and sexual characteristics. As you can see, both the rate and timing of these different aspects of growth are independent.

The Nervous System and Brain: The Foundations of Development

When Rina was born, she was the first baby among her parents' circle of friends. These young adults marveled at the infant, oohing and aahing at every sneeze and smile and whimper, trying to guess at their meaning. Whatever feelings, movements, and thoughts Rina was experiencing, they

were all brought about by the same complex network: the infant's nervous system. The *nervous system* is composed of the brain and the nerves that extend throughout the body.

Neurons are the basic cells of the nervous system. Figure 5-4 shows the structure of an adult neuron. Like all cells in the body, neurons have a cell body containing a nucleus. But unlike other cells, neurons have a distinctive ability: They can communicate with other cells, using a cluster of fibers called *dendrites* at one end. Dendrites receive messages from other cells. At their opposite end, neurons have a long extension called an *axon*, the part of the neuron that carries messages destined for other neurons. Neurons do not actually touch

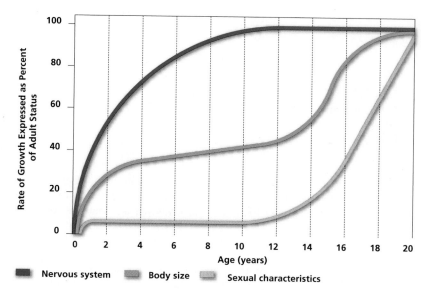

FIGURE 5-3 Maturation Rates

Different body systems mature at different rates. For instance, the nervous system is highly developed during infancy, while body size is considerably less developed. The development of sexual characteristics lags even more, maturing at adolescence. Do you think this pattern is universal among all species, or is it unique to humans?

(*Source:* Bornstein & Lamb, 1992a)

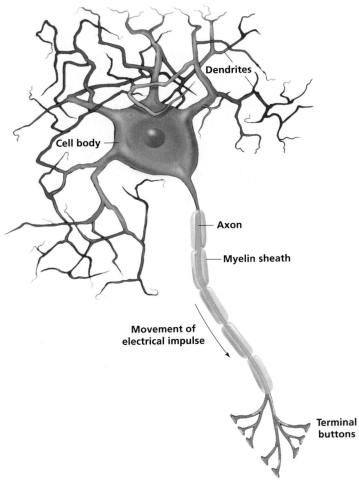

FIGURE 5-4 The Neuron

The basic element of the nervous system, the neuron is composed of a number of components.
(*Source:* Van de Graaff, 2000)

one another. Rather, they communicate with other neurons by means of chemical messengers, *neurotransmitters*, that travel across the small gaps, known as **synapses**, between neurons.

Although estimates vary, infants are born with between 100 and 200 billion neurons. To reach this number, neurons multiply at an amazing rate prior to birth. In fact, at some points in prenatal development, cell division creates some 250,000 additional neurons every minute.

At birth, most neurons in an infant's brain have relatively few connections to other neurons. During the first 2 years of life, however, a baby's brain will establish billions of new connections between neurons. Furthermore, the network of neurons becomes increasingly complex, as illustrated in Figure 5-5. The intricacy of neural connections continues to

increase throughout life. In fact, in adulthood a single neuron is likely to have a minimum of 5,000 connections to other neurons or other body parts.

Synaptic Pruning Babies are actually born with many more neurons than they need. In addition, although synapses are formed throughout life, based on our changing experiences, the billions of new synapses infants form during the first 2 years are more numerous than necessary. What happens to the extra neurons and synaptic connections?

Like a farmer who, in order to strengthen the vitality of a fruit tree, prunes away unnecessary branches, brain development enhances certain capabilities in part by a "pruning down" of unnecessary neurons. Neurons that do not become interconnected with other neurons as the infant's experience of the world increases become unnecessary. They eventually die out, increasing the efficiency of the nervous system.

As unnecessary neurons are being reduced, connections between remaining neurons are expanded or eliminated as a result of their use or disuse during the baby's experiences. If a baby's experiences do not stimulate certain nerve connections, these, like unused neurons, are eliminated—a process called *synaptic pruning*. The result of synaptic pruning is to allow established neurons to build more elaborate communication networks with other neurons. Unlike most other aspects of growth, then, the development of the nervous system proceeds most effectively through the loss of cells (Johnson, 1998; Mimura, Kimoto, & Okada, 2003; Iglesias et al., 2005).

After birth, neurons continue to increase in size. In addition to growth in dendrites, the axons of neurons become coated with **myelin**, a fatty substance that, like the insulation on an electric wire, provides protection and speeds the transmission of nerve impulses. So, even though many neurons are lost, the increasing size and complexity of the remaining ones contribute to impressive brain growth. A baby's brain triples its weight during the first 2 years of life, and it reaches more than three-fourths of its adult weight and size by the age of 2.

The neurons also reposition themselves as they grow, becoming arranged by function. Some move into the **cerebral cortex**, the upper layer of the brain, while others move to *subcortical levels*, which are below the cerebral cortex. The subcortical levels, which regulate such fundamental activities as breathing and heart rate, are the most fully developed at birth. As time passes, however, the cells in the cerebral cortex, which are responsible for higher-order processes such as thinking and reasoning, become more developed and interconnected. Although the brain is protected by the bones of the skull, it is highly sensitive to some forms of injury. One particularly devastating injury comes from a form of child abuse called *shaken baby syndrome* in which an infant is shaken by a caretaker, usually out of frustration or anger due to a baby's crying. Shaking can lead the brain to rotate within the skull, causing blood vessels to tear and

Plasticity The degree to which a developing structure or behavior is modifiable due to experience

Sensitive period A specific, but limited, time, usually early in an organism's life, during which the organism is particularly susceptible to environmental influences relating to some particular facet of development

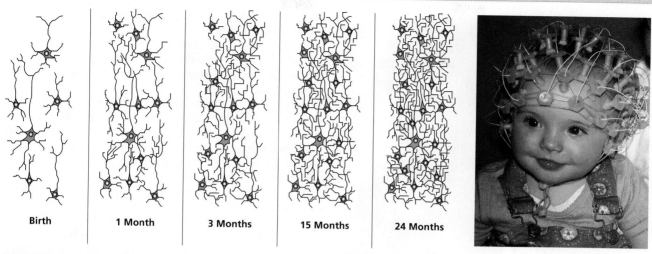

| Birth | 1 Month | 3 Months | 15 Months | 24 Months |

FIGURE 5-5 Neuron Networks

Over the first 2 years of life, networks of neurons become increasingly complex and interconnected. Why are these connections important? (*Source:* Conel, 1930/1963)

destroying the intricate connections between neurons. The results can be devastating, leading to severe medical problems, long-term physical and learning disabilities, and often death (Miehl, 2005; Gerber & Coffman, 2007; Jayawant & Parr, 2007).

Environmental Influences on Brain Development

Brain development, much of which unfolds automatically because of genetically predetermined patterns, is also strongly susceptible to environmental influences. In fact, the brain's **plasticity**, the degree to which a developing structure or behavior is modifiable due to experience, is relatively great for the brain. For instance, as we've seen, an infant's sensory experience affects both the size of individual neurons and the structure of their interconnections.

Consequently, compared with those brought up in more enriched environments, infants raised in severely restricted settings are likely to show differences in the brain's structure and weight (Cicchetti, 2003; Cirulli, Berry, & Alleva, 2003; Couperus & Nelson, 2006).

Work with nonhumans has helped reveal the nature of the brain's plasticity. Studies have compared rats raised in an unusually visually stimulating environment to those raised in more typical and less interesting cages. Results of such research show that areas of the brain associated with vision are both thicker and heavier for the rats reared in enriched settings (Black & Greenough, 1986; Cynader, 2000; Degroot, Wolff, & Nomikos, 2005).

On the other side of the coin, environments that are unusually barren or in some way restricted may impede the brain's development. Again, work with nonhumans provides some intriguing data. In one study, kittens were fitted with goggles that restricted their vision so that they could view only vertical lines (Hirsch & Spinelli, 1970). When the cats grew up and had their goggles removed, they were unable to see horizontal lines, although they saw vertical lines perfectly well. Analogously, kittens whose goggles restricted their vision of vertical lines early in life were effectively blind to vertical lines during their adulthood—although their vision of horizontal lines was accurate.

On the other hand, when goggles are placed on older cats who have lived relatively normal lives as kittens, such results are not seen after the goggles are removed. The conclusion is that there is a sensitive period for the development of vision. As we noted in Chapter 1, a **sensitive period** is a specific, limited time, usually early in an organism's life, during which the organism is particularly susceptible to environmental influences relating to some particular facet of development. A sensitive period may be associated with a behavior—such as the development of full vision—or with the development of a structure of the body, such as the configuration of the brain (Uylings, 2006).

The existence of sensitive periods raises several important issues. For one thing, it suggests that unless an infant receives a certain level of early environmental stimulation during a sensitive period, the infant may suffer damage or fail to develop capabilities that can never be fully remedied. If this is true, providing successful later intervention for such children may prove to be particularly challenging (Gottlieb & Blair, 2004).

The opposite question also arises: Does an unusually high level of stimulation during sensitive periods produce developmental gains beyond what a more commonplace level of stimulation would provide?

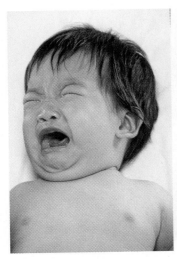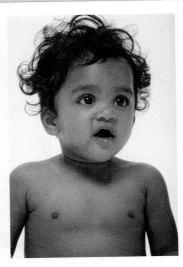

Infants cycle through various states, including crying and alertness. These states are integrated through bodily rhythms.

Such questions have no simple answers. Determining how unusually impoverished or enriched environments affect later development is one of the major questions addressed by developmental researchers as they try to find ways to maximize opportunities for developing children.

In the meantime, many developmentalists suggest that there are many simple ways parents and caregivers can provide a stimulating environment that will encourage healthy brain growth. Cuddling, playing, and talking and singing to babies will help enrich their environment. In addition, holding children and reading to them is important, as it simultaneously engages multiple senses, including vision, hearing, and touch (Lafuente et al., 1997; Garlick, 2003).

Integrating the Bodily Systems: The Life Cycles of Infancy

If you happen to overhear new parents discuss their newborns, chances are one or several bodily functions will be the subject. In the first days of life, infants' body rhythms—waking, eating, sleeping, urination, and defecation—govern the infant's behavior, often at seemingly random times.

These most basic activities are controlled by a variety of bodily systems. Although each of these individual behavioral patterns probably is functioning quite effectively, it takes some time and effort for infants to integrate the separate behaviors. In fact, one of the neonate's major missions is to make its individual behaviors work in harmony, helping it, for example, to sleep through the night (Ingersoll & Thoman, 1999; Waterhouse & DeCoursey, 2004).

Rhythms and States One of the most important ways that behavior becomes integrated is through the development of various **rhythms**, which are repetitive, cyclical patterns of behavior. Some rhythms are immediately obvious, such as the change from wakefulness to sleep. Others are more subtle, but still easily noticeable, such as breathing and sucking patterns. Still other rhythms may require careful observation to be noticed.

For instance, newborns may go through periods in which they jerk their legs in a regular pattern every minute or so. Although some of these rhythms are apparent just after birth, others emerge slowly over the 1st year as the neurons of the nervous system become increasingly integrated (Groome et al., 1997; Thelen & Bates, 2003).

One of the major body rhythms is that of an infant's **state**, the degree of awareness it displays to both internal and external stimulation. As can be seen in Table 5-2, such states include various levels of wakeful behaviors, such as alertness, fussing, and crying, and different levels of sleep as well. Each change in state brings about an alteration in the amount of stimulation required to get the infant's attention (Balaban, Snidman, & Kagan, 1997; Diambra & Menna-Barretio, 2004).

Some of the different states that infants experience produce changes in electrical activity in the brain. These changes are reflected in different patterns of electrical *brain waves*, which can be measured by a device called an *electroencephalogram (EEG)*. Starting at 3 months before birth, these brain wave patterns are relatively irregular. However, by the time an infant reaches the age of 3 months, a more mature pattern emerges and the brain waves become more regular (Burdjalov, Baumgart, & Spitzer, 2003; Thordstein et al., 2006).

Sleep: Perchance to Dream? At the beginning of infancy, the major state that occupies a baby's time is sleep—much to the relief of exhausted parents, who often regard sleep as a welcome respite from caregiving responsibilities. On average, newborn infants sleep some 16 to 17 hours a day. However, there are wide variations. Some sleep more than 20 hours, while others sleep as little as 10 hours a day (Peirano, Algarin, & Uauy, 2003; Buysse, 2005).

Infants sleep a lot, but you probably shouldn't ever wish to "sleep like a baby." The sleep of infants comes in fits and starts. Rather than covering one long stretch, sleep initially comes in spurts of around 2 hours, followed by periods of wakefulness. Because of this, infants—and their sleep-deprived parents—are "out of sync" with the rest of the world, for whom sleep comes at night and wakefulness during the day (Groome et al., 1997; Burnham et al., 2002). Most babies do not sleep through the night for several months. Parents' sleep is interrupted, sometimes several times a night, by the infant's cries for food and physical contact.

Luckily for their parents, infants gradually settle into a more adultlike pattern. After a week, babies sleep a bit more at night and are awake for slightly longer periods during the day. Typically, by the age of 16 weeks infants begin to sleep as

TABLE 5-2 Primary Behavioral States

States	Characteristics	Percentage of Time When Alone in State
Awake States		
Alert	Attentive or scanning, the infant's eyes are open, bright, and shining.	6.7
Nonalert waking	Eyes are usually open, but dull and unfocused. Varied, but typically high motor activity.	2.8
Fuss	Fussing is continuous or intermittent, at low levels.	1.8
Cry	Intense vocalizations occurring singly or in succession.	1.7
Transition States Between Sleep and Waking		
Drowse	Infant's eyes are heavy-lidded, but opening and closing slowly. Low level of motor activity.	4.4
Daze	Open, but glassy and immobile eyes. State occurs between episodes of Alert and Drowse. Low level of activity.	1.0
Sleep–wake transition	Behaviors of both wakefulness and sleep are evident. Generalized motor activity; eyes may be closed, or they open and close rapidly. State occurs when baby is awakening.	1.3
Sleep States		
Active sleep	Eyes closed; uneven respiration; intermittent rapid eye movements. Other behaviors: smiles, frowns, grimaces, mouthing, sucking, sighs, and sigh-sobs.	50.3
Quiet sleep	Eyes are closed and respiration is slow and regular. Motor activity limited to occasional startles, sigh-sobs, or rhythmic mouthing.	28.1
Transitional Sleep State		
Active–quiet transition sleep	During this state, which occurs between periods of Active Sleep and Quiet Sleep, the eyes are closed and there is little motor activity. Infant shows mixed behavioral signs of Active Sleep and Quiet Sleep.	1.9

(*Source:* Adapted from Thoman & Whitney, 1990)

much as 6 continuous hours at night, and daytime sleep falls into regular naplike patterns. Most infants sleep through the night by the end of the 1st year, and the total amount of sleep they need each day is down to about 15 hours (Thoman & Whitney, 1989; Mao et al., 2004).

Hidden beneath the supposedly tranquil sleep of infants is another cyclic pattern. During periods of sleep, infants' heart rates increase and become irregular, their blood pressure rises, and they begin to breathe more rapidly (Montgomery-Downs & Thomas, 1998). Sometimes, although not always, their closed eyes begin to move in a back-and-forth pattern, as if they were viewing an action-packed scene. This period of active sleep is similar, although not identical, to the **rapid eye movement (REM) sleep** that is found in older children and adults and is associated with dreaming.

Infants sleep in spurts, often making them out of sync with the rest of the world.

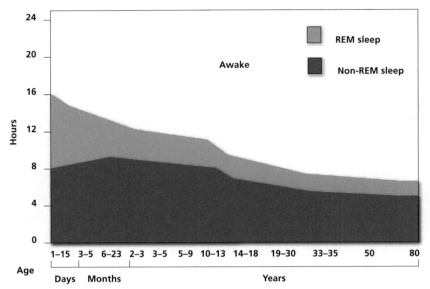

FIGURE 5-6 REM Sleep Through the Life Span

As we age, the proportion of REM sleep increases as the proportion of non-REM sleep declines. In addition, the total amount of sleep falls as we get older.
(Adapted from Roffwarg, Muzio, & Dement, 1966)

At first, this active, REM-like sleep takes up around one-half of an infant's sleep, compared with just 20% of an adult's sleep (see Figure 5-6). However, the quantity of active sleep quickly declines, and by the age of 6 months, amounts to just one-third of total sleep time (Coons & Guilleminault, 1982; Burnham et al., 2002; Staunton, 2005).

The appearance of active sleep periods that are similar to REM sleep in adults raises the intriguing question of whether infants dream during those periods. No one knows the answer, although it seems unlikely. First of all, young infants do not have much to dream about, given their relatively limited experiences. Furthermore, the brain waves of sleeping infants appear to be qualitatively different from those of adults who are dreaming. It is not until the baby reaches 3 or 4 months of age that the wave patterns become similar to those of dreaming adults, suggesting that young infants are not dreaming during active sleep—or at least are not doing so in the same way as adults do (McCall, 1979; Parmelee & Sigman, 1983; Zampi, Fagioli, & Salzarulo, 2002).

Then what is the function of REM sleep in infants? Although we don't know for certain, some researchers think it provides a means for the brain to stimulate itself—a process called *autostimulation* (Roffwarg, Muzio, & Dement, 1966). Stimulation of the nervous system would be particularly important in infants, who spend so much time sleeping and relatively little time in alert states.

Infants' sleep cycles seem largely prepro-grammed by genetic factors, but environmental influences also play a part. For instance, both long- and short-term stressors in infants' environments (such as a heat wave) can affect their sleep patterns. When environmental circumstances keep babies awake, sleep, when at last it comes, is apt to be less active (and quieter) than usual (Halpern, MacLean, & Baumeister, 1995; Goodlin-Jones, Burnham, & Anders, 2000).

Cultural practices also affect infants' sleep patterns. For example, among the Kipsigis of Africa, infants sleep with their mothers at night and are allowed to nurse whenever they wake. In the daytime, they accompany their mothers during daily chores, often napping while strapped to their mothers' backs. Because they are often out and on the go, Kipsigis infants do not sleep through the night until much later than babies in Western societies, and for the first 8 months of life, they seldom sleep longer than 3 hours at a stretch. In comparison, 8-month-old infants in the United States may sleep as long as 8 hours at a time (Super & Harkness, 1982; Anders & Taylor, 1994; Gerard, Harris, & Thach, 2002).

SIDS: The Unanticipated Killer

For a tiny percentage of infants, the rhythm of sleep is interrupted by a deadly affliction: sudden infant death syndrome, or SIDS. **Sudden infant death syndrome (SIDS)** is a disorder in which seemingly healthy infants die in their sleep. Put to bed for a nap or for the night, an infant simply never wakes up.

SIDS strikes about 1 in 1,000 infants in the United States each year. Although it seems to occur when the normal patterns of breathing during sleep are interrupted, scientists have been unable to discover why that might happen. It is clear that infants don't smother or choke; they die a peaceful death, simply ceasing to breathe.

Although no reliable means for preventing the syndrome has been found, the American Academy of Pediatrics now suggests that babies sleep on their backs rather than on their sides or stomachs—called the *back-to-sleep* guideline. In addition, they suggest that parents consider giving their babies a pacifier during naps and bedtime (Task Force on Sudden Infant Death Syndrome, 2005).

The number of deaths from SIDS has decreased significantly since these guidelines were developed (see Figure 5-7). Still, SIDS is the leading cause of death in children under the age of 1 year (Eastman, 2003; Daley, 2004; Blair, et al., 2006). Some infants are more at risk for SIDS than are others. For instance, boys and African Americans are at greater risk. In addition, low birthweight and low Apgar scores found at birth are associated with SIDS, as is having a mother who smokes during pregnancy. Some evidence also suggests that a brain defect that affects breathing may produce SIDS. In a small number of cases, child abuse may be the actual cause. Still, there is no clear-cut factor that explains why some infants die from the syndrome. SIDS is found in children of every race and socioeconomic group and in children who have had no apparent health problems (Fleming, Tsogt, & Blair, 2006; Howard, Kirkwood, & Latinovic, 2006; Paterson et al., 2007).

From a social worker's perspective:

What are some cultural or subcultural influences that might affect parents' willingness to accept recommendations from physicians and other experts?

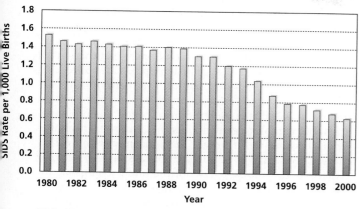

FIGURE 5-7 Declining Rates of SIDS

In the United States, SIDS rates have dropped dramatically as parents have become more informed and put babies to sleep on their backs instead of their stomachs.

(*Source:* American SIDS Institute, based on data from the Centers for Disease Control and the National Centers for Health Statistics, 2004)

Many hypotheses have been suggested to explain why infants die from SIDS. These include such problems as undiagnosed sleep disorders, suffocation, nutritional deficiencies, problems with reflexes, and undiagnosed illness. Still, the actual cause of SIDS remains elusive (Hunt & Hauck, 2006; Lipsitt, 2003; Fleming, Tsogt, & Blair, 2006).

Because parents are unprepared for the death of an infant from SIDS, the event is particularly devastating. Parents often feel guilt, fearing that they were neglectful or somehow contributed to their child's death. Such guilt is unwarranted, since nothing has been identified so far that can invariably prevent SIDS (Krueger, 2006).

REVIEW ↵ **mydevelopmentlab**

1. _____ are the basic cells of the nervous system.

   Answer: Neurons

2. _____ is the degree to which a developing structure or behavior is modifiable due to experience.

   Answer: Plasticity

3. One of the most important ways behavior becomes integrated is through the development of various body _____, which are repetitive, cyclical patterns of behavior.

   Answer: rhythms

4. At the beginning of infancy, _____ is the major state that occupies a baby's time.

   Answer: sleep

*To see more review questions, log on to MyDevelopmentLab.

Motor Development

Suppose you were hired by a genetic engineering firm to redesign newborns and were charged with replacing the current version with a new, more mobile one. The first change you'd probably consider in carrying out this (luckily, fictitious) job would be in the conformation and composition of the baby's body.

The shape and proportions of newborn babies are simply not conducive to easy mobility. Their heads are so large and heavy that young infants lack the strength to raise them. Because their limbs are short in relation to the rest of the body, their movements are further impeded. Furthermore, their bodies are mainly fat, with a limited amount of muscle; the result is that they lack strength.

Fortunately, it doesn't take too long before infants begin to develop a remarkable amount of mobility. In fact, even at birth they have an extensive repertoire of behavioral possibilities brought about by innate reflexes, and their range of motor skills grows rapidly during the first 2 years of life.

Reflexes: Our Inborn Physical Skills

When her father pressed 3-day-old Christina's palm with his finger, she responded by tightly winding her small fist around his finger and grasping it. When he moved his finger upward, she held on so tightly that it seemed he might be able to lift her completely off her crib mattress.

The Basic Reflexes In fact, her father was right: Christina probably could have been lifted in this way. The reason for her resolute grip was activation of one of the dozens of

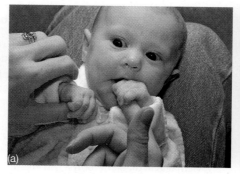
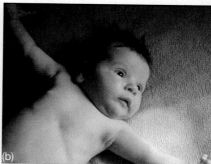
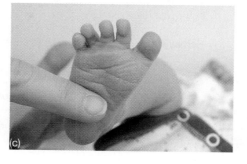

Infants show (a) the rooting and grasping reflexes, (b) the startle reflex, and (c) the Babinski reflex.

Reflexes unlearned, organized involuntary responses that occur automatically in the presence of certain stimuli

reflexes with which infants are born. **Reflexes** are unlearned, organized, involuntary responses that occur automatically in the presence of certain stimuli. Newborns enter the world with a repertoire of reflexive behavioral patterns that help them adapt to their new surroundings and serve to protect them.

As we can see from the list of reflexes in Table 5-3, many reflexes clearly represent behavior that has survival value, helping to ensure the well-being of the infant. For instance, the *swimming reflex* makes a baby who is lying face down in a body of water paddle and kick in a sort of swimming motion. The obvious consequence of such behavior is to help the baby move from danger and survive until a caregiver can come to its rescue. Similarly, the *eye-blink reflex* seems designed to protect the eye from too much direct light, which might damage the retina.

Given the protective value of many reflexes, it might seem beneficial for them to remain with us for our entire lives. In fact, some do: The eye-blink reflex remains functional throughout the full life span. On the other hand, quite a few reflexes, such as the swimming reflex, disappear after a few months. Why should this be the case?

Researchers who focus on evolutionary explanations of development attribute the gradual disappearance of reflexes to the increase in voluntary control over behavior that occurs as infants become more able to control their muscles. In addition, it may be that reflexes form the foundation for future, more complex behaviors. As these more intricate behaviors become well learned, they encompass the earlier reflexes (Myklebust & Gottlieb, 1993; Lipsitt, 2003). It may be that reflexes stimulate parts of the brain responsible for more complex behaviors, helping them develop. For example, some researchers argue that exercise of the stepping reflex helps the brain's cortex later develop the ability to walk. As evidence, developmental psychologist Philip R. Zelazo and his colleagues conducted a study in which they provided 2-week-old infants practice in walking for four sessions of 3 minutes each over a 6-week period. The results showed that

TABLE 5-3	Some Basic Reflexes in Infants		
Reflex	**Approximate Age of Disappearance**	**Description**	**Possible Function**
Rooting reflex	3 weeks	Neonate's tendency to turn its head toward things that touch its cheek.	Food intake
Stepping reflex	2 months	Movement of legs when held upright with feet touching the floor.	Prepares infants for independent locomotion
Swimming reflex	4–6 months	Infant's tendency to paddle and kick in a sort of swimming motion when lying face down in a body of water.	Avoidance of danger
Moro reflex	6 months	Activated when support for the neck and head is suddenly removed. The arms of the infant are thrust outward and then appear to grasp onto something.	Similar to primates' protection from falling
Babinski reflex	8–12 months	An infant fans out its toes in response to a stroke on the outside of its foot.	Unknown
Startle reflex	Remains in different form	An infant, in response to a sudden noise, flings out its arms, arches its back, and	Protection
Eye-blink reflex	Remains	Rapid shutting and opening of eye on exposure to direct light.	Protection of eye from direct light
Sucking reflex	Remains	Infant's tendency to suck at things that touch its lips.	Food intake
Gag reflex	Remains	An infant's reflex to clear its throat.	Prevents choking

the children who had the walking practice actually began to walk unaided several months earlier than those who had had no such practice. Zelazo suggests that the training produced stimulation of the stepping reflex, which in turn led to stimulation of the brain's cortex, readying the infant earlier for independent locomotion (Zelazo et al., 1993; Zelazo, 1998).

Do these findings suggest that parents should make out-of-the-ordinary efforts to stimulate their infant's reflexes? Probably not. Although the evidence shows that intensive practice may produce an earlier appearance of certain motor activities, there is no evidence that the activities are performed qualitatively any better in practiced infants than in unpracticed infants. Furthermore, even when early gains are found, they do not seem to produce an adult who is more proficient in motor skills.

In fact, structured exercise may do more harm than good. According to the American Academy of Pediatrics, structured exercise for infants may lead to muscle strain, fractured bones, and dislocated limbs, consequences that far outweigh the unproven benefits that may come from the practice (American Academy of Pediatrics, 1988).

Ethnic and Cultural Differences and Similarities in Reflexes

Although reflexes are, by definition, genetically determined and universal throughout all infants, there are actually some cultural variations in the ways they are displayed. For instance, consider the *Moro reflex* (often called the *startle response*), which is activated when support for the neck and head is suddenly removed. The Moro reflex consists of the infant's arms thrusting outward and then appearing to seek to grasp onto something. Most scientists feel that the Moro reflex represents a leftover response that we humans have inherited from our nonhuman ancestors. The Moro reflex is an extremely useful behavior for monkey babies, who travel about by clinging to their mothers' backs. If they lose their grip, they fall down unless they are able to grasp quickly onto their mother's fur—using a Moro-like reflex (Prechtl, 1982; Zafeiriou, 2004).

The Moro reflex is found in all humans, but it appears with significantly different vigor in different children. Some differences reflect cultural and ethnic variations (Freedman, 1979). For instance, Caucasian infants show a pronounced response to situations that produce the Moro reflex. Not only do they fling out their arms, but also they cry and respond in a generally agitated manner. In contrast, Navajo babies react to the same situation much more calmly. Their arms do not flail out as much, and they cry only rarely.

In some cases, reflexes can serve as helpful diagnostic tools for pediatricians. Because reflexes emerge and disappear on a regular timetable, their absence—or presence—at a given point of infancy can provide a clue that something may be amiss in an infant's development. (Even for adults, physicians include reflexes in their diagnostic bag of tricks, as anyone knows who has had his or her knee tapped with a rubber mallet to see if the lower leg jerks forward.)

Reflexes evolved because they had, at one point in humankind's history, survival value. For example, the sucking reflex automatically helps infants obtain nourishment, and the rooting reflex helps it search for the presence of a nipple. In addition, some reflexes also serve a social function, promoting caregiving and nurturance. For instance, Christina's father, who found his daughter gripping his finger tightly when he pressed her palm, probably cares little that she is simply responding with an innate reflex. Instead, he will more likely view his daughter's action as responsiveness to him, a signal perhaps of increasing interest and affection on her part. As we will see in Chapter 6, when we discuss the social and personality development of infants, such apparent responsiveness can help cement the growing social relationship between an infant and her caregivers.

Motor Development in Infancy: Landmarks of Physical Achievement

Probably no physical changes are more obvious—and more eagerly anticipated—than the increasing array of motor skills that babies acquire during infancy. Most parents can remember their child's first steps with a sense of pride and awe in how quickly he changed from a helpless infant, unable even to roll over, into a person who could navigate quite effectively in the world.

Gross Motor Skills Even though the motor skills of newborn infants are not terribly sophisticated, at least compared with attainments that will soon appear, young infants still are able to accomplish some kinds of movement. For instance, when placed on their stomachs they wiggle their arms and legs and may try to lift their heavy heads. As their strength increases, they are able to push hard enough against the surface on which they are resting to propel their bodies in different directions. They often end up moving backward rather than forward, but by the age of 6 months they become rather accomplished at moving themselves in particular directions. These initial efforts are the forerunners of crawling, in which babies coordinate the motions of their arms and legs and propel themselves

This 5-month-old girl demonstrates her gross motor skills.

By 4 months of age, infants are able to reach toward an object with some degree of precision.

Dynamic systems theory
A theory of how motor skills
develop and are coordinated

forward. Crawling appears typically between 8 and 10 months. (Figure 5-8 provides a summary of some of the milestones of normal motor development.)

Walking comes later. At around the age of 9 months, most infants are able to walk by supporting themselves on furniture, and half of all infants can walk well by the end of their 1st year of life.

At the same time infants are learning to move around, they are perfecting the ability to remain in a stationary sitting position. At first, babies cannot remain seated upright without support. But they quickly master this ability, and most are able to sit without support by the age of 6 months.

Fine Motor Skills As infants are perfecting their gross motor skills, such as sitting upright and walking, they are also making advances in their fine motor skills. For instance, by the age of 3 months, infants show some ability to coordinate the movements of their limbs.

Furthermore, although infants are born with a rudimentary ability to reach toward an object, this ability is neither very sophisticated nor very accurate, and it disappears around the age of 4 weeks. A different, more precise, form of reaching reappears at 4 months. It takes some time for infants to coordinate successful grasping after they reach out, but in fairly short order they are able to reach out and hold on to an object of interest (Claxton, Keen, & McCarty, 2003).

The sophistication of fine motor skills continues to grow. By the age of 11 months, infants are able to pick up objects as small as marbles—something caregivers need to be concerned about, because the next place such objects often go next is the mouth. By the time they are 2 years old, children can carefully hold a cup, bring it to their lips, and take a drink without spilling a drop.

Grasping, like other motor advances, follows a sequential developmental pattern in which simple skills are combined with more sophisticated ones. For example, infants first begin picking things up with their whole hand. As they get older, they use a *pincer grasp*, where thumb and index finger meet to form a circle. The pincer grasp allows for considerably more precise motor control.

3.2 months: rolling over	3.3 months: grasping rattle	5.9 months: sitting without support	7.2 months: standing while holding on
8.2 months: grasping with thumb and finger	11.5 months: standing alone well	12.3 months: walking well	14.8 months: building tower of two cubes
16.0 months: placing pegs in a board	16.6 months: walking up steps	23.8 months: jumping in place	33.0 months: copies circle

FIGURE 5-8 Milestones of Motor Development

Fifty percent of children are able to perform each skill at the month indicated in the figure. However, the specific timing at which each skill appears varies widely. For example, one-quarter of children are able to walk well at 11.1 months; by 14.9 months, 90% of children are walking well. Is knowledge of such average benchmarks helpful or harmful to parents?

(Adapted from Frankenburg et al., 1992)

Dynamic Systems Theory: How Motor Development Is Coordinated

Although it is easy to think about motor development in terms of a series of individual motoric achievements, the reality is that each of these skills does not develop in a vacuum. Each skill (such as a baby's ability to pick up a spoon and guide it to her lips) advances in the context of other motor abilities (such as the ability to reach out and lift the spoon in the first place). Furthermore, as motor skills are developing, so also are nonmotoric skills such as visual capabilities.

Developmentalist Esther Thelen has created an innovative theory to explain how motor skills develop and are coordinated. **Dynamic systems theory** describes how motor behaviors are assembled. By "assembled," Thelen means the coordination of a variety of skills that develop in a child, ranging from the development of an infant's muscles, its perceptual abilities and nervous system, as well as its motivation to carry out particular motor activities, and support from the environment (Thelen, 2002; Thelen & Bates, 2003; Gershkoff-Stowe & Thelen, 2004).

Norms The average performance of a large sample of children of a given age

Brazelton Neonatal Behavioral Assessment Scale (NBAS) A measure designed to determine infants' neurological and behavioral responses to their environment

According to dynamic systems theory, motor development in a particular sphere, such as beginning to crawl, is not just dependent on the brain initiating a "crawling program" that permits the muscles to propel the baby forward. Instead, crawling requires the coordination of muscles, perception, cognition, and motivation. The theory emphasizes how children's exploratory activities, which produce new challenges as they interact with their environment, lead them to advancements in motor skills.

Dynamic systems theory is noteworthy for its emphasis on a child's own motivation (a cognitive state) in advancing important aspects of motor development. For example, infants need to be motivated to touch something out of their reach to develop the skills they need to crawl to it. The theory also may help explain individual differences in the emergence of motor abilities in different children, which we consider next.

Developmental Norms: Comparing the Individual to the Group

Keep in mind that the timing of the milestones in motor development that we have been discussing is based on norms. **Norms** represent the average performance of a large sample of children of a given age. This measure permits comparisons between a particular child's performance on a particular behavior and the average performance of the children in the norm sample.

For instance, one of the most widely used techniques to determine infants' normative standing is the **Brazelton Neonatal Behavior Assessment Scale (NBAS)**, a measure designed to determine infants' neurological and behavioral responses to their environment.

The NBAS provides a supplement to the traditional Apgar test (discussed in Chapter 3) that is given immediately following birth. Taking about 30 minutes to administer, the NBAS includes 27 separate categories of responses that constitute four general aspects of infants' behavior: interactions with others (such as alertness and cuddliness); motor behavior; physiological control (such as the ability to be soothed after being upset); and responses to stress (Brazelton, 1973, 1990; M. Davis & Emory, 1995; Canals, Fernandez-Ballart, & Esparo, 2003).

Although the norms provided by scales such as the NBAS are useful in making broad generalizations about the timing of various behaviors and skills, they must be interpreted with caution. Because norms are averages, they mask substantial individual differences in the times when children attain various achievements. For example, some children, like Josh, whose first steps were described earlier, may be ahead of the norm. Other perfectly healthy children may be a bit behind the norm. Norms also may hide the fact that the sequence in which various behaviors are achieved may differ somewhat from one child to another.

Norms are useful only to the extent that they are based on data from a large, heterogeneous, culturally diverse sample of children. Unfortunately, many of the norms on which developmental researchers have traditionally relied have been based on groups of infants who are predominantly Caucasian and from the middle- and upper-socioeconomic strata. The reason: much of the research was conducted on college campuses, using the children of graduate students and faculty.

This limitation would not be critical if no differences existed in the timing of development in children from different cultural, racial, and social groups. But they do. For example, as a group, African American babies show more rapid motor development than Caucasian babies throughout infancy. Moreover, there are significant variations related to cultural factors, as we discuss next (Gartstein et al., 2003; deOnis et al., 2007).

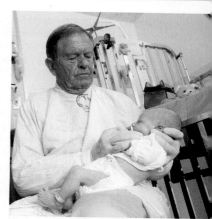

T. Berry Brazelton devised the Brazelton Neonatal Behavioral Assessment Scale (NBAS), which measures infants' neurological and behavioral responses.

DEVELOPMENTAL DIVERSITY

The Cultural Dimensions of Motor Development

Among the Ache people, who live in the rain forest of South America, infants face an early life of physical restriction. Because the Ache lead a nomadic existence, living in a series of tiny camps in the rain forest, open space is at a premium. Consequently, for the first few years of life, infants spend nearly all their time in direct physical contact with their mothers. Even when they are not physically touching their mothers, they are permitted to venture no more than a few feet away.

Infants among the Kipsigis people, who live in a more open environment in rural Kenya, Africa, lead quite a different existence. Their lives are filled with activity and exercise. Parents seek to teach their children to sit up, stand, and walk from the earliest days of infancy. For example, very young infants are placed in shallow holes in the ground designed to keep them in an upright position. Parents begin to teach their children to walk starting at the 8th week of life. The infants are held with their feet touching the ground, and they are pushed forward.

Clearly, the infants in these two societies lead very different lives (Super, 1976; Kaplan & Dove, 1987). But do the relative lack of early motor stimulation for Ache infants and the efforts of the Kipsigis to encourage motor development really make a difference?

The answer is both yes and no. It's yes, in that Ache infants tend to show delayed motor development, relative both to Kipsigis infants and to children raised in Western societies. Although their social abilities are no different, Ache children tend to begin walking at around 23 months, about a year later than the typical child in the United States. In contrast, Kipsigis children, who are encouraged in their motor development, learn to sit up and walk several weeks earlier, on average, than U.S. children.

In the long run, however, the differences among Ache, Kipsigis, and Western children disappear. By late childhood, about age 6, there is no evidence of differences in general, overall motor skills among Ache, Kipsigis, and Western children.

As we see with the Ache and Kipsigis babies, variations in the timing of motor skills seem to depend in part on parental expectations of what is the "appropriate" schedule for the emergence of specific skills. For instance, one study examined the motor skills of infants who lived in the same city in England, but whose mothers varied in ethnic origin. In the research, English, Jamaican, and Indian mothers' expectations were first assessed regarding several markers of their infants' motor skills. The Jamaican mothers expected their infants to sit and walk significantly earlier than the time frame denoted by English and Indian mothers—and the actual emergence of these activities was in line with their expectations. The source of the Jamaican infants' earlier mastery seemed to lie in the treatment of the children by their parents. For instance, Jamaican mothers gave their children practice in stepping quite early in infancy (Hopkins & Westra, 1989, 1990).

In sum, cultural factors help determine the time at which specific motor skills appear. Activities that are an intrinsic part of a culture are more apt to be purposely taught to infants in that culture, leading to the potential of their earlier emergence (Nugent, Lester, & Brazelton, 1989).

It is not all that surprising that children in a given culture who are expected by their parents to master a particular skill, and who are taught components of that skill from an early age, are more likely to be proficient in that skill earlier than are children from other cultures with no such expectations and no such training. The larger question, however, is whether the earlier emergence of a basic motor behavior in a given culture has lasting consequences for specific motor skills and for achievements in other domains. On this issue, the jury is still out.

One thing that is clear, however, is that there are certain limitations on how early a skill can emerge. It is physically impossible for 1-month-old infants to stand and walk, regardless of the encouragement and practice they may get within their culture. Consequently, parents who are eager to accelerate their infants' motor development should be cautioned not to hold overly ambitious goals. In fact, they might well ask themselves whether it matters if an infant acquires a motor skill a few weeks earlier than his or her peers.

The most reasonable answer is "no." Although some parents may take pride in a child who walks earlier than other babies (just as some parents may be concerned over a delay of a few weeks), in the long run the timing of this activity will probably make no difference. ────────────────────⬤

Nutrition in Infancy: Fueling Motor Development

Rosa sighed as she sat down to nurse the baby—again. She had fed 5-week-old Juan about every hour today, and he still seemed hungry. Some days, it seemed like all she did was breast-feed her baby. "Well, he must be going through a growth spurt," she decided, as she settled into her favorite rocking chair and put the baby to her nipple.

The rapid physical growth that occurs during infancy is fueled by the nutrients that infants receive. Without proper nutrition, infants cannot reach their physical potential, and they may suffer cognitive and social consequences as well (Tanner & Finn-Stevenson, 2002; Costello, Compton, & Keeler, 2003; Gregory, 2005).

Although there are vast individual differences in what constitutes appropriate nutrition—infants differ in terms of growth rates, body composition, metabolism, and activity levels—some broad guidelines do hold. In general, infants should consume about 50 calories per day for each pound they weigh—an allotment that is twice the suggested caloric intake for adults (Dietz & Stern, 1999; Skinner et al., 2004).

Typically, though, it's not necessary to count calories for infants. Most infants regulate their caloric intake quite effectively on their own. If they are allowed consume as much they seem to want, and not pressured to eat more, they will do fine.

Malnutrition *Malnutrition*, the condition of having an improper amount and balance of nutrients, produces several results, none good. For instance, malnutrition is more common among children living in many developing countries than it is among children who live in more industrialized, affluent countries. Malnourished children in these countries begin to show a slower growth rate by the age of 6 months. By the time they reach the age of 2 years, their height and weight are only 95% the height and weight of children in more industrialized countries.

Children who have been chronically malnourished during infancy later score lower on IQ tests and tend to do less well in school. These effects may linger even after the children's diet has improved substantially (Grantham-McGregor, Ani, & Fernald, 2001; Ratanachu-Ek, 2003).

The problem of malnutrition is greatest in underdeveloped countries, where overall 10% of infants are severely malnourished. In some countries the problem is especially severe. For example, 37% of North Korean children are chronically malnourished, suffering moderate to severe malnutrition (World Food Programme, 2008; also see Figure 5-9).

Problems of malnourishment are not restricted to developing countries, however. In the United States, some 13 million children—17%—live in poverty, which puts them at risk for malnutrition. In fact, the proportion of children living in low-income families has risen since 2000. Overall, some 20% of families who have children 3 years old and younger live in poverty, and 44% are classified as low income. And, as we can see in Figure 5-10, the poverty rates are even higher for Latino, African American, and American Indian families (Duncan & Brooks-Gunn, 2000; Douglas-Hall & Chau, 2007).

Because of social service programs, children in the United States rarely become severely malnourished, but children living in poverty remain susceptible to *undernutrition*, in which there is some deficiency in diet. In fact, as many as a quarter of 1- to 5-year-old children in the United States have diets that fall below the minimum caloric intake recommended by nutritional experts. Although the consequences are not as severe as those of malnutrition, undernutrition also has long-term costs. For instance, cognitive development later in childhood is affected by even mild to moderate undernutrition (Sigman, 1995; Pollitt et al., 1996; Tanner & Finn-Stevenson, 2002).

Severe malnutrition during infancy may lead to several disorders. Malnutrition during the 1st year can produce *marasmus*, a disease in which infants stop growing. Marasmus, attributable to a severe deficiency in proteins and calories, causes the body to waste away and ultimately results in death. Older children are susceptible to *kwashiorkor*, a disease in which a child's stomach, limbs, and face swell with water. To a casual observer, it appears that a child with kwashiorkor is actually chubby. However, this is an illusion: The child's body is in fact struggling to make use of the few nutrients that are available.

From an educator's perspective: What might be some of the reasons that malnourishment, which slows physical growth, also harms IQ scores and school performance? How might malnourishment affect education in Third-World countries?

In some cases, infants who receive sufficient nutrition behave as if they have been deprived of food. Looking as though they suffer from marasmus, they are underdeveloped, listless, and apathetic. The real cause, though, is emotional: They lack sufficient love and emotional support. In such cases, known as **nonorganic failure to thrive**, children stop growing not for biological reasons but due to a lack of stimulation and attention from their parents. Usually occurring by the age of 18 months, nonorganic failure to thrive can be reversed through intensive parent training or by placing children in a foster home where they can receive emotional support.

Obesity It is clear that malnourishment during infancy has potentially disastrous consequences for an infant. Less clear, however, are the effects of *obesity*, defined as weight greater than 20% above the average for a given height. Although there is no clear correlation between obesity during infancy and obesity at the age of 16 years, some research suggests that overfeeding during infancy may lead to the creation of an excess of fat cells, which remain in the body throughout life and may predispose a person to be overweight. In fact, weight gains during infancy are associated with weight at age 6. Other research shows an association between obesity after the age of 6 and adult obesity, suggesting that obesity in babies ultimately may be found to be associated with adult weight problems. A clear link between overweight babies and overweight adults, however, has not yet been found (Toschke et al., 2004; Dennison et al., 2006; Stettler, 2007).

Although the evidence linking infant obesity to adult obesity is inconclusive, what is apparent is that the societal view that "a fat baby is a healthy baby" is not necessarily

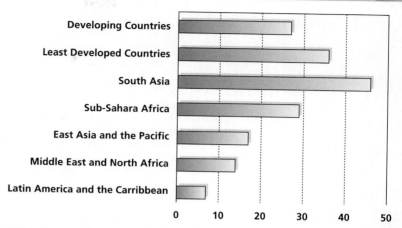

FIGURE 5-9 Underweight Children

The percentage of children under 5 years who are moderately or severely underweight.
(*Source:* UNICEF, *The State of the World's Children*, 2005)

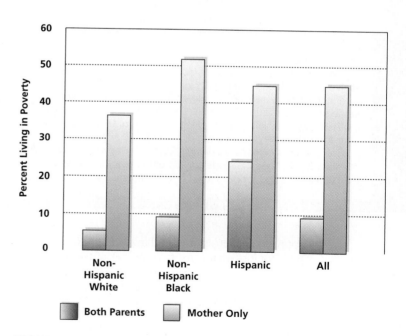

FIGURE 5-10 Children Living in Poverty

The incidence of poverty among children under the age of 3 is particularly high in minority and single-parent households. (Figures are shown only for single mothers, and not fathers, because 97% of all children under 3 who live with a single parent live with their mothers; only 3% live with their fathers.)
(*Source:* National Center for Children in Poverty at the Joseph L. Mailman School of Public Health of Columbia University, 2007)

correct. Given the lack of clarity regarding infant obesity, parents should concentrate less on their baby's weight and more on providing appropriate nutrition. During the period of infancy, concerns about weight need not be central, as long as infants are provided with an

Fast-Food Babies

At 20 pounds and 27 inches long, Zachary Miller was a happy and healthy, but not especially active, baby. "The pediatrician told me, 'The big ones don't like to move,'" says Zach's mom, Ellie. "She told me to put him on the floor and on his tummy as often as possible. He hates that. But it does get him to push up on his arms and roll over."

At 7 months, Zach was already overweight. (Sachs, 2006, p. 112).

Childhood obesity is on the rise, and as Zachary Miller's story suggests, the problem sometimes begins at a very early age. Children of overweight parents are particularly at risk of becoming overweight themselves, but heredity seems to be only part of the explanation. At issue is what children are eating in their first years of life—or rather, what their parents are feeding them (Flegal et al., 2006; Breen, Plomin, & Wardle, 2006; Mennella, Kennedy, & Beauchamp, 2006).

Research shows that children's food preferences are determined early on. One study that tracked children's eating habits over a period of 6 years found that the strongest predictor of preferred foods at age 8 was preferred foods at age 4, and moreover that children were more likely to accept new foods before age 4 than after that time. In other words, children develop their taste for certain foods at an early age and then tend to stick with those foods as they get older (Skinner et al., 2002).

But the real issue is what children are developing a taste for: The same study also found that children tended to like foods that their mothers liked, which is unsurprising—the mothers tended not to offer foods that they themselves did not like.

So what kinds of foods are parents feeding their young children? Another study examined the foods actually eaten over the course of a day by 3,000 infants and toddlers aged 4 to 24 months. Some of the findings were startling: Infants as young as 7 months were being fed adult diets. About a quarter of infants and toddlers between 7 and 24 months were eating no vegetables and about the same proportion were eating no fruits. Even among the children who were eating vegetables, French fries topped the list for toddlers over 18 months—and it was in the top three vegetables for infants between 9 and 12 months. By 8 months, nearly half of infants were already consuming desserts or sweetened drinks. By 24 months, a majority of toddlers were eating pastries and nearly half were drinking sweetened drinks (Fox et al., 2004).

These findings reveal a problem with how we are feeding our children in the critical early years, when they are developing food preferences and eating habits that will likely remain with them through adulthood. Convenience foods that are high in sugar and fat but low in nutrients may be a significant component of parents' diets, but if parents provide these same foods to their young children, they may be paving the way to a lifetime of unhealthful dietary habits. Experts recommend that such foods be offered to infants and toddlers sparingly, if at all. Better options include fruits, vegetables, or grains in place of snack foods, and water, milk, or pure fruit juices in place of sweetened drinks. Providing these foods may take extra planning and effort on the part of parents—especially when they are foods that parents don't particularly like themselves; experts agree that doing so is essential to stem the growing problem of childhood obesity (O'Dea & Wilson, 2006; Linsday et al., 2006; Sallis & Glanz, 2006).

- If you were to advise new parents on the right and wrong foods to offer their newborn child, what would you tell them?
- Why might parents be inclined to serve their young children unhealthful adult foods? Why might they not be serving the children more fruits and vegetables instead?

appropriate diet, as discussed in the *From Research to Practice* box. But just what constitutes proper nutrition? Probably the biggest question revolves around whether infants should be breast-fed or given a formula of commercially processed cow's milk with vitamin additives, as we consider next.

Breast or bottle? Although infants receive adequate nourishment from breast- or bottle-feeding, most authorities agree that "breast is best."

Breast or Bottle?

Fifty years ago, if a mother asked her pediatrician whether breast-feeding or bottle-feeding was better, she would have received a simple and clear-cut answer: Bottle-feeding was the preferred method. Starting around the 1940s, the general belief among child-care experts was that breast-feeding was an obsolete method that put children unnecessarily at risk.

With bottle-feeding, the argument went, parents could keep track of the amount of milk their baby was receiving and could thereby ensure that the child was taking in sufficient nutrients. In contrast, mothers who breast-fed their babies could never be certain just how much milk their infants were getting. Use of the bottle was also supposed to help mothers keep their feedings to a rigid schedule of one bottle every 4 hours, the recommended procedure at that time. Today, however, a mother would get a very different answer to the same question. Child-care authorities agree: For the first 12 months of life, there is no better food for an infant than breast milk. Breast milk not only contains all the nutrients necessary for growth, but it also seems to offer some degree of immunity to a variety of childhood diseases, such as respiratory illnesses, ear infections, diarrhea, and allergies (see Figure 5-11). Breast milk is more easily digested than cow's milk or formula, and it is sterile, warm, and convenient for the mother to dispense. There is even some evidence that breast milk may enhance cognitive growth, leading to high adult intelligence (American Academy of Pediatrics, 2005; Der, Batty, & Deary, 2006; Ferguson & Molfese, 2007).

Breast-feeding also offers significant emotional advantages for both mother and child. Most mothers report that the experience of breast-feeding brings about feelings of well-being and intimacy with their infants, perhaps because of the production of endorphins in mothers' brains. Breast-fed infants are also more responsive to their mothers' touch and their mothers' gaze during feeding, and they are calmed and soothed by the experience. As we see in Chapter 6, this mutual responsiveness may lead to healthy social development (Gerrish & Mennella, 2000; Zanardo et al., 2001).

Breast-feeding may even be advantageous to mothers' health. For instance, research suggests that women who breast-feed may have lower rates of ovarian cancer and breast cancer prior to menopause. Furthermore, the hormones produced during breast-feeding help shrink the uteruses of women following birth, enabling their bodies to return more quickly to a prepregnancy state. These hormones also may inhibit ovulation, reducing (but not eliminating) the chance of becoming pregnant, and thereby help space the birth of additional children (Altemus et al., 1995; Ma et al., 2006; Kim et al., 2007).

Breast-feeding is not a cure-all for infant nutrition and health, and the millions of individuals who have been raised on formula should not be concerned that they have suffered irreparable harm. (In fact, recent research suggests that infants fed enriched formula show better cognitive development than those using traditional formula.) But it does continue to be clear that the popular slogan used by groups advocating the use of breast-feeding is right on target: "Breast is Best" (Birch et al., 2000; Auestad et al., 2003; Rabin, 2006).

Social Patterns in Breast-Feeding Although it has several advantages, only about 70% of all new mothers in the United States employ breast-feeding. Issues of age, social status, and race influence the decision whether to breast-feed. The rates of breast-feeding are highest among women who are older, have better education, are of higher socioeconomic status, and have social or cultural support. Connected to these factors, breast-feeding among Caucasian mothers in the United States occurs at a significantly higher rate than that for African American mothers. Globally, countries in which there is significant social and governmental support for breast-feeding have higher rates of breast-feeding than in the United States. For example, almost all mothers in the Scandinavian countries of Norway, Denmark, and Sweden

breast-feed (Forste, Weiss, & Lippincott, 2001; Alvarez, 2003; Greve, 2003; Merewood, 2006; see Figure 5-11).

If authorities are in agreement about the benefits of breast-feeding, why in so many cases do women not breast-feed? In some cases, they can't. Some women have difficulties producing milk, while others are taking some type of medicine or have an infectious disease such as AIDS that could be passed on to their infants through breast milk. Sometimes infants are too ill to nurse successfully. And in many cases of adoption, where the birth mother is unavailable after giving birth, the adoptive mother has no choice but to bottle-feed.

For some women, the decision not to breast-feed is based on practical considerations. Women who hold jobs outside the home may not have sufficiently flexible schedules to breast-feed their infants. This problem is particularly true with less affluent women who may have less control over their schedules. Such problems may account for the lower rate of breast-feeding among mothers of lower socioeconomic status, who may lack social support for breast-feeding (Cardala et al., 2003; Click, 2006; Johnston & Esposito, 2007).

Education is also an issue: Some women simply do not receive adequate information and advice regarding the advantages of breast-feeding, and choose to use formula because they think it is the best choice. Indeed, some hospitals may inadvertently encourage the use of formula by including it in the gift packets new mothers receive as they leave the hospital.

In developing countries, the use of formula is particularly problematic. Because formula often comes in powdered form that must be mixed with water, pollution of the local water supply can make using formula particularly dangerous. Poverty-stricken parents may dilute formula too much

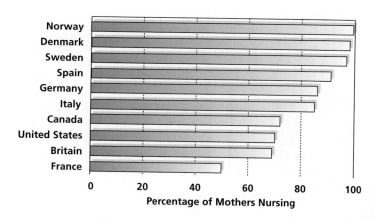

FIGURE 5-11 Nursing Mothers

Norway and other European countries lead the way in the percentage of mothers who breast-feed their newborns. What social changes in the United States might encourage more mothers to breast-feed?

(*Source:* La Leche League International, 2003)

Sensation The physical stimulation of the sense organs

Perception The sorting out, interpretation, analysis, and integration of stimuli involving the sense organs and brain

"I forgot to say I was breast-fed."

because they can't afford to buy the proper amounts, leading to problems with infant malnutrition or undernutrition.

Educational, social, and cultural support for breast-feeding is particularly important. Women need to be educated about the health advantages of breast-feeding and be given specific information on just how to do it. Although breast-feeding is a natural act, mothers require a bit of practice to learn how to hold the baby properly and position the nipple correctly, so the baby can "latch on." Mothers may also need help dealing with such potential problems as sore nipples.

Introducing Solid Foods: When and What?

Although pediatricians agree that breast milk is the ideal initial food, at some point infants require more nutriments than breast milk alone can provide. The American Academy of Pediatrics and the American Academy of Family Physicians suggest that babies can start solids at around 6 months, although they aren't needed until 9 to 12 months of age (American Academy of Pediatrics, 1997; American Academy of Family Physicians, 1997).

Solid foods should be introduced into an infant's diet gradually, one at a time, to allow awareness of the child's preferences and allergies. Most often, cereal comes first followed by strained fruits. Vegetables and other foods typically are introduced next, although the order varies significantly from one infant to another.

Infants generally start eating solid foods at around 4 to 6 months, gradually working their way up to a variety of foods.

The timing of *weaning*, the gradual cessation of breast- or bottle-feeding, varies greatly. In developed countries such as the United States, weaning frequently occurs as early as 3 or 4 months. On the other hand, some mothers continue breast-feeding for 2 or 3 years. The American Academy of Pediatrics recommends that infants be fed breast milk for the first 12 months (American Academy of Pediatrics, 1997; Sloan et al., 2008).

REVIEW ↵ **mydevelopmentlab**

1. _____ are unlearned, organized involuntary responses that occur automatically in the presence of certain stimuli.

   Answer: Reflexes

2. Infants are able to accomplish different types of gross _____ movement including lifting their heads, propelling themselves, crawling, and eventually walking.

   Answer: motor

3. _____ represent the average performance of a large sample of children of a given age.

   Answer: Norms

4. _____, the condition of having an improper amount and balance of nutrients, can lead to a slower growth rate by age 6 months, lower IQ scores, and poorer performance in school.

   Answer: Malnutrition

To see more review questions, log on to MyDevelopmentLab.

The Develoment of the Senses

William James, one of the founding fathers of psychology, believed the world of the infant is a "blooming, buzzing confusion" (James, 1890/1950). Was he right?

In this case, James's wisdom failed him. The newborn's sensory world does lack the clarity and stability that we can distinguish as adults, but day by day the world grows increasingly comprehensible as the infant's ability to sense and perceive the environment develops. In fact, babies appear to thrive in an environment enriched by pleasing sensations.

The processes that underlie infants' understanding of the world around them are sensation and perception. **Sensation** is the physical stimulation of the sense organs, and **perception** is the mental process of sorting out, interpreting, analyzing, and integrating stimuli from the sense organs and brain.

The study of infants' capabilities in the realm of sensation and perception challenges the ingenuity of investigators.

A neonate's view of the world is limited to 8 to 14 inches. Objects beyond that distance are fuzzy.

A month after birth, newborns' vision has improved, but still lacks clarifying detail.

By 3 months, objects are seen with clarity.

As we'll see, researchers have developed a number of procedures for understanding sensation and perception in different realms.

Visual Perception: Seeing the World

From the time of Lee Eng's birth, everyone who met him felt that he gazed at them intently. His eyes seemed to meet those of visitors. They seemed to bore deeply and knowingly into the faces of people who looked at him.

How good in fact was Lee's vision, and what, precisely, could he make out of his environment? Quite a bit, at least up close. According to some estimates, a newborn's distance vision ranges from 20/200 to 20/600, which means that an infant can only see with accuracy visual material up to 20 feet that an adult with normal vision is able to see with similar accuracy from a distance of between 200 and 600 feet (Haigth, 1991).

These figures indicate that infants' distance vision is one-tenth to one-third that of the average adult's. This isn't so bad, actually: The vision of newborns provides the same degree of distance acuity as the uncorrected vision of many adults who wear eyeglasses or contact lenses. (If you wear glasses or contact lenses, remove them to get a sense of what an infant can see of the world; see the accompanying set of photos.) Furthermore, infants' distance vision grows increasingly acute. By 6 months of age, the average infant's vision is already 20/20—in other words, identical to that of adults (Aslin, 1987; Cavallini et al., 2002).

Other visual abilities grow rapidly. For instance, *binocular vision*, the ability to combine the images coming to each eye to see depth and motion, is achieved at around 14 weeks. Before then, infants do not integrate the information from each eye.

Depth perception is a particularly useful ability, helping babies acknowledge heights and avoid falls. In a classic study by developmental psychologists Eleanor Gibson and Richard Walk (1960) infants were placed on a sheet of heavy glass. A checkered pattern appeared under one half of the glass sheet, making it seem that the infant was on a stable floor. However, in the middle of the glass sheet, the pattern dropped down several feet, forming an apparent "visual cliff." The question Gibson and Walk asked was whether infants would willingly crawl across the cliff when called by their mothers (see Figure 5-12).

FIGURE 5-12 Visual Cliff

The "visual cliff" experiment examines the depth perception of infants. Most infants in the age range of 6 to 14 months cannot be coaxed to cross the cliff, apparently responding to the fact that the patterned area drops several feet.

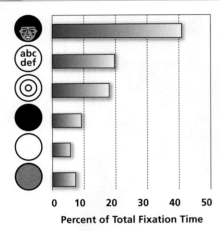

FIGURE 5-13 Preferring Complexity

In a classic experiment, researcher Robert Fantz found that 2- and 3-month-old infants preferred to look at more complex stimuli.

(Adapted from R.L. Fantz, 1961)

The results were unambiguous. Most of the infants in the study, who ranged in age from 6 to 14 months, could not be coaxed over the apparent cliff. Clearly the ability to perceive depth had already developed in most of them by that age. On the other hand, the experiment did not pinpoint when depth perception emerged, because only infants who had already learned to crawl could be tested. But other experiments, in which infants of 2 and 3 months were placed on their stomachs above the apparent floor and above the visual cliff, revealed differences in heart rate between the two positions (Campos, Langer, & Krowitz, 1970).

Still, it is important to keep in mind that such findings do not permit us to know whether infants are responding to depth itself or merely to the *change* in visual stimuli that occurs when they are moved from a lack of depth to depth.

Infants also show clear visual preferences, preferences that are present from birth. Given a choice, infants reliably prefer to look at stimuli that include patterns than to look at simpler stimuli (see Figure 5-13). How do we know? Developmental psychologist Robert Fantz (1963) created a classic test. He built a chamber in which babies could lie on their backs and see pairs of visual stimuli above them. Fantz could determine which of the stimuli the infants were looking at by observing the reflections of the stimuli in their eyes.

Fantz's work was the impetus for a great deal of research on the preferences of infants, most of which points to a critical conclusion: Infants are genetically preprogrammed to prefer particular kinds of stimuli. For instance, just minutes after birth they show preferences for certain colors, shapes, and configurations of various stimuli. They prefer curved over straight lines, three-dimensional figures to two-dimensional ones, and human faces to nonhuman faces. Such capabilities may be a reflection of the existence of highly specialized cells in the brain that react to stimuli of a particular pattern, orientation, shape, and direction of movement (Rubenstein, Kalakanis, & Langlois, 1999; Hubel & Wiesel, 1979, 2004; Kellman & Arterberry, 2006).

However, genetics is not the sole determinant of infant visual preferences. Just a few hours after birth, infants have already learned to prefer their own mother's face to other faces. Similarly, between the ages of 6 and 9 months, infants become more adept at distinguishing among the faces of humans, whereas they become less able to distinguish faces of members of other species (see Figure 5-14). They also distinguish

FIGURE 5-14 Distinguishing Faces

Examples of faces used in a study that found that 6-month-old infants distinguished human or monkey faces equally well, whereas 9-month-olds were less adept at distinguishing monkey faces than they were human faces.

(*Source:* Pascalis, de Haan, & Nelson, 2002, p. 1322)

between male and female faces. Such findings provide another clear piece of evidence of how heredity and environmental experiences are woven together to determine an infant's capabilities (Pascalis, de Haan, & Nelson, 2002; Turati et al., 2006; Ramsey-Rennels & Langlois, 2006; Valenti, 2006).

Auditory Perception: The World of Sound

What is it about a mother's lullaby that helps soothe a crying, fussy baby? Some clues emerge when we look at the capabilities of infants in the realm of auditory sensation and perception.

Infants hear from the time of birth—and even before. As we noted in Chapter 2, the ability to hear begins prenatally. Even in the womb, the fetus responds to sounds outside of its mother. Furthermore, infants are born with preferences for particular sound combinations (Schellenberg & Trehub, 1996; Trehub, 2003).

Because they have had some practice in hearing before birth, it is not surprising that infants have reasonably good auditory perception after they are born. In fact, infants actually are more sensitive to certain very high and very low frequencies than adults are—a sensitivity that seems to increase during the first 2 years of life. On the other hand, infants are initially less sensitive than adults to middle-range frequencies. Eventually, however, their capabilities within the middle range improve (Werner & Marean, 1996; Fernald, 2001).

It is not fully clear what leads to the improvement during infancy in sensitivity to mid-frequency sounds, although it may be related to the maturation of the nervous system. More puzzling is why, after infancy, children's ability to hear very high and low frequencies gradually declines. One explanation may be that exposure to high levels of noise may diminish capacities at the extreme ranges (Trehub et al., 1988, 1989; Stewart, Scherer, & Lehman, 2003).

In addition to the ability to detect sound, infants need several other abilities in order to hear effectively. For instance, *sound localization* permits us to pinpoint the direction from which a sound is emanating. Compared to adults, infants have a slight handicap in this task because effective sound localization requires the use of the slight difference in the times at which a sound reaches our two ears. Sound that we hear first in the right ear tells us that the source of the sound is to our right. Because infants' heads are smaller than those of adults, the difference in timing of the arrival of sound at the two ears is less than it is in adults, so they have difficulty determining from which direction sound is coming.

However, despite the potential limitation brought about by their smaller heads, infants' sound localization abilities are actually fairly good even at birth, and they reach adult levels of success by the age of 1 year. Interestingly, their improvement is not steady: Although we don't know why, studies show that the accuracy of sound localization actually declines between birth and 2 months of age, but then begins to increase (Clifton, 1992; Litovsky & Ashmead, 1997; Fenwick & Morrongiello, 1998).

Infants can discriminate groups of different sounds, in terms of their patterns and other acoustical characteristics quite well. For instance, infants as young as 6 months old can detect the change of a single note in a six-tone melody. They also react to changes in musical key and rhythm. In sum, they listen with a keen ear to the melodies of lullabies sung to them by their mothers and fathers (Trehub, 2003; Phillips-Silver & Trainor, 2005; Masataka, 2006).

Even more important to their ultimate success in the world, young infants are capable of making the fine discriminations that their future understanding of language will require (Bijeljac-Babic, Bertoncini, & Mehler, 1993). For instance, in one classic study, a group of 1- to 5-month-old infants sucked on nipples that activated a recording of a person saying "ba" every time they sucked (Eimas et al., 1971). At first, their interest in the sound made them suck vigorously. Soon, though, they became acclimated to the sound (through a process called *habituation*, discussed in Chapter 3) and sucked with less energy. On the other hand, when the experimenters changed the sound to "pa," the infants immediately showed new interest and sucked with greater vigor once again. The clear conclusion: Infants as young as 1 month old could make the distinction between the two similar sounds (Eimas et al., 1971; Goodman & Nusbaum, 1994; J.L. Miller & Eimas, 1995).

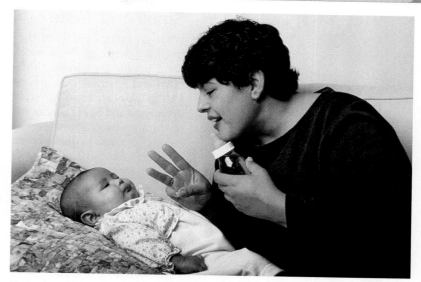

By the age of 4 months, infants are able to discriminate their own names from other, similar-sounding words

Even more intriguingly, young infants are able to discriminate one language from another. By the age of 4 1/2 months, infants are able to discriminate their own names from other, similar-sounding words. By the age of 5 months, they can distinguish the difference between English and Spanish passages, even when the two are similar in meter, number of syllables, and speed of recitation. In fact, some evidence suggests that even 2-day-olds show preferences for the language spoken by those around them over other languages (Mandel, Jusczyk, & Pisoni, 1995; Rivera-Gaxiola, Silva-Pereyra, & Kuhl, 2005; Kuhl, 2006).

Given their ability to discriminate a variation in speech as slight as the difference between two consonants, it is not surprising that infants can distinguish different people on the basis of voice. In fact, from an early age they show clear preferences for some voices over others. For instance, in one experiment newborns were allowed to suck a nipple that turned on a recording of a human voice reading a story. The infants sucked significantly longer when the voice was their mothers' than when the voice was that of a stranger (DeCasper & Fifer, 1980; Fifer, 1987).

How do such preferences arise? One hypothesis is that prenatal exposure to the mother's voice is the key. As support for this conjecture, researchers point to the fact that newborns do not show a preference for their fathers' voices over other male voices. Furthermore, newborns prefer listening to melodies sung by their mothers before they were born to melodies that were not sung before birth. It seems, then, that the prenatal exposure to their mothers' voices—although muffled by the liquid environment of the womb—helps shape infants' listening preferences (DeCasper & Prescott, 1984; Vouloumanos & Werker, 2007; Rosen & Iverson, 2007).

Smell and Taste

What do infants do when they smell a rotten egg? Pretty much what adults do—crinkle their noses and generally look unhappy. On the other hand, the scent of bananas and butter produces a pleasant reaction on the part of infants (Steiner, 1979; Pomares, Schirrer, & Abadie, 2002).

The sense of smell is so well developed, even among very young infants, that at least some 12- to 18-day-old babies can distinguish their mothers on the basis of smell alone. For instance, in one experiment infants sniffed gauze pads worn under the arms of adults the previous evening. Infants who were being breast-fed were able to distinguish their mothers' scent from that of other adults. In contrast, those who were being bottle-fed were unable to make the distinction. Moreover, both breast-fed and bottle-fed infants were unable to distinguish their fathers on the basis of odor (Porter, Balogh, & Malkin, 1988; Mizuno & Ueda, 2004; Allam, Marlier, & Schaal, 2006).

Infants' sense of smell is so well developed that they can distinguish their mothers on the basis of smell alone.

Infants seem to have an innate sweet tooth (even before they have teeth!), and they show facial expressions of disgust when they taste something bitter. Very young infants smile when a sweet-tasting liquid is placed on their tongues. They also suck harder at a bottle if it is sweetened. Because breast milk has a sweet taste, it is possible that this preference may be part of our evolutionary heritage, retained because it offered a survival advantage. Infants who preferred sweet tastes may have been more likely to ingest sufficient nutrients and to survive than those who did not (Steiner, 1979; Rosenstein & Oster, 1988; Porges & Lipsitt, 1993).

Infants also develop taste preferences based on what their mothers drank while they were in the womb. For instance, one study found that women who drank carrot juice while pregnant had children who had a preference for the taste of carrots during infancy (Mennella, 2000).

Sensitivity to Pain and Touch

When Eli Rosenblatt was 8 days old, he participated in the ancient Jewish ritual of circumcision. As he lay nestled in his father's arms, the foreskin of his penis was removed. Although Eli shrieked in what seemed to his anxious parents as pain, he soon settled down and went back to sleep. Others who had watched the ceremony assured his parents that at Eli's age babies don't really experience pain, at least not in the same way that adults do.

Were Eli's relatives accurate in saying that young infants don't experience pain? In the past, many medical practitioners would have agreed. In fact, because they assumed that infants didn't experience pain in truly bothersome ways, many physicians routinely carried out medical procedures, and even some forms of surgery, without the use of pain killers or anesthesia. Their argument was that the risks from the use of anesthesia outweighed the potential pain that the young infants experienced.

Contemporary Views on Infant Pain Today, however, it is widely acknowledged that infants are born with the capacity to experience pain. Obviously, no one can be sure whether the experience of pain in children is identical to that in adults, any more than we can tell whether an adult friend who complains of a headache is experiencing pain that is more or less severe than our own pain when we have a headache.

What we do know is that that pain produces distress in infants. Their heartbeat increases, they sweat, show facial expressions of discomfort, and change the intensity and tone of crying when they are hurt (Simons et al., 2003; Warnock & Sandrin, 2004).

Touch is one of the most highly developed sensory systems from the time of birth.

There appears to be a developmental progression in reactions to pain. For example, a newborn infant who has her heel pricked for a blood test responds with distress, but it takes her several seconds to show the response. In contrast, only a few months later, the same procedure brings a much more immediate response. It is possible that the delayed reaction in infants is produced by the relatively slower transmission of information within the newborn's less-developed nervous system (Anand & Hickey, 1992; Axia, Bonichini, & Benini, 1995; Puchalski & Hummel, 2002).

Research with rats suggests that exposure to pain in infancy may lead to a permanent rewiring of the nervous system resulting in greater sensitivity to pain during adulthood. Such findings indicate that infants who must undergo extensive, painful medical treatments and tests may be unusually sensitive to pain when older (Ruda et al., 2000; Taddio, Shah, & Gilbert-MacLeod, 2002).

In response to increasing support for the notion that infants experience pain and that its effects may be long lasting, medical experts now endorse the use of anesthesia and painkillers during surgery for even the youngest infants. According to the American Academy of Pediatrics, painkilling drugs are appropriate in most types of surgery—including circumcision (Sato et al., 2007; Urso, 2007).

Responding to Touch   It clearly does not take the sting of pain to get an infant's attention. Even the youngest infants respond to gentle touches, such as a soothing caress, which can calm a crying, fussy infant (Hertenstein & Campos, 2001; Hertenstein, 2002).

In fact, touch is one of the most highly developed sensory systems in a newborn, and it is also one of the first to develop; there is evidence that by 32 weeks after conception, the entire body is sensitive to touch. Furthermore, several of the basic reflexes present at birth, such as the rooting reflex, require touch sensitivity to operate: An infant must sense a touch near the mouth in order to seek automatically a nipple to suck (Haith, 1986).

Infants' abilities in the realm of touch are particularly helpful in their efforts to explore the world. Several theorists have suggested that one of the ways children gain information about the world is through touching. As mentioned earlier, at the age of 6 months, infants are apt to place almost any object in their mouths, apparently taking in data about its configuration from their sensory responses to the feel of it in their mouths (Ruff, 1989).

In addition, as we first discussed in Chapter 3, touch plays an important role in an organism's future development, for it triggers a complex chemical reaction that assists infants in their efforts to survive. For example, gentle massage stimulates the production of certain chemicals in an infant's brain that instigate growth. Periodic massage is also helpful in treating several kinds of medical conditions, including premature delivery and the effects of

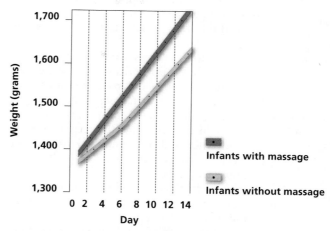

FIGURE 5-15 Effect of Massage on Weight Gain

The weight gain of premature infants who were systematically massaged is greater than those who did not receive the massage. How can this phenomenon be explained?
(*Source:* Field, 1988)

prenatal exposure to AIDS or cocaine. Furthermore, massage is beneficial for infants and even older children whose mothers are depressed and for those who suffer from burns, cancer, asthma, and a variety of other medical conditions (Field, Diego, Hernandez-Reif, 2006, 2007; Field, Hernandez-Reif, & Diego, 2006; Diego, Field, & Hernandez-Reif, 2008).

In one study that illustrates the benefits of massage, a group of preterm infants who were massaged for 15 minutes three times a day gained weight some 50% faster than a group of preterm infants of the same age who were not stroked (see Figure 5-15). The massaged infants also were more active and responsive to stimuli. Ultimately, the preterm infants who were massaged were discharged earlier from the hospital, and the costs of their medical care were significantly lower than for infants in the unmassaged group (Field, 1995; Hernandez-Reif, Deigo, & Field, 2007).

Multimodal Perception: Combining Individual Sensory Inputs

When Eric Pettigrew was 7 months old, his grandparents presented him with a squeaky rubber doll. As soon as he saw it, he reached out for it, grasped it in his hand, and listened as it squeaked. He seemed delighted with the gift.

One way of considering Eric's sensory reaction to the doll is to focus on each of the senses individually: what the doll looked like to Eric, how it felt in his hand, and what it

Multimodal approach to perception The approach that considers how information that is collected by various individual sensory systems is integrated and coordinated

Affordances The action possibilities that a given situation or stimulus provides

From a health-care worker's perspective:

Persons who are born without the use of one sense sometimes develop unusual abilities in one or more other senses. What can health-care professionals do to help infants who are lacking in a particular sense?

sounded like. In fact, this approach has dominated the study of sensation and perception in infancy.

However, let's consider another approach: We might examine how the various sensory responses are integrated with one another. Instead of looking at each individual sensory response, we could consider how the responses work together and are combined to produce Eric's ultimate reaction. The **multimodal approach to perception** considers how information that is collected by various individual sensory systems is integrated and coordinated.

Although the multimodal approach is a relatively recent innovation in the study of how infants understand their sensory world, it raises some fundamental issues about the development of sensation and perception. For instance, some researchers argue that sensations are initially integrated with one another in the infant, while others maintain that the infant's sensory systems are initially separate and that brain development leads to increasing integration (Lickliter & Bahrick, 2000; De Gelder, 2000; Lewkowicz, 2002).

We do not know yet which view is correct. However, it does appear that by an early age infants are able to relate what they have learned about an object through one sensory channel to what they have learned about it through another. For instance, even 1-month-old infants are able to recognize by sight objects that they have previously held in their mouths but never seen (A.N. Meltzoff, 1981; Steri & Spelke, 1988). Clearly, some cross-talk between various sensory channels is already possible a month after birth.

Infants' abilities at multimodal perception showcase the sophisticated perceptual abilities of infants, which continue to grow throughout the period of infancy. Such perceptual growth is aided by infants' discovery of **affordances**, the options that a given situation or stimulus provides. For example, infants learn that they might potentially fall when walking down a steep ramp—that is, the ramp *affords* the possibility of falling. Such knowledge is crucial as infants make the transition from crawling to walking. Similarly, infants learn that an object shaped in a certain way can slip out of their hands if not grasped correctly. For example, Eric is learning that his toy has several affordances: He can grab it and squeeze it, listen to it squeak, and even chew comfortably on it if he is teething (McCarty & Ashmead, 1999; Flom & Bahrick, 2007; Wilcox et al., 2007).

Becoming an Informed Consumer of Development

Exercising Your Infant's Body and Senses

Recall how cultural expectations and environments affect the age at which various physical milestones, such as the first step, occur. Although most experts feel attempts to accelerate physical and sensory–perceptual development yield little advantage, parents should ensure that their infants receive sufficient physical and sensory stimulation. There are several specific ways to accomplish this goal:

- Carry a baby in different positions—in a backpack, in a frontpack, or in a football hold with the infant's head in the palm of your hand and its feet lying on your arm. This lets the infant view the world from several perspectives.

- Let infants explore their environment. Don't contain them too long in a barren environment. Let them crawl or wander around—after first making the environment "childproof" by removing dangerous objects.

- Engage in "rough-and-tumble" play. Wrestling, dancing, and rolling around on the floor—if not violent—are activities that are fun and that stimulate older infants' motor and sensory systems.

- Let babies touch their food and even play with it. Infancy is too early to start teaching table manners.

- Provide toys that stimulate the senses, particularly toys that can stimulate more than one sense at a time. For example, brightly colored, textured toys with movable parts are enjoyable and help sharpen infants' senses.

REVIEW mydevelopmentlab

1. _____ is the physical stimulation of the sense organs.

Answer: Sensation

2. _____ is the process of sorting out, interpreting, analyzing, and integrating stimuli involving the sense organs and the brain.

Answer: Perception

3. _____ vision, the ability to combine the images coming to each eye to see depth and motion, is achieved at around 14 weeks.

Answer: Binocular

4. The _____ approach to perception considers how information that is collected by various individual sensory systems is integrated and coordinated.

Answer: multimodal

To see more review questions, log on to MyDevelopmentLab.

CASE STUDY

The Case of... One Step at a Time

Lila Jackson was thrilled to find a mom-and-baby group when she moved to Atlanta with her 6-month-old son, Danny. The women were friendly and Lila relished having other new moms with kids the same age.

But she was troubled by the undercurrent of competition among several of the moms. One woman in particular trumpeted her daughter's latest triumph at every get-together. Little Cora began crawling at 6 months. By 8 months, she was cruising the room, using furniture for support. At 10 months, she took her first independent steps.

Lila began to despair. Danny, at 10 months, had only recently started crawling. He struggled to pull up to a standing position, but then he plopped down. Lila wondered if he'd ever walk, and she worried that the seemingly huge gap between his development and Cora's meant that something was seriously wrong.

Then Lila read a study which claimed that children who were given regular practice stepping in early infancy walked sooner than other children. Although Danny was well past the age cited in the study, Lila began a rigorous program of practice walking. Holding his hands, she marched Danny around

the house three times a day for a total of 45 minutes, righting him each time he sagged. After a week of this routine, Danny broke down sobbing when Lila reached for his hand. He lay on the floor and refused to stand up. Frightened, Lila stopped the practice.

1. Do you think Lila's concern about Danny's development is justified? Why or why not?

2. What could you tell Lila about the range of normal physical development in infancy that might dispel her fears?

3. Why do you think Lila's program of regular practice walking did not work the way she had hoped?

4. What might Lila do to support Danny's gross motor development without causing him distress?

5. What are the disadvantages of comparing a child's development to that of his or her peers? What might Lila say to herself the next time her friends' comments start to worry her?

◄ Looking Back

How do the human body and nervous system develop?

- Human babies grow rapidly in height and weight, especially during the first 2 years of life.

- Major principles that govern human growth include the cephalocaudal principle, the proximodistal principle, the principle of hierarchical integration, and the principle of the independence of systems.

- The nervous system contains a huge number of neurons, more than will be needed as an adult. For neurons to survive and become useful, they must form interconnections with other neurons based on the infant's experience of the world. "Extra" connections and neurons that are not used are eliminated as an infant develops.

Does the environment affect the pattern of development?

- Brain development, largely predetermined genetically, also contains a strong element of plasticity—a susceptibility to environmental influences.

- Many aspects of development occur during sensitive periods when the organism is particularly susceptible to environmental influences.

What developmental tasks must infants accomplish in this period?

- One of the primary tasks of the infant is the development of rhythms—cyclical patterns that integrate individual behaviors. An important rhythm pertains to the infant's state—the degree of awareness it displays to stimulation.

- Reflexes are unlearned, automatic responses to stimuli that help newborns survive and protect themselves. Some reflexes also have value as the foundation for future, more conscious behaviors.

- The development of gross and fine motor skills proceeds along a generally consistent timetable in normal children, with substantial individual and cultural variations.

How does nutrition affect physical development?

- Adequate nutrition is essential for physical development. Malnutrition and undernutrition affect physical aspects of growth and also may affect IQ and school performance.

- Breast-feeding has distinct advantages over bottle-feeding, including the nutritional completeness of breast milk, its provision of a degree of immunity to certain childhood diseases, and its easy digestibility. In addition, breast-feeding offers significant physical and emotional benefits to both child and mother.

What sensory capabilities do infants possess?

- Sensation, the stimulation of the sense organs, differs from perception, the interpretation and integration of sensed stimuli.

- Infants' visual and auditory perception are rather well developed, as are the senses of smell and taste. Infants use their highly developed sense of touch to explore and experience the world. In addition, touch plays an important role in the individual's future development, which is only now being understood. ■

Epilogue

In this chapter, we discussed the nature and pace of infants' physical growth, the pace of less obvious growth in the brain and nervous system, and in the increasing regularity of infants' patterns and states.

We next looked at motor development, the development and uses of reflexes, the role of environmental influences on the pace and shape of motor development, and the importance of nutrition.

We closed the chapter with a look at the senses, and the infant's ability to to combine data from multiple sensory sources.

Turn back for a moment to the Prologue of this chapter, about a baby's first steps, and answer these questions.

1. Which principle or principles of growth (i.e., cephalocaudal, proximodistal, hierarchical integration, independence of systems) account for the progression of physical activities that precede Josh's first steps?

2. What conclusions about Josh's future physical development can be drawn based on the fact that his first steps

occurred approximately 2 months early? Can conclusions be drawn about his future cognitive development? Why?

3. In walking at 10 months of age, Josh outpaced his brother Jon by 4 months. Does this fact have any implications for the comparative physical or cognitive abilities of the two brothers? Why?

4. Do you think anything changed in the environment between the time Jon and Josh were born that might account for their different "first step" schedules? If you were researching this question, what environmental factors would you look for?

5. Why were Josh's parents so pleased and proud about his accomplishment, which is, after all, a routine and universal occurrence? What are the cultural factors that exist in the United States that make the "first steps" milestone so significant?

Key Terms and Concepts

cephalocaudal principle (p. 104)
proximodistal principle (p. 105)
principle of hierarchical
    integration (p. 105)
principle of the independence
    of systems (p. 105)
neuron (p. 105)
synapse (p. 106)
myelin (p. 106)
cerebral cortex (p. 106)

plasticity (p. 107)
sensitive period (p. 107)
rhythms (p. 108)
state (p. 108)
rapid eye movement (REM)
    sleep (p. 109)
sudden infant death syndrome
    (SIDS) (p. 110)
reflexes (p. 112)
dynamic systems theory (p. 114)

norms (p. 115)
Brazelton Neonatal Behavioral
    Assessment Scale
    (NBAS) (p. 115)
nonorganic failure to thrive (p. 117)
sensation (p. 120)
perception (p. 120)
multimodal approach to
    perception (p. 126)
affordances (p. 126)

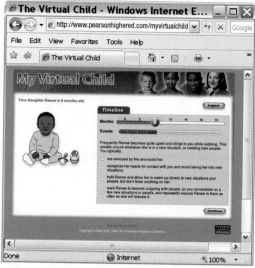

What decisions would you make while raising a child? What would the consequences of those decisions be?

Find out by logging onto **My Virtual Child** and raising your child from birth to 18 years.

chapter six

Cognitive Development in Infancy

PROLOGUE: THE ELECTRIC NANNY

Thomas Bausman, 2, and his brother Jake, 10 months, are typical American babies. Every day, Thomas settles down to watch two hours of television, while Jake sits in front of the set for an hour, the national average for their respective ages. Their favorite thing to watch, by far? *Baby Einstein*. Anita Bausman could not be more pleased with her children's preference. Jake, she reports, learned colors, numbers, and his love of robots from the popular videos, which are filled with puppets, animals, and moving objects, often set to classical music. "It's not just turning on Nickelodeon," Bausman says. "It's educational and beneficial. I know he's happy watching, and I can pop in and point out something on-screen, then go deal with the laundry." (Paul, 2006, p. 104).

▶ Looking Ahead

Can infants really become miniature Einsteins by watching educational media? What concepts are babies as young as 10-month-old Jake Bausman actually grasping, and what intellectual abilities remain undeveloped at that age? Can an infant's cognitive development really be accelerated through intellectual stimulation, or does the process unfold on its own timetable despite the best efforts of parents to hasten it?

Such questions go the heart of the nature of memory in infancy. Clearly, infants remember *some* information, because without memory they would be unable to

speak, recognize others, or, more generally, show the enormous advances in cognitive development that occurs throughout infancy.

We address these and related questions in this chapter as we consider cognitive development during the first years of life. Our examination focuses on the work of developmental researchers who seek to understand how infants develop their knowledge and understanding of the world. We first discuss the work of Swiss psychologist Jean Piaget, whose theory of developmental stages served as a highly influential impetus for a considerable amount of work on cognitive development. We look at both the limitations and the contributions of this important developmental specialist.

We then cover more contemporary views of cognitive development, examining information processing approaches that seek to explain how cognitive growth occurs. After considering how learning takes place, we examine memory in infants and the ways in which infants process, store, and retrieve information. We discuss the controversial issue of the recollection of events that occurred during infancy. We also address individual differences in intelligence.

Finally, we consider language, the cognitive skill that permits infants to communicate with others. We look at the roots of language in prelinguistic speech and trace the milestones indicating the development of language skills in the progression from baby's first words to phrases and sentences. We also look at the characteristics of adults' communication addressed to infants, characteristics that are surprisingly similar across different cultures.

After reading this chapter, you'll be able to answer these questions:

- *What are the fundamental features of Piaget's theories of cognitive development?*
- *How do infants process information?*
- *How is infant intelligence measured?*
- *By what processes do children learn to use language?*
- *How do children influence adults' language?*

Piaget's Approach to Cognitive Development

Olivia's dad is wiping up the mess around the base of her high chair—for the third time today! It seems to him that 14-month-old Olivia takes great delight in dropping food from the high chair. She also drops toys, spoons, anything it seems, just to watch how it hits the floor. She almost appears to be experimenting to see what kind of noise or what size of splatter is created by each different thing she drops.

Swiss psychologist Jean Piaget (1896–1980) probably would have said that Olivia's dad is right in theorizing that Olivia is conducting her own series of experiments to learn more about the workings of her world. Piaget's views of the ways infants learn could be summed in a simple equation: *Action = Knowledge.*

Piaget argued that infants do not acquire knowledge from facts communicated by others, nor through sensation and perception. Instead, Piaget suggested that knowledge is the product of direct motor behavior. Although many of his basic explanations and propositions have been challenged by subsequent research, as we discuss later, the view that in significant ways infants learn by doing remains unquestioned (Piaget, 1952, 1962, 1983; Bullinger, 1997).

Swiss psychologist Jean Piaget

Key Elements of Piaget's Theory

As we first noted in Chapter 2, Piaget's theory is based on a stage approach to development. He assumed that all children pass through a series of four universal stages in a fixed order from birth through adolescence: sensorimotor, preoperational, concrete operational, and formal operational. He also suggested that movement from one stage to the next occurred when a child reaches an appropriate level of physical maturation *and* is exposed to relevant experiences. Without such experience, children are assumed to be incapable of reaching their cognitive potential. Some approaches to cognition focus on changes in the *content* of children's knowledge about the world, but Piaget argued that it was critical to also consider the changes in the *quality* of children's knowledge and understanding as they move from one stage to another.

For instance, as they develop cognitively, infants experience changes in their understanding about what can and cannot occur in the world. Consider a baby who participates in an experiment during which she is exposed to three identical versions of her mother all at the same time, thanks to some well-placed mirrors. A 3-month-old infant will interact happily with each of these images of mother. However, by 5 months of age, the child becomes quite agitated at the sight of multiple mothers. Apparently by this time the child has figured out that she has but one mother, and viewing three at a time is thoroughly alarming (Bower, 1977). To Piaget, such reactions indicate that a baby is beginning to master principles regarding the way the world operates, indicating that she has begun to construct a mental sense of the world that she didn't have 2 months earlier.

Piaget believed that the basic building blocks of the way we understand the world are mental structures called **schemes**, organized patterns of functioning, that adapt and change with mental development. At first, schemes are related to physical, or sensorimotor, activity, such as picking up or reaching for toys. As children develop, their schemes move to a mental level, reflecting thought. Schemes are similar to computer software: They direct and determine how data from the world, such as new events or objects, are considered and dealt with (Achenbach, 1992; Rakison & Oakes, 2003).

If you give a baby a new cloth book, for example, he or she will touch it, mouth it, perhaps try to tear it or bang it on the floor. To Piaget, each of these actions may represent a scheme, and they are the infant's way of gaining knowledge and understanding of this new object. Adults, on the other hand, would use a different scheme upon encountering the book. Rather than picking it up and putting it in their mouths or banging it on the floor, they would probably be drawn to the letters on the page, seeking to understand the book through the meaning of the printed words—a very different approach.

Piaget suggested that two principles underlie the growth in children's schemes: assimilation and accommodation. **Assimilation** is the process by which people understand an experience in terms of their current stage of cognitive development and way of thinking. Assimilation occurs, then, when a stimulus or event is acted upon, perceived, and understood in accordance with existing patterns of thought. For example, an infant who tries to suck on any toy in the same way is assimilating the objects to her existing sucking scheme. Similarly, a child who encounters a flying squirrel at a zoo and calls it a "bird" is assimilating the squirrel to his existing scheme of bird.

In contrast, when we change our existing ways of thinking, understanding, or behaving in response to encounters with new stimuli or events, **accommodation** takes place. For instance, when a child sees a flying squirrel and calls it "a bird with a tail," he is beginning to *accommodate* new knowledge, modifying his scheme of bird.

Piaget believed that the earliest schemes are primarily limited to the reflexes with which we are all born, such as sucking and rooting. Infants start to modify these simple early schemes almost immediately, through the processes of assimilation and accommodation, in response to their

exploration of the environment. Schemes quickly become more sophisticated as infants become more advanced in their motor capabilities—to Piaget, a signal of the potential for more advanced cognitive development. Because Piaget's sensorimotor stage of development begins at birth and continues until the child is about 2 years old, we consider it here in detail. (In future chapters, we'll discuss development during the later stages.)

The Sensorimotor Period: Six Substages of Cognitive Development

Piaget suggests that the **sensorimotor stage**, the initial major stage of cognitive development, can be broken down into six substages. These are summarized in Table 6-1. It is important to keep in mind that although the specific substages of

TABLE 6-1		Piaget's Six Substages of the Sensorimotor Stage		
Substage	Age	Description		Example
Substage 1: Simple reflexes	First month of life	During this period, the various reflexes that determine the infant's interactions with the world are at the center of its cognitive life.		The sucking reflex causes the infant to suck at anything placed in its lips.
Substage 2: First habits and primary circular reactions	From 1 to 4 months	At this age infants begin to coordinate what were separate actions into single, integrated activities.		An infant might combine grasping an object with sucking on it, or staring at something with touching it.
Substage 3: Secondary circular reactions	From 4 to 8 months	During this period, infants take major strides in shifting their cognitive horizons beyond themselves and begin to act on the outside world.		A child who repeatedly picks up a rattle in her crib and shakes it in different ways to see how the sound changes is demonstrating her ability to modify her cognitive scheme about shaking rattles.
Substage 4: Coordination of secondary circular reactions	From 8 to 12 months	In this stage, infants begin to use more calculated approaches to producing events, coordinating several schemes to generate a single act. They achieve object permanence during this stage.		An infant will push one toy out of the way to reach another toy that is lying, partially exposed, under it.
Substage 5: Tertiary circular reactions	From 12 to 18 months	At this age infants develop what Piaget regards as the deliberate variation of actions that bring desirable consequences. Rather than just repeat enjoyable activities, infants appear to carry out miniature experiments to observe the consequences.		A child will drop a toy repeatedly, varying the position from which he drops it, carefully observing each time to see where it falls.
Substage 6: Beginnings of thought	From 18 months to 2 years	The major achievement of Substage 6 is the capacity for mental representation or symbolic thought. Piaget argued that only at this stage can infants imagine where objects that they cannot see might be.		Children can even plot in their heads unseen trajectories of objects, so that if a ball rolls under a piece of furniture, they can figure out where it is likely to emerge on the other side.

the sensorimotor period may at first appear to unfold with great regularity, as though infants reach a particular age and smoothly proceed into the next substage, the reality of cognitive development is somewhat different. First, the ages at which infants actually reach a particular stage vary a good deal among different children. The exact timing of a stage reflects an interaction between the infant's level of physical maturation and the nature of the social environment in which the child is being raised. Consequently, although Piaget contended that the order of the substages does not change from one child to the next, he admitted that the timing can and does vary to some degree.

Piaget viewed development as a more gradual process than the notion of different stages might seem to imply. Infants do not go to sleep one night in one substage and wake up the next morning in the next one. Instead, there is a rather gradual and steady shifting of behavior as a child moves toward the next stage of cognitive development. Infants also pass through periods of transition, in which some aspects of their behavior reflect the next higher stage while other aspects indicate their current stage (see Figure 6-1).

Substage 1: Simple Reflexes
The first substage of the sensorimotor period is *Substage 1: Simple reflexes*, encompassing the first month of life. During this time, the various inborn reflexes, described in Chapters 4 and 5, are at the center of a baby's physical and cognitive life, determining the nature of his or her interactions with the world. For example, the sucking reflex causes the infant to suck at anything

placed in his or her lips. This sucking behavior, according to Piaget, provides the newborn with information about objects—information that paves the way to the next substage of the sensorimotor period.

At the same time, some of the reflexes begin to accommodate the infant's experience with the nature of the world. For instance, an infant who is being breast-fed, but who also receives supplemental bottles, may start to change the way he or she sucks, depending on whether a nipple is on a breast or on a bottle.

Substage 2: First Habits and Primary Circular Reactions
Substage 2: First habits and primary circular reactions, the second substage of the sensorimotor period, occurs from 1 to 4 months of age. In this period, infants begin to coordinate what were separate actions into single, integrated activities. For instance, an infant might combine grasping an object with sucking on it, or staring at something while touching it.

If an activity engages a baby's interests, he or she may repeat it over and over, simply for the sake of continuing to experience it. Olivia's "experiments" with gravity while in her high chair are an example of this. This repetition of a chance motor event helps the baby start building cognitive schemes through a process known as a *circular reaction*. *Primary circular reactions* are schemes reflecting an infant's repetition of interesting or enjoyable actions, just for the enjoyment of doing them. Piaget referred to these schemes as *primary* because the activities they involve focus on the infant's own body. Thus, when an infant first puts his thumb in his mouth and begins to suck, it is a mere chance event. However, when he repeatedly sucks his thumb in the future, it represents a primary circular reaction, which he is repeating because the sensation of sucking is pleasurable.

Substage 3: Secondary Circular Reactions
Substage 3: Secondary circular reactions are more purposeful. According to Piaget, this third stage of cognitive development in infancy occurs from 4 to 8 months of age. During this period, infants begin to act upon the outside world. For instance, infants now seek to repeat enjoyable events in their environments if they happen to produce them through chance activities. A child who repeatedly picks up a rattle in her crib and shakes it in different ways to see how the sound changes is demonstrating her ability to modify her cognitive scheme about shaking rattles. She is engaging in what Piaget calls secondary circular reactions.

Secondary circular reactions are schemes regarding repeated actions that bring about a desirable consequence. The major difference between primary circular reactions and secondary circular reactions is whether the infant's activity is focused on the infant and his or her own body (primary circular reactions), or involves actions relating to the world outside (secondary circular reactions).

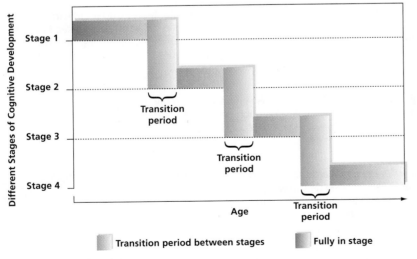

FIGURE 6-1 Transitions

Infants do not suddenly shift from one stage of cognitive development to the next. Instead, Piaget argues that there is a period of transition in which some behavior reflects one stage, while other behavior reflects the more advanced stage. Does this gradualism argue against Piaget's interpretation of stages?

During the third substage, babies' vocalization increases substantially as infants come to notice that if they make noises, other people around them will respond with noises of their own. Similarly, infants begin to imitate the sounds made by others. Vocalization becomes a secondary circular reaction that ultimately helps lead to the development of language and the formation of social relationships.

Substage 4: Coordination of Secondary Circular Reactions

One of the major leaps forward in *Substage 4: Coordination of secondary circular reactions,* which lasts from around 8 months to 12 months. Before this stage, behavior involved direct action on objects. When something happened by chance that caught an infant's interest, she attempted to repeat the event using a single scheme. However, in Substage 4, infants begin to employ **goal-directed behavior**, in which several schemes are combined and coordinated to generate a single act to solve a problem. For instance, they will push one toy out of the way to reach another toy that is lying, partially exposed, under it. They also begin to anticipate upcoming events. For instance, Piaget tells of his son Laurent, who at 8 months "recognizes by a certain noise caused by air that he is nearing the end of his feeding and, instead of insisting on drinking to the last drop, he rejects his bottle . . ." (Piaget, 1952, pp. 248–249).

Infants' newfound purposefulness, their ability to use means to attain particular ends, and their skill in anticipating future circumstances, owe their appearance in part to the developmental achievement of object permanence that emerges in Substage 4. **Object permanence** is the realization that people and objects exist even when they cannot be seen. It is a simple principle, but its mastery has profound consequences.

Piaget suggests that infants increasingly seek to repeat enjoyable events by acting on their environment.

Consider, for instance, 7-month-old Chu, who has yet to learn the idea of object permanence. Chu's father shakes a rattle in front of him, then takes the rattle and places it under a blanket. To Chu, who has not mastered the concept of object permanence, the rattle no longer exists. He will make no effort to look for it.

Several months later, when he is in Substage 4, the story is quite different (see Figure 6-2). This time, as soon as his father places the rattle under the blanket, Chu tries to toss the cover aside, eagerly searching for the rattle. Chu clearly has learned that the object continues to exist even when it cannot be seen. For the infant who achieves an understanding of object permanence, then, out of sight is decidedly not out of mind.

Before Object Permanence

After Object Permanence

FIGURE 6-2
Object Permanence

Before an infant has understood the idea of object permanence, he will not search for an object that has been hidden right before his eyes. But several months later, he will search for it, illustrating that he has attained object permanence. Why would the concept of object permanence be important to a caregiver?

Linda G. Miller

Education: Auburn University at Montgomery, Alabama: B.S. in education, M.A. in education, and Ph.D. in education.

Position: Author, with Mary Jo Gibbs, *Making Toys for Infants and Toddlers: Using Ordinary Stuff for Extraordinary Play.* Adjunct Professor of Education, Auburn University at Montgomery, Alabama

Home: Wetumpka, Alabama

Watching an infant play, one might think the child is randomly swatting various toys and objects, but research has found that children as young as infants not only interact with toys but also develop cognitively. According to educator and author, Linda Miller, the young infant is very aware and sensitive of his or her background.

"Young children enjoy high-contrast colors, but brighter colors tend to over-stimulate all children, not just infants," Miller said. "From research we have found that background colors such as beige are best. It's important to have the color in the activity instead of the environment. You don't want to have bright red walls, but rather have a red carpet where activity takes place," she added.

Because toys can be a variety of shapes, safety issues are of extreme importance with providing an infant with any toy.

"Infants are exploring their environments at all times," Miller noted, "and initially they explore with their mouths. It is also important not to have toys appropriate for older children in a younger child's environment."

Miller added that it is also important to introduce enough new toys to retain interest, but enough of the older ones to maintain familiarity. "You wouldn't want to change cuddle toys every week," she said.

A major component in the development of an infant's cognitive abilities is to develop a connection with a familiar adult, and toys can be one way of achieving this.

"With a connection to a familiar adult, young children feel safe and connected in the world and that feeling can sustain them into adulthood," Miller said. "Triangulation can be used to interact with a child in which the adult interacts with the new toy and then introduces it to the child. The child then plays with the toy and the adult."

Dramatic play with items such as cuddle toys, dolls, and even hats can help in developing the child's connectedness with a familiar adult.

Miller also notes the importance of literacy in infant development.

"It is very important to have books for young children and model that behavior," she explained. "Literacy begins at a very young age. The rhythm of the way sentences begin and end, and the visual things associated with books are important.

"Songs and rhymes have also been found to be important," Miller added. "Some research has suggested that reading difficulties later in life can be linked to the absence of these songs and rhymes."

The attainment of object permanence extends not only to inanimate objects but to people too. It gives Chu the security that his father and mother still exist even when they have left the room. This awareness is likely a key element in the development of social attachments, which we consider in Chapter 7. The recognition of object permanence also feeds infants' growing assertiveness: As they realize that an object taken away from them doesn't just cease to exist but is merely somewhere else, their only-too-human reaction may be to want it back—and quickly.

Although the understanding of object permanence emerges in Substage 4, it is only a rudimentary understanding. It takes several months for the concept to be fully comprehended, and infants continue for several months to make certain kinds of errors relating to object permanence. For instance, they often are fooled when a toy is hidden first under one blanket and then under a second blanket. In seeking out the toy, Substage 4 infants most often turn to the first hiding place, ignoring the second blanket under which the toy is currently located—even if the hiding was done in plain view. (For a more on the role of play and toys

from a toy designer's perspective, see the *Careers in Child Development* interview.)

Substage 5: Tertiary Circular Reactions *Substage 5: Tertiary circular reactions* is reached at around the age of 12 months and extends to 18 months. As the name of the stage indicates, during this period infants develop what Piaget labeled *tertiary circular reactions*, schemes regarding the deliberate variation of actions that bring desirable consequences. Rather than just repeating enjoyable activities, as they do with secondary circular reactions, infants appear to carry out miniature experiments to observe the consequences.

For example, Piaget observed his son Laurent dropping a toy swan repeatedly, varying the position from which he dropped it, carefully observing each time to see where it fell. Instead of just repeating the action each time (as in a secondary circular reaction), Laurent made modifications in the situation to learn about their consequences. As you may recall from our discussion of research methods in Chapter 2, this behavior represents the essence of the scientific method: An experimenter varies a situation in a laboratory to learn

Mental representation
An internal image of a past event
or object

Deferred imitation   An act in
which a person who is no longer
present is imitated by children

the effects of the variation. To infants in Substage 5, the world is their laboratory, and they spend their days leisurely carrying out one miniature experiment after another. Olivia, the baby described earlier who enjoyed dropping things from her high chair, is another little scientist in action.

What is most striking about infants' behavior during Substage 5 is their interest in the unexpected. Unanticipated events are treated not only as interesting but also as something to be explained and understood. Infants' discoveries can lead to newfound skills, some of which may cause a certain amount of chaos, as Olivia's dad realized while cleaning up around her high chair.

Substage 6: Beginnings of Thought   The final stage of the sensorimotor period is *Substage 6: Beginnings of thought*, which lasts from around 18 months to 2 years. The major achievement of Substage 6 is the capacity for mental representation, or symbolic thought. A **mental representation** is an internal image of a past event or object. Piaget argued that by this stage infants can imagine where objects might be that they cannot see. They can even plot in their heads unseen pathways of objects, so if a ball rolls under a piece of furniture, they can figure out where it is likely to emerge on the other side.

Because of children's new abilities to create internal representations of objects, their understanding of causality also becomes more sophisticated. For instance, consider Piaget's description of his son Laurent's efforts to open a gate:

> Laurent tries to open a garden gate but cannot push it forward because it is held back by a piece of furniture. He cannot account either visually or by any sound for the cause that prevents the gate from opening, but after having tried to force it he suddenly seems to understand; he goes around the wall, arrives at the other side of the gate, moves the armchair which holds it firm, and opens it with a triumphant expression. (Piaget, 1954, p. 296)

The attainment of mental representation also permits another important development: the ability to pretend. Using the skill of what Piaget refers to as **deferred imitation**, in which a person who is no longer present is imitated later, children are able to pretend that they are driving a car, feeding a doll, or cooking dinner long after they have witnessed such scenes played out in reality. To Piaget, deferred imitation provided clear evidence that children form internal mental representations.

Appraising Piaget: Support and Challenges

Most developmental researchers would probably agree that in many significant ways, Piaget's descriptions of how cognitive development proceeds during infancy are quite accurate (Harris, 1987; Marcovitch, Zelazo, & Schmuckler, 2003). Yet,

With the attainment of the cognitive skill of deferred imitation, children are able to imitate people and scenes they have witnessed in the past.

there is substantial disagreement over the validity of the theory and many of its specific predictions.

Let's start with what is clearly correct about the Piagetian approach. Piaget was a masterful reporter of children's behavior, and his descriptions of growth during infancy remain a monument to his powers of observation. Furthermore, literally thousands of studies have supported Piaget's view that children learn much about the world by acting on objects in their environment. Finally, the broad outlines sketched out by Piaget of the sequence of cognitive development and the increasing cognitive accomplishments that occur during infancy are generally accurate (Gratch & Schatz, 1987; Kail, 2004).

On the other hand, specific aspects of the theory have come under increasing scrutiny—and criticism—in the decades since Piaget carried out his pioneering work. For example, some researchers question the stage conception that forms the basis of Piaget's theory. Although, as we noted earlier, even Piaget acknowledged that children's transitions between stages are gradual, critics contend development proceeds in a much more continuous fashion. Rather than showing major leaps of competence at the end of one stage and the beginning of the next, improvement comes in more gradual increments, growing step-by-step in a skill-by-skill manner.

For instance, developmental researcher Robert Siegler suggests that cognitive development proceeds not in stages but in "waves." According to him, children don't one day drop a mode of thinking and the next take up a new form. Instead, there is an ebb and flow of cognitive approaches that children use to understand the world. One day children may use one form of cognitive strategy, while another day they may choose a less advanced strategy—moving back and forth over a period of time. Although one strategy may be used most frequently at a given age, children still may have access to alternative ways of thinking. Siegler thus sees cognitive development as being in constant flux (R. Siegler, 2003; Opfer & Siegler, 2007).

Other critics dispute Piaget's notion that cognitive development is grounded in motor activities. They charge that Piaget overlooked the importance of the sensory and perceptual systems that are present from a very early age in infancy—systems about which Piaget knew little, because so much of the research illustrating how sophisticated they are even in infancy was done relatively recently. Studies of children born without arms and legs (due to their mothers' ill-advised use of teratogenic drugs during pregnancy, as described in Chapter 3) show that such children display normal cognitive development, despite their lack of practice with motor activities, further evidence that the connection Piaget made between motor development and cognitive development was exaggerated (Decarrie, 1969; Butterworth, 1994).

To bolster their views, Piaget's critics also point to more recent studies that cast doubt on Piaget's view that infants are incapable of mastering the concept of object permanence until they are close to a year old. For instance, some work suggests that younger infants did not appear to understand object permanence because the techniques used to test their abilities were not sensitive enough to their true capabilities (Krojgaard, 2005; Walden et al., 2007; Baillargeon, 2004, 2008).

It may be that a 4-month-old doesn't search for a rattle hidden under a blanket because she hasn't learned the motor skills necessary to do the searching—not because she doesn't understand that the rattle still exists. Similarly, the apparent inability of young infants to comprehend object permanence may reflect more about their memory deficits than their lack of understanding of the concept: The memories of young infants may be poor enough that they simply do not recall the earlier concealment of the toy. In fact, when more age-appropriate tasks were employed, some researchers found indications of object permanence in children as young as 3 1/2 months (Aguiar & Baillargeon, 2002; Wang, Baillargeon, & Paterson, 2005).

Other types of behavior likewise seem to emerge earlier than Piaget suggested. For instance, recall the ability of neonates to imitate basic facial expressions of adults just hours after birth, as we discussed in Chapter 3. The presence of such skill at such an early age contradicts Piaget's view that initially infants are able to imitate only behavior that they see in others, using parts of their own body that they can plainly view—such as their hands and feet. In fact, facial imitation suggests that humans may be born with a basic, innate capability for imitating

others' actions, a capability that depends on certain kinds of environmental experiences, but one that Piaget believed develops later in infancy (Meltzoff & Moore, 2002; Lepage & Théret, 2007; Legerstee & Markova, 2008).

Piaget's work also seems to describe children from developed, Western countries better than those in non-Western cultures. For instance, some evidence suggests cognitive skills emerge on a different timetable for children in non-Western cultures than for children living in Europe and the United States. Infants raised in the Ivory Coast of Africa, for example, reach the various substages of the sensorimotor period at an earlier age than do infants reared in France (Dasen et al., 1978). This is not altogether surprising, because parents in the Ivory Coast tend to emphasize motor skills more heavily than do parents in Western societies, thereby providing greater opportunity for practice of those skills (Dasen et al., 1978; Rogoff & Chavajay, 1995; Mistry & Saraswathi, 2003).

Despite these problems regarding Piaget's view of the sensorimotor period, even his most passionate critics concede that he has provided us with a masterful description of the broad outlines of cognitive development during infancy. His failings seem to be in underestimating the capabilities of younger infants and in his claims that sensorimotor skills develop in a consistent, fixed pattern. Still, his influence has been enormous, and although the focus of many contemporary developmental researchers has shifted to newer information-processing approaches that we discuss next, Piaget remains a towering and pioneering figure in the field of development (Fischer & Hencke, 1996; Roth, Slone, & Dar, 2000; Kail, 2004).

REVIEW ↵ mydevelopmentlab

1. Piaget's theory of cognitive development is based on a _____ approach, in which development proceeds in a fixed order from birth.

   Answer: stage

2. According to Piaget, _____ is the process by which people understand an experience in terms of their current stage of cognitive development and way of thinking.

   Answer: assimilation

3. The first stage of development, according to Piaget, is the _____ stage.

   Answer: sensorimotor

4. Cognitive skills among children in _____-_____ cultures appear to emerge on a different timetable from children living in the United States and Europe.

   Answer: non-Western

To see more review questions, log on to MyDevelopmentLab.

From a child-care worker's perspective:

In general, what are some implications for child-rearing practices according to Piaget's observations about the ways children gain an understanding of the world? Would you use the same child-rearing approaches for a child growing up in a non-Western culture? Why or why not?

Information-Processing Approaches to Cognitive Development

Amber Nordstrom, 3 months old, breaks into a smile as her brother Marcus stands over her crib, picks up a doll, and makes a whistling noise through his teeth. In fact, Amber never seems to tire of Marcus's efforts at making her smile, and soon whenever Marcus appears and simply picks up the doll, her lips begin to curl into a smile.

Clearly, Amber remembers Marcus and his humorous ways. But how does she remember him? And how much else can Amber remember?

To answer questions such as these, we need to diverge from the road that Piaget laid out for us. Rather than seeking to identify the universal, broad milestones in cognitive development through which all infants pass, as Piaget tried to do, we must consider the specific processes by which individual babies acquire and use the information to which they are exposed. We need, then, to focus less on the qualitative changes in infants' mental lives and consider more closely their quantitative capabilities.

Information-processing approaches to cognitive development seek to identify the way that individuals take in, use, and store information. According to this approach, the quantitative changes in infants' abilities to organize and manipulate information represent the hallmarks of cognitive development.

Taking this perspective, cognitive growth is characterized by increasing sophistication, speed, and capacity in information processing. Earlier, we compared Piaget's idea of schemes to computer software, which directs how a computer deals with data from the world. We might compare the information-processing perspective on cognitive growth to the improvements that come from the use of more efficient programs that lead to increased speed and sophistication in the processing of information. Information-processing approaches, then, focus on the types of "mental programs" that people use when they seek to solve problems (Siegler, 1998; Cohen and Cashon, 2003).

Encoding, Storage, and Retrieval: The Foundations of Information Processing

Information processing has three basic aspects: encoding, storage, and retrieval (see Figure 6-3). *Encoding* is the process by which information is initially recorded in a form

usable to memory. Infants and children—indeed, all people—are exposed to a massive amount of information; if they tried to process it all, they would be overwhelmed. Consequently, they encode selectively, by picking and choosing the information to which they will pay attention.

Even if someone has been exposed to the information initially and has encoded it in an appropriate way, there is still no guarantee that he or she will be able to use it in the future. Information must also have been stored in memory adequately. *Storage* refers to the placement of material into memory. Finally, success in using the material in the future depends on retrieval processes. *Retrieval* is the process by which material in memory storage is located, brought into awareness, and used.

We can use our comparison to computers again here. Information-processing approaches suggest that the processes of encoding, storage, and retrieval are analogous to different parts of a computer. Encoding can be thought of as a computer's keyboard, through which one inputs information; storage is the computer's hard drive, where information is stored; and retrieval is analogous to software that accesses the information for display on the screen. Only when all three processes are operating—encoding, storage, and retrieval—can information be processed.

Automatization   In some cases, encoding, storage, and retrieval are relatively automatic, while in other cases they are deliberate. *Automatization* is the degree to which an activity requires attention. Processes that require relatively little attention are automatic; processes that require relatively large amounts of attention are controlled. For example, some activities such as walking, eating with a fork, or reading may be automatic for you, but at first they required your full attention.

Automatic mental processes help children in their initial encounters with the world by enabling them to easily and "automatically" process information in particular ways. For instance, by the age of 5, children automatically encode information in terms of frequency. Without a lot of attention to counting or tallying, they become aware, for example, of how often they have encountered various people, permitting them to differentiate familiar from unfamiliar people (Hasher & Zacks, 1984).

Furthermore, without intending to and without being aware of it, infants and children develop a sense of how often different stimuli are found together simultaneously. This permits them to develop an understanding of *concepts*, categorizations of objects, events, or people that share common

Encoding (initial recording of information)

Storage (information saved for future use)

Retrieval (recovery of stored information)

FIGURE 6-3
Information Processing

The process by which information is encoded, stored, and retrieved.

properties. For example, by encoding the information that four legs, a wagging tail, and barking are often together, we learn very early in life to understand the concept of "dog." Children—as well as adults—are rarely aware of how they learn such concepts, and they are often unable to articulate the features that distinguish one concept (such as a dog) from another (such as cat). Instead, learning tends to occur automatically.

Some of the things we learn automatically are unexpectedly complex. For example, infants have the ability to learn subtle statistical patterns and relationships; these results are consistent with a growing body of research showing that the mathematical skills of infants are surprisingly good. Infants as young as 5 months are able to calculate the outcome of simple addition and subtraction problems. In a study by developmental psychologist Karen Wynn, infants first were shown an object—a 4-inch-high Mickey Mouse statuette (see Figure 6-4). A screen was then raised, hiding the statuette. Next, the experimenter showed the infants a second, identical Mickey Mouse, and then placed it behind the same screen (Wynn, 1992, 1995, 2000).

Finally, depending on the experimental condition, one of two outcomes occurred. In the "correct addition" condition, the screen dropped, revealing the two statuettes (analogous to 1 + 1 = 2). But in the "incorrect addition" condition, the screen dropped to reveal just one statuette (analogous to the incorrect 1 + 1 = 1).

Because infants look longer at unexpected occurrences than at expected ones, the researchers examined the pattern of infants' gazes under the different conditions. In support of the notion that infants can distinguish between correct and incorrect addition, the infants in the experiment gazed longer at the incorrect result than at the correct one, indicating they expected a different number of statuettes. In a similar procedure, infants also looked longer at incorrect subtraction problems than at correct ones. The conclusion: Infants have rudimentary mathematical skills that enable them to understand whether a quantity is accurate or not.

The results of this research suggest that infants have an innate grasp of certain basic mathematical functions and statistical patterns. This inborn proficiency is likely to form the basis for learning more complex mathematics and statistical relationships later in life (Gelman & Gallistel, 2004; vanMarle & Wynn, 2006; McCrink & Wynn, 2004, 2007).

We turn now to several aspects of information processing, focusing on memory and individual differences in intelligence.

Memory During Infancy: They Must Remember This . . .

Simona Young spent her infancy with virtually no human contact. For up to 20 hours each day, she was left alone in a crib in a squalid Romanian orphanage. Cold bottles of milk were propped above her small body, which she clutched to get nourishment. She rocked back and forth, rarely feeling any soothing touch or hearing words of comfort. Alone in her bleak surroundings, she rocked back and forth for hours on end.

Simona's story, however, has a happy ending. After being adopted by a Canadian couple when she was two, Simona's life is now filled with the usual activities of childhood involving friends, classmates, and above all, a loving family. In fact, now, at age six, she can remember almost nothing of her miserable life in the orphanage. It is as if she has entirely forgotten the past (Blakeslee, 1995, p. C1).

How likely is it that Simona truly remembers nothing of her infancy? And if she ever does recall her first 2 years of life, how accurate will her memories be? To answer these questions, we need to consider the qualities of memory that exist during infancy.

Memory Capabilities in Infancy Certainly, infants have **memory** capabilities, defined as the process by which information is initially recorded, stored, and retrieved. As we've seen, infants can distinguish new stimuli from old stimuli, and this implies that some memory of the old must be present. Unless the infants had some memory of an original stimulus, it would be impossible for them to recognize that a new stimulus differed from the earlier one (Newcombe, Drummey, & Lie, 1995).

However, infants' capability to recognize new stimuli from old stimuli tells us little about how age brings about changes in the capacities of memory and in its fundamental nature. Do infants' memory capabilities increase as they get older? The answer is clearly affirmative. In one study, infants

FIGURE 6-4
Mickey Mouse Math

Researcher Karen Wynn found that 5-month-olds like Michelle Follet, pictured here, reacted differently according to whether the number of Mickey Mouse statuettes they saw represented correct or incorrect addition. Do you think this ability is unique to humans? How would an educator explain the uniqueness of this ability?

were taught that they could move a mobile hanging over the crib by kicking their legs (see Figure 6-5). It took only a few days for 2-month-old infants to forget their training, but 6-month-old infants still remembered for as long as 3 weeks (Rovee-Collier, 1993, 1999).

Furthermore, infants who were later prompted to recall the association between kicking and moving the mobile showed evidence that the memory continued to exist even longer. Infants who had received just two training sessions lasting 9 minutes each still recalled about a week later, as illustrated by the fact that they began to kick when placed in the crib with the mobile. Two weeks later, however, they made no effort to kick, suggesting that they had forgotten entirely.

But they hadn't: When the babies saw a reminder—a moving mobile—their memories were apparently reactivated. In fact, the infants could remember the association, following prompting, for as long as an additional month (Sullivan, Rovee-Collier, & Tynes, 1979). Other evidence confirms these results, suggesting that hints can reactivate memories that at first seem lost, and that the older the infant, the more effective such prompting is (Rovee-Collier, Hayne, & Columbo, 2001; Hildreth, Sweeney, & Rovee-Collier, 2003).

Is infant memory qualitatively different from that in older children and adults? Researchers generally believe that information is processed similarly throughout the life span, even though the kind of information being processed changes and different parts of the brain may be used. According to memory expert Carolyn Rovee-Collier, people, regardless of their age, gradually lose memories, although, just like babies, they may regain them if reminders are provided. Moreover, the more times a memory is retrieved, the more enduring the memory becomes (Barr, Marrott, & Rovee-Collier, 2003; Galluccio & Rovee-Collier, 2006; Hsu & Rovee-Collier, 2006).

The Duration of Memories Although the processes that underlie memory retention and recall seem similar throughout the life span, the quantity of information stored and recalled does differ markedly as infants develop. Older infants can retrieve information more rapidly and they can remember it longer. But just how long? Can memories from infancy be recalled, for example, after babies grow up?

Researchers disagree on the age from which memories can be retrieved. Although early research supported the notion of **infantile amnesia**, the lack of memory for experiences occurring prior to 3 years of age, more recent research shows that infants do retain memories. For example, Nancy Myers and her colleagues conducted an experiment in which they showed 6-month-old children an unusual series of events, such as intermittent periods of light and dark and unusual sounds. When the children were later tested at the age of 1 1/2 years or 2 1/2 years, they had some memory of the earlier experience. Other research indicates that infants show memory for behavior and situations that they have seen only once

(Myers, Clifton, & Clarkson, 1987; M. L. Howe, Courage, & Edison, 2004; Neisser, 2004).

Such findings are consistent with evidence that the physical trace of a memory in the brain appears to be relatively permanent, suggesting that memories, even from infancy, may be enduring. However, memories may not be easily or accurately retrieved. For example, memories are susceptible to interference from other, newer information, which may displace or block out the older information, thereby preventing its recall.

One reason why infants appear to remember less may be because language plays a key role in determining the way in which memories from early in life can be recalled: Older children and adults may only be able to report memories using the vocabulary that they had available at the time of the initial event, when the memories were stored. Because their vocabulary at the time of initial storage may have been quite limited, they are unable to describe the event later in life, even though it is actually in their memories (Adler, Gerhardstein, & Rovee-Collier, 1998; Bauer et al., 2000; Simcock & Hayne, 2002).

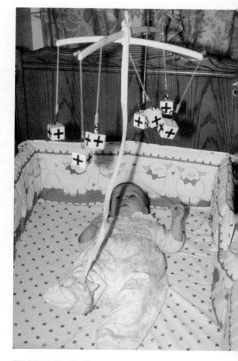

FIGURE 6-5
Early Signs of Memory

Infants who had learned the association between a moving mobile and kicking showed surprising recall ability if they were exposed to a reminder of the early memory.

The question of how well memories formed during infancy are retained in adulthood remains not fully answered. Although infants' memories may be highly detailed and can be enduring if the infants experience repeated reminders, it is still not clear how accurate those memories remain over the course of the life span. In fact, early memories are susceptible to misrecollection if people are exposed to related but contradictory information following the initial formation of the memory. Not only does such new information potentially impair recall of the original material, but also the new material may be inadvertently incorporated into the original memory, thereby corrupting its accuracy (Bauer, 1996; DuBreuil, Garry, & Loftus, 1998; Cordón et al., 2004).

In sum, although it is at least theoretically possible for memories to remain intact from a young age—if subsequent experiences do not interfere with their recollection—in most cases memories of personal experiences in infancy do not last into adulthood. Furthermore, evidence from brain scans shows that the prefrontal cortex and parts of the hippocampus of the brain—areas of the brain important to memory—do not begin to mature until 20 to 24 months of age. Current findings suggest that memories are not accurate prior around 2 years of age (Howe, 2003; Howe et al., 2004; Bauer, 2007).

Developmental quotient
An overall developmental score that relates to performance in four domains: motor skills, language use, adaptive behavior, and personal–social behavior

Bayley Scales of Infant Development   A measure that evaluates an infant's development from 2 to 42 months

The Cognitive Neuroscience of Memory   Some of the most exciting research on the development of memory is coming from studies of the neurological basis of memory. Advances in brain-scan technology, as well as studies of adults with brain damage, suggest that there are two separate systems involved with long-term memory. These two systems, called explicit memory and implicit memory, retain different sorts of information. *Explicit memory* is conscious memory that can be recalled intentionally. In comparison, *implicit memory* is memory that is recalled unconsciously. Implicit memory consists of motor skills, habits, and activities that can be remembered without conscious cognitive effort, such as how to ride a bike or climb a stairway.

Explicit and implicit memory emerge at different rates and involve different parts of the brain. Earliest memories seem to be implicit, and they involve the cerebellum and brain stem. The forerunner of explicit memory involves the hippocampus, but true explicit memory doesn't emerge until the second half of the 1st year. When explicit memory does emerge, it involves an increasing number of areas of the cortex of the brain (Bauer, 2004; Squire & Knowlton, 2005; Bauer, 2007).

Individual Differences in Intelligence: Is One Infant Smarter Than Another?

Maddy Rodriguez is a bundle of curiosity and energy. At 6 months of age, she cries heartily if she can't reach a toy, and when she sees a reflection of herself in a mirror, she gurgles and seems, in general, to find the situation quite amusing.

Jared Lynch, at 6 months, is a good deal more inhibited than Maddy. He doesn't seem to care much when a ball rolls out of his reach, losing interest in it rapidly. And, unlike Maddy, when he sees himself in a mirror, he pretty much ignores the reflection.

As anyone who has spent any time at all observing more than one baby can tell you, not all infants are alike. Some are full of energy and life, apparently displaying a natural-born curiosity, while others seem, by comparison, somewhat less interested in the world around them. Does this mean that such infants differ in intelligence?

Answering questions about how and to what degree infants vary in their underlying intelligence is not easy. Although it is clear that different infants show significant variations in their behavior, the issue of just what types of behavior may be related to cognitive ability is complicated. Interestingly, the examination of individual differences among infants was

Determining what is meant by intelligence in infants represents a major challenge for developmentalists.

the initial approach taken by developmental specialists to understand cognitive development, and such issues still represent an important focus within the field.

What Is Infant Intelligence?   Before we can address whether and how infants may differ in intelligence, we need to consider what is meant by the term *intelligence*. Educators, psychologists, and other experts on development have yet to agree upon a general definition of intelligent behavior, even among adults. Is it the ability to do well in scholastic endeavors? Proficiency in business negotiations? Competence in navigating across treacherous seas, such as that shown by peoples of the South Pacific, who have no knowledge of Western navigational techniques?

It is even more difficult to define and measure intelligence in infants than it is in adults. Do we base it on the speed with which a new task is learned through classical or operant conditioning? How fast a baby becomes habituated to a new stimulus? The age at which an infant learns to crawl or walk? Even if we are able to identify particular behaviors that seem to differentiate one infant from another in terms of intelligence during infancy, we need to address a further, and probably more important, issue: How well do measures of infant intelligence relate to eventual adult intelligence?

Clearly, such questions are not simple, and no simple answers have been found. However, developmental specialists have devised several approaches (summarized in Table 6-2) to illuminate the nature of individual differences in intelligence during infancy.

Developmental Scales   Developmental psychologist Arnold Gesell formulated the earliest measure of infant development, which was designed to distinguish normally developing babies from atypically developing ones (Gesell, 1946). Gesell based his scale on examinations of hundreds of babies. He compared their performance at different ages to learn what behaviors were most common at a particular age. If an infant varied significantly from the norms of a given age, he or she was considered to be developmentally delayed or advanced.

Following the lead of researchers who sought to quantify intelligence through a specific score (known as an intelligence quotient, or IQ, score), Gesell (1946) devised a developmental quotient, or DQ. The **developmental quotient** is an overall developmental score that relates to performance in four domains: motor skills (for example, balance and sitting), language use, adaptive behavior (such as alertness and exploration), and personal–social (for example, adequately feeding and dressing oneself).

Later researchers have created other developmental scales. For instance, Nancy Bayley developed one of the most widely used measures for infants. The **Bayley Scales of Infant Development** evaluate an infant's development from 2 to 42 months. The Bayley Scales focus on the areas of mental and motor abilities. The mental scale focuses on the senses, perception, memory, learning, problem solving, and language, while the motor scale evaluates fine- and gross-motor skills (see Table 6-3). Like Gesell's approach, the Bayley Scales yield a developmental quotient. A child who scores at an average level—meaning average performance for other children at the same age—receives a score of 100 (Bayley, 1969; Black & Matula, 1999; Gagnon & Nagle, 2000).

The virtue of approaches such as those taken by Gesell and Bayley is that they provide a good snapshot of an infant's current developmental level. Using these scales, we can tell in an objective manner whether a particular infant falls behind or is ahead of his or her same-age peers. They are particularly useful tools in identifying infants who are substantially behind their peers, and who therefore need immediate special attention (Culbertson & Gyurke, 1990; Aylward & Verhulst, 2000).

TABLE 6-2	Approaches Used to Detect Differences in Intelligence During Infancy
Developmental quotient	Formulated by Arnold Gesell, the developmental quotient is an overall developmental score that relates to performance in four domains: motor skills (balance and sitting), language use, adaptive behavior (alertness and exploration), and personal–social behavior.
Bayley Scales of Infant Development	Developed by Nancy Bayley, the Bayley Scales of Infant Development evaluate an infant's development from 2 to 42 months. The Bayley Scales focus on two areas: mental (senses, perception, memory, learning, problem solving, and language) and motor abilities (fine- and gross-motor skills).
Visual-recognition memory measurement	Measures of visual-recognition memory (the memory of and recognition of a stimulus that has been previously seen) also relate to intelligence. The more quickly an infant can retrieve a representation of a stimulus from memory, the more efficient, presumably, is that infant's information processing.

TABLE 6-3	Sample Items From the Bayley Scales of Infant Development	
Age	Mental Scale	Motor Scale
2 months	Turns head to sound Reacts to disappearance of face	Holds head erect/steady for 15 seconds Sits with support
6 months	Lifts cup by handle Looks at pictures in book	Sits alone for 30 seconds Grasps foot with hands
12 months	Builds tower of 2 cubes Turns pages of book	Walks with help Grasps pencil in middle
17–19 months	Imitates crayon stroke Identifies objects in photo	Stands alone on right foot Walks up stairs with help
23–25 months	Matches pictures Imitates a 2-word sentence	Laces 3 beads Jumps distance of 4 inches
38–42 months	Names 4 colors Uses past tense Identifies gender	Copies circle Hops twice on 1 foot Walks down stairs, alternating feet

(*Source:* Bayley, N. 7 1993. *Bayley Scales of Infant Development* [BSID-II] 2nd ed., San Antonio, IX: The Psychological Corporation)

From a nurse's perspective:

In what ways is the use of such developmental scales as Gesell's or Bayley's helpful? In what ways is it dangerous? How would you maximize the helpfulness and minimize the danger if you were advising a parent?

What such scales are not useful for is predicting a child's future course of development. A child whose development is identified by these measures as relatively slow at the age of 1 year will not necessarily display slow development at age 5, or 12, or 25. The association between most measures of behavior during infancy and adult intelligence, then, is minimal (Molfese & Acheson, 1997; Murray et al., 2007).

Because of the difficulties in using developmental scales to obtain measures of infant intelligence that are related to later intelligence, investigators have turned in the last decade to other techniques that may help assess intelligence in a meaningful way. Some have proven to be quite useful.

Information-Processing Approaches to Individual Differences in Intelligence

When we speak of intelligence in everyday parlance, we often differentiate between "quick" individuals and those who are "slow." Actually, according to research on the speed of information processing, such terms hold some truth. Contemporary approaches to infant intelligence suggest that the speed with which infants process information may correlate most strongly with later intelligence, as measured by IQ tests administered during adulthood (S. A. Rose & Feldman, 1997; Sigman, Cohen, & Beckwith, 1997).

How can we tell whether or not a baby is processing information quickly or not? Most researchers use habituation tests. Infants who process information efficiently ought to be able to learn about stimuli more quickly. Consequently, we would expect that they would turn their attention away from a given stimulus more rapidly than those who are less efficient at information processing, leading to the phenomenon of habituation. Similarly, measures of *visual-recognition memory,* the memory and recognition of a stimulus that has been previously seen, also relate to IQ. The more quickly an infant can retrieve a representation of a stimulus from memory, the more efficient, presumably, is that infant's information processing (Canfield et al., 1997; Rose, Jankowski, & Feldman, 2002; Robinson & Pascalis, 2005).

Research using an information-processing framework clearly suggests a relationship between information processing efficiency and cognitive abilities: Measures of how quickly infants lose interest in stimuli that they have previously seen, as well as their responsiveness to new stimuli, correlate moderately well with later measures of intelligence. Infants who are more efficient information processors during the 6 months following birth tend to have higher intelligence scores between 2 and 12 years of age, as well as higher scores on other measures of cognitive competence (Sigman, Cohen, & Beckwith, 2000; Rose, Feldman, & Jankowski, 2004; Fagan, Holland, & Wheeler, 2007).

Other research suggests that abilities related to the *multimodal approach to perception,* which we considered in Chapter 5, may offer clues about later intelligence. For instance, the ability to identify a stimulus that previously has been experienced through only one sense by using another sense (called *cross-modal transference*) is associated with intelligence. A baby who is able to recognize by sight a screwdriver that she has previously only touched, but not seen, is displaying cross-modal transference. Research has found that the degree of cross-modal transference displayed by an infant at age 1—which requires a high level of abstract thinking—is associated with intelligence scores several years later (Rose, Feldman, & Jankowski, 1999, 2004).

Although information processing efficiency and cross-modal transference abilities during infancy relate moderately well to later IQ scores, we need to keep in mind two qualifications. First, even though there is an association between early information processing capabilities and later measures of IQ, the correlation is only moderate in strength. Other factors, such as the degree of environmental stimulation, also play a crucial role in helping to determine adult intelligence. Consequently, we should not assume that intelligence is somehow permanently fixed in infancy.

Second, and perhaps even more important, intelligence measured by traditional IQ tests relates to a particular type of intelligence, one that emphasizes abilities that lead to academic, and certainly not artistic or professional, success. Consequently, predicting that a child may do well on IQ tests later in life is not the same as predicting that the child will be successful later in life.

Despite these qualifications, the relatively recent finding that an association exists between efficiency of information processing and later IQ scores does suggest some consistency of cognitive development across the life span. Whereas the earlier reliance on scales such as the Bayley led to the misconception that little continuity existed, the more recent information-processing approaches suggest that cognitive development unfolds in a more orderly, continuous manner from infancy to the later stages of life.

Assessing Information-Processing Approaches

The information-processing perspective on cognitive development during infancy is very different from that held by Piaget. Rather than focus on broad explanations of the *qualitative* changes that occur in infants' capabilities, as Piaget does, information processing looks at *quantitative* change. Piaget sees cognitive growth occurring in fairly sudden spurts; information processing sees more gradual, step-by-step growth. (Think of the difference between a track-and-field runner leaping hurdles versus a slow but steady marathon racer.)

Because information-processing researchers consider cognitive development in terms of a collection of individual skills, they are often able to use more precise measures of cognitive ability, such as processing speed and memory

Do Educational Media for Infants Enhance Their Cognitive Development?
Taking the Einstein Out of *Baby Einstein*

Jetta is 11 months old, with big eyes, a few pearly teeth—and a tiny index finger that can already operate electronic entertainment devices.

"We own everything electronic that's educational—LeapFrog, *Baby Einstein*, everything," said her mother, Naira Soibatian. "She has an HP laptop, bigger than mine. I know one leading baby book says, very simply, it's a waste of money. But there's only one thing better than having a baby, and that's having a smart baby. And at the end of the day, what can it hurt? She learns things, and she loves them." (Lewin, 2005, p. A1)

Naira Soibatian's philosophy captures the sentiments of many parents, who believe that exposing infants to educational media like the *Baby Einstein* series of videos may be beneficial to their cognitive growth. For instance, one survey found that about half the parents agreed that educational media are "very important" contributors to their children's intellectual development. And there is certainly a wide variety of products to try, ranging from DVDs to computer games and electronic devices, that are marketed with claims of having educational value. But one important question for parents is whether their infant children are really deriving any benefit from these products—and if they are not, is it truly a safe assumption that they such products are completely harmless (Wartella et al., 2004)?

A report from the Kaiser Family Foundation reveals that the marketing of educational media for infants is far outpacing the research on its effectiveness. In fact, practically no such research evidence exists. One part of the reason is the difficulty in conducting such research experimentally; much of the limited evidence is based on correlational studies that cannot rule out such factors as natural intelligence or parental education—or even discern true benefits of the media exposure from normal cognitive development over time (Garrison & Christakis, 2005).

Another part of the reason for the lack of research on the effectiveness of electronic media is that companies producing such products are reluctant to test the claims that their products are of value. Although they do conduct research on whether children can understand the media well enough to use it, their research on actual beneficial outcomes is very limited. Quite simply, they find that outcome research doesn't affect their sales nearly as much as the entertainment value of their products does. And they seem to have a point, because parents are buying and using their products

despite the lack of scientific evidence. For example, another Kaiser Family Foundation report revealed that babies as young as 6 months are spending over one and a half hours a day on average with television, video, and other on-screen media (Rideout et al., 2003).

But there may be reason to think that an overreliance on educational media products can actually be harmful. Consider the research of language expert Patricia Kuhl, who helped recognize the unique language learning abilities of infants. Kuhl has found that infants don't learn language from rote repetition, such as on an audiotape. Nine-month-old American infants who interacted with Mandarin-speaking adults acquired a sensitivity to the sounds of the Mandarin language—but not so for infants who were exposed to the language through audio and video media. Social interaction seems to be a critical part of language learning. Without social context, the language lessons were little more than meaningless noise to the infants. Other research also shows that very young children learn better from live demonstrations than they do from videotapes (Kuhl, Tsao, & Liu, 2003; Anderson & Pempek, 2005; Krcmar, Grela, & Lin, 2007).

What constitutes appropriate use of educational media for infants? Developmentalists agree that such materials are no replacement for learning that comes from social interaction, and they caution against allowing educational media use to supplant other activities such as free play and interaction with caregivers. On the other hand, if educational media are replacing other passive media-based activities used to keep a child entertained—such television lacking an educational component—then their use may be reasonable. In addition, because education media products often have at least one advantage over run-of-the-mill educational television: They typically include printed inserts, parent guides, and other resources to facilitate the kind of parent–child interaction that is known to benefit infants' cognitive development (Garrison & Christakis, 2005; Arnold & Colburn, 2007).

- Do you think that educational media for infants is worth a try, despite the lack of scientific research supporting its use? Why? Under what conditions might its use actually have undesirable consequences?

- Why do you think parents generally do not seem to be concerned about the lack of scientific evidence for the effectiveness of educational media for infants?

recall, than proponents of Piaget's approach. Still, the very precision of these individual measures makes it harder to get an overall sense of the nature of cognitive development, something at which Piaget was a master. It's as if information-processing approaches focus more on the individual pieces of the puzzle of cognitive development, while Piagetian approaches focus more on the whole puzzle.

Ultimately, both Piagetian and information-processing approaches are critical in providing an account of cognitive development in infancy. Coupled with advances in the biochemistry of the brain and theories that consider the effects of social factors on learning and cognition (which we'll discuss in the next chapter), the two help us paint a full picture of cognitive development. (Also see the *From Research to Practice* box.)

R E V I E W ↵ mydevelopmentlab

1. _____-_____ approaches to cognitive development seek to identify the way that individuals take in, use, and store information.

Answer: Information-processing

2. The duration of infants' _____, the process in which information is recorded, stored, and retrieved, is controversial.

Answer: memory

3. _____ is the process by which material in memory storage is located, brought into awareness, and used.

Answer: Retrieval

4. The _____ _____ is an overall developmental score that relates to performance in motor skills, language use, adaptive behavior, and personal–social domains.

Answer: developmental quotient

* To see more review questions, log on to MyDevelopmentLab.

The Roots of Language

Vicki and Dominic were engaged in a friendly competition over whose name would be the first word their baby, Maura, said. "Say 'mama,'" Vicki would coo, before handing Maura over to Dominic for a diaper change. Grinning, he would take her and coax, "No, say 'daddy.'" Both parents ended up losing—and winning—when Maura's first word sounded more like "baba," and seemed to refer to her bottle.

Mama. No. Cookie. Dad. Jo. Most parents can remember their baby's first word, and no wonder. It's an exciting moment, this emergence of a skill that is, arguably, unique to human beings

But those initial words are just the first and most obvious manifestations of language. Many months earlier, infants began to understand the language used by others to make sense of the world around them. How does this linguistic ability develop? What is the pattern and sequence of language development? And how does the use of language transform the cognitive world of infants and their parents? We consider these questions, and others, as we address the development of language during the first years of life.

The Fundamentals of Language: From Sounds to Symbols

Language, the systematic, meaningful arrangement of symbols, provides the basis for communication. But it does more than this: It is closely tied to the way we think and understand the world. It enables us to reflect on people and objects and to convey our thoughts to others.

Language has several formal characteristics that must be mastered as linguistic competence is developed. They include:

- *Phonology.* Phonology refers to the basic sounds of language, called *phonemes,* that can be combined to produce words and sentences. For instance, the "a" in "mat" and the "a" in "mate" represent two different phonemes in English. Although English employs just 40 phonemes to create every word in the language, other languages have as many as 85 phonemes—and some as few as 15 (Akmajian, Demers, & Harnish, 1984).

- *Morphemes.* A morpheme is the smallest language unit that has meaning. Some morphemes are complete words, while others add information necessary for interpreting a word, such as the endings "-s" for plural and "-ed" for past tense.

- *Semantics.* Semantics are the rules that govern the meaning of words and sentences. As their knowledge of semantics develops, children are able to understand the subtle distinction between "Ellie was hit by a ball" (an answer to the question of why Ellie doesn't want to play catch) and "A ball hit Ellie" (used to announce the current situation).

In considering the development of language, we need to distinguish between linguistic *comprehension,* the understanding of speech, and linguistic *production,* the use of language to communicate. One principle underlies the relationship between the two: Comprehension precedes production. An 18-month-old may be able to understand a complex series of directions ("pick up your coat from the floor and put it on the chair by the fireplace") but may not yet have strung more than two words together when speaking for herself. Throughout infancy comprehension also outpaces production. For instance, during infancy, comprehension of words expands at a rate of 22 new words a month, while production of words increases at a rate of about 9 new words a

Although we tend to think of language in terms of the production of words and then groups of words, infants can begin to communicate linguistically well before they say their first word.

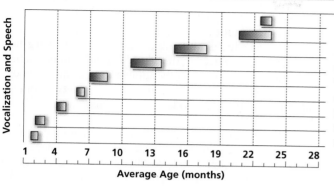

Vocalization and Speech

Uses first pronoun, phrase, sentence
Uses two words in combination
Says five words or more
Says first word
Two syllables with repetition of first: "ma-ma," "da-da"
Clear vocalization of several syllables
Babbling
Cooing
One syllable

Average Age (months)

FIGURE 6-6

Comprehension Precedes Production

Throughout infancy, the comprehension of speech precedes the production of speech.

(*Source:* Adapted from Bornstein & Lamb, 1992a)

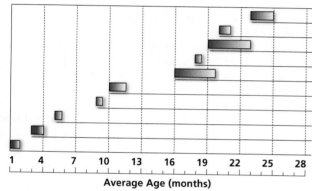

Language Comprehension

Understands two prepositions: "in," "under"
Repeats things said
Names a picture in a book: "dog"
Understands a simple question
Understands a prohibition
Responds to simple commands
Understands gestures and responds to "bye-bye"
Discriminates between friendly and angry talking
Vocalizes to social stimulation
Responds and attends to speaking voice

Average Age (months)

month, once talking begins (Benedict, 1979; Tincoff & Jusczyk, 1999; Rescorla, Alley, & Christine, 2001; see Figure 6-6).

Early Sounds and Communication

Spend 24 hours with even a very young infant and you will hear a variety of sounds: cooing, crying, gurgling, murmuring, and assorted types of other noises. These sounds, although not meaningful in themselves, play an important role in linguistic development, paving the way for true language (Bloom, 1993; O'Grady & Aitchison, 2005).

Prelinguistic communication is communication through sounds, facial expressions, gestures, imitation, and other nonlinguistic means. When a father responds to his daughter's "ah" with an "ah" of his own, and then the daughter repeats the sound, and the father responds once again, they are engaged in prelinguistic communication. Clearly, the "ah" sound has no particular meaning. However, its repetition, which mimics the give-and-take of conversation, teaches the infant something about turn-taking and the back-and-forth of communication (V. Reddy, 1999).

Babbling is universal, done in the same way across all cultures.

The most obvious manifestation of prelinguistic communication is babbling. **Babbling**—making speechlike but meaningless sounds—starts at the age of 2 or 3 months and continues until around the age of 1 year. When they babble, infants repeat the same vowel sound over and over, changing the pitch from high to low (as in "ee-ee-ee," repeated at different pitches). After the age of 5 months, the sounds of babbling begin to expand, reflecting the addition of consonants (such as "bee-bee-bee-bee").

Babbling is a universal phenomenon, accomplished in the same way throughout all cultures. While they are babbling, infants spontaneously produce all of the sounds found in every language, not just the language they hear people around them speaking.

In fact, even deaf children display their own form of babbling: Infants who cannot hear and who are exposed to sign language babble with their hands instead of their voices, and their gestural babbling is analogous to the verbal babbling of children who can speak. Furthermore, as shown in Figure 6-7, the areas of the brain activated during the production of hand gestures are

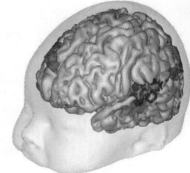

FIGURE 6-7

Infant's Speech Processing

The fMRI scan of a 3-month-old infant shows speech processing activity similar to that of an adult, suggesting there may be an evolutionary basis to language,

(*Source:* Dehaene-Lambertz, Hertz-Pannier, & Dubois, 2006)

similar to the areas activated during speech production, suggesting that spoken language may have evolved from gestural language (Corballis, 2000, 2002; Holoway & Petitto, 2002; Senghas, Kita, & Özyürek, 2004; Petitto et al., 2004).

Babbling typically follows a progression from simple to more complex sounds. Although exposure to the sounds of a particular language does not seem to influence babbling initially, eventually experience does make a difference. By the age of 6 months, babbling reflects the sounds of the language to which infants are exposed (Blake & de Boysson-Bardies, 1992). The difference is so noticeable that even untrained listeners can distinguish among babbling infants raised in cultures in which French, Arabic, or Cantonese languages are spoken. Furthermore, the speed at which infants begin homing in on their own language is related to the speed of later language development (Oller et al., 1997; Tsao, Liu, & Kuhl, 2004).

There are other indications of prelinguistic speech. For instance, consider 5-month-old Marta, who spies her red ball just beyond her reach. After reaching for it and finding that she is unable to get to it, she makes a cry of anger that alerts her parents that something is amiss, and her mother hands it to her. Communication has occurred.

Four months later, when Marta faces the same situation, she no longer bothers to reach for the ball and doesn't respond in anger. Instead, she holds out her arm in the direction of the ball, and with great purpose, seeks to catch her mother's eye. When her mother sees the behavior, she knows just what Marta wants. Clearly, Marta's communicative skills—although still prelinguistic—have taken a leap forward.

Even these prelinguistic skills are supplanted in just a few months, when the gesture gives way to a new communicative skill: producing an actual word. Marta's parents clearly hear her say "ball."

By the age of two, most children use two-word phrases, such as "ball play."

First Words

When a mother and father first hear their child say "Mama" or "Dada," or even "baba," Maura, the baby described earlier in this section's first word, it is hard to be anything but delighted. But their initial enthusiasm may be dampened a bit when they find that the same sound is used to ask for a cookie, a doll, and a ratty old blanket.

First words generally are spoken somewhere around the age of 10 to 14 months, but may occur as early as 9 months of age. Linguists differ on just how to recognize that a first word has actually been uttered. Some say it is when an infant clearly understands words and can produce a sound that is close to a word spoken by adults, such as a child who uses "mama" for any request she may have. Other linguists use a stricter criterion for the first word; they restrict "first word" to cases in which children give a clear, consistent name to a person, event, or object. In this view, "mama" counts as a first word only if it is consistently applied to the same person, seen in a variety of situations and doing a variety of things, and is not used to label other people (Hollich et al., 2000; Masataka, 2003).

Although there is disagreement over when we can say a first word has been uttered, no one disputes that once an infant starts to produce words, vocabulary increases at a rapid rate. By the age of 15 months, the average child has a vocabulary of 10 words and methodically expands until the one-word stage of language development ends at around 18 months of age. Once that happens, a sudden spurt in vocabulary occurs. In just a short period—a few weeks somewhere between 16 and 24 months of age—there is an explosion of language, in which a child's vocabulary typically increases from 50 to 400 words (Gleitman & Landau, 1994; Fernald et al., 1998; Nazzi & Bertoncini, 2003).

As you can see from the list in Table 6-4, the first words in children's early vocabularies typically regard objects and things, both animate and inanimate. Most often they refer to people or objects who constantly appear and disappear ("Mama"), to animals ("kitty"), or to temporary states ("wet"). These first words are often **holophrases**, one-word utterances that stand for a whole phrase, whose meaning depends on the particular context in which they are used. For instance, a youngster may use the phrase "ma" to mean, depending on the context, "I want to be picked up by Mom" or "I want something to eat, Mom" or "Where's Mom?" (Dromi, 1987; O'Grady & Aitchison, 2005).

Culture has an effect on the type of first words spoken. For example, unlike North American English-speaking infants, who are more apt to use nouns initially, Chinese Mandarin-speaking infants use more verbs than nouns. On the other hand, by the age of 20 months, there are remarkable cross-cultural similarities in the types of words spoken. For example, a comparison of 20-month-olds in Argentina, Belgium, France, Israel, Italy, and the Republic of Korea found that children's vocabularies in every culture contained greater proportions of nouns than other classes of words (Tardif, 1996; Bornstein, Cote, & Maital, 2004).

First Sentences

When Aaron was 19 months old, he heard his mother coming up the back steps, as she did every day just before dinner. Aaron turned to his father and distinctly said, "Ma come." In stringing those two words together, Aaron took a giant step in his language development.

The explosive increase in vocabulary that comes at around 18 months is accompanied by another accomplishment: the linking together of individual words into sentences that convey a single thought. Although there is a good deal of variability in the time at which children first create

Telegraphic speech Speech in which words not critical to the message are left out

TABLE 6-4	The Top 50: The First Words Children Understand and Speak		
		Comprehension Percentage	Production Percentage
1. *Nominals (Words referring to "things")*			
Specific (people, animals, objects)		56	61
		17	11
General (words referring to all members of a category)		39	50
Animate (objects)		9	13
Inanimate (objects)		30	37
Pronouns (e.g., this, that, they)		1	2
2. *Action words*		36	19
Social action games (e.g., peek-a-boo)		15	11
Events (e.g., "eat")		1	NA
Locatives (locating or putting something in specific location)		5	1
General action and inhibitors (e.g., "don't touch")		15	6
3. *Modifiers*		3	10
Status (e.g., "all gone")		2	4
Attributes (e.g., "big")		1	3
Locatives (e.g., "outside")		0	2
Possessives (e.g., "mine")		1	1
4. *Personal–social*		5	10
Assertions (e.g., "yes")		2	9
Social expressive (e.g., "bye-bye")		4	1

Note: Percentage refers to percentage of children who include this type of word among their first 50 words.
(*Source:* Adapted from Benedict, 1979)

two-word phrases, it is generally around 8 to 12 months after they say their first word.

The linguistic advance represented by two-word combinations is important because the linkage not only provides labels for things in the world but also indicates the relations between them. For instance, the combination may declare something about possession ("Mama key") or recurrent events ("Dog bark"). Interestingly, most early sentences don't represent demands or even necessarily require a response. Instead, they are often merely comments and observations about events occurring in the child's world (Halliday, 1975; O'Grady & Aichison, 2005).

Two-year-olds using two-word combinations tend to employ particular sequences that are similar to the ways in which adult sentences are constructed. For instance, sentences in English typically follow a pattern in which the subject of the sentence comes first, followed by the verb, and then the object ("Josh threw the ball"). Children's speech most often uses a similar order, although not all the words are initially included. Consequently, a child might say "Josh threw" or "Josh ball" to indicate the same thought. What is

significant is that the order is typically not "threw Josh" or "ball Josh," but rather the usual order of English, which makes the utterance much easier for an English speaker to comprehend (Brown, 1973; Hirsh-Pasek & Michnick-Golinkoff, 1995; Masataka, 2003).

Although the creation of two-word sentences represents an advance, the language used by children still is by no means adultlike. As we've just seen, 2-year-olds tend to leave out words that aren't critical to the message similar to the way we might write a telegram for which we were paying by the word. For that reason, their talk is often called **telegraphic speech**. Rather than saying, "I showed you the book," a child using telegraphic speech might say, "I show book." "I am drawing a dog" might become "Drawing dog" (see Table 6-5).

Early language has other characteristics that differentiate it from the language used by adults. For instance, consider Sarah, who refers to the blanket she sleeps with as "blankie." When her Aunt Ethel gives her a new blanket, Sarah refuses to call the new one a "blankie," restricting the word to her original blanket.

Underextension The overly restrictive use of words, common among children just mastering spoken language

Overextension The overly broad use of words, overgeneralizing their meaning

Referential style A style of language use in which language is used primarily to label objects

Expressive style A style of language use in which language is used primarily to express feelings and needs about oneself and others

Learning theory approach The theory that language acquisition follows the basic laws of reinforcement and conditioning

TABLE 6-5 Children's Imitation of Sentences Showing Decline of Telegraphic Speech

	Eve, 25.5 Months	Adam, 28.5 Months	Helen, 30 Months	Ian, 31.5 Months	Jimmy, 32 Months	June, 35.5 Months
I showed you the book.	I show book.	(I show) book.	C	I show you the book.	C	Show you the book.
I am very tall.	(My) tall.	I (very) tall.	I very tall.	I'm very tall.	Very tall.	I very tall.
It goes in a big box.	Big box.	Big box.	In big box.	It goes in the box.	C	C
I am drawing a dog.	Drawing dog.	I draw dog.	I drawing dog.	Dog.	C	C
I will read the book.	Read book.	I will read book.	I read the book.	I read the book.	C	C
I can see a cow.	See cow.	I want see cow.	C	Cow.	C	C
I will do that again.	Do-again.	I will that again.	I do that.	I again.	C	C

C = correct imitation.
(*Source:* Adapted from R. Brown & Fraser, 1963)

Sarah's inability to generalize the label of "blankie" to blankets in general is an example of **underextension**, using words too restrictively, which is common among children just mastering spoken language. Underextension occurs when language novices think that a word refers to a specific instance of a concept, instead of to all examples of the concept (Caplan & Barr, 1989; Masataka, 2003).

As infants like Sarah grow more adept with language, the opposite phenomenon sometimes occurs. In **overextension**, words are used too broadly, overgeneralizing their meaning. For example, when Sarah refers to buses, trucks, and tractors as "cars," she is guilty of overextension, making the assumption that any object with wheels must be a car. Although overextension reflects speech errors, it also shows that advances are occurring in the child's thought processes: The child is beginning to develop general mental categories and concepts (Johnson & Eilers, 1998; McDonough, 2002).

Infants also show individual differences in the style of language they use. For example, some use a **referential style**, in which language is used primarily to label objects. Others tend to use an **expressive style**, in which language is used primarily to express feelings and needs about oneself and others (Bates et al., 1994; Nelson, 1996; Bornstein, 2000).

Language styles reflect, in part, cultural factors. For example, mothers in the United States label objects more frequently than do Japanese mothers, encouraging a more referential style of speech. In contrast, mothers in Japan are more apt to speak about social interactions, encouraging a more expressive style of speech (Fernald & Morikawa, 1993).

The Origins of Language Development

The immense strides in language development during the preschool years raise a fundamental question: How does proficiency in language come about? Linguists are deeply divided on how to answer this question.

Learning Theory Approaches: Language as a Learned Skill One view of language development emphasizes the basic principles of learning. According to the **learning theory approach**, language acquisition follows the basic laws of reinforcement and conditioning discussed in Chapter 1 (Skinner, 1957). For instance, a child who articulates the word "da" may be hugged and praised by her father, who jumps to the conclusion that she is referring to him. This reaction reinforces the child, who is more likely to repeat the word. In sum, the learning theory perspective on language acquisition suggests that children learn to speak by being rewarded for making sounds that approximate speech. Through the process of *shaping*, language becomes more and more similar to adult speech.

However, there's a problem with the learning theory approach; it doesn't seem to adequately explain how children acquire the rules of language as readily as they do. For instance, young children are reinforced when they make errors. Parents are apt to be just as responsive if their child says, "Why the dog won't eat?" as they are if the child phrases the question more correctly ("Why won't the dog eat?"). Both forms of the question are understood correctly, and both elicit the same response; reinforcement is provided for both correct and incorrect language usage. Under such circumstances, learning theory is hard-put to explain how children learn to speak properly.

Children are also able to move beyond specific utterances they have heard, and produce novel phrases, sentences, and constructions, an ability that also cannot be explained by learning theory. Furthermore, children can apply linguistic rules to nonsense words. In one study, 4-year-old children heard the nonsense verb "to pilk" in the sentence "the bear is pilking the horse." Later, when asked what was happening to the horse, they responded by placing the nonsense verb in the correct tense and voice: "He's getting pilked by the bear."

Nativist Approaches: Language as an Innate Skill

Such conceptual difficulties with the learning theory approach have led to the development of an alternative, championed by the linguist Noam Chomsky and known as the nativist approach (1991, 1999). The **nativist approach** argues that there is a genetically determined, innate mechanism that directs the development of language. According to Chomsky, people are born with an innate capacity to use language, which emerges, more or less automatically, due to maturation.

Chomsky's analysis of different languages suggests that all the world's languages share a similar underlying structure, which he calls **universal grammar**. In this view, the human brain is wired with a neural system called the **language-acquisition device**, or **LAD**, that both permits the understanding of language structure and provides a set of strategies and techniques for learning the particular characteristics of the language to which a child is exposed. In this view, language is uniquely human, made possible by a genetic predisposition to both comprehend and produce words and sentences (Hauser, Chomsky, & Fitch, 2002; Lidz & Gleitman, 2004; Stromswold, 2006).

Support for Chomsky's nativist approach comes from identification of a specific gene related to speech production. Further support comes from research showing that language processing in infants involves brain structures similar to those in adult speech processing, suggesting an evolutionary basis to language (see Figure 6-7; Wade, 2001; Monaco, 2005; Dehaene-Lambertz, Hertz-Pannier, & Dubois, 2006).

The view that language is an innate ability unique to humans also has its critics. For instance, some researchers argue that certain primates are able to learn at least the basics of language, an ability that calls into question the uniqueness of the human linguistic capacity. Others point out that although humans may be genetically primed to use language, language use still requires significant social experience in order for it to be used effectively (MacWhinney, 1991; Savage-Rumbaugh et al., 1993; Goldberg, 2004).

The Interactionist Approaches

Neither the learning theory nor the nativist perspective fully explains language acquisition. As a result, some theorists have turned to a theory that combines both schools of thought. The *interactionist perspective* suggests that language development is produced through a combination of genetically determined predispositions and environmental circumstances that help teach language.

The interactionist perspective accepts that innate factors shape the broad outlines of language development. However, interactionists also argue that the specific course of language development is determined by the language to which children are exposed and the reinforcement they receive for using language in particular ways. Social factors are considered to be key to development, because the motivation provided by one's membership in a society and culture and one's interactions with others leads to the use of language and the growth of language skills (Dixon, 2004; Yang, 2006).

Just as there is support for some aspects of learning theory and nativist positions, the interactionist perspective has also received some support. We don't know, at the moment, which of these positions will ultimately provide the best explanation. More likely, different factors play different roles at different times during childhood. The full explanation for language acquisition, then, remains to be found.

Speaking to Children: The Language of Infant-Directed Speech

Say the following sentence aloud: Do you like the apple sauce?

Now pretend that you are going to ask the same question of an infant, and speak it as you would for a young child's ears.

Chances are several things happened when you translated the phrase for the infant. First of all, the wording probably changed, and you may have said something like, "Does baby like the applesauce?" At the same time, the pitch of your voice probably rose, your general intonation most likely had a singsong quality, and you probably separated your words carefully.

Infant-Directed Speech The shift in your language was due to your use of **infant-directed speech**, a style of speech that characterizes much of the verbal communication directed toward infants. This type of speech pattern used to be called *motherese*, because it was assumed that it applied only to mothers. However, that assumption was wrong, and the gender-neutral term *infant-directed speech* is now used more frequently.

Infant-directed speech, also known as "motherese," includes the use of short, simple sentences and is spoken using a pitch higher than that used with older children and adults.

Infant-directed speech is characterized by short, simple sentences. Pitch becomes higher, the range of frequencies increases, and intonation is more varied. There is also repetition of words, and topics are restricted to items that are assumed to be comprehensible to infants, such as concrete objects in the baby's environment.

Sometimes infant-directed speech includes amusing sounds that are not even words, imitating the prelinguistic speech of infants. In other cases, it has little formal structure, but is similar to the kind of telegraphic speech that infants use as they develop their own language skills.

Infant-directed speech changes as children become older. Around the end of the 1st year, infant-directed speech takes on more adultlike qualities. Sentences become longer and more complex, although individual words are still spoken slowly and deliberately. Pitch is also used to focus attention on particularly important words.

Infant-directed speech plays an important role in infants' acquisition of language. As discussed next, infant-directed speech occurs all over the world, though there are cultural variations. Newborns prefer such speech to regular language, a fact that suggests that they may be particularly receptive to it. Furthermore, some research suggests that babies who are exposed to a great deal of infant-directed speech early in life seem to begin to use words and exhibit other forms of linguistic competence earlier (Englund & Behne, 2006; Soderstrom, 2007; Werker et al., 2007).

DEVELOPMENTAL DIVERSITY

Is Infant-Directed Speech Similar in All Cultures?

Do mothers in the United States, Sweden, and Russia speak the same way to their infants?

In some respects, they clearly do. Although the words themselves differ across languages, the way the words are spoken to infants is quite similar. According to a growing body of research, there are basic similarities across cultures in the nature of infant-directed speech (Papousek & Papousek, 1991; Rabain-Jamin & Sabeau-Jouannet, 1997; Werker et al., 2007).

Consider, for instance, the comparison in Table 6-6 of the major characteristics of speech directed at infants used by native speakers of English and Spanish. Of the 10 most frequent features, 6 are common to both: exaggerated intonation, high pitch, lengthened vowels, repetition, lower volume, and instructional emphasis (i.e., heavy stress on certain key words (such as emphasizing the word "ball" in the sentence, "No, that's a *ball*") (Blount, 1982). Similarly, mothers in the United States, Sweden, and Russia all exaggerate and elongate the pronunciation of the three vowel sounds of "ee," "ah," and "oh" when speaking to infants in similar ways, despite differences in the languages in which the sounds are used (Kuhl et al., 1997).

TABLE 6-6	The Most Common Features of Infant-Directed Speech
English	**Spanish**
1. Exaggerated intonation	1. Exaggerated intonation
2. Breathiness	2. Repetition
3. High pitch	3. High pitch
4. Repetition	4. Instructional
5. Lowered volume	5. Attentionals
6. Lengthened vowel	6. Lowered volume
7. Creaky voice	7. Raised volume
8. Instructional	8. Lengthened vowel
9. Tenseness	9. Fast tempo
10. Falsetto	10. Personal pronoun substitution

(*Source:* Adapted from Blount, 1982)

Even deaf mothers use a form of infant-directed speech: When communicating with their infants, deaf mothers use sign language at a significantly slower tempo than when communicating with adults, and they frequently repeat the signs (Swanson, Leonard, & Gandour, 1992; Masataka, 1996, 1998, 2000).

The cross-cultural similarities in infant-directed speech are so great, in fact, that they appear in some facets of language specific to particular types of interactions. For instance, evidence comparing American English, German, and Mandarin Chinese speakers shows that in each of the languages, pitch rises when a mother is attempting to get an infant's attention or produce a response, while pitch falls when she is trying to calm an infant (Papousek & Papousek, 1991).

Why do we find such similarities across very different languages? One hypothesis is that the characteristics of infant-directed speech activate innate responses in infants. As we have noted, infants seem to prefer infant-directed speech over adult-directed speech, suggesting that their perceptual systems may be more responsive to such characteristics. Another explanation is that infant-directed speech facilitates language development, providing cues as to the meaning of speech before infants have developed the capacity to understand the meaning of words (Kuhl et al., 1997; Trainor & Desjardins, 2002; Falk, 2004).

Despite the similarities in the style of infant-directed speech across diverse cultures, there are some important cultural differences in the *quantity* of speech that infants hear from their parents. For example, although the Gusii of Kenya care for their infants in an extremely close, physical way, they speak to them less than American parents do (LeVine, 1994).

There are also some stylistic differences related to cultural factors in the United States. A major factor, it seems, might be gender.

Gender Differences

To a girl, a bird is a "birdie," a blanket a "blankie" and a dog a "doggy." To a boy, a bird is a "bird," a blanket a "blanket," and a dog a "dog."

At least that's what parents of boys and girls appear to think, as illustrated by the language they use toward their sons and daughters. Virtually from the time of birth, the language parents employ with their children differs depending on the child's sex, according to research conducted by developmental psychologist Jean Berko Gleason (Gleason et al., 1994; Gleason & Ely, 2002).

Gleason found that, by the age of 32 months, girls hear twice as many diminutives (words such as "kitty" or "dolly" instead of "cat" or "doll") as boys hear. Although the use of diminutives declines with increasing age, their use consistently remains higher in speech directed at girls than in that directed at boys (see Figure 6-8).

Parents also are more apt to respond differently to children's requests depending on the child's gender. For instance, when turning down a child's request, mothers are likely to respond with a firm "no" to a male child, but to soften the blow to a female child by providing a diversionary response ("Why don't you do this instead?") or by somehow making the refusal less direct. Consequently, boys tend to hear firmer, clearer language, while girls are exposed to

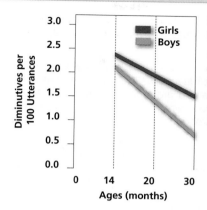

FIGURE 6-8 Diminishing Diminutives

While the use of diminutives toward both male and female infants declines with age, they are consistently used more often in speech directed at females. What do you think is the cultural significance of this? (*Source:* Gleason et al., 1991)

warmer phrases, often referring to inner emotional states (Perlmann & Gleason, 1990).

Do such differences in language directed at boys and girls during infancy affect their behavior as adults? There is no direct evidence that plainly supports such an association, but men and women do use different sorts of language as adults. For instance, as adults, women tend to use more tentative, less assertive language, such as "Maybe we should try to go to a movie," than men ("I know, let's go to a movie!"). Although we don't know whether these differences are a reflection of early linguistic experiences, such findings are certainly intriguing (Tenenbaum & Leaper, 2003; Hartshorne & Ullman, 2006; Plante et al., 2006).

From an educator's perspective: What are some implications of differences in the ways adults speak to boys and girls? How might such speech differences contribute to later differences not only in speech but also in attitudes?

Becoming an Informed Consumer of Development

What Can You Do to Promote Infants' Cognitive Development?

All parents want their children to reach their full cognitive potential, but sometimes efforts to reach this goal take a bizarre path. For instance, some parents spend hundreds of dollars enrolling in workshops with titles such as "How to Multiply Your Baby's Intelligence" and buying books with titles such as *How to Teach Your Baby to Read* (Doman & Doman, 2002).

Do such efforts ever succeed? Although some parents swear they do, there is no scientific support for the effectiveness of such programs. For example, despite the many cognitive skills of infants, no infant can actually read. Furthermore, "multiplying" a baby's intelligence is impossible, and such organizations as the American Academy of Pediatrics and the American Academy of Neurology have denounced programs that claim to do so.

On the other hand, certain things can be done to promote cognitive development in infants. The following suggestions, based upon findings of developmental researchers, offer a starting point (Gopnik, Meltzoff, & Kuhl, 2000; Cabrera, Shannon, & Tamis-LeMonda, 2007):

- *Provide infants the opportunity to explore the world.* As Piaget suggests, children learn by doing, and they need the opportunity to explore and probe their environment. Make sure the environment contains a variety of toys, books, and other sources of stimulation.

- *Be responsive to infants on both a verbal and a nonverbal level.* Try to speak *with* babies, as opposed to *at* them. Ask questions, listen to their responses, and provide further communication (Merlo, Bowman, & Barnett, 2007.)

- *Read to your infant.* Although they may not understand the meaning of your words, they will respond to your tone of voice and the intimacy provided by the activity. Reading

together also is associated with later literacy skills and begins to create a lifelong reading habit. In fact, the American Academy of Pediatrics recommends daily reading to children starting at the age of 6 months (American Academy of Pediatrics, 1997; Reutzel, Fawson, & Smith, 2006; Weigel, Martin, & Bennett, 2006).

- *Keep in mind that you don't have to be with an infant 24 hours a day.* Just as infants need time to explore their world on their own, parents and other caregivers need time off from child-care activities.

- *Don't push infants and don't expect too much too soon.* Your goal should not be to create a genius; it should be to provide a warm, nurturing environment that will allow an infant to reach his or her potential. ●

One important way to encourage cognitive development in infants is to read to them.

CASE STUDY

The Case of... The Deedio Mystery

Like most parents, Karen Muller was excited when her 10-month old daughter, Lisa, said her first word. She was especially-pleased that the word was "Mama." In the next 3 months, Lisa added more new words: kitty, baba (bottle), Dada, hi, cookie, and bus.

Karen waited eagerly for Lisa to begin putting words together, but the baby seemed content with her one-word utterances. Then, around 15 months, Lisa added some surprising new words: Mammia, Daddio, Meemia, and Deedio. Karen understood that Mammia and Daddio referred to her and Lisa's father, and she thought Meemia might be a reference to Lisa herself, but the new "fancy" labels puzzled her, and "Deedio" was a complete mystery. Also, Lisa did not use these new words in direct relation to the people they named, but in a seemingly abstract manner. For example, she said "Daddio" when her father was nowhere in sight.

Lisa's new words remained puzzling until one day, at about 18 months, as she and Karen were getting ready to go to the park, Lisa pointed to her own shoes and said, "Meemia." Then she pointed to her older brother's shoes and said, "Deedio." Karen realized two things instantly: Deedio was Lisa's brother David, and the use of "ia" and "io" endings on the familiar terms for her family and self indicated ownership.

Over the next month, Karen listened carefully to Lisa when she used these words. Daddy was still "Dada" when he was in sight, but Lisa began using two-word sentences, saying things like "Daddio coat" and "Meemia baby" (for her doll). The mystery of Deedio had been satisfactorily solved.

1. How would you explain to Karen the cognitive advance that was likely occurring in Lisa as she began using "Mammia," "Daddio," "Meemia," and "Deedio," even though, initially, these were one-word utterances?

2. Do you think Lisa's initial use of "Meemia" or "Daddio" could be considered telegraphic speech? Why or why not?

3. How might Karen have gone about investigating Lisa's meaning for words like "Mammia" and "Deedio" before the baby began using two-word sentences?

4. Do you think infants ever utter nonsense words, or does each word have a concrete meaning to the baby? Explain your response in terms of what we know about infant language acquisition.

5. How can a parent influence an infant's language development? In what ways is the parent's influence limited?

◀ Looking Back

What are the fundamental features of Piaget's theories of cognitive development?

Jean Piaget's stage theory asserts that children pass through stages of cognitive development in a fixed order. The stages represent changes not only in the quantity of infants' knowledge but also in the quality of that knowledge.

- According to Piaget, all children pass gradually through the four major stages of cognitive development (sensorimotor, preoperational, concrete operational, and formal operational) and their various substages when they are at an appropriate level of maturation and are exposed to relevant types of experiences.

- In the Piagetian view, children's understanding grows through assimilation of their experiences into their current way of thinking or through accommodation of their current way of thinking to their experiences.

- During the sensorimotor period (birth to about 2 years), with its six substages, infants progress from the use of simple reflexes through the development of repeated and integrated actions that gradually increase in complexity to the ability to generate purposeful effects from their actions. By the end of the sixth substage of the sensorimotor period, infants are beginning to engage in symbolic thought.

How do infants process information?

- Information-processing approaches to the study of cognitive development seek to learn how individuals receive, organize, store, and retrieve information. Such approaches differ from Piaget's by considering quantitative changes in children's abilities to process information.

- Infants have memory capabilities from their earliest days, although the accuracy of infant memories is a matter of debate.

How is infant intelligence measured?

- Traditional measures of infant intelligence, such as Gesell's developmental quotient and the Bayley Scales of Infant Development, focus on average behavior observed at particular ages in large numbers of children.
- Information-processing approaches to assessing intelligence rely on variations in the speed and quality with which infants process information.

By what processes do children learn to use language?

- Prelinguistic communication involves the use of sounds, gestures, facial expressions, imitation, and other nonlinguistic means to express thoughts and states. Prelinguistic communication prepares the infant for speech.
- Infants typically produce their first words between the ages of 10 and 14 months. At around 18 months of age, children typically begin to link words together into primitive sentences that express single thoughts. Beginning speech is characterized by the use of holophrases, telegraphic speech, underextension, and overextension.
- The learning theory approach to language acquisition assumes that adults and children use basic behavioral processes—such as conditioning, reinforcement, and shaping—in language learning. A different approach proposed by Chomsky holds that humans are genetically endowed with a language-acquisition device, which permits them to detect and use the principles of universal grammar that underlie all languages.

How do children influence adults' language?

- Adult language is influenced by the children to whom it is addressed. Infant-directed speech takes on characteristics, surprisingly invariant across cultures, that make it appealing to infants and probably encourage language development.
- Adult language also exhibits differences based on the gender of the child to whom it is directed, which may have effects that emerge later in life. ■

Epilogue

In this chapter we looked at infants' cognitive development from perspectives ranging from Piaget to information-processing theory. We examined infant learning, memory, and intelligence, and we concluded the chapter with a look at language.

Before we proceed to social and personality development in the next chapter, turn back to the Prologue of this chapter, about Jake Bausman's apparent eagerness to view *Baby Einstein* and other education media, and answer the following questions.

1. Is Anita Bausman correct to assume that her infant son Jake is "happy watching" educational videos just because he eagerly spends time in front of the television?

2. If a certain minimum amount of stimulation is necessary for an infant's cognitive development, does that necessarily mean that extra stimulation will accelerate the process?

3. In what ways might Anita Bausman unwittingly be limiting Jake's cognitive development if she relies too heavily on *Baby Einstein* videos to keep him occupied?

4. Do Anita Bausman's claims about the benefits to Jake of *Baby Einstein* videos ring true, or do they seem exaggerated? How might Jake's true intellectual capacity be more accurately assessed?

Key Terms and Concepts

scheme (p. 132)
assimilation (p. 132)
accommodation (p. 133)
sensorimotor stage (of cognitive
  development) (p. 133)
goal-directed behavior (p. 135)
object permanence (p. 135)
mental representation (p. 137)
deferred imitation (p. 137)
information-processing
  approaches (p. 139)

memory (p. 140)
infantile amnesia (p. 141)
developmental quotient (p. 142)
Bayley Scales of Infant
  Development (p. 142)
language (p. 146)
babbling (p. 147)
holophrases (p. 148)
telegraphic speech (p. 149)
underextension (p. 150)
overextension (p. 150)

referential style (p. 150)
expressive style (p. 150)
learning theory approach (p. 150)
nativist approach (p. 151)
universal grammar (p. 151)
language-acquisition
  device (LAD) (p. 151)
infant-directed speech (p. 151)

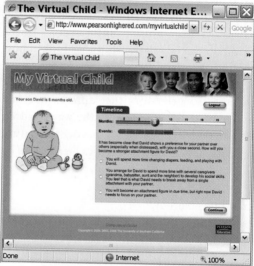

What decisions would you make while raising a child? What would the consequences of those decisions be?

Find out by logging onto **My Virtual Child** and raising your child from birth to 18 years.

chapter seven

Social and Personality Development in Infancy

PROLOGUE: THE VELCRO CHRONICLES

It was during the windy days of March that the problem in the child care center first arose. Its source: 10-month-old Russell Ruud. Otherwise a model of decorum, Russell had somehow learned how to unzip the Velcro chin strap to his winter hat. He would remove the hat whenever he got the urge, seemingly oblivious to the potential health problems that might follow.

But that was just the start of the real difficulty. To the chagrin of the teachers in the child care center, not to speak of the children's parents, soon other children were following his lead, removing their own caps at will.

Russell's mother, made aware of the anarchy at the child care center—and the other parents' distress over Russell's behavior—pleaded innocent. "I never showed Russell how to unzip the Velcro," claimed his mother, Judith Ruud, an economist with the Congressional Budget Office in Washington, D.C. "He learned by trial and error, and the other kids saw him do it one day when they were getting dressed for an outing." (Goleman, 1993, C10)

By then, though, it was too late for excuses: Russell, it seems, was an excellent teacher. Keeping the children's hats on their heads proved to be no easy task. Even more ominous was the thought that if the infants could master the Velcro straps on their hats, would they soon be unfastening the Velcro straps on their shoes and removing *them*?

▶ Looking Ahead

As babies like Russell show us, children are sociable from a very early age. This anecdote also demonstrates one of the side benefits of infants' participation in child care, and something research has begun to suggest: Through their social interactions, babies acquire new skills and abilities from more "expert" peers.

Infants, as we will see, have an amazing capacity to learn from other children, and their interactions with others can play a central role in their developing social and emotional worlds.

In this chapter we consider social and personality development in infancy. We begin by examining the emotional lives of infants, considering which emotions they feel and how well they can read others' emotions. We also look at how others' responses shape infants' own reactions, and how babies view their own and others' mental lives.

We then turn to infants' social relationships. We look at how they forge bonds of attachment and the ways they interact with family members and peers.

Finally, we cover the characteristics that differentiate one infant from another and discuss differences in the way children are treated depending on their gender. We'll consider the nature of family life and discuss how it differs from earlier eras. The chapter closes with a look at the advantages and disadvantages of infant child care outside the home, a child-care option that today's families increasingly employ.

After reading this chapter, you will be able to answer these questions:

- *Do infants experience emotions?*
- *What sort of mental lives do infants have?*
- *What is attachment in infancy and how does it affect a person's future social competence?*
- *What roles do other people play in infants' social development?*
- *What individual differences distinguish one infant from another?*
- *How does nonparental child care impact infants?*

Forming the Roots of Sociability

Germaine smiles when he catches a glimpse of his mother. Tawanda looks angry when her mother takes away the spoon that she is playing with. Sydney scowls when a loud plane flies overhead.

A smile. A look of anger. A scowl. The emotions of infancy are written all over a baby's face. Yet do infants experience emotions in the same way that adults do? When do they become capable of understanding what others are experiencing emotionally? And how do they use others' emotional states to make sense of their environment? We consider some of these questions as we seek to understand how infants develop emotionally and socially.

Emotions in Infancy: Do Infants Experience Emotional Highs and Lows?

Anyone who spends any time at all around infants knows they display facial expressions that seem indicative of their emotional states. In situations in which we expect them to be happy, they seem to smile; when we might assume they are frustrated, they show anger; and when we might expect them to be unhappy, they look sad.

In fact, these basic facial expressions are remarkably similar across the most diverse cultures. Whether we look at babies in India, the United States, or the jungles of New Guinea, the expression of basic emotions is the same (see Figure 7-1). Furthermore, the nonverbal expression of emotion, called *nonverbal encoding,* is fairly consistent among people of all ages. These consistencies have led researchers to conclude that we are born with the capacity to display basic emotions (Scharfe, 2000; Sullivan & Lewis, 2003; Ackerman & Izard, 2004).

Infants display a fairly wide range of emotional expressions. According to research on what mothers see in their children's nonverbal behavior, almost all think that by the age of 1 month, their babies have expressed interest and joy. In addition, 84% of mothers think their infants have expressed anger, 75% surprise, 58% fear, and 34% sadness. Research using the *Maximally Discriminative Facial Movement Coding System (MAX),* developed by psychologist Carroll Izard, also finds that interest, distress, and disgust are present at birth, and that other emotions emerge over the next few months (see Figure 7-2; Izard, 1982; Sroufe, 1996; Benson, 2003).

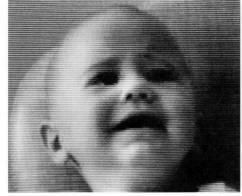

FIGURE 7-1

Universals in Facial Expressions

Across every culture, infants show similar facial expressions relating to basic emotions. Do you think such expressions are similar in nonhuman animals?

Although infants display similar kinds of emotions, the degree of emotional expressivity varies among infants. Children in different cultures show reliable differences in emotional expressiveness, even during infancy. For example, by the age of 11 months, Chinese infants are generally less expressive than European, American, and Japanese infants (Eisenberg et al., 2000; Camras, Meng, & Ujiie, 2002).

Experiencing Emotions

Does the capability of infants to express emotions nonverbally in a consistent, reliable manner mean that they actually *experience* emotions, and—if they do—is the experience similar to that of adults?

The fact that children display nonverbal expressions in a manner similar to that of adults does not necessarily mean that their actual experience is identical. In fact, if the nature of such displays is innate, or inborn, it is possible that facial expressions can occur without any accompanying awareness of our emotional experience. Nonverbal expressions, then, might be emotionless in young infants, in much the same way that your knee reflexively jerks forward when a physician taps it, without the involvement of emotions (Soussignan et al., 1997).

However, most developmental researchers do not think this is the case: They argue that the nonverbal expressions of infants represent actual emotional experiences. In fact, emotional expressions may not only reflect emotional experiences but also help regulate the emotion itself.

It now seems clear that infants are born with an innate repertoire of emotional expressions, reflecting basic emotional states such as happiness and sadness. As infants and children grow older, they expand and modify these basic expressions and become more adept at controlling their nonverbal behavioral expressions. For example, they eventually may learn that by smiling at the right time, they can increase the chances of getting their own way. In addition to *expressing* a wider variety of emotions, as children develop they also *experience* a wider array of emotions (Izard et al., 2003; Buss & Kiel, 2004).

Although infants do appear to experience emotions, the range of emotions at birth is fairly restricted. However, as they get older, infants both display and experience a wider range of increasingly complex emotions.

The advances in infants' emotional lives are made possible by the increasing sophistication of their brain. Initially, the differentiation of emotions occurs as the cerebral cortex becomes operative in the first 3 months of life. By the age of 9 or 10 months, the structures that make up the limbic system (the site of emotional reactions) begin to grow. The limbic system starts to work in tandem with the frontal lobes, allowing for an increased range of emotions (Davidson, 2003; Schore, 2003; Swain et al., 2007).

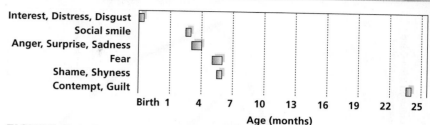

FIGURE 7-2 Emergence of Emotional Expressions

Emotional expressions emerge at roughly these times. Keep in mind that expressions in the first few weeks after birth do not necessarily reflect particular inner feelings.

Stranger Anxiety and Separation Anxiety

"She used to be such a friendly baby," thought Erika's mother. "No matter who she encountered, she had a big smile. But almost on the day she turned 7 months old, she began to react to strangers as if she were seeing a ghost. Her face crinkles up with a frown, and she either turns away or stares at them with suspicion. And she doesn't want to be left with anyone she doesn't already know. It's as if she has undergone a personality transplant."

What happened to Erika is, in fact, quite typical. By the end of the 1st year, infants often develop both stranger anxiety and separation anxiety. **Stranger anxiety** is the caution and wariness displayed by infants when encountering an unfamiliar person. Such anxiety typically appears in the second half of the 1st year.

What brings on stranger anxiety? Here, too, brain development, and the increased cognitive abilities of infants, plays a role. As infants' memory develops, they are able to separate the people they know from the people they don't. The same cognitive advances that allow them to respond so positively to those people with whom they are familiar also give them the ability to recognize those who are unfamiliar. Furthermore, between 6 and 9 months of age, infants begin trying to make sense of their world, and are starting to anticipate and predict events. When something happens that they don't expect—such as the appearance of an unknown person—they experience fear. It's as if an infant has a question but is unable to answer it (Volker, 2007).

Although stranger anxiety is common after the age of 6 months, significant differences exist between children. Some infants, particularly those who have a lot of experience with strangers, tend to show less anxiety than those whose experience with strangers is limited. Furthermore, not all strangers evoke the same reaction. For instance, infants tend to show less anxiety with female strangers than with male strangers. In addition, they react more positively to strangers who are children than to strangers who are adults, perhaps because their size is less intimidating (Swingler, Sweet, & Carver, 2007; Murray et al., 2007).

Separation anxiety
The distress displayed by infants
when a customary care provider
departs

Social smile   Smiling in
response to other individuals

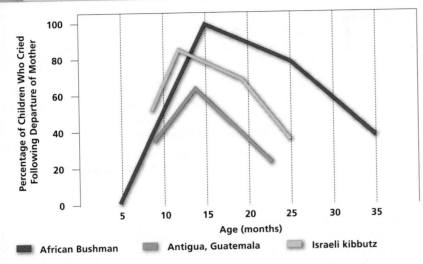

FIGURE 7-3 Separation Anxiety

Separation anxiety, the distress displayed by infants when their usual care provider
leaves their presence, is a universal phenomenon beginning at around the age of
7 or 8 months. It peaks at around the age of 14 months and then begins to decline.
Does separation anxiety have survival value for humans?

(*Source:* Kagan, Kearsley, & Zelazo, 1978)

Separation anxiety is the distress displayed by infants when a customary care provider departs. Separation anxiety, which is also universal across cultures, usually begins at about 7 or 8 months (see Figure 7-3). It peaks around 14 months, and then decreases. Separation anxiety is largely attributable to the same reasons as stranger anxiety. Infants' growing cognitive skills allow them to ask reasonable questions, but they may be questions that they are too young to understand the answer to: "Why is my mother leaving?" "Where is she going?" and "Will she come back?"

Stranger anxiety and separation anxiety represent important social progress. They reflect both cognitive advances and the growing emotional and social bonds between infants and their caregivers—bonds that we'll consider later in the chapter when we discuss infants' social relationships.

Smiling   As Luz lay sleeping in her crib, her mother and father caught a glimpse of the most beautiful smile crossing her face. Her parents were sure that Luz was having a pleasant dream. Were they right?

Probably not. The earliest smiles expressed during sleep probably have little meaning, although no one can be absolutely sure. By 6 to 9 weeks babies begin to smile reliably at the sight of stimuli that

When infants smile at a person
rather than a nonhuman
stimulus, they are displaying a
social smile.

please them, including toys, mobiles, and—to the delight of parents—people. The first smiles tend to be relatively indiscriminate, as infants first begin to smile at the sight of almost anything they find amusing. However, as they get older, they become more selective with their smiles.

A baby's smile in response to another person, rather than to nonhuman stimuli, is considered a **social smile**. As babies get older, their social smiles become directed toward particular individuals, not just anyone. By the age of 18 months, social smiling, directed more toward mothers and other caregivers, becomes more frequent than smiling directed toward nonhuman objects. Moreover, if an adult is unresponsive to a child, the amount of smiling decreases. By the end of their 2nd year children are quite purposefully using smiling to communicate their positive emotions, and they are sensitive to the emotional expressions of others (Carver, Dawson, & Panagiotides, 2003; Bigelow & Rochat, 2006; Fogel et al., 2006).

Decoding Others' Facial and Vocal Expressions

In Chapter 4, we discussed the possibility that neonates can imitate adults' facial expressions even minutes after birth. Although their imitative abilities certainly do not imply that they can understand the meaning of others' facial expressions, such imitation does pave the way for *nonverbal decoding* abilities, which begin to emerge fairly soon. Using these abilities, infants can interpret others' facial and vocal expressions that carry emotional meaning. For example, they can tell when a caregiver is happy to see them and can pick up on worry or fear in the faces of others (Bornstein & Arterberry, 2003; Hernandez-Reif et al., 2006; Striano & Vaish, 2006).

Infants seem to be able to discriminate vocal expressions of emotion at a slightly earlier age than they can interpret facial expressions. Although relatively little attention has been given to infants' perception of vocal expressions, it does appear that they are able to discriminate happy and sad vocal expressions at the age of 5 months (Soken & Pick, 1999; Montague & Walker-Andrews, 2002).

Scientists know more about the sequence in which nonverbal facial decoding ability progresses. In the first 6 to 8 weeks, infants' visual precision is sufficiently limited that they cannot pay much attention to others' facial expressions. But they soon begin to discriminate among different facial expressions of emotion and even seem to be able to respond to differences in emotional intensity conveyed by facial expressions. They also respond to unusual facial expressions. For instance, they show distress when their mothers pose bland, unresponsive, neutral facial expressions (Adamson & Frick, 2003; Bertin & Striano, 2006).

By the time they reach the age of 4 months, infants may already have begun to understand the emotions that lie behind the facial and vocal expressions of others. How do we know this? One important clue comes from a study in which 7-month-old infants were shown a pair of facial expressions relating to joy and sadness, and simultaneously heard a

Social referencing
The intentional search for information about others' feelings to help explain the meaning of uncertain circumstances and events

Self-awareness
Knowledge of oneself

vocalization representing either joy (a rising tone of voice) or sadness (a falling tone of voice). When the facial expression matched the tone, infants paid more attention, suggesting that they had at least a rudimentary understanding of the emotional meaning of facial expressions and voice tones (Kahana-Kalman & Walker-Andrews, 2001; Kochanska & Aksan, 2004; Grossmann, Striano, & Friederici, 2006).

In sum, infants learn early both to produce and to decode emotions, and they begin to learn the effect of their own emotions on others. Such abilities play an important role not only in helping them experience their own emotions, but—as we see next—in using others' emotions to understand the meaning of ambiguous social situations (Buss & Kiel, 2004).

Social Referencing: Feeling What Others Feel

> Twenty-three-month-old Stephania watches as her older brother Eric and his friend Chen argue loudly with each other and begin to wrestle. Uncertain of what is happening, Stephania glances at her mother. Her mother, though, wears a smile, knowing that Eric and Chen are just playing. On seeing her mother's reaction, Stephania smiles too, mimicking her mother's facial expression.

Like Stephania, most of us have been in situations in which we feel uncertain. In such cases, we sometimes turn to others to see how they are reacting. This reliance on others, known as social referencing, helps us decide what an appropriate response ought to be.

Social referencing is the intentional search for information about others' feelings to help explain the meaning of uncertain circumstances and events. Like Stephania, we use social referencing to clarify the meaning of a situation and so to reduce our uncertainty about what is occurring.

Social referencing first occurs around the age of 8 or 9 months. It is a fairly sophisticated social ability: Infants need it not only to understand the significance of others' behavior, by using such cues as their facial expressions, but also to understand the meaning of those behaviors within the context of a specific situation (Mumme & Fernald, 2003; de Rosnay, et al., 2006; Carver & Vaccaro, 2007).

Infants make particular use of facial expressions in their social referencing, the way Stephania did when she noticed her mother's smile. For instance, in one study infants were given an unusual toy to play with. The amount of time they played with it depended on their mothers' facial expressions. When their mothers displayed disgust, they played with it significantly less than when their mothers appeared pleased. Furthermore, when given the opportunity to play with the same toy later, the infants remained reluctant to play with it, despite the mothers' now neutral-appearing facial reactions, suggesting that parental attitudes may have lasting consequences (Hornik & Gunnar, 1988; Hertenstein & Campos, 2004).

Two Explanations of Social Referencing

Although it is clear that social referencing begins fairly early in life, researchers are still not certain how it operates. It may be that observing someone else's facial expression brings about the emotion the expression represents. That is, an infant who views someone looking sad may come to feel sad herself, and her behavior may be affected. On the other hand, it may be the case that viewing another's facial expression simply provides information. In this case, the infant does not experience the particular emotion represented by another's facial expression; she simply uses the display as data to guide her own behavior.

Both explanations for social referencing have received some support in research studies, and so we still don't know which is correct. What we do know is that social referencing is most likely to occur when a situation breeds uncertainty and ambiguity. Furthermore, infants who reach the age when they are able to use social referencing become quite upset if they receive conflicting nonverbal messages from their mothers and fathers. For example, if a mother shows with her facial expressions that she is annoyed with her son for knocking over a carton of milk, while his grandmother sees it as cute and smiles, the child receives two contradictory messages. Such mixed messages can be a real source of stress for an infant (Stenberg, 2003; Vaish & Striano, 2004).

The Development of Self: Do Infants Know Who They Are?

> Elysa, 8 months old, crawls past the full-length mirror that hangs on a door in her parents' bedroom. She barely pays any attention to her reflection as she moves by. On the other hand, her cousin Brianna, who is almost 2 years old, stares at herself in the mirror as she passes and laughs as she notices, and then rubs off, a smear of jelly on her forehead.

Perhaps you have had the experience of catching a glimpse of yourself in a mirror and noticing a hair out of place. You probably reacted by attempting to push the unruly hair back into place. Your reaction shows more than that you care about how you look. It implies that you have a sense of yourself, the awareness and knowledge that you are an independent social entity to which others react, and that you attempt to present this to the world in ways that reflect favorably upon you.

However, we are not born with the knowledge that we exist independently from others and the larger world. Very young infants do not have a sense of themselves as individuals; they do not recognize themselves in photos or mirrors. However, the roots of **self-awareness**, knowledge of oneself,

> **From a child-care provider's perspective:**
> In what situations do adults rely on social referencing to work out appropriate responses? How might social referencing be used to influence parents' behavior toward their children?

Theory of mind Knowledge and beliefs about how the mind works and how it affects behavior

Empathy An emotional response that corresponds to the feelings of another person

begin to grow at around the age of 12 months. We know this from a simple but ingenious experimental technique. An infant's nose is secretly colored with a dab of red powder, and the infant is seated in front of a mirror. If infants touch their noses or attempt to wipe off the rouge, we have evidence that they have at least some knowledge of their physical characteristics. For them, this awareness is one step in developing an understanding of themselves as independent objects. For instance, Brianna, in the example at the beginning of this section showed her awareness of her independence when she tried to rub the jam off her forehead (Asendorpf, Warkentin, & Baudonniere, 1996; Rochat, 2004).

Although some infants as young as 12 months seem startled on seeing the rouge spot, for most a reaction does not occur until between 17 and 24 months of age. It is also around this age that children begin to show awareness of their own capabilities. For instance, infants who participate in experiments when they are between the ages of 23 and 25 months sometimes begin to cry if the experimenter asks them to imitate a complicated sequence of behaviors involving toys, although they readily accomplish simpler sequences. Their reaction suggests that they are conscious that they lack the ability to carry out difficult tasks and are unhappy about it—a reaction that provides a clear indication of self-awareness (Legerstee, 1998; Asendorpf, 2002).

Children's cultural upbringing also impacts the development of self-recognition. For instance, Greek children—who experience parenting practices that emphasize autonomy and separation—show self-recognition at an earlier age than children from Cameroon in Africa. In the Cameroonian culture, parenting practices emphasize body contact and warmth, leading to more interdependence between infants and parents, and ultimately, later development of self-recognition (Keller, Voelker, & Yovsi, 2005).

In general, by the age of 18 to 24 months, infants in Western cultures have developed at least an awareness of their own physical characteristics and capabilities, and they understand that their appearance is stable over time. Although it is not clear how far this awareness extends, it is becoming increasingly evident that infants have not only a basic understanding of themselves but also the beginnings of an understanding of how the mind operates—what has come to be called a "theory of mind," which we discuss next (Forrester, 2001; Fogel, de Koeyer, & Bellagamba, 2002; Nielsen, Dissanayake, & Kashima, 2003; Lewis & Ramsay, 2004).

Theory of Mind: Infants' Perspectives on the Mental Lives of Others—and Themselves

What are infants' thoughts about thinking? According to developmental psychologist John Flavell, infants begin to understand certain things about their own and others' mental processes at quite an early age. Flavell has investigated children's **theory of mind**, their knowledge and beliefs about how the mind works and how it influences behavior. Theories of mind are the explanations that children use to explain how others think.

For instance, cognitive advances during infancy that we discussed in Chapter 6 permit older infants to come to see people in very different ways from other objects. They learn to see other people as *compliant agents,* beings similar to themselves who behave under their own power and who have the capacity to respond to infants' requests. Eighteen-month-old Chris, for example, has come to realize that he can ask his father to get him more juice (Rochat, 1999, 2004).

In addition, children's capacity to understand intentionality and causality grows during infancy. They begin to understand that others' behaviors have some meaning and that the behaviors they see people enacting are designed to accomplish particular goals, in contrast to the "behaviors" of inanimate objects. For example, a child comes to understand that his father has a specific goal when he is in the kitchen making sandwiches. In contrast, his father's car is simply parked in the driveway, having no mental life or goal (Ahn, Gelman, & Amsterlaw, 2000; Zimmer, 2003).

Another piece of evidence for infants' growing sense of mental activity is that by the age of 2, infants begin to demonstrate the rudiments of empathy. **Empathy** is an emotional response that corresponds to the feelings of another person. At 24 months of age, infants sometimes comfort others or show concern for them. In order to do this, they need to be aware of the emotional states of others. For example, 1-year-olds are able to pick up emotional cues by observing the behavior of an actress on television (Gauthier, 2003; Mumme & Fernald, 2003).

Further, during their 2nd year, infants begin to use deception, both in games of "pretend" and in outright attempts

Research suggests that this 18-month-old is exhibiting a clearly developed sense of self.

to fool others. A child who plays "pretend" and who uses falsehoods must be aware that others hold beliefs about the world—beliefs that can be manipulated. In short, by the end of infancy children have developed the rudiments of their own personal theory of mind. It helps them understand the actions of others and it affects their own behavior (van der Mark et al., 2002).

1. _____ anxiety typically appears around 6 months while separation anxiety usually begins at about 7 or 8 months.

Answer: Stranger

2. _____ _____, which first occurs around the age of 8 or 9 months, is the intentional search for information about others' feelings to help explain the meaning of uncertain circumstances and events.

Answer: Social referencing

3. A child's _____ _____ _____ is her knowledge and beliefs about the mental world.

Answer: theory of mind

*To see more review questions, log on to MyDevelopmentLab.

Forming Relationships

Louis Moore became the center of attention on the way home [from the hospital]. His father brought Martha, age 5, and Tom, age 3, to the hospital with him when Louis and his mother were discharged. Martha rushed to see "her" new baby and ignored her mother. Tom clung to his mother's knees in the reception hall of the hospital.

A hospital nurse carried Louis to the car. . . . The two older children immediately climbed over the seat and swamped mother and baby with their attention. Both children stuck their faces into his, smacked at him, and talked to him. They soon began to fight over him with loud voices. The loud argument and the jostling of his mother upset Louis, and he started to cry. He let out a wail that came like a shotgun blast into the noisy car. The children quieted immediately and looked with awe at this new infant. His insistent wails drowned out their bickering. He had already asserted himself in their eyes. Martha's lip quivered as she watched her mother attempt to comfort Louis, and she added her own soft cooing in imitation of her mother. Tom squeezed even closer to his mother, put his thumb in his mouth, and closed his eyes to shut out the commotion (Brazelton, 1983, p. 48).

The arrival of a newborn brings a dramatic change to a family's dynamics. No matter how welcome a baby's birth, it causes a fundamental shift in the roles that people play within the family. Mothers and fathers must start to build a relationship with their infant, and older children must adjust to the presence of a new member of the family and build their own alliance with their infant brother or sister.

Although the process of social development during infancy is neither simple nor automatic, it is crucial: The bonds that grow between infants and their parents, siblings, family, and others provide the foundation for a lifetime's worth of social relationships.

Attachment: Forming Social Bonds

The most important aspect of social development that takes place during infancy is the formation of attachment. **Attachment** is the positive emotional bond that develops between a child and a particular, special individual. When children experience attachment to a given person, they feel pleasure when they are with them and feel comforted by their presence at times of distress. The nature of our attachment during infancy affects how we relate to others throughout the rest of our lives (Waters, 2005; Hofer, 2006).

To understand attachment, the earliest researchers turned to the bonds that form between parents and children in the nonhuman animal kingdom. For instance, ethologist Konrad Lorenz (1965) observed newborn goslings, who have an innate tendency to follow their mother, the first moving object to which they typically are exposed after birth. Lorenz found that goslings whose eggs were raised in an incubator and who viewed him just after hatching would follow his

The bonds that children forge with others during infancy play a crucial role throughout their lives.

Ainsworth Strange Situation
A sequence of staged episodes
that illustrate the strength of
attachment between a child and
(typically) his or her mother

Secure attachment pattern
A style of attachment in which
children use the mother as a kind
of home base and are at ease
when she is present; when she
leaves, they become upset and
go to her as soon as she returns

FIGURE 7-4
Monkey Mothers Matter

Harlow's research showed that monkeys
preferred the warm, soft "mother" over the
wire "monkey" that provided food.

every movement, as if he were their mother. As we discussed in Chapter 4, he labeled this process *imprinting:* behavior that takes place during a critical period and involves attachment to the first moving object that is observed.

Lorenz's findings suggested that attachment was based on biologically determined factors, and other theorists agreed. For instance, Freud theorized that attachment grew out of a mother's ability to satisfy a child's oral needs.

It turns out, however, that the ability to provide food and other physiological needs may not be as crucial as Freud and other theorists first thought. In a classic study, psychologist Harry Harlow gave infant monkeys the choice of cuddling a wire "monkey" that provided food or a soft, terry cloth monkey that was warm but did not provide food (see Figure 7-4). Their preference was clear: Baby monkeys spent most of their time clinging to the cloth monkey, although they made occasional expeditions to the wire monkey to nurse. Harlow suggested that the preference for the warm cloth monkey provided *contact comfort* (Harlow & Zimmerman, 1959; Blum, 2002).

Harlow's work illustrates that food alone is not the basis for attachment. Given that the monkeys' preference for the soft cloth "mothers" developed some time after birth, these findings are consistent with the research we discussed in Chapter 4, showing little support for the existence of a critical period for bonding between human mothers and infants immediately following birth.

The earliest work on human attachment, which is still highly influential, was carried out by British psychiatrist John Bowlby (1951, 2007). In Bowlby's view, attachment is based primarily on infants' needs for safety and security—their

genetically determined motivation to avoid predators. As they develop, infants come to learn that their safety is best provided by a particular individual. This realization ultimately leads to the development of a special relationship with that individual, who is typically the mother. Bowlby suggested that this single relationship with the primary caregiver is qualitatively different from the bonds formed with others, including the father—a suggestion that, as we'll see later, has been a source of some disagreement.

According to Bowlby, attachment provides a home base. As children become more independent, they can progressively roam farther away from their secure base.

Developmental psychologist Mary Ainsworth built on Bowlby's theorizing to develop a widely used experimental technique to measure attachment (Ainsworth et al., 1978). The **Ainsworth Strange Situation** consists of a sequence of staged episodes that illustrate the strength of attachment between a child and (typically) his or her mother. The "strange situation" follows this general eight-step pattern: (1) The mother and baby enter an unfamiliar room; (2) the mother sits down, leaving the baby free to explore; (3) an adult stranger enters the room and converses first with the mother and then with the baby; (4) the mother exits the room, leaving the baby alone with the stranger; (5) the mother returns, greeting and comforting the baby, and the stranger leaves; (6) the mother departs again, leaving the baby alone; (7) the stranger returns; and (8) the mother returns and the stranger leaves (Ainsworth et al., 1978).

Infants' reactions to the various aspects of the Strange Situation vary considerably, depending on the nature of their attachment to their mothers. One-year-olds typically show one of four major patterns—securely attached, avoidant, ambivalent, and disorganized-disoriented (summarized in Table 7-1). Children who have a **secure attachment pattern** use the mother as the home base that Bowlby described. These children seem at ease in the Strange Situation as long as their mothers are present. They explore independently, returning to her occasionally. Although they may or may not appear upset when she leaves, securely attached children immediately go to her when she returns and seek contact. Most North American children—about two-thirds—fall into the securely attached category.

In this illustration of the strange situation, the infant first explores the playroom on his own, as long as his mother is present. But when she leaves, he begins to cry. On her return, however, he is immediately comforted and stops crying. The conclusion: He is securely attached.

Avoidant attachment pattern A style of attachment in which children do not seek proximity to the mother; after the mother has left, they seem to avoid her when she returns as if they are angered by her behavior

Ambivalent attachment pattern A style of attachment in which children display a combination of positive and negative reactions to their mothers; they show great distress when the mother leaves, but upon her return they may simultaneously seek close contact but also hit and kick her

Disorganized-disoriented attachment pattern A style of attachment in which children show inconsistent, often contradictory behavior, such as approaching the mother when she returns but not looking at her; they may be the least securely attached children of all

TABLE 7-1   Classifications of Infant Attachment

Label	Classification Criteria			
	Seeking Proximity with Caregiver	Maintaining Contact with Caregiver	Avoiding Proximity with Caregiver	Resisting Contact with Caregiver
Avoidant	Low	Low	High	Low
Secure	High	High (if distressed)	Low	Low
Ambivalent	High	High (often preseparation)	Low	High
Disorganized-disoriented	Inconsistent	Inconsistent	Inconsistent	Inconsistent

(*Source:* From E. Walters, 1963)

In contrast, children with an **avoidant attachment pattern** do not seek proximity to the mother, and after she has left, they typically do not seem distressed. Furthermore, they seem to avoid her when she returns. It is as if they are indifferent to her behavior. Some 20% of 1-year-old children are in the avoidant category.

Children with an **ambivalent attachment pattern**, display a combination of positive and negative reactions to their mothers. Initially, ambivalent children are in such close contact with the mother that they hardly explore their environment. They appear anxious even before the mother leaves, and when she does leave, they show great distress. But upon her return, they show ambivalent reactions, seeking to be close to her but also hitting and kicking, apparently in anger. About 10% to 15% of 1-year-olds fall into the ambivalent classification (Cassidy & Berlin, 1994).

Although Ainsworth identified only three categories, a more recent expansion of her work finds that there is a fourth category: disorganized-disoriented. Children who have a **disorganized-disoriented attachment pattern** show inconsistent, contradictory, and confused behavior. They may run to the mother when she returns but not look at her, or seem initially calm and then suddenly break into angry weeping. Their confusion suggests that they may be the least securely attached children of all. About 5% to 10% of children fall into this category (Mayseless, 1996; Cole, 2005).

A child's attachment style would be of only minor consequence were it not for the fact that the quality of attachment between infants and their mothers has significant consequences for relationships at later stages of life. For example, boys who are securely attached at the age of 1 year show fewer psychological difficulties at older ages than do avoidant or ambivalent children. Similarly, children who are securely attached as infants tend to be more socially and emotionally competent later, and others view them more positively. Adult romantic relationships are associated with the kind of attachment style developed during infancy

(Aviezer, Sagi, & Resnick, 2002; Mikulincer & Shaver, 2005; Simpson et al., 2007).

On the other hand, we cannot say that children who do not have a secure attachment style during infancy invariably experience difficulties later in life, nor that those with a secure attachment at age 1 always have good adjustment later on. In fact, some evidence suggests that children with avoidant and ambivalent attachment—as measured by the Strange Situation—do quite well (Weinfield, Sroufe, & Egeland, 2000; Lewis, Feiring, & Rosenthal, 2000; Fraley & Spieker, 2003).

In cases in which the development of attachment has been severely disrupted, children may suffer from *reactive attachment disorder,* a psychological problem characterized by extreme problems in forming attachments to others. In young children, it can be displayed in feeding difficulties, unresponsiveness to social overtures from others, and a general failure to thrive. Reactive attachment disorder is rare and typically the result of abuse or neglect (Vasa & Pine, 2006; Hardy, 2007).

Many Ainsworth, who devised the Strange Situation to measure attachment.

Producing Attachment: The Roles of the Mother and Father

As 5-month-old Annie cries passionately, her mother comes into the room and gently lifts her from her crib. After just a few moments, as her mother rocks Annie and speaks softly, Annie's cries cease, and she cuddles in her mother's arms. But the moment her mother places her back in the crib, Annie begins to wail again, leading her mother to pick her up once again.

The pattern is familiar to most parents. The infant cries, the parent reacts, and the child responds in turn. Such seemingly insignificant sequences as these, repeatedly occurring in the lives of infants and parents, help pave the way for the development of relationships between children, their parents, and the rest of the social world. We'll consider how each of the major caregivers and the infant play a role in the development of attachment.

Mothers and Attachment Sensitivity to their infants' needs and desires is the hallmark of mothers of securely attached infants. Such a mother tends to be aware of her child's moods, and she takes into account her child's feelings as they interact. She is also responsive during face-to-face interactions, provides feeding "on demand," and is warm and affectionate to her infant (Thompson, Easterbrooks, & Padilla-Walker, 2003; McElwain & Booth-LaForce, 2006).

It is not a matter of responding in just any fashion to their infants' signals that separates mothers of securely attached and insecurely attached children. Mothers of secure infants tend to provide the appropriate level of response. In fact, research has shown that overly responsive mothers are just as likely to have insecurely attached children as underresponsive mothers. In contrast, mothers whose communication involves *interactional synchrony,* in which caregivers respond to infants appropriately and both caregiver and child match emotional states, are more likely to produce secure attachment (Kochanska, 1998; Hane, Feldstein, & Dernetz, 2003).

Research showing the correspondence between mothers' sensitivity to their infants and the security of the infants' attachment is consistent with Ainsworth's arguments that at-tachment depends on how mothers react to their infants' emotional cues. Ainsworth suggests that mothers of securely attached infants respond rapidly and positively to their infants. For example, Annie's mother responds quickly to her cries by cuddling and comforting her. In contrast, the way for mothers to produce insecurely attached infants, according to Ainsworth, is to ignore the child's behavioral cues, to behave inconsistently with them, and to ignore or reject their social efforts. For example, picture a child who repeatedly and unsuccessfully tries to gain her mother's attention by calling or turning and gesturing from her stroller while her mother, engaged in conversation, ignores her. This baby is likely to be less securely attached than a child whose mother acknowledges her child more quickly and consistently.

But how does a mother learn to respond to her infant? One source is her own mother's example. Mothers typically respond to their infants based on their own attachment styles. As a result, there is substantial similarity in attachment patterns from one generation to the next (Peck, 2003).

It is important to realize that a mother's (and others') behavior toward an infant is at least in part a reaction to the child's ability to provide effective cues. A mother may not be able to respond effectively to a child whose own behavior is unrevealing, misleading, or ambiguous. For instance, children who clearly display their anger or fear or unhappiness will be easier to read—and to respond to effectively—than are children whose behavior is ambiguous. Consequently, the kind of signals an infant sends may in part determine how successfully the mother will respond.

Fathers and Attachment Up to now we've barely touched on one of the key players involved in the upbringing of a child: the father. If you looked at the early theorizing and research on attachment, you'd find little mention of the father and his potential contributions to the life of the infant (Tamis-LeMonda & Cabrera, 1999). There are at least two reasons for this absence. First, John Bowlby, who provided the initial theory of attachment, suggested that there was something unique about the mother–child relationship. He believed the mother was uniquely equipped, biologically, to provide sustenance for the child, and he concluded that this capability led to the development of a special relationship between mothers and children. Second, the early work on attachment was influenced by the traditional social views of the time, which considered it "natural" for the mother to be the primary caregiver, while the father's role was to work outside the home to provide for his family.

Several factors led to the demise of this view. Since the time of the initial studies, societal norms changed and fathers began to take a more active child-rearing role. More important, it became increasingly clear from research findings that—despite societal norms that relegated fathers to secondary child-rearing roles—some infants formed their primary initial relationship with their fathers (Volling & Belsky, 1992; Lewis & Lamb, 2003).

The differences in the ways that fathers and mothers play with their children occur even in families in which the father is the primary caregiver. Based on this observation, how does culture affect attachment?

In addition, a growing body of research has shown that fathers' expressions of nurturance, warmth, affection, support, and concern are extremely important to their children's emotional and social well-being. In fact, certain kinds of psychological disorders, such as substance abuse and depression, have been found to be related more to the father's than to the mother's behavior (Tamis-LeMonda & Cabrera, 2002; Veneziano, 2003; Parke, 2004; Roelofs et al., 2006).

Infants' social bonds extend beyond their parents, especially as they grow older. For example, one study found that although most infants formed their first primary relationship with one person, around one-third had multiple relationships, and it was difficult to determine which attachment was primary. Furthermore, by the time the infants were 18 months old, most had formed multiple relationships. In sum, infants may develop attachments not only to their mothers but to a variety of others as well (Silverstein & Auerbach, 1999; Booth, Kelly, & Spieker, 2003).

Are There Differences in Attachment to Mothers and Fathers? Although infants are fully capable of forming attachments to both mother and father—as well as to other individuals—the nature of attachment between infants and mothers, on the one hand, and infants and fathers, on the other, is not identical. For example, when they are in unusually stressful circumstances, most infants prefer to be soothed by their mothers rather than by their fathers (Thompson, Easterbrooks, & Padilla-Walker, 2003; Schoppe-Sullivan et al., 2006).

One reason for qualitative differences in attachment involves the differences in what fathers and mothers do with their children. Mothers spend a greater proportion of their time feeding and directly nurturing their children. In contrast, fathers spend more time, proportionally, playing with infants. Most fathers do contribute to child care: Surveys show that 95% say they do some child-care chores every day. But on average they still do less than mothers. For instance, 30% of fathers with spouses who work do 3 or more hours of daily child care. In comparison, 74% of employed married mothers spend 3 hours every day in child-care activities (Grych & Clark, 1999; Kazura, 2000; Whelan & Lally, 2002).

The way that fathers play with their babies is often quite different from that of mothers. Fathers engage in more physical, rough-and-tumble activities with their children. In contrast, mothers play traditional games such as peekaboo and games with more verbal elements (Paquette, Carbonneau, & Dubeau, 2003).

These differences in the ways that fathers and mothers play with their children occur even in the minority of families in the United States in which the father is the primary caregiver. Moreover, the differences occur in diverse cultures: Fathers in Australia, Israel, India, Japan, Mexico, and even in the Aka Pygmy tribe in central Africa all engage more in play than in caregiving, although the amount of time they spend with their infants varies widely. For instance, Aka fathers spend more time caring for their infants than do members of

any other known culture; they hold and cuddle their babies at a rate some five times higher than anywhere else in the world (Roopnarine, 1992; Bronstein, 1999; Hewlett & Lamb, 2002).

These similarities and differences in child-rearing practices across different societies raise an important question: How does culture affect attachment?

DEVELOPMENTAL DIVERSITY

Does Attachment Differ Across Cultures?

John Bowlby's observations of the biologically motivated efforts of the young of other species to seek safety and security were the basis for his views on attachment. His theory suggests that seeking attachment is biologically universal, and is a trait that we should find in other species and among humans of all cultures.

However, research has shown that human attachment is not as culturally universal as Bowlby predicted. Certain attachment patterns seem more likely among infants of particular cultures. For example, one study of German infants showed that most fell into the avoidant category. Other studies, conducted in Israel and Japan, have found a smaller proportion of infants who were securely attached than were identified in the United States. Finally, comparisons of Chinese and Canadian children show that Chinese children are more inhibited than Canadians in the Strange Situation (Takahashi, 1986; Chen et al., 1998; Rothbaum et al., 2000). Do such findings suggest that we should abandon the notion that attachment is a universal biological tendency?

Japanese parents seek to avoid separation and stress during infancy and do not foster independence. As a result, Japanese children often have the appearance of being less securely attached according to the Strange Situation, but using other measurement techniques they may well score higher in attachment.

Mutual regulation model
The model in which infants and parents learn to communicate emotional states to one another and to respond appropriately

Reciprocal socialization
A process in which infants' behaviors invite further responses from parents and other caregivers, which in turn bring about further responses from the infants

Not necessarily. While it is possible that Bowlby's claim that the desire for attachment is universal was too strongly stated, most of the data on attachment have been obtained by using the Ainsworth Strange Situation, which may not be the most appropriate measure in non-Western cultures. For example, Japanese parents seek to avoid separation and stress during infancy, and they don't strive to foster independence to the same degree as parents do in many Western societies. Because of their relative lack of prior experience in separation, then, infants placed in the Strange Situation may experience unusual stress—producing the appearance of less secure attachment in Japanese children. If a different measure of attachment were used, one that might be administered later in infancy, more Japanese infants could likely be classified as secure (Nakagawa, Lamb, & Miyaki, 1992; Vereijken et al., 1997; Dennis, Cole, & Zahn-Waxler, 2002).

Attachment is now viewed as susceptible to cultural norms and expectations. Cross-cultural and within-cultural differences in attachment reflect the nature of the measure employed and the expectations of various cultures. Some developmental specialists suggest that attachment should be viewed as a general tendency, but one that varies in the way it is expressed according to how actively caregivers in a society seek to instill independence in their children. Secure attachment, as defined by the Western-oriented Strange Situation, may be seen earliest in cultures that promote independence, but may be delayed in societies in which independence is a less important cultural value (Rothbaum et al., 2000; Rothbaum, Rosen, & Ujiie, 2002). ————————

Infant Interactions: Developing a Working Relationship

Research on attachment is clear in showing that infants may develop multiple attachment relationships, and that over the course of time the specific individuals with whom the infant is primarily attached may change. These variations in attachment highlight the fact that the development of relationships is an ongoing process, not only during infancy, but throughout our lifetimes.

Which processes underlie the development of relationships during infancy? One answer comes from studies that examine how parents interact with their children. For instance, across almost all cultures, mothers behave in typical ways with their infants. They tend to exaggerate their facial and vocal expressions—the nonverbal equivalent of the infant-directed speech that they use when they speak to infants (as we discussed in Chapter 6). Similarly, they often imitate their infants' behavior, responding to distinctive sounds and movements by

From a social worker's perspective:

Imagine you are a social worker visiting a foster home. It is 11 A.M. You find the breakfast dishes in the sink and books and toys all over the floor. The infant you have placed in the home is happily pounding on pots and pans as his foster mother claps time. The kitchen floor is gooey under the baby's high chair. What is your assessment?

repeating them. There are even types of games, such as peek-aboo, itsy-bitsy spider, and patty-cake, that are nearly universal (Harrist & Waugh, 2002; Kochanska, 1997; 2002).

According to the **mutual regulation model**, it is through these sorts of interactions that infants and parents learn to communicate emotional states to one another and to respond appropriately. For instance, in patty-cake, both infant and parent act jointly to regulate turn-taking behavior, with one individual waiting until the other completes a behavioral act before starting another. Consequently, at the age of 3 months, infants and their mothers have about the same influence on each other's behavior. Interestingly, by the age of 6 months, infants have more control over turntaking, although by the age of 9 months both partners once again become roughly equivalent in terms of mutual influence (Tronick, 2003).

The use of facial expressions is one of the ways infants and parents signal each other when they interact. As we saw earlier in this chapter, even very young infants are able to read, or decode, the facial expressions of their caregivers, and they react to those expressions. Studies have shown that an infant, whose mother displays a stony, immobile facial expression, will react by making a variety of sounds, gestures, and facial expressions of her own in response to such a puzzling situation—and possibly to elicit some new response from her mother. Infants also show more happiness themselves when their mothers appear happy, and they look at their mothers longer. On the other hand, infants are apt to respond with sad looks and to turn away when their mothers display unhappy expressions (Crockenberg & Leerkes, 2003; Reissland & Shepherd, 2006).

In short, the development of attachment in infants does not merely represent a reaction to the behavior of the people around them. Instead, there is a process of **reciprocal socialization**, in which infants' behaviors invite further responses from parents and other caregivers. In turn, the caregivers' behaviors bring about a reaction from the child, continuing the cycle. Recall, for instance, Annie, the baby who kept crying to be picked up when her mother put her in her crib. Ultimately, the actions and reactions of parents and child lead to an increase in attachment, forging and strengthening bonds between infants and caregivers as babies and caregivers communicate their needs and responses to each other. Figure 7-5 summarizes the sequence of infant–caregiver interaction (Kochanska & Aksan, 2004; Spinrad & Stifter, 2006).

Infants' Sociability with Their Peers: Infant–Infant Interaction

How sociable are infants with other children? Although it is clear that they do not form friendships in the traditional sense, babies do react positively to the presence of peers from early in life, and they engage in rudimentary forms of social interaction.

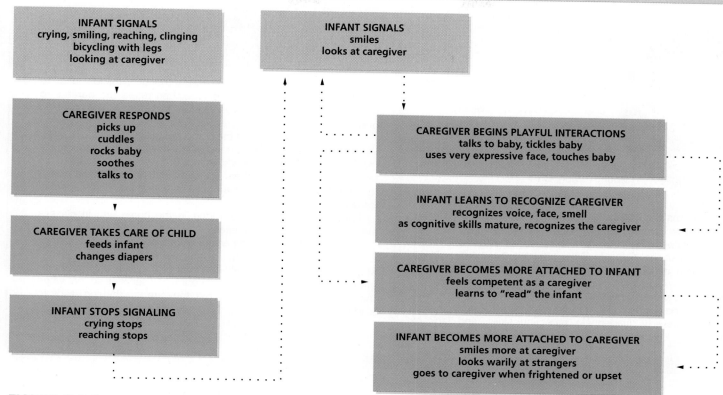

FIGURE 7-5 Sequence of Infant–Caregiver Interaction

The actions and reactions of caregivers and infants influence each other in complex ways. Do you think a similar pattern shows up in adult–adult interactions?

(*Source:* Adapted from Bell & Ainsworth, 1972; Tomlinson-Keasey, 1985)

Infants' sociability is expressed in several ways. From the earliest months of life, they smile, laugh, and vocalize while looking at their peers. They show more interest in peers than in inanimate objects and pay greater attention to other infants than they do to a mirror image of themselves. They also begin to show preferences for peers with whom they are familiar compared with those they do not know. For example, studies of identical twins show that twins exhibit a higher level of social behavior toward each other than toward an unfamiliar infant (Eid et al., 2003).

Infants' level of sociability generally rises with age. Nine- to 12-month-olds mutually present and accept toys, particularly if they know each other. They also play social games, such as peekaboo or crawl-and-chase. Such behavior is important, as it serves as a foundation for future social exchanges in which children will try to elicit responses from others and then offer reactions to those responses. These kinds of exchanges are important to learn, since they continue into adulthood. For example, someone who says, "Hi, what's up?" may be trying to elicit a response to which he or she can then reply (Endo, 1992; Eckerman & Peterman, 2001).

Finally, as infants age, they begin to imitate each other. Such imitation serves a social function and can also be a powerful teaching tool. For example, recall the story of 10-month-old Russell Ruud in the chapter Prologue, who showed the other children in his child-care center how he could remove his hat by unfastening its Velcro straps, and soon had others following his lead (Jones, 2007).

According to Andrew Meltzoff, a developmental psychologist at the University of Washington, Russell's ability to impart this information is only one example of how so-called expert babies are able to teach skills and information to other infants. According to the research of Meltzoff and his colleagues, the abilities learned from these expert's example are retained and later utilized to a remarkable degree. Learning by exposure starts early in life. Recent evidence shows that even 7-week-old infants can perform delayed imitation of a novel stimulus to which they have earlier been exposed, such as an adult sticking the tongue out the side of the mouth (Barr & Hayne, 1999, Meltzoff & Moore, 1994, 1999; Meltzoff, 2002).

CAREERS in CHILD DEVELOPMENT

Joyce Meyers

Education: Capital University, Columbus, Ohio: B.S.W.

Position: Social worker and service coordinator for the Help Me Grow program, Knox County Health Department, Mount Vernon, Ohio

Home: Mount Vernon, Ohio

Not all newborns and infants have access to the proper care needed for good development nor do they get the opportunity to participate in a preschool. For those who don't, social workers such as Joyce Meyers of the Help Me Grow program make sure that as many of them as possible receive the best care and attention available.

"We live in a small county that is mostly rural," says Meyers, who carries a caseload of 46 children, "and many of the issues we deal with involve poverty, inadequate parenting skills, and lack of education."

Meyers tries to assess a child's home situation and to identify what the problems are. She then refers the parents to the appropriate service organization to address the specific problems.

"When we initially go into the home, we make two or three visits, for a comprehensive assessment," she explains. "We try to identify the issues that need to be addressed. But we have to be cautious because in some cases there are so many issues that the parent may be overwhelmed. We then have to determine the top-priority issues."

Parenting education is provided in the home and in classes available at a local health center.

"We also make sure the parents have a health-care provider for themselves and their children. If not, we will find one for them," Meyers points out. "Basically, the goal of the Help Me Grow program is to provide health and developmental services so that when the children reach the age of three, they are healthy and ready to start preschool."

To some developmentalists, the capacity of young children to engage in imitation suggests that imitation may be inborn. In support of this view, research has identified a class of neurons in the brain that seems related to an innate ability to imitate. *Mirror neurons* are neurons that fire not only when an individual enacts a particular behavior but also when the individual simply observes *another* organism carrying out the same behavior (Falck-Ytter, 2006; Lepage & Théret, 2007).

For example, research on brain functioning shows activation of the inferior frontal gyrus both when an individual carries out a particular task and also when observing another individual carrying out the same task. Mirror neurons may help infants understand others' actions and to develop a theory of mind. Dysfunction of mirror neurons may be related to the development of disorders involving children's theory of mind as well as autism, a psychological disorder involving significant emotional and linguistic problems (Dapretto et al., 2006; Kilner, Friston, & Frith, 2007).

The idea that through exposure to other children, infants learn new behaviors, skills, and abilities has several implications. For one thing, it suggests that interactions between infants provide more than social benefits; they may have an impact on children's future cognitive development

as well. Even more important, these findings illustrate that infants may benefit from participation in child-care centers (which we consider later in this chapter). Although we don't know for sure, the opportunity to learn from their peers may prove to be a lasting advantage for infants in group child-care settings.

REVIEW ⏎ mydevelopmentlab

1. _____ is the positive emotional bond that develops between a child and a particular, special individual.

   Answer: Attachment

2. One-year-olds show four major attachment patterns: _____, avoidant, ambivalent, and disorganized-disoriented.

   Answer: secure

3. According to the _____ _____ model, infants and parents learn to communicate emotional states to one another and to respond appropriately.

   Answer: mutual regulation

To see more review questions, log on to MyDevelopmentLab.

Personality The sum total of the enduring characteristics that differentiate one individual from another

Erikson's theory of psychosocial development The theory that considers how individuals come to understand themselves and the meaning of others'—and their own—behavior

Trust-versus-mistrust stage According to Erikson, the period during which infants develop a sense of trust or mistrust, largely depending on how well their needs are met by their caregivers

Autonomy-versus-shame-and-doubt stage The period during which, according to Erikson, toddlers (aged 18 months to 3 years) develop independence and autonomy if they are allowed the freedom to explore, or shame and self-doubt if they are restricted and overprotected

Temperament Patterns of arousal and emotionality that are consistent and enduring characteristics of an individual

Differences Among Infants

Lincoln was a difficult baby, his parents both agreed. For one thing, it seemed like they could never get him to sleep at night. He cried at the slightest noise, a problem since his crib was near the windows facing a busy street. Worse yet, once he started crying, it seemed to take forever to calm him down again. One day his mother, Aisha, was telling her mother-in-law, Mary, about the challenges of being Lincoln's mom. Mary recalled that her own son, Lincoln's father Malcom, had been much the same way. "He was my first child, and I thought this was how all babies acted. So, we just kept trying different ways until we found out how he worked. I remember, we put his crib all over the apartment until we finally found out where he could sleep, and it ended up being in the hallway for a long time. Then his sister, Maleah, came along, and she was so quiet and easy, I didn't know what to do with my extra time!"

As the story of Lincoln's family shows, babies are not all alike, and neither are their families. In fact, as we'll see, some of the differences among people seem to be present from the moment we are born. The differences among infants include overall personality and temperament, and differences in the lives they lead—differences based on their gender, the nature of their families, and the ways in which they are cared for.

Personality Development: The Characteristics That Make Infants Unique

The origins of **personality**, the sum total of the enduring characteristics that differentiate one individual from another, stem from infancy. From birth onward, infants begin to show unique, stable traits and behaviors that ultimately lead to their development as distinct, special individuals (Caspi, 2000; Kagan, 2000; Shiner, Masten, & Roberts, 2003).

According to psychologist Erik Erikson, whose approach to personality development we first discussed in Chapter 2, infants' early experiences are responsible for shaping one of the key aspects of their personalities: whether they will be basically trusting or mistrustful.

Erikson's theory of psychosocial development considers how individuals come to understand themselves and the meaning of others'—and their own—behavior (Erikson, 1963). The theory suggests that developmental change occurs throughout people's lives in eight distinct stages, the first of which occurs in infancy.

According to Erikson, during the first 18 months of life, we pass through the **trust-versus-mistrust stage**. During this period, infants develop a sense of trust or mistrust, largely depending on how well their needs are met by their caregivers. Mary's attention to Malcom's needs, in the example above, probably helped him develop a basic sense of trust

in the world. Erikson suggests that if infants are able to develop trust, they experience a sense of hope, which permits them to feel as if they can fulfill their needs successfully. On the other hand, feelings of mistrust lead infants to see the world as harsh and unfriendly, and they may have later difficulties in forming close bonds with others.

During the end of infancy, children enter the **autonomy-versus-shame-and-doubt stage**, which lasts from around 18 months to 3 years. During this period, children develop independence and autonomy if parents encourage exploration and freedom within safe boundaries. However, if children are restricted and overly protected, they feel shame, self-doubt, and unhappiness.

Erikson argues that personality is primarily shaped by infants' experiences. However, as we discuss next, other developmentalists concentrate on consistencies of behavior that are present at birth, even before the experiences of infancy. These consistencies are viewed as largely genetically determined and as providing the raw material of personality.

According to Erikson, children from 18 months to 3 years develop independence and autonomy if parents encourage exploration and freedom, within safe boundaries. What does Erikson theorize if children are restricted and overly protected at this stage?

Temperament: Stabilities in Infant Behavior

Sarah's parents thought there must be something wrong. Unlike her older brother Josh, who had been so active as an infant that he seemed never to be still, Sarah was much more placid. She took long naps and was easily soothed on those relatively rare occasions when she became agitated. What could be producing her extreme calmness?

The most likely answer: The difference between Sarah and Josh reflected differences in temperament. As we first discussed in Chapter 3, **temperament** encompasses patterns of arousal and emotionality that are consistent and enduring characteristics of an individual (Rothbart, Ahadi, & Evans, 2000; Kochanska, 2004).

Temperament refers to how children behave, as opposed to what they do or why they do it. Infants show temperamental differences in general disposition from the time of birth, initially being largely due to genetic factors, and temperament is fairly stable well into adolescence. On the other hand, temperament is not fixed and unchangeable: Child-rearing practices can modify temperament significantly. In fact, some children show little consistency in temperament from one age to another (McCrae et al., 2000; Rothbart, Derryberry, & Hershey, 2000; Rothbart & Derryberry, 2002).

Temperament is reflected in several dimensions of behavior. One central dimension is *activity level*, which reflects

Easy babies Babies who have a positive disposition; their body functions operate regularly, and they are adaptable

Difficult babies Babies who have negative moods and are slow to adapt to new situations; when confronted with a new situation, they tend to withdraw

Slow-to-warm babies Babies who are inactive, showing relatively calm reactions to their environment; their moods are generally negative, and they withdraw from new situations, adapting slowly

the degree of overall movement. Some babies (like Sarah and Maleah, in the earlier examples) are relatively placid, and their movements are slow and almost leisurely. In contrast, the activity level of other infants (like Josh) is quite high, with strong, restless movements of the arms and legs.

Another important dimension of temperament is the nature and quality of an infant's mood, and in particular a child's *irritability*. Like Lincoln, who was described in the example at the beginning of this section, some infants are easily disturbed and cry readily, while others are relatively easygoing. Irritable infants fuss a great deal, and they are easily upset. They are also difficult to soothe when they do begin to cry. Such irritability is relatively stable: Infants who are irritable at birth remain irritable at the age of 1, and even at age 2 they are still more easily upset than those infants who were not irritable directly following birth (Worobey & Bajda, 1989). (Other aspects of temperament are listed in Table 7-2.)

Categorizing Temperament: Easy, Difficult, and Slow-to-Warm Babies Because temperament can be viewed along so many dimensions, some researchers have asked whether there are broader categories that can be used to describe children's overall behavior. According to Alexander Thomas and Stella Chess, who carried out a large-scale study of a group of infants that has come to be known as the *New York Longitudinal Study* (Thomas & Chess, 1980), babies can be described according to one of several profiles:

- **Easy babies** have a positive disposition. Their body functions operate regularly, and they are adaptable. They are generally positive, showing curiosity about new situations, and their emotions are moderate or low in intensity. This category applies to about 40% (the largest number) of infants.

- **Difficult babies** have more negative moods and are slow to adapt to new situations. When confronted with a new situation, they tend to withdraw. About 10% of infants belong in this category.

- **Slow-to-warm babies** are inactive, showing relatively calm reactions to their environment. Their moods are generally negative, and they withdraw from new situations, adapting slowly. Approximately 15% of infants are slow-to-warm.

As for the remaining 35%, they cannot be consistently categorized. These children show a variety of combinations of characteristics. For instance, one infant may have relatively sunny moods, but react negatively to new situations, or another may show little stability of any sort in terms of general temperament.

TABLE 7-2   Dimensions of Temperament

Dimension	Definition
Activity level	Proportion of active time periods to inactive time periods
Approach–withdrawal	The response to a new person or object, based on whether the child accepts the new situation or withdraws from it
Adaptability	How easily the child is able to adapt to changes in his or her environment
Quality of mood	The contrast of the amount of friendly, joyful, and pleasant behavior with unpleasant, unfriendly behavior
Attention span and persistence	The amount of time the child devotes to an activity and the effect of distraction on that activity
Distractibility	The degree to which stimuli in the environment alter behavior
Rhythmicity (regularity)	The regularity of basic functions such as hunger, excretion, sleep, and wakefulness
Intensity of reaction	The energy level or reaction of the child's response
Threshold of responsiveness	The intensity of stimulation needed to elicit a response

(*Source:* Thomas, Chess, & Birch, 1968)

Goodness-of-fit The notion that development is dependent on the degree of match between children's temperament and the nature and demands of the environment in which they are being raised

Gender The sense of being male or female

The Consequences of Temperament: Does Temperament Matter?

One obvious question to emerge from the findings of the relative stability of temperament is whether a particular kind of temperament is beneficial. The answer seems to be that no single type of temperament is invariably good or bad. Instead, children's long-term adjustment depends on the **goodness-of-fit** of their particular temperament with the nature and demands of the environment in which they find themselves. For instance, children with a low activity level and low irritability may do particularly well in an environment in which they are left to explore on their own and are allowed largely to direct their own behavior. In contrast, high-activity-level, highly irritable children may do best with greater direction, which permits them to channel their energy in particular directions (Thomas & Chess, 1980; Strelau, 1998; Schoppe-Sullivan et al., 2007). Mary, the grandmother in the earlier example, found ways to adjust the environment for her son, Malcom. Malcom and Aisha may need to do the same for their own son, Lincoln.

Some research does suggest that certain temperaments are, in general, more adaptive than others. For instance, difficult children are more likely to show behavior problems by school age than those who were classified in infancy as easy children. But not all difficult children experience problems. The key determinant seems to be the way parents react to their infant's difficult behavior. If they react by showing anger and inconsistency—responses that their child's difficult, demanding behavior readily evokes—then the child is ultimately more likely to experience behavior problems. On the other hand, parents who display more warmth and consistency in their responses are more likely to have a child who avoids later problems (Thomas, Chess, & Birch, 1968; Teerikangas et al., 1998; Pauli-Pott, Mertesacker, & Bade, 2003).

Furthermore, temperament seems to be at least weakly related to infants' attachment to their adult caregivers. For example, infants vary considerably in how much emotion they display nonverbally. Some are "poker-faced," showing little expressivity, while others' reactions tend to be much more easily decoded. More expressive infants may provide more discernible cues to others, thereby easing the way for caregivers to be more successful in responding to their needs and facilitating attachment (Feldman & Rimé, 1991; Seifer, Schiller, & Sameroff, 1996; Meritesacker, Bade, & Haverkock, 2004).

Cultural differences also have a major influence on the consequences of a particular temperament. For instance, children who would be described as "difficult" in Western cultures actually seem to have an advantage in the East African Masai culture. The reason? Mothers offer their breast to their infants only when they fuss and cry; therefore, the irritable, more difficult infants are apt to receive more nourishment than the more placid, easy infants. Particularly when environmental conditions are bad, such as during a drought, difficult babies may have an advantage (deVries, 1984; Gartstein et al., 2007).

The Biological Basis of Temperament

Recent approaches to temperament grow out of the framework of behavioral genetics that we discussed in Chapter 3. From this perspective, temperamental characteristics are seen as inherited traits that are fairly stable during childhood and across the entire life span. These traits are viewed as making up the core of personality and playing a substantial role in future development.

Such a view supports the consistency of such traits as *physiological reactivity*. This is a characteristic of temperament that corresponds to the level of physiological reactivity that is exhibited in response to a novel stimulus. High reactivity, which has been termed *inhibition to the unfamiliar*, is exhibited as shyness.

There is a clear biological basis underlying inhibition to the unfamiliar, in which any novel stimulus produces a rapid increase in heartbeat, blood pressure, and pupil dilation, as well as high excitability of the brain's limbic system. For example, people who were categorized as inhibited at 2 years of age show high reactivity in their brain's amygdala in adulthood when viewing unfamiliar faces. The shyness associated with this physiological pattern seems to continue through childhood and even into adulthood (Arcus, 2001; Schwartz et al., 2003; Propper & Moore, 2006).

Gender: Boys in Blue, Girls in Pink

"It's a boy." "It's a girl."

One of these two statements, or some variant, is probably the first announcement made after the birth of a child. From the moment of birth, girls and boys are treated differently. Their parents send out different kinds of birth announcements. They are dressed in different clothes and wrapped in different-colored blankets. They are given different toys (Bridges, 1993; Coltrane & Adams, 1997; Serbin et al., 2001).

Parents play with boy and girl babies differently: From birth, fathers tend to interact more with sons, while mothers interact more with daughters. Because, as we noted earlier in the chapter, mothers and fathers play in different ways (with fathers typically engaging in more physical, rough-and-tumble activities and mothers in traditional games such as peekaboo), male and female infants are clearly exposed to different styles of activity and interaction from their parents (Laflamme, Pomerleau, & Malcuit, 2002; Clearfield & Nelson, 2006; Parke, 2007).

The behavior exhibited by girls and boys is interpreted in very different ways by adults. For instance, when researchers showed adults a video of an infant whose name was given as either "John" or "Mary," adults perceived "John" as adventurous and inquisitive, while "Mary" was fearful and anxious although it was the same baby performing a single set of behaviors (Condry & Condry, 1976). Clearly, adults view the behavior of children through the lens of gender. **Gender** refers to our sense of being male or female. The term *gender* is often used to mean the same thing as "sex," but they terms are not the same. *Sex* typically refers to sexual anatomy and sexual

From a social worker's perspective: What might a social worker seeking to find a good home for a foster child look for when evaluating potential foster parents?

behavior, while gender refers to the social perceptions of maleness or femaleness. All cultures prescribe *gender roles* for males and females, but these roles differ greatly between cultures.

Gender Differences

There is a considerable amount of disagreement over both the extent and causes of such gender differences, even though most agree that boys and girls do experience at least partially different worlds based on gender. Some gender differences are fairly clear from the time of birth. For example, male infants tend to be more active and fussier than female infants. Boys' sleep tends to be more disturbed than that of girls. Boys grimace more, although no gender difference exists in the overall amount of crying. There is also some evidence that male newborns are more irritable than female newborns, although the findings are inconsistent (Eaton & Enns, 1986; Guinsburg et al., 2000).

Differences between male and female infants, however, are generally minor. In fact, in most ways infants seem so similar that usually adults cannot discern whether a baby is a boy or girl, as the "John" and "Mary" video research shows. Furthermore, it is important to keep in mind that there are much larger differences among individual boys and among individual girls than there are, on average, between boys and girls (Crawford & Unger, 2004).

Gender Roles

Gender differences emerge more clearly as children age and become increasingly influenced by the gender roles that society sets out for them. For instance, by the age of 1 year, infants are able to distinguish between males and females. Girls at this age prefer to play with dolls or stuffed animals, while boys seek out blocks and trucks. Often, of course, these are the only options available to

them, due to the choices their parents and other adults have made in the toys they provide (Serbin et al., 2001; Cherney, Kelly-Vance, & Glover, 2003).

Children's preferences for certain kinds of toys are reinforced by their parents. In general, however, parents of boys are more apt to be concerned about their child's choices than are parents of girls. Boys receive more reinforcement for playing with toys that society deems appropriate for boys and this reinforcement increases with age. On the other hand, a girl playing with a truck is viewed with considerably less concern than a boy playing with a doll might be. Girls who play with toys seen as masculine by society are less discouraged for their behavior than boys who play with toys seen as feminine (Leaper, 2002; Martin, Ruble, & Szkrybalo, 2002; Schmalz & Kerstetter, 2006; Hill & Flom, 2007).

By the time they reach the age of 2, boys behave more independently and less compliantly than girls. Much of this behavior can be traced to parental reactions to earlier behavior. For instance, when a child takes his or her first steps, parents tend to react differently, depending on the child's gender: Boys are encouraged more to go off and explore the world, while girls are hugged and kept close. It is hardly surprising, then, that by the age of 2, girls tend to show less independence and greater compliance (Kuczynski & Kochanska, 1990; Poulin-Dubois, Serbin, & Eichstedt, 2002).

Societal encouragement and reinforcement do not, however, completely explain differences in behavior between boys and girls. For example, as we'll discuss further in Chapter 10, one study examined girls who were exposed before birth to abnormally high levels of *androgen*, a male hormone, because their mothers unwittingly took a drug containing the hormone while pregnant. Later, these girls were more likely to play with toys stereotypically preferred by boys (such as cars) and less likely to play with toys stereotypically associated with girls (such as dolls). Although there are many alternative explanations for these results—you can probably think of several yourself—one possibility is that exposure to male hormones affected the brain development of the girls, leading them to favor toys that involve certain kinds of preferred skills (Levine et al., 1999; Mealey, 2000; Servin et al., 2003).

In sum, differences in behavior between boys and girls begin in infancy, and—as we will see in future chapters—continue throughout childhood (and beyond). Although gender differences have complex causes, representing some combination of innate, biologically related factors and environmental factors, they play a profound role in the social and emotional development of infants.

Family Life in the 21st Century

A look back at television shows of the 1950s finds a world of families portrayed in a way that today seems oddly old-fashioned and quaint: mothers and fathers, married for years, and their good-looking children making their way in a world that seems to have few, if any, serious problems.

Parents of girls who play with toys related to activities typically associated with boys are apt to be less concerned than parents of boys who play with toys typically associated with girls.

As we discussed in Chapter 1, even in the 1950s such a view of family life was overly romantic and unrealistic. Today, however, it is broadly inaccurate, representing only a minority of families in the United States. A quick review tells the story:

- The number of single-parent families has increased dramatically in the last 2 decades, as the number of two-parent households has declined. One-third of all families with children are headed by single parents. Nearly a quarter of children live with only their mothers, 5% live with only their fathers, and 5% live with neither of their parents (U.S. Bureau of the Census, 2000; ChildStats.gov, 2007).

- The average size of families is shrinking. Today, on average, there are 2.6 persons per household, compared to 2.8 in 1980. The number of people living in nonfamily households (without any relatives) is close to 30 million.

- Although the number of adolescents giving birth has declined substantially over the last 5 years, there are still half a million births to teenage women, the vast majority of whom are unmarried.

- Close to 50% of children under the age of 3 are cared for by other adults while their parents work, and more than half of mothers of infants work outside the home.

- One in three children lives in low-income households in the United States. The rates are even higher for African American and Hispanic families, and for single-parent families of young children. More children under 3 live in poverty than do older children, adults, or the elderly. Furthermore, the proportion of children living in low-income families began rising in 2000, reversing a decade of decline (Federal Interagency Forum on Child and Family Statistics, 2003; National Center for Children in Poverty, 2005).

At the very least, these statistics suggest that many infants are being raised in environments in which substantial stressors are present. Such stress makes it unusually difficult task to raise children—which is never easy, even under the best circumstances.

On the other hand, society is adapting to the new realities of family life in the 21st century. Several kinds of social support exist for the parents of infants, and society is evolving new institutions to help in their care. One example is the growing array of child-care arrangements available to help working parents, as we discuss in the *From Research to Practice* box.

Becoming an Informed Consumer of Development

Choosing the Right Infant-Care Provider

One finding that clearly emerges from research conducted on the consequences of infant child-care programs is that its benefits, such as peer learning, greater social skills, and greater independence, occur only when the care is of high quality. But what distinguishes high-quality child care from low-caliber

programs? The American Psychological Association suggests that parents consider these questions in choosing a program (Zigler & Styfco, 1994; Love et al., 2003; deSchipper et al., 2006):

- Are there enough providers? A desirable ratio is one adult for every three infants, although one to four can be adequate.

- Are group sizes manageable? Even with several providers, a group of infants should not be larger than eight.

- Has the center complied with all governmental regulations, and is it licensed?

- Do the people providing the care seem to like what they are doing or is offering child care just a way to earn money? What is their motivation? Is child care just a temporary job, or is it a career? Are they experienced? Do they seem happy in the job?

- What do the caregivers do during the day? Do they spend their time playing with, listening and talking to, and paying attention to the children? Do they seem genuinely interested in the children, rather than merely going through the motions of caring for them? Is there a television on constantly?

- Are the children safe and clean? Does the environment allow infants to move around safely? Is the equipment and furniture in good repair? Do the providers adhere to the highest levels of cleanliness? After changing a baby's diaper, do providers wash their hands?

- What training do the providers have in caring for children? Do they demonstrate a knowledge of the basics of infant development and an understanding of how normal children develop? Do they seem alert to signs that development may depart from normal patterns?

- Finally, is the environment happy and cheerful? Child care is not just a babysitting service: For the time an infant is there, it is the child's whole world. You should feel fully comfortable and confident that the child-care center is a place where your infant will be treated as an individual.

- In addition to following these guidelines, you may contact the National Association for the Education of Young Children, from which you can get the name of a resource and referral agency in your area. Go their Web site at http://www.naeyc.org or call (800) 424-2460. ●

REVIEW ↵ mydevelopmentlab

1. According to Erikson, during the first 18 months of life, infants pass through the _____ - _____ - _____ stage.
   Answer: trust-versus-mistrust

2. _____ encompasses patterns of arousal and emotionality that are consistent and enduring characteristics of an individual.
   Answer: Temperament

3. _____ is one's sense of being male or female.
   Answer: Gender

To see more review questions, log on to MyDevelopmentLab.

How Does Infant Child Care Affect Later Development?

For most of the years my two kids were in child care, I worried about it. Did that weird day-care home where my daughter stayed briefly as a toddler do irreparable harm? Was my son irretrievably damaged by that child-care center he disliked? (Shellenbarger, 2003, p. D1).

Every day, parents ask themselves questions like these. The issue of how infant child care affects later development is a pressing one for many parents, who, because of economic, family, or career demands, leave their children to the care of others for a portion of the day. In fact, almost two-thirds of all children between 4 months and 3 years of age spend time in nonparental child care. Overall, more than 80% of infants are cared for by people other than their mothers at some point during their 1st year of life. The majority of these infants begin child care outside the home before the age of 4 months and are enrolled for almost 30 hours per week (Federal Interagency Forum on Child and Family Statistics, 2003; NICHD, 2006; also see Figure 7-6). What effects do such arrangements have on later development?

Although the answer is largely reassuring, the newest research to come from the massive, long-term Study of Early Child Care and Youth Development, the longest-running examination of child care ever conducted, suggests that there may be unanticipated consequences to long-term participation in day care.

First the good news. According to most of the evidence, high-quality child care outside the home produces only minor differences from home care in most respects, and may even enhance certain aspects of development. For example, research finds little or no

High-quality infant child care seems to produce only minor differences from home care in most respects, and some aspects of development may even be enhanced. What aspects of development might be enhanced by participation in infant child care outside the home?

difference in the strength or nature of parental attachment bonds of infants who have been in high-quality child care compared with infants raised solely by their parents (NICHD Early Child Care Research Network, 1997, 2001; Vandell et al., 2005).

In addition to the direct benefits from involvement in child care outside the home, there are indirect benefits. For example, children in lower income households and those whose mothers are single may benefit from the educational and social experiences available through quality child care, as well as from the higher income produced by parental employment (Harvey, 1999; Love et al., 2003; NICHD Early Child Care Research Network, 2003a).

Furthermore, children who participate in Early Head Start—a program that serves at-risk infants and toddlers in high-quality child-care centers—can solve problems better, pay greater attention to others, and use language more effectively than low-income children who do not participate in the program. In addition, Head Start parents (who are also involved in the program) benefit from their own participation. Participating parents talk and read more to their children, and they are less likely to spank them. Likewise, children who receive good, responsive child care were more like to play well with other children (NICHD Early Child Care Research Network, 2001; Maccoby & Lewis, 2003; Loeb et al., 2004).

On the other hand, some of the findings on participation in child care outside the home are less positive. Infants may be somewhat less secure when they are placed in low-quality child care, if they are placed in multiple child-care arrangements, or if their mothers are relatively insensitive and unresponsive. In addition, children who spend long hours in outside-the-home child-care situations have a lower ability to work independently

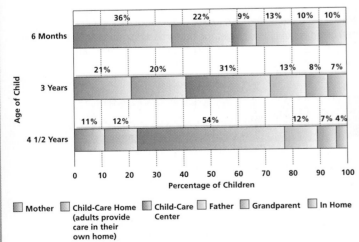

FIGURE 7-6 Where Are Children Cared For?

According to a major study by the National Institute of Child Health and Human Development, children spent more time in some kind of child care outside the home or family as they get older

(*Source:* NICHD, 2006)

and have less effective time-management skills (Vandell et al., 2005).

The newest research, which focused on preschoolers, finds that children who spend 10 or more hours a week in group child care for a year or more have an increased probability of being disruptive in class, and that the effect continues through the sixth grade. Although the increase in the likelihood of acting disruptive is not substantial—every year spent in a child-care center resulted in a 1% higher score on a standardized measure of problem behavior completed by teachers—the results were quite reliable (Belsky et al., 2007).

In sum, the ballooning body of research finds that the effects of participation in group child care are neither unambiguously positive or unambiguously negative. What is clear, though, is that the *quality* of child care is critical. Ultimately, more research is needed on just who makes use of child care and how it is used by members of different segments of society to more fully understand its consequences (NICHD Early Child Care Research Network, 2005; Marshall, 2004; deSchipper et al., 2006; Belsky, 2006).

- If you were to offer advice to a new mother and father about the potential effects of child care on their newborn, what would you tell them, based on research findings?

- What steps would you take to identify a quality child-care center in your own town or city?

CASE STUDY

The Case of... The Long Goodbye

Elena Ross and her husband, Hwang Chen, were delighted to resume their prebaby custom of going out for Sunday brunch. A friend of Elena's who had just returned to the area had proposed a child-care swap: She would look after the Ross-Chen's 8-month-old daughter, Hannah, and they would look after her son Greg, age 2, on alternating Sundays.

Greg was easy. He asked a lot of delightful questions and he played nicely around Hannah, often making the baby laugh. Elena and Hwang smiled, anticipating the upcoming Sundays of newspapers and chat over omelets at their favorite restaurant.

But when Elena placed Hannah in her friend's arms that first Sunday, the baby's face crumpled. Startled, Elena watched as Hannah began to cry, then howl. Her friend cuddled the baby, smiling and cooing into the tearful face, but Hannah's howls escalated. Finally, Elena took her daughter and went to a quiet room to nurse her. Hannah calmed immediately and nursed contentedly. But when Elena tried again to give Hannah to her friend, the baby resumed fussing. "Just go," her friend advised. "She'll calm down as soon as you're gone." Uncertain whether she should leave, Elena was finally convinced by Hwang to go. "I'm sure she'll stop crying," he said. But when the couple returned 2 hours later, Hannah was still howling, and her friend, though cheerful, was clearly exhausted.

The Hwang-Chens tried twice more to leave Hannah with Elena's friend, but each time the baby sobbed, only breaking into a wispy smile at her mother's return. They finally had to give up the arrangement. Sunday brunch just wasn't going to happen.

1. What steps might Elena have taken to make Hannah's experience more comfortable before she left her with the friend that first Sunday morning?

2. How would you explain Hannah's sudden outburst to Elena, in terms of infant social development?

3. What thoughts or questions might be going through Hannah's mind as her mother places her in the arms of her friend?

4. Would you advise Elena to put off leaving Hannah with another caretaker until the baby's older? Why or why not?

5. Not all children exhibit outbursts like Hannah's when meeting strangers or being parted from their mother. Do different parting behaviors suggest specific differences in children's environments, such as differences or in parenting style? Why or why not?

Do infants experience emotions?

- Infants display a variety of facial expressions, which are similar across cultures and appear to reflect basic emotional states.
- By the end of the 1st year, infants often develop both stranger anxiety, wariness around an unknown person, and separation anxiety, distress displayed when a customary care provider departs.
- Early in life, infants develop the capability of nonverbal decoding: determining the emotional states of others based on their facial and vocal expressions.
- Through social referencing, infants from the age of 8 or 9 months use the expressions of others to clarify ambiguous situations and learn appropriate reactions to them.

What sort of mental lives do infants have?

- Infants begin to develop self-awareness at about the age of 12 months.
- They also begin to develop a theory of mind at this time: knowledge and beliefs about how they and others think.

What is attachment in infancy, and how does it affect a person's future social competence?

- Attachment, a strong, positive emotional bond that forms between an infant and one or more significant persons, is a crucial factor in enabling individuals to develop social relationships.
- Infants display one of four major attachment patterns: securely attached, avoidant, ambivalent, and disorganized-disoriented. Research suggests an association between an infant's attachment pattern and his or her adult social and emotional competence.

What roles do other people play in infants' social development?

- Mothers' interactions with their babies are particularly important for social development. Mothers who respond effectively to their babies' social overtures appear to contribute to the babies' ability to become securely attached.
- Through a process of reciprocal socialization, infants and caregivers interact and affect one another's behavior, which strengthens their mutual relationship.
- From an early age, infants engage in rudimentary forms of social interaction with other children, and their level of sociability rises as they age.

What individual differences distinguish one infant from another?

- The origins of personality, the sum total of the enduring characteristics that differentiate one individual from another, arise during infancy.
- Temperament encompasses enduring levels of arousal and emotionality that are characteristic of an individual. Temperamental differences underlie the broad classification of infants into easy, difficult, and slow-to-warm categories.
- As infants age, gender differences become more pronounced, mostly due to environmental influences. Differences are accentuated by parental expectations and behavior.

How does nonparental child care impact infants?

- Child care is a societal response to the changing nature of the family. If it is of high quality, it can be beneficial to the social development of children, fostering social interaction and cooperation. ■

Epilogue

The road infants travel as they develop as social individuals is long and winding. We saw in this chapter that infants begin decoding and encoding emotions early, using social referencing and eventually developing a "theory of mind." We also considered how the attachment patterns that infants display can have long-term effects, influencing even what kind of parent the child eventually becomes. In addition to examining Erik Erikson's theory of psychosocial development, we also discussed temperament and explored the nature and causes of gender differences. We concluded with a discussion of infant child-care options.

Return to the Prologue of this chapter depicting Russell Ruud's Velcro discovery, and answer the following questions.

1. Is this episode evidence of self-awareness on the part of Russell or his child-care companions? Why or why not?

2. What role do you think social referencing might have played in this scenario? If Russell's care providers had reacted negatively, would this have stopped the other children from imitating Russell?

3. How does this story relate to the sociability of infants?

4. Can we form any opinion about Russell's personality based on this event? Why or why not?

5. Do you think Russell's actions might have brought a different response from his adult care providers if he had been a girl? Would the response from his peers have been different? Why or why not?

Key Terms and Concepts

stranger anxiety (p. **161**)
separation anxiety (p. **162**)
social smile (p. **162**)
social referencing (p. **163**)
self-awareness (p. **163**)
theory of mind (p. **164**)
empathy (p. **164**)
attachment (p. **165**)
Ainsworth Strange Situation (p. **166**)
secure attachment pattern (p. **166**)

avoidant attachment pattern (p. **167**)
ambivalent attachment
　　pattern (p. **167**)
disorganized-disoriented attachment
　　pattern (p. **167**)
mutual regulation model (p. **170**)
reciprocal socialization (p. **170**)
personality (p. **173**)
Erikson's theory of psychosocial
　　development (p. **173**)

trust-versus-mistrust
　　stage (p. **173**)
autonomy-versus-shame-
　　and-doubt stage (p. **173**)
temperament (p. **173**)
easy babies (p. **174**)
difficult babies (p. **174**)
slow-to-warm babies (p. **174**)
goodness-of-fit (p. **175**)
gender (p. **175**)

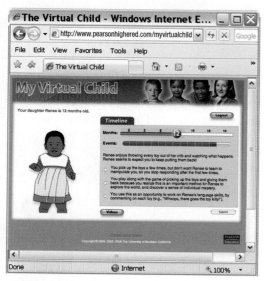

What decisions would you make while raising a child? What would the consequences of those decisions be?

Find out by logging onto **My Virtual Child** and raising your child from birth to 18 years.

▶ ▶ ▶ Putting It All Together

2 Infancy

Physical, Cognitive, and Social and Personality Development in Infancy

Four-month-old Alex was a model infant in almost every respect. However, there was one aspect of his behavior that posed a dilemma: how to respond when he woke up in the middle of the night and cried despondently. It usually was not a matter of being hungry, because typically he had been fed recently. And it was not caused by his diaper being soiled, because usually that had been changed recently. Instead, it seemed that Alex just wanted to be held and entertained, and when he wasn't, he cried and shrieked dramatically until someone came to him.

What decisions would you make while raising a child? What would the consequences of those decisions be?

Find out by logging onto **My Virtual Child** and raising your child from birth to 18 years.

● From a **Parent's** Perspective

What strategies would you use in dealing with Alex? Would you go to him every time he cried? Or, would you try to wait him out, perhaps setting a time limit before going to him?

HINT **Review pages 173–175**

Your response?

● From a **Nurse's** Perspective

How would you recommend that Alex's caregivers deal with the situation? Are there any dangers that the caregivers should be aware of?

HINT **Review pages 173–175**

Your response?

Infancy

Physical Development:

- Alex has developed various rhythms (repetitive, cyclical patterns of behavior) that are responsible for the change from sleep to wakefulness (p. 108)

- Alex sleeps in spurts of around 2 hours, followed by periods of wakefulness until about 16 weeks of age, when he will begin to sleep for as many as 6 continuous hours (p. 108)

- Since infants' sense of touch is one of their most highly developed senses (and one of the earliest to develop), Alex will respond to gentle touches; such as a soothing caress, which can calm crying, fussy infants (p. 124)

Cognitive Development:

- Infants learn that their behavior (crying) can produce a desired effect (someone holding and entertaining him) (p. 132)

- As Alex's brain develops, he is able to separate people he knows from people he doesn't; this is why he responds so positively when someone he knows comes to comfort him during the night (p. 139)

Social and Personality Development:

- Alex has developed attachment (the positive emotional bond with particular individuals) to those who care for him (p. 165)

- In order to feel secure, Alex needs to know that his caregivers will provide an appropriate response to the signals he is sending (p. 170)

- Part of Alex's temperament is that he is irritable. Irritable infants fuss a great deal and are easily upset; they are also difficult to soothe when they do begin to cry (p. 174)

- Since irritability is relatively stable, Alex will continue to display this temperament at age 1 and even at age 2 (p. 174)

From an **Educator's** Perspective

Suppose Alex spends a few hours every weekday afternoon in day care. If you were a child-care provider, how would you deal with Alex if he wakes up from naps soon after falling asleep?

HINT **Review pages 108–110**

Your response?

From **Your** Perspective

How would you deal with Alex? What factors would affect your decision? Based on your reading, how do you think Alex will respond?

HINT: **Review pages 125–127**

Your response?

8

Physical Development in the Preschool Years

PROLOGUE: AARON

Aaron, a wildly energetic preschooler who has just turned 3, was trying to stretch far enough to reach the jar of cookies that he spied sitting on the kitchen counter. Because the jar was just beyond his grasp, he pushed a chair from the kitchen table over to the counter and climbed up.

He still couldn't reach the cookies from the chair, so Aaron climbed onto the kitchen counter and crawled over to the cookie jar. He pried the lid off the jar, thrust his hand in, pulled out a cookie, and began to munch on it.

But not for long. His curiosity getting the better of him, he grabbed another cookie and began to work his body along the counter toward the sink. He climbed in, twisted the cold water faucet to the "on" position, and happily splashed in the cold water.

Aaron's father, who had left the room for only a moment, returned to find Aaron sitting in the sink, soaked, with a contented smile on his face.

▶ Looking Ahead

Three years ago, Aaron could not even lift his head. Now he can move with confidence—pushing furniture, opening jars, turning knobs, and climbing on chairs. These advances in mobility are challenging to parents, who must rise to a whole new level of vigilance in order to prevent injuries, the greatest threat to preschoolers' physical well-being. (Think what would have happened if Aaron had turned on the hot water, rather than the cold, when he reached the sink.)

The preschool period is an exciting time in children's lives. In one sense, the preschool years mark a time of

preparation: a period spent anticipating and getting ready for the start of a child's formal education, through which society will begin the process of passing on its intellectual tools to a new generation.

But it is a mistake to take the label "preschool" too literally. The years between 3 and 6 are hardly a mere way station in life, an interval spent waiting for the next, more important period to start. Instead, the preschool years are a time of tremendous change and growth, where physical, intellectual, and social development proceeds at a rapid pace.

In this chapter, we focus on the physical changes that occur during the preschool years. We begin by considering the nature of growth during those years. We discuss the rapid changes in the body's weight and height, as well as developmental changes in the brain and its neural byways. We also consider some intriguing findings relating to the ways the brain functions in terms of gender and culture.

Next, we focus on health and wellness in the preschool years. After discussing the nutritional needs of preschoolers, we examine the risk of illness and injury that they face. We also look at the grimmer side of some children's lives: child abuse and psychological maltreatment.

The chapter ends with a discussion of the development of gross and fine motor skills. We consider the significant changes that occur in motor performance during the preschool period and what these changes allow children to accomplish. We also look at the impact of being right- or left-handed and discuss how artistic abilities develop during the preschool years.

After reading this chapter, you'll be able to answer the following questions:

- *What changes in the body and the brain do children experience in the preschool years?*
- *What are the nutritional needs of preschool children, and what causes obesity?*
- *What threats to their health and wellness do preschool children experience?*
- *What are child abuse and psychological maltreatment, what factors contribute to them, and can anything be done about them?*
- *In what ways do children's gross and fine motor skills develop during the preschool years?*
- *How do handedness and artistic expression develop during these years?*

Physical Growth

It is an unseasonably warm spring day at the Cushman Hill Preschool, one of the first nice days after a long winter. The children in Mary Scott's class have happily left their winter coats in the classroom and they are excitedly playing outside. Jessie plays a game of catch with Germaine, and Sarah and Molly are climbing up the slide. Craig and Marta chase one another, while Jesse and Bernstein try, with gales of giggles, to play leapfrog. Virginia and Ollie sit across from eachother on the teeter-totter, successively bumping it so hard into the

ground that they both are in danger of being knocked off. Erik, Jim, Scott, and Paul race around the perimeter of the playground, running for the sheer joy of it.

These same children, now so active and mobile, were unable even to crawl or walk just a few years ago; just how far they have developed is apparent when we look at the specific changes they have undergone in their size, shape, and physical abilities.

The Growing Body

Two years after birth, the average child in the United States weighs 25 to 30 pounds and is close to 36 inches tall—around half the height of the average adult. Children grow steadily during the preschool period, and by the time they are 6 years old, they weigh, on average, about 46 pounds and stand 46 inches tall (see Figure 8-1).

Individual Differences in Height and Weight These averages mask great individual differences in height and weight. For instance, 10% of 6-year-olds weigh 55 pounds or more, and 10% weigh 36 pounds or less. Furthermore, average differences in height and weight between boys and girls increase during the preschool years. Although at age 2 the differences are relatively small, during the preschool years boys start becoming taller and heavier, on average, than girls.

Global economics also affect these averages. Profound differences in height and weight exist among children in economically developed countries and those in developing countries. The better nutrition and health care received by children in developed countries translates into significant

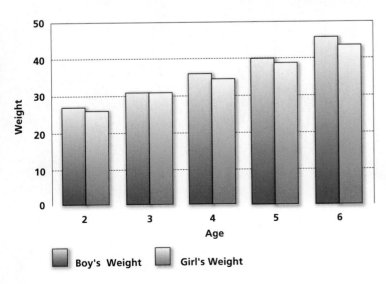
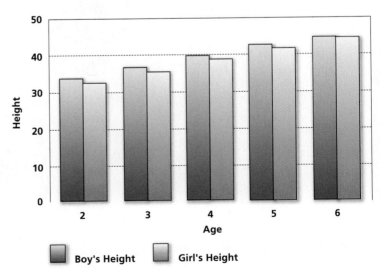

FIGURE 8-1 Gaining Height and Weight

The preschool years are marked by steady increases in height and weight. The figures show the median point for boys and girls at each age, in which 50% of children in each category are above this height or weight level and 50% are below it.

(*Source:* National Center for Health Statistics, 2000)

Myelin Protective insulation
that surrounds parts of neurons

Lateralization The process
whereby certain functions are
located more in one hemisphere
of the brain than in the other

differences in growth. For instance, the average Swedish 4-year-old is as tall as the average 6-year-old in Bangladesh (United Nations, 1991; Leathers & Foster, 2004).

Differences in height and weight reflect economic factors within the United States as well. For instance, children in families whose incomes are below the poverty level are more likely to be unusually shorter than children raised in more affluent homes (Barrett & Frank, 1987; Ogden et al., 2002).

Changes in Body Shape and Structure If we compare the bodies of a 2-year-old and a 6-year-old, we find that the bodies vary not only in height and weight, but also in shape. During the preschool years, boys and girls become less chubby and roundish and grow more slender. They begin to burn off some of the fat they have carried from their infancy, and they no longer have a pot-bellied appearance. Moreover, their arms and legs lengthen, and the size relationship between the head and the rest of the body becomes more adultlike. In fact, by the time children reach 6 years of age, their proportions are quite similar to those of adults.

The changes in size, weight, and appearance we see during the preschool years are only the tip of the iceberg. Internally, other physical changes are occurring. Children grow stronger as their muscle size increases and their bones become sturdier. The sense organs continue their development. For instance, the *eustachian tube* in the ear, which carries sounds from the external part of the ear to the internal part, moves from a position that is almost parallel to the ground at birth to a more angular position. This change sometimes leads to an increase in the frequency of earaches during the preschool years.

The Growing Brain

The brain grows at a faster rate than does any other part of the body. Two-year-olds who have received proper nutrients have brains that are about three-fourths the size and weight of an adult brain. By age 5, children's brains are 90% the weight of an average adult brain. In comparison, the average 5-year-old's total body weight is just 30% of the average adult's body weight (Schuster & Ashburn, 1986; Nihart, 1993; House, 2007).

Why does the brain grow so rapidly? One reason is an increase in the number of interconnections among cells, as we saw in Chapter 5. These interconnections allow for more complex communication between neurons, and they permit the rapid growth of cognitive skills that we discuss later in the chapter. In addition, the amount of myelin—the protective insulation that surrounds parts of neurons—increases, which speeds the transmission of electrical impulses along brain cells but also adds to brain weight. This rapid brain growth not only allows for increased cognitive abilities, but also helps in the development of more sophisticated fine and gross motor skills (Dalton & Bergenn, 2007).

By the end of the preschool period, some parts of the brain have undergone particularly significant growth. For example, the *corpus callosum,* a bundle of nerve fibers that connect the two hemispheres of the brain, becomes considerably thicker, developing as many as 800 million individual fibers that help coordinate brain functioning between the two hemispheres.

In contrast, children who are malnourished show delays in brain development. For example, severely malnourished children develop less myelin to protect their neurons (Hazin, Alves, & Rodrigues Falbo, 2007).

Brain Lateralization The two halves of the brain also begin to become increasingly differentiated and specialized. **Lateralization**, the process in which certain functions are located more in one hemisphere than in the other, becomes more pronounced during the preschool years.

For most people, the left hemisphere concentrates on tasks that necessitate verbal competence, such as speaking, reading, thinking, and reasoning. The right hemisphere develops its own strengths, especially in nonverbal areas such as comprehension of spatial relationships, recognition of patterns and drawings, music, and emotional expression (Koivisto & Revonsuo, 2003; Pollak, Holt, & Wismer Fries, 2004; Watling & Bourne, 2007; see Figure 8-2).

Each of the two hemispheres also begins to process information in a slightly different manner. Whereas the left hemisphere considers information sequentially, one piece of data at a time, the right hemisphere processes information in a more global manner, reflecting on it as a whole (Ansaldo, Arguin, & Roch-Locours, 2002; Holowka & Petitto, 2002).

Although there is some specialization of the hemispheres, in most respects the two hemispheres act in tandem. They are interdependent, and the differences between the two are minor. Even the hemispheric specialization in certain tasks is not absolute. In fact, each hemisphere can perform most of the tasks of the other. For example, the right hemisphere does some language processing and plays an important role in language comprehension (Corballis, 2003; Hutchinson, Whitman, & Abeare, 2003; Hall, Neal, & Dean, 2008).

Furthermore, the brain has remarkable resiliency. In another example of human plasticity, if the hemisphere that specializes in a particular type of information is damaged, the other hemisphere can take up the slack. For instance, when young children suffer brain damage to the left side of the brain (which specializes in verbal processing) and

From a health-care worker's perspective:

How might biology and environment combine to affect the physical growth of a child adopted as an infant from a developing country and reared in a more industrialized one?

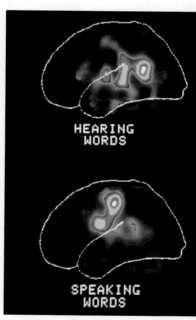

HEARING WORDS

SPEAKING WORDS

FIGURE 8-2 Brain Activity

This series of PET scans of the brain shows that activity in the right or left hemisphere of the brain differs according to the task in which a person is engaged. How might educators use this finding in their approach to teaching?

initially lose language capabilities, the linguistic deficits are often not permanent. In such cases, the right side of the brain pitches in and may be able to compensate substantially for the damage to the left hemisphere (Shonen et al., 2005; Kolb & Gibb, 2006).

There are also individual differences in lateralization. For example, many of the 10% of people who are left-handed or ambidextrous (able to use both hands interchangeably) have language centered in their right hemispheres or have no specific language center (Compton & Weissman, 2002; Isaacs et al., 2006). Even more intriguing are differences in lateralization related to gender and culture, as we consider next.

DEVELOPMENTAL DIVERSITY

Are Gender and Culture Related to the Brain's Structure?

Among the most controversial findings relating to the specialization of the hemispheres of the brain is evidence that lateralization is related to gender and culture. For instance, starting during the 1st year of life and continuing in the preschool years, boys and girls show some hemispheric differences associated with lower body reflexes and the processing of auditory information. Boys also clearly tend to show greater specialization of language in the left hemisphere; among females, language is more evenly divided between the two hemispheres. Such differences may help explain why—as we'll see later in the chapter—girls' language development proceeds at a more rapid pace during the preschool years than does boys' language development (Gur et al., 1982; Grattan et al., 1992; Bourne & Todd, 2004).

According to psychologist Simon Baron-Cohen, the differences between male and female brains may help explain the puzzling riddle of autism, the profound developmental disability that produces language deficits and great difficulty in interacting with others. Baron-Cohen argues that children with autism (who are predominately male) have what he calls an "extreme male brain." The extreme male brain, while relatively good at systematically sorting out the world, is poor at understanding the emotions of others and experiencing empathy for others' feelings. To Baron-Cohen, individuals with an extreme male brain have traits associated with the normal male brain, but display the traits to such an extent that their behavior is viewed as autistic (Baron-Cohen, 2003, 2005; Ingudomnukul et al., 2007).

Although Baron-Cohen's theory is quite controversial, it is clear that some kind of gender differences exist in lateralization. But we still don't know the extent of the differences, and why they occur. One explanation is genetic: Female brains and male brains are predisposed to function in slightly different ways. Such a view is supported by data suggesting that there are minor structural differences between males' and females' brains. For instance, a section of the corpus callosum is proportionally larger in women than in men. Furthermore, studies conducted among other species, such as primates, rats, and hamsters, have found size and structural differences in the brains of males and females (Witelson, 1989; Highley et al., 1999; Matsumoto, 1999).

However, before we accept a genetic explanation for the differences between female and male brains, we need to consider an equally plausible alternative: It may be that verbal abilities emerge earlier in girls because girls receive greater encouragement for verbal skills than boys do. For instance, even as infants, girls are spoken to more than boys (Beal, 1994). Such higher levels of verbal stimulation may produce growth in particular areas of the brain that does not occur in boys. Consequently, environmental factors rather than genetic ones may lead to the gender differences we find in brain lateralization.

Culture and Brain Lateralization Is the culture in which one is raised related to brain lateralization? Some research suggests it is. For instance, native speakers of Japanese process information related to vowel sounds primarily in the left hemisphere of the brain. In comparison, North and South Americans and Europeans—as well as people of Japanese ancestry who learn Japanese as a second language—process vowel sounds primarily in the brain's right hemisphere.

The explanation for this cultural difference in processing of vowels seems to rest on the nature of the Japanese language. Specifically, the Japanese language allows for the expression of complex concepts using only vowel sounds. Consequently, a specific type of brain lateralization may develop while learning and using Japanese at a relatively early age (Tsunoda, 1985; Hiser & Kobayashi, 2003).

This explanation, which is speculative, does not rule out the possibility that some type of subtle genetic difference may also be at work in determining the difference in lateralization. Once again, then, we find that teasing out the relative impact of heredity and environment is a challenging task. ————

The Links Between Brain Growth and Cognitive Development

Neuroscientists are just beginning to understand the ways in which brain development is related to cognitive development. For example, it appears that there are periods during childhood in which the brain shows unusual growth spurts, and these periods are linked to advances in cognitive abilities. One study that measured electrical activity in the brain across the life span found unusual spurts at between 1 1/2 and 2 years, a time when language abilities increase rapidly. Other spurts occurred around other ages when cognitive advances are particularly intense (see Figure 8-3; Fischer & Rose, 1995).

Other research has suggested that increases in myelin, the protective insulation that surrounds parts of neurons, may be related to preschooler's growing cognitive capabilities. For example, myelination of the reticular formation, an area of the brain associated with attention and concentration, is completed by the time children are about 5 years old. This may be associated with children's growing attention spans as they approach school age. The improvement in memory that occurs during the preschool years may also be associated with myelination: During the preschool years, myelination is completed in the hippocampus, an area associated with memory (Rolls, 2000).

Nightmare A vivid bad dream, usually occurring toward morning

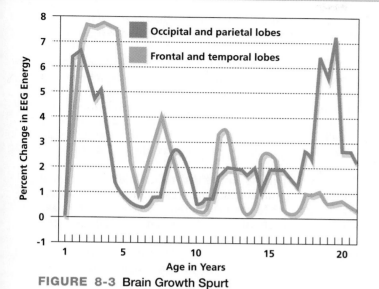

FIGURE 8-3 Brain Growth Spurt

According to one study, electrical activity in the brain has been linked to advances in cognitive abilities at various stages of life. In this graph, activity increases dramatically between 18 and 24 months, a period during which language rapidly develops.
(*Source:* Fischer & Rose, 1995)

We do not yet know the direction of causality. (Does brain development produce cognitive advances, or do cognitive accomplishments fuel brain development?) However, it is clear that increases in our understanding of the physiological aspects of the brain will eventually have important implications for parents and teachers.

Sensory Development

The increasing development of the brain permits improvements in the senses during the preschool period. For instance, brain maturation leads to better control of eye movements and focusing. Still, preschoolers' eyes are not as capable as they will be in later stages of development. Specifically, preschool-age children are unable to easily and precisely scan groupings of small letters, as is required when reading small print. Consequently, preschoolers who start to read often focus on just the initial letter of a word and guess at the rest—leading, as you might expect, to relatively frequent errors. It is not until they are approximately 6 years of age that children can effectively focus and scan. Even at this point, however, they still don't have the capabilities of adults (Willows, Kruk, & Corcos, 1993).

Preschool-age children also begin a gradual shift in the way they view objects made up of multiple parts. For instance, consider the rather unusual vegetable-fruit-bird combination shown in Figure 8-4. Rather than identifying it as a bird, as most adults do, preschool-age children see the figure in terms of the parts that make it up ("carrots" and "cherries" and "a pear"). Not until they reach middle childhood, about the age of 7 or 8,

do they begin to look at the figure in terms of both its overall organization and its parts ("a bird made of fruit").

Preschoolers' judgments of objects may reflect the way in which their eyes move when perceiving figures (Zaporozhets, 1965). Until the age of 3 or 4, preschoolers devote most of their looking to the insides of two-dimensional objects they are scanning, concentrating on the internal details and largely ignoring the perimeter of the figure. In contrast, 4- and 5-year-olds begin to look more at the surrounding boundaries of the figure, and at 6 and 7 years of age, they look at the outside systematically, with far less scanning of the inside. The result is a greater awareness of the overall organization of the figure.

Of course, vision is not the only sense that improves during the preschool period. For instance, *auditory acuity*, or the sharpness of hearing, improves as well. However, because hearing is more fully developed at the start of the preschool period, the improvement is not as significant as with vision.

One area in which preschoolers' auditory acuity does show some deficits is in their ability to isolate specific sounds when many sounds are heard simultaneously (Moores & Meadow-Orlans, 1990). This deficiency may account for why some preschoolers are easily distracted by competing sounds in group situations such as classrooms.

FIGURE 8-4 Sensory Development

Preschool-age children who view this odd vegetable-fruit-bird combination focus on the components that make it up. Not until they reach middle childhood do they begin to look at the figure as a whole in addition to its parts.
(*Source:* Elkind, 1978)

Sleep

No matter how tired they may be, some active preschoolers find it difficult to make the transition from the excitement of the day to settling down for a night's rest. This may lead to friction between caregivers and preschoolers over bedtime. Children may object to being told to sleep, and it may take them some time before they are able to fall asleep.

Although most children settle down fairly easily and drift off into sleep, for some, sleep presents a real problem. As many as 20% to 30% of preschoolers may take more than an hour to fall asleep. Furthermore, they may wake in the night and call to their parents for comfort (Morgenthaler et al., 2006).

Once they do get to sleep, most preschoolers sleep fairly soundly through the night. However, between 10% and 50% of children ages 3 to 5 experience nightmares, with the frequency higher in boys than in girls. **Nightmares** are vivid bad dreams, usually occurring toward morning. Although an occasional nightmare is no cause for concern, when they occur repeatedly and cause a child anxiety during waking hours, they may be indicative of a problem (Pagel, 2000).

Night terrors produce intense physiological arousal and cause a child to wake up in an intense state of panic. After waking from a night terror, children are not easily comforted, and they cannot say why they are so disturbed and cannot recall having a bad dream. But the following morning, they cannot remember anything about the incident. Night terrors are much less frequent than nightmares, occurring in just 1% to 5% of children (Bootzin et al., 1993).

REVIEW ↵ mydevelopmentlab

1. Brain _____, in which certain functions are located more in one hemisphere than the other, becomes more pronounced during the preschool years.

   Answer: lateralization

2. The protective insulation that surrounds parts of neurons, called _____, may be related to a preschooler's growing cognitive capabilities.

   Answer: myelin

3. _____ _____ produce intense physiological arousal and cause a child to wake up in an intense state of panic.

   Answer: Night terrors

To see more review questions, log on to MyDevelopmentLab.

Health and Wellness

For the average child in the United States, a runny nose due to the common cold is the most frequent—and happily, the most severe—health problem during the preschool years. In fact, the majority of children in the United States are quite healthy during this period. The major threats to health and wellness come not from disease but, as we will see, from injuries due to accidents.

Nutrition: Eating the Right Foods

Because the rate of growth during the preschool period is slower than during infancy, preschoolers need less food to maintain their growth. The change in food consumption may be so noticeable that parents sometimes worry that their preschooler is not eating enough. However, children tend to be adept at maintaining an appropriate intake of food, if they are provided with nutritious meals. In fact, anxiously encouraging children to eat more than they seem to want may lead them to increase their food intake beyond an appropriate level.

Ultimately, some children's food consumption can become so high as to lead to **obesity**, which is defined as a body weight more than 20% above the average weight for a person of a given age and height. The prevalence of obesity among older preschoolers has increased significantly since the mid-1980s (Canning et al., 2007; Sigmund et al., 2007; Wake et al., 2007). (We'll discuss the causes of obesity in Chapter 11.)

How do parents ensure that their children have good nutrition without turning mealtimes into a tense, adversarial situation? In most cases, the best strategy is to make sure that a variety of foods, low in fat and high in nutritional content, is available. Foods that have a relatively high iron content are particularly important: Iron deficiency anemia, which causes chronic fatigue, is one of the prevalent nutritional problems in developed countries such as the United States. High-iron foods include dark green vegetables (such as broccoli), whole grains, and some kinds of meat (Drewett, 2007).

Because preschool children, like adults, will not find all foods equally appealing, children should be given the opportunity to develop their own natural preferences. As long as their overall diet is adequate, no single food is indispensable. Exposing children to a wide variety of foods by encouraging them to take just one bite of new foods are often a relatively low stress way of expanding children's diets (Shapiro, 1997).

Minor Illnesses of Preschoolers

The average preschooler has 7 to 10 minor colds and other minor respiratory illnesses in each of the years from age 3 to 5. Although the sniffles and coughs that are the symptoms of such illnesses are certainly distressing to children, the unpleasantness is usually not too severe and the illnesses usually last only a few days (Kalb, 1997).

Actually, such minor illnesses may offer some unexpected benefits: Not only may they help children build up immunity to more severe illnesses to which they may be exposed in the future, but also they may provide some emotional benefits. Specifically, some researchers argue that minor illness permits children to understand their bodies better. It also may permit them to learn coping skills that will help them deal more effectively with future, more severe diseases. Furthermore, it gives them the ability to better understand what others who are sick are going through. This ability to put oneself in another's shoes, known as empathy, may teach children to be more sympathetic and better caretakers (Notaro, Gelman, & Zimmerman, 2002; Raman & Winer, 2002; Williams & Binnie, 2002).

Providing preschoolers with a variety of foods helps ensure good nutrition.

Major Illnesses

The preschool years were not always a period of relatively good health. Before the discovery of vaccines and the routine immunization of children, the preschool period was a dangerous time. Even today, this period is risky in many parts of the world and in certain lower socioeconomic segments of the U.S. population (Ripple & Zigler, 2003).

Why does the United States, the richest nation in the world, provide less than ideal health care for its children? The U.S. cultural tradition is that children are the complete responsibility of their parents, not of the government or of other individuals. What this means is that socioeconomic factors prevent some children from getting good health care and that members of minority groups, which tend to have less disposable income, suffer from inferior care (see Figure 8-5).

In other cultures, however, child rearing is regarded more as a shared, collective responsibility. Until the United States gives greater priority to the health of its children, the country will continue to lag behind in the effectiveness of its child care (Clinton, 1996).

Cancer and AIDS

The most frequent major illness to strike preschoolers is cancer, particularly in the form of leukemia. Leukemia causes the bone marrow to produce an excessive amount of white blood cells, inducing severe anemia and, potentially, death. Although just 2 decades ago a diagnosis of leukemia was the equivalent of a death sentence, today the story is quite different. Due to advances in treatment, more than 70% of victims of childhood leukemia survive (Ford & Martinez-Ramirez, 2006; Brown et al., 2008).

One childhood disease that presents a more discouraging picture is childhood AIDS, or acquired immune deficiency syndrome. Children with this disease face many difficulties. For instance, even though there is virtually no risk of spreading the disease through everyday contact, children with AIDS may be shunned by others. Furthermore, because their parents may suffer from the disease themselves (children with AIDS typically have contracted the disease prenatally from their mothers) there are often severe disruptions in the family due to a parent's death. On the other hand, treatment options are expanding and the number of cases of AIDS in children is declining due to increasing use of drugs that reduce prenatal transmission from mothers to children (Plowfield, 2007).

Reactions to Hospitalization

For ill preschoolers who must spend time in the hospital, the experience is quite difficult. The most frequent reaction of 2- to 4-year-olds is anxiety, most typically brought about by the separation from their parents. At slightly older ages, preschoolers may become upset because they interpret their hospitalization, on some level, as desertion or rejection by

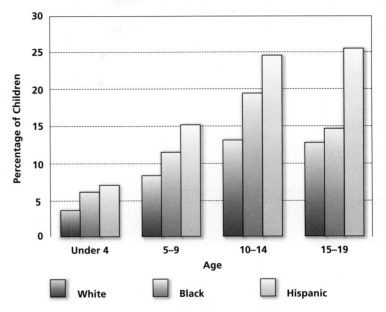

FIGURE 8-5 Children with No Physician Visits in the Past Year

In every age group, more Black and Hispanic children than White children did not have a single visit to a physician during the previous year. From a social worker's perspective, what could you do to help minority children have better access to health care?

(*Source:* Health Resources and Services Administration, 2001)

their family. Their anxiety may result in the development of new fears, such as fear of the dark or of hospital staff (Taylor, 1991).

One of the ways that hospitals deal with the anxieties of young patients is to allow a parent to stay with the child for lengthy periods of time or, in some cases, permitting parents to spend the night on a cot in the child's room. But it does not have to be a parent who can alleviate a child's fears: Assigning children a "substitute mother," a nurse or other care provider who is supportive and nurturing, can go a long way toward reducing children's concerns. In addition, providing older children with the opportunity to participate in decisions about their care leads to anxiety reduction (Branstetter, 1969; Runeson, Martenson, & Enskar, 2007).

Emotional Illness

Although physical illness is typically a minor problem during the preschool years, an increasing number of children are being treated with drugs for emotional disorders such as depression. In fact, the use of drugs such as antidepressants and stimulants has grown significantly (see Figure 8-6). Although it is not clear why the increase has occurred, some experts believe that parents and preschool teachers may be seeking a quick fix for behavior problems that may, in fact, represent normal difficulties (Colino, 2002; Zito, 2002; Leckman & King, 2007).

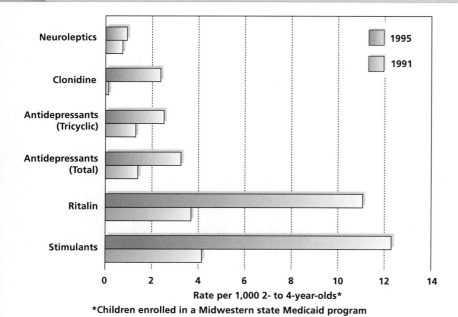

FIGURE 8-6 Numbers of Preschool Children Taking Medication for Behavioral Problems

Although there is no clear explanation why the use of stimulants and antidepressants has increased among children, some experts believe medication is being used as a quick-fix solution for behavior problems that may in fact be normal difficulties in growing up. From an educator's perspective, how would you go about determining the extent of a behavioral problem in a child?

(*Source:* Zito et al., 2000)

Injuries: Playing It Safe

The greatest risk that preschoolers face comes from neither illness nor nutritional problems but from accidents: Before the age of 10, children have twice the likelihood of dying from an injury than from an illness. Annually, children in the United States have a 1 in 3 chance of receiving an injury that requires medical attention (National Safety Council, 2007; Field & Behrman, 2003).

Preschoolers' high level of physical activity and their curiosity increase the risk of injury.

The danger of injuries during the preschool years is in part a result of the children's high levels of physical activity. A 3-year-old might think that it is perfectly reasonable to climb on an unsteady chair to get something that is out of reach, and a 4-year-old might enjoy holding on to a low tree branch and swinging her legs up and down. It is this physical activity, in combination with the curiosity and lack of judgment that also characterize this age group, which makes preschoolers so accident-prone (MacInnes & Stone, 2008).

Furthermore, some children are more apt to take risks, and such preschoolers are more likely to be injured than are their more cautious peers. Boys, who are more active than girls and tend to take more risks, have a higher rate of injuries. Ethnic differences, probably due to the variation in cultural norms concerning how closely children need to be supervised, can also be seen in accident rates. Asian American children in the United States, who tend to be supervised particularly strictly by their parents, have one of the lowest accident rates for children. Economic factors also play a role. Children raised under conditions of poverty in urban areas, whose inner-city neighborhoods may contain more hazards than more affluent areas, are two times more likely to die of injuries than those children living in affluence (Morrongiello, 1997; Morrongiello, Midgett, & Stanton, 2000; Morrongiello & Hogg, 2004).

Preschoolers face a wide range of dangers. Injuries come from falls; burns from stoves and fires; from drowning in bathtubs indoors, or in standing water outdoors; and from suffocation in places such as abandoned refrigerators. Auto accidents also account for a large number of injuries. Finally, children face injuries from poisonous substances, such as household cleaners.

Parents and caregivers of preschoolers can take several precautions to prevent injuries, although, as we've seen, none of these measures eliminate the need for close supervision. Caregivers can start by "child proofing" preschoolers' homes and classrooms, placing covers on electrical outlets and child locks on cabinets where poisons are kept, are good examples. Child car seats and bike helmets can help prevent injuries in an accident. Parents and teachers also need to be aware of the dangers from long-term hazards, such as lead poisoning.

Lead Poisoning Risk Children also face injuries from poisonous substances such as household cleaners and lead paint. For example, 14 million children are at risk for lead poisoning due to exposure to potentially toxic levels of lead. Although there are stringent restrictions on the amount of lead permitted in paint and gasoline, lead is found on painted walls and window frames—particularly in older homes; in gasoline; in ceramics; in lead-soldered pipes; and in trace amounts in dust and water. People who live in areas of substantial air pollution due to automobile and truck traffic may also be exposed to high levels of lead. The U.S. Department of Health and Human Services has called lead poisoning the most hazardous health threat to children under the age of 6 (Lanphear, 1998; Duncan & Brooks-Gunn, 2000).

Poor children are particularly susceptible to lead poisoning, and the results of poisoning tend to be worse for them than for children from more affluent families. Children living in poverty are more apt to reside in housing that

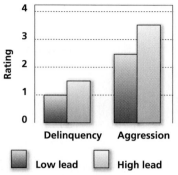

FIGURE 8-7
The Consequences of Lead Poisoning

High levels of lead have been linked to higher levels of antisocial behavior, including aggression and delinquency in school-age children. What roles can social workers and health-care workers play in preventing lead poisoning among children? (*Source:* Needleman et al., 1996)

contains peeling and chipping lead paint or to live near heavily trafficked urban areas with high levels of air pollution. At the same time, many families living in poverty may be less stable and unable to provide consistent opportunities for intellectual stimulation that might serve to offset some of the cognitive problems caused by the poisoning (Evans & Gard, 2005).

Even tiny amounts of lead can permanently harm children. Exposure to lead has been linked to lower intelligence, problems in verbal and auditory processing, and both hyperactivity and distractibility. High lead levels have also been linked to increased levels of antisocial behavior, including aggression and delinquency in school-age children (see Figure 8-7). At yet higher levels of exposure, lead poisoning results in illness and death (Schwartz & Stewart, 2007; Brown, 2008).

Reducing the Risks   Although we can never completely prevent exposure to dangerous substances such as lead, accidents, and injuries, the risks can be reduced. Poisons, medicines, household cleaners, and other potentially dangerous substances can be removed from the house or kept under lock and key, and parents can strap their children into car seats whenever they take them along for a ride. Because drowning can occur in just a few inches of water and in a short time, young children should never be left unattended in the bathtub. Finally, children can be taught basic safety rules from the earliest age. Ultimately, adults need to concentrate on "injury control" rather than focus on preventing "accidents," which implies a random act in which no one is at fault (Schwebel & Gaines, 2007).

Child Abuse and Psychological Maltreatment: The Grim Side of Family Life

The figures are gloomy and disheartening: In the United States, at least five children are killed by their parents or caretakers every day, and 140,000 others are physically injured every year. Around 3 million children in the United States are victims of

child abuse, the physical and psychological maltreatment or neglect of children. The abuse takes several forms, ranging from actual physical abuse to psychological mistreatment (see Figure 8-8; Maas, Herrenkohl, & Sousa, 2008).

Physical Abuse   Child abuse can occur in any household, regardless of economic well-being or the social status of the parents. It is most frequent in families living in stressful environments. Poverty, single-parenthood, and higher than average levels of marital conflict help create such environments. Stepfathers are more likely to commit abuse against stepchildren than genetic fathers are against their own offspring. Child abuse is also more likely when there is a history of violence between spouses (Litrownik, Newton, & Hunter, 2003; Osofsky, 2003; Evans, 2004; Herrenkohl et al., 2008). (Table 8-1 lists some of the warning signs of abuse.)

Abused children are more likely to be fussy, resistant to control, and not readily adaptable to new situations. They have more headaches and stomachaches, experience more bedwetting, are generally more anxious, and may show developmental delays. Three- and 4-year-olds, as well as 15- to 17-year-olds, are the most likely to be abused by their parents (Straus & Gelles, 1990; Ammerman & Patz, 1996; Haugaard, 2000).

As you consider this information about the characteristics of abused children, keep in mind that labeling children as being at higher risk for receiving abuse does not make them responsible for their abuse; the family members who

The urban environment in which poor children often live makes them especially susceptible to lead poisoning.

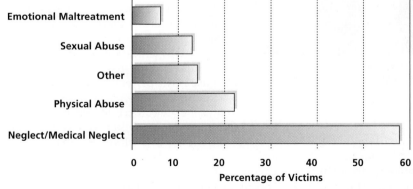

Note: Percentage may total more that 100% because some states report more than one type of maltreatment per victim; *N* = 572,943 victims in 31 states.

FIGURE 8-8 Child Abuse

Although neglect is the most frequent form of abuse, other types of abuse are also prevalent. How can caregivers and educators, as well as health-care and social workers, take the lead in identifying child abuse before it becomes serious? (*Source:* Health Resources and Services Administration, 2001)

Cycle-of-violence hypothesis
The theory that abuse and neglect that children suffer predispose them as adults to abuse and neglect their own children

Psychological maltreatment Harm to children's behavioral, cognitive, emotional, or physical functioning that is caused by parents or other caregivers who use verbal or psychological abuse, hurtful actions, exploitation, or neglect

TABLE 8-1	What Are the Warning Signs of Child Abuse?

Because child abuse is typically a secret crime, identifying the victims of abuse is particularly difficult. Still, there are several signs in a child that indicate that he or she is the victim of violence (Robbins, 1990):

- Visible, serious injuries that have no reasonable explanation
- Bite or choke marks
- Burns from cigarettes or immersion in hot water
- Feelings of pain for no apparent reason
- Fear of adults or care providers
- Inappropriate attire in warm weather (long sleeves, long pants, high-necked garments)—possibly to conceal injuries to the neck, arms, and legs
- Extreme behavior—highly aggressive, extremely passive, extremely withdrawn
- Fear of physical contact

If you suspect a child is a victim of aggression, it is your responsibility to act. Call your local police or the department of social services in your city or state, or call Childhelp U.S.A at 1-800-422-4453. Talk to a teacher or a member of the clergy. Remember, by acting decisively you can literally save someone's life.

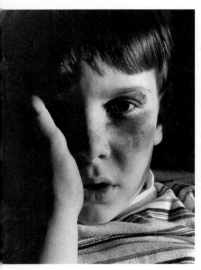

Each year, more than 3 million children in the United States are victims of child abuse.

From a social worker's perspective:

If a society's emphasis on family privacy contributes to the prevalence of child abuse, what sorts of social policies regarding privacy do you think are appropriate? Why?

carry out the abuse are at fault. Statistical findings simply suggest that children with such characteristics are more at risk of being the recipients of family violence.

Why does physical abuse occur? Most parents certainly do not intend to hurt their children. In fact, most parents who abuse their children later express bewilderment and regret about their own behavior.

One reason for child abuse is the vague demarcation between permissible and impermissible forms of physical punishment. The line between "spanking" and "beating" is not clear, and spankings begun in anger can escalate easily into abuse. (As we discuss in the *From Research to Practice* box, the use of physical punishment of any sort is not recommended by child-care experts.)

Another factor that leads to high rates of abuse is the privacy in which child care is conducted in Western societies. In many other cultures child rearing is seen as the joint responsibility of several people and even of the society as a whole. In most Western cultures—and particularly in the United States—children are raised in private, isolated households. Because child care is seen as the sole responsibility of the parent, other people are typically not available to help out when a parent's patience is tested.

Sometimes abuse is the result of an adult's unrealistically high expectations regarding children's abilities to be quiet and compliant at a particular age. Children's failure to meet these unrealistic expectations may provoke abuse (Peterson, 1994).

Frequently, those who abuse children were themselves abused as children. According to the **cycle of violence hypothesis**, the abuse and neglect that children suffer predispose them as adults to abuse and neglect their own children (Miller-Perrin & Perrin, 1999; Widom, 2000; Heyman & Slep, 2002).

According to this hypothesis, victims of abuse have learned from their childhood experiences that violence is an appropriate and acceptable form of discipline. Violence may be perpetuated from one generation to another, as each generation learns to behave abusively (and fails to learn the skills needed to solve problems and instill discipline without resorting to physical violence) through its participation in an abusive, violent family (Blumenthal, 2000; Ethier, Couture, & Lacharite, 2004; Craig & Sprang, 2007).

Being abused as a child does not inevitably lead to abuse of one's own children. In fact, statistics show that only about one-third of adults who were abused or neglected as children abuse their own children; the remaining two-thirds do not turn out to be child abusers. Clearly, suffering abuse as a child is not the full explanation for child abuse in adults (Cicchetti, 1996; Straus & McCord, 1998).

Psychological Maltreatment Children may also be the victims of more subtle forms of mistreatment. **Psychological maltreatment** occurs when parents or other caregivers harm children's behavioral, cognitive, emotional, or physical functioning. It may occur through either overt behavior or neglect (Higgins & McCabe, 2003; Arias, 2004).

For example, abusive parents may frighten, belittle, or humiliate their children, thereby intimidating and harassing them. Children may be made to feel like disappointments or failures, or they may be constantly reminded that they are a burden to their parents. Parents may tell their children that they

FROM RESEARCH to PRACTICE
Spanking: Why the Experts Say "No"

According to surveys, the majority of parents in the United States believe that spanking is not just acceptable, but often necessary and desirable. Almost half of mothers with children younger than 4 years of age have spanked their child in the previous week, and close to 20% of mothers believe it is appropriate to spank a child less than 1 year of age (Springen, 2000; Straus, Gelles, & Steinmetz, 2003; Gagné et al., 2007).

This view is at odds with the experts. There is increasing scientific evidence that spanking should be avoided. Although physical punishment may produce immediate compliance—children typically stop the behavior spanking is meant to end—there are a number of serious long-term side effects. For example, spanking is associated with lower quality of parent–child relationships, poorer mental health for both child and parent, higher levels of delinquency, and more antisocial behavior. In addition, children who experience higher levels of spanking are less able to develop their own inner sense of right and wrong than are those who have been the recipients of lower amounts of spanking. Spanking also teaches children that violence is an acceptable solution to problems by serving as a model of violent, aggressive behavior (Gershoff, 2002; Kazdin & Benjet, 2003; Durant, 2008).

Culture plays a key role in the nature and incidence of spanking. Austria, Germany, Israel, and Sweden outlaw any form of physical punishment directed toward a child, including spanking. In many other countries, such as China, there are strong social norms against hitting children, and spanking is rare. There is a high incidence of spanking in the United States, where a belief in the importance of individual freedom fosters a social climate in which family life—including physical punishment of children—is viewed as a matter of private, personal choice (Gershoff, 2002; Kim & Hong, 2007).

Despite the consensus view of child development on the negative consequences of spanking, it is also clear that not all spanking is the same. Although child developmentalists, physicians, and other experts unanimously agree that severe, sustained spankings that are routinely administered produce the most negative effects, the research evidence for the negative effects of occasional, mild, and non-injurious spankings is more mixed. For instance, parents who spank their children more also hug their children less, read to them less, and play with them less than those who use spanking less frequently. They also are more physiologically volatile, reacting more quickly to stress. It's possible, then, that spanking itself is not the cause of the problems associated with spanking, but that those who spank their children more tend to engage in a variety of behaviors that result in negative outcomes for their children (Benjet & Kazdin, 2003; Martorell & Bugental, 2006; McLoyd et al., 2007; Durant, 2008).

Even mild spanking can easily escalate into more severe spanking. Furthermore, there are a variety of techniques that are at least as effective, and often more so, than spanking for obtaining children's compliance (such as use of time-out periods). The negative consequences of spanking, and the effectiveness of nonphysical alternatives, have led the American Academy of Pediatrics to advise that spanking is not an appropriate disciplinary technique (American Academy of Pediatrics, 1998, 2002; Kazdin & Benjet, 2003; Gullotta & Blau, 2008).

- How might you go about educating parents about the dangers of spanking?

- Are there any circumstances in which it is appropriate for a teacher or school administrator to spank a child? What might they be?

wish they had never had children and specifically that they wish that their children had never been born. Children may be threatened with abandonment or even death. In other instances, older children may be exploited. They may be forced to seek employment and then to give their earnings to their parents.

In other cases of psychological maltreatment, the abuse takes the form of neglect. In **child neglect**, parents ignore their children or are emotionally unresponsive to them. In such cases, children may be given unrealistic responsibilities or may be left to fend for themselves.

No one is certain how much psychological maltreatment occurs each year because figures separating psychological maltreatment from other types of abuse are not routinely gathered. Most maltreatment occurs in the privacy of people's homes. Furthermore, psychological maltreatment typically causes no physical damage, such as bruises or broken bones, which could alert physicians, teachers, and other authorities. Consequently, many cases of psychological maltreatment probably are not

identified. However, it is clear that profound neglect that involves children who are unsupervised or uncared for is the most frequent form of psychological maltreatment (Hewitt, 1997).

What are the consequences of psychological maltreatment? Some children are sufficiently resilient to survive the abuse and will grow into psychologically healthy adults. In many cases, however, lasting damage results. For example, psychological maltreatment has been associated with low self-esteem, lying, misbehavior, and underachievement in school. In extreme cases, it can produce criminal behavior, aggression, and murder. In other instances, children who have been psychologically maltreated become depressed and even commit suicide (Shonk & Cicchetti, 2001; Eigsti & Cicchetti, 2004; Koenig, Cicchetti, & Rogosch, 2004).

One reason that psychological maltreatment—as well as physical abuse—produces so many negative consequences is that the brains of victims undergo permanent changes due

Resilience The ability to overcome circumstances that place a child at high risk for psychological or physical damage

CAREERS *in* CHILD DEVELOPMENT

Debra A. Littler

Education: B.A. Psychology, Arizona State University; Master of Counseling, Arizona State University

Position: Clinical Director, Child Crisis Center, Mesa Arizona

More than 3 million children a year are victims of child abuse. To deal with this epidemic, many organizations across the country are dedicated to the prevention of child abuse and to providing a safe haven for children who have been abused. Among them is the nonprofit Child Crisis Center in Mesa, Arizona.

The Center has served more than 10,000 children, from birth through 12 years of age, over the past 25 years. The goal of the Center is to prevent child abuse by supporting and strengthening families and providing a safe environment for children to heal and grow. With 40 beds, it provides emergency shelter for children who have experienced child abuse.

According to the Center's clinical director, Debra Littler, "Children come to the Center through two pathways. One is through the state Child Protection Services, where children have been removed from their caretakers because of substantiated or alleged abuse.

"The other way is where the child is taken for a minimum 24-hour stay, an early prevention and intervention so the child is not at further risk," she added. "This is usually the result of a family crisis such as homelessness or incarceration."

Littler's counseling responsibilities range from when a child enters the clinic to when he or she leaves.

"I see newly admitted children who have behavioral and/or emotional distress of some type," Littler said, "and they need to be told information which may be traumatic, difficult, or significant in some way. For example, I might have to tell a child they are leaving for a foster home without their sibling, or talk to a child about a parent's incarceration."

"We provide 24/7 caregiving in a homelike environment," Littler noted, "and we have counselors provide one-to-one counseling. We use a child-directed play therapy in fully equipped playrooms where children see a counselor at least once a week and often more frequently.

"Many children come in with serious behavioral problems and we work from a cognitive behavioral model, depending on age, to have the child learn more appropriate ways of expressing feelings," she said.

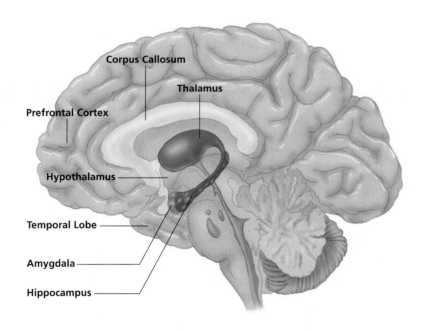

FIGURE 8-9 Abuse Alters the Brain

The limbic system, comprised of the hippocampus and amygdala, can be permanently altered as a result of childhood abuse.

(*Source:* Teicher, 2002, p. 71)

to the abuse (see Figure 8-9). For example, childhood maltreatment can lead to reductions in the size of the amygdala and hippocampus in adulthood. The fear and terror produced by abuse may also lead to permanent changes in the brain due to overexcitation of the limbic system, which is involved in the regulation of memory and emotion, leading to antisocial behavior during adulthood (Teicher et al., 2002, 2003; Bremmer, 2003).

Resilience: Overcoming the Odds

For many children, childhood is a difficult time. According to the United Nations Children's Fund, more than a billion children—one out of every two of the world's children—experience intense deprivation due to war, HIV and AIDS, or poverty. More than 640 million children live in homes with mud floors or under extremely overcrowded conditions. Close to 30,000 children die every day, often from preventable causes. Two million children, most of them girls, are involved in commercial sex industries (United Nations Children's Fund, 2004).

Yet not all children succumb to the adversity that life dishes out to them. In fact, some do surprisingly well, considering the types of problems they have encountered. What enables some children to overcome stress and trauma that may scar others for life?

The answer appears to be a quality that psychologists have termed resilience. **Resilience** is the ability to overcome circumstances that place a child at high risk for psychological or physical damage, such as extremes of poverty, prenatal stress, or homes that are racked with violence or other forms of social disorder. Several factors seem to reduce and, in certain cases, eliminate some children's reactions to difficult circumstances that produce profoundly negative consequences in others (Luthar, Cicchetti, & Becker, 2000; Trickett, Kurtz, & Pizzigati, 2004; Bonanno & Mancini, 2007).

According to developmental psychologist Emmy Werner, resilient children tend to have temperaments that evoke positive responses from a wide variety of caregivers. They tend to be affectionate, easygoing, and good-natured. They are easily soothed as infants, and they are able to elicit care from the most nurturant people in any environment in which they find themselves. In a sense, then, resilient children are successful in making their own environments by drawing out behavior in others that is necessary for their own development (Werner & Smith, 2002).

Similar traits are associated with resilience in older children. The most resilient school-age children are those who are socially pleasant, outgoing, and have good communication skills. They tend to be relatively intelligent, and they are independent, feeling that they can shape their own fate and are not dependent on others or luck (Curtis & Cichetti, 2003; Kim & Cicchetti, 2003; Mathiesen & Prior, 2006).

The characteristics of resilient children suggest ways to improve the prospects of children who are at risk from a variety of developmental threats. For instance, in addition to decreasing their exposure to factors that put them at risk in the first place, we need to increase their competence by teaching them ways to deal with their situation. In fact, programs that have been successful in helping especially vulnerable children have a common thread: They provide competent and caring adult models who can teach the children problem-solving skills and help them to communicate their needs to those who are in a position to help them (Maton, Schellenbach, & Leadbeater, 2004; Brazier & Duff, 2005; Ortega, Beauchemin, & Kaniskan, 2008).

Becoming an Informed Consumer of Development

Keeping Preschoolers Healthy

There's no way around it: Even the healthiest preschooler occasionally gets sick. Social interactions with others ensure that illnesses are going to be passed from one child to another.

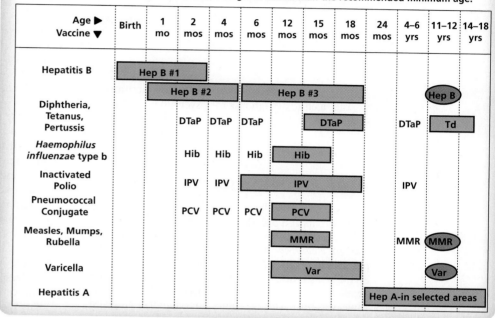

TABLE 8-2

Vaccines are listed under routinely recommended ages. Bars indicate range of recommended ages for immunization. Any dose not given at the recommended age should be given as a "catch-up" immunization at any subsequent visit when indicated and feasible. Ovals indicate vaccines to be given if previously recommended doses were missed or given earlier than the recommended minimum age.

However, some diseases are preventable, and others can be minimized if simple precautions are taken:

- Preschoolers should eat a well-balanced diet containing the proper nutrients, particularly foods with sufficient protein. (The recommended energy intake for children ages 2 to 4 is about 1,300 calories a day; for those ages 4 to 6, it is around 1,700 calories a day.) Because preschoolers' stomachs are small, they may need to eat as often as five to seven times a day.

- Children should get as much sleep as they wish. Being run-down from lack of either nutrition or sleep makes children more susceptible to illness.

- Children should avoid contact with others who are ill. Although they may not understand the concept of germs and contagion (Solomon & Cassimatis, 1999), children should be told to wash their hands after playing with other kids who are obviously sick.

- Ensure that children follow an appropriate schedule of immunizations. As illustrated in Table 8-2, current recommendations are that a child should have received nine different vaccines and other preventive medicines in five to seven separate visits to the doctor.

- Finally, if a child does get ill, remember this: Minor illnesses during childhood sometimes provide immunity to more serious illnesses later on.

1. _____ is body weight that is more than 20% above the average weight for a person of a given age and height.

Answer: Obesity

2. The greatest risk that preschoolers face comes not from illness but from _____.

Answer: accidents

3. _____ is the ability to overcome circumstances that place a child at high risk for psychological or physical damage.

Answer: Resilience

To see more review questions, log on to MyDevelopmentLab.

Motor Development

Anya sat in the sandbox at the park, chatting with the other parents and playing with her two children, 5-year-old Nicholai and 13-month-old Sofia. While she chatted, she kept a close eye on Sofia, who sometimes would still put sand in her mouth if she wasn't stopped. Today, however, Sofia seemed content to run the sand through her hands and try to put it into a bucket. Nicholai, meanwhile, was busy with two other boys, rapidly filling and emptying the other sand buckets to build an elaborate sand city, which they would then destroy with toy trucks.

When children of different ages gather at a playground, it's easy to see that preschool children have come a long way in their motor development since infancy. Both their gross and fine motor skills have become increasingly refined. Sofia, for example, is still mastering putting sand into a bucket, while her brother, Nicholai, uses that skill easily as part of his larger goal of building a sand city.

Gross Motor Skills

By the time they are 3 years old, children have mastered a variety of skills: jumping, hopping on one foot, skipping, and running. By ages 4 and 5, their skills have become honed as they have gained greater control over their muscles. For instance, at age 4 they can throw a ball with enough accuracy that a friend can catch it, and by age 5 they can toss a ring and have it land on a peg 5 feet away. Five-year-olds can learn to ride bikes, climb ladders, and ski downhill—activities that all require considerable coordination (Clark & Humphrey, 1985). Table 8-3 summarizes major gross motor skills that emerge during the preschool years.

Activity Level The advances in gross motor skills are related to brain development and myelination of neurons in areas of the brain related to balance and coordination. Another reason motor skills develop at such a rapid clip during the preschool years is that children spend a great deal of time practicing them. During this period, the general level of activity is extraordinarily high: Preschoolers seem to be perpetually in motion. In fact, the activity level is higher at age 3 than at any other point in the entire life span. In addition, as they age, preschoolers increase in general physical agility (Poest et al., 1990; Planinsec, 2001).

Despite generally high activity levels, there are also significant variations among children. Some differences are related to inherited temperament. Due to temperamental factors, children who are unusually active during infancy tend to continue in this way during the preschool years, whereas those who are relatively docile during infancy generally remain fairly docile during those years. Furthermore, monozygotic (identical) twins tend to show more similar activity levels than do dizygotic twins, a fact that suggests the importance of genetics in determining activity level (Wood et al., 2007).

Of course, genetics is not the sole determinant of preschoolers' activity levels. Environmental factors, such as a

TABLE 8-3	Major Gross Motor Skills in Early Childhood	
3-Year-Olds	**4-Year-Olds**	**5-Year-Olds**
Cannot turn or stop suddenly or quickly	Have more effective control of stopping, starting, and turning	Start, turn, and stop effectively in games
Jump a distance of 15 to 24 inches	Jump a distance of 24 to 33 inches	Can make a running jump of 28 to 36 inches
Ascend a stairway unaided, alternating the feet	Descend a long stairway alternating the feet, if supported	Descend a long stairway alternating the feet
Can hop, using largely an irregular series of jumps with some variations added	Hop 4 to 6 steps on one foot	Easily hop a distance of 16 feet

(*Source:* C. Corbin, 1973)

parent's style of discipline and, more broadly, a particular culture's view of what is appropriate and inappropriate behavior, also play a role. Some cultures are fairly lenient in allowing preschoolers to play vigorously, whereas others are considerably more restrictive.

Ultimately, a combination of genetic and environmental factors determines just how active a child will be. But the preschool period generally represents the most active time of the child's entire life.

Gender Differences in Gross Motor Skills Girls and boys differ in several aspects of gross motor coordination. In part, this difference is produced by variations in muscle strength, which is somewhat greater in boys than in girls. For instance, boys can typically throw a ball better and jump higher. Furthermore, boys' overall activity levels are generally greater than girls' (Eaton & Yu, 1989; Pelligrini & Smith, 1998).

Although they are not as strong as boys and have lower overall activity levels, girls generally surpass boys in tasks that involve the coordination of their arms and legs. For instance, at the age of 5, girls are better than boys at performing jumping jacks and balancing on one foot (Cratty, 1979).

The differences among preschoolers on some tasks involving gross motor skills are due to a number of factors. In addition to genetically determined differences in strength and activity levels, social factors likely play a role. As we will discuss further in Chapter 10, gender increasingly determines the sorts of activities that are seen by society as appropriate for girls and appropriate for boys. For instance, if the games that are considered acceptable for preschool boys tend to involve gross motor skills more than the games deemed appropriate for girls, boys will have more practice than girls in gross motor activities and ultimately be more proficient in them (Golombok & Fivush, 1994; Yee & Brown, 1994).

During the preschool years, children grow in both gross and fine motor skills.

Regardless of their gender, however, children typically show significant improvement in their gross motor skills during the preschool years. Such improvement permits them by the time they are 5 to climb ladders, play follow-the-leader, and snowboard with relative ease.

Fine Motor Skills

At the same time that gross motor skills are developing, children are progressing in their ability to use fine motor skills, which involve smaller, more delicate body movements. Fine motor skills encompass such varied activities as using a fork and spoon, cutting with scissors, tying one's shoelaces, and playing the piano.

The skills involved in fine motor movements require a good deal of practice, as anyone knows who has watched a 4-year-old struggling painstakingly to copy letters of the alphabet. Yet fine motor skills show clear developmental patterns (see Table 8-4).

From an educator's perspective: How might culture influence activity level in children? What might the long-term effects be on children influenced in this way?

TABLE 8-4 — Fine Motor Skills in Early Childhood

3-Year-Olds	4-Year-Olds	5-Year-Olds
Cuts paper	Folds paper into triangles	Folds paper into halves and quarters
Pastes using finger	Prints name	Draws triangle, rectangle, circle
Builds bridge with three blocks	Strings beads	Uses crayons effectively
Draws ○ and +	Copies X	Creates clay objects
Draws doll	Builds bridge with five blocks	Copies letters
Pours liquid from pitcher without spilling	Pours from various containers	Copies two short words
Completes simple jigsaw puzzle	Opens and positions clothespins	

At the age of 3, children can undo their clothes when they go to the bathroom, they can put a simple jigsaw puzzle together, and they can fit blocks of different shapes into matching holes. However, they do not show much polish in accomplishing such tasks; for instance, they may try to force puzzle pieces into place.

By the age of 4, their fine motor skills are considerably better. For example, they can fold paper into triangular designs and print their name with a crayon. And by the time they are 5, most children are able to hold and manipulate a thin pencil properly.

Another aspect of muscular skills—one that parents of toddlers often find most problematic—is bowel and bladder control. As we see next, the timing and nature of toilet training is a controversial issue.

Potty Wars: When—and How— Should Children Be Toilet Trained?

Ann Wright, of University Park, Maryland, woke up on a sweltering night in June at 3 A.M., her head spinning as she reenacted the previous day's parenting trauma: She and her husband, Oliver, had told their 4-year-old daughter, Elizabeth, on Thursday night that it was time for her to stop using her pull-up training pants. For the next 18 1/2 hours, the girl had withheld her urine, refusing to use the toilet.

"We had been talking to her for months about saying goodbye to the pull-ups, and she seemed ready," says Wright. "But on the day of the big break she refused to sit on the toilet. Two hours before she finally went, she was crying and constantly moving, clearly uncomfortable."

Eventually the child wet herself. (Gerhardt, 1999)

Few child-care issues raise so much concern among parents as toilet training. And on few issues are there so many opposing opinions from experts and laypersons. Often the various viewpoints are played out in the media and even take on political overtones. On the one hand, for instance, the well-known pediatrician T. Berry Brazelton (1997; Brazelton et al., 1999) suggests a flexible approach to toilet training, advocating that it be put off until the child shows signs of readiness. On the other hand, psychologist John Rosemond (2007), known primarily for his media advocacy of a conservative, traditional stance to child rearing, argues for a more rigid approach, saying that toilet training should be done early and quickly.

What is clear is that the age at which toilet training takes place has been rising over the past few decades. For example, in 1957, fully 92% of children were toilet trained by the age of 18 months. In 1999, only 25% were toilet trained at that age, and just 60% at 36 months. Two percent were still not toilet-trained at the age of 4 (Goode, 1999).

The current guidelines of the American Academy of Pediatrics support Brazelton's position, suggesting that there is no single time to begin toilet training and that training should begin only when children show that they are ready. Children have no bladder or bowel control until the age of 12 months and only slight control for 6 months after that. Although some children show signs of readiness for toilet training between 18 and 24 months, some are not ready until 30 months or older (American Academy of Pediatrics, 1999b; Stadtler, Gorski, & Brazelton, 1999).

The signs of readiness include staying dry at least 2 hours at a time during the day or waking up dry after naps; regular and predictable bowel movements; an indication, through facial expressions or words, that urination or a bowel movement is about to occur; the ability to follow simple directions; the ability to get to the bathroom and undress alone; discomfort with soiled diapers; asking to use the toilet or potty chair; and the desire to wear underwear. Furthermore, children must be ready not only physically but also emotionally, and if they show strong signs of resistance to toilet training, like Elizabeth in our example, toilet training should be put off (American Academy of Pediatrics, 1999b).

Even after children are toilet trained during the day, it often takes months or years before they are able to achieve

Among the signs that a child is ready to give up diapers is evidence that he or she is able to follow directions and can get to the bathroom and undress on his or her own.

control at night. Around three-quarters of boys and most girls are able to stay dry after the age of 5 years.

Complete toilet training eventually occurs in almost all children as they mature and attain greater control over their muscles. However, delayed toilet training can be a cause for concern if a child is upset about it or if it makes the child a target of ridicule from siblings or peers. In such cases, several types of treatments have proved effective. In particular, treatments in which children are rewarded for staying dry or are awakened by a battery device that senses when they have wet the bed are often effective (American Psychiatric Association, 1994).

Handedness: Separating Righties From Lefties

How do preschoolers decide which hand to hold the pencil in as they work on their copying and other fine motor skills? For many, their choice was established soon after birth.

By the end of the preschool years, most children show a clear preference for the use of one hand over the other—the development of **handedness**. Actually, some signals of future handedness are seen early in infancy, when infants may show a preference for one side of the body over the other. By the age of 7 months, some infants seem to favor one hand by grabbing more with it than the other. Many children, however, show no preference until the end of the preschool years (Saudino & McManus, 1998; Segalowitz; & Rapin, 2003).

By the age of 5, most children display a clear tendency to use one hand over the other, with 90% being right-handed and 10% left-handed. More boys than girls are left-handed.

Much speculation has been devoted to the meaning of handedness, fueled in part by long-standing myths about the sinister nature of left-handedness. (The word *sinister* itself is derived from a Latin word meaning "on the left.") In Islamic cultures, for instance, the left hand is generally used when going to the toilet, and it is considered uncivilized to serve food with that hand. In Christian art, portrayals of the devil often show him as left-handed.

However, there is no scientific basis for myths that suggest that there is something wrong with being left-handed. In fact, some evidence exists that left-handedness may be associated with certain advantages. For example, a study of 100,000 students who took the Scholastic Assessment Test (SAT) showed that 20% in the highest scoring category were left-handed, double the proportion of left-handed people in the general population. Such gifted individuals as Michelangelo, Leonardo da Vinci, Benjamin Franklin, and Pablo Picasso were left-handed (Bower, 1985).

Although some educators of the past tried to force left-handed children to use the right hand, particularly when learning to write, thinking has changed. Most teachers now encourage children to use whichever hand they prefer. Still, most left-handed people will agree that the design of desks, scissors, and most other everyday objects favors the right-handed. In fact, the world is so "right biased" that it may prove to be a dangerous place for lefties: Left-handed people have more accidents and are at greater risk of dying younger than right-handed people (Ellis & Engh, 2000; Bhushan & Khan, 2006; Dutta & Mandal, 2006).

Art: The Picture of Development

It is a basic feature of many kitchens: the refrigerator covered with recent art created by the children of the house. Yet the art that children create is far more important than mere kitchen decoration. Developmentalists suggest that art plays an important role in honing fine motor skills and several other aspects of development.

At the most basic level, the production of art involves practice with tools such as paintbrushes, crayons, pencils, and markers. As preschoolers learn to manipulate these tools, they gain motor control skills that will help them as they learn to write.

But art also teaches several important lessons. For example, children learn the importance of planning, restraint, and self-correction. When 3-year-olds pick up a brush, they tend to swish it across the page, with little thought of the ultimate product. By the time they are 5, however, children spend more time thinking about and planning the final product. They are more likely to have a goal in mind when they start out, and when they are finished, they examine their creation to see how successful they have been. Older children will also produce the same artwork over and over, seeking to overcome their previous errors and improve the final product.

According to developmental psychologist Howard Gardner, the rough, unformed art of preschoolers represents the equivalent of linguistic babbling in infants. He argues that the random marks that young preschoolers make contain all the building blocks of more sophisticated creations that will be produced later (Gardner, 1989; Golumb, 2002, 2003).

Other researchers suggest that children's art proceeds through a series of stages during the preschool years (Kellogg, 1970). The first is the *scribbling* stage, in which the end product appears to be random scrawls across a paper. But this is not the case: Instead, scribbles can be categorized, consisting of 20 distinct types, such as horizontal lines and zigzags.

The *shape* stage, which is reached around the age of 3, is marked by the appearance of shapes such as squares and circles. In this stage, children draw shapes of various sorts,

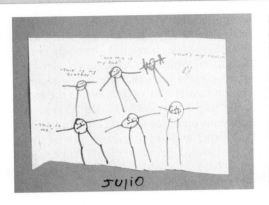

FIGURE 8-10 Art of Development

As preschoolers enter the pictorial stage between the ages of 4 and 5, their drawings begin to approximate recognizable objects.

as well as X's and plus signs. After reaching this stage, they soon move into the *design* stage, which is characterized by the ability to combine more than one simple shape into a more complex one.

Finally, children enter the *pictorial* stage between the ages of 4 and 5. At this point, drawings begin to approximate recognizable objects (see Figure 8-10).

The depiction of recognizable real-world objects, known as representational art, may appear to be a substantial advance over previous art, and adults often strongly encourage its creation. However, in some respects this change to representational art is regrettable, for it marks a shift in focus away from an interest in form and design. Because form and design are important—and in some ways essential—a focus on representation may ultimately have disadvantages. As the great artist Pablo Picasso once remarked, "It has taken me a whole lifetime to learn to draw like children" (Winner, 1989).

REVIEW ↵ mydevelopmentlab

1. Examples of _____ _____ skills encompass learning how to tie one's shoelaces, playing the piano, and using a fork and spoon.

   Answer: fine motor.

2. By the end of the preschool years, most children show _____, which is a clear preference for the use of one hand over the other.

   Answer: handedness

3. The stages of artistic expression include, shape, design, and the _____ stage.

   Answer: pictorial

To see more review questions, log on to MyDevelopmentLab.

CASE STUDY

The Case of... Girls Don't

Jessalyn Palmer's father Dave was baffled. Jessalyn, nearly 5, had been denied admission to the "Ropes & Branches" course at a Native American camp she wanted to attend, and had been assigned instead to "Beads and Baskets."

Jessalyn didn't want to make necklaces and baskets; she wanted to tie knots and make rope ladders and fashion slings and fly from branch to branch with the boys in Ropes & Branches. She had always been an active child, heedless of her body and happy to laugh off any hurts or bruises she earned as a result.

Dave Palmer begged the couple who ran the camp to allow Jessalyn to switch courses, but they were adamant. It would be too dangerous for her. It demanded too much brute strength and agility. Girls were better at finger skills like weaving and beading. Jessalyn would hurt herself on the ropes. They couldn't risk that.

Dave was certain they were exaggerating the risk. The camp was well staffed and had a perfect safety record. He protested that Jessalyn was as strong and agile as any boy in the course and her risk was no greater than theirs. But the owners were unmoved. When the husband remarked "Girls don't tie knots," Dave sensed that this was more than a personal judgment. The camp owners, he knew, were good and fair people, but perhaps their Native American heritage was guiding their decision.

Caught between culture and his daughter's disappointment, Dave didn't know what to do.

1. Given what you know about boys' and girls' physical characteristics at age 5, how can Dave make a case that Jessalyn's strength and agility matched those of the boys her age in the camp?

2. Could the camp owners be right about assigning Jessalyn to Beads & Baskets based on girls' superior fine motor skills? Are they justified in denying her admission to the more physical course that boys usually take?

3. What more would you need to know to decide fairly if Jessalyn would be as safe as the boys in the camp in Ropes & Branches? What policy change, if any, would you urge the owners to introduce?

4. If Jessalyn asks why she can't do Ropes & Branches, how should Dave answer? Should he tell her the truth behind the owners' decision or hide it?

5. If the owners don't change their minds, what would you advise Dave to do?

◄ Looking Back

What changes in the body and the brain do children experience in the preschool years?

- Children's physical growth during the preschool period proceeds steadily. Variations in height and weight reflect individual differences, gender, and economic status.

- In addition to gaining height and weight, the body of the preschooler undergoes changes in shape and structure. Children grow more slender, and their bones and muscles strengthen.

- Brain growth is particularly rapid during the preschool years, with the number of interconnections among cells and the amount of myelin around neurons increasing greatly. Through the process of lateralization, the two halves of the brain begin to specialize in somewhat different functions. However, despite lateralization, the two hemispheres function as a unit and in fact differ only slightly.

- There is some evidence that the structure of the brain differs by gender and culture. For instance, boys and girls show some hemispheric differences in lower body reflexes, the processing of auditory information, and language. Furthermore, some studies suggest that such structural features as the processing of vowel sounds may show cultural differences.

- Brain development permits improvements in sensory processing during the preschool years, including better control of eye movements and focusing and improved visual perception and auditory acuity.

- Although most children sleep well at night, sleep presents real difficulties for some. Sleep-related problems include nightmares and night terrors.

What are the nutritional needs of preschool children, and what causes obesity?

- Preschoolers need less food than they did in the early years. Primarily, they require balanced nutrition. If parents and caregivers provide a variety of healthful foods, children will generally achieve an appropriate intake of nutrients.

- Obesity is caused by both genetic and environmental factors. Parents and caregivers can wield strong environmental influence in this area. They may override their own child's innate tendencies and natural controls toward food and instead substitute their own interpretation of what the child should eat.

What threats to their health and wellness do preschool children experience?

- Children in the preschool years generally experience only minor illnesses, but they are susceptible to some dangerous diseases, including childhood leukemia and AIDS.

- In the economically developed world, immunization programs have largely controlled most life-threatening diseases for this age group. However, this is not the case in economically disadvantaged sectors of the world.

- Preschool children are at greater risk from accidents than from illness or nutritional problems in industrialized societies. The danger is due partly to children's high activity levels and partly to environmental hazards, such as lead poisoning.

What are child abuse and psychological maltreatment, what factors contribute to them, and can anything be done about them?

- Child abuse may take physical forms, but it may also be more subtle. Psychological maltreatment may involve neglect of parental responsibilities, emotional negligence, intimidation or humiliation, unrealistic demands and expectations, or exploitation of children.

- Child abuse occurs with alarming frequency in the United States and other countries, especially in stressful home environments. Firmly held notions regarding family privacy and norms that support the use of physical punishment in child rearing contribute to the high rate of abuse.

- The cycle-of-violence hypothesis points to the likelihood that persons who were abused as children may turn into abusers as adults.

- Resilience is a personal characteristic that permits some children at risk for abuse to overcome their dangerous situations. Resilient children tend to be affectionate, easygoing, and able to elicit a nurturant response from people in their environment.

In what ways do children's gross and fine motor skills develop during the preschool years?

- Gross motor skills advance rapidly during the preschool years, a time when the activity levels of children are at their peak. Genetic and cultural factors affect how active a given child will be.

- During these years, gender differences in gross motor skill levels begin to emerge clearly, with boys displaying increased strength and higher activity levels, and girls showing greater coordination of arms and legs. Both genetic and social factors probably play a role in determining these differences.

- Fine motor skills also develop during the preschool years, with increasingly delicate movements being mastered through extensive practice.

How do handedness and artistic expression develop during these years?

- Handedness asserts itself, with the great majority of children showing a clear preference for the right hand by the end of the preschool years.

- The meaning of handedness is unclear, but the right-handed have certain practical advantages because of the "right bias" of the world.

- The development of artistic expression progresses during the preschool years through the scribbling, shape, design, and pictorial stages. Artistic expression entails the development of important related skills, including planning, restraint, and self-correction. ∎

Epilogue

We saw in this chapter the enormous physical changes that accompany the move from infancy into the preschool years. Beginning with the growth of their bodies, both in weight and height, preschoolers make enormous physical strides. Although they face threats to their health from sickness and accidental injury, for the most part children are healthy, energetic, inquisitive, and master an impressive list of physical accomplishments during the preschool years.

Before we move on to a discussion of children's cognitive development, turn back to this chapter's Prologue, which describes Aaron's excursion across the kitchen counter and into the sink (with a stop along the way at the cookie jar). Consider these questions:

1. Why, specifically, do you think Aaron climbed up on the counter? Was it merely to get a cookie?

2. What gross and fine motor skills were involved in Aaron's journey across the counter and into the sink?

3. What dangers did Aaron face in this incident?

4. What could Aaron's father, who had left the room for only a moment, have done to prevent Aaron from climbing into the sink?

Key Terms and Concepts

lateralization (p. 187)
myelin (p. 187)
nightmare (p. 189)
night terror (p. 190)

obesity (p. 190)
child abuse (p. 193)
cycle-of-violence hypothesis (p. 194)
psychological maltreatment (p. 194)

child neglect (p. 195)
resilience (p. 196)
handedness (p. 200)

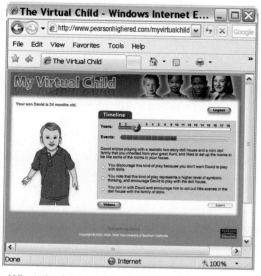

What decisions would you make while raising a child? What would the consequences of those decisions be?

Find out by logging onto **My Virtual Child** and raising your child from birth to 18 years.

chapter nine

Cognitive Development in the Preschool Years

PROLOGUE: FIRST DAY

The night before my younger child, Will, started kindergarten, neither he nor I could sleep. Mingled with his excitement was, I imagined, concern over some of the worries that he had expressed to my husband and me: Would he be smart enough? Would he be able to read? Would there be enough time at school to play? Similar doubts haunted my own dreams like the Wild Things; I wondered whether I should have left Will in preschool for another year (with an August birthday, he would be one of the youngest in his class), whether his skills would be as advanced as the other children's, whether his teacher would appreciate his charms, tolerate his mishaps, and love him no matter what, as we do—and how I would survive without a little one at my heels.

The next morning, I helped Will get dressed in the new outfit that we had bought weeks earlier and carefully laid out the night before. To avoid last-minute panic, I'd packed his favorite lunch and his backpack the night before. After a photo session, we set off together. Although he clutched my hand on the walk to the classroom, Will lined up with his classmates as if he had been doing it for years, and trotted into the class with nary a backward glance (Fishel, 1993, p. 165).

► Looking Ahead

For both preschoolers and their parents, the experience of attending school for the first time produces a combination of apprehension, exhilaration, and anticipation. It marks the start of an intellectual, as well as social, journey that will continue for many years and shape the development of children in significant ways.

In this chapter we focus on the cognitive and linguistic growth that occurs during the preschool years. We begin by examining the major approaches to cognitive development, including Piaget's theory, information-processing approaches, and the increasingly influential view of cognitive development proposed by Russian developmental psychologist Lev Vygotsky that focuses on culture and the social aspects of learning.

We then turn to the important advances in language development that occur during the preschool years. We consider several different explanations for the rapid increase in language abilities that characterizes the preschool period and consider the effects that poverty has on language development.

Finally, we discuss two of the major factors that influence cognitive development during the preschool years: schooling and the media. We consider the different types of child-care and preschool programs, and we end with a discussion of how exposure to television and computers affect preschool viewers.

After reading this chapter, you'll be able to answer the following questions:

- *How does Piaget interpret cognitive development during the preschool years?*
- *How do information-processing approaches and Vygotsky's theory explain cognitive development?*
- *How do children's linguistic abilities develop in the preschool years, and what is the importance of early linguistic development?*
- *What kinds of preschool educational programs are available in the United States, and what effects do they have?*
- *What effects do television and computers have on preschoolers?*

Intellectual Development

Three-year-old Sam was talking to himself. As his parents listened with amusement from another room, they could hear him using two very different voices. "Find your shoes," he said in a low voice. "Not today. I'm not going. I hate the shoes," he said in a higher-pitched voice. The lower voice answered, "You are a bad boy. Find the shoes, bad boy." The higher-voiced response was "No, no, no."

Sam's parents realized that he was playing a game with his imaginary friend, Gill. Gill was a bad boy who often disobeyed his mother, at least in Sam's imagination. In fact, according to Sam's musings, Gill often was guilty of the very same misdeeds for which his parents blamed Sam.

In some ways, the intellectual sophistication of 3-year-olds is astounding. Their creativity and imagination leap to new heights, their language is increasingly sophisticated, and they reason and think about the world in ways that would have been impossible even a few months earlier. But what underlies the dramatic advances in intellectual development that start in the preschool years and continue throughout that period? We can consider several approaches, starting with a look at Piaget's findings on the cognitive changes that occur during the preschool years.

Piaget's Stage of Preoperational Thinking

The Swiss psychologist Jean Piaget, whose stage approach to cognitive development we discussed in Chapter 6, saw the preschool years as a time of both stability and great change. He suggests that the preschool years fit entirely into a single stage of cognitive development—the preoperational stage—which lasts from the age of 2 years until around 7 years.

During the **preoperational stage**, children's use of symbolic thinking grows, mental reasoning emerges, and the use of concepts increases. Seeing Mom's car keys may prompt a question, "Go to store?" as the child comes to see the keys as a symbol of a car ride. In this way, children become better at representing events internally, and they grow less dependent on the use of direct sensorimotor activity to understand the world around them. Yet they are still not capable of **operations**: organized, formal, logical mental processes. It is only at the end of the preoperational stage that the ability to carry out operations comes into play.

According to Piaget, a key aspect of preoperational thought is **symbolic function**, the ability to use a mental symbol, a word, or an object to stand for or represent something that is not physically present. For example, during this stage, preschoolers can use a mental symbol for a car (the word *car*), and they likewise understand that a small toy car is representative of the real thing. Because of their ability to use symbolic function, children have no need to get behind the wheel of an actual car to understand its basic purpose and use.

The Relation Between Language and Thought

Symbolic function is at the heart of one of the major advances that occurs in the preoperational period: the increasingly sophisticated use of language. As we discuss later in this chapter, children make substantial progress in language skills during the preschool period.

Piaget suggests that language and thinking are tightly interconnected and that the advances in language that occur during the preschool years reflect several improvements over the type of thinking that is possible during the earlier sensorimotor period. For instance, thinking embedded in sensorimotor activities is relatively slow, since it depends on actual movements of the body that are bound by human physical limitations. In contrast, the use of symbolic thought, such as the development of an imaginary friend, allows preschoolers to represent actions symbolically, permitting much greater speed.

Even more important, the use of language allows children to think beyond the present to the future. Consequently, rather than being grounded in the immediate here-and-now, preschoolers can imagine future possibilities through language in the form of sometimes elaborate fantasies and daydreams.

Do the improved language abilities of preschoolers lead to improvements in thinking, or is it the other way around, where the improvements in thinking during the preoperational period lead to enhancements in language ability? This question—whether thought determines language or language determines thought—is one of the enduring and most controversial questions within the field of psychology. Piaget's answer is that language grows out of cognitive advances, rather than the other way around. He argues that improvements during the earlier sensorimotor period are necessary for language development and that continuing growth in cognitive ability during the preoperational period provides the foundation for language ability.

Centration: What You See Is What You Think

Place a dog mask on a cat and what do you get? According to 3- and 4-year-old preschoolers, a dog. To them, a cat with a dog mask ought to bark like a dog, wag its tail like a dog, and eat dog food. In every respect, the cat has been transformed into a dog (deVries, 1969).

To Piaget, the root of this belief is centration, a key element, and limitation, of the thinking of children in the preoperational period. **Centration** is the process of concentrating on one limited aspect of a stimulus and ignoring other aspects.

Preschoolers are unable to consider all available information about a stimulus. Instead, they focus on superficial, obvious elements that are within their sight. These external elements come to dominate preschoolers' thinking, leading to inaccuracy in thought.

Conservation The knowledge that quantity is unrelated to the arrangement and physical appearance of objects

Consider what happens when preschoolers are shown two rows of buttons, one with 10 buttons that are spaced closely together, and the other with 8 buttons spread out to form a longer row (see Figure 9-1). If asked which of the rows contains more buttons, children who are 4 or 5 years old usually choose the row that looks longer, rather than the one that actually contains more buttons. This occurs in spite of the fact that children this age know quite well that 10 is more than 8.

The cause of the children's mistake is that the visual image of the longer row dominates their thinking. Rather than taking into account their understanding of quantity, they focus on appearance. To a preschooler, appearance is everything. Preschoolers' focus on appearances might be related to another aspect of preoperational thought, the lack of conservation.

Conservation: Learning That Appearances Are Deceiving

Consider the following scenario:

Four-year-old Jaime is shown two drinking glasses of different shapes. One is short and broad; the other, tall and thin. A teacher half-fills the short, broad glass with apple juice. The teacher then pours the juice into the tall, thin glass. The juice fills the tall glass almost to the brim. The teacher asks Jaime a question: Is there more juice in the second glass than there was in the first?

If you view this as an easy task, so do children like Jaime. They have no trouble answering the question. However, they almost always get the answer wrong.

Most 4-year-olds respond that there is more apple juice in the tall, thin glass than there was in the short, broad one. In fact, if the juice is poured back into the shorter glass, they are quick to say that there is now less juice than there was in the taller glass (see Figure 9-2).

The reason for the error in judgment is that children of this age have not mastered conservation. **Conservation** is the knowledge that quantity is unrelated to the arrangement and physical appearance of objects. Because they are unable to conserve, preschoolers can't understand that changes in one dimension (such as a change in appearance) does not necessarily mean that other dimensions (such as quantity) change. For example, children who do not yet understand

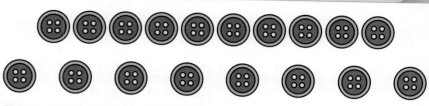

FIGURE 9-1 Which Row Contains More Buttons?

When preschoolers are shown these two rows and asked the question of which row has more buttons, they usually respond that the lower row of buttons contains more, because it looks longer. They answer in this way even though they know quite well that 10 is greater than 8. Do you think an educator could teach preschoolers to answer correctly?

the principle of conservation feel quite comfortable in asserting that the amount of liquid changes as it is poured between glasses of different sizes. They simply are unable to realize that the transformation in appearance does not imply a transformation in quantity.

The lack of conservation also manifests itself in children's understanding of area, as illustrated by Piaget's cow-in-the field problem (Piaget, Inhelder, & Szymanska, 1960). In the problem, two sheets of green paper, equal in size, are shown to a child, and a toy cow is placed in each field. Next, a toy barn is placed in each field, and children are asked which cow has more to eat. The typical—and, so far, correct—response is that the cows have the same amount.

In the next step, a second toy barn is placed in each field. But in one field, the barns are placed adjacent to each other, while in the second field, they are separated from each other. Children who have not mastered conservation usually say that the cow in the field with the adjacent barns has more grass to eat than the cow in the field with the separated barns. In contrast, children who can conserve answer, correctly, that the amount available is identical. (Some other conservation tasks are shown in Figure 9-3.)

Why do children in the preoperational stage make errors on tasks that require conservation? Piaget suggests that the main reason is that their tendency toward centration prevents them from focusing on the relevant features of the

a

b

FIGURE 9-2 Which Glass Contains More?

Most 4-year-old children believe that the amount of liquid in the two glasses in **a** differ because of the differences in the containers' shapes, even though they may have seen equal amounts of liquid being poured into each **b**.

Transformation The process whereby one state is changed into another

Type of Conservation	Modality	Change in Physical Appearance	Average Age Invariance Is Grasped
Number	Number of elements in a collection 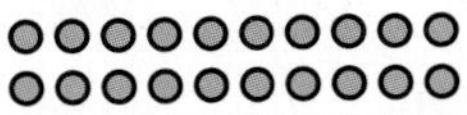	Rearranging or dislocating elements 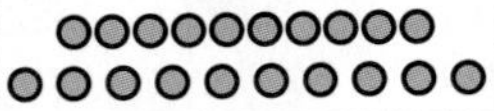	6–7 years
Substance (mass)	Amount of a malleable substance (e.g., clay or liquid) 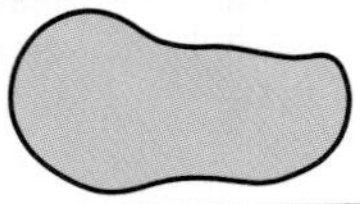	Altering shape 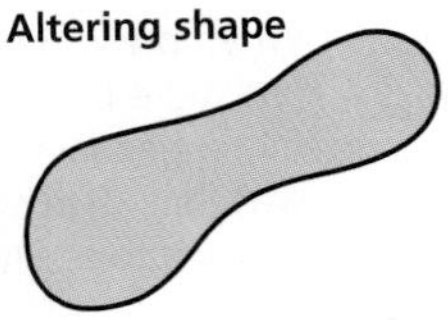	7–8 years
Length	Length of a line or object 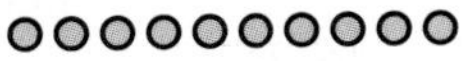	Altering shape or configuration 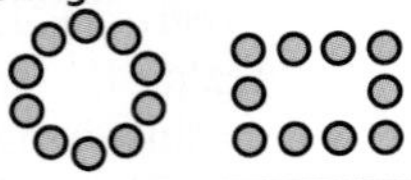	7–8 years
Area	Amount of surface covered by a set of plane figures 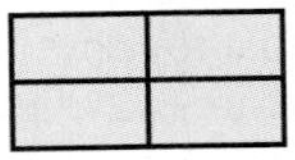	Rearranging the figures 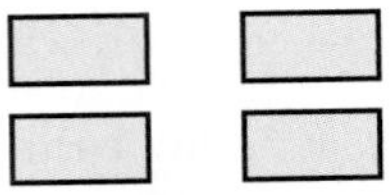	8–9 years
Weight	Weight of an object 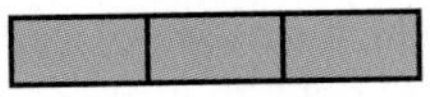	Altering shape 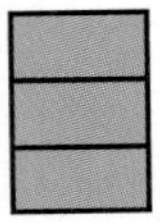	9–10 years
Volume	Volume of an object (in terms of water displacement) 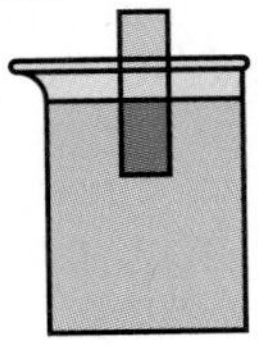	Altering shape 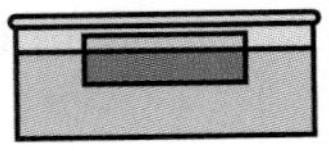	14–15 years

FIGURE 9-3
Common Tests of Children's Understanding of the Principle of Conservation

From the perspective of an educator, why would knowledge of a child's level of conservation be important?

situation. Furthermore, they cannot follow the sequence of transformations that accompanies changes in the appearance of a situation.

Incomplete Understanding of Transformation A preoperational, preschool child who sees several worms during a walk in the woods may believe that they are all the same worm. The reason: She views each sighting in isolation and is unable to form an idea about the transformation it would take for the worm to move quickly from one sighting to the next. She cannot yet realize that worms can't transform themselves into creatures that can do that.

As Piaget used the term, **transformation** is the process in which one state is changed into another. For instance, adults know that if a pencil that is held upright is allowed to fall down, it passes through a series of successive stages until it reaches its final, horizontal resting spot (see Figure 9-4). In contrast, children in the preoperational period are unable to envision or recall the successive transformations that the pencil followed in moving from the upright to the horizontal position. If asked to reproduce the sequence in a drawing, they draw the pencil upright and lying down, with nothing in between. Basically, they ignore the intermediate steps.

Egocentric thought Thinking that does not take the viewpoints of others into account

Intuitive thought Thinking that reflects preschoolers' use of primitive reasoning and their avid acquisition of knowledge about the world

Egocentrism: The Inability to Take Others' Perspectives

Another hallmark of the preoperational period is egocentric thinking. **Egocentric thought** is thinking that does not take into account the viewpoints of others. Preschoolers do not understand that others have different perspectives from their own. Egocentric thought takes two forms: the lack of awareness that others see things from a different physical perspective and the failure to realize that others may hold thoughts, feelings, and points of view that differ from theirs. (Note what egocentric thought does *not* imply: that preoperational children intentionally think in a selfish or inconsiderate manner.)

Egocentric thinking is what is behind children's lack of concern over their nonverbal behavior and the impact it has on others. For instance, a 4-year-old who is given an unwanted gift of socks when he was expecting something more desirable may frown and scowl as he opens the package, unaware that his face can be seen by others, and may reveal his true feelings about the gift (Feldman, 1992).

Egocentrism lies at the heart of several types of behavior during the preoperational period. For instance, preschoolers may talk to themselves, even in the presence of others, and at times they simply ignore what others are telling them. Rather than being a sign of eccentricity, such behavior illustrates the egocentric nature of preoperational children's thinking: the lack of awareness that their behavior acts as a trigger to others' reactions and responses. Consequently, a considerable amount of verbal behavior on the part of preschoolers has no social motivation behind it but is meant for the preschoolers' own consumption.

Similarly, egocentrism can be seen in hiding games with children during the preoperational stage. In a game of hide-and-seek, 3-year-olds may attempt to hide by covering their faces with a pillow—even though they remain in plain view. Their reasoning: If they cannot see others, others cannot see them. They assume that others share their view.

The Emergence of Intuitive Thought

Because Piaget labeled the preschool years as the "*preoperational period,*" it is easy to assume that this is a period of marking time, waiting for the more formal emergence of operations. As if to support this view, many of the characteristics of the preoperational period highlight deficiencies, cognitive skills that the preschooler has yet to master. However, the preoperational period is far from idle. Cognitive development proceeds steadily, and in fact several new types of ability emerge. A case in point: the development of intuitive thought.

Intuitive thought refers to preschoolers' use of primitive reasoning and their avid acquisition of knowledge about the world. From about age 4 through age 7, children's curiosity blossoms. They constantly seek out the answers to a wide variety of questions, asking, "Why?" about nearly everything. At the same time, children may act as if they are authorities on particular topics, feeling certain that they have the

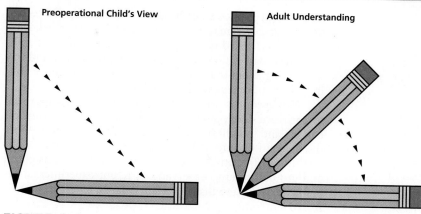

Preoperational Child's View

Adult Understanding

FIGURE 9-4
The Falling Pencil

Children in Piaget's preoperational stage do not understand that as a pencil falls from the upright to the horizontal position, it moves through a series of intermediary steps. Instead, they think that there are no intermediate steps in the change from the upright to horizontal position.

correct—and final—word on an issue. If pressed, they are unable to explain how they know what they know. In other words, their intuitive thought leads them to believe that they know answers to all kinds of questions, but there is little or no logical basis for this confidence in their understanding of the way the world operates. This may lead a preschooler to state authoritatively that airplanes can fly because they move their wings up and down like a bird, even if they have never seen an airplane's wings moving in that way.

In the late stages of the preoperational period, children's intuitive thinking does have certain qualities that prepare them for more sophisticated forms of reasoning. For instance, preschoolers come to understand that pushing harder on the pedals makes a bicycle move faster, or that pressing a button on a remote control makes the television change channels. By the end of the preoperational stage, preschoolers begin to understand the notion of *functionality*, the idea that actions, events, and outcomes are related to one another in fixed patterns. Children also begin to show an awareness of the concept of identity in the later stages of the preoperational period. *Identity* is the understanding that certain things stay the same, regardless of changes in shape, size, and appearance.

For instance, knowledge of identity allows one to understand that a lump of clay contains the same amount of clay regardless of whether it is clumped into a ball or stretched out like a snake. Comprehension of identity is necessary for children to develop an understanding of conservation, the ability to understand that quantity is not related to physical appearances, as we discussed earlier. Piaget regarded children's development of conservation as a skill that marks the transition from the preoperational period to the next stage, concrete operations, which we will discuss in Chapter 12.

Evaluating Piaget's Approach to Cognitive Development Piaget, a masterful observer of children's behavior, provided a detailed portrait of preschoolers' cognitive abilities. The broad outlines of his approach provide a useful way of thinking about the progressive advances in cognitive ability that occur during the preschool years.

However, it is important to consider Piaget's approach to cognitive development within the appropriate historical context and in light of more recent research findings. As we discussed in Chapter 6, his theory is based on extensive observations of relatively few children. Despite his insightful and groundbreaking observations, recent experimental investigations suggest that in certain regards, Piaget underestimated children's capabilities.

Consider Piaget's views of how children in the preoperational period understand numbers. He contended that preschoolers' thinking is seriously handicapped, as evidenced by their performance on tasks involving conservation and *reversibility*, the understanding that a transformation can be reversed to return something to its original state. Yet more recent experimental work suggests otherwise. For instance, developmental psychologist Rochel Gelman (2006) has found that children as young as 3 can easily tell the difference between rows of two and three toy animals, regardless of the animals' spacing. Older children are able to note differences in number, and can perform tasks such as identifying which of two numbers is larger, thus indicating that they understand some rudiments of addition and subtraction problems (Vilette, 2002; McCrink & Wynn, 2007).

Based on such evidence, Gelman concludes that children have an innate ability to count, one akin to the ability to use language that some theorists see as universal and genetically determined. Such a conclusion is clearly at odds with Piagetian notions, which suggest that children's numerical abilities do not blossom until after the preoperational period.

Some developmentalists (particularly those who favor the information-processing approach, as we'll see later in the chapter) also believe that cognitive skills develop in a more continuous manner than Piaget's stage theory implies. They believe that rather than thought changing in quality, as Piaget argues, developmental changes are more quantitative in nature, improving gradually. The underlying processes that produce cognitive skill are regarded by such critics as undergoing only minor changes with age.

There are further difficulties with Piaget's view of cognitive development. His contention that conservation does not emerge until the end of the preoperational period, and in some cases even later, has not stood up to careful experimental scrutiny. Children can be taught to answer correctly on conservation tasks following certain training and experiences. The fact that one can improve children's performance on these tasks argues against the Piagetian view that children in the preoperational period have not reached a level of cognitive maturity that would permit them to understand conservation (Siegler, 1998).

Clearly, children are more capable at an earlier age than Piaget's account would lead us to believe. Why did Piaget underestimate children's cognitive abilities? One answer is that his questioning of children used language that was too difficult to allow children to answer in a way that would provide a true picture of their skills. In addition, as we've seen, Piaget tended to concentrate on preschoolers' *deficiencies* in thinking, focusing his observations on children's lack of logical thought. By focusing more on children's competence, more recent theorists have found increasing evidence for a surprising degree of capability in preschoolers.

Information-Processing Approaches to Cognitive Development

Even as an adult, Paco has clear recollections of his first trip to a farm, which he took when he was 3 years old. He was visiting his godfather, who lived in Puerto Rico, and the two of them went to a nearby farm. Paco recounts seeing what seemed like hundreds of chickens, and he clearly recalls his fear of the pigs, who seemed huge, smelly, and frightening. Most of all, he recalls the thrill of riding on a horse with his godfather.

That Paco has a clear memory of his farm trip is not surprising: Most people have unambiguous, and seemingly accurate, memories dating as far back as the age of 3. But are the processes used to form memories during the preschool years similar to those that operate later in life? More broadly, what general changes in the processing of information occur during the preschool years?

Information-processing approaches focus on changes in the kinds of "mental programs" that children use when approaching problems. They view the changes that occur in children's cognitive abilities during the preschool years as analogous to the way a computer program becomes more sophisticated as a programmer modifies it on the basis of experience. In fact, for many child developmentalists, information-processing approaches represent the dominant, most comprehensive, and ultimately the most accurate explanation of how children develop cognitively (Siegler, 1994; Lacerda, von Hofsten, & Heimann, 2001).

We'll focus on two areas that highlight the approach taken by information-processing theorists: understanding of numbers and memory development during the preschool years.

Preschoolers' Understanding of Numbers As we saw earlier, one of the flaws critics have noticed in Piaget's theory is that preschoolers have a greater understanding of numbers than Piaget thought. Researchers using information-processing approaches to cognitive development have found increasing evidence for the sophistication of preschoolers' understanding of numbers. The average preschooler is able not only to count, but to do so in a fairly systematic, consistent manner (Siegler, 1998).

Autobiographical memory
Memory of particular events from
one's own life

Scripts Broad representations
in memory of events and the
order in which they occur

For instance, developmental psychologist Rochel Gelman suggests that preschoolers follow a number of principles in their counting. When shown a group of several items, they know they should assign just one number to each item and that each item should be counted only once. Moreover, even when they get the *names* of numbers wrong, they are consistent in their usage. For instance, a 4-year-old who counts three items as "1, 3, 7" will say "1, 3, 7" when counting another group of different items. And she will probably say that there are 7 items in the group, if asked how many there are (Gelman & Gallistel, 2001; Gelman, 2006).

In short, preschoolers may demonstrate a surprisingly sophisticated understanding of numbers, although their understanding is not totally precise. Still, by the age of 4, most are able to carry out simple addition and subtraction problems by counting, and they are able to compare different quantities quite successfully (Donlan, 1998; Gilmore & Spelke, 2008).

Memory: Recalling the Past Think back to your own earliest memory. If you are like Paco, described earlier, and most other people too, it probably is of an event that occurred after the age of 3. **Autobiographical memory**, memory of particular events from one's own life, achieves little accuracy until after 3 years of age. Accuracy then increases gradually and slowly throughout the preschool years (De Roten, Favez, & Drapeau, 2004; Nelson & Fivush, 2004).

Preschool children's recollections of events that happened to them are sometimes, but not always, accurate. For instance, 3-year-olds can remember central features of routine occurrences, such as the sequence of events involved in eating at a restaurant fairly well. In addition, preschoolers are typically accurate in their responses to open-ended questions, such as "What rides did you like best at the amusement park?" (Price & Goodman, 1990; Wang, 2007).

The accuracy of preschoolers' memories is partly determined by how soon the memories are assessed. Unless an event is particularly vivid or meaningful, it is not likely to be remembered at all. Moreover, not all autobiographical memories last into later life. For instance, a child may remember the first day of kindergarten 6 months or a year later, but later in life might not remember that day at all.

Memories are also affected by cultural factors. For example, Chinese college students' memories of early childhood are more likely to be unemotional and reflect activities involving social roles, such as working in their family's store. In contrast, U.S. college students' earliest memories are more emotionally elaborate and focus on specific events such as the birth of a sibling (Wang, 2004, 2007).

Not only do preschoolers' autobiographical memories fade, but also what is remembered may not be wholly accurate. For example, if an event happens often, such as a trip to a grocery store, it may be hard to remember one specific time it happened. Preschoolers' memories of familiar events are often organized in terms of **scripts**,

broad representations in memory of events and the order in which they occur.

For example, a young preschooler might represent eating in a restaurant in terms of a few steps: talking to a waitress, getting the food, and eating. With age, the scripts become more elaborate: getting in the car, being seated at the restaurant, choosing food, ordering, waiting for the meal to come, eating, ordering dessert, and paying for the food. Because events that are frequently repeated tend to be melded into scripts, particular instances of a scripted event are recalled with less accuracy than those that are unscripted in memory (Fivush, Kuebli, & Clubb, 1992; Sutherland, Pipe, & Schick, 2003).

There are other reasons why preschoolers may not have entirely accurate autobiographical memories. Because they have difficulty describing certain kinds of information, such as complex causal relationships, they may oversimplify recollections. For example, a child who has witnessed an argument between his grandparents may only remember that grandma took the cake away from grandpa, not the discussion of his weight and cholesterol that led up to the action. And, as we consider next, preschoolers' memories are also susceptible to the suggestions of others. This is a special concern when children are called upon to testify in legal situations, such as when abuse is suspected, as we discuss next.

How specific and accurate will these preschoolers' memories of this event be in the future?

Forensic Developmental Psychology: Bringing Child Development to the Courtroom

I was looking and then I didn't see what I was doing and it got in there somehow.... The mousetrap was in our house because there's a mouse in our house.... The mousetrap is down in the basement, next to the firewood.... I was playing a game called "Operation" and then I went downstairs and said to Dad, "I want to eat lunch," and then it got stuck in the mousetrap.... My daddy was down in the basement collecting firewood. . . . [My brother] pushed me [into the mousetrap].... It happened yesterday. The mouse was in my house yesterday. I caught my finger in it yesterday. I went to the hospital yesterday (Ceci & Bruck, 1993, p. A23).

Despite the detailed account by this 4-year-old boy of his encounter with a mousetrap and subsequent trip to the hospital, there's a problem: The incident never happened, and the memory is entirely false.

The conviction of preschool teacher Kelly Michaels for sexually molesting several preschool children may have been the result of leading questions posed to the children.

The 4-year-old's explicit recounting of a mousetrap incident that had not actually occurred was the product of a study on children's memory. Each week for 11 weeks, the 4-year-old boy was told, "You went to the hospital because your finger got caught in a mousetrap. Did this ever happen to you?"

The 1st week, the child quite accurately said, "No. I've never been to the hospital." But by the 2nd week, the answer changed to, "Yes, I cried." In the 3rd week, the boy said, "Yes. My mom went to the hospital with me." By the 11th week, the answer had expanded to the quote on the previous page (Ceci & Bruck, 1993; Bruck & Ceci, 2004).

The research study that elicited the child's false memories is part of a new and rapidly growing field within child development: forensic developmental psychology. *Forensic developmental psychology* focuses on the reliability of children's autobiographical memories in the context of the legal system. It considers children's abilities to recall events in their lives and the reliability of children's courtroom accounts where they are witnesses or victims (Bruck & Ceci, 2004).

The embellishment of a completely false incident is characteristic of the fragility, impressionability, and inaccuracy of memory in young children. Young children may recall things quite mistakenly, but with great conviction, contending that events occurred when they never really happened, and forgetting events that *did* occur.

Children's memories are susceptible to the suggestions of adults asking them questions. This is particularly true of preschoolers, who are considerably more vulnerable to suggestion than either adults or school-age children. Preschoolers are also more prone to make inaccurate inferences about the reasons behind others' behavior and are less able to draw appropriate conclusions based on their knowledge of a situation (e.g., "He was crying because he didn't like the sandwich."). (Principe & Ceci, 2002; Ceci, Fitneva, & Gilstrap, 2003; Loftus, 2004).

Of course, preschoolers recall many things accurately; as we discussed earlier in the chapter, children as young as 3 recall some events in their lives without distortion. However, not all recollections are accurate, and some events that are recalled with seeming accuracy never actually occurred.

The error rate for children is heightened when the same question is asked repeatedly. False memories—of the type reported by the 4-year-old who "remembered" going to the hospital after his finger was caught in a mousetrap—in fact may be more persistent than actual memories. In addition, when questions are highly suggestive (that is, when questioners attempt to lead a person to particular conclusions), children are more apt to make mistakes in recall (Powell, Thomson, & Ceci, 2003; Bruck & Ceci, 2004; Loftus & Bernstein, 2005).

How can children be questioned to produce the most accurate recollections? One way is to question them as soon as possible after an event has occurred. The longer the time between the actual event and questioning, the less firm are children's recollections. Furthermore, more specific questions are answered more accurately than more general ones. ("Did you go downstairs with Brian?") Asking the questions outside of a courtroom is also preferable, as the courtroom setting can be intimidating and frightening (Ceci & Bruck, 2007; Melnyk, Crossman, & Scullin, 2007; London et al., 2008; also see Table 9-1).

TABLE 9-1	Eliciting Accurate Recollections From Children
Recommended Practice	
Play Dumb. INTERVIEWER *Now that I know you a little better, tell me why you are here today.*	
Ask Follow-up Questions. CHILD *Bob touched my private.* INTERVIEWER *Tell me everything about that.*	
Encourage Children to Describe Events. INTERVIEWER *Tell me everything that happened at Bob's house from the beginning to the end.*	
Avoid Suggesting That Interviewers Expect Descriptions of Particular Kinds of Events.	
Avoid Offering Rewards or Expressing Disapproval.	

(*Source:* Poole & Lamb, 1998)

Information-Processing Theories in Perspective

According to information-processing approaches, cognitive development consists of gradual improvements in the ways people perceive, understand, and remember information. With age and practice, preschoolers process information more efficiently and with greater sophistication, and they are able to handle increasingly complex problems. In the eyes of proponents of information-processing approaches, it is these quantitative advances in information processing—and not the qualitative changes suggested by Piaget—that constitute cognitive development (Case & Okamoto, 1996; Goswami, 1998; Zhe & Siegler, 2000).

For supporters of information-processing approaches, the reliance on well-defined processes that can be tested, with relative precision, by research is one of the perspective's most important features. Rather than relying on concepts that are somewhat vague, such as Piaget's notions of assimilation and accommodation, information-processing approaches provide a comprehensive, logical set of concepts.

For instance, as preschoolers grow older, they have longer attention spans, can monitor and plan what they are attending to more effectively, and become increasingly aware of their cognitive limitations. As we discussed earlier in this chapter, these advances may be due to brain development. Such increasing attentional abilities place some of Piaget's findings in a different light. For instance, increased attention allows older children to attend to both the height *and* the width of tall and short glasses into which liquid is poured. This permits them to understand that the amount of liquid in the glasses stays the same when it is poured back and forth. Preschoolers, in contrast, are unable to attend to both dimensions simultaneously, and thus are less able to conserve (Miller & Seier, 1994; Hudson, Sosa, & Shapiro, 1997).

Proponents of information-processing theory have also been successful in focusing on important cognitive processes to which alternative approaches traditionally have paid little attention, such as the contribution of mental skills like memory and attention to children's thinking. They suggest that information processing provides a clear, logical, and full account of cognitive development.

Yet information-processing approaches have their detractors, who raise significant points. For one thing, the focus on a series of single, individual cognitive processes leaves out of consideration some important factors that appear to influence cognition. For instance, information-processing theorists pay relatively little attention to social and cultural factors—a deficiency that the approach we'll consider next attempts to remedy.

An even more important criticism is that information-processing approaches "lose the forest for the trees." In other words, information-processing approaches pay so much attention to the detailed, individual sequence of processes that compose cognitive processing and development that they never adequately paint a whole, comprehensive picture of cognitive development—which Piaget clearly did quite well.

Developmentalists using information-processing approaches respond to such criticisms by saying that their model of cognitive development has the advantage of being precisely stated and capable of leading to testable hypotheses. They also argue that there is far more research supporting their approach than there is for alternative theories of cognitive development. In short, they suggest that their approach provides a more accurate account than any other.

Information-processing approaches have been highly influential over the past several decades. They have inspired a tremendous amount of research that has helped us gain some insights into how children develop cognitively.

Vygotsky's View of Cognitive Development: Taking Culture Into Account

As her daughter watches, a member of the Chilcotin Indian tribe prepares a salmon for dinner. When the daughter asks a question about a small detail of the process, the mother takes out another salmon and repeats the entire process. According to the tribal view of learning, understanding and comprehension can come only from grasping the total procedure, and not from learning about the individual subcomponents of the task (Tharp, 1989).

The Chilcotin view of how children learn about the world contrasts with the prevalent view of Western society, which assumes that only by mastering the separate parts of a problem can one fully comprehend it. Do differences in the ways particular cultures and societies approach problems influence cognitive development? According to Russian developmental psychologist Lev Vygotsky, who lived from 1896 to 1934, the answer is a clear "yes."

Vygotsky viewed cognitive development as a result of social interactions in which children learn through guided participation, working with mentors to solve problems. Instead of concentrating on individual performance, as Piaget's and many alternative approaches do, Vygotsky's increasingly influential view focuses on the social aspects of development and learning.

Vygotsky saw children as apprentices, learning cognitive strategies and other skills

Russian developmental psychologist Lev Vygotsky proposed that the focus of cognitive development should be on a child's social and cultural world, as opposed to the Piagetian approach, which concentrates on individual performance.

From an educator's perspective:

If children's cognitive development is dependent on interactions with others, what obligations does society have regarding such social settings as preschools and neighborhoods?

from adult and peer mentors who not only present new ways of doing things, but also provide assistance, instruction, and motivation. Consequently, he focused on the child's social and cultural world as the source of cognitive development. According to Vygotsky, children gradually grow intellectually and begin to function on their own because of the assistance that adult and peer partners provide (Vygotsky, 1926/1997; Tudge & Scrimsher, 2003).

Vygotsky contends that the nature of the partnershipbetween developing children and adults and peers is determined largely by cultural and societal factors. For instance, culture and society establish the institutions, such as preschools and play groups that promote development by providing opportunities for cognitive growth. Furthermore, by emphasizing particular tasks, culture and society shape the nature of specific cognitive advances. Unless we look at what is important and meaningful to members of a given society, we may seriously underestimate the nature and level of cognitive abilities that ultimately will be attained (Tappan, 1997; Schaller & Crandall, 2004).

For example, children's toys reflect what is important and meaningful in a particular society. In Western society, preschoolers commonly play with toy wagons, automobiles, and other vehicles, in part reflecting the mobile nature of the culture.

Societal expectations about gender also play a role in how children come to understand the world. For example, one study conducted at a science museum found that parents provided more detailed scientific explanations to boys than to girls at museum displays. Such differences in level of explanation may lead to more sophisticated understanding of science in boys and ultimately may produce later gender differences in science learning (Crowley et al., 2001).

Vygotsky's approach is therefore quite different from that of Piaget. Where Piaget looked at developing children

and saw junior scientists, working by themselves to develop an independent understanding of the world, Vygotsky saw cognitive apprentices, learning from master teachers the skills that are important in the child's culture. Where Piaget saw preschoolers who were egocentric, looking at the world from their own, limited vantage point, Vygotsky saw preschoolers as using others to gain an understanding of the world.

In Vygotsky's view, then, children's cognitive development is dependent on interaction with others. Vygotsky argued that it is only through partnership with other people—peers, parents, teachers, and other adults—that children can fully develop their knowledge, thinking processes, beliefs, and values (Fernyhough, 1997; Edwards, 2004).

The Zone of Proximal Development and Scaffolding: Foundations of Cognitive Development Vygotsky proposed that children's cognitive abilities increase through exposure to information that is new enough to be intriguing, but not too difficult for the child to contend with. He called this the **zone of proximal development**, or ZPD, the level at which a child can almost, but not fully, perform a task independently, but can do so with the assistance of someone more competent. When appropriate instruction is offered within the zone of proximal development, children are able to increase their understanding and master new tasks. In order for cognitive development to occur, then, new information must be presented—by parents, teachers, or more skilled peers—within the zone of proximal development. For example, a preschooler might not be able to figure out by herself how to get a handle to stick on the clay pot she's building, but she could do it with some advice from her child-care teacher (Chaiklin, 2003; Kozulin, 2004; Zuckerman & Shenfield, 2007).

The concept of the zone of proximal development suggests that even though two children might be able to achieve the same amount without help, if one child receives aid, he or she may improve substantially more than the other. The greater the improvement that comes with help, the larger is the zone of proximal development (see Figure 9-5).

The assistance or structuring provided by others has been termed *scaffolding*. **Scaffolding** is the support for learning and problem solving that encourages independence and growth (Puntambekar & Hübscher, 2005).

To Vygotsky, the process of scaffolding not only helps children solve specific problems, but also aids in the development of their overall cognitive abilities. Scaffolding takes its name from the scaffolds that are put up to aid in the construction of a building and then are removed once the building is complete. In education, scaffolding involves, first of all, helping children think about and frame a task in an appropriate manner. In addition, a parent or teacher is likely to provide clues to task completion that are appropriate to the child's level of development and to model behavior that can lead to completion of the task. As in construction, the scaffolding that more competent

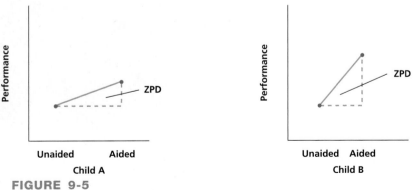

FIGURE 9-5

Sample Zones of Proximal Development (ZPDs) for Two Children

Although the two children's performance is similar when working at a task without aid, the second child benefits more from aid and therefore has a larger ZPD. Is there any way to measure a child's ZPD? Can it be enlarged?

people provide, which facilitates the completion of identified tasks, is removed once children are able to solve a problem on their own (Warwick & Maloch, 2003; Taumoepeau & Ruffman, 2008).

To illustrate how scaffolding operates, consider the following conversation between mother and son:

MOTHER: Do remember how you helped me make the cookies before?

CHILD: No.

MOTHER: We made the dough and put it in the oven. Do you remember that?

CHILD: When Grandma came?

MOTHER: Yes, that's right. Would you help me shape the dough into cookies?

CHILD: OK.

MOTHER: Can you remember how big we made the cookies when Grandma was here?

CHILD: Big.

MOTHER: Right. Can you show me how big?

CHILD: We used the big wooden spoon.

MOTHER: Good boy, that's right. We used the wooden spoon, and we made big cookies. But let's try something different today by using the ice cream scoop to form the cookies.

Although this conversation isn't particularly sophisticated, it illustrates the practice of scaffolding. The mother is supporting her son's efforts, and she gets him to respond conversationally. In the process, she not only expands her son's abilities by using a different tool (the scoop instead of the spoon), she models how conversations proceed.

In some societies parental support for learning differs by gender. In one study, Mexican mothers were found to provide more scaffolding than fathers. A possible explanation is that mothers may be more aware of their children's cognitive abilities than are fathers (Tenenbaum & Leaper, 1998; Tamis-LeMonda & Cabrera, 2002).

One key aspect of the aid that more accomplished individuals provide to learners comes in the form of cultural tools. *Cultural tools* are actual, physical items (e.g., pencils, paper, calculators, computers, and so forth), as well as an intellectual and conceptual framework for solving problems. The intellectual and conceptual framework available to learners includes the language that is used within a culture, its alphabetical and numbering schemes, its mathematical and scientific systems, and even its religious systems. These cultural tools provide a structure that can be used to help children define and solve specific problems, as well as an intellectual point of view that encourages cognitive development.

For example, consider the cultural differences in how people talk about distance. In cities, distance is usually measured in blocks ("the store is about 15 blocks away"). To a child from a rural background, such a unit of measurement is meaningless, and more meaningful distance-related terms may be used, such as yards, miles, such practical rules of thumb as "a stone's throw," or references to known distances and landmarks ("about half the distance to town"). To make matters more complicated, "how far" questions are sometimes answered in terms not of distance, but of time ("it's about 15 minutes to the store"), which will be understood variously to refer to walking or riding time, depending on context—and, if riding time, to different forms of riding. For some children the ride to the store will be conceived of as being by ox cart, for others, by bicycle, bus, canoe, or automobile, again depending on cultural context. The nature of the tools available to children to solve problems and perform tasks is highly dependent on the culture in which they live.

Evaluating Vygotsky's Contributions

Vygotsky's view—that the specific nature of cognitive development can be understood only by taking into account cultural and social context—has become increasingly influential in the last decade. In some ways, this is surprising, in light of the fact that Vygotsky died over 7 decades ago at the young age of 37 (Winsler, 2003; Gredler & Shields, 2008).

Several factors explain Vygotsky's growing influence. One is that until recently he was largely unknown to developmentalists. His writings are only now becoming widely disseminated in the United States due to the growing availability of good English translations. In fact, for most of the 20th century Vygotsky was not widely known even within his native land. His work was banned for some time, and it was not until the breakup of the Soviet Union that it became freely available in the formerly Soviet countries. Thus, Vygotsky, long hidden from his fellow developmentalists, only emerged onto the scene long after his death.

Even more important, though, is the quality of Vygotsky's ideas. They represent a consistent theoretical system and help explain a growing body of research attesting to the importance of social interaction in promoting cognitive development. The idea that children's comprehension of the world is an outcome of their interactions with their parents, peers, and other members of society is both appealing and well supported by research findings. It is also consistent with a growing body of multicultural and cross-cultural research, which finds evidence that cognitive development is shaped, in part, by cultural factors (Daniels, 1996; Scrimsher & Tudge, 2003).

Of course, not every aspect of Vygotsky's theorizing has been supported, and he can be criticized for a lack of precision in his conceptualization of cognitive growth. For instance, such broad concepts as the zone of proximal development are not terribly precise, and they do not always lend themselves to experimental tests.

Furthermore, Vygotsky was largely silent on how basic cognitive processes such as attention and memory develop and how children's natural cognitive capabilities unfold.

TABLE 9-2 Comparison of Piaget's Theory, Information-Processing Theories, and Vygotsky's Approach to Cognitive Development

	Piaget	Information Processing	Vygotsky
Key concepts	Stages of cognitive development; qualitative growth from one stage to another	Gradual, quantitative improvements in attention, perception, understanding, and memory	Culture and social context drive cognitive development
Role of stages	Heavy emphasis	No specific stages	No specific stages
Importance of social factors	Low	Low	High
Educational perspective	Children must have reached a given stage of development for specific types of educational interventions to be effective.	Education is reflected in gradual increments in skills.	Education is very influential in promoting cognitive growth; teachers serve as facilitators.

Because of his emphasis on broad cultural influences, he did not focus on how individual bits of information are processed and synthesized. These processes, which must be taken into account if we are to have a complete understanding of cognitive development, are more directly addressed by information-processing theories.

Still, Vygotsky's melding of the cognitive and social worlds of children has been an important advance in our understanding of cognitive development. We can only imagine what his impact would have been if he had lived a longer life. (See Table 9-2 for a comparison of Piaget's theory, information-processing theories, and Vygotskian approaches.)

REVIEW ↵ mydevelopmentlab

1. During the _____ period children's use of symbolic thinking grows, mental reasoning emerges, and the use of concepts increases.

    Answer: preoperational

2. Vygotsky argues that the focus of cognitive development should be on a child's _____ and cultural world.

    Answer: social

3. The _____ _____ _____ _____ is the level at which a child can almost, but not fully, perform a task independently, but can do so with the assistance of someone more competent.

    Answer: zone of proximal development

To see more review questions, log on to MyDevelopmentLab.

The Growth of Language

I tried it out and it was very great!

This is a picture of when I was running through the water with Mommy.

Where you are going when I go to the fireworks with Mommy and Daddy?

I didn't know creatures went on floats in pools.

We can always pretend we have another one.

And the teacher put it up on the counter so no one could reach it.

I really want to keep it while we're at the park.

You need to get your own ball if you want to play "hit the tree."

When I grow up and I'm a baseball player, I'll have my baseball hat, and I'll put it on, and I'll play baseball (Schatz, 1994, p. 179).

Listen to Ricky, at the age of 3. In addition to recognizing most letters of the alphabet, printing the first letter of his name, and writing the word "HI," he is readily capable of producing the complex sentences quoted above.

During the preschool years, children's language skills reach new heights of sophistication. They begin the period with reasonable linguistic capabilities, although with significant gaps in both comprehension and production. In fact, no one would mistake the language used by a 3-year-old for that of an adult. However, by the end of the preschool years, they can hold their own with adults, both comprehending and producing language that has many of the qualities of adults' language. How does this transformation occur?

Syntax The combining of words and phrases to form meaningful sentences

Language Development During the Preschool Years

Language blooms so rapidly between the late-twos and the mid-threes that researchers have yet to understand the exact pattern. What is clear is that sentence length increases at a steady pace, and the ways in which children at this age combine words and phrases to form sentences—known as **syntax**—doubles each month. By the time a preschooler is 3, the various combinations reach into the thousands (see Table 9-3 for an example of one child's growth in the use of language; Wheeldon, 1999, Pinker, 2005).

TABLE 9-3 Growing Speech Capabilities

Over the course of just a year, the sophistication of the language of a boy named Adam increased amazingly, as these speech samples show.

Age	Sentences Produced
2 years, 3 months	Play checkers. Big drum. I got horn. A bunny-rabbit walk.
2 years, 4 months	See marching bear go? Screw part machine. That busy bulldozer truck.
2 years, 5 months	Now put boots on. Where wrench go? Mommy talking 'bout lady. What that paper clip doing?
2 years, 6 months	Write a piece of paper. What that egg doing? I lost a shoe. No, I don't want to sit seat.
2 years, 7 months	Where piece a paper go? Ursula has a boot on. Going to see kitten. Put the cigarette down. Dropped a rubber band. Shadow has hat just like that. Rin Tin Tin don't fly, Mommy.
2 years, 8 months	Let me get down with the boots on. Don't be afraid a horses. How tiger be so healthy and fly like kite? Joshua throw like a penguin.
2 years, 9 months	Where Mommy keep her pocketbook? Show you something funny. Just like turtle make mud pie.
2 years, 10 months	Look at that train Ursula brought. I simply don't want put in chair. You don't have paper. Do you want little bit, Cromer? I can't wear it tomorrow.
2 years, 11 months	That birdie hopping by Missouri in bag. Do want some pie on your face? Why you mixing baby chocolate? I finish drinking all up down my throat. I said why not you coming in? Look at that piece of paper and tell it. Do you want me tie that round? We going turn light on so you can't see.
3 years, 0 months	I going come in fourteen minutes. I going wear that to wedding. I see what happens. I have to save them now. Those are not strong mens. They are going sleep in wintertime. You dress me up like a baby elephant.
3 years, 1 month	I like to play with something else. You know how to put it back together. I gon' make it like a rocket to blast off with. I put another one on the floor. You went to Boston University? You want to give me some carrots and some beans? Press the button and catch it, sir. I want some other peanuts. Why you put the pacifier in his mouth? Doggies like to climb up.
3 years, 2 months	So it can't be cleaned? I broke my racing car. Do you know the light wents off? What happened to the bridge? When it's got a flat tire it's need a go to the station. I dream sometimes. I'm going to mail this so the letter can't come off. I want to have some espresso. The sun is not too bright. Can I have some sugar? Can I put my head in the mailbox so the mailman can know where I are and put me in the mailbox? Can I keep the screwdriver just like a carpenter keep the screwdriver?

(*Source:* Pinker, 1994)

This is a wug.

Now there is another one. There are two of them. There are two _____ .

FIGURE 9-6 Appropriate Formation of Words

Even though preschoolers—like the rest of us—are unlikely to have ever before encountered a wug, they are able to produce the appropriate word to fill in the blank (which, for the record, is *wugs*).

(*Source:* Adapted from Berko, 1958)

In addition to the increasing complexity of sentences, there are enormous leaps in the number of words children use. By age 6, the average child has a vocabulary of around 14,000 words. To reach this number, preschoolers acquire vocabulary at a rate of nearly one new word every 2 hours, 24 hours a day. They manage this feat through a process known as **fast mapping**, in which new words are associated with their meaning after only a brief encounter (Ganger & Brent, 2004; Gershkoff-Stowe & Hahn, 2007; Krcmar, Grela, & Lin, 2007).

By the age of 3, preschoolers routinely use plurals and possessive forms of nouns (such as "boys" and "boy's"), employ the past tense (adding "-ed" at the end of words), and use articles ("the" and "a"). They can ask, and answer, complex questions ("Where did you say my book is?" and "Those are trucks, aren't they?").

Preschoolers' skills extend to the appropriate formation of words that they have never before encountered. For example, in one classic experiment, preschool children were shown cards with drawings of a cartoon-like bird, such as those shown in Figure 9-6 (Berko, 1958). The experimenter told the children that the figure was a "wug," and then showed them a card with two of the cartoon figures. "Now there are two of them," the children were told, and they were then asked to supply the missing word in the sentence, "There are two _____" (the answer to which, as *you* no doubt know, is "wugs").

Not only did children show that they knew rules about the plural forms of nouns, but they understood possessive forms of nouns and the third-person singular and past-tense forms of verbs—all for words that they never had previously encountered, since they were nonsense words with no real meaning (O'Grady & Aitchison, 2005).

Preschoolers also learn what *cannot* be said as they acquire the principles of grammar. **Grammar** is the system of rules that determine how our thoughts can be expressed. For instance, preschoolers come to learn that "I am sitting" is correct, while the similarly structured "I am knowing [that]" is incorrect. Although they still make frequent mistakes of one sort or another, 3-year-olds follow the principles of grammar most of the time. Some errors are very noticeable—such as the use of "mens" and "catched"—but these errors are actually quite rare, occurring between one-tenth of a percent and 8% of the time. Put another way,

young preschoolers are correct in their grammatical constructions more than 90% of the time (deVilliers & deVilliers, 1992; Pinker, 1994; Guasti, 2002).

Private Speech and Social Speech In even a short visit to a preschool, you're likely to notice some children talking to themselves during play periods. A child might be reminding a doll that the two of them are going to the grocery store later, or another child, while playing with a toy racing car, might speak of an upcoming race. In some cases, the talk is sustained, as when a child, working on a puzzle, says things like, "This piece goes here. . . . Uh-oh, this one doesn't fit. . . . Where can I put this piece? . . . This can't be right."

Some developmentalists suggest that **private speech**, speech by children that is spoken and directed to themselves, performs an important function. For instance, Vygotsky suggested that private speech is used as a guide to behavior and thought. By communicating with themselves through private speech, children are able to try out ideas, acting as their own sounding boards. In this way, private speech facilitates children's thinking and helps them control their behavior. (Have you ever said to yourself, "Take it easy" or "Calm down" when trying to control your anger over some situation?) In Vygotsky's view, then, private speech ultimately serves an important social function, allowing children to solve problems and reflect upon difficulties they encounter. He also suggested that private speech is a forerunner to the internal dialogues that we use when we reason with ourselves during thinking (Winsler, De Leon, & Wallace, 2003).

In addition, private speech may be a way for children to practice the practical skills required in conversation, also known as *pragmatics*. **Pragmatics** is the aspect of language relating to communicating effectively and appropriately with others. The development of pragmatic abilities permits children to understand the basics of conversations—turn-taking, sticking to a topic, and what should and should not be said, according to the conventions of society. When children are taught that the appropriate response to receiving a gift is "thank you," or that they should use different language in various settings (on the playground with their friends versus in the classroom with their teacher), they are learning the pragmatics of language.

The preschool years also mark the growth of social speech. **Social speech** is speech directed toward another person and meant to be understood by that person. Before the age of 3, children may seem to be speaking only for their own entertainment, apparently uncaring whether anyone else can understand. However, during the preschool years, children begin to direct their speech to others, wanting others to listen and becoming frustrated when they cannot make themselves understood. As a result, they begin to adapt their speech to others through pragmatics, as discussed above. Recall that Piaget contended that most speech during the preoperational period was egocentric: Preschoolers were seen as taking little account of the effect their speech was having on others. However, more recent experimental evidence suggests that children are somewhat more adept in taking others into account than Piaget initially suggested.

How Living in Poverty Affects Language Development

The language that preschoolers hear at home has profound implications for future cognitive success, according to results of a landmark series of studies by psychologists Betty Hart and Todd Risley (Hart & Risley, 1995; Hart, 2000, 2004). The researchers studied the language used over a 2-year period by a group of parents of varying levels of affluence as they interacted with their children. Their examination of some 1,300 hours of everyday interactions between parents and children produced several major findings:

- The greater the affluence of the parents, the more they spoke to their children. As shown in Figure 9-7, the rate at which language was addressed to children varied significantly according to the economic level of the family.

- In a typical hour, parents classified as professionals spent almost twice as much time interacting with their children as parents who received welfare assistance.

- By the age of 4, children in families that received welfare assistance were likely to have been exposed to some 13 million fewer words than those in families classified as professionals.

- The kind of language used in the home differed among the various types of families. Children in families that received welfare assistance were apt to hear prohibitions ("no" or "stop," for example) twice as frequently as those in families classified as professionals.

Ultimately, the study found that the type of language to which children were exposed was associated with their performance on tests of intelligence. The greater the number and variety of words children heard, for instance, the better their performance at age 3 on a variety of measures of intellectual achievement.

Although the findings are correlational, and thus cannot be interpreted in terms of cause-and-effect, they clearly suggest the importance of early exposure to language, in terms of both quantity and variety. They also suggest that intervention programs that teach parents to speak to their children more often and use more varied language may be useful in alleviating some of the potentially damaging consequences of poverty.

The research is also consistent with an increasing body of evidence that family income and poverty have powerful consequences for children's general cognitive development and behavior. By the age of 5, children raised in poverty tend to have lower IQ scores and perform less well on other measures of cognitive development than children raised in affluence. Furthermore, the longer children live in poverty, the more severe are the consequences. Poverty not only

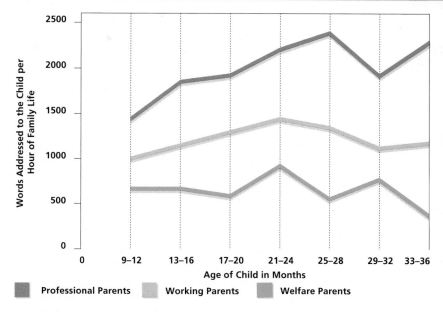

FIGURE 9-7 Different Language Exposures

Parents at differing levels of affluence provide different language experiences. Professional parents and working parents address more words to their children, on average, than parents on welfare. Why do you think this is so?
(*Source:* B. Hart & Risley, 1995, p. 239)

reduces the educational resources available to children, it also has such negative effects on *parents* that it limits the psychological support they can provide their families. In short, the consequences of poverty are severe, and they linger (Ramey & Ramey, 1998; Whitehurst & Fischel, 2000; Bornstein & Bradley, 2003).

From a social worker's perspective: What do you think are the underlying reasons for differences between poor and more affluent households in the use of language, and how do such language differences affect a family's social interactions?

REVIEW ↵ mydevelopmentlab

1. The way in which words and phrases are combined to form sentences, known as _____, increases at a steady pace during the preschool years.

    Answer: syntax

2. _____ _____ is speech by children that is spoken and directed to themselves.

    Answer: Private speech

3. _____ is the aspect of language relating to communicating effectively and appropriately with others.

    Answer: Pragmatics

To see more review questions, log on to MyDevelopmentLab.

Schooling and Society

It's a Thursday afternoon at Unitel Studio on Ninth Avenue, where *Sesame Street* is taping its nineteenth season. Hanging back in the wings is a newcomer on the set, a compact young woman with short blonde hair named Judy Sladky. Today is her screen test. Other performers come to New York aspiring to be actresses, dancers, singers, comedians. But Sladky's burning ambition is to be Alice, a shaggy mini-mastodon who will make her debut later this season as the devoted baby sister of Aloysius Snuffleupagus, the biggest creature on the show (Hellman, 1987, p. 50).

Ask almost any preschooler, and she or he will be able to identify Snuffleupagus, as well as Big Bird, Bert, Ernie, and a host of other characters as the members of the cast of *Sesame Street*, the most successful television show in history targeted at preschoolers, with a daily audience in the millions.

However, preschoolers do more than watch TV. Many spend a good portion of their day involved in some form of child-care setting outside their own homes, designed, in part, to enhance their cognitive development. What are the consequences of these activities? We turn now to a consideration of how early childhood education and television and other media are related to preschool development.

Early Childhood Education: Taking the *Pre-* Out of the Preschool Period

The term *preschool period* is something of a misnomer: Almost three-quarters of children in the United States are enrolled in some form of care outside the home, much of which is designed either explicitly or implicitly to teach skills that will enhance intellectual as well as social abilities (see Figure 9-8). One important reason for this increase is the rise in the number of families in which both parents work outside the home. For instance, a high proportion of fathers work outside the home, and close to 60% of women with children under 6 are employed, most of them full time (Borden, 1998; Tamis-LeMonda & Cabrera, 2002).

However, there is another cause, one less tied to the practical considerations of child care: Developmentalists have found increasing evidence that children can benefit substantially from involvement in some form of educational activity before they enroll in formal schooling, which typically takes place at age 5 or 6 in the United States. When compared to children who stay at home and have no formal educational involvement, those children enrolled in *good* preschools experience clear cognitive and social benefits (Campbell, Ramey, & Pungello, 2002; Friedman, 2004; National Association for the Education of Young Children, 2005).

The Varieties of Early Education The variety of early education alternatives is vast. Some outside-the-home care for children is little more than babysitting, while other options are designed to promote intellectual and social advances. Among the major choices of the latter type are the following:

- *Child-care centers* typically provide care for children all day, while their parents are at work. (Child-care centers were previously referred to as *day-care centers*. However, because a significant number of parents work nonstandard schedules and therefore require care for their children at times other than the day, the preferred label has changed to child-care centers.)

  Although many child-care centers were first established as safe, warm environments where children could be cared for and could interact with other children, today their purpose tends to be broader, aimed at providing some form of intellectual stimulation. Still, their primary purpose tends to be more social and emotional than cognitive.

- Some child care is provided in *family child-care centers*, small operations run in private homes. Because centers in some areas are unlicensed, the quality of care can be uneven, and parents should consider whether a family child-care center is licensed before enrolling their children. In contrast, providers of center-based care, which is offered in institutions such as school classrooms, community centers, and churches and synagogues, are typically licensed and regulated by governmental authorities. Because teachers in such programs are more often trained professionals than those who provide family child care, the quality of care is often higher.

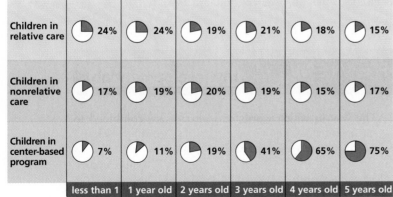

Percentage of Children in Each Age Group*	less than 1	1 year old	2 years old	3 years old	4 years old	5 years old
Children in relative care	24%	24%	19%	21%	18%	15%
Children in nonrelative care	17%	19%	20%	19%	15%	17%
Children in center-based program	7%	11%	19%	41%	65%	75%

*Columns do not add up to 100 because some children participated in more than one type of day care.

FIGURE 9-8 Care Outside the Home

Approximately 75% of children in the United States are enrolled in some form of care outside the home—a trend that is the result of more parents being employed full time. Evidence suggests that children can benefit from early childhood education. What role might a caregiver provide that can help the educational development of a child? (*Source:* National Center for Education Statistics, 1997)

- *Preschools* are explicitly designed to provide intellectual and social experiences for children. They tend to be more limited in their schedules than family care centers, typically providing care for only 3 to 5 hours per day. Because of this limitation, preschools mainly serve children from middle and higher socioeconomic levels, in cases where parents don't need to work full time.

  Like child-care centers, preschools vary enormously in the activities they provide. Some emphasize social skills, while others focus on intellectual development. Some do both.

  For instance, Montessori preschools, which use a method developed by Italian educator Maria Montessori, employ a carefully designed set of materials to create an environment that fosters sensory, motor, and language development through play. Children are provided with a variety of activities to choose from, with the option of moving from one to another (Gutek, 2003).

  Similarly, in the Reggio Emilia preschool approach—another Italian import—children participate in what is called a "negotiated curriculum" that emphasizes the joint participation of children and teachers. The curriculum builds on the interests of children, promoting their cognitive development through the integration of the arts and participation in week-long projects (Hong & Trepanier-Street, 2004; Rankin, 2004).

- *School child care* is provided by some local school systems in the United States. Almost half the states in the United States fund prekindergarten programs for 4-year-olds, often aimed at disadvantaged children. Because they typically are staffed by better trained teachers than less-regulated child-care centers, school child-care programs are often of higher quality than other early education alternatives. (For more on preschool programs from the perspective of a caregiver, see the *Careers in Child Development* interview.)

The Effectiveness of Child Care How effective are such programs? Most research suggests that preschoolers enrolled in child-care centers show intellectual development that at least matches that of children at home, and often is better. For instance, some studies find that preschoolers in child care are more verbally fluent, show memory and comprehension advantages, and even achieve higher IQ scores than at-home children. Other studies find that early and long-term participation in child care is particularly helpful for children from impoverished home environments or who are otherwise at risk (Campbell, Ramey, & Pungello, 2002; Clarke-Stewart & Allhusen, 2002; Vandell, 2004).

Similar advantages are found for social development. Children in high-quality programs tend to be more self-confident, independent, and knowledgeable about the social world in which they live than those who do not participate. On the other hand, not all the outcomes of outside-the-home care are positive: Children in child care have been found to be less polite, less compliant, less respectful of adults, and sometimes more competitive and aggressive than their peers. Furthermore, children who spend more than 10 hours a week in preschools have a slightly higher likelihood of being disruptive in class extending through the sixth grade (Clarke-Stewart & Allhusen, 2002; NICHD Early Child Care Research Network, 2003a; Belsky et al., 2007).

Another way to consider the effectiveness of child care is to take an economic approach. For instance, one study of prekindergarten education in Texas found that every dollar invested in high-quality preschool programs produced $3.50 in benefits. Benefits included increased graduation rates, higher earnings, savings in juvenile crime, and reductions in child welfare costs (Aguirre et al., 2006).

It is important to keep in mind that not all early childhood care programs are equally effective. As we observed of infant child care in Chapter 7, one key factor is program *quality*: High-quality care provides intellectual and social benefits, while low-quality care not only is unlikely to furnish benefits, but poor programs actually may harm children (Maccoby & Lewis, 2003; Votruba-Drzal, Coley, & Chase-Lansdale, 2004; NICHD Early Child Care Research Network, 2006).

The Quality of Child Care How can we define "high quality"? Several characteristics are important; they are analogous to those that pertain to infant child care (see Chapter 7). The major characteristics of high-quality include the following (Vandell, Shumow, & Posner, 2005; Layzer & Goodson, 2006; Leach et al., 2008; Rudd, Cain, & Saxon, 2008):

- The care providers are well trained.
- The child-care center has an appropriate overall size and ratio of care providers to children. Single groups should not have many more than 14 to 20 children, and there should be no more than five to ten 3-year-olds per caregiver, or seven to ten 4- or 5-year-olds per caregiver.
- The curriculum of a child-care facility is not left to chance, but is carefully planned out and coordinated among the teachers.
- The language environment is rich, with a great deal of conversation.
- The caregivers are sensitive to children's emotional and social needs, and they know when, and when not, to intervene.
- Materials and activities are age appropriate.
- Basic health and safety standards are followed.

No one knows how many programs in the United States can be considered "high quality," but there are many fewer than desirable. In fact, the United States lags behind almost every other industrialized country in the quality of its child care as well as in its quantity and affordability (Zigler & Finn-Stevenson, 1995; Scarr, 1998; Muenchow & Marsland, 2007).

DEVELOPMENTAL DIVERSITY

Preschools Around the World: Why Does the United States Lag Behind?

In France and Belgium, access to preschool is a legal right. In Sweden and Finland, the governments provide child care to preschoolers whose parents work. Russia has an extensive system of state-run *yasli-sads,* nursery schools and kindergartens, attended by 75% of children age 3 to 7 in urban areas.

In contrast, the United States has no coordinated national policy on preschool education—or on the care of children in general. There are several reasons for this. For one, decisions about education have traditionally been left to the states and local school districts. For another, the United States has no tradition of teaching preschoolers, unlike other countries in which preschool programs have existed for decades. Finally, the status of preschools in the United States has been traditionally low. Consider, for instance, that preschool and nursery school teachers are the lowest paid of all teachers. (Teacher salaries increase as the age of students rises. Thus, college and high school teachers are paid most, while preschool and elementary school teachers are paid least.)

Preschools also differ significantly from one country to another according to the views that different society's hold of the purpose of early childhood education (Lamb et al., 1992). For instance, in a cross-country comparison of preschools in China, Japan, and the United States, researchers found that parents in the three countries view the purpose of preschools very differently. Whereas parents in China tend to see preschools primarily as a way of giving children a good start academically, Japanese parents view them primarily as a way of giving children the opportunity to be members of a group. In the United States, in comparison, parents regard the primary purpose of preschools as making children more independent and self-reliant, although obtaining a good academic start and having group experience are also important (see Figure 9-9; Huntsinger et al., 1997; Johnson et al., 2003). ⎯⎯⎯⎯⎯⎯⎯⎯⎯

"I didn't realize how much I needed to get away from that daycare grind."

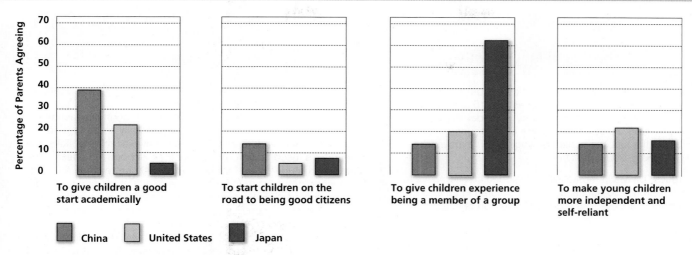

FIGURE 9-9 The Purpose of Preschool

To parents in China, Japan, and the United States, the main purpose of preschools is very different. Whereas parents in China see preschools mainly as a way of giving children a good start academically, parents in Japan see them primarily as a means of giving children the experience of being a member of a group. In contrast, parents in the United States view preschools as a way of making children more independent, although obtaining a good academic start and group experience are also important. As a preschool educator, how would you interpret these findings?

(*Source:* Adapted from Tobin, Wu, & Davidson, 1989)

Preparing Preschoolers for Academic Pursuits: Does Head Start Truly Provide a Head Start?

Although many programs designed for preschoolers focus primarily on social and emotional factors, some are geared primarily toward promoting cognitive gains and preparing preschoolers for the more formal instruction they will experience when they start kindergarten. In the United States, the best-known program designed to promote future academic success is Head Start. Born in the 1960s when the United States declared a War on Poverty, the program has served over 13 million children and their families. The program, which stresses parental involvement, was designed to serve the "whole child," including children's physical health, self-confidence, social responsibility, and social and emotional development (Zigler & Styfco, 2004; Love, Chazen-Cohen, & Raikes, 2007).

Whether Head Start is seen as successful or not depends on the lens through which one is looking. If, for instance, the program is expected to provide long-term increases in IQ scores, it is a disappointment. Although graduates of Head Start programs tend to show immediate IQ gains, these increases do not last.

On the other hand, it is clear that Head Start is meeting its goal of getting preschoolers ready for school. Preschoolers who participate in Head Start are better prepared for future schooling than those who do not take part. Furthermore, graduates of Head Start programs have better future school adjustment than their peers, and they are less likely to be in special education classes or to be retained in grade. Finally, some research suggests that Head Start graduates even show higher academic performance at the end of high school, although the gains are modest (Schnur & Belanger, 2000; Brooks-Gunn, 2003; Kronholz, 2003).

In addition to Head Start programs, other types of preschool readiness programs also provide advantages throughout the school years. Studies show that those who participate and graduate from such preschool programs are less likely to repeat grades, and they complete school more frequently than those who are not in the programs. Preschool readiness programs also appear to be cost-effective. According to a cost–benefit analysis of one readiness program, for every dollar spent on the program, taxpayers saved seven dollars by the time the graduates reached the age of 27 (Schweinhart, Barnes, & Weikart, 1993; Friedman, 2004; Gormley et al., 2005).

The most recent comprehensive evaluation of early intervention programs, suggests that, taken as a group, they can provide significant benefits, and that government funds invested early in life may ultimately lead to a reduction in future costs. For instance, compared with children who did not participate in early intervention programs, participants in various programs showed gains in emotional or cognitive development, better educational outcomes, increased economic self-sufficiency, reduced levels of criminal activity, and improved health-related behaviors. Although not every

FROM RESEARCH to PRACTICE

The Montessori Approach: Is It Effective?

In immaculately ordered and naturally lit classrooms, materials play a prominent role. Children ages 3 to 6 pick their tools—a wet sponge, a textured globe, a model dinosaur skeleton—and work quietly, either alone or in groups of two or three. Down the hall, their peers do yoga on 10 mats in the library (MacDonald, 2007, p. 9D).

In the early 1900s, Dr. Maria Montessori developed an alternative to the traditional approach to educating young children in an effort to improve educational access to the poor. Montessori rejected traditional methods such as tests and grades because she felt they fostered competition and discouraged collaborative learning. Instead, she embraced self-directed exploration and discovery through hands-on, active learning. Montessori education emphasizes children's active participation in their own learning. In Montessori schools, teachers act more as facilitators within multiage classrooms where pupils engage in individual and small-group activities that help them learn social skills as well as academic lessons (Montessori, 1964).

Montessori argued that the traditional educational approach treated children as adults and that her method was better tailored to the distinctive ways in which children think and learn. Thousands of private schools in the United States employ the Montessori method, and Montessori programs are available at several hundred public schools.

While Montessori education is clearly a different experience from the traditional classroom, does it in fact produce better educational outcomes for children? Recent research provides compelling evidence that it does.

Researchers Angeline Lillard and Nicole Else-Quest compared two groups of 3- to 6-year-old children: One group was completing the primary level of education at a Montessori school while the other group was completing the equivalent level at various non-Montessori schools (mainly urban public schools). These two groups were known to be equivalent before they entered their respective schools, as they had all originally applied for admission to the Montessori school, with admission being determined by a random lottery. Consequently, any differences between the groups on outcome measures could be attributed to the different educational programs (Lillard & Else-Quest, 2006).

The researchers examined a variety of cognitive–academic and social–behavioral skills that are generally important to life success. To examine differences in cognitive–academic skills, the researchers used a test that measures school readiness. The Montessori students performed significantly better than the non-Montessori group on standardized measures of reading and math skill. Moreover, the Montessori students performed better on a test of executive function that involved applying different decision rules in a card-sorting task.

The benefits weren't just academic, either. The children were asked their solutions to several social problems (such as a child not sharing a playground swing). The children from the Montessori school were significantly more likely than those from the comparison school group to make appeals to justice or fairness in trying to persuade the problem child to do the right thing. On the playground, Montessori children were more likely to engage in positive shared play and less likely to engage in ambiguous rough play, such as wrestling. Finally, Montessori children were more likely to show an understanding of false beliefs, a milestone in development that we will discuss in Chapter 10.

Further research is needed to determine what specific components of a Montessori education are responsible for producing these beneficial outcomes. Still, taking the Montessori approach as a whole, the advantages it produces over traditional educational programs are compelling evidence of its effectiveness.

- Can you think of any potential drawbacks to Montessori education? Would it be appropriate for every pupil? Keep in mind that in this comparison, all of the parents originally wanted their children to attend a Montessori school. What about children whose parents aren't as supportive of the Montessori method?

- In what ways does the Montessori method relate to Vygotsky's view of cognitive development?

program produced all these benefits, and not every child benefited to the same extent, the results of the evaluation suggested that the potential benefits of early intervention can be substantial (NICHD Early Child Care Research Network & Duncan, 2003; Love et al., 2006; Barnard, 2007; Izard et al., 2008).

Of course, traditional programs such as Head Start, which emphasize academic success brought about by traditional instruction, are not the only approach to early intervention that has proven effective. As we consider in the *From Research to Practice* box, Montessori schools, which have their own unique philosophy and approach, have also proven valuable.

Are We Pushing Children Too Hard and Too Fast?

Not everyone agrees that programs that seek to enhance academic skills during the preschool years are a good thing. In fact, according to developmental psychologist David Elkind, U.S. society tends to push children so rapidly that they begin to feel stress and pressure at a young age (Elkind, 1994b).

Elkind argues that academic success is largely dependent upon factors out of parents' control, such as inherited abilities and a child's rate of maturation. Consequently, children of a particular age cannot be expected to master educational material without taking into account their current level of cognitive development. In short, children require **developmentally appropriate educational practice**, which is education that is

"Say, Dad, think you could wrap it up? I have a long day tomorrow."

based on both typical development and the unique characteristics of a given child (Robinson & Stark, 2005).

Rather than arbitrarily expecting children to master material at a particular age, Elkind suggests that a better strategy is to provide an environment in which learning is encouraged, but not pushed. By creating an atmosphere in which learning is facilitated—for instance, by reading to preschoolers—parents will allow children to proceed at their own pace rather than at one that pushes them beyond their limits (van Kleeck & Stahl, 2003).

Although Elkind's suggestions are appealing—it is certainly hard to disagree that increases in children's anxiety levels and stress should be avoided—they are not without their detractors. For instance, some educators have argued that pushing children is largely a phenomenon of the middle and higher socioeconomic levels, possible only if parents are relatively affluent. For poorer children, whose parents may not have substantial resources available to push their children nor the easy ability to create an environment that promotes learning, the benefits of formal programs that promote learning are likely to outweigh their drawbacks.

Learning From the Media: Television and the Internet

Television—and, more recently, the Internet and computers—play a central role in many U.S. households. Television, in particular, is one of the most potent and widespread stimuli to which children are exposed, with the average preschooler watching more than 21 hours of TV a week. More than a third of households with children 2 to 7 years of age say that television is on "most of the time" in their homes. In comparison, preschoolers spend

three-quarters of an hour reading on the average day (see Figure 9-10; Robinson & Bianchi, 1997; Roberts et al., 1999; Bryant & Bryant, 2001, 2003).

Computers are also are becoming influential in the lives of preschoolers. Seventy percent of preschoolers between the ages of 4 and 6 have used a computer, and a quarter of them use one every day. Those who use a computer spend an average of an hour a day, and the majority use it by themselves. With help from their parents, almost one-fifth have sent an e-mail (Rideout, Vandewater, & Wartella, 2003).

It's too early to know the effects of computer usage—or of other new media such as video games—on preschoolers. However, there is a wealth of research on the consequences of viewing television, as we begin to consider next (Pecora, Murray, & Wartella, 2007).

From the perspective of an educator: Should the United States develop a more encouraging and more supportive preschool policy? If so, what sort of policy? If not, why not?

Controlling TV Exposure   Despite the introduction of a number of high-quality educational programs over the past decade, many children's programs are not of high quality or are not appropriate for a preschool audience. Accordingly, the American Academy of Pediatrics recommends that exposure to television should be limited. They suggest that until the age of 2, children watch *no* television, and after that age, no more than 1 to 2 hours of quality programming each day (American Academy of Pediatrics, 1999b).

[Bar graph: Hours on y-axis (0 to 4)]

Watching TV and videos: 3:09 total (watching their own shows 1:59; in the room when parents watch TV :43; watching videos :29)

Reading: :45

Using a computer: :11

Playing video games: :08

Times are presented in hours:minutes. Numbers cannot be summed to calculate children's total media-use time because they may have used more than one medium at a time. Reading includes amount of time children are read to.

FIGURE 9-10 Television Time

Although 2- to 7-year-olds spend more time reading than playing video games or using a computer, they spend the most time watching television. As an educator, how would you instill interest in children to read more?
(*Source:* V. J. Rideout et al., 1999)

One reason for restricting children's viewing of television relates to the inactivity it produces. Preschoolers who watch more than 2 hours per day of television and videos (or use computers for significant amounts of time) have a significantly higher risk of obesity than those who watch less (Mendoza, Zimmerman, & Christakis, 2007; Jordan & Robinson, 2008).

Furthermore, when they do watch television, preschool children often do not fully understand the plots of the stories they are viewing, particularly in longer programs. They are unable to recall significant story details after viewing a program, and the inferences they make about the motivations of characters are limited and often erroneous. Moreover, preschool children may have difficulty separating fantasy from reality in television programming, with some believing, for example, that there is a real Big Bird living on *Sesame Street* (Wright et al., 1994).

Preschool-age children exposed to advertising on television are not able to critically understand and evaluate the messages to which they are exposed. Consequently, they are likely to fully accept advertisers' claims about a product. The likelihood of children believing advertising messages is so high that the American Psychological Association has recommended that advertising targeting children under the age of 8 be restricted (Kunkel et al., 2004; Pine, Wilson, & Nash, 2007).

In short, the world to which preschoolers are exposed on TV is imperfectly understood and unrealistic. On the other hand, as they get older and their information-processing capabilities improve, preschoolers' understanding of the material they see on television improves. They remember things more accurately, and they become better able to focus on the central message of a show. This improvement suggests that the powers of the medium of television may be harnessed to bring about cognitive gains—exactly what the producers of *Sesame Street* set out to do (Singer & Singer, 2000; Crawley, Anderson, & Santomero, 2002; Berry, 2003).

Sesame Street: A Teacher in Every Home? *Sesame Street* is the most popular educational program for children in the United States. Almost half of all preschoolers in the United States watch the show, and it is broadcast in almost 100 different countries and in 13 foreign languages. Characters like Big Bird and Elmo have become familiar throughout the world to both adults and preschoolers (Bickham, Wright, & Huston, 2000; Cole, Arafat, & Tidhar, 2003; Moran, 2006).

Sesame Street was devised with the express purpose of providing an educational experience for preschoolers. Its specific goals include teaching letters and numbers, increasing vocabulary, and teaching preliteracy skills. Has *Sesame Street* achieved its goals? Most evidence suggests that it has.

For example, a 2-year longitudinal study compared three groups of 3- and 5-year-olds: those who watched cartoons or other programs, those who watched the same amount of *Sesame Street,* and those who watched little or no TV. Children who watched *Sesame Street* had significantly larger vocabularies than those who watched other programs or those who watched little television. These findings held regardless of the children's gender, family size, and parent education and attitudes. Such findings are consistent with earlier evaluations of the program, which concluded that viewers showed dramatic improvements in skills that were directly taught, such as alphabet recitation, and improvements in other areas that were not directly taught, such as reading words (Rice et al., 1990; McGinn, 2002).

Formal evaluations of the show find that preschoolers living in lower income households who watch the show are better prepared for school, and they perform significantly higher on several measures of verbal and mathematics ability at ages 6 and 7 than those who do not watch it. Furthermore, viewers of *Sesame Street* spend more time reading than nonviewers. And by the time they are 6 and 7, viewers of *Sesame Street* and other educational programs tend to be better readers and judged more positively by their teachers. The findings for *Sesame Street* are mirrored for other educationally oriented shows such as *Dora the Explorer* and *Blue's Clues* (Augustyn, 2003; Linebarger & Walker, 2005).

On the other hand, *Sesame Street* has not been without its critics. For instance, some educators claim the frenzied pace at which different scenes are shown makes viewers less receptive to the traditional forms of teaching that they will experience when they begin school. However, careful evaluations of the program find no evidence that viewing *Sesame Street* leads to declines in enjoyment of traditional schooling. Indeed, the most recent findings regarding *Sesame Street* and other informative programs like it show quite positive outcomes for viewers (Wright et al., 2001; Fisch, 2004).

Becoming an Informed Consumer of Development

Promoting Cognitive Development in Preschoolers: From Theory to the Classroom

We have considered the notion that one focus of the preschool period should be on promoting future academic success, and we have also discussed the alternative view that pushing children too hard academically may be hazardous to their well-being.

There is, however, a middle ground. Drawing on research conducted by developmental psychologists who examine cognitive development during the preschool years (Reese & Cox, 1999), we can make several suggestions for parents and preschool teachers who wish to improve the academic readiness of children without creating undue stress. Among them are the following:

- Parents and teachers should be aware of the stage of cognitive development, with its capabilities and limitations, that each individual child has reached. Unless they are aware of a child's current level of development, it will be impossible to provide appropriate materials and experiences.

- Instruction should be at a level just slightly higher than each student's current level of cognitive development. With too little novelty, children will be bored; with too much, they will be confused.

- Instruction should be individualized as much as possible. Because children of the same age may be at different levels of cognitive development, curriculum materials that are prepared individually stand a better chance of success.

- Opportunities for social interaction—both with other students and with adults—should be provided. By receiving feedback from others and observing how others react in given situations, preschoolers learn new approaches and new ways of thinking about the world.

- Let students make mistakes. Cognitive growth often flows from confronting and correcting errors.

- Because cognitive development can occur only when children have achieved the appropriate level of maturation, preschoolers should not be pushed too far ahead of their current state of cognitive development.

- Read to children. Children learn from hearing stories read to them, and it can motivate them to learn to read themselves.

1. _____ preschools, developed in Italy, employ a carefully designed set of materials to create an environment that fosters sensory, motor, and language development through play.

   Answer: Montessori

2. A key factor in the effects of preschools are their level of _____.

   Answer: quality

3. David Elkind argues children require _____ _____ _____ practices, which are based on both typical development and the unique characteristics of a given child.

   Answer: developmentally appropriate educational

To see more review questions, log on to MyDevelopmentLab.

CASE STUDY

The Case of... The Secret Reader

Della Faison had handled the situation badly. As an assistant teacher in an urban preschool, she had been concerned that one of her students, Lawson Ellings, showed little interest in books and story time. She knew that Lawson's mother was a single parent who worked two jobs, and she wanted to encourage the mother to try harder to help Lawson value reading.

The next time she chatted with Mrs. Ellings, she mentioned how important it was for Lawson to take an active interest in academics, to be exposed to books in the home, and to develop an enjoyment of books and learning. When Mrs. Ellings asked what she meant, she explained that Lawson never joined reading circle and never picked a book to look through, choosing instead to play with Legos and trucks and other physical toys.

Della noticed that Mrs. Ellings paused before answering. "Thank you for your concern, Ms. Faison, but Lawson probably doesn't sit in reading circle because he is a shy boy who likes to be by himself most of the time. And he may not choose your books because he's read most of them already. I take him to the library every Wednesday evening and Saturday morning, no matter how tired I am, and I read to him and let him read to me. He's been through nearly every book in the preschool section. He may want to play with Legos because we don't have any of those at home."

Della didn't know what to say.

1. Had Della interpreted Lawson's classroom decisions accurately? Why had she made the interpretation that she had?

2. Is it plausible for a preschooler like Lawson to have a "secret reading life"? Could he really have the language skills to read books at his age?

3. Should Della still be concerned about Lawson's reading? Should she quietly test his abilities one-on-one?

4. Is it possible for an academically able student to emerge from circumstances like Lawson's? Why or why not? What factors might affect his academic achievement?

◄ Looking Back

How does Piaget interpret cognitive development during the preschool years?

- During the stage that Piaget has described as preoperational, children are not yet able to engage in organized, formal, logical thinking. However, their development of symbolic function permits quicker and more effective thinking as they are freed from the limitations of sensorimotor learning.

- According to Piaget, children in the preoperational stage engage in intuitive thought for the first time, actively applying rudimentary reasoning skills to the acquisition of world knowledge.

How do information-processing approaches and Vygotsky's theory explain cognitive development?

- A different approach to cognitive development is taken by proponents of information-processing theories, who focus on preschoolers' storage and recall of information and on quantitative changes in information-processing abilities (such as attention).

- Lev Vygotsky proposed that the nature and progress of children's cognitive development are dependent on the children's social and cultural context.

How do children's linguistic abilities develop in the preschool years, and what is the importance of early linguistic development?

- Children rapidly progress from two-word utterances to longer, more sophisticated expressions that reflect their growing vocabularies and emerging grasp of grammar.

- The development of linguistic abilities is affected by socioeconomic status. The result can be lowered linguistic—and ultimately academic—performance by poorer children.

What kinds of preschool educational programs are available in the United States, and what effects do they have?

- The United States lacks a coordinated national policy on preschool education. The major federal initiative in U.S. preschool education has been the Head Start program, which has yielded mixed, although promising, results.

- Early childhood educational programs—center-based, school-based, or preschool—can lead to cognitive and social advances.

What effects do television and computers have on preschoolers?

- The effects of exposure to television and other media sources, such as computers, are mixed. Although preschoolers' constant exposure to situations that are not representative of the real world have raised concerns, they can attain cognitive advances from programs such as *Sesame Street*. ∎

Epilogue

In this chapter, we looked at children in the preschool years. We discussed cognitive development from the Piagetian perspective, with its description of the characteristics of thought in the preoperational stage, and from the perspective of information-processing theorists and Lev Vygotsky. We then discussed the burst in linguistic ability that occurs during the preschool years. We concluded with a discussion of preschool education and the influence of television and computers on preschoolers' development.

Return to the Prologue, which describes Will's preparation for his first day of kindergarten, and answer these questions.

1. According to Piaget, what sorts of understandings—and limitations to his understandings—will Will have as he enters school?

2. Can you discuss from an information-processing perspective the likely course of Will's cognitive development during his preschool years? What most likely changed as he progressed toward kindergarten, and why?

3. In what ways is kindergarten likely to affect Will's sense of the pragmatics of language that govern communications with others?

4. To what aspects of the school "culture" that Will is joining do Vygotsky's theories apply? What features of the typical kindergarten program would a follower of Vygotsky emphasize?

Key Terms and Concepts

preoperational stage (p. 208)
operations (p. 208)
symbolic function (p. 208)
centration (p. 208)
conservation (p. 209)
transformation (p. 210)
egocentric thought (p. 211)

intuitive thought (p. 211)
autobiographical memory (p. 213)
scripts (p. 213)
zone of proximal development
    (ZPD) (p. 216)
scaffolding (p. 216)
syntax (p. 219)

fast mapping (p. 220)
grammar (p. 220)
private speech (p. 220)
pragmatics (p. 220)
social speech (p. 220)
developmentally appropriate
    educational practice (p. 226)

What decisions would you make while raising a child? What would the consequences of those decisions be?

Find out by logging onto **My Virtual Child** and raising your child from birth to 18 years.

chapter ten

10 Social and Personality Development in the Preschool Years

PROLOGUE: THE GATHERING

Sandy Rossoff was cooking for a family get-together and was delighted that her 3-year-old daughter, Sarah, was happily playing in the living room. Ten minutes later, Sandy peeked in. The room had been transformed from order into chaos. Sarah had upended her play table, draped a blanket over it to make a tent, and strewn toys and crayons all over the floor. She had also removed all the cushions from the sofa and chairs, making them into a mountain perfect for a headlong jump.

"Oh, no, Sarah! Guests are coming. We need to clean up," Sandy said as she frantically started picking up debris. But when she put the table back on its legs and began to heap toys onto it, Sarah tipped it over again. "Noooo, Mommy," she implored. "I *need* to mess." (Greenspan, 1997, p. 96)

► Looking Ahead

Sarah Rossoff's assertion that she needed to make a mess, whether literally true or not, does clearly signify something quite important: her growing sense of who she is. During the preschool years, children's sense of themselves as distinct individuals begins to grow, and it colors their relationships with others.

In this chapter, we address social and personality development during the preschool period, a time of enormous growth and change. We

begin by examining how preschool-age children continue to form a sense of self, focusing on how they develop their self-concepts. We especially examine issues of self relating to gender, a central aspect of children's views of themselves and others.

Preschoolers' social lives are the focus of the next part of the chapter. We look at how children play with one another, examining the various types of play. We consider how parents and other authority figures use discipline to shape children's behavior.

Finally, we examine two key aspects of preschool-age children's social behavior: moral development and aggression. We consider how children develop a notion of right and wrong and how that development can lead them to be helpful to others. We also look at the other side of the coin—aggression—and examine the factors that lead preschool-age children to behave in a way that hurts others. We end on an optimistic note: considering how we may help preschool-age children to be more moral and less aggressive individuals.

After reading this chapter, you'll be able to answer these questions:

- *How do preschool-age children develop a concept of themselves?*
- *How do children develop their sense of racial identity and gender?*
- *In what sorts of social relationships do preschool-age children engage?*
- *What sorts of disciplinary styles do parents employ, and what effects do they have?*
- *How do children develop a moral sense?*
- *How does aggression develop in preschool-age children?*

232

Forming a Sense of Self

Although the question "Who am I?" is not explicitly posed by most preschool-age children, it underlies a considerable amount of development during the preschool years. During this period, children wonder about the nature of the self, and the way they answer the "Who am I?" question may affect them for the rest of their lives.

Psychosocial Development: Resolving the Conflicts

Mary-Alice's preschool teacher raised her eyebrows slightly when the 4-year-old took off her coat. Mary-Alice, usually dressed in well-matched play suits, was a medley of prints. She had on a pair of flowered pants, along with a completely clashing plaid top. The outfit was accessorized with a striped headband, socks in an animal print, and Mary-Alice's polka-dotted rain boots. Mary-Alice's mom gave a slightly embarrassed shrug. "Mary-Alice got dressed all by herself this morning," she explained as she handed over a bag containing spare shoes, just in case the rain boots became uncomfortable during the day.

Psychoanalyst Erik Erikson may well have praised Mary-Alice's mother for helping Mary-Alice develop a sense of initiative (if not of fashion). The reason: Erikson (1963) suggested that, during the preschool years, children face a key conflict relating to psychosocial development that involves the development of initiative.

As we discussed in Chapter 7, **psychosocial development** encompasses changes both in individuals' understanding of themselves and their understanding of others' behavior. According to Erikson, society and culture present the developing person with particular challenges, which shift as people age. Erikson believed that people pass through eight distinct stages, each characterized by a crisis or conflict that the person must resolve. Our experiences as we try to resolve these conflicts lead us to develop ideas about ourselves that can last for the rest of our lives.

In the early part of the preschool period, children are ending the autonomy-versus-shame-and-doubt stage, which lasts from around 18 months to 3 years. In this period, children either become more independent and autonomous if their parents encourage exploration and freedom or they experience shame and self-doubt if they are restricted and over-protected.

The preschool years largely encompass what Erikson called the **initiative-versus-guilt stage**, which lasts from around age 3 to age 6. During this period, children's views of themselves change as

From a child-care provider's perspective:
How would you relate Erikson's stages of trust versus mistrust, autonomy versus shame and doubt, and initiative versus guilt to the issue of secure attachment discussed in an earlier chapter?

preschool-age children face conflicts between, on the one hand, the desire to act independently of their parents and do things on their own, and, on the other hand, the guilt that comes from failure when they don't succeed. They are eager to do things on their own ("Let *me* do it" is a popular refrain among preschoolers"), but they feel guilt if their efforts fail. They come to see themselves as persons in their own right, and they begin to make decisions on their own.

Parents, such as Mary-Alice's mother, who react positively to this transformation toward independence can help their children resolve the opposing feelings that are characteristic of this period. By providing their children with opportunities to act self-reliantly, while still giving them direction and guidance, parents can support and encourage their children's initiative. On the other hand, parents who discourage their children's efforts to seek independence may contribute to a sense of guilt that persists throughout their lives as well as affects their self-concept, which begins to develop during this period.

Self-Concept in the Preschool Years: Thinking About the Self

If you ask preschool-age children to specify what makes them different from other kids, they readily respond with answers like, "I'm a good runner" or "I like to color" or "I'm a big girl." Such answers relate to **self-concept**—their identity, or their set of beliefs about what they are like as individuals (Brown, 1998; Tessor, Felson, & Suls, 2000; Marsh, Ellis, & Craven, 2002).

The statements that describe children's self-concepts are not necessarily accurate. In fact, preschool children typically overestimate their skills and knowledge across all domains of expertise. Consequently, their view of the future is quite rosy: They expect to win the next game they play, to beat all opponents in an upcoming race, to write great stories when they grow up. Even when they have just experienced failure at a task, they are likely to expect to do well in the future. This optimistic view is held, in part, because they have not yet started to compare themselves and their performance against others. Their inaccuracy is also helpful, freeing them to take chances and try new activities (Dweck, 2002; Wang, 2004).

Preschool-age children's view of themselves also reflects the way their particular culture considers the self. For example, many Asian societies tend to have a **collectivistic orientation**, promoting the notion of interdependence. People in such cultures tend to regard themselves as parts of a larger social network in which they are interconnected with and responsible to others. In contrast, children in Western cultures are more likely to develop a view of the self reflecting an **individualistic orientation** that emphasizes personal identity and the uniqueness of the individual. They are more apt to see themselves as self-contained and autonomous, in competition with others for scarce resources. Consequently, children in Western cultures are more likely to focus on what sets them apart from others—what makes them special.

Such views pervade a culture, sometimes in subtle ways. For instance, one well-known saying in Western cultures states that "the squeaky wheel gets the grease." Preschoolers who are exposed to this perspective are encouraged to gain the attention of others by standing out and making their needs known. On the other hand, children in Asian cultures are exposed to a different perspective; they are told that "the nail that stands out gets pounded down." This perspective suggests to preschoolers that they should attempt to blend in and refrain from making themselves distinctive (Dennis et al., 2002; Lehman, Chiu, & Schaller, 2004; Wang, 2004).

Preschoolers' developing self-concepts can also be affected by their culture's attitudes toward various racial and ethnic groups, As we'll see next, preschoolers' awareness of their ethnic or racial identity develops slowly, and is subtly influenced by the attitudes of the people, schools, and other cultural institutions with which they come into contact in their community.

The view of the self that preschoolers develop depends in part on the culture in which they grow up.

DEVELOPMENTAL DIVERSITY

Developing Racial and Ethnic Awareness

The preschool years mark an important turning point for children. Their answer to the question of who they are begins to take into account their racial and ethnic identity.

For most preschool-age children, racial awareness comes relatively early. Certainly, even infants are able to distinguish different skin colors; their perceptual abilities allow for such color distinctions quite early in life. However, it is only later that children begin to attribute meaning to different racial characteristics.

By the time they are 3 or 4 years of age, preschool-age children notice differences among people based on skin color, and they begin to identify themselves as a member of a particular group such as "Hispanic" or "Black." Although early in the preschool years they do not realize that ethnicity and race are enduring features of who they are, later they progressively begin to develop an understanding of the significance that society places on ethnic and racial membership (Hall & Rowan, 2003; Cross & Cross, 2008; Quintana & McKown, 2008).

Some preschoolers have mixed feelings about their racial and ethnic identity. Some experience **race dissonance**, the phenomenon in which minority children indicate preferences for majority values or people. For instance, some studies find that as many as 90 percent of African American children, when asked about their reactions to drawings of Black and White children, react more negatively to the drawings of Black children than to those of White children. However, these negative reactions did not translate into lower self-esteem for the African American subjects. Instead, their preferences appear to be a result of the powerful influence of the dominant White culture, rather than a disparagement of their own racial characteristics (Holland, 1994; Quintana, 2007).

Ethnic identity emerges somewhat later than racial identity, because it is usually less conspicuous than race. For instance, in one study of Mexican American ethnic awareness, preschoolers displayed only a limited knowledge of their ethnic identity. However, as they became older, they grew more aware of the significance of their ethnicity. Preschoolers who were bilingual, speaking both Spanish and English, were most apt to be aware of their ethnic identity. Ultimately, both race and ethnicity play a significant role in the development of children's overall identities (Bernal, 1994; Quintana et al., 2006).

Gender Identity: Developing Femaleness and Maleness

Boys' awards: Very Best Thinker, Most Eager Learner, Most Imaginative, Most Enthusiastic, Most Scientific, Best Friend, Mr. Personality, Hardest Worker, Best Sense of Humor.

Girls' awards: All-Around Sweetheart, Sweetest Personality, Cutest Personality, Best Sharer, Best Artist, Biggest Heart, Best Manners, Best Helper, Most Creative.

What's wrong with this picture? To one parent, whose daughter received one of the girls' awards during a kindergarten graduation ceremony, quite a bit. While the girls were getting pats on the back for their pleasing personalities, the boys were receiving awards for their intellectual and analytic skills (Deveny, 1994).

Such a situation is not rare: Girls and boys often live in very different worlds. Differences in the ways males and females are treated begin at birth, continue during the preschool years, and as we'll see later, extend into adolescence and beyond (Martin & Ruble, 2004; Bornstein et al., 2008).

Gender, the sense of being male or female, is well established by the time children reach the preschool years. (As we first noted in Chapter 7, the terms *gender* and *sex* do not mean the same thing. *Sex* typically refers to sexual anatomy and sexual behavior, while *gender* refers to the perception of maleness or femaleness related to membership in a given society.) By the age of 2, children consistently label themselves and those around them as male or female (Raag, 2003; Campbell, Shirley, & Candy, 2004).

One way gender shows up is in play. Preschool boys spend more time than girls in rough-and-tumble play, while preschool girls spend more time than boys in organized games and role-playing. During this time boys begin to play more with boys, and girls play more with girls, a trend that increases during middle childhood. Girls begin to prefer same-sex playmates a little earlier than boys. They first have a clear preference for interacting with other girls at age 2, while boys don't show much preference for same-sex playmates until age 3 (Martin & Fabes, 2001; Raag, 2003).

Such same-sex preferences appear in many cultures. For instance, studies of kindergartners in mainland China show no examples of mixed-gender play. Similarly, gender "outweighs" ethnic variables when it comes to play: A Hispanic boy would rather play with a White boy than with a Hispanic girl (Whiting & Edwards, 1988; Aydt & Corsaro, 2003).

Preschool-age children often have very strict ideas about how boys and girls are supposed to act. In fact, their expectations about gender-appropriate behavior are even more gender-stereotyped than those of adults and may be less flexible during the preschool years than at any other point in the life span. Beliefs in gender stereotypes become increasingly pronounced up to age 5, and although they become somewhat less rigid by age 7, they do not disappear. In fact, the gender stereotypes held by preschoolers resemble those held by traditional adults in society (Serbin, Poulin-Dubois, & Eichstedt, 2002; Lam & Leman, 2003; Ruble et al., 2007).

And what is the nature of preschoolers' gender expectations? Like adults, preschoolers expect that males are more apt to have traits involving competence, independence, forcefulness, and competitiveness. In contrast, females are viewed as more likely to have traits such as warmth, expressiveness, nurturance, and submissiveness. Although these are expectations, and say nothing about the way that men and women actually behave, such expectations provide the lens through which preschool-age children view the world and affect preschoolers' behavior as well as the way they interact with peers and adults (Blakemore, 2003; Gelman, Taylor, & Nguyen, 2004).

The prevalence and strength of preschoolers' gender expectations, and differences in behavior between boys and girls, have proven puzzling. Why should gender play such a powerful role during the preschool years (as well as during the rest of the life span)? Developmentalists have proposed several explanations.

Biological Perspectives on Gender   Since gender relates to the sense of being male or female, and sex refers to the physical characteristics that differentiate males and females, it would hardly be surprising to find that the biological characteristics associated with sex might themselves lead to gender differences. This has been shown to be true.

Hormones are one sex-related biological characteristic that have been found to affect gender-based behaviors. Girls exposed to unusually high levels of *androgens* (male hormones) prenatally are more likely to display behaviors associated with male stereotypes than are their sisters who were not exposed to androgens (Hines et al., 2002; Servin, Nordenstrom, & Larsson, 2003; Knickmeyer & Baron-Cohen, 2006).

Furthermore, androgen-exposed girls preferred boys as playmates and spent more time than other girls playing with toys associated with the male role, such as cars and trucks. Similarly, boys exposed prenatally to atypically high levels of female hormones are apt to display more behaviors that are stereotypically female than is usual (Servin et al., 2003).

Moreover, biological differences exist in the structure of female and male brains. For instance, part of the *corpus callosum*, the bundle of nerves that connects the hemispheres of the brain, is proportionally larger in women than in men. To some theoreticians, evidence such as this suggests that gender differences may be produced by biological factors like hormones (Westerhausen et al., 2004).

Before accepting such contentions, however, it is important to note that alternative explanations abound. For example, it may be that the corpus callosum is proportionally larger in women as a result of certain kinds of experiences that influence brain growth in particular ways. We know, as discussed in Chapter 6, that girls are spoken to more than boys as infants, which might produce certain kinds of brain development. If this is true, environmental experience produces biological change—and not the other way around. Other developmentalists see gender differences as serving the biological goal of survival of the species through reproduction. Basing their work on an evolutionary approach, these theorists suggest that our male ancestors who showed more stereotypically masculine qualities, such as forcefulness and competitiveness, may have been able to attract females who were able to provide them with hardy offspring. Females who excelled at stereotypically feminine tasks, such as nurturing, may have been valuable partners because they could increase the likelihood that children would survive the dangers of childhood (Browne, 2006; Ellis, 2006).

As in other domains that involve the interaction of inherited biological characteristics and environmental influences, it is difficult to attribute behavioral characteristics unambiguously to biological factors. Because of this problem, we must consider other explanations for gender differences.

Psychoanalytic Perspectives   You may recall from Chapter 1 that Freud's psychoanalytic theory suggests that we move through a series of stages related to biological urges.

Identification The process in which children attempt to be similar to their parent of the same sex, incorporating the parent's attitudes and values

Gender identity The perception of oneself as male or female

Gender schema A cognitive framework that organizes information relevant to gender

To Freud, the preschool years encompass the *phallic stage*, in which the focus of a child's pleasure relates to genital sexuality.

Freud argued that the end of the phallic stage is marked by an important turning point in development: the Oedipal conflict. According to Freud, the *Oedipal conflict* occurs at around the age of 5, when the anatomical differences between males and females become particularly evident. Boys begin to develop sexual interests in their mothers, viewing their fathers as rivals.

As a consequence, boys conceive a desire to kill their fathers—just as Oedipus did in the ancient Greek tragedy. However, because they view their fathers as all-powerful, boys develop a fear of retaliation, which takes the form of *castration anxiety*. In order to overcome this fear, boys repress their desires for their mothers and instead begin to identify with their fathers, attempting to be as similar to them as possible. **Identification** is the process in which children attempt to be similar to their same-sex parent, incorporating the parent's attitudes and values.

Girls, according to Freud, go through a different process. They begin to feel sexual attraction toward their fathers and experience *penis envy*—a view that not unexpectedly has led to accusations that Freud viewed women as inferior to men. In order to resolve their penis envy, girls ultimately identify with their mothers, attempting to be as similar to them as possible.

In the cases of both boys and girls, the ultimate result of identifying with the same-sex parent is that the children adopt their parents' gender attitudes and values. In this way, says Freud, society's expectations about the ways females and males "ought" to behave are perpetuated into new generations.

You may find it difficult to accept Freud's elaborate explanation of gender differences. So do most developmentalists, who believe that gender development is best explained by other mechanisms. In part, they base their criticisms of Freud on the lack of scientific support for his theories.

For example, children learn gender stereotypes much earlier than the age of 5. Furthermore, this learning occurs even in single-parent households. However, some aspects of psychoanalytic theory have been supported, such as findings indicating that preschool-age children whose same-sex parents support sex-stereotyped behavior tend to demonstrate that behavior also. Still, far simpler processes can account for this phenomenon, and many developmentalists have searched for explanations of gender differences other than Freud's (Martin & Ruble, 2004).

Social Learning Approaches

As their name implies, social learning approaches see children as learning gender-related behavior and expectations by observing others. Children watch the behavior of their parents, teachers, siblings, and even peers. A little boy sees the glory of a major league baseball player and becomes interested in sports. A little girl watches her high-school neighbor practicing cheerleading moves and begins to try them herself. The observation of the

rewards that these others attain for acting in a gender-appropriate manner leads the child to conform to such behavior themselves (Rust et al., 2000).

Books and the media, and in particular television and video games, also play a role in perpetuating traditional views of gender-related behavior from which preschoolers may learn. Analyses of the most popular television shows, for example, find that male characters outnumber female characters by 2 to 1. Furthermore, females are more apt to appear with males, whereas female–female relationships are relatively uncommon (Calvert et al., 2003).

Television also presents men and women in traditional gender roles. Television shows typically define female characters in terms of their relationships with males. Females are more likely to appear as victims than males. They are less likely to be presented as productive or as decision-makers, and more likely to be portrayed as characters interested in romance, their homes, and their families. Such models, according to social learning theory, are apt to have a powerful influence on preschoolers' definitions of appropriate behavior (Wright et al., 1995; Scharrer et al., 2006; Hust, Brown, & L'Engle, 2008).

According to social learning approaches, children observe the behavior of adults of the same sex as themselves and come to imitate it.

In some cases, learning of social roles does not involve models, but occurs more directly. For example, most of us have heard preschool-age children being told by their parents to act like a "little girl" or "little man." What this generally means is that girls should behave politely and courteously, or that boys should be tough and stoic—traits associated with society's traditional stereotypes of men and women. Such direct training sends a clear message about the behavior expected of a preschool-age child (Leaper, 2002).

Cognitive Approaches

In the view of some theorists, one aspect of the desire to form a clear sense of identity is the desire to establish a **gender identity**, a perception of oneself as male or female. To do this, children develop a **gender schema**, a cognitive framework that organizes information relevant to gender (Barbera, 2003; Martin, 2000; Martin & Ruble, 2004).

Gender schemas are developed early in life and serve as a lens through which preschoolers view the world. For instance, preschoolers use their increasing cognitive abilities to develop

Gender constancy The fact that people are permanently males or females, depending on fixed, unchangeable biological factors

TABLE 10-1	Four Approaches to Gender Development	
Perspective	**Key Concepts**	**Applying the Concepts to Preschool Children**
Biological	Our ancestors who behaved in ways that are now stereotypically feminine or masculine may have been more successful in reproducing. Brain differences may lead to gender differences.	Girls may be genetically "programmed" by evolution to be more expressive and nurturing, whereas boys are "programmed" to be more competitive and forceful. Hormone exposure before birth has been linked to both boys' and girls' behaving in ways typically expected of the other gender.
Psychoanalytic	Gender development is the result of identification with the same-sex parent, achieved by moving through a series of stages related to biological urges.	Girls and boys whose parents of the same sex behave in stereotypically masculine of feminine ways are likely to do so, too, perhaps because they identify with those parents.
Social learning	Children learn gender-related behavior and expectations from their observation of others' behavior.	Children notice that other children and adults are rewarded for behaving in ways that conform to standard gender stereotypes, and are sometimes punished for violating those stereotypes.
Cognitive	Through the use of gender schemas, developed early in life, preschoolers form a lens through which they view the world. They use their increasing cognitive abilities to develop "rules" about what is appropriate for males and females.	Preschoolers are more rigid in their rules about proper gender behavior than are people at other ages, perhaps because they have just developed gender schemas that don't yet permit much variation from stereotypical expectations.

"rules" about what is right and what is inappropriate for males and females. Thus, some girls decide that wearing pants is inappropriate for a female and apply the rule so rigidly that they refuse to wear anything but dresses. Or a preschool boy may reason that since makeup is typically worn by females, it is inappropriate for him to wear makeup even when he is in a preschool play and all the other boys and girls are wearing it.

According to *cognitive-developmental theory*, proposed by Lawrence Kohlberg, this rigidity is in part a reflection of preschoolers' understanding of gender (Kohlberg, 1966). Rigid gender schemas are influenced by the preschooler's erroneous beliefs about sex differences. Specifically, young preschoolers believe that sex differences are based not on biological factors but on differences in appearance or behavior. Employing this view of the world, a girl may reason that she can be a father when she grows up, or a boy may think he could turn into a girl if he put on a dress and tied his hair in a ponytail. However, by the time they reach the age of 4 or 5, children develop an understanding of **gender constancy**, the awareness that people are permanently males or females, depending on fixed, unchangeable biological factors.

Interestingly, research on children's growing understanding of gender constancy during the preschool period indicates that it has no particular effect on gender-related behavior. In fact, the appearance of gender schemas occurs well before children understand gender constancy. Even young preschool-age children assume that certain behaviors are appropriate—and others are not—on the basis of stereotypic views of gender (Martin, Ruble, & Szkrybalo, 2002; Martin & Ruble, 2004; Ruble et al., 2007).

Like the other approaches to gender development (summarized in Table 10-1), the cognitive perspective does not imply that differences between the two sexes are in any way improper or inappropriate. Instead, it suggests that preschoolers should be taught to treat others as individuals. Furthermore, preschoolers need to learn the importance of fulfilling their own talents, acting as individuals and not as representatives of a particular gender.

REVIEW ↵ mydevelopmentlab

1. During the _____-versus-_____ stage, Erikson says children's views of themselves change as preschool-age children face conflicts between, on the one hand, the desire to act independently of their parents and do things on their own, and, on the other hand, the guilt that comes from failure when they don't succeed.

Answer: initiative-versus-guilt

2. _____-_____ is a child's identity or set of beliefs about what they are like as individuals.

Answer: Self-concept

3. _____ identity is the perception of oneself as male or female.

Answer: Gender

To see more review questions, log on to MyDevelopmentLab.

Friends and Family: Preschoolers' Social Lives

When Juan was 3, he had his first best friend, Emilio. Juan and Emilio, who lived in the same apartment building in San Jose, were inseparable. They played incessantly with toy cars, racing them up and down the apartment hallways until some of the neighbors began to complain about the noise. They pretended to read to one another, and sometimes they slept over at each other's home—a big step for a 3-year-old. Neither boy seemed more joyful than when he was with his *best friend*—the term each used for the other.

An infant's family can provide nearly all the social contact he or she needs. As preschoolers, however, many children, like Juan and Emilio, begin to discover the joys of friendship with their peers. Although they may expand their social circles considerably, parents and family nevertheless remain very influential in the lives of preschoolers. Let's take a look at both these sides of preschoolers' social development, friends and family.

The Development of Friendships

Most social activity before the age of 3 involves simply being in the same place at the same time, without real social interaction. However, around the age of 3, children begin to develop real friendships like that shared by Juan and Emilio, as peers come to be seen as individuals who hold some special qualities and rewards. While preschoolers' relations with adults reflect children's needs for care, protection, and direction, their relations with peers are based more on the desire for companionship, play, and fun.

As preschoolers age, their ideas about friendship gradually evolve. They come to view friendship as a continuing state, a stable relationship that takes place not just in the immediate moment, but also offers the promise of future activity (Harris, 2000; Hay, Payne, & Chadwick, 2004).

The quality and kinds of interactions children have with friends changes during the preschool period. For 3-year-olds, the focus of friendship is the enjoyment of carrying out shared activities—doing things together and playing jointly, as when Juan and Emilio played with their toy cars in the hallway. Older preschoolers, however, pay more attention to abstract concepts such as trust, support, and shared interests (Park, Lay, & Ramsay, 1993). Throughout the preschool years, playing together remains an important part of all friendships. Like friendships, these play patterns change during the preschool years.

Playing by the Rules: The Work of Play

In Rosie Graiff's class of 3-year-olds, Minnie bounces her doll's feet on the table as she sings softly to herself. Ben pushes his toy car across the floor, making motor noises. Sarah chases Abdul around and around the perimeter of the room.

Play is more than what children of preschool age do to pass the time. Instead, play helps preschoolers develop in important ways. In fact, the American Academy of Pediatrics states that play is essential for the cognitive, physical, social, and emotional well-being of children and youth. The United Nations High Commission for Human Rights maintains that play is a basic right of every child (Lindsey & Colwell, 2003; Blundon & Schaefer, 2006; Samuelsson & Johansson, 2006; Ginsburg et al., 2007).

As preschoolers get older, their conception of friendship evolves and the quality of their interactions changes.

Categorizing Play   At the beginning of the preschool years, children engage in **functional play**—simple, repetitive activities typical of 3-year-olds. Functional play may involve objects, such as dolls or cars, or repetitive muscular movements like skipping, jumping, or rolling and unrolling a piece of clay. Functional play, then, involves doing something simply for the sake of being active rather than wanting to create some end product (Bober, Humphry, & Carswell, 2001; Kantrowitz & Evans, 2004).

As children get older, functional play declines. By the time they are 4, children become involved in a more sophisticated form of play. In **constructive play** children manipulate objects to produce or build something. A child who builds a house out of Legos or puts a puzzle together is involved in constructive play: He or she has an ultimate goal—to produce something. Such play is not necessarily aimed at creating something novel, since children may repeatedly build a house of blocks, let it fall into disarray, and then rebuild it.

Constructive play gives children a chance to test their developing physical and cognitive skills and to practice their fine muscle movements. They gain experience in solving problems about the ways and the sequences in which things fit together. They also learn to cooperate with others—a development we observe as the social nature of play shifts during the preschool period. Consequently, it's important for adults who care for preschoolers to provide a variety of toys that allow for both functional and constructive play (Edwards, 2000; Shi, 2003; Love & Burns, 2006).

The Social Aspects of Play   If two preschoolers are sitting at a table side by side, each putting a different puzzle together, are they engaged jointly in play?

According to pioneering work done by Mildred Parten (1932), the answer is yes. She suggests that these preschoolers are engaged in **parallel play**, in which children play with similar toys, in a similar manner, but do not interact with each other. Parallel play is typical for children during the

> **From an educator's perspective:** How might a nursery school teacher encourage a shy child to join a group of preschoolers who are playing?

Onlooker play
Action in which children simply watch others at play but do not actually participate themselves

Associative play
Play in which two or more children interact by sharing or borrowing toys or materials, although they do not do the same thing

Cooperative play
Play in which children genuinely interact with one another, taking turns, playing games, or devising contests

In parallel play, children play with similar toys, in a similar manner, but don't necessarily interact with one another.

early preschool years. Preschoolers also engage in another form of play, a highly passive one: onlooker play. In **onlooker play**, children simply watch others at play, but do not actually participate themselves. They may look on silently, or they may make comments of encouragement or advice.

As they get older, however, preschool-age children engage in more sophisticated forms of social play that involve a greater degree of interaction. In **associative play** two or more children actually interact with one another by sharing or borrowing toys or materials, although they do not do the same thing. In **cooperative play**, children genuinely play with one another, taking turns, playing games, or devising contests. (The various types of play are summarized in Table 10-2.)

Usually, associative and cooperative play do not typically become common until children reach the end of the preschool years. But children who have had substantial preschool experience are more apt to engage in more social forms of behavior, such as associative and cooperative play,

TABLE 10-2 Preschoolers' Play

Type of Play	Description	Examples
General Categories		
Functional play	Simple, repetitive activities typical of 3-year-olds. May involve objects or repetitive muscular movements.	Moving dolls or cars repetitively. Skipping, jumping, rolling or unrolling a piece of clay.
Constructive play	More sophisticated play in which children manipulate objects to produce or build something. Developed by age 4, constructive play lets children test physical and cognitive skills and practice fine muscle movements.	Building a doll house or car garage out of Legos, putting together a puzzle, making an animal out of clay.
Social Aspects of Play (Parten's Categories)		
Parallel play	Children use similar toys in a similar manner at the same time, but do not interact with each other. Typical of children during the early preschool years.	Children sitting side by side, each playing with his or her own toy car, putting together his or her own puzzle, or making an individual clay animal.
Onlooker play	Children simply watch others at play but do not actually participate. They may look on silently or make comments of encouragement or advice. Common among preschoolers and helpful when a child wishes to join a group already at play.	One child watches as a group of others play with dolls, cars, or clay; build with Legos; or work on a puzzle together.
Associative play	Two or more children interact, sharing or borrowing toys or materials, although they do not do the same thing.	Two children, each building his or her own Lego garage, may trade bricks back and forth.
Cooperative play	Children genuinely play with one another, taking turns, playing games, or devising contests.	A group of children working on a puzzle may take turns fitting in the pieces. Children playing with dolls or cars may take turns making the dolls talk or may agree on rules to race the cars.

Does Play Promote Brain Development?

As Janet took a lump of soft clay and pounded it into the shape of a long, curly snake, Franklin moved a toy truck across a tabletop so quickly that it flew off the side. He laughed, quickly picked it up off the floor, and repeatedly made it fly off the table while his friend Jason watched and giggled himself. At another table, Helena pretended to read a book, quietly talking to herself as she flipped from one page to another.

A growing amount of research suggests that play like this, found in preschool classrooms around the world, goes well beyond simply fun and games. In fact, play not only leads to increases in self-control and the ability to plan ahead, but it may even promote the development of the brain.

According to Adele Diamond, a developmental researcher at the University of British Columbia, play may help children learn self-regulation skills by teaching them the importance of controlling their impulses. By playing games in which they must plan out strategies, they learn the importance of planning ahead and regulating their emotions (Diamond & Amso, 2008).

Even more intriguing, some researchers believe that play helps the brain to develop and become more sophisticated. Based on experiments with nonhumans, neuroscientist Sergio Pellis has found not only that certain sorts of damage to the brain leads to abnormal sorts of play, but that depriving animals of the ability to play effects the course of brain development (Pellis & Pellis, 2007).

For instance, in one experiment, Pellis and his colleagues observed rats under two different conditions. In the control condition, a juvenile target rat was housed with three other young females, allowing them to engage in the equivalent of rat play. In the experimental condition, the young target rats were housed with three adult females. Although young rats caged with adults don't have the opportunity to play, they do encounter social experiences with the adults, who will groom and touch them. When Pellis examined the brains of the rats, he found that the play-deprived rats showed deficiencies in the development of their prefrontal cortex (Pellis & Pellis, 2007; Henig, 2008).

Although it's a big leap from rat play to toddler play, the results of the study do suggest the significance of play in promoting brain and cognitive development. Ultimately, play may be one of the engines that fuels the intellectual development of preschoolers.

- What are the best ways to incorporate play in preschoolers' lives?

- Based on these new research findings, what would you say to educators who reduce the amount of recess for budgetary reasons or to include more time for academic subjects?

---

fairly early in the preschool years than are those with less experience (Brownell, Ramani, & Zerwas, 2006; Dyer & Moneta, 2006).

Solitary and onlooker play continue in the later stages of the preschool period. There are simply times when children prefer to play by themselves. And when newcomers join a group, one often successful strategy for becoming part of the group is to engage in onlooker play, waiting for an opportunity to join the play more actively (Lindsey & Colwell, 2003).

The nature of pretend, or make-believe, play also changes during the preschool period. In some ways, pretend play becomes increasingly *un*realistic—and even more imaginative—as preschoolers change from using only realistic objects to using less concrete ones. Thus, at the start of the preschool period, children may pretend to listen to a radio only if they actually have a plastic radio that looks realistic. Later, however, they are more likely to use an entirely different object, such as a large cardboard box, as a pretend radio (Bornstein et al., 1996).

Russian developmentalist Lev Vygotsky (1930/1978) argued that pretend play, particularly if it involves social play, is an important means for expanding preschool-age children's cognitive skills. Through make-believe play, children are able to "practice" activities (like pretending to use a computer or read a book) that are a part of their particular culture and broaden their understanding of the way the world functions. (For more on the links between play and cognitive development, see the *From Research to Practice* box.)

"We've done a lot of important playing here today."

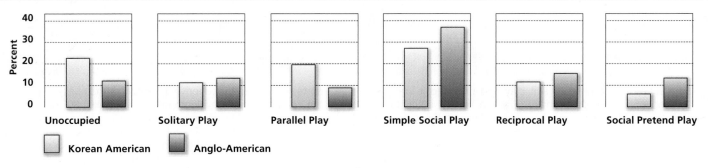

FIGURE 10-1 Comparing Play Complexity

An examination of Korean American and Anglo-American preschoolers' play complexity finds clear differences in patterns of play. How would a child-care provider explain this conclusion?
(*Source:* Adapted from Farver, Kim, & Lee-Shin, 1995)

Culture also affects children's styles of play. For example, Korean American children engage in a higher proportion of parallel play than their Anglo-American counterparts, while Anglo-American preschoolers are involved in more pretend play (see Figure 10-1; Farver, Kim, & Lee-Shin, 1995; Farver & Lee-Shin, 2000; Bai, 2005).

Preschoolers' Theory of Mind: Understanding What Others Are Thinking

One reason behind the changes in children's play is the continuing development of preschoolers' theory of mind. As we first discussed in Chapter 7, *theory of mind* refers to knowledge and beliefs about how the mind operates. Using their theory of mind, preschool children are able to come up with explanations for how *others* think and reasons for why they behave the way they do.

One of the main reasons for children's emerging play and social skills is that during the preschool years, children increasingly can see the world from others' perspectives. Even children as young as 2 are able to understand that others have emotions. By the age of 3 or 4, preschoolers can distinguish between something in their minds and physical actuality. For instance, 3-year-olds know that they can imagine something that is not physically present, such as a zebra, and that others can do the same. They can also pretend that something has happened and react as if it really had occurred, a skill that becomes part of their imaginative play. And they know that others have the same capability (Cadinu & Kiesner, 2000; Mauritzson & Saeljoe, 2001; Andrews, Halford, & Bunch, 2003).

Preschool-age children also become more insightful regarding the motives and reasons behind people's behavior. They begin to understand that their mother is angry because she was late for an appointment, even if they themselves haven't seen her be late. Furthermore, by the age of 4, preschool-age children's understanding that people can be fooled and mistaken by physical reality (such as magic tricks involving sleight-of-hand) becomes surprisingly sophisticated. This increase in understanding helps children become more socially skilled as they gain insight into what others are thinking (Fitzgerald & White, 2002; Eisbach, 2004).

There are limits, however, to 3-year-olds' theory of mind. Although they understand the concept of "pretend" by the age of 3, their understanding of "belief" is still not complete. The difficulty experienced by 3-year-olds in comprehending "belief" is illustrated by their performance on the *false belief* task. In the false belief task, preschoolers are shown a doll named Maxi who places chocolate in a cabinet and then leaves. After Maxi is gone, though, his mother moves the chocolate somewhere else.

After viewing these events, a preschooler is asked where Maxi will look for the chocolate when he returns. Three-year-olds answer (erroneously) that Maxi will look for it in the new location. In contrast, 4-year-olds correctly realize that Maxi has the erroneous false belief that the chocolate is still in the cabinet, and that's where he will look for it (Ziv & Frye, 2003; Flynn, O'Malley, & Wood, 2004; Amsterlaw & Wellman, 2006; Brown & Bull, 2007).

By the end of the preschool years, most children easily solve false belief problems. One group has considerable difficulties throughout their lifetimes: children with autism. *Autism* is a psychological disorder that produces significant language and emotional difficulties. Children with autistic find it particularly hard to relate to others, in part because they find it difficult to understand what others are thinking. Occurring in about 4 in 10,000 people, particularly males, autism is characterized by a lack of connection to other people, even parents, and an avoidance of interpersonal situations. Individuals with autism are bewildered by false belief problems no matter how old they are (Begeer et al., 2003: Heerey, Keltner, & Capps, 2003; Ropar, Mitchell, Ackroyd, 2003).

The Emergence of Theory of Mind What factors are involved in the emergence of theory of mind? Certainly, brain maturation is an important factor. As myelination

Authoritarian parents Parents who are controlling, punitive, rigid, and cold and whose word is law; they value strict, unquestioning obedience from their children and do not tolerate expressions of disagreement

Permissive parents Parents who provide lax and inconsistent feedback and require little of their children

Authoritative parents Parents who are firm, setting clear and consistent limits, but try to reason with their children, explaining why they should behave in a particular way

within the frontal lobes becomes more pronounced, preschoolers develop more emotional capacity involving self-awareness. In addition, hormonal changes seem to be related to emotions that are more evaluative in nature (Davidson, 2003; Schore, 2003).

Developing language skills are also related to the increasing sophistication of children's theory of mind. In particular, the ability to understand the meaning of words such as *think* and *know* is important in helping preschool-age children understand the mental lives of others (Astington & Baird, 2005; Farrant, Fletcher, & Maybery, 2006).

As much as the child's developing theory of mind promotes more engaged social interactions and play, the process is reciprocal: Opportunities for social interaction and make-believe play are also critical in promoting the development of theory of mind. For example, preschool-age children with older siblings (who provide high levels of social interaction) have more sophisticated theories of mind than those without older siblings. In addition, abused children show delays in their ability to correctly answer the false belief task, in part due to reduced experience with normal social interaction (Watson, 2000; Cicchetti et al., 2003, 2004; McAlister & Peterson, 2006).

Cultural factors also play an important role in the development of theory of mind and the interpretations that children bring to bear on others' actions. For example, children in more industrialized Western cultures may be more likely to see others' behavior as due to the kind of people they are, a function of the person's personal traits and characteristics ("She won the race because she is really fast.") In contrast, children in non-Western cultures may see others' behavior as produced by forces that are less under their personal control ("She won the race because she was lucky.") (Tardif, Wellman, & Cheung, 2004; Wellman et al., 2006; Liu et al., 2008).

Preschoolers' Family Lives

Four-year-old Benjamin was watching TV while his mom cleaned up after dinner. After a while, he wandered in and grabbed a towel, saying, "Mommy, let me help you do the dishes." Surprised by this unprecedented behavior, she asked him, "Where did you learn to do dishes?"

"I saw it on *Leave It to Beaver*," he replied, "Only it was the dad helping. Since we don't have a dad, I figured I'd do it."

For an increasing number of preschool-age children, life does not mirror what we see in reruns of old sitcoms. Many face the realities of an increasingly complicated world. For instance, as we noted in Chapter 7 and will discuss in greater detail in Chapter 13, children are increasingly likely to live with only one parent. In 1960, less than 10% of all children under the age of 18 lived with one parent. In 2000, a single parent headed 21% of White families, 35% of Hispanic families, and 55% of African American families.

Still, for most children the preschool years are not a time of upheaval and turmoil. Instead, the period encompasses a

growing interaction with the world at large. As we've seen, for instance, preschoolers begin to develop genuine friendships with other children, in which close ties emerge. One central factor leading preschoolers to develop friendships comes when parents provide a warm, supportive home environment. Strong, positive relationships between parents and children encourage children's relationships with others (Sroufe, 1994; Howes, Galinsky, & Kontos, 1998). How do parents nurture that relationship?

Effective Parenting: Teaching Children Desired Behavior

While she thinks no one is looking, Maria goes into her brother Alejandro's bedroom, where he has been saving the last of his Halloween candy. Just as she takes his last Reese's Peanut Butter Cup, the children's mother walks into the room and immediately takes in the situation.

If you were Maria's mother, which of the following reactions seems most reasonable?

1. Tell Maria that she must go to her room and stay there for the rest of the day and that she is going to lose access to her favorite blanket, the one she sleeps with every night and during naps.

2. Mildly tell Maria that what she did was not such a good idea and that she shouldn't do it in the future.

3. Explain why her brother Alejandro was going to be upset and tell her that she must go to her room for an hour as punishment.

4. Forget about it and let the children sort it out themselves.

Each of these four alternative responses represents one of the major parenting styles identified by Diana Baumrind (1971, 1980) and later updated by Eleanor Maccoby and colleagues (Baumrind, 1971, 1980; Maccoby & Martin, 1983).

Authoritarian parents respond as in the first alternative. They are controlling, punitive, rigid, cold. Their word is law, and they value strict, unquestioning obedience from their children. They also do not tolerate expressions of disagreement.

Permissive parents, in contrast, provide lax and inconsistent feedback, as in the second alternative. They require little of their children, and they don't see themselves as holding much responsibility for how their children turn out. They place little or no limits or control on their children's behavior.

Authoritative parents are firm, setting clear and consistent limits. Although they tend to be relatively strict, like authoritarian parents, they are loving and emotionally supportive. They also try to reason with their children, giving explanations for why they should behave in a particular way ("Alejandro is going to be upset."), and communicating the rationale for any punishment they may impose. Authoritative parents encourage their children to be independent.

Uninvolved parents Parents who show virtually no interest in their children, displaying indifferent, rejecting behavior

Finally, **uninvolved parents** show virtually no interest in their children, displaying indifferent, rejecting behavior. They are detached emotionally and see their role as no more than feeding, clothing, and providing shelter for their child. In its most extreme form, uninvolved parenting results in *neglect*, a form of child abuse. (The four patterns are summarized in Table 10-3.)

Does the particular style of discipline that parents use result in differences in children's behavior? The answer is very much yes—although, as you might expect, there are many exceptions (Snyder, Cramer, & Alfrank, 2005; Arredondo et al., 2006; Simons & Conger, 2007; Hoeve et al., 2008):

- Children of authoritarian parents tend to be withdrawn, showing relatively little sociability. They are not very friendly, often behaving uneasily around their peers. Girls who are raised by authoritarian parents are especially dependent on their parents, whereas boys are unusually hostile.

- Permissive parents have children who, in many ways, share the undesirable characteristics of children of authoritarian parents. Children with permissive parents tend to be dependent and moody, and they are low in social skills and self-control.

- Children of authoritative parents fare best. They generally are independent, friendly with their peers, self-assertive, and cooperative. They have strong motivation to achieve, and they are typically successful and likable. They regulate their own behavior effectively, both in terms of their relationships with others and emotional self-regulation.

  Some authoritative parents also display several characteristics that have come to be called *supportive parenting*, including parental warmth, proactive teaching, calm discussion during disciplinary episodes, and interest and involvement in children's peer activities. Children whose parents engage in such supportive parenting show better adjustment and are better protected from the consequences of later adversity they may encounter (Pettit, Bates, & Dodge, 1997; Belluck, 2000; Kaufmann et al., 2000).

- Children whose parents show uninvolved parenting styles are the worst off. Their parents' lack of involvement disrupts their emotional development considerably, leading them to feel unloved and emotionally detached, and impedes their physical and cognitive development as well.

TABLE 10-3 Parenting Styles

How Demanding Parents Are of Children ▶	Demanding	Undemanding
How Responsive Parents Are to a Child ▼	Authoritative	Permissive
Highly Responsive	**Characteristics:** firm, setting clear and consistent limits **Relationship with Children:** Although they tend to be relatively strict, like authoritarian parents, they are loving and emotionally supportive and encourage their children to be independent. They also try to reason with their children, giving explanations for why they should behave in a particular way, and communicate the rationale for any punishment they may impose.	**Characteristics:** lax and inconsistent feedback **Relationship with Children:** They require little of their children, and they don't see themselves as holding much responsibility for how their children turn out. They place little or no limits or control on their children's behavior.
	Authoritarian	Uninvolved
Low Responsive	**Characteristics:** controlling, punitive, rigid, cold **Relationship with Children:** Their word is law, and they value strict, unquestioning obedience from their children. They also do not tolerate expressions of disagreement.	**Characteristics:** displaying indifferent, rejecting behavior **Relationship with Children:** They are detached emotionally and see their role as only providing food, clothing, and shelter. In its extreme form, this parenting style results in neglect, a form of child abuse.

(*Source:* Based on Baumrind, 1971; Maccoby & Martin, 1983)

While such classification systems are useful ways of categorizing and describing parents' behavior, they are not a recipe for success. Parenting and growing up are more complicated than that! For instance, in a significant number of cases the children of authoritarian and permissive parents develop quite successfully.

Furthermore, most parents are not entirely consistent: Although the authoritarian, permissive, authoritative, and uninvolved patterns describe general styles, sometimes parents switch from their dominant mode to one of the others. For instance, when a child darts into the street, even the most laid-back and permissive parent is likely to react in a harsh, authoritarian manner, laying down strict demands about safety. In such cases, authoritarian styles may be most effective (Holden & Miller, 1999; Eisenberg & Valiente, 2002; Gershoff, 2002).

Cultural Differences in Child-Rearing Practices It's important to keep in mind that the findings regarding child-rearing styles we have been discussing are chiefly applicable to Western societies. The style of parenting that is most successful may depend quite heavily on the norms of a particular culture—and what parents in a particular culture are taught regarding appropriate child-rearing practices (Giles-Sims & Lockhart, 2005; Dwairy et al., 2006; Hulei, Zevenbergen, & Jacobs, 2006; Rudy & Grusec, 2006; Keller et al., 2008).

For example, the Chinese concept of *chiao shun* suggests that parents should be strict, firm, and in tight control of their children's behavior. Parents are seen to have a duty to train their children to adhere to socially and culturally desirable standards of behavior, particularly those manifested in good school performance. Children's acceptance of such an approach to discipline is seen as a sign of parental respect (Wu, Robinson, & Yang, 2002; Ng, Pomerantz, & Lam, 2007).

Parents in China are typically highly directive with their children, pushing them to excel and controlling their behavior to a considerably higher degree than parents typically do in Western countries. And it works: Children of Asian parents tend to be quite successful, particularly academically (Steinberg, Dornbusch, & Brown, 1992; Nelson et al., 2006).

In contrast, U.S. parents are generally advised to use authoritative methods and explicitly to avoid authoritarian measures. Interestingly, it wasn't always this way. Until World War II, the point of view that dominated the advice in literature was authoritarian, apparently founded on Puritan religious influences that suggested that children had "original sin" or that they needed to have their wills broken (Smuts & Hagen, 1985).

In short, the child-rearing practices that parents are urged to follow reflect cultural perspectives about the nature of children as well as about the appropriate role of parents and their support system. No single parenting pattern or style is likely to be universally appropriate, nor will it invariably produce successful children (Wang & Tamis-LeMonda, 2003; Chang Pettit, & Katsurada, 2006).

Becoming an Informed Consumer of Development

Disciplining Children

The question of how best to discipline children has been raised for generations. Answers from current developmentalists include the following advice (Brazelton & Sparrow, 2003; Flouri, 2005; Mulvaney & Mebert, 2007):

- **For most children in Western cultures, authoritative parenting works best.** Parents should be firm and consistent, providing clear direction for desirable behavior. Authoritative disciplinarians provide rules, but they explain why those rules make sense, using language that children can understand.

- **Spanking is never an appropriate discipline technique,** according to the American Academy of Pediatrics. Not only is spanking less effective than other techniques in curbing undesirable behavior, but it leads to additional, unwanted outcomes, such as the potential for more aggressive behavior (American Academy of Pediatrics, 1998).

- **Use time-out for punishment.** in which children are removed from a situation in which they have misbehaved and are not permitted to engage in enjoyable activities for a set period of time.

- **Tailor parental discipline to the characteristics of the child and the situation.** Try to keep the child's particular personality in mind, and adapt discipline to it.

- **Use routines (such as a bath routine or a bedtime routine) to avoid conflict.** For instance, bedtime can be the source of a nightly struggle between a resistant child and an insistent parent. Parental strategies for gaining compliance that involve making the situation predictably enjoyable—such as routinely reading a bedtime story or engaging in a nightly "wrestling" match with the child—can help defuse potential battles.

REVIEW ↵ **mydevelopmentlab**

1. Functional play is the simple, repetitive activities seen among 3-year-olds. By the time children are 4, they are engaging in _____ play, manipulating objects to produce or build something.

   Answer: constructive

2. _____ _____ _____, which refers to knowledge and beliefs about how the mind operates, becomes increasingly sophisticated during the preschool years.

   Answer: Theory of mind

3. The discipline style that seems most effective is _____ parenting.

   Answer: authoritative

To see more review questions, log on to MyDevelopmentLab.

Moral Development and Aggression

During snack time at preschool, playmates Jan and Meg inspected the goodies in their lunch boxes. Jan found two appetizing cream-filled cookies. Meg's snack offered less tempting carrot and celery sticks. As Jan began to munch on one of her cookies, Meg looked at the cut-up vegetables and burst into tears. Jan responded to Meg's distress by offering her companion one of her cookies, which Meg gladly accepted. Jan was able to put herself in Meg's place, understand Meg's thoughts and feelings, and act compassionately (Katz, 1989, p. 213).

In this short scenario we see many of the key elements of morality, as it is played out among preschool-age children. Changes in children's views of what is ethically right and what is the right way to behave are an important element of growth during the preschool years.

At the same time, the kind of aggression displayed by preschoolers is also changing. We can consider the development of morality and aggression as two sides of the coin of human conduct, and both involve a growing awareness of others.

Developing Morality: Following Society's Rights and Wrongs

Moral development, refers to changes in people's sense of justice and of what is right and wrong, and in their behavior related to moral issues. Developmentalists have considered moral development in terms of children's reasoning about morality, their attitudes toward moral lapses, and their behavior when faced with moral issues. In the process of studying moral development, several approaches have evolved.

Piaget believed that at the heteronomous morality stage, this child would feel that the degree to which she had done the wrong thing is directly related to the number of items broken.

Piaget's View of Moral Development Child psychologist Jean Piaget was one of the first to study questions of moral development. He suggested that moral development, like cognitive development, proceeds in stages (Piaget, 1932). The earliest stage is a broad form of moral thinking he called *heteronomous morality*, in which rules are seen as invariant and unchangeable.

During this stage, which lasts from about age 4 through age 7, children play games rigidly, assuming that there is one, and only one, way to play and that every other way is wrong. At the same time, though, preschool-age children may not even fully grasp game rules. Consequently, a group of children may be playing together, with each child playing according to a slightly different set of rules. Nevertheless, they enjoy playing with others. Piaget suggests that every child may "win" such a game, because winning is equated with having a good time, as opposed to truly competing with others.

This rigid heteronomous morality is ultimately replaced by two later stages of morality: incipient cooperation and autonomous cooperation. As its name implies, in the *incipient cooperation stage,* which lasts from around age 7 to age 10, children's games become more clearly social. Children learn the actual formal rules of games, and they play according to this shared knowledge. Consequently, rules are still seen as largely unchangeable. There is a "right" way to play the game, and preschool children play according to these formal rules.

It is not until the *autonomous cooperation stage,* which begins at about age 10, that children become fully aware that formal game rules can be modified if the people who play them agree. The later transition into more sophisticated forms of moral development—which we will consider in Chapter 15—also is reflected in school-age children's understanding that rules of law are created by people and are subject to change according to the will of people.

Until these later stages are reached, however, children's reasoning about rules and issues of justice is bounded in the concrete. For instance, consider the following two stories:

> A little boy who is called John is in his room. He is called to dinner. He goes into the dining room. But behind the door there was a chair, and on the chair there was a tray with fifteen cups on it. John couldn't have known there was all this behind the door. He goes in, the door knocks against the tray, bang go the fifteen cups, and they all get broken!
>
> Once there was a little boy whose name was Marcello. One day when his mother was out he tried to get some jam out of the cupboard. He climbed up on to a chair and stretched out his arm. But the jam was too high up and he couldn't reach it and have any. But while he was trying to get it he knocked over a cup. The cup fell down and broke. (Piaget, 1932, p. 122)

Piaget found that a preschool child in the heteronomous morality stage judges the child who broke the 15 cups worse than the one who broke just 1. In contrast, children who have moved beyond the heteronomous morality stage consider the child who broke the 1 cup naughtier. The reason: Children in the heteronomous morality stage do not take *intention* into account.

Prosocial behavior Helping
behavior that benefits others

Abstract modeling
The process in which modeling
paves the way for the
development of more general
rules and principles

Empathy The understanding
of what another individual feels

Children in the heteronomous stage of moral development also believe in immanent justice. *Immanent justice* is the notion that rules that are broken earn immediate punishment. Preschool children believe that if they do something wrong, they will be punished instantly—even if no one sees them carrying out their misdeeds. In contrast, older children understand that punishments for misdeeds are determined and meted out by people. Children who have moved beyond the heteronomous morality stage have come to understand that one must make judgments about the severity of a transgression based on whether the person intended to do something wrong.

Evaluating Piaget's Approach to Moral Development

Recent research suggests that although Piaget was on the right track in his description of how moral development proceeds, his approach suffers from the same problem we encountered in his theory of cognitive development. Specifically, Piaget underestimated the age at which children's moral skills are honed.

It is now clear that preschool-age children understand the notion of intentionality by about age 3, and this allows them to make judgments based on intent at an earlier age than Piaget supposed. Specifically, when provided with moral questions that emphasize intent, preschool children judge someone who is intentionally bad as more "naughty" than someone who is unintentionally bad, but who creates more objective damage. Moreover, by the age of 4, they judge intentional lying to be wrong (Yuill & Perner, 1988; Bussey, 1992).

Social Learning Approaches to Morality

Social learning approaches to moral development stand in stark contrast to Piaget's approach. While Piaget emphasizes how limitations in preschoolers' cognitive development lead to particular forms of moral *reasoning,* social learning approaches focus more on how the environment in which preschoolers operate produces **prosocial behavior**, helping behavior that benefits others (Eisenberg, 2004; Spinrad, Eisenberg, & Bernt, 2007).

Social learning approaches build upon the behavioral approaches that we first discussed in Chapter 1. They acknowledge that some instances of children's prosocial behavior stem from situations in which they have received positive reinforcement for acting in a morally appropriate way. For instance, when Claire's mother tells her she has been a "good girl" for sharing a box of candy with her brother Dan, Claire's behavior has been reinforced. As a consequence, she is more likely to engage in sharing behavior in the future.

However, social learning approaches go a step further, arguing that not all prosocial behavior has to be directly performed and subsequently reinforced for learning to occur. According to social learning approaches, children also learn moral behavior more indirectly by observing the behavior of others, called models (Bandura, 1977). Children imitate models who receive reinforcement for their behavior, and ultimately they learn to perform the behavior themselves. For example, when Claire's friend Jake watches Claire share her candy with her brother, and Claire is praised for her behavior, Jake is more likely to engage in sharing behavior himself at some later point.

Quite a few studies illustrate the power of models and of social learning more generally in producing prosocial behavior in preschool-age children. For example, experiments have shown that children who view someone behaving generously or unselfishly are apt to follow the model's example, subsequently behaving in a generous or unselfish manner themselves when put in a similar situation. The opposite also holds true: If a model behaves selfishly, children who observe such behavior tend to behave more selfishly themselves (Hastings et al., 2007).

Not all models are equally effective in producing prosocial responses. For instance, preschoolers are more apt to model the behavior of warm, responsive adults than of adults who appear colder (Yarrow, Scott, & Waxler, 1973; Bandura, 1977). Furthermore, models viewed as highly competent or high in prestige are more effective than others.

Children do more than simply mimic unthinkingly behavior that they see rewarded in others. By observing moral conduct, they are reminded of society's norms about the importance of moral behavior as conveyed by parents, teachers, and other powerful authority figures. They notice the connections between particular situations and certain kinds of behavior. This increases the likelihood that similar situations will elicit similar behavior in the observer.

Consequently, modeling paves the way for the development of more general rules and principles in a process called **abstract modeling**. Rather than always modeling the particular behavior of others, older preschoolers begin to develop generalized principles that underlie the behavior that they observe. After observing repeated instances in which a model is rewarded for acting in a morally desirable way, children begin the process of inferring and learning the general principles of moral conduct (Bandura, 1991).

Empathy and Moral Behavior

According to some developmentalists, **empathy**—the understanding of what another individual feels—lies at the heart of some kinds of moral behavior. The roots of empathy grow early. One-year-old infants cry when they hear other infants crying. By 2 and 3, toddlers will offer gifts and spontaneously share toys with other children and adults, even if they are strangers (Zahn-Wexler & Radke-Yarrow, 1990).

During the preschool years, empathy continues to grow. Some theorists believe that increasing empathy—as well as other positive emotions, such as sympathy and admiration—leads children to behave in a more moral fashion. In addition, some negative emotions, such as anger at an unfair situation or shame over previous transgressions, also may promote moral behavior (Valiente, Eisenberg, & Fabes, 2004; Decety & Jackson, 2006).

"Have you been a moral child?"

The notion that negative emotions may promote moral development is one that Freud first suggested in his theory of psychoanalytic personality development that we first discussed in Chapter 2. Freud argued that a child's *superego,* the part of the personality that represents societal do's and don'ts, is developed through resolution of the *Oedipal conflict.* Children come to identify with their same-sex parent, incorporating that parent's standards of morality in order to avoid unconscious guilt raised by the Oedipal conflict.

Whether or not we accept Freud's account of the Oedipal conflict and the guilt it produces, his theory is consistent with more recent findings. These suggest that preschoolers' attempts to avoid experiencing negative emotions sometimes lead them to act in more moral, helpful ways. For instance, one reason children help others is to avoid the feelings of personal distress that they experience when they are confronted with another person's unhappiness or misfortune (Valiente, Eisenberg, & Fabes, 2004; Eisenberg, Valiente, & Champion, 2004).

Aggression and Violence in Preschoolers: Sources and Consequences

Four-year-old Duane could not contain his anger and frustration anymore. Although he usually was mild mannered, when Eshu began to tease him about the split in his pants and kept it up for several minutes, Duane finally snapped. Rushing over to Eshu, Duane pushed him to the ground and began to hit him with

his small, closed fists. Because he was so distraught, Duane's punches were not terribly effective, but they were severe enough to hurt Eshu and bring him to tears before the preschool teachers could intervene.

Aggression among preschoolers is quite common, though attacks such as this are not. The potential for verbal hostility, shoving matches, kicking, and other forms of aggression is present throughout the preschool years, although the degree to which aggression is acted out changes as children become older.

Eshu's taunting was also a form of aggression. **Aggression** is intentional injury or harm to another person. Infants don't act aggressively; it is hard to contend that their behavior is *intended* to hurt others, even if they inadvertently manage to do so. In contrast, by the time they reach preschool age, children demonstrate true aggression.

During the early preschool years, some of the aggression is addressed at attaining a desired goal, such as getting a toy away from another person or using a particular space occupied by another person. Consequently, in some ways the aggression is inadvertent, and minor scuffles may in fact be a typical part of early preschool life. It is the rare child who does not demonstrate at least an occasional act of aggression.

On the other hand, extreme and sustained aggression is a cause of concern. In most children, the amount of aggression declines as they move through the preschool years as does the frequency and average length of episodes of aggressive behavior (Persson, 2005).

The child's personality and social development contribute to this decline in aggression. Throughout the preschool years, children become better at controlling the emotions that they are experiencing. **Emotional self-regulation** is the capability to adjust emotions to a desired state and level of intensity. Starting at age 2, children are able to talk about their feelings, and they engage in strategies to regulate them. As they get older, they develop more effective strategies, learning to better cope with negative emotions. In addition to their increasing self-control, children are also, as we've seen, developing sophisticated social skills. Most learn to use language to express their wishes, and they become increasingly able to negotiate with others (Eisenberg & Zhou, 2000; Philippot & Feldman, 2004).

Despite these typical declines in aggression, some children remain aggressive throughout the preschool period. Furthermore, aggression is a relatively stable characteristic: The most aggressive preschoolers tend to be the most aggressive children during the school-age years, and the least aggressive preschoolers tend to be the least aggressive school-age children (Tremblay, 2001; Schaeffer, Petras, & Ialongo, 2003).

Boys typically show higher levels of physical, instrumental aggression than girls. **Instrumental aggression** is aggression motivated by the desire to obtain a concrete goal, such as wanting to play with a desirable toy that another child is enjoying.

On the other hand, although girls show lower levels of instrumental aggression, they may be just as aggressive but in different ways from boys. Girls are more likely to practice **relational aggression**, which is nonphysical aggression that is intended to hurt another person's feelings. Such aggression may be demonstrated through name-calling, withholding friendship, or simply saying mean, hurtful things that make the recipient feel bad (Underwood, 2003; Werner & Crick, 2004; Murray-Close, Ostrov, & Crick, 2006, 2007; Ostrov & Crick, 2007).

The Roots of Aggression

How can we explain the aggression of preschoolers? Some theoreticians suggest that to behave aggressively is an instinct, part and parcel of the human condition. For instance, Freud's psychoanalytic theory suggests that we all are motivated by sexual and aggressive instincts (Freud, 1920). According to ethologist Konrad Lorenz, an expert in animal behavior, animals—including humans—share a fighting instinct that stems from primitive urges to preserve territory, maintain a steady supply of food, and weed out weaker animals (Lorenz, 1966, 1974).

Similar arguments are made by evolutionary psychologists, scientists who consider the biological roots of social behavior. They argue that aggression leads to increased opportunities to mate, improving the likelihood that one's genes will be passed on to future generations. In addition, aggression may help to strengthen the species and its gene pool as a whole, because the strongest survive. Ultimately, then, aggressive instincts promote the survival of one's genes to pass on to future generations.

Although instinctual explanations of aggression are logical, most developmentalists believe they are not the whole story. Not only do instinctual explanations fail to take into account the increasingly sophisticated cognitive abilities that humans develop as they get older, but they also have relatively little experimental support. Moreover, they provide little guidance in determining when and how children, as well as adults, will behave aggressively, other than noting that aggression is an inevitable part of the human condition. Consequently, developmentalists have turned to other approaches to explain aggression and violence.

Social Learning Approaches to Aggression

The day after Duane lashed out at Eshu, Lynn, who had watched the entire scene, got into an argument with Ilya. They verbally bickered for a while, and suddenly Lynn balled her hand into a fist and tried to punch Ilya. The preschool teachers were stunned: It was rare for Lynn to get upset, and she had never displayed aggression before.

Aggression, both physical and verbal, is present throughout the preschool period.

Is there a connection between the two events? Most of us would answer yes, particularly if we subscribed to the view, suggested by social learning approaches, that aggression is largely a learned behavior. Social learning approaches to aggression contend that aggression is based on observation and prior learning. To understand the causes of aggressive behavior, then, we should look at the system of rewards and punishments that exists in a child's environment.

Social learning approaches to aggression emphasize how social and environmental conditions teach individuals to be aggressive. These ideas grow out of behavioral perspectives, which suggest that aggressive behavior is learned through direct reinforcement. For instance, preschool-age children may learn that they can continue to play with the most desirable toys by aggressively refusing their classmates' requests for sharing. In the parlance of traditional learning theory, they have been reinforced for acting aggressively (by continued use of the toy), and they are more likely to behave aggressively in the future.

But social learning approaches suggest that reinforcement also comes in less direct ways. A good deal of research suggests that exposure to aggressive models leads to increased aggression, particularly if the observers are themselves angered, insulted, or frustrated. For example, Albert Bandura and his colleagues illustrated the power of models in a classic study of preschool-age children (Bandura, Ross, & Ross, 1963). One group of children watched a film of an adult playing aggressively and violently with a Bobo doll (a large, inflated plastic clown designed as a punching bag for children that always returns to an upright position after being pushed down). In comparison, children in another situation watched a film of an adult playing sedately with a

FIGURE 10-2 Modeling Aggression

This series of photos is from Albert Bandura's classic Bobo doll experiment, designed to illustrate social learning of aggression. The photos clearly show how the adult model's aggressive behavior (in the first row) is imitated by children who had viewed the aggressive behavior (second and third rows).

set of Tinkertoys (see Figure 10-2). Later the preschool-age children were allowed to play with a number of toys, which included both the Bobo doll and the Tinkertoys. But first the children were led to feel frustration by being refused the opportunity to play with a favorite toy.

As predicted by social learning approaches, the preschool-age children modeled the behavior of the adult. Those who had seen the aggressive model playing with the Bobo doll were considerably more aggressive than those who had watched the calm, unaggressive model playing with the Tinkertoys.

Later research has supported this early study, and it is clear that exposure to aggressive models increases the likelihood that aggression on the part of observers will follow. These findings have profound consequences, particularly for children who live in communities in which violence is prevalent. For instance, one-third of the children in some urban neighborhoods have seen a homicide, and two-thirds have seen a serious assault. Such frequent exposure to violence certainly increases the probability that observers will behave aggressively themselves (Farver & Frosch, 1996; Farver et al., 1997; Evans, 2004).

Viewing Violence on TV: Does It Matter? Even the majority of preschool-age children who are not witnesses to real-life violence are typically exposed to aggression via the medium of television. Children's television programs actually contain higher levels of violence (69%) than other types of programs (57%). In an average hour, children's programs contain more than twice as many violent incidents than other types of programs (see Figure 10-3; Wilson, 2002).

This high level of televised violence and Bandura's and others' research findings on modeling violence raise a significant question: Does viewing aggression increase the likelihood that children (and later, adults) will enact actual—and ultimately deadly—aggression? It is hard to answer the question definitively, primarily because scientists are unable to conduct true experiments outside laboratory settings.

Although it is clear that laboratory observation of aggression on television leads to higher levels of aggression, evidence showing that real-world viewing of aggression is associated with subsequent aggressive behavior is correlational. (Think, for a moment, of what would be required to conduct a true experiment involving children's viewing habits. It would be necessary to control children's viewing of television in their

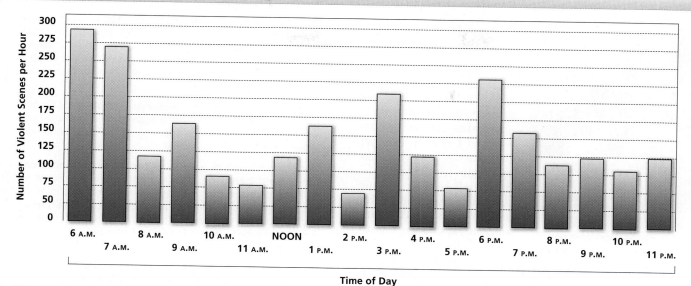

FIGURE 10-3 Televised Acts of Violence

A survey of the violence shown on the major TV networks and several cable channels in Washington, DC., on one particular weekday found acts of violence during every time period. From the perspective of an educator, do you think depictions of violence on TV should be regulated? Why or why not?

(*Source:* Center for Media and Public Affairs, 1995)

homes for extended periods, exposing some to a steady diet of violent shows and others to nonviolent ones—something that most parents would not agree to.)

Despite the fact, then, that the results are primarily correlational, the overwhelming weight of research evidence is clear in suggesting that observation of televised aggression does lead to subsequent aggression. Longitudinal studies have found that children's preferences for violent television shows at age 8 are related to the seriousness of criminal convictions by age 30. Other evidence supports the notion that observation of media violence can lead to a greater readiness to act aggressively, a tendency toward bullying, and an insensitivity to the suffering of victims of violence (Huesmann, Moise-Titus, & Podolski, 2003; Anderson et al., 2003; Slater, Henry, & Swaim, 2003; Ostrov, Gentile, & Crick, 2006).

Television is not the only source of media violence. Many video games contain a significant amount of aggressive behavior, and children are playing such games at high rates. For example, 14% of children 3 and younger and around 50% of those 4 to 6 play video games. Because research conducted with adults shows that playing violent video games is associated with behaving aggressively, children who play video games containing violence may be at higher risk for behaving aggressively (Funk, Buchman, & Jenks, 2003; Rideout, Vandewater, & Wartella, 2003; Anderson et al., 2004; Barlett, Harris, & Baldassaro, 2007).

Fortunately, social learning principles that lead preschoolers to learn aggression from television and video games suggest ways to reduce the negative influence of the medium. For

instance, children can be explicitly taught to view violence with a more skeptical, critical eye. Being taught that violence is not representative of the real world, that the viewing of violence can affect them negatively, and that they should refrain from imitating the behavior they have seen on television can help children interpret the violent programs differently and be less influenced by them (Persson & Musher-Eizenman, 2003; Donnerstein, 2005).

Furthermore, just as exposure to aggressive models leads to aggression, observation of *non* aggressive models can *reduce* aggression. Preschoolers don't learn from others only how to be aggressive; they can also learn how to avoid confrontation and to control their aggression, as we'll discuss later.

Cognitive Approaches to Aggression: The Thoughts Behind Violence Two children, waiting for their turn in a game of kickball, inadvertently knock into one another. One child's reaction is to apologize; the other's is to shove, saying angrily, "Cut it out."

Despite the fact that each child bears the same responsibility for the minor event, very different reactions result. The first child interprets the event as an accident, while the second sees it as a provocation and reacts with aggression.

The cognitive approach to aggression suggests that the key to understanding moral development is to examine preschoolers' interpretations of others' behavior and of the environmental context in which a behavior occurs. According

From an educator's perspective:
How might a preschool teacher or parent help protect children from violence in the programs they watch?

Social learning explanations of aggression suggest that children seeing aggression on television can prompt them to act aggressively.

to developmental psychologist Kenneth Dodge and his colleagues, some children are more prone than others to assume that actions are aggressively motivated. They are unable to pay attention to the appropriate cues in a situation and unable to interpret the behaviors in a given situation accurately. Instead, they often erroneously assume that what is happening is related to others' hostility. Subsequently, in deciding how to respond, they base their behavior on their inaccurate interpretation of behavior. In sum, they may behave aggressively in response to a situation that never in fact existed (Petit & Dodge, 2003).

For example, consider Jake, who is drawing at a table with Gary. Jake reaches over and takes a red crayon that Gary had just decided he was going to use next. Gary is instantly certain that the Jake "knew" that he was going to use the red crayon, and that Jake is taking it just to be mean. With this interpretation in mind, Gary hits Jake for "stealing" his crayon.

Although the cognitive approach to aggression provides a description of the process that leads some children to behave aggressively, it is less successful in explaining how certain children come to be inaccurate perceivers of situations in the first place. Furthermore, it fails to explain why such inaccurate perceivers so readily respond with aggression, and why they assume that aggression is an appropriate and even desirable response.

On the other hand, cognitive approaches to aggression are useful in pointing out a means to reduce aggression: By teaching preschool-age children to be more accurate interpreters of a situation, we can induce them to be less prone to view others' behavior as motivated by hostility, and consequently less likely to respond with aggression themselves. The guidelines presented in *Becoming an Informed Consumer of Development* are based on the various theoretical perspectives on aggression and morality that we've discussed in this chapter.

Becoming an Informed Consumer of Development

Increasing Moral Behavior and Reducing Aggression in Preschool-Age Children

The various points of view on the causes of aggression have yielded several approaches to encourage preschoolers' moral conduct and reduce their aggression. Here are some of the most practical strategies (Bor & Bor, 2004):

- **Provide opportunities for preschool-age children to observe others acting in a cooperative, helpful, prosocial manner.** Encourage them to interact with peers in joint activities in which they share a common goal. Such cooperative activities can teach the importance and desirability of working with, and helping, others.

- **Do not ignore aggressive behavior.** Parents and teachers should intervene when they see aggression in preschoolers, and send a clear message that aggression is an unacceptable means to resolve conflicts.

- **Help preschoolers devise alternative explanations for others' behavior.** This is particularly important for children who are prone to aggression and who may be apt to view others' conduct as more hostile than it actually is. Parents and teachers should help such children see that the behavior of their peers has several possible interpretations.

- **Monitor preschoolers' television viewing, particularly the violence that they view.** There is good evidence that observation of televised aggression results in subsequent increases in children's levels of aggression. At the same time, encourage preschoolers to watch particular shows that are designed, in part, to increase the level of moral conduct, such as *Sesame Street, Dora the Explorer, Mr. Rogers' Neighborhood,* and *Barney.*

- **Help preschoolers understand their feelings.** When children become angry—and all children do—they need to learn how to manage their feelings in a constructive manner. Tell them specific things they can do to improve the situation ("I see you're really angry with Jake for not giving you a turn. Don't hit him, but tell him you want a chance to play with the game.")

- **Explicitly teach reasoning and self-control.** Preschoolers can understand the rudiments of moral reasoning, and they should be reminded why certain behaviors are desirable. For instance, explicitly saying "If you take all the cookies, others will have no dessert" is preferable to saying, "Good children don't eat all the cookies."

REVIEW ↵ mydevelopmentlab

1. _____ behavior is helping behavior that benefits others.

Answer: Prosocial

2. Observation of a _____ who is rewarded for prosocial behavior can lead to prosocial behavior on the part of the observer.

Answer: model

3. The understanding of what others feel is called _____.

Answer: empathy

To see more review questions, log on to MyDevelopmentLab.

CASE STUDY

The Case of... The Wrong Role Models?

Jim Martell has been watching his son Jason carefully. Because Jim runs a business 90 minutes from home, his wife Tessa, who works right in the neighborhood, has had primary responsibility for raising Jason, and Jim has been growing steadily more worried over the 4 years of Jason's life.

First it was Jason's quiet voice and shy, gentle mannerisms. Then it was his quiet insistence on getting a doll for Christmas at age 3, which Jim felt he had at least managed to sabotage by picking a G.I. Joe. Of course, Jim's anxiety mounted when Jason spent more time dressing Joe in different outfits than making him run around, blowing things up. Then it was Jason's love of drawing and making clay models instead of playing with the neat toy guns and sports gear that Jim brought home for him.

Jim has long believed that his big mistake was letting Tessa place Jason in a local day care where all the other kids are girls. Jim is convinced that this environment has influenced Jason's choices and made him more feminine. He is hoping that next year Jason's kindergarten class will have more boys in it so his son can escape from the undue pressure to conform to a girl's lifestyle.

1. Given what you know about gender differences in preschoolers, are Jim's worries about Jason's mannerisms and habits justified? Why or why not?

2. Jim attributes Jason's behaviors to environmental influences. Could genetics also be a factor? Can the relative influences of nature and nurture be determined accurately?

3. If Jason attended an all-boys day care, would his behavior and preferences necessarily be different? Why or why not?

4. Which perspective—biological, psychoanalytic, social learning, or cognitive—provides the most satisfying explanation for Jason's behavior? Why?

5. Do you think Jim is right that exposure to boys in kindergarten will change Jason's behavior? If so, how might this work?

◄ Looking Back

How do preschool-age children develop a concept of themselves?

- According to Erik Erikson, preschool-age children initially are in the autonomy-versus-shame-and-doubt stage (18 months to 3 years) in which they develop independence and mastery over their physical and social worlds, or feel shame, self-doubt, and unhappiness. Later, in the initiative-versus-guilt stage (ages 3 to 6), preschool-age children face conflicts between the desire to act independently and the guilt that comes from the unintended consequences of their actions.

- Preschoolers' self-concepts are formed partly from their own perceptions and estimations of their characteristics, partly from their parents' behavior toward them, and partly from cultural influences.

How do children develop a sense of racial identity and gender?

- Preschool-age children form racial attitudes largely in response to their environment, including parents and other influences. Gender differences emerge early in the preschool years as children form expectations—which generally conform to social stereotypes—about what is appropriate and inappropriate for each sex.

- The strong gender expectations held by preschoolers are explained in different ways by different theorists. Some point to genetic factors as evidence for a biological explanation of gender expectations. Freud's psychoanalytic theories use a framework based on the subconscious. Social learning theorists focus on environmental influences, including parents, teachers, peers, and the media, while cognitive theorists propose that children form gender schemas, cognitive frameworks that organize information that the children gather about gender.

In what sorts of social relationships and play do preschool-age children engage?

- Preschool social relationships begin to encompass genuine friendship, involve trust and endure over time.

- Older preschoolers engage in more constructive play than functional play. They also engage in more associative and cooperative play than younger preschoolers, who do more parallel and onlooker playing.

What sorts of disciplinary styles do parents employ, and what effects do they have?

- Disciplinary styles differ both individually and culturally. In the United States and other Western societies, parents' styles tend to be mostly authoritarian, permissive, uninvolved, and authoritative, the last regarded as the most effective.

- Children of authoritarian and permissive parents may develop dependency, hostility, and low self-control, while children of uninvolved parents may feel unloved and emotionally detached. Children of authoritative parents tend to be more independent, friendly, self-assertive, and cooperative.

How do children develop a moral sense?

- Piaget believed that preschool-age children are in the heteronomous morality stage of moral development, characterized by a belief in external, unchangeable rules of conduct and sure, immediate punishment for all misdeeds.

- In contrast, social learning approaches to morality emphasize interactions between environment and behavior in moral development in which models of behavior play an important role in development.

- Some developmentalists believe that moral behavior is rooted in a child's development of empathy. Other emotions, including the negative emotions of anger and shame, may also promote moral behavior.

How does aggression develop in preschool-age children?

- Aggression, which involves intentional harm to another person, begins to emerge in the preschool years. As children age and improve their language skills, acts of aggression typically decline in frequency and duration.

- Some ethologists, such as Konrad Lorenz, believe that aggression is simply a biological fact of human life. This belief is held also by many sociobiologists, who focus on competition within species to pass genes on to the next generation.

- Social learning theorists focus on the role of the environment, including the influence of models and social reinforcement as factors influencing aggressive behavior.

- The cognitive approach to aggression emphasizes the role of interpretations of the behaviors of others in determining aggressive or nonaggressive responses. ■

Epilogue

In this chapter we examined the social and personality development of preschool-age children, including their development of self-concept. We looked at the social relationships of preschool-age children and the changing nature of play. We considered typical styles of parental discipline and their effects later in life. We discussed the development of a moral sense from several developmental perspectives, and we concluded with a discussion of aggression.

Before moving on to the next chapter, take a moment to reread the Prologue to this chapter, about Sarah Rossoff's living room "tent," and answer the following questions.

1. How does Sarah Rossoff's "need to mess" relate to Erikson's autonomy-versus-shame-and-doubt stage of moral development?

2. Can you think of a response to this situation that a parent might make that would reinforce Sarah's emerging cultural stereotypes about gender? Can you think of a different response that would reinforce a more androgynous identity?

3. Can you analyze Sarah's activity in terms of "play," as it is discussed by developmentalists? If Sarah were playing with a friend, what characteristics do you think their play would have?

4. How would parents react to this situation using each of the three disciplinary styles typical in the United States (i.e., authoritarian, permissive, and authoritative) react to this situation? Which response do you think is most appropriate? Why?

5. How might you design an experiment around a situation like this one, focusing on how social models affect a child's compliance with his or her mother's instructions to clean up a room? What would be your hypothesis? What variable would you manipulate (i.e., your independent variable)? What variable would you measure (i.e., your dependent variable)?

Key Terms and Concepts

psychosocial development (p. 234)

initiative-versus-guilt stage (p. 234)

self-concept (p. 234)

collectivistic orientation (p. 234)

individualistic orientation (p. 234)

race dissonance (p. 235)

identification (p. 237)

gender identity (p. 237)

gender schema (p. 237)

gender constancy (p. 238)

functional play (p. 239)

constructive play (p. 239)

parallel play (p. 239)

onlooker play (p. 240)

associative play (p. 240)

cooperative play (p. 240)

authoritarian parents (p. 243)

permissive parents (p. 243)

authoritative parents (p. 243)

uninvolved parents (p. 244)

moral development (p. 246)

prosocial behavior (p. 247)

abstract modeling (p. 247)

empathy (p. 247)

aggression (p. 248)

emotional self-regulation (p. 248)

instrumental aggression (p. 248)

relational aggression (p. 249)

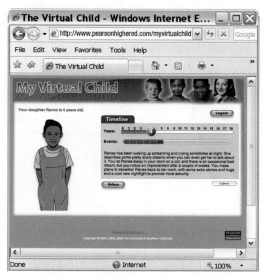

What decisions would you make while raising a child? What would the consequences of those decisions be?

Find out by logging onto **My Virtual Child** and raising your child from birth to 18 years.

3

The Preschool Years

Physical, Cognitive, and Social and Personality Development in the Preschool Years

At the beginning of the preschool years, some children may initially be shy and passive in social situations with peers. They do not always understand the dynamics of social interaction with other children and they may not yet have the skills to stand up for themselves or to solve problems that arise. As preschoolers become older, however, they improve their ability to navigate the complex social dynamics of peer interaction. Older preschoolers can use their new-found moral sense, together with their evolving language skills, to successfully participate in more complex interactions, and to solve problems that arise in a social context.

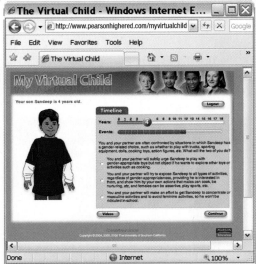

What decisions would you make while raising a child? What would the consequences of those decisions be?

Find out by logging onto **My Virtual Child** and raising your child from birth to 18 years.

● From a **Parent's** Perspective

How would you help a shy preschooler become more assertive, both at home and at school? How would you help him prepare to deal with bullies in preschool and with older siblings at home?

HINT **Review pages 239–241**

Your response?

● From a **Social Worker's** Perspective

How would you help the parents of a preschooler provide appropriate kinds of discipline? How would you help them to optimize their home environment to promote physical, cognitive, and social development for their children?

HINT **Review pages 243–245**

Your response?

The Preschool Years

Physical Development

- Preschoolers grow bigger, heavier, and stronger during these years (p. 186)
- Their brains grow, and with it their cognitive abilities, including the ability to plan and to use language as a tool (p. 187)
- Preschoolers learn to use and control their gross and fine motor skills (p. 198)

Cognitive Development

- During the preschool years, a child's memory capabilites increase. (p. 213)
- Preschoolers watch others, and learn from peers and from adults how to handle different situations (p. 215)
- Preschoolers use their growing language skills to function more effectively (p. 218)

Social and Personality Development

- Preschool-age children use play as a way to grow socially, cognitively, and physically (p. 239)
- A preschooler learns the rules of play, such as turn-taking and playing fairly (p. 239)
- They also develop theories of mind that help them to understand what others may be thinking (p. 242)
- They develop the beginnings of a sense of justice and moral behavior (p. 246)
- They are eventually able to adjust their emotions to a desired intensity level and can use language to express their wishes and to deal with others (p. 252)

From an **Educator's** Perspective

What strategies would you use to promote cognitive and social development? How would you deal with instances of bullying in your preschool classroom, both in terms of children who were victimized as well as dealing with the bully?

HINT **Review pages 248–252**

Your response?

From **Your** Perspective

What would you do to promote a preschooler's development? What specific advice would you give to parents and teachers regarding how to help a preschooler overcome his shyness and learn to interact more effectively with other children?

HINT **Review pages 239–241**

Your response?

chapter eleven

Physical Development in Middle Childhood

PROLOGUE: SUZANNE McGUIRE

It was a hot summer day in Atlanta, the kind when most adults are moving slowly through the heavy, humid air. But not 8-year-old Suzanne McGuire. She was a study in motion as she rounded the corner from third base to home plate, a look of triumph on her face.

A few moments earlier, she was waiting for the pitcher to throw the ball. At her first and second turns at bat, Suzanne had struck out, and she was still feeling unhappy and a bit humiliated by her performance.

Now, though, the pitch looked perfectly positioned, and she swung at it with a combination of confidence and high hope. As if by magic, the bat connected with the ball, lobbing it in a lazy arc well beyond the left fielder. It was a home run—and it created a moment that she would never forget.

▶ Looking Ahead

Suzanne McGuire has come a long way from the preschooler she was only a few years earlier, for whom running quickly in a coordinated fashion was a challenge and successfully hitting an incoming pitch an impossibility.

Middle childhood is characterized by a procession of moments such as these, as children's physical, cognitive, and social skills ascend to new heights. In this chapter we focus on the physical aspects of middle childhood, both in typical children and in children with special needs. Beginning at age 6 and continuing to the start of adolescence at around age 12, middle childhood is often referred to as the "school years" because it marks the beginning of formal education for most children. Sometimes the physical and cognitive growth that occurs during middle childhood is gradual; other times it is sudden; but always it is remarkable.

We begin our consideration of middle childhood by examining physical and motor development. We discuss how children's bodies change and the twin problems of malnutrition and—the other side of the coin—childhood obesity. Next we turn to motor development. We discuss the growth of gross and fine motor skills and the role that physical competence plays in children's lives. We also discuss threats to children's safety, including a new risk that enters the home through the personal computer.

The chapter ends with a discussion of some of the special needs that affect the sensory and physical abilities of exceptional children. It concludes by focusing on the question of how children with special needs should be integrated into society.

In sum, after reading this chapter, you will be able to answer the following questions:

- *In what ways do children grow during the school years, and what factors influence their growth?*
- *What are the nutritional needs of school-age children, and what are some causes and effects of improper nutrition?*
- *What sorts of health threats do school-age children face?*
- *What are the characteristics of motor development during middle childhood, and what advantages do improved physical skills bring?*
- *What safety threats affect school-age children, and what can be done about them?*
- *What sorts of special needs manifest themselves in the middle-childhood years, and how can they be met?*

The Growing Body

Cinderella, dressed in yella,
Went upstairs to kiss her fellah
But she made a mistake and kissed a snake.
How many doctors did it take?
One, two, . . .

Variations of 6 inches in height between children of the same age are not unusual and are well within the normal range.

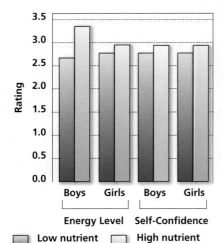

FIGURE 11-1 Nutritional Benefits

Children who received higher levels of nutrients had more energy and felt more self-confident than those whose nutritional intake was lower. How might a social worker use this information?
(*Source:* Adapted from Barrett & Radke-Yarrow, 1985)

While the other girls chanted the classic jump-rope rhyme, Kat proudly displayed her newly developed ability to jump backward. In second grade, Kat was starting to get quite good at jumping rope. In first grade, she had not been able to master it. But over the summer, she had spent many hours practicing, and now that practice seemed to be paying off.

As Kat is gleefully experiencing, middle childhood is the time when children make great physical strides, mastering all kinds of new skills as they grow bigger and stronger. How does this progress occur?

Physical Development

Slow but steady.

If three words could characterize the nature of growth during middle childhood, it would be these. Especially when compared to the swift growth during the first 5 years of life and the remarkable growth spurt characteristic of adolescence, middle childhood is relatively tranquil. But the body has not shifted into neutral. Physical growth continues, although at a more steady pace than it did during the preschool years.

Height and Weight Changes

While they are in elementary school, children in the United States grow, on average, 2 to 3 inches a year. By the age of 11, the average height for girls is 4 feet, 10 inches and the average height for boys is slightly shorter at 4 feet, 9 1/2 inches. This is the only time during the life span when girls are, on average, taller than boys. This height difference reflects the slightly more rapid physical development of girls, who start their adolescent growth spurt around the age of 10.

Weight gain follows a similar pattern. During middle childhood, both boys and girls gain around 5 to 7 pounds a year. Weight is also redistributed. As the rounded look of "baby fat" disappears, children's bodies become more muscular and their strength increases.

These average height and weight increases disguise significant individual differences, as anyone who has seen a line of fourth graders walking down a school corridor has doubtless noticed. It is not unusual to see children of the same age who are 6 or 7 inches apart in height.

Nutrition: Links to Overall Functioning

The level of nutrition that children receive during their lives significantly affects many aspects of their behavior. For instance, longitudinal studies over many years in Guatemalan villages show that children's nutritional backgrounds are related to several dimensions of social and emotional functioning at school age. Children who had received more nutrients were more involved with their peers, showed more positive emotion, had less anxiety, and had more moderate activity levels than their peers who had received less adequate nutrition (Barrett & Frank, 1987; see Figure 11-1).

Not only does good nutrition promote the growth of strong bones, but it is also related to the development of healthy teeth. During middle childhood, the majority of adult teeth replace the primary teeth of early childhood. Starting at around the age of 6, the primary teeth fall out at the rate of about four per year until the age of 11.

Nutrition is also linked to cognitive performance. For instance, children who are well nourished perform better on tests of verbal abilities and other cognitive measures than those who have mild to moderate undernutrition. Malnutrition may influence cognitive development by dampening children's curiosity, responsiveness, and motivation to learn (Brown & Pollitt, 1996; Drewett, 2007).

Cultural Patterns of Growth Most children in North America receive sufficient nutrients to grow to their full potential. In other parts of the world, however, inadequate nutrition and disease take their toll, producing children who are shorter and who weigh less than they would if they had sufficient nutrients.

For example, children in poorer areas of cities such as Calcutta, Hong Kong, and Rio de Janeiro are smaller than their counterparts in affluent areas of the same cities. In the United States, most variations in height and weight are the result of different people's unique genetic inheritance, including genetic factors relating to racial and ethnic background. For instance, children from Asian and Oceanic Pacific backgrounds tend to be shorter, on average, than those with northern and central European heritages. In addition, the rate of growth during childhood is generally more rapid for Blacks than for Whites (Deurenberg, Deurenberg-Yap, Guricci, 2002; Deurenberg et al., 2003).

Of course, even within particular racial and ethnic groups, there is significant variation between individuals. Moreover, we cannot attribute racial and ethnic differences solely to genetic factors, because dietary customs as well as possible variations in levels of affluence also may contribute to the differences. In addition, severe stress—brought on by factors such as parental conflict or alcoholism—can affect the functioning of the pituitary gland, thereby affecting growth (Koska et al., 2002).

Promoting Growth With Hormones: Should Short Children Be Made to Grow?

Because being tall is considered an advantage by most members of U.S. society, parents frequently worry about their children's growth if their children are short. Some parents react by giving their children artificial human growth hormones that can make short children grow taller than they naturally would (Sandberg & Voss, 2002; Lagrou et al., 2008).

Should children be given such drugs? The question is a relatively new one: Artificial hormones to promote growth have become available only in the last 2 decades. Although tens of thousands of children who have insufficient natural growth hormone are taking such drugs, some observers question whether shortness is a serious enough problem to warrant the use of the drug. Certainly, one can function well in society without being tall. Furthermore, the drug is costly and has potentially dangerous side effects. In some cases, the drug may lead to the premature onset of puberty, which may—ironically—restrict later growth.

On the other hand, there is no denying that artificial growth hormones are effective in increasing children's height, in some cases adding well over a foot in height to extremely short children, placing them within normal height ranges. Ultimately, until long-term studies of the safety of such treatments are completed, parents and medical personnel must carefully weigh the pros and cons before administering the drug to children (Gohlke & Stanhope, 2002; Heyman et al., 2003; Ogilvy-Stuart & Gleeson, 2004).

Childhood Obesity

When Ruthellen's mother asks if she would like a piece of bread with her meal, Ruthellen replies that she better not—she thinks that she may be getting fat. Ruthellen, who is of normal weight and height, is 6 years old.

Children in poorer areas of cities, such as these youngsters in Calcutta, are shorter and weigh less than those raised in more affluent places.

Although height can be of concern to both children and parents during middle childhood, maintaining the appropriate weight is an even greater worry for some. In fact, concern about weight can border on an obsession, particularly among girls. For instance, many 6-year-old girls worry about becoming "fat," and some 40% of 9- and 10-year-olds are trying to lose weight. Why? Their concern is most often the result of the U.S. preoccupation with being slim, which permeates every sector of society (Schreiber et al., 1996; Greenwood & Pietromonaco, 2004).

In spite of this widely held view that thinness is a virtue, increasing numbers of children are becoming obese. *Obesity* is defined as body weight that is more than 20% above the average for a person of a given age and height. By this definition, one in eight of U.S. children is obese—a proportion that has tripled since the 1960s (see Figure 11-2; Brownlee, 2002; Dietz, 2004; Mann, 2005).

The costs of childhood obesity last a lifetime. Children who are obese are more likely to be overweight as adults, as well as having a greater risk of heart disease, diabetes, and other diseases. In fact, some scientists believe that an epidemic of obesity may be leading to a decline in life span in the United States (Freedman et al., 2004; Olshansky et al., 2005; Pietrobelli, Espinoza, & DeCristofaro, 2008).

Obesity is caused by a combination of genetic and environmental factors. Particular inherited genes are related

From a health-care provider's perspective: Under what circumstances would you recommend the use of a growth hormone? Is shortness primarily a physical or a cultural problem?

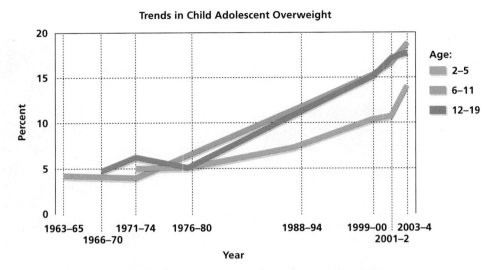

Trends in Child Adolescent Overweight

Age:
- 2–5
- 6–11
- 12–19

Note: Overweight is defined as BMI ≥ gender- and weight-specific 95th percentile from the 2000CDC Growth Charts.

FIGURE 11-2 Obesity in Children

Obesity in children of all ages has risen dramatically over the past 4 decades. (*Source:* National Center for Health Statistics, 2001)

"Remember when we used to have to fatten the kids up first?"

to obesity and predispose certain children to be overweight. For example, adopted children tend to have weights that are more similar to those of their birth parents than to those of their adoptive parents (Whitaker et al., 1997; Bray, 2008).

But it is not just a matter of a genetic predisposition that leads to weight problems. Poor diets also contribute to obesity. Despite recommendations regarding what foods are necessary for a balanced, nutritious diet, most children eat too few fruits and vegetables and more fats and sweets than experts recommend (see Figure 11-3).

Another major factor in childhood obesity is a lack of exercise. School-age children, by and large, tend to engage in relatively little exercise and are not particularly fit. For instance, around 40% of boys aged 6 to 12 are unable to do more than one pull-up, and a quarter of them can't do any. Furthermore, school fitness surveys reveal that children in the United States have shown little or no improvement in the amount of exercise they get, despite national efforts to increase the level of fitness of school-age children. From the ages of 6 to 18, boys decrease their physical activity by 24% and girls by 36% (Moore, Gao, & Bradlee, 2003; Stork & Sanders, 2008).

Why, when our visions of childhood include children running happily on school playgrounds, playing sports, and chasing one another in games of tag, is the actual level of exercise relatively low? One answer is that many kids are inside their homes, watching television and computer screens. Such sedentary activities not only keep children from exercising, but they often snack while viewing TV, playing video games, or surfing the Web. (Rideout, Vandewater, & Wartella, 2003; Tartamella, Herscher, & Woolston, 2005; Jenvey, 2007; Pardee et al., 2007).

Furthermore, many children return from school to homes without adult supervision because their parents are at work. In such situations, parents may prohibit their children from leaving the home for safety reasons, meaning that the youngsters are unable to engage in exercise even if they wanted to (Murphy & Polivka, 2007; Speroni, Earley, & Atherton, 2007).

Treating Obesity Regardless of what causes a child to become obese, treatment is tricky, because creating too strong a concern about food and dieting must be avoided. Children need to learn to control their eating themselves. Parents who are particularly controlling and directive regarding their children's eating may produce children who lack internal controls to regulate their own food intake (Wardle, Guthrie, & Sanderson, 2001; Okie, 2005).

One strategy is to control the food that is available in the home. By filling the cupboards and refrigerator with healthy foods—and keeping high-caloric, highly processed foods out of the house—children are essentially forced to eat a healthy diet. Furthermore, avoiding fast foods, which are high in calories and fats, is important (Campbell,

Crawford, & Ball, 2006; Lindsay et al., 2006; Hoerr, Murashima, & Keast, 2008).

In most cases, the goal of treatment for obesity is to temporarily maintain a child's current weight through an improved diet and increased exercise, rather than actually seeking to lose weight. In time, obese children's normal growth in height will result in their weight becoming more normal.

MyPyramid for Kids reminds you to be physically active every day, or most days, and to make healthy food choices. Every part of the new symbol has a message for you. Can you figure it out?

Be Physically Active Every Day
The person climbing the stairs reminds you to do something active every day, like running, walking the dog, playing, swimming, biking, or climbing lots of stairs.

Eat More From Some Food Groups Than From Others
Did you notice that some of the color stripes are wider than others? The different sizes remind you to choose more foods from the food groups with the widest stripes.

Choose Healthier Foods From Each Group
Why are the colored stripes wider at the bottom of the pyramid? Every food group has foods that you should eat more often than others; these foods are at the bottom of the pyramid.

Every Color Every Day
The colors orange, green, red, yellow, blue, and purple represent the five different food groups plus oils. Remember to eat foods from all food groups every day.

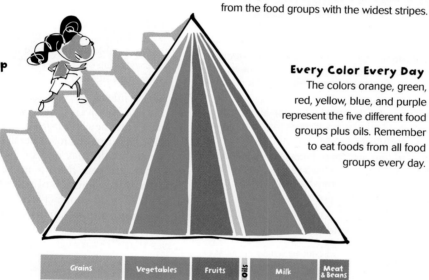

Grains | Vegetables | Fruits | Oils | Milk | Meat & Beans

Make Choices That Are Right for You
MyPyramid.gov is a Web site that will give everyone in the family personal ideas on how to eat better and exercise more.

Take One Step at a Time
You do not need to change overnight what you eat and how you exercise. Just start with one new, good thing, and add a new one every day.

FIGURE 11-3
A Balanced Diet

According to the U.S. Department of Agriculture, this is the ideal food distribution for a 10-year-old who engages in 30 to 60 minutes of exercise most days. However, the diet of most 10-year-olds is quite different, with far fewer fruits and vegetables and more fats and sugars—a situation that can lead to an increase in obesity. What suggestions would you make to the parents of children who are not eating appropriately?
(*Source:* U.S. Department of Agriculture, 2005)

MyPyramid.gov
STEPS TO A HEALTHIER YOU

U.S. Department of Agriculture
Food and Nutrition Service
September 2005
FNS-388

USDA

TEAM
NUTRITION • USDA
teamnutrition.usda.gov

USDA is an equal opportunity provider and employer.

Becoming an Informed Consumer of Development

Keeping Children Fit

Sam works all week at a desk and gets no regular physical exercise. On weekends he spends many hours sitting in front of the TV, often snacking on sodas and sweets. Both at home and at restaurants, his meals feature high-calorie, fat-saturated foods. (Segal & Segal, 1992, p. 235)

Although this sketch could apply to many adult men and women, Sam is actually a 6-year-old. He is one of many school-age children in the United States who get little or no regular exercise and who are consequently physically unfit and at risk for obesity and other health problems.

Several things can be done to encourage children to become more physically active (Tyre & Scelfo, 2003; Okie, 2005):

- **Make exercise fun.** In order for children to build the habit of exercising, they need to find it enjoyable. Activities that keep children on the sidelines or that are overly competitive may give children with inferior skills a lifelong distaste for exercise.

- **Be an exercise role model.** Children who see that exercise is a regular part of the lives of their parents, teachers, or adult friends may come to think of fitness as a regular part of their lives, too.

- **Gear activities to the child's physical level and motor skills.** For instance, use child-size equipment that can make participants feel successful.

- **Encourage the child to find a partner.** It could be a friend, a sibling, or a parent. Exercising can involve a variety of activities, such as roller skating or hiking, but almost all activities are carried out more readily if someone else is doing them too.

- **Start slowly.** Sedentary children—those who aren't used to regular physical activity—should start off gradually. For instance, they could start with 5 minutes of exercise a day, 7 days a week. Over 10 weeks, they could move toward a goal of 30 minutes of exercise 3 to 5 days a week.

- **Urge participation in organized sports activities, but do not push too hard.** Not every child is athletically inclined, and pushing too hard for involvement in organized sports may backfire. Make participation and enjoyment the goals of such activities, not winning.

- **Don't make physical activity, such as jumping jacks or push-ups, a punishment for unwanted behavior.** Instead, schools and parents should encourage children to participate in organized programs that seek to involve children in ways that are enjoyable.

Health During Middle Childhood

Imani was miserable. Her nose was running, her lips were chapped, and her throat was sore. Although she had been able to stay home from school and spend the day watching old reruns on TV, she still felt that she was suffering mightily.

Despite her misery, Imani's situation is not so bad. She'll get over the cold in a few days and be no worse for having experienced it. In fact, she may be a little *better* off, for she is now immune to the specific cold germs that made her ill in the first place.

Imani's cold may end up being the most serious illness that she gets during middle childhood. For most children, this is a period of robust health, and most of the ailments they do contract tend to be mild and brief. Routine immunizations during childhood have produced a considerably lower incidence of the life-threatening illnesses that 50 years ago claimed the lives of a significant number of children.

However, illness is not uncommon. For instance, more than 90% of children are likely to have at least one serious medical condition over the 6-year period of middle childhood, according to the results of one large survey. And although most children have short-term illnesses, about one in nine has a chronic, persistent condition, such as repeated migraine headaches. And some illnesses are actually becoming more prevalent (Dey & Bloom, 2005).

Asthma Asthma is among the diseases that have shown a significant increase in prevalence in recent decades. **Asthma** is a chronic condition characterized by periodic attacks of wheezing, coughing, and shortness of breath. More than 5% of U.S. children suffer from the disorder, and worldwide there are 150 million sufferers (Doyle, 2000; Johnson, 2003; Dey & Bloom, 2005; see Figure 11-4).

Asthma occurs when the airways leading to the lungs constrict, partially blocking the passage of air. Because the airways are obstructed, more effort is needed to push air

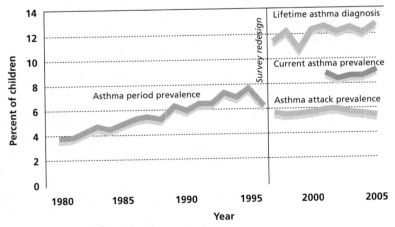

Asthma Prevalence by Age in America, 1980–2005

Percent of children (y-axis: 0, 2, 4, 6, 8, 10, 12, 14)
Year (x-axis: 1980, 1985, 1990, 1995, 2000, 2005)

Survey redesign

Asthma period prevalence

Lifetime asthma diagnosis

Current asthma prevalence

Asthma attack prevalence

FIGURE 11-4 Rising Rates of Asthma

Since the early 1980s, the rate of asthma among children has almost doubled. A number of factors explain the rise, including increased air pollution and better means of detecting the disease. (Note that the way in which the incidence of asthma was surveyed changed in 1997.)

(*Source:* Akinbami, 2006)

through them, making breathing more difficult. As air is forced through the obstructed airways, it makes the whistling sound called wheezing.

Not surprisingly, children are often exceedingly frightened by asthma attacks, and the anxiety and agitation produced by their breathing difficulties may actually make the attack worse. In some cases, breathing becomes so difficult that further physical symptoms develop, including sweating, an increased heart rate, and—in the most severe cases—blueness in the face and lips due to a lack of oxygen.

Asthma attacks are triggered by a variety of factors. Among the most common are respiratory infections (such as colds or flu), allergic reactions to airborne irritants (such as pollution, cigarette smoke, dust mites, and animal dander and excretions), stress, and exercise. Sometimes even a sudden change in air temperature or humidity is enough to bring on an attack (Juhn et al., 2005; Li et al., 2005; Noonan & Ward, 2007).

Although asthma can be serious, treatment is increasingly effective for those who suffer from the disorder. Some children who experience frequent asthma attacks use a small aerosol container with a special mouthpiece to spray drugs into the lungs. Other patients take tablets or receive injections (Israel, 2005).

One of the most puzzling questions about asthma is why more and more children are suffering from it. Some researchers suggest that increasing air pollution has led to the rise; others believe that cases of asthma that might have been missed in the past are being identified more accurately. Still others have suggested that exposure to "asthma triggers," such as dust, may be increasing because new buildings are more weatherproof—and therefore less drafty—than older ones, and consequently the flow of air within them is more restricted.

Finally, poverty may play an indirect role. Children living in poverty have a higher incidence of asthma than is found in other children, probably due to poorer medical care and less sanitary living conditions. For instance, poor youngsters are more likely than more affluent ones to be exposed to triggering factors that are associated with asthma, such as dust mites, cockroach feces and body parts, and rodent feces and urine (Johnson, 2003; Caron, Gjelsvik, & Buechner, 2005).

Psychological Disorders

Jackson had always been a quiet child, and had, since his days as a toddler, seemed less exuberant than most other children. But when his third-grade teacher called his parents to report that Jackson seemed increasingly withdrawn from his classmates and had to be coaxed into going out to the playground, the parents thought they might have a serious problem on their hands. They took Jackson to a psychologist, who diagnosed Jackson as suffering from *childhood depression*.

For years most people neglected the symptoms of childhood depression, and even today parents and teachers may overlook its presence. In part, their neglect is due to the fact that its symptoms are not entirely consistent with the ways adults express depression. Rather than being manifested in a profound sadness or hopelessness, a negative outlook on life, and, in extreme cases, suicidal thoughts, as adult depression is, childhood depression may instead be characterized by the expression of exaggerated fears, clinginess, or avoidance of everyday activities. In older children, childhood depression may produce sulking, school problems, and even acts of delinquency (Katon et al., 2008).

Disorders such as childhood depression are hardly rare. Yet psychological disorders are a common problem: One in five children and adolescents has a psychological disorder that produces at least some impairment. For example, about 5% of preteens suffer from childhood depression, and 13% of children between the ages of 9 and 17 experience an anxiety disorder. The incidence of some kinds of disorders, such as bipolar disorder, have increased significantly in recent years, although it is unclear whether the rise is due to an actual increase in the disorder or to changes in diagnostic criteria (Kalb, 2003; Goodwin et al., 2007; Holtmann, Bölte, & Poustka, 2008).

Like adult psychological disorders, childhood disorders can be treated effectively through a variety of approaches. In addition to psychological counseling, drugs are sometimes prescribed, although their use is controversial, as we discuss in the *From Research to Practice* box.

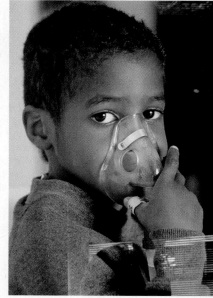

The incidence of asthma, a chronic respiratory condition, has increased dramatically over the past several decades.

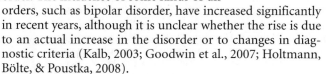

REVIEW ↵ mydevelopmentlab

1. _____ but steady characterizes the nature of growth during middle childhood.

    Answer: Slow

2. The adequacy of _____ children experience during their lives significantly affects many aspects of their behavior.

    Answer: nutrition

3. _____ is defined as body weight that is more than 20% above the average for a person of a given age and height.

    Answer: Obesity

To see more review questions, log on to MyDevelopmentLab.

Motor Development and Safety

When my son's friend Owen was 9 years old, everybody at school knew the shameful truth about him: He was a whiz at math but a lousy football player.

Nobody was more aware of this than Owen. "He knew he wasn't as good at sports as the others," says his mother, Cheryl. "It really got him down. Even when we told him, 'You have to get out there, you have to try,' as soon as he made a mistake, he would just walk away. Owen's schoolwork was good, so he felt okay about himself. But because he didn't play sports, he didn't have as many friends as most kids did."

Then one day, just after he turned 10, when Owen happened to be at a nearby mall, he saw a demonstration of a martial art called tae kwon do. "That's what I want to do," he immediately told his mother. "Can you sign me up?"

He now takes lessons several times a week, and according to Cheryl, the changes are remarkable. "Owen's mood has improved, he's sleeping better, he's even better about doing homework," she says. "And when he got his yellow belt, he was over the moon." (Heath, 1994, pp. 127–128)

During middle childhood, children's athletic abilities play an important role in determining how they see themselves, as well as how they are viewed by others. This is also a time when such physical proficiencies develop substantially.

Motor Skills: Continuing Improvement

Watching a schoolyard softball player pitch a ball past a batter to the catcher or a third-grade runner reach the finish line in a race, it is hard not to be struck by the huge strides that these children have made since the more awkward days of preschool. Both gross and fine motor skills improve significantly during the middle-childhood years.

Gross Motor Skills One important improvement in gross motor skills is in the realm of muscle coordination. For instance, most school-age children can readily learn to ride a bike, ice-skate, swim, and skip rope, skills that earlier they could not perform well (see Figure 11-5).

Do boys and girls differ in their motor skills? Years ago, developmentalists contended that gender differences in gross motor skills become increasingly pronounced during these years, with boys outperforming girls (Espenschade, 1960). However, more recent research casts some doubt on this claim. When comparisons are made between boys and girls who regularly take part in similar activities such as softball, gender variations in gross motor skills are found to be minimal (Jurimae & Saar, 2003).

During middle childhood, children master many types of skills that earlier they could not perform well, such as riding a bike, ice-skating, swimming, and skipping rope. Is this true for children in all cultures?

6 Years	7 Years	8 Years	9 Years	10 Years	11 Years	12 Years
Girls superior in accuracy of movement; boys superior in more forceful, less complex acts. Can throw with the proper weight shift and step. Acquire the ability to skip.	Can balance on one foot with eyes closed. Can walk on a 2-inch-wide balance beam without falling off. Can hop and jump accurately into small squares (hopscotch). Can correctly execute a jumping-jack exercise.	Can grip objects with 12 pounds of pressure. Can engage in alternate rhythmical hopping in a 2-2, 2-3, or 3-3 pattern. Girls can throw a small ball 33 feet; boys can throw a small ball 59 feet. The number of games participated in by both sexes is the greatest at this age.	Girls can jump vertically 8.5 inches over their standing height plus reach; boys can jump vertically 10 inches. Boys can run 16.6 feet per second and throw a small ball 41 feet; girls can run 16 feet per second and throw a small ball 41 feet.	Can judge and intercept directions of small balls thrown from a distance. Both girls and boys can run 17 feet per second.	Boys can achieve standing broad jump of 5 feet; girls can achieve standing broad jump of 4.5 feet.	Can achieve high jump of 3 feet.

FIGURE 11-5 Gross Motor Skills Developed Between the Ages of 6 and 12 Years

Why would it be important that a social worker be aware of this period of development?
(*Source:* Adapted from Cratty, 1979, p. 222)

Fine motor skills, such as typing on a keyboard, improve during early and middle childhood.

What accounts for the discrepancy in earlier observations? Performance differences were probably found because of differences in motivation and expectations. Society told girls that they would do worse than boys in sports, and the girls' performance reflected that message.

Today, however, society's message has changed, at least officially. For instance, the American Academy of Pediatrics suggests that boys and girls should engage in the same sports and games and that they can do so together in mixed-gender groups. There is no reason to separate the sexes in physical exercise and sports until puberty, when the smaller size of females begins to make them more susceptible to injury in contact sports (Raudsepp & Liblik, 2002; Vilhjalmsson & Kristjansdottir, 2003; American Academy of Pediatrics, 1999, 2004).

Fine Motor Skills Typing at a computer keyboard, writing in cursive with pen or pencil, drawing detailed pictures—these are just some of the accomplishments that depend on improvements in fine motor coordination that occur during early and middle childhood. Children 6 and 7 years old are able to tie their shoes and fasten buttons; by age 8, they can use each hand independently; and by 11 and 12, they can manipulate objects with almost as much dexterity as they will possess in adulthood.

One of the reasons for advances in fine motor skills is that the amount of myelin in the brain increases significantly between the ages of 6 and 8. As you'll recall from Chapter 3, *myelin* provides protective insulation around parts of nerve cells. Because increased levels of myelin raise the speed at which electrical impulses travel between neurons, messages can reach muscles more rapidly and control them better.

The Social Benefits of Physical Competence Is Matt, a fifth grader who is a clear standout on his Saturday-morning soccer team, more popular as a result of his physical talents?

He may well be. According to a long history of research on the topic, school-age children who perform well physically are often more accepted and better liked by their peers than are those who perform less well (Pintney, Forlands, & Freedman, 1937; Branta, Lerner, & Taylor, 1997).

However, the link between physical competence and popularity is considerably stronger for boys than for girls. The reason for this sex difference most likely relates to differing societal standards for appropriate male and female behavior. Despite the increasing evidence that girls and boys do not differ substantially in athletic performance, a lingering "physical toughness" standard still exists for males but not

for females. Regardless of age, males who are bigger, stronger, and more physically competent are seen as more desirable than males who are smaller, weaker, and less physically competent. In contrast, standards for females are less supportive of physical success. In fact, women receive less admiration for physical prowess than men do throughout the life span. Although these societal standards may be changing, with women's participation in sports activities becoming more frequent and valued, gender biases remain (Burn, 1996; Bowker, Gabdois, & Shannon, 2003).

Although the social desirability of athletically proficient boys increases throughout elementary school and continues into secondary school, at some point the positive consequences of motor ability begin to diminish. Presumably, other traits become increasingly important in determining social attractiveness—some of which we'll discuss in Chapter 13.

Furthermore, it is difficult to sort out the extent that advantages from exceptional physical performance are due to actual athletic competence, as opposed to being a result of earlier maturation. Boys who physically mature at a more rapid pace than their peers or who happen to be taller, heavier, and stronger tend to perform better at athletic activities due to their relative size advantage. Consequently, it may be that early physical maturity is ultimately of greater consequence than physical skills per se.

Still, it is clear that athletic competence and motor skills in general play a notable role in school-age children's lives. However, it is important to help children avoid overemphasizing the significance of physical ability. Participation in sports should be fun, not something that separates one child from another or raises children's and parents' anxiety levels. Consequently, it is important to match the sport to a child's level of development. When the skills required by participation in a sport go beyond children's physical and mental capabilities, they may feel inadequate and frustrated (American Academy of Pediatrics, 2001).

In fact, some forms of organized sports, such as Little League baseball, are sometimes criticized for the emphasis they may place on winning at any cost. When children feel that success in sports is the sole goal, the pleasure of playing the game is diminished, particularly for children who are not naturally athletic and do not excel (Weber, 2005).

In sum, the goals of participation in sports and other physical activities should be to maintain physical fitness, to learn physical skills, and to become comfortable with one's body. And in addition to these goals, children should have fun in the process.

Threats to Children's Safety, Offline and Online

The increasing independence and mobility of school-age children give rise to new safety issues. In fact, the rate of injury for children increases between the ages of 5 and 14 (see Figure 11-6). Furthermore, boys are more apt to be injured than girls, probably because their overall level of physical activity is greater (Noonan, 2003a).

Accidents   The increased mobility of school-age children is a source of several kinds of accidents. For instance, children who regularly walk to school on their own, of whom many are traveling such a distance alone for the first time in their lives, face the risk of being hit by cars and trucks. Because of their lack of experience, they may misjudge distances when calculating just how far they are from an oncoming vehicle. Furthermore, bicycle accidents pose an increasing risk, particularly as children more frequently venture out onto busy roads (Schnitzer, 2006).

The most common source of injury to children is automobile accidents. Auto crashes annually kill 5 out of every 100,000 children between the ages 5 and 9. Fires and burns, drowning, and gun-related deaths follow in frequency (Field & Behrman, 2002; Schiller & Bemedel, 2004).

Two ways to reduce auto and bicycle injuries are to use seat belts consistently inside the car and to wear appropriate protective gear when bike riding. Bicycle helmets have significantly reduced head injuries, and in many localities their use is mandatory. Similar protection is available for other outside activities; for example, knee and elbow pads and helmets have proven to be important sources of injury reduction for roller-blading, skateboarding, and snowboarding (American Academy of Pediatrics Committee on Accident and Poison Prevention, 1990; Lee, Schofer, & Koppelman, 2005).

Safety in Cyberspace   A contemporary threat to the safety of school-age children comes from the World Wide Web. Cyberspace makes available material that many parents find objectionable (Brant, 2003).

This father offers feedback to his daughter, who is a goalie on her ice hockey team. In some organized sports, pressure to win is significant.

Although computer software developers are developing programs that will block particular computer sites, most experts feel that the most reliable safeguard is close supervision by parents. According to the National Center for Missing and Exploited Children (2002), a nonprofit organization that works with the U.S. Department of Justice, parents should warn their children never to provide personal information, such as

From an educator's perspective:

Do you think using blocking-software or computer chips to screen potentially offensive content on the Internet is a practical idea? A good idea? Are such controls the best way to keep children safe in cyberspace?

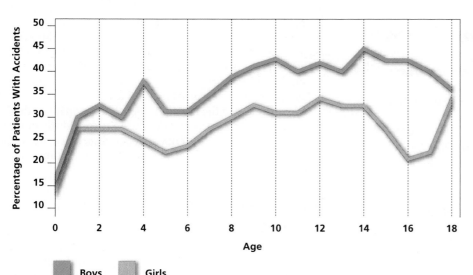

Boys   **Girls**

FIGURE 11-6 Comparative Injury Rates Between Girls and Boys

As children become more independent and more mobile, their rate of injury increases.
(*Source:* Schor, 1987)

TABLE 11-1 Online Safety Rules

The following rules for children to follow have been compiled by the National Center for Missing and Exploited Children, a nonprofit group, and the Interactive Services Association, an industry group.

- Do not give personal information such as your address, telephone number, parent's work address or telephone number, or the name and location of your school.
- Tell your parents if something that you come across online makes you feel uncomfortable.
- Never agree to get together with someone you "meet" online without your parents' permission. If your parents agree to the meeting, be sure the meeting is in a public place and that you bring them along.
- Never respond to messages or bulletin board items that are suggestive, obscene, belligerent, threatening, or make you feel uncomfortable. Give a copy of such messages to your parents and have them forward it to your Internet service provider.
- Never send pictures of yourself or any other personal material to a friend you meet online without telling your parents first.
- Follow the rules that your parents set for your online activities.
- There are places on the Internet that are for adults only. If you find yourself in one of those areas, LEAVE and go to one of the cool places on the Internet for kids.

(*Source:* National Center for Missing and Exploited Children, 1994)

home addresses or telephone numbers, to people on public computer "bulletin boards" or in chat rooms. In addition, children should not be allowed to hold face-to-face meetings with people they meet via computer, at least not without a parent present.

We do not yet have statistics that provide a true sense of the risk presented by exposure to cyberspace. But certainly a potential hazard exists, and parents must offer their children guidance in the use of this computer resource. It would be erroneous to think that just because children are in the supposed safety of their own rooms, logged on to home computers, they are truly protected (Mitchell, Finkelhor, & Walak, 2007; Willard, 2007; Table 11-1 provides some online safety rules for children).

REVIEW ↵ mydevelopmentlab

1. During middle childhood, children make significant improvements in muscle _____.

   Answer: coordination

2. The increase in _____ in the brain that occurs between ages 6 and 8 is one of the reasons for advances in fine motor skills.

   Answer: myelin

3. The most frequent source of injury to children is _____-related accidents followed by fires and burns, drowning, and gun-related deaths.

   Answer: automobile

To see more review questions, log on to MyDevelopmentLab.

Children With Special Needs

Andrew Mertz was a very unhappy little boy. . . . Third grade was a disaster, the culmination of a crisis that had been building since he entered kindergarten in suburban Maryland. He couldn't learn to read, and he hated school. "He would throw temper tantrums in the morning because he didn't want to go," recalls his mother, Suzanne. The year before, with much prodding from Suzanne, the school had authorized diagnostic tests for Andrew. The results revealed a host of brain processing problems that explained why he kept mixing up letters and sounds. Andrew's problem now had a label—he was officially classified as learning disabled—and he was legally entitled to help. (Wingert & Kantrowitz, 1997)

Andrew joined millions of other children who are classified as learning disabled, one of several types of special needs that children can have. Although every child has different specific capabilities, children with *special needs* differ significantly from typical children in terms of physical attributes or learning abilities. Furthermore, their needs present major challenges for both care providers and teachers.

We turn now to the most prevalent exceptionalities that affect children of normal intelligence: sensory difficulties, learning disabilities, and attention-deficit disorders. (We will consider the special needs of children who are significantly below and above average in Chapter 12.)

Sensory Difficulties: Visual, Auditory, and Speech Problems

Anyone who has temporarily lost his or her eyeglasses or a contact lens has had a glimpse of how difficult even rudimentary, everyday tasks must be for those with sensory impairments. To function with less than typical vision, hearing, or speech can be a tremendous challenge.

Visual impairment can be considered in both a legal and an educational sense. The definition of legal impairment is quite straightforward: *Blindness* is visual acuity of less than 20/200 after correction (meaning the inability to see even at 20 feet what a typical person can see at 200 feet), while *partial sightedness* is visual acuity of less than 20/70 after correction.

Even if a person is not so impaired as to be legally blind, their visual problems may still seriously affect their schoolwork. For one thing, the legal criterion pertains solely to distance vision, while most educational tasks require close-up vision. In addition, the legal definition does not consider abilities in the perception of color, depth, and light—all of which might influence a student's educational success. About 1 student in 1,000 requires special education services relating to a visual impairment.

Most severe visual problems are identified fairly early, but it sometimes happens that an impairment goes undetected. Visual problems can also emerge gradually as children develop physiologically and changes occur in the visual apparatus of the eye. Parents and teachers need to be aware of the signals of visual problems in children. Frequent eye irritation (redness, sties, or infection), continual blinking and facial contortions when reading, holding reading material unusually close to the face, difficulty in writing, and frequent headaches, dizziness, or burning eyes are some of the signs of visual problems.

Auditory impairments can also cause academic problems, and they can produce social difficulties as well, since considerable peer interaction takes place through informal conversation. Hearing loss, which affects some 1% to 2% of the school-age population, is not simply a matter of not hearing enough. Rather, auditory problems can vary along a number of dimensions (Yoshinaga-Itano, 2003; Smith, Bale, & White, 2005).

In some cases of hearing loss, the child's hearing is impaired at only a limited range of frequencies, or pitches. For example, the loss may be great at pitches in the normal speech range yet quite minor in other frequencies, such as those of very high or low sounds. A child with this kind of loss may require different levels of amplification at different frequencies; a hearing aid that indiscriminately amplifies all frequencies equally may be ineffective because it will amplify the sounds the person can hear to an uncomfortable degree.

How a child adapts to this impairment depends on the age at which the hearing loss begins. If the loss of hearing occurs in infancy, the effects will probably be much more severe than if it occurs after the age of 3. Children who have had little or no exposure to the sound of language are unable to understand or produce oral language themselves. On the other hand, loss of hearing after a child has learned language will not have as serious consequences on subsequent linguistic development.

Severe and early loss of hearing is also associated with difficulties in abstract thinking. Because hearing-impaired children may have limited exposure to language, they may have trouble mastering abstract concepts that can be understood fully only through the use of language and its nuances. On the other hand, concrete concepts that can be illustrated visually may be more readily comprehended. For example, it is difficult to explain the concept of "freedom" or "soul" without use of language (Butler & Silliman, 2003; Marschark, 2003; Marschark, Spencer, & Newsom, 2003).

Auditory difficulties are sometimes accompanied by speech impairments, one of the most public types of exceptionality: Every time the child speaks aloud, the impairment is obvious to listeners. In fact, the definition of **speech impairment** suggests that speech is impaired when it deviates so much from the speech of others that it calls attention to itself, interferes with communication, or produces maladjustment in the speaker. In other words, if a child's speech sounds impaired, it probably is. Speech impairments are present in around 3% to 5% of the school-age population (Bishop & Leonard, 2001).

Stuttering, which involves a substantial disruption in the rhythm and fluency of speech, is the most common speech impairment. Despite extensive research, no specific cause has been identified. Sporadic stuttering in not unusual in young children—and occasionally occurs in normal adults—but chronic stuttering can be a severe problem. Not only does stuttering hinder communication but it can produce embarrassment and stress in children, who may become inhibited from conversing with others and speaking aloud in class (Whaley & Parker, 2000; Altholz & Golensky, 2004).

Parents and teachers can adopt several strategies for dealing with stuttering. For instance, attention should not be drawn to the stuttering. Furthermore, children should be given sufficient time to finish what they begin to say, no matter how protracted the statement becomes. It does not help stutterers to finish their sentences for them or otherwise correct their speech (Ryan, 2001).

Like Andrew Mertz, who was described at the beginning of this section, some 1 in 10 school-age children are labeled as having learning disabilities. **Learning disabilities** are characterized by difficulties in the acquisition and use of listening, speaking, reading, writing, reasoning, or mathematical abilities. A somewhat ill-defined, grab-bag category, learning disabilities are diagnosed when there is a discrepancy between children's actual academic performance and their apparent potential to learn (Lerner, 2002; Bos & Vaughn, 2005).

Such a broad definition encompasses a wide and extremely varied range of difficulties. For instance, some children suffer from *dyslexia*, a reading disability that can result

Attention deficit hyperactivity disorder (ADHD) A learning disability marked by inattention, impulsiveness, a low tolerance for frustration, and a great deal of inappropriate activity

Seven-year-old Dusty Nash's high energy level and short attention span are due to attention-deficit hyperactivity disorder (ADHD), which occurs in 3% to 5% of the school-age population.

in the misperception of letters during reading and writing, unusual difficulty in sounding out letters, confusion between left and right, and difficulties in spelling. Although dyslexia is not fully understood, one likely explanation for the disorder is a problem in the part of the brain responsible for breaking words into the sound elements that make up language (Paulesu et al., 2001; McGough, 2003; Lachmann et al., 2005).

The causes of learning disabilities in general are not well understood. Although they are generally attributed to some form of brain dysfunction, probably due to genetic factors, some experts suggest that they are produced by such environmental causes as poor early nutrition or allergies (Shaywitz, 2004).

Attention-Deficit/Hyperactivity Disorder

Dusty Nash, an angelic-looking blond child of 7, awoke at five one recent morning in his Chicago home and proceeded to throw a fit. He wailed. He kicked. Every muscle in his 50-pound body flew in furious motion. Finally, after about 30 minutes, Dusty pulled himself together sufficiently to head downstairs for breakfast. While his mother bustled about the kitchen, the hyperkinetic child pulled a box of Kix cereal from the cupboard and sat on a chair.

But sitting still was not in the cards this morning. After grabbing some cereal with his hands, he began kicking the box, scattering little round corn puffs across the room. Next he turned his attention to the TV set, or rather, the table supporting it. The table was covered with checkerboard Con-Tact paper, and Dusty began peeling it off. Then he became intrigued with the spilled

cereal and started stomping it to bits. At this point his mother interceded. In a firm but calm voice she told her son to get the stand-up dust pan and broom and clean up the mess. Dusty got out the dust pan but forgot the rest of the order. Within seconds he was dismantling the plastic dust pan, piece by piece. His next project: grabbing three rolls of toilet paper from the bathroom and unraveling them around the house

It was only 7:30 A.M. (Wallis, 1994, p. 43).

Seven-year-old Dusty Nash's high energy and low attention span is due to attention-deficit/hyperactivity disorder, which occurs in 3% to 5% of the school-age population.

Attention deficit hyperactivity disorder, or **ADHD,** is marked by inattention, impulsiveness, a low tolerance for frustration, and generally, a great deal of inappropriate activity. All children show such traits some of the time, but for those diagnosed with ADHD, such behavior is common and interferes with their home and school functioning (American Academy of Pediatrics, 2000a; Nigg, 2001; Whalen et al., 2002).

What are the most common signs of ADHD? It is often difficult to distinguish between children who simply have a high level of activity and those with ADHD. Some of the most common symptoms include:

- persistent difficulty in finishing tasks, following instructions, and organizing work
- inability to watch an entire television program
- frequent interruption of others or excessive talking
- a tendency to jump into a task before hearing all the instructions
- difficulty in waiting or remaining seated
- fidgeting, squirming

Because there is no simple test to identify whether a child has ADHD, it is hard to know for sure how many children have the disorder. Most estimates put the number between 3% to 7% of those under the age of 18. Only a trained clinician can make an accurate diagnosis following an extensive evaluation of the child and supplemental interviews with parents and teachers (Sax & Kautz, 2003).

The treatment of children with ADHD has been a source of considerable controversy. Because it has been found that doses of Ritalin or Dexadrine (which, paradoxically, are stimulants) reduce activity levels in hyperactive children, many physicians routinely prescribe drug treatment (Volkow et al., 2001; Kaplan et al., 2004; HMHL, 2005; Schachar et al., 2008).

Although in many cases such drugs are effective in increasing attention span and compliance, in some cases the side effects (such as irritability, reduced appetite, and depression) are considerable, and the long-term health consequences of this treatment are unclear. It is also true that though the drugs often help scholastic performance in the short run, the long-term evidence for continuing

Least restrictive environment
The setting most similar to that of children without special needs

Mainstreaming An educational approach in which exceptional children are integrated as much as possible into the traditional educational system and are provided with a broad range of educational alternatives

improvement is mixed. In fact, some studies suggest that after a few years, children treated with drugs do not perform academically any better than untreated children with ADHD. Nonetheless the drugs are being prescribed with increasing frequency (see Figure 11-7; Marshall, 2000; Zernike & Petersen, 2001; Mayes & Rafalovich, 2007; Rose, 2008).

In addition to the use of drugs for treating ADHD, behavior therapy is often employed. With behavior therapy, parents and teachers are trained in techniques for improving behavior, primarily involving the use of rewards (such as verbal praise) for desired behavior. In addition, teachers can increase the structure of classroom activities and use other class management techniques to help children with ADHD, who have great difficulty with unstructured tasks. (Parents and teachers can receive support from the Children and Adults with Attention-Deficit/Hyperactivity Disorder organization at www.chadd.org.)

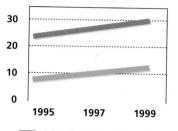

FIGURE 11-7
Overprescribing Drugs?

The number of children being given drugs for psychological disorders has increased significantly.
(*Source:* U.S. Surgeon General, 2000)

■ **Stimulants like Ritalin®**

■ **Antidepressants like Prozac®**

DEVELOPMENTAL DIVERSITY

Mainstreaming and Full Inclusion of Children With Special Needs

Are exceptional children best served by providing specialized services that separate them from their peers who do not have special needs, or do they benefit more from being integrated with their peers to the fullest extent?

If you had asked that question 3 decades ago, the answer would have been simple: Exceptional children were assumed to do best when removed from their regular classes and placed in a class taught by a special-needs teacher. Such classes often accommodated a hodgepodge of afflictions (emotional difficulties, severe reading problems, and physical disabilities such as multiple sclerosis). In addition, they kept students segregated from the regular educational process.

However, that changed when Congress passed Public Law 94-142, the Education for All Handicapped Children Act, in the mid-1970s. The intent of the law was to ensure that children with special needs received a full education in the **least restrictive environment**, the setting most similar to that of children without special needs (Handwerk, 2002; Swain, 2004).

In practice, the law has meant that children with special needs must be integrated into regular classrooms and regular activities to the greatest extent possible, as long as doing so is educationally beneficial. Children are to be isolated from the regular classroom only for subjects that are specifically affected by their exceptionality; for all other subjects, they are to be taught with nonexceptional children in regular classrooms. Of course, some children with severe handicaps still need a mostly or entirely separate education, depending on the extent of their condition. But the goal of the law is to integrate exceptional children and typical children to the fullest extent possible (Burns, 2003).

This educational approach to special education, designed to end the segregation of exceptional students as much as possible, has come to be called "mainstreaming." In **mainstreaming**, exceptional children are integrated as much as possible into the traditional educational system and are provided with a broad range of educational alternatives.

Mainstreaming was meant to provide a mechanism to equalize the opportunities available to all children. Its objective was to ensure that all persons, regardless of ability or disability, had—to the greatest extent possible— opportunities to choose their goals on the basis of a full education, enabling them to obtain a fair share of life's rewards (Burns, 2003).

To some extent, the benefits extolled by proponents of mainstreaming have been realized. However, classroom teachers must receive substantial support for

Mainstreaming of exceptional children into traditional educational systems has provided opportunities that were previously denied.

CAREERS in CHILD DEVELOPMENT

Valerie Patterson

Education: Western Washington University, Bellingham, Washington: B.A. in psychology; City University, Tacoma, Washington: M.A. in special education

Position: Special education teacher, Sajhalie Junior High School, Federal Way, Washington

Home: Sumner, Washington

Individualized attention and close communication with parents have helped create a welcoming environment for students with special needs at Sajhalie Junior High School in Federal Way, Washington, according to special education teacher Valerie Patterson. Patterson presides over a class of nine students, aged 12 to 16, with moderate to severe disabilities. In addition to herself, Patterson has four paraeducators who assist in giving the students essential one-on-one attention.

To better provide for the needs of each student, educators and parents conduct a comprehensive assessment before school begins, Patterson notes.

"Each year, we meet with the parents of the students and prepare an individualized education plan, or IEP, setting up specific goals and objectives for each student," she explains. "We then add in specific skills, such as dealing with money, time management, following schedules—anything that is relative to the real world.

"The IEP can also be changed as the child progresses," she adds, "and as the child becomes more independent, we go back to the IEP for the next step."

According to Patterson, parents are constantly kept in touch through the progress reports on IEP goals and daily communication logs.

"We have an open-door policy for parents—they can come in at any time," Patterson says. "Information goes home every day on the progress of their children. We try to talk with parents on what their child did over the weekend to help us prepare for the coming week."

Since Sajhalie Junior High operates under a full-inclusion policy, every attempt is made to integrate special-needs students with the general student body.

"The whole class goes to an integrated physical education class," Patterson points out. "In addition, some kids attend other classes, and everyone eats in the cafeteria together."

From an educator's perspective:

What are the advantages of mainstreaming and full inclusion? What challenges do they present? Are there situations in which you would not support mainstreaming and full inclusion?

mainstreaming to be effective. It is not easy to teach a class in which students' abilities vary greatly. Furthermore, providing the necessary support for children with special needs is expensive, and sometimes budgetary tensions exist that pit parents of children with special needs against parents of nonexceptional children (Jones, 2004; Waite, Bromfield, & McShane, 2005).

The benefits of mainstreaming have led some professionals to promote an alternative educational model known as full inclusion. **Full inclusion** is the integration of all students, even those with the most severe disabilities, into regular classes. In such a system, separate special education programs would cease to operate. Full inclusion is controversial, and it remains to be seen how widespread the practice will become (Jacobson, Foxx, & Mulick, 2005; Spence-Cochran & Pearl, 2006; Begeny & Martens, 2007).

REVIEW ↵ mydevelopmentlab

1. _____ impairment, which involves the loss of hearing or some aspect of hearing, affects 1 to 2% of school-age children.

   Answer: Auditory

2. _____ is the most common speech impairment.

   Answer: Stuttering

3. _____ _____, difficulties in the acquisition and use of listening, speaking, reading, writing, reasoning, or mathematical abilities, occur in approximately 2.6 million school-age children in the United States.

   Answer: Learning disabilities

To see more review questions, log on to MyDevelopmentLab.

CASE STUDY

The Case of... The Too-Tight Tights

Zoe Hallstrom had always dreamed of becoming a professional dancer. She had trained in ballet starting at age 5, but modern dance was her favorite. She loved the slinky black leotards and footless tights the girls wore. They looked so cool.

Now that Zoe was 9, her teacher felt she was ready for Modern Level I in the upcoming year. Her mom paid the deposit on the class, and Zoe went home dreaming she would be the next Twyla Tharp.

But when September came, she begged off her first class. The new leotard and tights remained in their packaging. Zoe had gained ten pounds over the summer and she hated the way she looked. "I'm fat!" Zoe wailed as she confronted herself in the mirror. She felt huge in comparison to some of the best dancers in the school, who she considered skinny.

To console herself, she went to see her best friend, Kara. The two girls split a box of donuts as they watched a DVD and played computer games. That night, both her parents were exhausted from a demanding work day so they ordered a large pizza with "the works." Zoe topped it off with a super-size soda. When she weighed herself a few days later, the scale showed she had added yet another pound over the previous week. Soon afterward, Zoe dropped her modern dance class.

1. How might Zoe's comparison of herself to the "skinny" girls at the ballet school affect how realistically she views her weight gain?

2. Why is Zoe's decision to drop modern dance a poor solution to her problem?

3. How can Zoe's parents help her make better eating choices?

4. What specific actions would you advise Zoe to take to improve her health, self-image, and general happiness?

◀ Looking Back

In what ways do children grow during the school years, and what factors influence their growth?

- The middle-childhood years are characterized by slow and steady growth, with children gaining, on average, about 5 to 7 pounds and 2 to 3 inches per year. Weight is redistributed as baby fat disappears.

- In part, growth is genetically determined, but societal factors such as affluence, dietary habits, nutrition, and disease also contribute significantly.

What are the nutritional needs of school-age children, and what are some causes and effects of improper nutrition?

- Adequate nutrition is important because of its contributions to growth, health, social and emotional functioning, and cognitive performance.

- Obesity is partially influenced by genetic factors but is also associated with children's failure to develop internal controls over eating, overindulgence in sedentary activities such as television viewing, and lack of physical exercise.

What sorts of health threats do school-age children face?

- The health of children in the school years is generally good, and few health problems arise. However, the incidence of some diseases that affect children, such as asthma, is increasing.

- School-age children can suffer from psychological disorders as well as physical ones, including childhood depression. Because childhood depression can lead to adult mood disorders or even to suicide, it should be taken seriously.

What are the characteristics of motor development during middle childhood, and what advantages do improved physical skills bring?

- During the middle-childhood years, great improvements occur in gross motor skills. Cultural expectations probably underlie most gross motor skill differences between boys and girls. Fine motor skills also develop rapidly.

- Physical competence is important for a number of reasons, some of which relate to self-esteem and confidence. Physical competence also brings social benefits during this period, especially for males.

What safety threats affect school-age children, and what can be done about them?

- Threats to safety in middle childhood relate mainly to children's increasing independence and mobility. Accidents account for most injuries, especially those related to automobiles, other vehicles (such as bicycles and skateboards), and sports. In most cases, the use of proper protective gear can greatly reduce injuries.

- An emerging area of potential danger for children is cyberspace. Unsupervised access to the Internet and the World Wide Web may permit children to explore offensive areas and come into contact with people who might take advantage of them.

What sorts of special needs manifest themselves in the middle-childhood years, and how can they be met?

- Visual, auditory, and speech impairments, as well as other learning disabilities, can lead to academic and social problems and must be handled with sensitivity and appropriate assistance.

- Learning disabilities, characterized by difficulties in the acquisition and use of listening, speaking, reading, writing, reasoning, or mathematical abilities, affect a small proportion of the population. Although the causes of learning disabilities are not well understood, some form of brain dysfunction seems to be involved.

- Children with attention-deficit/hyperactivity disorder exhibit another form of special need characterized by inattention, impulsiveness, failure to complete tasks, lack of organization, and excessive amounts of uncontrollable activity. Treatment of ADHD with drugs is controversial because of unwanted side effects and doubts about long-term consequences.

- Children with exceptionalities are generally placed today in the least restrictive environment, typically the regular classroom. Mainstreaming and full inclusion can benefit exceptional students by permitting them to focus on their strengths and gain useful skills of social interaction. ■

Epilogue

Physical development during middle childhood has been the focus of this chapter. Beginning with a look at how children's height and weight increases during this period, we then examined gross and fine motor development, considering the importance of physical competence. Finally, we discussed children with special needs in the areas of sensory and physical abilities.

Before leaving this chapter, return for a moment to the description of Suzanne McGuire's home run in the Prologue. Consider the following questions:

1. What kinds of physical abilities permitted Suzanne to play baseball? How had these abilities changed as she moved from the preschool period into middle childhood? What abilities does she probably still lack, given her developmental stage?

2. What advice would you have given Suzanne's parents regarding modeling and competition to encourage Suzanne to engage in physical exercise?

3. How can the ideas of fun and competition be reconciled in sports? Can organized competitive sports be fun for both physically competent and less competent individuals? Why or why not?

4. If children have special needs that reduce their physical abilities, should they be encouraged to participate in sports with other children, and if so, under what circumstances should that participation occur?

Key Terms and Concepts

asthma (p. 264)
visual impairment (p. 271)
auditory impairment (p. 271)
speech impairment (p. 271)

stuttering (p. 271)
learning disabilities (p. 271)
attention-deficit/hyperactivity
disorder (ADHD) (p. 272)

least restrictive environment
(p. 273)
mainstreaming (p. 273)
full inclusion (p. 274)

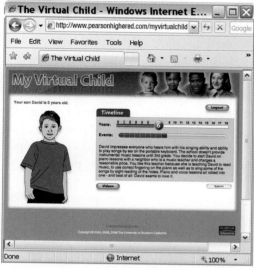

What decisions would you make while raising a child? What would the consequences of those decisions be?

Find out by logging onto **My Virtual Child** and raising your child from birth to 18 years.

Cognitive Development in Middle Childhood

PROLOGUE: LA-TOYA PANKEY AND *THE WITCHES*

There are few books in La-Toya Pankey's apartment on 102nd Street near Amsterdam Avenue in Manhattan, and even fewer places for an 8-year-old girl to steal away to read them.

There is no desk, no bookshelf, no reading lamp or even a bureau in La-Toya's small room, one of only two bedrooms in the apartment she shares with seven other people: her mother, her five sisters, and her infant brother.

At night, there is little light, save a couple of bare bulbs mounted on the peeling, beige walls. And there are few places to sit, except a lone, wooden chair at a battered kitchen table, which La-Toya must wait her turn to occupy.

Yet there was La-Toya, on a rainy evening earlier this month, leaning against that table and reading aloud, flawlessly, to her mother from the Roald Dahl classic *The Witches,* which she had borrowed from the makeshift library in her third-grade classroom. (Steinberg, 1997, p. B1)

► Looking Ahead

It was a significant moment for La-Toya. It marked a shift from the first-grade-level books that she had previously chosen to read to a far more challenging one, written at a grade level 2 years above her own.

Middle childhood is characterized by a procession of moments such as these as children's cognitive skills ascend to new heights. In this chapter, we consider the cognitive advances made by children during middle childhood. After beginning with Piaget's explanation for intellectual development, we turn to information-processing approaches. We

discuss the development of memory and how memory can be improved.

Next we turn to the important strides that occur in language development during the middle-childhood years. We focus on increases in linguistic skill and examine the consequences of bilingualism, the use of more than one language to communicate. We then discuss schooling and the ways in which society transmits knowledge, beliefs, values, and wisdom to a new generation. We consider such topics as how children explain their academic performance and how teachers' expectations can affect student achievement.

Finally, the chapter ends by focusing on intelligence. It highlights what developmentalists mean when they speak of intelligence, how intelligence is related to school success, and the ways in which children differ from one another in terms of intelligence.

In sum, after reading this chapter, you will be able to answer the following questions:

- *In what ways do children develop cognitively during the years of middle childhood?*
- *How does language develop during the middle-childhood period, and what special circumstances pertain to children for whom English is not the first language?*
- *What trends are affecting schooling worldwide and in the United States?*
- *What kinds of subjective factors contribute to academic outcomes?*
- *How can intelligence be measured, what are some issues in intelligence testing, and how are children who fall outside the normal range of intelligence educated?*

Cognitive and Language Development

Jared's parents were delighted when he came home from kindergarten one day and explained that he had learned why the sky was blue. He talked about the Earth's atmosphere—although he didn't pronounce the word correctly—and how tiny bits of moisture in the air reflected the sunlight. Although his explanation had rough edges (he couldn't quite grasp what the atmosphere was), he still had the general idea, and that, his parents felt, was quite an achievement for their 5-year-old.

Fast-forward 6 years. Jared, now age 11, had already spent an hour laboring over his evening's homework. After completing a two-page worksheet on multiplying and dividing fractions, he had begun work on his U.S. Constitution project. He was taking notes for his report, which would explain what political factions had been involved in the writing of the document and how the Constitution had been amended since its creation.

Jared is not alone in having made vast intellectual advances during middle childhood. During this period, children's cognitive abilities broaden, and they become increasingly able to understand and master complex skills. At the same time, though, their thinking is still not fully adultlike.

What are the advances, and the limitations, in thinking during childhood? Next we discuss several psychological perspectives that explain what goes on cognitively during middle childhood.

Piagetian Approaches to Cognitive Development

Let's return for a moment to Jean Piaget's view of the preschooler, which we considered in Chapter 9. From Piaget's perspective, the preschooler thinks *preoperationally.* This type of thinking is largely egocentric, and preoperational children lack the ability to use *operations*—organized, formal, logical mental processes.

The Rise of Concrete Operational Thought According to Piaget, all this changes during the concrete operational period, which coincides with the school years. The **concrete operational stage**, which occurs between 7 and 12 years of age, is characterized by the active and appropriate use of logic.

Concrete operational thought involves applying *logical thinking* to concrete problems. For instance, when children in the concrete operational stage are confronted with a conservation problem (such as determining whether the amount of liquid poured from one container to another container of a different shape stays the same), they use cognitive and logical processes to answer, and are no longer influenced solely by appearance. They are able to reason correctly that because none of the liquid has been lost, the amount stays the same. Because they are less egocentric, they can take multiple aspects of a situation into account, an ability known as **decentering**. Jared, the sixth grader described earlier, was using his decentering skills to consider the views of the different factions involved in creating the U.S. Constitution.

The shift from preoperational thought to concrete operational thought does not happen overnight, of course. During the 2 years before children move firmly into the concrete operational period, they shift back and forth between preoperational and concrete operational thinking. For instance, they typically pass through a period when they can answer conservation problems correctly but can't articulate why they did so. When asked to explain the reasoning behind their answers, they may respond with an unenlightening, "Because."

However, once concrete operational thinking is fully engaged, children show several cognitive advances representative of their logical thinking. For instance, they attain the concept of *reversibility,* which is the notion that processes transforming a stimulus can be reversed, returning it to its original form. Grasping reversibility permits children to understand that a ball of clay that has been squeezed into a long, snakelike rope can be returned to its original state. More abstractly, it allows school-age children to understand that if 3 plus 5 equals 8, then 5 plus 3 also equals 8—and later during this period of development, that 8 minus 3 equals 5.

Concrete operational thinking also permits children to understand such concepts as the relationship between time, speed, and distance, comprehending, for example, that an increase in speed can compensate for greater distance in a journey. For instance, consider the problem shown in Figure 12-1, in which two cars start and finish at the same points in the same amount of time but travel different routes. Children who are just entering the concrete operational period reason that the cars are traveling at the

Cognitive development makes substantial advances in middle childhood.

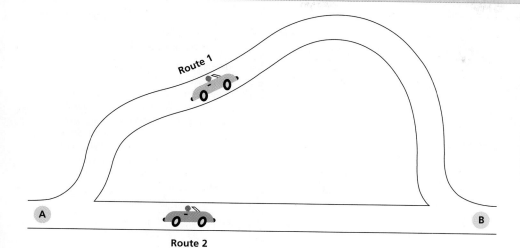

Route 1

A

Route 2

B

FIGURE 12-1 Sample Problem in Concrete Operational Thinking

After being told that the two cars traveling Routes 1 and 2 start and end their journeys in the same amount of time, children who are just entering the concrete operational period still reason that the cars are traveling at the same speed. Later, however, they reach the correct conclusion that the car traveling the longer route must be moving at a higher speed if it starts and ends its journey at the same time as the car traveling the shorter route.

same speed. However, between the ages of 8 and 10, children begin to draw the right conclusion: that the car traveling the longer route must be moving faster if it arrives at the finish point at the same time as the car traveling the shorter route.

Despite the advances that occur during the concrete operational stage, children still experience one critical limitation in their thinking. They remain tied to concrete, physical reality. Furthermore, they are unable to understand truly abstract or hypothetical questions or ones that involve formal logic.

Piaget in Perspective: Piaget Was Right; Piaget Was Wrong As we learned in our prior consideration of Piaget's views in Chapters 6 and 9, researchers following in Piaget's footsteps have found much to cheer about, as well as much to criticize.

Piaget was a virtuoso observer of children, and his many books contain pages of brilliant, careful observations of children at work and play. Furthermore, his theories have powerful educational implications, and many schools employ principles derived from his views to guide the nature and presentation of instructional materials (Flavell, 1996; Siegler & Ellis, 1996; Brainerd, 2003).

In some ways, then, Piaget's approach was quite successful in describing cognitive development. At the same time, though, critics have raised justifiable objections to his approach. As we have noted before, many researchers argue that Piaget underestimated children's capabilities, in part because of the limited nature of the miniexperiments he conducted. When a broader array of experimental tasks is used, children show less consistency within stages than Piaget would predict (Siegler, 1994; Bjorklund, 1997b).

Furthermore, Piaget seems to have misjudged the age at which children's cognitive abilities emerge. As might be expected from our earlier discussions of Piaget's stages,

increasing evidence suggests that children's capabilities emerge earlier than Piaget envisioned. Some children show evidence of a form of concrete operational thinking before the age of 7, the time at which Piaget suggested these abilities first appear.

The opposite phenomenon also seems to occur: Cross-cultural research implies that some children never leave the preoperational stage, failing to master conservation and to develop concrete operations. For example, pioneering work by Patricia Greenfield (1966) found that among the Wolof children in Senegal, a West African country, only half of children ages 10 to 13 understood conservation of liquid. Studies in other non-Western areas such as the jungles of New Guinea and Brazil and remote villages in Australia confirmed her findings: When a broad sample of children are studied—children who have had very different experiences from the Western European children on whom Piaget based his theory—not everyone reaches the concrete operational stage (Dasen, 1977). It appears, then, that Piaget's claims that his stages provided a universal description of cognitive development were exaggerated.

Still, we cannot dismiss the Piagetian approach. Although some early cross-cultural research seemed to imply that children in certain cultures never left the preoperational stage, failing to master conservation and to develop concrete operations, more recent research suggests otherwise. For instance, with proper training in conservation, children in non-Western cultures who do not conserve can readily learn to do so. For instance, in one study, urban Australian children—who develop concrete operations on the same timetable as Piaget suggested—were compared to rural Aborigine children, who typically do not demonstrate an understanding of conservation at the age of 14 (Dasen, Ngini, & Lavallée, 1979). When the rural Aborigine children were given training, they showed conservation skills similar to their urban counterparts, although with a time lag of around 3 years (see Figure 12-2).

Memory The process by which information is initially recorded, stored, and retrieved

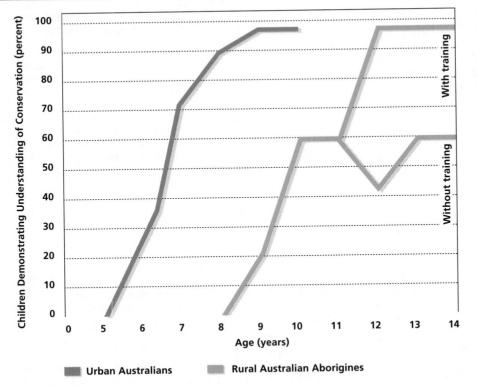

FIGURE 12-2 Understanding of Conservation Among Urban and Aboriginal Australian Children

Rural Australian Aborigine children trail their urban counterparts in the development of their understanding of conservation. With training, they later catch up, but without training, around half of 14-year-old Aborigines do not understand conservation. What types of teaching programs might an educator provide to help the development of conservation?

■ Urban Australians   ■ Rural Australian Aborigines

Furthermore, when children are interviewed by researchers from their own culture, who know the language and customs of the culture well and who use reasoning tasks that are related to domains important to the culture, the children are considerably more likely to display concrete operational thinking (Nyiti, 1982; Jahoda, 1983). Ultimately, such research suggests that Piaget was right when he argued that concrete operations were universally achieved during middle childhood. Although school-age children in some cultures may differ from Westerners in the demonstration of certain cognitive skills, the most probable explanation of the difference is that the non-Western children have had different sorts of experiences from those that permit children in Western societies to perform well on Piagetian measures of conservation and concrete operations. The progress of cognitive development, then, cannot be understood without looking at the nature of a child's culture (Beilin & Pufall, 1992; Mishra, 1997; Lau, Lee, & Chiu, 2004).

Information Processing in Middle Childhood

It is a significant achievement for first-graders to learn basic math tasks, such as addition and subtraction of single-digit numbers, as well as the spelling of simple words such as *dog* and *run*. But by the time they reach the sixth grade, children are able to work with fractions and decimals, like the fractions worksheet that Jared, the boy in the example at the start of this section, completed for his sixth-grade homework. They can also spell more complex words such as *exhibit* and *residence.*

According to *information-processing approaches,* children become increasingly sophisticated in their handling of information. Like computers, they can process more data as the size of their memories increases and the "programs" they use to process information become increasingly sophisticated (Kail, 2003; Zelazo et al., 2003).

Memory As we saw in Chapter 6, **memory** in the information-processing model is the ability to encode, store, and retrieve information. For a child to remember a piece of information, the three processes must all function properly. Through *encoding,* the child initially records the information in a form usable to memory. Children who were never taught that 5 plus 6 equals 11 or who didn't pay attention when they were exposed to this fact will never be able to recall it. They never encoded the information in the first place.

But mere exposure to a fact is not enough; the information also has to be *stored.* In our example, the information that 5 plus 6 equals 11 must be placed and maintained in the memory system. Finally, proper functioning of memory requires that material that is stored in memory must be *retrieved.* Through retrieval, material in memory storage is located, brought into awareness, and used.

According to the *three-system approach to memory* that has dominated our understanding of memory, there are three different memory storage systems or stages that describe how information is processed in order for it to be recalled (Atkinson & Shiffrin, 1968, 1971). *Sensory memory* refers to the initial, momentary storage of information that lasts only an instant. Sensory memory records an exact replica of the stimulus. In the second stage, *short-term memory* (also known as *working memory*), information is stored for 15 to 25 seconds according to its meaning. Finally, the third type of storage system is *long-term memory,* in which information is stored relatively permanently, although it may be difficult to retrieve.

During middle childhood, short-term memory capacity improves significantly. For instance, children are increasingly able to hear a string of digits ("1-5-6-3-4") and then repeat the string in reverse order ("4-3-6-5-1"). At the start of the preschool period, they can remember and reverse only about two digits; by the beginning of adolescence, they can perform the task with as many as six digits (Cowan, Saults, & Elliot, 2002; Towse & Cowan, 2005).

Memory capacity may shed light on another issue in cognitive development. Some developmental psychologists suggest that the difficulty children experience in solving conservation problems during the preschool period may stem from memory limitations (Siegler & Richards, 1982). They argue that young children simply may not be able to recall all the necessary pieces of information that enter into the correct solution of conservation problems.

Metamemory, an understanding about the processes that underlie memory, also emerges and improves during middle childhood. By the time they enter first grade and their theory of mind becomes more sophisticated, children have a general notion of what memory is, and they are able to understand that some people have better memories than others (Cherney, 2003; Ghetti et al., 2008).

School-age children's understanding of memory becomes more sophisticated as they grow older and increasingly engage in *control strategies*—conscious, intentionally used tactics to improve cognitive processing. For instance, school-age children are aware that rehearsal, the repetition of information, is a useful strategy for improving memory, and they increasingly employ it over the course of middle childhood. Similarly, they progressively make more effort to organize material into coherent patterns, a strategy that permits them to recall it better. For instance, when faced with remembering a list including cups, knives, forks, and plates, older school-age children are more likely to group the items into coherent patterns—cups and plates, forks and knives—than are children just entering the school-age years (Sang, Miao, & Deng, 2002).

Similarly, children in middle childhood increasingly use *mnemonics* (pronounced *nee-mah-niks*), which are formal techniques for organizing information in a way that makes it more likely to be remembered. For instance, they may learn that the spaces on the music staff spell the word *FACE* or learn the rhyme "Thirty days hath September, April, June, and November . . ." to try to recall the number of days in each month (Bellezza, 2000; Carney & Levin, 2003; Sprenger, 2007).

Improving Memory Can children be trained to be more effective in the use of control strategies? Definitely. School-age children can be taught to use particular mnemonic strategies, although such teaching is not a simple matter. For instance, children need to know not only how to use a memory strategy but also when and where to use it most effectively.

Take, for example, an innovative technique called the *key word strategy*, which can help students learn the vocabulary of a foreign language, the capitals of the states, or other information in which two sets of words or labels are paired. In the keyword strategy, one word is paired with another that sounds like it (Wyra, Lawson, & Hungi, 2007).

Memory requires three steps: encoding, storing, and retrieving material.

For instance, in learning foreign language vocabulary, a foreign word is paired with a common English word that has a similar sound. The English word is the keyword. Thus, to learn the Spanish word for duck (*pato,* pronounced *pot-o*), the keyword might be "pot"; for the Spanish word for horse (*caballo,* pronounced *cob-eye-yo*), the keyword might be "eye." Once the keyword is chosen, children then form a mental image of the two words interacting with one another. For instance, a student might use an image of a duck taking a bath in a pot to remember the word *pato,* or a horse with bulging eyes to remember the word *caballo.*

Other memory strategies include *rehearsal,* consistent repetition of information that children wish to remember; *organization,* which is placing material into categories (such as coastal states or types of food); and *cognitive elaboration,* in which mental images are linked with information that someone wants to recall. For example, in trying to remember where Cape Cod is on a map of Massachusetts, an 8-year-old might think of a muscle-bound Pilgrim to link the image of the shape of Cape Cod (which looks something like a flexing, curved arm) with its location. Whatever memory strategies children use, they use such strategies more often and more effectively as they get older.

Vygotsky's Approach to Cognitive Development and Classroom Instruction

Recall from Chapter 9 that Russian developmentalist Lev Vygotsky proposed that cognitive advances occur through exposure to information within a child's *zone of*

Students working in cooperative groups benefit from the insights of others.

proximal development (ZPD). The ZPD is the level at which a child can almost, but not quite, understand or perform a task unassisted.

Vygotsky's approach has been particularly influential in the development of several classroom practices based on the proposition that children should actively participate in their educational experiences. In this approach, classrooms are seen as places where children should have the opportunity to experiment and try out new activities (Vygotsky, 1926/1997; Gredler & Shields, 2008).

According to Vygotsky, education should focus on activities that involve interaction with others. Both child–adult and child–child interactions can provide the potential for cognitive growth. The nature of the interactions must be carefully structured to fall within each individual child's zone of proximal development.

Several current and noteworthy educational innovations have borrowed heavily from Vygotsky's work. For example, *cooperative learning*, in which children work together in groups to achieve a common goal, incorporates several aspects of Vygotsky's theory. Students working in cooperative groups benefit from the insights of others, and if they get off on the wrong track, they may be brought back to the correct course by others in their group. On the other hand, not every peer is equally helpful to members of a cooperative learning group: As Vygotsky's approach would imply, individual children benefit most when at least some of the other members of the group are more competent at the task and can act as experts (Slavin, 1995; DeLisi, 2006).

Reciprocal teaching is another educational practice that reflects Vygotsky's approach to cognitive

From an educator's perspective:

How might a teacher use Vygotsky's approach to teach 10-year-olds about colonial America?

development. *Reciprocal teaching* is a technique to teach reading comprehension strategies. Students are taught to skim the content of a passage, raise questions about its central point, summarize the passage, and finally predict what will happen next. A key to this technique is its reciprocal nature and its emphasis on giving students a chance to take on the role of teacher. In the beginning, teachers lead students through the comprehension strategies. Gradually, students progress through their zones of proximal development, taking more and more control over use of the strategies, until the students are able to take on a teaching role. The method has shown impressive success in raising reading comprehension levels, particularly for students experiencing reading difficulties (Greenway, 2002; Takala, 2006).

Language Development: What Words Mean

If you listen to what school-age children say to one another, their speech, at least at first hearing, sounds not too different from that of adults. However, the apparent similarity is deceiving. The linguistic sophistication of children, particularly at the start of the school-age period—still requires refinement to reach adult levels of expertise.

Mastering the Mechanics of Language Vocabulary continues to increase during the school years at a fairly rapid clip. For instance, the average 6-year-old has a vocabulary of from 8,000 to 14,000 words, whereas the vocabulary grows by another 5,000 words between the ages of 9 and 11.

School-age children's mastery of grammar also improves. For instance, the use of the passive voice is rare during the early school-age years (as in "The dog was walked by Jon," compared with the active-voice "Jon walked the dog"). Six- and 7-year-olds only infrequently use conditional sentences, such as "If Sarah will set the table, I will wash the dishes." However, over the course of middle childhood, the use of both passive voice and conditional sentences increases. In addition, children's understanding of *syntax*, the rules that indicate how words and phrases can be combined to form sentences, grows during middle childhood.

By the time they reach first grade, most children pronounce words quite accurately. However, certain *phonemes*—units of sound—remain troublesome. For instance, the ability to pronounce *j, v, th,* and *zh* sounds develops later than the ability to pronounce other phonemes.

School-age children also may have difficulty decoding sentences when the meaning depends on *intonation*, or tone of voice. For example, consider the sentence, "George gave a book to David and he gave one to Bill." If the word "he" is emphasized, the meaning is "George gave a book to David and David gave a different book to Bill." But if the intonation emphasizes the word "and," then the meaning changes to "George gave a book to David and George also gave a book

Metalinguistic awareness
An understanding of one's own
use of language

Bilingualism The ability to
speak two languages

to Bill." School-age children cannot easily sort out subtleties such as these (Wells, Peppé, & Goulandris, 2004).

In addition to language skills, conversational skills also develop during middle childhood. Children become more competent in their use of *pragmatics,* the rules governing the use of language to communicate in a given social setting.

For example, although children are aware of the rules of conversational turn-taking at the start of the early childhood period, their use of these rules is sometimes primitive. Consider the following conversation between 6-year-olds Yonnie and Max:

YONNIE: My dad drives a FedEx truck.
MAX: My sister's name is Molly.
YONNIE: He gets up really early in the morning.
MAX: She wet her bed last night.

Later, however, conversations show more give-and-take, with the second child actually responding to the comments of the first. For instance, this conversation between 11-year-olds Mia and Josh reflects a more sophisticated mastery of pragmatics:

MIA: I don't know what to get Claire for her birthday.
JOSH: I'm getting her earrings.
MIA: She already has a lot of jewelry.
JOSH: I don't think she has that much.

Metalinguistic Awareness One of the most significant developments in middle childhood is children's increasing understanding of their own use of language or **metalinguistic awareness.** By the time children are 5 or 6 years of age, they understand that language is governed by a set of rules. Whereas in the early years they learn and comprehend these rules implicitly, during middle childhood, children come to understand them more explicitly (Benelli et al., 2006; Saiegh-Haddad, 2007).

Metalinguistic awareness helps children achieve comprehension when information is fuzzy or incomplete. For instance, when preschoolers are given ambiguous or unclear information, such as directions for how to play a complicated game, they rarely ask for clarification, and they tend to blame themselves if they do not understand. By the time they reach the age of 7 or 8, children realize that miscommunication may be due to factors attributable not only to themselves but also to the person communicating with them. Consequently, school-age children are more likely to ask for clarification of information that is unclear to them (Apperly & Robinson, 2002).

How Language Promotes Self-Control The growing sophistication of their language helps school-age children control their behavior. For instance, in one experiment, children were told that they could have one marshmallow treat if they chose to eat one immediately but two treats if they

The increase in metalinguistic skills during middle childhood allows children to enter into the give-and-take of conversation more successfully.

waited. Most of the children, who ranged in age from 4 to 8, chose to wait, but the strategies they used while waiting differed significantly.

The 4-year-olds often chose to look at the marshmallows while waiting, a strategy that was not terribly effective. In contrast, 6- and 8-year-olds used language to help them overcome temptation, although in different ways. The 6-year-olds spoke and sang to themselves, reminding themselves that if they waited, they would get more treats in the end. The 8-year-olds focused on aspects of the marshmallows that were not related to taste, such as their appearance, which helped them to wait.

In short, children used "self-talk" to help regulate their own behavior. Furthermore, the effectiveness of their self-control grew as their linguistic capabilities increased.

Bilingualism: Speaking in Many Tongues

For picture day at New York's P.S. 217, a neighborhood elementary school in Brooklyn, the notice to parents was translated into 5 languages. That was a nice gesture, but insufficient: More than 40 percent of the children are immigrants whose families speak any one of 26 languages, ranging from Armenian to Urdu. (Leslie, 1991, p. 56)

From the smallest towns to the biggest cities, the voices with which children speak are changing. Nearly one in five people in the United States speaks a language other than English at home, a percentage that is growing. **Bilingualism**—the use of more than one language—is growing increasingly common (Shin & Bruno, 2003; Graddol, 2004; see Figure 12-3).

Number of Speakers
(by county)

- 0
- 1 – 99
- 100 – 499
- 500 – 999
- 1,000 – 4,999
- 5,000 – 19,999
- 20,000 – 49,999
- 50,000 – 99,999
- 100,000 – 499,999
- 500,000 – 999,999
- 1,000,000 – 3,500,000

0   838 Miles

Alaska

0   738 Miles

0   82 Miles

Hawaii

FIGURE 12-3 The Top 10 Languages Other Than English Spoken in the United States

These figures show the number of U.S. residents over the age of 5 who speak a language other than English at home. With increases in the number and variety of languages spoken in the United States, what types of approaches might an educator use to meet the needs of bilingual students?
(*Source:* Modern Language Association, www.mla.org/census_map,2005. Based on data from U.S. Census Bureau, 2000)

Children who enter school with little or no English proficiency must learn both the standard curriculum and the language in which that curriculum is taught. One approach to educating non-English speakers is *bilingual education,* in which children are initially taught in their native language, while at the same time learning English.

With bilingual instruction, students are able to develop a strong foundation in basic subject areas using their native language. The ultimate goal of bilingual education programs is to gradually increase students' English proficiency while maintaining or improving skills in their native language.

Bilingual education, in which children are initially taught in their native language while at the same time learning English, is one approach to educating non-English speakers.

An alternative approach is to immerse students in English as quickly as possible, teaching solely in that language, and providing only minimal instruction in a student's native language. To proponents of this approach, initially teaching students in a language other than English hinders students' efforts to learn English and slows their integration into society. Consequently, the emphasis is on English instruction.

The drawback to immersion approaches is that it can make it more difficult for students to learn new skills if those skills are being taught in a second language. For example, consider the difficulty of a student who must learn fractions in second language to which she has been exposed for only a few months (Pearson, 2007).

Both bilingual and immersion approaches have been highly politicized, with some politicians arguing in favor of "English-only" laws, while others urge school systems to respect the challenges faced by nonnative speakers by offering some instruction in their native language. Still, the psychological research is clear in suggesting that knowing more than one language offers several cognitive advantages. Because they have a wider range of linguistic possibilities to choose from as they assess a situation, speakers of two languages show greater cognitive flexibility. They can solve problems with greater creativity and versatility. Furthermore, learning in one's native tongue is associated with higher self-esteem in minority students (Barker, Giles, & Noels, 2001; Lesaux & Siegel, 2003; Chen & Bond, 2007).

Bilingual students often have greater metalinguistic awareness, understanding the rules of language more explicitly, and show great cognitive sophistication. They even may score higher on tests of intelligence, according to some research. Furthermore, brain scans comparing bilingual individuals with those who speak only one language find differences suggesting different types of brain activation (Swanson, Saez, & Gerber, 2004; Carlson & Meltzoff, 2008; Kovelman, Baker, & Petitto, 2008).

Finally, because many linguists contend that universal processes underlie language acquisition, as we noted in Chapter 5, instruction in a native language may enhance instruction in a second language. In fact, many educators believe that second-language learning should be a regular part of elementary schooling for all children (Kecskes & Papp, 2000; McCardle & Hoff, 2006).

REVIEW ↵ mydevelopmentlab

1. Piaget assumed that school-age children are in the _____ _____ period.

   Answer: concrete operational

2. _____, an understanding about the processes that underlie memory, emerges and improves during middle childhood.

   Answer: Metamemory

3. Children who are _____ often have a greater metalinguistic awareness, and can understand the rules of language more explicitly.

   Answer: bilingual

To see more review questions, log on to MyDevelopmentLab.

Schooling: The Three Rs (and More) of Middle Childhood

As the eyes of the six other children in his reading group turned to him, Glenn shifted uneasily in his chair. Reading had never come easily to him, and he always felt anxious when it was his turn to read aloud. But as his teacher nodded in encouragement, he plunged in, hesitantly at first, then gaining momentum as he read the story about a mother's first day on a new job. He found that he could read the passage quite nicely, and he felt a surge of happiness and pride at his accomplishment. When he was done, he broke into a broad smile as his teacher said simply, "Well done, Glenn."

Small moments such as these, repeated over and over, make—or break—a child's educational experience. Schooling marks a time when society formally attempts to transfer to new generations its accumulated body of knowledge, beliefs, values, and wisdom. The success with which this transfer is managed determines, in a very real sense, the future fortunes of the world.

Schooling Around the World: Who Gets Educated?

In the United States, as in most developed countries, a primary school education is both a universal right and a legal requirement. Virtually all children are provided with a free education through the 12th grade.

Children in other parts of the world are not so fortunate. More than 160 million of the world's children do not have access to even a primary school education. An additional 100 million children do not progress beyond a level comparable to our elementary school education, and close to a billion individuals (two-thirds of them women) are illiterate throughout their lives (International Literacy Institute, 2001; see Figure 12-4).

In almost all developing countries, fewer females than males receive formal education, a discrepancy found at every level of schooling. Even in developed countries, women lag behind men in their exposure to science and technology. These differences reflect widespread and deeply held cultural and parental biases that favor males over females. Educational levels in the United States are more nearly equal between men and women, and especially in the early years of school, boys and girls share equal access to educational opportunities.

What Makes Children Ready for School?

Many parents have a hard time deciding exactly when to enroll their children in school for the first time. Do children who are younger than most of the other children in their grade suffer as a result of the age difference? According to traditional wisdom, the answer is yes. Because younger children are assumed to be slightly less advanced developmentally than their peers, it has been assumed that such children would be at a competitive disadvantage. In some cases, teachers recommended that students delay entry into kindergarten in order to cope better academically and emotionally (Noel & Newman, 2008).

However, a massive study conducted by developmental psychologist Frederick Morrison contradicts the traditional view. He found that children who are among the youngest in first grade progress at the same rate as the oldest. Although they were slightly behind older first-graders in reading, the difference was negligible. It was also clear that parents who chose to hold their children back in kindergarten, thereby ensuring that they would be among the oldest in first grade and after, were not doing their children a favor. These older children did no better than their younger classmates (Morrison, Smith, & Dow-Ehrensberger, 1995; Vecchiotti, 2003; Morrison, Bachman, & Connor, 2005).

Other research has even identified some delayed negative reaction to delayed entry. For example, one longitudinal study examined adolescents whose entrance into kindergarten was delayed by a year. Even though many seemed to show no ill effects from the delay during elementary school, during adolescence a surprising number of these children had emotional and behavioral problems (Byrd, Weitzman, & Auinger, 1997; Stipek, 2002).

In short, delaying children's entry into school does not necessarily provide an advantage and in some cases may actually be harmful. Ultimately, age per se is not a critical indicator of when children should begin school. Instead, the start of formal schooling is more reasonably tied to overall developmental readiness, the product of a complex combination of several factors.

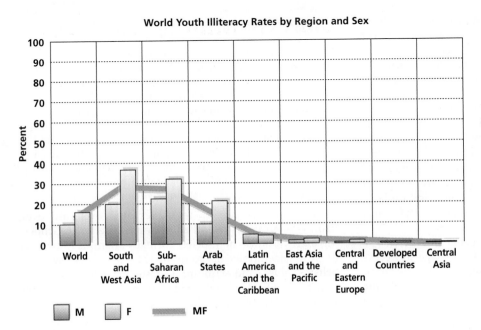

World Youth Illiteracy Rates by Region and Sex

M   F   MF

FIGURE 12-4
Plague of Illiteracy

Illiteracy remains a significant problem worldwide, particularly for women. Across the world, close to a billion people are illiterate throughout their lives.
(*Source:* UNESCO, 2006)

Becoming an Informed Consumer of Development

Creating an Atmosphere That Promotes School Success

What makes children succeed in school? Although there are many factors, some of which we discuss in the next chapter, there are several practical steps that can be taken to maximize children's chances of success. These are a few suggestions:

- *Promote a "literacy environment."* Parents should read to their children and familiarize them with books and reading. Adults should provide reading models so that children see that reading is an important activity in the lives of the adults with whom they interact.

- *Talk to children.* Discuss events in the news, talk about their friends, and share hobbies. Getting children to think about and discuss the world around them is one of the best preparations for school.

- *Provide a place for children to work.* This can be a desk, a corner of a table, or an area of a room. What's important is that it be a separate, designated area.

- *Encourage children's problem-solving skills.* To solve a problem, they should learn to (a) identify their goal, what they know, and what they don't know; (b) design and carry out a strategy; and (c) evaluate their result.

Reading: Learning to Decode the Meaning Behind Words

The efforts of La-Toya Pankey (described in the chapter Prologue) to improve her reading are no small matter, for there is no other task that is more fundamental to schooling than learning to read. Reading involves a significant number of skills, from low-level cognitive skills (the identification of single letters and associating letters with sounds) to higher level skills (matching written words with meanings located in long-term memory and using context and background knowledge to determine the meaning of a sentence).

Reading Stages   Development of reading skill generally occurs in several broad and frequently overlapping stages (Chall, 1992; see Table 12-1). In *Stage 0*, which lasts from birth to the start of first grade, children learn the essential prerequisites for reading, including identification of the letters in the alphabet, sometimes writing their names, and reading a few very familiar words (such as their own names or *stop* on a stop sign).

Stage 1 brings the first real type of reading, but it largely involves *phonological recoding* skill. At this stage, which usually encompasses the first and second grade, children can sound out words by blending the letters together. Children also complete the job of learning the names of letters and the sounds that go with them.

In *Stage 2,* typically around second and third grades, children learn to read aloud with fluency. However, they do not attach much meaning to the words, because the effort involved in simply sounding out words is usually so great that relatively few cognitive resources are left over to process the meaning of the words. La-Toya's flawless reading of *The Witches* shows that she has reached at least this stage of reading development. The next period, *Stage 3,* extends from fourth to eighth grades. Reading becomes a means to an end—in particular, a way to learn. Whereas earlier reading was an accomplishment in and of itself, by this point children use reading to learn about the world. However, even at this age, understanding gained from reading is not complete. For instance, one limitation children have at this stage is that they are able to comprehend information only when it is presented from a single perspective.

In the final period, *Stage 4,* children are able to read and process information that reflects multiple points of view. This ability, which begins during the transition into high school, permits children to develop a far more sophisticated understanding of material. This explains why great works of

TABLE 12-1	Development of Reading Skills	
Stage	Age	Key Characteristics
0	Birth to start of first grade	Learns prerequisites for reading, such as identification of the letters
1	First and second grades	Learns phonological recoding skills; starts reading
2	Second and third grades	Reads aloud fluently, but without much meaning
3	Fourth to eighth grade	Uses reading as a means for learning
4	Eighth grade and beyond	Understands reading in terms of reflecting multiple points of view

(*Source:* Based on Chall, 1979)

literature are not read at an earlier stage of education. It is not so much that younger children do not have the vocabulary to understand such works (although this is partially true); it is that they lack the ability to understand the multiple points of view that sophisticated literature invariably presents.

How Should We Teach Reading? Educators have long been engaged in an ongoing debate regarding the most effective means of teaching reading. At the heart of this debate is a disagreement about the nature of the mechanisms by which information is processed during reading. According to proponents of *code-based approaches to reading,* reading should be taught by presenting the basic skills that underlie reading. Code-based approaches emphasize the components of reading, such as the sounds of letters and their combinations—phonics—and how letters and sounds are combined to make words. They suggest that reading consists of processing the individual components of words, combining them into words, and then using the words to derive the meaning of written sentences and passages (Vellutino, 1991; Jimenez & Guzman, 2003; Rego, 2006).

In contrast, some educators argue that reading is taught most successfully by using a whole-language approach. In *whole-language approaches to reading,* reading is viewed as a natural process, similar to the acquisition of oral language. According to this view, children should learn to read through exposure to complete writing—sentences, stories, poems, lists, charts, and other examples of actual uses of writing. Instead of being taught to sound out words, children are encouraged to make guesses about the meaning of words based on the context in which they appear. Through such a trial-and-error approach, children come to learn whole words and phrases at a time, gradually becoming proficient readers (Shaw, 2003; Sousa, 2005; Donat, 2006).

A growing body of data, based on careful research, suggests that code-based approaches to reading instruction is superior to whole-language approaches. For example, one study found that a group of children tutored in phonics for a year not only improved substantially in their reading, compared to a group of good readers, but that the neural pathways involved in reading became closer to that of good readers (see Figure 12-5; Shaywitz et al., 2004).

Based on research such as this, the National Reading Panel and National Research Council now support reading instruction using code-based approaches. Their position signals that an end may be near to the debate over which approach to teaching reading is most effective (Rayner et al., 2002).

Educational Trends: Beyond the Three *R*s

Schooling in the 21st century is very different from what it was as recently as a decade ago. In fact, U.S. schools are experiencing a return to the educational fundamentals embodied in the traditional three *R*s (reading, writing, and arithmetic). The

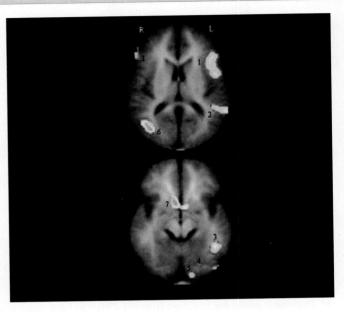

FIGURE 12-5

Students with reading difficulties who were tutored in phonics showed improved reading proficiency and increased activity in brain areas related to skilled reading.
(*Source:* Shaywitz et al., 2004)

focus on the fundamentals marks a departure from educational trends of prior decades when the emphasis was on their social well-being and on allowing students to choose study topics on the basis of their interests instead of following a set curriculum (Schemo, 2003; Yinger, 2004).

Elementary school classrooms today also stress individual accountability, both for teachers and for students. Teachers are more likely to be held responsible for their students' learning, and both students and teachers are more likely to be required to take tests, developed at the state or national level, to assess their competence. As we discuss in the *From Research to Practice* box, pressures on students to succeed have grown (McDonnell, 2004).

As the U.S. population has become more diverse, elementary schools have also paid increased attention to issues involving student diversity and multiculturalism. And with good reason: Cultural, as well as language, differences affect students socially and educationally. The demographic makeup of students in the United States is undergoing an extraordinary shift. For instance, the proportion of Hispanics will in all likelihood more than double in the next 50 years. Moreover, by the year 2050, non-Hispanic Caucasians will likely become a minority of the total population of the United States U.S. Bureau of Census, 2001; see Figure 12-6). Consequently, educators have been increasingly serious about multicultural concerns. As we see next, the goals for educating students from different cultures have changed significantly over the years and are still being debated today (Brock et al., 2007).

FROM RESEARCH to PRACTICE
Making the Grade: Are We Pushing Too Hard?

Brian and Tiffany Aske of Oakland, California, desperately want their daughter, Ashlyn, to succeed in first grade. . . . When they started Ashlyn in kindergarten last year, they had no reason to worry. A bright child with twinkling eyes, Ashlyn was eager to learn, and the neighborhood school had a great reputation. But by November, Ashlyn, then 5, wasn't measuring up. No matter how many times she was tested, she couldn't read the 130-word list her teacher gave her: words like "our," "house" and "there." She became so exhausted and distraught over homework—including a weekly essay on "my favorite animal" or "my family vacation"—that she would put her head down on the dining-room table and sob. "She would tell me, 'I can't write a story, Mama. I just can't do it,'" said Tiffany. (Tyre, 2006, p. 34)

The No Child Left Behind Act of 2002 aimed to ensure that all children would be able to read by the time they reached the third grade. The law requires school principals to meet this goal or risk losing their jobs and their school funding. While the intentions of this law may have been good, an unforeseen outcome in some cases has been so much focus on reading that other important topics such as social studies, music, and activities such as recess are excluded from the school day. Worse, some schools' reading programs have become so intense that a number of children are simply burning out (Abril & Gault, 2006; Paige, 2006; Sunderman, 2008).

Once, kindergarten was a time for finger painting, story time, and free play; now, children are increasingly beginning reading lessons at that level. Frequent testing to ensure that children are meeting short-term and long-term literacy goals has become more commonplace. The experience of failure—and of competitive pressure to be at the top of the class—is hitting children at younger ages than before.

One trend that has many parents and educators concerned is an increase in the amount of homework assigned. A study conducted by the Institute for Social Research at University of Michigan determined that children are spending a lot more time on academics today than they did 20 years ago. The time spent in school for children ages 6 to 8 has increased from about 5 hours to about 7 hours per weekday. Time spent studying and reading has increased over that time period, while play time, sports, and other outdoor activities have decreased (Juster, Ono, & Stafford, 2004).

But is the extra homework worth the cost? While time spent on homework is associated with greater academic achievement in secondary school, the relationship gets less strong for the lower grades; below grade 5, the relationship disappears. Experts explain this finding in terms of younger children's inability to tune out distractions, as well as their yet undeveloped study skills. Moreover, research with older children shows that more homework is not necessarily better. In fact, some research indicates that the benefits of homework may reach a plateau beyond which additional time spent on homework produces no further benefits (Cooper & Valentine, 2001; Trautwein et al., 2006).

Some educational experts fear that the social and emotional development of children are taking a back seat to literacy education, and that the pressure, the testing, the accelerated programs, and the time spent in school—as well as in after-school programs and on homework—are robbing kids of opportunities to just be kids. Some parents, such as the Askes, are worried that their children are just becoming frustrated and discouraged with learning (Kohn, 2006).

Ultimately, the Askes found their own solution to the pressure that Ashlyn was facing: They moved to a different state where Ashlyn could attend a less-intense public school that offered more more flexibility and less pressure.

- Why might it be the case that students who spend a lot of time doing homework tend not to have better academic success than students who spend a moderate amount of time?

- Do you agree with the Askes that the challenges Ashlyn was facing were excessive? Why do you think more parents aren't expressing the same concerns?

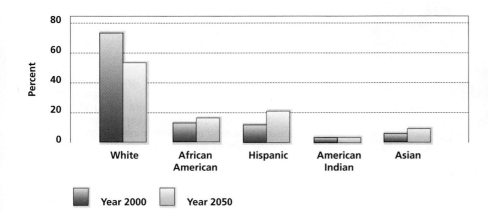

FIGURE 12-6 The Changing Face of America

Current projections of the population makeup of the United States show that by the year 2050, the proportion of non-Hispanic Whites will decline as the proportion of minority group members increases. What will be some of the impacts on social workers as the result of changing demographics?
(*Source:* U.S. Bureau of the Census, 2001)

Multicultural education
Education in which the goal is to help students from minority cultures develop competence in the culture of the majority group while maintaining positive group identities that build on their original cultures

Cultural assimilation model
The view of American society as a "melting pot" in which all cultures are amalgamated

Pluralistic society model
The concept that American society is made up of diverse, coequal cultures that should preserve their individual features

Bicultural identity
The maintenance of one's original cultural identity while becoming integrated into the majority culture

DEVELOPMENTAL DIVERSITY

Multicultural Education

Since the earliest period of formal education in the United States, classrooms have been populated by individuals from a broad range of backgrounds and experiences. Yet it is only relatively recently that variations in student backgrounds have been viewed as one of the major challenges—and opportunities—that educators face.

In fact, the diversity of background and experience in the classroom relates to a fundamental objective of education, which is to provide a formal mechanism to transmit the information a society deems important. As the famous anthropologist Margaret Mead (1942, p. 633) once said, "In its broadest sense, education is the cultural process, the way in which each newborn human infant, born with a potentiality for learning greater than that of any other mammal, is transformed into a full member of a specific human society, sharing with the other members of a specific human culture."

Culture, then, can be thought of as a set of behaviors, beliefs, values, and expectations shared by members of a particular society. But although culture is often thought of in a relatively broad context (as in "Western culture" or "Asian culture"), it is also possible to focus on particular *subcultural* groups within a larger, more encompassing culture. For example, we can consider particular racial, ethnic, religious, socioeconomic, or even gender groups in the United States as manifesting characteristics of a subculture.

Membership in a cultural or subcultural group might be of only passing interest to educators were it not for the fact that students' cultural backgrounds have a substantial impact on the way that they—and their peers—are educated. In fact, in recent years, a considerable amount of thought has gone into establishing multicultural education, a form of education in which

Pupils and teachers exposed to a diverse group can gain a better understanding of the world and greater sensitivity to the values and needs of others. What are some ways of developing greater sensitivity in the classroom?

the goal is to help minority students develop competence in the culture of the majority group while maintaining positive group identities that build on their original cultures (Nieto, 2005).

Cultural Assimilation or Pluralistic Society? Multicultural education developed in part as a reaction to a cultural assimilation model, in which the goal of education is to assimilate individual cultural identities into a unique, unified American culture. In practical terms, this meant, for example, that non-English-speaking students were discouraged from speaking their native tongues and were totally immersed in English.

In the early 1970s, however, educators and members of minority groups began to suggest that the cultural assimilation model ought to be replaced by a pluralistic society model. According to this conception, American society is made up of diverse, coequal cultural groups that should preserve their individual cultural features.

The pluralistic society model grew in part from the belief that teachers, by emphasizing the dominant culture and discouraging students who were nonnative speakers from using their native tongues, had the effect of devaluing minority subcultural heritages and lowering those students' self-esteem. Instructional materials, such as readers and history lessons, inevitably feature culture-specific events and understandings, children who never saw examples representing their own cultural heritage might never be exposed to important aspects of their backgrounds. For example, English-language texts rarely present some of the great themes that appear throughout Spanish literature and history (such as the search for the Fountain of Youth and the Don Juan legend). Hispanic students immersed in such texts might never come to understand important components of their own heritage.

Ultimately, educators began to argue that the presence of students representing diverse cultures enriched and broadened the educational experience of all students. Pupils and teachers exposed to people from different backgrounds could better understand the world and gain greater sensitivity to the values and needs of others (Gurin, Nagda, & Lopez, 2004; Zirkel & Cantor, 2004).

Fostering a Bicultural Identity. Most educators agree that the pluralistic society model is the most valid one for schooling and that minority children should be encouraged to develop a bicultural identity. They recommend that school systems encourage children to maintain their original cultural identities while they integrate themselves into the dominant culture. This view suggests that an individual can live as a member of two cultures, with two cultural identities, without having to choose one over the other (Lu, 2001; Oyserman et al., 2003; Vyas, 2004).

The best way to achieve this goal of biculturalism is not clear. Consider, for example, children who enter a school speaking only Spanish. The traditional "melting-pot" technique would be to immerse the children in classes taught in English while providing a crash course in English-language instruction (and little else) until the children demonstrate a suitable level of proficiency. Unfortunately, the traditional approach has a considerable drawback: Until the children master English, they fall further and further behind their peers who entered school already knowing English.

More contemporary approaches emphasize a bicultural strategy in which children are encouraged to maintain simultaneous membership in more than one culture. In the case of

Spanish-speaking children, for example, instruction begins in the child's native language and shifts as rapidly as possible to include English. At the same time, the school conducts a program of multicultural education for all students, in which teachers present material on the cultural backgrounds and traditions of all the students in the school. Such instruction is designed to enhance the self-image of speakers from both majority and minority cultures (Bracey, Bamaca, & Umana-Taylor, 2004).

Although most educational experts favor bicultural approaches, the general public does not always agree. For instance, the national "English-only" movement mentioned earlier has as one of its goals the prohibition of school instruction in any language other than English. Whether such a perspective will prevail remains to be seen.

Should Schools Teach Emotional Intelligence?

In many elementary schools, the hottest topic in the curriculum has little to do with the traditional three *R*s. Instead, a significant educational trend for educators in many elementary schools throughout the United States is the use of techniques to increase students' **emotional intelligence**, the set of skills that underlie the accurate assessment, evaluation, expression, and regulation of emotions (Mayer, Salovey, & Caruso, 2000; Mayer, 2001; Hastings, 2004; Fogarty, 2008).

Psychologist Daniel Goleman (2005) argues that emotional literacy should be a standard part of the school curriculum. He points to several programs that succeed in teaching students to manage their emotions more effectively. For instance, in one program, children are provided with lessons in empathy, self-awareness, and social skills. In another, children are taught about caring and friendship as early as first grade through exposure to stories (Fasano & Pellitteri, 2006).

Programs meant to increase emotional intelligence have not been met with universal acceptance. Critics suggest that the nurturance of emotional intelligence is best left to students' families and that schools ought to concentrate on more traditional curriculum matters. Others suggest that adding emotional intelligence to an already crowded curriculum may reduce time spent on academics. Finally, some critics argue that there is no well-specified set of criteria for what constitutes emotional intelligence, and consequently it is difficult to develop appropriate, effective curriculum materials (Roberts, Zeidner, & Matthews, 2001).

Still, most people consider emotional intelligence worthy of nurturance. It is clear that emotional intelligence is quite different from the traditional conceptions of intelligence that we consider in the next section of the chapter. The goal of emotional intelligence training is to produce people who are not only cognitively sophisticated but also able to manage their emotions effectively (Matthews, Zeidner, & Roberts, 2002; Brackett & Katulak, 2007; Ulutas & Ömeroglu, 2007).

Expectation Effects: How Teachers' Expectancies Influence Their Students

Suppose you were an elementary school teacher and were told that certain children in your class were expected to bloom intellectually in the coming year. Would you treat them differently from the children who were not so designated?

You probably would treat them differently, according to the results of a classic but controversial study. Teachers do, in fact, treat children for whom they have expectations of improvement differently from those for whom they have no such expectations (Rosenthal & Jacobson, 1968). In the experiment, elementary school teachers were told at the beginning of a new school year that based on test results, five children in their classes would be likely to "bloom" in the upcoming year. In reality, however, the information was bogus: The names of the children had been picked at random, although the teachers didn't know that. At the end of the year, the children completed an intelligence test that was identical to one taken a year earlier. The results showed that clear differences existed in the intellectual growth of the so-called bloomers, compared with that of the other members of their classes. Those randomly designated as likely to make significant gains did, in fact, improve more than the other children.

When the findings of the experiment, reported in a book titled *Pygmalion in the Classroom,* were published, they caused an immediate stir among educators—and among the public at large. The reason for this furor was the implication of the results: If merely holding high expectations is sufficient to bring about gains in achievement, wouldn't holding low expectations lead to slowed achievement? And because teachers may sometimes hold low expectations for children from lower socioeconomic and minority backgrounds, did this mean that children from such backgrounds were destined to show low achievement throughout their educational careers?

Although the original experiment has been criticized on methodological and statistical grounds (Wineburg, 1987), enough subsequent evidence has been amassed to make it clear that the expectations of teachers are communicated to their students and can in fact bring about the expected performance. The phenomenon has come to be called the **teacher expectancy effect**—the cycle of behavior in which a teacher transmits an expectation about a

The expectations of parents and teachers have a significant effect on student performance.

> **From an educator's perspective:**
> Should one goal of instruction be to foster cultural assimilation for children from other cultures? Why or why not?

Homeschooling, a growing educational practice, has both advantages and drawbacks.

child and thereby actually brings about the expected behavior (Rosenthal, 2002; Rubie-Davies, 2007; Tenenbaum & Ruck, 2007; Anderson-Clark, Green, & Henley, 2008; see Figure 12-7).

The teacher expectancy effect can be viewed as a special case of a broader concept known as the *self-fulfilling prophecy,* in which a person's expectation is capable of bringing about an outcome. For instance, physicians have long known that providing patients with placebos (pills with no active ingredients) can sometimes "cure" them simply because the patients expect the medicine to work.

In the case of teacher expectancy effects, the basic explanation seems to be that teachers, after forming an initial expectation about a child's ability—often inappropriately based on such factors as previous school records, physical appearance, gender, or even race—transmit their expectation to the child through a complex series of verbal and nonverbal cues. These communicated expectations in turn indicate to the child what behavior is appropriate, and the child behaves accordingly (Carpenter, Flowers, & Mertens, 2004; Gewertz, 2005; Trouilloud et al., 2006; McKown & Weinstein, 2008).

Homeschooling: Living Rooms as Classrooms

At 9 A.M. on a Wednesday, Damon Buchanan, 9 years old, sits on the couch going through one of his morning rituals: reading the horoscopes in the newspaper. In the kitchen his brothers, Jacob, age 7, and Logan, age 4, are performing one of their "experiments": dropping action figures and Fisher-Price toys into glasses of water, then freezing them. Another day of school has begun.

For students like the Buchanan brothers, there is no distinction between their living room and classroom, because they are among the close to 1 million students who are homeschooled. *Homeschooling* is a major educational phenomenon in which students are taught, by their parents, in their own homes.

There are a number of reasons why parents may choose to school their children at home. Some parents feel their children will thrive with the one-to-one attention that homeschooling can bring, whereas they might get lost in a larger public school. Other parents are dissatisfied with the nature of instruction and teachers in their local public schools and feel that they can do a better job teaching their children. And some parents engage in homeschooling for religious reasons, wishing to impart a particular religious ideology (and avoid exposing their children to aspects of the popular culture and values with which they disagree) that would be impossible in a public school (Bauman, 2001; Dennis, 2004; Isenberg, 2007).

Homeschooling clearly works, in the sense that children who have been homeschooled generally do as well on standardized tests as students who have been educated traditionally. In addition, their acceptance rate into college appears to be no different from that of traditionally schooled children (Lattibeaudiere, 2000; Lauricella, 2001; Lines, 2001).

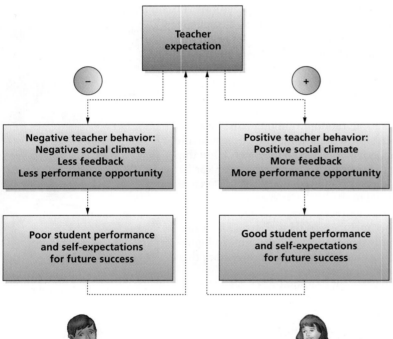

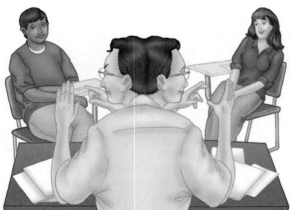

FIGURE 12-7 Teacher Expectations and Student Performance

Teachers' expectations about their students—positive or negative—can actually bring about positive or negative performance from their students. How does this relate to what we know about self-esteem?

However, the apparent academic success of children schooled at home does not mean that homeschooling, per se, is effective, because parents who choose to homeschool their children may be more affluent or have the kind of well-structured family situation in which children would succeed no matter what kind of schooling they had. In contrast, parents in dysfunctional and disorganized families are unlikely to have the motivation or interest to homeschool their children. For children from families like these, the demands and structure of a traditional school may be a good thing.

Critics of homeschooling argue that it has considerable drawbacks. For example, the social interaction involving groups of children that is inherent in classrooms in traditional schools is largely missing for homeschooled children. Learning in an at-home environment, while perhaps strengthening family ties, hardly provides an environment that reflects the diversity of U.S. society. Furthermore, even the best-equipped home is unlikely to have sophisticated science and technology that is available at many schools. Finally, most parents do not have the preparation of well-trained teachers, and their teaching methods may be unsophisticated. Although parents may be successful in teaching subject areas in which their child is already interested, they may have more difficulty teaching subjects that their child seeks to avoid (Cai, Reeve, & Robinson, 2002; Lois, 2006).

Because homeschooling is relatively new, few controlled experiments have been conducted examining its effectiveness. More research needs to be done to determine how and when homeschooling is an effective means to educate children.

REVIEW ↵ mydevelopmentlab

1. In Stage _____ reading, which typically occurs around second and third grade, children learn to read aloud with fluency.

   Answer: 2

2. In _____-_____ approaches to reading, reading is taught by presenting the basic skills that underlie reading.

   Answer: code-based

3. _____ _____ is a form of education in which the goal is to help minority students develop competence in the culture of the majority group while maintaining positive group identities that build on their original cultures

   Answer: Multicultural education

To see more review questions, log on to MyDevelopmentLab.

Intelligence: Determining Individual Strengths

Why should you tell the truth? How far is Los Angeles from New York? A table is made of wood; a window of _____.

As 10-year-old Hyacinth sat hunched over her desk, trying to answer a long series of questions like these, she tried to guess the point of the test she was taking in her fifth-grade classroom. Clearly, the test didn't cover material that her teacher, Ms. White-Johnston, had talked about in class.

"What number comes next in this series: 1, 3, 7, 15, 31, _____?"

As she continued to work her way through the questions, she gave up trying to guess the rationale for the test. She'd leave that to her teacher, she sighed to herself. Rather than attempt to figure out what it all meant, she simply tried to do her best on the individual test items.

Hyacinth was taking an intelligence test. She might be surprised to learn that she was not alone in questioning the meaning and import of the items on the test. Intelligence test items are painstakingly prepared, and intelligence tests show a strong relationship to success in school (for reasons we soon discuss). Many developmentalists, however, would admit to harboring their own doubts as to whether questions such as those on Hyacinth's test are entirely appropriate to the task of assessing intelligence.

Understanding just what is meant by the concept of intelligence has proven to be a major challenge for researchers interested in delineating what separates intelligent from unintelligent behavior. Although nonexperts have their own conceptions of intelligence (one survey found, for instance, that laypersons believe that intelligence consists of three components: problem-solving ability, verbal ability, and social competence), it has been more difficult for experts to concur (Sternberg et al., 1981). Still, a general definition of intelligence is possible: **Intelligence** is the capacity to understand the world, think with rationality, and use resources effectively when faced with challenges (Wechsler, 1975).

Part of the difficulty in defining intelligence stems from the many—and sometimes unsatisfactory—paths that have been followed over the years in the quest to distinguish more intelligent people from less intelligent ones. To understand how researchers

French educator Alfred Binet originated the intelligence test.

Mental age The typical intelligence level found for people of a given chronological age

Chronological (physical) age A person's age according to the calendar

Intelligence quotient (IQ) A score that expresses the ratio between a person's mental and chronological ages

have approached the task of assessing intelligence by devising *intelligence tests,* we need to consider some of the historical milestones in the area of intelligence.

Intelligence Benchmarks: Differentiating the Intelligent From the Unintelligent

The Paris school system was faced with a problem at the turn of the 20th century: A significant number of children were not benefiting from regular instruction. Unfortunately, these children—many of whom we would now call mentally retarded—were generally not identified early enough to shift them to special classes. The French minister of instruction approached psychologist Alfred Binet with this problem and asked him to devise a technique for the early identification of students who might benefit from instruction outside the regular classroom.

Binet's Test Binet tackled his task in a thoroughly practical manner. His years of observing school-age children suggested to him that previous efforts to distinguish intelligent from unintelligent students—some of which were based on reaction time or keenness of sight—were off the mark. Instead, he launched a trial-and-error process in which items and tasks were administered to students who had been previously identified by teachers as being either "bright" or "dull." Tasks that the bright students completed correctly and the dull students failed to complete correctly were retained for the test. Tasks that did not discriminate between the two groups were discarded. The result of this process was a test that reliably distinguished students who had previously been identified as fast or slow learners.

Binet's pioneering efforts in intelligence testing left several important legacies. The first was his pragmatic approach to the construction of intelligence tests. Binet did not have theoretical preconceptions about what intelligence was. Instead, he used a trial-and-error approach to psychological measurement that continues to serve as the predominant approach to test construction today. His definition of intelligence as *that which his test measured* has been adopted by many modern researchers, and it is particularly popular among test developers, who respect the widespread utility of intelligence tests but wish to avoid arguments about the underlying nature of intelligence.

Binet's legacy extends to his linking intelligence and school success. Binet's procedure for constructing an intelligence test ensured that intelligence—defined as performance on the test—and school success would be virtually one and the same. Thus, Binet's intelligence test, and today's tests that follow in Binet's footsteps, have become reasonable indicators of the degree to which students possess attributes that contribute to successful school performance. On the other hand, they do not provide useful information regarding

a vast number of other attributes that are largely unrelated to academic proficiency, such as social skills or personality characteristics.

Finally, Binet developed a procedure of linking each intelligence test score with a **mental age**, the age of the children taking the test who, on average, achieved that score. For example, if a 6-year-old girl received a score of 30 on the test, and this was the average score received by 10-year-olds, her mental age would be considered 10 years. Similarly, a 15-year-old boy who scored a 90 on the test—thereby matching the mean score for 15-year-olds—would be assigned a mental age of 15 years (Wasserman & Tulsky, 2005).

Although assigning a mental age to students provides an indication of whether they are performing at the same level as their peers, it does not permit adequate comparisons among students of different **chronological (physical) ages.** By using mental age alone, for instance, it would be assumed that a 15-year-old responding with a mental age of 17 years would be as bright as a 6-year-old responding with a mental age of 8 years, when actually the 6-year-old would be showing a much greater *relative* degree of brightness.

A solution to this problem comes in the form of the **intelligence quotient (IQ)**, a score that takes into account a student's mental *and* chronological age. The traditional method of calculating an IQ score uses the following formula, in which MA stands for mental age and CA stands for chronological age:

$$\text{IQ score} = \frac{\text{MA}}{\text{CA}} \times 100$$

As a bit of trial-and-error with this formula demonstrates, people whose mental age (MA) is equal to their chronological age (CA) will always have an IQ of 100. Furthermore, if the chronological age exceeds the mental age—implying below-average intelligence—the score will be below 100; and if the chronological age is lower than the mental age—suggesting above-average intelligence—the score will be above 100. Using this formula, we can return to our earlier example of a 15-year-old who scores at a 17-year-old mental age. This student's IQ is 17/15 × 100, or 113. In comparison, the IQ of a 6-year-old scoring at a mental age of 8 is 8/6 × 100, or 133—a higher IQ score than the 15-year-old's.

Although the basic principles behind the calculation of an IQ score still hold, scores today are calculated in a more mathematically sophisticated manner and are known as *deviation IQ scores.* The average deviation IQ score remains set at 100, but tests are now devised so that the degree of deviation from this score permits the calculation of the proportion of people who have similar scores. For instance, approximately two-thirds of all people fall within 15 points of the average score of 100, achieving scores between 85 and 115. As scores rise or fall beyond this range, the percentage of people in the same score category drops significantly (see Figure 12-8).

Measuring IQ: Present-Day Approaches to Intelligence

Since the time of Binet, tests of intelligence have become increasingly accurate measures of IQ. Most of them can still trace their roots to his original work in one way or another. For example, one of the most widely used tests, the **Stanford–Binet Intelligence Scale, Fifth Edition (SB5)**, began as an American revision of Binet's original test. The test consists of a series of items that vary according to the age of the person being tested. For instance, young children are asked to answer questions about everyday activities or to copy complex figures. Older people are asked to explain proverbs, solve analogies, and describe similarities between groups of words. The test is administered orally, and test-takers are given progressively more difficult problems until they are unable to proceed.

The **Wechsler Intelligence Scale for Children, Fourth Edition (WISC-IV)** is another widely used intelligence test. The test (which stems from its adult counterpart, the *Wechsler Adult Intelligence Scale*) provides separate measures of verbal and performance (or nonverbal) skills, as well as a total score. As you can see from the sample items in Figure 12-9, the verbal tasks are traditional word problems testing skills such as understanding a passage, whereas typical nonverbal tasks are copying a complex design, arranging pictures in a logical order, and assembling objects. The separate portions of the test allow for easier identification of any specific problems a test taker may have. For example, significantly higher scores on the performance part of the test than on the verbal part may indicate difficulties in linguistic development (Zhu & Weiss, 2005).

The **Kaufman Assessment Battery for Children, Second Edition (KABC-II)** takes a different approach from the Stanford–Binet and WISC-IV. In it, children are tested on their ability to integrate different kinds of stimuli simultaneously and to use step-by-step thinking. A special virtue of the KABC-II is its flexibility. It allows the person giving the test to use alternative wording or gestures, or even to pose questions in a different language, in order to maximize a test taker's performance. This capability of the KABC-II makes testing more valid and equitable for children to whom English is a second language (Kaufman et al., 2005).

What do the IQ scores derived from IQ tests mean? For most children, IQ scores are reasonably good predictors of their school performance. That's not surprising, given that the initial impetus for the development of intelligence tests was to identify children who were having difficulties in school (Sternberg & Grigorenko, 2002).

But when it comes to performance outside of academic spheres, the story is different. For instance, although people with higher IQ scores are apt to finish more years of schooling, once this is statistically controlled for, IQ scores are not closely related to income and later success in life.

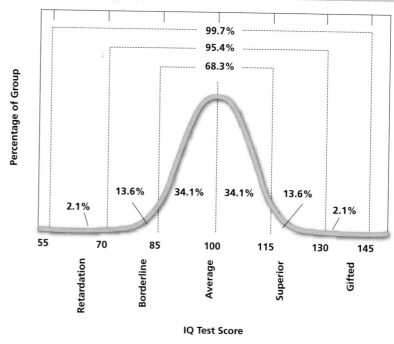

FIGURE 12-8 IQ Scores

The most common and average IQ score is 100, with 68.3% of all people falling within 15 points of 100. About 95% of the population has scores that are within 30 points above or below 100; fewer than 3% score below 55 or above 145.

A number of different tests are used to measure intelligence.

Fluid intelligence
Intelligence that reflects information processing capabilities, reasoning, and memory

Crystallized intelligence
The accumulation of information, skills, and strategies that people have learned through experience and that they can apply in problem-solving situations

Triarchic theory of intelligence
The belief that intelligence consists of three aspects of information processing: the componential element, the experiential element, and the contextual element

Furthermore, IQ scores are frequently inaccurate when it comes to predicting a particular individual's future success. For example, two people with different IQ scores may both finish their bachelor's degrees at the same college, and the person with a lower IQ might end up with a higher income and a more successful career. Because of these difficulties with traditional IQ scores, researchers have turned to alternative approaches to intelligence (McClelland, 1993).

From an educator's perspective:
Does Howard Gardner's theory of multiple intelligences suggest that classroom instruction should be modified from an emphasis on the traditional three *R*s of reading, writing, and arithmetic?

What IQ Tests Don't Tell: Alternative Conceptions of Intelligence

The intelligence tests used most frequently in school settings today are based on the idea that intelligence is a single factor, a unitary mental ability. This one main attribute has commonly been called *g* (Spearman, 1927; Lubinski, 2004). The *g* factor is assumed to underlie performance on every aspect of intelligence, and it is the *g* factor that intelligence tests presumably measure.

However, many theorists dispute the notion that intelligence is one-dimensional. Some developmentalists suggest that, in fact two kinds of intelligence exist: fluid intelligence and crystallized intelligence. **Fluid intelligence** reflects information-processing capabilities, reasoning, and memory. For example, a student asked to group a series of letters according to some criterion or to remember a set of numbers would be using fluid intelligence.

In contrast, **crystallized intelligence** is the accumulation of information, skills, and strategies that people have learned through experience that they can apply in problem-solving situations. A student would likely be relying on crystallized intelligence to solve a puzzle or deduce the solution to a mystery, in which it was necessary to draw on past experience (Alfonso, Flanagan, & Radwan, 2005; McGrew, 2005).

Other theorists divide intelligence into an even greater number of parts. For example, psychologist Howard Gardner suggests that we have eight distinct intelligences, each relatively independent (see Figure 12-10). Gardner suggests that these separate intelligences operate not in isolation, but together, depending on the type of activity in which we are engaged (Gardner, 2000, 2003; Chen & Gardner, 2005; Gardner & Moran, 2006).

The Russian psychologist Lev Vygotsky, whose approach to cognitive development we first discussed in Chapter 2, had a very different approach to intelligence. He suggested that to assess intelligence, we should look not only at those cognitive processes that are fully developed but also at those that are currently being developed. To do this, Vygotsky contended that assessment tasks should involve cooperative interaction between the individual who is being assessed and the person who is doing the assessment—a process called *dynamic assessment.* In short, intelligence is seen as being reflected not only in how children can perform on their own but also in terms of how well they perform when helped by adults (Vygotsky, 1927/1976; Lohman, 2005).

Taking yet another approach, psychologist Robert Sternberg (1990, 2003a) suggests that intelligence is best thought of in terms of information processing. In this view, the way in which people store material in memory and later use it to solve intellectual tasks provides the most precise conception of intelligence. Rather than focusing on the various subcomponents that make up the *structure* of intelligence, information-processing approaches examine the *processes* that underlie intelligent behavior (Floyd, 2005).

Studies of the nature and speed of problem-solving processes show that people with higher intelligence levels differ from others not only in the number of problems they ultimately are able to solve but also in their method of solving the problems. People with high IQ scores spend more time on the initial stages of problem solving, retrieving relevant information from memory. In contrast, those who score lower on traditional IQ tests tend to spend less time on the initial stages, instead skipping ahead and making less informed guesses. The processes used in solving problems, then, may reflect important differences in intelligence (Sternberg, 2005).

Sternberg's work on information-processing approaches to intelligence has led him to develop the **triarchic theory of intelligence**. According to this model, intelligence consists of three aspects of information processing: the componential element, the experiential element, and the contextual element. The componential aspect of intelligence reflects how efficiently people can process and analyze information. Efficiency in these areas allows people to infer relationships among different parts of a problem, solve the problem, and then evaluate their solution. People who are strong on the componential element score highest on traditional tests of intelligence (Sternberg, 2005).

The *experiential* element is the insightful component of intelligence. People who have a strong experiential element can easily compare new material with what they already know and can combine and relate facts that they already know in novel and creative ways. Finally, the *contextual* element of intelligence concerns practical intelligence, or ways of dealing with the demands of the everyday environment.

In Sternberg's view, people vary in the degree to which each of these three elements is present. Our level of success at any given task reflects the match between the task and our own specific pattern of strength on the three components of intelligence (Sternberg, 2003b, 2008).

NAME	GOAL OF ITEM	EXAMPLE
VERBAL SCALE		
Information	Assess general information	How many nickels make a dime?
Comprehension	Assess understanding and evaluation of social norms and past experience	What is the advantage of keeping money in the bank?
Arithmetic	Assess math reasoning through verbal problems	If two buttons cost 15 cents, what will be the cost of a dozen buttons?
Similarities	Test understanding of how objects or concepts are alike, tapping abstract reasoning	In what way are an hour and a week alike?
PERFORMANCE SCALE		
Digit symbol	Assess speed of learning	Match symbols to numbers using key. 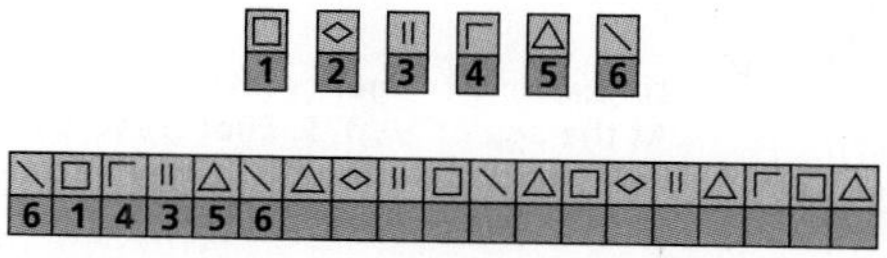
Picture completion	Visual memory and attention	Identify what is missing. 
Object assembly	Test understanding of relationship of parts to wholes	Put pieces together to form a whole. 

FIGURE 12-9 Measuring Intelligence

The Wechsler Intelligence Scale for Children (WISC-IV) includes items such as these. What do such items cover? What do they miss?

1. *Musical intelligence* (skills in tasks involving music). Case example:
When he was 3, Yehudi Menuhin was smuggled into the San Francisco Orchestra concerts by his parents. The sound of Louis Persinger's violin so entranced the youngster that he insisted on a violin for his birthday and Louis Persinger as his teacher. He got both. By the time he was 10 years old, Menuhin was an international performer.

2. *Bodily kinesthetic intelligence* (skills in using the whole body or various portions of it in the solution of problems or in the construction of products or displays, exemplified by dancers, athletes, actors, and surgeons). Case example:
Fifteen-year-old Babe Ruth played third base. During one game, his team's pitcher was doing poorly and Babe loudly criticized him from third base. Brother Mathias, the coach, called out, "Ruth, if you know so much about it, *you* pitch!" Babe was surprised and embarrassed because he had never pitched before, but Brother Mathias insisted. Ruth said later that at the very moment he took the pitcher's mound, he *knew* he was supposed to be a pitcher.

3. *Logical mathematical intelligence* (skills in problem solving and scientific thinking). Case example:
Barbara McClintock won the Nobel Prize in medicine for her work in microbiology. She describes one of her breakthroughs, which came after thinking about a problem for half an hour: "Suddenly I jumped and ran back to the [corn]field. At the top of the field, [the others were still at the bottom] I shouted, 'Eureka, I have it!'"

4. *Linguistic intelligence* (skills involved in the production and use of language). Case example:
At the age of 10, T. S. Eliot created a magazine called *Fireside*, to which he was the sole contributor. In a 3-day period during his winter vacation, he created eight complete issues.

5. *Spatial intelligence* (skills involving spatial configurations, such as those used by artists and architects). Case example:
Navigation around the Caroline Islands...is accomplished without instruments....During the actual trip, the navigator must envision mentally a reference island as it passes under a particular star and from that he computes the number of segments completed, the proportion of the trip remaining, and any corrections in heading.

6. *Interpersonal intelligence* (skills in interacting with others, such as sensitivity to the moods, temperaments, motivations, and intentions of others). Case example:
When Anne Sullivan began instructing the deaf and blind Helen Keller, her task was one that had eluded others for years. Yet, just 2 weeks after beginning her work with Keller, Sullivan achieved a great success. In her words, "My heart is singing with joy this morning. A miracle has happened! The wild little creature of 2 weeks ago has been transformed into a gentle child."

7. *Intrapersonal intelligence* (knowledge of the internal aspects of oneself; access to one's own feelings and emotions). Case example:
In her essay "A Sketch of the Past," Virginia Woolf displays deep insight into her own inner life through these lines, describing her reaction to several specific memories from her childhood that still, in adulthood, shock her: "Though I still have the peculiarity that I receive these sudden shocks, they are now always welcome; after the first surprise, I always feel instantly that they are particularly valuable. And so I go on to suppose that the shock-receiving capacity is what makes me a writer."

8. *Naturalist intelligence* (ability to identify and classify patterns in nature). Case example:
In prehistoric periods, hunter-gatherers required naturalist intelligence in order to identify what types of plants were edible.

FIGURE 12-10 Gardner's Eight Intelligences

Howard Gardner has theorized that there are eight distinct intelligences, each relatively independent of one another. How do you fit into this categorization?

(*Source:* Adapted from Walters & Gardner, 1986)

Group Differences in IQ

A jontry is an example of a
(a) rulpow
(b) flink
(c) spudge
(d) bakwoe

If you were to find an item composed of nonsense words such as this on an intelligence test, your immediate—and quite legitimate—reaction would likely be to complain. How could a test that purports to measure intelligence include test items that incorporate meaningless terminology?

Yet for some people, the items actually used on traditional intelligence tests might appear equally nonsensical. To take a hypothetical example, suppose children living in rural areas were asked details about subways, while those living in urban areas were asked about the mating practices of sheep. In both cases, we would expect that the previous experiences of test takers would have a substantial effect on their ability to answer the questions. And if questions about such matters were included on an IQ test, the test could rightly be viewed as a measure of prior experience rather than of intelligence.

Although the questions on traditional IQ tests are not so obviously dependent on test takers' prior experiences, our examples, cultural background, and experiences do have the potential to affect intelligence-test scores. In fact, many educators suggest that traditional measures of intelligence are subtly biased in favor of White, upper- and middle-class students, and against groups with different cultural experiences (Ortiz & Dynda, 2005).

Explaining Racial Differences in IQ

The issue of how cultural background and experience influence IQ-test performance has led to considerable debate among researchers. The debate has been fueled by the finding that IQ scores of certain racial groups are consistently lower, on average, than the IQ scores of other groups. For example, the mean score of African Americans tends to be about 15 IQ points lower than the mean score of Whites—although the measured difference varies a great deal depending on the particular IQ test employed (Fish, 2001; Maller, 2003).

The question that emerges from such differences, of course, is whether they reflect actual differences in intelligence or, instead, are caused by bias in the intelligence tests themselves in favor of majority groups and against minorities. For example, if Whites perform better on an IQ test than African Americans do because they have a greater familiarity with the language used in the test items, the test hardly can be said to provide a fair measure of the intelligence of African Americans. Similarly, an intelligence test that solely used African American vernacular English could not be considered an impartial measure of intelligence for Whites.

The question of how to interpret differences among intelligence scores of different cultural groups lies at the heart of one of the major controversies in child development: To what degree is an individual's intelligence determined by heredity and to what degree by environment? The issue is important because of its social implications. For instance, if intelligence is primarily determined by heredity and is therefore largely fixed at birth, attempts to alter cognitive abilities later in life, such as schooling, will meet with limited success. On the other hand, if intelligence is largely environmentally determined, modifying social and educational conditions is a more promising strategy for bringing about increases in cognitive functioning (Weiss, 2003).

The Bell Curve Controversy Although investigations into the relative contributions of heredity and environment to intelligence have been conducted for decades, the smoldering debate became a raging fire with the publication of a book by Richard J. Herrnstein and Charles Murray (1994), titled *The Bell Curve*. In the book, Herrnstein and Murray argue that the average 15-point IQ difference between Whites and African Americans is due primarily to heredity rather than to environment. Furthermore, they argue that this IQ difference accounts for the higher rates of poverty, lower employment, and higher use of welfare among minority groups as compared with majority groups.

The conclusions reached by Herrnstein and Murray (1994) raised a storm of protest, and many researchers who examined the data reported in the book came to conclusions that were quite different. Most developmentalists and psychologists responded by arguing that the racial differences in measured IQ can be explained by environmental differences between the races. In fact, when a variety of indicators of economic and social factors are statistically taken into account simultaneously, mean IQ scores of Black and White children turn out to be quite similar. For instance, children from similar middle-class backgrounds, whether African American or White, tend to have similar IQ scores (Brooks-Gunn, Klebanov, & Duncan, 1996; Alderfer, 2003).

Furthermore, critics maintained that there is little evidence to suggest that IQ is a cause of poverty and other social ills. In fact, some critics suggested, as mentioned earlier in this discussion, that IQ scores were unrelated in meaningful ways to later success in life (Nisbett, 1994; Reifman, 2000; Sternberg, 2005).

Finally, members of cultural and social minority groups may score lower than members of the majority group due to the nature of the intelligence tests themselves. It is clear that traditional intelligence tests may discriminate against minority groups who have not had exposure to the same environment as majority group members.

Most traditional intelligence tests are constructed using White, English-speaking, middle-class populations as their test subjects. As a result, children from different cultural backgrounds may perform poorly on the tests—not because they are less intelligent, but because the tests use questions that are culturally biased in favor of majority group members.

**Mental retardation
(intellectual disability)**
A significantly subaverage level
of intellectual functioning that
occurs with related limitations
in two or more skill areas

In fact, a classic study found that in one California school district, Mexican American students were 10 times more likely than Whites to be placed in special education classes (Mercer, 1973; Hatton, 2002).

More recent findings show that nationally, twice as many African American students as White students are classified as mildly retarded, a difference that experts attribute primarily to cultural bias and poverty. Although certain IQ tests (such as the System of Multicultural Pluralistic Assessment [SOMPA]) have been designed to be equally valid regardless of the cultural background of test takers, no test can be completely without bias (Reschly, 1996; Sandoval et al., 1998; Hatton, 2002).

In short, most experts in the area of IQ were not convinced by *The Bell Curve* contention that differences in group IQ scores are largely determined by genetic factors. Still, we cannot put the issue to rest, largely because it is impossible to design a definitive experiment that can determine the cause of differences in IQ scores among members of different groups. (Thinking about how such an experiment might be designed shows the futility of the entire One cannot ethically assign children to different living conditions to find the effects of environment, nor would one wish to genetically control or alter intelligence levels in unborn children.)

Today, IQ is seen as the product of both nature and nurture interacting with one another in a complex manner. Rather than seeing intelligence as produced by either genes or experience, genes are seen to affect experiences, and experiences are viewed as influencing the expression of genes. For instance, psychologist Eric Turkheimer has found evidence that although environmental factors play a larger role in influencing the IQ of poor children, genes are more influential in the IQ of affluent children (Turkheimer et al., 2003).

Children with intellectual disability (formerly known as mental retardation) are often educated in classes with typical children and perform well.

Ultimately, it may be less important to know the absolute degree to which intelligence is determined by genetic and environmental factors than it is to learn how to improve children's living conditions and educational experiences. By enriching the quality of children's environments, we will be in a better position to permit all children to reach their full potential and to maximize their contributions to society, whatever their individual levels of intelligence (Posthuma & de Geus, 2006).

Falling Below and Above Intelligence Norms

Although Connie kept pace with her classmates in kindergarten, by the time she reached first grade she was academically the slowest in almost every subject. It was not that she didn't try, but rather that it took her longer than other students to catch on to new material, and she regularly required special attention to keep up with the rest of the class.

Yet in some areas she excelled: When asked to draw or produce something with her hands, she not only matched her classmates' performance but exceeded it, producing beautiful work that was much admired by her classmates. Although the other students in the class felt that there was something different about Connie, they were hard-pressed to identify the source of the difference, and in fact they didn't spend much time pondering the issue.

Connie's parents and teacher, though, knew what made her special. Extensive testing in kindergarten had shown that Connie's intelligence was well below normal, and she was officially classified as a special-needs student.

Below the Norm: Mental Retardation (Intellectual Disability) Approximately 1% to 3% of the school-age population is considered to have mental retardation. **Mental retardation** (or, as it is increasingly called, *intellectual disability*) is characterized by significant limitations in intellectual functioning and in adaptive behavior involving conceptual, social, and practical skills (AAMR, 2002).

Although limitations in intellectual functioning can be measured in a relatively straightforward manner using standard IQ tests, it is more difficult to determine how to gauge limitations in adaptive behavior. Ultimately, this imprecision leads to a lack of uniformity in the ways experts apply the label of "intellectual disability." Furthermore, it has resulted in significant variation in the abilities of people who are categorized as mentally retarded. Accordingly, people with mental retardation range from those who can be taught to work and function with little special attention to those who are virtually untrainable and who never develop speech or basic motor skills such as crawling or walking.

Mild retardation Intellectual disability with IQ scores in the range of 50 or 55 to 70

Moderate retardation Intellectual disability with IQ scores from around 35 or 40 to 50 or 55

Severe retardation Intellectual disability with IQ scores that range from around 20 or 25 to 35 or 40

Profound retardation Intellectual disability with IQ scores below 20 or 25

Gifted and talented Showing evidence of high performance capability in intellectual, creative, or artistic areas, in leadership capacity, or in specific academic fields

Degrees of Intellectual Disability About 90% of individuals with mental retardation have relatively minor levels of deficits. Classified with **mild retardation**, they score in the range of 50 or 55 to 70 on IQ tests. Typically, their retardation is not even identified before they reach school, although their early development is often slower than average. Once they enter elementary school, their retardation and their need for special attention usually become apparent, as it did with Connie, the first grader profiled at the beginning of this discussion. With appropriate training, these students can ultimately reach a third- to sixth-grade educational level, and although they cannot carry out complex intellectual tasks, they are able to hold jobs and function independently and successfully.

Intellectual and adaptive limitations become more apparent, however, at more extreme levels of mental retardation. People whose IQ scores range from around 35 or 40 to 50 or 55 are classified with **moderate retardation**. Accounting for 5% to 10% of those classified as intellectually disabled, the moderately retarded display distinctive behavior early in their lives. They are slow to develop language skills, and their motor development is also affected. Regular schooling is usually not effective in training people with moderate retardation to acquire academic skills because generally they are unable to progress beyond the second-grade level. Still, they are capable of learning occupational and social skills, and they can learn to travel independently to familiar places. Typically, they require moderate levels of supervision.

At the most significant levels of retardation—in individuals with **severe retardation** (IQs ranging from around 20 or 25 to 35 or 40) and **profound retardation** (IQs below 20 or 25)—the ability to function is severely limited. Usually, such people produce little or no speech, have poor motor control, and may need 24-hour nursing care. At the same time, though, some people with severe retardation are capable of learning basic self-care skills, such as dressing and eating, and they may even develop the potential to become partially independent as adults. Still, the need for relatively high levels of care continues throughout the life span, and most individuals with severe and profound retardation are institutionalized for a large part of their lives.

Above the Norm: The Gifted and Talented

Before her second birthday, Audry Walker recognized sequences of five colors. When she was 6, her father, Michael, overheard her telling a little boy: "No, no, no, Hunter, you don't understand. What you were seeing was a flashback."

At school, Audry quickly grew bored as the teacher drilled letters and syllables until her classmates caught on. She flourished, instead, in a once-a-week class for gifted and talented children where she could learn as fast as her nimble brain could take her. (Schemo, 2004, p. A18)

It sometimes strikes people as curious that the gifted and talented are considered to have a form of exceptionality. Yet, the 3% to 5% of school-age children who are gifted and talented present special challenges of their own.

Which students are considered to be **gifted and talented**? Little agreement exists among researchers on a single definition of this rather broad category of students. However, the federal government considers the term *gifted* to include "children who give evidence of high-performance capability in areas such as intellectual, creative, artistic, leadership capacity, or specific academic fields, and who require services or activities not ordinarily provided by the school in order to fully develop such capabilities" (Sec. 582, P.L.97-35). Intellectual capabilities, then, represent only one type of exceptionality; unusual potential in areas outside the academic realm are also included in the concept. Gifted and talented children have so much potential that they, no less than students with low IQs, warrant special concern—although special school programs for them are often the first to be dropped when school systems face budgetary problems (Robinson, Zigler, & Gallagher, 2000; Schemo, 2004; Mendoza, 2006).

Despite the stereotypic description of the gifted—particularly those with exceptionally high intelligence—as being unsociable, poorly adjusted, and neurotic, most research suggests that highly intelligent people tend to be outgoing, well adjusted, and popular (Howe, 2004; Bracken & Brown, 2006; Shaunessy et al., 2006).

For instance, one landmark, long-term study of 1,500 gifted students, which began in the 1920s, found that not only were the gifted smarter than average, but also they were healthier, better coordinated, and psychologically better adjusted than their less intelligent classmates. Furthermore, their lives played out in ways that most people would envy. The subjects received more awards and distinctions, earned more money, and made many more contributions in art and literature than the average person. For instance, by the time they had reached the age of 40, they had collectively produced more than 90 books, 375 plays and short stories, and 2,000 articles, and they had registered more than 200 patents. Perhaps not surprisingly, they reported greater satisfaction with their lives than did the nongifted (Sears, 1977; Reis & Renzulli, 2004).

Yet, being gifted and talented is no guarantee of success in school, as we can see if we consider the particular components of the category. For example, the verbal abilities that allow the eloquent expression of ideas and feelings can equally permit the expression of glib and persuasive statements that happen to be inaccurate. Furthermore, teachers

Acceleration The provision of special programs that allow gifted students to move ahead at their own pace, even if this means skipping to higher grade levels

Enrichment Approach through which students are kept at grade level but are enrolled in special programs and given individual activities to allow greater depth of study on a given topic

may sometimes misinterpret the humor, novelty, and creativity of unusually gifted children, and see their intellectual fervor to be disruptive or inappropriate. And peers are not always sympathetic: Some very bright children try to hide their intelligence in an effort to fit in better with other students (Swiatek, 2002).

Educating the Gifted and Talented Educators have devised two approaches to teaching the gifted and talented: acceleration and enrichment. **Acceleration** allows gifted students to move ahead at their own pace, even if this means skipping to higher grade levels. The materials that students receive under acceleration programs are not necessarily different from what other students receive, they simply are provided at a faster pace (Smutny, Walker, & Meckstroth, 2007).

An alternative approach is **enrichment**, through which students are kept at grade level but are enrolled in special programs and given individual activities to allow greater depth of study on a given topic. In enrichment, the material provided to gifted students differs not only in the timing of its presentation but also in its sophistication. Thus, enrichment materials are designed to provide an intellectual challenge to the gifted student, encouraging higher order thinking (Worrell, Szarko, & Gabelko, 2001; Rotigel, 2003).

Acceleration programs can be remarkably effective. Most studies have shown that gifted students who begin school even considerably earlier than their age mates do as well as or better than those who begin at the traditional age. One of the best illustrations of the benefits of acceleration is the "Study of Mathematically Precocious Youth," an ongoing program at Vanderbilt University. In this program, seventh and eighth graders who have unusual abilities in mathematics participate in a variety of special classes and workshops. The results have been nothing short of sensational, with students successfully completing college courses and sometimes even enrolling in college early. Some students have even graduated from college before the age of 18 (Lubinski & Benbow, 2001, 2006; Webb, Lubinski, & Benbow, 2002).

REVIEW ↵ **mydevelopmentlab**

1. _____ is the capacity to understand the world, think with rationality, and use resources effectively when faced with challenges.

Answer: Intelligence

2. _____ _____ is characterized by significant limitations in intellectual functioning and in adaptive behavior involving conceptual, social, and practical skills.

Answer: Mental retardation (or intellectual disability)

3. _____ _____ _____ children usually have high intellectual capabilities but also typically excel in other domains outside the academic realm.

Answer: Gifted and talented

*To see more review questions, log on to MyDevelopmentLab.

CASE STUDY

The Case of... The Risky Bet

Sarah Canton, a second-grade practicum teacher, was assigned the midlevel reading group. Since the group was small, she asked the reading specialist if she could add a student from the specialist's group—the children considered to be struggling.

The specialist reluctantly agreed to let Sarah put Maria Gonzales, age 8, in the midlevel group. "She will fall behind and feel worse about herself," the specialist warned. But Sarah had observed Maria, a shy girl, closely and felt she was capable of achieving more if appropriately challenged.

Sarah sat next to Maria the first week. The girl loved the attention and eagerly followed the lessons though she answered only when called upon. Sarah made sure to ask Maria questions she knew the girl could manage successfully.

The next week, Sarah moved among the children. She began asking Maria questions that required the girl to think a bit beyond the knowledge she possessed. She also asked Maria to interpret a poem the girl loved. Her interpretation was original and heartfelt, and the other children gave her positive feedback. Maria began raising her hand when Sarah asked for volunteers.

By the third week, Maria was posing questions in her reading journal and answering the other children's questions. Reading one-on-one with her, Sarah realized Maria's reading had jumped three levels. She continued to find links to Maria's interests and knowledge to advance the girl's understanding. When the marking period ended, Maria had made the most progress and was now reading above grade level. Best of all, she was writing poetry and stories of her own.

1. How might Sarah have gone about deciding what "appropriate challenge" meant for Maria?

2. What considerations may have prompted Sarah's decisions to sit next to Maria for the first week and, initially, to restrict her questions to those she was certain Maria already had the knowledge to answer successfully?

3. Do you think Sarah was putting Maria at risk when she asked her to interpret a poem for the group? Why or why not?

4. How did the posing of questions for the group in her reading journal, and answering the other children's questions support Maria's growth as a reader?

5. What is the significance of Sarah's efforts to find links in the reading lessons to Maria's interests and current knowledge? Explain your thinking in terms of Vygotsky's theory of cognitive development.

◄ Looking Back

In what ways do children develop cognitively during the years of middle childhood?

- According to Piaget, school-age children enter the concrete operational period and for the first time become capable of applying logical thought processes to concrete problems.

- According to information-processing approaches, children's intellectual development in the school years can be attributed to substantial increases in memory capacity and the sophistication of the "programs" children can handle.

- Vygotsky recommends that students focus on active learning through child–adult and child–child interactions that fall within each child's zone of proximal development.

How does language develop during the middle-childhood period, and what special circumstances pertain to children for whom English is not the first language?

- The language development of children in the school years is substantial, with improvements in vocabulary, syntax, and pragmatics. Children learn to control their behavior through linguistic strategies, and they learn more effectively by seeking clarification when they need it.

- Bilingualism can be beneficial in the school years. Children who are taught all subjects in their first language with simultaneous instruction in English appear to experience few deficits and several linguistic and cognitive advantages.

What trends are affecting schooling worldwide and in the United States?

- Schooling, which is available to nearly all children in most developed countries, is not as accessible to children, especially girls, in many less developed countries.
- The development of reading skills, which are fundamental to schooling, generally occurs in several stages. Research suggests that code-based (phonics) approaches are superior to whole-language approaches.
- Multiculturalism and diversity are significant issues in U.S. schools, where the melting-pot society, in which minority cultures were assimilated to the majority culture, is being replaced by the pluralistic society, where individual cultures maintain their own identities while participating in the definition of a larger culture.

What kinds of subjective factors contribute to academic outcomes?

- The expectancies of others, particularly teachers, can produce outcomes that conform to those expectancies by leading students to modify their behavior.

- Emotional intelligence is the set of skills that permit people to manage their emotions effectively.

How can intelligence be measured, what are some issues in intelligence testing, and how are children who fall outside the normal range of intelligence educated?

- Intelligence testing has traditionally focused on factors that differentiate successful academic performers from unsuccessful ones. The intelligence quotient (IQ) reflects the ratio of a person's mental age to his or her chronological age. Other conceptualizations of intelligence focus on different types of intelligence or on different aspects of information processing.
- The question of whether there are racial differences in IQ, and how to explain those differences, is highly controversial.
- Research shows that children who are above or below the norm benefit from special educational programs. ■

Epilogue

In this chapter, we discussed children's cognitive development during the middle-childhood years, tracing its development through the different lenses provided by Piaget, information-processing approaches, and Vygotsky. We noted the increased capabilities that children develop during middle childhood in the areas of memory and language, both of which facilitate and support gains in many other areas.

We then looked at some aspects of schooling worldwide. We touched on such trends as the reemphasis on the academic basics, the great debate on reading instruction, and the changing picture for multicultural education and diversity.

Finally, we concluded the chapter with an examination of the controversial issue of intelligence: how it is defined, how it is tested, how IQ-test differences are interpreted, and how children who fall significantly below or above the intellectual norm are educated and treated.

Look back to the chapter Prologue, about La-Toya Pankey's development of reading skills, and answer the following questions:

1. Judging from the cues provided in the Prologue, how would you have estimated La-Toya's chances for academic success before you learned about her ability to read? Why?

2. If you wished to isolate the factors in La-Toya's genetic or environmental background that contributed to her interest and ability in reading, how would you proceed? Which factors would you examine? What questions would you ask?

3. Given her circumstances, what threats to academic accomplishment does La-Toya still face? What advantages does she seem to have?

4. Discuss La-Toya's situation in light of the premises of the authors of *The Bell Curve*. If La-Toya succeeds academically, outperforming students of higher socioeconomic status, how would the authors explain this phenomenon? How do you explain it?

Key Terms and Concepts

concrete operational stage (p. 280)
decentering (p. 280)
memory (p. 282)
metamemory (p. 283)
metalinguistic awareness (p. 285)
bilingualism (p. 285)
multicultural education (p. 292)
cultural assimilation model
    (p. 292)
pluralistic society model (p. 292)
bicultural identity (p. 292)
emotional intelligence (p. 293)
teacher expectancy effect (p. 293)

Intelligence (p. 295)
mental age (p. 296)
chronological (physical) age (p. 296)
intelligence quotient (IQ) (p. 296)
Stanford–Binet Intelligence Scale,
    Fifth Edition (SB5) (p. 297)
Wechsler Intelligence Scale for
    Children, Fourth Edition (WISC-IV)
    (p. 297)
Kaufman Assessment Battery for
    Children, Second Edition (KABC-II)
    (p. 297)
fluid intelligence (p. 298)

crystallized intelligence (p. 298)
triarchic theory of intelligence
    (p. 298)
mental retardation (intellectual
    disability) (p. 302)
mild retardation (p. 303)
moderate retardation (p. 303)
severe retardation (p. 303)
profound retardation (p. 303)
gifted and talented (p. 303)
acceleration (p. 304)
enrichment (p. 304)

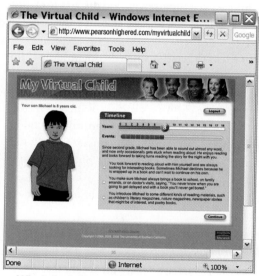

What decisions would you make while
raising a child? What would the
consequences of those decisions be?

Find out by logging onto **My Virtual Child**
and raising your child from birth to 18 years.

chapter thirteen

Social and Personality Development in Middle Childhood

PROLOGUE: PLAY TIME

On a bright weekday afternoon, six boys are playing under the endless Nevada sky. Bryan and Christopher Hendrickson are third graders, 9-year-old twins, and as on so many afternoons, their garage is headquarters.

The twins, their younger brother, Andrew, and three friends pull two enormous boxes from the garage—one each from a recently purchased washer and dryer—and set to work transforming them.

"We're making our spaceship," says Bryan. "With guns included."

Why does the spaceship need guns?

"For evil, don't you know?" says Bryan. He sprays machine gun sounds.

As the sun sets, an ever-larger clan of kids, now including the twins' older sister, Lindsay, invades the backyard. The boxes become forts, the group divides in two, and a furious round of capture-the-stuffed-tiger ensues . . .

Around 6 o'clock, mom Judy summons all the kids—now nearly a dozen—inside for dinner of pizza and juice. Later, the game resumes for another hour or so by moonlight before exhausting itself. Some children wander home. Others are picked up by their parents. (Fishman, 1999, p. 56)

▶ Looking Ahead

For Bryan and Christopher, afternoons like these represent more than just a way of passing time. They also pave the way for the formation of friendships and social relationships, a key developmental task during middle childhood.

In this chapter, we focus on social and personality development during middle childhood. It is a time when children's views of themselves undergo significant changes, they form new bonds with friends and family, and they become increasingly attached to social institutions outside the home.

We start our consideration of personality and social development during middle childhood by examining the changes that occur in the ways children see themselves. We discuss how they view their personal characteristics, and we examine the complex issue of self-esteem.

Next, the chapter turns to relationships during middle childhood. We discuss the stages of friendship and the ways gender and ethnicity affect how and with whom children interact. We also examine how to improve children's social competence.

The last part of the chapter explores the central societal institution in children's lives: the family. We consider the consequences of divorce, self-care children, and the phenomenon of group care.

After reading this chapter, you will be able to answer the following questions:

- *In what ways do children's views of themselves change during middle childhood?*
- *Why is self-esteem important during these years?*
- *What sorts of relationships and friendships are typical of middle childhood?*
- *How do gender and ethnicity affect friendships?*
- *How do today's diverse family and care arrangements affect children?*

The Developing Self

Nine-year-old Karl Haglund is perched in his eagle's nest, a tree house built high in the willow that grows in his backyard. Sometimes he sits there alone among the tree's spreading branches, his face turned toward the sky, a boy clearly enjoying his solitude. . . .

This morning Karl is busy sawing and hammering. "It's fun to build," he says. "I started the house when I was 4 years old. Then when I was about 7, my dad built me this platform. 'Cause all my places were falling apart and they were crawling with carpenter ants. So we destroyed them and then built me a deck. And I built on top of it. It's stronger now. You can have privacy here, but it's a bad place to go when it's windy 'cause you almost get blown off." (Kotre & Hall, 1990, p. 116)

Karl's growing sense of competence is reflected in the passage above, as he describes how he and his father built his tree house. Conveying what psychologist Erik Erikson calls "industriousness," Karl's quiet pride in his accomplishment illustrates one of the ways in which children's views of themselves evolve.

Psychosocial Development in Middle Childhood: Industry Versus Inferiority

According to Erik Erikson, whose approach to psychosocial development we last discussed in Chapter 10, middle childhood is very much about competence. Lasting from roughly age 6 to age 12—the period in which children are in elementary school—the **industry-versus-inferiority stage** is characterized by a focus on efforts to meet the challenges presented by parents, peers, school, and the other complexities of the modern world.

As they move through middle childhood, school presents enormous challenges. Children must direct their energies to mastering what they are presented in school, which encompasses an enormous body of information, while also making a place for themselves in their social worlds. They increasingly work with others in group activities and must navigate among different social groups and roles, including relationships involving teachers, friends, and families.

Success in the industry-versus-inferiority stage brings with it feelings of mastery and proficiency and a growing sense of competence, like those expressed by Karl when he talks about his building experience. On the other hand, difficulties in this stage lead to feelings of failure and inadequacy. As a result, children may withdraw both from academic pursuits, showing less interest and motivation to excel, and from interactions with peers.

Children such as Karl may find that attaining a sense of industry during the middle childhood years has lasting consequences. For example, one study examined how childhood industriousness and hard work were related to adult behavior by following a group of 450 men over a 35-year period, starting in early childhood (Vaillant & Vaillant, 1981). The men who were most industrious and hard-working during childhood were most successful as adults, both in occupational attainment and in their personal lives. In fact, childhood industriousness was more closely associated with adult success than was intelligence or family background.

According to Erik Erikson, middle childhood encompasses the industry-versus-inferiority stage, characterized by a focus on meeting the challenges presented by the world.

As children become older, they begin to characterize themselves in terms of their psychological attributes (such as being a responsible and nurturing individual) as well as their physical achievements.

Understanding One's Self: A New Response to "Who Am I?"

During middle childhood, children continue their efforts to answer the question "Who am I?" as they seek to understand the nature of the self. Although the question does not yet have the urgency it will assume in adolescence, elementary-school-age children still seek to pin down their place in the world.

The Shift in Self-Understanding From the Physical to the Psychological Children are on a quest for self-understanding during middle childhood. Helped by the cognitive advances that we discussed in the previous chapter, such as growing understanding of theory of mind and increased information-processing capabilities, children begin to view themselves less in terms of external, physical attributes and more in terms of psychological traits (Marsh & Ayotte, 2003; Sotiriou & Zafiropoulou, 2003; Lerner, Theokas, & Jelicic, 2005).

For instance, 6-year-old Carey describes herself as "a fast runner and good at drawing"—both characteristics dependent on skill in external activities relying on motor skills. In contrast, 11-year-old Meiping characterizes herself as "pretty smart, friendly, and helpful to my friends." Meiping's view of herself is based on psychological characteristics, inner traits that are more abstract than the younger child's descriptions. The use of inner traits to determine self-concept results from the child's increasing cognitive skills, a development that we discussed in Chapter 12.

In addition to shifting focus from external characteristics to internal, psychological traits, children's views of who they are become less simplistic and have greater complexity. In Erikson's view, children are seeking endeavors where they can be successfully industrious. As they get older, children discover that they may be good at some things and not so good at others. Ten-year-old Ginny, for instance, comes to understand that she is good at arithmetic but not very good at spelling; 11-year-old Alberto determines that he is good at softball but doesn't have the stamina to play soccer very well.

Children's self-concepts also become divided into personal and academic spheres. In fact, as can be seen in Figure 13-1, children evaluate themselves in four major areas, and each of these areas can be broken down even further. For instance, the nonacademic self-concept includes the components of physical appearance, peer relations, and physical ability. Academic self-concept is similarly divided. Research on students' self-concepts in English, mathematics, and nonacademic realms has found that the separate self-concepts are not always correlated, although there is overlap among them. For example, a child who sees herself as a star math student is not necessarily going to feel she is great at English (Marsh & Ayotte, 2003; Marsh & Hau, 2004).

From an educator's perspective: If industriousness is a more accurate predictor of future success than IQ, how might an individual's industriousness be improved? Should this be a focus of schooling?

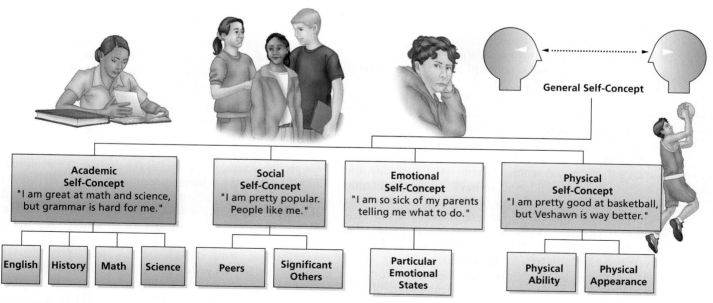

FIGURE 13-1 Looking Inward: The Development of Self

As children get older, their views of themselves become more differentiated, composed of several personal and academic spheres. What cognitive changes make this possible?
(*Source:* Adapted from Shavelson, Hubner, & Stanton, 1976)

Social comparison
The desire to evaluate one's own behavior, abilities, expertise, and opinions by comparing them to those of others

Self-esteem An individual's overall and specific positive and negative self-evaluation

Social Comparison If someone asks you how good you are at math, how would you respond? Most of us would compare our performance to others who are roughly of the same age and educational level. It is unlikely that we'd answer the question by comparing ourselves either to Albert Einstein or to a kindergartner just learning about numbers.

Elementary-school-age children begin to follow the same sort of reasoning when they seek to understand how able they are. When they were younger, they tended to consider their abilities in terms of some hypothetical standard, making a judgment that they are good or bad in an absolute sense. Now they begin to use social comparison processes, comparing themselves to others, to determine their levels of accomplishment during middle childhood (Weiss, Ebbeck, & Horn, 1997).

Social comparison is the desire to evaluate one's own behavior, abilities, expertise, and opinions by comparing them to those of others. According to a theory first suggested by psychologist Leon Festinger (1954), when concrete, objective measures of ability are lacking, people turn to *social reality* to evaluate themselves. Social reality refers to understanding that is derived from how others act, think, feel, and view the world.

But who provides the most adequate comparison? When they cannot objectively evaluate their ability, children during middle childhood increasingly look to others who are similar to themselves (Suls & Wills, 1991; Summers, Schallert, & Ritter, 2003).

Downward Social Comparison Although children typically compare themselves to similar other children, in some cases—particularly when their self-esteem is at stake—they choose to make *downward social comparisons* with others who are obviously less competent or successful (Vohs & Heatherton, 2004; Hui et al., 2006).

Downward social comparison protects children's self-esteem. By comparing themselves to those who are less able, children ensure that they will come out on top and thereby preserve an image of themselves as successful.

Downward social comparison helps explain why some students in elementary schools with generally low achievement levels are found to have stronger academic self-esteem than very capable students in schools with high achievement levels. The reason seems to be that students in the low-achievement schools observe others who are not doing terribly well academically, and they feel relatively good by comparison. In contrast, students in the high-achievement schools may find themselves competing with a more academically proficient group of students, and their perception of their performance may suffer in comparison. At least in terms of self-esteem, then, it is better to be a big fish in a small pond than a small fish in a big one (Borland & Howsen, 2003; Marsh & Hau, 2004).

Self-Esteem: Developing a Positive—or Negative—View of Oneself

Children don't dispassionately view themselves just in terms of an itemization of physical and psychological characteristics. Instead, they make judgments about themselves as being good or bad in particular ways. **Self-esteem** is an individual's overall and specific positive and negative self-evaluation. Whereas self-concept reflects beliefs and cognitions about the self (*I am good at trumpet; I am not so good at social studies*), self-esteem is more emotionally oriented (*Everybody thinks I'm a nerd*) (Davis-Kean & Sandler, 2001; Bracken & Lamprecht, 2003).

Self-esteem develops in important ways during middle childhood. As we noted previously, children increasingly compare themselves to others, and as they do, they assess how well they measure up to society's standards. In addition, they increasingly develop their own internal standards of success, and they can see how well they compare to those. One of the advances that occurs during middle childhood is that, like self-concept, self-esteem becomes increasingly differentiated. At the age of 7, most children have self-esteem that reflects a global, fairly simple view of themselves. If their overall self-esteem is positive, they believe that they are relatively good at all things. Conversely, if their overall self-esteem is negative, they feel that they are inadequate at most things (Lerner et al., 2005; Harter, 2006).

As children progress into the middle-childhood years, however, their self-esteem is higher for some areas and lower in others. For example, a boy's overall self-esteem may be composed of positive self-esteem in some areas (such as the positive feelings he gets from his artistic ability) and more negative self-esteem in others (such as the unhappiness he feels over his athletic skills).

Change and Stability in Self-Esteem Generally, overall self-esteem increases during middle childhood, with a brief decline around the age of 12. Although there are probably several reasons for the decline, the main one appears to be the school transition that typically occurs around this age: Students leaving elementary school and entering either middle school or junior high school show a decline in self-esteem, which then gradually rises again (Twenge & Campbell, 2001; Robins & Trzesniewski, 2005).

Children with chronically low self-esteem face a tough road, in part because their self-esteem becomes enmeshed in a cycle of failure that grows increasingly difficult to break. Assume, for instance, that Harry, a student with chronically low self-esteem, is facing an important test. Because of his low self-esteem, he expects to do poorly. As a consequence, he is quite anxious—so anxious that he is unable to concentrate well and study effectively.

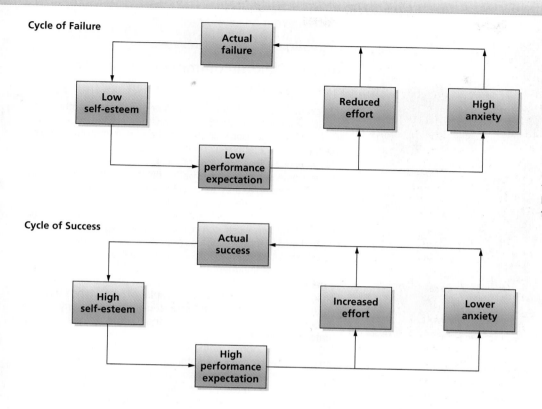

Cycle of Failure

Actual failure → Low self-esteem → Low performance expectation → Reduced effort → High anxiety → Actual failure

Cycle of Success

Actual success → High self-esteem → High performance expectation → Increased effort → Lower anxiety → Actual success

FIGURE 13-2 Cycles of Self-Esteem

Because children with low self-esteem may expect to do poorly on a test, they may experience high anxiety and not work as hard as those with higher self-esteem. As a result, they actually do perform badly on the test, which in turn confirms their negative view of themselves. In contrast, those with high self-esteem have more positive expectations, which lead to lower anxiety and higher motivation. As a consequence, they perform better, reinforcing their positive self-image. How would a teacher help students with low self-esteem break out of their negative cycle?

Furthermore, he may decide not to study much, because he figures that if he's going to do badly anyway, why bother studying?

Ultimately, of course, Harry's high anxiety and lack of effort bring about the result he expected: He does poorly on the test. This failure, which confirms Harry's expectation, reinforces his low self-esteem, and the cycle of failure continues (see Figure 13-2).

On the other hand, students with high self-esteem travel a more positive path, entering a cycle of success. Having higher expectations leads to increased effort and lower anxiety, increasing the probability of success. In turn, this helps affirm their higher self-esteem that began the cycle.

Parents can help break the cycle of failure by promoting their child's self-esteem. The best way to do this is through the use of the *authoritative* child-rearing style that we discussed in Chapter 10. Authoritative parents are warm and emotionally supportive, while still setting clear limits for their children's behavior. In contrast, other parenting styles have less positive effects on self-esteem. Parents who are highly punitive and controlling send a message to their children that they are untrustworthy and unable to make good decisions—a message that can undermine children's sense of adequacy. Highly indulgent parents, who indiscriminately praise and reinforce their children regardless of their actual performance, can create a false sense of self-esteem in their

children, which ultimately may be just as damaging to children (DeHart, Pelham, & Tennen, 2006; Rudy & Grusec, 2006; Bender et al., 2007).

Race and Self-Esteem If you were a member of a racial group whose members routinely experienced prejudice and discrimination, it seems reasonable to predict that your self-esteem would be affected. Early research confirmed that hypothesis and found that African Americans had lower self-esteem than Whites. For example, a set of pioneering studies a generation ago found that African American children shown Black and White dolls preferred the White dolls over the Black ones (Clark & Clark, 1947). The interpretation that was drawn from the study: The self-esteem of the African American children was low.

However, more recent research has shown these early assumptions to be overstated. The picture is more complex regarding relative levels of self-esteem among members of different racial and ethnic groups. For example, although White children initially show higher self-esteem than Black children, Black children begin to show slightly higher self-esteem than White children around the age of 11. This shift occurs as African American children become more identified with their racial group and increasingly view the positive aspects of their group membership (Gray-Little & Hafdahl, 2000; Oyserman et al., 2003; Tatum, 2007).

In pioneering research conducted, African American girls' preference for White dolls was viewed as an indication of low self-esteem. More recent evidence, however, suggests that White and African American children show little difference in self-esteem.

Are the Children of Immigrant Families Well-Adjusted?

Immigration to the United States has risen significantly in the last 30 years. More than 13 million children in the United States are either foreign born or the children of immigrants—some one-fifth of the total population of children.

How well are these children of immigrants faring? Quite well. In fact, in some ways they are better off than their nonimmigrant peers. For example, they tend to have equal or better grades in school than do children whose parents were born in the United States. Psychologically, they also do quite well, showing similar levels of self-esteem when compared to nonimmigrant children, although they do report feeling less popular and less in control of their lives (Harris, 2000; Kao, 2000; Driscoll, Russell, & Crockett, 2008).

Why is the adjustment of immigrant children to U.S. culture so generally positive? One answer is that often their socioeconomic status is relatively higher. In spite of stereotypes that immigrant families come from lower social classes, many in fact are well educated and come to the United States seeking greater opportunities.

But socioeconomic status is only part of the story. Even the immigrant children who are not financially well off are often more highly motivated to succeed and place greater value on education than do children in nonimmigrant families. In addition, many immigrant children come from societies that emphasize collectivism, and consequently they may feel more obligation and duty toward their family to succeed. Finally, their country of origin may give some immigrant children a strong enough cultural identity to prevent them from adopting undesirable "American" behaviors—such as materialism or selfishness (Fuligni & Yoshikawa, 2003; Suárez-Orozco & Suárez-Orozco, 2008).

During the middle-childhood years, it thus appears that children in immigrant families typically do quite well in the United States. The story is less clear, however, when immigrant children reach adolescence and adulthood. Research is just beginning to clarify how effectively immigrants cope over the course of the life span (Portes & Rumbaut, 2001; Fuligni & Fuligni, 2007).

Hispanic children also show an increase in self-esteem toward the end of middle childhood, although even in adolescence their self-esteem still trails that of Whites. In contrast, Asian American children show the opposite pattern: Their self-esteem in elementary school is higher than that of Whites and Blacks, but by the end of childhood, their self-esteem is lower than that of Whites (Twenge & Crocker, 2002; Umana et al., 2002; Tropp & Wright, 2003; Verkuyten, 2008).

One explanation for the complex relationship between self-esteem and minority-group status comes from *social identity theory*. According to the theory, members of a minority group are likely to accept the negative views held by a majority group only if they perceive that there is little realistic possibility of changing the power and status differences between the groups. If minority group members feel that prejudice and discrimination can be reduced, and they blame society, and not themselves, for the prejudice, self-esteem should not differ between majority and minority groups (Tajfel & Turner, 2004).

In fact, as group pride and ethnic awareness on the part of minority group members has grown, differences in self-esteem among members of different ethnic groups have narrowed. This trend has further been supported by an increased sensitivity to the importance of multiculturalism Negy, Shreve, & Jensen, 2003; Lee, 2005; Tatum, 2007).

1. According to Erikson, children in middle childhood are in the _____-_____-_____ stage.

   Answer: industry-versus-inferiority

2. In the middle-childhood years, children begin to use social comparison and self-concepts based on _____ rather than physical characteristics.

   Answer: psychological

3. _____-_____ is an individual's overall and specific positive and negative self-evaluation.

   Answer: Self-esteem

To see more review questions, log on to MyDevelopmentLab.

Relationships: Building Friendship in Middle Childhood

In Lunch Room Number Two, Jamillah and her new classmates chew slowly on sandwiches and sip quietly on straws from cartons of milk. . . . Boys and girls look timidly at the strange faces across the table from them, looking for someone who might play with them in the schoolyard, someone who might become a friend.

For these children, what happens in the schoolyard will be just as important as what happens in the school. And when they're out on the playground, there will be no one to protect them. No child will hold back to keep from beating them at a game, humiliating them in a test of skill, or harming them in a fight. No one will run interference or guarantee membership in a group. Out on the playground, it's sink or swim. No one automatically becomes your friend. (Kotre & Hall, 1990, pp. 112–113)

As Jamillah and her classmates demonstrate, friendship comes to play an increasingly important role during middle childhood. Children grow progressively more sensitive to the importance of friends, and building and maintaining friendships becomes a large part of children's social lives.

Friends influence children's development in several ways. For instance, friendships provide children with information about the world and other people, as well as about themselves. Friends provide emotional support that allows children to respond more effectively to stress. Having friends makes a child less likely to be the target of aggression, and it can teach children how to manage and control their emotions and help them interpret their own emotional experiences (Berndt, 2002).

Friendships in middle childhood also provide a training ground for communicating and interacting with others. They also can foster intellectual growth by increasing a child's range of experiences (Harris, 1998; Nangle & Erdley, 2001; Gifford-Smith & Brownell, 2003).

Although friends and other peers become increasingly influential throughout middle childhood, they are not more important than parents and other family members. Most developmentalists believe that children's psychological functioning and their development in general are the product of a combination of factors, including peers and parents (Harris, 2000; Vandell, 2000; Parke, Simpkins, & McDowell, 2002). For that reason, we talk more about the influence of family later in this chapter.

Stages of Friendship: Changing Views of Friends

During middle childhood, a child's conception of the nature of friendship undergoes some profound changes. According to developmental psychologist William Damon, a child's

Immigrant children tend to fare quite well in the United States, partly because many come from societies that emphasize collectivism and consequently may feel more obligation and duty to their family to succeed. What are some other cultural differences that can support the success of immigrant children?

view of friendship passes through three distinct stages (Damon & Hart, 1988).

Stage 1: Basing Friendship on Others' Behaviors In the first stage, which ranges from around 4 to 7 years of age, children see friends as others who like them and with whom they share toys and other activities. They view the children with whom they spend the most time as their friends. For instance, a kindergartner who was asked "How do you know that someone is your best friend?" responded in this way:

> I sleep over at his house sometimes. When he's playing ball with his friends he'll let me play. When I slept over, he let me get in front of him in 4-squares. He likes me. (Damon, 1983, p. 140)

What children in this first stage don't do much of, however, is take others' personal qualities into consideration. For instance, they don't see their friendship as being based on their peers' unique positive personal traits. Instead, they use a very concrete approach to deciding who is a friend, primarily dependent upon others' behavior. They like those who share and with whom they can share, while they don't like those who don't share, who hit, or who don't play with them. In sum, in the first stage, friends are viewed largely in terms of presenting opportunities for pleasant interactions.

Stage 2: Basing Friendship on Trust In the next stage, however, children's view of friendship becomes more complicated. Lasting from around age 8 to age 10, this stage covers a period in which children take others' personal qualities

Social competence
The collection of social skills that permit individuals to perform successfully in social settings

Mutual trust is considered the centerpiece of friendship during middle childhood.

and traits as well as the rewards they provide into consideration. But the centerpiece of friendship in this second stage is mutual trust. Friends are seen as those who can be counted on to help out when they are needed. This means that violations of trust are taken very seriously, and friends cannot make amends for such violations just by engaging in positive play, as they might at earlier ages. Instead, the expectation is that formal explanations and formal apologies must be provided before a friendship can be reestablished.

Stage 3: Basing Friendship on Psychological Closeness The third stage of friendship begins toward the end of middle childhood, from 11 to 15 years of age. During this period, children begin to develop the view of friendship that they hold during adolescence. Although we discuss this perspective in detail in Chapter 16, the main criteria for

friendship shift toward intimacy and loyalty. Friendship at this stage is characterized by feelings of closeness, usually brought on by sharing personal thoughts and feelings through mutual disclosure. They are also somewhat exclusive. By the time they reach the end of middle childhood, children seek out friends who will be loyal, and they come to view friendship not so much in terms of shared activities but in terms of the psychological benefits that friendship brings.

Children also develop clear ideas about which behaviors they seek in their friends—and which they dislike. As can be seen in Table 13-1, fifth and sixth graders most enjoy others who invite them to participate in activities and who are helpful, both physically and psychologically. In contrast, displays of physical or verbal aggression, among other behaviors, are disliked.

Individual Differences in Friendship: What Makes a Child Popular?

Children's friendships typically sort themselves out according to popularity. More popular children tend to form friendships with more popular individuals, while less popular children are more likely to have friends who are less popular. Popularity is also related to the number of friends a child has: More popular children are more apt to have a greater number of friends than those with lower popularity. In addition, more popular children are more likely to form *cliques*, groups that are viewed as exclusive and desirable, and they tend to interact with a greater number of other children.

Why is it that some children are the schoolyard equivalent of the life of the party, while others are social isolates whose overtures toward their peers are dismissed or disdained? To answer this question, developmentalists have considered the personal characteristics of popular children.

What Personal Characteristics Lead to Popularity?

Popular children share several personality characteristics. They are usually helpful, cooperating with others on joint projects. Popular children are also funny, tend to have good senses of humor, and typically appreciate others' attempts at humor. Compared with children who are less popular, they are better able to read others' nonverbal behavior and understand others' emotional experiences. They also can control their nonverbal behavior more effectively, thereby presenting themselves well. In short, popular children are high in **social competence**, the collection of individual social skills that permit individuals to perform successfully in social settings (Feldman, Tomasian, & Coats, 1999).

Although generally popular children are friendly, open, and cooperative, one subset of popular boys displays an array of negative behaviors, including being aggressive,

TABLE 13-1	Most-Liked and Least-Liked Behaviors That Children Note in Their Friends, in Order of Importance
Most-Liked Behaviors	**Least-Liked Behaviors**
Having a sense of humor	Verbal aggression
Being nice or friendly	Expressions of anger
Being helpful	Dishonesty
Being complimentary	Being critical or criticizing
Inviting one to participate in games, etc.	Being greedy or bossy
Sharing	Physical aggression
Avoiding unpleasant behavior	Being annoying or bothersome
Giving one permission or control	Teasing
Providing instructions	Interfering with achievements
Loyalty	Unfaithfulness
Performing admirably	Violating of rules
Facilitating achievements	Ignoring others

(*Source*: Adapted from Zarbatany, Hartmann, & Rankin, 1990)

disruptive, and causing trouble. Despite these behaviors, they may be viewed as cool and tough by their peers, and they are often remarkably popular. This popularity may occur in part because they are seen as boldly breaking rules that others feel constrained to follow (Farmer, Estell, & Bishop, 2003; Cillessen & Mayeux, 2004; Andreou, 2006).

Social Problem-Solving Abilities   Another factor that relates to children's popularity is their skill at social problem-solving. **Social problem-solving** refers to the use of strategies for solving social conflicts in ways that are satisfactory both to oneself and to others. Because social conflicts among school-age children are a not infrequent occurrence—even among the best of friends—successful strategies for dealing with them are an important element of social success (Rose & Asher, 1999; Murphy & Eisenberg, 2002).

According to developmental psychologist Kenneth Dodge, successful social problem-solving proceeds through a series of steps that correspond to children's information-processing strategies (see Figure 13-3). Dodge argues that the manner in which children solve social problems is a consequence of the decisions that they make at each point in the sequence (Dodge, Lansford, & Burks, 2003; Lansford et al., 2006).

By carefully delineating each of the stages, Dodge provides a means by which interventions can be targeted toward a specific child's deficits. For instance, some children routinely misinterpret the meaning of other children's behavior (Step 2), and then respond according to their misinterpretation.

Suppose Max, a fourth grader, is playing a game with Will. While playing the game, Will begins to get angry because he is losing and complains about the rules. If Max is not able to understand that much of Will's anger is frustration at not winning, he is likely to react in an angry way himself, defending the rules, criticizing Will, and making the situation worse. If Max interprets the source of Will's anger more accurately, Max may be able to behave in a more effective manner, perhaps by reminding Will, "Hey, you beat me at Connect Four," thereby defusing the situation.

Generally, children who are popular are better at interpreting the meaning of others' behavior accurately. Furthermore, they possess a wider inventory of techniques for dealing with social problems. In contrast, less popular children tend to be less effective at understanding the causes of others' behavior, and because of this their reactions to others may be inappropriate. In addition, their strategies for dealing with social problems are more limited; they sometimes simply don't know how to apologize or help someone who is unhappy feel better (Rose & Asher, 1999; Rinaldi, 2002).

Unpopular children may become victims of a phenomenon known as *learned helplessness*. Because they don't understand the root causes of their unpopularity, children may feel that they have little or no ability to improve their situation. As a result, they may simply give up and not even try to become more involved with their peers. In turn, their learned helplessness becomes a self-fulfilling prophecy, reducing the

A variety of factors lead some children to be unpopular and socially isolated from their peers.

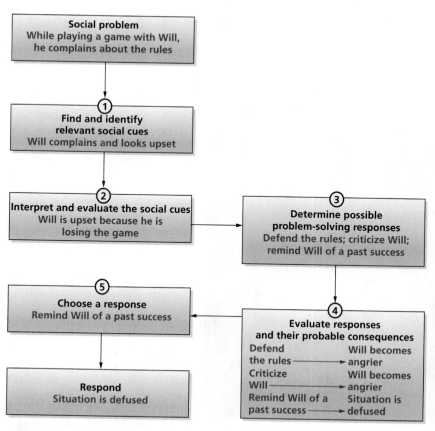

FIGURE 13-3 Problem-Solving Steps

Children's problem solving proceeds through several steps involving different information-processing strategies. In what ways might an educator use children's problem-solving skills as a learning tool?
(*Source:* Adapted from Dodge, 1985)

chances that they will become more popular in the future (Seligman, 2007; Aujoulat, Luminet, & Deccache, 2007).

Teaching Social Competence   Can anything be done to help unpopular children learn social competence? Happily, the answer appears to be yes. Several programs have been developed to teach children a set of social skills that seem to underlie general social competence. For example, in one experimental program, a group of unpopular fifth and sixth graders were taught how to hold a conversation with friends. They were taught ways to disclose material about themselves, to learn about others by asking questions, and to offer help and suggestions to others in a nonthreatening way.

Compared with a group of children who did not receive such training, the children who were in the experiment interacted more with their peers, held more conversations, developed higher self-esteem, and—most critically—were more accepted by their peers than before training (Asher & Rose, 1997; Bierman, 2004.)

Gender and Friendships: The Sex Segregation of Middle Childhood

Girls rule; boys drool.
Boys are idiots. Girls have cooties.
Boys go to college to get more knowledge; girls go to Jupiter to get more stupider.

Though same-sex groupings dominate in middle childhood, when boys and girls do make occasional forays into each others' territory, there are often romantic overtones. Such behavior has been termed "border work."

Those are the views of some boys and girls regarding members of the opposite sex during the elementary school years. Avoidance of the opposite sex becomes quite pronounced during those years, to the degree that the social networks of most boys and girls consist almost entirely of same-sex groupings (Adler, Kless, & Adler, 1992; Lewis & Phillipsen, 1998; McHale, Dariotis, & Kauh, 2003).

Interestingly, the segregation of friendships according to gender occurs in almost all societies. In nonindustrialized societies, same-gender segregation may be the result of the types of activities that children engage in. For instance, in many cultures, boys are assigned one type of chore and girls another (Whiting & Edwards, 1988). Participation in different activities may not provide the whole explanation for sex segregation, however; even children in

more developed countries, who attend the same schools and participate in many of the same activities, still tend to avoid members of the other gender.

When boys and girls make occasional forays into the other gender's territory, the action often has romantic overtones. For instance, girls may threaten to kiss a boy, or boys might try to lure girls into chasing them. Such behavior, termed *border work*, helps emphasize the clear boundaries that exist between the two sexes. In addition, it may pave the way for future interactions that do involve romantic or sexual interests, when school-age children reach adolescence and cross-sex interactions become more socially endorsed (Beal, 1994).

The lack of cross-gender interaction in the middle-childhood years means that boys' and girls' friendships are restricted to members of their own sex. Furthermore, the nature of friendships within these two groups is quite different (Lansford & Parker, 1999; Rose, 2002).

Boys typically have larger networks of friends than do girls, and they tend to play in groups, rather than pair off. Differences in status within the group are usually quite pronounced, with an acknowledged leader and members falling into particular levels within the hierarchy. Because of the fairly rigid rankings that represent the relative social power of those in the group, known as the **dominance hierarchy**, members of higher status can safely question and oppose children lower in the hierarchy (Beal, 1994; Pedersen et al., 2007).

Boys tend to be concerned with their place in the dominance hierarchy, and they attempt to maintain their status and improve on it. This makes for a style of play known as restrictive. In *restrictive play*, interactions are interrupted when a child feels that his status is challenged. Thus, a boy who feels that he is unjustly challenged by a peer of lower status may attempt to end the interaction by scuffling over a toy or otherwise behaving assertively. Consequently, boys' play tends to come in bursts, rather than in more extended, tranquil episodes (Benenson & Apostoleris, 1993; Estell et al., 2008).

The language of friendship used among boys reflects their concern over status and challenge. For instance, consider this conversation between two boys who were good friends:

CHILD 1: Why don't you get out of my yard?
CHILD 2: Why don't you *make* me get out the yard?
CHILD 1: I *know* you don't want that.
CHILD 2: You're not gonna make me get out the yard cuz you can't.
CHILD 1: Don't force me.
CHILD 2: You can't. Don't force me to hurt you (*snickers*). (Goodwin, 1990, p. 37)

Friendship patterns among girls are quite different. Rather than having a wide network of friends, school-age girls focus on one or two "best friends" who are of relatively equal status. In contrast to boys, who seek out status differences, girls profess to avoid differences in status, preferring to maintain friendships at equal-status levels.

Conflicts among school-age girls are usually solved through compromise, by ignoring the situation, or by giving in, rather than by seeking to make one's own point of view prevail. In sum, the goal is to smooth over disagreements, making social interaction easy and nonconfrontational (Goodwin, 1990; Noakes & Rinaldi, 2006).

The motivation of girls to solve social conflict indirectly does not stem from a lack of self-confidence or from apprehension over the use of more direct approaches. In fact, when school-age girls interact with other girls who are not considered friends or with boys, they can be quite confrontational. However, among friends their goal is to maintain equal-status relationships—ones lacking a dominance hierarchy (Beale, 1994; Zahn-Waxler et al., 2008).

The language used by girls tends to reflect their view of relationships. Rather than blatant demands ("Give me the pencil"), girls are more apt to use language that is less confrontational and directive. Girls tend to use indirect forms of verbs, such as "Let's go to the movies" or "Would you want to trade books with me?" rather than "I want to go to the movies" or "Let me have these books" (Goodwin, 1990; Besag, 2006).

Cross-Race Friendships: Integration In and Out of the Classroom

Are friendships color-blind? For the most part, the answer is no. Children's closest friendships tend largely to be with others of the same race. In fact, as children age there is a decline in the number and depth of friendships outside their own racial group. By the time they are 11 or 12 years old, it appears that African American children become particularly aware of and sensitive to the prejudice and discrimination directed toward members of their race. At that point, they are more likely to make distinctions between members of

As children age, the number of and depth of friendships outside their own racial group tend to decline. What are some ways in which schools can foster mutual acceptance?

ingroups (groups to which people feel they belong) and members of outgroups (groups to which people do not perceive membership) (Bigler, Jones, & Lobliner, 1997; Aboud, Mendelson, & Purdy, 2003; Aboud & Sankar, 2007).

For instance, when third graders from one long-integrated school were asked to name a best friend, around one-fourth of White children and two-thirds of African American children chose a child of the other race. In contrast, by the time they reached tenth grade, fewer than 10% of Whites and 5% of African Americans named a different-race best friend (Asher, Singleton, & Taylor, 1982; McGlothlin & Killen, 2005).

On the other hand, although they may not choose each other as best friends, Whites and African Americans—as well as members of other minority groups—can show a high degree of mutual acceptance. This pattern is particularly true in schools with ongoing integration efforts. This makes sense: A good deal of research supports the notion that contact between majority and minority group members can reduce prejudice and discrimination (Hewstone, 2003; Quintana, 2008a, b).

From a social worker's perspective:

How might it be possible to decrease the segregation of friendships along racial lines? What factors would have to change in individuals or in society?

Schoolyard—and Cyber-Yard—Bullies

Alex hung with a popular crowd, had a quick wit, and got good grades. He was small for his age, so his father says he taught the boy "how to punch and hold his own. I thought he was doing okay." But for Alex the threat wasn't physical. Unknown to his parents, a group of girls at his school in Chesapeake, Va., had been taunting him for about a month through instant messages, teasing him about his size and challenging him to perform physical activities he couldn't accomplish, like running around the school track in a certain time or jumping across a ditch.

Alex spent many hours chatting online in his bedroom. Other kids knew he was thinking about taking his own life, his mother says. "They were trying to dare him to commit suicide, thinking it was a big joke." (Meadows, 2005, p. 153)

It was no joke. One afternoon, Alex took his grandfather's shotgun and killed himself.

Alex is not alone in facing the torment of bullying, whether it comes at school or on the Internet. Almost 85% of girls and 80% of boys report experiencing some form of harassment in school at least once, and 160,000 U.S. schoolchildren stay home from school each day because they are afraid of being bullied. Others encounter bullying on the Internet, which may be even more painful because often the bullying is done anonymously or may involve public postings (Harmon, 2004; Dehue, Bolman, & Völlink, 2008; Slonje & Smith, 2008; Smith et al., 2008).

Those children who experience frequent bullying are most often loners who are fairly passive. They often cry easily, and they tend to lack the social skills that might otherwise defuse a bullying situation. For example, they are unable to think of humorous comebacks to bullies' taunts. But though children such as these are more likely to be bullied, even children without these characteristics occasionally are bullied during their school careers: Some 90% of middle-school students report being bullied at some point in their time at school, beginning as early as the preschool years (Crick, Casas, & Ku, 1999; Ahmed & Braithwaite, 2004; Li, 2006, 2007).

About 10% to 15% of students bully others at one time or another. About half of all bullies come from abusive homes—meaning, of course, that half don't. Bullies tend to watch more television containing violence, and they misbehave more at home and at school than do nonbullies. When their bullying gets them into trouble, they may try to lie their way out of the situation, and they show little remorse for their victimization of others. Furthermore, bullies, compared with their peers, are more likely to break the law as adults. Although bullies are sometimes popular among their peers, some ironically become victims of bullying themselves (Kaltiala-Heino et al., 2000; Haynie et al., 2001; Ireland & Archer, 2004).

Becoming an Informed Consumer of Development

Increasing Children's Social Competence

Building and maintaining friendships is critical in children's lives. Is there anything that parents and teachers can do to increase children's social competence?

The answer is a clear yes. Among the strategies that can work are the following:

- Encourage social interaction. Teachers can devise ways in which children are led to take part in group activities, and parents can encourage membership in such groups as Brownies and Cub Scouts or participation in team sports.

- Teach listening skills to children. Show them how to listen carefully and respond to the underlying meaning of a communication as well as its overt content.

- Make children aware that people display emotions and moods nonverbally and that consequently they should pay attention to others' nonverbal behavior, not only to what they are saying on a verbal level.

- Teach conversational skills, including the importance of asking questions and self-disclosure. Encourage students to use "I" statements in which they clarify their own feelings or opinions, and avoid making generalizations about others.

- Don't ask children to choose teams or groups publicly. Instead, assign children randomly: It works just as well in ensuring a distribution of abilities across groups and avoids the public embarrassment of a situation in which some children are chosen last.

1. _____ _____ is the collection of social skills that permit individuals to perform successfully in social settings.

   Answer: Social competence

2. The use of strategies for solving social conflicts in ways that are satisfactory both to oneself and to others is known as _____ _____ - _____.

   Answer: social problem-solving

3. The _____ _____ are the rankings that represent the relative social power of those in a group.

   Answer: dominance hierarchy

To see more review questions, log on to MyDevelopmentLab.

The Family

Tamara's mother, Brenda, waited outside the door of her second-grade classroom for the end of the school day. Tamara came over to greet her mother as soon as she spotted her.

"Mom, can Anna come over to play today?" Tamara demanded. Brenda had been looking forward to spending some time alone with Tamara, who had spent the last 3 days at her dad's house. But, Brenda reflected, Tamara hardly ever got to ask kids over after school, so she agreed to the request.

Unfortunately, it turned out today wouldn't work for Anna's family, so they tried to find an alternate date. "How about Thursday?" Anna's mother suggested. Before Tamara could reply, her mother reminded her, "You'll have to ask your dad. You're at his house that night." Tamara's expectant face fell. "OK," she mumbled.

How will Tamara's adjustment be affected from dividing her time between the two homes where she lives with her divorced parents? What about the adjustment of her friend, Anna, who lives with both her parents, both of whom work outside the home? These are just a few of the questions we need to consider as we look at the ways that children's schooling and home life affect their lives during middle childhood.

Families: The Changing Home Environment

The original plot goes like this: First comes love. Then comes marriage. Then comes Mary with a baby carriage. But now there's a sequel: John and Mary break up. John moves in with Sally and her two boys. Mary takes the baby Paul. A year later Mary meets Jack, who is divorced with three children. They get married. Paul, barely 2 years old, now has a mother, a father, a step-mother, a stepfather, and five stepbrothers and stepsisters—as well as four sets of grandparents (biological and step) and countless aunts and uncles. And guess what? Mary's pregnant again. (Katrowitz & Wingert, 1990, p. 24)

We've already noted in earlier chapters the changes that have occurred in the structure of the family over the last few decades. With an increase in the number of parents who both work outside of the home, a soaring divorce rate, and a rise in single-parent families, the environment faced by children passing through middle childhood in the 21st century is very different from that faced by prior generations.

One of the biggest challenges facing children and their parents is the increasing independence that characterizes children's behavior during middle childhood. During this period, children move from being almost completely controlled by their parents to having increasing control of their own destinies—or at least their everyday conduct. Middle childhood, then, is a period of **coregulation** in which children and parents jointly control behavior. Increasingly, parents provide broad, general guidelines for conduct, whereas children have control over their everyday behavior. For instance, parents may urge their daughter to buy a balanced, nutritious school lunch each day, but their daughter's decision to regularly buy pizza and two desserts is very much her own.

Family Life

During the middle years of childhood, children spend significantly less time with their parents than in earlier years. Still, parents remain the major influence in their children's lives, and they are seen as providing essential assistance, advice, and direction (Furman & Buhrmester, 1992; Parke, 2004).

Siblings also have an important influence on children during middle childhood, for good and for bad. Although brothers and sisters can provide support, companionship, and a sense of security, they can also be a source of strife.

Sibling rivalry can occur, with siblings competing or quarreling with one another. Such rivalry can be most intense when siblings are similar in age and of the same sex. Parents may intensify sibling rivalry by being perceived as favoring one child over another. Such perceptions may or may not be accurate. For example, older siblings may be permitted more freedom, which the younger sibling may interpret as favoritism. In some cases, perceived favoritism not only leads to sibling rivalry, but may damage the self-esteem of the younger sibling. On the other hand, sibling rivalry is not inevitable, as we discuss in the accompanying *From Research to Practice* box (Branje et al., 2004; McHale, Kim, & Whiteman, 2006; Li et al., 2007).

What about children who have no siblings? As an only-child, although there is no opportunity to develop sibling rivalry, they also miss out on the benefits that siblings can bring. Generally, despite the stereotype that only-children are spoiled and self-centered, the reality is that they are as

Sibling rivalry occurs when brothers and sisters compete or fight with one another.

well-adjusted as children with brothers and sisters. In fact, in some ways, only-children are better adjusted, often having higher self-esteem and stronger motivation to achieve. This is particularly good news for parents in China, where a strict one-child policy is in effect. Studies there show that Chinese only-children often academically outperform children with siblings (Mino & Wang, 2003).

When Both Parents Work Outside the Home: How Do Children Fare?

In most cases, children whose parents both work full time outside the home fare quite well. Children whose parents are loving, are sensitive to their children's needs, and provide appropriate substitute care typically develop no differently from children in families in which one of the parents does not work (Harvey, 1999).

The good adjustment of children whose mothers and fathers both work relates to the psychological adjustment of the parents, especially mothers. In general, women who are satisfied with their lives tend to be more nurturing with their children. When work provides a high level of satisfaction, then, mothers who work outside of the home may be more psychologically supportive of their children. Thus, it is not so much a question of whether a mother chooses to work full time, to stay at home, or to arrange some combination of the two. What matters is how satisfied she is with the choices she has made (Barnett & Rivers, 1992; Gilbert, 1994; Haddock & Rattenborg, 2003).

Although we might expect that children whose parents both work would spend comparatively less time with their parents than children with one parent at home full time, research suggests otherwise. Children with mothers

Learning to Get Along: How Children Are Influenced by their Siblings

Alejandra and Sofia Romero, 5-year-old fraternal twins growing up in New York City, entered the world at almost the same instant but have gone their own ways ever since—at least in terms of temperament. Alejandra has more of a tolerance—even a taste—for rules and regimens. Sofia. . . . distinguished herself as the looser, less disciplined of the two. Sofia is also the more garrulous, and Alejandra eventually became the more taciturn. "Sofia served as their mouthpiece," says Lisa Dreyer, 39, the girls' mother, "and Alejandra was perfectly happy to let her do it." (Kluger, 2006, p. 52)

Siblings Alejandra and Sofia Romero couldn't be more different. But like other siblings, they share a special relationship with one another—one that will likely last a lifetime. Unlike our relationships with peers and parents, sibling relationships are likely to endure across the life span. Developmental scientists are uncovering the ways in which early relationships between siblings shape the ways in which we relate to others as well as the choices we make later in life (McHale, Kim, & Whiteman, 2006).

What are relationships with siblings like? Romanticized notions of brotherly love aside, siblings in middle childhood bicker and fight a lot—as often as one conflict every 20 minutes or so (Kramer, Perozynski, & Chung, 1999). But beyond the fighting, the jealousy, and the jostling for attention, sibling relationships have a special quality that sets them apart: Unlike friends or spouses, people can't choose their siblings. The influence of siblings is unsurprising when you consider just how much time is spent together in childhood and even into adolescence—more time, in fact, than is spent with friends, teachers, and other family members. Strategies learned for getting along with one's siblings, especially in terms of resolving conflicts, seem to carry over into later social settings. For example, children who negotiate well with their siblings in early childhood enjoy better relations with their teachers and classmates in middle childhood, whereas destructive conflict solving between siblings is associated with continued aggressiveness in boys (Vondra et al., 1999; Garcia et al., 2000; Criss & Shaw, 2005).

Older children also can function as role models for their younger sibling, but not always in a positive way. For example, younger

sisters of teenage mothers are more than four times as likely to become teenage mothers themselves. But younger children can also learn what *not* to do from an older sibling—and it may not simply be because they learned from the older child's mistakes. In some cases, they seem to be more motivated by distinguishing themselves from their big brother or sister.

For example, one study of childhood smoking found that while children take after their older siblings in picking up the habit, their tendency to do so is weaker the closer they are in age (and presumably, the more motivated they therefore are to distinguish themselves). Consequently, big brothers and big sisters seem to inspire behavior in their younger siblings in two ways: often by emulation, but sometimes in the opposite direction to set themselves apart (Bard & Rodgers, 2003; East & Khoo, 2005).

The desire to be different from an older sibling—a phenomenon called *de-identification*—also influences gender-role behavior. In one study, children with opposite-sex siblings tended not only to adhere more closely to gender-linked traits themselves but also to have friends who did as well. Specifically, boys with sisters tended to choose friends who were more masculine and more focused on shared activities, while girls with brothers tended to choose friends who were more feminine in terms of preferring emotional closeness and intimacy (Updegraff, McHale, & Crouter, 2000; McHale et al., 2004; Whiteman, McHale, & Crouter, 2007).

But while having an opposite-sex sibling may exaggerate same-gender identification in childhood, it also seems to improve cross-gender relations later in life. In one study, college students were put together in opposite-sex pairs and given a chance to casually interact. When they later rated the quality of these interactions, the students who had older, opposite sex siblings were rated as more interactive and more likable by their opposite-sex conversation partners (Ickes & Turner, 1983; Updegraff, McHale, & Crouter, 2000).

- What might determine whether a child chooses to model an older sibling's behavior or to de-identify with him or her?

- Why might sibling relationships have a more pronounced effect than peer relationships on how children learn to get along with others?

and fathers who work full time spend essentially the same amount of time with family, in class, with friends, and alone as children in families where one parent stays at home (Richards & Duckett, 1994; Gottfried, Gottfried, & Bathurst, 2002).

What are children doing during the day? The activities that take the most time are sleeping and school. The next most frequent activities are watching television and playing, followed closely by personal care and eating. This has changed little over the past 20 years (see Figure 13-4). What has changed is the amount of time spent in supervised, structured settings. In 1981, 40% of a child's day was free

time; by the late 1990s, only 25% of a child's day was unscheduled (Hofferth & Sandberg, 1998).

Home and Alone: What Do Children Do?

When 10-year-old Johnetta Colvin comes home after finishing a day at Martin Luther King Elementary School, the first thing she does is grab a few cookies and turn on the computer. She takes a quick look at her e-mail, and then goes over to the television and typically spends the next hour watching. During commercials, she takes a look at her homework.

What she doesn't do is chat with her parents, neither of whom are there.

She's home alone.

Johnetta is a **self-care child**, the term for children who let themselves into their homes after school and wait alone until their parents return from work. She is far from unique. Some 12% to 14% of children in the United States between the ages of 5 and 12 spend some time alone after school, without adult supervision (Lamorey, Robinson, & Rowland, 1998; Berger, 2000).

In the past, concern about self-care children centered on their lack of supervision and the emotional costs of being alone. In fact, such children were previously called *latchkey children*, raising connotations of sad, pathetic, and neglected children. However, a new view of self-care children is emerging. According to sociologist Sandra Hofferth, given the hectic schedule of many children's lives, a few hours alone may provide a helpful period of decompression. Furthermore, it may provide the opportunity for children to develop a greater sense of autonomy (Hofferth & Sandberg, 2001).

Research has identified few differences between self-care children and children who return to homes with parents. Although some children report negative experiences while at home by themselves (such as loneliness), they do not seem emotionally damaged by the experience. In addition, if they stay at home by themselves rather than "hang out" unsupervised with friends, they may avoid involvement in activities that can lead to difficulties (Long & Long, 1983; Belle, 1999; Goyette-Ewing, 2000).

In sum, the consequences of being a self-care child are not necessarily harmful. In fact, children may develop an enhanced sense of independence and competence. Furthermore, the time spent alone provides an opportunity to work uninterrupted on homework and school or personal projects. In fact, children with employed parents may have higher self-esteem because they feel they are contributing to the household in significant ways (Goyette-Ewing, 2000).

Divorce

Having divorced parents, like Tamara, the second grader who was described earlier, is no longer very distinctive. Only around half the children in the United States spend their entire childhoods living in the same household with both their parents. The rest will live in single-parent homes or with stepparents, grandparents, or other nonparental relatives; and some will end up in foster care (Harvey & Fine, 2004).

How do children react to divorce? The answer depends on how soon you ask the question following a divorce as well as how old the children are at the time of the divorce. Immediately after a divorce, both children and parents may show several types of psychological maladjustment for a period

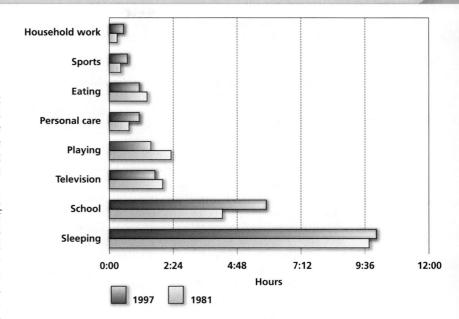

FIGURE 13-4 How Children Spend Their Time

Whereas the amount of time children spend on certain activities has remained constant over the years, the time spent on others, such as playing and eating, have shown significant changes. What might account for these changes? (*Source:* Hofferth & Sandberg, 1998)

that may last from 6 months to 2 years. For instance, children may be anxious, experience depression, or show sleep disturbances and phobias. Even though children most often live with their mothers following a divorce, the quality of the mother–child relationship declines in the majority of cases, often because children see themselves caught in the middle between their mothers and fathers (Holyrod & Sheppard, 1997; Wallerstein, Lewis, & Blakeslee, 2000; Amato & Afifi, 2006; Juby et al., 2007).

During the early stage of middle childhood, children whose parents are divorcing often blame themselves for the breakup. By the age of 10, children feel pressure to choose sides, taking the position of either the mother or the father. Because of this, they experience some degree of divided loyalty (Shaw, Winslow, & Flanagan, 1999).

Although researchers agree that the short-term consequences of divorce can be quite difficult, the longer term consequences are less clear. Some studies have found that 18 months to 2 years later, most children begin to return to their predivorce state of psychological adjustment. For many children, there are minimal long-term consequences (Hetherington & Kelly, 2002; Guttmann & Rosenberg, 2003; Harvey & Fine, 2004).

From a health-care worker's perspective: How might the development of self-esteem in middle childhood be affected by a divorce? Can constant hostility and tension between parents lead to a child's health problems?

On the other hand, there is evidence that the fallout from divorce lingers. For example, twice as many children of divorced parents enter psychological counseling as children from intact families (although sometimes counseling is mandated by a judge as part of the divorce). In addition, people who have experienced parental divorce are more at risk for experiencing divorce themselves later in life (Wallerstein et al., 2000; Amato & Booth, 2001; Wallerstein & Resnikoff, 2005; Huurre, Junkkari, & Aro, 2006).

How children react to divorce depends on several factors. One is the economic standing of the family the child is living with. In many cases, divorce brings a decline in both parents' standards of living. When this occurs, children may be thrown into poverty (Ozawa & Yoon, 2003).

In other cases, the negative consequences of divorce are less severe because the divorce reduces the hostility and anger in the home. If the household before the divorce was overwhelmed by parental strife—as is the case in around 30% of divorces—the greater calm of a postdivorce household may be beneficial to children. This is particularly true for children who maintain a close, positive relationship with the parent with whom they do not live (Davies et al., 2002).

For some children, then, divorce is an improvement over living with parents who have an intact but unhappy marriage, high in conflict. But in about 70% of divorces, the predivorce level of conflict is not high, and children in these households may have a more difficult time adjusting to divorce (Amato & Booth, 1997).

Based on current trends, almost three-quarters of American children will spend some portion of their lives in a single-parent family. What are some possible consequences for a child raised in a single-parent household?

Single-Parent Families

Almost one-fourth of all children under the age of 18 in the United States live with only one parent. If present trends continue, almost three-fourths of American children will spend some portion of their lives in a single-parent family before they are 18 years old. For minority children, the numbers are even higher: Almost 60% of African American children and 35% of Hispanic children under the age of 18 live in single-parent homes (U.S. Bureau of the Census, 2000; see Figure 13-5).

In rare cases, death is the reason for single parenthood. More frequently, no spouse was ever present (i.e., the mother never married), the spouses have divorced, or the spouse is absent. In the vast majority of cases, the single parent who is present is the mother.

What consequences are there for children living in homes with just one parent? This is a difficult question to answer. Much depends on whether a second parent was present earlier and the nature of the parents' relationship at that time. Furthermore, the economic status of the single-parent family plays a role in determining the consequences for children. Single-parent families are often less well-off financially than two-parent families, and living in relative poverty has a negative impact on children (Davis, 2003; Harvey & Fine, 2004).

In sum, the impact of living in a single-parent family is not, by itself, invariably negative or positive. Given the large number of single-parent households, the stigma that once existed toward such families has largely declined. The ultimate consequences for children depend on a variety of factors that accompany single parenthood, such as the economic status of the family, the amount of time that the parent is able to spend with the child, and the degree of stress in the household.

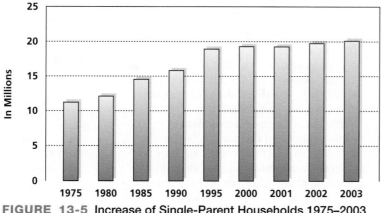

FIGURE 13-5 Increase of Single-Parent Households 1975–2003

Although the number of children living with single parents increased dramatically for several decades, it has leveled off in recent years. (*Source:* U.S. Bureau of the Census, September 15, 2004)

Blended family A remarried couple that has at least one stepchild living with them

Multigenerational Families

Some households consist of several generations, in which children, parents, and grandparents live together. The presence of multiple generations in the same house can make for a rich living experience for children, who experience the influence of both their parents and their grandparents. On the other hand, multigenerational families also have the potential for conflict, with several adults acting as disciplinarians without coordinating what they do.

The prevalence of three-generation families who live together is greater among African Americans than among Caucasians. In addition, African American families, which are more likely than White families to be headed by single parents, often rely substantially on the help of grandparents in everyday child care, and cultural norms tend to be highly supportive of grandparents taking an active role (Crowther & Rodriguez, 2003; Oberlander, Black, & Starr, 2007; Pittman & Boswell, 2007).

Blended families result when previously married mothers and fathers marry.

Blended Families

For many children, the aftermath of divorce includes the subsequent remarriage of one or both parents. In fact, more than 10 million households in the United States contain at least one spouse who has remarried. More than 5 million remarried couples have at least one stepchild living with them in what have come to be called **blended families**. Overall, 17% of all children in the United States live in blended families (U.S. Bureau of the Census, 2001; Bengtson et al., 2004).

Living in a blended family is challenging for the children involved. Often there is a fair amount of *role ambiguity,* in which roles and expectations are unclear. Children may be uncertain about their responsibilities, how to behave toward stepparents and stepsiblings, and how to make a host of decisions that have wide-ranging implications for their role in the family. For instance, a child in a blended family may have to choose which parent to spend each vacation and holiday with, or to decide between the conflicting advice coming from a biological parent and a stepparent (Dainton, 1993; Cath & Shopper, 2001; Belcher, 2003).

In many cases, however, school-age children in blended families often do surprisingly well. In comparison to adolescents, who have more difficulties, school-age children often adjust relatively smoothly to blended arrangements, for several reasons. For one thing, the family's financial situation is often improved after a parent remarries. In addition, in a blended family there are more people to share the burden of household chores. Finally, the simple fact that the family contains more individuals increases the opportunities for social interaction (Greene, Anderson, & Hetherington, 2003; Hetherington & Elmore, 2003).

On the other hand, not all children adjust well to life in a blended family. Some find the disruption of routine and of established networks of family relationships difficult. For

instance, a child who is used to having her mother's complete attention may find it difficult to observe her mother showing interest and affection to a stepchild. The most successful blending of families occurs when the parents create an environment that supports children's self-esteem and creates a climate in which all family members feel a sense of togetherness. Generally, the younger the children, the easier the transition is within a blended family (Sage, 2003; Jeynes, 2006, 2007; Kirby, 2006).

Families With Gay and Lesbian Parents

An increasing number of children have two mothers or two fathers. Estimates suggest there are between 1 and 5 million families headed by two lesbians or two gay parents in the United States, and some 6 million children have lesbian or gay parents (Patterson & Friel, 2000; Patterson, 2007).

A growing body of research on the effects of same-sex parenting on children shows that children in lesbian and gay households develop similarly to the children of heterosexual families. Their sexual orientation is unrelated to that of their parents; their behavior is no more or less gender typed; and they seem equally well-adjusted (Patterson, 2002, 2003; Parke, 2004; Fulcher, Sutfin, & Patterson, 2008).

Furthermore, children of lesbian and gay parents and children of heterosexual parents have similar relationships with their peers. They also relate to adults—both those who are gay and straight—no differently from children whose parents are heterosexual. And when they reach adolescence, their romantic relationships and sexual behavior are no different from those of adolescents living with opposite-sex parents (Golombok et al., 2003; Wainright, Russell, & Patterson, 2004).

In short, there is little developmental difference between children whose parents are gay and lesbian and those whose parents are heterosexual. What is clearly different for children with same-sex parents is the possibility of discrimination and prejudice due to their parents' homosexuality. As U.S. citizens engage in an ongoing and highly politicized debate regarding the legality of gay and lesbian marriage, children of such unions may feel singled out and victimized because of societal stereotypes and discrimination. (We consider more about gay and lesbian relationships in Chapter 16.)

Race and Family Life

Although there are as many types of families as there are individuals, research does find some consistencies related to race (Parke, 2004). For example, African American families often have a particularly strong sense of family. Members of African American families are frequently willing to offer welcome and support to extended family members in their homes. Because there is a relatively high level of female-headed households among African Americans, the social and economic support of extended family often is critical. In addition, there is a relatively high proportion of families headed by older adults, such as grandparents, and some studies find that children in grandmother-headed households are particularly well-adjusted (McLoyd et al., 2000; Smith & Drew, 2002; Taylor, 2002).

Hispanic families also often stress the importance of family life, as well as community and religious organizations. Children are taught to value their ties to their families, and they come to see themselves as a central part of an extended family. Ultimately, their sense of who they are becomes tied to the family. Hispanic families also tend to be relatively larger, with an average size of 3.71, compared to 2.97 for Caucasian families and 3.31 for African American families (Cauce & Domenech-Rodriguez, 2000; U.S. Census Bureau, 2003; Halgunseth, Ispa, & Rudy, 2006).

Although relatively little research has been conducted on Asian American families, emerging findings suggest that fathers are more apt to be powerful figures, maintaining discipline. In keeping with the more collectivist orientation of Asian cultures, children tend to believe that family needs have a higher priority than personal needs, and males, in particular, are expected to care for their parents throughout their lifetimes (Ishi-Kuntz, 2000).

Poverty and Family Life

Regardless of race, children living in families who are economically disadvantaged face significant hardships. Poor families have fewer basic everyday resources, and there are more disruptions in children's lives. For example, parents may be forced to look for less expensive housing or may move the entire household in order to find employment. The results frequently are family environments in which parents are less responsive to their children's needs and provide less social support (Evans, 2004).

The stress of difficult family environments, along with other stress in the lives of poor children—such as living in unsafe neighborhoods with high rates of violence and attending inferior schools—ultimately takes its toll. Economically disadvantaged children are at risk for poorer academic performance, higher rates of aggression, and conduct problems. In addition, declines in economic well-being have been linked to mental health problems (Solantaus, Leinonen, & Punamaki, 2004; Sapolsky, 2005; Morales & Guerra, 2006).

Group Care: Orphanages in the 21st Century

The term *orphanage* evokes images of pitiful youngsters clothed in rags, eating porridge out of tin cups, and housed in huge, prisonlike institutions. The reality today is different. Even the term *orphanage* is rarely used, having been replaced by *group home* or *residential treatment center*. Typically housing a relatively small number of children, group homes are used for children whose parents are no longer able to

Although the orphanages of the early 1900s were crowded and institutional (left), today the equivalent, called group homes or residential treatment centers (right), are much more pleasant.

care for them adequately. They are typically funded by a combination of federal, state, and local aid.

Group care has grown significantly in the last decade. In fact, in the 5-year period from 1995 to 2000, the number of children in foster care increased by more than 50%. Today, over 500,000 children in the United States live in foster care (Roche, 2000; Jones-Harden, 2004; Bruskas, 2008).

About three-fourths of children in group care are victims of neglect and abuse. Each year, 300,000 are removed from their homes. Most of them can be returned to their homes following intervention with their families by social service agencies. But the remaining one-fourth are so psychologically damaged due to abuse or other causes that once they are placed in group care, they are likely to remain there throughout childhood. Children who have developed severe problems, such as high levels of aggression or anger, have difficulty finding adoptive families, and it is often difficult to find even temporary foster families who are able to cope with their emotional and behavioral problems (Bass, Shields, & Behrman, 2004; Chamberlain et al., 2006).

Although some politicians have suggested that an increase in group care is a solution to complex social problems associated with unwed mothers who become dependent on welfare, experts in providing social services and psychological treatment are not so sure. For one thing, group homes cannot always consistently provide the support and love potentially available in a family setting. Moreover, group care is hardly cheap: It can cost some $40,000 per year to support a child in group care—about 10 times the cost of maintaining a child in foster care or on welfare (Roche, 2000; Allen & Bissell, 2004).

Other experts argue that group care is neither inherently good nor bad. Instead, the consequences of living away from one's family may be quite positive, depending on the particular characteristics of the staff of the group home and whether child- and youth-care workers are able to develop an effective, stable, and strong emotional bond with a specific child. On the other hand, if a child is unable to form a meaningful relationship with a worker in a group home, the results may well be harmful (Hawkins-Rodgers, 2007; Knorth et al., 2008; Table 13-2 shows the personal characteristics of the best—and worst—child- and youth-care workers).

TABLE 13-2 Personal Characteristics of the Best and Worst Child- and Youth-Care Workers

Best Workers	Worst Workers
Flexible	Exhibit pathology
Mature	Selfish
Integrity	Defensive
Good judgment	Dishonest
Common sense	Abusive
Appropriate values	Abuse drugs/alcohol
Responsible	Uncooperative
Good self-image	Poor self-esteem
Self-control	Rigid
Responsive to authority	Irresponsible
Interpersonally adept	Critical
Stable	Passive–aggressive
Unpretentious	Inappropriate boundaries
Predictable/consistent	Unethical
Nondefensive	Authoritarian/coercive
Nurturant/firm	Inconsistent/unpredictable
Self-aware	Avoidant
Empowering	Don't learn from experience
Cooperative	Poor role model
Good role model	Angry/explosive

(*Source:* Adapted from Shealy, 1995)

REVIEW ↵ mydevelopmentlab

1. The term for children who let themselves into their homes after school and stay alone until their parents return from work is _____-_____.

Answer: self-care

2. _____ families encompass married couples who have at least one stepchild living with them.

Answer: Blended

3. The development of children growing up in families with same-sex parents is _____ to that of children of heterosexual families.

Answer: similar

*To see more review questions, log on to MyDevelopmentLab.

CASE STUDY

The Case of... The Failed Star

Jake Stoddard appeared to be a typical 10-year-old boy. He earned Bs in school, except in composition where he struggled to get his ideas on paper. He played trumpet in the school band, and was the right fielder on his Little League team. Yes, Jake seemed an average boy to everyone—except his parents.

"You're a star, Jake. You're a winner," his parents reminded him daily. For his birthday, his dad had given him an expensive bat. "A pro deserves the best, Jake."

But Jake knew he wasn't a star, no matter how many times his parents said so. And comparing himself to the other kids, he didn't feel like a winner. Until fourth grade, Jake had tried to succeed in school, but this year he had faced facts. Writing was tough for him. He would never be as good as Mark or Beth. So why try?

Though his batting was okay, his coach had already warned him about his fielding. "I like you, Jake, but if your fielding doesn't improve you may not make the team next year," the coach said. Jake mumbled a thanks and wandered away. If he was lousy in the field, and couldn't bat like Tim or Will, maybe he should just give up the game. Then the music teacher pulled him aside. "Jake, I think maybe the trumpet isn't for you. Would you like to try another instrument?"

Jake didn't try another instrument. Instead, he continued to carry the trumpet to school. He didn't want his parents to know their "star" had failed yet again.

1. How does Jake's comparing himself to other children reflect typical social and personality development in middle childhood?

2. What parenting style do Jake's parents seem to have adopted, and how is this affecting Jake's view of himself?

3. Why doesn't Jake believe his parents when they say he's a star and a winner? How might they change their parenting style to promote genuine self-esteem in Jake?

4. How do you see Jake's self-concept affecting the decisions he makes?

5. What specific actions would you advise Jake to take that might change his self-concept and raise his self-esteem?

◀ Looking Back

In what ways do children's views of themselves change during middle childhood?

- According to Erikson, children in the middle-childhood years are in the industry-versus-inferiority stage, focusing on achieving competence and responding to a wide range of personal challenges.

- Children in the middle-childhood years begin to view themselves in terms of psychological characteristics and to differentiate their self-concepts into separate areas. They use social comparison to evaluate their behavior, abilities, expertise, and opinions.

Why is self-esteem important during these years?

- Children in these years are developing self-esteem; those with chronically low self-esteem can become trapped in a cycle of failure in which low self-esteem feeds on itself by producing low expectations and poor performance.

What sorts of relationships and friendships are typical of middle childhood?

- Children's understanding of friendship passes through stages, from a focus on mutual liking and time spent together through the consideration of personal traits and the rewards that friendship provides to an appreciation of intimacy and loyalty.

- Popularity in children is related to traits that underlie social competence. Because of the importance of social interactions and friendships, developmental researchers have engaged in efforts to improve social problem-solving skills and the processing of social information.

How do gender and ethnicity affect friendships?

- Boys and girls in middle childhood increasingly prefer same-gender friendships. Male friendships are characterized by groups, clear dominance hierarchies, and restrictive play. Female friendships tend to involve one or two close relationships, equal status, and a reliance on cooperation.

- Cross-race friendships diminish in frequency as children age. Equal-status interactions among members of different racial groups can lead to improved understanding, mutual respect and acceptance, and a decreased tendency to stereotype.

How do today's diverse family and care arrangements affect children?

- Children in families in which both parents work outside the home generally fare well. Self-care children who fend for themselves after school may develop independence and a sense of competence and contribution.

- Immediately after a divorce, the effects on children in the middle-childhood years can be serious, depending on the financial condition of the family and the hostility level between spouses before the divorce.

- The consequences of living in a single-parent family depend on the financial condition of the family and, if there had been two parents, the level of hostility that existed between them. Blended families present challenges to the child but can also offer opportunities for increased social interaction.

- Children in group care often have been victims of neglect and abuse. Many can be helped and placed with their own or other families, but about 25% of them will spend their childhood years in group care. ■

Epilogue

In this chapter we considered social and personality development in the middle-childhood years and examined self-esteem. During middle childhood, children develop and rely on deeper relationships and friendships, and we discussed the ways that gender and race can affect friendships. We also saw that the changing nature of family arrangements can affect social and personality development, as can the ways children and teachers explain school successes and failures.

Return to the chapter Prologue, describing a typical afternoon of play at Bryan and Christopher Hendrickson's house, and answer the following questions.

1. In what ways do the Hendrickson twins' activities exemplify Erikson's industry-versus-inferiority stage of development?

2. How does the children's play with the boxes differ from the way they would have played during the preschool years?

3. What would you expect is the basis of the friendship between the twins and the other kids in the Prologue?

4. What educated guesses can you make about the popularity, status, and social competence of the twins based on the information in the Prologue?

Key Terms and Concepts

industry-versus-inferiority stage (p. 310)
social comparison (p. 312)
self-esteem (p. 312)
social competence (p. 316)
social problem-solving (p. 317)

dominance hierarchy (p. 318)
coregulation (p. 321)
self-care children (p. 323)
blended family (p. 325)

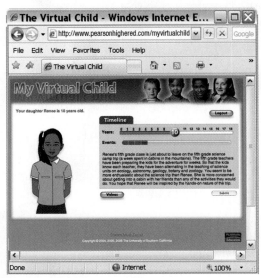

What decisions would you make while raising a child? What would the consequences of those decisions be?

Find out by logging onto **My Virtual Child** and raising your child from birth to 18 years.

4

Middle Childhood

Physical, Cognitive, and Social Personality Development in Middle Childhood

Children entering middle childhood are poised to make great strides in every area of their development. Gross and fine motor skills improve dramatically, and their cognitive development enables them to apply their new skills to the pursuit of more complex tasks, such as reading and sports. However, sensory difficulties and deficits in cognitive and/or physical capabilities can interfere with reading and writing. Being singled out can lead to children being ignored—and even bullied—by some of their peers. With proper treatment, children's physical and social skills can advance to match their cognitive abilities. This can help them become more engaged in their schoolwork and increasingly open to friendships.

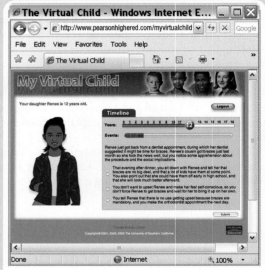

What decisions would you make while raising a child? What would the consequences of those decisions be?

Find out by logging onto **My Virtual Child** and raising your child from birth to 18 years.

● From a **Parent's** Perspective

What strategies would you use to help a child overcome his difficulties and function effectively? How would you bolster his self-esteem?

HINT **Review pages 312–314**

Your response?

● From a **Health-Care** Provider's Perspective

How might you respond to a child's vision and motor problems? What if her parents refuse to believe that there is anything physically wrong with her? How would you convince them to get treatment for their child?

HINT **Review pages 270–271, 273–274**

Your response?

Middle Childhood

Physical Development

- Steady growth and increased abilities characterize a child's physical development in these years (p. 260)
- Gross and fine motor skills develop as muscle coordination improves and new skills are practiced (p. 266)
- Sensory problems can interfere with schoolwork and create social difficulties (p. 270)

Cognitive Development

- Intellectual abilities such as language and memory become more advanced in middle childhood (p. 284)
- Reading fluently with appropriate comprehension is a key academic task for a child during this period (p. 289)
- Many components and types of intelligence are displayed, and the development of intellectual skills is aided by social interactions (p. 295)

Social and Personality Development

- In this period, a child masters many of the challenges presented by school and peers, which take on central importance in his life (p. 310)
- The development of self-esteem is particularly crucial; when a child feels he is inadequate, his self-esteem suffers (p. 312)
- A child's friendships help provide emotional support and foster intellectual growth (p. 315)

From an **Educator's** Perspective

How would you deal with a child's difficulties in reading and writing? What would you do to help integrate him into his class and encourage friendships with his classmates? What would you recommend in terms of educational specialists to deal with his problems?

HINT **Review pages 287–290**

Your response?

From **Your** Perspective

What would you do if your child had physical disabilities that could prevent him or her from progressing in school? How would you encourage your child? How would you deal with your child's frustration with falling behind in school?

HINT **Review pages 270–274**

Your response?

Physical Development in Adolescence

PROLOGUE: THE CRUELEST CUT

He arrived 10 minutes before his fate, so Filip Olsson stood outside Severna Park High School and waited for coaches to post the cut list for the boys' soccer team.

Olsson, a sophomore, wanted desperately to make the junior varsity, but he also wanted justification for a long list of sacrifices. His family had rearranged a trip to Sweden so he could participate in a preparatory soccer camp; he'd crawled out of bed at 5:30 A.M. for two weeks of camp and tryouts and forced down Raisin Bran; he'd sweated off five pounds and pulled his hamstring.

Finally, a coach walked by holding a list, and Olsson followed him into the high school. He walked back out two minutes later, his hands shoved deep into his pockets and his eyes locked on the ground.

"It felt," he said later, "like a punch in the stomach." (Saslow, 2005, p. A1)

▶ Looking Ahead

For adolescents like Filip Olsson, their physical abilities are closely tied to who they are and how they view themselves. No wonder: The physical changes that occur during adolescence are so drastic that it is hard for adolescents to avoid viewing—and sometimes defining—themselves, in large part, in terms of their bodies.

Adolescence is the developmental stage that lies between childhood and adulthood. It is generally viewed as starting just before the teenage years and ending just after them. A transitional stage, adolescents no longer are considered children, but not yet adults. It is a time of considerable physical and psychological growth and change.

This chapter focuses on physical growth during adolescence. We begin by considering the extraordinary physical maturation that occurs during adolescence, triggered by the onset of puberty. We then discuss the consequences of early and late maturation and how they differ for males and females. We also consider nutrition during adolescence. After discussing the causes—and consequences—of obesity, we discuss eating disorders, which are surprisingly common during the period.

We then turn to stress and coping. We examine the causes of stress during adolescence, as well as the short- and long-term consequences of stress. We also consider ways for adolescents to control, reduce, and cope with stressors in their lives.

The chapter concludes with a discussion of several of the major threats to adolescents' well-being. We focus on drug, alcohol, and tobacco use, as well as on sexually transmitted infections.

After reading this chapter, you will be able to answer the following questions:

- *What physical changes do adolescents experience?*
- *What are the consequences of early and late maturation?*
- *What are the nutritional needs and concerns of adolescents?*
- *What are the effects of stress, and what can be done about it?*
- *What are some threats to the well-being of adolescents?*
- *What dangers do adolescent sexual practices present, and how can these dangers be avoided?*

Physical Maturation

For the male members of the Awa tribe, the beginning of adolescence is signaled by an elaborate and—to Western eyes—gruesome ceremony marking the transition from childhood to adulthood. The boys are whipped for 2 or 3 days with sticks and prickly branches. Through the whipping, the boys atone for their previous infractions and honor tribesmen who were killed in warfare. But that's just for starters; the ritual continues for days more.

Most of us probably feel gratitude that we did not have to endure such physical trials when we entered adolescence. But members of Western cultures do have their own rites of passage into adolescence, admittedly less fearsome, such as bar mitzvahs and bat mitzvahs at age 13 for Jewish boys and girls, and confirmation ceremonies in many Christian denominations (Herdt, 1998; Eccles, Templeton, & Barber, 2003; Hoffman, 2003).

Regardless of the nature of the ceremonies celebrated by various cultures, their underlying purpose tends to be similar from one culture to the next: symbolically celebrating the onset of the physical changes that turn a child's body into an adult body capable of reproduction. With these changes the child exits childhood and arrives at the doorstep of adulthood.

Growth During Adolescence: The Rapid Pace of Physical and Sexual Maturation

In only a few months, adolescents can grow several inches and require an entirely new wardrobe as they are transformed—at least in physical appearance—from children to young adults. One aspect of this transformation is the **adolescent growth spurt**, a period of very rapid growth in height and weight. On average, boys grow 4.1 inches a year, and girls, 3.5 inches a year. Some adolescents grow as much as 5 inches in a single year (Tanner, 1972; Caino et al., 2004).

Boys' and girls' adolescent growth spurts begin at different times. As you can see in Figure 14-1, girls begin their spurts around age 10, while boys start at about age 12. During the 2-year period starting at age 11, girls tend to be taller than boys. But by the age of 13, boys, on average, are taller than girls—a state of affairs that persists for the remainder of the life span.

Puberty: The Start of Sexual Maturation

Puberty, the period during which the sexual organs mature, begins when the pituitary gland in the brain signals other glands in children's bodies to begin producing the sex

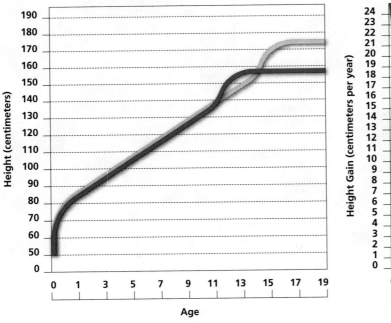
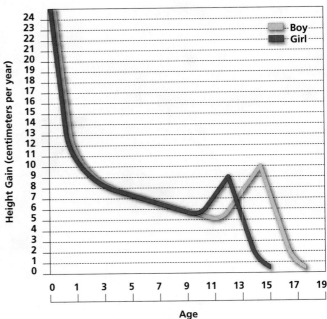

FIGURE 14-1 Growth Patterns

Patterns of growth are depicted in two ways. The figure on the left shows height at a given age, whereas the figure on the right shows the height increase that occurs from birth through the end of adolescence. Notice that girls begin their growth spurt around age 10; boys, about 2 years later. However, by the age of 13, boys tend to be taller than girls. Why is it important that educators be aware of the social consequences of being taller or shorter than average for boys and girls?

(*Source:* Adapted from Cratty, 1986)

hormones, *androgens* (male hormones) or *estrogens* (female hormones), at adult levels. (Males and females produce both types of sex hormones, but males have a higher concentration of androgens, and females a higher concentration of estrogens.) The pituitary gland also signals the body to increase production of growth hormones that interact with the sex hormones to cause the growth spurt and puberty. In addition, the hormone *leptin* appears to play a role in the start of puberty.

Like the growth spurt, puberty begins earlier for girls than for boys. Girls start puberty at around 11 or 12 years of age, and boys begin at around 13 or 14 years of age. However, there are wide variations among individuals. For example, some girls begin puberty as early as 7 or 8 years of age or as late as 16 years of age.

Note the changes that have occurred in just a few years in these pre- and postpuberty photos of the same boy.

Puberty in Girls It is not clear why puberty begins at a particular time. What is clear is that environmental and cultural factors play a role. For example, **menarche**, the onset of menstruation and probably the most obvious signal of puberty in girls, varies greatly in different parts of the world. In poorer, developing countries, menstruation begins later than it does in more economically advantaged countries. Even within wealthier countries, girls in more affluent groups begin to menstruate earlier than do less affluent girls (see Figure 14-2).

Consequently, it appears that girls who are better nourished and healthier are more apt to start menstruation at an earlier age than those who suffer from malnutrition or chronic disease. In fact, some studies have suggested that weight or the proportion of fat to muscle in the body plays a critical role in the timing of menarche. For example, in the United States, athletes with a low percentage of body fat may start menstruating later than less active girls. Conversely, obesity—which results in an increase in the secretion of leptin,

a hormone associated with the onset of menstruation—leads to earlier puberty (Richards, 1996; Vizmanos & Marti-Henneberg, 2000; Woelfle, Harz, & Roth, 2007).

Other factors can affect the timing of menarche. For instance, environmental stress due to such factors as parental divorce or high levels of family conflict can bring about an early onset (Kaltiala-Heino, Kosunen, & Rimpela, 2003; Ellis, 2004; Belsky et al., 2007).

Girls begin their growth spurt several years earlier than boys, leading to significant disparities in mixed-gender settings.

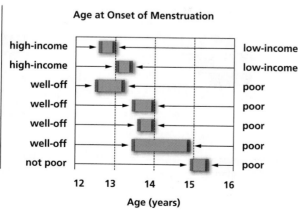

Age at Onset of Menstruation

USA (African descent)	high-income		low-income
USA (European descent)	high-income		low-income
Hong Kong	well-off		poor
Tunis	well-off		poor
Baghdad	well-off		poor
South Africa (Bantu, urban)	well-off		poor
Transkei reserve (Bantu, rural)	not poor		poor

12 13 14 15 16

Age (years)

FIGURE 14-2 Onset of Menstruation

The onset of menstruation occurs earlier in more economically advantaged countries than in poorer nations. But even in wealthier countries, girls living in more affluent circumstances begin to menstruate earlier than those living in less affluent situations.

(*Source:* Adapted from Eveleth & Tanner, 1976)

Over the past 100 years or so, girls in the United States and other cultures have been experiencing puberty at earlier ages. Near the end of the 19th century, menstruation began, on average, around age 14 or 15, compared with today's age 11 or 12. Other indicators of puberty, such as the age at which adult height and sexual maturity are reached, have also appeared at earlier ages, probably due to reduced disease and improved nutrition (Posner, 2006; Cesario & Hughes, 2007).

The earlier start of puberty is an example of a significant **secular trend**, a pattern of change occurring over several generations. Secular trends occur when a physical characteristic changes over the course of several generations, such as earlier onset of menstruation or increased height that has occurred as a result of better nutrition over the centuries.

Menstruation is just one of several changes in puberty that are related to the development of primary and secondary sex characteristics. **Primary sex characteristics** are associated with the development of the organs and structures of the body that directly relate to reproduction. In contrast, **secondary sex characteristics** are the visible signs of sexual maturity that do not involve the sex organs directly.

In girls, the development of primary sex characteristics involves changes in the vagina and uterus. Secondary sex characteristics include the development of breasts and pubic hair. Breasts begin to grow at about age 10, and pubic hair begins to appear at about age 11. Underarm hair appears about 2 years later.

For some girls, indications of puberty start unusually early. One of seven Caucasian girls develops breasts or pubic hair by age 8. Even more surprisingly, the figure is one out of two for African American girls. The reasons for this earlier onset of puberty are unclear, and the demarcation between normal and abnormal onset of puberty is a point of controversy among specialists (Lemonick, 2000; Endocrine Society, 2001; Ritzen, 2003).

Puberty in Boys Boys' sexual maturation follows a somewhat different course. The penis and scrotum begin to grow at an accelerated rate at around the age of 12, reaching adult size about 3 or 4 years later. As boys' penises enlarge, other primary sex characteristics are developing with enlargement of the prostate gland and seminal vesicles, which produce semen (the fluid that carries sperm). A boy's first ejaculation, known as *spermarche*, usually occurs around the age of 13, more than a year after the body has begun producing sperm. At first, the semen contains relatively few sperm, but the amount of sperm increases significantly with age. Secondary sex characteristics are also developing. Pubic hair begins to grow at around the age of 12, followed by the growth of underarm and facial hair. Finally, boys' voices deepen as the vocal cords become longer and the larynx becomes larger. (Figure 14-3 summarizes the changes that occur in sexual maturation during early adolescence.)

The surge in production of hormones that triggers the start of adolescence also may lead to rapid swings in mood. For example, boys may have feelings of anger and annoyance that are associated with higher hormone levels. In girls, the emotions produced by hormone production are somewhat different: Higher levels of hormones are associated with anger and depression (Buchanan, Eccles, & Becker, 1992).

Body Image: Reactions to Physical Changes in Adolescence

Unlike infants, who also undergo extraordinarily rapid growth, adolescents are well aware of what is happening to their bodies, and they may react with horror or joy, spending long periods in front of mirrors. Few, though, are neutral about the changes they are witnessing.

Some of the changes of adolescence do not show up in physical changes, but carry psychological weight. In the past,

FIGURE 14-3 The Changes of Sexual Maturation During Adolescence

Changes in sexual maturation occur for both males and females primarily during early adolescence.
(*Source:* Adapted from Tanner, 1978)

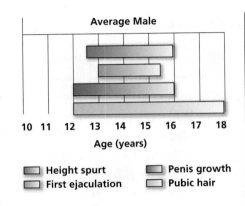

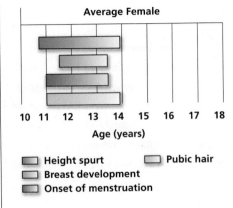

girls tended to react to menarche with anxiety because Western society tended to emphasize the more negative aspects of menstruation, such as the potential of cramps and messiness. Today, however, society's view of menstruation tends to be more positive, in part because menstruation has been demystified and discussed more openly (for instance, television commercials for tampons are commonplace). As a consequence, menarche is typically accompanied by an increase in self-esteem, a rise in status, and greater self-awareness, as adolescent girls see themselves as becoming adults (Johnson, Roberts, & Worell, 1999; Matlin, 2003).

A boy's first ejaculation is roughly equivalent to menarche in a girl. However, although girls generally tell their mothers about the onset of menstruation, boys rarely mention their first ejaculation to their parents or even to their friends (Stein & Reiser, 1994). Why? One reason is that girls require tampons or sanitary napkins, and mothers provide them. It also may be that boys see the first ejaculation as an indication of their budding sexuality, an area about which they are quite uncertain and therefore reluctant to discuss with others.

Menstruation and ejaculations occur privately, but changes in body shape and size are quite public. Consequently, teenagers entering puberty frequently are embarrassed by the changes that are occurring. Girls, in particular, are often unhappy with their new bodies. Ideals of beauty in many Western countries call for an unrealistic thinness that is quite different from the actual shape of most women. Puberty brings a considerable increase in the amount of fatty tissue, as well as enlargement of the hips and buttocks—a far cry from the slenderness that society seems to demand (Unger & Crawford, 2004; McCabe & Ricciardelli, 2006; Cotrufo et al., 2007).

How children react to the onset of puberty depends in part on when it happens. Girls and boys who mature either much earlier or much later than most of their peers are especially affected by the timing of puberty.

The Timing of Puberty: Consequences of Early and Late Maturation

Why does it matter when a boy or girl reaches puberty? There are social consequences of early or late maturation. And as we shall see, social consequences are very important to adolescents.

Early Maturation   For boys, early maturation is largely a plus. Early maturing boys tend to be more successful at athletics, presumably because of their larger size. They also tend to be more popular and to have a more positive self-concept.

On the other hand, early maturation in boys does have a downside. Boys who mature early are more apt to have difficulties in school, and they are more likely to become involved in delinquency and substance abuse. The reason: Their larger size makes it more likely that they will seek out the company of older boys who may involve them in activities that are inappropriate for their age. Furthermore, although early maturers are more responsible and cooperative in later life, they are also more conforming and lacking in humor. Overall, though, the pluses seem to outweigh the minuses for early maturing boys (Taga, Markey, & Friedman, 2006; Costello et al., 2007; Lynne et al., 2007; van Jaarsveld et al., 2007).

The story is a bit different for early maturing girls. For them, the obvious changes in their bodies—such as the development of breasts—may lead them to feel uncomfortable and different from their peers. Moreover, because girls, in general, mature earlier than boys do, early maturation tends to come at a very young age in the girl's life. Early maturing girls may have to endure ridicule from their less mature classmates (Franko & Striegel-Moore, 2002; Olivardia & Pope, 2002; Mendle, Turkheimer, & Emery, 2007).

On the other hand, early maturation is not a completely negative experience for girls. Girls who mature earlier tend to be sought after more as potential dates, and their popularity may enhance their self-concepts. This attention has a price, however. They may not be socially ready to participate in the kind of one-on-one dating situations that most girls deal with at a later age, and such situations may be psychologically challenging for early maturing girls. Moreover, the conspicuousness of their deviance from their later maturing classmates may have a negative effect, producing anxiety, unhappiness, and depression (Kaltiala-Heino, Kosunen, & Rimpela, 2003).

Cultural norms and standards regarding how women should look play a big role in how girls experience early maturation. For instance, in the United States, the notion of female sexuality is looked on with a degree of ambivalence, being promoted in the media yet frowned on socially. Girls who appear "sexy" attract both positive and negative attention.

Consequently, unless a young girl who has developed secondary sex characteristics early can handle the disapproval she may encounter when she conspicuously displays her growing sexuality, the outcome of early maturation may be negative. In countries in which attitudes about sexuality are more liberal, the results of early maturation may be more positive. For example, in cultures that have a more open view

Boys who mature early tend to be more successful in athletics and have a more positive self-concept. Why might there be a downside to early maturation?

From an educator's perspective:

Why do you think the passage to adolescence is regarded in many cultures as a significant transition that calls for unique ceremonies?

of sex, early maturing girls have higher self-esteem than do such girls in the United States. Furthermore, the consequences of early maturation vary even within the United States, depending on the views of girls' peer groups and on prevailing community standards regarding sex (Petersen, 2000; Güre, Uçanok, & Sayil, 2006).

Late Maturation As with early maturation, the situation with late maturation is mixed, although in this case boys fare worse than girls. For instance, boys who are smaller and lighter than their more physically mature peers tend to be viewed as less attractive. Because of their smaller size, they are at a disadvantage when it comes to sports activities. Furthermore, boys are expected to be bigger than their dates, so the social lives of late-maturing boys may suffer. Ultimately, if these difficulties lead to a decline in self-concept, the disadvantages of late maturation for boys could extend well into adulthood. More positively, coping with the challenges of late maturation may actually help males in some ways. Late-maturing boys grow up to have several positive qualities such as assertiveness and insightfulness, and they are more creatively playful than early maturers (Kaltiala-Heino, Kosunen, & Rimpela, 2003).

The picture for late-maturing girls is actually quite positive. In the short-term, girls who mature later may be overlooked in dating and other mixed-sex activities during junior high school and middle school, and they may have relatively low social status. However, by the time they are in the 10th grade and have begun to mature visibly, late-maturing girls' satisfaction with themselves and their bodies may be greater than that of early maturers. In fact, late-maturing girls may end up with fewer emotional problems. The reason? Late-maturing girls are more apt to fit the societal ideal of a slender, "leggy" body type than early maturers, who tend to look heavier in comparison (Kaminaga, 2007; Leen-Feldner, Reardon, & Hayward, 2008).

In sum, the reactions to early and late maturation present a complex picture. As we have seen repeatedly, we need to take into consideration the complete constellation of factors affecting individuals in order to understand their development. Some developmentalists suggest that other factors, such as changes in peer groups; family dynamics; and particularly, schools and other societal institutions, may be more pertinent in determining an adolescent's behavior than the presence of early and later maturation, or the effects of puberty in general (Dorn, Susman, & Ponirakis, 2003; Stice, 2003; Mendle, Turkheimer, & Emery, 2007).

Obesity has become the most common nutritional concern during adolescence. In addition to issues of health, what are some psychological concerns about obesity in adolescence?

Nutrition and Food: Fueling the Growth of Adolescence

A rice cake in the afternoon, an apple for dinner. That was Heather Rhodes's typical diet her freshman year at St. Joseph's College in Rensselaer, Indiana, when she began to nurture a fear (exacerbated, she says, by the sudden death of a friend) that she was gaining weight. But when Rhodes, now 20, returned home to Joliet, Illinois, for summer vacation a year and a half ago, her family thought she was melting away. "I could see the outline of her pelvis in her clothes . . ." says Heather's mother . . . , so she and the rest of the family confronted Heather one evening, placing a bathroom scale in the middle of the family room. "I told them they were attacking me and to go to hell," recalls Heather, who nevertheless reluctantly weighed herself. Her 5'7" frame held a mere 85 pounds—down 22 pounds from her senior year in high school. "I told them they rigged the scale," she says. It simply didn't compute with her self-image. "When I looked in the mirror," she says, "I thought my stomach was still huge and my face was fat." (Sandler, 1994, p. 56)

Heather's problem: a severe eating disorder, anorexia nervosa. As we have seen, the cultural ideal of slim and fit favors late-developing girls. But when those developments do occur, how do girls, and increasingly, boys, cope when the image in the mirror deviates from the ideal presented in the popular media?

The rapid physical growth of adolescence is fueled by an increase in food consumption. Particularly during the growth spurt, adolescents eat substantial quantities of food, increasing their intake of calories rather dramatically. During the teenage years, the average girl requires some 2,200 calories a day, and the average boy, 2,800.

Of course, not just any calories help nourish adolescents' growth. Several key nutrients are essential, in particular, calcium and iron. The calcium provided by milk helps bone growth, which may prevent the later development of osteoporosis—the thinning of bones—that affects 25% of women later in their lives. Similarly, iron is necessary to prevent iron-deficiency anemia, an ailment that is common in teenagers.

For most adolescents, the major nutritional issue is ensuring the consumption of a sufficient balance of appropriate foods. Two extremes of nutrition can be a major concern for a substantial minority and can create a real threat to health. Obesity and eating disorders (like the one afflicting Heather Rhodes) are among the most prevalent problems.

Obesity The most common nutritional concern during adolescence is obesity. One in 5 adolescents is overweight, and 1 in 20 can be formally classified as obese (body weight

Anorexia nervosa A severe and potentially life-threatening eating disorder in which individuals refuse to eat, while denying that their behavior or skeletal appearance is out of the ordinary

Bulimia An eating disorder that primarily afflicts adolescent girls and young women, characterized by binges on large quantities of food followed by purges of the food through vomiting or the use of laxatives

that is more than 20% above average). Moreover, the proportion of female adolescents who are classified as obese increases over the course of adolescence (Brook & Tepper, 1997; Kimm et al., 2002; Critser, 2003).

Although adolescents are obese for the same reasons as younger children, the psychological consequences may be particularly severe during a time of life when body image is of special concern. Furthermore, the potential health consequences of obesity during adolescence are also problematic. For instance, obesity taxes the circulatory system, and it increases the likelihood of high blood pressure and diabetes. Finally, obese adolescents stand an 80% chance of becoming obese adults (Blaine, Rodman, & Newman, 2007; Goble, 2008; Wang et al., 2008).

Lack of exercise is one of the main culprits. One survey found that by the end of the teenage years, most females get virtually no exercise outside of physical education classes in school. In fact, the older they are, the less exercise female adolescents engage in. The problem is particularly pronounced for older Black female adolescents, more than half of whom who report *no* physical exercise outside of school, compared with about one-third of White adolescents who report no exercise (see Figure 14-4; Kimm et al., 2002; Burke et al., 2006; Deforche, De Bourdeaudhuij, & Tanghe, 2006; Delva, O'Malley, & Johnston, 2006).

Why do adolescent women get so little exercise? It may reflect a lack of organized sports or good athletic facilities for women. It may even be the result of lingering cultural norms suggesting that athletic participation is more the realm of boys than of girls.

There are additional reasons for the high rate of obesity during adolescence. One is the availability of fast foods, which deliver large portions of high calorie, high fat cuisine

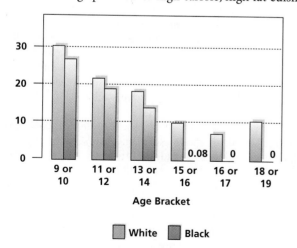

FIGURE 14-4 Decline in Physical Activity

Physical activity among both White and Black adolescent females declines substantially over the course of adolescence. What might be the reasons for this decline?
(*Source:* Kimm et al., 2002)

at prices adolescents can afford. In addition, many adolescents spend a significant proportion of their leisure time inside their homes watching television, playing video games, and surfing the Web. Such sedentary activities not only keep adolescents from exercising, but they often are accompanied by snacks of junk foods (Delmas et al., 2007; Krebs et al., 2007; Bray, 2008).

Anorexia Nervosa and Bulimia The fear of fat and desire to avoid obesity sometimes becomes so strong that it turns into a problem. For instance, Heather Rhodes suffered from **anorexia nervosa**, a severe eating disorder in which individuals refuse to eat. Their troubled body image leads them to deny that their behavior and skeletal appearance are out of the ordinary.

Anorexia is a dangerous psychological disorder; some 15% to 20% of its victims literally starve themselves to death. It primarily afflicts women between the ages of 12 and 40; those most susceptible are intelligent, successful, and attractive White adolescent girls from affluent homes. Anorexia is increasingly becoming a problem for boys. About 10% of victims are male, a percentage that is swelling and is associated with the use of steroids (Robb & Dadson, 2002; Jacobi et al., 2004; Ricciardelli & McCabe, 2004; Crisp et al., 2006).

Even though they eat little, anorexics are often focused on food. They may go shopping often, collect cookbooks, talk about food, or cook huge meals for others. Although they may be incredibly thin, their body images are so distorted that they see their reflections in mirrors as disgustingly fat and try to lose more and more weight. Even when they look like skeletons, they are unable to see what they have become.

Bulimia, another eating disorder, is characterized by *bingeing*, eating large quantities of food, followed by *purging* of the food through vomiting or the use of laxatives. Bulimics may eat an entire gallon of ice cream or a whole package of tortilla chips. But after such a binge, sufferers experience powerful feelings of guilt and depression, and they intentionally rid themselves of the food.

Although the weight of a person with bulimia remains fairly normal, the disorder is quite hazardous. The constant vomiting and diarrhea of the binge-and-purge cycles may produce a chemical imbalance that can lead to heart failure. Furthermore, it produces damage to the throat, mouth, and teeth.

This young woman suffers from anorexia nervosa, a severe eating disorder in which people refuse to eat while denying that their behavior and appearance are out of the ordinary.

The exact reasons for the occurrence of eating disorders are not clear, although several factors appear to be implicated. Dieting often precedes the development of eating disorders, as even normal-weight individuals are spurred on by societal standards of slenderness to seek to lower their weight. The feelings of control and success may encourage them to lose more and more weight. Furthermore, girls who mature earlier than their peers and who have a higher level of body fat are more susceptible to eating disorders during later adolescence as they try to bring their maturing bodies back into line with the cultural standard of a thin, boyish physique. Adolescents who are clinically depressed are also more likely to develop eating disorders later, perhaps seeking to withhold from themselves (Pratt, Phillips, & Greydanus, 2003; Walcott, Pratt, & Patel, 2003; Giordana, 2005).

Some experts suggest that a biological cause lies at the root of both anorexia nervosa and bulimia. In fact, twin studies suggest there are genetic components to the disorders. In addition, hormonal imbalances sometimes occur in sufferers (Kaye et al., 2004; Kump et al., 2007; Wade et al., 2008).

Other attempts to explain the eating disorders emphasize psychological and social factors. For instance, some experts suggest that the disorders are a result of perfectionistic, overdemanding parents or by-products of other family difficulties. Culture also plays a role. Anorexia nervosa, for instance, is found only in cultures that idealize slender female bodies. Because in most places such a standard does not hold, anorexia is not prevalent outside the United States (Haines & Neumark-Sztainer, 2006; Harrison & Hefner, 2006).

For example, anorexia is virtually nonexistent in all of Asia, with two interesting exceptions: the upper classes of both Japan and Hong Kong, where Western influence is greatest. Furthermore, anorexia nervosa is a fairly recent disorder. It was rarely seen in the 17th and 18th centuries, when the ideal of the female body was a plump corpulence. The increasing number of boys with anorexia in the United States may be related to a growing emphasis on a muscular male physique that features little body fat (Mangweth, Hausmann, & Walch, 2004; Makino et al., 2006; Greenberg, Cwikel, & Mirsky, 2007).

Because anorexia nervosa and bulimia are thought to be products of both biological and environmental causes, treatment typically involves a mix of approaches. For instance, both psychological therapy and dietary modifications are likely to be needed for successful treatment. In more extreme cases, hospitalization may be necessary (Robergeau, Joseph, & Silber, 2006; Rossi et al., 2007; Wilson, Grilo, & Vitousek, 2007).

Brain Development and Thought: Paving the Way for Cognitive Growth

Adolescence brings greater independence. Teenagers tend to assert themselves more and more. This independence is, in part, the result of changes in the brain that pave the way for the significant advances that occur in cognitive abilities during adolescence, as we consider in the next part of the chapter. As the number of neurons (the cells of the nervous system) continue to grow, and their interconnections become richer and more complex, adolescent thinking also becomes more sophisticated (Thompson & Nelson, 2001; Toga & Thompson, 2003; Petanjek et al., 2008).

The brain produces an oversupply of gray matter during adolescence that is later pruned back at the rate of 1% to 2% per year. Myelination—the process in which nerve cells are insulated by a covering of fat cells—increases and continues to make the transmission of neural messages more efficient. Both the pruning process and increased myelination contribute to the growing cognitive abilities of adolescents (Sowell et al., 2001, 2003).

One specific area of the brain that undergoes considerable development throughout adolescence is the prefrontal cortex, which is not fully developed until the early 20s. The *prefrontal cortex* is the part of the brain that allows people to think, evaluate, and make complex judgments in a uniquely human way. It underlies the increasingly complex intellectual achievements that are possible during adolescence.

During adolescence, the prefrontal cortex becomes increasingly efficient in communicating with other parts of the brain. This helps build a communication system within the brain that is more distributed and sophisticated, permitting the different areas of the brain to process information more effectively (Scherf, Sweeney, & Luna, 2006; Hare et al., 2008).

The prefrontal cortex, the area of the brain responsible for impulse control, is biologically immature during adolescence, leading to some of the risky and impulsive behavior associated with people in this age group.

The prefrontal cortex also provides for impulse control. Rather than simply reacting to emotions such as anger or rage, an individual with a fully developed prefrontal cortex is able to inhibit the desire for action that stems from such emotions.

Because the prefrontal cortex is biologically immature during adolescence, the ability to inhibit impulses is not fully developed (see Figure 14-5). This brain immaturity may lead to some of the risky and impulsive behaviors that are characteristic of adolescence (Weinberger, 2001; Steinberg & Scott, 2003; Eshel et al., 2007).

Adolescent brain development also produces changes in regions involving dopamine sensitivity and production. As a result of these alterations, adolescents may become less susceptible to the effects of alcohol, and it requires more drinks to for adolescents to experience its reinforcing qualities—leading to higher alcohol intake. In addition, alterations in dopamine sensitivity may make adolescents more sensitive to stress, leading to further alcohol use (Spear, 2002).

The Immature Brain Argument: Too Young for the Death Penalty?

Just after 2 A.M. on September 9, 1993, Christopher Simmons, 17, and Charles Benjamin, 15, broke into a trailer south of Fenton, Missouri, just outside of St. Louis. They woke Shirley Ann Crook, a 46-year-old truck driver who was inside, and proceeded to tie her up and cover her eyes and mouth with silver duct tape. They then put her in the back of her minivan, drove her to a railroad bridge and pushed her into the river below, where her body was found the next day. Simmons and Benjamin later confessed to the abduction and murder, which had netted them $6. (Raeburn, 2004, p. 26)

This horrific case sent Benjamin to life in prison, and Simmons was given the death penalty. But Simmons' lawyers appealed, and ultimately the U.S. Supreme Court ruled that he—and anyone else under the age of 18—could not be executed because of their youth.

Among the evidence that the Supreme Court weighed in its decision was evidence from neuroscientists and child developmentalists that the brains of adolescents were still developing in important ways and that therefore they lacked judgment because of this brain immaturity. According to this reasoning, adolescents are not fully capable of making reasonable decisions because their brains are not yet wired like those of adults.

The argument that adolescents may not be as responsible for their crimes stems from research showing that the brain continues to grow and mature during the teenage years, and sometimes beyond. For example, neurons that make up unnecessary gray matter of the brain begin to disappear during adolescence. In its place, the volume of white matter of the brain begins to increase. The decline in gray matter and increase in white matter permits more sophisticated, thoughtful cognitive processing (Beckman, 2004).

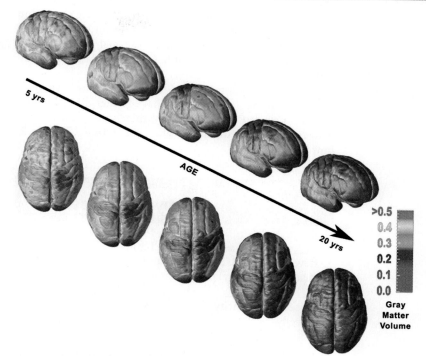

FIGURE 14-5 Continuing Brain Maturation

Even in the late teenage years, gray matter is replaced throughout the cortex. (*Source:* Beckman, 2004)

For instance, when the frontal lobes of the brain contain more white matter, they are better at restraining impulsivity and censoring emotional outbursts.

In adolescents, that censoring process may not occur as efficiently. As a result, teenagers may act impulsively, responding with emotion rather than reason. Furthermore, adolescents' ability to foresee the consequences of their actions may also be hindered as a result of their less mature brains.

Are the brains of adolescents so immature that teenage offenders should receive less harsh punishment for their crimes than those with older, and therefore more mature, brains? It is not a simple question, and the answer probably will come more from those studying morality than from scientists (Aronson, 2007).

Sleep Deprivation

With increasing academic and social demands placed upon them, adolescents go to bed later and get up earlier. As a result, they often lead their lives in something of a sleep-deprived daze.

The sleep deprivation comes at a time when adolescents' internal clocks shift. Older adolescents in particular experience the need to go to bed later and to sleep later in the morning, and they require 9 hours of sleep each night to feel

Stress The physical response to events that threaten or challenge us

Psychosomatic disorders Medical problems caused by the interaction of psychological, emotional, and physical difficulties

rested. Because they typically have early morning classes but don't feel sleepy until late at night, they end up getting far less sleep than their bodies crave (National Sleep Foundation, 2002; Dorofaeff & Denny, 2006; Fuligni & Hardway, 2006).

Sleep deprivation takes its toll. Sleepy teens have lower grades, are more depressed, and have greater difficulty controlling their moods. In addition, they are a great risk for auto accidents (Fredriksen et al., 2004; Teixeira, Fischer, & Lowden, 2006).

REVIEW ↵ mydevelopmentlab

1. _____ sex characteristics are associated with the development of the organs and structures of the body that directly relate to reproduction. In contrast, _____ sex characteristics are the visible signs of sexual maturity that do not involve the sex organs directly.

   Answer: Primary; secondary

2. For girls, _____ maturation initially offers increased popularity, but they may also experience embarrassment over the changes occurring in their bodies. On the other hand, it is a more positive experience for boys.

   Answer: early

3. _____ _____ is a severe eating disorder in which individuals refuse to eat.

   Answer: Anorexia nervosa

To see more review questions, log on to MyDevelopmentLab.

Stress and Coping

It was only 10:34 A.M., and already Jennifer Jackson had put in what seemed like a full day. After getting up at 6:30 A.M., she studied a bit for an American history exam scheduled later in the afternoon. She gulped down breakfast as she studied and then headed off to the campus bookstore, where she worked part time.

Her car was in the shop with some undiagnosed ailment, so she had to take the bus. The bus was late, so Jennifer didn't have time to stop off at the library before work to pick up the reserved book she needed. Making a mental note to try to get the book at lunchtime (although she thought it probably wouldn't be available by then), she sprinted from the bus to the store, arriving a few minutes late. Although her supervisor didn't say anything, she looked irritated as Jennifer explained why she was late. Feeling that she needed to make amends, Jennifer volunteered to sort invoices—a task that she, and everyone else, hated. As she sorted the invoices, she also answered the phone and jumped up to serve a steady stream of customers who were placing special orders. When the phone rang at 10:34 A.M., it was her garage mechanic telling her that the car repair would cost several hundred dollars—a sum she did not have.

If you were to monitor Jennifer Jackson's heart rate and blood pressure, you wouldn't be shocked to find that both were higher than normal. You also wouldn't be surprised if she reported experiencing stress.

Few of us need much of an introduction to **stress,** the response to events that threaten or challenge us. Stress is a part of nearly everyone's existence, and most people's lives are crowded with events and circumstances, known as *stressors,* that produce threats to our well-being. Stressors need not be unpleasant events: Even the happiest events, such as obtaining admission to a sought-after college or graduating from high school, can produce stress for adolescents.

Stress produces several outcomes. Most immediate is typically a biological reaction, as certain hormones, secreted by the adrenal glands, cause a rise in heart rate, blood pressure, respiration rate, and sweating. In some situations, these immediate effects may be beneficial because they produce an "emergency reaction" in the sympathetic nervous system that prepares people to defend themselves from a sudden, threatening situation. A person challenged by a snarling, ferocious dog, for instance, would want all the bodily preparedness possible to deal with the emergency situation.

However, long-term, continuous exposure to stressors may result in a reduction of the body's ability to deal with stress. As stress-related hormones are constantly secreted, the heart, blood vessels, and other body tissues may deteriorate. As a consequence, people become more susceptible to diseases as their ability to fight off germs declines (Schneiderman, 1983; Kiecolt-Glaser & Glaser, 1986; Cohen, Tyrrell, & Smith, 1993).

Origins of Stress: Reacting to Life's Challenges

Although stress is experienced long before adolescence, it becomes particularly wearing during the teenage years, and it can produce formidable costs (see Figure 14-6). Over the long run, the constant wear-and-tear caused by the physiological arousal that occurs as the body tries to fight off stress produces negative effects. For instance, headaches, backaches, skin rashes, indigestion, chronic fatigue, sleep disturbances, and even the common cold are stress-related illnesses (Kiecolt-Glaser & Glaser, 1991; Cohen et al., 1993; Reid et al., 2002).

Stress may also lead to **psychosomatic disorders,** medical problems caused by the interaction of psychological, emotional, and physical difficulties. For instance, ulcers, asthma, arthritis, and high blood pressure may—although not invariably—be produced or worsened by stress (Siegel & Davis, 2008).

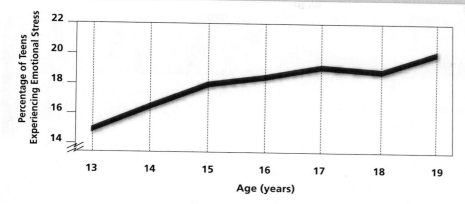

FIGURE 14-6 Teenage Stress

Teenage students may experience stress concerning where they will work in the future and at what kind of job. What can health-care workers look for as signs of stress among adolescents?
(*Source:* National Longitudinal Study of Adolescent Health, 2000)

Stress may even cause more serious, even life-threatening illnesses. According to some research, the greater the number of stressful events a person experiences over the course of a year, the more likely he or she is to have a major illness (see Table 14-1; Holmes & Rahe, 1967; Alverdy, Zaborina, & Wu, 2005).

Before you start calculating whether you are overdue for a major illness, however, keep in mind some important

---

TABLE 14-1 How Stressed Are You?

Test your level of stress by answering these questions, and adding the score from each box. Questions apply to the last month only. The key below will help you determine the extent of your stress.

1. How often have you been upset because of something that happened unexpectedly?
   0 = never, 1 = almost never, 2 = sometimes, 3 = fairly often, 4 = very often

2. How often have you felt that you were unable to control the important things in your life?
   0 = never, 1 = almost never, 2 = sometimes, 3 = fairly often, 4 = very often

3. How often have you felt nervous and "stressed"?
   0 = never, 1 = almost never, 2 = sometimes, 3 = fairly often, 4 = very often

4. How often have you felt confident about your ability to handle your personal problems?
   4 = never, 3 = almost never, 2 = sometimes, 1 = fairly often, 0 = very often

5. How often have you felt that things were going your way?
   4 = never, 3 = almost never, 2 = sometimes, 1 = fairly often, 0 = very often

6. How often have you been able to control irritations in your life?
   4 = never, 3 = almost never, 2 = sometimes, 1 = fairly often, 0 = very often

7. How often have you found that you could not cope with all the things that you had to do?
   0 = never, 1 = almost never, 2 = sometimes, 3 = fairly often, 4 = very often

8. How often have you felt that you were on top of things?
   4 = never, 3 = almost never, 2 = sometimes, 1 = fairly often, 0 = very often

9. How often have you been angered because of things that were outside your control?
   0 = never, 1 = almost never, 2 = sometimes, 3 = fairly often, 4 = very often

10. How often have you felt difficulties were piling up so high that you could not overcome them?
    0 = never, 1 = almost never, 2 = sometimes, 3 = fairly often, 4 = very often

How You Measure Up

Stress levels vary among individuals—compare your total score to the averages below:

AGE		GENDER	
18–29	14.2	Men	12.1
30–44	13.0	Women	13.7
45–54	12.6		
55–64	11.9		
65 & over	12.0		

MARITAL STATUS

Widowed	12.6
Married or living with	12.4
Single or never wed	14.1
Divorced	14.7
Separated	16.6

(*Source:* Cohen, Kamarack, & Mermelstein, 1983.)

Coping Efforts to control, reduce, or tolerate the threats and challenges that lead to stress

FROM RESEARCH to PRACTICE
Bullies and Their Victims: The Lingering Stress

Of the many different stress-provoking events that occur in adolescence, being the victim of bullying is one of the most stressful. Nearly a third of all adolescents have been bullied at some point, and as many as 10% are chronically victimized. Bullying includes aggressive and hurtful acts such as name-calling, rejection, teasing, threats, and physical harm. Given that such experiences provoke negative emotions, are uncontrollable, and directly affect adolescents' lives in important ways, it's hardly surprising that being bullied is associated with anxiety, depression, and low self-worth, among other negative psychological outcomes (Hawker & Boulton, 2000; Nansel et al., 2001; Pepler et al., 2008).

Although bullying declines in frequency with age, some victims continue to be bullied throughout later adolescence and even into adulthood, where the workplace replaces the playground as a place of fear and intimidation. To understand the long-term outcomes of bullying, psychologist Matthew Newman and his colleagues explored the psychological effects during later adolescence of being bullied earlier in life. Researchers were specifically interested in how the experience of being bullied in high school continued to affect adolescents after they made the transition to college (Smith, Singer, & Hoel, 2003; Newman, Holden, & Delville, 2005).

University undergraduates provided data on their experiences with bullying in high school and prior to high school, as well as on a variety of stress symptoms they were currently experiencing as college students. They found that the prevalence of bullying changed over time as adolescents transitioned into high school. For example, one-third of the participants reported being bullied occasionally during the time before high school, and over another quarter of

them reported frequent bullying during that period. But the frequency dropped off in high school, where a quarter of the participants experienced occasional bullying and fewer than 10% were bullied frequently.

Most important, the stress that college students currently reported was related to bullying experiences before college. Students who had been bullied more in high school reported more stress symptoms in college; interestingly, even students who had been bullied more *before* high school reported more stress symptoms in college (despite the fact that a wide majority of them reported that the bullying had decreased or stopped during high school).

Clearly, the harmful effects of being bullied during adolescence persist for years, emerging as stress symptoms after the bullied adolescent's transition to college. Furthermore, the relationship between being bullied in adolescence and increased stress in college was most pronounced for students who felt the most isolated. Students who were bullied frequently in high school but nevertheless did not feel isolated from others were less likely to continue to be affected into college. This finding underscores the importance of social support as a valuable coping resource (Holt & Espelage, 2007; Carney, 2008).

- Why might being bullied be such a powerfully stressful experience for adolescents?

- Do you think that the greater stress that bullied students feel in college is a direct consequence of being bullied or that it results indirectly from a loss of social support?

limitations to the research. Not everyone who experiences high stress becomes ill, and the weights given to particular stressors probably vary from one person to the next. Furthermore, there is a kind of circularity to such enumerations of stressors: Because the research is correlational, it is possible that someone who has a major illness to begin with is more likely to experience some of the stressors on the list. For example, a person may have lost a job because of the effects of an illness, rather than develop an illness because of the loss of a job. Still, the list of stressors does provide a way to consider how most people react to various potentially stressful events in their lives. (Also see the *From Research to Practice* box.)

Meeting the Challenge of Stress

Some adolescents are better than others at **coping**, making efforts to control, reduce, or tolerate the threats and challenges that lead to stress. What is the key to successful coping?

Some individuals use *problem-focused coping*, by which they attempt to manage a stressful problem or situation by directly changing the situation to make it less stressful. For example, a high school student who is having academic difficulties may speak to his teachers and ask that they extend the deadlines for assignments, or a worker who is dissatisfied with her job assignment can ask that she be assigned other tasks.

Other adolescents employ *emotion-focused coping*, which involves the conscious regulation of emotion. For instance, a teenager who is having problems getting along with her boss in her after-school job may tell herself that she should look at the bright side: At least she has a job in the first place (Folkman & Moskowitz, 2007; Karademas, 2007; Vingerhoets, Nyklicek, & Denollet, 2008).

Coping is also aided by the presence of *social support*, assistance and comfort supplied by others. Turning to others in the face of stress can provide both emotional support (in the form of a shoulder to cry on) and practical, tangible support (such as an advance of one's allowance) (Boehmer, Linde, & Freund, 2005; Schwarzer & Knoll, 2007).

Finally, even if adolescents don't consciously cope with stress, some psychologists suggest that they may unconsciously use defensive coping mechanisms that aid in stress reduction. *Defensive coping* involves the unconscious use of strategies that distort or deny the true nature of a situation. For instance, a person may deny the seriousness of a threat, trivialize a life-threatening illness, or tell himself that academic failure on a series of tests is unimportant. The problem with such defensive coping is that it does not deal with the reality of the situation but merely avoids or ignores the problem.

Becoming an Informed Consumer of Development

Coping With Stress

Although no single formula can cover all cases of stress, some general guidelines can help everyone cope with the stress that is part of life. Among them are the following:

- Seek control over the situation producing the stress. Putting yourself in charge of a situation that is producing stress can take you a long way toward coping with it.

- Redefine the "threat" as a "challenge." Changing the definition of a situation can make it seem less threatening. "Look for the silver lining" isn't bad advice.

- Get social support. Almost any difficulty can be faced more easily with the help of others. Friends, family members, and even telephone hotlines staffed by trained counselors can provide significant support. (For help in identifying appropriate hotlines, the U.S. Public Health Service maintains a master toll-free number that can provide phone numbers and addresses of many national groups. Call 800-336-4794.)

- Use relaxation techniques. Procedures that reduce the physiological arousal brought about by stress can be particularly effective. A variety of techniques produce relaxation, such as transcendental meditation, Zen, yoga, progressive muscle relaxation, and even hypnosis; these have been shown to be effective in reducing stress. One that works particularly well, devised by physician Herbert Benson (1993), is illustrated in Table 14-2.

- Exercise! Vigorous exercise not only leads to greater fitness and health but also helps cope with stress and can lead to a sense of psychological well-being.

- Keep in mind that a life without *any* stress at all would be a dull one. Stress is a natural part of life, and successfully coping with it can be a gratifying experience.

From a health-care provider's perspective: Are there periods of life that are relatively stress free, or do people of all ages experience stress? Do stressors differ from age to age?

TABLE 14-2 **How to Produce the Relaxation Response**

Some general advice on regular practice of the relaxation response:

- Try to find 10 to 20 minutes in your daily routine; before breakfast is a good time.
- Sit comfortably.
- For the period you will practice, try to arrange your life so you won't have distractions. Put on the answering machine, and ask someone else to watch the kids.
- Time yourself by glancing periodically at a clock or watch (but don't set an alarm). Commit yourself to a specific length of practice, and try to stick to it.

There are several approaches to eliciting the relaxation response. Here is one standard set of instructions:

Step 1. Pick a focus word or short phrase that's firmly rooted in your personal belief system. For example, a nonreligious individual might choose a neutral word like *one* or *peace* or *love*. A Christian person desiring to use a prayer could pick the opening words of Psalm 23, *The Lord is my shepherd;* a Jewish person could choose *Shalom*.

Step 2. Sit quietly in a comfortable position.

Step 3. Close your eyes.

Step 4. Relax your muscles.

Step 5. Breathe slowly and naturally, repeating your focus word or phrase silently as you exhale.

Step 6. Throughout, assume a passive attitude. Don't worry about how well you're doing. When other thoughts come to mind, simply say to yourself, "Oh, well," and gently return to the repetition.

Step 7. Continue for 10 to 20 minutes. You may open your eyes to check the time, but do not use an alarm. When you finish, sit quietly for a minute or so, at first with your eyes closed and later with your eyes open. Then do not stand for 1 or 2 minutes.

Step 8. Practice the technique once or twice a day.

(*Source:* Benson, H. 1993)

Addictive drugs Drugs that produce a biological or psychological dependence in users, leading to increasingly powerful cravings for them

REVIEW ↵ mydevelopmentlab

1. _____ is the response to events that threaten or challenge us.

   Answer: Stress

2. In _____-_____ coping, adolescents attempt to manage a stressful problem or situation by directly changing the situation to make it less stressful.

   Answer: problem-focused

3. Medical problems caused by the interaction of psychological, emotional, and physical difficulties are known as _____ disorders.

   Answer: psychosomatic

To see more review questions, log on to MyDevelopmentLab.

Threats to Adolescents' Well-Being

Like most parents, I had thought of drug use as something you worried about when your kids got to high school. Now I know that, on the average, kids begin using drugs at 11 or 12, but at the time that never crossed our minds. Ryan had just begun attending mixed parties. He was playing Little League. In the eighth grade, Ryan started getting into a little trouble—one time he and another fellow stole a fire extinguisher, but we thought it was just a prank. Then his grades began to deteriorate. He began sneaking out at night. He would become belligerent at the drop of a hat, then sunny and nice again. . . .

It wasn't until Ryan fell apart at 14 that we started thinking about drugs. He had just begun McLean High School, and to him, it was like going to drug camp every day. Back then, everything was so available. He began cutting classes—a common tip-off—but we didn't hear from the school until he was flunking everything. It turned out that he was going to school for the first period, getting checked in, then leaving and smoking marijuana all day. (Shafer, 1990, p. 82)

Ryan's parents learned that marijuana was not the only drug Ryan was using. As his friends later admitted, Ryan was what they called a "garbage head." He would try anything. Despite efforts to curb his use of drugs, he never succeeded in stopping. He died at the age of 16, hit by a passing car after wandering into the street during an episode of drug use.

Few cases of adolescent drug use produce such extreme results, but the use of drugs, as well as other kinds of substance use and abuse, is one of several kinds of threats to health during adolescence, usually one of the healthiest periods of life. Although the extent of risky behavior is difficult to gauge, preventable problems such as drug, alcohol, and tobacco use, as well as sexually transmitted diseases, represent serious threats to adolescents' health and well-being.

Illegal Drugs

How common is illegal drug use during adolescence? Very. For instance, the most recent annual survey of nearly 50,000 U.S. students shows that almost 50% of high school seniors and almost 20% of eighth graders report having used marijuana within the past year. Although marijuana usage (as well as use of other drugs) has declined over the last few years, the data on drug use still represent substantial adolescent involvement (Johnston, Bachman, & O'Malley, 2003; see Figure 14-7).

Adolescents have a variety of reasons for using drugs. Some use them for the pleasurable experience drugs supposedly provide. Others use them to try to escape from the pressures of everyday life, however temporarily. Some adolescents try drugs simply for the thrill of doing something illegal. The alleged drug use of well-known celebrities may also contribute. Finally, peer pressure plays a role: Adolescents, as we'll discuss in greater detail in Chapter 16, are particularly susceptible to the perceived standards of their peer groups (Jenkins, 1996; Bogenschneider et al., 1998; Urberg, Luo, & Pilgrim, 2003).

The use of illegal drugs is dangerous in several respects. For instance, some drugs are addictive. **Addictive drugs** are those that produce a biological or psychological dependence in users, leading to increasingly powerful cravings for them.

Despite declines in usage over the past several years marijuana use continues to be fairly common among older adolescents.

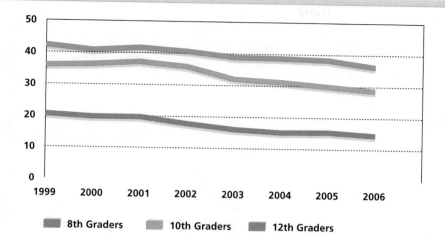

FIGURE 14-7 Downward Trend in Marijuana Use

According to an annual survey, the proportion of students reporting marijuana use over the past 12 months has decreased since 1999. What might account for the decline in drug use?
(*Source:* Johnston et al., 2006)

When drugs produce a biological addiction, their presence in the body becomes so common that the body is unable to function in their absence. Furthermore, addiction causes actual physical—and potentially lingering—changes in the nervous system. In such cases, drug intake no longer may provide a "high," but may be necessary simply to maintain the perception of everyday normalcy (Cami & Farré, 2003; Munzar, Cami, & Farré, 2003).

In addition to physical addiction, drugs also can produce psychological addiction. In such cases, people grow to depend on drugs to cope with the everyday stress of life. If drugs are used as an escape, they may prevent adolescents from confronting, and potentially solving, the problems that led them to drug use in the first place. Finally, drugs may be dangerous because even casual users of less hazardous drugs can escalate to more dangerous forms of substance abuse (Toch, 1995; Segal & Stewart, 1996).

Alcohol: Use and Abuse

Three-fourths of college students have something in common: They've consumed at least one alcoholic drink during the last 30 days. More than 40% say they've had five or more drinks within the past 2 weeks, and some 16% drink 16 or more drinks per week. High school students, too, are drinkers: 75% of high school seniors report having had an alcoholic drink in the last year, and in some subgroups—such as male athletes—the proportion of drinkers is even higher. Almost a quarter of eighth graders report being drunk at least once in their lives (Johnston, O'Malley, & Bachman, 2002; Ford, 2007).

Binge drinking is a particular problem on college campuses. Binge drinking is defined for men as drinking five or more drinks in one sitting; for women, who tend to weigh less and whose bodies absorb alcohol less efficiently, binge drinking is defined as four drinks in one sitting. Surveys find that almost half of male college students and over 40%

of female college students say they participated in binge drinking during the previous 2 weeks (Harrell & Karim, 2008; see Figure 14-8).

Binge drinking affects even those who don't drink or drink very little. Two-thirds of lighter drinkers reported that they had been disturbed by drunken students while sleeping or studying. Around a third had been insulted or humiliated by a drunken student, and 25% of women said they had been the target of an unwanted sexual advance by a drunk classmate (Wechsler, & Nelson, 2001; Wechsler et al., 2002).

About half of all college students engage in binge drinking.

Alcoholics People who have learned to depend on alcohol and are unable to control their drinking

CAREERS *in* CHILD DEVELOPMENT

Daniel W. Prior

Education: Evangel College, Springfield, Missouri: B.S. in psychology and sociology; Pittsburg State University, Pittsburg, Kansas: M.S. in psychology; Kansas State University, Manhattan, Kansas: Ph.D. in counseling psychology

Position: Program manager/counselor, The Pathway Home

Home: Anchorage, Alaska

Although substance abuse cuts across all age groups, adolescents are particularly vulnerable to the threats posed by drugs, alcohol, and tobacco. As a result, treatment centers such as the Pathway Home in Anchorage, Alaska, have been established to deal with the problems and help youth get back on track with their lives.

According to program manager Daniel Prior, the Pathway Home serves a maximum of 30 Alaskan Native youth in an environment that offers care and support.

"Most of the youth that come here have a co-occurring disorder, meaning they have a substance abuse issue and some mental health issues as well," Prior noted. "As a result, we believe in creating an environment that offers a lot of nurturance and personal growth.

"For example, the building was designed as a open structure, since many of the kids are used to being outdoors a lot," he said.

"We found that environmental factors are critical, since adolescents like a lot of freedom."

The approach taken to help adolescents at the Pathway Home is based on psychologist Abraham Maslow's hierarchy of motivational needs. Maslow suggested that certain basic needs must be satisfied before more sophisticated, higher order needs can be fulfilled. In his view, the most basic are physiological needs, safety and security needs, and the need for love and a sense of belongingness.

"Based on Maslow's theory, the first needs we address are physiological needs," said Prior. "Because kids come in influenced by various unhealthy substances, we strive to get them on a balanced diet and physically fit. This usually takes 2 to 3 months.

"The second of Maslow's needs are safety and security needs. Here we work hard to help them set boundaries, teaching them how to stay safe and how not to engage in risky behaviors," Prior added. "Finally, to address love and belongingness needs, we teach them how to have a meaningful relationship since many, because of trauma, are suspicious and skeptical of authority and others."

In addition to counseling services, the Pathway Home provides an in-house school that includes shops to teach the residents how to work with their hands. In addition, courses are offered on the Alaskan Native culture.

"Many youth come in with mixed identity issues," Prior explained. "We offer a significant cultural program that teaches young people the good aspects of their culture with emphasis on native drumming, dancing, and singing."

FIGURE 14-8 Binge Drinking Among College Students

For men, binge drinking was defined as consuming five or more drinks in one sitting; for women, the total was four or more. Why is binge drinking popular?
(*Source:* Wechsler et al., 2003)

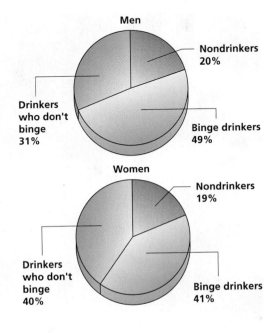

Why do adolescents start to drink? There are many reasons. For some—especially male athletes, whose rate of drinking tends to be higher than that of the adolescent general population—drinking is seen as a way of proving they can drink as much as anybody. Others drink for the same reason that some use drugs: It releases inhibitions and tension and reduces stress. Many begin because the conspicuous examples of drunkenness strewn around campus causes them to assume that everyone is drinking heavily, something known as the *false consensus effect* (Pavis, Cunningham-Burley, & Amos, 1997; Nelson & Wechsler, 2003; Weitzman, Nelson & Wechsler, 2003).

For some adolescents, alcohol use becomes a habit that cannot be controlled. **Alcoholics**, those with alcohol problems, learn to depend on alcohol and are unable to control their drinking. They also become increasingly able to tolerate alcohol, and therefore need to drink ever-larger amounts of liquor in order to bring about the effects they crave. Some drink throughout the day, whereas others go on binges in which they consume huge quantities of alcohol.

The reasons that some people, no matter their age, become alcoholics is not fully known. Genetics plays a role: Alcoholism runs in families. On the other hand, not all alcoholics have family members with alcohol problems. For those adolescents, alcoholism may be triggered by efforts to deal with the stress that having an alcoholic parent or family member can cause (Berenson, 2005; Clarke et al., 2008).

Of course, identifying the origins of an adolescent's existing problems with alcohol or drugs are less important than getting him help. Parents, teachers, and friends can help a teen address the problem—if they know that there *is* a problem. How can concerned friends and family members ascertain if an adolescent they know is having difficulties with alcohol or drugs? Some of the telltale signs are described next.

Becoming an Informed Consumer of Development

Hooked on Drugs or Alcohol?

Although it is not always easy to determine if an adolescent has a drug or alcohol abuse problem, there are some signals. Among them:

- Drug-related magazines or slogans on clothing
- Conversation and jokes that are preoccupied with drugs
- Hostility discussing drugs
- Collection of beer cans
- Signs of physical deterioration
- Memory lapses, short attention span, difficulty concentrating
- Poor physical coordination; slurred or incoherent speech
- Unhealthy appearance; indifference to hygiene and grooming
- Bloodshot eyes; dilated pupils
- Dramatic changes in school performance
- Marked downturn in grades—not just from C's to F's, but from A's to B's and C's; assignments not completed
- Increased absenteeism or tardiness
- Changes in behavior
- Chronic dishonesty (lying, stealing, and cheating); trouble with the police
- Changes in friends; evasiveness in talking about new ones
- Possession of large amounts of money
- Increasing and inappropriate anger, hostility, irritability, secretiveness
- Reduced motivation, energy, self-discipline, self-esteem
- Diminished interest in extracurricular activities and hobbies

(Adapted from Franck & Brownstone, 1991, pp. 593–594)

If an adolescent—or anyone else, for that matter—fits any of these descriptors, help is probably needed. A good place to start is a national hotline run by the National Institute on Drug Abuse at 800–662–4357 or its Web site at www.nida.nih.gov. In addition, individuals who need advice can find a local listing for Alcoholics Anonymous in the telephone book.

Tobacco: The Dangers of Smoking

Most adolescents are well aware of the dangers of smoking, but many still indulge in it. Recent figures show that, overall, a smaller proportion of adolescents smoke than in prior decades, but the numbers remain substantial; and within certain groups the numbers are increasing. Smoking is on the rise among girls, and in several countries, including Austria, Norway, and Sweden, the proportion of girls who smoke is higher than the proportion of boys. There are racial differences, as well: White children and children in lower socioeconomic status households are more likely to experiment with cigarettes and to start smoking earlier than African American children and children living in higher socioeconomic status households. Also, significantly more White males of high school age smoke than do African American males in high school, although the differences have narrowed in recent years (Harrell et al., 1998; Stolberg, 1998; Baker, Brandon, & Chassin, 2004).

Increasing numbers of film actors are depicted as smokers, leading to the perception that smoking is not only acceptable but also desirable.

From a health-care provider's perspective: Why do adolescents' increased cognitive abilities, including the ability to reason and to think experimentally, fail to deter them from irrational behavior such as drug and alcohol abuse, tobacco use, and unsafe sex practices? How might you use these abilities to design a program to help prevent these problems?

Smoking is becoming a habit that is harder and harder to maintain. There are growing social sanctions against it. It's becoming more difficult to find a comfortable place to smoke: More places, including schools and places of business, have become "smoke free." Even so, a good number of adolescents still smoke, despite knowing the dangers of smoking and of secondhand smoke. Why, then, do adolescents begin to smoke and maintain the habit?

One reason is that for some adolescents, smoking is seen as an adolescent rite of passage, a sign of growing up. In addition, seeing influential models, such as film stars, parents, and peers smoking increases the chances that an adolescent will take up the habit. Cigarettes are also very addictive. Nicotine, the active chemical ingredient of cigarettes, can produce biological and psychological dependency very quickly. Although one or two cigarettes generally do not usually produce a lifetime smoker, it takes only a little more to start the habit. In fact, people who smoke as few as 10 cigarettes early in their lives stand an 80% chance of becoming habitual smokers (Kodl & Mermelstein, 2004; Wills, Resko, & Ainette, 2004; West, Romero, & Trinidad, 2007; Tucker et al., 2008).

DEVELOPMENTAL DIVERSITY

Selling Death: Pushing Smoking to the Less Advantaged

In Dresden, Germany, three women in miniskirts offer passersby a pack of Lucky Strikes and a leaflet that reads "You just got hold of a nice piece of America." Says a local doctor, "Adolescents time and again receive cigarettes at such promotions."

A Jeep decorated with the Camel logo pulls up to a high school in Buenos Aires. A woman begins handing out free cigarettes to 15- and 16-year-olds during their lunch recess.

At a video arcade in Taipei, free American cigarettes are strewn atop each game. At a disco filled with high school students, free packs of Salems are on each table. (Ecenbarger, 1993, p. 50)

If you are a cigarette manufacturer and you find that the number of people using your product is declining, what do you do? American companies

Krista Blake contracted AIDS at the age of 16. She later died from the disease.

have sought to carve out new markets by turning to the least advantaged groups of people, both at home and abroad. For instance, in the early 1990s the R.J. Reynolds tobacco company designed a new brand of cigarettes it named "Uptown." The advertising used to herald its arrival made clear who the target was: African Americans living in urban areas (Quinn, 1990). Because of subsequent protests, the tobacco company withdrew "Uptown" from the market.

In addition to seeking new converts in the United States, tobacco companies aggressively recruit adolescent smokers abroad. In many developing countries the number of smokers is still low. Tobacco companies are seeking to increase this number through marketing strategies designed to hook adolescents on the habit by means of free samples. In addition, in countries where American culture and products are held in high esteem, advertising suggests that the use of cigarettes is an American—and consequently prestigious—habit (Sesser, 1993).

The strategy is effective. For instance, in some Latin American cities as many as 50% of teenagers smoke. According to the World Health Organization, smoking will prematurely kill some 200 million of the world's children and adolescents, and overall, 10% of the world's population will die because of smoking (Ecenbarger, 1993).

Sexually Transmitted Infections: One Risk of Sex

In the fall of 1990, Krista Blake was 18 and looking forward to her first year at Youngstown State University in Ohio. She and her boyfriend were talking about getting married. Her life was, she says, "basic, white-bread America." Then she went to the doctor, complaining about a backache, and found out she had the AIDS virus.

Blake had been infected with HIV, the virus that causes AIDS, two years earlier by an older boy, a hemophiliac. "He knew that he was infected, and he didn't tell me," she says. "And he didn't do anything to keep me from getting infected, either." (Becahy, 1992, p. 49)

AIDS Krista Blake, who contracted AIDS at the age of 16 and who later died from the disease, was not alone. *Acquired immunodeficiency syndrome (AIDS)* is one of the leading causes of death among young people across the globe. AIDS has no cure, and although it can be treatable with a "cocktail" of powerful drugs, the worldwide death toll from the disease is significant.

Because AIDS is spread primarily through sexual contact, it is classified as a **sexually transmitted infection (STI)**. Although it began as a problem that primarily affected homosexuals, it has spread to other populations, including heterosexuals and intravenous drug users. Minorities have been particularly hard hit: African Americans and Hispanics account for some 40% of AIDS cases, although they make up only 18% of the population. Already, 25 million people have died from AIDS, and people living with the disease number 33 million worldwide (Quinn & Overbaugh, 2005; UNAIDS, 2007).

AIDS and Adolescent Behavior

It is no secret how AIDS is transmitted—through the exchange of bodily fluids, including semen and blood. AIDS awareness has resulted in an increase in the use of condoms during sexual intercourse, and people are less likely to engage in casual sex with new acquaintances (Everett et al., 2000; Hoppe et al., 2004a, b). But the temptation to think that "It can't hurt this one time," is always there. The use of safer sex practices is far from universal. As we discussed earlier in the chapter, teens are prone to feel invulnerable and are therefore more likely to engage in risky behavior, believing their chance of contracting AIDS is minimal. This is particularly true when adolescents perceive that their partner is "safe"—someone they know well and with whom they are involved in a relatively long-term relationship (Raffaelli & Crockett, 2003; Tinsley, Lees, & Sumartojo, 2004; Haley & Vasquez, 2008).

Unfortunately, unless an individual knows the complete sexual history and AIDS status of a partner, unprotected sex remains risky business. And learning a partner's complete sexual history is difficult. Not only is it embarrassing to ask, but partners may not be accurate reporters, whether from ignorance of their own exposure, embarrassment, a sense of privacy, or simple forgetfulness.

Short of abstinence, there is no certain way to avoid AIDS. There are things you can do to make sex safer; these are listed in Table 14-3.

Other Sexually Transmitted Infections

Although AIDS is the deadliest of sexually transmitted diseases, there are a number of other STIs that are far more common (see Figure 14-9). In fact, one out of four adolescents

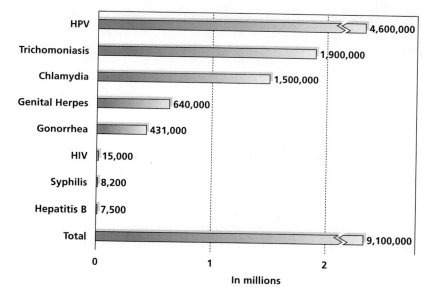

FIGURE 14-9 Sexually Transmitted Infections (STIs) Among Adolescents

Why are adolescents in particular in danger of contracting an STI? (*Sources:* Alan Guttmacher Institute, 1993a; Weinstock, Berman & Cates, 2004)

contracts an STI before graduating from high school. Overall, around 2.5 million teenagers contract an STI, such as the ones listed here, each year (Weinstock, Berman, & Cates, 2004).

Chlamydia, a bacterial disease, is the most common STI. Initially it has few symptoms, but later it causes burning urination and a discharge from the penis or vagina. It can lead to pelvic inflammation and even to sterility. Chlamydial infections can be treated successfully with antibiotics. Too often, adolescents are not aware of chlamydia,

Although most adolescents are well aware of the importance of safer sex practices, their feelings of invulnerability sometimes lead them to believe that their chances of contracting a sexually transmitted disease are minimal—especially when they are well acquainted with their partner.

cycle repeats itself. When the sores appear, the disease, for which there is no cure, is contagious (Farrell, 2005).

Several other STIs are frequent among adolescents. *Trichomoniasis,* an infection in the vagina or penis, is caused by a parasite. Initially without symptoms, it can eventually cause a painful discharge. *Gonorrhea* and *syphilis* are the STIs that have been recognized for the longest time; cases were recorded by ancient historians. Until the advent of antibiotics, both diseases were deadly; today both can be treated quite effectively.

Contracting an STI not only is an immediate problem during adolescence but also could become a problem later in life. Some diseases increase the chances of future infertility and cancer.

REVIEW ↵ mydevelopmentlab

1. _____ drugs are those that produce a biological or psychological dependence in users.

   Answer: Addictive

2. _____, those with alcohol problems, learn to depend on alcohol and are unable to control their drinking. They also become increasingly able to tolerate alcohol, and therefore need to drink ever-larger amounts of liquor in order to bring about the effects they crave.

   Answer: Alcoholics

3. Diseases that are spread through sexual contact are known as _____ _____ _____.

   Answer: sexually transmitted infections

*To see more review questions, log on to MyDevelopmentLab.

and those who have heard of it may be unaware of the serious problems it causes (Fayers et al., 2003; Centers for Disease Control, 2004).

Another common STI is *genital herpes,* a virus not unlike the cold sores that sometimes appear around the mouth. The first symptoms of herpes are often small blisters or sores around the genitals, which may break open and become quite painful. Although the sores may heal after a few weeks, the disease often recurs after an interval, and the

CASE STUDY

The Case of... Too Much, Too Soon

The first day Joanna wore a bra to school was the most humiliating time in her life. One boy in her class wrote something embarrassing about the size of her breasts on the school sidewalk, and another snapped her bra strap as they stood in line at the cafeteria. Joanna, age 10, went home crying that afternoon.

Two years later, when Joanna started middle school, she faced a very different challenge. She was now fully mature physically and the boys had developed an open interest in girls. Considered the "hottest" girl in her class, Joanna never lacked for a date for the school dance or the movies. Boys four and five years older than her expressed interest.

At first, Joanna reveled in all the attention. Boys desired her and many of the girls envied her. Within months, however, Joanna grew unhappy, then anxious. The boys, especially the older ones, were putting a great deal of pressure on her to go further sexually than she felt comfortable with, and the girls were spreading nasty rumors about her.

Joanna came to hate her voluptuous body and she decided to do something about it. She stopped eating breakfast, consumed only an apple at lunch, and pushed the food around on her plate at dinner. By the start of eighth grade, Joanna had dropped 20 pounds and her breasts and hips had disappeared.

Metacognition	**Adolescent egocentrism**	**Imaginary audience**	**Personal fables** The view
The knowledge that people have about their own thinking processes and their ability to monitor their cognition	A state of self-absorption in which the world is viewed from one's own point of view	Fictitious observers who pay as much attention to adolescents' behavior as they do themselves	held by some adolescents that what happens to them is unique, exceptional, and shared by no one else

metacognition. **Metacognition** is the knowledge that people have about their own thinking processes and their ability to monitor their cognition. Although school-age children can use some metacognitive strategies, adolescents are much more adept at understanding their own mental processes.

For example, as adolescents improve their understanding of their own memory capacity, they get better at gauging how long they need to study a particular kind of material to memorize it for a test. Furthermore, they can judge when they have fully memorized the material with considerably more accuracy than they could when they were younger. These improvements in metacognitive abilities permit adolescents to comprehend and master school material more effectively (Nelson, 1994; Kuhn, 2000; Desoete, Roeyers, & De Clercq, 2003).

These new abilities also can make adolescents particularly introspective and self-conscious—two hallmarks of the period which, as we see next, may produce a high degree of egocentrism.

Egocentrism in Thinking: Adolescents' Self-Absorption

Carlos thinks of his parents as "control freaks." He cannot figure out why his parents insist that, when he borrows their car, he call home and let them know where he is. Jeri is thrilled that Molly bought earrings just like hers, thinking it is the ultimate compliment, even though it's not clear that Molly even knew that Jeri had a similar pair when she bought them. Lu is upset with his biology teacher, Ms. Sebastian, for giving a long, difficult midterm exam on which he didn't do well.

Adolescents' newly sophisticated metacognitive abilities enable them to readily imagine that others are thinking about them, and they may construct elaborate scenarios about others' thoughts. It is also the source of the egocentrism that sometimes dominates adolescents' thinking. **Adolescent egocentrism** is a state of self-absorption in which the world is viewed as focused on oneself. This egocentrism makes adolescents highly critical of authority figures such as parents and teachers, unwilling to accept criticism, and quick to find fault with others' behavior (Greene, Krcmar, & Rubin, 2002; Alberts, Elkind, & Ginsberg, 2007).

The kind of egocentrism we see in adolescence helps explain why adolescents sometimes perceive that they are the focus of everyone else's attention. In fact, adolescents may develop what has been called an **imaginary audience**, fictitious observers who pay as much attention to the adolescents' behavior as adolescents do themselves.

The imaginary audience is usually perceived as focusing on the one thing that adolescents think most about: themselves. Unfortunately, these scenarios may suffer from the same kind of egocentrism as the rest of their thinking. For instance, a student sitting in a class

may be sure a teacher is focusing on her, and a teenager at a basketball game is likely to be convinced that everyone around is focusing on the pimple on his chin.

Egocentrism leads to a second distortion in thinking: the notion that one's experiences are unique. Adolescents develop **personal fables**, the view that what happens to them is unique, exceptional, and shared by no one else. For instance, teenagers whose romantic relationships have ended may feel that no one has ever experienced the hurt they feel, that no one has ever been treated so badly, that no one can understand what they are going through.

Adolescents' egocentrism leads to the belief that what happens to them is unique and to feelings of invulnerability—producing risky behavior.

Personal fables also may make adolescents feel invulnerable to the risks that threaten others. Much adolescent risk-taking may well be traced to the personal fables they construct for themselves. They may think that there is no need to use condoms during sex because, in the personal fables they construct, pregnancy and sexually transmitted infections such as AIDS only happen to other kinds of people, not to them. They may drive after drinking, because their personal fables paint them as careful drivers, always in control (Greene et al., 2000; Vartanian, 2000; Aalsma, Lapsley, & Flannery, 2006).

From a social worker's perspective: In what ways does adolescent egocentrism complicate adolescents' social and family relationships? Do adults entirely outgrow egocentrism and personal fables?

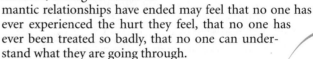

REVIEW ↵ mydevelopmentlab

1. According to Piaget, the _____ _____ stage is the stage at which people develop the ability to think abstractly.

    Answer: formal operational

2. According to the _____-_____ perspective general intelligence remains stable during adolescence, but dramatic improvements evolve in the specific mental abilities that underlie intelligence.

    Answer: information-processing

3. Adolescent _____ is a state of self-absorption in which the world is viewed from one's own point of view.

    Answer: egocentrism

To see more review questions, log on to MyDevelopmentLab.

Moral Development

Your wife is near death from an unusual kind of cancer. One drug exists that the physicians think might save her—a form of radium that a scientist in a nearby city has recently developed. The drug, though, is expensive to manufacture, and the scientist is charging 10 times what the drug costs him to make. He pays $1,000 for the radium and charges $10,000 for a small dose. You have gone to everyone you know to borrow money, but you can get together only $2,500—one quarter of what you need. You've told the scientist that your wife is dying and asked him to sell it more cheaply or let you pay later. But the scientist has said, "No, I discovered the drug and I'm going to make money from it." In desperation, you consider breaking into the scientist's laboratory to steal the drug for your wife. Should you do it?

According to developmental psychologist Lawrence Kohlberg and his colleagues, the answer that adolescents give to this question reveals central aspects of their sense of morality and justice. He suggests that people's responses to moral dilemmas such as this one reveal the stage of moral development they have attained—and yield information about their general level of cognitive development (Kohlberg, 1984; Colby & Kohlberg, 1987).

Kohlberg's Approach to Moral Development

Kohlberg contends that people pass through a series of stages as their sense of justice evolves and in the kind of reasoning they use to make moral judgments. Primarily due to cognitive characteristics that we discussed earlier, younger school-age children tend to think either in terms of concrete, unvarying rules ("It is always wrong to steal" or "I'll be punished if I steal") or in terms of the rules of society ("Good people don't steal" or "What if everyone stole?").

By the time they reach adolescence, however, individuals are able to reason on a higher plane, typically having reached Piaget's stage of formal operations. They are capable of comprehending abstract, formal principles of morality, and they consider cases such as the one presented previously in terms of broader issues of morality and of right and wrong ("Stealing may be acceptable if you are following your own conscience and doing the right thing").

Kohlberg suggests that moral development emerges in a three-level sequence, which is further subdivided into six stages (see Table 15-1). At the lowest level, *preconventional morality* (Stages 1 and 2), people follow rigid rules based on punishments or rewards. For example, a student at the preconventional level might evaluate the moral dilemma posed in the story by saying that it was not worth stealing the drug because if you were caught, you would go to jail.

In the next level, that *of conventional morality* (Stages 3 and 4), people approach moral problems in terms of their own position as good, responsible members of society. Some at this level would decide *against* stealing the drug because they think they would feel guilty or dishonest for violating social norms. Others would decide *in favor* of stealing the drug because if they did nothing in this situation, they would be unable to face others. All of these people would be reasoning at the conventional level of morality.

Finally, individuals using *postconventional morality* (Stages 5 and 6) invoke universal moral principles that are considered broader than the rules of the particular society in which they live. People who feel that they would condemn themselves if they did not steal the drug because they would not be living up to their own moral principles would be reasoning at the postconventional level.

Kohlberg's theory proposes that people move through the periods of moral development in a fixed order and that they are unable to reach the highest stage until adolescence, due to deficits in cognitive development that are not overcome until then. However, not everyone is presumed to reach the highest stages: Kohlberg found that postconventional reasoning is relatively rare (Hedgepeth, 2005).

Although Kohlberg's (1984) theory provides a good account of the development of moral judgments, the links with moral behavior are less strong. Still, students at higher levels of moral reasoning are less likely to engage in antisocial behavior at school (such as breaking school rules) and in the community (engaging in juvenile delinquency) (Richards et al., 1992; Langford, 1995; Carpendale, 2000).

Furthermore, one experiment found that 15% of students who reasoned at the postconventional level of morality—the highest category—cheated when given the opportunity, although they were not as likely to cheat as those at lower levels, where more than half of the students cheated. Clearly, though, knowing what is morally right does not always mean acting that way (Killen & Hart, 1995; Snarey, 1995; Hart, Burock, & London, 2003).

Kohlberg's theory has also been criticized because it is based solely on observations of members of Western cultures. In fact, cross-cultural research finds that members of more industrialized, technologically advanced cultures move through the stages more rapidly than members of nonindustrialized countries. Why? One explanation is that Kohlberg's higher stages are based on moral reasoning involving governmental and societal institutions like the police and court system. In less industrialized areas, morality may be based more on relationships among people in a particular village. In short, the nature of morality may differ in diverse cultures, and Kohlberg's theory is more suited for Western cultures (Snarey, 1995).

An aspect of Kohlberg's theory that has proved even more problematic is the difficulty it has explaining *girls'*

TABLE 15-1 Kohlberg's Sequence of Moral Reasoning

Level	Stage	SAMPLE MORAL REASONING	
		In Favor of Stealing	Against Stealing
LEVEL 1 **Preconventional morality:** At this level, the concrete interests of the individual are considered in terms of rewards and punishments.	**STAGE 1** Obedience and punishment orientation: At this stage, people stick to rules in order to avoid punishment, and obedience occurs for its own sake.	"If you let your wife die, you will get in trouble. You'll be blamed for not spending the money to save her, and there'll be an investigation of you and the druggist for your wife's death."	"You shouldn't steal the drug because you'll get caught and sent to jail if you do. If you do get away, your conscience will bother you thinking how the police will catch up with you at any minute."
	STAGE 2 Reward orientation: At this stage, rules are followed only for a person's own benefit. Obedience occurs because of rewards that are received.	"If you do happen to get caught, you could give the drug back and you wouldn't get much of a sentence. It wouldn't bother you much to serve a little jail term, if you have your wife when you get out."	"You may not get much of a jail term if you steal the drug, but your wife will probably die before you get out, so it won't do much good. If your wife dies, you shouldn't blame yourself; it isn't your fault; she has cancer."
LEVEL 2 **Conventional morality:** At this level, people approach moral problems as members of society. They are interested in pleasing others by acting as good members of society.	**STAGE 3** "Good boy" morality: Individuals at this stage show an interest in maintaining the respect of others and doing what is expected of them.	"No one will think you're bad if you steal the drug, but your family will think you're an inhuman husband if you don't. If you let your wife die, you'll never be able to look anybody in the face again."	"It isn't just the druggist who will think you're a criminal; everyone else will, too. After you steal the drug, you'll feel bad thinking how you've brought dishonor on your family and yourself; you won't be able to face anyone again."
	STAGE 4 Authority and social-order-maintaining morality: People at this stage conform to society's rules and consider that "right" is what society defines as right.	"If you have any sense of honor, you won't let your wife die just because you're afraid to do the only thing that will save her. You'll always feel guilty that you caused her death if you don't do your duty to her."	"You're desperate and you may not know you're doing wrong when you steal the drug. But you'll know you did wrong after you're sent to jail. You'll always feel guilty for your dishonesty and law breaking."
LEVEL 3 **Postconventional morality:** At this level, people use moral principles, which are seen as broader than those of any particular society.	**STAGE 5** Morality of contract, individual rights, and democratically accepted law: People at this stage do what is right because of a sense of obligation to laws which are agreed on within society. They perceive that laws can be modified as part of changes in an implicit social contract.	"You'll lose other people's respect, not gain it, if you don't steal. If you let your wife die, it will be out of fear, not out of reasoning. So you'll just lose self-respect and probably the respect of others, too."	"You'll lose your standing and respect in the community and violate the law. You'll lose respect for yourself if you're carried away by emotion and forget the long-range point of view."
	STAGE 6 Morality of individual principles and conscience: At this final stage, a person follows laws because they are based on universal ethical principles. Laws that violate the principles are disobeyed.	"If you don't steal the drug, and if you let your wife die, you'll always condemn yourself for it afterward. You won't be blamed and you'll have lived up to the outside rule of the law, but you won't have lived up to your own standards of conscience."	"If you steal the drug, you won't be blamed by other people, but you'll condemn yourself because you won't have lived up to your own conscience and standards of honesty."

(*Source*: Adapted from Kohlberg, 1969)

moral judgments. Because the theory initially was based largely on data from males, some researchers have argued that it does a better job describing boys' moral development than girls' moral development. This would explain the surprising finding that women typically score at a lower level than men do on tests of moral judgments using Kohlberg's stage sequence. This result has led to an alternative account of moral development for girls.

These students exemplify Gilligan's stage of moral development in which violence against others (as well as oneself) is viewed as immoral.

Gilligan's Approach to Moral Development: Gender and Morality

Psychologist Carol Gilligan (1987, 1996) has suggested that differences in the ways boys and girls are raised in our society lead to basic distinctions in how men and women view moral behavior. According to her, boys view morality primarily in terms of broad principles such as justice or fairness, whereas girls see it in terms of responsibility toward individuals and willingness to sacrifice themselves to help specific individuals within the context of particular relationships. Compassion for individuals, then, is a more prominent factor in moral behavior for women than it is for men (Gilligan, Lyons, & Hammer, 1990; Gump, Baker, & Roll, 2000).

Gilligan views morality as developing among females in a three-stage process (summarized in Table 15-2). In the first stage,

Carol Gilligan argues that boys and girls view morality differently, with boys seeing it primarily in terms of broad principles and girls considering it in terms of personal relationships and responsibility toward individuals.

called "orientation toward individual survival," females first concentrate on what is practical and best for them, gradually making a transition from selfishness to responsibility, in which they think about what would be best for others. In the second stage, termed "goodness as self-sacrifice," females begin to think that they must sacrifice their own wishes to what other people want.

Ideally, women make a transition from "goodness" to "truth," in which they take into account their own needs plus those of others. This transition leads to the third stage,

TABLE 15-2	Gilligan's Three States of Moral Development for Women	
Stage	**Characteristics**	**Example**
Stage 1 Orientation toward individual survival	Initial concentration is on what is practical and best for self. Gradual transition from selfishness to responsibility, which includes thinking about what would be best for others.	A first grader may insist on playing only games of her own choosing when playing with a friend.
Stage 2 Goodness as self-sacrifice	Initial view is that a woman must sacrifice her own wishes to what other people want. Gradual transition from "goodness" to "truth," which takes into account needs of both self and others.	Now older, the same girl may believe that to be a good friend, she must play the games her friend chooses, even if she herself doesn't like them.
Stage 3 Morality of nonviolence	A moral equivalence is established between self and others. Hurting anyone—including one's self—is seen as immoral. Most sophisticated form of reasoning, according to Gilligan.	The same girl may realize that both friends must enjoy their time together and look for activities that both she and her friend can enjoy.

"morality of nonviolence," in which women come to see that hurting anyone is immoral—including hurting themselves. This realization establishes a moral equivalence between themselves and others and represents, according to Gilligan, the most sophisticated level of moral reasoning.

It is obvious that Gilligan's sequence of stages is quite different from Kohlberg's, and some developmentalists have suggested that her rejection of Kohlberg's work is too sweeping and that gender differences are not as pronounced as first thought (Colby & Damon, 1987). For instance, some researchers argue that both males and females use similar "justice" and "care" orientations in making moral judgments. Clearly, the question of how boys and girls differ in their moral orientations, as well as the nature of moral development in general, is far from settled (Haviv & Leman, 2002; Tangney & Dearing, 2002; Weisz & Black, 2002; Jorgensen, 2006).

REVIEW ↵ mydevelopmentlab

1. At Kohlberg's lowest level of moral development, _____ morality, people follow unvarying rules based on rewards and punishments.

Answer: preconventional

2. Although Kohlberg's theory provides a good account of the development of moral judgments, it is less adequate in predicting moral _____.

Answer: behavior

3. In Gilligan's second stage of moral development, which she terms _____ _____ _____ - _____, females begin to think that they must sacrifice their own wishes to what other people want, ultimately making the transition from "goodness" to "truth," in which they take into account their own needs plus the needs of others.

Answer: goodness as self-sacrifice

To see more review questions, log on to MyDevelopmentLab.

Schooling and Cognitive Development

I Love Middle School!!!!!!! none of my old friends are really in my classes though (ok I have some in gym and Steph in get the facs but that's only like 1 class per person) but Joe just happened to be in 4 of my classes so I spend 5 periods of every day with him, sitting by him in 3 of them. he's gotten nicer though, kinda. anyway I LOVE MIDDLE SCHOOL!!!!! it's the greatest. and plus there's Vivi who is sick right now but I have my last 3 periods with her and Morgan... I love Latin too it's so much fun and I love my teacher Mrs. Whittaker. She's the best.

From 4th grade till the summer before 6th grade I was depressed. it was in 6th grade that I decided that I needed to live. I figured that since I was moving to middle school I might be able to sort of start over. however, that was not the case. my brothers had by this point stopped messing with me for the most part. but school was horrible I was the kid that everyone picked on. that lasted for 2 years until I realized that if I stopped reacting to being made fun of people stopped making fun of me. so throughout middle school I was a loner. I had a lot of people who would claim to be my friends but they would still make fun of me so I became a loner.

If nothing else, middle school evokes strong feelings on the part of adolescents, as these excerpts from two adolescents' blogs illustrate. That's hardly surprising, given that the transition from elementary school to middle school comes at time when students are changing radically along a variety of dimensions.

The Transition From Elementary School to Middle School

The transition from elementary school into secondary education is a normative transition, meaning it is a part of the life of almost all adolescents in the United States. However, the fact that nearly everyone is doing it doesn't make it easy. The transition can be particularly difficult because of the physical, intellectual, and social changes that are occurring at about the same time.

After leaving elementary school, most students enter a *middle school,* which typically comprises grades 6 to 8. At the same time, most adolescents are beginning puberty and coming to grips with the changes taking place in their bodies. Furthermore, their thinking is becoming more sophisticated, and their relationships with their family and friends are becoming far more complicated than ever before.

For most adolescents, middle schools provide a very different educational structure from the one they grew accustomed to in elementary school. Rather than spending the day in a self-contained classroom, students move from one class to another. Not only must they adapt to the demands of different teachers, but their classmates may be different in every class period: And those classmates may be more heterogeneous and diverse than those they encountered in their elementary schools.

Furthermore, because they are the youngest and least experienced, students in middle school enter an environment in which they suddenly find themselves at the bottom of the status hierarchy. Coming from elementary schools in which they were at the top of that status hierarchy (and at which they were physically and cognitively so different from the kindergarteners and first graders who occupied the bottom level), students can find the middle-school experience alarming and sometimes damaging.

In addition, middle schools are typically larger in physical size and student population than most elementary schools. These factors alone makes the transition to middle school more difficult. A significant amount of research demonstrates quite clearly that students do better, both academically and psychologically, in smaller, less bureaucratic educational settings (Lee & Burkam, 2003; Ready, Lee, & Welner, 2004).

On the other hand, the overall record of middle schools has been harshly criticized. For example, consider these facts (Juvonen et al., 2004):

- Over half of eighth graders do not achieve proficiency in reading, math, and science according to national standards.

- In comparison to their peers in other countries, eighth graders rank in 12th place academically, which places them below average. In some cases, students from the United States who did better than their international peers in elementary school actually declined in rank when they entered middle school. For instance, in fourth grade, U.S. students are average in math and science compared to their international peers; 4 years later, when they enter eighth grade, they score below the international average. Furthermore, compared to students in other industrialized countries, U.S. students score lower on standardized math and science tests (see Figure 15-1; Organization for Economic Cooperation and Development [OECD], 2005).

- The proportion of middle school students who suffer from emotional problems is higher for students in the United States than for students in all 11 of the other countries examined by the World Health Organization. Middle school students exhibit higher rates of depression in the United States, a greater degree of disengagement with school, and a greater desire to drop out of school than do students of the same age in other countries.

- Even when middle school students report feeling connected to their peers and their school, it does not lead to greater academic achievement. In fact, the link between social–emotional climate and academic success is weak at best, according to carefully conducted research (Williamson & Johnston, 1999).

- Middle schools often do not do a good job in preparing students for the rigors of high school. For example, although once rated first in the percentage of the population graduating from high school, the United States has dropped to 24th among industrialized countries. Only 78% of U.S. high school students graduate—a rate considerably lower than that of other developed countries (Organization for Economic Cooperation and Development [OECD], 1998, 2001).

Although such findings suggest that middle schools have not been up to the task of educating young adolescents, it's important to keep in mind that the findings don't necessarily mean that students in middle schools fare worse than students in other school configurations. There are only a limited

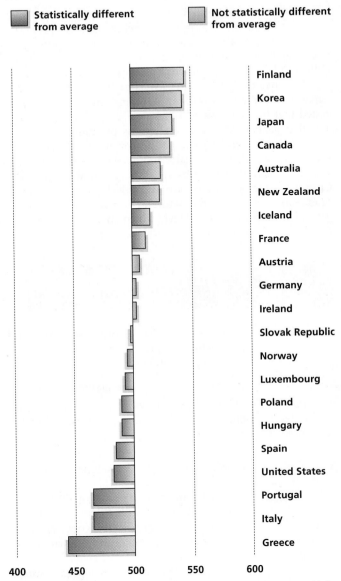

Statistically different from average

Not statistically different from average

Finland
Korea
Japan
Canada
Australia
New Zealand
Iceland
France
Austria
Germany
Ireland
Slovak Republic
Norway
Luxembourg
Poland
Hungary
Spain
United States
Portugal
Italy
Greece

400   450   500   550   600

FIGURE 15-1 Not at the Top of the Class: Lagging U.S. Math Performance

When compared to the math performance of students across the world, U.S. students perform at below-average levels.
(*Source:* Adapted from OECD, 2005)

number of studies that compare outcomes in schools with different grade configurations. While some evidence suggests that students in some traditional configurations, such as the kindergarten-through-eighth-grade pattern, may outperform students following the elementary-to-middle-school progression, the data are far from conclusive (Yecke, 2005).

Furthermore, in many cases, the philosophy behind the middle school movement—such as a focus on discovery learning—never was fully implemented. In fact, many school

Homeschooling: An Alternative to Traditional Schools

Amanda Crosswhite is part of a school of 1,702 students. But when she goes to class, it's one-on-one with her mother.

Sharon Crosswhite has been home-schooling Amanda, 9, for three years and her son, Adam, 17, for two years.

"I had always wanted to try this experience," said Sharon Crosswhite, 48. "I was just getting a little disillusioned with the public school...."

[Adam,] a high school senior . . . takes classes at Palomar College in San Marcos while continuing with high school subjects taught by his mother.

"He wasn't doing all that great in high school," Crosswhite said, adding it was Adam's choice to be home-schooled. "He's done a real turnaround. I think a big part of that is because I know what the assignments are." (Lepper, 2006, p. NC-8).

For students like the Crosswhite siblings, there is no distinction between their living room and classroom, because they are among the close to 1 million students who are homeschooled. *Homeschooling* is a major educational phenomenon in which students are taught not by teachers in schools, but by their parents in their own homes.

There are a number of reasons why parents may choose to school their adolescents at home. Some parents feel their children will thrive with the one-to-one attention that homeschooling can bring, whereas they might get lost in a larger public school. Other parents are dissatisfied with the nature of the instruction and the quality of the teachers in their public schools and feel that they can do a better job teaching their children. And some parents engage in homeschooling for religious reasons, wishing to impart particular religious beliefs and practices that would not be provided in a public school and hoping to avoid exposing their children to values and aspects of the popular culture with which they disagree (Dennis, 2004; Green & Hoover-Dempsey, 2007; Isenberg, 2007).

Homeschooling clearly works, in the sense that adolescents who have been homeschooled score generally as well on standardized tests as students who have been educated traditionally. In addition, their college acceptance rate appears to be no different from that of traditionally schooled students, and they seem as well adjusted in college as their counterparts (Lauricella, 2001; Lines, 2001; Bolle, Wessel, & Mulvihill, 2007).

However, the apparent academic success of adolescents schooled at home does not mean that homeschooling, per se, is effective, because parents who choose to homeschool their children may be more affluent or have the kind of well-structured family situation in which children would succeed no matter what kind of schooling they had. In contrast, parents in dysfunctional and disorganized families are unlikely to have the motivation or interest to homeschool

Homeschooling is an increasingly popular alternative to traditional schools.

their children. For adolescents from families like these, the demands and structure of a formal school are probably a good thing.

Critics of homeschooling argue that it has considerable drawbacks. For example, the social interaction with groups of adolescents that is inherent in classrooms in traditional schools is largely missing for homeschooled students. Learning in an at-home environment, while perhaps strengthening family ties, hardly provides an environment that reflects the diversity of U.S. society. Furthermore, even the best-equipped home is unlikely to have the sophisticated science materials and educational technology that are available at many schools. Finally, most parents do not have the preparation of well-trained teachers, and their teaching methods may be unsophisticated. Although parents may be successful in teaching subject areas in which their child is already interested, they may have more difficulty teaching subjects that their child seeks to avoid (Cai, Reeve, & Robinson, 2002; Apple, 2007).

Because homeschooling is relatively new, few controlled experiments have been conducted to examine its effectiveness. More research is needed to clarify how and when homeschooling is an effective way to educate adolescents.

- Do you think adolescents who are homeschooled may face social problems when they attend college due to their lack of social interaction with other adolescents? Why?

districts replaced large junior high schools with large middle schools and otherwise made only minimal changes, which was hardly a fair test of the middle-school philosophy (Roeser, Eccles, & Sameroff, 2000; Wigfield & Eccles, 2002; Wallis, 2005).

The challenges faced by students in middle schools have led adolescents and their parents to seek alternatives. We discuss one in the *From Research to Practice* box.

Socioeconomic Status and School Performance: Individual Differences in Achievement

All students are entitled to the same opportunity in the classroom, but it is very clear that certain groups have more educational advantages than others. One of the most telling indicators of this reality is the relationship between educational achievement and socioeconomic status (SES).

Middle- and high-SES students, on average, earn higher grades, score higher on standardized tests of achievement, and complete more years of schooling than do students from lower SES homes. Of course, this disparity does not start in adolescence; the same findings hold for children in lower grades. However, by the time students are in high school, the effects of socioeconomic status become even more pronounced (Farah et al., 2006; Horton-Ikard & Weismer, 2007; Frederickson & Petrides, 2008).

Why do students from middle- and high-SES homes show greater academic success? There are several reasons. For one thing, children living in poverty lack many of the advantages enjoyed by other children. Their nutrition and health may be less adequate. Often living in crowded conditions and attending inadequate schools, they may have few places to do homework. Their homes may lack the books and computers commonplace in more economically advantaged households (Prater, 2002; Chiu & McBride-Chang, 2006).

For these reasons, students from impoverished backgrounds may be at a disadvantage from the day they begin their schooling. As they grow older, their school performance may continue to lag, and in fact their disadvantage may snowball. Because later school success builds heavily on basic skills that are presumably learned early in school, children who experience such problems in the primary grades may find themselves falling increasingly behind the academic eight ball as adolescents (Huston, 1991; Philips et al., 1994; Biddle, 2001).

Ethnic and Racial Differences in School Achievement

Achievement differences between ethnic and racial groups are significant, and they paint a troubling picture of American education. For instance, data on school achievement indicate that, on average, African American and Hispanic students tend to perform at lower levels, receive lower grades, and score lower on standardized tests of achievement than Caucasian students (see Figure 15-2). In contrast, Asian American students tend to receive higher grades than Caucasian students (National Center for Educational Statistics, 2003).

What is the source of such ethnic and racial differences in academic achievement? Clearly, much of the difference is due to socioeconomic factors: Because more African American and Hispanic families live in poverty, their economic disadvantage may be reflected in their school performance. In fact, when we take socioeconomic levels into account by comparing different ethnic and racial groups at the same socioeconomic level, achievement differences diminish, but they do not vanish (Luster & McAdoo, 1994; Meece & Kurtz-Costes, 2001; Cokley, 2003).

Anthropologist John Ogbu (1988, 1992) argues that members of certain minority groups may perceive school success as relatively unimportant. They may believe that societal prejudice in the workplace will dictate that they will not succeed, no matter how much effort they expend. The conclusion is that hard work in school will have no eventual payoff.

Ogbu suggests that members of minority groups who enter a new culture voluntarily are more likely to be successful in school than those who are brought into a new culture against their will. For instance, he notes that Korean children who are the sons and daughters of voluntary immigrants to the United States tend to be, on average, quite successful in school. On the other hand, Korean children in Japan, whose parents were forced to immigrate during World War II and work as forced laborers, tend to do relatively poorly in school. The reason for the disparity? The process of involuntary immigration apparently leaves lasting scars, reducing the motivation to succeed in subsequent generations. Ogbu suggests that in the United States, the involuntary immigration,

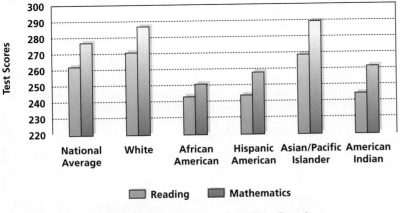

FIGURE 15-2 Achievement Test Results

Racial discrepancies between groups are apparent on a national test of reading and math achievement administered to a sample of 150,000 eighth graders.
(*Source:* NAEP, 2003)

as slaves, of the ancestors of many African American students might be related to their motivation to succeed (Ogbu, 1992; Gallagher, 1994).

Concerns about the educational performance of students have led to considerable efforts to improve schooling. No educational reform has had greater impact than the *No Child Left Behind Act,* which we discuss next.

Achievement Testing in High School: Will No Child Be Left Behind?

A student was shot dead by a classmate during lunch period outside Frank W. Ballou Senior High. It didn't come as much of a surprise to anyone at the school, in this city's most crime-infested ward. Just during the current school year, one boy was hacked by a student with an ax, a girl was badly wounded in a knife fight with another female student, five fires were set by arsonists, and an unidentified body was dumped next to the parking lot. (Suskind, 1994, p. 1; 1999)

Can schools like this be turned around, providing not only a safe environment but also one that ensures an excellent education for every student? Most definitely, according to the thinking behind the passage of the *No Child Left Behind Act,* a comprehensive law designed to improve school performance across the United States.

The *No Child Left Behind Act,* passed by Congress in 2002, requires every U.S. state to design and administer achievement tests that students must pass in order to graduate from high school. In addition, schools themselves are graded so that the public is aware of which schools have the best (and worst) test results. The basic idea behind the mandatory testing programs in the *No Child Left Behind Act* is to ensure that students graduate with a minimum level of proficiency. Proponents suggest that students—and teachers—will be motivated by the tests and that overall educational standards will be raised (Jehlen & Winans, 2005; Watkins, 2008; Opfer, Henry, & Mashburn, 2008).

In addition, schools that are successful will attract more students (and funding), while nonperforming schools will either improve or, essentially be driven out of business and shut down due to a loss of accreditation. The law allows parents to transfer their children to more effective public schools if their local school is not doing a good job (Lewis & Haug, 2005; Phelps, 2005; Haney, 2008).

Critics of the Act (and other forms of mandatory standardized testing) argue that a number of unintended negative consequences will result from implementation of the law. To ensure that the maximum numbers of students pass the tests, they suggest that instructors are driven to "teach to the test," meaning that they focus on the content of the tests to the exclusion of material that is not test biased. In this view, approaches to teaching designed to foster creativity and critical thinking may be discouraged by the emphasis on testing (Thurlow, Lazarus, & Thompson, 2005; Linn, 2008; Koretz, 2008).

In addition, mandatory high-stakes tests raise the anxiety level for students, potentially leading to poor performance, and students who might have performed well throughout their schooling face the possibility of not graduating if they do poorly on the test. Moreover, because students from lower socioeconomic and ethnic and racial minority backgrounds and those with special needs fail tests disproportionately, critics, have argued that mandatory testing programs may be inherently biased (Samuels, 2005; Yeh, 2008).

Although the *No Child Left Behind Act* has been controversial from the time of its passage, one part of the law has received nearly universal approval. Specifically, the law provides funding to help determine what educational practices and programs have been proven to be effective based on scientific research. Although there is disagreement over what constitutes proof of best educational practices, developmental and educational researchers have welcomed the emphasis on research (Chatterji, 2004; Sunderman, 2008).

Media and Technology Use by Adolescents

Dominique Jones, 12, of Los Angeles, likes to IM her friends before school to find out what they plan to wear. "You'll get IMs back that say things like 'Oh, my God, I'm wearing the same shoes!' After school we talk about what happened that day, what outfits we want to wear the next day." (Wallis, 2006, p. 55)

Instant Messaging (IMing) is only one of the enormous variety of media and technologies available to adolescents, ranging from more traditional sorts, such as radio and television, to newer forms, such as Instant Messaging, cell phones, and MP3 players. And adolescents make use of them—to a staggering degree.

According to a comprehensive survey using a sample of boys and girls 8 to 18 years old conducted by the Kaiser Family Foundation (a well-respected think tank), young people spend an average of 6.5 hours a day with media. Furthermore, because around a quarter of the time they are using more than one form of medium simultaneously, they are actually being exposed to the equivalent of 8.5 hours per day (Rideout, Roberts, & Foehr, 2005; Boneva et al., 2006; Jordan et al., 2007; see Figure 15-3).

In fact, these figures probably underestimate media use by teenagers for at least two reasons. First, the sample included preteens, many of whom likely have less opportunity and access to media than do older youth. Second, the survey was conducted in 2003 and 2004, meaning that some technologies, such as Instant Messaging, were not as widespread as they are now. It seems reasonable, then, that media use is even more extensive than initially found in the survey.

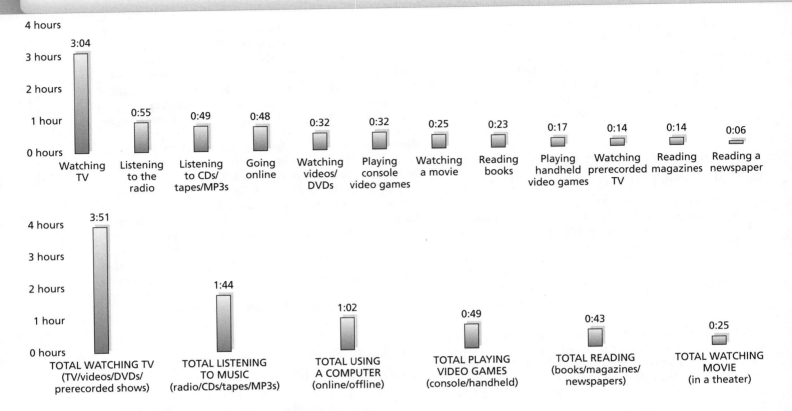

FIGURE 15-3 Time Spent with Media in a Typical Day

One comprehensive study by the Kaiser Family Foundation has shown that young people spend more than 6.5 hours a day interacting with various media.
(*Source*: Rideout et al., 2005)

These varied media play a number of significant functions in adolescents' lives. Not only do media provide entertainment and information, but they also help adolescents cope with the stress of everyday life. Losing oneself in a television show or CD can be a way of escaping from one's current problems.

In addition, the media provide models and a sense of norms that are operating among other adolescents. Teenagers watching popular music programs on MTV not only are exposed to major musical artists, but they can view how their peers in the audience look, dress, and behave (Arnett, 1995; Head, 2005).

Part-Time Work: Students on the Job

For most high school students, school is sandwiched between one or more part-time jobs. In fact, most 16- and 17-year-olds work at some sort of job, and 38% of 15-year-olds have regular employment during the school year (Employment Policies Institute, 2000; National Center for Education Statistics, 2001).

Working offers several advantages. In addition to providing funds for recreational activities and sometimes necessities, it helps students learn responsibility, gives practice with the ability to handle money, and can help teach workplace skills. Students also can develop good work habits that may help them do better academically. Finally, participation in jobs and paid internships can help students understand the nature of work in specific employment settings.

However, there are also significant drawbacks to work. Many jobs that are available to high school students are high on drudgery and low on transferable skills. Employment also may prevent students from participating in extracurricular activities such as sports. Because organized activities have been shown to enhance adolescent development, the inability to participate is a downside of work (Danish, Taylor, & Fazio, 2006).

The most troubling consequence of high school employment is that school performance is negatively related to the number of hours a student works: Generally, the more hours on the job, the lower a student's grades. One reason for this relationship is that there are only 24 hours in each day, and with fewer free hours, students are unable to devote enough time to their studies. But it is also possible that students who work a greater number of hours are more psychologically invested in their work than in high school—an explanation called the *primary orientation model*. Consequently, their motivation to do well academically is lower (Warren, 2002; Warren, Lee, & Cataldi, 2004).

A premature focus on work also may cause some adolescents to experience a phenomenon known as pseudomaturity. *Pseudomaturity* involves an unusually early entry into adult roles before an adolescent is developmentally ready to assume them. Some adolescents, particularly those who do not have strong ties to school or their peers, may see early entry into adulthood as a desirable escape from their current roles, and this may provide them with great satisfaction. In such cases, working many hours at a job may be a way for such adolescents to escape from current sources of stress. In other situations, however, socioeconomic pressures force adolescents into pseudomaturity (Staff, Mortimer, & Uggen, 2004).

In short, the consequences of high school students working are mixed. For some students, particularly those who work a limited number of hours each work, the advantages of working can be substantial. On the other hand, for those who work long hours, employment is likely to hinder academic performance.

Dropping Out of School

Although most students complete high school, some half-million students each year drop out prior to graduating. The consequences of dropping out are severe. High school dropouts earn 42% less than high school graduates, and the unemployment rate for dropouts is 50%.

Adolescents who leave school do so for a variety of reasons. Some leave because of pregnancy or problems with the English language. Some leave for economic reasons, needing to support themselves or their families (Christle, Jolivette, & Nelson, 2007; Lessard et al., 2008).

Dropout rates differ according to gender and ethnicity (see Figure 15-4). Males are more likely than females to drop out of school. In addition, although the drop out rate for all ethnicities has been declining somewhat over the last 2 decades, Hispanics and African American students still are more likely to leave high school before graduating than are non-Hispanic White students. On the other hand, not all minority groups show higher dropout rates: Asians, for instance, drop out at a lower rate than do Caucasians (National Center for Educational Statistics, 2003).

Poverty plays a large role in determining whether a student completes high school. Students from lower income households are three times more likely to drop out than are

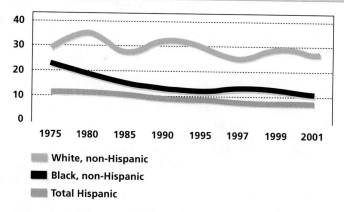

FIGURE 15-4 Dropout Rates and Ethnicity

In spite of the fact that dropout rates have been falling for all ethnic groups, Hispanic and African American students are still more likely not to graduate. How can social workers and educators work together to reduce high school dropout rates?

(*Source:* National Center for Education Statistics, 2003)

those from middle- and upper-income households. Because economic success is so dependent on education, dropping out often perpetuates a cycle of poverty (National Center for Education Statistics, 2002).

College: Pursuing Higher Education

For Enrico Vasquez, there was never any doubt: He was headed for college. Enrico, the son of a wealthy Cuban immigrant who had made a fortune in the medical supply business after fleeing Cuba 5 years before Enrico's birth, had had the importance of education constantly drummed into him by his family. In fact, the question was never whether he would go to college, but what college he would be able to get into. As a consequence, Enrico found high school to be a pressure cooker: Every grade and extracurricular activity was evaluated in terms of its helping or hindering his chances of admission to a good college.

Armando Williams's letter of acceptance to Dallas County Community College is framed on the wall of his mother's apartment. To her, the letter represents nothing short of a miracle, an answer to her prayers. Growing up in a neighborhood infamous for its drugs and drive-by shootings, Armando had always been a hard worker and a "good boy," in his mother's view. But when he was growing up, she never even entertained the possibility of his making it to college. To see him reach this stage in his education fills her with joy.

Whether a student's enrollment seems almost inevitable or signifies a triumph over the odds, attending college is a significant accomplishment. Although students already enrolled may feel that college attendance is nearly universal, this is not the case at all: Nationwide, only a minority of high school graduates enter college.

Who Goes to College?   As in the U.S. population as a whole, U.S. college students are primarily White and middle class. Although nearly 69% of White high school graduates enter college, only 61% of African American and 47% of Hispanic graduates do so (see Figure 15-5). Even more striking, although the absolute number of minority students enrolled in college has increased, the overall *proportion* of the minority population that does enter college has decreased over the past decade—a decline that most education experts attribute to changes in the availability of financial aid (U.S. Bureau of the Census, 1998, 2000).

Furthermore, the proportion of students who enter college but ultimately never graduate is substantial. Only around 40% of those who start college finish 4 years later with a degree. Although about half of those who don't receive a degree in 4 years eventually do finish, the other half never obtain a college degree. For minorities, the picture is even worse: The national dropout rate for African American college students stands at 70% (Minorities in Higher Education, 1995; American College Testing Program, 2001).

These observations notwithstanding, the number of students traditionally classified as "minorities" attending college is rising dramatically, and ethnic and racial minorities make up an increasingly larger proportion of the college population. Already at some colleges, such as the University of California at Berkeley, Whites have shifted from the majority to the minority as diversity among the students has increased significantly. These trends, reflecting changes in the racial and ethnic composition of the United States, are significant, because higher education remains an important way for families to improve their economic well-being.

Gender and College

I registered for a calculus course my first year at De-Pauw. Even twenty years ago I was not timid, so on the very first day I raised my hand and asked a question. I still have a vivid memory of the professor rolling his eyes, hitting his head with his hand in frustration, and announcing to everyone, "Why do they expect me to teach calculus to girls?" I never asked another question. Several weeks later I went to a football game, but I had forgotten to bring my ID. My calculus professor was at the gate checking IDs, so I went up to him and said, "I forgot my ID but you know me, I'm in your class." He looked right at me and said, "I don't remember you in my class." I couldn't believe that someone who changed my life and whom I remember to this day didn't even recognize me. (Sadker & Sadker, 1994, p. 162)

Although such incidents of blatant sexism are less likely to occur today, prejudice and discrimination directed at women are still a fact of college life. For instance, the next time you are in class, consider the gender of your classmates and the subject matter of the class. Although men and women attend college in roughly equal numbers, there is significant variation in the classes they take. Classes in education and the social sciences, for instance, typically have a larger proportion of women than men; and classes in engineering, the physical sciences, and mathematics tend to have more men than women.

The gender gap is also apparent when we look at college instructors. Although the number of female faculty members has increased, there is still evidence of discrimination. For example, the more prestigious the institution, the fewer the proportion of women who have attained the highest rank. The situation is even more pronounced in the fields of math, science, and engineering, where women are significantly underrepresented (Wilson, 2004).

The persistent differences in gender distribution across subject areas likely reflect the powerful influence of gender stereotypes that operate throughout the world of education

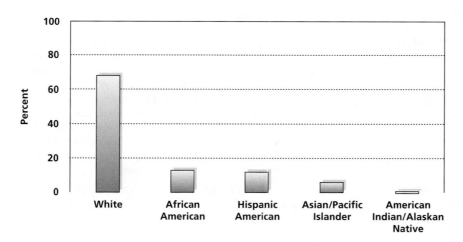

FIGURE 15-5 College Participation by High School Graduates

The proportion of African Americans and Hispanics who enter college after graduating from high school is lower than the proportion of Whites.

(*Source: The Condition of Education 2004,* National Center for Education Statistics, 2004)

Even though they may be unaware of it, both male and female professors treat men and women in their classes differently. For example, they typically call on men in class more frequently than women.

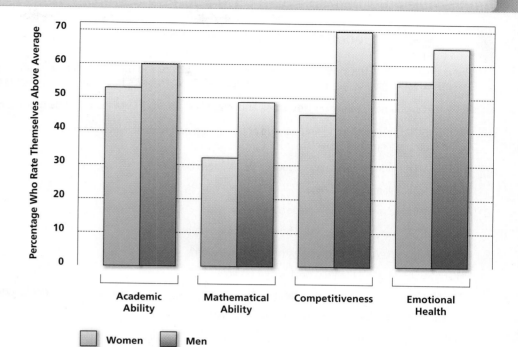

FIGURE 15-6 Self-Assessments in Various Categories by Male and Female College Students

During their first year of college, men are more likely than women to view themselves as above average in areas relevant to academic success. How can educators be made more aware of this problem, and how might it be addressed? (*Source:* Sax et al., 2000)

and beyond. For instance, when women in their first year of college are asked to name a likely career choice, they are much less apt to choose careers that have traditionally been dominated by men, such as engineering or computer programming, and more likely to choose professions that have traditionally been populated by women, such as nursing and social work (Avalon, 2003; White & White, 2006).

Male and female college students also have different expectations regarding their areas of competence. For instance, one survey asked first-year college students whether they were above or below average on a variety of traits and abilities. As can be seen in Figure 15-6, men were more likely than women to think of themselves as above average in overall academic and mathematical ability, competitiveness, and emotional health.

Both male and female college professors treat men and women differently in their classes, even though the different treatment is largely unintentional and often the professors are unaware of their actions. For instance, professors call on men in class more frequently than on women, and they make more eye contact with men than with women. Furthermore, male students are more likely than women to receive extra help from their professors. Finally, the male students often receive more positive reinforcement for their comments than female students do—exemplified by the startling illustration in Table 15-3 (Epperson, 1988; American Association of University Women, 1992; Sadker & Sadker, 1994, 2005).

The diversity of students attending college is rising dramatically, although enrollment of minority students still lags proportionately to the enrollment of Whites.

TABLE 15-3 Gender Bias in the Classroom

The course on the U.S. Constitution is required for graduation, and more than 50 students, approximately half male and half female, file in. The professor begins by asking if there are questions on next week's midterm. Several hands go up.

BERNIE: Do you have to memorize names and dates in the book? Or will the test be more general?

PROFESSOR: You do have to know those critical dates and people. Not every one but the important ones. If I were you, Bernie, I would spend time learning them. Ellen?

ELLEN: What kind of short-answer questions will there be?

PROFESSOR: All multiple choice.

ELLEN: Will we have the whole class time?

PROFESSOR: Yes, we'll have the whole class time. Anyone else?

BEN (calling out): Will there be an extra-credit question?

PROFESSOR: I hadn't planned on it. What do you think?

BEN: I really like them. They take some of the pressure off. You can also see who is doing extra work.

PROFESSOR: I'll take it under advisement, Charles?

CHARLES: How much of our final grade is this?

PROFESSOR: The midterm is 25 percent. But remember, class participation counts as well. Why don't we begin?

The professor lectures on the Constitution for twenty minutes before he asks a question about the electoral college. The electoral college is not as hot a topic as the midterm, so only four hands are raised. The professor calls on Ben.

BEN: The electoral college was created because there was a lack of faith in the people. Rather than have them vote for the president, they voted for the electors.

PROFESSOR: I like the way you think. (He smiles at Ben, and Ben smiles back.) Who could vote? (Five hands go up, five out of fifty.) Angie?

ANGIE: I don't know if this is right, but I thought only men could vote.

BEN (calling out): That was a great idea. We began going downhill when we let women vote. (Angie looks surprised but says nothing. Some of the students laugh, and so does the professor. He calls on Barbara.)

BARBARA: I think you had to be pretty wealthy, own property—

JOSH (not waiting for Barbara to finish, calls out): That's right. There was a distrust of the poor, who could upset the democracy. But if you had property, if you had something at stake, you could be trusted not to do something wild. Only property owners could be trusted.

PROFESSOR: Nice job, Josh. But why do we still have electors today? Mike?

MIKE: Tradition, I guess.

PROFESSOR: Do you think it's tradition? If you walked down the street and asked people their views of the electoral college, what would they say?

MIKE: Probably they'd be clueless. Maybe they would think that it elects the Pope. People don't know how it works.

PROFESSOR: Good, Mike. Judy, do you want to say something? (Judy's hand is at "half-mast," raised but just barely. When the professor calls her name, she looks a bit startled.)

JUDY (speaking very softly): Maybe we would need a whole new constitutional convention to change it. And once they get together to change that, they could change anything. That frightens people, doesn't it? (As Judy speaks, a number of students fidget, pass notes, and leaf through their books; a few even begin to whisper.)

(*Source:* Sadker & Sadker, 1994)

The different treatment of men and women in the classroom has led some educators to argue in favor of single-sex education for women. They point to evidence that the rate of participation and ultimately the success of women in the sciences is greater for graduates of women's colleges than for graduates of coeducational institutions. Furthermore, some research suggests that women who attend same-sex colleges may show higher self-esteem than those attending coeducational colleges, although the evidence is not entirely consistent on this count (Mael, 1998; Sax, 2005).

Why might women do better in single-sex environments? One reason is that they receive more attention than they would in coeducational settings, where professors are affected, however inadvertently, by societal biases. In addition, women's colleges tend to have more female professors than coeducational institutions, and they thereby provide more role models for women. Finally, women attending women's colleges may receive more encouragement for participation in nontraditional subjects such as mathematics and science than those in coeducational colleges (Robinson & Gillibrand, 2004; Kinzie et al., 2007).

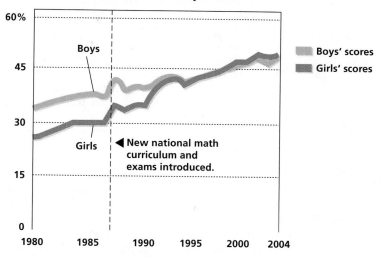

Percentage of English boys and girls earning passing grades of A through C on the state math exam for 18-year-olds

FIGURE 15-7 The New Math

After the introduction of a new math curriculum and exams in England, girls' and boys' performance began to converge. (*Source:* Department for Education and Skills, England 2004)

DEVELOPMENTAL DIVERSITY

Overcoming Gender and Racial Barriers to Achievement

In her 10th-grade math class, Frankie Teague dimmed the lights, switched on soothing music, and handed each student a white board and a marker. Then, she projected an arithmetic problem onto a screen at the front of the room.

"As soon as you get the answer, hold up your board," she said, setting off a round of squeaky scribbling. The simple step of having students hold up their work, instead of raising their hands or shouting out the answer, gives a leg up to a group of pupils who have long lagged in math classes—girls. (Whalen & Begley, 2005, p. A1)

This simple innovation is part of a large-scale, and ultimately successful, effort to improve the teaching of math in English schools. Although meant to benefit all children, it has had an unintended result: erasing a gender gap that favored boys over girls in math performance.

As illustrated in Figure 15-7, the introduction of the new math curriculum in the late 1980s brought about a rise in overall math exam scores. But the rise was more pronounced for girls, and today girls outperform boys on some standardized math tests.

What changes in the curriculum led to the improvement in performance? Teachers were taught to be on the alert for gender stereotyping in their courses, and they were encouraged to include girls in discussions more vigorously. In addition, gender stereotypes were removed from textbooks. Classrooms were made "safer" for girls by discouraging students

Women choosing traditionally male fields such as math and science can overcome even long-standing societal stereotypes if they are convinced that others like them.

from shouting out answers and by encouraging girls more directly to participate. Tests were changed, too, to give partial credit when students write out their thinking—something that benefited girls, who tend to be more methodical when working on test items.

Academic Performance and Stereotype Threat

From an educator's perspective:

Why might descendants of people who were forced to immigrate to a country be less successful academically than those who came voluntarily? What approaches might be used to overcome this obstacle?

Research on gender stereotypes suggests that the curricular changes adopted in England are moving in the right direction. For instance, consider this fact: When women take college classes in math, science, and engineering, they are more likely to do poorly than are men who enter college with the same level of preparation and identical SAT scores. Strangely, however, this phenomenon does not hold true for other areas of the curriculum, where men and women perform at similar levels.

According to psychologist Claude Steele, the reason has to do with women's acceptance of society's stereotypes about achievement in particular domains. Steele suggests that women are no strangers to society's dominant view that some subjects are more appropriate areas of study for women than others are. In fact, the pervasiveness of the stereotype makes women who attempt to achieve in traditionally "inappropriate" fields highly vulnerable (Suzuki & Aronson, 2005; Goff, Steele, & Davies, 2008).

Specifically, because of the strength and pervasiveness of such stereotypes, the performance of women seeking to achieve in nontraditional fields may be hindered as they are distracted by worries about the failure that society predicts for them. In some cases, a woman may decide that failure in a male-dominated field, because it would confirm societal stereotypes, would be so unpalatable that the struggle to succeed is not worth the effort. In that instance, the woman may not even try very hard.

But there is a bright side to Steele's analysis: If women can be convinced that societal stereotypes regarding achievement are invalid, their performance might well improve. And in fact, this is just what Steele found in a series of experiments he conducted at the University of Michigan and Stanford University (Steele, 1997).

In one study, male and female college students were told they would be taking two math tests: one in which there were gender differences—men supposedly performed better than women—and a second in which there were no gender differences. In reality, the tests were entirely similar, drawn from the same pool of difficult items. The reasoning behind the experimental manipulation was that women would be vulnerable to societal stereotypes on a test that they thought supported those stereotypes but would not be vulnerable on a test supposedly lacking gender differences.

The results fully supported Steele's reasoning. When the women were told there were gender differences in the test, they greatly underperformed the men. But when they were told there were no gender differences, they performed virtually the same as the men.

In short, the evidence from this study and others clearly suggests that women are vulnerable to expectations regarding their future success, whether the expectations come from societal stereotypes or from information about the prior performance of women on similar tasks. More encouraging, the evidence suggests that if women can be convinced that others have been successful in given domains, they may overcome even long-standing societal stereotypes (Croizet et al., 2004; Davies, Spencer, & Steele, 2005; Good, Aronson, & Harder, 2008).

We should also keep in mind that women are not the only group susceptible to society's stereotyping. Members of minority groups, such as African Americans and Hispanic Americans, are also vulnerable to stereotypes about academic success. In fact, Steele suggests that African Americans may "disidentify" with academic success by putting forth less effort on academic tasks and generally downgrading the importance of academic achievement. Ultimately, such disidentification may act as a self-fulfilling prophecy, increasing the chances of academic failure (Perry, Steele, & Hilliard, 2003; Ryan & Ryan, 2005; Davis, Aronson, & Salinas, 2006; Kellow & Jones, 2008).

REVIEW ⏎ mydevelopmentlab

1. _____ is a major educational phenomenon in which students are taught not by teachers in schools, but by their parents in their own homes.

   Answer: Homeschooling

2. _____ involves an unusually early entry into adult roles before an adolescent is developmentally ready to assume them.

   Answer: Pseudomaturity

3. The rate of participation and ultimately the success of women in the sciences is greater for graduates of _____-_____ colleges.

   Answer: single-sex

To see more review questions, log on to MyDevelopmentLab.

Picking an Occupation: Choosing Life's Work

Some people know from childhood that they want to be physicians or actors or go into business, and they follow direct paths toward that goal. For others, the choice of a career is very much a matter of chance, of turning to the want ads and seeing what's available.

Regardless of how a career is chosen, it is unlikely to be the only career that people will have during the course of their lifetimes. As technology alters the nature of work at a rapid pace, changing careers at least once, and sometimes several times, is likely to be the norm in the 21st century.

Fantasy period According to Ginzberg, the period of life when career choices are made—and discarded—without regard to skills, abilities, or available job opportunities

Tentative period The second stage of Ginzberg's theory, spanning adolescence, in which people begin to think in pragmatic terms about the requirements of various jobs and how their own abilities might fit with those requirements

Realistic period The stage in late adolescence and early adulthood during which people explore career options through job experience or training, narrow their choices, and eventually make a commitment to a career

Communal professions Occupations associated with relationships

Agentic professions Occupations associated with getting things accomplished

Ginzberg's Three Periods

According to Eli Ginzberg (1972), people generally move through several stages in choosing a career. In the **fantasy period**, which lasts until around age 11, career choices are made—and discarded—without regard to skills, abilities, or available job opportunities. Instead, choices are made solely on the basis of what sounds appealing. Thus, a child may decide that she wants to be a veterinarian, despite the fact that she is allergic to dogs and cats.

People begin to take practical considerations into account during the tentative period, which spans adolescence. During the **tentative period**, people begin to think in pragmatic terms about the requirements of various jobs and how their own abilities might fit with those requirements. They also consider their personal values and goals, exploring how well a particular occupation might satisfy them. Finally, in early adulthood, people enter the **realistic period**, in which they explore specific career options either through actual experience on the job or through training for a profession. They begin to narrow their choices to a few alternative careers and eventually make a commitment to a particular one.

Holland's Six Personality Types

Although the three stages make intuitive sense, the stage approach oversimplifies the process of choosing a career. Consequently, some researchers suggest that it is more fruitful to examine the match between job seekers' personality types and career requirements. For example, according to researcher John Holland (1973, 1987; Gottfredson & Holland, 1990; Donohue, 2007), certain personality types match particularly well with certain careers. Specifically, he suggests that six personality types are important in career choice:

- *Realistic:* These people are down-to-earth, practical problem solvers who are physically strong, but their social skills are mediocre. They make good farmers, laborers, and truck drivers.

- *Intellectual:* Intellectual types are oriented toward the theoretical and the abstract. Although not particularly good with people, they are well suited to careers in math and science.

- *Social:* The traits associated with the social personality type are related to verbal skills and interpersonal relations. Social types are good at working with people and consequently make good salespersons, teachers, and counselors.

- *Conventional:* Conventional individuals prefer highly structured tasks. They make good clerks, secretaries, and bank tellers.

- *Enterprising:* These individuals are risk takers and take-charge types. They are good leaders and may be particularly effective as managers or politicians.

- *Artistic:* Artistic types use art to express themselves, and they often prefer the world of art to interactions with people. They are best suited to occupations involving art.

Of course, not everyone fits neatly into one particular personality type. Furthermore, there are certainly exceptions to the typology, with jobs being held successfully by people who don't have the predicted personality. Still, the theory forms the foundation of several instruments designed to assess the occupational options for which a given person is particularly suited (Randahl, 1991).

Gender and Career Choices: Women's Work

WANTED: Full-time employee for small family firm. DUTIES: Including but not limited to general cleaning, cooking, gardening, laundry, ironing and mending, purchasing, bookkeeping and money management. Child care may also be required. HOURS: Avg. 55/wk but standby duty required 24 hours/day, 7 days/wk. Extra workload on holidays. SALARY AND BENEFITS: No salary, but food, clothing, and shelter provided at employer's discretion; job security and benefits depend on continued good will of employer. No vacation. No retirement plan. No opportunities for advancement. REQUIREMENTS: No previous experience necessary, can learn on the job. Only women need apply. (Unger & Crawford, 1992, p. 446)

Just 2 decades ago, many women entering early adulthood assumed that this admittedly exaggerated job description matched the work for which they were best suited and to which they aspired: housewife. Even those women who sought work outside the home were relegated to certain professions. For instance, until the 1960s, employment ads in newspapers throughout the United States were almost always divided into two sections: "Help Wanted: Male" and "Help Wanted: Female." The men's job listings encompassed such professions as police officer, construction worker, and legal counsel; the women's listings were for secretaries, teachers, cashiers, and librarians.

The breakdown of jobs deemed appropriate for men and women reflected society's traditional view of what the two genders were best suited for. Traditionally, women were considered most appropriate for **communal professions**, occupations associated with relationships. In contrast, men were perceived as best suited for **agentic professions**. Agentic professions are associated with getting things accomplished. It is probably no coincidence that communal professions typically have lower status and lower salaries than agentic professions (Eagly & Steffen, 1984, 1986).

Although discrimination based on gender is far less blatant today than it was several decades ago—it is now illegal, for instance, to advertise a position specifically for a man or a woman—remnants of traditional gender-role prejudice persist. One reflection of this is illustrated by the

CAREERS *in* CHILD DEVELOPMENT

Amy Aspengren

Education: B.A. Business Administration, Ohio University, Athens Ohio; M.A. Labor and Human Resources, Ohio State University, Columbus, Ohio; M.A. School Counseling, University of Dayton, Dayton, Ohio.

Position: Project Counselor, Upper Arlington High School, Upper Arlington, Ohio

Home: Upper Arlington, Ohio

Getting through high school and graduating is a milestone for many students. But equally important is what students will be doing with their future, and this is where career counselors can offer guidance as to the best path to pursue.

For Amy Aspengren, who sees 25 students during the course of a week at Upper Arlington High School, counseling can range from helping students meet graduation requirements to offering guidance to four-year colleges and universities.

"I work in changing areas and with different numbers of students based on current needs," Aspengren said. "Currently I'm working with at-risk seniors who need assistance with graduation requirements."

Guidance at Upper Arlington, with a student population of close to 2,000, begins in the 9th grade, followed by a personality assessment in the 10th grade that offers career suggestions, according to Aspengren.

"Students are also encouraged to find summer work and internships that would give them insight into possible careers," she added. "Some students transition to career centers starting their junior year."

There are always students who are uncertain about what path to take and Aspengren offers several suggestions on helping students find the right direction.

"We ask them what are their interests, priorities, and how do they see themselves in five years," she said. "We also talk about their personality profile and the careers it suggests."

A more specific approach involves doing what Aspengren calls a "Reality Check" income analysis.

"This is a program done through our state education site," she explained. "Students choose things they want in their life, and the income analysis determines what income they need to support that lifestyle. It then suggests different careers to consider. We also discuss about the impact of *not* choosing a career plan."

Ultimately the decision is up to the student. "All you can do is present the information to them," Aspengren said. "Discussing the impact of their decisions can help them understand the implications, but the decision needs to be theirs."

discrepancy between women's and men's salaries. As shown in Figure 15-8, in 97% of the occupations for which data have been collected, women's weekly earnings are less than men's. On average, women earn 77 cents for every dollar that men earn. Moreover, women who are members of minority groups do even worse: African American women earn 65 cents for every dollar men make, while for Hispanic women the figure is 54 cents (U.S. Bureau of the Census, 2006).

Nevertheless, despite status and pay that are often lower than men's, more women are working outside the home than ever before. Between 1950 and 2000, the percentage of the female population ages 16 and older in the U.S. labor force overall increased from around 35% to 60%. Today, women make up around 46% of the workforce. Almost all women expect to earn a living, and almost all do at some point in their lives. Furthermore, in about one-half of U.S. households, women earn about as much as their husbands (Lewin, 1995; Women's Bureau, 2002).

In addition, opportunities for women are in many ways considerably greater today than they were in earlier years. Women are more likely to be physicians, lawyers, insurance agents, and bus drivers than they were in the past. However, within specific job categories, sex discrimination still occurs. For example, female bus drivers are more apt to have part-time school bus routes, whereas men hold better paying

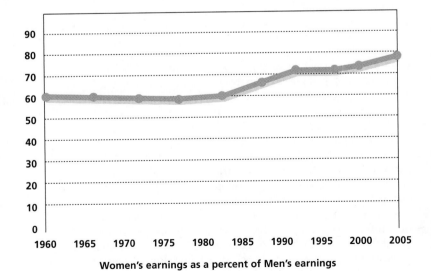

Women's earnings as a percent of Men's earnings

FIGURE 15-8 The Gender Wage Gap

Women's weekly earnings as a percentage of men's has increased since 1979 but still is only slightly more than 75% and has remained steady in recent years.
(*Source:* U.S. Bureau of the Census, 2006)

Discrimination based on gender is less blatant than it once was, but it remains a potent force. However, strides have been made in many professions.

full-time routes in cities. Similarly, female pharmacists are more likely to work in hospitals, while men work in higher paying jobs in retail stores (Unger & Crawford, 2004).

Women and minorities in high-status, visible professional roles still often hit what has come to be called the "glass ceiling." The glass ceiling is an invisible barrier in an organization that prevents individuals from being promoted beyond a certain level because of discrimination. It operates subtly, and the people responsible for keeping the glass ceiling in place may not even be aware of how their actions perpetuate discrimination against women and minorities. For instance, a male supervisor in the oil exploration business may conclude that a particular task is "too dangerous" for a female employee. As a consequence of his decision, he may be preventing female candidates for the job from obtaining the experience they need to get promoted (Reid, Miller, & Kerr, 2004; Stroh, Langlands, & Simpson, 2004; Probert, 2005).

Becoming an Informed Consumer of Development

Choosing a Career

One of the greatest challenges people face in late adolescence is making a decision that will have lifelong implications: the choice of a career. Although there is no single correct choice—most people can be happy in any of several different jobs—the options can be daunting. Here are some guidelines for at least starting to come to grips with the question of what occupational path to follow.

- Systematically evaluate a variety of choices. Libraries and the Internet contain a wealth of information about potential career paths, and most colleges and universities have career centers that can provide occupational data and guidance.

- Know yourself. Evaluate your strengths and weaknesses, perhaps by completing a questionnaire at a college career center that can provide insight into your interests, skills, and values.

- Create a "balance sheet" listing the potential gains and losses that you will incur from a particular profession. First, list the gains and losses that you will experience directly, and then list the gains and losses for others. Next, write down the projected social approval or disapproval you are likely to receive from others. By systematically evaluating a set of potential careers according to each of these criteria, you will be in a better position to compare different possibilities.

- "Try out" different careers through paid or unpaid internships. By experiencing a job firsthand, interns are able to get a better sense of what an occupation is truly like.

- Remember that if you make a mistake, you can change careers. In fact, people today increasingly change careers in early adulthood or even beyond. No one should feel locked into a decision made earlier in life.

As we've seen throughout this book, people develop substantially as they age, and this development continues beyond adolescence through the entire life span. It is reasonable to expect that shifting values, interests, abilities, and life circumstances might make a different career more appropriate later in life than the one chosen in late adolescence.

From an educator's perspective: Some people advocate same-sex (and even same-ethnicity) high schools and colleges as a way to combat the disadvantages of discrimination. Why might this be effective? What drawbacks do you see?

REVIEW ↵ mydevelopmentlab

1. Ginzberg suggested that people move through three stages when choosing a career: the fantasy period, the _____ period, and the realistic period.

   Answer: tentative

2. According to John Holland, certain personality types match with certain careers. He suggested six personality types: realistic, intellectual, social, _____ , enterprising, and artistic.

   Answer: conventional

3. Traditionally, women were considered appropriate for communal professions and men were considered appropriate for _____ professions.

   Answer: agentic

To see more review questions, log on to MyDevelopmentLab.

CASE STUDY

The Case of... The Frustrated Fantasy

Jared Mulford, 16, began his college search in a state of high excitement. A bright, creative student, he had already aced three AP classes and planned to take more. He was also editor of the school paper and a member of the debating team. Jared loved to lie on his bed and imagine how Harvard, Princeton, and Yale would fight over him.

To Jared's annoyance, his school college counselor did not share his vision. "It's fine to dream of Harvard, but you should pick some safety schools, Jared. You may need them."

Jared seethed at such advice. Hadn't he skipped a grade in elementary school? Wasn't he slated to be the high school valedictorian? And he was sure to get perfect SAT scores, so why bother applying to any schools but the best?

The first shock came when he received his SAT scores. Though they were quite high, they were not perfect. "Pick some safety schools," his counselor repeated. But Jared ignored her and applied only to his dream trio. His last editorial in the school paper had won a local award. He knew he was destined for special things.

Then the real shocks started hitting. First, Harvard rejected him, then Yale. Still, Jared clung to his dream until, at last, in early April, he heard from Princeton. No go.

As his friends began planning what they would take to college and arranged their freshman courses, Jared grew depressed. He had nowhere to go.

1. How do Jared's thoughts and actions reflect the egocentrism that is so typical of adolescents?

2. Why might Jared still cling to his dreams after Harvard and Yale have rejected him?

3. Is Jared's view of himself realistic? What is Jared overlooking when he fantasizes about the elite colleges fighting over him?

4. Do you think Jared's refusal to accept his college counselor's advice demonstrates growth in his cognitive abilities? Why or why not?

5. If you were Jared's college counselor, how would you have prepared him to better understand and assess the reality of his situation?

◄ Looking Back

How does cognitive development proceed during adolescence?

- Cognitive growth during adolescence is rapid, with gains in abstract thinking, reasoning, and the ability to view possibilities in relative rather than in absolute terms.

- Adolescence coincides with Piaget's formal operations period of development, when people begin to engage in abstract thought and experimental reasoning.

- According to information-processing approaches, cognitive growth during adolescence is gradual and quantitative, involving improvements in memory capacity, mental strategies, and other aspects of cognitive functioning.

- Another major area of cognitive development is the growth of metacognition, which permits adolescents to monitor their thought processes and to accurately assess their cognitive capabilities.

What aspects of cognitive development cause difficulties for adolescents?

- Hand in hand with the development of metacognition is the growth of adolescent egocentrism, a self-absorption that makes it hard for adolescents to accept criticism and tolerate authority figures.

- Adolescents may play to an imaginary audience of critical observers, and they may develop personal fables, which emphasize the uniqueness of their experiences and supposed invulnerability to risks.

Through what stages does moral development progress during childhood and adolescence?

- Adolescents develop morally as well as in other ways. According to Lawrence Kohlberg, people pass through three major levels and six stages of moral development as their sense of justice and their moral reasoning evolve.

- According to Kohlberg, levels of moral development encompass preconventional morality (motivated by rewards and punishments), conventional morality (motivated by social reference), and postconventional morality (motivated by a sense of universal moral principles)—a level that may be reached during adolescence but that many people never attain.

- Although Kohlberg's theory provides a good account of moral judgments, it is less adequate in predicting moral behavior.

- There appear to be gender differences in moral development not reflected in Kohlberg's work. Carol Gilligan has sketched out an alternative progression for girls, from an orientation toward individual survival through goodness as self-sacrifice to the morality of nonviolence.

What factors affect adolescent school performance?

- School achievement is linked with socioeconomic status, race, and ethnicity. Many academic achievement differences are due to socioeconomic factors, but other factors also play a part: attributional patterns regarding success factors and belief systems regarding the link between school success and success in life.

Who attends college, and how is the college experience different for men and women?

- The proportion of White high school graduates that enter and complete college is larger than that of African American or Hispanic high school graduates. Nevertheless, minority students make up an increasingly larger proportion of the U.S. college population each year.

- The college experience differs for men and women. Differences are evident in courses and majors chosen and in expectations for financial success upon graduation. The differences appear to be attributable to gender stereotypes that operate in college to affect teachers' and students' expectations.

How do adolescents make career choices, and what influence do ethnicity and gender have on career opportunities?

- According to Eli Ginzberg, people proceed through stages as they consider careers, from the fantasy period, in which dream choices are made without regard to practical factors, through the tentative period, which spans adolescence and involves pragmatic thought about job requirements and personal abilities and goals, to the realistic period of early adulthood, in which career options are explored through actual experience and training. Other theories of career choice, such as John Holland's, link personality characteristics and career options.

- Career choice and attitudes and behaviors on the job are influenced by gender. Traditionally, women have been associated with communal professions, which tend to be lower paid; and men, with agentic professions, which pay better.

- Women and minorities in professional roles may find themselves hitting the *glass ceiling*, an invisible barrier in an organization that prevents career advancement beyond a certain level because of conscious or unconscious discrimination. ■

Epilogue

This chapter focused on the cognitive advances that occur during adolescence. We began by considering Piagetian and information-processing approaches to cognitive development and then saw how adolescents' self-absorption occurs in part because of the state of their cognitive abilities. We then turned to moral development, focusing on moral reasoning and males' and females' different conceptions of morality. Finally, we looked at school performance and its relationship to cognitive development.

Before moving on to the next chapter, return to the Prologue and consider these questions:

1. What aspects of early adolescent development are apparent in the description of a day at the Fritsche Middle School?

2. How might these adolescents be different in 2 or 3 years when they reach later adolescence?

3. Some educators, politicians, and parents believe that middle school (and high school) should focus more on core academic subjects than on the diffuse variety of arts and music courses described in the Prologue. What do you think of this idea? ○

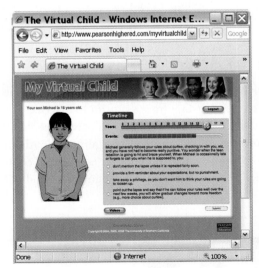

What decisions would you make while raising a child? What would the consequences of those decisions be?

Find out by logging onto **My Virtual Child** and raising your child from birth to 18 years.

Key Terms and Concepts

formal operational stage (p. **358**)
information-processing perspective (p. **360**)
metacognition (p. **361**)
adolescent egocentrism (p. **361**)
imaginary audience (p. **361**)

personal fables (p. **361**)
fantasy period (p. **377**)
tentative period (p. **377**)
realistic period (p. **377**)
communal professions (p. **377**)
agentic professions (p. **377**) ○

16

Social and Personality Development in Adolescence

PROLOGUE: AGAINST THE TIDE

Lucian Schulte had always planned to wait until he was married to have sex, but that was before a warm night a couple of years ago when the green-eyed, lanky six-footer found himself with an unexpected opportunity. "She was all for it," says Lucian, now 18. "It was like, 'Hey, let's give this a try.'" The big event was over in a hurry and lacked any sense of intimacy. "In movies, if people have sex, it's always romantic," he says. "Physically, it did feel good, but emotionally, it felt really awkward. It was not what I expected it to be."

Lucian, raised Roman Catholic, was plagued by guilt. "I was worried that I'd given myself to someone and our relationship was now a lot more serious than it was before," he says. "It was like, 'Now, what is she going to expect from me?'" Lucian worried, too, about disease and pregnancy. He promised himself never again.

Lucian, now an engineering major at the University of Alberta in Canada, is a "renewed virgin." His parents are strong proponents of chastity, and he attended school-sponsored abstinence classes. But the messages didn't hit home until he'd actually had sex.... He has dated since his high-school affair, and is now hoping a particular cute coed from Edmonton will go out with him. "But I'll try to restrict myself to kissing," he says. (Ali & Scelfo, 2002, p. 61)

▶ Looking Ahead

We'll probably never know whether Lucian Schulte will be successful in his quest to abstain from sex prior to marriage. But the issues of sexuality that he is grappling with are those that virtually every adolescent thinks about at one point or another.

Despite the reputation of adolescence as a time of confusion and rebellion, most teenagers pass through the period without much turmoil. Although adolescents may "try on" different roles and flirt with activities that their parents find objectionable, the majority find adolescence an exciting time during which friendships grow, intimate relationships develop, and their sense of themselves deepens.

This is not to say that the transitions adolescents pass through are not challenging. As we shall see in this chapter, where we discuss personality and social development, adolescence brings about major changes in the ways in which individuals must deal with the world.

We begin by considering how adolescents form their views of themselves. We look at self-concept, self-esteem, and identity development. We also examine two major psychological difficulties: depression and suicide.

Next, we discuss relationships during adolescence. We consider how adolescents reposition themselves within the family and how the influence of family members declines in some spheres as peers take on new importance. We also examine the ways in which adolescents interact with their friends and the ways in which popularity is determined.

Finally, the chapter considers dating and sexual behavior. We look at the role of dating and close relationships in adolescents' lives, and we consider sexual behavior and the standards that govern adolescents' sex lives. We conclude by looking at teenage pregnancy and at programs that seek to prevent unwanted pregnancy.

After reading this chapter, you will be able to answer these questions:

- *How does the development of self-concept, self-esteem, and identity proceed during adolescence?*

- *What dangers do adolescents face as they deal with the stresses of adolescence?*
- *How does the quality of relationships with family and peers change during adolescence?*
- *What are gender, race, and ethnic relations like in adolescence?*
- *What does it mean to be popular and unpopular in adolescence, and how do adolescents respond to peer pressure?*
- *What are the functions and characteristics of dating during adolescence?*
- *How does sexuality develop in the adolescent years?*

Identity: Asking "Who Am I?"

Thirteen is a hard age, very hard. A lot of people say you have it easy, you're a kid, but there's a lot of pressure being 13—to be respected by people in your school, to be liked, always feeling like you have to be good. There's pressure to do drugs, too, so you try not to succumb to that. But you don't want to be made fun of, so you have to look cool. You gotta wear the right shoes, the right clothes. (Carlos Quintana, 1998, p. 66)

The thoughts of 13-year-old Carlos Quintana demonstrate a clear awareness—and self-consciousness—regarding his newly forming place in society and life. During adolescence, questions like "Who am I?" and "Where do I belong in the world?" begin to take a front seat.

Why should issues of identity become so important during adolescence? One reason is that adolescents' intellectual capacities become more adultlike. They are able to see how they stack up to others and become aware that they are individuals, apart not just from their parents, but from all others. The dramatic physical changes during puberty make adolescents acutely conscious of their own bodies and aware that others are reacting to them in ways to which they are unaccustomed. Whatever the cause, adolescence often brings substantial changes in teenagers' self-concepts and self-esteem—in sum, their notions of their own identity.

Self-Concept: What Am I Like?

Ask Valerie to describe herself, and she says, "Others look at me as laid-back, relaxed, and not worrying too much. But really, I'm often nervous and emotional."

The fact that Valerie distinguishes others' views of her from her own perceptions represents a developmental advance of adolescence. In childhood, Valerie would have characterized herself according to a list of traits that would not differentiate her view of herself and others' perspectives.

However, adolescents are able to make the distinction, and when they try to describe who they are, they take both their own and others' views into account (Cole et al., 2001; Updegraff et al., 2004).

This broader view of themselves is one aspect of adolescents' increasing understanding of who they are. They can see various aspects of the self simultaneously, and this view of the self becomes more organized and coherent. They look at the self from a psychological perspective, viewing traits not as concrete entities but as abstractions (Adams, Montemayor, & Gullotta, 1996). For example, teenagers are more likely than younger children to describe themselves in terms of their ideology (saying something like, "I'm an environmentalist") than in terms of physical characteristics (such as, "I'm the fastest runner in my class").

In some ways, however, this broader, more multifaceted self-concept is a mixed blessing, especially during the earlier years of adolescence. At that time, adolescents may be troubled by the multiple aspects of their personalities. During the beginning of adolescence, for instance, teenagers may want to view themselves in a certain way ("I'm a sociable person and love to be with people"), and they may become concerned when their behavior is inconsistent with that view ("Even though I want to be sociable, sometimes I can't stand being around my friends and just want to be alone"). By the end of adolescence, however, teenagers find it easier to accept that different situations elicit different behaviors and feelings (Trzesniewski, Donnellan, & Robins, 2003; Hitlin, Brown, & Elder, 2006).

Self-Esteem: How Do I Like Myself?

Knowing who you are and *liking* who you are two different things. Although adolescents become increasingly accurate in understanding who they are (their self-concept), this knowledge does not guarantee that they like themselves (their self-esteem) any better. In fact, their increasing accuracy in understanding themselves permits them to see themselves fully—warts and all. It's what they do with these perceptions that leads them to develop a sense of their self-esteem.

The same cognitive sophistication that allows adolescents to differentiate various aspects of the self also leads them to evaluate those aspects in different ways (Chan, 1997; J. Cohen, 1999). For instance, an adolescent may have high self-esteem in terms of academic performance, but lower self-esteem in terms of relationships with others. Or it may be just the opposite, as articulated by this teenage girl:

How much do I *like* the kind of person I am? Well, I like some things about me, but I don't like others. I'm glad that I'm popular since it's really important to me to have friends. But in school I don't do as well as the really smart kids. That's OK, because if you're too smart you'll lose your friends. So being smart is just not that important. Except to my parents. I feel like I'm letting them down when I don't do as well as they want. (Harter, 1990b, p. 364)

Gender Differences in Self-Esteem

What determines an adolescent's self-esteem? Several factors make a difference. One is gender: Particularly during early adolescence, girls' self-esteem tends to be lower and more vulnerable than that held by boys (Byrne, 2000; Miyamoto et al., 2000; Ah-Kion, 2006).

One reason is that, compared to boys, girls tend to be more concerned about physical appearance and social success—in addition to academic achievement. Although boys are also concerned about these things, their attitudes are often more casual. In addition, societal messages suggesting that female academic achievement is a roadblock to social success can put girls in a difficult bind: If they do well academically, they jeopardize their social success. No wonder that the self-esteem of adolescent girls is more fragile than that of boys (Unger, 2001; Ricciardelli & McCabe, 2003; Ata, Ludden, & Lally, 2007).

Although self-esteem is typically higher in adolescent boys than in girls, boys do have vulnerabilities of their own. For example, society's stereotypical gender expectations may lead boys to feel that they should be confident, tough, and fearless all the time. Boys facing difficulties, such as not making a sports team or experiencing rejection from a girl they want to go out with, are likely to feel not only miserable about the defeat they face but also incompetent, because they don't measure up to the stereotype expectations (Pollack, 1999; Pollack, Shuster, & Trelease, 2001).

Socioeconomic Status and Race Differences in Self-Esteem

Socioeconomic status (SES) and race also influence self-esteem. Adolescents of higher SES generally have higher self-esteem than those of lower SES, particularly during middle and later adolescence. It may be that the social status factors that especially enhance one's standing and self-esteem—such as having more expensive clothes or a car—become more conspicuous in the later periods of adolescence (Van Tassel-Baska et al., 1994).

Race and ethnicity also play a role in self-esteem, but their impact has lessened as prejudicial treatment of minorities has eased. Early studies argued that minority status would lead to lower self-esteem, and this was initially supported by research. African Americans and Hispanics, researchers' explained, had lower self-esteem than did Caucasians because prejudicial attitudes in society made them feel disliked and rejected, and this feeling was incorporated into their self-concepts. More recent research paints a different picture. Most findings suggest that African American adolescents differ little from Whites in their levels of self-esteem (Harter, 1990b). Why should this be? One explanation is that social movements within the African American community that bolster racial pride help support African American adolescents. In fact, research finds that a stronger sense of racial identity is related to a higher level of self-esteem in African Americans and Hispanics (Phinney, Lochner, & Murphy, 1990; Gray-Little & Hafdahl, 2000; Verkuyten, 2003).

Another reason for overall similarity in self-esteem levels between adolescents of different racial groups is that teenagers in general focus their preferences and priorities on those aspects of their lives at which they excel. Consequently, African American youths may concentrate on the things that they find most satisfying and gain self-esteem from being successful at them (Gray-Little & Hafdahl, 2000; Yang & Blodgett, 2000; Phinney, 2005).

Finally, self-esteem may be influenced not by race alone, but by a complex combination of factors. For instance, some developmentalists have considered race and gender simultaneously, coining the term *ethgender* to refer to the joint influence of race and gender. One study that simultaneously

Identity-versus-identity-confusion stage The period during which teenagers seek to determine what is unique and distinctive about themselves

took both race and gender into account found that African American and Hispanic males had the highest levels of self-esteem, while Asian and Native American females had the lowest levels (Romero & Roberts, 2003; Saunders, Davis, & Williams, 2004; Biro et al., 2006).

Research has revealed that minority status does not necessarily lead to low self-esteem. In fact, a strong sense of racial identity is tied to higher levels of self-esteem.

Identity Formation: Change or Crisis?

According to Erik Erikson, whose theory we last discussed in Chapter 13, the search for identity inevitably leads some adolescents into substantial psychological turmoil as they encounter the adolescent identity crisis (Erikson, 1963). Erikson's theory regarding this stage, which is summarized with his other stages in Table 16-1, suggests teenagers try to figure out what is unique and distinctive about themselves—something they are able to do with increasing sophistication because of the cognitive gains that occur during adolescence.

Erikson argues that adolescents strive to discover their particular strengths and weaknesses and the roles they can best play in their future lives. This discovery process often involves "trying on" different roles or choices to see if they fit an adolescent's capabilities and views about himself or herself. Through this process, adolescents seek to understand who they are by narrowing and making choices about their personal, occupational, sexual, and political commitments. Erikson call this the **identity-versus-identity-confusion stage**.

In Erikson's view, adolescents who stumble in their efforts to find a suitable identity may go off course in several ways. They may adopt socially unacceptable roles as a way of expressing what they do *not* want to be, or they may have difficulty forming and maintaining long-lasting close personal relationships. In general, their sense of self becomes "diffuse," failing to organize around a central, unified core identity.

TABLE 16-1 A Summary of Erikson's Stages

Stage	Approximate Age	Positive Outcomes	Negative Outcomes
1. Trust-versus-mistrust	Birth–1.5 years	Feelings of trust from environmental support	Fear and concern regarding others
2. Autonomy-versus-shame-and-doubt	1.5–3 years	Self-sufficiency if exploration is encouraged	Doubts about self, lack of independence
3. Initiative-versus-guilt	3–6 years	Discovery of ways to initiate actions	Guilt from actions and thoughts
4. Industry-versus-inferiority	6–12 years	Development of sense of competence	Feelings of inferiority, no sense of mastery
5. Identity-versus-identity-confusion	Adolescence	Awareness of uniqueness of self, knowledge of role to be followed	Inability to identify appropriate roles in life
6. Intimacy-versus-isolation	Early adulthood	Development of loving, sexual relationships and close friendships	Fear of relationships with others
7. Generativity-versus-stagnation	Middle adulthood	Sense of contribution to continuity of life	Trivialization of one's activities
8. Ego-integrity-versus-despair	Late adulthood	Sense of unity in life's accomplishments	Regret over lost opportunities of life

(*Source*: Erikson, 1963)

On the other hand, those who are successful in forging an appropriate identity set a course that provides a foundation for future psychosocial development. They learn their unique capabilities and believe in them, and they develop an accurate sense of who they are. They are prepared to set out on a path that takes full advantage of what their unique strengths permit them to do (Blustein & Palladino, 1991; Archer & Waterman, 1994; Allison & Schultz, 2001).

Societal Pressures and Reliance on Friends and Peers   As if teenagers' self-generated identity issues were not difficult enough, societal pressures are also high during the identity-versus-identity-confusion stage, as any student knows who has been repeatedly asked by parents and friends "What's your major?" and "What are you going to do when you graduate?" Adolescents feel pressure to decide whether their post–high school plans include work or college and, if they choose work, which occupational track to follow. Up to this point in their development, their educational lives have been pretty much programmed by U.S. society, which lays out a universal educational track. However, the track ends at high school, and consequently, adolescents face difficult choices about which of several possible future paths they will follow (Kidwell et al., 1995).

During this period, adolescents increasingly rely on their friends and peers as sources of information. At the same time, their dependence on adults declines. As we discuss later in the chapter, this increasing dependence on the peer group enables adolescents to forge close relationships. Comparing themselves to others helps them clarify their own identities.

This reliance on peers to help adolescents define their identities and learn to form relationships is the link between this stage of psychosocial development and the next stage Erikson proposed, known as intimacy-versus-isolation. It also relates to the subject of gender differences in identity formation. When Erikson developed his theory, he suggested that males and females move through the identity-versus-identity-confusion period differently. He argued that males are more likely to proceed through the social development stages in the order they are shown in Table 16-1, developing a stable identity before committing to an intimate relationship with another person. In contrast, he suggested that females reverse the order, seeking intimate relationships and then defining their identities through these relationships. These ideas largely reflect the social conditions at the time he was writing, when women were less likely to go to college or establish their own careers and instead often married early. Today, however, the experiences of boys and girls seem relatively similar during the identity-versus-confusion period.

Psychological Moratorium   Because of the pressures of the identity-versus-identity-confusion period, Erikson suggested that many adolescents pursue a "psychological moratorium." The *psychological moratorium* is a period during

During the identity-versus-identity-confusion stage, American teenagers seek to understand who they are by narrowing and making choices about their personal, occupational, sexual, and political commitments. Can this stage be applied to teenagers in other cultures? Why or why not?

which adolescents take time off from the upcoming responsibilities of adulthood and explore various roles and possibilities. For example, many college students take a semester or year off to travel, work, or find some other way to examine their priorities.

On the other hand, many adolescents cannot, for practical reasons, pursue a psychological moratorium involving a relatively leisurely exploration of various identities. Some adolescents, for economic reasons, must work part time during the year school and then take jobs immediately after graduation from high school. As a result, they have little time to experiment with identities and engage in a psychological moratorium. Does this mean such adolescents will be psychologically damaged in some way? Probably not. In fact, the satisfaction that can come from successfully holding a part-time job while attending school may be a sufficient psychological reward to outweigh the inability to try out various roles.

Limitations of Erikson's Theory   One criticism that has been raised regarding Erikson's theory is that he uses male identity development as the standard against which to compare female identity. In particular, he saw males as developing intimacy only after they have achieved a stable identity, which is viewed as the normative pattern. To critics, Erikson's view is based on male-oriented concepts of individuality and competitiveness. In an alternative conception, psychologist Carol Gilligan has suggested that women develop identity through the establishment of relationships. In this view, a

Identity achievement
The status of adolescents who commit to a particular identity following a period of crisis during which they consider various alternatives

Identity foreclosure
The status of adolescents who prematurely commit to an identity without adequately exploring alternatives

Moratorium The status of adolescents who may have explored various identity alternatives to some degree, but have not yet committed themselves

Identity diffusion The status of adolescents who consider various identity alternatives, but never commit to one or never even consider identity options in any conscious way

TABLE 16-2 Marcia's Four Categories of Adolescent Development

		Commitment	
		Present	Absent
CRISIS/EXPLORATION	**PRESENT**	Identity achievement "I love animals, I'm going to become a vet."	Moratorium "I'm going to work at the mall while I figure out what to do next."
	ABSENT	Identity foreclosure "I'm going into law, just like Mom."	Identity diffusion "I don't have a clue."

(*Source:* Marcia, 1980)

Teenagers who have successfully attained what James Marcia termed identity achievement tend to be the most psychologically healthy and *show* higher achievement motivation than adolescents of any other status.

key component of a woman's identity is the building of caring networks between herself and others (Gilligan, 2004; Kroger, 2006).

Marcia's Approach to Identity Development: Updating Erikson

Using Erikson's theory as a springboard, psychologist James Marcia suggests that identity can be seen in terms of which of two characteristics—crisis or commitment—is present or absent. *Crisis* is a period of identity development in which an adolescent consciously chooses between various alternatives and makes decisions. *Commitment* is psychological investment in a course of action or an ideology. We can see the difference between an adolescent who careens from one activity to another, with nothing lasting more than a few weeks, compared with one who becomes totally absorbed in volunteer work at a homeless shelter (Peterson, Marcia, & Carpendale, 2004; Marcia, 2007).

After conducting lengthy interviews with adolescents, Marcia proposed four categories of adolescent identity (see Table 16-2).

1. **Identity achievement.** Teenagers within this identity status have successfully explored and thought through who they are and what they want to do. Following a period of crisis during which they considered various alternatives, these adolescents have committed to a

particular identity. Teens who have reached this identity status tend to be the most psychologically healthy, and are higher in achievement motivation and moral reasoning than adolescents of any other status.

2. **Identity foreclosure.** These are adolescents who have committed to an identity, but who did not do it by passing through a period of crisis in which they explored alternatives. Instead, they accepted others' decisions about what was best for them. Typical adolescents in this category are a son who enters the family business because it is expected of him, and a daughter who decides to become a physician simply because her mother is one. Although foreclosers are not necessarily unhappy, they tend to have what can be called "rigid strength": Happy and self-satisfied, they also have a high need for social approval and tend to be authoritarian.

3. **Moratorium.** Although adolescents in the moratorium category have explored various alternatives to some degree, they have not yet committed themselves. As a consequence, Marcia suggests, they show relatively high anxiety and experience psychological conflict. On the other hand, they are often lively and appealing, seeking intimacy with others. Adolescents of this status typically settle on an identity, but only after something of a struggle.

4. **Identity diffusion.** Adolescents in this category neither explore nor commit to consider various alternatives. They tend to be flighty, shifting from one thing to the next. Although they may seem carefree, according to Marcia, their lack of commitment impairs their ability to form close relationships. In fact, they are often socially withdrawn.

It is important to note that adolescents are not necessarily stuck in one of the four categories. In fact, some move back and forth between moratorium and identity achievement in what has been called a "MAMA" cycle (**m**oratorium—identity **a**chievement—**m**oratorium—identity **a**chievement). For instance, even though a forecloser may have settled on a career path during early adolescence with little active decision making, he or she may reassess the choice later and move into another category. For some individuals, then, identity formation may take place beyond the period of adolescence. However, identity gels in the late teens and early 20s for most people (Meeus, 2003; Kroger, 2000, 2007).

Identity, Race, and Ethnicity

Although the path to forming an identity is often difficult for adolescents, it presents a particular challenge for members of racial and ethnic groups that have traditionally been discriminated against. Society's contradictory values are one part of the problem. On the one hand, these adolescents are told that society should be color blind, that race and ethnic background should not matter in terms of opportunities and achievement, and that if they do achieve, society will accept them. Based on a traditional *cultural assimilation model,* this view holds that individual cultural identities should be assimilated into a unified culture in the United States—the proverbial melting-pot model.

On the other hand, the *pluralistic society model* suggests that U.S. society is made up of diverse, coequal cultural groups that should preserve their individual cultural features. The pluralistic society model grew in part from the belief that the cultural assimilation model denigrates the cultural heritage of minorities and lowers their self-esteem. According to this view, then, racial and ethnic factors become a central part of adolescents' identity and are not submerged in an attempt to assimilate into the majority culture.

There is a middle ground. Minority group members can form a *bicultural identity* in which they draw from their own cultural identity while integrating themselves into the dominant culture. This view suggests that an individual can live as a member of two cultures, with two cultural identities, without having to choose one over the other (LaFromboise, Coleman, & Gerton, 1993; Shi & Lu, 2007). The choice of a bicultural identity is increasingly common. In fact, the number of individuals who think of themselves as belonging to more than one race is considerable, according to data from the 2000 U.S. Census (see Figure 16-1; Schmitt, 2001).

The process of identity formation is not simple for anyone and may be doubly complicated for minority group members. Racial and ethnic identity takes time to form, and for some individuals it may occur over a prolonged period. Still, the ultimate result can be the formation of a rich, multifaceted identity (Nadal, 2004; Umana-Taylor & Fine, 2004; Quintana, 2007; Jensen, 2008).

FIGURE 16-1 Increase in Bicultural Identity

On the 2000 Census, almost 7 million people indicated they were multiracial.

(*Source:* U.S. Bureau of the Census, 2000)

Depression and Suicide: Psychological Difficulties in Adolescence

Brianne Camilleri had it all: Two involved parents, a caring older brother, and a comfortable home near Boston. But that didn't stop the overwhelming sense of hopelessness that enveloped her in ninth grade. "It was like a cloud that followed me everywhere," she says. "I couldn't get away from it."

Brianne started drinking and experimenting with drugs. One Sunday she was caught shoplifting at a local store and her mother, Linda, drove her home in what Brianne describes as a "piercing silence." With the clouds in her head so dark she believed she would never see light again, Brianne went straight for the bathroom and swallowed every Tylenol and Advil she found—a total of 74 pills. She was only 14, and she wanted to die. (Wingert & Kantrowitz, 2002, p. 54)

From a guidance counselor's perspective: Are there stages in Marcia's theory of development that may be more difficult to achieve for adolescents who live in poverty? Why?

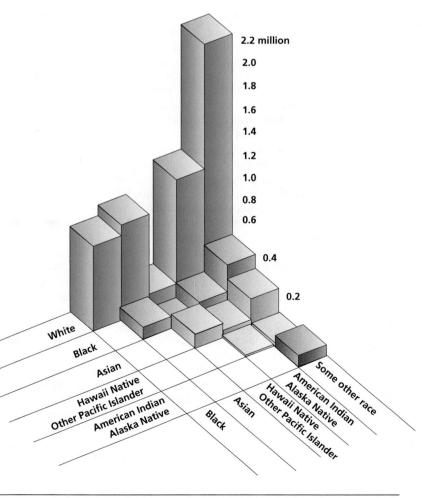

Between 25% to 40% of girls and 20% to 35% of boys experience occasional episodes of depression during adolescence, although the incidence of major depression is far lower.

Although by far the majority of teenagers weather the search for identity—as well as the other challenges presented by the period—without major psychological difficulties, a number of adolescents some find this period particularly stressful. Some, in fact, develop severe psychological problems. Two of the most serious are adolescent depression and suicide.

Adolescent Depression No one is immune to periods of sadness and bad moods, and adolescents are no exception. The end of a relationship, failure at an important task, the death of a loved one—all may produce profound feelings of sadness, loss, and grief. In situations such as these, depression is a fairly typical reaction.

How common are feelings of depression in adolescence? More than one-fourth of adolescents report feeling so sad or hopeless for 2 or more weeks in a row that they stop doing their normal activities. Almost two-thirds of teenagers say they have experienced such feelings at one time or another. On the other hand, only a small minority of adolescents—some 3%—experience *major depression,* a full-blown psychological disorder in which depression is severe and lingers for long periods (Grunbaum, 2001; Galambos, Leadbeater, & Barker, 2004).

Research has found gender, ethnic, and racial differences in the incidence of depression. As is the case among adults, adolescent girls, on average, experience depression more often than do boys. Some studies have found that African American adolescents have higher rates of depression than White adolescents, although not all research supports this conclusion. Native Americans, too, have higher rates of depression (Stice, Presnell, & Bearman, 2001; Jacques & Mash, 2004; Hightower, 2005; Li, DiGiuseppe, & Froh, 2006).

In cases of severe, long-term depression, biological factors are often involved. Although some adolescents seem to be genetically predisposed to experience depression, environmental and social factors relating to the extraordinary changes in the social lives of adolescents are also important influences. An adolescent who experiences the death of a loved one, for example, or one who grows up with an alcoholic or depressed parent, is at a higher risk of depression. In addition, being unpopular, having few close friends, and experiencing rejection are associated with adolescent depression (Lau & Kwok, 2000; Goldsmith et al., 2002; Eley, Liang, & Plomin, 2004; Zalsman et al., 2006).

One of the most puzzling questions about depression is why its incidence is higher among girls than boys. There is little evidence that depression is linked to hormone differences or to a particular gene. Instead, some psychologists speculate that stress is more pronounced for girls than for boys in adolescence due to the many, sometimes conflicting demands of the traditional female gender role. Recall, for instance, the situation of the adolescent girl who was quoted in our discussion of self-esteem. She is worried about doing well in school and about being popular. If she feels that academic success undermines her popularity, she is placed in a difficult bind that can leave her feeling helpless. Added to this is the fact that traditional gender roles still give higher status to men than to women (Nolen-Hoeksema, 2003; Gilbert, 2004; Hyde, Mezulis, & Abramson, 2008).

The generally higher levels of depression in girls during adolescence may reflect gender differences in ways of coping with stress, rather than gender differences in mood. Girls may be more apt than boys to react to stress by turning inward, thereby experiencing a sense of helplessness and hopelessness. In contrast, boys more often react by externalizing the stress and acting more impulsively or aggressively, or by turning to drugs and alcohol (Hankin & Abramson, 2001; Winstead & Sanchez, 2005; Wisdom et al., 2007; Wu et al., 2007).

Adolescent Suicide The rate of adolescent suicide in the United States has tripled in the last 30 years. In fact, 1 teenage suicide occurs every 90 minutes, for an annual rate of 12.2 suicides per 100,000 adolescents. Moreover, the reported rate may actually understate the true number of suicides; parents and medical personnel are often reluctant to report a death as suicide, preferring to label it an accident. Even with underreporting, suicide is the third most common cause of death in the 15- to 24-year-old age group, after accidents and homicide. It is important to keep in mind, however, that although the rate of suicide for adolescents has risen more than for other age groups, the highest rate of suicide is found in the period of late adulthood (Grunbaum et al., 2002; Joe & Marcus, 2003; Conner & Goldston, 2007).

In adolescence, the rate of suicide is higher for boys than for girls, although girls *attempt* suicide more frequently. Suicide attempts among males are more likely to result in death because of the methods they use: Boys tend to use more violent means, such as guns, while girls are more apt to choose the more peaceful strategy of drug overdose. Some estimates suggest that there are as many as 200 attempted suicides by both sexes for every successful one (Joseph, Reznik, & Mester, 2003; Dervic et al., 2006).

The reasons behind the increase in adolescent suicide over past decades are unclear. The most obvious explanation is that the stress experienced by teenagers has increased, leading those who are most vulnerable to be more likely to commit suicide. But why should stress have increased only for adolescents, given that the suicide rate for other segments of the population has remained fairly stable over the same time period?

Although we are not yet sure why adolescent suicide has increased, it is clear that certain factors heighten the risk of suicide. One factor is depression. Depressed teenagers who are experiencing a profound sense of hopelessness are at greater risk of committing suicide (although most depressed individuals do not commit suicide). In addition, social inhibition, perfectionism, and a high level of stress and anxiety are related to a greater risk of suicide. The easy availability of guns—which is more prevalent in the United States than in other industrialized nations—also contributes to the suicide rate (Goldston, 2003; Zalsman, Levy, & Shoval, 2008).

In addition to depression, some cases of suicide are associated with family conflicts, and relationship or school difficulties. Some stem from a history of abuse and neglect. The rate of suicide among drug and alcohol abusers is also relatively high. As can be seen in Figure 16-2, teens who called in to a hotline because they were thinking of killing themselves mentioned several other factors as well (Lyon et al., 2000; Bergen, Martin, & Richardson, 2003; Wilcox, Conner, & Caine, 2004).

Some suicides appear to be caused by exposure to the suicide of others. In *cluster suicide*, one suicide leads to attempts by others to kill themselves. For instance, some high schools have experienced a series of suicides following a well-publicized case. As a result, many schools have established crisis intervention teams to counsel students when one student commits suicide (Haas, Hendin, & Mann, 2003; Arenson, 2004; Insel & Gould, 2008).

There are several warning signs that should sound an alarm regarding the possibility of suicide. Among them:

- Direct or indirect talk about suicide, such as "I wish I were dead" or "You won't have me to worry about any longer"
- School difficulties, such as missed classes or a decline in grades
- Making arrangements as if preparing for a long trip, such as giving away prized possessions or arranging for the care of a pet

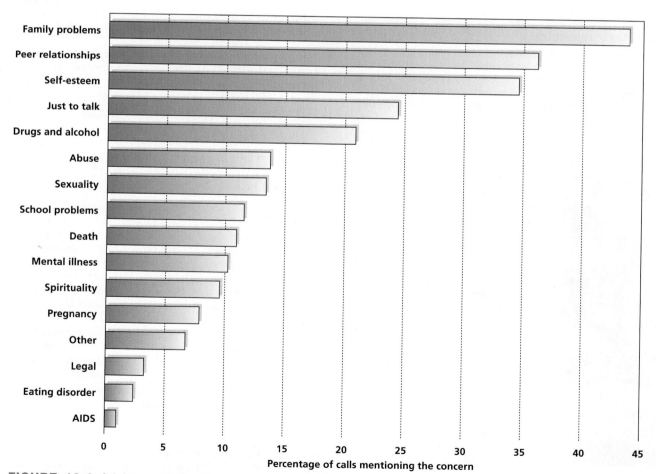

FIGURE 16-2 Adolescent Difficulties

Family, peer relationships, and self-esteem problems were most often mentioned by adolescents contemplating suicide, according to a review of phone calls to a telephone help line.
(*Source:* Boehm & Campbell, 1995)

- Writing a will
- Loss of appetite or excessive eating
- General depression, including a change in sleeping patterns, slowness and lethargy, and uncommunicativeness
- Dramatic changes in behavior, such as a shy person suddenly acting outgoing
- Preoccupation with death in music, art, or literature

Becoming an Informed Consumer of Development

Adolescent Suicide: How to Help

If you suspect that an adolescent, or anyone else for that matter, is contemplating suicide, don't stand idly by. Act! Here are several suggestions:

- Talk to the person, listen without judging, and allow the person to talk things through.

- Talk specifically about suicidal thoughts, asking such questions as: Does the person have a plan? Has he or she bought a gun? Where is it? Has he or she stockpiled pills? Where are they? The Public Health Service notes that, "contrary to popular belief, such candor will not give a person dangerous ideas or encourage a suicidal act."

- Evaluate the situation, trying to distinguish between general upset and more serious danger, as when suicide plans *have* been made. If the crisis is acute, *do not leave the person alone*.

Contrary to popular belief, talking about suicide does not encourage it. In fact, it actually combats it by providing supportive feedback and breaking down the sense of isolation many suicidal people have.

- Be supportive, let the person know you care, and try to break down his or her feelings of isolation.

- Take charge of finding help, without concern about invading the person's privacy. Do not try to handle the problem alone; get professional help immediately.

- Make the environment safe, removing from the premises (not just hiding) weapons such as guns, razors, scissors, medication, and other potentially dangerous household items.

- Do not keep suicide talk or threats secret; these are calls for help and require immediate action.

- Do not challenge, dare, or use verbal shock treatment on the person in an effort to make them realize the errors in their thinking. These can have tragic effects.

- Make a contract with the person, getting a promise or commitment, preferably in writing, not to make any suicidal attempt until you have talked further.

- Don't be overly reassured by a sudden improvement of mood. Such seemingly quick recoveries sometimes reflect the relief of finally having decided to commit suicide or the temporary release from talking to someone, but most likely the underlying problems will not have been resolved.

For immediate help with a suicide-related problem, call 800-784-2433 or 800-621-4000 for national hotlines staffed with trained counselors.

Relationships: Family and Friends

Slim and dark, with a passing resemblance to actress Demi Moore, Leah is dressed up and ready to go to the first real formal dance of her life. True, the smashing effect of her short beaded black dress is marred slightly by the man's shirt she insists on wearing to cover her bare shoulders. And she is in a sulk. Her boyfriend, Sean Moffitt, is four minutes late, and her mother, Linda, refuses to let her stay out all night at a coed sleepover party after the dance....

Leah's father, George, suggests a 2 A.M. curfew: Leah hoots incredulously. Sean pitches the all-nighter, stressing that the party will be chaperoned. Leah's mother has already talked to the host's mother, mortifying Leah with her off-hand comment that a coed sleepover seemed "weird." Rolling her eyes, Leah persists: "It's not like anybody's really going to sleep!" (E. Graham, 1995, p. B1)

The social world of adolescents is considerably wider than that of younger children. As adolescents' relationships with people outside the home grow increasingly important, their interactions with their families evolve and take on a new, and sometimes difficult, character (Collins, Gleason, & Sesma, 1997; Collins & Andrew, 2004).

Family Ties: Changing Relations With Relations

When Paco Lizzagara entered junior high school, his relationship with his parents changed drastically. What had been a good relationship had become tense by the middle of seventh grade. Paco felt his parents always seemed to be "on his case." Instead of giving him more freedom, which he felt he deserved at age 13, they actually seemed to be becoming more restrictive.

Paco's parents would probably see things differently. They would likely suggest that they were not the source of the tension in the household—Paco was. From their point of view, Paco, with whom they'd established what seemed to be a close, stable, loving relationship throughout much of his childhood, suddenly seemed transformed. They felt he was shutting them out of his life, and when he did speak with them, it was merely to criticize their politics, their dress, their preferences in TV shows. To his parents, Paco's behavior was upsetting and bewildering.

The Quest for Autonomy Parents are sometimes angered, and even more frequently puzzled, by adolescents' conduct. Children who have previously accepted their parents' judgments, declarations, and guidelines begin to question—and sometimes rebel against—their parents' views of the world.

One reason for these clashes are the shifting roles both children and parents must deal with during adolescence. Adolescents increasingly seek **autonomy**, independence, and a sense of control over their lives. Most parents intellectually realize that this shift is a normal part of adolescence, representing one of the primary developmental tasks of the period, and in many ways they welcome it as a sign of their children's growth. However, in many cases the day-to-day realities of their adolescent's increasing autonomy may prove difficult for them to deal with (Smetana, 1995). But understanding this growing independence intellectually and agreeing to allow a teen to attend a party when no parents will be present are two different things. To the adolescent, her parents' refusal indicates a lack of trust or confidence. To the parent, it's simple good sense: "I trust you," they may say. "It's everyone else who will be there that I worry about."

In most families, teenagers' autonomy grows gradually over the course of adolescence. For instance, one study of changes in adolescents' views of their parents found that increasing autonomy led them to perceive parents less in idealized terms and more as persons in their own right. For example, rather than see their parents as authoritarian disciplinarians mindlessly reminding them to do their homework, they may come to see their parents' emphasis on excelling in school as evidence of parental regrets about their own lack of education and a wish to see their children have more options in life. At the same time, adolescents come to depend more on themselves and to feel more like separate individuals (see Figure 16-3).

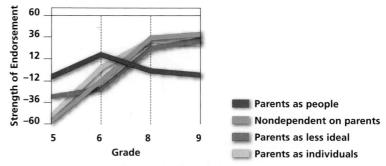

FIGURE 16-3 Changing Views of Parents

As adolescents become older, they come to perceive their parents in less idealized terms and more as individuals. What effect is this likely to have on family relations?
(*Source:* Adapted from Steinberg & Silverberg, 1986)

The increase in adolescent autonomy changes the relationship between parents and teenagers. At the start of adolescence, the relationship tends to be asymmetrical: Parents hold most of the power and influence over the relationship. By the end of adolescence, however, power and influence have become more balanced, and parents and children end up in a more symmetrical, or egalitarian, relationship. Power and influence are shared, although parents typically retain the upper hand.

Culture and Autonomy The degree of autonomy that is eventually achieved varies from one family and one child to the next. Cultural factors play an important role. In Western societies, which tend to value individualism, adolescents seek autonomy at a relatively early stage of adolescence. In contrast, Asian societies are collectivistic; they promote the idea that the well-being of the group is more important than that of the individual. In such societies, adolescents' aspirations to achieve autonomy are less pronounced (Kim et al., 1994; Raeff, 2004).

Adolescents from different cultural backgrounds also vary in the degree of obligation to their family that they feel. Those in more collectivistic cultures tend to feel greater obligation to their families, in terms of fulfilling their expectations about their duty to provide assistance, show respect, and support their families in the future, than those from more individualistic societies. In such societies, the push for autonomy is less strong, and the

In collectivistic societies, the well-being of the group is promoted as more important than individual autonomy.

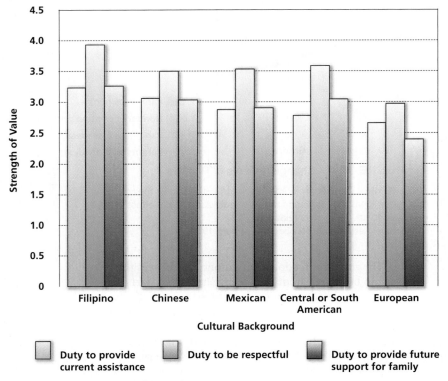

FIGURE 16-4 Family Obligations

Adolescents from Asian and Latin American groups feel a greater sense of respect and obligation toward their families than do those adolescents with European backgrounds.

(*Source:* Fuligni, Tseng, & Lam, 1999)

timetable during which autonomy is expected to develop is slower (see Figure 16-4; Chao, 2001; Fuligni & Zhang, 2004; Leung, Pe-Pua, & Karnilowicz, 2006).

For example, when asked at what age an adolescent would be expected to carry out certain behaviors (such as going to a concert with friends), adolescents and parents provide different answers depending on their cultural background. In comparison to Asian adolescents and parents, Caucasian adolescents and parents indicate an earlier timetable, anticipating greater autonomy at an earlier age (Feldman & Wood, 1994).

Does the more extended timetable for the development of autonomy in more collectivistic cultures have negative consequences for adolescents in those cultures? Apparently not. The more important factor is the degree of match between cultural expectations and developmental patterns. What probably matters most is how well the development of autonomy matches societal expectations, not the specific timetable of autonomy (Zimmer-Gembeck & Collins, 2003; Updegraff et al., 2006).

In addition to cultural factors affecting autonomy, gender also plays a role. Male adolescents generally are permitted

more autonomy at an earlier age than are female adolescents. The encouragement of male autonomy is consistent with traditional male stereotypes, in which males are perceived as more independent and females, conversely, more dependent on others. In fact, parents who hold traditional stereotypical views of gender are less likely to encourage their daughters' autonomy (Bumpus, Crouter, & McHale, 2001).

The Myth of the Generation Gap Teen movies often depict adolescents and their parents with totally opposing points of view about the world. For example, the parent of an environmentalist teen might turn out to own a polluting factory. These exaggerations are often funny because we assume there is a kernel of truth in them, in that parents and teenagers often don't see things the same way. According to this argument, there is a **generation gap**, a deep divide between parents and children in attitudes, values, aspirations, and worldviews.

The reality, however, is quite different. The generation gap, when it exists, is really quite narrow. Adolescents and their parents tend to see eye to eye in a variety of domains. Republican parents generally have Republican children; members of Evangelical Christian churches have children who espouse similar views; parents who advocate for abortion rights have children who are pro-choice. On social, political, and religious issues, parents and adolescents tend to be in synch, and children's worries mirror those of their parents. Adolescents' concerns about society's problems (see Figure 16-5) are ones with which most adults would probably agree (Flor & Knap, 2001; Knafo & Schwartz, 2003; Smetana, 2005).

As we've said, most adolescents and their parents get along quite well. Despite their quest for autonomy and independence, most adolescents have deep love, affection, and respect for their parents—and parents feel the same way about their children. Although some parent–adolescent relationships are seriously troubled, the majority of relationships are more positive than negative and, as such, help adolescents avoid the kind of peer pressure we discuss later in the chapter (Gavin & Furman, 1996; Resnick et al., 1997; Black, 2002).

Even though adolescents spend decreasing amounts of time with their families in general, the amount of time they spend alone with each parent remains remarkably stable across adolescence (see Figure 16-6). In short, there is no evidence suggesting that family problems are worse during adolescence than at any other stage of development (Larson et al., 1996; Granic, Hollenstein, & Dishion, 2003).

Conflicts With Parents Of course, if most adolescents get along with their parents most of the time, that means some of the time they don't. No relationships are always sweetness and light. Parents and teens may hold similar attitudes about social and political issues, but they often hold different views on matters of personal taste, such as music preferences and styles of dress. Also, as we've seen, parents and children may run into disagreements when children seek to achieve autonomy and independence sooner than parents feel is right. Consequently, parent–child conflicts are more likely to occur during adolescence, particularly during the early stages, although it's important to remember that not every family is affected to the same degree (Arnett, 2000; Smetana, Daddis, & Chuang, 2003).

Why should conflict be greater during early adolescence than at later stages of the period? According to developmental psychologist Judith Smetana, the reason involves differing definitions of, and rationales for, appropriate and inappropriate conduct. Parents may feel, for instance, that getting one's ear pierced in three places is inappropriate because society traditionally deems it inappropriate. On the other hand, adolescents may view the issue in terms of personal choice (Smetana, 2005, 2006).

Furthermore, the newly sophisticated reasoning of adolescents (discussed in the previous chapter) leads teenagers to think about parental rules in more complex ways. Arguments that might be convincing to a school-age child ("Do it because I tell you to do it") are less compelling to an adolescent.

The argumentativeness and assertiveness of early adolescence at first may lead to an increase in conflict, but in many ways these qualities play an important role in the evolution of parent–child relationships. Although parents may initially react defensively to the challenges that their children present, and may grow inflexible and rigid, in most cases they eventually come to realize that their children *are* growing up and that they want to support them in that process.

FIGURE 16-5 What's the Problem?

Adolescents' views of society's ills are ones with which their parents would likely agree. (*Source:* PRIMEDIA/Roper National Youth Survey, 1999)

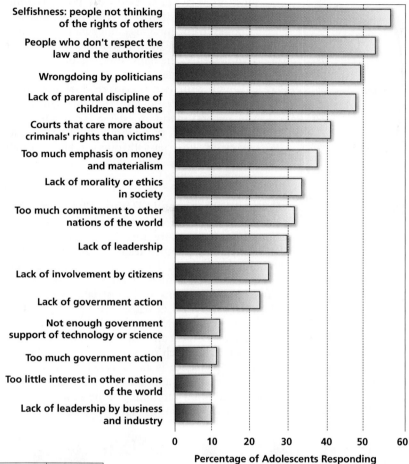

FIGURE 16-6 Time Spent by Adolescents With Parents

Despite their quest for autonomy and independence, most adolescents have deep love, affection, and respect for their parents, and the amount of time they spend alone with each parent (the lower two segments) remains remarkably stable across adolescence. (*Source:* Larson, Richards, Moneta, Holmbeck, & Duckett, 1996)

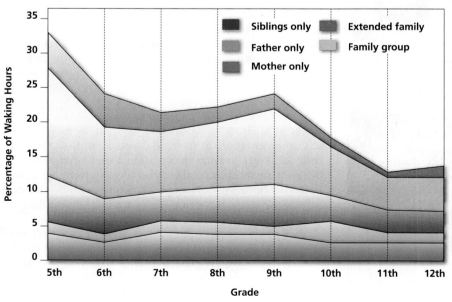

Reference groups
Groups of people with whom
one compares oneself

**From
a social
worker's
perspective:**

In what ways do you
think parents with different styles—authoritarian,
authoritative, permissive,
and uninvolved—react to
attempts to establish au-
tonomy during adoles-
cence? Are the styles
of parenting different
for a single parent?
Are there cultural
differences?

As parents come to see that their adolescent children's arguments are often compelling and not so unreasonable, and that their daughters and sons can in fact be trusted with more freedom, they become more yielding, allowing (and per-haps even encouraging) independence. As this process occurs during the middle stages of adolescence, the combativeness of early ado-lescence declines.

Of course, this pattern does not apply for all adolescents. Although the majority of teenagers maintain stable relations with their parents throughout adolescence, as many as 20% pass through a fairly rough time (Dryfoos, 1990; Dmitrieva, Chen & Greenberger, 2004).

Cultural Differences in Parent–Child Conflicts During Adolescence Although parent–child con-flicts are found in every culture, there does seem to be less conflict between parents and their teenage children in "tradi-tional," preindustrial cultures. Teens in such traditional cul-tures also experience fewer mood swings and instances of risky behavior than do teens in industrialized countries (Arnett, 2000; Nelson, Badger, & Wu, 2004).

Why? The answer may relate to the degree of indepen-dence that adolescents expect and adults permit. In more in-dustrialized societies, in which the value of individualism is typically high, independence is an expected component of adolescence. Consequently, adolescents and their parents must negotiate the amount and timing of the adolescent's in-creasing independence—a process that often leads to strife.

In contrast, in more traditional societies, individualism is not valued as highly, and therefore adolescents are less in-clined to seek out independence. With diminished inde-pendence seeking on the part of adolescents, the result is less parent–child conflict (Dasen, 2000, 2002).

Relationships With Peers: The Importance of Belonging

In the eyes of many parents, the most fitting symbols of ado-lescence are the cell phone or perhaps the computer, on which incessant instant messaging occurs. For many of their sons and daughters, communicating with friends is experi-enced as an indispensable lifeline, sustaining ties to individ-uals with whom they may have already spent many hours earlier in the day.

The seemingly compulsive need to communicate with friends demonstrates the role that peers play in adoles-cence. Continuing the trend that began in middle child-hood, adolescents spend increasing amounts of time with their peers, and the importance of peer relationships grows as well. In fact, there is probably no period of life in which peer relationships are as important as they are in adoles-cence.

Social Comparison Peers become more important for a number of reasons in adolescence. For one thing, they pro-vide each other with the opportunity to compare and evalu-ate opinions, abilities, and even physical changes—a process called *social comparison*. Because physical and cognitive changes of adolescence are so unique to this age group and so pronounced, especially during the early stages of puberty, adolescents turn increasingly to others who share, and con-sequently can shed light on, their own experiences (Schutz, Paxton, & Wertheim, 2002; Rankin, Lane, & Gibbons, 2004).

Parents are unable to provide social comparison. Not only are they well beyond the changes that adolescents un-dergo, but also adolescents' questioning of adult authority and their motivation to become more autonomous make parents, other family members, and adults in general inade-quate and invalid sources of knowledge. Who is left to pro-vide such information? Peers.

Reference Groups As we have said, adolescence is a time of experimentation, of trying out new identities, roles, and conduct. Peers provide information about what roles and behavior are most acceptable by serving as a reference group. **Reference groups** are groups of people with whom one compares oneself. Just as a professional ballplayer is likely to compare his performance against that of other professional players, so do teenagers compare themselves to those who are similar to them.

Reference groups present a set of *norms*, or standards, against which adolescents can judge their abilities and social success. An adolescent need not even belong to a group for it

Reference groups of peers provide norms for social comparison.

Cliques Groups of from 2 to 12 people whose members have frequent social interactions with one another

Crowds Groups larger than cliques, composed of individuals who share particular characteristics but who may not interact with one another

Sex cleavage Sex segregation in which boys interact primarily with boys and girls primarily with girls

to serve as a reference group. For instance, unpopular adolescents may find themselves belittled and rejected by members of a popular group, yet use that more popular group as a reference group (Berndt, 1999).

Cliques and Crowds: Belonging to a Group

One of the consequences of the increasing cognitive sophistication of adolescents is the ability to group others in more discriminating ways. Consequently, even if they do not belong to the group they use for reference purposes, adolescents typically are part of some identifiable group. Rather than defining people in concrete terms relating to what they do ("football players" or "musicians") as a younger school-age child might, adolescents use more abstract terms packed with greater subtleties ("jocks" or "skaters" or "stoners") (Brown, 2004).

There are actually two types of groups to which adolescents tend to belong: cliques and crowds. **Cliques** are groups of from 2 to 12 people whose members have frequent social interactions with one another. In contrast, **crowds** are larger, comprising individuals who share particular characteristics but who may not interact with one another. For instance, "jocks" and "nerds" are representative of crowds found in many high schools.

Membership in particular cliques and crowds is often determined by the degree of similarity with members of the group. One of the most important dimensions of similarity relates to substance use; adolescents tend to choose friends who use alcohol and other drugs to the same extent that they do. Their friends are also often similar in terms of their academic success, although this is not always true. For instance, during early adolescence, attraction to peers who are particularly well behaved seems to decrease, whereas, at the same time, those who behave more aggressively become more attractive (Bukowski, Sippola, & Newcomb, 2000; Kupersmidt & Dodge, 2004).

The emergence of distinct cliques and crowds during adolescence reflects in part the increased cognitive capabilities of adolescents. Group labels are abstractions, requiring teens to make judgments of people with whom they may interact only rarely and of whom they have little direct knowledge. It is not until mid-adolescence that teenagers are sufficiently sophisticated cognitively to make the subtle judgments that underlie distinctions between different cliques and crowds (Burgess & Rubin, 2000; Brown & Bradford, 2003).

Gender Relations

As children enter adolescence from middle childhood, their groups of friends are composed almost universally of same-sex individuals. Boys hang out with boys; girls hang out with girls. Technically, this sex segregation is called the **sex cleavage**.

However, the situation changes as members of both sexes enter puberty. Boys and girls experience the hormonal surge that marks puberty and causes the maturation of the sex organs (see Chapter 14). At the same time, societal pressures suggest that the time is appropriate for romantic involvement. These developments lead to a change in the ways adolescents view the opposite sex. Where a 10-year-old is likely to see every member of the other sex as "annoying" and "a pain," heterosexual teenage boys and girls begin to regard each other with greater interest in terms of both personality and sexuality. (For gays and lesbians, pairing off holds its own complexities, as we discuss later when we consider adolescent dating.)

As they move into puberty, boys' and girls' cliques, which previously had moved along parallel but separate tracks, begin to converge. Adolescents begin to attend boy–girl dances or parties, although most of the time the boys still spend their time with boys, and the girls with girls (Richards et al., 1998).

A little later, however, adolescents increasingly spend time with members of the other sex. New cliques emerge, composed of both males and females. Not everyone participates initially: Early on, the teenagers who are leaders of the same-sex cliques and who have the highest status lead the way. Eventually, however, most adolescents find themselves in cliques that include boys and girls.

Cliques and crowds undergo yet another transformation at the end of adolescence: They become less influential and may dissolve as a result of the increased pairing off that occurs.

DEVELOPMENTAL DIVERSITY

Race Segregation: The Great Divide of Adolescence

When Philip McAdoo, a [student] at the University of North Carolina, stopped one day to see a friend who worked on his college campus, a receptionist asked if he would autograph a basketball for her son. Because he was African American and tall, "she just assumed that I was on the basketball team," recounted McAdoo.

Jasme Kelly, an African American sophomore at the same college, had a similar story to tell. When she went to see a friend at a fraternity house, the student who answered the door asked if she was there to apply for the job of cook.

White students, too, find racial relations difficult and in some ways forbidding. For instance, Jenny Johnson, a white 20-year-old junior, finds even the most basic conversation with African American classmates difficult. She describes a conversation in which African American friends "jump at my throat because I used the word 'black' instead of African American. There is just such a huge barrier that it's really hard . . . to have a normal discussion." (Sanoff & Minerbrook, 1993, p. 58). ●

The pattern of race segregation found at the University of North Carolina is repeated over and over in schools and colleges throughout the United States: Even when they attend

Controversial adolescents	Rejected adolescents	Neglected adolescents
Children who are liked by some peers and disliked by others	Children who are actively disliked, and whose peers may react to them in an obviously negative manner	Children who receive relatively little attention from their peers in the form of either positive or negative interactions

Adolescents who have had extensive interactions with members of different races are more likely to have friends of different races.

If minority-group members experience less academic success, they may find themselves in classes with proportionally fewer majority-group members. Similarly, majority students may be in classes with few minority students. Such class assignment practices, then, may inadvertently maintain and promote racial and ethnic segregation. This pattern would be particularly prevalent in schools where rigid academic tracking is practiced, with students assigned to "low," "medium," and "high" tracks depending on their prior achievement (Lucas & Behrends, 2002).

The lack of contact among students of different racial and ethnic backgrounds in school may also reflect prejudice, both perceived and real, toward members of other groups. Students of color may feel that the White majority is prejudiced, discriminatory, and hostile, and they may prefer to stick to same-race groups. Conversely, White students may assume that minority group members are antagonistic and unfriendly. Such mutually destructive attitudes reduce the likelihood that meaningful interaction can take place (Phinney, Ferguson, & Tate, 1997; Tropp, 2003).

Is this sort of voluntary segregation along racial and ethnic lines found during adolescence inevitable? No. Adolescents who have interacted regularly and extensively with those of different races earlier in their lives are more likely to have friends of different races. Schools that actively promote contact among members of different ethnicities in classes help create an environment in which cross-race friendships can flourish (Hewstone, 2003).

Still, the task is daunting. Many societal pressures act to keep members of different races from interacting with one another. Peer pressure, too, may encourage this as some cliques may actively promote norms that discourage group members from crossing racial and ethnic lines to form new friendships.

desegregated schools with significant ethnic and racial diversity, people of different ethnicities and races interact very little. Moreover, even if they have a friend of a different ethnicity within the confines of a school, most adolescents don't interact with that friend outside of school (DuBois & Hirsch, 1990).

It doesn't start out this way. During elementary school and even during early adolescence, there is a fair amount of integration among students of differing ethnicities. However, by middle and late adolescence, the amount of segregation is striking (Shrum, Cheek, & Hunter, 1988; Spencer & Dornbusch, 1990; Spencer, 1991; Ennett & Bauman, 1996).

Why should racial and ethnic segregation be the rule, even in schools that have been desegregated for some time? One reason is that minority students may actively seek support from others who share their minority status (where "minority" is used in its sociological sense to indicate a subordinate group whose members lack power, compared to members of a dominant group). By associating primarily with other members of their own group, members of minority groups are able to affirm their own identity.

Members of different racial and ethnic groups may be segregated in the classroom as well. As we discussed in Chapter 13, members of groups that have been historically discriminated against tend to experience less school success than do members of the majority group. It may be that ethnic and racial segregation in high school is based not on ethnicity itself, but on academic achievement.

Popularity and Rejection

Most adolescents have well-tuned antennae when it comes to determining who is popular and who is not. In fact, for some teenagers, concerns over popularity—or lack of it—may be a central focus of their lives.

Actually, the social world of adolescents is divided not only into popular and unpopular individuals; the differentiations are more complex (see Figure 16-7). For instance, some adolescents are controversial; in contrast to *popular* adolescents, who are mostly liked, **controversial adolescents** are liked by some and disliked by others. For example, a controversial adolescent may be highly popular within a particular group such as the string orchestra, but not popular among other classmates. Furthermore, there are **rejected adolescents**, who are uniformly disliked, and **neglected adolescents**, who are neither liked nor disliked. Neglected adolescents are the forgotten student—the ones whose status is so low that they are overlooked by almost everyone.

In most cases, popular and controversial adolescents tend to be similar in that their overall status is higher, whereas

Peer pressure The influence of one's peers to conform to their behavior and attitudes

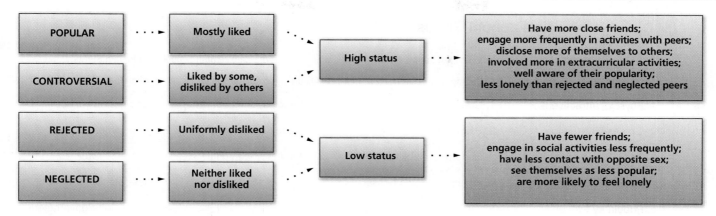

FIGURE 16-7 The Social World of Adolescence

An adolescent's popularity can fall into one of four categories, depending on the opinions of his or her peers. Popularity is related to differences in status, behavior, and adjustment.

rejected and neglected adolescents share a generally lower status. Popular and controversial adolescents have more close friends, engage more frequently in activities with their peers, and disclose more about themselves to others than do less popular students. They are also more involved in extracurricular school activities. In addition, they are well aware of their popularity, and they are less lonely than their less popular classmates (Englund et al., 2000; Farmer et al., 2003; Zettergren, 2004; Becker & Luthar, 2007).

In contrast, the social world of rejected and neglected adolescents is considerably less pleasant. They have fewer friends, engage in social activities less frequently, and have less contact with the opposite sex. They see themselves—accurately, it turns out—as less popular, and they are more likely to feel lonely.

What is it that determines status in high school? As illustrated in Table 16-3, men and women have different perceptions. For example, college men suggest that physical attractiveness is the most important factor in determining high school girls' status, whereas college women believe it is a high school girl's grades and intelligence (Suitor, Minyard, & Carter, 2001).

Conformity: Peer Pressure in Adolescence

Whenever Aldos Henry said he wanted to buy a particular brand of sneakers or a certain style of shirt, his parents complained that he was just giving in to peer pressure and told him to make up his own mind about things.

In arguing with Aldos, his parents were subscribing to a view of adolescence that is quite prevalent in U.S. society: that teenagers are highly susceptible to **peer pressure**, the influence of one's peers to conform to their behavior and attitudes. Were his parents correct?

The research suggests that it all depends. In some cases, adolescents are highly susceptible to the influence of their peers. For instance, when considering what to wear, whom to date, and what movies to see, adolescents are apt to follow the lead of their peers. Wearing the right clothes, down to the right brand of the right clothes, sometimes can be a ticket to membership in a popular group. It shows you know what's what. On the other hand, when it comes to many nonsocial matters, such as choosing a career path or trying to solve a problem, they are more likely to turn to an experienced adult (Phelan, Yu, & Davidson, 1994).

In short, particularly in middle and late adolescence, teenagers turn to those they see as experts on a given dimension. If they have social concerns, they turn to the people most

Unpopular adolescents fall into several categories. Controversial adolescents are liked by some and disliked by others, rejected adolescents are uniformly disliked, and neglected adolescents are neither liked nor disliked.

Undersocialized delinquents
Adolescent delinquents who are
raised with little discipline or with
harsh, uncaring parental
supervision

TABLE 16-3 High School Status

| What Makes High School Girls High in Status | | What Makes High School Boys High in Status | |
According to College Men	According to College Women	According to College Men	According to College Women
1. Physical attractiveness	1. Grades/intelligence	1. Participation in sports	1. Participation in sports
2. Grades/intelligence	2. Participation in sports	2. Grades/intelligence	2. Grades/intelligence
3. Participation in sports	3. General sociability	3. Popularity with girls	3. General sociability
4. General sociability	4. Physical attractiveness	4. General sociability	4. Physical attractiveness
5. Popularity with boys	5. Clothes	5. Car	5. School clubs/government

Note: Students at the following universities were asked in which ways adolescents in their high schools had gained prestige with their peers: Louisiana State University, Southeastern Louisiana University, State University of New York at Albany, State University of New York at Stony Brook, University of Georgia, and the University of New Hampshire.

(*Source:* Suitor et al., 2001)

As they grow more confident of their own decisions, adolescents become less likely to conform to peers and parents.

likely to be experts—their peers. If the problem is one about which parents or other adults are most likely to have expertise, teenagers tend to turn to them for advice and are most susceptible to their opinions (Young & Ferguson, 1979; Perrine & Aloise-Young, 2004).

Overall, then, it does not appear that susceptibility to peer pressure suddenly soars during adolescence. Instead, adolescence brings about a change in the people to whom an individual conforms. Whereas children conform fairly consistently to their parents during childhood, in adolescence, conformity shifts to the peer group, in part because pressures to conform to peers increase as adolescents seek to establish their identity apart from their parents.

Ultimately, however, adolescents conform less to both peers *and* adults as they develop increasing autonomy over their lives. As they grow in confidence and in the ability to make their own decisions, adolescents are more apt to remain independent and to reject pressures from others, no matter who those others are. Before they learn to resist the urge to conform to their peers, however, teenagers may get into trouble, often along with their friends (Crockett & Crouter, 1995; Steinberg & Monahan, 2007). (For a look at a growing problem among adolescents, see the *From Research to Practice* box.)

Juvenile Delinquency: The Crimes of Adolescence

Adolescents, along with young adults, are more likely to commit crimes than any other age group. This is a misleading statistic in some respects: because certain behaviors (such as drinking) are illegal for adolescents but not for older individuals, it is rather easy for adolescents to break the law by doing something that would be legal if they were a few years older. But even when such crimes are disregarded, adolescents are disproportionately involved in violent crimes, such as murder, assaults, and rape, and in property crimes involving theft, robbery, and arson.

Although the number of violent crimes committed by U.S. adolescents over the past decade has shown a decline of 40%, probably due to the strength of the economy, delinquency among some teenagers remains a significant problem. Overall, 16% of all arrests for serious crimes involved a person under the age of 18.

Why do adolescents become involved in criminal activity? Some offenders, known as **undersocialized delinquents**, are adolescents who are raised with little discipline or with harsh, uncaring parental supervision. Although they are influenced by their peers, these children have not been socialized appropriately by their parents and were not taught standards of conduct to regulate their own behavior. Undersocialized delinquents typically begin criminal activities at an early age, well before the onset of adolescence.

Undersocialized delinquents share several characteristics. They tend to be relatively aggressive and violent fairly early in life, characteristics that lead to rejection by peers and academic failure. They also are more likely to have been diagnosed with attention-deficit disorder as children, and they

Socialized delinquents
Adolescent delinquents who know and subscribe to the norms of society and who are fairly normal psychologically

FROM RESEARCH to PRACTICE

Know When to Fold 'Em: The Growing Problem of Online Gambling

Greg Hogan Jr., a 19-year-old Lehigh University sophomore, was on tilt—the poker term for a spell of insanity that often follows a run of bad luck—for months now. Alone at the computer, usually near the end of one of his long online gambling sessions, the thought "I'm on tilt" would occur to him. "Dude," he'd tell himself, "you gotta stop." These thoughts sounded the way a distant fire alarm sounds in the middle of a warm bath. He would ignore them and go back to playing poker. "The side of me that said, 'Just one more hand,' was the side that always won," he reported months later. "I couldn't get away from it, not until all my money was gone." In a little more than a year, he had lost $7,500 playing poker online. (Schwartz, 2006, p. 52)

Greg Hogan's addiction to Internet gambling shortly came to an end when, in desperation, he held up a local bank and was quickly caught and arrested. While the ending of Hogan's story may be extreme, the events that sent him down the path of self-destruction are becoming alarmingly common among adolescent males.

A survey conducted by the Annenberg Public Policy Center found that adolescent gambling—especially on card games—is on the rise. The rate of monthly card playing among 14- to 22-year-old males rose from 35% to 42% between 2004 and 2005—an increase of 20% in just 1 year. The rate was even higher among men in college: some 50%. Over 1 million young people—mostly males—currently use online gambling sites at least once a month (Annenberg Public Policy Center, 2005, 2006).

Adolescent card players were particularly likely to report gambling on the Internet—a phenomenon that more than doubled in the same 1-year period. This trend is troubling, in part because gamblers who use the Internet for gaming are more than three times as likely as gamblers using non-Internet gaming venues to exhibit serious levels of problematic or pathological gambling. In addition, the Annenberg Center study showed that over half of young people who gambled at least once a week reported at least one symptom of problem gambling, with card players reporting more symptoms than other kinds of gamblers (Ladd & Petry, 2002).

Whether Internet venues foster more serious gambling problems or merely tend to attract people who already have such problems remains unclear. For example, one study of female gamblers found that gambling was associated with higher levels of hyperactivity at age 6 and higher levels of drug use within the prior year. Other research finds that problem gambling is associated with greater drug and alcohol problems, as well as engaging in unprotected sex (Huang et al., 2007; Martins et al., 2007).

Easy access to the Internet as well its anonymity make online gambling a behavior in which it is easy to become involved, and to keep it secret from others. It's much easier for adolescents to hide a gambling problem from friends and family when they never have to leave their dorm room (Wood, Williams, & Lawton, 2007).

- Why might gambling be particularly problematic among adolescents in college?

- Why do you think male adolescents are more attracted to gambling than are female adolescents?

tend to be less intelligent than average (Henry et al., 1996; Silverthorn & Frick, 1999; Rutter, 2003).

Undersocialized delinquents often suffer from psychological difficulties, and as adults fit a psychological pattern called antisocial personality disorder. They are relatively unlikely to be successfully rehabilitated, and many undersocialized delinquents live on the margins of society throughout their lives (Rönkä & Pulkkinen, 1995; Lynam, 1996; Frick et al., 2003).

A larger group of adolescent offenders are socialized delinquents. **Socialized delinquents** know and subscribe to the norms of society; they are fairly normal psychologically. For them, transgressions committed during adolescence do not lead to a life of crime. Instead, most socialized delinquents pass through a period during adolescence when they engage in some petty crimes (such as shoplifting), but they do not continue lawbreaking into adulthood.

Socialized delinquents are typically highly influenced by their peers, and their delinquency often occurs in groups. In addition, some research suggests that parents of socialized delinquents supervise their children's behavior less closely than do other parents. But like other aspects of adolescent behavior, these minor delinquencies are often a result of giving in to group pressure or seeking to establish one's identity as an adult (Fletcher et al., 1995; Thornberry & Krohn, 1997).

REVIEW mydevelopmentlab

1. Adolescents increasingly seek _____, independence and a sense of control over their lives.

   Answer: autonomy

2. The influence of one's peers to conform to their behavior and attitudes is known as _____ _____.

   Answer: peer pressure

3. _____ delinquents are adolescents who are raised with little discipline or with harsh, uncaring parental supervision.

   Answer: Undersocialized

To see more review questions, log on to MyDevelopmentLab.

Dating, Sexual Behavior, and Teenage Pregnancy

It took him almost a month, but Sylvester Chiu finally got up the courage to ask Jackie Durbin to go to the movies. It was hardly a surprise to Jackie, though. Sylvester had first told his friend Erik about his resolve to ask Jackie out, and Erik had told Jackie's friend Cynthia about Sylvester's plans. Cynthia, in turn, had told Jackie, who was primed to say "yes" when Sylvester finally did call.

Welcome to the complex world of dating, an important and changing ritual of adolescence. We consider dating, as well as several other aspects of adolescents' relationships with one another, in the remainder of the chapter.

Dating: Close Relationships in the 21st Century

When and how adolescents begin to date is determined by cultural factors that change from one generation to another. Until fairly recently, exclusively dating a single individual was seen as something of a cultural ideal, viewed in the context of romance. In fact, society often encouraged dating in adolescence, in part as a way for adolescents to explore relationships that might eventually lead to marriage. Today, some adolescents believe that the concept of dating is outmoded and limiting, and in some places the practice of *hooking up*—a vague term that covers everything from kissing to sexual intercourse—is viewed as more appropriate. Despite changing cultural norms, dating remains the dominant form of social interaction that leads to intimacy among adolescents (Denizet-Lewis, 2004; Manning, Giordano, & Longmore, 2006; Bogle, 2008).

The Functions of Dating Although on the surface dating is part of a pattern of courtship that can potentially lead to marriage, it actually serves other functions as well, especially early on. Dating is a way to learn how to establish intimacy with another individual. It can provide entertainment and, depending on the status of the person one is dating, prestige. It even can be used to develop a sense of one's own identity (Zimmer-Gembeck, & Gallaty, 2006; Friedlander, Connolly, & Pepler, 2007).

Just how well dating serves such functions, particularly the development of psychological intimacy, is an open question. What specialists in adolescence do know, however, is surprising: Dating in early and middle adolescence is not terribly successful at facilitating intimacy. On the contrary, dating is often a superficial activity in which the participants so rarely let down their guards that they never become truly close and never expose themselves emotionally to each other. Psychological intimacy may be lacking even when sexual activity is part of the relationship (Collins, 2003; Furman & Shaffer, 2003).

Just how well dating serves to further such functions as the development of psychological intimacy is still an open question.

True intimacy becomes more common during later adolescence. At that point, the dating relationship may be taken more seriously by both participants, and it may be seen as a way to select a mate and as a potential prelude to marriage.

For homosexual adolescents, dating presents special challenges. In some cases, blatant homophobic prejudice expressed by classmates may lead gays and lesbians to date members of the other sex in efforts to fit in. If they do seek relationships with other gays and lesbians, they may find it difficult to find partners, who may not openly express their sexual orientation. Homosexual couples who do openly date face possible harassment, making the development of a relationship all the more difficult (Savin-Williams, 2003a, b).

Dating, Race, and Ethnicity Culture influences dating patterns among adolescents of different racial and ethnic groups, particularly those whose parents have immigrated to the United States from other countries. Parents may try to control their children's dating behavior in an effort to preserve their culture's traditional values or to ensure that their child dates within his or her racial or ethnic group.

For example, Asian parents may be especially conservative in their attitudes and values, in part because they themselves may have had no experience of dating. (In many cases, the parents' marriage was arranged by others, and the entire concept of dating is unfamiliar.) They may insist that dating be conducted with chaperones, or not at all. As a consequence, they may find themselves involved in substantial conflict with their children (Hamon & Ingoldsby, 2003; Kibria, 2003; Hoelter, Axinn, & Ghimire, 2004).

Sexual Relationships

The hormonal changes of puberty bring the maturation of the sexual organs and a new range of feelings and possibilities in relations with others: sexuality. Sexual behavior and thoughts are among the central concerns of adolescents. Almost all adolescents think about sex, and many think about it a good deal of the time (Kelly, 2001; Ponton, 2001).

Masturbation The first type of sex in which adolescents engage is often solitary sexual self-stimulation or **masturbation**. By the age of 15, some 80% of teenage boys and 20% of teenage girls report that they have masturbated. The frequency of masturbation in males occurs more in the early teens and then begins to decline, whereas in females, the frequency is lower initially and increases throughout adolescence. In addition, patterns of masturbation frequency show differences according to race. For example, African American men and women masturbate less than Whites do (Oliver & Hyde, 1993; Schwartz, 1999; Hyde & DeLamater, 2003).

Although masturbation is widespread, it still may produce feelings of shame and guilt. There are several reasons for this. One is that adolescents may believe that masturbation signifies the inability to find a sexual partner—an erroneous assumption, because statistics show that three-fourths of married men and 68% of married women report masturbating between 10 and 24 times a year (Hunt, 1974; Davidson, Darling, & Norton, 1995).

For some, there is also a sense of shame about masturbation, the result of a lingering legacy of misguided views of masturbation. For instance, 19th-century physicians and laypersons warned of horrible effects of masturbation, including "dyspepsia, spinal disease, headache, epilepsy, various kinds of fits . . . impaired eyesight, palpitation of the heart, pain in the side and bleeding at the lungs, spasm of the heart, and sometimes sudden death" (Gregory, 1856). Suggested remedies included bandaging the genitals, covering them with a cage, tying the hands, male circumcision without anesthesia (so that it might better be remembered), and for girls, the administration of carbolic acid to the clitoris. One physician, J. W. Kellogg, believed that certain grains would be less likely to provoke sexual excitation—leading to his invention of corn flakes (Hunt, 1974; Michael et al., 1994).

The reality of masturbation is different. Today, experts on sexual behavior view it as a normal, healthy, and harmless activity. In fact, some suggest that it provides a useful way to learn about one's own sexuality (Hyde & DeLamater, 2003; Levin, 2007).

Sexual Intercourse Although it may be preceded by many different types of sexual intimacy, including deep kissing, massaging, petting, and oral sex, sexual intercourse remains a major milestone in the perceptions of most adolescents. Consequently, the main focus of researchers investigating sexual behavior has been on the act of heterosexual intercourse.

The average age at which adolescents first have sexual intercourse has been steadily declining over the last 50 years, and about one in five adolescents have had sex before the age of 15. Overall, around half of adolescents begin having intercourse between the ages of 15 and 18, and at least 80% have had sex before the age of 20 (see Figure 16-8). At the same time, though, many teenagers are postponing sex, and the number of adolescents who say they have never had sexual intercourse increased by nearly 10% from 1991 to 2001, largely as a response to the threat of infection by the virus that causes AIDS (Seidman & Reider, 1994; Centers for Disease Control & Prevention, 1998; NCPYP, 2003).

It is impossible to consider sexual activities without also looking at the societal norms governing sexual conduct. The prevailing norm several decades ago was the *double standard* in which premarital sex was considered permissible for males but not for females. Women were told by

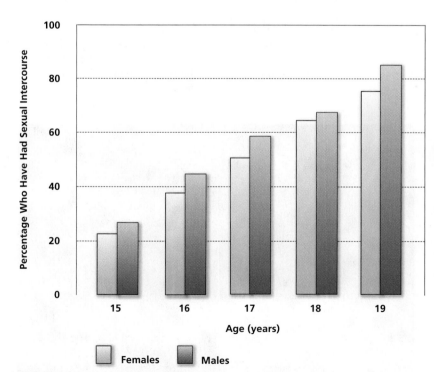

FIGURE 16-8 Adolescents and Sexual Activity

The age at which adolescents have sexual intercourse for the first time is declining, and 80% have had sex before the age of 20.
(*Source:* Kantrowitz & Wingert, 1999)

society that "nice girls don't," whereas men heard that premarital sex was permissible—although they should be sure to marry virgins.

Today, however, the double standard has begun to give way to a new norm, called *permissiveness with affection.* According to this standard, premarital intercourse is viewed as permissible for both men and women if it occurs in the context of a long-term, committed, or loving relationship (Hyde & Delamater, 2003; Earle et al., 2007).

The demise of the double standard is far from complete, however. Attitudes toward sexual conduct are still typically more lenient for males than for females, even in relatively socially liberal cultures. And in some cultures, the standards for men and women are quite distinct. For example, in North Africa, the Middle East, and the majority of Asian countries, most women conform to societal norms suggesting that they abstain from sexual intercourse until they are married. In Mexico, where there are strict standards against premarital sex, males are also considerably more likely than females to have premarital sex. In contrast, in sub-Saharan Africa, women are more likely to have sexual intercourse prior to marriage, and intercourse is common for unmarried teenage women (Johnson et al., 1992; Peltzer & Pengpid, 2006; Wellings et al., 2006; Ghule, Balaiah, & Joshi, 2007).

The Decline in Teen Pregnancy

Night has eased into day, but it is all the same for Tori Michel, 17. Her 5-day-old baby, Caitlin, has been fussing for hours, though she seems finally to have settled into the pink-and-purple car seat on the living-room sofa. "She wore herself out," explains Tori, who lives in a two-bedroom duplex in this St. Louis suburb with her mother, Susan, an aide to handicapped adults. "I think she just had gas."

Motherhood was not in Tori's plans for her senior year at Fort Zumwalt South High School—not until she had a "one-night thing" with James, a 21-year-old she met through friends. She had been taking birth-control pills but says she stopped after breaking up with a long-term boyfriend. "Wrong answer," she now says ruefully. (Gleick, Reed, & Schindehette, 1994)

Feedings at 3:00 A.M., diaper changes, and visits to the pediatrician are not part of most people's vision of adolescence. Yet, every year, more than 800,000 adolescents in the United States give birth. For these teenagers, life becomes increasingly challenging as they struggle with the demands of parenthood while still facing the complexities of adolescence.

The good news, though, is that the number of teenage pregnancies is declining. In the last 10 years, the teenage birthrate has dropped 30%. Births to African American teenagers have shown the steepest decline, with births down by more than 40% in a decade. Overall, the pregnancy rate of teenagers is 43 births per 1,000, a historic low (see Figure 16-9; Centers for Disease Control and Prevention, 2003).

This 16-year-old mother and her child are representative of a major social problem: teenage pregnancy. Why is teenage pregnancy a greater problem in the United States than in other countries?

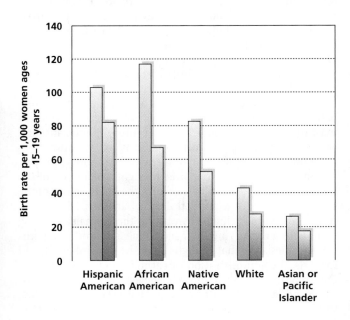

FIGURE 16-9 Teenage Pregnancy Rates

The rate of teenage pregnancy in the United States has declined significantly over the last decade among all ethnic groups. (*Source:* Centers for Disease Control, 2003)

Several factors explain the drop in teenage pregnancies:

- New initiatives have raised awareness among teenagers of the risks of unprotected sex. For example, about two-thirds of high schools in the United States have established comprehensive sex education programs (Villarosa, 2003).

- The rates of sexual intercourse among teenagers has declined. The percentage of teenage girls who have ever had sexual intercourse dropped from 51% to 43% between 1991 and 2001.

- The use of condoms and other forms of contraception has increased. For example, 57% of sexually active high school students reported using condoms.

- Substitutes for sexual intercourse may be more prevalent. For example, some research shows as rates of oral sex increase, rates of sexual intercourse decline (Bernstein, 2004).

The Challenges of Teenage Pregnancy   Even with the decline in the birth rate for U.S. teens, the rate of teenage pregnancy in the United States is 2 to 10 times higher compared to that of other industrialized countries. For example, teenagers in the United States are twice as likely to become pregnant as Canadian teenagers, four times as likely as French adolescents, and six times more likely than Swedish teenagers (Singh & Darroch, 2000).

The results of an unintended pregnancy can be devastating to both mother and child. In comparison to earlier times, teenage mothers today are much less likely to be married. In a high percentage of cases, mothers care for their children without the help of the father. Without financial or emotional support, a mother may have to abandon her own education, and consequently she may be relegated to unskilled, poorly paying jobs for the rest of her life. In other cases, she may develop long-term dependency on welfare. An adolescent mother's physical and mental health may suffer as she faces unrelenting stress due to continual demands on her time (Manlove et al., 2004; Lall, 2007).

These difficulties affect the children of teenage mothers as well. They are more likely to suffer from poor health and to show poorer school performance when compared to children of older mothers. Later, they are more likely to become teenage parents themselves, creating a cycle of pregnancy and poverty from which it is very difficult to extricate themselves (Carnegie Task Force, 1994; Spencer, 2001; East, Reyes, & Horn, 2007).

Virginity Pledges   One thing that apparently *hasn't* led to a reduction in teenage pregnancies is asking adolescents to take a virginity pledge. Public pledges to refrain from premarital sex—a centerpiece of some forms of sex education—have a mixed record. Initial studies of virginity pledges were promising, showing that adolescents who took a pledge to defer sexual intercourse until marriage delayed sex about 18 months longer than those who had never taken such a pledge (Bearman & Bruckner, 2001).

But even this early research called virginity pledges into question. For example, the effectiveness of pledging depended on a student's age. For older adolescents (18 years old and above), taking a pledge had no effect. Pledges were effective only for 16- and 17-year-olds. Furthermore, the pledges worked only when a minority of people in a school took such a pledge. When more than 30% took such a pledge, the effectiveness of the pledge diminished substantially.

The reason for this surprising finding relates to why virginity pledges might work: They offer adolescents a sense of identity, similar to the way joining a club does. When a minority of students take a virginity pledge, they feel part of a special group, and they are more likely to adhere to the norms of that group—in this case, remaining a virgin. In contrast, if a majority of students take a pledge of virginity, the pledge becomes less unique and adherence is less likely.

Most recent research finds that virginity pledges are ineffective. For example, in one study of 12,000 teenagers, 88% reported eventually having sexual intercourse before marriage, although taking a pledge did delay the start of sex (Bearman et al., 2004).

Because abstinence programs have not been successful, some researchers have called for more comprehensive education programs to replace ones that focus on abstinence as the only option. Most parents and teachers agree that abstinence education should be emphasized, but that information on contraception and safer sex practices should be included as well. Research supports these beliefs: While abstinence-only programs and programs that include contraception education do not clearly differ in their effects on adolescents' sexual activity, the addition of contraception education does improve adolescents' understanding and use of birth-control strategies (Manlove et al., 2002; Bennett & Assefi, 2005; Giami et al., 2006; Santelli et al., 2006).

Safer Choices, a two-year program for adolescents in high school, is one such program that combines encouragement of abstinence with education on contraceptive use. Its goals are to reduce the number of students who are sexually active while in high school and to increase condom usage in students who do have sex by addressing adolescent sexual activity on multiple fronts. The program attempts to modify students' attitudes and norms about sexual behavior, abstinence, and condom use (including adolescents' perceived barriers to condom use). It also addresses students' confidence in their ability to refuse sex, to discuss safer sex with their partners, and to use a condom; and it teaches students about the risks of contracting sexually transmitted infections. Finally, the program seeks to improve students' communication with their parents about sex (Advocates for Youth, 2003; Kirby et al., 2004).

From a health-care provider's perspective: A parent asks you how to prevent her 14-year-old son from engaging in sexual activity until he is older. What would you tell her?

Sexual Orientation: Heterosexuality, Homosexuality, and Bisexuality

When we consider adolescents' sexual development, the most frequent pattern is *heterosexuality,* sexual attraction and behavior directed to the other sex. Yet some teenagers are *homosexual,* in which their sexual attraction and behavior is oriented to members of their own sex. (Many male homosexuals prefer the term *gay,* and female homosexuals, the label *lesbian,* because they refer to a broader array of attitudes and lifestyle than the term *homosexual,* which focuses on the sexual act.) Other people find they are *bisexual,* or sexually attracted to people of both sexes.

Many teens experiment with homosexuality. At one time or another, around 20% to 25% of adolescent boys and 10% of adolescent girls have at least one same-sex sexual encounter. In fact, homosexuality and heterosexuality are not completely distinct sexual orientations. Alfred Kinsey, a pioneer sex researcher, argued that sexual orientation should be viewed as a continuum in which "exclusively homosexual" is at one end, and "exclusively heterosexual" is at the other (Kinsey, Pomeroy, & Martin, 1948). In between are people who show both homosexual and heterosexual behavior. Although accurate figures are difficult to obtain, most experts believe that between 4% and 10% of both men and women are exclusively homosexual during extended periods of their lives (McWhirter, Sanders, & Reinisch, 1990; Michael et al., 1994; Diamond, 2003a, 2003b; Russell & Consolacion, 2003).

The determination of sexual orientation is further complicated by distinctions between sexual orientation and gender identity. Although sexual orientation relates to the object of one's sexual interests, *gender identity* is the gender a person believes he or she is psychologically. Sexual orientation and gender identity are not necessarily related

The stresses of adolescence are magnified for homosexuals, who often face societal prejudice. Eventually, however, most adolescents come to grips with their sexual orientation, as these students at a symposium exemplify.

to one another: A man who has a strong masculine gender identity may be attracted to other men. Consequently, the extent to which men and women enact traditional "masculine" or "feminine" behavior is not necessarily related to their sexual orientation or gender identity (Hunter & Mallon, 2000).

Some people feel they have been born the wrong physical sex, believing, for example, that they are women trapped in men's bodies. These *transgendered* individuals may pursue sexual reassignment surgery, a prolonged course of treatment in which they receive hormones and reconstructive surgery so they are able to take on the physical characteristics of the other sex.

What Determines Sexual Orientation? The factors that induce people to develop as heterosexual, homosexual, or bisexual are not well understood. Evidence suggests that genetic and biological factors may play an important role. Studies of twins shows that identical twins are more likely to be homosexual than are pairs of siblings who don't share their genetic makeup. Other research finds that various structures of the brain are different in homosexuals and heterosexuals, and hormone production also seems to be linked to sexual orientation (Rahman & Wilson, 2003; Kraemer et al., 2006; Ellis et al., 2008; Santtila et al., 2008).

Other researchers have suggested that family or peer environmental factors play a role. For example, Freud argued that homosexuality was the result of inappropriate identification with the opposite-sex parent (Freud, 1922/1959). The difficulty with Freud's theoretical perspective and other, similar perspectives that followed is that there simply is no evidence to suggest that any particular family dynamic or child-rearing practice is consistently related to sexual orientation. Similarly, explanations based on learning theory, which suggest that homosexuality arises because of rewarding, pleasant homosexual experiences and unsatisfying heterosexual ones, do not appear to be the complete answer (Isay, 1990; Golombok & Tasker, 1996).

In short, there is no accepted explanation of why some adolescents develop a heterosexual orientation, and others a homosexual orientation. Most experts believe that sexual orientation develops out of a complex interplay of genetic, physiological, and environmental factors (LeVay & Valente, 2003).

What is clear is that adolescents who find themselves attracted to members of the same sex may face a more difficult time than do other teens. Our society still harbors great ignorance and prejudice regarding homosexuality, persisting in the belief that people have a choice in the matter—which they do not. Gay and lesbian teens may be rejected by their family or peers, or even harassed and assaulted if they are open about their orientation. The result is that adolescents who find themselves to be homosexual are at greater risk for depression, and suicide rates are significantly higher for homosexual adolescents than for heterosexual adolescents (Koh & Ross, 2006; Lester, 2006; Eisenberg & Resnick, 2006; Silenzio et al., 2007).

Ultimately, though, most people are able to come to grips with their sexual orientation and become comfortable with it. Although lesbians, gays, and bisexuals may experience mental health difficulties as a result of stress, prejudice, and discrimination they face, homosexuality is not considered a psychological disorder by any of the major psychological or medical associations. All of them endorse efforts to reduce discrimination against homosexuals (van Wormer & McKinney, 2003; Davison, 2005; Russell & McGuire, 2006).

CASE STUDY

The Case of... Too Much of a Good Thing

Marcia Wilder was the eldest child in a close-knit family of five. Her parents took pride in the fact that the family spent all their weekends together, hiking, gardening, or going to the movies. They assumed this would always be true, and Marcia herself was happy to bask in so much familial love—until the year she turned 13. That was the year she entered middle school and her whole world changed.

Marcia discovered she had lots of interests. She joined the stage crew at her school and painted scenery for student productions. She took a photography course and began spending her afternoons in the school's darkroom, printing the photos she had taken of friends. She started babysitting 2 nights a week for the neighbors. On weekends, she went to the mall and the movies with friends.

"We never see you anymore," her parents complained. At first, Marcia shrugged it off, but when her parents began to criticize everything from the clothes she wore to the music she preferred, she got annoyed. When they began scrutinizing her friends and calling her cell phone every hour to see who she was with and where she was at, she became enraged. "You just won't let me have a life!" she shouted when

they demanded she cancel plans with friends to spend weekend time with the family. Deep down, Marcia knew her parents loved her and she still loved them, but increasingly she felt a strong need to escape their complaints and restraints.

1. How do the changes in Marcia reflect normal social development in adolescence?

2. What specific advice would you give Marcia's parents to help ease the conflict with their daughter?

3. Do you feel Marcia is exercising an appropriate level of autonomy and independence for her age? Why or why not?

4. Given what we know about social and personality development in adolescence, what changes would you expect to occur in Marcia's relationship with her parents over the next 5 years?

5. Do you think Marcia and her parents are experiencing a true generation gap? Why or why not?

◄ Looking Back

How does the development of self-concept, self-esteem, and identity proceed during adolescence?

- During adolescence, self-concept differentiates to encompass others' views as well as one's own and to include multiple aspects simultaneously. Differentiation

of self-concept can cause confusion as behaviors reflect a complex definition of the self.

- Adolescents also differentiate their self-esteem, evaluating particular aspects of themselves differently.

- According to Erik Erikson, adolescents are in the identity-versus-identity-confusion stage, seeking to discover their individuality and identity. They may become confused and exhibit dysfunctional reactions, and they may rely on friends and peers for help and information more than on adults.
- James Marcia identifies four identity statuses that individuals may experience in adolescence and in later life: identity achievement, identity foreclosure, identity diffusion, and moratorium.
- The formation of an identity is challenging for members of racial and ethnic minority groups, many of whom appear to be embracing a bicultural identity approach.

What dangers do adolescents face as they deal with the stresses of adolescence?

- Many adolescents have feelings of sadness and hopelessness, and some experience major depression. Biological, environmental, and social factors contribute to depression, and there are gender, ethnic, and racial differences in its rate of occurrence.
- The rate of adolescent suicide is rising, with suicide now the third most common cause of death in the 15- to 24-year-old bracket.

How does the quality of relationships with family and peers change during adolescence?

- Adolescents' quest for autonomy often brings confusion and tension to their relationships with their parents, but the actual "generation gap" between parents' and teenagers' attitudes is usually small.
- Peers are important during adolescence because they provide social comparison and reference groups against which to judge social success. Relationships among adolescents are characterized by the need to belong.

What are gender, race, and ethnic relations like in adolescence?

- During adolescence, boys and girls begin to spend time together in groups and, toward the end of adolescence, to pair off.

- In general, segregation among people of different races and ethnicities increases in middle and late adolescence, even in schools with a diverse student body.

What does it mean to be popular and unpopular in adolescence, and how do adolescents respond to peer pressure?

- Degrees of popularity during adolescence include popular and controversial adolescents (on the high end of popularity) and neglected and rejected adolescents (on the low end).
- Peer pressure is not a simple phenomenon. Adolescents conform to their peers in areas in which they feel their peers are expert, and to adults in areas of adult expertise. As adolescents grow in confidence, their conformity to both peers and adults declines.
- Although most adolescents do not commit crimes, adolescents are disproportionately involved in criminal activities. Juvenile delinquents can be categorized as undersocialized or socialized delinquents.

What are the functions and characteristics of dating during adolescence?

- During adolescence, dating provides intimacy, entertainment, and prestige. Achieving psychological intimacy, difficult at first, becomes easier as adolescents mature, gain confidence, and take relationships more seriously.

How does sexuality develop in the adolescent years?

- For most adolescents, masturbation is often the first step into sexuality. The age of first intercourse, which is now in the teens, has declined as the double standard has faded and the norm of permissiveness with affection has gained ground. However, as more and more adolescents have become aware of the threat of STIs and AIDS, the rate of sexual intercourse has declined.
- Sexual orientation develops out of a complex interplay of genetic, physiological, and environmental factors. ■

Epilogue

We concluded our consideration of adolescence in this chapter, looking at social and personality issues. Self-concept, self-esteem, and identity develop during adolescence and can be a period of self-discovery. We looked at adolescents' relationships with family and peers, and at gender, race, and ethnic relations during adolescence. Our discussion concluded with a look at dating, sexuality, and sexual orientation.

Return to the chapter Prologue and recall the experience of Lucian Schulte, who felt guilty about his first sexual encounter and resolved to remain celibate until marriage. Consider the following questions.

1. What do you think motivated Lucian to experiment with sex despite his desire to wait until marriage?

2. Lucian says his first sexual experience turned out differently from what he had expected. What consequences did Lucian fail to take into account?

3. What effect do you think Lucian's religious upbringing, his parents' values, and his abstinence classes had on his sexual activity?

4. What tentative conclusions can you draw about how Lucian's personality relates to his notions about sexuality? How typical does he seem to be?

Key Terms and Concepts

identity-versus-identity-confusion stage (p. 386)
identity achievement (p. 388)
identity foreclosure (p. 388)
moratorium (p. 388)
identity diffusion (p. 388)
autonomy (p. 393)

generation gap (p. 394)
reference groups (p. 396)
cliques (p. 397)
crowds (p. 397)
sex cleavage (p. 397)
controversial adolescents (p. 398)

rejected adolescents (p. 398)
neglected adolescents (p. 398)
peer pressure (p. 399)
undersocialized delinquents (p. 400)
socialized delinquents (p. 401)
masturbation (p. 403)

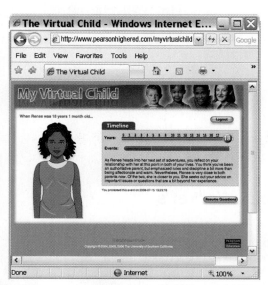

What decisions would you make while raising a child? What would the consequences of those decisions be?

Find out by logging onto **My Virtual Child** and raising your child from birth to 18 years.

5

Adolescence

Physical, Cognitive, and Social and Personality Development in Adolescence

An adolescent can change from being a seemingly "together" teenager into a troubled young adolescent, and then into an increasingly confident and independent late adolescent. Early in adolescence, the struggle to define oneself can lead to some decidedly unwise decisions. An adolescent may dabble with drugs and alcohol. Depression and suicide are also high risks for this age group. Adolescents seeking help for their difficulties may kick their bad habits, begin to work on their self-concept, and enter into a positive relationship with family and friends.

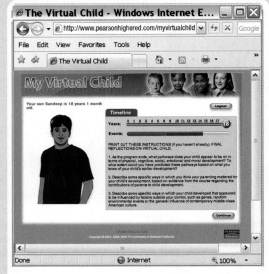

What decisions would you make while raising a child? What would the consequences of those decisions be?

Find out by logging onto **My Virtual Child** and raising your child from birth to 18 years.

⬤ From a **Parent's** perspective

What warning signs should parents watch for to protect their adolescent from depression and suicide? What can they do when an adolescent is depressed or seems at risk for suicide?

HINT **Review pages 389–392**

Your Response?

⬤ From a **Social Worker's** perspective

When an adolescent shows a definite decline in academic performance, are the symptoms likely to be interpreted differently depending on whether the adolescent comes from an affluent or an impoverished background? Why? How can a professional care provider avoid being inappropriately influenced by socioeconomic status?

HINT **Review pages 368–369**

Your Response?

Adolescence

From an **Educator's** perspective

What signals might a teacher observe in a student's classroom performance to suggest that she has a drug problem? What steps might the teacher take?

HINT **Review pages 346–349**

Your Response?

From **Your** perspective

If a friend was depressed and possibly suicidal, what advice and support would you give her? What warning signs indicating suicidal tendencies would you look for?

HINT **Review pages 389–392**

Your Response?

Glossary

Abstract modeling   The process in which modeling paves the way for the development of more general rules and principles (Ch. 10)

Acceleration   The provision of special programs that allow gifted students to move ahead at their own pace, even if this means skipping to higher grade levels (Ch. 12)

Accommodation   Changes in existing ways of thinking that occur in response to encounters with new stimuli or events (Ch. 6)

Addictive drugs   Drugs that produce a biological or psychological dependence in users, leading to increasingly powerful cravings for them (Ch. 14)

Adolescence   The developmental stage between childhood and adulthood (Ch. 14)

Adolescent egocentrism   A state of self-absorption in which the world is viewed from one's own point of view (Ch. 15)

Adolescent growth spurt   A period of very rapid growth in height and weight during adolescence (Ch. 14)

Affordances   The action possibilities that a given situation or stimulus provides (Ch. 5)

Agentic professions   Occupations associated with getting things accomplished (Ch. 15)

Aggression   Intentional injury or harm to another person (Ch. 10)

Ainsworth Strange Situation   A sequence of staged episodes that illustrate the strength of attachment between a child and (typically) his or her mother (Ch. 7)

Alcoholics   People who have learned to depend on alcohol and are unable to control their drinking (Ch. 14)

Ambivalent attachment pattern   A style of attachment in which children display a combination of positive and negative reactions to their mothers; they show great distress when the mother leaves, but upon her return they may simultaneously seek close contact but also hit and kick her (Ch. 7)

Amniocentesis   The process of identifying genetic defects by examining a small sample of fetal cells drawn by a needle inserted into the amniotic fluid surrounding the unborn fetus (Ch. 3)

Anorexia nervosa   A severe and potentially life-threatening eating disorder in which individuals refuse to eat, while denying that their behavior or skeletal appearance is out of the ordinary (Ch. 14)

Anoxia   A restriction of oxygen to the baby, lasting a few minutes during the birth process, which can produce brain damage (Ch. 4)

Apgar scale   A standard measurement system that looks for a variety of indications of good health in newborns (Ch. 4)

Applied research   Research meant to provide practical solutions to immediate problems (Ch. 2)

Artificial insemination   A process of fertilization in which a man's sperm is placed directly into a woman's vagina by a physician (Ch. 3)

Assimilation   The process in which people understand an experience in terms of their current stage of cognitive development and way of thinking (Ch. 6)

Associative play   Play in which two or more children interact by sharing or borrowing toys or materials, although they do not do the same thing (Ch. 10)

Asthma   A chronic condition characterized by periodic attacks of wheezing, coughing, and shortness of breath (Ch. 11)

Attachment   The positive emotional bond that develops between a child and a particular individual (Ch. 7)

Attention deficit hyperactivity disorder (ADHD)   A learning disability marked by inattention, impulsiveness, a low tolerance for frustration, and a great deal of inappropriate activity (Ch. 11)

Auditory impairment   A special need that involves the loss of hearing or some aspect of hearing (Ch. 11)

Authoritarian parents   Parents who are controlling, punitive, rigid, and cold and whose word is law; they value strict, unquestioning obedience from their children and do not tolerate expressions of disagreement (Ch. 10)

Authoritative parents   Parents who are firm, setting clear and consistent limits, but try to reason with their children, explaining why they should behave in a particular way (Ch. 10)

Autobiographical memory   Memory of particular events from one's own life (Ch. 9)

Autonomy   Having independence and a sense of control over one's life (Ch. 16)

Autonomy-versus-shame-and-doubt stage   The period during which, according to Erikson, toddlers (aged 18 months to 3 years) develop independence and autonomy if they are allowed the freedom to explore, or shame and self-doubt if they are restricted and overprotected (Ch. 7)

Avoidant attachment pattern   A style of attachment in which children do not seek proximity to the mother; after the mother has left, they seem to avoid her when she returns as if they are angered by her behavior (Ch. 7)

Babbling   Making speechlike but meaningless sounds (Ch. 6)

Bayley Scales of Infant Development   A measure that evaluates an infant's development from 2 to 42 months (Ch. 6)

Behavior modification   A formal technique for promoting the frequency of desirable behaviors and decreasing the incidence of unwanted ones (Ch. 2)

Behavioral genetics   The study of the effects of heredity on behavior (Ch. 3)

Behavioral perspective   The approach to the study of development that suggests that the keys to understanding development are observable behavior and outside stimuli in the environment (Ch. 2)

Bicultural identity   The maintenance of one's original cultural identity while becoming integrated into the majority culture (Ch. 12)

Bilingualism   The ability to speak two languages (Ch. 12)

Bioecological approach   The perspective suggesting that different levels of the environment simultaneously influence every biological organism (Ch. 2)

Blended family   A remarried couple that has at least one stepchild living with them (Ch. 13)

Bonding   Close physical and emotional contact between parent and child during the period immediately following birth, argued by some to affect later relationship strength (Ch. 4)

Brazelton Neonatal Behavioral Assessment Scale (NBAS) A measure designed to determine infants' neurological and behavioral responses to their environment (Ch. 5)

Bulimia   An eating disorder that primarily afflicts adolescent girls and young women, characterized by binges on large quantities of food followed by purges of the food through vomiting or the use of laxatives (Ch. 14)

Case studies   Extensive, in-depth interviews with a particular individual or small group of individuals (Ch. 2)

Centration   The process of concentrating on one limited aspect of a stimulus and ignoring other aspects (Ch. 9)

Cephalocaudal principle   The principle that growth follows a pattern that begins with the head and upper body parts and then proceeds down to the rest of the body (Ch. 5)

Cerebral cortex   The upper layer of the brain (Ch. 5)

Cesarean delivery   A birth in which the baby is surgically removed from the uterus, rather than traveling through the birth canal (Ch. 4)

Child abuse   The physical or psychological maltreatment or neglect of children (Ch. 8)

Child development   The field that involves the scientific study of the patterns of growth, change, and stability that occur from conception through adolescence (Ch. 1)

Child neglect   Ignoring one's children or being emotionally unresponsive to them (Ch. 8)

Chorionic villus sampling (CVS)   A test used to find genetic defects that involves taking samples of hairlike material that surrounds the embryo (Ch. 3)

Chromosomes   Rod-shaped portions of DNA that are organized in 23 pairs (Ch. 3)

Chronological (physical) age   A person's age according to the calendar (Ch. 12)

Classical conditioning   A type of learning in which an organism responds in a particular way to a neutral stimulus that normally does not bring about that type of response (Ch. 2 & 4)

Cliques   Groups of from 2 to 12 people whose members have frequent social interactions with one another (Ch. 16)

Cognitive development   Development involving the ways that growth and change in intellectual capabilities influence a person's behavior (Ch. 1)

Cognitive neuroscience approaches   Approaches to the study of cognitive development that focus on how brain processes are related to cognitive activity (Ch. 2)

Cognitive perspective   The approach to the study of development that focuses on the processes that allow people to know, understand, and think about the world (Ch. 2)

Cohort   A group of people born at around the same time in the same place (Ch. 1)

Collectivistic orientation   A philosophy that promotes the notion of interdependence (Ch. 10)

Communal professions   Occupations associated with relationships (Ch. 15)

Concrete operational stage   The period of cognitive development between 7 and 12 years of age, characterized by the active and appropriate use of logic (Ch. 12)

Conservation   The knowledge that quantity is unrelated to the arrangement and physical appearance of objects (Ch. 9)

Constructive play   Play in which children manipulate objects to produce or build something (Ch. 10)

Contextual perspective   The perspective that considers the relationship between individuals and their physical, cognitive, personality, social, and physical worlds (Ch. 2)

Continuous change   Gradual development in which achievements at one level build on those of previous levels (Ch. 1)

Control group   The group in an experiment that receives either no treatment or an alternative treatment (Ch. 2)

Controversial adolescents   Children who are liked by some peers and disliked by others (Ch. 16)

Cooperative play   Play in which children genuinely interact with one another, taking turns, playing games, or devising contests (Ch. 10)

Coping   Efforts to control, reduce, or tolerate the threats and challenges that lead to stress (Ch. 14)

Coregulation   A period in which parents and children jointly control children's behavior (Ch. 13)

Correlational research   Research that seeks to identify whether an association or relationship between two factors exists (Ch. 2)

Critical period   A specific time during development when a particular event has its greatest consequences (Ch. 1)

Cross-sectional research   Research in which people of different ages are compared at the same point in time (Ch. 2)

Crowds   Groups larger than cliques, composed of individuals who share particular characteristics but who may not interact with one another (Ch. 16)

Crystallized intelligence   The accumulation of information, skills, and strategies that people have learned through experience and that they can apply in problem-solving situations (Ch. 12)

Cultural assimilation model   The view of American society as a "melting pot" in which all cultures are amalgamated (Ch. 12)

Cycle-of-violence hypothesis   The theory that abuse and neglect that children suffer predispose them as adults to abuse and neglect their own children (Ch. 8)

Decentering   The ability to take multiple aspects of a situation into account (Ch. 12)

Deferred imitation   An act in which a person who is no longer present is imitated by children (Ch. 6)

Dependent variable   The variable in an experiment that is measured and is expected to change as a result of the experimental manipulation (Ch. 2)

Developmental quotient   An overall developmental score that relates to performance in four domains: motor skills, language use, adaptive behavior, and personal–social behavior (Ch. 6)

Developmentally appropriate educational practice   Education that is based on both typical development and the unique characteristics of a given child (Ch. 9)

Difficult babies   Babies who have negative moods and are slow to adapt to new situations; when confronted with a new situation, they tend to withdraw (Ch. 7)

Discontinuous change   Development that occurs in distinct steps or stages, with each stage bringing about behavior that is assumed to be qualitatively different from behavior at earlier stages (Ch. 1)

Disorganized-disoriented attachment pattern   A style of attachment in which children show inconsistent, often contradictory behavior, such as approaching the mother when she returns but not looking at her; they may be the least securely attached children of all (Ch. 7)

Dizygotic twins   Twins who are produced when two separate ova are fertilized by two separate sperm at roughly the same time (Ch. 3)

DNA (deoxyribonucleic acid) molecules   The substance that genes are composed of that determines the nature of every cell in the body and how it will function (Ch. 3)

Dominance hierarchy   Rankings that represent the relative social power of those in a group (Ch. 13)

Dominant trait   The one trait that is expressed when two competing traits are present (Ch. 3)

Down syndrome   A disorder produced by the presence of an extra chromosome on the 21st pair; once referred to as mongolism (Ch. 3)

Dynamic systems theory   A theory of how motor skills develop and are coordinated (Ch. 5)

Easy babies   Babies who have a positive disposition; their body functions operate regularly, and they are adaptable (Ch. 7)

Egocentric thought   Thinking that does not take the viewpoints of others into account (Ch. 9)

Embryonic stage   The period from 2 to 8 weeks following fertilization during which significant growth occurs in the major organs and body systems (Ch. 3)

Emotional intelligence   The set of skills that underlie the accurate assessment, evaluation, expression, and regulation of emotions (Ch. 12)

Emotional self-regulation   The capability to adjust one's emotions to a desired state and level of intensity (Ch. 10)

Empathy   An emotional response that corresponds to the feelings of another person (Ch. 7)

Empathy   The understanding of what another individual feels (Ch. 10)

Enrichment   Approach through which students are kept at grade level but are enrolled in special programs and given individual activities to allow greater depth of study on a given topic (Ch. 12)

Episiotomy   An incision sometimes made to increase the size of the opening of the vagina to allow the baby to pass (Ch. 4)

Erikson's theory of psychosocial development   The theory that considers how individuals come to understand themselves and the meaning of others'—and their own—behavior (Ch. 7)

Evolutionary perspective   The theory that seeks to identify behavior that is the result of our genetic inheritance from our ancestors (Ch. 2)

Experiment   A process in which an investigator, called an experimenter, devises two different experiences for subjects or participants (Ch. 2)

Experimental research   Research designed to discover causal relationships between various factors (Ch. 2)

Expressive style   A style of language use in which language is used primarily to express feelings and needs about oneself and others (Ch. 6)

Fantasy period   According to Ginzberg, the period of life when career choices are made—and discarded—without regard to skills, abilities, or available job opportunities (Ch. 15)

Fast mapping   The process in which new words are associated with their meaning after only a brief encounter (Ch. 9)

Fertilization   The process by which a sperm and an ovum—the male and female gametes, respectively—join to form a single new cell (Ch. 3)

Fetal alcohol effects (FAE)   A condition in which children display some, although not all, of the problems of fetal alcohol syndrome due to the mother's consumption of alcohol during pregnancy (Ch. 3)

Fetal alcohol syndrome (FAS)   A disorder caused by the pregnant mother consuming substantial quantities of alcohol during pregnancy, potentially resulting in mental retardation and delayed growth in the child (Ch. 3)

Fetal monitor   A device that measures the baby's heartbeat during labor (Ch. 4)

Fetal stage   The stage that begins at about 8 weeks after conception and continues until birth (Ch. 3)

Fetus   A developing child, from 8 weeks after conception until birth (Ch. 3)

Field study   A research investigation carried out in a naturally occurring setting (Ch. 2)

Fluid intelligence Intelligence that reflects information processing capabilities, reasoning, and memory (Ch. 12)

Formal operational stage The stage at which people develop the ability to think abstractly (Ch. 15)

Fragile X syndrome A disorder produced by injury to a gene on the X chromosome, producing mild to moderate mental retardation (Ch. 3)

Full inclusion The integration of all students, even those with the most severe disabilities, into regular classes and all other aspects of school and community life (Ch. 11)

Functional play Play that involves simple, repetitive activities typical of 3-year-olds (Ch. 10)

Gametes The sex cells from the mother and father that form a new cell at conception (Ch. 3)

Gender constancy The fact that people are permanently males or females, depending on fixed, unchangeable biological factors (Ch. 10)

Gender identity The perception of oneself as male or female (Ch. 10)

Gender schema A cognitive framework that organizes information relevant to gender (Ch. 10)

Gender The sense of being male or female (Ch. 7)

Generation gap A divide between parents and adolescents in attitudes, values, aspirations, and worldviews (Ch. 16)

Genes The basic unit of genetic information (Ch. 3)

Genetic counseling The discipline that focuses on helping people deal with issues relating to inherited disorders (Ch. 3)

Genotype The underlying combination of genetic material present (but not outwardly visible) in an organism (Ch. 3)

Germinal stage The first, and shortest, stage of the prenatal period, which takes place during the first 2 weeks following conception (Ch. 3)

Gifted and talented Showing evidence of high performance capability in intellectual, creative, or artistic areas, in leadership capacity, or in specific academic fields (Ch. 12)

Goal-directed behavior Behavior in which several schemes are combined and coordinated to generate a single act to solve a problem (Ch. 6)

Goodness-of-fit The notion that development is dependent on the degree of match between children's temperament and the nature and demands of the environment in which they are being raised (Ch. 7)

Grammar The system of rules that determine how thoughts can be expressed (Ch. 9)

Habituation The decrease in the response to a stimulus that occurs after repeated presentations of the same stimulus (Ch. 4)

Handedness A clear preference for the use of one hand over the other (Ch. 8)

Heterozygous Inheriting from parents different forms of a gene for a given trait (Ch. 3)

Holophrases One-word utterances that stand for a whole phrase, whose meaning depends on the particular context in which they are used (Ch. 6)

Homozygous Inheriting from parents similar genes for a given trait (Ch. 3)

Hypothesis A prediction stated in a way that permits it to be tested (Ch. 2)

Identification The process in which children attempt to be similar to their parent of the same sex, incorporating the parent's attitudes and values (Ch. 10)

Identity achievement The status of adolescents who commit to a particular identity following a period of crisis during which they consider various alternatives (Ch. 16)

Identity diffusion The status of adolescents who consider various identity alternatives, but never commit to one or never even consider identity options in any conscious way (Ch. 16)

Identity foreclosure The status of adolescents who prematurely commit to an identity without adequately exploring alternatives (Ch. 16)

Identity-versus-identity-confusion stage The period during which teenagers seek to determine what is unique and distinctive about themselves (Ch. 16)

Imaginary audience Fictitious observers who pay as much attention to adolescents' behavior as they do themselves (Ch. 15)

In vitro fertilization (IVF) A procedure in which a woman's ova are removed from her ovaries, and a man's sperm are used to fertilize the ova in a laboratory (Ch. 3)

Independent variable The variable in an experiment that is manipulated by researchers (Ch. 2)

Individualistic orientation A philosophy that emphasizes personal identity and the uniqueness of the individual (Ch. 10)

Industry-versus-inferiority stage According to Erikson, the period from ages 6 to 12 characterized by a focus on efforts to attain competence in meeting the challenges presented by parents, peers, school, and the other complexities of the modern world (Ch. 13)

Infant mortality Death within the first year of life (Ch. 4)

Infant-directed speech A type of speech directed toward infants, characterized by short, simple sentences (Ch. 6)

Infantile amnesia The lack of memory for experiences that occurred prior to 3 years of age (Ch. 6)

Infertility The inability to conceive after 12 to 18 months of trying to become pregnant (Ch. 3)

Information-processing approaches Approaches to the study of cognitive development that seek to identify the ways individuals take in, use, and store information (Ch. 2)

Information-processing approaches The model that seeks to identify the way that individuals take in, use, and store information (Ch. 6)

Information-processing perspective The model that seeks to identify the way that individuals take in, use, and store information (Ch. 15)

Initiative-versus-guilt stage According to Erikson, the period during which children aged 3 to 6 years experience conflict between independence of action and the sometimes negative results of that action (Ch. 10)

Instrumental aggression   Aggression motivated by a desire to obtain a concrete goal (Ch. 10)

Intelligence quotient (IQ)   A score that expresses the ratio between a person's mental and chronological ages (Ch. 12)

Intelligence   The capacity to understand the world, think rationally, and use resources effectively when faced with challenges (Ch. 12)

Intuitive thought   Thinking that reflects preschoolers' use of primitive reasoning and their avid acquisition of knowledge about the world (Ch. 9)

Kaufman Assessment Battery for Children, Second Edition (KABC-II)   An intelligence test that measures children's ability to integrate different stimuli simultaneously and step-by-step thinking (Ch. 12)

Klinefelter's syndrome   A disorder resulting from the presence of an extra X chromosome that produces underdeveloped genitals, extreme height, and enlarged breasts (Ch. 3)

Laboratory study   A research investigation conducted in a controlled setting explicitly designed to hold events constant (Ch. 2)

Language   The systematic, meaningful arrangement of symbols, which provides the basis for communication (Ch. 6)

Language-acquisition device (LAD)   A neural system of the brain hypothesized to permit understanding of language (Ch. 6)

Lateralization   The process whereby certain functions are located more in one hemisphere of the brain than in the other (Ch. 8)

Learning disabilities   Difficulties in the acquisition and use of listening, speaking, reading, writing, reasoning, or mathematical abilities (Ch. 11)

Learning theory approach   The theory that language acquisition follows the basic laws of reinforcement and conditioning (Ch. 6)

Least restrictive environment   The setting most similar to that of children without special needs (Ch. 11)

Longitudinal research   Research in which the behavior of one or more individuals is measured as the subjects age (Ch. 2)

Low-birthweight infants   Infants who weigh less than 2,500 grams (around 5 1/2 pounds) at birth (Ch. 4)

Mainstreaming   An educational approach in which exceptional children are integrated as much as possible into the traditional educational system and are provided with a broad range of educational alternatives (Ch. 11)

Masturbation   Sexual self-stimulation (Ch. 16)

Maturation   The process of the predetermined unfolding of genetic information (Ch. 1)

Memory   The process by which information is initially recorded, stored, and retrieved (Ch. 6, 12)

Menarche   The onset of menstruation (Ch. 14)

Mental age   The typical intelligence level found for people of a given chronological age (Ch. 12)

Mental representation   An internal image of a past event or object (Ch. 6)

Mental retardation (intellectual disability)   A significantly subaverage level of intellectual functioning that occurs with related limitations in two or more skill areas (Ch. 12)

Metacognition   The knowledge that people have about their own thinking processes and their ability to monitor their cognition (Ch. 15)

Metalinguistic awareness   An understanding of one's own use of language (Ch. 12)

Metamemory   An understanding about the processes that underlie memory that emerges and improves during middle childhood (Ch. 12)

Mild retardation   Intellectual disability with IQ scores in the range of 50 or 55 to 70 (Ch. 12)

Moderate retardation   Intellectual disability with IQ scores from around 35 or 40 to 50 or 55 (Ch. 12)

Monozygotic twins   Twins who are genetically identical (Ch. 3)

Moral development   The maturation of people's sense of justice, of what is right and wrong, and their behavior in connection with such issues (Ch. 10)

Moratorium   The status of adolescents who may have explored various identity alternatives to some degree, but have not yet committed themselves (Ch. 16)

Multicultural education   Education in which the goal is to help students from minority cultures develop competence in the culture of the majority group while maintaining positive group identities that build on their original cultures (Ch. 12)

Multifactorial transmission   The determination of traits by a combination of genetic and environmental factors in which a genotype provides a range within which a phenotype may be expressed (Ch. 3)

Multimodal approach to perception   The approach that considers how information that is collected by various individual sensory systems is integrated and coordinated (Ch. 5)

Mutual regulation model   The model in which infants and parents learn to communicate emotional states to one another and to respond appropriately (Ch. 7)

Myelin   A fatty substance that helps insulate neurons and speeds the transmission of nerve impulses (Ch. 15)

Myelin   Protective insulation that surrounds parts of neurons (Ch. 8)

Nativist approach   The theory that a genetically determined, innate mechanism directs language development (Ch. 6)

Naturalistic observation   Studies in which researchers observe some naturally occurring behavior without intervening or making changes in the situation (Ch. 2)

Neglected adolescents   Children who receive relatively little attention from their peers in the form of either positive or negative interactions (Ch. 16)

Neonate   The term used for newborns (Ch. 4)

Neuron   The basic nerve cell of the nervous system (Ch. 5)

Night terror   An intense physiological arousal that causes a child to awaken in a state of panic (Ch. 8)

Nightmare   A vivid bad dream, usually occurring toward morning (Ch. 8)

Nonorganic failure to thrive   A disorder in which infants stop growing due to a lack of stimulation and attention as the result of inadequate parenting (Ch. 5)

Norms   The average performance of a large sample of children of a given age (Ch. 5)

Obesity   A body weight more than 20% higher than the average weight for a person of a given age and height (Ch. 8)

Object permanence   The realization that people and objects exist even when they cannot be seen (Ch. 6)

Onlooker play   Action in which children simply watch others at play but do not actually participate themselves (Ch. 10)

Operant conditioning   A form of learning in which a voluntary response is strengthened or weakened, depending on its association with positive or negative consequences (Ch. 2, 4)

Operations   Organized, formal, logical mental processes (Ch. 9)

Overextension   The overly broad use of words, overgeneralizing their meaning (Ch. 6)

Parallel play   Action in which children play with similar toys, in a similar manner, but do not interact with each other (Ch. 10)

Peer pressure   The influence of one's peers to conform to their behavior and attitudes (Ch. 16)

Perception   The sorting out, interpretation, analysis, and integration of stimuli involving the sense organs and brain (Ch. 5)

Permissive parents   Parents who provide lax and inconsistent feedback and require little of their children (Ch. 10)

Personal fables   The view held by some adolescents that what happens to them is unique, exceptional, and shared by no one else (Ch. 15)

Personality development   Development involving the ways that the enduring characteristics that differentiate one person from another change over the life span (Ch. 1)

Personality   The sum total of the enduring characteristics that differentiate one individual from another (Ch. 7)

Phenotype   An observable trait; the trait that actually is seen (Ch. 3)

Physical development   Development involving the body's physical makeup, including the brain, nervous system, muscles, and senses and the need for food, drink, and sleep (Ch. 1)

Placenta   A conduit between the mother and fetus, providing nourishment and oxygen via the umbilical cord (Ch. 3)

Plasticity   The degree to which a developing behavior or physical structure is modifiable (Ch. 1)

Plasticity   The degree to which a developing structure or behavior is modifiable due to experience (Ch. 5)

Pluralistic society model   The concept that American society is made up of diverse, coequal cultures that should preserve their individual features (Ch. 12)

Polygenic inheritance   Inheritance in which a combination of multiple gene pairs is responsible for the production of a particular trait (Ch. 3)

Postmature infants   Infants still unborn 2 weeks after the mother's due date (Ch. 4)

Pragmatics   The aspect of language relating to communicating effectively and appropriately with others (Ch. 9)

Preoperational stage   According to Piaget, the stage that lasts from ages 2 to 7 during which children's use of symbolic thinking grows, mental reasoning emerges, and the use of concepts increases (Ch. 9)

Preterm infants   Infants who are born prior to 38 weeks after conception (also known as premature infants) (Ch. 4)

Primary sex characteristics   Characteristics that are associated with the development of the organs and structures of the body that directly relate to reproduction (Ch. 14)

Principle of hierarchical integration   The principle that simple skills typically develop separately and independently but are later integrated into more complex skills (Ch. 5)

Principle of the independence of systems   The principle that different body systems grow at different rates (Ch. 5)

Private speech   Spoken language that is not intended for others and is commonly used by children during the preschool years (Ch. 9)

Profound retardation   Intellectual disability with IQ scores below 20 or 25 (Ch. 12)

Prosocial behavior   Helping behavior that benefits others (Ch. 10)

Proximodistal principle   The principle that development proceeds from the center of the body outward (Ch. 5)

Psychoanalytic theory   The theory proposed by Freud that suggests that unconscious forces act to determine personality and behavior (Ch. 2)

Psychodynamic perspective   The approach to the study of development that states behavior is motivated by inner forces, memories, and conflicts of which a person has little awareness or control (Ch. 2)

Psychological maltreatment   Harm to children's behavioral, cognitive, emotional, or physical functioning that is caused by parents or other caregivers who use verbal or psychological abuse, hurtful actions, exploitation, or neglect (Ch. 8)

Psychophysiological methods   A research approach that focuses on the relationship between physiological processes and behavior (Ch. 2)

Psychosexual development   According to Freud, a series of stages that children pass through in which pleasure, or gratification, is focused on a particular biological function and body part (Ch. 2)

Psychosocial development   According to Erikson, development that encompasses changes both in the understandings individuals have of themselves as members of society and in their comprehension of the meaning of others' behavior (Ch. 10)

Psychosomatic disorders   Medical problems caused by the interaction of psychological, emotional, and physical difficulties (Ch. 14)

Puberty   The period of maturation during which the sexual organs mature (Ch. 14)

Race dissonance   The phenomenon in which minority children indicate preferences for majority values or people (Ch. 10)

Rapid eye movement (REM) sleep   The period of sleep that is found in older children and adults and is associated with dreaming (Ch. 5)

Realistic period   The stage in late adolescence and early adulthood during which people explore career options through job experience or training, narrow their choices, and eventually make a commitment to a career (Ch. 15)

Recessive trait   A trait within an organism that is present, but is not expressed (Ch. 3)

Reciprocal socialization   A process in which infants' behaviors invite further responses from parents and other caregivers, which in turn bring about further responses from the infants (Ch. 7)

Reference groups   Groups of people with whom one compares oneself (Ch. 16)

Referential style   A style of language use in which language is used primarily to label objects (Ch. 6)

Reflexes   Unlearned, organized involuntary responses that occur automatically in the presence of certain stimuli (Ch. 4 & 5)

Rejected adolescents   Children who are actively disliked, and whose peers may react to them in an obviously negative manner (Ch. 16)

Relational aggression   Nonphysical aggression that is intended to hurt another person's psychological well-being (Ch. 10)

Resilience   The ability to overcome circumstances that place a child at high risk for psychological or physical damage (Ch. 8)

Rhythms   Repetitive, cyclical patterns of behavior (Ch. 5)

Sample   A group of participants chosen for an experiment (Ch. 2)

Scaffolding   The support for learning and problem solving that encourages independence and growth (Ch. 9)

Scheme   An organized pattern of sensorimotor functioning (Ch. 6)

Scientific method   The process of posing and answering questions using careful, controlled techniques that include systematic, orderly observation and the collection of data (Ch. 2)

Scripts   Broad representations in memory of events and the order in which they occur (Ch. 9)

Secondary sex characteristics   The visible signs of sexual maturity that do not involve the sex organs directly (Ch. 14)

Secular trend   A statistical tendency observed over several generations (Ch. 14)

Secure attachment pattern   A style of attachment in which children use the mother as a kind of home base and are at ease when she is present; when she leaves, they become upset and go to her as soon as she returns (Ch. 7)

Self-awareness   Knowledge of oneself (Ch. 7)

Self-care children   Children who let themselves into their homes after school and wait alone until their caretakers return from work; previously known as latchkey children (Ch. 13)

Self-concept   A person's identity or set of beliefs about what one is like as an individual (Ch. 10)

Self-esteem   An individual's overall and specific positive and negative self-evaluation (Ch. 13)

Sensation   The physical stimulation of the sense organs (Ch. 5)

Sensitive period   A specific time when organisms are particularly susceptible to certain kinds of stimuli in their environment (Ch. 1)

Sensitive period   A specific, but limited, time, usually early in an organism's life, during which the organism is particularly susceptible to environmental influences relating to some particular facet of development (Ch. 5)

Sensorimotor stage (of cognitive development)   Piaget's initial major stage of cognitive development, which can be broken down into six substages (Ch. 6)

Separation anxiety   The distress displayed by infants when a customary care provider departs (Ch. 7)

Sequential studies   Studies in which researchers examine members of a number of different age groups at several points in time (Ch. 2)

Severe retardation   Intellectual disability with IQ scores that range from around 20 or 25 to 35 or 40 (Ch. 12)

Sex cleavage   Sex segregation in which boys interact primarily with boys and girls primarily with girls (Ch. 16)

Sexually transmitted infection (STI)   An infection that is spread through sexual contact (Ch. 14)

Sickle-cell anemia   A blood disorder that gets its name from the shape of the red blood cells in those who have it (Ch. 3)

Slow-to-warm babies   Babies who are inactive, showing relatively calm reactions to their environment; their moods are generally negative, and they withdraw from new situations, adapting slowly (Ch. 7)

Small-for-gestational-age infants   Infants who, because of delayed fetal growth, weigh 90% (or less) of the average weight of infants of the same gestational age (Ch. 4)

Social comparison   The desire to evaluate one's own behavior, abilities, expertise, and opinions by comparing them to those of others (Ch. 13)

Social competence   The collection of social skills that permit individuals to perform successfully in social settings (Ch. 13)

Social development   The way in which individuals' interactions with others and their social relationships grow, change, and remain stable over the course of life (Ch. 1)

Social problem-solving   The use of strategies for solving social conflicts in ways that are satisfactory both to oneself and to others (Ch. 13)

Social referencing   The intentional search for information about others' feelings to help explain the meaning of uncertain circumstances and events (Ch. 7)

Social smile   Smiling in response to other individuals (Ch. 7)

Social speech   Speech directed toward another person and meant to be understood by that person (Ch. 9)

Social-cognitive learning theory   An approach to the study of development that emphasizes learning by observing the behavior of another person, called a model (Ch. 2)

Socialized delinquents   Adolescent delinquents who know and subscribe to the norms of society and who are fairly normal psychologically (Ch. 16)

Sociocultural theory   An approach that emphasizes how cognitive development proceeds as a result of social interactions between members of a culture (Ch. 2)

Speech impairment   Speech that deviates so much from the speech of others that it calls attention to itself, interferes with communication, or produces maladjustment in the speaker (Ch. 11)

Stanford–Binet Intelligence Scale, Fifth Edition (SB5)   A test that consists of a series of items that vary according to the age of the person being tested (Ch. 12)

State   The degree of awareness an infant displays to both internal and external stimulation (Ch. 5)

States of arousal   Different degrees of sleep and wakefulness through which newborns cycle, ranging from deep sleep to great agitation (Ch. 4)

Stillbirth   The delivery of a child who is not alive, occurring in fewer than 1 delivery in 100 (Ch. 4)

Stranger anxiety   The caution and wariness displayed by infants when encountering an unfamiliar person (Ch. 7)

Stress   The physical response to events that threaten or challenge us (Ch. 14)

Stuttering   Substantial disruption in the rhythm and fluency of speech; the most common speech impairment (Ch. 11)

Sudden infant death syndrome (SIDS)   The unexplained death of a seemingly healthy baby (Ch. 5)

Survey research   Research in which a group of people chosen to represent some larger population are asked questions about their attitudes, behavior, or thinking on a given topic (Ch. 2)

Symbolic function   According to Piaget, the ability to use a mental symbol, a word, or an object to represent something that is not physically present (Ch. 9)

Synapse   The gap at the connection between neurons, through which neurons chemically communicate with one another (Ch. 5)

Syntax   The combining of words and phrases to form meaningful sentences (Ch. 9)

Tay-Sachs disease   A disorder that produces blindness and muscle degeneration prior to death; there is no treatment (Ch. 3)

Teacher expectancy effect   The phenomenon whereby an educator's expectations for a given child actually bring about the expected behavior (Ch. 12)

Telegraphic speech   Speech in which words not critical to the message are left out (Ch. 6)

Temperament   Patterns of arousal and emotionality that represent consistent and enduring characteristics in an individual (Ch. 3 & 7)

Tentative period   The second stage of Ginzberg's theory, spanning adolescence, in which people begin to think in pragmatic terms about the requirements of various jobs and how their own abilities might fit with those requirements (Ch. 15)

Teratogen   A factor that produces a birth defect (Ch. 3)

Theoretical research   Research designed specifically to test some developmental explanation and expand scientific knowledge (Ch. 2)

Theories   Explanations and predictions concerning phenomena of interest, providing a framework for understanding the relationships among an organized set of facts or principles (Ch. 2)

Theory of mind   Knowledge and beliefs about how the mind works and how it affects behavior (Ch. 7)

Transformation   The process whereby one state is changed into another (Ch. 9)

Treatment group   The group in an experiment that receives the treatment (Ch. 2)

Treatment   A procedure applied by an experimental investigator based on two different experiences devised for subjects or participants (Ch. 2)

Triarchic theory of intelligence   The belief that intelligence consists of three aspects of information processing: the componential element, the experiential element, and the contextual element (Ch. 12)

Trust-versus-mistrust stage   According to Erikson, the period during which infants develop a sense of trust or mistrust, largely depending on how well their needs are met by their caregivers (Ch. 7)

Ultrasound sonography   A process in which high-frequency sound waves scan the mother's womb to produce an image of the unborn baby, whose size and shape can then be assessed (Ch. 3)

Underextension   The overly restrictive use of words, common among children just mastering spoken language (Ch. 6)

Undersocialized delinquents   Adolescent delinquents who are raised with little discipline or with harsh, uncaring parental supervision (Ch. 16)

Uninvolved parents   Parents who show virtually no interest in their children, displaying indifferent, rejecting behavior (Ch. 10)

Universal grammar   Noam Chomsky's theory that all the world's languages share a similar underlying structure (Ch. 6)

Very-low-birthweight infants Infants who weigh less than 1,250 grams (around 2 1/4 pounds) or, regardless of weight, have been in the womb fewer than 30 weeks (Ch. 4)

Visual impairment Difficulties in seeing that may include blindness or partial sightedness (Ch. 11)

Wechsler Intelligence Scale for Children, Fourth Edition (WISC-IV) A test for children that provides separate measures of verbal and performance (nonverbal) skills, as well as a total score (Ch. 12)

X-linked genes Genes that are considered recessive and located only on the X chromosome (Ch. 3)

Zone of proximal development (ZPD) According to Vygotsky, the level at which a child can almost, but not fully, comprehend or perform a task without assistance (Ch. 9)

Zygote The new cell formed by the process of fertilization (Ch. 3)

Aalsma, M., Lapsley, D., & Flannery, D. (2006, April). Personal fables, narcissism, and adolescent adjustment. *Psychology in the Schools, 43,* 481–491.

AAMR (American Association on Mental Retardation). (2002). *Mental retardation: Definition, classification, and systems of support.* Washington, DC: Author.

Aboud, F., & Sankar, J. (2007, September). Friendship and identity in a language-integrated school. *International Journal of Behavioral Development, 31,* 445–453.

Aboud, F., Mendelson, M., & Purdy, K. (2003). Cross-race peer relations and friendship quality. *International Journal of Behavioral Development, 27,* 165–173.

Abril, C., & Gault, B. (2006, March). The state of music in the elementary school: The principal's perspective. *Journal of Research in Music Education, 54,* 6–20.

Achenbach, T. A. (1992). Developmental psychopathology. In M. H. Bornstein & M. E. Lamb (Eds.). *Developmental psychology: An advanced textbook.* Hillsdale, NJ: Erlbaum.

Ackerman, B. P., & Izard, C. E. (2004). Emotion cognition in children and adolescents: Introduction [Special issue]. *Journal of Experimental Child Psychology, 89,* 271–275.

Acocella, J. (2003, August 18 & 25). Little people. *The New Yorker,* 138–143.

Adams, G. R., Montemayor, R., & Gullotta, T. P. (Eds.). (1996). *Psychosocial development during adolescence.* Thousand Oaks, CA: Sage.

Adams, R. J., Mauer, D., & Davis, M. (1986). Newborns' discrimination of chromatic from achromatic stimuli. *Journal of Experimental Child Psychology, 41,* 267–281.

Adamson, L., & Frick, J. (2003). The still face: A history of a shared experimental paradigm. *Infancy, 4,* 451–473.

Adler, P. A., Kless, S. J., & Adler, P. (1992). Socialization to gender roles: Popularity among elementary school boys and girls. *Sociology of Education, 65,* 169–187.

Adler, S. A., Gerhardstein, P., & Rovee-Collier, C. K. (1998). Levels-of-processing effects in infant memory? *Child Development, 69,* 280–284.

Advocates for Youth. (2003). *Science and success: Sex educations and other programs that work to prevent teen pregnancy, HIV & sexually transmitted infections.* Washington DC. Retrieved March 4, 2006, from http://www.advocatesforyouth.org/publications/ScienceSuccess.pdf.

Aguiar, A., & Baillargeon, R. (2002). Developments in young infants' reasoning about occluded objects. *Cognitive Psychology, 45,* 267–336.

Ah-Kion, J. (2006, June). Body image and self-esteem: A study of gender differences among mid-adolescents. *Gender & Behaviour, 4,* 534–549.

Ahmed, E., & Braithwaite, V. (2004). Bullying and victimization: Cause for concern for both families and schools. *Social Psychology of Education, 7,* 35–54.

Ahn, W., Gelman, S., & Amsterlaw, J. (2000). Causal status effect in children's categorization. *Cognition, 76,* B35–B43.

Ainsworth, M. D. S., Blehar, M. C., Waters, E., & Wall, S. (1978). *Patterns of attachment: A psychological study of the strange situation.* Hillsdale, NJ: Erlbaum.

Aitken, R. J. (1995, July 7). The complexities of conception, *Science, 269,* 39–40.

Akinbami, L.J. (2006, December 12). The state of childhood asthma, United States, 1980–2005. *Advance Data from Vital and Health Statistics,* No. 381. Hyattsville, MD: National Center for Health Statistics.

Akmajian, A., Demers, R. A., & Harnish, R. M. (1984). *Linguistics.* Cambridge, MA: MIT Press.

Albers, L. L., & Krulewitch, C. J. (1993). Electronic fetal monitoring in the United States in the 1980s. *Obstetrics & Gynecology, 82,* 8–10.

Alberts, A., Elkind, D., & Ginsberg, S. (2007, January). The personal fable and risk-taking in early adolescence. *Journal of Youth and Adolescence, 36,* 71–76.

Alderfer, C. (2003). The science and nonscience of psychologists' responses to *The Bell Curve. Professional Psychology: Research & Practice, 34,* 287–293.

Ales, K. L., Druzin, M. L., & Santini, D. L. (1990). Impact of advanced maternal age on the outcome of pregnancy. *Surgery, Gynecology & Obstetrics, 171,* 209–216.

Alexander, G. M., & Hines, M. (2002). *Evolution and Human Behavior, 23,* 467–479.

Alfonso, V. C., Flanagan, D. P., & Radwan, S. (2005). The impact of the Cattell-Horn-Carroll theory on test development and interpretation of cognitive and academic abilities. In D. P. Flanagan & P. L. Harrison (Eds.), *Contemporary intellectual assessment: Theories, tests, and issues.* New York: Guilford Press.

Ali, L., and Scelfo, J. (2002, December 9). Choosing virginity. *Newsweek,* 6–64.

Allam, M., Marlier, L., & Schaal, B. (2006). Learning at the breast: Preference formation for an artificial scent and its attraction against the odor of maternal milk. *Infant Behavior & Development, 29,* 308–321.

Allen, M., & Bissell, M. (2004). Safety and stability for foster children: The policy context. *Future of Children, 14,* 49–74.

Allison, A. C. (1954). Protection afforded by sickle cell trait against subtertian malarial infection. *British Medical Journal, 1,* 290–294.

Allison, B., & Schultz, J. (2001). Interpersonal identity formation during early adolescence. *Adolescence, 36,* 509–523.

Altemus, M., Deuster, P. A., Galliven, E., Carter, C. S., & Gold, P. W. (1995). Suppression of hypothalamic pituitary adrenal axis responses to stress in lactating women. *Journal of Clinical Endocrinology and Metabolism, 80,* 2954–2959.

Altholz, S., & Golensky, M. (2004). Counseling, support, and advocacy for clients who stutter. *Health & Social Work, 29,* 197–205.

Alvarez-Leon, E. E., Roman-Vinas, B., & Serra-Majem, L. (2006). Dairy products and health: A review of the epidemiological evidence. *British Journal of Nutrition, 96*, Supplement, S94–S99.

Alverdy, J., Zaborina, O., & Wu, L. (2005). The impact of stress and nutrition on bacterial–host interactions at the intestinal epithelial surface. *Current Opinion in Clinical Nutrition and Metabolic Care, 8*, 205–209.

Amato, P., & Afifi, T. (2006, February). Feeling caught between parents: Adult children's relations with parents and subjective well-being. *Journal of Marriage and Family, 68*, 222–235.

Amato, P., & Booth, A. (1997). *A generation at risk.* Cambridge, MA: Harvard University Press.

American Academy of Family Physicians. (2002). *Position paper on neonatal circumcision.* Leawood, KS: American Academy of Family Physicians.

American Academy of Pediatrics. (1988). Infant exercise programs. *Pediatrics, 82*, 800–825.

American Academy of Pediatrics. (1997). Breast-feeding and the use of human milk. *Pediatrics, 100*, 1035–1039.

American Academy of Pediatrics. (1998, April). Guidance for effective discipline. *Pediatrics, 101*, 723–728.

American Academy of Pediatrics. (1999a). *Circumcision: Information for parents.* Washington, DC: Author.

American Academy of Pediatrics. (1999b). Media education. *Pediatrics, 104*, 341–343.

American Academy of Pediatrics. (2000). *Circumcision: Information for parents.* Washington, DC: Author.

American Academy of Pediatrics. (2001). Organized sports for children and preadolescents. *Pediatrics, 107*, 1459–1462.

American Academy of Pediatrics. (2004, June 3). Sports programs. Retrieved June 3, 2004, from http://www.medem.com/medlb/article_detaillb_for_printer.cfm?article_ID=ZZZD2QD5M7C&sub_cat=405.

American Academy of Pediatrics Committee on Fetus and Newborn. (2004). Hospital stay for healthy term newborns. *Pediatrics, 113*, 1434–2436.

American Academy of Pediatrics. (2005). Breastfeeding and the use of human milk: Policy Statement. *Pediatrics, 115*, 496–506.

American Association of University Women. (1992). *How schools shortchange women: The AAUW report.* Washington, DC: Author.

American College of Medical Genetics. (2006). *Genetics in Medicine, 8* (5), Supplement.

American College of Obstetricians and Gynecologists. (2002). *Guidelines for perinatal care.* Washington, DC: Author.

American College Testing Program. (2001). *National dropout rates.* Iowa City: Author.

American Psychiatric Association. (1994). *Diagnostic and statistical manual of mental disorders* (4th ed.). Washington, DC: Author.

American Psychological Association. (2008). Ethical principles of psychologists and code of conduct. In D.N. Bersoff (Ed.), *Ethical conflicts in psychology* (4th Ed). Washington, DC: American Psychological Association.

American Psychological Association Reproductive Choice Working Group. (2000). *Reproductive choice and abortion: A resource packet.* Washington, DC: American Psychological Association.

American SIDS Institute. (2004). Statistics on SIDS, based on data from the Centers for Disease Control and Prevention and the National Center for Health Statistics. Marietta, GA: American SIDS Institute.

Amitai, Y., Haringman, M., Meiraz, H., Baram, N., & Leventhal, A. (2004). Increased awareness, knowledge and utilization of preconceptional folic acid in Israel following a national campaign. *Preventive Medicine: An International Journal Devoted to Practice and Theory, 39*, 731–737.

Ammerman, R. T., & Patz, R. J. (1996). Determinants of child abuse potential: Contribution of parent and child factors. *Journal of Clinical Child Psychology, 25*, 300–307.

Amsterlaw, J., & Wellman, H. (2006). Theories of mind in transition: A microgenetic study of the development of false belief understanding. *Journal of Cognition and Development, 7*,139–172.

Anand, K. J. S., & Hickey, P. R. (1992). Halothane–morphine compared with high-dose sufentanil for anesthesia and post-operative analgesia in neonatal cardiac surgery. *New England Journal of Medicine, 326*, 1–9.

Anders, T. F., & Taylor, T. (1994). Babies and their sleep environment. *Children's Environments, 11*, 123–134.

Andersen, S. L., & Navalta, C. P. (2004). Altering the course of neurodevelopment: A framework for understanding the enduring effects of psychotropic drugs: Developmental aspects of addiction [Special issue]. *Journal of Developmental Neuroscience, 22*, 423–440.

Anderson, C. A., Funk, J. B., & Griffiths, M. D. (2004). Contemporary issues in adolescent video game playing: Brief overview and introduction to the special issue. *Journal of Adolescence, 27*,1–3.

Anderson, C., Berkowitz, L., Donnerstein, E., Huesmann, L., Johnson, J., Linz, D., et al. (2003). The influence of media violence on youth. *Psychological Science in the Public Interest, 4*, 81–110.

Anderson, D., & Pempek, T. (2005). Television and very young children. *American Behavioral Scientist, 48*, 505–522.

Anderson-Clark, T., Green, R., & Henley, T. (2008, March). The relationship between first names and teacher expectations for achievement motivation. *Journal of Language and Social Psychology, 27*, 94–99.

Andreou, E. (2006, July). Social preference, perceived popularity and social intelligence: Relations to overt and relational aggression. *School Psychology International, 27*, 339–351.

Andrews, G., Halford, G., & Bunch, K. (2003). Theory of mind and relational complexity. *Child Development, 74*, 1476–1499.

Anisfeld, M. (1996). Only tongue protrusion modeling is matched by neonates. *Developmental Review, 16*, 149–161.

Ansaldo, A.I., Arguin, M., & Roch-Locours. (2002). The contribution of the right cerebral hemisphere to the recovery from aphasia: a single longitudinal case study. *Brain Language, 82*, 206–22.

Apperly, I., & Robinson, E. (2003). When can children handle referential opacity? Evidence for systematic variation in 5- and 6-year-old children's reasoning about beliefs and belief reports. *Journal of Experimental Child Psychology, 85*, 297–311.

Archer, S. L., & Waterman, A. S. (1994). Adolescent identity development: Contextual perspectives. In C. B. Fisher & R. M. Lerner (Eds.), *Applied developmental psychology.* New York: McGraw-Hill.

Arcus, D. (2001). Inhibited and uninhibited children: Biology in the social context. In T. D. Wachs & G. A. Kohnstamm (Eds.), *Temperament in context.* Mahwah, NJ: Erlbaum.

Arenson, K. W. (2004, December 4). Worried colleges step up efforts over suicide. *The New York Times,* p. A1.

Arias, I. (2004). The legacy of child maltreatment: Long-term health consequences for women. *Journal of Women's Health, 13,* 468–473.

Ariès, P. (1962). *Centuries of childhood.* New York: Knopf.

Armstrong, V., Brunet, P., He, C., Nishimura, M., Poole, H., & Spector, F. (2006). What is so Critical?: A Commentary on the reexamination of critical periods. *Developmental Psychobiology, 48,* 326–331.

Arnett, J. J. (2000). Emerging adulthood: A theory of development from the late teens through the 20s. *American Psychologist, 55,* 469–480.

Arnett, J.J. (1995). Adolescents; uses of media for self-socialization. *Journal of Youth and Adolescence, 24,* 519–534.

Aronson, J. D. (2007), Brain imaging, culpability and the juvenile death penalty. *Psychology, Public Policy, and Law, 13,* 115–142.

Arseneault, L., Moffitt, T. E., & Caspi, A. (2003). Strong genetic effects on cross-situational antisocial behavior among 5-year-old children according to mothers, teachers, examiner–observers, and twins' self-reports. *Journal of Child Psychology and Psychiatry and Allied Disciplines, 44,* 832–848.

Arseneault, L., Tremblay, R. E., Boulerice, B., & Saucier, J.-F. (2002). Obstetrical complications and violent delinquency: Testing two developmental pathways. *Child Development, 73,* 496–508.

Asendorpf, J. (2002). Self-awareness, other-awareness, and secondary representation. In A. Meltzoffa & W. Prinz (Eds.), *The imitative mind: Development, evolution, and brain bases.* New York: Cambridge University Press.

Asendorpf, J. B., Warkentin, V., & Baudonniere, P. (1996). Self-awareness and other-awareness II: Mirror self-recognition, social contingency awareness, and synchronic imitation. *Developmental Psychology, 32,* 313–321.

Asher, S. R., & Rose, A. J. (1997). Promoting children's social–emotional adjustment with peers. In P. Salovey & D. J. Sluyter (Eds.), *Emotional development and emotional intelligence: Educational implications* (pp. 196–230). New York: Basic Books.

Asher, S. R., Singleton, L. C., & Taylor, A. R. (1982). *Acceptance vs. friendship.* Paper presented at the meeting of the American Research Association, New York.

Aslin, R. N. (1987). Visual and auditory development in infancy. In J. D. Osofsky (Ed.), *Handbook of infant development* (2nd ed.). New York: Wiley.

Ata, R., Ludden, A., & Lally, M. (2007, November). The effects of gender and family, friends, and media influences on eating behaviors and body image during adolescence. *Journal of Youth and Adolescence, 36,* 1024–1037.

Atkinson, R.C., & Shiffrin, R.M. (1971). The control of short-term memory. *Scientific American, 225,* 82–90.

Auestad, N., Scott, D. T., Janowsky, J. S., Jacobsen, C., Carroll, R. E., Montalto, M. B., et al. (2003). Visual cognitive and language assessments at 39 months: A follow-up study of children fed formulas containing long-chain polyunsaturated fatty acids to 1 year of age. *Pediatrics, 112,* e177–e183.

Augustyn, M. (2003). "G" is for growing. Thirty years of research on children and *Sesame Street. Journal of Developmental and Behavioral Pediatrics, 24,* 451.

Aujoulat, I., Luminet, O., Deccache, E. (2007). The perspective of patients on their experience of powerlessness. *Qualitative Health Research, 17,* 772–785.

Aviezer, O., Sagi, A., & Resnick, G. (2002). School competence in young adolescence: Links to early attachment relationships beyond current self-perceived competence and representations of relationships. *International Journal of Behavioral Development, 26,* 397–409.

Axia, G., Bonichini, S., & Benini, F. (1995). Pain in infancy: Individual differences. *Perceptual and Motor Skills, 81,* 142.

Aydt, H., & Corsaro, W. (2003). Differences in children's construction of gender across culture: An interpretive approach. *American Behavioral Scientist, 46,* 1306–1325.

Aylward, G. P., & Verhulst, S. J. (2000). Predictive utility of the Bayley Infant Neurodevelopmental Screener (BINS) risk status classifications: Clinical interpretation and application. *Developmental Medicine & Child Neurology, 42,* 25–31.

Ayoub, N. C. (2005, February 25). A pleasing birth: Midwives and maternity care in the Netherlands. *Chronicle of Higher Education,* p. 9.

Bacchus, L., Mezey, G., & Bewley, S. (2006). A qualitative exploration of the nature of domestic violence in pregnancy. *Violence Against Women, 12,* 588–604.

Bader, A. P. (1995). Engrossment revisited: Fathers are still falling in love with their newborn babies. In J. L. Shapiro, M. J. Diamond, & M. Grenberg (Eds.), *Becoming a father.* New York: Springer.

Baer, J. S., Sampson, P. D., Barr, H. M., Connor, P. D., & Streissguth, A. P. (2003). A 21-year longitudinal analysis of the effects of prenatal alcohol exposure on young adult drinking. *Archives of General Psychiatry, 60,* 377–385.

Bai, L. (2005). Children at play: A childhood beyond the Confucian shadow. *Childhood: A Global Journal of Child Research, 12,* 9–32.

Bailey, J. M., Kirk, K. M., Zhu, G., Dunne, M. P., & Martin, N.G. (2000). Do individual differences in sociosexuality represent genetic or environmentally contingent strategies? Evidence from the Australian twin registry. *Journal of Personality and Social Psychology, 78,* 537–545.

Baillargeon, R. (2008). Innate ideas revisited: For a principle of persistence in infants' physical reasoning. *Perspectives on Psychological Science, 3,* 2–13.

Baker, J., Mazzeo, S., & Kendler, K. (2007). Association between broadly defined bulimia nervosa and drug use disorders: Common genetic and environmental influences. *International Journal of Eating Disorders, 40,* 673–678.

Baker, T., Brandon, T., & Chassin, L. (2004). Motivational influences on cigarette smoking. *Annual Review of Psychology, 55,* 463–491.

Balaban, M. T., Snidman, N., & Kagan, J. (1997). Attention, emotion, and reactivity in infancy and early childhood. In P. J. Lang, R. F. Simons, & M. T. Balaban (Eds.), *Attention and orienting: Sensory and motivational processes.* Mahwah, NJ: Erlbaum.

Ballen, L., & Fulcher, A. (2006). Nurses and doulas: Complementary roles to provide optimal maternity care. *Journal of Obstetric, Gynecologic, & Neonatal Nursing: Clinical Scholarship for the Care of Women, Childbearing Families, & Newborns, 35,* 304–311.

Bamshad, M. J., & Olson, S. E. (2003, December). Does race exist? *Scientific American,* pp. 78–85.

Bandura, A. (1977). *Social learning theory.* Englewood Cliffs, NJ: Prentice Hall.

Bandura, A. (1991). Social cognitive theory of moral thought and action. In W. M. Kurtines & J. L. Gewirtz (Eds.), *Handbook of moral behavior and development.* Hillsdale, NJ: Erlbaum.

Bandura, A. (1994). Social cognitive theory of mass communication. In J. Bryant & D. Zillmann (Eds.), *Media effects: Advances in theory and research.* Hillsdale, NJ: Erlbaum.

Bandura, A. (2002). Social cognitive theory in cultural context [Special issue]. *Applied Psychology: An International Review, 51,* 269–290.

Bandura, A., Grusec, J. E., & Menlove, F. L. (1967). Vicarious extinction of avoidance behavior. *Journal of Personality and Social Psychology, 5,* 16–23.

Bandura, A., Ross, D., & Ross, S. (1963). Vicarious extinction of avoidance behavior. *Journal of Personality and Social Psychology, 67,* 601–607.

Baptista, T., Aldana, E., Angeles, F., & Beaulieu, S. (2008). Evolution theory: An overview of its applications in psychiatry. *Psychopathology, 41,* 17–27.

Barberá, E. (2003). Gender schemas: Configuration and activation processes. *Canadian Journal of Behavioural Science, 35,* 176–180.

Barker, V., Giles, H., & Noels, K. (2001). The English-only movement: A communication analysis of changing perceptions of language vitality. *Journal of Communication, 51,* 3–37.

Barlett, C., Harris, R., & Baldassaro, R. (2007). Longer you play, the more hostile you feel: Examination of first person shooter video games and aggression during video game play. *Aggressive Behavior, 33,* 486–497.

Barnett, R. C., & Rivers, C. (1992). The myth of the miserable working woman. *Working Woman, 2,* 62–65, 83–85.

Baron-Cohen, S. (2003). *The essential difference: Men, women and the extreme male brain.* London: Allen Lane/Penguin.

Baron-Cohen, S. (2005). Testing the extreme male brain (EMB) theory of autism: Let the data speak for themselves. *Cognitive Neuropsychiatry, 10,* 77–81.

Barr, R. G., & Hayne, H. (1999). Developmental changes in imitation from television during infancy. *Child Development, 70,* 1067–1081.

Barr, R., Marrott, H., & Rovee-Collier, C. (2003). The role of sensory preconditioning in memory retrieval by preverbal infants. *Learning & Behavior, 31,* 111–123.

Barrett, D. E., & Frank, D. A. (1987). *The effects of undernutrition on children's behavior.* New York: Gordon & Breach.

Barrett, D. E., & Radke-Yarrow, M. R. (1985). Effects of nutritional supplementation on children's responses to novel, frustrating, and competitive situations. *American Journal of Clinical Nutrition, 42,* 102–120.

Barton, R. (2007). Use of medication in children with psychiatric disorders. *Journal of Community Practice, 80,* 42, 44.

Bass, S., Shields, M. K., & Behrman, R. E. (2004). Children, families, and foster care: Analysis and recommendations. *The Future of Children, 14,* 5–30.

Bates, E., Marchman, V., Thal, D., Fenson, L., Dale, P., Reznick, J. S., et al. (1994). Developmental and stylistic variation in the composition of the early vocabulary. *Journal of Child Language, 21,* 85–123.

Bauer, P. J. (1996). What do infants recall of their lives? Memory for specific events by 1- to 2-year-olds. *American Psychologist, 51,* 29–41.

Bauer, P. J. (2004). Getting explicit memory off the ground: Steps toward construction of a neuro-developmental account of changes in the first two years of life [Social issue]. *Developmental Review: Memory Development in the New Millennium, 24,* 347–373.

Bauer, P. J., (2007) Recall in infancy: A neurodevelopmental account. *Current Directions in Psychological Science, 16,* 142–146.

Bauer, P. J., Wenner, J. A., Dropik, P. L., & Wewerka, S. S. (2000). Parameters of remembering and forgetting in the transition from infancy to early childhood. With commentary by Mark L. Howe. *Monographs of the Society for Research in Child Development, 65,* 4.

Bauman, K. J. (2001, March 29–31). *Home schooling in the United States: Trends and characteristics* (Working Paper No. 53). Paper presented at the annual meeting of the Population Association of America, Washington, DC.

Baumrind, D. (1971). Current patterns of parental authority. *Developmental Psychology Monographs, 4* (1, Pt. 2).

Baumrind, D. (1980). New directions in socialization research. *Psychological Bulletin, 35,* 639–652.

Bayley, N. (1969). *Manual for the Bayley Scales of Infant Development.* New York: The Psychological Corporation.

Bayley, N. (1993). *Bayley Scales of Infant Development (BSID-II)* (2nd ed.). San Antonio: Psychological Corporation.

Beal, C. R. (1994). *Boys and girls: The development of gender roles.* New York: McGraw-Hill.

Bearman, P., & Bruckner, H. (2004). *Study on teenage virginity pledge.* Paper presented at meeting of the National STD Prevention conference, Philadelphia, PA.

Bearman, P., & Bruckner, H. (2004). *Study on teenage virginity pledge.* Paper presented at meeting of the National STD Prevention Conference, Philadelphia, PA.

Beauchaine, T. P. (2003). Taxometrics and developmental psychopathology [Special issue]. *Development and Psychopathology, 15,* 501–527.

Becahy, R. (1992, August 3). AIDS epidemic. *Newsweek,* pp. 49.

Becker, B., & Luthar, S. (2007, March). Peer-perceived admiration and social preference: Contextual correlates of positive peer regard among suburban and urban adolescents. *Journal of Research on Adolescence, 17,* 117–144.

Beckman, M. (2004, July 30). Neuroscience: Crime, culpability, and the adolescent brain. *Science,* pp. 305, 596–599.

Begeny, J., & Martens, B. (2007, March). Inclusionary education in Italy: A literature review and call for more empirical research. *Remedial and Special Education, 28,* 80–94.

Begley, S. (1995, July 10). Deliver, then depart. *Newsweek,* p. 62.

Beilin, H., & Pufall, P. (Eds.). (1992). *Piaget's theory: Prospects and possibilities.* Hillsdale, NJ: Erlbaum.

Belcher, J. R. (2003). Stepparenting: Creating and recreating families in America today. *Journal of Nervous & Mental Disease, 191,* 837–838.

Belkin, L. (1999, July 25). Getting the girl. *The New York Times Magazine,* pp. 26–35.

Bell, A., & Weinberg, M. S. (1978). *Homosexuality: A study of diversities among men and women.* New York: Simon & Schuster.

Belle, D. (1999). *The after-school lives of children: Alone and with others while parents work.* Mahwah, NJ: Erlbaum.

Bellezza, F. S. (2000). Mnemonic devices. In A. E. Kazdin (Ed.), *Encyclopedia of psychology* Vol. 5, pp. 286–287. Washington, DC: American Psychological Association.

Belluck, P. (2000, October 18). New advice for parents: Saying "That's great!" may not be. *The New York Times,* p. A14.

Belsky, J. (2006). Early child care and early child development: Major findings from the NICHD Study of Early Child Care. *European Journal of Developmental Psychology, 3,* 95–110.

Belsky, J., Vandell, D. L., Burchinal, M., Clarke-Stewart, A. K., McCartney, K., & Owen, M. T. (2007). Are there long-term effects of early child care? *Child Development, 78,* 188–193.

Bender, H., Allen, J., McElhaney, K., Antonishak, J., Moore, C.,Kelly, H., et al. (2007, December). Use of harsh physical discipline and developmental outcomes in adolescence. *Development and Psychopathology, 19,* 227–242.

Benedict, H. (1979). Early lexical development: Comprehension and production. *Journal of Child Language, 6,* 183–200.

Benelli, B., Belacchi, C., Gini, G., & Lucangeli, D. (2006, February). "To define means to say what you know about things": The development of definitional skills as metalinguistic acquisition. *Journal of Child Language, 33,* 71–97.

Benenson, J. F., & Apostoleris, N. H. (1993, March). *Gender differences in group interaction in early childhood.* Paper presented at the biennial meeting of the Society for Research in Child Development, New Orleans.

Bengtson, V. L., Acock, A. C., Allen, K. R., & Dilworth-Anderson, P. (Eds.). (2004). *Sourcebook of family theory and research.* Thousand Oaks, CA: Sage.

Benjamin, J., Ebstein, R. P., & Belmaker, R. H. (2002). Personality genetics, 2002 [Special issue]. *Israel Journal of Psychiatry and Related Sciences, 39,* 271–219.

Benjet, C., & Kazdin, A. E. (2003). Spanking children: The controversies, findings and new directions. *Clinical Psychology Review, 23,* 197–224.

Bennet, S., & Assefi, N. (2005). School-based teenage pregnancy prevention programs: A systematic review of randomized controlled trials. *Journal of Adolescent Health, 36,* 72–81.

Bennett, A. (1992, October 14). Lori Schiller emerges from the torments of schizophrenia. *The Wall Street Journal,* pp. A1, A10.

Benson, E. (2003, March). 'Goo, gaa, grr?' *Monitor on Psychology,* 50–51.

Benson, H. (1993). The relaxation response. In D. Goleman & J. Guerin (Eds.), *Mind–body medicine: How to use your mind for better health.* Yonkers, NY: Consumer Reports Publications.

Berenbaum, S. A., & Bailey, J. M. (2003). Effects on gender identity of prenatal androgens and genital appearance: Evidence from girls with congenital adrenal hyperplasia. *Journal of Clinical Endocrinology and Metabolism, 88,* 1102–1106.

Berenson, P. (2005). *Understand and treat alcoholism.* New York: Basic Books.

Bergen, H., Martin, G., & Richardson, A. (2003). Sexual abuse and suicidal behavior: A model constructed from a large community sample of adolescents. *Journal of the American Academy of Child & Adolescent Psychiatry, 42,* 1301–1309.

Berger, L. (2000, April 11). What children do when home and alone. *The New York Times,* p. F8.

Bergmann, R. L., Bergmann, K. E., & Dudenhausen, J. W. (2008). Undernutrition and growth restriction in pregnancy. *Nestle Nutritional Workshop Series; Pediatrics Program, 61,* 103–121.

Berko, J. (1958). The child's learning of English morphology. *Word, 14,* 150–177.

Bernal, M. E. (1994, August). *Ethnic identity of Mexican American children.* Address at the annual meeting of the American Psychological Association, Los Angeles.

Berndt, T. J. (1999). Friends' influence on students' adjustment to school. *Educational Psychologist, 34,* 15–28.

Bernstein, N. (2004, March 7). Behind fall in pregnancy, a new teenage culture of restraint. *The New York Times,* pp. 1, 20.

Berry, G. L. (2003). Developing children and multicultural attitudes: The systemic psychosocial influences of television portrayals in a multimedia society. *Cultural Diversity and Ethnic Minority Psychology, 9,* 360–366.

Bertin, E., & Striano, T. (2006, April). The still-face response in newborn, 1.5-, and 3-month-old infants. *Infant Behavior & Development, 29,* 294–297.

Besag, Valerie E. (2006). *Understanding girls' friendships, fights and feuds: A practical approach to girls' bullying.* Maidenhead, BRK, England: Open University Press/McGraw-Hill Education.

Bhushan, B., & Khan, S. (2006, September). Laterality and accident proneness: A study of locomotive drivers. *Laterality: Asymmetries of body, brain and cognition, 11,* 395–404.

Bickham, D. S., Wright, J. C., & Huston, A. C. (2000). Attention, comprehension and the educational influences of television. In D. G. Singer & J. L. Singer (Eds.) Handbook of children and Media. Thousand Oaks, Ca: Sage.

Biddle, B. J. (2001). *Social class, poverty, and education.* London: Falmer Press.

Bierman, K. L. (2004). *Peer rejection: Developmental processes and intervention strategies.* New York: Guilford Press.

Bigelow, A., & Rochat, P. (2006). Two-month-old infants' sensitivity to social contingency in mother–infant and stranger–infant interaction. *Infancy, 9,* 313–325.

Bigler, R. S., Jones, L. C., & Lobliner, D. B. (1997). Social categorization and the formation of intergroup attitudes in children. *Child Development, 68,* 530–543.

Bijeljac-Babic, R., Bertoncini, J., & Mehler, J. (1993). How do 4-day-old infants categorize multisyllabic utterances? *Developmental Psychology, 29,* 711–721.

Birch, E. E., Garfield, S., Hoffman, D. R., Uauy, R., & Birch, D. G. (2000). A randomized controlled trail of early dietary supply of long-chain polyunsaturated fatty acids and mental development in term infants. *Developmental Medicine and Child Neurology, 42,* 174–181.

Biro, F., Striegel-Moore, R., Franko, D., Padgett, J., & Bean, J.(2006, October). Self-esteem in adolescent females. *Journal of Adolescent Health, 39,* 501–507.

Bishop, D. V. M., & Leonard, L. B. (Eds.). (2001). *Speech and language impairments in children: Causes, characteristics, intervention and outcome.* Philadelphia, PA: Psychology Press.

Bjorklund, D. (2006). Mother knows best: Epigenetic inheritance, maternal effects, and the evolution of human intelligence. *Developmental Review, 26,* 213–242.

Bjorklund, D. F. (1997a). In search of a metatheory of cognitive development (or Piaget is dead and I don't feel so good myself). *Child Development, 68,* 144–148.

Bjorklund, D. F. (1997b). The role of immaturity in human development. *Psychological Bulletin, 122,* 153–169.

Black, J. E., & Greenough, W. T. (1986). Induction of pattern in neural structure by experience: Implication for cognitive development. In M. E. Lamb, A. L. Brown, & B. Rogoff (Eds.), *Advances in developmental psychology* (Vol. 4). Hillsdale, NJ: Erlbaum.

Black, K. (2002). Associations between adolescent-mother and adolescent-best friend interactions. *Adolescence, 37,* 235–253.

Black, M. M., & Matula, K. (1999). *Essentials of Bayley Scales of Infant Development II assessment.* New York: Wiley.

Blaine, B. E., Rodman, J., & Newman, J. M. (2007). Weight loss treatment and psychological well-being: A review and meta analysis. *Journal of Health Psychology, 12,* 66–82.

Blair, P., Sidebotham, P., Berry, P., Evans, M., & Fleming, P. (2006). Major epidemiological changes in sudden infant death syndrome: A 20-year population-based study in the UK. *Lancet, 367,* 314–319.

Blake, J., & de Boysson-Bardies, B. (1992). Patterns in babbling: A cross-linguistic study. *Journal of Child Language, 19,* 51–74.

Blakemore, J. (2003). Children's beliefs about violating gender norms: Boys shouldn't look like girls, and girls shouldn't act like boys. *Sex Roles, 48,* 411–419.

Blakeslee, S. (1995, August 29). In brain's early growth, timetable may be crucial. *The New York Times,* pp. C1, C3.

Blass, E. M., Ganchrow, J. R., & Steiner, J. E. (1984). Classical conditioning in newborn humans 2–48 hours of age. *Infant Behavior and Development, 7,* 223–235.

Block, J. S., Weinstein, J., & Seitz, M. (2005). School and parent partnerships in the preschool years. In D. Zager (Ed.), *Autism spectrum disorders: Identification, education, and treatment* (3rd ed.). Mahwah, NJ: Erlbaum.

Bloom, L. (1993). *The transition from infancy to language: Acquiring the power of expression.* New York: Cambridge University Press.

Blount, B. G. (1982). Culture and the language of socialization: Parental speech. In D. A. Wagner & H. W. Stevenson (Eds.), *Cultural perspectives on child development.* San Francisco: Freeman.

Blumenthal, S. (2000). Developmental aspects of violence and the institutional response. *Criminal Behaviour & Mental Health, 10,* 185–198.

Blundon, J., & Schaefer, C. (2006). The role of parent–child play in children's development. *Psychology and Education: An InterdisciplinaryJournal, 43,* 1–10.

Blustein, D. I., & Palladino, D. E. (1991). Self and identity in late adolescence: A theoretical and empirical integration. *Journal of Adolescent Research, 6,* 437–453.

Bober, S., Humphry, R., & Carswell, H. (2001). Toddlers' persistence in the emerging occupations of functional play and self-feeding. *American Journal of Occupational Therapy, 55,* 369–376.

Boehm, K. E., & Campbell, N. B. (1995). Suicide: A review of calls to an adolescent peer listening phone service. *Child Psychiatry & Human Development, 26*(1), pp. 61–66.

Boehmer, U., Linde, R., & Freund, K. M. (2005). Sexual minority women's coping and psychological adjustment after a diagnosis of breast cancer. *Journal of Women's Health, 14,* 213–224.

Bogenschneider, K., Wu, M.Y., Raffaelli, M., & Tsay, J. C. (1998). Parent influences on adolescent peer orientation and substance use: The interface of parenting practices and values. *Child Development, 69,* 1672–1688.

Bogle, K. A. (2008). "Hooking Up": What educators need to know. *The Chronicle of Higher Education, 54,* A32

Bolle, M. B., Wessel, R. D., & Mulvihill, T. M. (2007). Transitional experiences of first-year college students who were homeschooled. *Journal of College Student Development, 48,* 637–654.

Bonanno, G., Galea, S., Bucciarelli, A., & Vlahov, D. (2006). Psychological resilience after disaster: New York City in the aftermath of the September 11th terrorist attack. *Psychological Science,17,* 181–186.

Bonke, B., Tibben, A., Lindhout, D., Clarke, A. J., & Stijnen, T. (2005). Genetic risk estimation by healthcare professionals. *Medical Journal of Autism, 182,* 116–118.

Bonnicksen, A. (2007). Oversight of assisted reproductive technologies: The last twenty years. *Reprogenetics: Law, policy, and ethical issues.* Baltimore, MD: Johns Hopkins University Press.

Bookstein, F. L., Sampson, P. D., Streissguth, A. P., & Barr, H. M. (1996). Exploiting redundant measurement of dose and developmental outcome: New methods from the behavioral teratology of alcohol. *Developmental Psychology, 32,* 404–415.

Booth, C., Kelly, J., & Spieker, S. (2003). Toddlers' attachment security to child-care providers: The safe and secure scale. *Early Education & Development, 14,* 83–100.

Bootzin, R. R., Manber, R., Perlis, M. L., Salvio, M., & Wyatt, J. K. (1993). Sleep disorders. In P. B. Sutker & H. E. Adams (Eds.), *Comprehensive handbook of psychopathology* (2nd ed.). New York: Plenum.

Bor, W., & Bor, W. (2004). Prevention and treatment of childhood and adolescent aggression and antisocial behaviour: A selective review. *Australian & New Zealand Journal of Psychiatry, 38,* 373–380.

Borden, M. E. (1998). *Smart start: The parents' complete guide to preschool education.* New York: Facts on File.

Bornstein, M., & Arterberry, M. (2003). Recognition, discrimination and categorization of smiling by 5-month-old infants. *Developmental Science, 6,* 585–599.

Bornstein, M. H. (2000). Infant into conversant: Language and nonlanguage processes in developing early communication. In N. Budwig & I. C. Uzgiris (Eds.), *Communication: An arena of development.* Westport, CT: Ablex Publishing.

Bornstein, M. H., & Bradley, R. H. (2003). *Socioeconomic status, parenting, and child development.* Mahwah, NJ: Erlbaum.

Bornstein, M. H., & Lamb, M. E. (1992a). *Development in infancy: An introduction.* New York: McGraw-Hill.

Bornstein, M. H., & Lamb, M. E. (1992b). *Developmental psychology: An advanced textbook.* Hillsdale, NJ: Erlbaum.

Bornstein, M. H., & Lamb, M. E. (Eds.). (2005). *Developmental science.* Mahwah, NJ: Erlbaum.

Bornstein, M. H., Haynes, O. M., O'Reilly, A. W., & Painter, K. M. (1996). Solitary and collaborative pretense play in early childhood: Sources of individual variation in the development of representational competence. *Child Development, 67,* 2910–2929.

Bornstein, M. H., Putnick, D. L., Suwalsky, T. D., & Gini, M.(2006). Maternal chronological age, prenatal and perinatal history, social support, and parenting of infants. *Child Development,77,* 875–892.

Bos, C. S., & Vaughn, S. S. (2005). *Strategies for teaching students with learning and behavior problems* (6th ed). Boston: Allyn & Bacon.

Bostwick, J. (2006, February). Do SSRIs cause suicide in children? The evidence is underwhelming. *Journal of Clinical Psychology, 62,* 235–241.

Bouchard, C., Tremblay, A., Despres, J. P., Nadeau, A., Lupien, P. J., Theriault, J., et al. (1990). The response to long-term overfeeding in identical twins. *New England Journal of Medicine, 322,* 1477–1482.

Bouchard, T. J., Jr. (1997, September/October). Whenever the twain shall meet. *The Sciences,* 52–57.

Bouchard, T. J., Jr. Genes, environment, and personality. *Science, 264,* 1700–1701.

Bouchard, T. J., Jr. (2004). Genetic influence on human psychological traits: A survey. *Current Directions in Psychological Science, 13,* 148–153.

Bouchard, T. J., Jr., & McGue, M. (1981). Familial studies of intelligence: A review. *Science, 264*, 1700–1701.

Bourne, V., & Todd, B. (2004). When left means right: An explanation of the left cradling bias in terms of right hemisphere specializations. *Developmental Science 7*, 19–24.

Bower, B. (1985). The left hand of math and verbal talent. *Science News, 127*, 263.

Bower, T. G. R. (1977). *A primer of infant development.* San Francisco: Freeman.

Bowlby, J. (1951). Maternal care and mental health. *Bulletin of the World Health Organization, 3*, 355–534.

Bowlby, R. (2007). Babies and toddlers in non-parental daycare can avoid stress and anxiety if they develop a lasting secondary attachment bond with one carer who is consistently accessible to them. [Special issue]. The Life and Work of John Bowlby: A Tribute to his Centenary. *Attachment & Human Development, 9*, 307–319.

Bracey, J., Bamaca, M., & Umana-Taylor, A. (2004). Examining ethnic identity and self-esteem among biracial and monoracial adolescents. *Journal of Youth & Adolescence, 33*, 123–132.

Bracken, B., & Brown, E. (2006, June). Behavioral identification and assessment of gifted and talented students. *Journal of Psychoeducational Assessment, 24*, 112–122.

Bracken, B., & Lamprecht, M. (2003). Positive self-concept: An equal opportunity construct. *School Psychology Quarterly, 18*, 103–121.

Brackett, M., & Katulak, N. (2007). Emotional intelligence in the classroom: skill-based training for teachers and students. *Applying emotional intelligence: A practitioner's guide* (pp. 1–27). New York: Psychology Press.

Brady, S. (2007). Young adults' media use and attitudes toward interpersonal and institutional forms of aggression. *Aggressive Behavior, 33*, 519–525.

Brainerd, C. (2003). Jean Piaget, learning research, and American education. In B. Zimmerman (Ed.), *Educational psychology: A century of contributions.* Mahwah, NJ: Erlbaum.

Branje, S. J. T., van Lieshout, C. F. M., van Aken, M. A. G., & Haselager, G. J. T. (2004). Perceived support in sibling relationships and adolescent adjustment. *Journal of Child Psychology and Psychiatry, 45*, 1385–1396.

Branstetter, E. (1969). The young child's response to hospitalization: Separation anxiety or lack of mothering care? *American Journal of Public Health, 59*, 92–97.

Branta, C. F., Lerner, J. V., & Taylor, C. S. (Eds.). (1997). *Physical activity and youth sports: Social and moral issues.* Mahwah, NJ: Erlbaum.

Bray, G. (2008). Causes of childhood obesity. *Obesity in childhood and adolescence, Vol 1: Medical, biological, and social issues* (pp. 25–57). Westport, CT: Praeger/Greenwood Publishing Group.

Brazelton, T. B. (1973). *The Neonatal Behavioral Assessment Scale.* Philadelphia: Lippincott.

Brazelton, T. B. (1983). *Infants and mothers: Differences in development* (Rev. ed.). New York: Dell.

Brazelton, T. B. (1990). Saving the bathwater. *Child Development, 61*, 1661–1671.

Brazelton, T. B. (1997). *Toilet training your child.* New York: Consumer Visions.

Brazelton, T. B., Christophersen, E. R., Frauman, A. C., Gorski, P. A., Poole. J. M., Stadtler, A. C., et al. (1999). Instruction, timeliness, and medical influences affecting toilet training. *Pediatrics, 103*, 1353–1358.

Brazelton, T. B., & Sparrow, J. D. (2003). *Discipline: The Brazelton way.* New York: Perseus.

Brazier, A., & Duff, A. J. A. (2005). Editorial: Working with childhood chronic illness: Psychosocial approaches. *Clinical Child Psychology & Psychiatry, 10*, 5–8.

Breedlove, G. (2005). Perceptions of social support from pregnant and parenting teens using community-based doulas. *Journal of Perinatal Education, 14*, 15–22.

Bremmer, J. D. (2003). Long-term effects of childhood abuse on brain and neurobiology. *Child Adolescent Psychiatric Clinics of North America, 12*, 271–292.

Bremner, G., & Fogel, A. (Eds.). (2004). *Blackwell handbook of infant development.* Malden, MA: Blackwell.

Bridges, J. S. (1993). Pink or blue: Gender-stereotypic perceptions of infants as conveyed by birth congratulations cards. *Psychology of Women Quarterly, 17*, 193–205.

Brock, C., Lapp, D., Flood, J., Fisher, D., & Han, K. (2007, July). Does homework matter? An investigation of teacher perceptions about homework practices for children from nondominant backgrounds. *Urban Education, 42*, 349–372.

Brody, N. (1993). Intelligence and the behavioral genetics of personality. In R. Plomin & G. E. McClearn (Eds.), *Nature, nurture, and psychology.* Washington, DC: American Psychological Association.

Bronfenbrenner, U. (1989). Ecological systems theory. In R. Vasta (Ed.), *Six theories of child development.* Greenwich, CT: JAI Press.

Bronfenbrenner, U. (2002). Preparing a world for the infant in the twenty-first century: The research challenge. In J. Goes-Pedro, J. K. Nugent, J. G. Young, & T. B. Brazelton, *The infant and family in the twenty-first century.* New York: Brunner-Routledge.

Bronfenbrenner, U., & Morris, P. (1998). The ecology of developmental processes. In W. Damon (Ed.), Handbook of child psychology: *Vol. 1. TTL* (5th ed., pp. XX). New York: Wiley.

Bronstein, P. (1999). Differences in mothers' and fathers' behaviors toward children: A cross-cultural comparison. In L. A. Peplau & S. C. De Bro (Eds.), *Gender, culture, and ethnicity: Current research about women and men.* Mountain View, CA: Mayfield.

Brook, U., & Tepper, I. (1997). High school students' attitudes and knowledge of food consumption and body image: Implications for school-based education. *Patient Education & Counseling, 30*, 282–288.

Brooks-Gunn, J. (2003). Do you believe in magic? What we can expect from early childhood intervention programs. *Social Policy Report, 17*, 1–16.

Brooks-Gunn, J., Klebanov, P. K., & Duncan, G. J. (1996). Ethnic differences in children's intelligence test scores: Role of economic deprivation, home environment, and maternal characteristics. *Child Development, 67*, 396–408.

Brown, B. (2004). Adolescents' relationship with peers. In R.M. Lerner & L. Stenberg (Eds.), *Handbook of Adolescent Psychology, 2nd Edition.* New York, NY: John Wiley & Sons.

Brown, C., Pikler, V., Lavish, L., Keune, K., & Hutto, C. (2008, January). Surviving childhood leukemia: Career, family, and future expectations. *Qualitative Health Research, 18*, 19–30.

Brown, J. D. (1998). *The self.* New York: McGraw-Hill.

Brown, J. L., & Pollitt, E. (1996, February). Malnutrition, poverty and intellectual development. *Scientific American*, pp. 38–43.

Brown, J. V., Bakeman, R., Coles, C. D., Platzman, K. A., & Lynch, M. E. (2004). Prenatal cocaine exposure: A comparison of 2-year-old children in prenatal and non-parental care. *Child Development, 75,* 1282–1295.

Brown, M. J. (2008). Childhood lead poisoning prevention: Getting the job done by 2010. *Journal of Environmental Health.* 7056–7057.

Brown, R. (1973). *A first language.* Cambridge, MA: Harvard University Press.

Brown, W. M., Hines, M., & Fane, B. A. (2002). Masculinzed finger-length patterns in human male and females with congenital adrenal hyperplasia. *Hormones and Behavior, 42,* 380–386.

Browne, K. (2006, March). Evolved sex differences and occupational segregation. *Journal of Organizational Behavior, 27,*143–162.

Brownlee, S. (2002, January 21). Too heavy, too young. *Time,* pp. 21–23.

Bruck, M., & Ceci, S. (2004). Forensic developmental psychology: Unveiling four common misconceptions. *Current Directions in Psychological Science, 13,* 229–232.

Brueggemann, I. (1999). Failure to meet ICPD goals will affect global stability, health of environment, and well-being, rights and potential of people. *Asian Forum News,* 8.

Brune, C., & Woodward, A. (2007). Social cognition and social responsiveness in 10-month-old infants. *Journal of Cognition and Development, 8,* 133–158.

Bruskas, D. (2008, May). Children in foster care: A vulnerable population at risk. *Journal of Child and Adolescent Psychiatric Nursing, 21,* 70–77.

Bryant, J., & Bryant, J. (2003). Effects of entertainment televisual media on children. In E. Palmer & B. Young (Eds.), *The faces of televisual media: Teaching, violence, selling to children.* Mahwah, NJ: Erlbaum.

Bryant, J., & Bryant, J. A. (Eds.). (2001). *Television and the American family* (2nd ed.). Mahwah, NJ: Erlbaum.

Buchanan, C. M., Eccles, J. S., & Becker, J. B. (1992). Are adolescents the victims of raging hormones? Evidence for activational effects of hormones on moods and behavior at adolescence. *Psychological Bulletin, 111,* 62–107.

Bukowski, W. M., Sippola, L. K., & Newcomb, A. F. (2000). Variations in patterns of attraction to same- and other-sex peers during early adolescence. *Developmental Psychology, 36,* 147–154.

Bullinger, A. (1997). Sensorimotor function and its evolution. In J. Guimon (Ed.), *The body in psychotherapy* (pp. 25–29). Basil, Switzerland: Karger.

Bumpus, M.F., Crouter, A.C., & McHale, S.M. (2001). Parental autonomy grating during adolescence: Exploring gender differences in context. *Developmental Psychology, 37,* 163–173.

Burd, L., Cotsonas-Hassler, T. M., Martsolf, J. T., & Kerbeshian, J. (2003). Recognition and management of fetal alcohol syndrome. *Neurotoxicological Teratology, 25,* 681–688.

Burdjalov, V. F., Baumgart, S., & Spitzer, A. R. (2003). Cerebral function monitoring: A new scoring system for the evaluation of brain maturation in neonates. *Pediatrics, 112,* 855–861.

Burgess, K. B., & Rubin, K. H. (2000). Middle childhood: Social and emotional development. In A. E. Kazdin (Ed.), *Encyclopedia of psychology, Vol. 5.* Washington, DC: American Psychological Association.

Burke, V., Beilin, L., Durkin, K., Stritzke, W., Houghton, S., & Cameron, C. (2006, November). Television, computer use, physical activity, diet and fatness in Australian adolescents. *International Journal of Pediatric Obesity, 1,* 248–255.

Burn, S. M. (1996). *The social psychology of gender.* New York: McGraw-Hill.

Burnham, M., Goodlin-Jones, B., & Gaylor, E. (2002). Nighttime sleep-wake patterns and self-soothing from birth to one year of age: A longitudinal intervention study. *Journal of Child Psychology & Psychiatry & Allied Disciplines, 43,* 713–725.

Burns, E. (2003). *A handbook for supplementary aids and services: A best practice and IDEA guide to enable children with disabilities to be educated with nondisabled children to the maximum extent appropriate.* Springfield, IL: Charles C. Thomas.

Bushman, B. J., & Anderson, C. A. (2002). Violent video games and hostile expectations: A test of the General Aggression Model. *Personality and Social Psychology Bulletin, 28,* 1679–1689.

Buss, D. M. (2003). The dangerous passion: Why jealousy is as necessary as love and sex: Book review. *Archives of Sexual Behavior, 32,* 79–80.

Buss, D. M., & Reeve, H. K. (2003). Evolutionary psychology and developmental dynamics: Comment on Lickliter and Honeycutt. *Psychological Bulletin, 129,* 848–853.

Buss, K. A., & Kiel, E. J. (2004). Comparison of sadness, anger, and fear facial expressions when toddlers look at their mothers. *Child Development, 75,* 1761–1773.

Bussey, K. (1992). Lying and truthfulness: Children's definition, standards, and evaluative reactions. *Child Development, 63,* 1236–1250.

Butler, K. G., & Silliman, E. R. (Eds.). (2002). *Speaking, reading, and writing in students with language and learning disabilities: New paradigms for research and practice.* Mahwah, NJ: Lawrence Erlbaum.

Butterworth, G. (1994). Infant intelligence. In J. Khalfa (Ed.), *What is intelligence? The Darwin College lecture series* (pp. 49–71). Cambridge, England: Cambridge University Press.

Buysse, D. J. (2005). Diagnosis and assessment of sleep and circadian rhythm disorders. *Journal of Psychiatric Practice, 11,* 102–115.

Byrd, R. S., Weitzman, M., & Auinger, P. (1997). Increased behavior problems associated with delayed school entry and delayed school progress. *Pediatrics, 100,* 654–661.

Byrne, B. (2000). Relationships between anxiety, fear, self-esteem, and coping strategies in adolescence. *Adolescence, 35,* 201–215.

Cabrera, N., Shannon, J., & Tamis-LeMonda, C. (2007). Fathers' influence on their children's cognitive and emotional development: From toddlers to pre-K. *Applied Developmental Science, 11,* 208–213.

Cadinu, M. R., & Kiesner, J. (2000). Children's development of a theory of mind. *European Journal of Psychology of Education, 15,* 93–111.

Cai, Y., Reeve., J. M., & Robinson, D. T. (2002). Home schooling and teaching style: Comparing the motivating styles of home school and public school teachers. *Journal of Educational Psychology, 94,* 372–380.

Caino, S., Kelmansky, D., Lejarraga, H., & Adamo, P. (2004). Short-term growth at adolescence in healthy girls. *Annals of Human Biology, 31,* 182–195.

Calhoun, F., & Warren, K. (2007). Fetal alcohol syndrome: Historical perspectives. *Neuroscience & Biobehavioral Reviews, 31,* 168–171.

Callister, L. C., Khalaf. I., Semenic, S., Kartehner, R., & Vehvilainen-Julkunen, K. (2003). The pain of childbirth: Perceptions of culturally diverse women. *Pain Management Nursing, 4,* 145–154.

Calvert, S. L., Kotler, J. A., Zehnder, S., & Shockey, E. (2003). Gender stereotyping in children's reports about educational and informational television programs. *Media Psychology, 5,* 139–162.

Cami, J., & Farré, M. (2003). Drug addiction. *New England Journal of Medicine, 349*, 975–986.

Campbell, A., Shirley, L., & Candy, J. (2004). A longitudinal study of gender-related cognition and behavior. *Developmental Science, 7*, 1–9.

Campbell, D., Scott, K., Klaus, M., & Falk, M. (2007). Female relatives or friends trained as labor doulas: Outcomes at 6 to 8 weeks postpartum. *Birth: Issues in Perinatal Care, 34*, 220–227.

Campbell, F., Ramey, C., & Pungello, E. (2002). Early childhood education: Young adult outcomes from the Abecedarian Project. *Applied Developmental Science, 6*, 42–57.

Campbell, K., Crawford, D., & Ball, K. (2006, August). Family food environment and dietary behaviors likely to promote fatness in 5–6-year-old children. *International Journal of Obesity, 30*, 1272–1280.

Campos, J. J., Langer, A., & Krowitz, A. (1970). Cardiac responses on the visual cliff in prelocomotor human infants. *Science, 170*, 196–197.

Camras, L., Meng, Z., & Ujiie, T. (2002). Observing emotion in infants: Facial expression, body behavior, and rater judgments of responses to an expectancy-violating event. *Emotion, 2*, 179–193.

Canals, J., Fernandez-Ballart, J., & Esparo, G. (2003). Evolution of Neonatal Behavior Assessment Scale scores in the first month life. *Infant Behavior & Development, 26*, 227–237.

Canfield, R. L., Smith, E. G., Breznyak, M. P., & Snow, K. L. (1997). Information processing through the first year of life: A longitudinal study using the visual expectation paradigm. With commentary by Richard N. Aslin, Marshall M. Hairth, Tara S. Wass, & Scott A. Adler. *Monographs of the Society for Research in Child Development, 62*(2, Serial No. 250).

Canning, P., Courage, M., Frizzell, L., & Seifert, T. (2007). Obesity in a provincial population of Canadian preschool children: Differences between 1984 and 1997 birth cohorts. *International Journal of Pediatric Obesity, 2*, 51–57.

Caplan, L. J., & Barr, R. A. (1989). On the relationship between category intensions and extensions in children. *Journal of Experimental Child Psychology, 47*, 413–429.

Carlson, S. M., & Meltzoff, A. N. (2008). Bilingual experience and executive functioning in young children. *Developmental Science, 11*, 282–298.

Carnegie Task Force on Meeting the Needs of Young Children. (1994). *Starting points: Meeting the needs of our youngest children.* New York: Carnegie Corporation.

Carney, J. V. (2008). Perceptions of bullying and associated trauma during adolescence. *Professional School Counseling, 11*, 179–188.

Carney, R. N. & Levin, J. R. (2003) Promoting higher order learning benefits by building lower-order mnemonic connections. *Applied Cognitive Psychology, 17*, 563–575.

Carpendale, J. I. M. (2000). Kohlberg and Piaget on stages and moral reasoning. *Developmental Review, 20*, 181–205.

Carpenter, D. M., H., Flowers, N., & Mertens, S. B. (2004). High expectations for every student. *Middle School Journal, 35*, 64.

Carver, L., & Vaccaro, B. (2007, January). 12-month-old infants allocate increased neural resources to stimuli associated with negative adult emotion. *Developmental Psychology, 43*, 54–69.

Carver, L., Dawson, G., & Panagiotides, H. (2003). Age-related differences in neural correlates of face recognition during the toddler and preschool years. *Developmental Psychobiology, 42*, 148–159.

Case, R. (1999). Conceptual development. In M. Bennett (Ed.), *Developmental psychology: Achievements and prospects.* Philadelphia, PA: Psychology Press.

Case, R., Demetriou, A., & Platsidou, M. (2001). Integrating concepts and tests of intelligence from the differential and developmental traditions. *Intelligence, 29*, 307–336.

Case, R., & Okamoto, Y. (1996). The role of central conceptual structures in the development of children's thought. *Monographs of the Society for Research in Child Development, 61*, v–265.

Caspi, A. (2000). The child is father of the man: Personality continuities from childhood to adulthood. *Journal of Personality and Social Psychology, 78*, 158–172.

Caspi, A., & Moffitt, T. E. (1993). *Continuity amidst change: A paradoxical theory of personality coherence.* Manuscript submitted for publication.

Cassidy, J., & Berlin, L. J. (1994). The insecure/ambivalent pattern of attachment: Theory and research. *Child Development, 65*, 971–991.

Cath, S., & Shopper, M. (2001). *Step-parenting: Creating and recreating families in America today.* Hillsdale, NJ: Analytic Press, Inc.

Cauce, A, Domenech-Rodriguez, M. (2002). Latino families: myths and realities. In J. M. Contreras, K. A., Kerns & A. M. Neal-Barnett, (Eds.). *Latino children and families in the United States.* Westport, CT: Praeger.

Cavallini, A., Fazzi, E., & Viviani, V. (2002). Visual acuity in the first two years of life in healthy term newborns: An experience with the Teller Acuity Cards. *Functional Neurology: New Trends in Adaptive & Behavioral Disorders, 17*, 87–92.

Ceci, S. J., & Bruck, M. (1993). The suggestibility of the child witness: A historical review and synthesis. *Psychological Bulletin, 113*, 403–439.

Ceci, S. J., Fitneva, S. A., & Gilstrap, L. L. (2003). Memory development and eyewitness testimony. In A. Slater & G. Bremner (Eds.), *An introduction to developmental psychology.* Malden, MA: Blackwell Publishers.

Celera Genomics: International Human Genome Sequencing Consortium. (2001). Initial sequencing and analysis of the human genome. *Nature, 409*, 860–921.

Center for Media and Public Affairs. (1995, April 7). Adaptation analysis of violent content of broadcast and cable television stations on Thursday.

Centers for Disease Control & Prevention. (2003). Rates of teenage pregnancy. *Vital and Health Statistics, Series 10, no. 219.* Washington, DC: U.S. Department of Health and Human Services.

Centers for Disease Control & Prevention (CDC). (2004, June 11). Suicide and attempted suicide. *MMWR, 53*, 471.

Centers for Disease Control and Prevention. (1998). *Youth risk behavior surveillance—United States, 1997.* Atlanta: Author.

Cesario, S., & Hughes, L. (2007, May). Precocious puberty: A comprehensive review of literature. *Journal of Obstetric, Gynecologic, & Neonatal Nursing: Clinical Scholarship for the Care of Women, Childbearing Families, & Newborns, 36*, 263–274.

Chaiklin, S. (2003). The zone of proximal development in Vygotsky's analysis of learning and instruction. In A. Kozulin & B. Gindis (Eds.), *Vygotsky's educational theory in cultural context.* New York: Cambridge University Press.

Chall, J. (1992). The new reading debates: Evidence from science, art, and ideology. *Teachers College Record, 94*, 315–328.

Chall, J. S. (1979). The great debate: Ten years later, with a modest proposal for reading stages. In L. B. Resnick & P. A. Weaver (Eds.), *Theory and practice of early reading.* Hillsdale, NJ: Erlbaum.

Chan, D. W. (1997). Self-concept and global self-worth among Chinese adolescents in Hong Kong. *Personality & Individual Differences, 22,* 511–520.

Chao, R. K. (2001). Extending research on the consequences of parenting style for Chinese Americans and European Americans. *Child Development, 72,* 1832–1843.

Chatterji, M. (2004). Evidence on "What works": An argument for extended-term mixed-method (ETMM) evaluation designs. *Educational Researcher, 33,* 3–14.

Chen, J., & Gardner, H. (2005). Assessment based on multiple-intelligences theory. In D. P. Flanagan & P. L. Harrison (Eds.), *Contemporary intellectual assessment: Theories, tests, and issues.* New York: Guilford Press.

Chen, S. X., & Bond, M. H. (2007). Explaining language priming effects: Further evidence for ethnic affirmation among Chinese-English bilinguals, *Journal of Language and Social Psychology, 26,* 398–406.

Chen, X., Hastings, P. D., Rubin, K. H., Chen, H., Cen, G., & Stewart, S. L. (1998). Child-rearing attitudes and behavioral inhibition in Chinese and Canadian toddlers: A cross-cultural study. *Developmental Psychology, 34,* 677–686.

Cherney, I. (2003). Young children's spontaneous utterances of mental terms and the accuracy of their memory behaviors: A different methodological approach. *Infant & Child Development, 12,* 89–105.

Cherney, I., Kelly-Vance, L., & Glover, K. (2003). The effects of stereotyped toys and gender on play assessment in children aged 18 to 47 months. *Educational Psychology, 23,* 95–105.

Cheung, A., Emslie, G., & Mayes, T. (2006, January). The use of antidepressants to treat depression in children and adolescents. *Canadian Medical Association Journal, 174,* 193–200.

Chiu, M., & McBride-Chang, C. (2006). Gender, Context, and Reading: A Comparison of Students in 43 Countries. *Scientific Studies of Reading, 10,* 331–362.

Chien, S., Bronson-Castain, K., Palmer, J., & Teller, D. (2006). Lightness constancy in 4-month-old infants. *Vision Research, 46,*2139–2148.

Child Health USA. (2005). U.S. Department of Health and Human Services, Health Resources and Services Administration, Maternal and Child Health Bureau. *Child health USA 2005.* Rockville, MD: U.S. Department of Health and Human Services.

Chomsky, N. (1968). *Language and mind.* New York: Harcourt Brace Jovanovich.

Chomsky, N. (1978). On the biological basis of language capacities. In G. A. Miller & E. Lennenberg (Eds.), *Psychology and biology of language and thought* (pp. 199–220). New York: Academic Press.

Chomsky, N. (1991). Linguistics and cognitive science: Problems and mysteries. In A. Kasher (Ed.), *The Chomskyan turn.* Cambridge, MA: Blackwell.

Chomsky, N. (1999). On the nature, use, and acquisition of language. In W. C. Ritchie & T. J. Bhatia (Eds.), *Handbook of child language acquisition.* San Diego: Academic Press.

Choy, C. M., Yeung, Q. S., Briton-Jones, C. M., Cheung, C. K., Lam, C. W., & Haines, C. J. (2002). Relationship between semen parameters and mercury concentrations in blood and in seminal fluid from subfertile males in Hong Kong. *Fertility and Sterility, 78,* 426–428.

Christle, C., Jolivette, K., & Nelson, M. (2007, November). School characteristics related to high school dropout rates. *Remedial and Special Education, 28,* 325–339.

Cicchetti, D. (1996). Child maltreatment: Implications for developmental theory and research. *Human Development, 39,* 18–39.

Cicchetti, D., Rogosch, F. A., Maughan, A., Toth, S., & Bruce, J. (2003). False belief understanding in maltreated children [Special issue]. *Journal of Development and Psychopathology, 15,* 1067–1091.

Cillessen, A. H. N., & Mayeux, L. (2004). From censure to reinforcement: Developmental changes in the association between aggression and social status. *Child Development, 75,* 147–163.

Cina, V., & Fellmann, F. (2006). Implications of predictive testing in neurodegenerative disorders. *Schweizer Archiv für Neurologie und Psychiatrie, 157,* 359–365.

Cirulli, F., Berry, A., & Alleva, E. (2003). Early disruption of the mother–infant relationship: Effects on brain plasticity and implications for psychopathology. *Neuroscience & Biobehavioral Reviews, 27,* 73–82.

Clark, J. E., & Humphrey, J. H. (Eds.). (1985). *Motor development: Current selected research.* Princeton, NJ: Princeton Book Company.

Clark, K. B., & Clark, M. P. (1947). Racial identification and preference in Negro children. In T. M. Newcomb & E. L. Hartley (Eds.), *Readings in social psychology.* New York: Holt, Rinehart & Winston.

Clark, R., Hyde, J. S., Essex, M. J., & Klein, M. H. (1997). Length of maternity leave and quality of mother–infant interactions. *Child Development, 68,* 364–383.

Clarke, T-K., Treutlein, J., Zimmermann, U. S., Kiefer, F., Skowronek, M. H., Rietschel, M., et al. (2008). HPA-axis activity in alcoholism: Examples for a gene–environment interaction. *Addiction Biology, 13,* 1–14.

Clarke-Stewart, K., & Allhusen, V. (2002). Nonparental caregiving. In M. Bomstein (Ed.), *Handbook of parenting: Vol. 3: Being and becoming a parent* (2nd ed.). Mahwah, NJ: Erlbaum.

Claxton, L. J., Keen, R., & McCarty, M. E. (2003). Evidence of motor planning in infant reaching behavior. *Psychological Science, 14,* 354–356.

Clearfield, M., & Nelson, N. (2006, January). Sex differences in mothers' speech and play behavior with 6-, 9-, and 14-month-old infants. *Sex Roles, 54,* 127–137.

Click, E. (2006). Developing a Worksite Lactation Program. *MCN: The American Journal of Maternal/Child Nursing, 31,* 313–317.

Clifton, R. (1992). The development of spatial hearing in human infants. In L. A. Werner & E. W. Rubel (Eds.), *Developmental psychoacoustics* (pp. 135–157). Washington, DC: American Psychological Association.

Clinton, H. (1996). *It takes a village and other lessons children teach us.* New York: Touchstone.

Cnattingius, S., Berendes, H., & Forman, M. (1993). Do delayed childbearers face increased risks of adverse pregnancy outcomes after the first birth? *Obstetrics and Gynecology, 81,* 512–516.

Cohen, J. (1999). Nurture helps mold able minds. *Science, 283,* 1832–1833.

Cohen, L., & Cashon, C. (2003). Infant perception and cognition. In R. Lerner & M. Easterbrooks (Eds.), *Handbook of psychology:* Vol. 6, *Developmental psychology* (pp. 267–291). New York: Wiley.

Cohen, P., Cohen, J., Kasen, S., Velez, C. N., Hartmark, C., Johnson, et al. (1993). An epidemiological study of disorders in late childhood and adolescence: I. Age- and gender-specific prevalence. *Journal of Child Psychology and Psychiatry and Allied Disciplines, 34,* 851–867.

Cohen, S., Kamarck, T., & Mermelstein, R. (1983). A global measure of perceived stress. *Journal of Health and Social Behavior, 24,* 385–396.

Cohen, S., Tyrell, D. A., & Smith, A. P. (1993). Negative life events, perceived stress, negative affect, and susceptibility to the common cold. *Journal of Personality and Social Psychology, 64,* 131–140.

Cokley, K. (2003). What do we know about the motivation of African American students? Challenging the "anti-intellectual" myth. *Harvard Educational Review, 73,* 524–558.

Colby, A., & Damon, W. (1987). Listening to a different voice: A review of Gilligan's in a different voice. In M. R. Walsh (Ed.), *The psychology of women.* New Haven, CT: Yale University Press.

Colby, A., & Kohlberg, L. (1987). *The measurement of moral judgment* (Vols. 1–2). New York: Cambridge University Press.

Cole, C. F., Arafat, C., & Tidhar, C. (2003). The educational impact of Rechov Sumsum/Shara'a Simsim: A *Sesame Street* television series to promote respect and understanding among children living in Israel, the West Bank and Gaza. *International Journal of Behavioral Development, 27,* 409–422.

Cole, D. A., Maxwell, S. E., Martin, J. M., Peeke, L. G., Seroczynski, A. D., Tram, J. M., et al. (2001). The development of multiple domains of child and adolescent self-concept: A cohort sequential longitudinal design. *Child Development, 72,* 1723–1746.

Cole, M. (1992). Culture in development. In M. H. Bernstein & M. E. Lamb (Eds.), *Developmental psychology: An advanced textbook* (3rd ed.). Hillsdale, NJ: Erlbaum.

Cole, S. A. (2005). Infants in foster care: Relational and environmental factors affecting attachment. *Journal of Reproductive & Infant Psychology, 23,* 43–61.

Colino, S. (2002, February 26). Problem kid or label? *The Washington Post,* p. HE01.

Collins, W. (2003). More than myth: The developmental significance of romantic relationships during adolescence. *Journal of Research on Adolescence, 13,* 1–24.

Collins, W. A., Gleason, T., & Sesma, A. (1997). Internalization, autonomy, and relationships: Development during adolescence. In J. E. Grusec & L. Kuczynski (Eds.), *Parenting and children's internalization of values: A handbook of contemporary theory.* New York: Wiley.

Collins, W., & Andrew, L. (2004). Changing relationships, changing youth: Interpersonal contexts of adolescent development. *Journal of Early Adolescence, 24,* 55–62.

Colom, R., Lluis-Font, J. M., & Andrés-Pueyo, A. (2005). The generational intelligence gains are caused by decreasing variance in the lower half of the distribution: Supporting evidence for the nutrition hypothesis. *Intelligence, 33,* 83–91.

Coltrane, S., & Adams, M. (1997). Children and gender. In T. Arendell (Ed.), *Contemporary parenting: Challenges and issues. Understanding families: Vol. 9,* (pp. 219–253). Thousand Oaks, CA: Sage.

Committee to Study the Prevention of Low Birthweight. (1985). *Preventing low birthweight.* Washington, DC: National Academy Press.

Compton, R., & Weissman, D. (2002). Hemispheric asymmetries in global–local perception: Effects of individual differences in neuroticism. *Laterality, 7,* 333–350.

Condry, J., & Condry, S. (1976). Sex differences: A study of the eye of the beholder. *Child Development, 47,* 812–819.

Conel, J. L. (1930/1963). *Postnatal development of the human cortex* (Vols 1–6). Cambridge, MA: Harvard University Press.

Conner, K., & Goldston, D. (2007, March). Rates of suicide among males increase steadily from age 11 to 21: Developmental framework and outline for prevention. *Aggression and Violent Behavior, 12*(2), 193–207.

Coons, S., & Guilleminault, C. (1982). Developments of sleep–wake patterns and non-rapid-eye-movement sleep stages during the first six months of life in normal infants. *Pediatrics, 69,* 793–798.

Cooper, H., & Valentine, J. (2001). Using research to answer practical questions about homework. *Educational Psychologist, 36,* 143–153.

Corballis, M. (2002). *From hand to mouth: The origins of language.* Princeton, NJ: Princeton University Press.

Corballis, M. C. (2000). How laterality will survive the millennium bug. *Brain & Cognition, 42,* 160–162.

Corballis, P. (2003). Visuospatial processing and the right-hemisphere interpreter. *Brain & Cognition, 53,* 171–176.

Corbin, C. (1973). *A textbook of motor development.* Dubuque, IA: Brown.

Cordes, S., Gelman, R., Gallistel, C.R., & Whalen, J. (2001 Dec). Variability signatures distinguish verbal from nonverbal counting for both large and small numbers. *Psychonomic Bulletin Review, 8,* 698–707.

Cordón, I. M., Pipe, M., Sayfan, L., Melinder, A., & Goodman, G. S. (2004). Memory for traumatic experiences in early childhood. *Developmental Review, 24,* 101–132.

Costello, E., Compton, S., & Keeler, G. (2003). Relationships between poverty and psychopathology: A natural experiment. *Journal of the American Medical Association, 290,* 2023–2029.

Costello, E., Sung, M., Worthman, C., & Angold, A. (2007, April). Pubertal maturation and the development of alcohol use and abuse. *Drug and Alcohol Dependence, 88,* S50–S59.

Côté, J. (2005). Editor's introduction. *Identity, 5,* 95–96.

Cotrufo, P., Cella, S., Cremato, F., & Labella, A. (2007, December). Eating disorder attitude and abnormal eating behaviours in a sample of 11–13-year-old school children: The role of pubertal body transformation. *Eating and Weight Disorders, 12,* 154–160.

Couperus, J., & Nelson, C. (2006). Early brain development and plasticity. *Blackwell handbook of early childhood development.* New York: Blackwell Publishing.

Courchesne, E., Carper, R., & Akshoomoff, N. (2003). Evidence of brain overgrowth in the first year of life in autism. *Journal of the American Medical Association, 290,* 337–344.

Couzin, J. (2002). Quirks of fetal environment felt decades later. *Science, 296,* 2167–2169.

Couzin, J. (2004, July 23). Volatile chemistry: Children and antidepressants. *Science, 305,* 468–470.

Cowan, N., Saults, J., & Elliot, E. (2002). The search for what is fundamental in the development of working memory. In R. Kail & H. Reese (Eds.), *Advances in child development and behavior* (Vol. 29). San Diego: Academic Press.

Craig, C., & Sprang, G. (2007, April). Trauma exposure and child abuse potential: Investigating the cycle of violence. *American Journal of Orthopsychiatry, 77,* 296–305.

Crane, E., & Morris, J. (2006). Changes in maternal age in England and Wales—Implications for Down syndrome. *Down Syndrome: Research & Practice, 10,* 41–43.

Cratty, B. (1979). *Perceptual and motor development in infants and children* (2nd ed.). Englewood Cliffs, NJ: Prentice Hall.

Cratty, B. (1986). *Perceptual and motor development in infants and children* (3rd ed.). Englewood Cliffs, NJ: Prentice Hall.

Crawford, M., & Unger, R. (2004). *Women and gender: A feminist psychology* (4th ed). New York: McGraw-Hill.

Crawley, A., Anderson, D., & Santomero, A. (2002). Do children learn how to watch television? The impact of extensive experience with *Blue's Clues* on preschool children's television viewing behavior. *Journal of Communication, 52,* 264–280.

Crick, N. R., Casas, J. G., & Ku, H. (1999). Relational and physical forms of peer victimization in preschool. *Developmental Psychology, 35,* 376–385.

Crisp, A., Gowers, S., Joughin, N., McClelland, L., Rooney, B., Nielsen, S., et al. (2006, May). Anorexia nervosa in males: Similarities and differences to anorexia nervosa in females. *European Eating Disorders Review, 14,* 163–167.

Critser, G. (2003). *Fat land: How Americans became the fattest people in the world.* Boston: Houghton Mifflin.

Crockenberg, S., & Leerkes, E. (2003). Infant negative emotionality, caregiving, and family relationships. In A. Crouter & A. Booth (Eds.), *Children's influence on family dynamics: The neglected side of family relationships* (pp. 57–78). Mahwah, NJ: Erlbaum.

Crockett, L. J., & Crouter, A. C. (Eds.). (1995). *Pathways through adolescence: Individual development in relation to social contexts.* Hillsdale, NJ: Erlbaum.

Croizet, J., Després, G., Gauzins, M., Huguet, P., Leyens, J., & Méot, A. (2004). Stereotype threat undermines intellectual performance by triggering a disruptive mental load. *Personality and Social Psychology Bulletin, 30,* 721–731.

Crowley, K., Callaman, M. A., Tenenbaum, H. R., & Allen, E. (2001). Parents explain more often to boys than to girls during shared scientific thinking. *Psychological Science, 12,* 258–261.

Crowther, M., & Rodriguez, R. (2003). A stress and coping model of custodial grandparenting among African Americans. In B. Hayslip & J. Patrick (Eds.), *Working with custodial grandparents.* New York: Springer.

Culbertson, J. L., & Gyurke, J. (1990). Assessment of cognitive and motor development in infancy and childhood. In J. H. Johnson & J. Goldman (Eds.), *Developmental assessment in clinical child psychology: A handbook* (pp. 100–131). New York: Pergamon Press.

Curtis, W. J., & Cicchetti, D. (2003). Moving research on resilience into the 21st century: Theoretical and methodological considerations in examining the biological contributors to resilience. *Development and Psychopathology, 15,* 126–131.

Cyna, A. M., Andrew, M. I., & McAuliffe, G. L. (2006). Antenatal self-hypnosis for labour and childbirth: A pilot study. *Anaestheology Intensive Care, 34,* 464–469.

Cynader, M. (2000). Strengthening visual connections. *Science, 287,* 1943–1944.

Dailard, C. (2001). Sex education: Politicians, parents, teachers and teens. *The Guttmacher Report on Public Policy (Alan Guttmacher Institute), 4,* 1–4. Retrieved March 4, 2006, from http://www.guttmacher.org/pubs/tgr/04/1/gr040109.pdf

Dainton, M. (1993). The myths and misconceptions of the stepmother identity. *Family Relations, 42,* 93–98.

Daley, K. C. (2004). Update on sudden infant death syndrome. *Current Opinion in Pediatrics, 16,* 227–232.

Dalton, T. C., & Bergenn, V. W. (2007). *Early experience, the brain, and consciousness: An historical and interdisciplinary synthesis.* Mahwah, N.J.: Lawrence Erlbaum.

Damon, W. (1983). *Social and personality development.* New York: Norton.

Damon, W., & Hart, D. (1988). *Self-understanding in childhood and adolescence.* New York: Cambridge University Press.

Daniels, H. (Ed.). (1996). *An introduction to Vygotsky.* New York: Routledge.

Danish, S. J., Taylor, T. E., & Fazio, R. J. (2006). Enhancing adolescent development through sports and leisure. In G. R. Adams & M. D. Berzonsky (Eds.), *Blackwell handbook of adolescence.* Malden, MA: Blackwell.

Dapretto, M., Davies, M. S., Pfeifer, J. H., Scott, A. A., Sigman, M., Bookhermer, S. Y., & Iacobon, M. (2006). Understanding emotions in others: Mirror neuron dysfunction in children with autism spectrum disorders. *Nature and Neuroscience, 9,* 28–30.

Dare, W. N., Noronha, C. C., Kusemiju, O. T., & Okanlawon, O. A. (2002). The effect of ethanol on spermatogenesis and fertility in male Sprague-Dawley rats pretreated with acetylsalicylic acid. *Nigeria Postgraduate Medical Journal, 9,* 194–198.

Dasen, P. R. (1977). Are cognitive processes universal? A contribution to cross-cultural Piagetian psychology. In N. Warren (Ed.), *Studies in cross-cultural psychology* (Vol. 1). New York: Academic Press.

Dasen, P. R. (2000). Rapid social change and the turmoil of adolescence: A cross-cultural perspective. *International Journal of Group Tensions, 29,* 17–49.

Dasen, P. R., Inhelder, B., Lavallée, M., & Retschitzki, J. (1978). *Naissance de l 'Intelligence chez l' enfant baoulé de Côte d'Ivoire.* Berne, Switzerland: Huber.

Dasen, P. R., Ngini, L., & Lavallée, M. (1979). Cross-cultural training studies of concrete operations. In L. H. Eckenberger, W. J. Lonner, & Y. H. Poortinga (Eds.), *Cross-cultural contributions to psychology.* Amsterdam: Swets & Zeilinger.

Dasen, P.R. (2000). Rapid social change and the turmoil of adolescence: A cross-cultural perspective. *World Psychology, 7,* 114–122.

Davidson, J. K., Darling, C. A., & Norton, L. (1995). Religiosity and the sexuality of women: Sexual behavior and sexual satisfaction revisited. *Journal of Sex Research, 32,* 235–243.

Davidson, R. J. (2003). Affective neuroscience: A case for interdisciplinary research. In F. Kessel & P. L. Rosenfields (Eds.), *Expanding the boundaries of health and social science: Case studies in interdisciplinary innovation.* London: Oxford University Press.

Davies, P. G., Spencer, S. L., & Steele, C. M. (2005). Clearing the air: Identity safety moderates the effects of stereotype threat on women's leadership aspirations. *Journal of Personality & Social Psychology, 88,* 276–287.

Davies, P. T., Harold, G. T., Goeke-Morey, M. C., & Cummings, E. M. (2002). Child emotional security and interparental conflict. *Monographs of the Society for Research in Child Development, 67.*

Davis, A. (2003). *Your divorce, your dollars: Financial planning before, during, and after divorce.* Bellingham, WA: Self-Counsel Press.

Davis, C., Aronson, J., & Salinas, M. (2006, November). Shades of threat: racial identity as a moderator of stereotype threat. *Journal of Black Psychology, 32,* 399–417.

Davis, M., & Emory, E. (1995). Sex differences in neonatal stress reactivity. *Child Development, 66,* 14–27.

Davis-Kean, P. E., & Sandler, H. M. (2001). A meta-analysis of measures of self-esteem for young children: A framework for future measures. *Child Development, 72,* 887–906.

Davison, G. C. (2005). Issues and nonissues in the gay-affirmative treatment of patients who are gay, lesbian, or bisexual. *Clinical Psychology: Science & Practice, 12,* 25–28.

De Casper, A. J., & Fifer, W. P. (1980). Of human bonding: Newborns prefer their mothers' voices. *Science, 208,* 1174–1176.

De Casper, A. J., & Prescott, P. (1984). Human newborns' perception of male voices: Preference, discrimination, and reinforcing value. *Developmental Psychobiology, 17,* 481–491.

De Casper, A. J., & Spence, M. J. (1986). Prenatal material speech influences newborns' perception of speech sounds. *Infant Behavior and Development, 9,* 133–150.

De Gelder, B. (2000). Recognizing emotions by ear and by eye. In R. D. Lane & L. Nadel (Eds.), *Cognitive neuroscience of emotion. Series in affective science.* New York: Oxford University Press.

de Rosnay, M., Cooper, P., Tsigaras, N., & Murray, L. (2006, August). Transmission of social anxiety from mother to infant: An experimental study using a social referencing paradigm. *Behaviour Research and Therapy, 44,* 1165–1175.

De Roten, Y., Favez, N., & Drapeau, M. (2003). Two studies on autobiographical narratives about an emotional event by preschoolers: Influence of the emotions experienced and the affective closeness with the interlocutor. *Early Child Development & Care, 173,* 237–248.

De St. Aubin, E., McAdams, D. P., & Kim, T. C. (Eds.) (2004). *The generative society: Caring for future generations.* Washington, DC: American Psychological Association.

De Vries, M. W. (1984). Temperament and infant mortality among the Masai of East Africa. American *Journal of Psychiatry, 141,* 1189–1194.

Decarrie, T. G. (1969). A study of the mental and emotional development of the thalidomide child. In B. M. Foss (Ed.), *Determinants of infant behavior* (Vol. 4). London: Methuen.

Decety, J., & Jackson, P. L. (2006). A social-neuroscience perspective on empathy. *Current Directions in Psychological Science,15,* 54–61.

Deforche, B., De Bourdeaudhuij, I., & Tanghe, A. (2006, May). Attitude toward physical activity in normal-weight, overweight and obese adolescents. *Journal of Adolescent Health, 38,* 560–568.

Degroot, A., Wolff, M. C., & Nomikos. G. G. (2005). How early experience matters in intellectual development in the case of poverty. *Preventative Science, 5,* 245–252.

Dehue, F., Bolman, C., & Völlink, T. (2008, April). Cyberbullying: Youngsters' experiences and parental perception. *CyberPsychology & Behavior, 11,* 217–223.

Dehaene-Lambertz, G., Hertz-Pannier, L., & Dubois, J. (2006). Nature and nurture in language acquisition: Anatomical and functional brain-imaging studies in infants. *Neurosciences, 29* [*Special issue: Nature and nurture in brain development and neurological ldisorders*], 367–373.

DeHart, T., Pelham, B., & Tennen, H. (2006, January). What lies beneath: Parenting style and implicit self-esteem. *Journal of Experimental Social Psychology, 42,* 1–17.

Dejin-Karlsson, E., Hanson, B. S., Oestergren, P. O., Sjoeberg, N. O., & Marsal, K. (1998). Does passive smoking in early pregnancy increase the risk of small-for-gestational-age infants? *American Journal of Public Health, 88,* 1523–1527.

Delaney, C. H. (1995). Rites of passage in adolescence. *Adolescence, 30,* 891–897.

DeLisi, 2006

DeLisi, L., & Fleischhaker, W. (2007). Schizophrenia research in the era of the genome, 2007. *Current Opinion in Psychiatry, 20,* 109–110.

Delmas, C., Platat, C., Schweitzer, B., Wagner, A., Oujaa, M., & Simon, C. (2007, October). Association between television in bedroom and adiposity throughout adolescence. *Obesity, 15,* 2495–2503.

Delva, J., O'Malley, P., & Johnston, L. (2006, October). Racial/ethnic and socioeconomic status differences in overweight and health-related behaviors among American students: National trends 1986–2003. *Journal of Adolescent Health, 39,* 536–545.

Denizet-Lewis, B. (2004, May 30). Friends, friends with benefits and the benefits of the local mall. *The New York Times Magazine,* pp. 30–35, 54–58.

Denmark, F. L., & Fernandez, L. C. (1993). Historical development of the psychology of women. In F. L. Denmark & M. A. Paludi (Eds.), *Psychology of women: A handbook of issues and theories.* Westport, CT: Greenwood Press.

Dennis, J. G. (2004). *Homeschooling high school: Planning ahead for college admission.* Cambridge, MA: Emerald Press.

Dennis, T. A., Cole, P. M., Zahn-Wexler, C., & Mizuta, I. (2002). Self in context: Autonomy and relatedness in Japanese and U.S. mother–preschooler dyads. *Child Development, 73,* 1803–1817.

Dennison, B., Edmunds, L., Stratton, H., & Pruzek, R. (2006). Rapid infant weight gain predicts childhood overweight. *Obesity, 14,* 491–499.

Department for Education and Skills, England. (2004). *Math performance of schoolchildren.* London: Department for Education and Skills.

Der, G., Batty, G., & Deary, I. (2006). Effect of breast feeding on intelligence in children: Prospective study, sibling pairs analysis, and meta-analysis. *BMJ: British Medical Journal, 333,* 723–732.

Dervic, K., Friedrich, E., Oquendo, M., Voracek, M., Friedrich, M., & Sonneck, G. (2006, October). Suicide in Austrian children and young adolescents aged 14 and younger. *European Child & Adolescent Psychiatry, 15,* 427–434.

Desoete, A., Roeyers, H., & De Clercq, A. (2003). Can offline metacognition enhance mathematical problem solving? *Journal of Educational Psychology, 95,* 188–200.

Deurenberg, P., Deurenberg-Yap, M., Foo, L. F., Schmidt, G., & Wang, J. (2003). Differences in body composition between Singapore Chinese, Beijing Chinese and Dutch children. *European Journal of Clinical Nutrition, 57,* 405–409.

Deurenberg, P., Deurenberg-Yap, M., & Guricci, S. (2002). Asians are different from Caucasians and from each other in their body mass index/body fat percent relationship. *Obesity Review, 3,* 141–146.

DeVader, S. R., Neeley, N. L., Myles, T. D., & Leet, T. L. (2007). Evaluation of gestational weight gain guidelines for women with normal prepregnancy body mass index. *Obstetrics and Gynecology, 110,* 745–751.

Deveny, K. (1994, December 5). Chart of kindergarten awards. *The Wall Street Journal,* p. Bl.

deVilliers, P. A., & deVilliers, J. G. (1992). Language development. In M. H. Bornstein & M. E. Lamb (Eds.), *Developmental psychology: An advanced textbook.* Hillsdale, NJ: Erlbaum.

Devlin, B., Daniels, M., & Roeder, K. (1997). The heritability of IQ. *Nature, 388,* 468–471.

DeVries, R. (1969). Constancy of generic identity in the years 3 to 6. *Monographs of the Society for Research in Child Development, 34*(3, Serial No. 127).

DeVries, R. (2005). *A pleasing birth*. Philadelphia, PA: Temple University Press.

Dey, A. N., & Bloom, B. (2005). Summary health statistics for U.S. children: National Health Interview Survey, 2003. *Vital Health Statistics 10, 223*, 1–78.

DeYoung, C., Quilty, L., & Peterson, J. (2007). Between facets and domains: 10 aspects of the Big Five. *Journal of Personality and Social Psychology, 93*, 880–896.

Diambra, L., & Menna-Barretio, L. (2004). Infradian rhythmicity in sleep/wake ratio in developing infants. *Chronobiology International, 21*, 217–227.

Diamond, L. (2003a). Love matters: Romantic relationships among sexual-minority adolescents. In P. Florsheim (Ed.), *Adolescent romantic relations and sexual behavior: Theory, research, and practical implications*. Mahwah, NJ: Erlbaum.

Diamond, L. (2003b). Was it a phase? Young women's relinquishment of lesbian/bisexual identities over a 5-year period. *Journal of Personality & Social Psychology, 84*, 352–364.

Dick, D. M., & Rose, R. J. (2002). Behavior genetics: What's new? What's next? *Current Directions in Psychological Science, 11*, 70–74.

Dick, D., Rose, R., & Kaprio, J. (2006). The next challenge for psychiatric genetics: Characterizing the risk associated with identified genes. *Annals of Clinical Psychiatry, 18*, 223–231.

Diego, M., Field, T., & Hernandez-Reif, M. (2008). Temperature increases in preterm infants during massage therapy. *Infant Behavior & Development, 31*, 149–152.

Dietz, W. (2004). Overweight in childhood and adolescence. *New England Journal of Medicine, 350*, 855–857.

Dietz, W. H., & Stern, L. (Eds.). (1999). *American Academy of Pediatrics guide to your child's nutrition: Making peace at the table and building healthy eating habits for life*. New York: Villard.

Dildy, G. A. Jackson, G. M., Fowers, G. R., Oshino, B. T., Varner, M. W., & Clark, S. C. (1996). Very advanced maternal age: Pregnancy after 45. *American Journal of Obstetrics and gynecology, 175*, 668–674.

DiMatteo, M. R., & Kahn, K. L. (1997). Psychosocial aspects of childbirth. In S. J. Gallant, G. P. Keita, & R. Royak-Schaler (Eds.), *Health care for women: Psychological, social, and behavioral influences*. Washington, DC: American Psychological Association.

DiPietro, J. A. (2004). The role of prenatal maternal stress in child development. *Current Directions in Psychological Science, 13*, 71–73.

DiPietro, J. A., Bornstein, M. H., & Costigan, K. A. (2002). What does fetal movement predict about behavior during the first two years of life? *Developmental Psychobiology, 40*, 358–371.

Dipietro, J. A., Costigan, K. A., Gurewitsch, E. D. (2005). Maternal psychophysiological change during the second half of gestation. *Biological Psychology, 69*, 23–39.

Dittman, M. (2005). Generational differences at work. *Monitor on Psychology, 36*, 54–55.

Dixon, R. A., & Lerner, R. M. (1999). History and systems in developmental psychology. In M. H. Bornstein & M. E. Lamb (Eds.), *Developmental psychology: An advanced textbook*. Mahwah, NJ: Erlbaum.

Dixon, W. E., Jr. (2004). There's a long, long way to go. *Psyc-CRITIQUES*. Washington, DC: American Psychological Association.

Dmitrieva, J., Chen, C., & Greenberger, E. (2004). Family relationships and adolescent psychosocial outcomes: Converging findings from Eastern and Western cultures. *Journal of Research on Adolescence, 14*, 425–447.

Dobson, V. (2000). The developing visual brain. *Perception, 29*, 1501–1503.

Dodge, K. A. (1985). A social information processing model of social competence in children. In M. Perlmutter (Ed.), *Minnesota Symposia on Child Psychology, 18*, 77–126.

Dodge, K. A., Lansford, J. E., & Burks, V. S. (2003). Peer rejection and social information-processing factors in the development of aggressive behavior problems in children. *Child Development, 74*, 374–393.

Doman, G., & Doman, J. (2002). *How to teach your baby to read*. Wyndmoor, PA: Gentle Revolution Press.

Dombrowski, S., Noonan, K., & Martin, R. (2007). Low birthweight and cognitive outcomes: Evidence for a gradient relationship in an urban, poor, African American birth cohort. *School Psychology Quarterly, 22*, 26–43.

Dominguez, H. D., Lopez, M. F., & Molina, J. C. (1999). Interactions between perinatal and neonatal associative learning defined by contiguous olfactory and tactile stimulation. *Neurobiology of Learning and Memory, 71*, 272–288.

Donat, D. (2006, October). Reading their way: A balanced approach that increases achievement. *Reading & Writing Quarterly: Overcoming Learning Difficulties, 22*, 305–323.

Dondi, M., Simion, F., & Caltran, G. (1999). Can newborns discriminate between their own cry and the cry of another newborn infant? *Developmental Psychology, 35*, 418–426.

Donlan, C. (1998). *The development of mathematical skills*. Philadelphia: Psychology Press.

Donnerstein, E. (2005, January). *Media violence and children: What do we know, what do we do?* Paper presented at the annual National Teaching of Psychology meeting, St. Petersburg Beach, FL.

Donohue, R. (2007, April). Examining career persistence and career change intent using the career attitudes and strategies inventory. *Journal of Vocational Behavior, 70*, 259–276.

Dorn, L., Susman, E., & Ponirakis, A. (2003). Pubertal timing and adolescent adjustment and behavior: Conclusions vary by rater. *Journal of Youth & Adolescence, 32*, 157–167.

Dorofaeff, T., & Denny, S. (2006, September). Sleep and adolescence. Do New Zealand teenagers get enough? *Journal of Paediatrics and Child Health, 42*, 515–520.

Doyle, L. W., Victorian Infant Collaborative Study Group. (2004). Neonatal intensive care at borderline viability—Is it worth it? *Early Human Development, 80*, 103–113.

Doyle, R. (2000, June). Asthma worldwide. *Scientific American*, pp. 28.

Doyle, R. (2004, April). By the numbers: A surplus of women. *Scientific American, 290*, 33.

Drewett, R. (2007). *The nutritional psychology of childhood*. New York: Cambridge University Press.

Drews, C. D., Murphy, C. C., Yeargin-Allsopp, M., & Decoufle, P. (1996). The relationship between idiopathic mental retardation and maternal smoking during pregnancy. *Pediatrics, 97*, 547–553.

Driscoll, A. K. Russell, S. T., Crockett, L. J. (2008). Parenting styles and youth well-being across immigrant generations. *Journal of Family Issues, 29*, 185–209.

Dromi, E. (1987). *Early lexical development*. Cambridge, England: Cambridge University Press.

Dryfoos, J. G. (1990). *Adolescents at risk: Prevalence and prevention*. New York: Oxford University Press.

DuBois, D. L., & Hirsch, B. J. (1990). School and neighborhood friendship patterns of blacks and whites in early adolescence. *Child Development, 61*, 524–536.

DuBreuil, S. C., Garry, M., & Loftus, E. F. (1998). Tales from the crib: Age regression and the creation of unlikely memories. In S. J. Lynn & K. M. McConkey (Eds.), *Truth in memory*. New York: Guilford Press.

Dudding, T. C., Vaizey, C. J., & Kamm, M. A. (2008). Obstetric anal sphincter injury: incidence, risk factors, and management. *Annals of Surgery, 247*, 224–237.

Duenwald, M. (2003, July 15). After 25 years, new ideas in the prenatal test tube. *The New York Times*, p. D5.

Duenwald, M. (2004, May 11). For couples, stress without a promise of success. *The New York Times*, p. D3.

Duncan, G. J., & Brooks-Gunn, J. (2000). Family poverty, welfare reform, and child development. *Child Development, 71*, 188–196.

Dunham, R. M., Kidwell, J. S., & Wilson, S. M. (1986). Rites of passage at adolescence: A ritual process paradigm. *Journal of Adolescent Research, 1*, 139–153.

Durik, A. M., Hyde, J. S., & Clark, R. (2000). Sequelae of cesarean and vaginal deliveries: Psychosocial outcomes for mothers and infants. *Developmental Psychology, 36*, 251–260.

Dutta, T., & Mandal, M. (2006, July). Hand preference and accidents in India. *Laterality: Asymmetries of Body, Brain and Cognition, 11*, 368–372.

Dwairy, M., Achoui, M., Abouserie, R., & Farah, A. (2006, May). Parenting styles, individuation, and mental health of Arab adolescents: A third cross-regional research study. *Journal of Cross-Cultural Psychology, 37*, 262–272.

Dweck, C. (2002). The development of ability conceptions. In A. Wigfield & J. Eccles (Eds.), *Development of achievement motivation*. San Diego: Academic Press.

Dyson, A. H. (2003). "Welcome to the jam": Popular culture, school literacy and making of childhoods. *Harvard Educational Review, 73*, 328–361.

Eagly, A. H., & Steffen, V. J. (1984). Gender stereotypes stem from the distribution of women and men into social roles. *Journal of Personality and Social Psychology, 46*, 735–754.

Earle, J., Perricone, P., Davidson, J., Moore, N., Harris, C., & Cotten, S. (2007, March). Premarital sexual attitudes and behavior at a religiously-affiliated university: Two decades of change. *Sexuality & Culture: An Interdisciplinary Quarterly, 11*, 39–61.

East, P., Reyes, B., & Horn, E. (2007, June). Association between adolescent pregnancy and a family history of teenage births. *Perspectives on Sexual and Reproductive Health, 39*, 108–115.

Eastman, Q. (2003, June 20). Crib death exoneration could usher in new gene tests. *Science, 300*, 1858.

Easton, J., Schipper, L., & Shackelford, T. (2007). Morbid jealousy from an evolutionary psychological perspective. *Evolution and Human Behavior, 28*, 399–402.

Eaton, W. O., & Enns, L. R. (1986). Sex differences in human motor activity level. *Psychological Bulletin, 100*, 19–28.

Eaton, W. O., & Yu, A. P. (1989). Are sex differences in child motor activity level a function of sex differences in maturational status? *Child Development, 60*, 1005–1011.

Ebmeier, K., Donaghey, C., & Steele, J. (2006, December). Recent developments and current controversies in depression. *Lancet, 367*, 153–167.

Ebstein, R. P., Novick, O., Umansky, R., Priel, B., Osher, Y., Blaine, D., et al. (1996). Dopamine D4 receptor exon III polymorphism associated with the human personality trait of novelty seeking. *Nature and Genetics, 12*, 78–80.

Eccles, J., Templeton, J., & Barber, B. (2003). Adolescence and emerging adulthood: The critical passage ways to adulthood. In M. Bornstein & L. Davidson (Eds.), *Well-being: Positive development across the life course*. Mahwah, NJ: Erlbaum.

Ecenbarger, W. (1993, April 1). America's new merchants of death. *The Reader's Digest*, p. 50.

Eckerman, G., & Peterman, K. (2001). Peers and infant social/communicative development. In G. Bremner & A. Fogel (Eds.), *Blackwell handbook of infant development* (pp. 326–350). Malden, MA: Blackwell.

Edwards, C. P. (2000). Children's play in cross-cultural perspective: A new look at the Six Cultures study. *Cross-Cultural Research: The Journal of Comparative Social Science, 34*, 318–338.

Edwards, S. (2005). Constructivism does not only happen in the individual: Sociocultural theory and early childhood education. *Early Child Development & Care, 17*, 37–47.

Eichstedt, J., Serbin, L., & Poulin-Dubois, D. (2002). Of bears and men: Infants' knowledge of conventional and metaphorical gender stereotypes. *Infant Behavior & Development, 25*, 296–310.

Eid, M., Riemann, R., Angleitner, A., & Borkenau, P. (2003). Sociability and positive emotionality: Genetic and environmental contributions to the covariation between different facets of extraversion. *Journal of Personality, 71*, 319–346.

Eiden, R., Foote, A., & Schuetze, P. (2007). Maternal cocaine use and caregiving status: Group differences in caregiver and infant risk variables. *Addictive Behaviors, 32*, 465–476.

Eigsti, I., & Cicchetti, D. (2004). The impact of child maltreatment on expressive syntax at 60 months. *Developmental Science, 7*, 88–102.

Eimas, P. D., Sigueland, E. R., Jusczyk, P., & Vigorito, J. (1971). Speech perception in infants. *Science, 171*, 303–306.

Eisbach, A. O. (2004). Children's developing awareness of diversity in people's trains of thought. *Child Development, 75*, 1694–1707.

Eisenberg, M., & Resnick, M. (2006, November). Suicidality among gay, lesbian and bisexual youth: The role of protective factors. *Journal of Adolescent Health, 39*, 662–668.

Eisenberg, N. (2004). Another slant on moral judgment. *PsycCRITIQUES*, pp. 12–15. Washington, DC: American Psychological, Association.

Eisenberg, N., Fabes, R. A., Guthrie, I. K., & Reiser, M. (2000). Dispositional emotionality and regulation: Their role in predicting quality of social functioning. *Journal of Personality and Social Psychology, 78*, 136–157.

Eisenberg, N., & Valiente, C. (2004). Empathy-related responding: Moral, social, and socialization correlates. In A. G. Miller (Ed.), *Social psychology of good and evil*. New York: Guilford Press.

Eisenberg, N., & Zhou, Q. (2000). Regulation from a developmental perspective. *Psychological Inquiry, 11*, 166–172.

Eley, T., Liang, H., & Plomin, R. (2004). Parental familial vulnerability, family environment, and their interactions as predictors of depressive symptoms in adolescents. *Child & Adolescent Social Work Journal, 21,* 298–306.

Eley, T. C., Bolton, D., O'Connor, T., Perrin, S., Smith, P., & Plomin, R. (2003). Phenotypic and genetic differentiation of anxiety-related behaviours in young children. *Journal of Child Psychology & Psychiatry, 44,* 945–960.

Eley, T. C., Lichtenstein, P., & Moffitt, T. E. (2003). A longitudinal behavioral genetic analysis of the etiology of aggressive and nonaggressive antisocial behavior. *Development and Psychopathology, 15,* 383–402.

Elkind, D. (1978). The children's reality: Three developmental themes. In S. Coren & L. M. Ward (Eds.), *Sensation and perception.* Hillsdale, NJ: Erlbaum.

Elkind, D. (1994a). *A sympathetic understanding of the child: Birth to sixteen* (3rd ed). Needham Heights, MA: Allyn & Bacon.

Elkind, D. (1994b). *Ties that stress: The new family imbalance.* Cambridge, MA: Harvard University Press.

Elkind, D. (1996). Inhelder and Piaget on adolescence and adulthood: A postmodern appraisal. *Psychological Science, 7,* 216–220.

Ellis, B. J. (2004). Timing of pubertal maturation in girls: An integrated life history approach. *Psychological Bulletin, 130,* 920–958.

Ellis, L. (2006, July). Gender differences in smiling: An evolutionary neuroandrogenic theory. *Physiology & Behavior, 88,* 303–308.

Ellis, L., & Engh, T. (2000). Handedness and age of death: New evidence on a puzzling relationship. *Journal of Health Psychology, 5,* 561–565.

Ellis, L., Ficek, C., Burke, D., & Das, S. (2008, February). Eye color, hair color, blood type, and the rhesus factor: Exploring possible genetic links to sexual orientation. *Archives of Sexual Behavior, 37,* 145–149.

Else-Quest, N. M., Hyde, J. S., & Clark, R. (2003). Breast-feeding, bonding, and the mother–infant relationship. *Merrill-Palmer Quarterly, 49,* 495–517.

Employment Policies Institute. (2000). *Correcting part-time misconceptions.* Washington, DC: Author.

Endo, S. (1992). Infant–infant play from 7 to 12 months of age: An analysis of games in infant–peer triads. *Japanese Journal of Child and Adolescent Psychiatry, 33,* 145–162.

Endocrine Society (2001, March 1). *The Endocrine Society and Lawson Wilkins Pediatric Endocrine Society call for further research to define precocious puberty.* Bethesda, MD: Endocrine Society.

Englund, K., & Behne, D. (2006). Changes in infant directed speech in the first six months. *Infant and Child Development, 15* (2), 139–160.

Englund, M. M., Levy, A. K., Hyson, D. M., & Sroufe, L. A. (2000). Adolescent social competence: Effectiveness in a group setting. *Child Development, 71,* 1049–1060.

Ennett, S. T., & Bauman, K. E. (1996). Adolescent social networks: School, demographic, and longitudinal considerations. *Journal of Adolescent Research, 11,* 194–215.

Ensenauer, R. E., Michels, V. V., & Reinke, S. S. (2005). Genetic testing: Practical, ethical, and counseling considerations. *Mayo Clinic Proceedings, 80,* 63–73.

Epperson, S. E. (1988, September 16). Studies link subtle sex bias in schools with women's behavior in the workplace. *The Wall Street Journal,* p. 19.

Erikson, E. H. (1963). *Childhood and society.* New York: Norton.

Erlandsson, K., Dsilna, A., Fagerberg, I., & Christensson, K. (2007). Skin-to-skin care with the father after cesarean birth and its effect on newborn crying and prefeeding behavior. *Birth: Issues in Perinatal Care, 34,* 105–114.

Eshel, N., Nelson, E. E., Blair, R. J., Pine, D. S., Ernst, M. (2007). Neural substrates of choice selection in adults and adolescents: Development of the ventrolateral prefrontal and anterior cingulated cortices. *Neuropsychologia, 45,* 1270–1279.

Estell, D. B., Jones, M. H., Pearl, R., Van Acker, R., Farmer, T. W., & Rodkin, P. C. (2008). Peer groups, popularity, and social preference: Trajectories of social functioning among students with and without learning disabilities. *Journal of Learning Disabilities, 41,* 5–14.

Ethier, L., Couture, G., & Lacharite, C. (2004). Risk factors associated with the chronicity of high potential for child abuse and neglect. *Journal of Family Violence, 19,* 13–24.

Evans, G. (2004). The environment of childhood poverty. *American Psychologist, 59,* 77–92.

Eveleth, P., & Tanner, J. (1976). *Worldwide variation in human growth.* New York: Cambridge University Press.

Everett, S. A., Warren, C. W., Santelli, J. S., Kann, L., Collins, J. L., & Kolbe, L. J. (2000). Use of birth control pills, condoms, and withdrawal among U.S. high school students. *Journal of Adolescent Health, 27,* 112–118.

Faith, M. S., Johnson, S. L., & Allison, D. B. (1997). Putting the behavior into the behavior genetics of obesity. *Behavior Genetics, 27,* 423–439.

Falk, D. (2004). Prelinguistic evolution in early hominids: Whence motherese? *Behavioral and Brain Sciences, 27,* 491–503.

Fangman, J. J., Mark, P. M., Pratt, L., Conway, K. K., Healey, M. L., Oswald, J. W., et al. (1994). Prematurity prevention programs: An analysis of successes and failures. *American Journal of Obstetrical Gynecology, 170,* 744–750.

Fantz, R. (1963). Pattern vision in newborn infants. *Science, 140,* 296–297.

Fantz, R. L. (1961). The origin of form perception. *Scientific American,* pp. 72–81.

Farah, M., Shera, D., Savage, J., Betancourt, L., Giannetta, J., Brodsky, N., et al. (2006, September). Childhood poverty: Specific associations with neurocognitive development. *Brain Research, 1110,* 166–174.

Farrell, E. F. (2005), July 15). To test or not to test? *The Chronicle of Higher Education,* A39–A40.

Farroni, T., Menon, E., Rigato, S., & Johnson, M. (2007). The perception of facial expressions in newborns. *European Journal of Developmental Psychology, 4,* 2–13.

Farver, J. M., & Frosch, D. L. (1996). L.A. stories: Aggression in preschoolers' spontaneous narratives after the riots of 1992. *Child Development, 67,* 19–32.

Farver, J. M., & Lee-Shin, Y. (2000). Acculturation and Korean-American children's social and play behavior. *Social Development, 9,* 316–336.

Farver, J. M., Kim, Y. K., & Lee-Shin, Y. (1995). Cultural differences in Korean- and Anglo-American preschoolers' social interaction and play behaviors. *Child Development, 66,* 1088–1099.

Farver, J. M., Welles-Nystrorn, B., Frosch, D. L., & Wimbarti, S. (1997). Toy stories: Aggression in children's narratives in the United States, Sweden, Germany, and Indonesia. *Journal of Cross-Cultural Psychology, 28,* 393–420.

Fasano, C., & Pellitteri, J. (2006). Infusing emotional learning into the school environment. *Emotionally intelligent school counseling* (pp. 65–79). Mahwah, NJ: Lawrence Erlbaum.

Fayers, T., Crowley, T., Jenkins, J. M., & Cahill, D. J. (2003). Medical student awareness of sexual health is poor. *International Journal STD/AIDS, 14,* 386–389.

Federal Interagency Forum on Child and Family Statistics. (2003). *America's Children: Key National Indicators of Well-Being, 2003.* Federal Interagency Forum on Child and Family Statistics, Washington, DC: U.S. Government Printing Office.

Feldhusen, J. (2003). Precocity and acceleration. *Gifted Education International, 17,* 55–58.

Feldman, R. S. (Ed.). (1992). *Applications of nonverbal behavioral theories and research.* Hillsdale, NJ: Erlbaum.

Feldman, R. S., & Rimé, B. (Eds.). (1991). *Fundamentals of nonverbal behavior.* Cambridge, England: Cambridge University Press.

Feldman, R. S., Tomasian, J., & Coats, E. J. (1999). Adolescents' social competence and nonverbal deception abilities: Adolescents with higher social skills are better liars. *Journal of Nonverbal Behavior, 23,* 237–249.

Feldman, R., & Masalha, S. (2007). The role of culture in moderating the links between early ecological risk and young children's adaptation. *Development and Psychopathology, 19,* 1–21.Helms, J. E., Jernigan, M., & Mascher, J. (2005). The meaning of race in psychology and how to change it: A methodological perspective. *American Psychologist, 60,* 27–36.

Feldman, R., Weller, A., Sirota, L., & Eidelman, A. I. (2003). Testing a family intervention hypothesis: The contribution of mother–infant skin-to-skin contact (kangaroo care) to family interaction, proximity, and touch. *Journal of Family Psychology, 17,* 94–107.

Feldman, S.S., & Wood, D.N. (1994). Parents' expectations for preadolescent sons' behavioral autonomy: A longitudinal study of correlates and outcomes. *Journal of Research on Adolescence, 4,* 45–70.

Fenwick, K. D., & Morrongiello, B. A. (1998). Spatial co-location and infants' learning of auditory–visual associations. *Behavior & Development, 21,* 745–759.

Ferguson, M., & Molfese, P. (2007). Breast-fed infants process speech differently from bottle-fed infants: Evidence from neuroelectrophysiology. *Developmental Neuropsychology, 31,* 337–347.

Fergusson, D. M., Horwood, L. J., & Ridder, E. M. (2006). Abortion in young women and subsequent mental health. *Journal of Child Psychology and Psychiatry, 47,* 16–24.

Fernald, A. (2001). Hearing, listening, and understanding: Auditory development in infancy. In G. Bremner & A. Fogel (Eds.), *Blackwell handbook of infant development.* Malden, MA: Blackwell.

Fernald, A., & Morikawa, H. (1993). Common themes and cultural variations in Japanese and American mothers' speech to infants. *Child Development, 64,* 637–656.

Fernald, A., Taeschner, T., Dunn, J., Papousek, M., Boysson-Bardies, B., & Fukui, I. (1998). A cross-language study of prosodic modifications in mothers' and fathers' speech to preverbal infants. *Journal of Child Language, 16,* 477–501.

Fernyhough, C. (1997). Vygotsky's sociocultural approach: Theoretical issues and implications for current research. In S. Hala (Ed.), *The development of social cognition* (pp. 65–92). Hove, England: Psychology Press/Erlbaum, Taylor & Francis.

Festinger, L. (1954). A theory of social comparison processes. *Human Relations, 7,* 117–140.

Field, M. J., & Behrman, R. E. (Eds.). (2002). *When children die.* Washington, DC: National Academies Press.

Field, T. M. (1982). Individual differences in the expressivity of neonates and young infants. In R. S. Feldman (Ed.), *Development of nonverbal behavior in children.* New York: Springer-Verlag.

Field, T. M. (Ed.). (1988). *Stress and coping across development.* Hillsdale, NJ: Erlbaum.

Field, T. M. (1995). Massage therapy for infants and children. *Journal of Developmental & Behavioral Pediatrics, 16,* 105–111.

Field, T. M. (2001). *Touch.* Cambridge, MA: MIT Press.

Field, T., & Walden, T. (1982). Perception and production of facial expression in infancy and early childhood. In H. Reese & L. Lipsitt (Eds.), *Advances in child development and behavior* (Vol. 16). New York: Academic Press.

Field, T., Diego, M., & Hernandez-Reif, M. (2007). Massage therapy research. *Developmental Review, 27,* 75–89.

Field, T. M., Greenberg, R., Woodson, R., Cohen, D., & Garcia, R. (1984). Facial expression during Brazelton neonatal assessments. *Infant Mental Health Journal, 5,* 61–71.

Field, T., Diego, M., & Hernandez-Reif, M. (2006). Prenatal depression effects on the fetus and newborn: A review. *Infant Behavior & Development, 29,* 445–455.

Finkbeiner, A. K. (1996). *After the death of a child: Living with loss through the years.* New York: The Free Press.

Finkelstein, D. L., Harper, D. A., & Rosenthal, G. E. (1998). Does length of hospital stay during labor and delivery influence patient satisfaction? Results from a regional study. *American Journal of Managed Care, 4,* 1701–1708.

Fisch, S. M. (2004). *Children's learning from educational television: Sesame Street and beyond.* Mahwah, NJ: Erlbaum.

Fischer, K. W., & Hencke, R. W. (1996). Infants' construction of actions m context: Piaget's contributions to research on early development. *Psychological Science, 7,* 204–210.

Fish, J. M. (Ed.). (2001). *Race and intelligence: Separating science from myth.* Mahwah, NJ: Erlbaum.

Fisher, C. B. (2004). Informed consent and clinical research involving children and adolescents: Implications of the revised APA ethics code and HIPAA. *Journal of Clinical Child & Adolescent Psychology, 33,* 832–839.

Fisher, C., Hauck, Y., & Fenwick, J. (2006). How social context impacts on women's fears of childbirth: A Western Australian example. *Social Science & Medicine, 63,* 64–75.

Fishman, C. (1999, May). Watching the time go by. *American Demographics,* 56–57.

Fitzgerald, D., & White, K. (2003). Linking children's social worlds: Perspective-taking in parent–child and peer contexts. *Social Behavior & Personality, 31,* 509–522.

Fitzgerald, H. (2006). Cross cultural research during infancy: Methodological considerations. *Infant Mental Health Journal, 27,* 612–617.

Fivush, R., Kuebli, J., & Clubb, P. A. (1992). The structure of events and event representations: A developmental analysis. *Child Development, 63,* 188–201.

Flavell, J. H. (1994). Cognitive development: Past, present, and future. In R. D. Parke, P. A. Ornstein, J. J. Rieser, & C. Zahn-Waxler (Eds.), *A century of developmental psychology.* Washington, DC: American Psychological Association.

Flavell, J. H. (1996). Piaget's legacy. *Psychological Science, 7,* 200–203.

Flegal, K.M., Tabak, C.J. & Ogden, C.L. (2006). Overweight in children: definitions and interpretation. *Health Education Research, 21,* 755–60.

Fleming, P., Tsogt, B., & Blair, P. (2006). Modifiable risk factors, sleep environment, developmental physiology and common polymorphisms: Understanding and preventing sudden infant deaths. *Early Human Development, 82,* 761–766.

Fletcher, A. C., Darling, N. E., Steinberg, L., & Dornbusch, S. M. (1995). The company they keep: Relation of adolescents' adjustment and behavior to their friends' perceptions of authoritative parenting in the social network. *Developmental Psychology, 31,* 300–310.

Flom, R., & Bahrick, L. (2007). The development of infant discrimination of affect in multimodal and unimodal stimulation: The role of intersensory redundancy. *Developmental Psychology,43,* 238–252.

Flor, D. L., & Knap, N. F. (2001). Transmission and transaction: Predicting adolescents' internalization of parental religious values. *Journal of Family Psychology, 15,* 627–645.

Flouri, E. (2005). *Fathering and child outcomes.* New York: Wiley.

Floyd, R. G. (2005). Information-processing approaches to interpretation of contemporary intellectual assessment instruments. In D. P. Flanagan & P. L. Harrison (Eds.), *Contemporary intellectual assessment: Theories, tests, and issues.* New York: Guilford Press.

Flynn, E., O'Malley, C., & Wood, D. (2004). A longitudinal, microgenetic study of the emergence of false belief understanding and inhibition skills. *Developmental Science, 7,* 103–115.

Fogarty, R. (2008). The intelligence-friendly classroom: It just makes sense. *Teaching for intelligence* (2nd ed., pp. 142–148). Thousand Oaks, CA, Corwin Press.

Fogel, A., de Koeyer, I., & Bellagamba, F. (2004). The dialogical self in the first two years of life: Embarking on a journey of discovery [Special issue]. *Theory & Psychology: The Dialogical Self, 125,* 191–205.

Fogel, A., Hsu, H., Shapiro, A., Nelson-Goens, G., & Secrist, C. (2006, May). Effects of normal and perturbed social play on the duration and amplitude of different types of infant smiles. *Developmental Psychology, 42,* 459–473.

Fok, W. Y., Chan, L. Y., Tsui, M. H., Leung, T. N., Lau, T. K., & Chung, T. K. (2005). When to induce labor for post-term? A study of induction at 41 weeks versus 42 weeks. *European Journal of Obstetrics and Gynecological Reproductive Biology, 125,* 206–210.

Folkman, S., & Moskowitz, J. T. (2007). Positive affect and meaning-focused coping during significant psychological stress. In M. Hewstone, H. A. W. Schut, J. B. F. De Wit, K. Van Den Bos, & M. S. S. (Eds.), *The scope of social psychology: Theory and applications.* New York: Psychology Press.

Fombonne, E., & Zinck, S. (2008). Psychopharmacological treatment of depression in children and adolescents. *Handbook of depression in children and adolescents* (pp. 207–223). New York: Guilford Press.

Ford, A. M., & Martinez-Ramirez, A. (2006). Therapeutic opportunities and targets in childhood leukemia, *Clinical and Translational Oncology. 8,* 560–565.

Ford, J. (2007, August). Alcohol use among college students: A comparison of athletes and nonathletes. *Substance Use & Misuse, 42,* 1367–1377.

Forrester, M. (2001). The embedding of the self in early interaction. *Infant & Child Development, 10,* 189–202.

Forste, R., Weiss, J., & Lippincott, E. (2001). The decision to breast-feed in the United States: Does race matter? *Pediatrics, 108,* 291–296.

Fowers, B. J., & Davidov, B. J. (2006). The virtue of multiculturalism: Personal transformation, character, and openness to the other. *American Psychologist, 61,* 581–594.

Fraley, R. C., & Spieker, S. J. (2003). Are infant attachment patterns continuously or categorically distributed? A taxometric analysis of strange situation behavior. *Developmental Psychology, 39,* 387–104.

Franck, I., & Brownstone, D. (1991). *The parent's desk reference.* New York: Prentice Hall.

Frankenburg, W. K., Dodds, J., Archer, P., Maschka, P., Edelman, N., & Shapiro, H. (1992). *The Denver II training manual.* Denver, CO: Denver Developmental Materials.

Franko, D., & Striegel-Moore, R. (2002). The role of body dissatisfaction as a risk factor for depression in adolescent girls: Are the differences black and white? *Journal of Psychosomatic Research, 53,* 975–983.

Frazier, L. M., Grainger, D. A., Schieve, L. A., & Toner, J. P. (2004). Follicle-stimulating hormone and estradiol levels independently predict the success of assisted reproductive technology treatment. *Fertility and Sterility, 82,* 834–840.

Frederickson, N., & Petrides, K. (2008). Ethnic, gender, and socio-economic group differences in academic performance and secondary school selection: A longitudinal analysis. *Learning and Individual Differences, 18,* 144–151.

Fredriksen, K., Rhodes, J., Reddy, R., & Way, N. (2004). Sleepless in Chicago: Tracking the effects of adolescent sleep loss during the middle school years. *Child Development, 75,* 84–95.

Freedman, D. G. (1979, January). Ethnic differences in babies. *Human Nature,* 15–20.

Freedman, D. S., Khan, L. K., Serdula, M. K., Dietz, W. H., Sriniasan, S. R., & Berenson, G. S. (2004). Inter-relationships among childhood BMI, childhood height, and adult obesity: The Bogalusa Heart Study. *International Journal of Obesity and Related Metabolic Disorders, 28,* 10–16.

Freud, S. (1920). *A general introduction to psychoanalysis.* New York: Boni & Liveright.

Freud, S. (1959). *Group psychology and the analysis of the ego.* London: Hogarth. (Original work published 1922)

Frick, P. J., Cornell, A. H., Bodin, S. D., Dane, H. A., Barry, C. T., & Loney, B. R. (2003). Callous-unemotional traits and developmental pathways to severe conduct problems. *Developmental Psychology, 39,* 246–260.

Friedlander, L. J., Connolly, J. A., Pepler, D. J. (2007). Biological, familial, and peer influences on dating in early adolescence. *Archives of Sexual Behavior, 36,* 821–830.

Friedman, D. E. (2004). *The new economics of preschool.* Washington, DC: Early Childhood Funders' Collaborative/NAEYC.

Frisch, M., Friis, S., Kjear, S. K., & Melbye, M. (1995). Falling incidence of penis cancer in an uncircumcised population (Denmark1943–90). *British Medical Journal, 311,* 1471.

Fulcher, M., Sutfin, E. L., & Patterson, C. J. (2008). Individual differences in gender development: Associations with parental sexual orientation, attitudes, and division of labor. *Sex Roles, 58,* 330–341.

Fuligni, A. J., Fuligni, A. S. (2007). Immigrant families and the educational development of their children. In J. E. Lansford, K. Deater-Deckard & M. H. Bornstein (Eds.), *Immigrant families in contemporary society.* New York: Guilford Press.

Fuligni, A. J., Tseng, V., & Lam, M. (1999). Attitudes toward family obligations among American adolescents with Asian, Latin American, and European backgrounds. *Child Development, 70,* 1030–1044.

Fuligni, A., & Hardway, C. (2006, September). Daily variation in adolescents' sleep, activities, and psychological well-being. *Journal of Research on Adolescence, 16,* 353–378.

Fuligni, A., & Yoshikawa, H. (2003). Socioeconomic resources, parenting, and child development among immigrant families. In M. Bomstein & R. Bradley (Eds.), *Socioeconomic status, parenting, and child development.* Mahwah, NJ: Erlbaum.

Fuligni, A., & Zhang, W. (2004). Attitudes toward family obligation among adolescents in contemporary urban and rural China. *Child Development, 75,* 180–192.

Funk, J., Buchman, D., & Jenks, J. (2003). Playing violent video games, desensitization, and moral evaluation in children. *Journal of Applied Developmental Psychology, 24,* 413–436.

Furman, W., & Buhrmester, D. (1992). Age and sex differences in perceptions of networks of personal relationships. *Child Development, 63,* 103–115.

Furman, W., & Shaffer, L. (2003). The role of romantic relationships in adolescent development. In P. Florsheim (Ed.), *Adolescent romantic relations and sexual behavior: Theory, research, and practical implications.* Mahwah, NJ: Elbaum.

Gagnon, S. G., & Nagle, R. J. (2000). Comparison of the revised and original versions of the Bayley Scales of Infant Development. *School Psychology International, 21,* 293–305.

Galambos, N., Leadbeater, B., & Barker, E. (2004). Gender differences in and risk factors for depression in adolescence: A 4-year longitudinal study. *International Journal of Behavioral Development, 28,* 16–25.

Gallagher, J. J. (1994). Teaching and learning: New models. *Annual Review of Psychology, 45,* 171–195.

Galluccio, L., & Rovee-Collier, C. (2006). Nonuniform effects of reinstatement within the time window. *Learning and Motivation, 37,* 1–17.

Ganger, J., & Brent, M. R. (2004). Reexamining the vocabulary spurt. *Developmental Psychology, 40,* 621–632.

Garcia, C., & Saewyc, E. (2007). Perceptions of mental health among recently immigrated Mexican adolescents. *Issues in Mental Health Nursing, 28,* 37–54.

Garcia, C., Bearer, E. L., & Lerner, R. M. (Eds.). (2004). *Nature and nurture: The complex interplay of genetic and environmental influences on human behavior and development.* Mahwah: Erlbaum.

Gardner, H. (2000). *Intelligence reframed: Multiple intelligences for the 21st century.* New York: Basic Books.

Gardner, H. (2003). Three distinct meanings of intelligence. In R. Steinberg & J. Lautrey (Eds.), *Models of intelligence: International perspectives.* Washington, DC: American Psychological Association.

Gardner, H. (2006). *Multiple intelligences: New horizons* (Rev. ed.). New York: Basic Books.

Gardner, H., & Moran, S. (2006). The science of multiple intelligences theory: a response to Lynn Waterhouse. *Educational Psychologist, 41,* 227–232.

Gardner, H., & Perkins, D. (1989). *Art, mind, and education: Research from Project Zero.* Champaign, IL: University of Illinois Press.

Garland, J. E. (2004). Facing the evidence: Antidepressant treatment in children and adolescents. *Canadian Medical Association Journal, 17,* 489–491.

Garlick, D. (2003). Integrating brain science research with intelligence research. *Current Directions in Psychological Science, 12,* 185–189.

Garrison, M., & Christakis, D. (2005). *A teacher in the living room? Educational media for babies, toddlers and preschoolers.* Menlo Park, CA: Kaiser Family Foundation.

Gartstein, M., Slobodskaya, H., & Kinsht, I. (2003). Cross-cultural differences in temperament in the first year of life: United States of America (US) and Russia. *International Journal of Behavioral Development, 27,* 316–328.

Gaulden, M. E. (1992). Maternal age effect: The enigma of Down syndrome and other trisomic conditions. *Mutation Research, 296,* 69–88.

Gauthier, Y. (2003). Infant mental health as we enter the third millennium: Can we prevent aggression? *Infant Mental Health Journal, 24,* 101–109.

Gavin, L. A., & Furman, W. (1996). Adolescent girls' relationships with mothers and best friends. *Child Development, 67,* 375–386.

Gazmrian, J. A., Petersen, R., Spitz, A. M., Goodwin, M. M., Saltzman, L. E., & Marks, J. S. (2000). Violence and reproductive health: Current knowledge and future research directions. *Maternal and Child Health Journal, 4,* 79–84.

Gazzaniga, M. S. Right-hemisphere language following brain bisection: A twenty-year perspective. *American Psychologist, 38,* 525–537.

Gee, H. (2004). *Jacob's ladder: The history of the human genome.* New York: Norton.

Gelman, R. (2006, August). Young natural-number arithmeticians. *Current Directions in Psychological Science, 15,* 193–197.

Gelman, R., & Gallistel, C. R. (2004, October 15). Language and the origin of numerical concepts. *Science, 306,* 441–443.

Gelman, S. A., Taylor, M. G., & Nguyen, S. (2004). Mother–child conversations about gender. *Monographs of the Society for Research in Child Development, 69.*

Gerard, C. M., Harris, K. A., & Thach, B. T. (2002). Spontaneous arousals in supine infants while swaddled and unswaddled during rapid eye movement and quiet sleep. *Pediatrics, 110,* 70.

Gerber, P., & Coffman, K. (2007). Nonaccidental head trauma in infants. *Child's Nervous System, 23,* 499–507.

Gerhardt, P. (1999, August 10). Potty training: How did it get so complicated? *Daily Hampshire Gazette,* p. Cl.

Gerrish, C. J., & Mennella, J. A. (2000). Short-term influence of breastfeeding on the infants' interaction with the environment. *Developmental Psychobiology, 36,* 40–48.

Gershkoff-Stowe, I., & Thelen, E. (2004). U-shaped changes in behavior: A dynamic systems perspective. *Journal of Cognition & Development, 5,* 88–97.

Gershkoff-Stowe, L., & Hahn, E. (2007). Fast mapping skills in the developing lexicon. *Journal of Speech, Language, and Hearing Research, 50,* 682–696.

Gershoff, E. (2002). Corporal punishment by parents and associated child behaviors and experiences: A meta-analytic and theoretical review. *Psychological Bulletin, 128,* 539–579.

Gesell, A. L. (1946). The ontogenesis of infant behavior. In L. Carmidiael (Ed.), *Manual of child psychology.* New York: Harper.

Gewertz, C. (2005, April 6). Training focuses on teachers' expectations. *Education Week, 24,* 1–3.

Ghetti, S., Lyons, K., Lazzarin, F., & Cornoldi, C. (2008, March). The development of metamemory monitoring during retrieval: The case of memory strength and memory absence. *Journal of Experimental Child Psychology, 99,* 157–181.

Ghule, M., Balaiah, D., & Joshi, B. (2007, September). Attitude towards premarital sex among rural college youth in Maharashtra, India. *Sexuality & Culture: An Interdisciplinary Quarterly, 11,* 1–17.

Giami, A., Ohlrichs, Y., Quilliam, S., Wellings, K., Pacey, S., & Wylie, K. (2006, November). Sex education in schools is insufficient to support adolescents in the 21st century. *Sexual and Relationship Therapy, 21,* 485–490.

Gibson, E. J., & Walk, R. D. (1960). The "visual cliff." *Scientific American, 202,* 64–71.

Gifford-Smith, M., & Brownell, C. (2003). Childhood peer relationships: Social acceptance, friendships, and peer networks. *Journal of School Psychology, 41,* 235–284.

Gilbert, L. A. (1994). Current perspectives on dual-career families. *Current Directions in Psychological Science, 3,* 101–105.

Gilbert, S. (2004, March 16). New clues to women veiled in black. *The New York Times,* p. D1.

Gilbert, W. M., Nesbitt. T. S., & Danielsen, B. (1999). Childbearing beyond age 40: Pregnancy outcome in 24,032 cases. *Obstetrics and Gynecology, 93,* 9–14.

Giles-Sims, J., & Lockhart, C. (2005). Culturally shaped patterns of disciplining children. *Journal of Family Issues, 26,* 196–218.

Gillespie, N. A., Cloninger, C., R., & Heath, A. C. (2003). The genetic and environmental relationship between Cloninger's dimensions of temperament and character. *Personality and Individual Differences, 35,* 1931–1946.

Gilligan, C. (1987). Adolescent development reconsidered. In C. E. Irwin (Ed.), *Adolescent social behavior and health.* San Francisco: Jossey-Bass.

Gilligan, C. (1996). The centrality of relationship in human development: A puzzle, some evidence, and a theory. In G. G. Noam & K. W. Fischer (Eds.), *Development and vulnerability in close relationships.* Hillsdale, NJ: Lawrence Erlbaum.

Gilligan, C. (2004). Recovering psyche: Reflections on life-history and history. *Annual of Psychoanalysis, 32,* 131–147.

Gilligan, C., Lyons, N. P., & Hammer, T. J. (Eds.). (1990). *Making connections.* Cambridge, MA: Harvard University Press.

Ginzberg, E. (1972). Toward a theory of occupational choice: A restatement. *Vocational Guidance Quarterly, 12,* 10–14.

Giordana, S. (2005). *Understanding eating disorders: Conceptual and ethical issues in the treatment of anorexia (Issues in Biomedical Ethics).* New York: Oxford University Press.

Gleason, J. B., Perlmann, R. U., Ely, R., & Evans, D. W. (1994). The babytalk register: Parents' use of diminutives. In J. L. Sokolov & C. E. Snow (Eds.), *Handbook of research in language development using CHILDES.* Mahwah, NJ: Erlbaum.

Gleason, J. B., Perlmann, R. Y., Ely, R., & Evans, D. W. (1991). The babytalk register: Parents' use of diminutives. In J. L. Sokolov, & C. E. Snow (Eds.), *Handbook of research in language development using CHILDES.* Hillsdale, NJ: Erlbaum.

Gleason, J., & Ely, R. (2002). Gender differences in language development. In A. McGillicuddy-De Lisi & R. De Lisi (Eds.), *Biology, society, and behavior: The development of sex differences in cognition* (pp. 127–154). Westport, CT: Ablex.

Gleick, E., Reed, S., & Schindehette, S. (1994, October 24). The baby trap. *People Weekly,* pp. 38–56.

Gleitman, L., & Landau, B. (1994). *The acquisition of the lexicon.* Cambridge, MA: Bradford.

Goble, M. (2008). Medical and psychological complications of obesity. *Obesity in childhood and adolescence, Vol 1: Medical, biological, and social issues* (pp. 229–269). Westport, CT: Praeger/Greenwood Publishing Group.

Goetz, A., & Shackelford, T. (2006). Modern application of evolutionary theory to psychology: Key concepts and clarifications. *American Journal of Psychology, 119,* 567–584.

Goff, P. A., Steele, C. M., Davies, P. G. (2008). The space between us: Stereotype threat and distance in interracial contexts. *Journal of Personality and Social Psychology, 94,* 91–107.

Gohlke, B. C., & Stanhope, R. (2002). Final height in psychosocial short stature: Is there complete catch-up? *Acta Paediatrica 91,* 961–965.

Goldberg, A. E. (2004). But do we need universal grammar? Comment on Lidz et al. *Cognition, 94,* 77–84.

Goldberg, J., Holtz, D., Hyslop, T., & Tolosa, J. E. (2002). Has the use of routine episiotomy decreased? Examination of episiotomy rates from 1983 to 2000. *Obstetrics and Genecology, 99,* 395–400.

Goldsmith, L. T. (2000). Tracking trajectories of talent: Child prodigies growing up. In R. C. Friedman, & B. M. Shore, (Eds.), et al. *Talents unfolding: Cognition and development.* Washington, DC: American Psychological Association.

Goldsmith, S. K., Pellmar, T. C., Kleinman, A. M., & Bunney, W. E. (2002). *Reducing suicide: A national imperative.* Washington, DC: The National Academies Press.

Goldston, D. B. (2003). *Measuring suicidal behavior and risk in children and adolescents.* Washington, DC: American Psychological Association.

Goleman, D. (1993, July 21). Baby sees, baby does, and classmates follow. *The New York Times,* p. C10.

Goleman, D. (2005). What makes a leader? In R. L. Taylor & W. E. Rosenbach (Eds.), *Military leadership: In pursuit of excellence* (5th ed.). Boulder, CO: Westview Press.

Golomb, C. (2002). *Child art in context.* Washington, DC: American Psychological Association.

Golomb, C. (2003). *The child's creation of a pictorial world* (2nd ed.). Mahwah, NJ: Erlbaum.

Golombok, S., & Fivush, R. (1994). *Gender development.* Cambridge, England: Cambridge University Press.

Golombok, S., & Tasker, F. (1996). Do parents influence the sexual orientation of their children? Findings from a longitudinal study of lesbian families. *Developmental Psychology, 32,* 3–11.

Golombok, S., Golding, J., Perry, B., Burston, A., Murray, C., Mooney-Somers, J., & Stevens, M. (2003). Children with lesbian parents: A community study. *Developmental Psychology, 39,* 20–33.

Golombok, S., Murray, C., Vasanti, J., MacCallum, F., & Lycett, E. (2004). Families created through surrogacy arrangements: Parent–child relationships in the 1st year of life. *Developmental Psychology, 40,* 400–411.

Good, C., Aronson, J., & Harder, J. (2008, January). Problems in the pipeline: Stereotype threat and women's achievement in high-level math courses. *Journal of Applied Developmental Psychology, 29,* 17–28.

Goode, E. (2004, February 3). Stronger warning is urged on antidepressants for teenagers. *The New York Times,* p. A12.

Goodlin-Jones, B. L., Burnham, M. M., & Anders, T. F. (2000). Sleep and sleep disturbances: Regulatory processes in infancy. In A. J. Sameroff, M. Lewis, & S. Miller (Eds.), *Handbook of developmental psychopathology* (2nd ed.). New York: Kluwer Academic/Plenum.

Goodman, J. C., & Nusbaum, H. C. (Eds.). (1994). *The development of speech perception.* Cambridge, MA: Bradford.

Goodwin, G. M., Anderson, I., Arango, C., Bowden, C.L., Henry, C., Mitchell, P. B., et al. (2008, May). ECNP consensus meeting: Bipolar depression. *Journal of European Neuropsychopharmacology*, 18, 535–549

Goodwin, M. H. (1990). Tactical uses of stories: Participation frameworks within girls' and boys' disputes. *Discourse Processes, 13*, 33–71.

Goodwin, R. D., Sourander, A., Duarte, C. S., Niemela, S., Multimaki, P., Mikolakaros, G., et al. (2008). Do mental health problems in childhood predict chronic physical conditions among males in early adulthood? Evidence from a community-based prospective study. *Psychological Medicine, 28*, 1–11.

Gopnik, A., Meltzoff, A. N., & Kuhl, P. K. (2000). *The scientist in the crib: What early learning tells us about the mind.* New York: HarperCollins.

Goren, J. L. (2008). Antidepressant use in pediatric populations. *Expert Opinion on Drug Safety, 7*, 223–225.

Gormley, W. T. Jr., Gayer, T., Phillips, D., & Dawson, B. (2005). The effects of universal pre-K on cognitive development. *Developmental Psychology, 41*, 872–84.

Goswami, U. (1998). *Cognition in children.* Philadelphia: Psychology Press.

Gottesman, I. I. (1991). *Schizophrenia genesis: The origins of madness.* New York: Freeman.

Gottfredson, G. D., & Holland, J. L. (1990). A longitudinal test of the influence of congruence: Job satisfaction, competency utilization, and counterproductive behavior. *Journal of Counseling Psychology, 37*, 389–398.

Gottfried, A., Gottfried, A., & Bathurst, K. (2002). Maternal and dual-earner employment status and parenting. In M. Bornstein (Ed.), *Handbook of parenting: Vol. 2. Biology and ecology of parenting.* Mahwah, NJ: Erlbaum.

Gottlieb, G. (2003). On making behavioral genetics truly developmental. *Human Development, 46*, 337–355.

Gottlieb, G., & Blair, C. (2004). How early experience matters in intellectual development in the case of poverty. *Preventive Science, 5*, 245–252.

Gould, S. J. (1977). *Ontogeny and phylogeny.* Cambridge, MA; Harvard University Press.

Goyette-Ewing, M. (2000). Children's after-school arrangements: A study of self-care and developmental outcomes. *Journal of Prevention & Intervention in the Community, 20*, 55–67.

Graham, E. (1995, February 9). Leah: Life is all sweetness and insecurity. *The Wall Street Journal*, p. Bl.

Graham, S. (1992). "Most of the subjects were white and middle class": Trends in published research on African Americans in selected APA journals. *American Psychologist, 47*, 629–639.

Granic, I., Hollenstein, T., & Dishion, T. (2003). Longitudinal analysis of flexibility and reorganization in early adolescence: A dynamic systems study of family interactions. *Developmental Psychology, 39*, 606–617.

Grantham-McGregor, S., Ani, C., & Fernald, L. (2001). The role of nutrition in intellectual development. In R. J. Steinberg & E. L. Grigorenko (Eds.), *Environmental effects on cognitive abilities.* Mahwah, NJ: Erlbaum.

Grantham-McGregor, S., Powell, C., Walker, S., Chang, S., & Fletcher, P. (1994). The long-term follow-up of severely malnourished children who participated in an intervention program. *Child Development, 65*, 428–439.

Gratch, G., & Schatz, J. A. (1987). Cognitive development: The relevance of Piaget's infancy books. In J. D. Osofsky (Ed.), *Handbook of infant development* (2nd ed.). New York: Wiley.

Grattan, M. P., De Vos, E. S., Levy, J., & McClintock, M. K. (1992). Asymmetric action in the human newborn: Sex differences in patterns of organization. *Child Development, 63*, 273–289.

Gray-Little, B., & Hafdahl, A. R. (2000). Factors influencing racial comparisons of self-esteem: A quantitative review. *Psychological Bulletin, 126*, 26–54.

Gredler, M., & Shields, C. (2008). *Vygotsky's legacy: A foundation for research and practice.* New York: Guilford Press.

Green, C. L., & Hoover-Dempsey, K. V. (2007). Why do parents home-school? A systematic examination of parental involvement. *Education and Urban Society, 39*, 264.

Greenberg, L., Cwikel, J., & Mirsky, J. (2007, January). Cultural correlates of eating attitudes: A comparison between native-born and immigrant university students in Israel. *International Journal of Eating Disorders, 40*, 51–58.

Greene, K., Krcmar, M., & Rubin, D. (2002). Elaboration in processing adolescent health messages: The impact of egocentrism and sensation seeking on message processing. *Journal of Communication, 52*, 812–831.

Greene, K., Krcmar, M., Walters, L. H., Rubin, D L., & Hale, J. L. (2000). Targeting adolescent risk-taking behaviors: The contribution of egocentrism and sensation-seeking. *Journal of Adolescence, 23*, 439–461.

Greene, S., Anderson, E., & Hetherington, E. (2003). Risk and resilience after divorce. In F. Walsh (Ed.), *Normal family processes: Growing diversity and complexity.* New York: Guilford.

Greenfield, P. M. (1966). On culture and conservation. In J. S. Bruner, R. R. Olver, & P. M. Greenfield (Eds.), *Studies in cognitive growth.* New York: Wiley.

Greenway, C. (2002). The process, pitfalls, and benefits of implementing a reciprocal teaching intervention to improve the reading comprehension of a group of year 6 pupils. *Educational Psychology in Practice, 18*, 113–137.

Greenwood, D. N., & Piertomonaco, P. R. (2004). The interplay among attachment orientation, idealized media images of women, and body dissatisfaction: A social psychological analysis. In I. J. Shrum (Ed.), *Psychology of entertainment media: Blurring the lines between entertainment and persuasion.* Mahwah, NJ: Erlbaum.

Gregory, K. (2005). Update on nutrition for preterm and full-term infants. *Journal of Obstetrics and Gynecological Neonatal Nursing, 34*, 98–108.

Gregory, S. (1856). *Facts for young women.* Boston.

Greve, T. (2003). Norway: The breast-feeding top of the world. *Midwifery Today International, 67*, 57–59.

Griffith, D. R., Azuma, S. D., & Chasnoff, I. J. (1994). Three-year outcome of children exposed prenatally to drugs. *Journal of the American Academy of Child and Adolescent Psychiatry, 33*, 20–27.

Grigorenko, E. (2003). Intraindividual fluctuations in intellectual functioning: Selected links between nutrition and the mind. In R. Sternberg & J. Lautrey (Eds.), *Models of intelligence: International perspectives.* Washington, DC: American Psychological Association.

Groome, L. J., Swiber, M. J., Atterbury, J. I., Bentz, L. S., & Holland, S. B. (1997). Similarities and differences in behavioral state organization during sleep periods in the prenatal infant before and after birth. *Child Development, 68*, 1–11.

Groopman, J. (1998, February 8). Decoding destiny. *The New Yorker*, pp. 42–47.

Gross, R. T., Spiker, D., & Haynes, C. W. (Eds.). (1997). *Helping low-birthweight, premature babies: The Infant Health and Development Program.* Stanford, CA: Stanford University Press.

Grunbaum, J. A., Kann, L., Kinchen, S. A., Williams, B., Ross, J. G., Lowry, R., et al. (2002). *Youth risk behavior surveillance—United States, 2001.* Atlanta, GA: Centers for Disease Control.

Grych, J. H., & Clark, R. (1999). Maternal employment and development of the father–infant relationship in the first year. *Developmental Psychology, 35,* 893–903.

Guasti, M. T. (2002). *Language acquisition: The growth of grammar.* Cambridge, MA: MIT Press.

Guerrini, I., Thomson, A., & Gurling, H. (2007). The importance of alcohol misuse, malnutrition and genetic susceptibility on brain growth and plasticity. *Neuroscience & Biobehavioral Reviews,31,* 212–220.

Guinsburg, R., de Araújo Peres, C., Branco de Almeida, M. F., Xavier Balda, R., Bereguel, R. C., Tonelotto, J., & Kopelman, B. I. (2000). Differences in pain expression between male and female newborn infants. *Pain, 85,* 127–133.

Gullotta, T. P., & Blau, G. M. (2008). *Handbook of childhood behavioral issues: Evidence-based approaches to prevention and treatment.* New York: Routledge/Taylor & Francis Group.

Gump, L. S., Baker, R. C., & Roll, S. (2000). Cultural and gender differences in moral judgment: A study of Mexican Americans and Anglo Americans. *Hispanic Journal of Behavioral Sciences, 22,* 78–93.

Gupta, A., & State, M. (2007). Recent advances in the genetics of autism. *Biological Psychiatry, 61,* 429–437.

Gur, R. C., Gur, R. E., Obrist, W. D. Hungerbuhkr, J. P., Younkin, D., Rosen, A. D., et al. (1982). Sex and handedness differences in cerebral blood flow during rest cognitive activity. *Science, 217,* 659–661.

Güre, A., Uçanok, Z., Sayil, M. (2006) The associations among perceived pubertal timing, parental relations and self-perception in Turkish adolescents. *Journal of Youth and Adolescence, 35,* 541–550.

Gutek, G. L. (2003). Maria Montessori: Contributions to educational psychology. In B. J. Zimmerman (Ed.), *Educational psychology: A century of contributions.* Mahwah, NJ: Erlbaum.

Guterl, F. (2002, November 11). What Freud got right. *Newsweek,* pp. 50–51.

Guttmann, J., & Rosenberg, M. (2003). Emotional intimacy and children's adjustment: A comparison between single-parent divorced and intact families. *Educational Psychology, 23,* 457–472.

Haas, A. P., Hendin, H., & Mann, J. J. (May, 2003). Suicide in college students. *Suicide in Youth* [Special issue]. *American Behavioral Scientist, 46,* pp. 1224–1240.

Hack, M., Flannery, D. J., Schluchter, M., Cartar, L., Borawski, E., & Klein, N. (2002). Outcomes in young adulthood for very low birth weight infants. *New England Journal of Medicine, 346,* 149–157.

Haddock, S., & Rattenborg, K. (2003). Benefits and challenges of dual-earning: Perspectives of successful couples. *American Journal of Family Therapy, 3J,* 325–144.

Haeffel, G., Getchell, M., Koposov, R., Yrigollen, C., DeYoung, C., af Klinteberg, B., et al. (2008). Association between polymorphisms in the dopamine transporter gene and depression: Evidence for a gene-environment interaction in a sample of juvenile detainees. *Psychological Science, 19,* 62–69.

Hahn, C.-S., & Di Pietro. J. A. (2001). In vitro fertilization and the family: Quality of parenting, family functioning, and child psychosocial adjustment. *Developmental Psychology, 37,* 37–48.

Haight, B. K. (1991). Psychological illness in aging. In E. M. Baines (Ed.), *Perspectives on gerontological nursing.* Newbury Park, CA: Sage.

Haight, W. L., & Black, J. E. (2002). A comparative approach to play: Cross-species and cross-cultural perspectives of play in development. *Human Development, 44,* 228–234.

Haines, J., & Neumark-Sztainer, D. (2006, December). Prevention of obesity and eating disorders: A consideration of shared risk factors. *Health Education Research, 21,* 770–782.

Haith, M. H. (1986). Sensory and perceptual processes in early infancy. *Journal of Pediatrics, 109,* 158–171.

Haith, M. H. (1991). Gratuity, perception-action integration, and future orientation in infant vision. In F. S. Kessel, M. H. Bornstein, & A. J. Sameroff (Eds.), *Contemporary constructions of the child: Essays in honor of William Kessen.* Hillsdale, NJ: Erlbaum.

Haley, M., Vasquez, J. (2008). A future in jeopardy: Sexuality issues in adolescence. In D. Capuzzi & D. R. Gross (Eds.), *Youth at risk: A prevention resource for counselors, teachers, and parents.* Alexandria, VA: American Counseling Association.

Halgunseth, L. C., Ispa, J. M., & Rudy, D. (2006). Parental control in Latino families: An integrated review of the literature. *Child Development, 77,* 1282–1297.

Hall, G. S. (1916). *Adolescence.* New York: Appleton. (Original work published 1904).

Hall, J., Neal, T., & Dean, R. (2008). Lateralization of cerebral functions. *The Neuropsychology Handbook* (3rd ed., pp. 183–214). New York: Springer.

Hall, R. E., & Rowan, G. T. (2003). Identity development across the life span: Alternative model for biracial Americans. *Psychology and Education: An Interdisciplinary Journal, 40,* 3–12.

Halliday, M. A. K. (1975). *Learning how to mean: Explorations in the development of language.* London: Arnold.

Halpern, L. F., MacLean, W. E., & Baumeister, A. A. (1995). Infant sleep–wake characteristics: Relation to neurological status and the prediction of developmental outcome. *Developmental Review, 15,* 255–291.

Hamon, R. R., & Ingoldsby, B. B. (Eds.). (2003). *Mate selection across cultures.* Thousand Oaks, CA: Sage.

Handwerk, M. L. (2002). Least restrictive alternative: Challenging assumptions and further implications. *Children's Services: Social Policy, Research, & Practice, 5,* 99–103.

Hane, A., Feldstein, S., & Dernetz, V. (2003). The relation between coordinated interpersonal timing and maternal sensitivity in 4-month-old infants. *Journal of Psycholinguistic Research, 32,* 525–539.

Hankin, B. L., & Abramson, L. Y. (2001). Development of gender differences in depression: An elaborated cognitive vulnerability–transactional stress theory. *Psychological Bulletin, 127,* 773–796.

Hanson, D. R., & Gottesman, I. I. (2005). Theories of schizophrenia: A genetic-inflammatory-vascular synthesis. *BMC Medical Genetics, 6,* 7.

Hare, T., Tottenham, N., Galvan, A., Voss, H., Glover, G., & Casey, B. (2008, May). Biological substrates of emotional reactivity and regulation in adolescence during an emotional go-nogo task. *Biological Psychiatry, 63,* 927–934.

Harlow, H. F., & Zimmerman, R. R. (1959). Affectional responses in the infant monkey. *Science, 130,* 421–432.

Harmon, A. (2004, August 26). Internet gives teenage bullies weapons to wound from afar. *The New York Times,* pp. A1, A21.

Harrell, J. S., Bangdiwala, S. I., Deng, S., Webb, J. P., & Bradley, C. (1998). Smoking initiation in youth: The roles of gender, race, socioeconomics, and developmental status. *Journal of Adolescent Health, 23,* 271–219.

Harrell, Z., & Karim, N. (2008, February). Is gender relevant only for problem alcohol behaviors? An examination of correlates of alcohol use among college students. *Addictive Behaviors, 33,* 359–365.

Harris, J. R. (1998). *The nurture assumption: Why children turn out the way they do.* New York: Free Press.

Harris, J. R. (2000). Socialization, personality development, and the child's environments: Comment on Vandell. *Developmental Psychology, 36,* 711–723.

Harris, J., Vernon, P., & Jang, K. (2007). Rated personality and measured intelligence in young twin children. *Personality and Individual Differences, 42,* 75–86.

Harris, P. L. (1987). The development of search. In P. Sallapatek & L. Cohen (Eds.), *Handbook of infant perception: From perception to cognition* (Vol. 2, pp. 155–207). Orlando, FL: Academic Press.

Harrison, K., & Hefner, V. (2006, April). Media exposure, current and future body ideals, and disordered eating among preadolescent girls: A longitudinal panel study. *Journal of Youth and Adolescence, 35,* 153–163.

Harrist, A., & Waugh, R. (2002). Dyadic synchrony: Its structure and function in children's development. *Developmental Review, 22,* 555–592.

Hart, B. (2000). A natural history of early language experience. *Topics in Early Childhood Special Education, 20,* 28–32.

Hart, B. (2004). What toddlers talk about. *First Language, 24,* 91–106.

Hart, B., & Risley, T. R. (1995). *Meaningful differences in the everyday experience of young American children.* Baltimore, MD: Paul Brookes.

Hart, D., Burock, D., & London, B. (2003). Prosocial tendencies, antisocial behavior, and moral development. In A. Slater & G. Bremner (Eds.), *An introduction to developmental psychology.* Maiden, MA: Blackwell.

Harter, S. (1990). Issues in the assessment of self-concept of children and adolescents. In A. LaGreca (Ed.), *Through the eyes of a child.* Boston: Allyn & Bacon.

Harter, S. (2006). The Development of Self-Esteem. *Self-esteem issues and answers: A sourcebook of current perspectives* (pp. 144–150). New York NY, US: Psychology Press.

Hartshorne, J., & Ullman, M. (2006). Why girls say 'holded' more than boys. *Developmental Science, 9,* 21–32.

Harvey, E. (1999). Short-term and long-term effects of early parental employment on children of the National Longitudinal Survey of Youth. *Developmental Psychology, 35,* 445–459.

Harvey, J. H., & Fine, M. A. (2004). *Children of divorce: Stories of loss and growth.* Mahwah, NJ: Erlbaum.

Hasher, L., & Zacks, R. T. (1984). Automatic processing of fundamental information: The case of frequency of occurrence. *American Psychologist, 39,* 1372–1388.

Haslam, C., & Lawrence, W. (2004). Health-related behavior and beliefs of pregnant smokers. *Health Psychology, 23,* 486–491.

Hastings, S. (2004, October 15). Emotional intelligence. *The Times Educational Supplement, London,* p. F1.

Haugaard, J. J. (2000). The challenge of defining child sexual abuse. *American Psychologist, 55,* 1036–1039.

Hauser, M., Chomsky, N., & Fitch, W. (2002). The faculty of language: What is it, who has it, and how did it evolve? *Science, 298,* 1569–1579.

Haviv, S., & Leman, P. (2002). Moral decision-making in real life: Factors affecting moral orientation and behavior justification. *Journal of Moral Education, 31,* 121–140.

Hawker, D., & Boulton, M. (2000). Twenty years' research on peer victimization and psychosocial maladjustment: A meta-analytic review of cross-sectional studies. *Journal of Child Psychology and Psychiatry, 41,* 441–455.

Hawkins-Rodgers, Y. (2007). Adolescents adjusting to a group home environment: A residential care model of reorganizing attachment behavior and building resiliency. *Children and Youth Services Review, 29,* 1131–1141.

Hay, D. F., Pawlby, S., & Angold, A. (2003). Pathways to violence in the children of mothers who were depressed postpartum. *Developmental Psychology, 39,* 1083–1094.

Hay, D., Payne, A., & Chadwick, A. (2004). Peer relations in childhood. *Journal of Child Psychology & Psychiatry & Allied Disciplines, 45,* 84–108.

Haynie, D. L., Nansel, T., Eitel, P., Crump, A. D., Saylor, K., Yu, K., et al. (2001). Bullies, victims, and bully/victims: Distinct groups of at-risk youth. *Journal of Early Adolescence, 21,* 29–49.

Hazin, A.N., Alves, J.G., & Rodrigues Falbo, A. (2007). The myelenation process in severely malnourished children: MRI findings. *International Journal of Neuroscience, 117,* 1209–14

Head, D. (2005). Young people, sex and the media: the facts of life? *Journal of Family Studies, 11,* 326–327.

Health eLine. (2003, June 26). Baby's injury points to danger of kids imitating TV. *Health eLine. Date verified by auth*

Health Resources and Services Administration. (2001). *Child Health USA, 2001.* Washington, DC: U.S. Department of Health and Human Services.

Healy, P. (2001, March 3). Data on suicides set off alarm. *Boston Globe,* p. B1.

Heath, A. C. (1994, February). Winning at sports. *Parents,* pp. 126–130.

Hedgepeth, E. (2005). Different lenses, different vision. *School Administrator, 62,* 36–39.

Heerey, E. A., Keltner, D., & Capps, L. M. (2003). Making sense of self-conscious emotion: Linking theory of mind and emotion in children with autism. *Emotion, 3,* 394–400.

Heimann, M. (Ed.). (2003). *Regression periods in human infancy.* Mahwah, NJ: Lawrence Erlbaum Associates.

Hellman, P. (1987, November 23). *Sesame Street* smart. *The New York Times,* pp. 49–53.

Henry, B., Caspi, A., Moffitt, T. E., & Silva, P. A. (1996). Temperamental and familial predictors of violent and nonviolent criminal convictions: Age 3 to 18. *Developmental Psychology, 32,* 614–623.

Herdt, G. H. (Ed.). (1998). *Rituals of manhood: Male initiation in Papua New Guinea.* Somerset, NJ: Transaction Books.

Hernandez-Reif, M., Diego, M., & Field, T. (2007). Preterm infants show reduced stress behaviors and activity after 5 days of massage therapy. *Infant Behavior & Development, 30,* 557–561.

Hernandez-Reif, M., Field, T., Diego, M., Vera, Y., & Pickens, J. (2006, January). Brief report: Happy faces are habituated more slowly by infants of depressed mothers. *Infant Behavior & Development,29*, 131–135.

Herrenkohl, T., Sousa, C., Tajima, E., Herrenkohl, R., & Moylan, C. (2008, April). Intersection of child abuse and children's exposure to domestic violence. *Trauma, Violence, & Abuse, 9*, 84–99.

Herrnstein, R. J., & Murray, C. (1994). *The Bell Curve: Intelligence and class structure in American life.* New York: Free Press.

Hertenstein, M. J. (2002). Touch: Its communicative functions in infancy. *Human Development, 45*, 70–94.

Hertenstein, M. J., & Campos, J. J. (2001). Emotion regulation via maternal touch. *Infancy, 2*, 549–566.

Heterelendy, F., & Zakar, T. (2004). Prostaglandins and the mymetrium and cervix. *Prostaglandins, Leukotrienes and Essential Fatty Acids, 70*, 207–222.

Hetherington, E., & Elmore, A. (2003). Risk and resilience in children coping with their parents' divorce and remarriage. In S. Luthar (Ed.), *Resilience and vulnerability: Adaptation in the context of childhood adversities.* New York: Cambridge University Press.

Hetherington, E. M., & Kelly, J. (2002). *For better or worse: Divorce reconsidered.* New York: Norton.

Hewitt. B. (1997, December 15). A day in the life. *People Magazine,* pp. 49–58.

Hewlett, B., & Lamb, M. (2002). Integrating evolution, culture and developmental psychology: Explaining caregiver–infant proximity and responsiveness in central Africa and the USA. In H. Keller & Y. Poortinga (Eds.), *Between culture and biology: Perspectives on ontogenetic development* (pp. 241–269). New York: Cambridge University Press.

Heyman, J. D., Breu, G., Simmons, M., & Howard, C. (2003, September 15). Drugs can make short kids grow but is it right to prescribe them? *People,* pp. 103–104.

Heyman, R., & Slep, A. M. (2002). Do child abuse and interparental violence lead to adulthood family violence? *Journal of Marriage & Family, 64*, 864–870.

Hietala, J., Cannon, T. D., & van Erp, T. G. M. (2003). Regional brain morphology and duration of illness in never-medicated first-episode patients with schizophrenia. *Schizophrenia, 64*, 79–81.

Higgins, D., & McCabe, M. (2003). Maltreatment and family dysfunction in childhood and the subsequent adjustment of children and adults. *Journal of Family Violence, 18*, 107–120.

Highley, J. R. Esiri, M. M., McDonald, B., Cortina-Borja, M., Herron, B. M., & Crow, T. J. (1999). The size and fibre composition of the corpus callosum with respect to gender and schizophrenia: A post-mortem study. *Brain, 122*, 99–110.

Hightower, J. R. R. (2005). Women and depression. In A. Barnes (Ed.), *Handbook of women, psychology, and the law.* New York: Wiley.

Hildreth, K., Sweeney, B., & Rovee-Collier, C. (2003). Differential memory-preserving effects of reminders at 6 months. *Journal of Experimental Child Psychology, 84*, 41–62.

Hines, M., Golombok, S., Rust, J., Johnston, K. J., & Golding, J. (2002). Testosterone during pregnancy and gender role behavior of preschool children: A longitudinal, population study. *Child Development, 73*, 1678–1687.

Hirsch, H. V., & Spinelli, D. N. (1970). Visual experience modifies distribution of horizontally and vertically oriented receptive fields in cats. *Science, 168*, 869–871.

Hirsh-Pasek, K., & Michnick-Golinkoff, R. (1995). *The origins of grammar: Evidence from early language comprehension.* Cambridge, MA: MIT Press.

Hiser, E., & Kobayashi, J. (2003). Hemisphere lateralization differences: A cross-cultural study of Japanese and American students in Japan. *Journal of Asian Pacific Communication, 13*, 197–229.

Hitlin, S., Brown, J. S., & Elder, G. H., Jr. (2006). Racial self-categorization in adolescence: Multiracial development and social pathways. *Child Development, 77*, 1298–1308.

Hoelter, L. F., Axinn, W. G., & Ghimire, D. J. (2004). Social change, premarital nonfamily experiences, and marital dynamics. *Journal of Marriage & Family, 66*, 1131–1151.

Hoerr, S., Murashima, M., & Keast, D. (2008). Nutrition and obesity. *Obesity in childhood and adolescence, Vol 1: Medical, biological, and social issues* (pp. 201–227). Westport, CT: Praeger/Greenwood Publishing Group.

Hofer, M. A. (2006). Psychobiological roots of early attachment. *Current Directions in Psychological Science, 15*, 84–88.

Hofferth, S. L., & Sandberg, J. (1998). *Changes in American children's time, 1981–1997.* Ann, Arbor, MI: University of Michigan Institute for Social Research.

Hofferth, S. L., & Sandberg, J. F. (2001). How American children spend their time. *Journal of Marriage and the Family, 63*, 295–308.

Hoffman, L. (2003). Why high schools don't change: What students and their yearbooks tell us. *High School Journal, 86*, 22–37.

Holden, G. W., & Miller, P. C. (1999). Enduring and different: A meta-analysis of the similarity in parents' child rearing. *Psychological Bulletin, 125*, 223–254.

Holland, J. L. (1973). *Making vocational choices: A theory of careers.* Englewood Cliffs, NJ: Prentice Hall.

Holland, J. L. (1987). Current status of Holland's theory of careers: Another perspective. *Career Development Quarterly, 36*, 24–30.

Holland, N. (1994, August). *Race dissonance—Implications for African American children.* Paper presented at the annual meeting of the American Psychological Association, Los Angeles.

Hollich, G. J., Hirsh-Pasek, K., Golinkoff, R. M., Brand, R. J., Brown, E. C., He, L., et al. (2000). Breaking the language barrier: An emergentist coalition model of the origins of word learning. *Monographs of the Society for Research in Child Development, 65*(3, Serial No. 262).

Hollingworth, H. L. (1943/1990). *Letta Stetter Hollingworth: A biography.* Boston: Anker.

Holmes, T. H., & Rahe, R. H. (1967). The social readjustment scale. *Journal of Psychosomatic Research, 11*, 251–261.

Holowaly, S., & Petitto, L. A. (2002). Left hemisphere cerebral specialization for babies while babbling. *Science, 287*, 1515.

Holowka, S., & Petitto, L.A. (2002). Left hemisphere cerebral specialization for babies while babbling. *Science, 297*, 1515.

Holt, M. K., Espelage, D. L. (2007). Perceived social support among bullies, victims, and bully victims. *Journal of Youth and Adolescence, 36*, 984–994.

Holtmann, M., Bolte, S., Poustka, F. (2008). Rapid increase in rates of bipolar diagnosis in youth: "True" bipolarity or misdiagnosed severe disruptive behavior disorders? *Archives of General Psychiatry, 65*, 477.

Holyrod, R., & Sheppard, A. (1997). Parental separation: Effects on children: Implications for services. *Child: Care, Health & Development, 23*, 369–378.

Honey, J. L., Bennett, P., & Morgan, M. (2003). Predicting postnatal depression. *Journal of Affective Disorders, 76*, 201–210.

Hong, S. B., & Trepanier-Street, M. (2004). Technology: A tool for knowledge construction in a Reggio Emilia inspired teacher education program. *Early Childhood Education Journal, 32*, 87–94.

Hopkins, B., & Westra, T. (1989). Maternal expectations of their infants' development: Some cultural differences. *Developmental Medicine and Child Neurology, 31*, 384–390.

Hopkins, B., & Westra, T. (1990). Motor development, maternal expectation, and the role of handling. *Infant Behavior and Development, 13*, 117–122.

Hopkins-Golightly, T., Raz, S., & Sander, C. (2003). Influence of slight to moderate risk for birth hypoxia on acquisition of cognitive and language function in the preterm infant: A cross-sectional comparison with preterm-birth controls. *Neuropsychology, 17*, 3–13.

Hoppe, M. J., Graham, L., Wilsdon, A., Wells, E. A., Nahom, D., & Morrison, D. M. (2004). Teens speak out about HIV/AIDS: Focus group discussions about risk and decision-making. *Journal of Adolescent Health, 35*, 27–35.

Hornik, R., & Gunnar, M. R. (1988). A descriptive analysis of infant social referencing. *Child Development, 59*, 626–634.

Horton-lkard, R., & Weismer, S. (2007, November). A preliminary examination of vocabulary and word learning in African American toddlers from middle and low socioeconomic status homes. *American Journal of Speech-Language Pathology, 16*, 381–392.

Hotelling, B. A., & Humenick, S. S. (2005). Advancing normal birth: organizations, goals, and research. *Journal of Perinatal Education, 14*, 40–48.

House, S. H. (2007). Nurturing the brain nutritionally and emotionally from before conception to late adolescence, *Nutritional Health, 19*, 143–61.

Howard, L.M., Kirkwood, G., & Latinovic, R. (2007). Sudden infant death syndrome and maternal depression. *Journal of Clinical Psychiatry, 68*, 1279–83.

Howe, M. J. (2004). Some insights of geniuses into the causes of exceptional achievement. In L. V. Shavinina & M. Ferrari (Eds.), *Beyond knowledge: Extracognitive aspects of developing high ability*. Mahwah, NJ: Erlbaum

Howe, M. L. (2003). Memories from the cradle. *Current Directions in Psychological Science, 12*, 62–65.

Howe, M. L., Courage, M. L., & Edison, S. C. (2004). When autobiographical memory begins. In S. Algarabel, A. Pitarque, T. Bajo, S. E. Gathercole, & M. A. Conway (Eds.), *Theories of memory* (Vol. 3). New York: Psychology Press.

Howes, C., Galinsky, E., & Kontos, S. (1998). Childcare caregiver sensitivity and attachment. *Social Development, 7*, 25–36.

Hsu, V., & Rovee-Collier, C. (2006). Memory reactivation in the second year of life. *Infant Behavior & Development, 29*, 91–107.

Hubel, D. H., & Wiesel, T. N. (1979). Brain mechanisms of vision. *Scientific American, 241*, 150–162.

Hubel, D. H., & Wiesel, T. N. (2004). *Brain and visual perception: The story of a 25-year collaboration*. New York: Oxford University Press.

Hudson, J. A., Sosa, B. B., & Shapiro, L. R. (1997). Scripts and plans: The development of preschool children's event knowledge and event planning. In S. L. Friedman & E. K. Scholnick (Eds.), *The developmental psychology of planning: Why, how and when do we plan* (pp. 77–102). Mahwah, NJ: Erlbaum.

Huesmann, L. R., Moise-Titus, J., & Podolski, C. L. (2003). Longitudinal relations between children's exposure to TV violence and their aggressive and violent behavior in young adulthood: 1977–1992. *Developmental Psychology, 39*, 201–221.

Hui, A., Lau, S., Li, C., Tong, T., & Zhang, J. (2006). A cross-societal comparative study of Beijing and Hong Kong children's self-concept. *Social Behavior and Personality, 34*, 511–524.

Huizink, A., & Mulder, E. (2006). Maternal smoking, drinking or cannabis use during pregnancy and neurobehavioral and cognitive functioning in human offspring. *Neuroscience & Biobehavioral Reviews, 30*, 24–41.

Huizink, A., Mulder, E., & Buitelaar, J. (2004). Prenatal stress and risk for psychopathology: Specific effects or induction of general susceptibility? *Psychological Bulletin, 130*, 115–142.

Hulei, E., Zevenbergen, A., & Jacobs, S. (2006, September). Discipline behaviors of Chinese American and European American mothers. *Journal of Psychology: Interdisciplinary and Applied,140*, 459–475.

Hunt, C., & Hauck, F. (2006). Sudden infant death syndrome. *Canadian Medical Association Journal, 174*, 1861–1869.

Hunt, M. (1974). *Sexual behaviors in the 1970s.* New York: Dell.

Hunt, M. (1993). *The story of psychology.* New York: Doubleday.

Hunter, J., & Mallon, G. P. (2000). Lesbian, gay, and bisexual adolescent development: Dancing with your feet tied together. In B. Greenej & G. L. Croom (Eds.), *Education, research, and practice in lesbian, gay, bisexual, and transgendered psychology: A resource manual* (Vol. 5). Thousand Oaks, CA: Sage.

Huntsinger, C. S., Jose, P. E., Liaw, F., & Ching, W.-D. (1997). Cultural differences in early mathematics learning: A comparison of Euro-American, Chinese-American, and Taiwan-Chinese families. *International Journal of Behavioral Development, 21*, 371–388.

Huston, A. (Ed.). (1991). *Children in poverty: Child development and public policy.* Cambridge, England: Cambridge University Press.

Hutchinson, A., Whitman, R., & Abeare, C. (2003). The unification of mind: Integration of hemispheric semantic processing. *Brain & Language, 87*, 361–368.

Hutton, P. H. (2004). *Phillippe Aries and the politics of French cultural history.* Amherst, MA: University of Massachusetts Press.

Huurre, T., Junkkari, H., & Aro, H. (2006, June). Long-term psychosocial effects of parental divorce: A follow-up study from adolescence to adulthood. *European Archives of Psychiatry and Clinical Neuroscience, 256*, 256–263.

Hyde, J. S., & DeLamater, J. D. (2003). *Understanding human sexuality* (8th ed). New York: McGraw-Hill.

Hyde, J., Mezulis, A., & Abramson, L. (2008, April). The ABCs of depression: Integrating affective, biological, and cognitive models to explain the emergence of the gender difference in depression. *Psychological Review, 115*, 291–313.

Hyssaelae, L., Rautava, P., & Helenius, H. (1995). Fathers' smoking and use of alcohol: The viewpoint of maternity health care clinics and well-baby clinics. *Family Practice, 12*, 22–27.

Iglesias, J., Eriksson, J., Grize, F., Tomassmi, M., & Villa, A. E. (2005). Dynamics of pruning in simulated large-scale spiking neural networks. *Biosystems, 79*, 11–20.

Ingersoll, E. W., & Thoman, E. B. (1999). Sleep/wake states of preterm infants: Stability, developmental change, diurnal variation, and relation with caregiving activity. *Child Development, 70*, 1–10.

Ingudomnukul, E., Baron-Cohen, S., Wheelwright, S., & Knickmeyer, R. (2007, May). Elevated rates of testosterone-related disorders in women with autism spectrum conditions. *Hormones and Behavior, 51,* 597–604.

Insel, B., & Gould, M. (2008, June). Impact of modeling on adolescent suicidal behavior. *Psychiatric Clinics of North America, 31,* 293–316.

International Human Genome Sequencing Consortium. (2001). Initial sequencing and analysis of the human genome. *Nature, 409,* 860–921.

Ireland, J. L., & Archer, J. (2004). Association between measures of aggression and bullying among juvenile young offenders. *Aggressive Behavior, 30,* 29–42.

Isaacs, K., Barr, W., Nelson, P., & Devinsky, O. (2006, June). Degree of handedness and cerebral dominance. *Neurology, 66,* 1855–1858.

Isay, R. A. (1990). *Being homosexual: Gay men and their development.* New York: Avon.

Isenberg, E. (2007). What have we learned about homeschooling?. *Peabody Journal of Education, 82,* 387–409.

Ishi-Kuntz, M. (2000). Diversity within Asian-American families. In D. H. Demo, K. R. Allen, & M. A. Fine (Eds.), *Handbook of family diversity.* New York: Oxford.

Israel, E. (2005). Introduction: The rise of the age of individualism—Variability in the pathobiology, response to treatment, and treatment outcomes in asthma. *Journal of Allergy and Clinical Immunology, 115,* S525.

Izard, J., Haines, C., Crouch, R., Houston, S., & Neill, N. (2003).Assessing the impact of the teaching of modelling: Some implications. In S. Lamon., W. Parker., & K. Houston (Eds.), *Mathematical modelling: A way of life: ICTMA 11.* Chichester, England: Horwood Publishing.

Jacobi, C., Hayward, C., de Zwaan, M., Kraemer, H. C., & Agras, W. S. (2004). Coming to terms with risk factors for eating disorders: Application of risk terminology and suggestions for a general taxonomy. *Psychological Bulletin, 130,* 19–65.

Jacobson, J. W., Foxx, R. M., & Mulick, J. A. (Eds.). *Controversial therapies for developmental disabilities: Fad, fashion and science in professional practice.* Mahwah, NJ: Erlbaum.

Jacques, H., & Mash, E. (2004). A test of the tripartite model of anxiety and depression in elementary and high school boys and girls. *Journal of Abnormal Child Psychology, 32,* 13–25.

Jahoda, G. (1980). Theoretical and systematic approaches in mass-cultural psychology. In H. C. Triandis & W. W. Lambert (Eds.), *Handbook of cross-cultural psychology* (Vol. 1). Needham Heights, MA: Allyn & Bacon.

Jahoda, G. (1983). European "lag" in the development of an economic concept: A study in Zimbabwe. *British Journal of Developmental Psychology, 1,* 113–120.

James, W. (1950). *The principles of psychology.* New York: Holt. (Original work published 1890)

Jayawant, S., & Parr, J. (2007). Outcome following subdural haemorrhages in infancy. *Archives of Disease in Childhood, 92,* 343–7.

Jehlen, A., & Winans, D. (2005). No child left behind—Myth or Truth? *NEA Today, 23,* 32–34.

Jenkins, J. E. (1996). The influence of peer affiliation and student activities on adolescent drug involvement. *Adolescence, 31,* 297–306.

Jensen, A. R. (2003). *Regularities in Spearman's Law of Diminishing Returns. Intelligence, 31,* 95–105.

Jensen, L. (2008). Coming of age in a multicultural world: Globalization and adolescent cultural identity formation. *Adolescent identities: A collection of readings* (pp. 3–17). New York: Analytic Press/Taylor & Francis Group.

Jenvey, V. (2007, December). The relationship between television viewing and obesity in young children: A review of existing explanations. *Early Child Development and Care, 177,* 809–820.

Jeynes, W. (2007). The impact of parental remarriage on children: a meta-analysis. *Marriage & Family Review, 40,* 75–102.

Jimenez, J., & Guzman, R. (2003). The influence of code-oriented versus meaning-oriented approaches to reading instruction on word recognition in the Spanish language. *International Journal of Psychology, 38,* 65–78.

Joe, S., & Marcus, S. (2003). Datapoints: Trends by race and gender in suicide attempts among U.S. adolescents, 1991–2001. *Psychiatric Services, 54,* 454.

Johannes, L. (2003, October 9). A better test for Down syndrome. *The Wall Street Journal,* pp. Dl, D3.

Johnson, A. M., Wadsworth, J., Wellings, K., & Bradshaw, S. (1992). Sexual lifestyles and HIV risk. *Nature, 360,* 410–412.

Johnson, D. (2003, September 22). Fighting for air. *Newsweek,* pp. 54–57.

Johnson, D. J., Jaeger, E., Randolph, S. M., Cauce, A. M., Ward, J., & National Institute of Child Health and Human Development: Early Child Care Research Network. (2003). Studying the effects of early child care experiences on the development of children of color in the United States: Toward a more inclusive research agenda. *Child Development, 74,* 1227–1244.

Johnson, J. L., Primas, P. J., & Coe, M. K. (1994). Factors that prevent women of low socioecoriomic status from seeking prenatal Care. *Journal of the American Academy of Nurse Practitioners, 6,* 105–111.

Johnson, K., & Eilers, A. (1998). Effects of knowledge and development on subordinate level categorization. *Cognitive Development, 13,* 515–545.

Johnson, M. H. (1998). The neural basis of cognitive development. In D. Kuhn & R. S. Siegler (Eds.), *Handbook of child psychology: Vol. 2: Cognition, perception, and language* (5th ed., pp. 1–49). New York: Wiley.

Johnson, N. G., Roberts, M. C., & Worell, J. (Eds.). (1999). *Beyond appearance: A new look at adolescent girls.* Washington, DC: American Psychological Association.

Johnston, L.D., Bachman, J.G., & O'Malley, P.M. (2006). *Monitoring the Future study.* Lansing: University of Michigan.

Johnston, M., & Esposito, N. (2007). Barriers and facilitators for breastfeeding among working women in the United States. *Journal of Obstetric, Gynecologic, & Neonatal Nursing: Clinical Scholarship for the Care of Women, Childbearing Families, & Newborns, 36,* 9–20.

Jones, Brown, & Aber, 2008.

Jones, S. (2006). Exploration or imitation? The effect of music on 4-week-old infants' tongue protrusions. *Infant Behavior & Development, 29,* 126–130.

Jones, S. S. (2007). Imitation in infancy: The development of mimicry. *Psychological Science, 18,* 593–599.

Jones-Harden, B. (2004). Safety and stability for foster children: A developmental perspective. *Future of Children, 14,* 31–48.

Joseph, H., Reznik, I., & Mester, R. (2003). Suicidal behavior of adolescent girls: Profile and meaning. *Israel Journal of Psychiatry & Related Sciences, 40,* 209–219.

Joseph, R. (1999). Environmental influences on neural plasticity, the limbic system, emotional development and attachment: A review. *Child Psychiatry & Human Development, 29,* 189–208.

Juby, H., Billette, J., Laplante, B., & Le Bourdais, C. (2007, September). Nonresident fathers and children: Parents' new unions and frequency of contact. *Journal of Family Issues, 28,* 1220–1245.

Juhn, Y. J., Sauver, J. S., Katusic, S., Vargas, D., Weaver, A., & Yungmger, J. (2005). The influence of neighborhood environment on the incidence of childhood asthma: A multilevel approach. *Social Science Medicine, 60,* 2453–2464.

Jurimae, T., & Saar, M. (2003). Self-perceived and actual indicators of motor abilities in children and adolescents. *Perception and Motor Skills, 97,* 862–866.

Juster, F., Ono, H., & Stafford F. (2004). *Changing times of American youth: 1981–2003.* Ann Arbor, MI: Institute for Social Research.

Juvonen, J., Le, V.-N., Kaganoff, T., Augustine, C. H., & Constand, L. (2004). *Focus on the wonder years: Challenges facing the American middle school.* Santa Monica, CA: Rand.

Kagan, J. (2000, October). Adult personality and early experience. *Harvard Mental Health Letter,* pp. 4–5.

Kagan, J. (2003). An unwilling rebel. In R. J. Steinberg (Ed.), *Psychologists defying the crowd: Stories of those who battled the establishment and won.* Washington, DC: American Psychological Association.

Kagan, J. (2003). An unwilling rebel. In R. J. Sternberg (Ed.), *Psychologists defying the crowd: Stories of those who battled the establishment and won.* Washington, DC: American Psychological Association.

Kagan, J., Arcus, D., & Snidman, N. (1993). The idea of temperament: Where do we go from here? In R. Plomin & G. E. McClearn (Eds.), *Nature, nurture, and psychology.* Washington, DC: American Psychological Association.

Kagan, J., Arcus, D., Snidman, N., Feng, W. Y., Hendler, J., & Greene, S. (1994). Reactivity in infants: A cross-national comparison. *Developmental Psychology, 30,* 342–345.

Kagan, J., Kearsley, R., & Zelazo, P. R. (1978). *Infancy: Its place in human development.* Cambridge, MA: Harvard University Press.

Kagan, J., & Snidman, N. (1991). Infant predictors of inhibited and uninhibited profiles. *Psychological Science, 2,* 40–44.

Kahana-Kalman, R., & Walker-Andrews, A. (2001). The role of person familiarity in young infants' perception of emotional expressions. *Child Development, 72,* 352–369.

Kail, R. V. (2003). Information processing and memory. In M. H. Bomstein & L. Davidson (Eds.), *Well-being: Positive development across the life course.* Mahwah, NJ: Erlbaum.

Kail, R. V. (2004). Cognitive development includes global and domain-specific processes [Special issue: 50th Anniversary Issue: Part II, The maturing of the human development sciences: Appraising past, present, and prospective agendas]. *Merrill-Palmer Quarterly, 50,* 445–455.

Kail, R., & Miller, C. (2006). Developmental change in processing speed: Domain specificity and stability during childhood and adolescence. *Journal of Cognition and Development, 7,* 119–137.

Kaiser, L. L., & Allen, L. American Dietetic Association. (2002). Position of the American Dietetic Association: Nutrition and lifestyle for a healthy pregnancy outcome. *Journal of the American Dietetic Association, 102,* 1479–1490.

Kalb, C. (1997, Spring/Summer). The top 10 health worries [Special issue]. *Newsweek,* pp. 42–43.

Kalb, C. (2003, March 10). Preemies grow up. *Newsweek,* pp. 50–51.

Kalb, C. (2004, January 26). Brave new babies. *Newsweek,* pp. 45–53.

Kalb, C. (2006, December 11). Peering into the future. *Newsweek,* 52.

Kaltiala-Heino, R., Kosunen, E., & Rimpela, M. (2003). Pubertal timing, sexual behavior and self-reported depression in middle adolescence. *Journal of Adolescence, 26,* 531–545.

Kaltiala-Heino, R., Rimpelae, M., Rantanen, P., & Rimpelae, A. (2000). Bullying at school—An indicator of adolescents at risk for mental disorders. *Journal of Adolescence, 23,* 661–674.

Kamerman, S. B. (2000a). From maternity to parental leave policies: Women's health employment, and child and family well-being. *The Journal of the Women's Medical Association, 55,* Table 1.

Kamerman, S. B. (2000b). Parental leave policies: An essential ingredient in early childhood education and care policies. *Social Policy Report 14,* Table 1.0.

Kaminaga, M. (2007). Pubertal timing and depression in adolescents. *Japanese Journal of Educational Psychology, 55,* 370–381.

Kantrowitz, B., & Wingert, P. (1999, May 10). How well do you know your kid? (teenagers need adult attention). *Newsweek, 133,* 36.

Kantrowitz, E. J., & Evans, G. W. (2004). The relation between the ratio of children per activity area and off-task behavior and type of play in day care centers. *Environment & Behavior, 36,* 541–557.

Kao, G. (2000). Psychological well-being and educational achievement among immigrant youth. In D. J. Hernandez (Ed.), *Children of immigrants: Health, adjustment, and public assistance.* Washington, DC: National Academy Press.

Kaplan, H., & Dove, H. (1987). Infant development among the Ache of Eastern Paraguay. *Developmental Psychology, 23,* 190–198.

Kaplan, S., Heiligenstein, J., West, S., Busner, J., Harder, D., Dittmann, R., et al. (2004). Efficacy and safety of atomoxetine in childhood attention-deficit/hyperactivity disorder with comorbid oppositional defiant disorder. *Journal of Attention Disorders, 8,* 45–52.

Karademas, E. C. (2007). Positive and negative aspects of well-being: Common and specific predictors. *Personality and Individual Differences, 43,* 277–287.

Kato, K., & Pedersen, N. L. (2005). Personality and coping: A study of twins reared apart and twins reared together. *Behavior Genetics, 35,* 147–158.

Katon, W., Russo, J., Richardson, L., McCauley, E., Lozano, P. (2008). Anxiety and depression screening for youth in a primary care population. *Ambulatory Pediatrics, 8,* 182–8.

Katrowitz, B., & Wingert, P. (1990, Winter/Spring). Step by step. *Newsweek Special Edition,* pp. 24–34.

Katz, L. G. (1989, December). Beginners' ethics. *Parents,* p. 213.

Kaufman, J. C., Kaufman, A. S., Kaufman-Singer, J., & Kaufman, N. L. (2005). The Kaufman Assessment Battery for Children—Second Edition and the Kaufman Adolescent and Adult Intelligence Test. In D. P. Flanagan & P. L. Harrison (Eds.), *Contemporary intellectual assessment: Theories, tests, and issues.* New York: Guilford Press.

Kaufmann, D., Gestert, E., Santa Lucia, R. C., Salcedo, O., Rendina-Gobioff, G., & Gadd, R. (2000). The relationship between parenting style and children's adjustment: The parents' perspective. *Journal of Child & Family Studies, 9,* 231–245.

Kaye, W. H., Devlin, B., Barbarich, N., Bulik, C. M., Thornton, L., Badanu, S. A., et al. (2004). Genetic analysis of bulimia nervosa: Methods and sample description. *Journal of Eating Disorders, 35,* 556–570.

Kazdin, A. E., & Behjet, C. (2003). Spanking children: Evidence and issues. *Current Directions in Psychological Science, 12,* 99–103.

Kazura, K. (2000). Fathers' qualitative and quantitative involvement: An investigation of attachment, play, and social interactions. *Journal of Men's Studies, 9,* 41–57.

Keating, D. P. (1980). Thinking processes in adolescence. In J. Adelson (Ed.), *Handbook of adolescent psychology.* New York: Wiley.

Kecskes, I., & Papp, T. (2000). *Foreign language and mother tongue.* Mahwah, NJ: Erlbaum.

Kellman, P., & Arterberry, M. (2006). Infant visual perception. In W. Damon & R. M. Lerner (Eds.), *Handbook of child psychology: Vol. 2, Cognition, perception, and language* (6th ed.). New York: John Wiley & Sons Inc.

Kellow, J., & Jones, B. (2008, February). The effects of stereotypes on the achievement gap: Reexamining the academic performance of African American high school students. *Journal of Black Psychology, 34,* 94–120.

Kelly, G. (2001). *Sexuality today: A human perspective* (7th ed.). New York: McGraw-Hill.

Kelly-Weeder, S., & Cox, C. (2007). The impact of lifestyle risk factors on female infertility. *Women & Health, 44,* 1–23.

Kennell, J. H. (2002). On becoming a family: Bonding and the changing patterns in baby and family behavior. In J. Gomes-Pedro & J. K. Nugent (Eds.), *The infant and family in the twenty-first century.* New York: Brunner-Routledge.

Kesler, S. (2007). Turner syndrome. *Child and Adolescent Psychiatric Clinics of North America, 16,* 709–722.

Kibria, N. (2003). *Becoming Asian American: Second-generation Chinese and Korean American identities.* Baltimore, MD: Johns Hopkins University Press.

Kidwell, J. S., Dunyam, R. M., Bacho, R. A., Pastorino, E., & Fortes, P. R. (1995). Adolescent identity exploration: A test of Erikson's theory of transitional crisis. *Adolescence, 30,* 785–793.

Kiecolt-Glaser, J. K., & Glaser, R. (1986). Behavioral influences on immune function: Evidence for the interplay between stress and health. In T. Field, P. McCabe, & N. Schneiderman (Eds.), *Stress and coping* (Vol. 2). Hillsdale, NJ: Erlbaum.

Kiecolt-Glaser, J. K., & Glaser, R. (1991). Psychosocial factors, stress disease, and immunity. In R. Ader, D. L. Felten, & N. Cohen (Eds.), *Psychoneuroimmunology.* San Diego, CA: Academic Press.

Killen, M., & Hart, D. (Eds.). (1995). *Morality in everyday life: Developmental perspectives.* New York: Cambridge University Press.

Kilner, J. M., Friston, J. J., & Frith, C. D. (2007). Predictive coding: An account of the mirror neuron system. *Cognitive Processes, 33,* 88–997.

Kim, E., Hong, S. (2007). First-generation Korean-American parents' perceptions of discipline, *Journal of Professional Nursing. 23,* 60–8.

Kim, J., & Cicchetti, D. (2003). Social self-efficacy and behavior problems in maltreated children. *Journal of Clinical Child & Adolescent Psychology, 32,* 106–117.

Kim, Y., & Stevens, J. H. (1987). The socialization of prosocial behavior in children. *Childhood Education, 63,* 200–206.

Kim, Y., Choi, J.Y., Lee, K.M., Park, S.K., Ahn, S.H., Noh, D.Y., et al. (2007). Dose-dependent protective effect of breast-feeding against breast cancer among ever-lactated women in Korea. *European Journal of Cancer Prevention, 16,* 124–9.

Kimball, J. W. (1983). *Biology* (5th ed.). Reading, MA: Addison-Wesley.

Kimm, S. Y., Glynn, N. W., Kriska, A. M., Barton, B. A., Kronsberg, S. S., Daniels, S. R., et al. (2000). Decline in physical activity in black girls and white girls during adolescence. *New England Journal of Medicine, 347,* 709–715.

Kinney, H. C., Randall, L. L., Sleeper, L. A., Willinger, M., Beliveau, R. A., Zec, N., et al. Serotonergic brainstem abnormalities in Northern Plains Indians with the sudden infant death syndrome. *Journal of Neuropathology and Experimental Neurology, 62,* 1178–1191.

Kinzie, J., Thomas, A., Palmer, M., Umbach, P., & Kuh, G. (2007, March). Women students at coeducational and women's colleges: How do their experiences compare? *Journal of College Student Development, 48,* 145–165.

Kirby, D., Baumler, E., Coyle, K., Basen-Engquist, K., Parcel, G., Harrist, R., & et al. (2004). The "safer choices" intervention: Its impact on the sexual behaviors of different subgroups of high school students. *Journal of Adolescent Health, 35,* 442–452.

Kirby, J. (2006, May). From single-parent families to stepfamilies: Is the transition associated with adolescent alcohol initiation? *Journal of Family Issues, 27,* 685–711.

Kirchengast, S., & Hartmann, B. (2003). Impact of maternal age and maternal somatic characteristics on newborn size. *American Journal of Human Biology, 15,* 220–228.

Kisilevsky, B., Mains, S., & Lee, K. (2003). Effects of experience on fetal voice recognition. *Psychological Science, 14,* 220–224.

Klaczynski, P. A. (2004). A dual-process model of adolescent development: Implications for decision making, reasoning, and identity. In R. V. Kail (Ed.), *Advances in child development and behavior* (Vol. 32). San Diego, CA: Elsevier Academic Press.

Klier, C. M., Muzik, M., Dervic, K., Mossaheb, N., Benesch, T., Ulm, B., & Zeller, M. (2007). The role of estrogen and progesterone in depression after birth. *Journal of Psychiatric Research, 41,* 273–279.

Knafo, A., & Schwartz, S. H. (2003). Parenting and accuracy of perception of parental values by adolescents. *Child Development, 73,* 595–611.

Knickmeyer, R., & Baron-Cohen, S. (2006, December). Fetal testosterone and sex differences. *Early Human Development, 82,* 755–760.

Knight, K. (1994, March). Back to basics. *Essence,* 122–138.

Knorth, E., Harder, A., Zandberg, T., & Kendrick, A. (2008, February). Under one roof: A review and selective meta-analysis on the outcomes of residential child and youth care. *Children and Youth Services Review, 30,* 123–140

Kochanska, G. (1998). Mother–child relationship, child fearfulness, and emerging attachment: A short-term longitudinal study. *Developmental Psychology, 34,* 480–490

Kochanska, G. (2002). Mutually responsive orientation between mothers and their young children: A context for the early development of conscience. *Current Directions in Psychological Science, 11,* 191–195.

Kochanska, G., & Aksan, N. (2004). Development of mutual responsiveness between parents and their young children. *Child Development, 75,* 1657–1676.

Kodl, M., & Mermelstein, R. (2004). Beyond modeling: Parenting practices, parental smoking history, and adolescent cigarette smoking. *Addictive Behaviors, 29,* 17–32.

Koenig, A., Cicchetti, D., & Rogosch, F. (2004). Moral development: The association between maltreatment and young childern's prosocial behaviors and moral transgressions. *Social Development, 13,* 97–106.

Koenig, L. B., McGue, M., Krueger, R. F., & Bouchard, T. J., Jr. (2005). Genetic and environmental influences on religiousness: Findings for retrospective and current religiousness ratings. *Journal of Personality, 73,* 471–488.

Kohlberg, L. (1966). A cognitive-developmental analysis of children's sex-role concepts and attitudes. In E. E. Maccoby (Ed.), *The development of sex differences*. Stanford, CA: Stanford University Press.

Kohlberg, L. (1969). Stage and sequence: The cognitive-developmental approach to socialization. In D. Goslin (Ed.), *Handbook of socialization theory and research*. Chicago: Rand McNally.

Kohlberg, L. (1984). *The psychology of moral development: Essays on moral development*. San Francisco: Harper & Row.

Kohn, A. (2006). *The homework myth: Why our kids get too much of a bad thing*. Cambridge, MA: Da Capo Press.

Koivisto, M., & Revonsuo, A. (2003). Object recognition in the cerebral hemispheres as revealed by visual field experiments. *Laterality: Asymmetries of Body, Brain & Cognition, 8,* 135–153.

Kolata, G. (May 11, 2004). The heart's desire. *The New York Times,* p. D1.

Kolb, B., & Gibb, R. (2006). Critical periods for functional recovery after cortical injury during development. *Reprogramming the cerebral cortex: Plasticity following central and peripheral lesions* (pp. 297–307). New York: Oxford University Press.

Koretz, D. (2008). The pending reauthorization of NCLB: An opportunity to rethink the basic strategy. In G. L. Sunderman (Ed.), *Holding NCLB accountable: Achieving, accountability, equity, & school reform*; Thousand Oaks, CA: Corwin Press.

Koroukian, S. M., Trisel, B., & Rimm, A. A. (1998). Estimating the proportion of unnecessary cesarean sections in Ohio using birth certificate data. *Journal of Clinical Epidemiology, 51,* 1327–1334.

Koshmanova, T. (2007). Vygotskian Scholars: Visions and Implementation of Cultural-Historical Theory. *Journal of Russian & East European Psychology, 45,* 61–95.

Koska, J., Ksinantova, L., Sebokova, E., Kvemansky, R., Klimes, I., Chrousps, G., et al. (2002). Endocrine regulation of subcutaneous fat metabolism during cold exposure in humans. *Annals of the New York Academy of Science, 967,* 500–505.

Kotre, J., & Hall, E. (1990). *Seasons of life*. Boston: Little, Brown.

Kovelman, I., Baker & S. A., Petitto, L. A. (2008). Bilingual and monolingual brains compared: A functional magnetic resonance imaging investigation of syntactic processing and a possible "neural signature" of bilingualism. *Journal of Cognitive Neuroscience, 20,* 153–169.

Kozulin, A. (2004). Vygotsky's theory in the classroom: Introduction. *European Journal of Psychology of Education, 19,* 3–7.

Kramer, M. S. (2003). The epidemiology of adverse pregnancy outcomes: An overview. *Journal of Nutrition, 133,* 1592S–1596S.

Krcmar, M., Grela, B., & Lin, K. (2007). Can toddlers learn vocabulary from television? An experimental approach. *Media Psychology, 10,* 41–63.

Krebs, N. F., Himes, J. H., Jacobson, D., Nicklas, T. A., Guilday, P., & Styne, D. (2007). Assessment of child and adolescent overweight and obesity [*Special issue*]. *Pediatrics, 120,* S193–S228.

Kroger, J. (2000). *Identity development: Adolescence through adulthood*. Thousand Oaks, CA: Sage.

Kroger, J. (2006). Identity development during adolescence. In G.R. Adams & M.D. Berzonsky (Eds.), Blackwell handbook of adolescence. Malden, MA: Blackwell Publishing.

Kroger, J. (2007). Why is identity achievement so elusive? *Identity, 7,* 331–348.

Krojgaard, P. (2005). Infants' search for hidden persons. *International Journal of Behavioral Development, 29,* 70–79.

Kronenfeld, J. J. (2002). *Health care policy: Issues and trends*. New York: Prager.

Kronholz, J. (2003, August 10). Trying to close the stubborn learning gap. *The Wall Street Journal,* pp. B1, B5.

Krueger, G. (2006, September). Meaning-making in the aftermath of sudden infant death syndrome. *Nursing Inquiry, 13,* 163–171.

Kuczynski, L., & Kochanska, G. (1990). Development of children's non-compliance strategies from toddlerhood to age 5. *Developmental Psychology, 26,* 398–408.

Kuhl, P. K., Andruski, J. E., Chistovich, I. A., Chistovieh, L. A., Kozhevnikova, E. V., Ryskina, V. L., et al. (1977, August 1). Cross-language analysis of phonetic units in language addressed to infants. *Science, 277,* 684–686.

Kuhl, P., Tsao, F.-M., & Liu, H.-M. (2003). Foreign language experience in infancy: Effects of short-term exposure and social interaction on phonetic learning. *Proceedings of the National Academy of Sciences, 100,* 9096–9101.

Kuhn, D. (2000). Metacognitive development. *Current Directions in Psychological Science, 9,* 178–181.

Kunkel, D., Wilcox, B. L., Cantor, J., Palmer, E., Linn, S., & Dowrick, P. (2004, February 20). *Report of the APA task force on advertising and children*. Washington, DC: American Psychological Association.

Kupersmidt, J. B., & Dodge, K. A. (Eds.). (2004). *Children's peer relations: From development to intervention*. Washington, DC: American Psychological Association.

La Leche League International. (2003). *Breastfeeding around the world*. Schaumburg, IL: La Leche League International.

Labouvie-Vief, G., & Diehl, M. (2000). Cognitive complexity and cognitive–affective integration: Related or separate domains of adult development? *Psychology & Aging, 15,* 490–504.

Lacerda, F., von Hofsten, C., & Heimann, M. (2001). *Emerging cognitive abilities in early infancy*. Mahwah, NJ: Erlbaum.

Lachmann, T., Berti, S., Kujala, T., & Schroger, E. (2005). Diagnostic subgroups of developmental dyslexia have different deficits in neural processing of tones and phonemes. *International Journal of Psychophysiology, 56,* 105–120.

Laditka, S., Laditka, J., & Probst, J. (2006). Racial and ethnic disparities in potentially avoidable delivery complications among pregnant Medicaid beneficiaries in South Carolina. *Maternal & Child Health Journal, 10,* 339–350.

Laflamme, D., Pomerleau, A., & Malcuit, G. (2002). A comparison of fathers' and mothers' involvement in childcare and stimulation behaviors during free-play with their infants at 9 and 15 months. *Sex Roles, 47,* 507–518.

LaFromboise, T., Coleman, H. L., & Gerton, J. (1993). Psychological impact of biculturalism: Evidence and theory. *Psychological Bulletin, 114,* 395–412.

Lafuente, M. J., Grifol, R., Segarra, J., & Soriano, J. (1997). Effects of the Firstart method of prenatal stimulation on psychomotor development: The first 6 months. *Pre- & PeriNatal Psychology, 11,* 151–162.

Lagrou, K., Froidecoeur, C., Thomas, M., Massa, G., Beckers, D., Craen, M., et al.

Lall, M. (2007, August). Exclusion from school: Teenage pregnancy and the denial of education. *Sex Education, 7,* 219–237.

Lam, V., & Leman, P. (2003). The influence of gender and ethnicity on children's inferences about toy choice. *Social Development, 12,* 269–287.

Lamb, M. E., Sternberg, K. J., Hwang, C. P., & Broberg, A. G. (Eds.). (1992). *Child care in context: Cross-cultural perspectives.* Hillsdale, NJ: Erlbaum.

Lamorey, S., Robinson, B. E., & Rowland, B. H. (1998). *Latchkey kids: Unlocking doors for children and their families.* Newbury Park, CA: Sage.

Langford, P. E. (1995). *Approaches to the development of moral reasoning.* Hillsdale, NJ: Erlbaum.

Lanphear, B. P. (1998). The paradox of lead poisoning prevention. *Science, 281,* 1617–1618.

Lansford, J. E., & Parker, J. G. (1999). Children's interactions in triads: Behavioral profiles and effects of gender and patterns of friendships among members. *Developmental Psychology, 35,* 80–93.

Lansford, J. E., Malone, P. S., Dodge, K. A., Crozier, J. C., Pettit, G. S., Bates, J. E. (2006). A 12-year prospective study of patterns of social information processing, problems and externalizing behaviors. *Journal of Abnormal Child Psychology, 34,* 715–724.

Larson, R. W., Richards, M. H., Moneta, G., Holmbeck, G., & Duckett, E. (1996). Changes in adolescents' daily interactions with their families from ages 10 to 18: Disengagement and transformation. *Developmental Psychology, 32,* 744–754.

Lattibeaudiere, V. H. (2000). An exploratory study of the transition and adjustment of former home-schooled students to college life. *Dissertation Abstracts International, 61A,* 2211.

Lau, I., Lee, S., & Chiu, C. (2004). Language, cognition, and reality: Constructing shared meanings through communication. In M. Schaller & C. Crandall (Eds.), *The psychological foundations of culture.* Mahwah, NJ: Erlbaum.

Lau, S., & Kwok, L. K. (2000). Relationship of family environment to adolescents' depression and self-concept. *Social Behavior & Personality, 28,* 41–50.

Laugharne, J., Janca, A., & Widiger, T. (2007). Posttraumatic stress disorder and terrorism: 5 years after 9/11. *Current Opinion in Psychiatry, 20,* 36–41.

Laurance, 2008

Lauricella, T. (2001, November). The education of a home schooler. *Smart Money,* pp. 115–121.

Lauter, J. L. (1998). Neuroimaging and the trimodal brain: Applications for developmental communication neuroscience. *Phoniatrica et Logopaedica, 50,* 118–145.

Layzer, J.I. & Goodson, B.D. (2006). The "quality" of early care and education settings: definitional and measurement issues. *Evaluation Review, 30,* 556–76.

Le Vay, S., & Valente, S. M. (2003). *Human Sexuality.* Sunderland, MA: Sinauer Associates.

Leaper, C. (2002). Parenting girls and boys. In M. Bornstein (Ed.), *Handbook of parenting: Vol. 1. Children and parenting* (2nd ed.). Mahwah, NJ: Erlbaum.

Leathers, H. D., & Foster, P. (2004). *The world food problem: Tackling causes of undernutrition in the third world.* Boulder, CO: Lynne Rienner Publishers.

Leckman, J., & King, R. (2007, September). A developmental perspective on the controversy surrounding the use of SSRIs to treat pediatric depression. *American Journal of Psychiatry, 164,* 1304–1306.

Lee, B. H., Schofer, J. L., & Koppelman, F. S. (2005). Bicycle safety helmet legislation and bicycle-related non-fatal injuries in California. *Accidental Analysis and Prevention, 37,* 93–102.

Lee, R. M. (2005). Resilience against discrimination: Ethnic identity and other-group orientation as protective factors for Korean Americans. *Journal of Counseling Psychology, 52,* 36–44.

Lee, V. E. & Burkam, D. T. (2003). Dropping out of high school: The role of school organization and structure. *American Educational Research Journal, 40,* 353–393.

Leen-Feldner, E. W., Reardon, L. E., Hayward, C. (2008). The relation between puberty and adolescent anxiety: Theory and evidence. In M. J. Zvolensky & J. A. J. Smits (Eds.), *Anxiety in health behaviors and physical illness* (pp. 155–179). New York: Springer Science + Business Media.

Legerstee, M. (1998). Mental and bodily awareness in infancy: Consciousness of self-existence. *Journal of Consciousness Studies, 5,* 627–644.

Legerstee, M., & Markova, G. (2008). Variations in 10-month-old infant imitation of people and things. *Infant Behavior & Development, 31,* 81–91.

Lehman, D., Chiu, C., & Schaller, M. (2004). Psychology and culture. *Annual Review of Psychology, 55,* 689–714.

Lemonick, M. D. (2000, October 30). Teens before their time. *Time, 67,* 68–74.

Lepage, J. F., & Théret, H. (2007). The mirror neuron system: Grasping others' actions from birth? *Developmental Science, 10,* 513–523.

Lepper, R. (2006, March 2). Home-school includes hands-on work. *The San Diego Union-Tribune,* NC-8.

Lerner, R. M. (2002). *Concepts and theories of human development* (3rd ed.). Mahwah, NJ: Erlbaum.

Lerner, R. M., Fisher, C. B., & Weinberg, R. A. (2000). Toward a science for and of the people: Promoting civil society through the application of developmental science. *Child Development, 71,* 11–20.

Lerner, R. M., Theokas, C., & Jelicic, H. (2005). Youth as active agents in their own positive development: A developmental systems perspective. In W. Greve, K. Rothermund, & D. Wentura (Eds.), *Adaptive self: Personal continuity and intentional self-development.* Ashland, OH: Hogrefe & Huber Publishers.

Lesaux, N. K., & Siegel, L. S. (2003). The development of reading in children who speak English as a second language. *Developmental Psychology, 39,* 1005–1019.

Leslie, C. (1991, February 11). Classrooms of Babel. *Newsweek,* pp. 56–57.

Lessard, A., Butler-Kisber, L., Fortin, L., Marcotte, D., Potvin, P., & Royer, É. (2008, February). Shades of disengagement: High school dropouts speak out. *Social Psychology of Education, 11,* 25–42.

Leung, C., Pe-Pua, R., & Karnilowicz, W. (2006, January). Psychological adaptation and autonomy among adolescents in Australia: A comparison of Anglo-Celtic and three Asian groups. *International Journal of Intercultural Relations, 30,* 99–118.

Leung, K. (2005). Cross-cultural variations in distributive justice perception [Special issue]. *Journal of Cross-Cultural Psychology, 36,* 6–8.

LeVine, R. (1994). *Child care and culture.* Cambridge: Cambridge University Press.

Levin, R. (2007, February). Sexual activity, health and well-being—the beneficial roles of coitus and masturbation. *Sexual and Relationship Therapy, 22,* 135–148.

Levine, S. C., Huttenlocher, J., Taylor, A., & Langrock, A. (1999). Early sex differences in spatial skill. *Developmental Psychology, 35,* 940–949.

Lewin, T. (1995, May 11). Women are becoming equal providers: Half of working women bring home half the household income. *The New York Times*, p. A14.

Lewis, B., Legato, M., & Fisch, H. (2006). Medical implications of the male biological clock. *JAMA: Journal of the American Medical Association, 296*, 2369–2371.

Lewis, C., & Lamb, M. (2003). Fathers' influences on children's development: The evidence from two-parent families. *European Journal of Psychology of Education, 18*, 211–228.

Lewis, D. M., & Haug, C. A. (2005). Aligning policy and methodology to achieve consistent across-grade performance standards. *Applied Measurements in Education, 18*, 11–34.

Lewis, J., & Elman, J. (2008). Growth-related neural reorganization and the autism phenotype: A test of the hypothesis that altered brain growth leads to altered connectivity. *Developmental Science, 11*, 135–155.

Lewis, M., Feiring, C., & Rosenthal, S. (2000). Attachment over time. *Child Development, 71*, 707–720.

Lewis, M., & Ramsay, D. (2004). Development of self-recognition, personal pronoun use, and pretend play during the 2nd year. *Child Development, 75*, 1821–1831.

Lewis, T. E., & Phillipsen, L. C. (1998). Interactions on an elementary school playground: Variations by age, gender, race, group size, and playground area. *Child Study Journal, 28*, 309–320.

Leyens, J. P., Camino, L., Parke, R. D., & Berkowitz, L. (1975). Effects of movie violence on aggression in a field setting as a function of group dominance and cohesion. *Journal of Personality and Social Psychology, 32*, 346–360.

Li, C., DiGiuseppe, R., & Froh, J. (2006, September). The roles of sex, gender, and coping in adolescent depression. *Adolescence, 41*, 409–415.

Li, Q. (2006, May). Cyberbullying in Schools: A research of gender differences. *School Psychology International, 27*, 157–170.

Li, Q. (2007, July). New bottle but old wine: A research of cyberbullying in schools. *Computers in Human Behavior, 23*, 1777–1791.

Li, Y. F., Laangholz, B., Salam, M. T., & Gilliland, F. D. (2005). Maternal and grandmaternal smoking patterns are associated with early childhood asthma. *Chest, 127*, 1232–1241.

Lickliter, R., & Bahrick, L. E. (2000). The development of infant intersensory perception: Advantages of a comparative convergent-operations approach. *Psychological Bulletin, 126*, 260–280.

Lidz, J., & Gleitman, L. R. (2004). Yes, we still need Universal Grammar: Reply. *Cognition, 94*, 85–93.

Lillard, A., & Else-Quest, N. (2006). The early years. Evaluating Montessori education. *Science, 313*, 1893-4.

Lindsay, A., Sussner, K., Kim, J., & Gortmaker, S. (2006, March). The role of parents in preventing childhood obesity. *The Future of Children, 16*, 169–186.

Lindsey, E., & Colwell, M. (2003). Preschoolers' emotional competence: Links to pretend and physical play. *Child Study Journal, 33*, 39–52.

Linebarger, D. L., & Walker, D. (2005). Infants' and toddlers' television viewing and language outcomes, *American Behavioral Scientist, 48*, 624–645.

Lines, P. M. (2001). Home schooling. *Eric Digest, EDO-EA-OI-08*, pp. 1–4.

Linn, R. L. (2008). Toward a more effective definition of adequate yearly progress. In G. L. Sunderman (Ed.), *Holding NCLB accountable: Achieving, accountability, equity, & school reform.* Thousand Oaks, CA: Corwin Press.

Lipsett, L. (2003). Crib death: A biobehavioral phenomenon? *Current Directions in Psychological Science, 12*, 164–170.

Lipsitt, L. P. (1986). Toward understanding the hedonic nature of infancy. In L. P. Lipsitt & J. H. Cantor (Eds.), *Experimental child psychologist: Essays and experiments in honor of Charles C. Spiker* (pp. 97–109). Hillsdale, NJ: Erlbaum.

Litovsky, R. Y., & Ashmead, D. H. (1997). Development of binaural and spatial hearing in infants and children. In R. H. Gilkey & T. R. Andersen (Eds.), *Binaural and spatial hearing in real and virtual environments* (pp. 571–592). Mahwah, NJ: Erlbaum.

Litrownik, A., Newton, R., & Hunter, W. (2003). Exposure to family violence in young at-risk children: A longitudinal look at the effects of victimization and witnessed physical and psychological aggression. *Journal of Family Violence, 18*, 59–73.

Liu, X., Lesniak, K. (2006). Progression in children's understanding of the matter concept from elementary to high school. *Journal of Research in Science Teaching, 43*, 320–347.

Lobel, M., & DeLuca, R. (2007). Psychosocial sequelae of cesarean delivery: Review and analysis of their causes and implications. *Social Science & Medicine, 64*, 2272–2284.

Loeb, S., Fuller, B., Kagan, S. L., & Carrol, B. (2004). Child care in poor communities: Early learning effects of type, quality and stability. *Child Development, 75*, 47–65.

Loewen, S. (2006). Exceptional intellectual performance: A neo-Piagetian perspective. *High Ability Studies, 17*, 159–181.

Loftus, E. F., & Bernstein, D. M. (2005). Rich false memories: The royal road to success. In A. F. Healy, *Experimental cognitive psychology and its applications.* Washington, DC: American Psychological Association.

Lohman, D. F. (2005). Reasoning abilities. In R. J. Sternberg & J. E. Pretz (Eds.), *Cognition and intelligence: Identifying the mechanisms of the mind.* New York: Cambridge University Press.

Lois, J. (2006, September). Role strain, emotion management, and burnout: Homeschooling mothers' adjustment to the teacher role. *Symbolic Interaction, 29*, 507–530.

Long, T., & Long, L. (1983). *Latchkey children.* New York: Penguin.

Lorenz, K. (1957). Companionship in bird life. In C. Scholler (Ed.), *Instinctive behavior.* New York: International Universities Press.

Lorenz, K. (1965). *Evolution and modification of behavior.* Chicago: University of Chicago Press.

Lorenz, K. (1966). *On aggression.* New York: Harcourt Brace Jovanovich.

Lorenz, K. (1974). *Civilized man's eight deadly sins.* New York: Harcourt Brace Jovanovich.

Lothian, J. (2005). *The official Lamaze guide: Giving birth with confidence.* Minnetonka, MN: Meadowbrook Press.

Love, J. M., Harrison, L., Sagi-Schwartz, A., van Ijzendoorn, M. H., Ross, C., Ungere, J. A., et al. (2003). Childcare quality matters: How conclusions may vary with context. *Child Development, 74*, 1021–1033.

Lu, M. C., Prentice, J., Yu, S. M., Inkelas, M., Lange, L. O., & Halfon, N. (2003). Childbirth education classes: Sociodemographic disparities in attendance and the association of attendance with breastfeeding initiation. *Maternal Child Health, 7*, 87–93.

Lu, X. (2001). Bicultural identity development and Chinese community formation: An ethnographic study of Chinese schools in Chicago. *Howard Journal of Communications, 12,* 203–220.

Lubinski, D. (2004). Introduction to the special section on cognitive abilities: 100 years after Spearman's (1904) "General Intelligence," objectively determined and measured." *Journal of Personality and Social Psychology, 86,* 96–111.

Lubinski, D., & Benbow, C. P. (2001). Choosing excellence. *American Psychologist, 56,* 76–77.

Lubinski, D., & Benbow, C. (2006, December). Study of mathematically precocious youth after 35 years: Uncovering antecedents for the development of math–science expertise. *Perspectives on Psychological Science, 1,* 316–345.

Lucas, S. R., & Berends, M. (2002). Sociodemographic diversity, correlated achievement, and de facto tracking. *Sociology of Education, 75,* 328–349.

Luster, T., & McAdoo, H. P. (1994). Factors related to the achievement and adjustment of young African American children. *Child Development, 65,* 1080–1094.

Luthar, S. S., Cicchetti, D., & Becker, B. (2000). The construct of resilience: A critical evaluation and guidelines for future work. *Child Development, 71,* 543–662.

Lynam, D. R. (1996). Early identification of chronic offenders: Who is the fledgling psychopath? *Psychological Bulletin, 120,* 209–234.

Lynch, M. E., Coles, C. D., & Corely, T. (2003). Examining delinquency in adolescents risk factors. *Journal of Studies on Alcohol, 64,* 678–686.

Lynne, S., Graber, J., Nichols, T., Brooks-Gunn, J., & Botvin, G.(2007, February). Links between pubertal timing, peer influences, and externalizing behaviors among urban students followed through middle school. *Journal of Adolescent Health, 40,* 35–44.

Lyon, M. E., Benoit, M., O'Donnell, R. M., Getson, P. R., Silber, T., & Walsh, T. (2000). Assessing African American adolescents' risk for suicide attempts: Attachment theory. *Adolescence, 35,* 121–134.

Lyons, M. J., Bar, J. L., & Kremen, W. S. (2002). Nicotine and familial vulnerability to schizophrenia: A discordant twin study. *Journal of Abnormal Psychology, 111,* 687–693.

Maas, C., Herrenkohl, T. I., & Sousa, C. (2008). Review of research on child maltreatment and violence in youth. *Trauma, Violence, Abuse, 9,* 56–67.

Maccoby, E. E., Lewis, C. C. (2003). Less day care or different day care? *Child Development, 74,* 1069–1075.

Maccoby, E. E., & Martin, J. A. (1983). Socialization in the context of the family: Parent–child interaction. In P. H. Mussen (Ed.) & E. M. Hetherington (Vol. Ed.), *Handbook of child psychology: Vol. 4. Socialization, personality, and social development* (4th ed., pp. 1–101). New York: Wiley.

MacDorman, M. F., Martin, J. A., Mathews, T. J., Hoyert, D. L., & Ventura, S. J. (2005). Explaining the 2001–02 infant mortality increase: Data from the linked birth/infant death data set. *National Vital Statistics Report, 53,* 1–22.

MacInnes, K., Stone, D. H. (2008). Stages of development and injury: An epidemiological survey of young children presenting to an emergency department. *BMC Public Health.*

MacPhee, D., Kreutzer, J. C., & Fritz, J. J. (1994). Infusing a diversity perspective into human development courses. *Child Development, 65,* 699–715.

MacWhinney, B. (1991). Connectionism as a framework for language acquisition. In J. Miller (Ed.), *Research on child language disorders.* Austin, TX: Pro-ed.

Mael, F. A. (1998). Single-sex and coeducational schooling: Relationships to socioemotional and academic development. *Review of Education Research, 68,* 101–129.

Makino, M., Hashizume, M., Tsuboi, K., Yasushi, M., & Dennerstein,L. (2006, September). Comparative study of attitudes to eating between male and female students in the People's Republic of China. *Eating and Weight Disorders, 11,* 111–117.

Maller, S. (2003). Best practices in detecting bias in nonverbal tests. In R. McCallum (Ed.), *Handbook of nonverbal assessment.* New York: Kluwer Academic/Plenum.

Mameli, M. (2007). Reproductive cloning, genetic engineering and the autonomy of the child: The moral agent and the open future. *Journal of Medical Ethics, 33,* 87–93.

Mandel, D. R., Jusczyk, P. W., & Pisoni, D. B. (1995). Infants' recognition of the sound patterns of their own names. *Psychological Science, 6,* 314–317.

Mangweth, B., Hausmann, A., & Walch, T. (2004). Body fat perception in eating-disordered men. *International Journal of Eating Disorders, 35,* 102–108.

Manlove, J., Terry-Humen, E., Romano Papillo, A., Franzetta, K., Williams, S., & Ryan, S. (2002*). Preventing teenage pregnancy, childbearing, and sexually transmitted diseases: What the research shows.* Washington, DC: Child Trends. Retrieved March 4, 2006, from http://www.childtrends.org/Files/K1Brief.pdf

Mann, C. C. (2005, March 18). Provocative study says obesity may reduce U.S. Life expectancy. *Science, 307,* 1716–1717.

Manning, M., & Hoyme, H. (2007). Fetal alcohol spectrum disorders: A practical clinical approach to diagnosis. *Neuroscience & Biobehavioral Reviews, 31,* 230–238.

Manning, W., Giordano, P., & Longmore, M. (2006, September).Hooking up: The relationship contexts of "nonrelationship" sex. *Journal of Adolescent Research, 21,* 459–483.

Mao, A., Burnham, M. M., Goodlin-Jones, B. L., Gaylor, E. E., & Anders, T. F. (2004). A comparison of the sleep–wake patterns of cosleeping and solitary-sleeping infants. *Child Psychiatry and Human Development, 35,* 95–105.

Marcia, J. E. (1980). Identity in adolescence. In J. Adelson (Ed.), *Handbook of adolescent psychology.* New York: Wiley.

Marcia, J. E. (2007). Theory and measure: The identity status interview. In M. Watzlawik & A. Born (Eds.), *Capturing identity: Quantitative and qualitative methods.* Lanham, MD: University Press of America.

Marcovitch, S., Zelazo, P., & Schmuckler, M. (2003). The effect of the number of A trials on performance on the A-not-B task. *Infancy, 3,* 519–529.

Marlier, L., Schaal, B., & Soussignan, R. (1998). Neonatal responsiveness to the odor of amniotic and lacteal fluids: A test of perinatal chemosensory continuity. *Child Development, 69,* 611–623.

Marschark, M. (2003). Interactions of language and cognition in deaf learners: From research to practice. *International Journal of Audiology, 42*(Suppl.), s41–s48.

Marschark, M., Spencer, P. E., & Newsom, C. A. (Eds.). (2003). *Oxford handbook of deaf students, language, and education.* London: Oxford University Press.

Marsh, H. W., & Hau, K. T. (2003). Big-fish-little-pond effect on academic self-concept. *American Psychologist, 58,* 364–376.

Marsh, H., & Ayotte, V. (2003). Do multiple dimensions of self-concept become more differentiated with age? The differential distinctiveness hypothesis. *Journal of Educational Psychology, 95*, 687–706.

Marsh, H., Ellis, L., & Craven, R. (2002). How do preschool children feel about themselves? Unraveling measurement and multidimensional self-concept structure. *Developmental Psychology, 38*, 376–393.

Marsh, H., & Hau, K. (2004). Explaining paradoxical relations between academic self-concepts and achievements: Cross-cultural generalizability of the internal/external frame of reference predictions across 26 countries. *Journal of Educational Psychology, 96*, 56–67.

Marshall, E. (2000). Duke study faults overuse of stimulants for children. *Science, 289*, 721.

Marshall, N. L. (2004). The quality of early child care and children's development. *Current Directions in Psychological Science, 13*, 165–168.

Martin, C. L. (2000). Cognitive theories of gender development. In T. Eckes & H. M. Trautner, (Eds.), *The developmental social psychology of gender.* Mahwah, NJ: Erlbaum.

Martin, C. L., & Ruble, D. (2004). Children's search for gender cues: Cognitive perspectives on gender development. *Current Directions in Psychological Science, 13*, 67–70.

Martin, C. L., Ruble, D. N., & Szkrybalo, J. (2002). Cognitive theories of early gender development. *Psychological Bulletin, 128*, 903–933.

Martin, C., & Fabes, R. (2001): The stability and consequences of young children's same-sex peer interactions. *Developmental Psychology, 37*, 431–446.

Martin, J. A., Hamilton, B. E., Sutton, P. D., Ventura, S. J., Menacker, F., & Munson, M. L. (2005). Births: Final data for 2003. *National Vital Statistics Reports, 54*, Table J, p. 21.

Martin, S., Li, Y., Casanueva, C., Harris-Britt, A., Kupper, L., & Cloutier, S. (2006). Intimate partner violence and women's depression before and during pregnancy. *Violence Against Women, 12*, 221–239.

Martorell, G. A., Bugental, D. B. (2006). Maternal variations in stress reactivity: Implications for harsh parenting practices with very young children. *Journal of Family Psychology, 20*, 641–647.

Masataka, N. (1996). Perception of motherese in a signed language by 6-month-old deaf infants. *Developmental Psychology, 32*, 874–879.

Masataka, N. (2000). The role of modality and input in the earliest stage of language acquisition: Studies of Japanese sign language. In C. Chamerlain & J. P. Morford (Eds.), *Language acquisition by eye.* Mahwah, NJ: Erlbaum.

Masataka, N. (2003). *The onset of language.* Cambridge, England: Cambridge University Press.

Masataka, N. (2006). Preference for consonance over dissonance by hearing newborns of deaf parents and of hearing parents. *Developmental Science, 9*, 46–50.

Masling, J. M., & Bornstein, R. F. (Eds.). (1996). *Psychoanalytic perspectives on developmental psychology.* Washington, DC: American Psychological Association.

Massaro, A., Rothbaum, R., & Aly, H. (2006). Fetal brain development: The role of maternal nutrition, exposures and behaviors. *Journal of Pediatric Neurology, 4*, 1–9.

Mathiesen, K., & Prior, M. (2006, December). The impact of temperament factors and family functioning on resilience processes from infancy to school age. *European Journal of Developmental Psychology, 3*, 357–387.

Matlin, M. (2003). From menarche to menopause: Misconceptions about women's reproductive lives. *Psychology Science, 45*, 10–122.

Maton, K. I., Schellenbach, C. J., Leadbeater, B. J., & Solarz, A. L. (Eds.). (2004). *Investing in children, youth, families and communities.* Washington, DC: American Psychological Association.

Matson, J., & LoVullo, S. (2008). A review of behavioral treatments for self-injurious behaviors of persons with autism spectrum disorders. *Behavior Modification, 32*, 61–76.

Matsumoto, A. (1999). *Sexual differentiation of the brain.* Boca Raton, FL: CRC Press.

Matthews, G., Zeidner, M., & Roberts, R. D. (2002). *Emotional intelligence: Science & myth.* Cambridge, MA: MIT Press.

Mattson, S., Calarco, K., & Lang, A. (2006). Focused and shifting attention in children with heavy prenatal alcohol exposure. *Neuropsychology, 20*, 361–369.

Mauritzson, U., & Saeljoe, R. (2001). Adult questions and children's responses: Coordination of perspectives in studies of children's theories of other minds. *Scandinavian Journal of Educational Research, 45*, 213–231.

Mayer, J. D. (2001). Emotion, intelligence, and emotional intelligence. In J. P. Forgas (Ed.), *Handbook of affect and social cognition.* Mahwah, NJ: Erlbaum.

Mayer, J. D., Salovey, P., & Caruso, D. R. (2000). Emotional intelligence as zeitgeist, as personality, and as a mental ability. In R. Bar-On, & J. D. A. Parker (Eds.), *The handbook of emotional intelligence: Theory, development, assessment, and application at home, school, and in the workplace.* San Francisco, CA: Jossey-Bass.

Mayes, L., Snyder, P., Langlois, E., & Hunter, N. (2007). Visuospatial working memory in school-aged children exposed in utero to cocaine. *Child Neuropsychology, 13*, 205–218.

Mayes, R., & Rafalovich, A. (2007, December). Suffer the restless children: The evolution of ADHD and paediatric stimulant use, 1900–80. *History of Psychiatry, 18*, 435–457.

Mayseless, O. (1996). Attachment patterns and their outcomes. *Human Development, 39*, 206–223.

Mazumdar et al., 2007

McCabe, M., & Ricciardelli, L. (2006, June). A prospective study of extreme weight change behaviors among adolescent boys and girls. *Journal of Youth and Adolescence, 35*, 425–434.

McCall, R. B. (1979). *Infants.* Cambridge, MA: Harvard University Press.

McCardle, P., & Hoff, E. (Eds.). (2006). *Childhood bilingualism: Research on infancy through school age*; Clevedon, Avon, U.K.: Multilingual Matters. Multilingual Matters Limited.

McCarty, M., & Ashmead, D. H. (1999). Visual control of reaching and grasping in infants. *Developmental Psychology, 35*, 620–631.

McClelland, D. C. (1993). Intelligence is not the best predictor of job performance. *Current Directions in Psychological Research, 2*, 5–8.

McCrae, R. R., Costa, P. T., Jr., Ostendorf, F., Angleitner, A., Hebikova, M., Avia, M. D., et al. (2000). Nature over nurture: Temperament, personality, and life span development. *Journal of Personality and Social Psychology, 78*, 173–186.

McCrink, K., & Wynn, K. (2004). Large-number addition and subtraction by 9-month-old infants. *Psychological Science, 15*, 776–782.

McCrink, K., & Wynn, K. (2007). Ratio abstraction by 6-month-old infants. *Psychological Science, 18*, 740–745.

McCullough, M., E., Tsang, J., & Brion, S. (2003). Personality traits in adolescence as predictors of religiousness in early maturity:

Findings from the Terman longitudinal study. *Personality & Social Psychology Bulletin, 29,* 980–991.

McCutcheon-Rosegg, S., Ingraham, E., & Bradley, R. A. (1996).*Natural childbirth the Bradley way: Revised edition.* New York: Plume Books.

McDonald, L., & Stuart-Hamilton, I. (2003). Egocentrism in older adults: Piaget's three mountains task revisited. *Educational Gerontology, 29,* 417–425.

McDonnell, L. M. (2004). *Politics, persuasion, and educational testing.* Cambridge, MA: Harvard University Press.

McDonough, L. (2002). Basic-level nouns: First learned but misunderstood. *Journal of Child Language, 29,* 357–377.

McElwain, N., & Booth-LaForce, C. (2006, June). Maternal sensitivity to infant distress and nondistress as predictors of infant–mother attachment security. *Journal of Family Psychology, 20,* 247–255.

McGinn, D. (2002, November 11). Guilt free TV. *Newsweek,* pp. 53–59.

McGlothlin, H., Killen, M. (2005). Children's perceptions of intergroup and intragroup similarity and the role of social experience. *Journal of Applied Developmental Psychology, 26,* 680–698.

McGough, R. (2003, May 20). MRIs take a look at reading minds. *The Wall Street Journal,* p. D8.

McGreal, D., Evans, B. J., & Burrows, G. D. (1997). Gender differences in coping following loss of a child through miscarriage or stillbirth: A pilot study. *Stress Medicine, 13,* 159–l65.

McGrew, K. S. (2005). The Cattell-Horn-Carroll theory of cognitive abilities: Past, present, and future. In D. P. Flanagan & P. L. Harrison (Eds.), *Contemporary intellectual assessment: Theories, tests, and issues.* New York: Guilford Press.

McGue, M., Bouchard, T. J., Jr., Iacono, W., & Lykken, D. T. (1993). Behavioral genetics of cognitive ability: A life-span perspective. In R. Plornin & G. E. McClearn (Eds.), *Nature, nurture, and psychology.* Washington, DC: American Psychological Association.

McGuffin, P., Riley, B., & Plomin, R. (2001). Toward behavioral genomics. *Science, 291,* 1223–1249.

McHale, J.P., Kuersten-Hogan, R., & Rao, N. (2004). Growing points for coparenting theory and research. *Journal of Adult Development, 11,* 135–141.

McHale, S. M., Kim, J-Y., & Whiteman, S. D. (2006). Sibling relationships in childhood and adolescence. In P. Noller & J. A.Feeney (Eds.), *Close relationships: Functions, forms and processes.* Hove, England: Psychology Press/Taylor & Francis.

McHale, S., Dariotis, J., & Kauh, T. (2003). Social development and social relationships in middle childhood. In R. Lerner & M. Easterbrooks (Eds.), *Handbook of psychology: Vol. 6. Developmental psychology.* New York: Wiley.

McKown, C., & Weinstein, R. (2008, June). Teacher expectations, classroom context, and the achievement gap. *Journal of School Psychology, 46,* 235–261.

McLoyd, V. C., Cauce, A. M., Takeuchi, D., & Wilson, L. (2000). Marital processes and parental socialization in families of color: A decade review of research. *Journal of Marriage and Family, 62,* 1070–l093.

McLoyd, V. C., Kaplan, R., Hardaway, C. R., Wood, D. (2007). Does endorsement of physical discipline matter? Assessing moderating influences on the maternal and child psychological correlates of physical discipline in African American families, *Journal of Family Psychology. 21,*165–175

McWhirter, D. P., Sanders, S., & Reinisch, J. M. (1990). *Homosexuality, heterosexuality: Concepts of sexual orientation.* New York: Oxford University Press.

Mead, M. (1942). *Environment and education,* a symposium held in connection with the fiftieth anniversary celebration of the Univeristy of Chicago. Chicago: University of Chicago Press.

Meadows, B. (2005, March 14). The Web: The bully's new playground. *People,* pp. 152–155.

Mealey, L. (2000). *Sex differences: Developmental and evolutionary strategies.* Orlando, FL: Academic Press.

Meece, J. L., & Kurtz-Costes, B. (2001). Introduction: The schooling of ethnic minority children and youth. *Educational Psychologist, 36,* 1–7.

Meeus, W. (2003). Parental and peer support, identity development and psychological well-being in adolescence. *Psychology: The Journal of the Hellenic Psychological Society, 10,* 192–201.

Mehran, K. (1997). Interferences in the move from adolescence to adulthood: The development of the male. In M. Laufer (Ed.), *Adolescent breakdown and beyond* (pp. 17–25). London: Karnac Books.

Meltzoff, A. (2002). Elements of a developmental theory of imitation. In A. Meltzoff & W. Prinz (Eds.), *The imitative mind: Development, evolution, and brain bases* (pp. 19–41). New York: Cambridge University Press.

Meltzoff, A. (2002). Elements of a developmental theory of imitation. In A. Meltzoff & W. Prinz (Eds.), *The imitative mind: Development, evolution, and brain bases*(pp. 19–41). New York: Cambridge University Press.

Meltzoff, A., & Moore, M. (2002). Imitation, memory, and the representation of persons. *Infant Behavior & Development, 25,* 39–61.

Meltzoff, A. N. (1981). Imitation, intermodal coordination and representation in early infancy. In G. Butterworth (Ed.), *Infancy and epistemology.* Brighton: Harvester Press.

Meltzoff, A. N., & Moore, M. K. (1977). Imitation official and manual gestures by human neonates. *Science, 198,* 75–78.

Mendle, J., Turkheimer, E., & Emery, R. (2007, June). Detrimental psychological outcomes associated with early pubertal timing in adolescent girls. *Developmental Review, 27,* 151–171.

Mendoza, C. (2006, September). Inside today's classrooms: Teacher voices on No Child Left Behind and the education of gifted children. *Roeper Review, 29,* 28–31.

Mennella, J.A., Kennedy, J.M. & Beauchamp, G.K. (2006). Vegetable acceptance by infants: effects of formula flavors. *Early Human Development, 82,* 463–8.

Mercer, J. R. (1973). *Labeling the mentally retarded.* Berkeley: University of California Press.

Merewood, A. (2006). Race, ethnicity, and breastfeeding. *Pediatrics, 118,* 1742–3.

Meritesacker, B., Bade, U., & Haverkock, A. (2004). Predicting maternal reactivity/sensitivity: The role of infant emotionality, maternal depressiveness/anxiety, and social support. *Infant Mental Health Journal, 25,* 47–61.

Merlo, L., Bowman, M., & Barnett, D. (2007). Parental nurturance promotes reading acquisition in low socioeconomic status children. *Early Education and Development, 18,* 51–69.

Mervis, J. (2004, June 11). Meager evaluations make it hard to find out what works. *Science, 304,* 1583.

Messer, S. B., & McWilliams, N. (2003). The impact of Sigmund Freud and the interpretation of dreams. In R. J. Sternberg (Ed.), *The anatomy of impact: What makes the great works of psychology great* (pp. 71–88). Washington, DC: American Psychological Association.

Michael, R. T., Gagnon, J. H., Laumann, E. O., & Kolata, G. (1994). *Sex in America: A definitive survey.* Boston: Little, Brown.

Miehl, N.J. (2005). Shaken baby syndrome. *Journal of Forensic Nursing, 1,* 111–7.

Miesnik, S., & Reale, B. (2007). A review of issues surrounding medically elective cesarean delivery. *Journal of Obstetric, Gynecologic, & Neonatal Nursing: Clinical Scholarship for the Care of Women, Childbearing Families, & Newborns, 36,* 605–615.

Mikhail, B. (2000). Prenatal care utilization among low-income African American women: *Journal of Community Health Nursing, 17,* 235–246.

Mikulincer, M., & Shaver, P. R. (2005). Attachment security, compassion, and altruism. *Current Directions in Psychological Science, 14,* 34–38.

Miles, R., Cowan, F., Glover, V., Stevenson, J., & Modi, N.(2006). A controlled trial of skin-to-skin contact in extremely preterm infants. *Early Human Development, 2*(7), 447–455.

Miller, E. M. (1998). Evidence from opposite-sex twins for the effects of prenatal sex hormones. In L. Ellis & L. Ebertz (Eds.), *Males, females, and behavior: Toward biological understanding.* Westport, CT: Praeger/Greenwood Publishing Group.

Miller, J. L., & Eimas, P. D. (1995). Speech perception: From signal to word. *Annual Review of Psychology, 46,* 467–492.

Miller, P. H., & Seier, W. L. (1994). *Strategy utilization deficiencies in children: When, where, and why.* San Diego: Academic Press.

Miller, S. A. (1998). *Developmental research methods* (2nd ed.). Upper Saddle River, NJ: Prentice Hall.

Miller-Perrin, C. L., & Perrin, R. D. (1999). *Child maltreatment: An introduction.* Thousand Oaks, CA: Sage.

Mimura, K., Kimoto, T., & Okada, M. (2003). Synapse efficiency diverges due to synaptic pruning following overgrowth. *Physical Reveiw E Statistical Nonlinear Soft Matter Physics, 68,* 124–131.

Mino, X., & Wang, W. (2003). A century of Chinese developmental psychology. *International Journal of Psychology, 38,* 258–273.

Minorities in Higher Education. (1995). *Annual status report on minorities in higher education.* Washington, DC: Author.

Mishra, R. C. (1997). Cognition and cognitive development. In J. W. Berry, P. R. Dasen, & T. S. Saraswathi (Eds.), *Handbook of cross-cultural psychology: Vol 2. Basic processes and human development* (2nd ed.). Needham Heights, MA: Allyn & Bacon.

Misri, S. (2007). Suffering in silence: The burden of perinatal depression. *The Canadian Journal of Psychiatry / La Revue canadienne de psychiatrie, 52,* 477–478.

Mistry, J., & Saraswathi, T. (2003). The cultural context of child development. In R. Lerner & M. Easterbrooks (Eds.), *Handbook of psychology: Vol. 6. Developmental psychology.* (pp. 267–291). New York: Wiley.

Mitchell, K., Finkelhor, D., & Wolak, J. (2007, August). Online requests for sexual pictures from youth: Risk factors and incident characteristics. *Journal of Adolescent Health, 41,* 196–203.

Mitchell, S. (2002). *American generations: Who they are, how they live, what they think.* Ithaca, NY: New Strategists Publications.

Miyamoto, R. H., Hishinuma, E. S., Nishimura, S. T., Nahulu, L. B., Andrade, N. N., & Goebert, D. A. (2000). Variation in self-esteem among adolescents in an Asian/Pacific-Islander sample. *Personality & Individual Differences, 29,* 13–25.

Mizuno, K., & Ueda, A. (2002). Antenatal olfactory learning influences infant feeding. *Early Human Development, 76,* 83–90.

Modern Language Association. (2005). www.mla.org/census_map. Based on data from the U.S. Census Bureau, 2000.

Moldin, S. O., & Gottesman, I. I. (1997). Genes, experience, and chance in schizophrenia—Positioning for the 21st century. *Schizophrenia Bulletin, 23,* 547–561.

Molfese, V. J., & Acheson, S. (1997). Infant and preschool mental and verbal abilities: How are infant scopes related to preschool scores? *International Journal of Behavioral Development. 20,* 595–607.

Molina, J. C., Spear, N. E., Spear, L. P., Mennella, J. A., & Lewis, M. J. (2007). The International society for developmental psychobiology 39th annual meeting symposium: Alcohol and development: beyond fetal alcohol syndrome. *Developmental Psychobiology, 49,* 227–242.

Monastra, V. (2008). The etiology of ADHD: A neurological perspective. *Unlocking the potential of patients with ADHD: A model for clinical practice.* Washington, DC, US: American Psychological Association.

Mongan, M. F. (2005). *HypnoBirthing: The Mongan method: A natural approach to a safe, easier, more comfortable birthing* (3rded.). Deerfield Beach, FL: Health Communications, Inc.

Montague, D., & Walker-Andrews, A. (2001). Peekaboo: A new look at infants' perception of emotion expressions. *Developmental Psychology, 37,* 826–838.

Montgomery-Downs, H., & Thomas, E. B. (1998). Biological and behavioral correlates of quiet sleep respiration rates infants. *Physiology and Behavior, 64,* 637–643.

Moon, C. (2002). Learning in early infancy. *Advances in Neonatal Care, 2,* 81–83.

Moore, K. L., & Persaud, T. V. N. (2003). *Before we were born* (6th ed., p. 36). Philadelphia, PA: Saunders.

Moore, L., Gao, D., & Bradlee, M. (2003). Does early physical activity predict body fat change throughout childhood? *Preventive Medicine: An International Journal Devoted to Practice & Theory, 37,* 10–17.

Moores, D., & Meadow-Orlans, K. (1990). *Educational and developmental aspects of deafness.* Washington, DC: Gallaudet University Press.

Morales, J. R., & Guerra, N. F. (2006). Effects of multiple context and cumulative stress on urban children's adjustment in elementary school. *Child Development, 77,* 907–923.

Morelli, G. A., Rogoff, B., Oppenheim, D., & Goldsmith, D. (1992). Cultural variation in infants' sleeping arrangements: Questions of independence. Special section: Cross-cultural studies of development. *Developmental Psychology, 28,* 604–613.

Morgenthaler, T., Owens, J., Alessi, C., Boehlecke, B., Brown, T., Coleman, J., et al. (2006, October). Practice parameters for behavioral treatment of bedtime problems and night wakings in infants and young children. *Sleep: Journal of Sleep and Sleep Disorders Research, 29,* 1277–1281.

Morice, A. (1998, February 27). Future moms, please note: Benefits vary. *The Wall Street Journal,* p. 15.

Morrison, F. J., Bachman, H. J., Connor, C. M. (2005) *Improving literacy in America: Guidelines from research.* New Haven, CT: Yale University Press.

Morrison, F. J., Smith, L., & Dow-Ehrensberger, M. (1995). Education and cognitive development: A natural experiment. *Developmental Psychology, 31,* 789–799.

Morrongiello, B., & Hogg, K. (2004). Mothers' reactions to children misbehaving in ways that can lead to injury: Implications for gender differences in children's risk taking and injuries. *Sex Roles, 50,* 103–118.

Morrongiello, B., Midgett, C., & Stanton, K. (2000). Gender biases in children's appraisals of injury risk and other children's risk-taking behaviors. *Journal of Experimental Child Psychology, 77*, 317–336.

Morrongiello, B. A. (1997). Children's perspectives on injury and close call experiences: Sex differences in injury-outcome process. *Journal of Pediatric Psychology, 22*, 499–512.

Mumme, D., & Fernald, A. (2003). The infant as onlooker: Learning from emotional reactions observed in a television scenario. *Child Development, 74*, 221–237.

Munzar, P., Cami, J., & Farré, M. (2003). Mechanisms of drug addiction. *New England Journal of Medicine, 349*, 2365–2365.

Murphy, B., & Eisenberg, N. (2002). An integrative examination of peer conflict: Children's reported goals, emotions, and behaviors. *Social Development, 11*, 534–557.

Murphy, M., Polivka, B. (2007). Parental perceptions of the schools' role in addressing childhood obesity. *The Journal of School Nursing, 23*, 40–46.

Murray, G., Jones, P., Kuh, D., & Richards, M. (2007). Infant developmental milestones and subsequent cognitive function. *Annals of Neurology, 62*, 128–136.

Murray, J. A., Terry, D. J., Vance, J. C., Battistutta, D., & Connolly, Y. (2000). Effects of a program of intervention on parental distress following infant death. *Death Studies, 4*, 275–305.

Murray, L., Cooper, P., Creswell, C., Schofield, E., & Sack, C. (2007). The effects of maternal social phobia on mother–*infant* interactions and *infant* social responsiveness. *Journal of Child Psychology and Psychiatry, 48*, 45–52.

Murray-Close, D., Ostrov, J., & Crick, N. (2007, December). A short-term longitudinal study of growth of relational aggression during middle childhood: Associations with gender, friendship intimacy, and internalizing problems. *Development and Psychopathology, 19*, 187–203.

Myklebust, B. M., & Gottlieb, G. L. (1993). Development of the stretch reflex in the newborn: Reciprocal excitation and reflex irradiation. *Child Development, 64*, 1036–1045.

Nadal, K. (2004). Filipino American identity development model. *Journal of Multicultural Counseling & Development, 32*, 45–62.

Nadeau, L., Boivin, M., Tessier, R., Lefebvre, F., & Robaey, P. (2001). Mediators of behavioral problems in 7-year-old children born after 24 to 28 weeks of gestation. *Journal of Developmental & Behavioral Pediatrics, 22*, 1–10.

Nadel, S., & Poss, J. (2007). Early detection of autism spectrum disorders: Screening between 12 and 24 months of age. *Journal of the American Academy of Nurse Practitioners, 19*, 408–417.

Nagy, E. (2006). From imitation to conversation: the first dialogues with human neonates. *Infant and Child Development, 15*, 223–232.

Nakagawa, M., Lamb, M. E., & Miyaki, K. (1992). Antecedents and correlates of the Strange Situation behavior of Japanese infants. *Journal of Cross-Cultural Psychology, 23*, 300–310.

Nangle, D. W., & Erdley, C. A. (Eds.). (2001). *The role of friendship in psychological adjustment*. San Francisco: Jossey-Bass.

Nansel, T. R., Overpeck, M., Pilla, R. S., Rua, W. J., Simons-Morton, B., & Scheidt, P. (2001). Bullying behaviors among US youth: Prevalence and association with psychosocial adjustment. *Journal of the American Medical Association, 285*, 2094.

National Campaign to Prevent Youth Pregnancy (NCPYP). (2003). *14 and younger: The sexual behavior of young adolescents*. Washington, DC.

National Center for Children in Poverty. (2005). *Basic facts about low-income children in the United States*. New York: National Center for Children in Poverty.

National Center for Education Statistics. (1997). *Digest of education statistics, 1997*. Washington, DC: U.S. Government Printing Office.

National Center for Education Statistics. (2002). *Dropout rates in the United States: 2000*. Washington, DC: NCES.

National Center for Educational Statistics. (2003). *Public high school dropouts and complete from the common core of data: School year 2000–01 statistical analysis report*. Washington, DC: NCES.

National Center for Education Statistics. (2004). *The Condition of Education, 2004*. Washington, DC: National Center for Education Statistics.

National Center for Health Statistics. (1997). *Asthma conditions of childern under 18*. Washington, DC: Public Health Service.

National Center for Health Statistics. (2000). *Health United States, 2000 with adolescent health chartbook*. Hyattsville, MD: Public Health Service.

National Center for Health Statistics (2001). *Obesity in children*. Washington, DC: National Center for Health Statistics.

National Center for Health Statistics (Infant and Child Health Studies Branch). (2003). *Rates of cesarean births*. Washington, DC: National Center for Health Statistics.

National Center for Health Statistics, 2003.

National Center for Health Statistics. (2006). National Hospital Discharge Survey: 2004 annual summary with detailed diagnosis and procedure data. *Vital and Health Statistics, 13*(162).

National Center for Missing and Exploited Children. (1994). *Safety guidelines for children*. Alexandria, VA: Author. Retrieved from http://www.missingkids.com./html/ncmec_default_ec_internetsafty.htm1.

National Coalition Against Domestic Violence (NCADC). (2003). *Poll finds domestic violence is women's main concern*. Denver, CO: NCADC.

National Institutes of Health. (2006, December 13). Adult male circumcision significantly reduces risk of acquiring HIV.NIH news release. Retrieved January 7, 2006 from http://www.nih.gov/news/pr/dec2006/niaid-13.htm.

National Longitudinal Study on Adolescent Health. (2000). *Teenage stress*. Chapel Hill, NC: Carolina Population Center.

National Safety Council. (1989). *Accident facts: 1989 edition*. Chicago: National Safety Council.

National Sleep Foundation. (2003). *Adolescents and sleep*. Washington, DC: National Sleep Foundation.

Nazzi, T., & Bertoncini, J. (2003). Before and after the vocabulary spurt: Two modes of word acquisition? *Developmental Science, 6*, 136–142.

Needleman, H. L., Riess, J. A., Tobin, M. J., Biesecker, G. E., & Greenhouse, J. B. (1996, February 7). Bone lead levels and delinquent behavior. *Journal of the American Medical Association, 2755*, 363–369.

Negy, C., Shreve, T., & Jensen, B. (2003). Ethnic identity, self-esteem, and ethnocentrism: A study of social identity versus multicultural theory of development. *Cultural Diversity & Ethnic Minority Psychology, 9*, 333–344.

Neisser, U. (2004). Memory development: New questions and old. *Developmental Review, 24*, 154–158.

Nelson, C. A. (1987). The recognition of facial expressions in the first two years of life: Mechanisms of development. *Child Development, 58*, 889–909.

Pedersen, S., Vitaro, F., Barker, E. D., Borge, A. I. H. (2007). The timing of middle-childhood peer rejection and friendship: Linking early behavior to early-adolescent adjustment. *Child Development, 78,* 1037–1051.

Peirano, P., Algarin, C., & Uauy, R. (2003). Sleep–wake states and their regulatory mechanisms throughout early human development. *Journal of Pediatrics, 143*(Suppl.), S70–S79.

Pelligrini, A. D., & Smith, P. K. (1998). Physical activity play: The nature and function of a neglected aspect of play. *Child Development, 69,* 577–598.

Peltonen, L., & McKusick, V. A. (2001, February 16). Dissecting the human disease in the postgenomic era. *Science, 291,* 1224–1229.

Peltzer, K., & Pengpid, S. (2006). Sexuality of 16- to17-year-old South Africans in the context of HIV/AIDS. *Social Behavior and Personality, 34,* 239–256.

Pennisi, E. (2000, May 19). And the gene number is . . .? *Science, 288,* 1146–1147.

Pepler, D., Jiang, D., Craig, W., Connolly, J. (2008). Developmental trajectories of bullying and associated factors. *Child Development, 79,* 325–338.

Perlmann, J., & Waters, M. (Eds.). (2002). *The new race question: How the census counts multiracial individuals.* New York: Russell Sage Foundation.

Perlmann, R. Y., & Gleason, J. B. (1990, July). *Patterns of prohibition in mothers' speech to children.* Paper presented at the Fifth International Congress for the Study of Child Language, Budapest, Hungary.

Perrine, N. E., & Aloise-Young, P. A. (2004). The role of self-monitoring in adolescents' susceptibility to passive peer pressure. *Personality and Individual Differences, 37,* 1701–1716.

Perry, T., Steele, C., & Hilliard, A., III. (2003). *Promoting high achievement among African-American students.* Boston: Beacon Press.

Persson, A., & Musher-Eizenman, D. R. (2003). The impact of a prejudice-prevention television program on young children's ideas about race. *Early Childhood Research Quarterly, 18,* 530–546.

Persson, G. E. B. (2005). Developmental perspectives on prosocial and aggressive motives in preschoolers' peer interactions. *International Journal of Behavioral Development, 29,* 80–91.

Petersen, A. (2000). A longitudinal investigation of adolescents' changing perceptions of pubertal timing. *Developmental Psychology, 36,* 37–43.

Peterson, D. M., Marcia, J. E., & Carpendale, J. I. M. (2004). Identity: Does thinking make it so? In C. Lightfoot, C. Lalonde, & M. Chandler (Eds.), *Changing conceptions of psychological life.* Mahwah, NJ: Erlbaum.

Peterson, L. (1994). Child injury and abuse-neglect: Common etiologies, challenges, and courses toward prevention. *Current Directions in Psychological Science, 3,* 116–120.

Petit, G., & Dodge, K. A. (2003). Violent children: Bridging development, intervention, and public policy. *Developmental Psychology, Special Issues: Violent Children, 39,* 187–188.

Petrou, S. (2006). Preterm birth—What are the relevant economic issues? *Early Human Development, 82*(2), 75–76.

Pettit, G. S., Bates, J. E., & Dodge, K. A. (1997). Supportive parenting, ecological context, and children's adjustment: A 7-year longitudinal study. *Child Development, 68,* 908–923.

Phelan, P., Yu, H. C., & Davidson, A. L. (1994). Navigating the psychosocial pressures of adolescence: The voices and experiences of high school youth. *American Educational Research Journal, 31,* 415–447.

Phelps, R. P. (2005). *Defending standardized testing.* Mahwah, NJ: Lawrence Erlbaum Associates.

Philippot, P., & Feldman, R. S. (Eds.). (2004). *The Regulation of Emotion.* Mahwah, NJ: Lawrence Erlbaum.

Phillips, D. A., Voran, M., Kisker, E., Howes, C., & Whitebook, M. (1994). Child care for children in poverty: Opportunity or inequity? *Child Development, 65,* 472–492.

Phillips-Silver, J. & Trainor, L. J. (2005). Feeling the beat: movement influences infant rhythm perception. *Science, 308,* 1430.

Phinney, J. S. (2005). Ethnic identity in late modern times: A response to Rattansi and Phoenix. *Identity, 5,* 187–194.

Phinney, J. S., Ferguson, D. L., & Tate, J. D. (1997). Intergroup attitudes among ethnic minority adolescents: A causal model. *Child Development, 68,* 955–969.

Phinney, J. S., Lochner, B., & Murphy, R. (1990). Ethnic identity development and psychological adjustment in adolescence. In A. Stiffman & L. Davis (Eds.), *Advances in adolescent mental health: Vol. 5. Ethnic issues.* Greenwich, CT: JAI Press.

Piaget, J. (1932). *The moral judgment of the child.* New York: Harcourt, Brace & World.

Piaget, J. (1952). *The origins of intelligence in children.* New York: International Universities Press.

Piaget, J. (1954). *The construction of reality in the child* (M. Cook, Trans.). New York: Basic Books.

Piaget, J. (1962). *Play, dreams and imitation in childhood.* New York: Norton.

Piaget, J. (1983). Piaget's theory. In W. Kessen (Ed.) & P. H. Mussen (Series Ed.), *Handbook of child psychology: Vol. 1. History, theory, and methods* (pp. 103–128). New York: Wiley.

Piaget, J., & Inhelder, B. (1958). *The growth of logical thinking from childhood to adolescence* (A. Parsons & S. Seagrin, Trans.). New York: Basic Books.

Piaget, J., Inhelder, B., & Szymanska, A. (1960). *The child's conception of geometry.* New York: Basic Books. (Original work published 1948.)

Pietrobelli, A., Espinoza, M. C., De Cristofaro, P. (2008) Childhood obesity: looking into the future. *Angiology, 59,* 305–335.

Pinker, S. (1994). *The language instinct.* New York: Morrow.

Pinker, S. (2005). So how does the mind work? *Mind & Language, 20,* 1–24.

Pintney, R., Forlands, F., & Freedman, H. (1937). Personality and attitudinal similarity among classmates. *Journal of Applied Psychology, 21,* 48–55.

Planinsec, J. (2001). A comparative analysis of the relations between the motor dimensions and cognitive ability of pre-school girls and boys. *Kinesiology, 33,* 56–68.

Plante, E., Schmithorst, V., Holland, S., & Byars, A. (2006). Sex differences in the activation of language cortex during childhood. *Neuropsychologia, 44,* 1210–1221.

Plomin, R. (1994a). Nature, nurture, and social development. *Social Development, 3,* 37–53.

Plomin, R. (1994b). The genetic basis of complex human behaviors. *Science, 264,* 1733–1739.

Plomin, R. (1994c). *Genetics and experience: The interplay between nature and nurture.* Newbury Park, CA: Sage.

Plomin, R., & Caspi, A. (1998). DNA and personality. *European Journal of Personality, 12*, 387–407.

Plomin, R., & Rutter, M. (1998). Child development, molecular genetics, and what to do with genes once they are found. *Child Development, 69*, 1223–1242.

Plowfield, L. A. (2007). HIV disease in children 25 years later. *Pediatric Nursing. 33* , 273, 274–278.

Poest, C. A., Williams, J. R., Witt, D. D., & Atwood, M. E. (1990). Challenge me to move: Large muscle development in young children. *Young Children, 45*, 4–10.

Polkinghome, D. E. (2005). Language and meaning: Data collection in qualitative research. Knowledge in context: Qualitative methods in counseling psychology research [Special issue]. *Journal of Counseling Psychology, 52*, 137–145.

Pollak, S., Holt, L., & Wismer Fries, A. (2004). Hemispheric asymmetries in children's perception of nonlinguistic human affective sounds. *Developmental Science, 7*, 10–18.

Pollack, W. (1999). *Real boys: Rescuing our sons from the myths of boyhood.* New York, NY: Owl Books.

Pollack, W., Shuster, T., & Trelease, J. (2001). *Real boys voices.* New York: Penguin.

Pollitt, E., Golub, M., Gorman, K., Grantham-McGregor, S., Levitsky, D., Schurch, B., et al. (1996). A reconceptualization of the effects of undernutrition on children's biological, psychosocial, and behavioral development. *Social Policy Report, 10*, 1–22.

Pomares, C. G., Schirrer, J., & Abadie, V. (2002). Analysis of the olfactory capacity of healthy children before language acquisition. *Journal of Developmental Behavior and Pediatrics, 23*, 203–207.

Ponton, L. E. (1999, May 10). Their dark romance with risk. *Newsweek,* pp. 55–58.

Poole, D. A., & Lamb, M. E. (1998). *Investigative interviews of children: A guide for helping professionals.* Washington, DC: American Psychological Association.

Porges, S. W., & Lipsitt, L. P. (1993). Neonatal responsivity to gustatory stimulation; The gustatory-vagal hypothesis. *Infant Behavior & Development, 16*, 487–494.

Porter, M., van Teijlingen, E., Yip, L., & Bhattacharya, S. (2007). Satisfaction with cesarean section: Qualitative analysis of open-ended questions in a large postal survey. *Birth: Issues in Perinatal Care, 34*, 148–154.

Porter, R. H., Bologh, R. D., & Malkin, J. W. (1988). Olfactory influences on mother–infant interactions. In C. Rovee-Collier & L. Lipsitt (Eds.), *Advances in infancy research* (Vol. 5). Norwood, NJ: Ablex.

Portes, A., & Rumbaut, R. (2001). *Legacies: The story of the immigrant second generation.* Berkeley: University of California Press.

Posner, R. (2006, March). Early menarche: A review of research on trends in timing, racial differences, etiology and psychosocial consequences. *Sex Roles, 54*, 315–322.

Posthuma, D., & de Geus, E. (2006, August). Progress in the molecular-genetic study of intelligence. *Current Directions in Psychological Science, 15*, 151–155.

Poulin-Dubois, D., Serbin, L., & Eichstedt, J. (2002). Men don't put on make-up: Toddlers' knowledge of the gender stereotyping of household activities. *Social Development, 11*, 166–181.

Poulton, R., & Caspi, A. (2005). Commentary: How does socioeconomic disadvantage during childhood damage health in adulthood? Testing psychosocial pathways. *International Journal of Epidemiology, 23*, 51–55.

Powell, M. B., Thomson, D. M., & Ceci, S. J. (2003). Children's memory of recurring events: Is the first event always the best remembered? *Applied Cognitive Psychology, 17*, 127–146.

Prater, L. (2002). African American families: Equal partners in general and special education. In F. Obiakor & A. Ford (Eds.), *Creating successful learning environments for African American learners with exceptionalities.* Thousand Oaks, CA: Corwin Press.

Pratt, H., Phillips, E., & Greydanus, D. (2003). Eating disorders in the adolescent population: Future directions. *Journal of Adolescent Research, 18*, 297–317.

Prechtl, H. F. R. (1982). Regressions and transformations during neurological development. In T. G. Bever (Ed.), *Regressions in mental development.* Hillsdale, NJ: Erlbaum.

Prescott, C., & Gottesman, I. (1993). Genetically mediated vulnerability to schizophrenia. *Psychiatric Clinics of North America, 16*, 245–267.

Prescott, C. A., Caldwell, C. B., Carey, G., Vogler, G. P., Trumbetta, S. L., & Gottesman, I. I. (2005). The Washington University Twin Study of alcoholism. *American Journal of Medical Genetics, B, Neuropsychiatric Genetics, 31.*

Pressley, M., & Schneider, W. (1997). *Introduction to memory development during childhood and adolescence.* Mahwah, NJ: Erlbaum.

Prezbindowski, A. K., & Lederberg, A. R. (2003). Vocabulary assessment of deaf and hard-of-hearing children from infancy through the preschool years. *Journal of Deaf Studies and Deaf Education, 8*, 383–400.

Price, D. W., & Goodman, G. S. (1990). Visiting the wizard: Children's memory for a recurring event. *Child Development, 61*, 664–680.

Price, R., & Gottesman, I. (1991). Body fat in identical twins reared apart: Roles for genes and environment. *Behavior Genetics, 21*, 1–7.

PRIMEDIA/Roper National Youth Survey. (1999). *Adolescents' view of society's ills.* Storrs, CT: Roper Center for Public Opinion Research.

Prince, M. (2000, November 13). How technology has changed the way we have babies. *The Wall Street Journal,* pp. R4, R13.

Principe, G. F., & Ceci, S. J. (2002). "I saw it with my own ears": The effects of peer conversations on preschoolers' reports of nonexperienced events. *Journal of Experimental Child Psychology, 83*, 1–25.

Probert, B. (2004). "I just couldn't fit in": Gender and unequal outcomes in academic careers. *Gender, Work & Organization, 72*, 50–72.

Propper, C., & Moore, G. (2006, December). The influence of parenting on infant emotionality: A multi-level psychobiological perspective. *Developmental Review, 26*, 427–460.

Puchalski, M., & Hummel, P. (2002). The reality of neonatal pain. *Advances in Neonatal Care, 2*, 245–247.

Puntambekar, S., & Hübscher, R. (2005). Tools for saffolding students in a complex learning environment: What have we gained and what have we missed? *Educational Psychologist, 40*, 1–12.

Pyszczynski, T., Solomon, S., & Greenberg, J. (2004). *In the wake of 9/11: The psychology of terror.* Washington, DC: American Psychological Association.

Quinn, M. (1990, January 29). Don't aim that pack at us. *Time,* p. 60.

Quintana, C. (1998, May 17). Riding the rails. *The New York Times Magazine,* pp. 22–24, 66.

Quintana, S. (2007, July). Racial and ethnic identity: Developmental perspectives and research. *Journal of Counseling Psychology, 54*, 259–270.

Quintana, S. M., & McKown, C. (Eds.). (2008). *Handbook of race, racism, and the developing child*. Hoboken, NJ: John Wiley & Sons.

Quintana, S. M., McKown, C., Cross, W. E., & Cross, T. B. (2008). *Handbook of race, racism, and the developing child*. S. M. Quintana & C. McKown (Eds). Hoboken, NJ: John Wiley & Sons Inc.

Raag, T. (2003). Racism, gender identities and young children: Social relations in a multi-ethnic, inner-city primary school. *Archives of Sexual Behavior, 32*, 392–393.

Rabain-Jamin, J., & Sabeau-Jouannet, E. (1997). Maternal speech to 4-month-old infant in two cultures: Wolof and French. *International Journal of Behavioral Development, 20*, 425–451.

Rabin, R. (2006, June 13). Breast-feed or else. *The New York Times*, p. D1.

Raeburn, P. (2004, October 1). Too immature for the death penalty? *The New York Times Magazine*, pp. 26–29.

Raeff, C. (2004). Within-culture complexities: Multifaceted and interrelated autonomy and connectedness characteristics in late adolescent selves. In M. E. Mascolo & J. Li (Eds.), *Culture and developing selves: Beyond dichotomization*. San Francisco, CA: Jossey-Bass.

Raffaelli, M., & Crockett, L. J. (2003). Sexual risk taking in adolescence: The role of self-regulation and attraction to risk. *Developmental Psychology, 39*, 1036–1046.

Rahman, Q., & Wilson, G. (2003). Born gay? The psychobiology of human sexual orientation. *Personality & Individual Differences, 34*, 1337–1382.

Rakison, D., & Oakes, L. (2003). *Early category and concept development: Making sense of the blooming, buzzing confusion*. London: Oxford University Press.

Raman, L., & Winer, G. (2002). Children's and adults' understanding of illness: Evidence in support of a coexistence model. *Genetic, Social, & General Psychology Monographs, 128*, 325–355.

Ramey, C. T., & Ramey, S. L. (1998). Early intervention and early experience. *American Psychologist, 53*, 109–120.

Ramsey-Rennels, J. L., & Langlois, J. H. (2006). Infants' differential processing of female and male faces. *Current Directions in Psychological Science, 15*, 59–62.

Randahl, G. J. (1991). A typological analysis of the relations between measured vocational interests and abilities. *Journal of Vocational Behavior, 38*, 333–650.

Rankin, B. (2004). The importance of intentional socialization among children in small groups: A conversation with Loris Malaguzzi. *Early Childhood Education Journal, 32*, 81–85.

Rankin, J., Lane, D., & Gibbons, F. (2004). Adolescent self-consciousness: Longitudinal age changes and gender differences in two cohorts. *Journal of Research on Adolescence, 14*, 1–21.

Ratanachu-Ek, S. (2003). Effects of multivitamin and folic acid supplementation in malnourished children. *Journal of the Medical Association of Thailand, 4*, 86–91.

Raudsepp, L., & Liblik, R. (2002). Relationship of perceived and actual motor competence in children. *Perception and Motor Skills, 94*, 1059–1070.

Rayner, K., Foorman, B. R., Perfetti, C. A., Pesetsky, D., & Seidenberg, M. S. (2002, March). How should reading be taught? *Scientific American*, pp. 85–91.

Ready, D. D., Lee, V. E., & Welner, K. G. (2004). Educational equity and school structure: School size, overcrowding, and schools-within-schools. *Teachers College Record, 106*, 1989–2014.

Reddy, V. (1999). Prelinguistic communication. In M. Barrett (Ed.), *The development of language* (pp. 25–50). Philadelphia: Psychology Press.

Reed, R. K. (2005). *Birthing fathers: The transformation of men in American rites of birth*. New Brunswick, NJ: Rutgers University Press.

Reese, E., & Cox, A. (1999). Quality of adult book reading affects children's emergent literacy. *Developmental Psychology, 35*, 20–28.

Rego, A. (2006). The alphabetic principle, phonics, and spelling: Teaching students the code. *Reading assessment and instruction for all learners* (pp. 118–162). New York: Guilford Press.

Reid, K. J., Zeldow, M., Teplin, L. A., McClelland, G. M., Atom, K. A., & Zee, P. C. (2002). *Steep habits of juvenile detainees in the Chicago area*. Paper presented at the annual meeting of the American Academy of Neurology, Denver.

Reid, M., Miller, W., & Kerr, E. (2004). Sex-based glass ceilings in U.S. state-level bureaucracies, 1987–1997. *Administration & Society, 36*, 377–405.

Reifman, A. (2000). Revisiting *The Bell Curve*. *Psycoloquy, 11*, 99.

Reiner, W. G., & Gearhart, J. P. (2004). Discordant sexual identity in some genetic males with cloacal exstrophy assigned to female sex at birth. *New England Journal of Medicine, 550*, 333–341.

Reis, S., & Renzulli, J. (2004). Current research on the social and emotional development of gifted and talented students: Good news and future possibilities. *Psychology in the Schools, 41*, 119–130.

Rennie, S., Muula, A., & Westreich, D. (2007). Male circumcision and HIV prevention: Ethical, medical and public health tradeoffs in low-income countries. *Journal of Medical Ethics, 33*, 357–361.

Reproductive Medicine Associates of New Jersey. (2002). *Older women and risks of pregnancy*. Princeton, NJ: American Society for Reproductive Medicine.

Reschly, D. J. (1996). Identification and assessment of students with disabilities. *Future of Children, 6*, 40–53.

Rescorla, L., Alley, A., & Christine, J. (2001). Word frequencies in toddlers' lexicons. *Journal of Speech, Language, & Hearing Research, 44*, 598–609.

Resnick, M. D., Bearman, P. S., Blum, R. W., Bauman, K. E., Harris, M. R., Jones, L., et al. (1997). Protecting adolescents from harm: Findings from the National Longitudinal Study on Adolescent Health. *Journal of the American Medical Association, 278*, 823–832.

Reutzel, D., Fawson, P., Smith J. (2006). Words to Go!: Evaluating a first-grade parent involvement program for "making" words at home. *Reading Research and Instruction* [serial online], *45*, 119–159.

Reyna, V. F. (1997). Conceptions of memory development with implications for reasoning and decision making. In R. Vasta (Ed.), *Annals of child development: A research annual* (Vol. 12, pp. 87–118). London: Jessica Kingsley.

Rhule, D. (2005). Take care to do no harm: Harmful interventions for youth problem behavior. *Professional Psychology: Research and Practice, 36*, 618–625.

Ricciardelli, L., & McCabe, M. (2003). Sociocultural and individual influences on muscle gain and weight loss strategies among adolescent boys and girls. *Psychology in the Schools, 40*, 209–224.

Ricciardelli, L. A., & McCabe, M. P. (2004). A biopsychosocial model of disordered eating and the pursuit of muscularity in adolescent boys. *Psychological Bulletin, 130*, 179–205.

Rice, M. L., Huston, A. C., Truglio, R., & Wright, J. (1990). Words from *Sesame Street*: Learning vocabulary while viewing. *Developmental Psychology, 26,* 421–428.

Richards, H. D., Bear, G. G., Stewart, A. L., & Norman, A. D. (1992). Moral reasoning and classroom conduct: Evidence of a curvilinear relationship. *Merrill-Palmer Quarterly, 38,* 176–190.

Richards, M. H., & Duckett, E. (1994). The relationship of maternal employment to early adolescent daily experience with and without parents. *Child Development, 65,* 225–236.

Richards, M. H., Crowe, P. A., Larson, R., & Swarr, A. (1998). Developmental patterns and gender differences in the experience of peer companionship during adolescence. *Child Development, 69,* 154–163.

Richards, M. P. M. (1996). The childhood environment and the development of sexuality. In C. J. K. Henry & S. J. Ulijaszek (Eds.), *Long-term consequences of early environment: Growth, development and the lifespan developmental perspective.* Cambridge, England: Cambridge University Press.

Richardson, K., & Norgate, S. (2007). A critical analysis of IQ studies of adopted children. *Human Development, 49,* 319–335.

Rideout, V., Roberts, D.F., & Foehr, U.G. (2005). *Generation M: Median in the lives of 8 to 18 year olds.* Menlo Park, CA: The Henry J. Kaiser Family Foundation.

Rideout, V. J., Vandewater, E. A., & Wartella, E. A. (2003). *Zero to six: Electronic media in the lives of infants, toddlers and preschoolers.* Menlo Park, CA: Henry J. Kaiser Foundation.

Rinaldi, C. (2002). Social conflict abilities of children identified as sociable, aggressive, and isolated: Developmental implications for children at-risk for impaired peer relations. *Developmental Disabilities Bulletin, 30,* 77–94.

Ripple, C., & Zigler, E. (2003). Research, policy, and the federal role in prevention initiatives for children. *American Psychologist, 58,* 482–490.

Ritzen, E. M. (2003). Early puberty: What is normal and when is treatment indicated? *Hormone Research, 60*(Suppl.), 31–34.

Rivera-Gaziola, M., Silva-Pereyra, J., & Kuhl, P. K. (2005). Brain potentials to native and non-native speech contrasts in 7- and 11-month-old American infants. *Developmental Science, 8,* 162–172.

Robb, A., & Dadson, M. (2002). Eating disorders in males. *Child & Adolescent Psychiatric Clinics of North America, 11,* 399–418.

Robbins, M. W. (1990, December 10). Sparing the child: How to intervene when you suspect abuse. *The New York Times Magazine,* pp. 42–53.

Robergeau, K., Joseph, J., & Silber, T. (2006, December). Hospitalization of children and adolescents for eating disorders in the state of New York. *Journal of Adolescent Health, 39,* 806–810.

Roberts, E. (2007). Extra embryos: The ethics of cryopreservation in Ecuador and elsewhere. *American Ethnologist, 34,* 181–199.

Roberts, R. D., Zeidner, M., & Matthews, G. (2001). Does emotional intelligence meet traditional standards for an intelligence? Some new data and conclusions. *Emotion, 1,* 196–231.

Roberts, R. E., Phinney, J. S., Masse, L. C., Chen, Y. R., Roberts, C. R., & Romero, A. (1999). The structure of ethnic identity of young adolescents from diverse ethnocultural groups. *Journal of Early Adolescence, 19,* 301–322.

Robins, R. W., & Trzesniewski, K. H. (2005). Self-esteem development across the lifespan. *Current Directions in Psychological Science, 14,* 158–162.

Robinson, A., & Stark, D. R. (2005). *Advocates in action.* Washington, DC: National Association for the Education of Young Children.

Robinson, A. J., & Pascalis, O. (2004). Development of flexible visual recognition memory in human infants. *Developmental Science, 7,* 527–533.

Robinson, G. E. (2004, April 16). Beyond nature and nurture. *Science, 304,* 397–399.

Robinson, J. P., & Bianchi, S. (1997, December). The children's hours. *American Demographics,* 20–23.

Robinson, N. M., Zigler, E., & Gallagher, J. J. (2000). Two tails of the normal curve; Similarities and differences in the study of mental retardation and giftedness. *American Psychologist, 55,* 1413–1421.

Robinson, W. P., & Gillibrand, E. (2004, May 14). Single-sex teaching and achievement in science. *International Journal of Science Education, 26,* 659.

Rochat, P. (2004). Emerging co-awareness. In G. Bremnery & A. Slater (Eds.), *Theories of infant development.* Maiden, MA: Blackwell.

Rochat, P. (Ed.). (1999). *Early social cognition: Understanding others in the first months of life.* Mahwah, NJ: Erlbaum.

Roche, T. (2000, November 13). The crisis of foster care. *Time,* pp. 74–82.

Roelofs, J., Meesters, C., Ter Huurne, M., Bamelis, L., & Muris, P. (2006, June). On the links between attachment style, parental rearing behaviors, and internalizing and externalizing problems in non-clinical children. *Journal of Child and Family Studies, 15,* 331–344.

Roeser, R. W., Eccles, J. S., & Sameroff, A. J. (2000). School as a context of early adolescents' academic and social-emotional development: A summary of research findings. *Elementary School Journal, 100,* 443–471.

Roffwarg, H. P., Muzio, J. N., & Dement, W. C. (1966). Ontogenic development of the human sleep–dream cycle. *Science, 152,* 604–619.

Rogan, J. (2007). How much curriculum change is appropriate? Defining a zone of feasible innovation. *Science Education, 91,* 439–460.

Rogers, S., & Willams, J. (2006). *Imitation and the social mind: Autism and typical development.* Guilford Press.

Rogoff, B., & Chavajay, P. (1995). What's become of research on the cultural basis of cognitive development? *American Psychologist, 50,* 859–877.

Rolls, E. (2000). Memory systems in the brain. *Annual Review of Psychology, 51,* 599–630.

Romero, A., & Roberts, R. (2003). The impact of multiple dimensions of ethnic identity on discrimination and adolescents' self-esteem. *Journal of Applied Social Psychology, 33,* 2288–2305.

Rönkä, A., & Pulkkinen, L. (1995). Accumulation of problems in social functioning in young adulthood: A developmental approach. *Journal of Personality and Social Psychology, 69,* 381–391.

Roopnarine, J. (1992). Father–child play in India. In K. MacDonald (Ed.), *Parent–child play.* Albany: State University of New York Press.

Ropar, D., Mitchell, P., & Ackroyd, K. (2003). Do children with autism find it difficult to offer alternative interpretations to ambiguous figures? *British Journal of Developmental Psychology, 21,* 387–395.

Rose, A. J. (2002). Co-rumination in the friendships of girls and boys. *Child Development, 73,* 1830–1843.

Rose, A. J., & Asher, S. R. (1999). Children's goals and strategies in response to conflicts within a friendship. *Developmental Psychology, 35,* 69–79.

Rose, S. (2008, January). Drugging unruly children is a method of social control. *Nature, 451,* 521.

Rose, S. A., & Feldman, J. F. (1997). Memory and speed: Their role in the relation of infant information processing to later IQ. *Child Development, 68,* 630–641.

Rose, S., Feldman, J., & Jankowski, J. (1999). Visual and auditory temporal processing, cross-modal transfer, and reading. *Journal of Learning Disabilities, 32,* 256–266.

Rose, S., Jankowski, J., & Feldman, J. (2002). Speed of processing and face recognition at 7 and 12 months. *Infancy, 3,* 435–55.

Rosen, S., & Iverson, P. (2007). Constructing adequate non-speech analogues: What is special about speech anyway? *Developmental Science, 10,* 165–168.

Rosenstein, D., & Oster, H. (1988). Differential facial responses to four basic tastes in newborns. *Child Development, 59,* 1555–1568.

Rosenthal, R. (2002). The Pygmalion effect and its mediating mechanisms. In J. Aronson (Ed.), *Improving academic achievement: Impact of psychological factors on education.* San Diego: Academic Press.

Rosenthal, R., & Jacobson, L. (1968). *Pygmalion in the classroom: Teacher expectation and pupils' intellectual development.* New York: Holt, Rinehart & Winston.

Ross, J., Stefanatos, G., & Roeltgen, D. (2007). Klinefelter syndrome. *Neurogenetic developmental disorders: Variation of manifestation in childhood.* Cambridge, MA: MIT Press.

Rossi, G., Balottin, U., Rossi, M., Chiappedi, M., Fazzi, E., & Lanzi, G. (2007, November). Pharmacological treatment of anorexia nervosa: A retrospective study in preadolescents and adolescents. *Clinical Pediatrics, 46,* 806–811.

Roth, D., Slone, M., & Dar, R. (2000). Which way cognitive development? An evaluation of the Piagetian and the domain-specific research programs. *Theory and Psychology, 10,* 353–373.

Rothbart, M., & Derryberry, D. (2002). Temperament in children. In C. von Hofsten & L. Backman (Eds.), *Psychology at the turn of the millennium: Vol. 2. Social, developmental, and clinical perspectives.* Florence, KY: Taylor & Frahces/Routledge.

Rothbart, M. K., Ahadi, S. A., & Evans, D. E. (2000). Temperament and personality: Origins and outcomes. *Journal of Personality and Social Psychology, 78,* 122–135.

Rothbart, M. K., Derryberry, D., & Hershey, K. (2000). Stability of temperament in childhood: Laboratory infant assessment to parent report at seven years. In V. J. Molfese & D. L. Molfese (Eds.), *Temperament and personality development across the life span.* Mahwah, NJ: Erlbaum.

Rothbaum, F., Rosen, K., & Ujiie, T. (2002). Family systems theory, attachment theory and culture. *Family Process, 41,* 328–350.

Rotigel, J. V. (2003). Understanding the young gifted child: Guidelines for parents, families, and educators. *Early Childhood Education Journal, 30,* 209–214.

Rovee-Collier, C. (1993). The capacity for long-term memory in infancy. *Current Directions in Psychological Science, 2,* 130–135.

Rovee-Collier, C. (1999). The development of infant memory. *Current Directions in Psychological Science, 8,* 80–85.

Rovee-Collier, C., Hayne, H., & Colombo, M. (2001). *The development of implicit and explicit memory.* Philadelphia: John Benjamins.

Rowe, D. C. (1994). *The effects of nurture on individual natures.* New York: Guilford.

Rubenstein, A. J., Kalakanis, L., & Langlois, J. H. (1999). Infant preferences for attractive faces: A cognitive explanation. *Developmental Psychology, 35,* 848–855.

Rubie-Davies, C. (2007, June). Classroom interactions: Exploring the practices of high- and low-expectation teachers. *British Journal of Educational Psychology, 77,* 289–306.

Ruda, M. A., Ling, Q.D., Hohmann, A. G., Peng, Y. B., & Tachibana, T. (2000, July 28). Altered nociceptive neuronal circuits after neonatal peripheral inflammation. *Science, 289,* 628–630.

Rudy, D., & Grusec, J. (2006, March). Authoritarian parenting in individualist and collectivist groups: Associations with maternal emotion and cognition and children's self-esteem. *Journal of Family Psychology, 20,* 68–78.

Ruff, H. A. (1989). The infant's use of visual and haptic information in the perception and recognition of objects. *Canadian Journal of Psychology, 43,* 302–319.

Runeson, I., Martenson, E., & Enskar, K. (2007). Children's knowledge and degree of participation in decision making when undergoing a clinical diagnostic procedure. *Pediatric Nursing, 33,* 505–511.

Russell, S., & Consolacion, T. (2003). Adolescent romance and emotional health in the United States: Beyond binaries. *Journal of Clinical Child & Adolescent Psychology, 32,* 499–508.

Russell, S., & McGuire, J. (2006). Critical mental health issues for sexual minority adolescents. *The crisis in youth mental health: Critical issues and effective programs, Vol. 2: Disorders in adolescence* (pp. 213–238). Westport, CT: Praeger/Greenwood Publishing Group.

Rust, J., Golombok, S., Hines, M., Johnston, K., & Golding, J., & ALSPAC Study Team. (2000). The role of brothers and sisters in the gender development of preschool children. *Journal of Experimental Child Psychology, 77,* 292–303.

Rustin, M. (2006). Infant observation research: What have we learned so far? *Infant Observation, 9,* 35–52.

Rutter, M. (2003). Commentary: Causal processes leading to antisocial behavior. *Developmental Psychology, 39,* 372–378.

Rutter, M. (2006). *Genes and behavior: Nature-nurture interplay explained.* New York: Blackwell Publishing.

Ryan, B. P. (2001). Programmed Therapy for Stuttering in Children and Adults; Charles C. Thomas, Spring, IL, 2001.

Ryan, K. E., & Ryan, A. M. (2005). Psychological process underlying stereotype threat and standardized math test performance. *Educational Psychologist, 40,* 53–63.

Sadker, D., & Sadker, M. (2005). *Teachers, schools, and society.* New York: McGraw-Hill.

Sadker, M., & Sadker, D. (1994). Failing at fairness: *How America's schools cheat girls.* New York: Scribner.

Saiegh-Haddad, E. (2007). Epilinguistic and metalinguistic phonological awareness may be subject to different constraints: Evidence from Hebrew. *First Language, 27,* 385–405.

Sales, B. D., & Folkman, S. (Eds.). (2000). *Ethics in research with human participants.* Washington, DC: American Psychological Association.

Sallis, J., & Glanz, K. (2006). The Role of Built Environments in Physical Activity, Eating, and Obesity in Childhood. *The Future of Children, 16,* 89–108.

Samet, J. H., DeMarini, D. M., & Malling, H. V. (2004, May 14). Do airborne particles induce heritable mutations? *Science, 304,* 971.

Samuels, C. A. (2005). Special educators discuss NCLB effect at national meeting. *Education Week, 24,* 12.

Samuelsson, I., & Johansson, E. (2006, January). Play and learning—inseparable dimensions in preschool practice. *Early Child Development and Care, 176,* 47–65.

Sandberg, D. E., & Voss, L. D. (2002). The psychosocial consequences of short stature: A review of the evidence. *Best Practice and Research Clinical Endocrinology and Metabolism, 16,* 449–463.

Sanderson, 2007

Sandler, B. (1994, January 31). First denial, then a near-suicidal plea: "Mom, I need your help." *People Weekly,* pp. 56–58.

Sandoval, J., Frisby, C. L., Geisinger, K. F., Scheuneman, J. D., & Grenier, J. R. (Eds.). (1998). *Test interpretation and diversity: Achieving equity in assessment.* Washington, DC: APA Books.

Sang, B., Miao, X., & Deng, C. (2002). The development of gifted and nongifted young children in metamemory knowledge. *Psychological Science (China), 25,* 406–409, 424.

Sanoff, A. P., & Minerbrook, S. (1993, April 19). Race on campus. *U.S. News & World Report,* 52–64.

Santelli, J., Ott, M., Lyon, M., Rogers, J., Summers, D., & Schleifer, R. (2006). Abstinence and abstinence-only education: A review of U.S. policies and programs. *Journal of Adolescent Health, 38,* 72–81.

Santtila, P., Sandnabba, N., Harlaar, N., Varjonen, M., Alanko, K., & von der Pahlen, B. (2008, January). Potential for homosexual response is prevalent and genetic. *Biological Psychology, 77,* 102–105.

Sapolsky, R. (2005, December). Sick of poverty. *Scientific American,* 93–99.

Saslow, E. (2005, August 22). High schools address the cruelest cut; Pressure to make team forces new methods upon imperfect process. The Washington Post, A01.

Sato, Y., Fukasawa, T., Hayakawa, M., Yatsuya, H., Hatakeyama, M., Ogawa, A., et al. (2007). A new method of blood sampling reduces pain for newborn infants: A prospective, randomized controlled clinical trial. *Early Human Development, 83,* 389–394.

Saudino, K., & McManus, I. C. (1998). Handedness, footedness, eyedness, and earedness in the Colorado Adoption Project. *British Journal of Developmental Psychology, 16,* 167–174.

Saunders, J., Davis, L., & Williams, T. (2004). Gender differences in self-perceptions and academic outcomes: A study of African American high school students. *Journal of Youth & Adolescence, 33,* 81–90.

Savage-Rumbaugh, E. S., Murphy, J., Sevcik, R. A., Brakke, K. E., Williams, S. L., & Rumbaugh, D. M. (1993). Language and comprehension in ape and child. *Monographs of the Society for Research in Child Development, 58*(3–4, Serial No. 233).

Savin-Williams, R. C. (2003a), Are adolescent same-sex romantic relationships on our radar screen? In P. Florsheim (Ed.), Adolescent romantic relations and sexual behavior: *Theory, research, and practical implications.* Mahwah, NJ: Erlbaum.

Savin-Williams, R. C. (2003b). Lesbian, gay, and bisexual youths' relationships with their parents. In L. Garnets & D. Kimme (Eds.), *Psychological perspectives on lesbian, gay, and bisexual experience* (2nd ed.). New York: Columbia University Press.

Sax, L. (2005, March 2). The promise and peril of single-sex public education. *Education Week, 24,* 48–51.

Sax, L., & Kautz, K. J. (2003). Who first suggests the diagnosis of attention-deficit/hyperactivity disorder? *Annals of Family Medicine. 1,* 171–174.

Sax, L. J., Astin, A. W., Korn, W. S., & Mahoney, K. M. (2000). *The American freshman: National norms for fall 2000.* Los Angeles: University of California, Higher Education Research Institute.

Scarr, S. (1993). Biological and cultural diversity: The legacy of Darwin for development. *Child Development, 64,* 1333–1353.

Scarr, S. (1998). American child care today. *American Psychologist, 53,* 95–108.

Scarr, S., & Carter-Saltzman, L. (1982). Genetics and intelligence. In R. J. Stemberg (Ed.), *Handbook of human intelligence* (pp. 792–896). Cambridge, England: Cambridge University Press.

Schachar, R., Ickowicz, A., Crosbie, J., Donnelly, G., Reiz, J., Miceli, P., et al. (2008, March). Cognitive and behavioral effects of multilayer-release methylphenidate in the treatment of children with attention-deficit/hyperactivity disorder. *Journal of Child and Adolescent Psychopharmacology, 18,* 11–24.

Schachter, E. P. (2005). Erikson meets the postmodern: Can classic identity theory rise to the challenge? *Identity, 5,* 137–160.

Schaeffer, C., Petras, H., & Lalongo, N. (2003). Modeling growth in boys' aggressive behavior across elementary school: Links to later criminal involvement, conduct disorder, and antisocial personality disorder. *Developmental Psychology, 39,* 1020–1035.

Schaller, M., & Crandall, C. S. (Eds.). (2004). *The Psychological Foundations of Culture.* Mahwah, NJ: Erlbaum.

Scharfe. E. (2000). Development of emotional expression, understanding, and regulation in infants and young children. In R. Bar-On & J. Parker (Eds.), *The handbook of emotional intelligence: Theory, development, assessment, and application at home, school, and in the workplace.* San Francisco: Jossey-Bass/Pfeiffer.

Scharrer, E., Kim, D., Lin, K., & Liu, Z. (2006). Working hard or hardly working? Gender, humor, and the performance of domestic chores in television commercials. *Mass Communication and Society, 9,* 215–238.

Schatz, M. (1994). *A toddler's life.* New York: Oxford University Press.

Schechter, T., Finkelstein, Y., & Koren, G. (2005). Pregnant "DES daughters" and their offspring. *Canadian Family Physician, 51,* 493–494.

Schellenberg, E. G., & Trehub, S. E. (1996). Natural musical intervals: Evidence from infant listeners. *Psychological Science, 7,* 212–211.

Schemo, D. J. (2003, November 13). Students' scores rise in math, not in reading. *The New York Times,* p. A2.

Schemo, D. J. (2004, March 2). Schools, facing tight budgets, leave gifted programs behind. *The New York Times,* pp. A1, A18.

Schempf, A. H., (2007). Illicit drug use and neonatal outcomes: A critical review. *Obstetrics and Gynecological Surveys, 62,* 745–757.

Scherf, K. S., Sweeney, J. A., & Luna, B. (2006). Brain basis of developmental change in visuospatial working memory. *Journal of Cognitive Neuroscience, 18,* 1045–1058.

Schiller, J. S., & Bemadel, L. (2004). Summary health statistics for the U.S. population: National Health Interview Survey, 2002. *Vital Health Statistics, 10,* 1–110.

Schmidt, M., Pekow, P., Freedson, P., Markenson, G., & Chasan-Taber, L. (2006). Physical activity patterns during pregnancy in a diverse population of women. *Journal of Women's Health, 15,* 909–918.

Schmitt, E. (2001, March 13). For 7 million people in census, one race category isn't enough. *The New York Times,* pp. A1, A14.

Schneiderman, N. (1983). Animal behavior models of coronary hearty disease. In D. S. Kranz, A. Baum, & J. E. Singer (Eds.), *Handbook of psychology and health* (Vol. 3). Hillsdale, NJ: Erlbaum.

Schnitzer, P.G. (2006). Prevention of unintentional childhood injuries. *American Family Physician, 74,* 1864–1869.

Schnur, E., & Belanger, S. (2000). What works in Head Start. In M. P. Kluger & G. Alexander (Eds.), *What works in child welfare*. Washington, DC: Child Welfare League of America.

Schöner, G., & Thelen, E. (2006). Using Dynamic Field Theory to Rethink Infant Habituation. *Psychological Review, 113*, 273–299.

Schoppe-Sullivan, S., Diener, M., Mangelsdorf, S., Brown, G.,McHale, J., & Frosch, C. (2006, July). Attachment and sensitivity in family context: The roles of parent and infant gender. *Infant and Child Development, 15*, 367–385.

Schoppe-Sullivan, S., Mangelsdorf, S., Brown, G., & Sokolowski, M. (2007, February). Goodness-of-fit in family context: Infant temperament, marital quality, and early coparenting behavior. *Infant Behavior & Development, 30*, 82–96.

Schor, E. L. (1987). Unintentional injuries: Patterns within families. *American Journal of the Diseases of Children, 141*, 1280.

Schore, A. (2003). Affect regulation and the repair of the self. New York: W. W. Norton.

Schreiber, G. B., Robins, M., Striegel-Moore, R., Obarzanek, M., Morrison, J. A., & Wright, D. J. (1996). Weight modification efforts reported by black and white preadolescent girls: National Heart, Lung, and Blood Institute Growth and Health Study. *Pediatrics, 98*, 63–70.

Schuetze, P., Eiden, R., & Coles, C. (2007). Prenatal cocaine and other substance exposure: Effects on infant autonomic regulation at 7 months of age. *Developmental Psychobiology, 49*, 276–289.

Schuster, C. S., & Ashburn, S. S. (1986). *The process of human development* (2nd ed.). Boston: Little, Brown.

Schutt, R. K. (2001). *Investigating the social world: The process and practice of research*. Thousand Oaks, CA: Sage.

Schutz, H., Paxton, S., & Wertheim, E. (2002). Investigation of body comparison among adolescent girls. *Journal of Applied Social Psychology, 32*, 1906–1937.

Schwartz, B. S., & Stewart, W. F. (2007). Lead and cognitive function in adults: A questions and answers approach to a review of the evidence for cause, treatment, and prevention, *International Review of Psychiatry. 19*, 671–92.

Schwartz, C. E., Wright, C. L., Shin, L. M., Kagan, J., & Rauch, S. L. (2003, June 20). Inhibited and uninhibited infants "grown up": Adult amygdalar response to novelty. *Science, 300*, 1952–1953.

Schwarzer, R., & Knoll, N. (2007). Functional roles of social support within the stress and coping process: A theoretical and empirical overview. *International Journal of Psychology, 42*, 243–252.

Schwebel, D. C., & Gaines, J. (2007). Pediatric unintentional injury: behavioral risk factors and implications for prevention. *Journal of Developmental and Behavioral Pediatrics. 28*, 245–254.

Schweinhart, L. J., Barnes, H. V., & Weikart, D. P. (1993). *Significant benefits: The High/Scope Perry Preschool Study through age 27 (Monographs of the High/Scope Educational Research Foundation, No. 10)*. Ypsilanti, MI: High/Scope Press.

Scrimsher, S., & Tudge, J. (2003). The teaching/learning relationship in the first years of school: Some revolutionary implications of Vygotsky's theory [Special issue]. *Early Education and Development, 14*, 293–312.

Sears, R. R. (1977). Sources of life satisfaction of the Terman gifted men. *American Psychologist, 32*, 119–129.

Segal, B. M., & Stewart, J. C. (1996). Substance use and abuse in adolescence: An overview. *Child Psychiatry & Human Development, 26*, 193–210.

Segal, J., & Segal, Z. (1992, September). No more couch potatoes. *Parents*, pp. 32–39.

Segall, M. H., Dasen, P. R., Berry, J. W., & Poortinga, Y. H. (1990). *Human behavior in global perspective*. Boston: Allyn & Bacon.

Segalowitz, S. J., & Rapin, I. (Eds.). (2003). *Child neuropsychology, Part 1*. Amsterdam, The Netherlands: Elsevier Science.

Seidman, S. N., & Rieder, R. O. (1994). A review of sexual behavior in the United States. *American Journal of Psychiatry, 151*, 330–341.

Seifer, R., Schiller, M., & Sameroff, A. J. (1996). Attachment, maternal sensitivity, and infant temperament during the first year of life. *Developmental Psychology, 32*, 12–25.

Seligman, M. E. P. (2007). Coaching and positive psychology. *Australian Psychologist, 42*, 266–267.

Senghas, A., Kita, S., & Özyürek, A. (2004, September, 17). Children creating core properties of language: Evidence from an emerging sign language in Nicaragua. *Science, 305*, 1779–1782.

Serretti, A., Calati, R., Ferrari, B., & De Ronchi, D. (2007). Personality and genetics. *Current Psychiatry Reviews, 3*, 147–159.

Servin, A., Nordenström, A., Larsson, A., & Bohlin, G. (2003). Prenatal androgens and gender-typed behavior: A study of girls with mild and severe forms of congenital adrenal hyperplasia. *Developmental Psychology, 39*, 440–450.

Sesser, S. (1993, September 13). Opium war redux. *The New Yorker*, pp. 78–89.

Shafer, R. G. (1990, March 12). An anguished father recounts the battle he lost—Trying to rescue a teenage son from drugs. *People Weekly*, pp. 81–83.

Shaffer, D., Bautista, C., Sateren, W., Sawe, F., Kiplangat, S., Miruka, A., et al. (2007). The protective effect of circumcision on HIV incidence in rural low-risk men circumcised predominantly by traditional circumcisers in Kenya: Two-Year Follow-Up of the Kericho HIV Cohort Study. *JAIDS Journal of Acquired Immune Deficiency Syndromes, 45*, 371–379.

Shapiro, L. (1997, Spring/Summer). Beyond an apple a day. *Newsweek Special Issue*, pp. 52–56.

Sharma, M. (2008. Twenty-first century pink or blue: How sex selection technology facilitates gendercide and what we can do about it. *Family Court Review, 46*, 198–215.

Shaunessy, E., Suldo, S., Hardesty, R., & Shaffer, E. (2006, December).School functioning and psychological well-being of international baccalaureate and general education students: A preliminary examination. *Journal of Secondary Gifted Education,17*, 76–89.

Shavelson, R., Hubner, J. J., & Stanton, J. C. (1976). Self-concept: Validation of construct interpretations. *Review of Educational Research, 46*, 407–441.

Shaw, D. S., Winslow, E. B., & Flanagan, C. (1999). A prospective study of the effects of marital status and family relations on young children's adjustment among African American and European American families. *Child Development, 70*, 742–755.

Shaw, M. L. (2003). Creativity and whole language. In J. Houtz, *The educational psychology of creativity*. Cresskill, NJ: Hampton Press.

Shaywitz, S. (2004). *Overcoming dyslexia: A new and complete science-based program for reading problems at any level*. New York: Vintage.

Shea, J. D. (1985). Studies of cognitive development in Papua New Guinea. *International Journal of Psychology, 20*, 33–61.

Shealy, C. N. (1995). From Boys Town to Oliver Twist: Separating fact from fiction in welfare reform and out-of-home placement of children and youth. *American Psychologist, 50,* 565–580.

Shelby & Vaske, 2008

Shellenbarger, S. (2003, January 9). Yes, that weird day-care center could scar your child, researchers say. *The Wall Street Journal,* p. D1.

Shi, L. (2003). Facilitating constructive parent–child play: Family therapy with young children. *Journal of Family Psychotherapy, 14,* 19–31.

Shi, X., & Lu, X. (2007, October). Bilingual and bicultural development of Chinese American adolescents and young adults: A comparative study. *Howard Journal of Communications, 18,* 313–333.

Shin, H. B., & Bruno. R. (2003). *Language use and English speaking ability: 2000.* Washington, DC: U.S. Census Bureau.

Shiner, R., Masten, A., & Roberts, J. (2003). Childhood personality foreshadows adult personality and life outcomes two decades later. *Journal of Personality, 71,* 1145–1170.

Shonk, S. M., & Cicchetti, D. (2001). Maltreatment, competency deficits, and risk for academic and behavioral maladjustment. *Developmental Psychology, 37,* 3–17.

Shrum, W., Cheek, N., Jr., & Hunter, S. M. (1988). Friendship in school: Gender and racial homophily. *Sociology of Education, 61,* 227–239.

Sieber, J. E. (2000). Planning research: Basic ethical decision-making. In B. D. Sales & S. Folkman (Eds.), *Ethics in research with human participants.* Washington, DC: American Psychological Association.

Siegel, L. J., & Davis, L. (2008). Somatic disorders. In R. J. Morris & T. R. Kratochwill (Eds.), *The practice of child therapy* (4th ed.). Mahwah, NJ: Lawrence Erlbaum.

Siegler, R. (2003). Thinking and intelligence. In M. Bornstein & L. Davidson (Eds.), *Well-being: Positive development across the life course* (pp. 311–320). Mahwah, NJ: Erlbaum.

Siegler, R. S. (1994). Cognitive variability: A key to understanding cognitive development. *Current Directions in Psychological Science, 3,* 1–5.

Siegler, R. S. (1998). *Children's thinking* (3rd ed.). Upper Saddle River, NJ: Prentice Hall.

Siegler, R. S., & Ellis, S. (1996). Piaget on childhood. *Psychological Science, 7,* 211–215.

Siegler, R. S., & Richards, D. (1982). The development of intelligence. In R. Sternberg (Ed.), *Handbook of human intelligence.* London: Cambridge University Press.

Sigman, M. (1995). Nutrition and child development: More food for thought. *Current Directions in Psychological Science, 4,* 52–55.

Sigman, M., Cohen, S. E., & Beckwith, L. (1997). Why does infant attention predict adolescent intelligence? *Infant Behavior & Development, 20,* 133–140.

Sigman, M., Cohen, S., & Beckwith, L. (2000). Why does infant attention predict adolescent intelligence? In D. Muir & A. Slater (Eds.), *Infant development: The essential readings* (pp. 239–253). Malden, MA: Blackwell Publishers.

Sigmund, E., De Ste Croix, M., Miklánková, L., & Frömel, K. (2007, December). Physical activity patterns of kindergarten children in comparison to teenagers and young adults. *European Journal of Public Health, 17,* 646–651.

Silenzio, V., Pena, J., Duberstein, P., Cerel, J., & Knox, K. (2007, November). Sexual orientation and risk factors for suicidal ideation and suicide attempts among adolescents and young adults. *American Journal of Public Health, 97,* 2017–2019.

Silverstein, L. B., & Auerbach, C. F. (1999). Deconstructing the essential father. *American Psychologist, 54,* 397–407.

Silverthorn, P., & Frick, P. J. (1999). Developmental pathways to antisocial behavior: The delayed-onset pathway in girls. *Developmental & Psychopathology, 11,* 101–126.

Simcock, G., & Hayne, H. (2002). Breaking the barrier? Children fail to translate their preverbal memories into language. *Psychological Science, 13,* 225–231.

Simmons, S. W., Cyna, A. M., Dennis, A. T., & Hughes, D. (2007). Combined spinal-epidural versus epidural analgesia in labour. *Cochrane Database and Systematic Review, 18,* CD003401.

Simons, S. H., van Dijk, M., Anand, K. S., Roofthooft, D., van Lingen, R. A., & Tibboel. D. (2003). Do we still hurt newborn babies? A prospective study of procedural pain and analgesia in neonates. *Archives of Pediatrics and Adolescence, 157,* 1058–1064.

Simpson, J., Collins, W., Tran, S., & Haydon, K. (2007, February). Attachment and the experience and expression of emotions in romantic relationships: A developmental perspective. *Journal of Personality and Social Psychology, 92,* 355–367.

Singer, D. G., & Singer, J. L. (Eds.). (2000). *Handbook of children and the media.* Thousand Oaks, CA: Sage.

Singer, L. T., Arendt, R., Minnes, S., Farkas, K., & Salvator, A. (2000). Neurobehavioral outcomes of cocaine-exposed infants. *Neurotoxicology & Teratology, 22,* 653–666.

Singh, S., & Darroch, J. E. (2000). Adolescent pregnancy and childbearing: Levels and trends in developed countries. *The Canadian Journal of Human Sexuality, 9,* 67.

Skinner, B. F. (1975). The steep and thorny road to a science of behavior. *American Psychologist, 30,* 42–49.

Skinner, J. D., Ziegler, P., Pac, S., & Devaney, B. (2004). Meal and snack patterns of infants and toddlers. *Journal of the American Dietary Association, 104,* s65–s70.

Slater, A., & Johnson, S. P. (1998). Visual sensory and perceptual abilities of the newborn: Beyond the blooming, buzzing confusion. In F. Simon & G. Butterworth (Eds.), *The development of sensory, motor and cognitive capacities in early infancy: From perception to cognition.* Philadelphia: Psychology Press.

Slater, A., Mattock, A., & Brown, E. (1990). Size constancy at birth: Newborn infants' responses to retinal and real size. *Journal of Experimental Child Psychology, 49,* 314–322.

Slater, M., Henry, K., & Swaim, R. (2003). Violent media content and aggressiveness in adolescents: A downward spiral model. *Communication Research, 30,* 713–736.

Slavin, R. E. (1995). Enhancing intergroup relations in schools: Cooperative learning and other strategies. In W. D. Hawley & A. W. Jackson (Eds.), *Toward a common destiny: Improving race and ethnic relations in America.* San Francisco: Jossey-Bass.

Sloan, S., Gildea, A., Stewart, M., Sneddon, H., & Iwaniec, D. (2008). Early weaning is related to weight and rate of weight gain in infancy. *Child: Care, Health and Development, 34,* 59–64.

Slonje, R., & Smith, P. (2008, April). Cyberbullying: Another main type of bullying? *Scandinavian Journal of Psychology, 49,* 147–154.

Smedley, A., & Smedley, B. D. (2005). Race as biology is fiction, racism as a social problem is real: Anthropological and historical perspectives on the social construction of race. *American Psychologist, 60,* 16–26.

Smetana, J. (2006). Social-cognitive domain theory: Consistencies and variations in children's moral and social judgments. *Handbook of moral development* (pp. 119–153). Mahwah, NJ: Lawrence Erlbaum.

Smetana, J., Daddis, C., & Chuang, S. (2003). "Clean your room!" A longitudinal investigation of adolescent–parent conflict and conflict resolution in middle–class African American families. *Journal of Adolescent Research, 18,* 631–650.

Smetana, J. G. (1995). Parenting styles and conceptions of parental authority during adolescence. *Child Development 66,* 299–316.

Smetana, J. G. (2005). Adolescent-parent conflict: Resistance and subversion as developmental process. In L. Nucci (Ed.), *Conflict, contradiction, and contrarian*

Smith, A., Fried, P., Hogan, M., & Cameron, I. (2006). Effects of prenatal marijuana on visuospatial working memory: An fMRI study in young adults. *Neurotoxicology and Teratology, 28,* 286–295.

Smith, P., & Drew, L. (2002). Grandparenthood. In M. Bornstein (Ed.), *Handbook of parenting: Vol. 3. Being and becoming a parent* (2nd ed., pp. 141–172). Mahwah, NJ: Erlbaum.

Smith, P. K., Mahdavi, J., Carvalho, M., Fisher, S., Russell, S., & Tippett, N. (2008). Cyberbullying: Its nature and impact in secondary school pupils. *Journal of Child Psychology and Psychiatry, 49,* 376–385.

Smith, P. K., Singer, M., & Hoel, H. (2003). Victimization in the school and the workplace: Are there any links? *British Journal of Psychology, 94,* 175–188.

Smith, R. J., Bale, J. F., Jr., & White, K. R. (2005, March 2). Sensorineural hearing loss in children. *Lancet, 365,* 879–890.

Smutny, J., Walker, S., & Meckstroth, E. (2007). *Acceleration for gifted learners, k–5.* Thousand Oaks, CA: Corwin Press.

Smuts, A. B., & Hagen, J. W. (1985). History of the family and of child development: Introduction to Part 1. *Monographs of the Society for Research in Child Development, 50*(4–5, Serial No. 211).

Snarey, J. R. (1995). In a communitarian voice: The sociological expansion of Kohlbergian theory, research, and practice. In W. M. Kurtines & J. L. Gerwirtz (Eds.), *Moral development: An introduction.* Boston: Allyn & Bacon.

Snyder, J., Cramer, A., & Alfrank, J. (2005). The contributions of ineffective discipline and parental hostile attributions of child misbehavior to the development of conduct problems at home and school. *Developmental Psychology, 41,* 30–41.

Soderstrom, M. (2007). Beyond babytalk: Re-evaluating the nature and content of speech input to preverbal infants. *Developmental Review, 27,* 501–532.

Soken, N. H., & Pick, A.D. (1999). Infants' perception of dynamic affective expressions: Do infants distinguish specific expressions? *Child Development. 70,* 1275–1282.

Solantaus, T., Leinonen, J., & Punamäki, R-L. (2004). Children's mental health in times of economic recession: Replication and extension of the family economic stress model in Finland. *Developmental Psychology, 40,* 412–429.

Solomon, G. E. A., & Cassimatis, N. L. (1999). On facts and conceptual systems: Young children's integration of their understandings of germs and contagion. *Developmental Psychology, 35,* 113–126.

Sorensen, T., Nielsen, G., Andersen, P., & Teasdale, T. (1988). Genetic and environmental influences on premature death in adult adoptees. *New England Journal of Medicine, 318,* 727–732.

Sotiriou, A., & Zafiropoulou, M. (2003). Changes of children's self-concept during transition from kindergarten to primary school. Psychology: *The Journal of the Hellenic Psychological Society, 10,* 96–118.

Sousa, D. A. (2004). How t*he brain learns to read.* Thousand Oaks, CA: Corwin Press.

Sousa, D. L. (2005). *How the brain learns to read.* Thousand Oaks, CA: Corwin Press.

Soussignan, R., Schaal, B., Marlier, L., & Jiang, T. (1997). Facial and autonomic responses to biological and artificial olfactory stimuli in human neonates: Re-examining early hedonic discrimination of odors. *Physiology and Behavior, 62,* 745–758.

Spear, L. P. (2002). The adolescent brain and the college drinker: Biological basis of propensity to use and misuse alcohol [Special issue]. *Journal of Studies on Alcohol, 14*(Suppl.), 71–81.

Spearman, C. (1927). *The abilities of man.* London: Macmillan.

Spence-Cochran, K., & Pearl, C. (2006). Moving toward full inclusion. *Life beyond the classroom: Transition strategies for young people with disabilities* (4th ed.) (pp. 133–164). Baltimore, MD: Paul H Brookes.

Spencer, M. B. (1991). Identity, minority development of. In R. M. Lerner, A. C. Petersen, & J. Brooks-Gunn (Eds.), *Encyclopedia of adolescence* (Vol. 1). New York: Garland.

Spencer, M. B., & Dornbusch, S. M. (1990). Challenges in studying minority youth. In S. Feldman & G. Elliott (Eds.), *At the threshold: The developing adolescent.* Cambridge, MA: Harvard University Press.

Spielman, D. A., & Staub, E. (2003). Reducing boy's aggression: Learning to fulfill basic needs constructively. In E. Staub (Ed.), *The Psychology of Good and Evil.* Cambridge, England: Cambridge University Press.

Spinrad, T. L., & Stifler, C. A. (2006). Toddlers' empathy-related responding to distress: predictions from negative emotionality and maternal behavior in infancy. *Inancy, 10,* 97–121.

Sprenger, M. (2007). *Memory 101 for educators.* Thousand Oaks, CA: Corwin Press.

Springen, K. (2000). The circumcision decision [Special issue: *Your Child.*] *Newsletter,* p. 50.

Squire, L. R., & Knowlton, B. J. (1995). Memory, hippocampus, and brain systems. In M. S. Gazzaniga (Ed.), *Cognitive neurosciences.* Cambridge, MA: MIT Press.

Sroufe, L. A. (1994). Pathways to adaptation and maladaptation: Psychopathology as developmental deviation. In D. Cicchetti (Ed.), *Developmental psychopathology: Past, present, and future.* Hillsdale, NJ: Erlbaum.

Sroufe, L. A. (1996). *Emotional development: The organization of emotional life in the early years.* New York: Oxford University Press.

Stadtler, A. C., Gorski, P. A., & Brazelton, T. B. (1999). Toilet training methods, clinical interventions, and recommendations. *Pediatrics, 103,* 1359–1361.

Staff, J., Mortimer, J. T., & Uggen, C. (2004). Work and leisure in adolescence. In R. M. Lerner & L. Steinberg (Eds.). *Handbook of adolescent psychology* (2nd ed.). NY: Wiley.

Staunton, H. (2005). Mammalian sleep. *Naturwissenschaften, 35,* 15.

Steele, C. M. (1997). A threat in the air: How stereotypes shape the intellectual identities and performance of women and African-Americans. *American Psychologist, 52,* 613–629.

Stein, J. H., & Reiser, L. W. (1994). A study of white middle-class adolescent boys' responses to "semenarche" (the first ejaculation). *Journal of Youth and Adolescence, 23,* 373–384.

Stein, Z., Susser, M., Saenger, G., & Marolla, F. (1975). *Famine and human development: The Dutch hunger winter of 1944–1945.* New York: Oxford University Press.

Steinberg, L. (1997, January 2). Turning words into meaning. *The New York Times,* pp. B1–B2.

Steinberg, L. D., & Scott, S. S. (2003). Less guilty by reason of adolescence: Developmental immaturity, diminished responsibility, and the juvenile death penalty. *American Psychologist, 58,* 1009–1018.

Steinberg, L., & Monahan, K. (2007, November). Age differences in resistance to peer influence. *Developmental Psychology, 43,* 1531–1543.

Steinberg, L., & Silverberg, S. (1986). The vicissitudes of autonomy in early adolescence. *Child Development, 57,* 841–851.

Steinberg, L., Dornbusch, S. M., & Brown, B. B. (1992). Ethnic differences in adolescent achievement: An ecological perspective. *American Psychologist, 47,* 723–729.

Steiner, J. E. (1979). Human facial expressions in response to taste and smell stimulation. *Advances in Child Development and Behavior, 13,* 257.

Steinhausen, H. C., & Spohr, H. L. (1998). Long-term outcome of children with fetal alcohol syndrome: Psychopathology, behavior, and intelligence. *Alcoholism, Clinical & Experimental Research, 22,* 334–338.

Stenberg, G. (2003). Effects of maternal inattentiveness on infant social referencing. *Infant & Child Development, 12,* 399–419.

Steri, A. O., & Spelke, E. S. (1988). Haptic perception of objects in infancy. *Cognitive Psychology, 20,* 1–23.

Sternberg, R. (2003a). A broad view of intelligence: The theory of successful intelligence. *Consulting Psychology Journal: Practice & Research, 55,* 139–154.

Sternberg, R. (2003b) Our research program validating the triarchic theory of successful intelligence: Reply to Gottfredson. *Intelligence, 31,* 399–413.

Sternberg, R. (2008, March). Applying psychological theories to educational practice. *American Educational Research Journal, 45,* 150–165.

Sternberg, R. J. (1990). *Metaphors of mind: Conceptions of the nature of intelligence.* Cambridge, England: Cambridge University Press.

Sternberg, R. J. (2005). The triarchic theory of successful intelligence. In D. P. Flanagan & P. L. Harrison (Eds.), *Contemporary intellectual assessment: Theories, tests, and issues.* New York: Guilford Press.

Sternberg, R. J., Conway, B. E., Ketron, J. L., & Bernstein, M. (1981). Peoples' conceptions of intelligence. *Journal of Personality and Social Psychology, 41,* 37–55.

Stettler, N. (2007). Nature and strength of epidemiological evidence for origins of childhood and adulthood obesity in the first year of life. *International Journal of Obesity, 31,* 1035–1043.

Stewart, M., Scherer, J., & Lehman, M. (2003). Perceived effects of high frequency hearing loss in a farming population. *Journal of the American Academy of Audiology, 14,* 100–108.

Stice, E. (2003). Puberty and body image. In C. Hayward (Ed.), *Gender differences at puberty.* New York: Cambridge University Press.

Stice, E., Presnell, K., & Bearman, K. (2001). Relation of early menarche to depression, eating disorders, substance abuse, and comorbid psychopathology among adolescent girls. *Developmental Psychology, 37,* 608–619.

Stipek, D. (2002). At what age should children enter kindergarten? A question for policy makers and parents. *Social Policy Report, 16,* 3–16.

Stolberg, S. G. (1998, April 3). Rise in smoking by young blacks erodes a success story in health. *The New York Times,* p. A1.

Stolberg, S. G. (1999, August 8). Black mothers' mortality rate under scrutiny. *The New York Times,* pp. 1, 18.

Storfer, M. (1990). *Intelligence and giftedness: The contributions of heredity and early environment.* San Francisco: Jossey-Bass.

Stork, S., & Sanders, S. (2008, January). Physical education in early childhood. *The Elementary School Journal, 108,* 197–206.

Straus, M. A., & Gelles, R. J. (Eds.). (1990). *Physical violence in American families.* New Brunswick, NJ: Transaction.

Straus, M. A., Gelles, R. J., & Steinmetz, S. K. (2003). The marriage license as a hitting license. In M. Silberman, *Violence and society: A reader.* Upper Saddle River, NJ: Prentice Hall.

Strelau, J. (1998). *Temperament: A psychological perspective.* New York: Plenum.

Straus, M. A., & McCord, J. (1998). Do physically punished children become violent adults? In S. Nolen-Hoeksema (Ed.), *Clashing views on abnormal psychology: A Taking Sides custom reader* (pp. 130–155). Guilford, CT: Dushkin/ McGraw-Hill.

Striano, T., & Vaish, A. (2006, November). Seven- to9-month-old infants use facial expressions to interpret others' actions. *British Journal of Developmental Psychology, 24,* 753–760.

Strobel, A., Dreisbach, G., Müller, J., Goschke, T., Brocke, B., & Lesch, K. (2007, December). Genetic variation of serotonin function and cognitive control. *Journal of Cognitive Neuroscience, 19,* 1923–1931.

Stroh, L, K., Langlands, C. L., & Simpson, P. A. (2004). Shattering the glass ceiling in the new millennium. In M. S. Stockdale & F. J. Crosby, *Psychology and management of workplace diversity.* Malden, MA: Blackwell.

Stromswold, K. (2006). Why aren't identical twins linguistically identical? Genetic, prenatal and postnatal factors. *Cognition, 101,* 333–384.

Suárez-Orozco, C., Suárez-Orozco., M. M. Todorova, I. (2008). *Learning a new land: Immigrant students in American society.* Cambridge, MA: Belknap Press/Harvard University Press.

Subotnik, R. (2006). Longitudinal studies: Answering our most important questions of prediction and effectiveness. *Journal for the Education of the Gifted, 29,* 379–383.

Sugarman, S. (1988). *Piaget's construction of the child's reality.* Cambridge, England: Cambridge University Press.

Suitor, J. J., Minyard, S. A., & Carter, R. S. (2001). "Did you see what I saw?" Gender differences in perceptions of avenues to prestige among adolescents. *Sociological Inquiry, 71,* 437–454.

Sullivan, K. (2000). *The anti-bullying handbook.* New York: Oxford University Press.

Sullivan, M., & Lewis, M. (2003). Contextual determinants of anger and other negative expressions in young infants. *Developmental Psychology, 39,* 693–705.

Sullivan, M. W., Rovee-Collier, C. K., & Tynes, D. M. (1979). A conditioning analysis of infant long-term memory. *Child Development, 50,* 152–162.

Suls, J., & Wills, T. A. (Eds.). (1991). *Social comparison: Contemporary theory and research.* Hillsdale, NJ: Erlbaum.

Sulzer-Azaroff, B., & Mayer, R. (1991). *Behavior analysis and lasting change.* New York: Holt.

Summers, J., Schallert, D., & Ritter, P. (2003). The role of social comparison in students' perceptions of ability: An enriched view of academic motivation in middle school students. *Contemporary Educational Psychology, 28,* 510–523.

Sunderman, G. L. (Ed.). (2008). *Holding NCLB accountable: Achieving, accountability, equity, & school reform.* Thousand Oaks, CA, US: Corwin Press.

Super, C. M. (1976). Environmental effects on motor development: A case of African infant precocity. *Developmental Medicine and Child Neurology, 18,* 561–576.

Super, C. M., & Harkness, S. (1982). The infant's niche in rural Kenya and metropolitan America. In L. Adler (Ed.), *Issues in cross-cultural research.* New York: Academic Press.

Suskind, R. (1994, September 24). Class struggle: Poor, black, and smart. *The New York Times,* p. A1.

Suskind, R. (1999). *A hope in the unseen: An American odyssey from the inner city to the Ivy League.* New York: Broadway Books.

Sutherland, R., Pipe, M., & Schick, K. (2003). Knowing in advance: The impact of prior event information on memory and event knowledge. *Journal of Experimental Child Psychology, 84,* 244–263.

Suzuki, L., & Aronson, J. (2005). The cultural malleability of intelligence and its impact on the racial/ethnic hierarchy. *Psychology, Public Policy, and Law, 11,* 320–327.

Swain, J. (2004). Is placement in the least restrictive environment a restricted debate? *PsycCRITIQUES,* p. 23–30.

Swain, J. E., Lorberbaum, J. P., Kose, S., & Strathearn, L., (2007). Brain basis of early parent–*infant* interactions: Psychology, physiology, and in vivo functional neuroimaging studies. *Journal of Child Psychology and Psychiatry, 48,* 262–287.

Swanson, H., Saez, L., & Gerber, M. (2004). Literacy and cognitive functioning in bilingual and nonbilingual children at or not at risk for reading disabilities. *Journal of Educational Psychology, 96,* 3–18.

Swanson, L. A., Leonard, L. B., & Gandour, J. (1992). Vowel duration in mothers' speech to young children. *Journal of Speech and Hearing Research, 35,* 617–625.

Swiatek, M. (2002). Social coping among gifted elementary school students. *Journal for the Education of the Gifted, 26,* 65–86.

Swingler, M. M., Sweet, M. A., & Carver, L. J. (2007). Relations between mother–child interaction and the neural correlates of face processing in 6-month-olds. *Infancy, 11,* 63–86.

Taddio, A., Shah, V., & Gilbert-MacLeod, C. (2002). Conditioning and hyperalgesia in newborns exposed to repeated heel lances. *Journal of the American Medical Association, 288,* 857–861.

Taga, K., Markey, C., & Friedman, H. (2006, June). A longitudinal investigation of associations between boys' pubertal timing and adult behavioral health and well-being. *Journal of Youth and Adolescence, 35,* 401–411.

Tajfel, H., & Turner, J. (2004). The social identity theory of intergroup behavior. In J.T. Jost & J. Sidanius (Eds.), *Political psychology: Key readings.* New York: Psychology Press.

Takahashi, K. (1986). Examining the Strange Situation procedure with Japanese mothers and 12-month-old infants. *Developmental Psychology, 22,* 265–270.

Takala, M. (2006, November). The effects of reciprocal teaching on reading comprehension in mainstream and special (SLI) education. *Scandinavian Journal of Educational Research, 50,* 559–576.

Tallandini, M., & Scalembra, C. (2006). Kangaroo mother care and mother–premature infant dyadic interaction. *Infant Mental Health Journal, 27,* 251–275.

Tamis-LeMonda, C. S. & Cabrera, N. (Eds.). (2002). *The handbook of father involvement: Multidisciplinary perspectives.* Mahwah, NJ: Lawrence Erlbaum.

Tan, H., Wen, S. W., Mark, W., Fung, K. F., Demissie, K., & Rhoads, G. G. (2004). The association between fetal sex and preterm birth in twin pregnancies. *Obstetrics and Gynecology, 103,* 327–332.

Tang, C., Wu, M., Liu, J., Lin, H., & Hsu, C. (2006). Delayed parenthoodand the risk of cesarean delivery—Is paternal age an independent risk factor? *Birth: Issues in Perinatal Care, 33,* 18–26.

Tangney, J., & Dearing, R. (2002). Gender differences in morality. In R. Bornstein & J. Masling (Eds.), *The psychodynamics of gender and gender role.* Washington, DC: American Psychological Association.

Tanner, E., & Finn-Stevenson, M. (2002). Nutrition and brain development: Social policy implications. *American Journal of Orthopsychiatry, 72,* 182–193.

Tanner, J. (1972). Sequence, tempo, and individual variation in growth and development of boys and girls aged twelve to sixteen. In J. Kagan & R. Coles (Eds.), *Twelve to sixteen: Early adolescence.* New York: Norton.

Tanner, J. M. (1978). *Education and physical growth* (2nd ed.). New York: International Universities Press.

Tappan, M. B. (1997). Language, culture and moral development: A Vygotskian perspective. *Developmental Review, 17,* 199–212.

Tardif, T. (1996). Nouns are not always learned before verbs: Evidence from Mandarin speakers' early vocabularies. *Developmental Psychology, 32,* 492–504.

Tardif, T., Wellman, H. M., & Cheung, K. M. (2004). False belief understanding in Cantonese-speaking children. *Journal of Child Language, 31,* 779–800.

Task Force on Sudden Infant Death Syndrome (2005). The changing concept of sudden infant death syndrome: Diagnostic coding shifts, controversies regarding the sleeping environment, and new variables to consider in reducing risk. *Pediatrics, 105,* 650–656.

Tatum, B. (2007). *Can we talk about race?: And other conversations in an era of school resegregation.* Boston: Beacon Press.

Taylor, D. M. (2002). *The quest for identity: From minority groups to Generation Xers.* Westport, CT: Praeger Publishers/ Greenwood.

Taylor, H. G., Klein, N., Minich, N. M., & Hack, M. (2000). Middle-school-age outcomes in children with very low birthweight. *Child Development, 71,* 1495–1511.

Taylor, S. E. (1991). *Health psychology* (2nd ed.). New York: McGraw-Hill.

Teerikangas, O. M., Aronen, E. T., Martin, R. P., & Huttunen, M. O. (1998). Effects of infant temperament and early intervention on the psychiatric symptoms of adolescents. *Journal of the American Academy of Child & Adolescent Psychiatry, 37,* 1070–1076.

Teicher, 2002

Teicher, M. H., Anderson, S. L., Polcari, A., Anderson, C. M., & Navalta, C. P. (2002). Developmental neurobiology of childhood stress and trauma. *Psychiatric Clinics of North America, 25,* 397–426.

Teicher, M. H., Anderson, S. L., Polcari, A., Anderson, C. M., Navalta, C. P., & Kim, D. M. (2003). The neurobiological consequences of early stress and childhood maltreatment. *Neuroscience and Biobehavioral Review, 27,* 33–44.

Teixeira, L., Fischer, F., & Lowden, A. (2006, August). Sleep deprivation of working adolescents—A hidden work hazard. *Scandinavian Journal of Work, Environment & Health, 32,* 328–330.

Tellegen, A., Lykken, D. T., Bouchard, T. J., Jr., Wilcox, K. J., Segal, N. L., & Rich, S. (1988). Personality similarity in twins reared apart and together. *Journal of Personality and Social Psychology, 54,* 1031–1039.

Tenenbaum, H., & Leaper, C. (2003). Parent–child conversations about science: The socialization of gender inequities? *Developmental Psychology, 39,* 34–47.

Tenenbaum, H. R., & Leaper, C. (1998). Gender effects on Mexican-descent parents' questions and scaffolding during toy play: A sequential analysis. *First Language, 18,* 129–147.

Tenenbaum, H., & Ruck, M. (2007, May). Are teachers' expectations different for racial minority than for European American students? A meta-analysis. *Journal of Educational Psychology, 99,* 253–273.

Terry, D. (1994, December 12). When the family heirloom is homicide. *The New York Times,* pp. A1, B7.

Terry, D. (2000, August, 11). U.S. child poverty rate fell as economy grew, but is above 1979 level. *The New York Times,* A10.

Terzidou, V. (2007). Preterm labour. Biochemical and endocrinological preparation for parturition. *Best Practices of Research in Clinical Obstetrics and Gynecology, 21,* 729–756.

Tessor, A., Felson, R. B., & Suls, J. M. (Eds.). (2000). *Psychological perspectives on self and identity.* Washington, DC: American Psychological Association.

Tharp, R. G. (1989). Psychocultural variables and constants: Effects on teaching and learning in schools: Special issue: Children and their development: Knowledge base, research agenda, and social policy application. *American Psychologist, 44,* 349–359.

Thelen, E. (2002). Motor development as foundation and future of developmental psychology. In W. W. Hartup, W. Willard, & R. K. Silbereisen (Eds.), *Growing points in developmental science: An introduction.* Philadelphia: Psychology Press.

Thelen, E., & Bates, E. (2003). Connectionism and dynamic systems: Are they really different? *Developmental Science, 6,* 378–391.

Thoman, E. B., & Whitney, M. P. (1989). Sleep states of infants monitored in the home: Individual differences, developmental trends, and origins of diurnal cyclicity. *Infant Behavior and Development, 12,* 59–75.

Thoman, E. B., & Whitney, M. P. (1990). Behavioral states in infants: Individual differences and individual analyses. In J. Colombo & J. Fagen (Eds.), *Individual differences in infancy: Reliability, stability, prediction* (pp. 113–136). Hillsdale, NJ: Erlbaum.

Thomas, A., & Chess, S. (1980). *The dynamics of psychological development.* New York: Brunner-Mazel.

Thomas, A., Chess, S., & Birch, H. G. (1968). *Temperament and behavior disorders in children.* New York: New York University Press.

Thomas, P. (1994, September 6). Washington's infant mortality rate, more than twice the U.S. average, reflects urban woes. *The Wall Street Journal,* A14.

Thomas, R. M. (2001). *Recent human development theories.* Thousand Oaks, CA: Sage.

Thompson, R., Easterbrooks, M., & Padilla-Walker, L. (2003). Social and emotional development in infancy. In R. Lerner & M. Easterbrooks (Eds.), *Handbook of psychology: vol. 6. Developmental psychology,* (pp. 91–112). New York: Wiley.

Thompson, R. A., & Nelson, C. A. (2001). Developmental science and the media. *American Psychologist, 56,* 5–15.

Thornberry, T. P., & Krohn, M. D. (1997). Peers, drug use, and delinquency. In D. M. Stoff, J. Breiling, & J. D. Maser (Eds.), *Handbook of antisocial behavior* (pp. 218–233). New York: Wiley

Thordstein, M., Lofgren, N., Flisberg, A., Lindecrantz, K. & Kjellmer, I. (2006). Sex differences in electrocortical activity in human neonates. *Neuroreport, 17,* 1165–8.

Thurlow, M. L., Lazarus, S. S., & Thompson, S. J. (2005). State policies on assessment participation and accommodations for students with disabilities. *Journal of Special Education, 38,* 232–240.

Tincoff, R., & Jusczyk, P. W. (1999). Some beginnings of word comprehension in 6-month-olds. *Psychological Science, 10,* 172–175.

Tinsley, B., Lees, N., & Sumartojo, E. (2004). Child and adolescent HIV risk: Familial and cultural perspectives. *Journal of Family Psychology, 18,* 208–224.

Tissaw, M. (2007). Making sense of neonatal imitation. *Theory & Psychology, 17,* 217-242.

Tobin, J. J., Wu, D. Y. H., & Davidson, D. H. (1989). *Preschool in three cultures: Japan, China, and the United States.* New Haven, CT: Yale University Press.

Toch, T. (1995, January 2). Kids and marijuana: The glamour is back. *U.S. News & World Report,* 12.

Toga, A. W., & Thompson, P. M. (2003). Temporal dynamics of brain anatomy. *Annual Review of Biomedical Engineering, 5,* 119–145.

Tolchinsky, L. (2003). *The cradle of culture and what children know about writing and numbers before being taught.* Mahwah, NJ: Lawrence Erlbaum.

Tomblin, J. B., Hammer, C. S., & Zhang, X. (1998). The association of prenatal tobacco use and SLI. *International Journal of Language and Communication Disorders, 33,* 357–368.

Tomlinson-Keasey, C. (1985). *Child development: Psychological, sociological, and biological factors.* Homewood, IL: Dorsey.

Tongsong, T., Iamthongin, A., Wanapirak, C., Piyamongkol, W., Sirichotiyakul, S., Boonyanurak, P., et al. (2005). Accuracy of fetal heart-rate variability interpretation by obstetricians using the criteria of the National Institute of Child Health and Human Development compared with computer-aided interpretation. *Journal of Obstetric and Gynaecological Research, 31,* 68–71.

Torvaldsen, S., Roberts, C. L., Simpson, J. M., Thompson, J. F., & Ellwood, D. A. (2006). Intrapartum epidural analgesia and breastfeeding: A prospective cohort study. *International Breastfeeding Journal, 24,* 1–24.

Toschke, A. M., Grote, V., Koletzko, B., & von Kries, R. (2004). Identifying children at high risk for overweight at school entry by weight gain during the first 2 years. *Archives of Pediatric Adolescence, 158,* 449–452.

Towse, J., & Cowan, N. (2005). Working memory and its relevance for cognitive development. In W. Schneider, R. Schumann-Hengsteler, & B. Sodian, *Young children's cognitive development: Interrelationships among executive functioning, working memory, verbal ability, and theory of mind.* Mahwah, NJ: Lawrence Erlbaum.

Trainor, L., and Desjardins, R. (2002). Pitch characteristics of infant-directed speech affect infants' ability to discriminate vowels. *Psychonomic Bulletin & Review, 9,* 335–340.

Trainor, L. J., Austin, C. M., & Desjardins, R. N. (2000). Is infant-directed speech prosody a result of the vocal expression of emotion? *Psychological Science, 11,* 188–195.

Trautwein, U., Lüdtke, O., Kastens, C., & Köller, O. (2006). Effort on homework in grades 5–9: Development, motivational antecedents, and the association with effort on classwork. *Child Development, 77,* 1094–1111.

Trehub, S. E., (2003). The developmental origins of musicality. *Nature Neuroscience, 6,* 669-673.

Trehub, S. E., Schneider, B. A., Morrongiello, B. A., & Thorpe, L. A. (1988). Auditory sensitivity in school-age children. *Journal of Experimental Child Psychology, 46,* 272–285.

Trehub, S. E., Schneider, B. A., Morrongiello, B. A., & Thorpe, L. A. (1989). Developmental changes in high-frequency sensitivity. *Audiology, 28,* 241–249.

Tremblay, R. E. (2001). The development of physical aggression during childhood and the prediction of later dangerousness. In G. F. Pinard & L. Pagani, (Eds.). *Clinical assessment of dangerousness: Empirical contributions.* New York: Cambridge University Press.

Trickett, P. K., Kurtz, D. A., & Pizzigati, K. (2004). Resilient outcomes in abused and neglected children: Bases for strength-based intervention and prevention policies. In K. I. Maton & C. J. Schellenbach, (Eds.), *Investing in children, youth, families and communities: Strength-based research and policy.* Washington, DC: American Psychological Associa-tion.

Tronick, E. (2003). Emotions and emotional communication in infants. In J. Raphael-Leff (Ed.), *Parent–infant psychodynamics: Wild things, mirrors and ghosts* (pp. 35–53). London: Whurr.

Tronick, E. Z., Thomas, R. B., & Daltabuit, M. (1994). The Quechua manta pouch: A caretaking practice for buffering the Peruvian infant against the multiple stressors of high altitude. *Child Development, 65,* 1005–1013.

Tropp, L. (2003). The psychological impact of prejudice: Implications for intergroup contact. *Group Processes & Intergroup Relations, 6,* 131–149.

Tropp, L., & Wright, S. (2003). Evaluations and perceptions of self, ingroup, and outgroup: Comparisons between Mexican American and European American children. *Self & Identity, 2,* 203–221.

Trouilloud, D., Sarrazin, P., Bressoux, P., & Bois, J. (2006, February). Relation between teachers' early expectations and students' later perceived competence in physical education classes: Autonomy–supportive climate as a moderator. *Journal of Educational Psychology, 98,* 75–86.

Trzesniewski, K. H., Donnellan, M. B., & Robins, R. W. (2003). Stability of self-esteem across the life span. *Journal of Personality and Social Psychology, 84,* 205–220.

Tsao, F. M., Liu, H. M., & Kuhl, P. K. (2004). Speech perception in infancy predicts language development in the second year of life: A longitudinal study. *Child Development, 75,* 1067–1084.

Tsunoda, T. (1985). *The Japanese brain: Uniqueness and universality.* Tokyo: Taishukan.

Tucker, J., Martínez, J., Ellickson, P., & Edelen, M. (2008, March). Temporal associations of cigarette smoking with social influences, academic performance, and delinquency: A four-wave longitudinal study from ages 13–23. *Psychology of Addictive Behaviors, 22,* 1–11.

Tudge, J., & Scrimsher, S. (2003). Lev S. Vygotsky on education: A cultural–historical, interpersonal, and individual approach to development. In B. Zimmerman (Ed.), *Educational psychology: A century of contributions.* Mahwah, NJ: Lawrence Erlbaum.

Turati, C., Cassia, V. M., Simion, F., & Leo, I. (2006). Newborns' face recognition: Role of inner and outer facial features. *Child Development, 77,* 297–311.

Turkheimer, E., Haley, A., Waldreon, M., D'Onofrio, B., & Gottesman, I. I. (2003). Socioeconomic status modifies heritability of IQ in young children. *Psychological Science, 14,* 623–628.

Twenge, J. M., & Campbell, W. K. (2001). Age and birth cohort differences in self-esteem: A cross-temporal meta-analysis. *Personality and Social Psychology Review, 5,* 321–344.

Twenge, J. M., & Crocker, J. (2002). Race and self-esteem: Meta-analyses comparing whites, blacks, Hispanics, Asians, and American Indians and comment on Gray-Little and Hafdahl (2000). *Psychological Bulletin, 128,* 371–408.

Twomey, J. (2006). Issues in genetic testing of children. *MCN: The American Journal of Maternal/Child Nursing, 31,* 156–163.

Tyre, P., & Scelfo, J. (2003, September 22). Helping kids get fit. *Newsweek,* 60–62.

U.S. Bureau of the Census. (2000). *Current population reports.* Washington, DC: U.S. Government Printing Office.

U.S. Bureau of the Census. (2001a). *Living arrangements of children.* Washington, DC: U.S. Government Printing Office.

U.S. Bureau of the Census. (2001b). *Statistical abstract of the United States, 2001.* Washington, DC: U.S. Government Printing Office.

U.S. Bureau of the Census. (2002). *Statistical abstract of the United States (122nd ed.).* Washington, DC: U.S. Government Printing Office.

U.S. Bureau of the Census. (2004). *Current Population Survey, 2004 Annual Social and Economic Supplement.* Washington, DC: U.S. Bureau of the Census.

U.S. Census Bureau. (2003). *Population reports.* Washington, DC: GPO.

U.S. Census Bureau. (1998). Poverty of educational attainment. Washington, DC: U.S. Census Bureau.

Ulutas, I., & Ömeroglu, E. (2007). The effects of an emotional intelligence education program on the emotional intelligence of children. *Social Behavior and Personality, 35,* 1365–1372.

Umana-Taylor, A. J., Diversi, M., & Fine, M. A. (2002). Ethnic identity and self-esteem of Latino adolescents: Distinctions among the Latino populations. *Journal of Adolescent Research,* 17, 303–327.

Umana-Taylor, A., & Fine, M. (2004). Examining ethnic identity among Mexican-origin adolescents living in the United States. Hispanic Journal of Behavioral Sciences, 26, 36–59.

Umana-Taylor, A., Diveri, M., & Fine, M. (2002). Ethnic identity and self-esteem among Latino adolescents: Distinctions among Latino populations. *Journal of Adolescent Research,* 17, 303–327.

Underwood, M. (2003). *Social aggression among girls.* New York: Guilford.

UNESCO. (2006). *Compendium of statistics on illiteracy.* Paris: Author.

Unger, R. K. (Ed.) (2001). *Handbook of the psychology of women and gender.* New York: Wiley.

Unger, R., & Crawford, M. (2004). *Women and gender: A feminist psychology* (4th ed.). New York, NY: McGraw-Hill.

UNICEF. (2005). *The state of the world's children.* New York: The United Nations Children's Fund U.S. Bureau of the Census.(2006). Women's earnings as a percentage of men's earnings:1960–2005. Historical Income Tables-People. Table P-40.Washington, DC: U.S. Bureau of the Census.

United Nations. (1990). *Declaration of the world summit for children.* New York: Author.

United Nations. (1991). *Declaration of the world summit for children.* New York: Author.

United Nations. (2004). *Hunger and the world's children*. New York: United Naitons.

Updegraff, K. A., Helms, H. M., McHale, S. M., Crouter, A. C., Thayer, S. M., & Sales, L. H. (2004). Who's the boss? Patterns for perceived control in adolescents' friendships. *Journal of Youth & Adolescence, 33*, 403–420.

Updegraff, K. A., McHale, S. M., Whiteman, S. D., Thayer, S.M., & Crouter, A. C. (2006). The nature and correlates of Mexican-American adolescents' time with parents and peers. *Child Development, 77*, 1470–1486.

Updegraff, K., McHale, S., & Crouter, A. (2000). Adolescents' sex-typed friendship experiences: Does having a sister versus a brother matter? *Child Development, 71*, 1597–1610.

Urberg, K., Luo, Q., & Pilgrim, C. (2003). A two-stage model of peer influence in adolescent substance use: Individual and relationship-specific differences in susceptibility to influence. *Addictive Behaviors, 28*, 1243–1256.

Uylings, H. (2006). Development of the human cortex and the concept of "critical" or "sensitive" periods. *Language Learning, 56*, 59–90.

Vaillant, G. E., & Vaillant, C. O. (1981). Natural history of male psychological health, X: Work as a predictor of positive mental health. *The American Journal of Psychiatry, 138*, 1433–1440.

Vaish, A., & Striano, T. (2004). Is visual reference necessary? Contributions of facial versus vocal cues in 12-month-olds' social referencing behavior. *Developmental Science, 7*, 261–269.

Valenti, C. (2006). Infant Vision Guidance: Fundamental Vision Development in Infancy. *Optometry and Vision Development, 37*, 147–155.

Valiente, C., Eisenberg, N., & Fabes, R. A. (2004). Prediction of children's empathy-related responding from their effortful control and parents' expressivity. *Developmental Psychology, 40*, 911–926.

van Balen, F. (1998). Development of IVF children. *Developmental Review, 18*, 30–46.

Van de Graaff, K. (2000). *Human anatomy* (5th ed.). New York: McGraw-Hill.

van der Mark, I., van Ijzendoorn, M., & Bakermans-Kranenburg, M. (2002). Development of empathy in girls during the second year of life: Associations with parenting, attachment, and temperament. *Social Development, 11*, 451–468.

van Jaarsveld, C., Fidler, J., Simon, A., & Wardle, J. (2007, October). Persistent impact of pubertal timing on trends in smoking, food choice, activity, and stress in adolescence. *Psychosomatic Medicine, 69*, 798–806.

van Kleeck, A., & Stahl, S. (2003). *On reading books to children: Parents and teachers*. Mahwah, NJ: Lawrence Erlbaum.

Van Tassel-Baska, J., Olszewski-Kubilius, P., & Kulieke, M. (1994). A study of self-concept and social support in advantaged and disadvantaged seventh and eighth grade gifted students. *Roeper Review, 16*, 186–191.

van Wormer, K., & McKinney, R. (2003). What schools can do to help gay/lesbian/bisexual youth: A harm reduction approach. *Adolescence, 38*, 409–420.

Vandell, D. L. (2000). Parents, peer groups, and other socializing influences. *Developmental Psychology, 36*, 699–710.

Vandell, D. L. (2004). Early child care: The known and the unknown. The maturing of human developmental sciences: Appraising past, present, and prospective agendas, [Special issue]. *Merrill-Palmer Quarterly, 50*, 387–414.

Vandell, D. L., Burchinal, M. R., Belsky, J., Owen, M. T., Friedman, S. L., Clarke-Stewart, A., McCartney, K., & Weinraub, M. (2005). *Early child care and children's development in the primary grades: Follow-up results from the NICHD Study of Early Child Care*. Paper presented at the biennial meeting of the Society for Research in Child Development, Atlanta, GA.

Vandell, D. L., Shumow, L., & Posner, J. (2005). After-school programs for low-income children: Differences in program quality. InJ. L. Mahoney, R. W. Larson, & J. S. Ecccles, *Organized activities as contexts of development: Extracurricular activities, after-school and community programs*. Mahwah, NJ: Lawrence Erlbaum Associates.

Vartanian, L. R. (2000). Revisiting the imaginary audience and personal fable constructs of adolescent egocentrism: A conceptual review. *Adolescence, 35*, 639–646.

Vasa, R. A., & Pine, D. S. (2006). Anxiety disorders. In C. A. Essau, *Child and adolescent psychopathology: Theoretical and clinical implications*. New York: Routledge.

Vaughn, V., McKay, R. J., & Behrman, R. (1979). *Nelson textbook of pediatrics* (11th ed.). Philadelphia: Saunders.

Vecchiotti, S. (2003). Kindergarten: An overlooked educational policy priority. *Social Policy Report*, 3–19.

Vedantam, S. (2004, April 23). Antidepressants called unsafe for children: Four medications singled out in analysis of many studies. *The Washington Post*, A03.

Vellutino, F. R. (1991). Introduction to three studies on reading acquisition: Convergent findings on theoretical foundations of code-oriented versus whole-language approaches to reading instruction. *Journal of Educational Psychology, 83*, 437–443.

Veneziano, R. (2003).The importance of paternal warmth. *Cross-Cultural Research: The Journal of Comparative Social Science, 37*, 265–281.

Vereijken, C. M., Riksen-Walraven, J. M., & Kondo-Ikemura, K. (1997). Maternal sensitivity and infant attachment security in Japan: A longitudinal study. *International Journal of Behavioral Development, 21*, 35–49.

Verkuyten, M. (2003). Positive and negative self-esteem among ethnic minority early adolescents: Social and cultural sources and threats. *Journal of Youth & Adolescence, 32*, 267–277.

Verkuyten, M. (2008). Perceived discrimination, ethnic minority identity, and self-esteem. *Handbook of race, racism, and the developing child* (pp. 339–365). Hoboken, NJ: John Wiley & Sons.

Vilette, B. (2002). Do young children grasp the inverse relationship between addition and subtraction? Evidence against early arithmetic. *Cognitive Development, 17*, 1365–1383.

Vilhjalmsson, R., & Kristjansdottir, G. (2003). Gender differences in physical activity in older children and adolescents: The central role of organized sport. *Social Science Medicine, 56*, 363–374.

Villarosa, L. (2003, December 23). More teenagers say no to sex, and experts are sure why. *The New York Times*, D6.

Vingerhoets, A., Nyklicek, I., & Denollet, J. (Eds.). (2008). *Emotion regulation: Conceptual and clinical issues*. New York: Springer Science + Business Media.

Vizmanos, B. & Marti-Henneberg, C. (2000). Puberty begins with a characteristic subcutaneous body fat mass in each sex. *European Journal of Clinical Nutrition, 54*, 203–206.

Vogel, G. (1997, June 13). Why the rise in asthma cases? *Science, 276*, 1645.

Vohs, K. D., & Heatherton, T. (2004). Ego threats elicits different social comparison process among high and low self-esteem people:

Implications for interpersonal perceptions. *Social Cognition, 22,* 168–191.

Volkow, N. D., Wang, G. J., Fowler, J. S., Logan, J., Gerasimov, M., Maynard, I., et al. (2001). Therapeutic doses of oral methylphenidate significantly increase extracellular dopamine in the human brain. *Journal of Neuroscience, 21,* 1–5.

Volling, B. L., & Belsky, J. (1992). The contribution of mother–child and father–child relationships to the quality of sibling interaction: A longitudinal study. *Child Development, 63,* 1209–1222.

Vouloumanos, A., & Werker, J. (2007). Listening to language at birth: Evidence for a bias for speech in neonates. *Developmental Science, 10,* 159–164.

Vyas, S. (2004). Exploring bicultural identities of Asian high school students through the analytic window of a literature club. *Journal of Adolescent & Adult Literacy, 48,* 12–18.

Vygotsky, L. S. (1926/1997). *Educational psychology.* Delray Beach, FL: St. Lucie Press.

Vygotsky, L. S. (1930/1978). *Mind in society: The development of higher mental processes.* Cambridge, MA: Harvard University Press. (Original works published 1930, 1933, and 1935.)

Wachs, T. (2002). Nutritional deficiencies as a biological context for development. In W. Hartup, W. Silbereisen, & K. Rainer (Eds.), *Growing Points in Developmental Science: An introduction.* Philadelphia: Psychology Press.

Wachs, T. D. (1992). *The nature of nurture.* Newbury Park, CA: Sage.

Wachs, T. D. (1993). The nature–nurture gap: What we have here is a failure to collaborate. In R. Plomin & G. E. McClearn (Eds.), *Nature, nurture, and psychology.* Washington, DC: American Psychological Association.

Wachs, T. D. (1996). Known and potential processes underlying developmental trajectories in childhood and adolescence. *Developmental Psychology, 32,* 796–801.

Wade, N. (2001, October 4). Researchers say gene is linked to language. *The New York Times,* p. A1.

Wade, T., Tiggemann, M., Bulik, C., Fairburn, C., Wray, N., & Martin, N. (2008, February). Shared temperament risk factors for anorexia nervosa: A twin study. *Psychosomatic Medicine, 70,* 239–244.

Wahlin, T. (2007). To know or not to know: A review of behaviour and suicidal ideation in preclinical Huntington's disease. *Patient Education and Counseling, 65,* 279–287.

Wainright, J. L., Russell, S. T., & Patterson, C. J. (2004). Psychosocial adjustment, school outcomes, and romantic relationships of adolescents with same-sex parents. *Child Development, 75,* 1886–1898.

Waite, S. J., Bromfield, C., & McShane, S. (2005). Successful for whom? A methodology to evaluate and inform inclusive activity in schools. *European Journal of Special Needs Education, 20,* 71–88.

Wake, M., Hardy, P., Canterford, L., Sawyer, M., & Carlin, J. (2007, July). Overweight, obesity and girth of Australian preschoolers: Prevalence and socio-economic correlates. *International Journal of Obesity, 31,* 1044–1051.

Wakefield, M., Reid, Y., & Roberts, L. (1998). Smoking and smoking cessation among men whose partners are pregnant: A qualitative study. *Social Science & Medicine, 47,* 657–664.

Walcott, D., Pratt, H., & Patel, D. (2003). Adolescents and eating disorders: Gender, racial, ethnic, sociocultural, and socioeconomic issues. *Journal of Adolescent Research, 18,* 223–243.

Walden, T., Kim, G., McCoy, C., & Karrass, J. (2007). Do you believe in magic? Infants' social looking during violations of expectations. *Developmental Science, 10,* 654–663.

Waldfogel, J. (2001). International policies toward parental leave and child care. *Caring for Infants and Toddlers, 11,* 99–111.

Walker, N. C., & O'Brien, B. (1999). The relationship between method of pain management during labor and birth outcomes. *Clinical Nursing Research, 8,* 119–134.

Walker, W.A., & Humphries, C. (2005). *The Harvard Medical School Guide to Healthy Eating during pregnancy.* New York: McGraw-Hill.

Walker, W.A., & Humphries, C. (2007, September 17). Starting the good life in the womb. *Newsweek,* pp. 56–57.

Wallerstein, J., & Resnikoff, D. (2005). Parental divorce and developmental progression: An inquiry into their relationship. In L. Gunsberg & P. Hymowitz, *A handbook of divorce and custody: Forensic, developmental, and clinical perspectives.* Hillsdale, NJ: Analytic Press.

Wallerstein, J. S., Lewis, J. M., & Blakeslee, S. (2000). *The unexpected legacy of divorce.* New York: Hyperion.

Wallis, C. (2006, March 27). The multitasking generation. *Time,* 48–55.

Wals, M., & Verhulst, F. (2005). Child and adolescent antecedents of adult mood disorders. *Current Opinion in Psychiatry, 18,* 15–19.

Walters, E., & Gardner, H. (1986). The theory of multiple intelligences: Some issues and answers. In R. J. Sternberg & R. K. Wagner (Eds.), *Practical intelligence.* New York: Cambridge University Press.

Wang, L., Chyen, D., Lee, S., & Lowry, R. (2008, May). The association between body mass index in adolescence and obesity in adulthood. *Journal of Adolescent Health, 42,* 512–518.

Wang, Q. (2004). The emergence of cultural self-constructs: Autobiographical memory and self-description in European American and Chinese children. *Developmental Psychology, 40,* 3–15.

Wang, Q. (2007, August). "Remember when you got the big, big bulldozer?" Mother–child reminiscing over time and across cultures. *Social Cognition, 25,* 455–471.

Wang, S., and Tamis-LeMonda, C. (2003). Do child-rearing values in Taiwan and the United States reflect cultural values of collectivism and individualism? *Journal of Cross-Cultural Psychology, 34,* 629–642.

Wang, S. H., Baillargeon, R., & Paterson, S. (2005). Detecting continuity violations in infancy: A new account and new evidence from covering and tube events. *Cognition, 95,* 129–173.

Wardle, F. (2007). Multiracial children in child development textbooks. *Early Childhood Education Journal, 35,* 253–259.

Wardle, J., Guthrie, C., & Sanderson, S. (2001). Food and activity preferences in children of lean and obese parents. *International Journal of Obesity & Related Metabolic Disorders, 25,* 971–977.

Warren J. R. (2002). Reconsidering the relationship between student employment and academic outcomes: A new theory and better data. *Youth & Society, 33,* 366–370.

Warren, J. R., Lee, J. C., & Cataldi, E. F. (2004). Teenage employment and high school completion. In D. Conley & K. Albright. (Eds.), *After the bell—Family background, public policy, and educational success.* London: Routledge.

Warwick, P., & Maloch, B. (2003). Scaffolding speech and writing in the primary classroom: A consideration of work with literature and science pupil groups in the USA and UK. *Reading: Literacy & Language, 37,* 54–63.

Wasserman, J. D., & Tulsky, D. S. (2005). The history of intelligence assessment. In D. P. Flanagan, & P. L. Harrison, (Eds.), *Contemporary intellectual assessment: Theories, tests, and issues.* New York: Guilford.

Waterhouse, J. M., & DeCoursey, P. J. (2004). Human circadian organization. In J. C. Dunlap & J. J. Loros (Eds.), *Chronobiology: Biological time-keeping.* Sunderland, MA: Sinauer.

Waterland, R. A., & Jirtle, R. L. (2004). Early nutrition, epigenetic changes at transposons and imprinted genes, and enhanced susceptibility to adult chronic diseases. *Nutrition,* 63–68.

Waters, E., Weinfield, N. S., & Hamilton, C. E. (2000). The stability of attchment security from infancy to adolescence and early adulthood: General discussion. *Child Development, 71,* 703–706.

Waters, L., & Moore, K. (2002). Predicting self-esteem during unemployment: The effect of gender financial deprivation, alternate roles and social support. *Journal of Employment Counseling, 39,* 171–189.

Watkins, R. (2008). Overview of federal education laws. In P. S. Jensen & K. Eaton (Eds.), *Improving children's mental health through parent empowerment: A guide to assisting families.* New York: Oxford University Press.

Watling, D., & Bourne, V. (2007, September). Linking children's neuropsychological processing of emotion with their knowledge of emotion expression regulation. *Laterality: Asymmetries of Body, Brain and Cognition, 12,* 381–396.

Watson, J. B. (1925). *Behaviorism.* New York: Norton.

Watson, J. B., & Rayner, R. (1920). Conditioned emotional reactions. *Journal of Experimental Psychology, 3,* 1–14.

Watson, J. K. (2000). Theory of mind and pretend play in family context (false belief). *Dissertation Abstracts International, 60B,* 3599.

Webb, R. M., Lubinski, D., & Benbow, C. P. (2002). Mathematically facile adolescents with math/science aspirations: New perspectives on their educational and vocational development. *Journal of Educational Psychology, 94,* 785–794.

Weber, B. (2005, February 25). From sidelines or in the rink, goalies are targets, even at 8. The *New York Times,* p. B1, B8.

Wechsler, D. (1975). Intelligence defined and undefined. *American Psychologist, 30,* 135–139.

Wechsler, H., Lee, J. E., Kuo, M., Seibring, M., Nelson, T. F., & Lee, H. (2002). Trends in college binge drinking during a period of increased prevention efforts: Findings from 4 Harvard School of Public Health college alcohol study surveys, 1993–2001. Journal of American College Health, 50, 208–217.

Wechsler, H., & Nelson, T. F. (2001). Binge drinking and the American college student: What's five drinks? *Psychology of Addictive Behaviors, 15,* 287–291.

Weigel, D., Martin, S., & Bennett, K. (2006). Contributions of the home literacy environment to preschool-aged children's emerging literacy and language skills. *Early Child Development and Care [serial online], 176,* 357–378.

Weinberg, R. A. (2004). The infant and the family in the twenty-first century. *Journal of the American Academy of Child & Adolescent Psychiatry, 43,* 115-116.

Weinberger, D. R. (2001, March 10). A brain too young for good judgment. *The New York Times,* p. D1.

Weinfield, N. S., Sroufe, L. A., & Egeland, B. (2000). Attachment from infancy to early adulthood in a high-risk sample: Continuity, discontinuity, and their correlates. *Child Development, 71,* 695–702.

Weinstock, H., Berman, S., & Cates, W., Jr. (2004). Sexually transmitted diseases among American youth: Incidence and prevalence estimates, 2000. *Perspectives on Sexual and Reproductive Health , 36,* 182–191.

Weiss, M. R., Ebbeck, V., & Horn. T. S. (1997). Children's self-perceptions and sources of physical competence information: A cluster analysis. *Journal of Sport and Exercise Psychology, 19,* 52–70.

Weiss, R. (2003, September 2). Genes' sway over IQ may vary with class. *The Washington Post,* A1.

Weisz, A., & Black, B. (2002). Gender and moral reasoning: African American youth respond to dating dilemmas. *Journal of Human Behavior in the Social Environment, 5,* 35–52.

Weitzman, E., Nelson, T., & Wechsler, H. (2003). Taking up binge drinking in college: The influences of person, social group, and environment. *Journal of Adolescent Health, 32,* 26–35.

Wellings, K., Collumbien, M., Slaymaker, E., Singh, S., Hodges, Z., Patel, D., et al. (2006, November). Sexual behaviour in context: A global perspective. *Lancet, 368,* 1706–1738.

Wells, B., Peppé, S., Goulandris, N. (2004). Intonation development from five to thirteen. *Journal of Child Language, 31,* 749–778.

Werker, J. F., Pons, F., Dietrich, C., Kajikawa, S., Fais, L., & Amano, S. (2007). Infant-directed speech supports phonetic category learning in English and Japanese. *Cognition, 103,* 147–162.

Werner, E. E., & Smith, R. S. (2002). Journeys from childhood to midlife: Risk, resilience and recovery. *Journal of Developmental and Behavioral Pediatrics, 23,* 456.

Werner, L. A., & Marean, G. C. (1996). *Human auditory development.* Boulder, CO: Westview Press.

Werner, N. E., & Crick, N. R. (2004). Maladaptive peer relationships and the development of relational and physical aggression during middle childhood. *Social Development, 13,* 495–514.

West, J. R., & Blake, C. A. (2005). Fetal alcohol syndrome: An assessment of the field. *Experimental Biology and Medicine, 230,* 354–356.

West, J., Romero, R., & Trinidad, D. (2007, August). Adolescent receptivity to tobacco marketing by racial/ethnic groups in California. *American Journal of Preventive Medicine, 33,* 121–123.

Westerhausen, R., Kreuder, F., Sequeira Sdos, S., Walter, C., Woerner, W., Wittling, R. A., et al. (2004). Effects of handedness and gender on macro- and microstructure of the corpus callosum and its subregions: a combined high-resolution and diffusion-tensor MRI study. *Brain Research and Cognitive Brain Research, 21,* 418–426.

Wexler, B. (2006). *Brain and culture: Neurobiology, ideology, and social change.* Cambridge, MA: MIT Press.

Whalen, C. K., Jamner, L. D., Henker, B., Delfino, R. J., & Lozano, J. M. (2002). The ADHD spectrum and everyday life: Experience sampling of adolescent moods, activities, smoking, and drinking. *Child Development, 73,* 209–227.

Whalen, J. & Begley, S. (2005, March 30). In England, girls are closing the gap with boys in math. *The Wall Street Journal,* A1.

Whaley, B. B., & Parker, R. G. (2000). Expressing the experience of communicative disability: Metaphors of persons who stutter. *Communication Reports, 13,* 115–125.

Wheeldon, L. R. (1999). *Aspects of language production.* Philadelphia: Psychology Press.

Whelan, T., & Lally, C. (2002). Paternal commitment and father's quality of life. *Journal of Family Studies, 8,* 181–196.

Whitaker, R. C., Wright, J. A., Pepe, M. S., Seidel, K. D., & Dietz, W. H. (1997, September 25). Predicting obesity in young adulthood from childhood and parental obesity. *The New England Journal of Medicine, 337,* 869–873.

Whitbourne, S. K., Zuschlag, M. K., Elliot, L. B., & Waterman, A. S. (1992). Psychosocial development in adulthood: A 22-year sequential study. *Journal of Personality and Social Psychology, 63,* 260–271.

White, M., & White, G. (2006, August). Implicit and explicit occupational gender stereotypes. *Sex Roles, 55,* 259–266.

Whitehurst, G. J., & Fischel, J. E. (2000). Reading and language impairments in conditions of poverty. In D. V. M. Bishop & L. B. Leonard (Eds.), *Speech and language impairments in children: Causes, characteristics, intervention, and outcome.* Philadelphia: Psychology Press.

Whiteman, S., McHale, S., & Crouter, A. (2007, November). Competing processes of sibling influence: Observational learning and sibling deidentification. *Social Development, 16,* 642–661.

Whiting, B. B., & Edwards, C. P. (1988). *Children of different worlds: The formation of social behavior.* Cambridge, MA: Harvard University Press.

Widom, C. S. (2000). Motivation and mechanisms in the "cycle of violence" In D. J. Hansen (Ed.), *Nebraska Symposium on Motivation Vol. 46, 1998: Motivation and child maltreatment* (Current theory and research in motivation series). Lincoln, NE: University of Nebraska Press.

Wilcox, H. C., Conner, K. R., & Caine, E. D. (2004). Association of alcohol and drug use disorders and completed suicide: An empirical review of cohort studies. *Drug & Alcohol Dependence, 76,* Special Issue: Drug Abuse and Suicidal Behavior, s11–s19.

Wilcox, T., Woods, R., Chapa, C., & McCurry, S. (2007). Multisensory exploration and object individuation in infancy. *Developmental Psychology, 43,* 479–495.

Wildberger, S. (2003, August). So you're having a baby. *Washingtonian,* 85–86, 88–90.

Willard, N. (2007). *Cyber-safe kids, cyber-savvy teens: Helping young people learn to use the Internet safely and responsibly.* San Francisco: Jossey-Bass.

Williams, J., & Binnie, L. (2002). Children's concept of illness: An intervention to improve knowledge. *British Journal of Health Psychology, 7,* 129–148.

Williams, J., & Ross, L. (2007). Consequences of prenatal toxin exposure for mental health in children and adolescents: A systematic review. *European Child & Adolescent Psychiatry, 16,* 243–253.

Williamson, R., & Johnston, J. H. (1999). Challenging orthodoxy: An emerging agenda for middle level reform. *Middle School Journal, 12,* 10–17.

Willows, D. M., Kruk, R. S., & Corcos, E. (Eds.). (1993). *Visual processes in reading and reading disabilities.* Hillsdale, NJ: Erlbaum.

Wills, T., Resko, J., & Ainette, M. (2004). Smoking onset in adolescence: A person-centered analysis with time-varying predictors. *Health Psychology, 23,* 158–167.

Wilson, B., et al. (2002). Violence in children's television programming: Assessing the risks. *Journal of Communication, 52,* 5–35.

Wilson, G., Grilo, C., & Vitousek, K. (2007, April). Psychological treatment of eating disorders. *American Psychologist, 62,* 199–216.

Wilson, R. (2004, December 3). Where the elite teach, it's still a man's world. *Chronicle of Higher Education, 51,* A8.

Wilson, S. L. (2003). Post-Institutionalization: The effects of early deprivation on development of Romanian adoptees. *Child & Adolescent Social Work Journal, 20,* 473-483.

Wineburg, S. S. (1987). The self-fulfillment of the self-fulfilling prophecy. *Educational Researcher, 16,* 28–37.

Winger, G., & Woods, J. H. (2004). *A handbook on drug and alcohol abuse: The biomedical aspects.* Oxford, England: Oxford University Press.

Wingert, P., & Kantrowitz, B. (1997, October 27). Why Andy couldn't read (Bright children who are also learning disabled). *Newsweek, 130,* 56.

Wingert, P., & Katrowitz, B. (2002, October 7). Young and depressed. *Newsweek,* 53–61

Winner, E. (1989). Development in the visual arts. In W. Damon (Ed.), *Child development today and tomorrow.* San Francisco: Jossey-Bass.

Winsler, A. (2003). Introduction to special issue: Vygotskian perspectives in early childhood education. *Early Education and Development. 14,* 253–269.

Winsler, A., De Leon, J. R., & Wallace, B. A. (2003). Private speech in preschool children: Developmental stability and change, across-task consistency, and relations with classroom behavior. *Journal of Child Language, 30,* 583–608.

Winstead, B.A., & Sanchez, J. (2005). Gender and Psychopathology. In J.E. Maddux, & G.A. Winstead (Eds.), *Psychopathology: Foundations for a contemporary understanding.* Mahwah, NJ: Lawrence Erlbaum Associates.

Wisdom, J., Rees, A., Riley, K., & Weis, T. (2007, April). Adolescents' perceptions of the gendered context of depression: "Tough" boys and objectified girls. *Journal of Mental Health Counseling, 29,* 144–162.

Witelson, S. (1989, March). *Sex differences.* Paper presented at the annual meeting of the New York Academy of Science, New York.

Woelfle, J. F., Harz, K., & Roth, C. (2007). Modulation of circulating IGF-I and IGFBP-3 levels by hormonal regulators of energy homeostasis in obese children. *Experimental and Clinical Endocrinology Diabetes, 115,* 17–23.

Wood, A. C., Saudino, K. J., Rogers, H., Asherson, P., & Kuntsi, J. (2007). Genetic influences on mechanically assessed activity level in children. *Journal of Child Psychology and Psychiatry. 48,* 695–702.

Wood, R. (1997). Trends in multiple births, 1938–1995. *Population Trends, 87,* 29–35.

Wood, R., Williams, R., & Lawton, P. (2007, June). Why do Internet gamblers prefer online versus land-based venues? Some preliminary findings and implications. *Journal of Gambling Issues, 20,* 235–252.

World Food Programme. (2008). *Where we work: Korea.* Rome: United Nations World Food Programme.

World Food Summit. (2002). *The spectrum of malnutrition.* New York: United Nations.

Worobey, J., & Bajda, V. M. (1989). Temperament ratings at 2 weeks, 2 months, and 1 year: Differential stability of activity and emotionality. *Developmental Psychology, 25,* 257–263.

Worrell, F., Szarko, J., & Gabelko, N. (2001). Multi-year persistence of nontraditional students in an academic talent development program. *Journal of Secondary Gifted Education, 12,* 80–89.

Wright, J. C., Huston, A. C., Murphy, K. C., St. Peters, M., Piñon, M., Scantlin, R., et al. (2001). The relations of early television viewing to school readiness and vocabulary of children from low-income families: The early window project. *Child Development, 72,* 1347–1366.

Wright, J. C., Huston, A. C., Reitz, A. L., & Piemyat, S. (1994). Young children's perceptions of television reality: Determinants and developmental differences. *Developmental Psychology, 30,* 229–239.

Wright, J. C., Huston, A. C., Truglio, R., Fitch, M., Smith, E., & Piemyat, S. (1995). Occupational portrayals on television: Children's role schemata, career aspirations, and perceptions of reality. *Child Development, 66,* 1706–1718.

Wright, R. (1995, March 13). The biology of violence. *The New Yorker,* 68–77.

Wu, P., Hoven, C., Okezie, N., Fuller, C., & Cohen, P. (2007). Alcohol abuse and depression in children and adolescents. *Journal of Child & Adolescent Substance Abuse, 17,* 51–69.

Wu, P., Robinson, C., & Yang, C. (2002). Similarities and differences in mothers' parenting of preschoolers in China and the United States. *International Journal of Behavioral Development, 26,* 481–491.

Wyer, R. (2004). The cognitive organization and use of general knowledge. In J. Jost & M. Banaji (Eds.) *Perspectivism in social psychology: The yin and yang of scientific progress.* Washington, DC: American Psychological Association.

Wynn, K. (1995). Infants possess a system of numerical knowledge. *Current Directions in Psychological Science, 4,* 172–177.

Wynn, K. (2000). Findings of addition and subtraction in infants are robust and consistent: Reply to Wakeley, Rivera, and Langer. *Child Development, 71,* 1535–1536.

Wyra, M., Lawson, M. J., Hungi, N. (2007). The mnemonic keyword method: The effects of bidirectional retrieval training and of ability to image on foreign language vocabulary recall. *Learning and Instruction, 17,* 360–371.

Yan, Z., & Fischer, K. (2002). Always under construction: Dynamic variations in adult cognitive microdevelopment. *Human Development, 45,* 141–160.

Yang, C. D. (2006). *The infinite gift: How children learn and unlearn the languages of the world.* New York: Scribner.

Yang, R., & Blodgett, B. (2000). Effects of race and adolescent decision-making on status attainment and self-esteem. *Journal of Ethnic & Cultural Diversity in Social Work, 9,* 135–153.

Yardley, J. (2001, July 2). Child-death case in Texas raises penalty questions. *The New York Times,* A1.

Yarrow, L. (1992, November). Giving birth: 72,000 moms tell all. *Parents,* 148–159.

Yarrow, M. R., Scott, P. M., & Waxler, C. Z. (1973). Learning concern for others. *Developmental Psychology, 8,* 240–260.

Yecke, C. P. (2005). *Mayhem in the middle.* Washington, DC: Thomas B. Fordham Institute.

Yee, M., & Brown, R. (1994). The development of gender differentiation in young children. *British Journal of Social Psychology, 33,* 183–196.

Yeh, S.S. (2008). High stakes testing and students with disabilities: Why federal policy needs to be changed. In E. L. Grigorenko (Ed.), *Educating individuals with disabilities: IDEIA 2004 and beyond.* New York: Springer.

Yinger, J. (Ed.). (2004). *Helping children left behind: State aid and the pursuit of educational equity.* Cambridge, MA: MIT Press.

Yoshinaga-Itano, C. (2003). From screening to early identification and intervention: Discovering predictors to successful outcomes for children with significant hearing loss. *Journal of Deaf Studies & Deaf Education, 8,* 11–30.

Young, H., & Ferguson, L. (1979). Developmental changes through adolescence in the spontaneous nomination of reference groups as a function of decision context. *Journal of Youth and Adolescence, 8,* 239–252.

Yu, M., & Stiffman, A. (2007). Culture and environment as predictors of alcohol abuse/dependence symptoms in American Indian youths. *Addictive Behaviors, 32,* 2253–2259.

Yuill, N., & Perner, J. (1988). Intentionality and knowledge in children's judgments of actor's responsibility and recipient's emotional reaction. *Developmental Psychology, 24,* 358–365.

Zafeiriou, D. I. (2004). Primitive reflexes and postural reactions in the neurodevelopmental examination. *Pediatric Neurology, 31,* 1–8.

Zahn-Waxler, C., & Radke-Yarrow, M. (1990). The origins of empathic concern. *Motivation and Emotion, 14,* 107–130.

Zahn-Waxler, C., Park, J., Usher, B., Belouad, F., Cole, P., & Gruber, R. (2008). Young children's representations of conflict and distress: A longitudinal study of boys and girls with disruptive behavior problems. *Development and Psychopathology, 20,* 99–119.

Zalsman, G., Levy, T., Shoval, G. (2008). Interaction of child and family psychopathology leading to suicidal behavior. *Psychiatric Clinics of North America, 31,* 237–246.

Zalsman, G., Oquendo, M., Greenhill, L., Goldberg, P., Kamali,M., Martin, A., et al. (2006, October). Neurobiology of depression in children and adolescents. *Child and Adolescent Psychiatric Clinics of North America, 15,* 843–868.

Zampi, C., Fagioli, I, & Salzarulo, P. (2002). Time course of EEG background activity level before spontaneous awakening in infants. *Journal of Sleep Research, 11,* 283-287.

Zanardo, V., Nicolussi, S., Favaro, F., Faggian, D., Plebani, M., Marzari, F. & Freato, F. (2001) Effect of postpartum anxiety on the colostral milk beta-endorphin concentrations of breastfeeding mothers. *Journal of Obstetrics and Gynaecology, 21,* 130–4.

Zaporozhets, A. V. (1965). The development of perception in the preschool child. *Monographs of the Society for Research in Child Development, 30,* 82–101.

Zarbatany, L., Hartmann, D. P., & Rankin, D. B. (1990). The psychological functions of preadolescent peer activities. *Child Development, 61,* 1067–1080.

Zauszniewski, J. A., & Martin, M. H. (1999). Developmental task achievement and learned resourcefulness in healthy older adults. *Archives of Psychiatric Nursing, 13,* 41–47.

Zeedyk, M., & Heimann, M. (2006). Imitation and socio-emotional processes: Implications for communicative development and interventions. *Infant and Child Development, 15,* 219–222.

Zelazo, P. R. (1998). McGraw and the development of unaided walking. *Developmental Review, 18,* 449–471.

Zernike, K., & Petersen, M. (2001, August 19). Schools' backing of behavior drugs comes under fire. *The New York Times,* 1, 28.

Zettergren, P. (2003). School adjustment in adolescence for previously rejected, average and popular children. *British Journal of Educational Psychology, 73,* 207–221.

Zhe, C., & Siegler, R. S. (2000). Across the Great Divide: Bridging the gap between understanding of toddlers' and older children's thinking. *Monographs of the Society for Research in Child Development, 65*(2, Serial No. 261).

Zhu, J., & Weiss, L. (2005). The Wechsler Scales. In D. P. Flanagan, & P. L. Harrison, (Eds.), *Contemporary intellectual assessment: Theories, tests, and issues.* New York, Guilford Press.

Zigler, E. F., & Styfco, S. J. (1994). Head Start: Criticism in a constructive context. *American Psychologist, 49,* 127–132.

Zimmer, C. (2003, 16 May). How the mind reads other minds. *Science, 300,* 1079–1080.

Zimmer-Gembeck, M. J., Gallaty, K. J. (2006). Hanging out or hanging in?: Young females' socioemotional functioning and the changing motives for dating and romance. In A. Columbus (Ed.), *Advances in psychology research: Vol. 44.* Hauppauge, NY: Nova Science.

Zimmer-Gembeck, M.J., & Collins, W.A. (2003). Autonomy development during adolescence. In G.R. Adams & M.D. Berzosky (Eds.), Blackwell handbook of adolescence). NY: Blackwell.

Zirkel, S., & Cantor, N. (2004). 50 years after *Brown v. Board of Education*: The promise and challenge of multicultural education. *Journal of Social Issues, 60,* 1–15.

Zito, J. (2002). Five burning questions. *Journal of Developmental & Behavioral Pediatrics, 23,* S23–S30.

Zito, J. M., Safer, D. J., dos Reis, S., Gardner, J. F., Boles, M., & Lynch, F. (2000). Trends in prescribing of psychotropic medications to preschoolers. *Journal of the American Medical Association, 283,* 1025–1030.

Ziv, M., & Frye, D. (2003). The relation between desire and false belief in children's theory of mind: No satisfaction? *Developmental Psychology, 39,* 859–876.

Zuckerman, M. (2003). Biological bases of personality. In T. Millon, & M. J. Lerner (Eds.), *Personality and Social Psychology: Vol. 5. Handbook of psychology.* New York: Wiley.

Zwelling, E. (2006). A challenging time in the history of Lamaze international: an interview with Francine Nichols. *Journal of Perinatal Education, 15,* 10–17.

Credits

Photos and Cartoons

Chapter 8　　Page 185 Robert W. Ginn; PhotoEdit Inc.; p. 187 Marcus E. Raichle, M.D.; Courtesy Marcus E. Raichle, M.D., Washington University Medical Center, from research based on S.E. Petersen et al., Positron emission tomographic studies of the cortical anatomy of single-word processing. Nature 331:585–589 (1988); p. 190 Laura Dwight Photography; p. 192 Chris Priest/Science Photo Library; Photo Researchers, Inc.; p. 193 G. Degrazia; Custom Medical Stock Photo, Inc.; p. 194 Frank Siteman; Frank Siteman; p. 196 Pamela Godfrey; Pamela Godfrey, Child Crisis Center, East Valley, Inc.; p. 199 (left) Charles Gupton; Stock Boston; p. 199 (right); Skjold Photographs; p. 200 Ellen Senisi; The Image Works.

Chapter 9　　Page 207 WireImageStock; Masterfile Stock Image Library; p. 209 Laura Dwight; Laura Dwight Photography; p. 209 Laura Dwight; Laura Dwight Photography; p. 213 Esbin-Anderson; The Image Works; p. 214 Mike Derer; AP Wide World Photos; p. 215 Felicia Martinez/PhotoEdit. Courtesy of Robert Solso; p. 223 Robert S. Feldman; p. 224 Bruce Eric Kaplan; © 2002 The New Yorker Collection, Bruce Eric Kaplan from cartoonbank.com. All Rights Reserved; p. 227 © 2002 The New Yorker Collection, Bernard Schoenbaum from cartoonbank.com. All Rights Reserved.

Chapter 10　　Page 232 Howard Shooter; Howard Shooter © Dorling Kindersley; p. 233 Nancy Sheehan; PhotoEdit Inc.; p. 235 The Image Works; p. 237 (top) Spencer Grant; Stock Boston; p. 237 (bottom) Myrleen Ferguson Cate; PhotoEdit Inc.; p. 239 J. Greenberg; The Image Works; p. 240 Arlene Collins; Arlene Collins; p. 241 ©The New Yorker Collection 2002 Bruce Eric Kaplan from cartoonbank.com. All Rights Reserved; p. 246 Michelle Bridwell; PhotoEdit Inc.; p. 248 M. Hamilton; © 2002 The New Yorker Collection, M. Hamilton from cartoonbank.com. All Rights Reserved; p. 249 Catherine Ursillo; Photo Researchers, Inc.; p. 250 Albert Bandura, D. Ross & S.A. Ross, Imitation of film-mediated aggressive models. "Journal of Abnormal and Social Psychology," 1963, 66. p. 8; p. 252 Mary Kate Denny; PhotoEdit Inc.; p. 256 David Mager; Pearson Learning Photo Studio.

Chapter 11　　Page 258 Lori Adamski Peek; Getty Images Inc.—Stone Allstock; p. 259 Ariel Skelley; © Ariel Skelley/ CORBIS All Rights Reserved; p. 260 Mary Kate Denny; PhotoEdit Inc.; p. 261 Ken Heyman; Woodfin Camp & Associates, Inc.; p. 262 ©The New Yorker Collection 2003 Christopher Weyant from cartoonbank.com. All Rights Reserved; p. 265 Lester Sloan; Woodfin Camp & Associates, Inc.; p. 267 Richard Hutchings; PhotoEdit Inc.; p. 268 David Young-Wolff; PhotoEdit Inc.; p. 269 Ozier Muhammad; Ozier Muhammad/*The New York Times*; p. 272 Jose Azel; Aurora Photos, Inc.; p. 273 Elizabeth Crews Photography; p. 274 Valerie Patterson Permission obtained for this author series: Feldman, 3/ed, 2004.

Chapter 12　　Page 279 Ellen B. Senisi; Ellen Senisi; p. 280 David Lassman/Syracuse Newspapers; The Image Works; p. 283 Laura Dwight; Laura Dwight Photography; p. 284 Michael Newman; PhotoEdit Inc.; p. 285 Bob Daemmrich; The Image Works; p. 287 Bob Daemmrich; The Image Works; p. 290 Shaywitz, et. al. 2004; p. 292 B. Daemmrich; The Image Works; p. 293 Elizabeth Crews; Elizabeth Crews Photography; p. 294 Mark Richards; PhotoEdit Inc.; p. 295 Corbis/Bettmann; p. 297 David Young-Wolff; PhotoEdit Inc.; p. 302 Richard Hutchings; Photo Researchers, Inc.

Chapter 13　　Page 309 Jim West; The Image Works; p. 310 (left) Robert Houser; Comstock Images; p. 310 (right) Myrleen Ferguson Cate;

PhotoEdit Inc.; p. 314 Lew Merrim; Photo Researchers, Inc.; p. 315 Richard Lord; The Image Works; p. 316 Bob Daemmrich; The Image Works; p. 317 Bob Daemmrich; Stock Boston; p. 318 Richard Hutchings; PhotoEdit Inc.; p. 319 Jeff Greenberg; PhotoEdit Inc.; p. 321 Rhoda Sidney; Pearson Education/PH College; p. 324 Robert Brenner; PhotoEdit Inc.; p. 325 Phil Borden; PhotoEdit Inc.; p. 326 (left); Corbis/Bettmann; p. 326 (right) Melchior DiGiacomo; Boys Town; p. 330 Amos Morgan; Getty Images, Inc.—Photodisc.

Chapter 14　　Page 333 Gordon, Larry Dale; Getty Images Inc.—Image Bank; p. 335 (top right) Ellen Senisi; The Image Works; p. 335 (top left) Ellen Senisi; The Image Works; p. 335 (bottom) David Young-Wolff; PhotoEdit Inc.; p. 337 Tony Freeman; PhotoEdit Inc.; p. 338 B. Daemmrich; The Image Works; p. 339 Express Newspaper; Getty Images/Time Life Pictures; p. 340 The Image Works; p. 346 Arlene Collins; Arlene Collins; p. 347 AP Photo/Victor R. Caivano; p. 348 Chris Arrend Photography; Southcentral Foundation; p. 349 David Appleby; Paramount/The Kobal Collection/David Appleby; p. 350 Roger Mastroianni; Roger Mastroianni; p. 352 Michael A. Keller Studios LTD.; Corbis/Stock Market.

Chapter 15　　Page 357 Nancy Richmond; © Nancy Richmond / The Image Works; p. 358 Kevin Radford; SuperStock, Inc.; p. 359 Bob Daemmrich; Stock Boston; p. 361 Christopher Brown; Stock Boston; p. 364 (left) Jerry Bauer; Photo by Jerry Bauer. Courtesy of Harvard Graduate School of Education; p. 364 (right) Lee Snider; The Image Works; p. 367 Chris Hondros; Getty Images, Inc.—Liaison; p. 373 (right) Doug Menuez; Getty Images, Inc.—PhotoDisc; p. 373 (left) Jose L. Pelaez; Corbis/Stock Market; p. 375 F. Pedrick; The Image Works; p. 378 Robert S. Feldman; p. 379 John W. McDonough; John W. McDonough/Sports Illustrated.

Chapter 16　　Page 358 Universal Press Syndicate; p. 383 Tony Freeman; PhotoEdit Inc.; p. 386 Michael Newman; PhotoEdit Inc.; p. 387 D. Young Wolff; PhotoEdit Inc.; p. 388 Jonathan Nourok; PhotoEdit Inc.; p. 390 G & M David de Lossy; Photodisc/Getty Images; p. 392 Mary Kate Denny; PhotoEdit Inc.; p. 393 Keren Su; Stock Boston; p. 396 N. Richmond; The Image Works; p. 398 Lori Adamski Peek; Getty Images Inc.—Stone Allstock; p. 399 David Young-Wolff; PhotoEdit Inc.; p. 400 Michael Newman; PhotoEdit Inc.; p. 402 Bill Aron; PhotoEdit Inc.; p. 404 Evan Johnson; Evan Johnson; p. 406 Paula Lerner; Woodfin Camp & Associates, Inc.; p. 410 Olivier Ribardiere; Olivier Ribardiere/ Taxi/Getty Images.

Maps　　Photodisc; Photodisc/Getty Images. Tony Freeman; PhotoEdit Inc. Dorling Kindersley; © Dorling Kindersley.

Figures and Tables

Chapter 2　　Figure 2-1: Adapted from W. Damon (ed.) *Handbook of Child Psychology* 5th ed., Vol I, John Wiley & Sons From Kopp, J. & Krakow, J.B. (1982). Child Development in the Social Context. Reading, MA: Addison Wesley Publishing Co. Reprinted by permission.

Chapter 3　　Figure 3-2: J.A. Martin & M.M. Park, "Trends in Twin & Triplet Births: 1980–1997," *National Vital Statistic Reports*, Sept. 14, 2007, 47, 1-17, Centers for Disease Control; Figure 3-5: J.W. Kimball, *Biology*, 5th ed., McGraw-Hill, 1984 from *Biology, 5th edition*, by J.W. Kimball. Copyright © 1984. Reprinted with permission; Figure 3-6: International Genome Sequencing Consortium, 2001; Figure 3-7: Samet, DeMarini,

Malling, *Science*, May 14, 2004, p. 971, adapted from N.M. Williams et al, *Journal Human Molecular Genetics*, 8, 1729 (1999) Reprinted with permission of Taina Litwak; Figure 3-9: T.J. Bouchard, M. McGue, "Familial Studies of Intelligence: A Review," *Science*, 1981, 264, pp. 1700–1701 Reprinted with permission of Dr. Matt McGue and Dr. Thomas Bouchard; Figure 3-10: Adapted from Tellegen et al. (1988), "Personality Similarity in Twins Reared Apart and Together," *Journal of Personality and Social Psychology*, 1988, 54, 1031–1039; Figure 3-11: I. I. Gotteman, *Schizophrenia Genesis: The Origins of Madness*, Freeman, 1991 from Schizophrenia Genesis: The Origins of Madness by Irving I. Gottesman © 1991 by W. H. Freeman and Company. Used by permisison; Figure 3-12: Moore, Persuad, *Before We are Born: Basic Embryology and Birth Defects*, Saunders, 2003 From *Before We Are Born: Basic Embryology and Birth Defects*, K.L Moore, T.V.N. Persaud. Saunders. Copyright © Elsevier 2003. Reprinted with permission; Figure 3-15: K.L. Moore, *Before We Are Born: Basic Embryology and Birth Defects*, W.B. Sauders, 1998, p. 96 From *Before We Are Born: Basic Embryology and Birth Defects*, K.L Moore, T.V.N. Persaud. Saunders. Copyright © Elsevier 2003. Reprinted with permission; Table 3-1: Adapted from P. McGuffin, B. Riley and R. Plomin, "Towards Behaviorial Genomics," *Science*, 291, 2/16/01, 1232–1249 From McGuffin, P., Riley, B., Plomin, R. (2001, Feb 16) "Towards Behavioral Genomics," *Science* 291, 1232–1249; Table 3-3: Human Genome Project, 1998, as seen at: http://www.ornl.gov/sci/techresources/human_genocide?medicine/genetests.shtml; Table 3-4: From J. Kagan, D. Arcus, N. Snidman, "The Idea of Temperament Where Do We Go From Here?" R. Plomin and G.E. McCleary, *Nature, Nurture & Psychology*, APA, 1993 J. Kagan, D. Arcus, N. Snidman, "The Idea of Temperament Where Do We Go From Here?", in R. Plmin & G.E. McCleary, *Nature, Nuture & Psychology*, APA, 1993. Reprinted with permission.

Chapter 4 Figure 4-2: D.L. Finkelstein, D.A. Harper, G.E. Rosenthal, "Does Hospital Stay During Labor and Deliver Influence Patient Satisfaction? Results from a regional study" *American Journal of Managed Care*, 4, 1998, 1701–1708 Adapted from Finkelstein, D.L., Harper, D.A., & Rosenthal, G.E. (1998). "Does Length of Hospital Stay During Labor and Delivery Influence Patient Satisfaction? Results from a Regional Study", *American Journal of Manged Care*, 4, 1701–1708; Figure 4-3: Adapted from the *National Center for Health Statistics*, (2001) Health United States, 2000 with Adolscent Health Chartbook, Hyattsville, MD; Figure 4-4: Adapted from Child Health Studies Branch (1997), *Survival Rates of Infants*, National Center for Health Statistics; Figure 4-6: *National Center for Health Statistics* (1997) "U.S. Infant Mortality Rates By Race of Mother: 1975–1996;" Table 4-1: V. Aphar, "A Proposal for a New Method of Evaluation in the Newborn Infant," *Current Research in Anesthesia and Analgesia*, 32, 1953, p. 260 "A Proposal for a New Method of Evaluation in the Newborn Infant," V. Apgar, *Current Research in Anesthesia and Analgesia*, 32, 1953, p. 260. Reprinted with permission of Wolters Kluwer; Table 4-2: Adapted from "Committee to Study the Prevention of Low Birthweight," *Preventing Low Birthweight*, 1985, National Academy Press from *Preventing Low Birthweight*, Copyright © 1985 by the National Academy Press. Permisson granted through the Copyright Clearance Center; Table 4-3: Kameran, S.B., "Maternity to Parental Leave Policies: Women's Health Employment and Child and Family Well-Being" from *The Journal for American Women's Medical Association* (Spring 2000), 55 Table 1 from S. B. Sameran "Parental Leave Policies" from *Social Policy Report*, (2000), 14, Table 1.0; Table 4-6: C.O. Eckerman, J.M. Oehler, "Very Low Birthweight Newborns and Parents as Early Social Partners," S.L. Friedman & M.B. Sigman, *The Psychological Development of Low-Birthweight Children*, Abex, 1992 Reprinted by permission of the author.

Chapter 5 Figure 5-1: B.J. Cratty, *Perceptual and Motor Development in Infants and Children*, 3rd Edition, Prentice Hall, 1979 From Cratty, B.J. (1979). Perceptual and Motor Development in Infants and Children. All rights reserved. Reprinted by permission of Allyn & Bacon; Figure 5-4: Van de Graaf, K., *Human Anatomy*, 5th Edition, McGraw-Hill, 2000, p. 339 From *Human Anatomy*, 5th Edition by K. Van de Graaf, McGraw-Hill, Copyright © 2000. Reprinted with permission; Figure 5-5: J.L. Conel, *Postnatal Development of the Human Cortex*, (Vol. 1-6), 1930/1963, Harvard University Press J. L. Colnel, *Postnatal Development of the Human Cortex*, (Vol. 1-6), 1930/1963, Harvard University Press. Reprinted with permission; Figure 5-7: Adapted from "SIDS Death and Infant Sleep Position," *National Institute for Child Health & Human Development* (1997); Figure 5-8: Adapted from W.K. Frankenburg, J. Dodds, P. Archer, H. Shapiro & B. Bresnick "The Denver II: A Major Revision and Restandarization of the Denver Screening Test," *Pediatrics* (1992), 89, pp. 91–97; Figure 5-9: UNICEF, *The State of the World's Children*; Figure 5-10: National Center for Children in Poverty at the Joseph L. Mailman School of Public Health of Columbia University. Analysis based on U.S. Bureau of the Census 2000 Current Population Survey; Figure 5-13: Adapted from R.L. Fantz, "The Origin of Form Perception," *Scientific American*, (1961), p. 72 Adaption used with permission of Alexander Semenocik. Original appeared in Fantz, R.L. (May 1661). "The Origin of Form Perception," *Scientific American*; Figure 5-14: O. Pascalis, M. deHaan & C.A. Nelson, "Is Face Processing Species Specific During the First Years of Life?" *Science*, May 17, 2002; Figure 5-15: T. Field, "Weight Gain on Premature Infants," *Pediatrics*, 77 (1986), p. 657 Reprinted with permission of the American Academy of Pediatrics.

Chapter 6 Figure 6-6: M.H. Bornstein, M.E. Lamb, eds., *Developmental Psychology: An Advanced Textbook*, Erlbaum, 1992, p. 135; Figure 6-7: Dehane Lamertz, Hertz-Pannier, & Dubois, 2006; Table 6-3: N. Bayley, *Bayley Scales of Infant Development*, Psychological Corporation; Simulated items similar to those in the *Bayley Scales of Infant Development-Second Edition (BSID-II)*. Copyright © 1993 by NCS Pearson, Inc. Reproduced with permission. All rights reserved. *"Bayley Scales of Infant Development"* is a trademark, in the United States and/or other countires, of Pearson Education, Inc. or its affiliates; Table 6-4: Adapted from H. Benedict, "Early Lexical Development: Comprehension and Production," *Journal of Child Language*, 6, 1079, pp. 182–200; From "Early Lexical Development: Comprehension and Production" by H. Benedict in *Journal of Child Language*, 1979, 6. Reprinted with permission of the Cambridge University Press; Table 6-5: R. Brown, C. Fraser, "The Acquisition of Syntax," C.N. Cofer & B. Musgrave (eds.) *Verbal Behaviour and Learning: Problems and Processes*, McGraw-Hill, 1963; Table 6-6: B.G. Blount, "Culture and the Language of Socialization: Parental Speech" D.A. Wagner & W. W. Stevenson eds., *Cultural Perspectives on Child Development*, Freeman 1982 from Cultural Perspectives on Child Development by Daniel A. Wagner and Harold W. Stevenson © 1982 by W. H. Freeman and Company. Used with permission.

Chapter 7 Figure 7-3: From F2.8 "Percentage of Childhood in Four Different Settings Who Cried Following Maternal Departure," J. Kagan, R.B. Kearsley & P.R. Zelazo, *Infancy, Its Place in Human Development*, Harvard University Press (1978), p. 107 "Percentage of Childhood in Four Different Settings Who Cried Following Maternal Departure," J. Kagan, R.B. Kearsley & P.R. Zelazo, *Infancy, Its Place in Human Development*, Harvard University Press. Copyright © 1978 Reprinted with permission; Figure 7-5: Adapted from S.M. Bell & M.D.S. Ainsworth, "Infant Crying and Maternal Responsiveness," *Child*

Development, 43, 1972, pp. 1171–1190 Used with permission of Dr. Carol Tomlinson-Keasey; Figure 7-6: National Child-care Research Network, *The NICHD Study of Child Care & Youth Development*, 2006, p. 20; Table 7-1: E. Waters, "The Reliability and Stability of Individual Differences in Infant-Mother Attachment," *Child Development*, 49, 1978, The Society for Research in Child Development, Inc. pp. 480–494 Adapted from Waters, E. "The Reliability and Stability of Individual Differences in Infant-Mother Attachment," in *Child Development*, 49, 1978, pp. 480–494. Reprinted with permission of The Society for Research in Child Development; Table 7-2: A. Thomas, S. Chess & H.G. Birch, "Temperament and Behavior Disorders in Children," New York University Press, 1968 Reprinted with permission of New York University Press.

Chapter 8 Figure 8-1: National Center for Health Statistics in Collaboration with the National Center for Prevention and Health Promotion; Figure 8-5: Washington D.C.: National Center for Health Statistics; Figure 8-6: J.M. Zito, D.J. Safer, S. dos Reis, J.F. Gardner, M. Boles & F. Lynch, "Trends in Prescribing of Psychotropic Medications to Preschoolers," *Journal of the American Medical Association*, 282, 2000, pp. 1025–1030 Reprinted with permission of the American Medical Association; Figure 8-7: H.L. Needleman, J.A. Reiss, M.J. Tobin, G.E. Biesecker, J.B. Greenhouse, "Bone Lead Levels and Delinquent Behavior," *Journal of American Medical Association*, 275, (1996, Feb. 7), pp. 363–369 Reprinted with permission of the American Medical Association; Figure 8-9: *Scientific American*, March 2002, p. 71 Reprinted by permission; Table 8-2: American Academy of Pediatrics, *Recommended Childhood Immunization Schedule*, United States, January–December 2001; Table 8-3: Adapted with permission from Charles C. Corbin: *A Textbook of Motor Development*. Dubuque, IA: Wm. C. Brown Publishers. Copyright © 1973, Times Mirror Higher Education Group, Inc., Dubuque, Iowa. All rights reserved. Used with permission of The McGraw-Hill Companies.

Chapter 9 Figure 9-6: Adapted from J. Berko, "The Child's Learning of English Morphology," *Word*, 14, (1958), pp. 150–177; Figure 9-7: B. Hart, T.R. Risley, *Meaningful Differences in the Everyday Experience of Young American Children*, Paul H. Brookes Publishing, 1995 from *Meaningful Differences in the Everyday Experience of Young American Children*, B. Hart, T.R. Risley, Paul H. Brookes Publishing Co., Inc., Baltimore, MD. Copyright © 1995. Reprinted with permission; Figure 9-8: U.S. Department of Education, National Center for Education Statistics; Figure 9-9: Based on J.J. Tobin, D.Y.H. Yu, D.D. Davidson, *Preschool in Three Cultures: Japan, China, and the United States*, Yale University Press, 1989, p. 192, T5-2 Based on J.J. Tobin, D.Y.H. Yu, D.D. Davidson, *Preschool in Three Cultures: Japan, China, and the United States*, Yale University Press Copyright © 1989. Reprinted with permission; Figure 9-10: V.J. Rideout, U.G. Foehr, D.F. Roberts, M. Brodie, "Kids and Media the New Millennium. A Kaiser Family Foundation Report," Nov. 1999, Henry J. Kaiser Family Foundation; Table 9-1: D. Poole, M. Lamb, *Investigative Interviews of Children: A Guide for Helping Professionals*, APA 1998; Table 9-3: S. Piner, *The Language Instinct*, William Morrow, 1994 Table "Growing Speech Capabilities" (p. 293) from *The Language Instinct* by Steven Pinker. Copyright © 1994 by Steven Pinker. Reprinted by permission of HarperCollins Publishers.

Chapter 10 Figure 10-1: J.M. Farver, Y.K. Kim & Y. Lee, "Cultural Differences in Korean and Anglo-American Preschoolers" Social Interaction and Play Behaviors, *Child Development*, 66, 1995, pp. 1088–1099 Reprinted with the permission of The Society for Research in Child Development, Inc.; Figure 10-3: Adaptation of analysis of vio-lent content of broadcast and cable television stations on Thursday, April 7, 1995. Center for Media and Public Affairs.

Chapter 11 Figure 11-1: D.E. Barrett, M.R. Radke-Yarrow, 1985, "Effects of Nutritional Supplementation on Children's Responses to Novel, Frustrating, and Competitive Situations," *American Journal of Clinical Nutrition*, 42, pp.102–120; Figure 11-3: From the U.S. Department of Agriculture and the NPD Group (1998). The Reality of Children's Diet. Port Washington, NY; NPD Group; Table 11-1: From *Child Safety on the Information Highway* by Lawrence J. Magrid, National Center for Missing & Exploited Children. These rules are from *Child Safety on the Information Highway* by Lawrence J. Magrid. They are reprinted with pemission of the National Center for Missing & Exploited Children (NCMEC). Copyright © NCMED 1994. All rights reserved.

Chapter 12 Figure 12-2: P. Dasen, P. Ngini, M. Lavallee, "Cross-Cultural Training Studies of Concrete Operations," in L.H. Eckenberger, W.J.Lonner, U.H. Poortinga (Eds.), *Cross-Cultural Contributions to Psychology*, Swets & Zeitlinger, 1079 from L.H. Eckenberger, W.J. Lonner & Y.H. Poortinga (eds), Cross-Cultural Contributions of Psychology. Amsterdam: Swets & Zeitlinger. Reprinted by permission; Figure 12-3: 3 MLA Maps, www.mla.org/censu_maps Reprinted by pemisson of the Modern Language Association; Figure 12-5: *Science* (Shaywitz, B.A., Shaywitz S.E., Blackburn B.A., Pugh K.R., Fulbright R.K., Skudlarski P., Mencl W.E., Constable, R.T., Holohan, J.M., Marchione K.E., Fletcher J.M., Lyon G.R., Gore J.C.) Reprinted with permission from Elsevier. Figure 12-9: Adapted from the Weschler Intelligence Scale for Children, 3rd edition. Copyright © 1990 by the Psychological Corporation. Simulated items similar to those in the Weschler Intelligence Scale (WISC-IV). Copyright © 1993 by NCS Pearson, Inc. Reproduced with permission. All rights reserved. "Weschler Intelligence Scale" is a trademark, in the United States and/or other countries, of Pearson Education, Inc. or its affiliates; Figure 12-10: E. Walters, E. Gardners, 1986. "The Theory of Intelligences: Some Issues and Answers." In R.J. 12/05 Sternber & R.K. Wagner, eds., Practical Intelligence. Cambridge University Press, 1985; Table 12-1: Adapted from Chall, J. S. (1979). "The Great Debate: Ten Years Later with a Modest Proposal for Reading Stages." In L. B. Resnick & P. A. Weaver (Eds.), *Theory and Practice of Early Reading*. Hillsdale, NJ: Lawrence Erlbaum Associates.

Chapter 13 Figure 13-1: Adapted from R. Shavelson, J.J. Hubner, J.C. Stanton, *Self-Concept: Validation of Construct Interpretations, Review of Educational Research*. 1976, 46, pp. 407–441; Figure 13-3: Adapted from Dodge, K. A. (1985). "A Social Information-Processing Model of Social Competence in Children." In M. Perlmutter (Ed.), Minnesota Symposia on Child Psychology (Vol.18), 77–126. Hillsdale, NJ: Erlbaum; Figure 13-4: From Hofferth, S., & Sandberg, J. F. (2001). "How American Children Spend Their Time." Journal of Marriage and the Family, 63, 2956–308. Copyright © 2001 by the National Council on Family Relations, 3989 Central Ave. NE. Suite 550, Minneapolis, MN 55421. Reprinted by permission; Figure 13-5: The U.S. Census Bureau, Sept. 14, 2004; Table 13-1: Adapted from L. Zarbatany, D.P. Harmann & D.B. Rankin, "The Psychological Functions of Preadolescents Peer Activities," *Child Development*, 2990, 61, pp. 1067–1180; Table 13-2: Adapted from Shealy, C. N. (1995). "Boy's Town to Oliver Twist: Separating Fact from Fiction in Welfare Reform and Out-of-Home Placement of Children and Youth." American Psychologist, 50, 5656–580. Copyright © 1995 by the American Psychological Association. Adapted with permission.

Arterberry, M., 122, 162
Asendorpf, J., 164
Asendorpf, J.B., 164
Ashburn, S.S., 187
Asher, S.R., 317, 318, 319
Asherson, P., 190
Ashmead, D.H., 123, 126
Aslin, R.N., 121
Assefi, N., 405
Astin, A.W., 373
Ata, R., 385
Atkinson, R.C., 283
Atom, K.A., 342
Atterbury, J.I., 108
Atterbury, J.L., 68
Atwood, M.E., 198
Auerbach, C.F., 169
Auestad, N., 119
Augustine, C.H., 366
Augustyn, M., 228
Auinger, P., 288
Aujoulat, I., 318
Austin, C.M., 97
Avia, M.D., 57, 173
Aviezer, O., 167
Axia, G., 125
Axinn, W.G., 403
Aydt, H., 236
Aylward, G.P., 143
Ayotte, V., 311
Ayoub, N.C., 82
Azuma, S.D., 71

B
Bacchus, L., 72
Bachman, H.J., 288
Bachman, J.G., 346, 347
Bacho, R., 387
Badanu, S., 340
Bade, U., 175
Bader, A.P., 84
Badger, S., 396
Baer, J.S., 71
Bahrick, L., 126
Bahrick, L.E., 126
Bai, L., 242
Bailey, J.M., 58, 66
Baillargeon, R., 138
Bajda, V.M., 174
Bakeman, R., 71
Baker, J., 51
Baker, R.C., 364
Baker, S.A., 287
Baker, T., 349
Bakermans-Kranenburg, M., 165
Balaban, M.T., 108
Balaiah, D., 404

Baldassaro, R., 13, 251
Bale, J.F., Jr., 271
Ball, K., 262–63
Ballen, L., 83
Balotti, U., 340
Bamaca, M., 293
Bamelis, L., 169
Bamsad, M.J., 7
Bandura, A., 22, 247, 249
Bangdiwala, S.I., 349
Baptista, T., 28
Bar, J.L., 62
Baram, N., 72
Barbarich, N., 340
Barber, B., 334
Barbera, E., 237
Barker, E., 390
Barker, E.D., 318
Barker, V., 287
Barlett, C., 13, 251
Barnard, W., 226
Barnes, H.V., 225
Barnes, J., 224
Barnett, D., 154, 322
Barnett, R.C., 321
Baron-Cohen, S., 66, 188, 236
Barr, H., 71
Barr, H.M., 69
Barr, R., 141
Barr, R.A., 150
Barr, R.G., 171
Barr, W., 188
Barrett, D.E., 187, 260
Barry, C.T., 401
Barton, B.A., 339
Barton, R., 266
Basen-Engquist, K., 405
Bass, S., 327
Bates, E., 108, 150
Bates, J.E., 244, 317
Bathurst, K., 322
Battistutta, D., 89
Batty, G., 119
Baudonniere. P., 164
Bauer, P.J., 141, 142
Bauman, K.E., 394, 398
Bauman, K.J., 294
Baumeister, A.A., 110
Baumgart, S., 71, 108
Baumler, E., 405
Baumrind, D., 243, 244
Bautista, C., 95
Bayley, N., 143
Beal, C.R., 188, 318
Beale, C.R., 319
Bean, J., 386
Bear, G.G., 362

Bearman, K., 390
Bearman, P., 405
Bearman, P.S., 394
Beauchaine, T., 11
Beauchamp, G.K., 118
Beauchemin, A., 197
Beaulieu, S., 28
Becahy, R., 350
Bech, B.H., 72
Becker, B., 197, 399
Becker, J.B., 336
Beckers, D., 261
Beckman, M., 341
Beckwith, L., 144
Begeer, S., 242
Begeny, J., 274
Beggs, A.H., 110
Begley, S., 83, 375
Behne, D., 152
Behrman, R., 47
Behrman, R.E., 192, 269, 327
Beilin, H., 282
Beilin, L., 339
Belacchi, C., 285
Belanger, S., 225
Belcher, J.R., 325
Beliveau, R.A., 69
Belkin, L., 48
Bell, S.M., 171
Bellagamba, F., 164
Belle, D., 323
Bellezza, F.S., 283
Belliveau, R.A., 110
Belluck, P., 244
Belmaker, R.H., 61
Belouad, F., 319
Belsky, J., 168, 178, 179, 224, 335
Bemadel, L., 269
Benbow, C., 304
Benbow, C.P., 304
Bender, H., 313
Benedict, H., 149
Benelli, B., 285
Benenson, J.F., 318
Benesch, T., 92
Bengtson, V.L., 325
Benini, F., 125
Benjamin, J., 61
Benjet, C., 195
Bennett, A., 62
Bennett, K., 154
Bennett, P., 92
Bennett, S., 405
Benoit, M., 391
Benson, E., 160
Benson, H., 345
Bentz, L.S., 68, 108

Brook, U., 339
Brooks-Gunn, J., 39, 90, 116, 192, 225, 301, 337
Brosh, H., 292, 313
Brown, B., 397
Brown, B.B., 245
Brown, C., 191
Brown, E., 94, 242, 303
Brown, E.C., 148
Brown, G., 169, 175
Brown, J., 237
Brown, J.D., 234
Brown, J.L., 260
Brown, J.S., 384
Brown, J.V., 71
Brown, M.J., 193
Brown, R., 149, 150, 159, 199
Brown, T., 189
Brown, W.M., 71
Browne, K., 236
Brownell, C., 314
Brownlee, S., 261
Brownstone, D., 349
Bruce, J., 243
Bruck, M., 213, 214
Bruckner, H., 405
Brueggemann, L., 82
Brune, C., 96
Brunet, P., 11
Bruno, R., 285
Brunswick, N., 272
Bruskas, D., 327
Bryant, J., 227
Bryant, J.A., 227
Bucciarelli, A., 8
Buchanan, C.M., 336
Buchman, D., 251
Buehler, J., 70
Buekens, P., 90
Bugental, D.B., 195
Buhrmester, D., 321
Buitelaar, J., 70
Bukowski, W.M., 397
Bulik, C., 340
Bulik, C.M., 340
Bull, R., 242
Bullinger, A., 132
Bumpus, M.F., 394
Bunch, K., 242
Bunney, W.E., 390
Burchinal, M., 179
Burchinal, M.R., 178, 179
Burd, L., 71
Burdjalov, V.F., 108
Burgess, K.B., 397
Burkam, D.T., 366
Burke, D., 406

Burke, V., 339
Burks, V.S., 317
Burn, S.M., 269
Burnham, M., 108, 110
Burnham, M.M., 109, 110
Burns, E., 273
Burns, M., 239
Burock, D., 362
Burrows, G.D., 89
Burston, A., 325
Bushman, B.J., 13
Busner, J., 272
Buss, D.M., 28
Buss, K.A., 161, 163
Bussey, K., 247
Butler, K.G., 271
Butler-Kisber, L., 371
Butterworth, G., 138
Buysee, D.J., 108
Byars, A., 153
Byrd, R.S., 288
Byrne, B., 385

C

Cabrera, N., 154, 169, 217, 222
Cadinu, M.R., 242
Cahill, D.J., 352
Cai, Y., 295, 367
Cain, D., 224
Caine, E.D., 391
Caino, S., 334
Calarco, K., 71
Calati, R., 61
Caldwell, C.B., 62
Calhoun, F., 71
Callaman, M.A., 216
Callister, L.C., 79
Caltran, G., 94
Calvert, S.L., 237
Cameron, C., 339
Cameron, I., 71
Cami, J., 347
Camino, L., 35
Campbell, A., 236
Campbell, D., 83
Campbell, F., 222, 223
Campbell, K., 262–63
Campbell, N.B., 391
Campbell, W.K., 312
Campos, J.J., 122, 125, 163
Camras, L., 161
Canals, J., 115
Candy, J., 236
Canfield, R.L., 144
Canning, P., 190
Cannon, T.D., 62

Canterford, L., 190
Cantor, J., 228
Cantor, N., 292
Caplan, L.J., 150
Caplovitz, A.G., 145
Capps, L.M., 242
Carbonneau, R., 169
Cardala, E.B., 119
Carey, G., 62
Carlin, J., 190
Carlson, S.M., 287
Carnegie Task Force on Meeting the Needs of
      Young Children, 405
Carnes, B.A., 261
Carney, J.V., 344
Carney, R.N., 283
Carpendale, J.I.M., 362, 388
Carpenter, D.M., 294
Carrier, S., 95
Carrol, B., 178
Carroll, R.E., 119
Carswell, H., 239
Cartar, L., 86
Carter, C.S., 119
Carter, R.S., 399
Carter-Saltzman, L., 60
Caruso, D.R., 293
Carvalho, M., 319
Carver, L., 162, 163
Carver, L.J., 161
Casanueva, C., 72
Casas, J.G., 320
Case, R., 24, 215, 360
Casey, B., 340
Cashon, C., 34, 94
Caspi, A., 61, 63, 173, 401
Cassia, V.M., 122
Cassidy, J., 167
Cassimatis, N.L., 197
Cataldi, E.F., 371
Cates, W., Jr., 351
Cath, S., 325
Cauce, A., 326
Cauce, A.M., 224, 326
Cauffman, E., 179
Cavallini, A., 121
Ceci, S., 214
Ceci, S.J., 213, 214
Celera Genomics: International Human
      Genome Sequencing Consortium, 50
Cella, S., 337
Cen, G., 169
Center for Media and Public Affairs, 251
Centers for Disease Control, 111, 352
Centers for Disease Control and Prevention,
      403, 404

Diego, M., 88, 125, 162
Diehl, M., 360
Diener, M., 169
Dietrich, C., 152
Dietz, W., 261
Dietz, W.H., 116, 261, 262
DiGiuseppe, R., 390
Dildy, G.A., 70
Dilworth-Anderson, P., 325
DiMatteo, M.R., 83
Ding, Y.S., 272
DiPietro, J.A., 66, 68, 70
Dishion, T., 394
Dissanayake, C., 164
Dittmann, M., 8
Dittmann, R., 272
Diversi, M., 314
Dixon, R.A., 10
Dixon, W.E., Jr., 151
Dmitrieva, J., 396
Dobson, V., 94
Dodds, J., 114
Dodge, K.A., 244, 252, 317, 397
Doman, G., 153
Doman, J., 153
Dombrowski, S., 86
Domenech-Rodriguez, M., 326
Dominguez, H.D., 95
Donaghey, C., 266
Donat, D., 290
Dondi, M., 94
Donlan, C., 213
Donnellan, M.B., 384
Donnelly, G., 272
Donnerstein, E., 32, 251
Donohue, R., 377
Dorn, L., 338
Dornbusch, S.M., 245, 398, 401
Dorofaeff, T., 342
dos Reis, S., 192
Dove, H., 14, 115
Dow-Ehrensberger, M., 288
Dowrick, P., 228
Doyle, L.W., 86
Doyle, R., 264
Drapeau, M., 213
Drapeau, S., 13, 195
Dreisbach, G., 25
Drew, L., 326
Drewett, R., 190, 260
Drews, C.D., 72
Driscoll, A.K., 314
Dromi, E., 148
Dropik, P.L., 141
Drummey, A.B., 140
Druzin, M.L., 70
Dryfoss, J.G., 396

Dsilna, A., 87
Duarte, C.S., 266
Dubas, J., 244
Dubeau, D., 169
Duberstein, P., 407
DuBois, D.L., 398
DuBois, J., 147, 151
DuBreuil, S.C., 141
Duckett, E., 322, 394, 395
Dudding, T.C., 79
Dudenhausen, J.W., 85, 88
Duenwald, M., 68
Duff, A.J.A., 197
Duncan, G.J., 90, 116, 192, 301
Dunn, J., 148
Dunne, M.P., 58
Dunyam, R.M., 387
Durant, J.E., 195
Durik, A.M., 89
Durkin, K., 339
Dutta, T., 201
Dwairy, M., 245
Dweck, C., 234
Dyer, S., 241
Dynda, A.M., 301
Dyson, A.H., 34

E

Eagly, A.H., 377
Earle, J., 404
East, P., 405
Easterbrooks, M., 168, 169
Eastman, Q., 110
Easton, J., 28
Eaton, W.O., 176, 199
Ebbeck, V., 312
Ebmeier, K., 266
Ebstein, R.P., 61
Eccles, J.S., 334, 336, 367
Ecenbarger, W., 350
Eckerman, C.O., 97
Eckerman, G., 171
Edelen, M., 350
Edelman, N., 114
Edison, S.C., 141
Edmunds, L., 117
Edwards, C.P., 216, 236, 239, 318
Edwards, S., 27
Egeland, B., 167
Eichstedt, J., 176, 236
Eid, M., 171
Eidelman, A.I., 87
Eiden, R., 71
Eigsti, I., 195
Eilers, A., 150
Eilers, R.E., 148
Eimas, P.D., 123

Eisbach, A.O., 242
Eisenberg, M., 407
Eisenberg, N., 161, 245, 247, 248, 317
Eitel, P., 320
Elder, G.H., 384
Eley, T., 390
Eley, T.C., 28, 61
Elkind, D., 189, 226, 359, 361
Ellickson, P., 350
Elliot, E., 283
Ellis, B.J., 335
Ellis, L., 201, 234, 236, 406
Ellis, S., 281
Ellwood, D.A., 83
Elman, J., 25
Elmore, A., 325
Else-Quest, N., 226
Else-Quest, N.M., 81
Ely, R., 153
Emery, R., 337, 338
Emory, E., 115
Employment Policies Institute, 370
Emslie, G., 266
Endo, S., 171
Endocrine Society, 336
Engh, T., 201
Englund, K., 152
Englund, M.M., 399
Ennett, S.T., 398
Enns, L.R., 176
Ensenauer, R.E., 54
Enskar, K., 191
Epperson, S.E., 373
Erdley, C.A., 314
Erikson, E.H., 19, 173, 386
Eriksson, J., 106
Erlandsson, K., 87
Ernst, M., 341
Eshel, N., 341
Esiri, M.M., 188
Esparo, G., 115
Espelage, D.L., 344
Espenschade, A., 267
Espinoza, M.C., 261
Esposito, N., 119
Essex, M.J., 90
Estell, D., 317, 399
Estell, D.B., 318
Ethier, L., 194
Evans, B.J., 89
Evans, D.E., 173
Evans, D.W., 153
Evans, G., 193, 250, 326
Evans, G.W., 239
Evans, M., 110
Eveleth, P., 335
Everett, S.A., 351

Kamm, M.A., 79
Kaniskan, R., 197
Kann, L., 351, 390
Kantrowitz, B., 270, 389, 403
Kantrowitz, E.J., 239
Kao, G., 314
Kaplan, H., 14, 115
Kaplan, R., 195
Kaplan, S., 272
Kaprio, J., 62
Karademas, E.C., 344
Karim, N., 347
Karnilowicz, W., 394
Karrass, J., 138
Kartehner, R., 79
Kärtner, J., 245
Kasen, S., 342
Kashima, Y., 164
Kastens, C., 291
Kato, K., 12
Katon, W., 265
Katrowitz, B., 321
Katsurada, E., 245
Katulak, N., 293
Katusic, S., 265
Katz, L.G., 246
Kaufman, A., 297
Kaufman, J.C., 297
Kaufman, N.L., 297
Kaufman-Singer, J., 297
Kaufmann, D., 244
Kauh, T., 318
Kautz, K.J., 272
Kaye, W.H., 340
Kazdin, A.E., 195
Kazura, K., 169
Kearsley, R., 162
Keast, D., 263
Keating, D., 359
Kecskes, I., 287
Keeler, G., 116
Keen, R., 114
Keller, H., 164, 245
Kellman, P., 122
Kellow, J., 376
Kelly, G., 403
Kelly, H., 313
Kelly, J., 169, 323
Kelly-Vance, L., 176
Kelly-Weeder, S., 67
Kelmansky, D., 334
Keltner, D., 242
Kemmelmeier, M., 292, 313
Kendler, K., 51
Kendrick, A., 327
Kennedy, J.M., 118
Kennell, J.H., 84

Kerr, E., 379
Kesler, S., 52
Kesmodel, U., 72
Ketron, J.L., 295
Keune, K., 191
Khalaf, I., 79
Khan, L.K., 261
Khan, S., 201
Kibria, N., 403
Kidwell, J.S., 387
Kiecolt-Glaser, J.K., 342
Kiefer, F., 349
Kiel, E.J., 161, 163
Kiely, J., 90
Kiesner, J., 242
Killen, M., 319, 362
Kilner, J.M., 172
Kim, D., 237
Kim, D.M., 196
Kim, E., 195
Kim, G., 138
Kim, J-Y., 321, 322
Kim, J., 118, 119, 197, 263
Kim, T.C., 19, 20
Kim, U., 393
Kim, Y.K., 242
Kimball, J.W., 50
Kimm, S.Y., 339
Kimoto, T., 106
Kinchen, S.A., 390
King, K., 226
King, R., 191
Kinney, H.C., 69, 110
Kinsey, A.C., 406
Kinsht, I., 115
Kinzie, J., 375
Kipangat, S., 95
Kirby, D., 405
Kirby, J., 325
Kirchengast, S., 70
Kirk, K.M., 58
Kirkwood, G., 110
Kisilevsky, B., 97
Kisker, E., 368
Kita, S., 148
Kjear, S.K., 95
Kjellmer, I., 108
Klaczynski, P.A., 359
Klaus, M., 83
Klebanov, P.K., 301
Klein, M.H., 90
Klein, N., 86
Kleinman, A.M., 390
Kless, S.J., 318
Klggitcibais, C., 393
Klier, C.M., 92
Klimes, I., 261

Klinteberg, B., 51
Knafo, A., 394
Knap, N.F., 394
Knickmeyer, R., 66, 188, 236
Knight, K., 81
Kno, K., 407
Knoll, N., 344
Knorth, E., 327
Knowlton, B.J., 142
Kobayashi, J., 188
Kochanska, G., 163, 168, 170, 173, 176
Kodl, M., 350
Koenig, A., 195
Koenig, L.B., 61
Kohlberg, L., 238, 362, 363
Kohn, A., 291
Koivisto, M., 187
Kolata, G., 68, 403, 406
Kolb, B., 188
Kolbe, L.J., 351
Koletko, B., 117
Köller, O., 291
Kondo-Ikemura, K., 170
Kontos, S., 243
Kopelman, B.I., 176
Koposov, R., 51
Koppelman, F.S., 269
Koren, G., 71
Koretz, D., 369
Korn, W.S., 373
Koroukian, S.M., 89
Kose, S., 161
Koshmanova, T., 28
Koska, J., 261
Kostovic, I., 340
Kosunen, E., 335, 337, 338
Kotler, J., 237
Kotre, J., 92, 310, 314
Kovelman, I., 287
Kozhevnikova, E.V., 152, 153
Kozulin, A., 216
Kraemer, H.C., 339, 406
Kramer, M.S., 70
Krauthamer-Ewing, E., 226
Krebs, N.F., 339
Kremar, M., 220, 361
Kremen, W.S., 62
Kreuder, F., 236
Kreutzer, J.C., 37
Kriska, A.M., 339
Kristjansdottir, G., 268
Kroger, J., 388, 389
Krohn, M.D., 401
Krojgaard, P., 138
Kromar, M., 145
Kronenfeld, J.J., 91
Kronholz, J., 225

Li, Q., 320
Li, S., 28
Li, Y., 72
Li, Y.F., 72, 265
Liang, H., 390
Liaw, F., 224
Liben, L.S., 235
Liblik, R., 268
Lichtenstein, P., 28
Lickliter, R., 126
Lidz, J., 151
Lie, E., 140
Lillard, A., 226
Lin, K., 145, 220, 237
Linde, R., 344
Lindecrantz, K., 108
Lindhout, D., 54
Lindsay, A., 118, 263
Lindsay, M., 70
Lindsey, E., 239, 241
Linebarger, D.L., 228
Lines, P.M., 294, 367
Ling, A.D., 125
Linn, R.L., 369
Linn, S., 228
Linz, D., 251
Lippincott, E., 119
Lipsitt, L., 111, 112
Lipsitt, L.P., 96, 124
Litovsky, R.Y., 123
Litrownik, A., 193
Little, R.E., 88
Liu, D., 243
Liu, H.-M., 145, 148
Liu, J., 89
Liu, X., 360
Liu, Z., 237
Lluis-Font, J.M., 32
Lobel, M., 89
Lobliner, D.B., 319
Lochner, B., 385
Lockhart, C., 245
Loeb, S., 178
Loeber, R., 244
Loewen, S., 24
Lofgren, N., 108
Loftus, E.F., 141, 214
Logan, J., 272
Lohman, D.F., 298
Lois, J., 295
London, B., 362
London, K., 214
Loney, B.R., 401
Long, L., 323
Long, T., 323
Longmore, M., 402
Lopez, G.F., 292

Lopez, M.F., 95
Lorberbaum, J.P., 161
Lorenz, K., 80, 165, 249
Lothian, J., 81
Lothian, S., 81
Love, A., 239
Love, J., 225, 226
Love, J.M., 177, 178
LoVullo, S., 22
Lowden, A., 342
Lowry, R., 339, 390
Lozano, J.M., 272
Lozano, P., 265
Lu, M.C., 82
Lu, X., 292, 389
Lubinski, D., 298, 304
Lucangeli, D., 285
Lucas, S.R., 398
Lucon, A.M., 67
Ludden, A., 385
Lüdtke, O., 291
Luminet, O., 318
Luna, B., 340
Luo, Q., 346
Lupien, P.J., 59
Lurye, L., 236, 238
Luster, T., 368
Lustig, R., 262
Luthar, S., 399
Luthar, S.S., 197
Lycett, E., 68
Lykken, D.T., 60, 61
Lynam, D.R., 401
Lynch, F., 192
Lynch, M.E., 71
Lynne, S., 337
Lyon, M., 405
Lyon, M.E., 391
Lyons, K., 283
Lyons, M.J., 62
Lyons, N.P., 364

M

Maas, C., 13, 193
MacCallum, F., 68
Maccoby, E.E., 178, 224, 243, 244
MacDorman, M.F., 89, 90
MacInnes, K., 192
MacLean, W.E., 110
MacPhee, D., 37
MacWhinney, B., 151
Mael, F.A., 375
Mahdavi, J., 319
Mahoney, K.M., 73
Mains, S., 97
Maital, S., 148
Makino, M., 340

Malcuit, G., 175
Malkin, J.W., 124
Malla, A.K., 62
Maller, S., 301
Malling, H.V., 51, 52
Mallon, G.P., 406
Malmberg, L., 224
Maloch, B., 217
Malone, P.S., 317
Mameli, M., 68
Manber, R., 190
Mandal, M., 201
Mandel, D.R., 123
Manganello, J., 369
Mangelsdorf, S., 169, 175
Mangweth, B., 340
Manlove, J., 405
Mann, C.C., 261
Mann, J.J., 391
Mann, K., 349
Manning, W., 402
Mao, A., 109
Marchman, V., 150
Marcia, J.E., 388
Marcotte, D., 371
Marcovitch, S., 137, 282
Marcus, S., 390
Marean, G.C., 122
Mark W., 87
Mark, P.M., 91
Markenson, G., 73
Markey, C., 337
Markova, G., 97, 138
Marks, J.S., 72
Marlier, L., 94, 124, 161
Marolla, F., 56
Marrott, H., 141
Marsal, K., 72
Marschark, M., 271
Marsh, H., 234, 311, 312
Marsh, H.W., 311, 312
Marshall, E., 273
Marshall, N.L., 179
Marsland, K., 224
Martens, B., 274
Martenson, E., 191
Marti-Henneberg, C., 335
Martin, A., 390
Martin, C., 236
Martin, C.E., 406
Martin, C.L., 176, 235, 237, 238
Martin, G., 391
Martin, J.A., 89, 90, 243, 244
Martin, J.M., 384
Martin, M.H., 20
Martin, N., 340
Martin, N.G., 58

Martin, R., 86
Martin, R.P., 175
Martin, S., 47, 72, 154
Martinez, J., 350
Martinez-Ramirez, A., 191
Martorell, G.A., 195
Marzari, F., 119
Masalha, S., 7
Masataka, N., 123, 148, 149, 150, 153
Mascher, J., 7
Maschka, P., 114
Mash, E., 390
Mashburn, A.J., 369
Masling, J.M., 18
Massa, G., 261
Massaro, A., 72
Masse, L.C., 227
Masten, A., 173
Mathews, T.J., 89, 90
Mathiesen, K., 197
Matlin, M., 337
Maton, K.I., 39, 197
Matson, J., 22
Matsumoto, A., 7, 188
Matthews, G., 293
Mattock, A., 94
Mattson, S., 71
Matula, K., 143
Mauer, D., 94
Maughan, A., 243
Mauritzson, U., 242
Maxwell, S.E., 384
Mayer, J.D., 293
Mayes, L., 71
Mayes, R., 273
Mayes, T., 266
Mayeux, L., 317
Maynard, I., 272
Mayseless, O., 167
Mazzeo, S., 51
McAdams, D.P., 19, 20
McAdoo, H.P., 368
McAuliffe, G.L., 82
McBride-Chang, C., 368
McCabe, M., 194, 337
McCabe, M.P., 339, 385
McCall, R.B., 110
McCardle, P., 287
McCartney, K., 178, 179
McCarty, M., 126
McCarty, M.E., 114
McCauley, E., 265
McClelland, D.C., 298
McClelland, G.M., 342
McClelland, L., 339
McClintock, M.K., 188
McCord, J., 194

McCoy, C., 138
McCrae, R.R., 57, 173
McCrink, K., 140, 212
McCrory, E., 272
McCullough, M.E., 38
McCurry, S., 126
McCutchen, A., 224
McCutcheon-Rosegg, S., 82
McDonald, B., 188
McDonald, L., 24
McDonnell, L.M., 290
McDonough, L., 150
McDowell, D., 314
McElkaney, K., 313
McElwain, N., 168
McGinn, D., 228
McGlothlin, H., 319
McGough, R., 272
McGreal, D., 89
McGrew, K.S., 298
McGue, M., 59, 60, 61
McGuire, J., 407
McGulfin, P., 51
McHale, J., 169
McHale, J.P., 322
McHale, S., 119, 318, 322
McHale, S.M., 321, 322, 384, 394
McKay, R.J., 47
McKinney, K., 405
McKinney, R., 407
McKown, C., 235, 294, 319
McKusick, V.A., 51
McLoyd, V.C., 195, 326
McManus, I.C., 201
McShane, K.E., 247
McShane, S., 274
McWhirter, D.P., 406
McWilliams, N., 20
Mead, M., 292
Meadow-Orlans, K., 189
Meadows, B., 319
Mealey, L., 176
Mebert, C., 245
Meckstroth, E., 304
Meece, J.L., 368
Meesters, C., 169
Meeus, W., 389
Mehler, J., 123
Mehran, K., 13
Meiraz, H., 72
Melancon, C., 13, 195
Melbye, M., 95
Melinder, A., 141
Melnyk, L., 214
Meltzoff, A., 138, 171
Meltzoff, A.N., 96, 126, 154, 171, 287
Menacker, F., 47

Mendelson, M., 319
Mendiola, L., 224
Mendle, J., 337, 338
Mendoza, C., 303
Mendoza, J.A., 228
Meng, Z., 161
Menlove, F.L., 22
Menna-Barretio, L., 108
Mennella, J., 124
Mennella, J.A., 71, 118, 119
Menon, E., 96
Méot, A., 376
Mercer, J.R., 302
Merewood, A., 119
Meritesacker, B., 175
Merlo, L., 154
Mermelstein, R., 343, 350
Mertens, S.B., 294
Mertesacker, B., 175
Mervis, J., 39
Messer, S.B., 20
Mester, R., 390
Met, Z., 187
Mezey, G., 72
Mezulis, A., 390
Miao, X., 283
Miceli, P., 272
Michael, R.T., 403, 406
Michels, V.V., 54
Michnick-Golinkoff, R., 149
Midgett, C., 192
Miehl, N.J., 107
Miesnik, S., 89
Mikhail, B., 90
Miklánková, L., 190
Mikolakaros, G., 266
Mikulincer, M., 167
Miles, R., 81, 86
Miller, C., 360
Miller, E.M., 71
Miller, J.L., 123
Miller, P.C., 245
Miller, P.H., 215
Miller, W., 379
Miller-Perrin, C.L., 194
Mimura, K., 106
Minerbrook, S., 397
Minich, N.M., 86
Minnes, S., 71
Mino, X., 321
Minorities in Higher Education, 372
Minyard, S.A., 399
Miranda, S.E., 119
Mirsky, J., 340
Miruka, A., 95
Mishra, R.C., 282
Misri, S., 92

Mistry, J., 138
Mitchell, K., 270
Mitchell, P., 242
Mitchell, P.B., 266
Mitchell, S., 8
Miyaki, K., 170
Miyamoto, R.H., 385
Mizuno, K., 124
Mizuta, I., 235, 270
Modern Language Association, 286
Modi, N., 81, 86
Moffitt, T.E., 28, 63, 401
Moilanen, I., 266
Moise-Titus, J., 251
Moldin, S.O., 52
Molfese, P., 119
Molfese, V.J., 144
Molina, J.C., 71, 95
Monahan, K., 400
Monastra, V., 62
Moneta, G., 241, 394, 395
Mongan, M., 82
Montague, D., 162
Montalto, M.B., 119
Montemayor, R., 384
Montgomery-Downs, H., 109
Moon, C., 96
Mooney-Somers, J., 325
Moore, C., 313
Moore, G., 57, 175
Moore, K.L., 64, 69
Moore, L., 262
Moore, M., 96, 138, 171
Moore, M.K., 96
Moore, N., 404
Moores, D., 189
Morales, J.R., 326
Moran, K.C., 228
Moran, S., 298
Moran, T., 92
Morelli, G.A., 7
Morgan, J., 226
Morgan, M., 92
Morgenthaler, T., 189
Morice, A., 90
Morikawa, H., 150
Morris, J., 52
Morris, P., 26
Morrison, D.M., 351
Morrison, F.J., 288
Morrison, J.A., 261
Morrongiello, B., 192
Morrongiello, B.A., 123, 192
Mortimer, J.T., 371
Mortweet, S.L., 22
Moskowitz, J.T., 344
Mossaheb, N., 92

Moylan, C., 193
Muenchow, S., 224
Mulder, E., 70, 71
Mulick, J.A., 274
Müller, J., 25
Muller, U., 282
Multimaki, P., 266
Mulvaney, M., 245
Mulvihill, T.M., 367
Mumme, D., 163, 164
Munson, M.L., 47
Munzar, P., 347
Murashima, M., 263
Muris, P., 169
Murphy, B., 317
Murphy, C.C., 72
Murphy, J., 151
Murphy, K.C., 228
Murphy, M., 262
Murphy, R., 385
Murray, C., 60, 68, 301, 325
Murray, G., 144, 161
Murray, J., 227
Murray, J.A., 89
Murray, L., 144, 163
Murray-Close, D., 249
Musher-Eizenman, D.R., 251
Muula, A., 95
Muzik, M., 92
Muzio, J.N., 110
Myers, N.A., 141
Myklebust, B.M., 112
Myles, T.D., 85

N

Nadal, K., 389
Nadeau, A., 59
Nadeau, L., 86
Nadel, S., 25
NAEP, 368
Nagda, B.A., 292
Nagle, R.J., 143
Nagy, E., 96
Nahom, D., 351
Nahulu, L.B., 385
Nakagawa, M., 170
Nangle, D.W., 314
Nansel, T., 320
Nansel, T.R., 344
Nash, A., 228
National Association for the Education of Young Children, 222
National Campaign to Prevent Youth Pregnancy (NCPYP), 403
National Center for Children in Poverty, 117, 177
National Center for Education Statistics, 222, 370, 371, 372

National Center for Educational Statistics, 368, 371
National Center for Health Statistics, 89, 95, 111, 262
National Center for Missing and Exploited Children, 269, 270
National Coalition Against Domestic Violence (NCADC), 13
National Institute of Child Health and Human Development: Early Child Care Research Network, 224
National Institutes of Health, 95
National Longitudinal Study of Adolescent Health, 343
National Safety Council, 192
National Sleep Foundation, 342
Navalta, C.P., 196, 266
Nazzi, T., 148
Neal, T., 187
Needleman, H.L., 193
Neelasri, C., 66
Neeley, N.L., 85
Negy, C., 314
Neill, N., 161
Neisser, U., 141
Nelson, C., 107
Nelson, C.A., 66, 122, 340
Nelson, E.E., 341
Nelson, K., 150, 213
Nelson, L., 396
Nelson, M., 371
Nelson, N., 175
Nelson, P., 188
Nelson, T., 347, 348
Nelson, T.F., 347
Nelson, T.O., 361
Nelson-Goens, G., 162
Nelson-Le Gall, S., 235
Nesbitt, T.S., 89
Nesheim, S., 70
Neumark-Sztainer, D., 340
Newcomb, A.F., 397
Newcombe, N., 140
Newman, J., 288
Newman, J.M., 339
Newman, M., 344
Newsom, C.A., 271
Newton, R., 193
Ng, F., 245
Ngini, L., 281
Nguyen, S., 236
NICHD Early Child Care Research Network, 178, 179, 224, 226
Nichols, T., 337
Nicklas, T.A., 339
Nicolussi, S., 119
Niederhofer, H., 66

Pellmar, T.C., 390
Peltonen, L., 51
Peltzer, K., 404
Pempek, T., 145
Pena, J., 407
Peng, Y.B., 125
Pengpid, S., 404
Pennisi, E., 46
Pepe, M.S., 262
Pepler, D., 344
Pepler, D.J., 402
Peppé, S., 285
Perez, M., 119
Perfetti, C.A., 290
Perlis, M.L., 190
Perlmann, J., 7
Perlmann, R., 153
Perlmann, R.Y., 153
Perner, J., 247
Perricone, P., 404
Perrin, R.D., 194
Perrine, N.E., 400
Perry, B., 325
Perry, T., 376
Persaud, T.V.N., 64
Persson, A., 251
Persson, G.E.B., 248
Pesetsky, D., 290
Peterman, K., 171
Petersen, A., 338
Petersen, M., 273
Petersen, R., 72
Peterson, B.S., 340
Peterson, D.M., 388
Peterson, J., 51
Peterson, L., 194
Petit, G., 252
Petitto, L.A., 148, 187, 287
Petras, H., 248
Petrides, K., 368
Petrou, S., 86
Pettit, G.S., 244, 317
Pettit, R., 245
Pfeifer, J.H., 172
Phelan, P., 399
Phelps, R.P., 369
Philippot, P., 248
Philips, D.A., 368
Phillips, D., 225
Phillips, E., 340
Phillips-Silver, J., 123
Phillipsen, L.C., 318
Phinney, J.S., 227, 385, 398
Piaget, J., 23, 132, 135, 137, 209, 246
Pick, A.D., 162
Pickens, J., 162
Piemyat, S., 228, 237

Piertomonaco, P.R., 261
Pietrobelli, A., 261
Piha, J., 266
Pikler, V., 191
Pilgrim, C., 346
Pilla, R.S., 344
Pine, D.S., 167, 341
Pine, K., 228
Pinker, S., 219, 220
Piñon, M., 228
Pintney, R., 269
Pipe, M., 141, 213
Pisoni, D.B., 123
Pittman, L., 325
Piyamongkol, W., 66
Pizzigati, K., 197
Planinsec, J., 198
Plante, E., 153
Platat, C., 339
Platsidou, M., 24
Platzman, K.A., 71
Plebani, M., 119
Plomin, R., 32, 38, 51, 52, 57, 61, 390
Plowfield, L.A., 191
Podolski, C.L., 251
Poest, C.A., 198
Polcari, A., 196
Polivka, B., 262
Polkinghome, D.E., 34
Pollack, W., 385
Pollak, S., 187
Pollitt, E., 117, 260
Pomares, C.G., 124
Pomerantz, E., 245
Pomerleau, A., 175
Pomeroy, W.B., 406
Ponirakis, A., 338
Pons, F., 152
Ponton, L.E., 403
Poole, D.A., 214
Poole, H., 11
Poole, J.M., 200
Poortinga, Y.H., 359
Pope, H., 337
Porges, S.W., 124
Porter, M., 89
Porter, R.H., 124
Portes, A., 314
Posner, J., 224
Posner, R., 336
Poss, J., 25
Posthuma, D., 302
Potvin, P., 371
Poulin-Dubois, D., 176, 236
Poulton, R., 63
Poustka, F., 265
Powell, C., 70

Powell, M.B., 214
Prater, L., 368
Pratt, H., 340
Pratt, L., 91
Prechtl, H.F.R., 113
Prentice, J., 82
Prescott, C., 62
Prescott, C.A., 62
Prescott, P., 123
Presnell, K., 390
Pressley, M., 360
Preud'homme, D., 262
Prezbindowski, A.K., 33
Price, D.W., 213
Price, R., 59
Price, R.J., Jr., 73
Priel, B., 61
Primas, P.J., 90
PRIMEDIA/Roper National Youth Survey, 395
Prince, M., 86
Principe, G.F., 214
Prior, M., 197
Probert, B., 379
Probst, J., 90
Propper, C., 57, 175
Pruzek, R., 117
Puchalski, M., 125
Pufall, P., 282
Punamaki, R-L., 326
Pungello, E., 222, 223
Puntambekar, S., 216
Purdy, K., 319
Putnick, D., 238
Putnick, D.L., 70
Pyszczynski, T., 13

Q

Quilliam, S., 405
Quilty, L., 51
Quinn, M., 350, 351
Quintana, C., 319
Quintana, C., 384
Quintana, S., 235, 389
Quintana, S.M., 235, 319

R

Raag, T., 236
Rabain-Jamin, J., 152
Rabin, R., 119
Radke-Yarrow, M., 247
Radke-Yarrow, M.R., 260
Radwan, S., 298
Raeburn, P., 341
Raeff, C., 393
Rafalovich, A., 273
Raffaelli, M., 346, 351
Rahe, R.H., 343

Schluchter, M., 86
Schmidt, G., 261
Schmidt, M., 73
Schmithorst, V., 153
Schmitt, E., 389
Schmuckler, M., 137
Schneider, B.A., 123
Schneider, W., 360
Schneiderman, N., 342
Schnitzer, P.G., 269
Schnur, E., 225
Schofer, J.L., 269
Schofield, E., 144
Schöner, G., 96
Schoppe-Sullivan, S., 169, 175
Schor, E.L., 269
Schore, A., 161, 243
Schreiber, G.B., 261
Schroder, R., 224
Schroger, E., 272
Schuetze, P., 71
Schultz, J., 387
Schumann, G., 349
Schurch, B., 117
Schuster, C.S., 187
Schutt, R.K., 32
Schutz, H., 396
Schwartz, B.S., 193
Schwartz, C.E., 175
Schwartz, I.M., 403
Schwartz, S.H., 394
Schwarzer, R., 344
Schwebel, D.C., 193
Schweiger, E., 236
Schweinhart, L.J., 225
Schweitzer, B., 339
Schwimmer, J., 262
Scott, A.A., 172
Scott, D., 119
Scott, K., 83
Scott, P., 247
Scott, S.S., 341
Scrimsher, S., 216, 217
Scullin, M., 214
Sears, R.R., 303
Sebokova, E., 261
Secrist, C., 162
Segal, B.M., 347
Segal, J., 264
Segal, N.L., 58, 61
Segal, Z., 264
Segall, M.H., 359
Segalowitz, S.J., 201
Segarra, J., 108
Seibring, M., 347
Seidel, K.D., 262
Seidenberg, M.S., 290

Seidman, S.N., 403
Seier, W.L., 215
Seifer, R., 175
Seifert, T., 190
Seitz, M., 13
Seligman, M.E.P., 318
Semenic, S., 79
Senghas, A., 148
Sequeira Sdos, S., 236
Serbin, A., 175, 176
Serbin, L., 176, 236
Serdula, M.K., 261
Seroczynski, A.D., 384
Serretti, A., 61
Servin, A., 176, 236
Sesma, A., 392
Sesser, S., 350
Sevcik, R.A., 151
Shackelford, T., 28
Shafer, R.G., 346
Shaffer, D., 95
Shaffer, E., 303
Shaffer, L., 402
Shah, V., 125
Shannon, J., 154
Shapiro, A., 162
Shapiro, H., 114
Shapiro, L., 190
Shapiro, L.R., 215
Sharma, M., 48
Shaunessy, E., 303
Shavelson, R., 311
Shaver, P.R., 167
Shaw, D.S., 323
Shaw, M.L., 290
Shaywitz, S., 272, 290
Shea, K.M., 88
Shealy, C.N., 327
Shellenbarger, S., 178
Shenfield, S., 216
Sheppard, A., 323
Shera, D., 368
Shi, L., 239
Shi, X., 389
Shields, C., 217, 284
Shields, M.K., 327
Shiffrin, R.M., 283
Shin, H.B., 285
Shin, L.M., 175
Shiner, R., 173
Shirley, L., 236
Shockey, E., 237
Shonk, S.M., 195
Shopper, M., 325
Shoval, G., 391
Shreve, T., 314
Shrout, P., 236, 238

Shrum, W., 398
Shumow, L., 224
Shuster, T., 385
Sidebotham, P., 110
Sieber, J.E., 41
Siegel, L.J., 342
Siegel, L.S., 287
Siegler, R., 138
Siegler, R.S., 212, 215, 281, 283, 360
Sierra, E.M., 119
Sigman, M., 117, 144, 172
Sigman, M.D., 110
Sigmund, E., 190
Sigueland, E.R., 123
Silber, T., 340, 391
Silenzio, V., 407
Silliman, E.R., 271
Silva, P.A., 401
Silva-Pereyra, J., 123
Silverberg, S., 393
Silverstein, L.B., 169
Silverthorn, P., 401
Simcock, G., 141
Simion, F., 94, 122
Simmons, M., 261
Simmons, S.W., 83
Simon, A., 337
Simon, C., 339
Simons, S.H., 124
Simons-Morton, B., 344
Simpkins, S., 314
Simpson, J., 167
Simpson, J.M., 83
Simpson, P.A., 379
Singer, D.G., 228
Singer, J.L., 228
Singer, L.T., 71
Singer, M., 344
Singh, S., 404, 405
Singleton, L.C., 319
Sippola, L.K., 397
Sirichotiyakul, S., 66
Sirota, L., 87
Sjoeberg, N.O., 72
Skinner, B.F., 150
Skinner, J.D., 116, 118
Skjaerven, R., 90
Skowronek, M.H., 349
Slater, A., 94
Slater, M., 251
Slavin, R.E., 284
Slaymaker, E., 404
Sleeper, L.A., 69
Slep, A.M., 194
Sloan, S., 120
Slobodskaya, H., 115
Slone, M., 138

Wardle, F., 7
Wardle, J., 262, 337
Warkentin, V., 164
Warnock, F., 124
Warren, C.W., 351
Warren, J.R., 371
Warren, K., 71
Wartella, E., 145, 227
Wartella, E.A., 227, 251, 262, 370
Warwick, P., 217
Washington Post, 85
Wasserman, J.D., 296
Waterhouse, J.M., 108
Waterland, R.A., 59
Waterman, A.S., 387
Waters, E., 165, 166
Waters, M., 7
Watkins, R., 369
Watling, D., 187
Watson, J.B., 21, 95
Watson, J.K., 243
Waugh, R., 170
Waxler, C.Z., 247
Way, N., 342
Weaver, A., 265
Webb, J.P., 349
Webb, R.M., 304
Weber, B., 269
Wechsler, D., 295
Wechsler, H., 347, 348
Wei, R., 187
Weigel, D., 154
Weikart, D.P., 225
Weinberg, M.K., 92
Weinberg, R.A., 38, 81
Weinberger, D.R., 341
Weinfeld, N.S., 167
Weinraub, M., 178, 179
Weinstein, J., 13
Weinstein, R., 294
Weinstock, H., 351
Weis, T., 390
Weismer, S., 368
Weiss, J., 119
Weiss, L., 297
Weiss, M.R., 312
Weiss, R., 301
Weissman, D., 188
Weisz, A., 365
Weitzman, E., 348
Weitzman, M., 288
Welcome, S.E., 340
Weller, A., 87
Welles-Nystron, B., 240
Wellings, K., 404, 405
Wellman, H., 242, 243
Wellman, H.M., 243

Wells, B., 285
Wells, E.A., 351
Welner, K.G., 366
Wen, S., 87
Wenner, J.A., 141
Werker, J., 123
Werker, J.F., 152
Werner, E.E., 197
Werner, L.A., 122
Werner, N.E., 249
Wertheim, E., 396
Wessel, R.D., 367
West, J., 350
West, S., 272
Westerhausen, R., 236
Westra, T., 116
Westreich, D., 95
Wewerka, S.S., 141
Wexler, B., 12
Whalen, C.K., 272
Whalen, J., 375
Whaley, B.B., 271
Wheeldon, L.R., 219
Wheeler, K., 144
Wheelwright, S., 188
Whelan, T., 169
Whitaker, R.C., 262
White, G., 373
White, K., 242
White, K.R., 271
White, M., 373
Whitebook, M., 368
Whitehurst, G.J., 221
Whiteman, S., 322
Whiteman, S.D., 321, 322, 394
Whiting, B.B., 236, 318
Whitman, R., 187
Whitney, M.P., 109
Widiger, T., 8
Widom, C.S., 194
Wiesel, T.N., 122
Wigfield, A., 367
Wilcox, A., 90
Wilcox, A.J., 88
Wilcox, B.L., 228
Wilcox, H.C., 391
Wilcox, K.J., 61
Wilcox, T., 126
Wildberger, S., 70
Willard, N., 270
Williams, B., 390
Williams, J., 71, 97, 190
Williams, J.R., 198
Williams, R., 401
Williams, S., 405
Williams, S.L., 151
Williams, T., 386

Williamson, R., 366
Willmger, M., 69
Willows, D.M., 189
Wills, T., 350
Wills, T.A., 312
Wilsdon, A., 351
Wilson, B., 250
Wilson, G., 340, 406
Wilson, L., 326
Wilson, P., 228
Wilson, R., 118, 372
Wilson, S.L., 34
Wimbarti, S., 250
Winans, D., 369
Wineburg, S.S., 293
Winer, G., 190
Winger, G., 69
Wingert, P., 270, 321, 389, 403
Winner, E., 202
Winsler, A., 27, 217, 220
Winslow, E.B., 323
Winstead, B.A., 390
Wisborg, K., 72
Wisdom, J., 390
Wismer, A., 187
Witelson, S., 188
Witt, D.D., 198
Wittchen, H.U., 266
Wittling, R.A., 236
Wittling, W., 236
Woelfle, J.F., 335
Woerner, W., 236
Wolak, J., 270
Wolff, M.C., 107
Wood, A.C., 198
Wood, D., 15, 242
Wood, D.N., 394
Wood, R., 47, 401
Woods, J.H., 69
Woods, R., 47, 126
Woodson, R., 96
Woodward, A., 96
Woolston, C., 262
Worell, J., 337
World Factbook, 85
World Food Programme, 116
Worobey, J., 174
Worrell, F., 304
Worthman, C., 337
Wray, N., 340
Wright, C.L., 175
Wright, D., 214, 261
Wright, J., 228
Wright, J.A., 262
Wright, J.C., 228, 237
Wright, R., 41
Wright, S., 314

Autism, 24, 25
  male vs. female brains, 188
Autobiographical memory, 213
Automatization, information processing, 139–40
Automobile accidents, during middle years, 269
Autonomous cooperation stage, 246
Autonomy, 393
  vs. shame-and-doubt stage, 173
Autostimulation, 110
Avoidant attachment pattern, 167
Axon, 105
AZT, pregnancy, 70

B
Babbling, 147–48
Baby
  biographies, 9
  difficult, 174
  easy, 174
  postmature, 88
  slow-to-warm, 174
Baby Einstein series of videos, 145
Back-to-sleep guideline, 110
Bandura, Albert, 22, 29t, 248
Barinski reflex, 111, 112
Baron-Cohen, Simon, 188
Bayley Scales of Infant Development, 142–43
Bayley, Nancy, 142
Behavior modification, 22
Behavioral genetics, 28, 50–51
Behavioral perspective, 21–22, 29, 42
  assessing, 22
Behavioral traits, genetic basis of, 51
Belgian preschools, 224
Bell Curve, The (Hernstein & Murray), 301
Bell curves, 301–2
Berkeley Growth and Guidance Studies, 10
Bicultural identity, 292, 389
Bicycle accidents, during middle years, 269
Bilingual education, 286–87
Bilingualism, 285–86
Binet's test, 296
Binet, Alfred, 9–10, 295, 296
Binge drinking, 347, 348
Bingeing, 339
Binocular vision, 121
Bioecological approach to development, 25–27
Bipolar disorder during middle childhood, 265
Birth
  complications of, 84–89
  first encounters upon, 93
  from fetus to neonate, 79–81
  labor, 78–79
  multiple, 46–47
Birth control pills, 71, 72
  pregnancy, 71

Birthing centers, family, 81
Birthing procedures, alternative, 81–82
Bisexuals, 406–7
Blended families, 325
Blindness, 271
Bobo doll and aggression, 250
Bodily kinesthetic intelligence, 300
Body
  proportions of, 66, 104
  structural and shape changes in, 187
Body image, 336–37
Bonding, 80–81
  by children, 165–67
Books, perpetuating gender roles, 237
Border work, 318
Bottle-feeding vs. breast-feeding, 118–20
Bowlby, John, 166, 168
Boys, puberty in, 336
Bradley Method, 82
Brain
  activity of, 187
  child abuse altering, 243
  culture, 188
  development in adolescence, 340–41
  development in infants, 107–8
  growing, 187–88
    linked with cognitive development, 188–89
    spurts in, 189
  lateralization of, 187–88
  play promoting development, 241
  structure of, gender and culture, 176
  waves, 108
Braxton-Hicks contractions, 78
Brazelton Neonatal Behavioral Assessment Scale (NBAS), 80, 115
Brazelton, T. Berry, 115
Breast-feeding
  social patterns in, 119–20
  vs. bottle-feeding, 118–20
Breech position, 89
Brinich, Judy Coleman, 27
Bronfenbrenner's approach to development, 25–26
Bronfenbrenner, Uric, 29
Brown, Louise, 2, 8
Bulimia, 339–40
Bullies, 319–20
  causing stress, 344
  cyber-year, 319
  schoolyard, 319

C
Caffeine, pregnancy, 72
Calvin, John, 61
Cancer in preschoolers, 191
Career, selection of, 379

Case studies, 34, 36
Castration anxiety, 237
CAT. See Computerized axial tomography (CAT) scan
Caucasian infants, mean behavioral scores for, 61
Causal relationships, 32
Cell, contents of human, 46
Centration, 208–9
Cephalocaudal principle, 104–5
Cerebral cortex, 106
Cervix, uterus, 78
Cesarean delivery, 88–89
  rate of, 89
Change
  continuous, 10
  developmental, measuring, 38–40
  discontinuous, 10
Chess, Stella, 174
Chiao shun, 245
Chickenpox in pregnancy, 70
Child abuse, 193–95
  altering brain, 196
  percentage of victims, 193
  warning signs of, 194
Child development, 4–15
  applying, 39
  approaches to, 6
  as a discipline, 9–10
  careers in, 27, 88, 136, 172, 196, 223, 274, 348
  future of, 12–13
  in 20th century, 9–10
  in courtroom, 213–14
  informed consumers, 14
  issues in, 10–12
  research strategies and challenges, 38–40
  scope, 5–7
Child neglect, 195
Child-rearing practices
  cultural differences in, 245
Childbirth, 98
  anesthesia for, 83
  approaches to, 81–84
  attendants, 82–83
  leave policies for, 91
  natural, 82
  pain-reducing drugs, 83
Child care
  effectiveness of, 223–24
  group, 178–79
    in the 21st century, 326–27
  infant, affecting later development, 178
  location of, 178
  outside home, 222
  quality of, 224
Child-care centers, 222
  family, 222

during early childhood, 199–200
during middle childhood, 268
of infants, 114
Finnish preschools, 224
First stage of labor, 78, 79
First-trimester screen, 53
Fixation, 19
Fluid intelligence, 298
fMRI. See Functional magnetic resonance imaging (fMRI) scan
Food
for adolescents, 338–40
solid, introduction of, 120
Forensic developmental psychology, 213–14
Formal operational stage, 23, 358
Formal operations
adolescence, 358–60
solving problems, 358–59
Formula for infants, 119–20
Fragile X syndrome, 52
French preschools, 224
Freud, Sigmund, 18, 29, 166, 248
psychoanalytic theory, 18–19, 236–37
stages of psychosexual development, 20
Friends
during preschool years, 239
identity, 387
in middle childhood, 315–20
of adolescents, 396–97
Friendship
behaviors in, 316
cross-race, 319
stages of, 315–16
Full inclusion, 273–74
Functional magnetic resonance imaging (fMRI) scan, 35
Functional play, 239, 240
Functionality, 211

G

Gag reflex, 112
Gambling, online, 401
Gamete intrafallopian transfer (GIFT), 67
Gametes, 46
Gardner's Eight Intelligences, 300
Gardner, Howard, 300
Gay parents, 325–26
Gender
adolescence, 397
and career choice, 377–79
and friendships, 318–19
autism, 188
barriers to achievement, 375–76
bias in classroom, 374
biological perspectives on, 236, 238
books, 237

child care, 176–77
cognitive approaches, 237–38
college, 372–75
constancy, 238
gross motor skills, 199, 267–68
identity, 237, 406
development during preschool years, 235–38
infants, 175–76
language, 153
morality, 364–65
psychoanalytic perspectives of, 236–37, 238
psychoanalytic perspectives on, 236–37
schema, 237–38
self-esteem, 385
social learning approaches, 237, 238
television, 237
video games, 237
wage gap, 378
Generation gap, 394
myth, 394
Generativity versus stagnation stage, 19
Genes, 46
sequence mapping, 50
tests, DNA-based, 55
therapy, 56
Genetic code, cracking, 50–51
Genetic counseling, 52–54
Genetic disorders
screening for, 54–55
Genetic factors, 11
Genetic information, transmission of, 49–50
Genetic testing, 44
Genetics, 44–75
and IQ, 59
behavioral, 50–51
intelligence, 59–60
obesity, 59
traits, 48–49
Genital herpes, 352
Genital stage of psychosexual development, 19
Genome, human, 50–51
Genotype, 48, 57
Germ line therapy, 56
Germinal stage, 64
Gesell, Arnold, 142
Gestational age and survival, 86
Gibson, Eleanor, 121
GIFT
See Gamete intrafallopian transfer (GIFT)
Gifted and talented, 303–4
educating, 304
Gilligan, Carol, 364
Ginzberg's three periods, 377
Ginzberg, Eli, 377
Girls, puberty in, 335–36

Goal-directed behavior, 135
Goleman, Daniel, 293
Gonorrhea, 70, 352
Goodness-of-fit, 175
Grammar, 220
universal, 151
Gross motor skills
during middle childhood, 267–68
gender differences in, 267–68
in early childhood, 198–99
of infants, 113–14
Group child care, 222–24
in the 21st century, 326–27
Group home, 326–27
Growth
cultural patterns of, 260–61
patterns of adolescence, 334
principles of, 104–5

H

Habituation, 96, 123
Hall, G. Stanley, 10
Handedness, 201
Harlow, Harry, 166
Head Start, 225–26
Head, decreasing proportions of, 65–66, 104
Hearing loss, 271
Hegger, Diana, 88
Height
in middle childhood, 260
individual differences in, 186–87
Height and weight growth, 104
Hemispheres, 66
Hemophilia, 50
inheriting, 50
Heredity, environment interaction, 55–63
Hernstein, Richard J., 301
Herodotus, 30
Heteronomous morality, 246
Heterozygous, 49
High school status, 400
Hippocampus, 142
Hispanic
and family life, 326
school achievement, 368
school dropouts, 372
self-esteem, 314, 385
vs. Latino, 7
History-graded influences, cohort, 8
Holland's six personality types, 377
Hollingworth, Leta Stetter, 10
Holophrases, 148
Home alone, 322–23
Home, group, 326–27
Homeschooling, 293, 294–95, 367
Homosexuals, 406–7

individual strengths, 293–94
infant
    defined, 142–43
    detecting differences in, 143
interpersonal, 300
intrapersonal, 300
linguistic, 300
logical mathematical, 300
measurement of, 297–99
musical, 300
naturalistic, 300
spatial, 300
triarchic theory of, 298
Intelligence norms, 302–4
Intelligence quotient (IQ), 142, 296
    genetics, 59–60
    group differences in, 301
    measuring, 296–97
    racial differences, 301–2
Intelligence tests, 296–97
Intensity of reaction, with temperament, 174
Intentionality, 246, 247
Interactionist approach, 151
Interactive synchrony, 168
Internet
    adolescents, 401
    preschoolers, 227
Interpersonal intelligence, 300
Intonation, 284
Intrapersonal intelligence, 300
Intuitive thought, 211
    emergence of, 211
IQ. See Intelligence quotient (IQ)
Irish infants, mean behavioral scores for, 61
Irritability, with temperament, 174
IVF. See In vitro fertilization
Izard, Carroll, 160

J

Japanese
    infant attachment, 169–70
    language, brain lateralization, 188
    parents, avoiding separation and stress during infancy, 169–70
    preschools, 224
    school achievement, 368
Jaundice, neonatal, 93
Jealousy, 28
Justice, immanent, 247
Juvenile delinquency, 400–1

K

Kagan, Jerome, 61
Karyotype, 53
Kaufman Assessment Battery for Children, Second Edition (KABC-II), 297
Kellogg, J.W., 403

Key word strategy, 283
Klinefelter's syndrome, 52
Knowing, 360
Kohlberg's sequence of moral reasoning, 363
Kohlberg, Lawrence, 238, 362
Koreans, school achievement, 368
Kwashiorkor, 117

L

Labor, 78–79, 98
    communication during, 84
    coping with, 84
    first stage of, 78, 79
    flexibility with, 84
    second stage of, 78, 79
    spousal support during, 84
    third stage of, 79
Laboratory study, 37
LAD. See Language-acquisition device
Lamaze classes, 81–82
Lamaze, Fernand, 81
Language
    as innate skill, 151
    as learned skill, 150–51
    different exposures to, 221
    fundamentals of, 146–50
    gender differences, 153
    growth of, 218–21
    Japanese, brain lateralization, 188
    mastering mechanics of, 284
    of infant-directed speech, 151–52
    poverty, 221
    promoting self-control, 285
    relationship to thought, 208
    roots of, 146–52
    top spoken in United States, 286
Language development
    in middle childhood, 284–87
    origins of, 150–51
Language-acquisition device (LAD), 151
Lanugo, 80
Latchkey children, 323
Late maturation, 338
Lateralization, 187–88
Latino vs. Hispanic, 7
Lead poisoning, 192
    risk among preschoolers, 192–93
Learned helplessness, 317–18
Learning
    cooperative, 284
    through imitation, 22
Learning disabilities, 271–72
Learning theory approach, 150–51
Learning theory, social-cognitive, 22
Least restrictive environment, 273
Left-handedness, 201
Leptin, 335

Lesbian parent, 325–26
Leukemia, 191
Leyens, Jacques-Philippe, 35
Lifespan approach, 11
    vs. focus on particular period, 11–12
Lifespan development, 28
    careers in, 88
Linguistic comprehension, precedes linguistic production, 146–47
Linguistic intelligence, 300
Littler, Debra A., 196
Locke, John, 9
Logical mathematical intelligence, 300
Logical thinking, 280
Long-term memory, in middle childhood, 283
Longitudinal research, 40
Longitudinal studies, measuring individual change, 38
Lorenz, Konrad, 28, 29, 165
Low birthweight infants, 86
    cause of, 87–88
    risk factors for, 87
Low-income households, in 21st century, 177
Luther, Martin, 61

M

Macrosystem, 26
Mainstreaming, 273–74
Major depression during adolescence, 390
Make-believe play, 241
Malnutrition in infants, 116–17
Mandatory testing, 369
Marasmus, 117
Marcia's four categories of adolescent development, 388–89
Marcia, James, 388
Marcus, Cyril, 59
Marijuana, 346
    pregnancy, 71
    use, 347
Maslow, Abraham, 348
Massage
    effect on infant weight gain, 125
    effect on infants with prenatal AIDS exposure, 125
    effect on infants with prenatal cocaine exposure, 125
Masturbation, 403
Math, adolescent performance in, 366, 375
Maturation, 12
Maximally Discriminative Facial Movement Coding System (MAX), 160
Meconium, 93
Media and technology use by adolescence, 369–70
Media violence, 251
Medieval Europe, children, 9

SOMPA. See System of Multicultural Pluralistic
    Assessment
Sonoembryology, 53
Sonogram, 53
Sound localization, 123
Sounds, early, 147–48
Spanking, 194–95, 245
Spatial intelligence, 300
Special needs, 270–74
Speech
    growing capabilities of, 219
    impairment, 271
    infant-directed, 151–52
        cultural effect, 152–53
        most common features of, 152
    private, 220
    social, 220–21
Sperm, 46, 64
Spermarche, 336
Spontaneous mutation, 51
Stagnation vs. generativity, 19
Stanford Studies of Gifted Children, 10
Stanford-Binet Intelligence Scale, Fifth Edition
    (SB5), 297
Startle reflex, 111, 112
    ethnic and cultural effects, 113
State of arousal, 97
States, 108
Stepping reflex, 112
Stillbirths, 89
Stimulants, overprescription of, 273
Stimulus, substitution, 21
Storage, information processing, 139
Strange situation, for infants, 161
Stranger anxiety, of infants, 161
Stress
    complications, 344–45
    coping with, 345–46
    in adolescence, 342–46
    origins of, 342–43
    questionnaire for, 343
Students. See College students
Stuttering, 271
Subcortical levels in brain, 106
Subjects, 35
Sucking reflex, 93, 112, 134
Sudden infant death syndrome (SIDS), 110–11
    declining rates of, 111
Suicide
    during adolescence, 390–92
    increased risk with antidepressants, 266
Superego, 19, 248
Supportive parenting, 244
Surrogate mothers, 68
Survey research, 34, 36, 43
Swallowing reflex, 93
Swedish preschools, 224

Swimming reflex, 112
Symbolic function, 208
Synapse, 106
Synaptic pruning, 106
Syntax, 219, 284
Syphilis, 352
    pregnancy, 70
System of Multicultural Pluralistic Assessment
    (SOMPA), 302

T

Tabula rasa, 9
Talented, 303–4
    educating, 304
Taste, infants, 124
Tay-Sachs disease, 52
Teacher expectancy effect, 293–94
Teaching, reciprocal, 284
Teenage pregnancy, 177, 404–5
    decline in, 404–5
    rates of, 404
Teenage stress, 343
Telegraphic speech, 149
    decline of, 150
Television
    perpetuating gender roles, 237
    violence on, 250–51
Television time, 227
    preschoolers, 227–28
Temperament, 56
    in infants, 173–75
        biological basis of, 175
        categorizing, 174
        consequences of, 175
        cultural differences, 175
        dimensions of, 174
        gender differences, 176
Tentative period, 377
Teratogen, 68–69
    sensitivity, 69
Terman, Lewis, 38
Thalidomide, pregnancy, 71
Theoretical research, 16–42, 43
Theories, 18, 20, 30, 31, 42
Theory of mind, 164–65
    preschool period, 242–43
Thinking, 360
    logical, 280
    postformal, 360
Third stage of labor, 79
Thought
    beginnings, 137
    intuitive, 211
        emergence of, 211
    propositional, 359
    symbolic, 208
Three-system approach to memory, 283

Threshold of responsiveness, with tempera-
    ment, 174
Time, spent by children, 323
Time-out for punishment, 245
Tobacco, 349–50
    pregnancy, 71–72
Toilet-training, 200–1
Total Request Live, 370
Touch, infants, 125, 126
Toys
    culture, 216
    gender roles, 236
Traditionalism, 61
Transformation, 210, 211
    incomplete understanding of, 210
Transgendered individuals, 406
Transition, labor, 78
Transverse position, 89
Treatment, 35
Treatment group, 35
Triarchic theory of intelligence, 298
Trichomoniasis, 352
Trust
    mutual, 316
    trust vs. mistrust stage of infants, 173
Turner syndrome, 52
Twin studies, 58–59
Twins
    dizygotic, 46
    monozygotic, 46

U

Ultrasound sonography, 53
Umbilical cord, 64
Unconscious, 18–19
Underextension, 150
Undernutrition in infants, 116–17
Undersocialized delinquents, 400–1
Underweight children, 117
Uninvolved parents, 244
Universal grammar, 151
Uterus, 64

V

Verbal scale, 299
Vernix, 80
Very low birthweight infants, 86–87
    medical costs for, 86
Video games
    violence, 251
Violence
    case study in, 42
    during preschool period, 248–52
    on television, 250–51
    prevention of, 13
Virginity pledges, 405
Vision, in newborns, 121–22

Visual cliff, 122
Visual impairment, 271
Visual perception, infants, 121–22
Visual-recognition memory measurement, 143, 144
Vocal expressions
  decoding, 162–63
Vygotsky's sociocultural theory, 27
  assessing, 28
Vygotsky's view of cognitive development, 215–16, 283–84
  evaluation of, 217–18
  vs. Piaget's theory and information processing, 218
Vygotsky, Lev, 27, 29, 220, 241, 298

W

Walk, Richard, 121
Walking epidural, for childbirth, 83

Watson, John B., 21, 29
Weaning, 120
Wechsler Adult Intelligence Scale, 297
Wechsler Intelligence Scale for Children, Fourth Edition (WISC-IV), 297, 299
Weight
  in middle childhood, 260
  individual differences in, 186–87
Werner, Emmy, 197
Whole-language approaches to reading, 290
Wire monkey mothers, 166
Women
  career choice, 377–79
  contributing to child development, 10
Words
  appropriate formation of, 220
  first, 148, 149
Work, part-time, adolescence, 370–71
Working memory, in middle childhood, 283

Working mothers, in 21st century, 177
Wynn, Karen, 140

X

X chromosome, 47
X-linked genes, 50

Y

Youth-care workers, characteristics of, 327

Z

Zelazo, Philip R., 112–13
Zone of proximal development (ZPD), 216–17, 283–84
Zygote, 46
Zygote intrafallopian transfer (ZIFT), 67

	Prenatal Period (conception to birth)	**Infancy and Toddlerhood** (birth to 3 years)
Physical Development 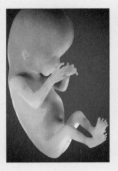	GERMINAL STAGE (fertilization to 2 weeks): • Cells divide rapidly. • Zygote attaches to uterine wall. EMBRYONIC STAGE (2 to 8 weeks): • Major organs and body systems grow. FETAL STAGE (8 weeks to birth): • Major organs become differentiated. • Fetus kicks and clenches fist, hears sounds outside the uterus. • Health can be affected by mother's diet, health, age, or substance use. • Reflexes emerge.	• Rapid height and weight gains. • Neurons grow and form interconnections in the brain. Some functions have "critical periods" for normal development. • Infants wiggle, push upward, sit up, crawl, and eventually walk. • Infants reach, grasp, and pick up small objects. • Vision is 20/20 by 6 months, with depth perception and recognition of patterns, faces, shapes, and colors. • Infants hear a wide range of frequencies, localize sound, and make sound distinctions that underlie language development.
Cognitive Development	• Intelligence is partly determined, and some psychological disorders may take root. • Cognitive functions can be affected by tobacco, alcohol, or drug use by mother.	• Infants begin to understand object permanence and "experiment" with the physical world. • Use of representations and symbols begins. • Information-processing speed increases. • Language develops rapidly through prelinguistic communication (babbling), use of single words to stand for whole ideas (holophrases), and telegraphic speech.
Social/Personality Development	• Some personality traits are partly determined genetically (e.g., neuroticism, extroversion). • Drug and alcohol use by mother can lead to irritability, difficulty dealing with multiple stimuli, and difficulty forming attachments in the child.	• Infants exhibit different temperaments and activity levels. • Facial expressions appear to reflect emotions; facial expressions of others are understood. • Toddlers begin to feel empathy. • A style of attachment to others emerges. 
Theories and Theorists	**Jean Piaget**	Sensorimotor stage
	Erik Erikson	Trust-versus-mistrust stage (birth–1½ yrs) Autonomy-versus-shame-and-doubt stage (1½–3 yrs)
	Sigmund Freud	Oral and anal stages
	Lawrence Kohlberg	Premoral period